Nathan D. Gru[illegible]

Reviewed

Pub. Ad. Rev.

(1952) 46 APSR 876 — Waldo

31 Pub. Ad. 35 (1953) — Spann — Thoughts on Admin. Case Study

(1955) 15 Pub. Ad. Rev. 115 — Somers, The Case Study Program: Where Do We Go From Here?

12 Pub. Ad. Rev. 197 (1952) — Wengert —

PUBLIC ADMINISTRATION AND POLICY DEVELOPMENT

COMMITTEE ON PUBLIC ADMINISTRATION CASES

April 1, 1948—June 30, 1951

CPAC POLICY COMMITTEE

(April 1, 1948—June 30, 1951)

Paul H. Appleby 1948-51
Merle Fainsod 1948-51
George A. Graham 1948-50
Edward H. Litchfield 1950-51
Arthur W. Macmahon 1949-51
Roscoe C. Martin 1949-51
Edward S. Mason 1949-51
Joseph E. McLean 1950-51
Paul M. O'Leary 1948-51
Don K. Price 1949-51
Wallace S. Sayre 1948-51
Donald H. Wallace 1948-51

CPAC EDITORIAL STAFF

Harold Stein 1948-51
Kathryn Smul Arnow 1948-51
Harvey C. Mansfield 1950

CPAC EDITORIAL ASSOCIATES

Phillips D. Carleton
Schuyler D. Hoslett
Norton E. Long

THE INTER-UNIVERSITY CASE PROGRAM

established July 1, 1951

ICP EXECUTIVE BOARD

Merle Fainsod
George A. Graham
Harvey C. Mansfield
Roscoe C. Martin
Emery E. Olson
Emmette S. Redford
Wallace S. Sayre
George A. Shipman
Lloyd M. Short
York Willbern

ICP EDITORIAL STAFF

Harold Stein
Kathryn Smul Arnow

THE INTER-UNIVERSITY CASE PROGRAM

Public Administration and Policy Development

A CASE BOOK

EDITED BY **Harold Stein** STAFF DIRECTOR OF THE INTER-UNIVERSITY CASE PROGRAM

NEW YORK HARCOURT, BRACE AND COMPANY 1952

[a·12·51]

The program of research of which this volume is an outgrowth was made possible by funds granted by the Carnegie Corporation of New York, and administered by The Committee on Public Administration Cases and its successor, The Inter-University Case Program. The Carnegie Corporation is not, however, the author, owner, publisher or proprietor of this publication, and has no responsibility for its contents.

PRINTED IN THE UNITED STATES OF AMERICA

CONTENTS

PART III RELATIONSHIPS

Relations with Legislatures

Relations with the Public

PUBLIC ADMINISTRATION AND POLICY DEVELOPMENT

CASE STUDIES IN PUBLIC ADMINISTRATION AND POLICY FORMATION
PUBLISHED BY THE INTER-UNIVERSITY CASE PROGRAM

*Cases marked with an asterisk are included in the present volume.

CPAC CASE STUDIES, 1948-1951 (previously published by the Committee on Public Administration Cases)

*The Air Search and Rescue Program. 1950	W. Scott Payne
*The Attack on the Cost of Living Index. 1951	Kathryn Smul Arnow
*The Battle of Blue Earth County. 1950, revised 1950	Paul N. Ylvisaker
*The Cambridge City Manager. 1951	Frank C. Abbott
The Consumers' Counsel. 1949, revised 1950	Kathryn Smul Arnow
*The Defense Plant Corporation. 1950	Clifford J. Durr
*The Disposal of the Aluminum Plants. 1948, revised 1952	Harold Stein
*The FBI Retirement Bill. 1949	Joseph F. Marsh, Jr.
The Feasibility Dispute. 1950	John Brigante
*The Foreign Service Act of 1946. 1949, revised 1952	Harold Stein
*Gotham in the Air Age. 1950, revised 1952	Herbert Kaufman
*Indonesian Assignment. 1950	Charles Wolf, Jr.
*The Kings River Project. 1949, revised 1950	Arthur A. Maass
The Latin American Proceeding. 1949	W. Scott Payne
*The Natural Cement Issue. 1950	Paul N. Ylvisaker
*The National Labor Relations Board Field Examiner. 1951	William H. Riker
*The Office of Education Library. 1950	Corinne Silverman
*The Reconversion Controversy. 1950	Jack W. Peltason
*The Sale of the Tankers. 1950, revised 1952	Louis W. Koenig
*Self-Insurance in the Treasury. 1949, revised 1952	Kathryn Smul Arnow
Smith and the OPA. 1950	Robert L. Gold
*The Transfer of the Children's Bureau. 1949, revised 1952	E. Drexel Godfrey, Jr.
*The TVA Ammonia Plant. 1950	Ellen St. Sure

ICP CASE SERIES, in progress, 1951-

1. The Firing of Pat Jackson. 1951	William H. Riker
*2. Cancellation of the Ration Stamps. 1952	Martin Kriesberg
*3. The Emergency Rubber Project. 1952	Martin Kriesberg
*4. The Glavis-Ballinger Dispute. 1952	Winifred McCulloch
*5. The Regional Director and the Press. 1952	
*6. Production Planning in the Patent Office. 1952	Arch Dotson
*7. The Rural Electrification Administration Personnel Report. 1952	Winifred McCulloch
*8. The Veterans' Gas Ration. 1952	William H. Riker

All the above case studies, in individual pamphlet form, are distributed by the Polygraphic Company of America, Inc., 310 East 45th Street, New York 17, New York.

INTRODUCTION On Public Administration and Public Administration Cases

PREFACE

This is a book of case studies, designed primarily for use in the teaching of public administration. The cases were not prepared or selected to prove or illustrate a specific theory of public administration, but rather to serve the more general function of permitting students and teachers—and other readers—to study some of the characteristic modes of behavior of public administrators (more particularly American public administrators) as they go about their task of making decisions.

These cases, by their very nature, illustrate a multitude of facets of public administration. What they can teach is, therefore, not subject to summary statement or doctrinal formulation. This Introduction is thus no short-hand substitute for the cases themselves. It is intended to outline: (1) the theoretical approach to public administration that underlies the book, (2) certain assumptions about methods of analyzing public administration, (3) the rationale of this particular case method, (4) the kind of teaching that the cases can aid, and (5) the history of the undertaking of which the book is an outgrowth.

Part I of this Introduction deals with the general theoretical concepts reflected in the cases. It is set down mainly in the form of conclusions, because a full rationalization and justification of this suggested approach to public administration would demand book-length treatment. Nevertheless, even in the absence of justification, these statements can serve the purpose of acquainting the reader with the attitudes and thinking of the authors and editors that are reflected throughout the finished product. To make effective use of the cases, the reader does not need to agree with all the reasoning of Part I; but it will be useful for him to understand the approach. He can then provide his own interpretation or re-interpretation of the cases with due allowance for the underlying assumptions.

Part II deals with the nature of the case method and its application to the study of public administration. It flows directly from the assumptions about the nature of public administration outlined in Part I and is in essence a continuation of that Part. Here again, the object is rather to make articulate what the cases represent than to argue a position. Each reader will have his own views on the validity of these conclusions about the functions and limitations of this kind of analysis of public administration; what is important in this, as in the first Part, is that the reader be enabled, by understanding what is intended, to make a more intelligent evaluation of the uses to which he can put the cases.

Part III carries on the discussion of the use of the case method in the study of public administration and relates it directly to the cases in this volume. It discusses some of the specific problems of case writing in terms of the more general considerations of theory and method outlined in the first two Parts.

Part IV offers suggestions on teaching with the cases. These suggestions are largely based on experiments carried on during the past five years. Up to the present there has been relatively little generally available case material specifically prepared for use in the teaching of public administration, and almost none like the cases in this volume. Teaching with cases presents certain problems and opportunities not present in other forms of instruction. Under the circumstances, some suggestions about appropriate teaching techniques may be welcome, for though teaching is a highly personal art, an account based on the experiences of other teachers can be helpful.

Part V is historical, and deals with the case-writing projects that preceded and led to the preparation and publication of this book. These projects are not without an interest of their own as examples of recent social science research; but the account given here is primarily designed to place this work in the larger stream of public administration research of which it is a part. The study of public administration as a defined field of research is still comparatively new but it has been developing so rapidly that the reader may be interested in this indication of the place of the present venture in the context of recent scholarly trends.

The reader will observe that in general there is an absence of documentation and annotation in all five Parts of the Introduction. This failure to give credit is not a sign that the ideas set forth are freshly minted. Every scholar will recognize the debt owed to unnamed predecessors both in the specialized field of public administration and more generally in the social sciences. Full annotation would submerge the text, partial annotation would be invidious; a general acknowledgment must suffice. But this general acknowledgment, in spite of its failure to give specific credit where so much credit is due, is none the less sincere.

I. AN APPROACH TO PUBLIC ADMINISTRATION

THE AREA OF PUBLIC ADMINISTRATION

There are many ways in which the phrase "public administration" can be defined: the words can be used to describe certain types of activities, or the activities of certain types of organizations, or some combination of the two. There is no sanctity about any of the numerous conventional definitions. One of the convenient ones, commonly used in the United States, defines "public administration" as the activities of the Executive Branch of our national government and of the comparable areas of state, local, and other governments. The subject matter of the case studies in this volume falls generally within this definition.

The chief advantage of adopting a purely descriptive definition is that it permits the analysis of all the activities of an important group of formal public organizations (i.e., government agencies), whereas under any functional definition some of these activities are excluded from the analysis. Yet the difficulties involved in this or any other simple descriptive definition are obvious. Judicial administration, for example, including the docketing and hearing of cases, assigning of judges, laying out of judicial districts, and so forth, is a public activity and is quite similar to many activities in executive agencies; its exclusion by definition, as in this book, is in the strict sense arbitrary; indeed, functionally judicial administration may be more easily thought of as "public administration" than the conduct of a manufacturing operation by the government. But difficulties of this kind, inherent in the process of descriptive definition, will prove unimportant if the reader remembers that the description is merely a matter of convenience and not intended to prove anything. More puzzling, perhaps, are the difficulties caused by uncertainties about the limits of public administration as defined. Even in our national government there are perennial arguments, for example, over the area of the Executive Branch: are the regulatory commissions part of the Executive Branch? or does public administration cover the President's campaign activities? Such questions arise with even greater frequency in a consideration of any government which does not maintain a formal constitutional tri-partite division of powers. Argument over these matters is useful for certain purposes, but it is fortunately irrelevant here. As a practical matter, the cases in this volume are centered on an easily recognizable area of activity. If, as the authors believe, this area is worth studying, the value of the cases is not affected by preferences for different definitions. No one will be inconvenienced if some of the cases deal with problems that seem to him peripheral or external to public administration; at worst they can be skipped. And since these cases deal with only a few of the innumerable problems of public administration, however defined, the exclusion of certain problems by definition will not impair the usefulness of a collection that makes no pretense of being complete in any event.

WAYS OF LOOKING AT PUBLIC ADMINISTRATION

Public administration in any developed government is a complex affair. It can be examined in terms of the people of which it is composed—several million in our national government; in terms of its groups—the economists, the New Dealers, the old gang; of its organization—departments and agencies and branches and units; of its legal framework—constitution, statutes, executive orders; of its procedures—filing systems, correspondence, conferences, memoranda, reports; of its techniques—management improvement, personnel classification, accounting controls. All these go to make up public administration; but these do not comprise all the activities of public administrators. Administrators are also deeply concerned with legislative and public relations, with program objectives and pressure groups, with public support and social ends; these too (as public administration is defined above) are part of public administration.

Historically most of the earlier academic studies of the field grew out of the study of public law—the official rules that govern the relations between administrators and the rest of the world. This is and always will be an essential aspect of the study of public administration; public administrators are bound by public law and are engaged in executing it (and in developing and formulating it, too); but public law by itself is insufficient for the analysis of public administration. Indeed, at its worst, the identification of the two would be akin to an attempt to arrive at an understanding of the working of the American government merely by reading the text of the Constitution and the statutes.

Other approaches are similarly essential and, in themselves, insufficient. Personnel—the people in government—are crucial to its operation. Since they are products of a society that induces certain norms of behavior, it is important for many purposes to study government as if the people in it were units amenable to aggregation and averaging and to general rather than specific analysis. But the behavior of individual administrators can also be studied, and usefully so, because personality can play a significant role in determining administrative action. In either way, the study of the persons in public administration is both imperative and inconclusive; for the environment that surrounds and conditions administration is only partially explicable in terms of the individuals on the job.

Organization—the specialization and formal assignment of functions—though occasionally, at one extreme, waved aside as irrelevant, is frequently treated as the sole or primary essence of public administration. Some writers seem almost to suggest that a set of organization charts is a fully valid explanation of governmental activity. The need for formal organization of any government is too obvious to require explanation: the fiscal affairs of the United States would hardly survive if every man and woman in the Treasury were merely told to pick up a pencil and pitch in on anything that interested him. And the very structure of a governmental organization can induce effective action or frustration. Yet those, for example, who have observed the abrupt changes in effectiveness of an agency with organization unchanged but with new personnel, or in a changing political environment, can testify that formal organization as such is only one part of public administration.

One of the realities that fulfills or frustrates the purposes of formal structure is informal organization. Within any formal organization there are inevitably informal groups, informal relationships, and work habits; though they lack official sanction, they exist and they are significant. The systematic identification and study of informal organization are fairly recent, and the term itself is relatively new; but identification and study did not create the fact, which is, of course, an inherent accompaniment of formal organization. Without the formal organization the informal vanishes (or, sometimes, in revolutionary eras, crystallizes, is formalized, and supersedes the old); but no formal organization runs entirely by the book without the help of these unwritten and unofficial work habits, groups, and relations.

Procedures are "the book" of organization, and the larger and more widely responsible the organization the greater the need for procedures. A government agency that fails to answer incoming mail in orderly fashion is headed for trouble; yet—and this is a point that specialists in public administration need especially to bear in mind—elaborate arrangements for controlling incoming and outgoing mail will serve no useful end unless the replies make sense.

Finally—and again we are in a field which is sometimes identified as the "whole" of public administration, because it is not in the bailiwick of the lawyers, the economists, *et al.*—the techniques of management become of ever-increasing importance with the increase in scale and complexity of governmental operations. Yet however refined the techniques, there is much they cannot achieve; no time and motion study can hope to evaluate the performance of the Secretary of State.

These are among the primary activities of public administrators that are ordinarily regarded as constituting the proper or basic concern of students of public administration. Conventionally, the other aspect of the public administrator's activities—the definition of his goals, his public and legislative relations, his dealings with pressure groups, and the like—has been regarded as somewhat alien to the study of public administration, has been held to be more properly a branch (or another branch) of political science. Clearly legislatures, pressure groups, and the other elements of society with which public administrators must deal have a life of their own that far transcends the boundaries of public administration as defined above; so, too, the ultimate goals of the administrator are largely set by others—the legislature, for example—so that the goals themselves constitute a field of inquiry that goes beyond public administration. What is essential is the study of the administrator's understanding of his objectives, and of his relations with his political environment; these are of crucial importance, and directly or indirectly they condition all administrative decisions. Like the internal aspects of public administration, they constitute only part of the administrator's problems; but to neglect them is to study public administration in a political vacuum—a realm where public administration does not exist.

TOWARD A SYNTHESIS

In very general terms, it can thus be said that the study of public administration in the past has frequently been approached in two quite different ways, and all too frequently with an assumption that the particular approach that has been adopted is the only approach. On the institutional side, a good many students have tended to pursue specialties like those touched on above as if the sum of the several specialties constituted the whole. Now these are not narrow specialties: their analysis has enlisted the services of all the social sciences; but if they are pursued individually, the many-sided aspects of public administration may be overlooked. On the political side, public administration has frequently been looked on rather as a side line, and sometimes cavalierly dismissed as negligible in comparison with large political movements. Thus in considerable part the study of public administration has tended to be both one-sided and fragmentary.

These tendencies toward narrowness of outlook and over-specialization in the study of public administration have not gone unnoticed or unchallenged. Scholars using a variety of intellectual devices have found it possible to take into account the many-sided character of public administration, while also managing to take advantage of the insights that can be obtained by the methods of analysis developed by specialists. Among the concepts that have been useful in broadening and deepening our understanding of public administration in this way have been the concept of public administration as process, and the concept of public administration as politics. These are two sides of the same coin; their particular usefulness lies in the fact that neither is restrictive and that the application of each leads naturally to the application of the other. The same act may be examined in terms of the process of public administration or in terms of the politics of public administration. Full understanding results from consideration under both heads.

PUBLIC ADMINISTRATION AS PROCESS

Change and movement are functions of all social organisms. Public administration—itself a society of men, operating under man-made laws, fulfilling human needs—is no exception to the rule. Insight into public administration requires an awareness of its dynamic character. A law is passed and an administrator is appointed; an agency is created; grants of authority are made; some people are satisfied, some not. Time passes. Practices are modified. The law is amended. The old agency is abolished; new grants of authority are made, old grants abandoned; new satisfactions and dissatisfactions arise.

This may sound simple; but it is enormously complex. Every verb—"passed," "appointed," "created," "made," "satisfied," "abolished," "abandoned"—is shorthand for a host of choices, decisions, actions of all sorts. "The old agency is abolished"; but its 150 employees do not die. Indeed, in modern administration they may not even change their desks or telephone extensions. The persistent coherence of the old groupings may be a source of strength, or weakness, or both, to the new administrators. It is as true today as when the sayings of Ecclesiastes were collected, that no administrative activity is so novel as to be totally without precedent; and none that persists indefinitely in precisely its original form, function, personnel, and relations.

The concept of public administration as process can thus be as broad as the whole of public administration; but while such an application of "process" can be useful (it is always wise to remember that change is the only constant in government), for present purposes the concept is more manageable if it is applied only to the internal functioning of public administration.

The cases in this volume are centered on the making of decisions. The problem of decision is no monopoly of administrators, public or private; sanity itself may be defined as the capacity for making rational choices. The making of decisions, whether in public or private life, whether in or out of an administrative context, always involves some of the same psychological processes. Most notable, perhaps, is the fact that decision itself is fundamentally a process rather than an act without temporal dimensions. We say, for example, that a particular act is part of a whole course of conduct; that it is a natural outgrowth of a man's early training; that anyone in a certain man's place would have done the same thing; and so forth. Phrases like these, and others that readily come to mind, all indicate that the understanding of a decision requires understanding of what came before as well as of the circumstances of the moment, that many of the decisions of today are in effect the consequences of yesterday's decisions. Indeed, when it is recalled that even a failure to act, deliberate or otherwise, constitutes a decision, the defining and dating of a decision may be no more than the satisfaction of a formal need. Every decision is part of a psychological and social process no matter how separable and definable it seems. Thus decision-making in all circumstances contains recurrent psychological elements: but decisions made in public administration have a special added character of their own. A few of these distinguishing characteristics require brief mention.

One is the primarily institutional character of decisions in public agencies. Each agency represents a specialization of function, and within each agency there is a further specialization. One of the problems of public administrators, therefore (more easily observed in large administrations because they are more formalized and specialized), is how to bring to bear on a decision all the relevant intellectual resources in or available to the agency. This indeed is one of the chief functions of a normal institutional practice like clearance, which is a cross-checking with various specialists; and of the basic structural device of hierarchy, which in this respect is a mechanism that permits an examination of a proposed decision from successive and broader perspectives. Only by understanding these fundamental institutional practices can the observer disentangle final responsibility for decision (legal, moral, political) from responsibility for participation in decision. Even more—only by understanding the process can the observer perceive the significance of responsibility for delegated decisions which the administrator never sees. The responsibility inheres in the process, not in the individual act. The analyst of public administration is thus constantly concerned with the effect of structural or procedural arrangements on administrative decisions, as is the administrator himself. In many public decisions only the technician can penetrate far into the technical substance; the task of administrator and analyst is to scrutinize and evaluate the flow of action.

Another distinctive characteristic of decision in public administration is the interplay between formal and informal processes. The institutional processes noted above are formal—official hierarchy, official procedures—but however great the effect of rank and official assignment of function, the process is also inevitably affected by a variety of matters that find no place in an official chart or manual. Professional groups have unwritten codes that transcend technical limits; dominant personalities are as significant in government as elsewhere; friendly or antagonistic relations color attitudes; the frailties and strengths of man, and even sheer chance, play a part. Thus the administrator operates in an active institutional environment; he is limited and guided in his actions by these circumstances. Yet, save for unforeseeable accident, they are not completely unchangeable. When we use terms like leadership and morale we are referring to the use made of the unofficial, the informal aspects of administration by the executive. But the process of manipulating the informal organization also contains both informal and formal aspects, for the administrator is bound by law and custom, as well as by his own personality, in his handling of his organization.

The analyst is thus confronted with the complex task of taking into account both formal and informal elements in public administration, and the interplay between the two. Only in the most minor and routine decisions, perhaps only in decisions of a purely ministerial character (issuance of a license on receipt of properly filled-out form and requisite fee, for example), are informal organization and procedures entirely irrelevant, and formal organization and procedures are invariably relevant. No matter how "personal" the decision, no matter what lack of clearance or hierarchical consideration, the very ability of the individual to make the decision is in some sense the product of organizational structure and official procedures.

These are the elements that go to make up the concept of public administration as process. Even though the concept be applied only to the internal workings of an administrative organization, it reveals public administration as a complex affair, replete with variables and intangibles. The task of the student in following these internal processes is both arduous and rewarding. He is following in the path of the administrator, but with an important difference. An effective administrator may work largely by intuition and must rely on insight; the student in going over the ground must also use insight, but it will be necessary for him to identify and define the elements that go to make up the process—elements that the administrator may know by feel but be unable to describe. The administrator, however, must act, must make decisions. The student can avoid this ultimate, painful end but he avoids it at his peril. Thorough understanding of public administration is possible only for those who are willing to undergo at least vicariously the pangs of decision.

PUBLIC ADMINISTRATION AS POLITICS

Many, perhaps most, of the insights gained from an understanding of public administration as process are insights that are also applicable to private administration as well. Yet there are differences between these two kinds of administration, the most important of which are derived, of course, from the political environment and purpose of the former.

In the United States, the study of public administration has been, and still is occasionally, confused by an attempt to define public administration in terms of the constitutional separation of powers. This has led to a series of meaningless and misleading generalizations, such as: "Congress creates policy, administrators carry it out," "the good public administrator pays no attention to politics," and so forth. Such artificial divisions (and other parallel ones) were, of course, not exclusively the result of treating public administration as a branch of public law; they were also in part the product of other intellectual currents, an over-simplified concept of a "neutral" civil service, for example. And these awkward conclusions were likewise supported by a parallel line of interpretation applied to business, involving a formal and strict separation of powers between stock holders, directors, and management. But the unreality of this doctrine as a definition of actual corporate behavior has become increasingly obvious, and the appeal to the supposed example of business no longer carries weight when used in an attempt to interpret the nature of public administration.

There were various reasons why the establishment of water-tight compartments for "administration" and "politics" persisted so long. Perhaps the most important is to be found in the ambiguities of the word "politics" itself. Naïvely, but honestly, it has occasionally been assumed, for example, that to admit the political nature of public administration is to abandon faith in a non-partisan civil service. "Politics," "politician," "political" are all slippery words. In the United States all of them tend to be used in a pejorative sense, though the connotation of the phrase "political science," if not universally enlivening, is at least honorable. In this situation the dictionary fails to enlighten.

Without attempting a formal definition, it can be said that the concept of public administration as politics as used here is designed particularly to refer to the administrator's understanding and pursuit of his objectives and his relations with the social environment outside his agency that affects or is capable of affecting its operations. This is obviously a rather special use of the phrase; the administrator also deals with the distribution of power and other political problems within his organization. But in this brief sketch, these matters are treated as part of public administration as process, so that the phrase "public administration as politics" in this particular context is given an essentially external orientation. The two concepts are, of course, complementary, and refer to two aspects of the same basic process.

It is in its political character that public administration tends to differ most decisively from private administration, and to vary most notably from one country, or even one jurisdiction within a country, to another. These differences are perhaps matters of degree not kind. All business is sensitive to a sort of constituency —its customers and prospective customers—and many businesses show an increasing tendency to give conscious thought to trade union, public, and governmental relations. Adaptations of this character are political in the sense in which the term is used here. Nevertheless, public administrators as a group are far more deeply affected than private administrators in making decisions by large, complex, often vaguely defined, social objectives and by the need for adjusting effectively to a highly complex environment composed of many forces, frequently conflicting—individuals, private associations, and the government itself.

A moment's reflection will show that variations in the tasks of public administrators are greatest in this area of external relations and final goals. While the British civil servant cannot be insensitive to public needs and desires, his formal line of responsibility is comparatively simple and direct, and his immediate relations with the outer world carefully defined. How different the problem of the administrator in our own national government. The Constitution, our customs and traditions, the size and complexity of our land and our society, produce cumulatively centrifugal pressures. Every executive agency, and many of its top administrators, have responsibilities to or toward the President, to a variety of control agencies either only partially or not at all under the President's discretionary supervision, ordinarily to at least four congressional committees, to Congress more generally, and to an indeterminate number of individual Congressmen and Senators; to the organized and unorganized constituencies of the agency; to pressure groups, public and private, local and national, powerful or merely persistent; frequently to the courts, and occasionally to a political party.

It is in this atmosphere that the administrator makes his decisions. It is perhaps arguable that all this is not as it should be, that while the administrator should be sensitive to public needs and desires, his direct line of responsibility should be reasonably clear and simple and he should be fairly free from the direct impact of the organized forces of American society. But that is another question. The individual administrator can do very little about changing the rules of the game; his task is to carry on his job under the rules as they exist, and the rules require him to deal with the forces that seek to deal with him.

Purely for purposes of discussion, it may be useful to distinguish two aspects of the administrator's adjustment to his political environment: the problem of survival and the problem of values. The problem of survival is omnipresent, though in fact the word "survival" tends to over-dramatize what occurs. In theory, an administrator who fails politically by antagonizing powerful groups may live to see the legislature repeal the law and thereby prevent the fulfillment of the public function he has been endeavoring to execute; but in practice this painful denouement, or even the anticipation of this painful denouement, is rare. Survival with disabilities is more usual. The administrator's job may be at stake—in some positions the job-holder may not even expect to be able to hold on very long—or some modification of the program (or curtailment of funds) may be involved, or both; on occasion the danger may lie in the possibility of transfer of function to another agency. And all these possible threats to what may be loosely called survival may come from a legislature such as Congress, for instance, or from an administrative superior such as the President, frequently acting on pressure from the general public or some specialized public.

Administrator, agency, program—all are subject to attack. But the reader should note that to phrase the question of survival in this way tends to assume the virtue of the administrator. For obvious reasons, most administrators normally assume their own virtue; but here the student must go his own way; for him, the virtue of the administrator cannot be assumed; it must be examined and evaluated.

Sometimes administrative survival is undermined by acts that clearly do the administrator no credit. There is no virtue in endangering person, agency, or program by clumsiness or tactlessness; there is no virtue (save perhaps for some special cases where the executive fulfills inescapable constitutional responsibilities in a way that incurs legislative disfavor) in cleaving to a policy that lacks any formal legislative sanction and meets with explicit legislative repugnance. But the usual case in this country is much harder: explicit legislative sanction and actual legislative repugnance—a law still on the books, but active objection to its energetic enforcement. What should the administrator do under such circumstances? (Throughout this discussion, opposition between administrator and superior can be substituted for the legislative-executive antithesis.)

No formula can provide the right answer to questions like this. Analysis and answer must follow two paths—tactics and values. Living with chief executive, legislature, pressure groups, and other elements in the political environment is a constant challenge to the administrator's tactical skill, and the components of that skill—timing, public relations, ability to mobilize friends, and the rest—are subject to analysis and evaluation.

The other aspect of survival—values—is also basic to the whole concept. For politics involves ethics and benefits and power; it is the resolution of the contending forces in society. In this light we see the administrator as an agent of society making choices that affect the well-being of society. With the increasing scope of government activity, the range of administrative discretion is enormously broadened. Pre-determined answers become increasingly less appropriate, and self-explanatory and self-executing standards more and more elusive. The administrator must rely on his own system of values—his feeling for what is right—his judgment of what to emphasize, or what to play down—his sense of justice and fair play. The fundamental safeguard against an administrator's arbitrary and unethical conduct is the fact that public administration, especially in a democracy, circumscribes the range of values which the administrator can observe. For the making of value judgments by the administrator is part and parcel of the whole system; every act of political response that can be weighed in terms of its significance for survival has value connotations as well. In our society and particularly in our national government, it is doubtful that any administrator can long survive, no matter how adroit a manipulator, if his decisions reflect values that are sharply at variance with the general standards of society or the goals which society seeks.

The consideration of values in administrative behavior is thus no mere academic exercise. Students of public administration must be concerned with values. They are observers and they should be capable of dispassionate observation; but ultimate neutrality with respect to administrative decisions is self-defeating. A lack of concern for the values of public administration is indicative of a lack of sensitivity; and an insensitive observer can never attain to more than a limited insight.

THE ANALYSIS OF PUBLIC ADMINISTRATION

In the preceding pages, the reader has been given a brief indication of two ways of looking at public administration—as process and as politics. For the sake of simplicity, the two have been treated as if they dealt with separable matters: the internal functioning of public administration and its external goals and relations. This distinction is useful for purposes of explanation, but it has limited validity. The decision to assign a new function to a particular agency is on the surface an internal governmental matter; but different assignments can lead to strikingly different functional and political consequences. Nor, on the other side, can an administrator operate in his political environment without affecting the internal operations of his agency. Important decisions by public administrators characteristically can, and should, be analyzed simultaneously in terms of both process and politics.

Concepts like process and politics when used in the study of public administration do not lead to the formulation of rules and principles that can provide the administrator with automatic guides to the right answer and permit the student to grade administrative decisions on some mathematical scale. Rather their function is to suggest the kinds of questions that can usefully be asked and the kind that are self-defeating. By encouraging a search for the multitudinous factors that may enter into administrative decisions, and the multitudinous consequences that flow from them, they tend to preclude simple answers to complex questions. We can have no effective understanding of public administration unless we keep in mind the wide range of considerations that are relevant to the administrator's behavior.

This range of considerations is indeed very wide. The student will even find it necessary at times to concern himself with considerations that the administrator did not or could not take into account. The student's use of such considerations must be handled carefully. The student may observe, for example, that a thoroughly informed decision on a particular matter may not be possible in advance of the receipt of certain census data; but if the administrator is compelled by some legal or other overriding requirement to act sooner, criticism of the decision because of the failure to use the data is beside the point (though criticism of the requirement may be valid). Thus, for any decision, the appropriate considerations are not necessarily those one would like to apply in the abstract. The very fact that the administrator must apportion his time means that the amount of personal attention he can devote to questions will vary from one problem to another. We oversimplify if we make the assumption that all problems can receive equally careful thought.

Thus the student of public administration must ask not only many different questions, but many different kinds of questions. He can, for example, usefully ask the kinds of questions that the philosophers would have asked—Plato, Aristotle, Hobbes, Bentham, Dewey, for example—and analyze decisions by casuistic or utilitarian or idealistic or other modes of inquiry:[1] was the decision conformable to the accepted rules and precedents? were the consequences of different alternatives duly weighed? was the decision based on some abstract principle of good conduct?

It is evident that ethical inquiries of this kind are intimately related to the modes of analysis that have been suggested earlier. The application of public law to a problem of decision is a form of casuistry; the utilitarian inquiry may relate to both survival and values; the appeal to an abstract ideal is one way of making, and justifying, a value judgment.

The different social sciences and disciplines make available another group of methods for the analysis of public administration. A lawyer may analyze a variety of illuminating matters, such as the powers and responsibilities of the administrator, of the chief executive, of the legislature. A social psychologist may explore the causes of public response to administrative action. A historian can reveal similarities and contrasts with events of the past. An economist may estimate the economic consequences of alternative administrative decisions. Others can express informed judgments on the effect of decisions by our government on friend and foe abroad. The relation of a particular decision to party structure in Congress can frequently be observed and occasionally predicted.

All these considerations, and a host of others, are clearly relevant to the problem of the administrator and to the problem of the student of administration. Yet to balance these considerations wisely is ultimately as much a question of values as of technical knowledge. No scientist as such can give the reader a precise definition of a phrase like "civilian control of the military" or construct a scale on which this element is given a specific rating to be compared with "efficiency" or some other element. A considered judgment on "civilian control" requires knowledge, but knowledge does not constitute the judgment.

The administrator and the student are thus on their own in the final step of making and evaluating administrative decisions. They can, by experience or study or both, become competent judges of trends set in motion by organizational structure and procedure; they may acquire a more than superficial insight into the reactions of men and the part played in those reactions by intellectual and social backgrounds; they may acquire skill in observing and predicting world or domestic mass political reactions. Without insights of this character, and without knowledge thus acquired, sound judgment will be no more than an accident. But sound judgment in this field does not include the ability to make absolute (or quasi-absolute) predictions such as are made in the physical sciences, nor to propound absolute standards for administrative decisions. Thus there are obvious limits on what can be learned.

Within these limits, characteristic of all the social sciences, the study of public administration remains fruitful for both student and administrator. For the administrator, a recognition of the recurrent elements in the different problems that he faces makes it easier for him to distinguish what is novel in each new situation, concentrate on the novel element, and find a suitable solution; this kind of knowledge is obtainable by the study of public administration. So, too, as has been suggested above, is an awareness of the essential interrelationship of politics and process. If substantive decisions, as they are called—i.e., decisions on program—are arrived at by wise and informed use of the resources of administration and by intelligent appreciation of the political environment, they are far more likely to be sound than if they are arrived at in hit-or-miss or doctrinaire fashion. A realization of the nature of public administration leads to a clarification of objectives and to a more sophisticated approach to those objectives in the midst of the pressures generated by society.

For both professional students and lay citizens who seek to understand why government officials behave as they do and to learn how to judge their decisions, the same general conclusions apply. In our society, characteristically, we complain about our government, we question its very justification for being; we match it against an ideal. We look to govern-

[1] In a forthcoming study by Dean Wayne A. R. Leys of Roosevelt College, *Ethics for Policy Decisions*, two of the case studies in this volume are made the subject of analysis by ethical techniques of inquiry.

ment officials for qualities that we do not forcefully demand of others, including those with whom the government does important business. The private citizen in his dealings with government is held responsible only for common honesty (whatever other qualities may be desirable); but to the humblest administrator we look for some breadth of consideration, some penetration in analysis, some concern for the future. We cannot sensibly ask that public administrators be prophets or saints or geniuses; we can and do ask that they use foresight and decency and intelligence in reaching their decisions.

PUBLIC ADMINISTRATION AND THE SOCIAL SCIENCES

Public administration occupies a rather special area in the social science field. It is an area of interest to many different specialists: political scientists, sociologists, psychologists, social psychologists, anthropologists, economists, lawyers, and historians. The striking enlargement of perspective which has characterized the study in recent years has largely come about from the impact of those who did not specialize in the study itself. This is cause for rejoicing rather than complaint, since each of these approaches has helped to deepen our understanding of the field. It is no rejection of these insights to say that there is a continued need for the study of public administration as such, the kind of study, for example, represented by the cases in this volume.

The phenomena of public administration apparently invite investigation by social scientists of all sorts. Interaction between the various disciplines and public administration is therefore particularly intense. Nevertheless, the modes of interaction are not peculiar to the field. Fundamentally, there are two ways in which the social sciences interact regardless of the particular subject matter. One consists of the direct application of the techniques developed in one of the branches to another. There are methods, for example, by which sociologists analyze and interpret social phenomena that can be applied to governmental activities. Sociologists have themselves applied their techniques to government in this way, as have students of public administration and political scientists who have learned sociological techniques. As has been said, this is all to the good: and an appropriate sense of competition among variously trained investigators will continue to result in deeper understanding and new insights.

There is, however, another form of interaction among the social sciences more subtle, more pervasive, more important in the long run than direct borrowings and formal interdisciplinary action. It is the form of interaction reflected in this Introduction—that general process of cultural absorption, which political scientists, like other people, undergo. It is hard to believe, for example, that any political scientist today observes and interprets the behavior of administrators exactly as he would have before the advent of Darwin, and Freud, and Sir James G. Frazer, and Keynes, even if he has not read a word that any of them has written. For they are among the men and women who have changed our whole way of looking at the world and society, and their ideas have helped to create the great gulf that lies between us and the eighteenth century, and even the nineteenth century. The cases in this book, no matter at what remove, bear a decisive imprint of the social studies of the past hundred years.

The identification of the nature of these changes in outlook is a task for the historian of ideas; but the student of public administration is concerned with the problem because our governmental institutions were in such large part crystallized in the eighteenth century. He must constantly bear in mind that it is usually his task to pour new wine into old bottles without spoiling the wine or breaking the bottles.

II. CASE METHOD AND THE ANALYSIS OF PUBLIC ADMINISTRATION

There are many techniques for analyzing public administration, and the concepts of public administration outlined in the preceding Part of this Introduction permit and even invite the use of many different analytic tools, of which the case method is only one. Furthermore, the particular case method used in this book is only one of several kinds of "case method," for the term has broad significance. Certain kinds of public administration cases, however useful, would not serve to develop the sort of understanding that is the objective of this book. The cases printed here represent a particular adaptation of the case method designed to illuminate both the internal process of public administration and its external political goals and environment. The discussion of methodology that follows is therefore intimately related to the discussion of theory that has gone before.

THE CASE METHOD

The word "case" and all the common phrases in which it is found—case report, case history, case study, case method—have a wide variety of meanings.[2] Common ground exists primarily in the inherent intellectual approach: examination of particulars prior to or as a part of generalization. However different the meaning of the word "case" to doctors and lawyers, the teaching and study of both law and medicine in the United States, each of which is so largely concerned with the examination of a large number of specific "cases," are examples of the same kind of pedagogy, and there are similarities in the practice of the two professions as well. The great contribution to medicine of Oliver Wendell Holmes the elder came as the result of, or at least in connection with his observation of repeated instances of post-natal illness. The contribution to law of Holmes the younger is found in his opinions and dissents in particular law cases. In each instance the fruitful generalization or the critical re-examination of an authoritative "principle" or "rule" arose in connection with the prior examination of the particular; naturally, neither the elder nor the younger Holmes approached his problem with a blank mind, but the precipitant was the concrete case.

Cases to the doctor and the social worker are part of the day's work. The case history (i.e., of a patient, a set of symptoms, the difficulties of a family group, and so forth) is primarily a working tool, which serves such very practical ends as ensuring continuity of treatment and facilitating diagnosis in the light of development rather than judgment from isolated symptoms. As such, it is a direct product of the state of the art and the training and ability of the particular doctor or social worker; how many doctors in 1900 would have noted down symptoms of psychic tension as relevant in describing a case of hay fever? To a large extent, medical case histories even in the developed form of articles are not expected to have more than illustrative value, and in text books they may well be included quite frankly as mere illustrations. As such they have a valid place in professional education: a medical student may be helped to recognize that a patient is suffering from yaws by virtue of having read a case description of the disease. But cases begin to "prove" something only when a whole series of cases can be made to yield useful statistical conclusions, or when (in medicine) a

[2] See, for example, a useful discussion of the significance of "case" in Anderson and Gaus, *Research in Public Administration* (Chicago, 1945) (Part 1, Anderson), pp. 48-52; see also footnote 5, below. Another helpful discussion of the use of the case method in research, in teaching, and in professional practice will be found in a recent article: Henry Reining, Jr., "Case Method and Public Personnel Administration," *Public Personnel Review XII* (July 1951), pp. 151-158; in this article Professor Reining discusses many of the problems treated in this Introduction.

single careful case study describes a series of experiments in a highly controlled environment where specific cause and specific effect can be isolated.

Law cases represent something quite different. As official authoritative decisions, they can, in the full sense of the word, be collected. Each judicial decision constitutes an act rather than a description. Each one constitutes the application of one or more formal generalizations to a set of facts available for observation under the rules of a rather rigid and highly conventionalized procedure. The task of the researcher is to discover "what" the judge decided, and to generalize on trends in decisions, i.e., to generalize on the habits of judges in applying or formulating generalized rules or principles of decision. Predictability is limited in the field of law because judicial personality bulks large and social trends are important. And the use of cases by lawyers is conditioned, again and again, by their responsibility for serving as advocates.

Still another form of case may be mentioned —the cases prepared by the Harvard Graduate School of Business Administration. These represent neither authoritative decisions nor accounts of what the case writer did or noted in the course of practicing his profession. The case writer is observer and historian, not a responsible participant in action. The cases are generally cast in narrative form, and tell of problems faced by businessmen: the focus is on decision. Over the years, a tremendous number of cases have been prepared under Business School auspices. No simple generalization about their character is possible, because the cases vary widely in both subject matter and technique. And the case reservoir is drawn on by many different teachers and for many different pedagogic objectives. Perhaps the most common denominator in the cases is the introduction of a problem of decision in a specified human environment and the most general objective is the training of students in making decisions in the kind of disorderly human situation that exists in the business world and is reproduced, as well as may be, in the case.

Some of these cases deal with major formal business decisions like plant location; here the student is generally expected to evaluate the substance of the decision. Other cases are more concerned with decision processes; and a considerable group of these center on problems of decision (frequently of a subdued, informal character) in small intimate groups. Cases of the latter type may include some scenes in vivid detail, with whole conversations quoted verbatim and in full (presumably these are written up after the event from recollection or notes); but in these cases the detail is generally limited to moments of personal contact, or selected letters, and is generally not supplied for a larger institutional background or movement. The Harvard Business School cases exist solely for teaching: unlike the medical, legal, and social work cases, questions of form and content are determined exclusively on pedagogic and analytic grounds; there are no operative rules of the game to be applied.

With the Business School cases we move closer to the cases in this volume. Both types deal with decisions made in an institutional context. The case is used to show the kind of problem in its particular institutional context and is designed to evoke a discussion of solutions that are possible, likely, and appropriate in that particular institutional (and political) environment.

THE USES OF PUBLIC ADMINISTRATION CASES

Like the business cases, but unlike the medical and legal cases, the cases in this volume are not a product or direct by-product of operating practice. They are written to serve educational ends. Several specific ends may be noted, in addition to whatever general pedagogic benefits can be gained by the use of material that requires the student to solve complex problems and make decisions.

The first is the development of an attitude toward public administration that has room for both dispassionate analysis and critical judgment. A most painful problem of public enlightenment in a democracy is to secure understanding of the fact that quick and easy answers to the government's problems are frequently more appealing than wise. A more intimate acquaintance with the laborious processes by which public decisions are made should, one hopes, lead to more balanced judgments on what governments do. What administrators say (and do) and what their friends or enemies say (and do) is more often designed to accomplish specific ends than to educate. But the intelligent interpretation of such sayings and doings is not feasible without an understanding of the processes of public administration of which they are end-products or by-products; the cases, by providing an opportunity for vicarious governmental experience, are designed to develop intelligent interpretation of governmental decisions and, more generally, of governmental behavior.

A second major function of the cases is to provide, as much as possible, a common ground on which to explore conflicting conclusions on administrative behavior in public organizations. An example may be helpful.

During and since the war there have been inconclusive debates on the merits of organizational devices like the Office of War Mobilization and the War Production Board used in the United States government for co-ordination of wartime economic mobilization. The debates are inconclusive for two reasons: partly because the debaters differ in the values they seek to affirm, partly because the knowledge each relies on is not, as they think, shared; each is actually relying on a different segment of knowledge (perhaps correct, perhaps incorrect) that he takes as the whole.

There is no device that provides a final cure for this latter difficulty; but the differences of view that arise from differences in understanding of what happened are reduced if the debaters can take a written case dealing with the Office of War Mobilization and the War Production Board and argue their generalizations on the basis of the text. There is still ample room for argument about the accuracy and completeness of the account and for divergent interpretations (as students and teachers can see in the classroom), but the chances of finding some area of common understanding are greater when the debaters can work from a rather full written account available to both.

A third, related goal may be identified as providing the means for suggesting and testing generalizations about behavior in public organizations. To revert to the example of co-ordination mentioned above: In reading one of the cases, a reader may note some of the operating difficulties encountered by a particular agency, say WPB, in attempting to co-ordinate the work of other agencies; he may note in the text certain structural and functional characteristics of WPB that appear to the author to have some relation to the operating problems. He begins to wonder if there is a causal relationship, if the same combination of structural and functional characteristics always produces the same results, or sets in motion the same tendencies. He may reject any specific suggestion of the author, but he is encouraged to provide an explanation of his own. In other words, in thinking about the events described in the case, the reader has begun to generalize. Further questioning and generalization may follow: for having reached a generalization about a causal relationship, albeit highly tentative, the next step for the reader is to consider whether the effects are controllable or not, or desirable or undesirable, and so forth. The reader does not (or should not) stop with the factual generalization because the effects he observes are not a matter of indifference; the functioning of government has inevitable social consequences, and for these the social scientist should have concern.

GENERALIZATION IN PUBLIC ADMINISTRATION

Generalizing is thus a constant process in the studying of public administration, and one of the objects of the cases is the encouragement of this process. But the limits and uses of generalization in this area of the social sciences deserve further examination.

Generalization in all branches of knowledge exhibits certain common characteristics: formulation of hypotheses from experience; the development of hypotheses into partial or, eventually, complete hypothetical systems; the testing of hypotheses by checking empirically on deductions drawn from them. But this kind of formulation conceals as much as it reveals; "hypothesis," "hypothetical system," "testing," "deduction" are not simple or unambiguous words. There are elements of identity in the mental process of chemist and psychologist; but what can properly be accepted as a "hypothesis" or "deduction" by one would be rejected by the other. To clarify the nature of the process in public administration (and elsewhere in the social sciences), it may be useful to begin with a brief look at the process in the physical sciences.

The General Theory of Relativity is one of the generalizations of the physical sciences. It constitutes, or is part of, an inclusive hypothetical system that is internally complete and logically consistent. The deductions that can be, and have been, made from it are expressible in mathematical terms of (to the layman) fantastic precision. These deductions are so definite and so precise that they made possible nuclear fission. Or, to take another example, again referred to in a layman's simplified terms, Mendelyeev's Periodic Table of the Elements: by deduction from this generalization, chemists predicted, correctly and precisely, the existence of certain then unknown elements, and their physical properties.

All this is a far cry from the work of the social scientist. His generalizations cannot be formed into a complete logically consistent system. His predictions usually cannot be expressed in mathematical terms, and if so formulated, are seldom absolutely certain and never absolutely precise, as the astronomer or physicist would define "precise." He must constantly qualify his statements by such phrases as "other things being equal," or "this will create a tendency toward," or "unless . . ." These are striking differences, whatever the identity in the mental processes of the different scientists.

The primary difference seems to be a question of manageable variables. At least to the layman it appears that the problems of physical science can be so isolated for practical purposes that all the relevant variables can be determined with precision. In dealing with the materials of the social sciences, the problems are so infinitely more complex that all the relevant variables cannot be effectively isolated or precisely determined. In consequence, generalization for the student of public administration is far less definitive than for the student of physics or chemistry.

There is a further important respect in which generalization differs in the two kinds of science. The facts of the physical scientists' world are essentially neutral and unaffected by criticism: no wars will be waged, no hearts broken over the digits set down when the value of π is determined to another hundred places past the decimal point; nor do the physical properties of uranium change when an article is written about them. But the facts with which the social scientist deals are in themselves loaded with values, and susceptible of reaction. Anyone who understands the term "Gross National Product" knows that its figures have immediate personal significance for him. The "facts" of legislative or administrative behavior can relieve or torture the mind; and publication of the "facts" may change the behavior. Mathematicians and physicists determined that the atomic bomb could be made; statesmen determined that it should be made and used. It is with decisions of statesmen that public administration is concerned.

Generalization in public administration must be understood and carried forward in these terms. As has been suggested earlier, generalization in this field is not to be judged solely as a tool for uncertain and imprecise predictions, however useful these qualified predictions may be. It also has other functions to serve. Material like these case studies can help, for example, to prevent what Santayana had in mind when he said: "Those who cannot remember the past are condemned to repeat it."

But students of public administration have attempted to push generalization even further —to raise generalization to the level of principles that constitute absolute rules of conduct. It has been said, for example, that no administrator should have more than six subordinates reporting to him. Overlooking the ambiguity of the word "reporting," one can hope that the principle is false because it is so clearly unattainable in any complex government. This "principle" seems to be based on the assumption that administration is a closed system in which all the administrator's time is used up within the institution and none devoted to external relations, and on the further assumption that all subordinates of an administrator have identical relations with each other and identical relations with the administrator. This is not the world of public administration outlined above in Part I nor, for that matter, is it the world of public administration that will be found in the cases. Perhaps it should be added that this principle of the Span of Control, as it is called, has real utility, if, but only if, it is not treated as an absolute rule subject to mathematical formulation.

The generalizations appropriate to the theoretical approach outlined above, and appropriate therefore to the cases in this volume, are much less absolute in character. They are both tentative and complex. They deal with tendencies and with values. Generalization is possible for both the internal stresses of the administrative process and for the strains of the political environment; but significant generalization about either possesses full validity only in the context supplied by the other.

The same conclusion is, of course, applicable to generalization in connection with the public administration cases in this volume. The critical point for the reader to bear in mind is that the cases (taken as a succession of events) do not convey a moral in themselves; each generalization derived from the cases represents the author speaking or the reader making a judgment. For the most part, the authors have refrained from stating conclusions, especially definitive conclusions, but they have attempted to point up the kinds of issues where (in their judgment) the effort to generalize will be fruitful. Unquestionably the reader is guided; but he is not coerced and certainly not deliberately pushed toward one specific judgment. If the cases are successful, readers will constantly check their previous generalizations, and will use the materials to improve their ability to observe and evaluate tendencies and consequences, and to make informed judgments; they will not arrive at a set of uniform judgments.

The kinds of judgments that are appropriate to these case materials are those that have been suggested above as appropriate to the study of public administration in general. Certainly they will not take the form of specific, fixed remedies for specific administrative ailments. There are ailments that are so purely technical in character in a particular administrative environment that precise technical cures can be specified; it is not in derogation of techniques that such problems and such solutions are absent from the cases. These cases deal with public administration more broadly construed. In this larger world, it is true that public administrators can be more effective than they are today, but they do not need, nor can the cases supply, pat formulae for their ills.

The cases will not serve as a trade manual; but this very limitation enlarges their sphere of relevance. They can deal with decisions in the traditional restricted technical world of public administration; they can also deal with decisions as part of the larger universes of process and politics. They can treat of decisions on program problems.

Cases can be used to describe the making of budgetary decisions, for example, or personnel decisions: What was the process by which the estimates of the Welfare Department were cut 10 per cent—who participated in the decision, what were the institutional surroundings, how did the attitudes of legislature, newspapers, and the general public enter in? But equally, and these subjects are also within the field of public administration, cases can be used to tell of program decisions. To sell or not to sell some government-owned tankers to applicants from other countries raises a variety of questions in foreign policy, in domestic economic policy, in military policy; it is a proper subject for study by diplomats, admirals, and economists, and by students of diplomacy, naval affairs, and economics. But it is also a problem in public administration. The making, unmaking, and remaking of this decision (it is described in one of the cases) was in fact constantly and overwhelmingly conditioned by the processes and politics that enter into the composition of public administration.

CASE COLLECTIONS: PROBLEMS OF COMPREHENSIVENESS AND CATEGORICAL ANALYSIS

The preceding section, dealing with the nature and limits of generalizations in public administration generally and in the cases in particular, is designed to be helpful in indicating what educational function a public administration case study, of the kind included in this book, can fulfill. The present section, dealing with related problems, will, it is hoped, cast some light on the uses and limitations of a collection of such cases.

It has been said above that under a broad concept of public administration, cases can deal with the whole broad range of decisions that administrators must make and not merely with those decisions that bear on the internal functioning of administration. But to say that all the activities of administrators are open for examination by cases is not the equivalent of saying that a sizable collection of cases, like the present one, has "comprehensive coverage."

Comprehensiveness is actually a highly elusive concept except where, as in the physical sciences, generalization can take the form of a self-contained logical system. For reasons that have already been suggested, in public administration such a system is beyond our grasp now and in any proximately foreseeable future. Indeed, the more rigorously defined and more logically complete the analytic device used in the study of public administration, the more the reader is left with a sense of incompleteness; for rigorous definition and logical completeness in analysis can be achieved only by the exclusion of a tremendous number of recognizable variables in a human situation—variables that are relevant for many other purposes. This is not a reflection on the utility of rigorous analysis in the social sciences, but an indication of the infinite gulf that separates any highly systematic set of insights from a theory of public administration that would place within an orderly scheme all the phenomena of governmental action.

There is thus no readymade framework to test the comprehensiveness of a collection of cases. It is obvious on the slightest reflection that neither this nor any other collection can possibly describe all decisions made even in any one government, nor all kinds of governmental decisions. Any collection of studies of governmental decisions can never hope to be more than a minute, an infinitesimal sample of the whole. Neither this collection, nor any other can represent more than an introduction to the field; and the adoption of a broadly comprehensive definition of public administration makes any sample proportionately small. While there is a value in having a case collection that does represent a varied sample (as is explained below), comprehensiveness in any formal sense is not and cannot be the objective of the collection.

There remains the further question of the relation of the collection of cases to the illumination of a set of categories. This is what legal case books seek to achieve. But law is a highly conventionalized discipline and its subject matter lends itself to categorization. Indeed, legal codification—the establishment of organized categories for the elements of formal law—is a highly developed art. In comparison with the law, public administration is a field in which every man is his own codifier and categorizer, and the categories adopted must be looked on as relatively evanescent.

Most books on public administration published in this country—textbooks in particular—deal with public administration in the United States, and only in minor degree with administration in other countries. Even limited in this fashion, there is always a striking selectivity in the materials presented and a lack of coherence in the categorical organization of the materials. Thus "Fiscal Management"—one of the old and respected categories—may bulk large in some volumes and disappear completely in others; "Identification and Morale" is a significant heading in one instance, non-existent elsewhere. And the same work that contains a chapter on "Administrative Responsibility" will also contain a chapter on "Personnel Classification"—although the two subjects represent quite different kinds of aspects of public administration; indeed they are not mutually exclusive and they are derived from two different types of idea-systems.

A collection of cases, like this book, is no more susceptible of analysis by a complete and logical system of categories than any other book on public administration. Superficially it is even less unified and coherent, for example, than the traditional textbook. Each case opens up a variety of aspects of a decision; each, therefore, can be looked on as a universe in itself; each one is subject to various forms of categorical analysis. The formal organization of the book (Part and Section headings) suggests the applicability of certain broad categories; and the topical index constitutes a kind of categorical cross-analysis of all the cases. But the categories themselves cannot be neatly classified, and alternative categories could be easily suggested. The listed categories should be looked on as a convenience for the reader; they are not comprehensive, and they cannot be organized into a formal, comprehensive, logical system.

In sum, therefore, this is a collection of cases that offers an incorrigible resistance to any highly systematic categorization. This may seem disconcerting, but it is not without its advantages. The more neatly the materials of history are cut to a particular predetermined pattern, the more sharply defined and therefore limited the uses that can be made of the account. For it is a significant phenomenon of the social sciences generally that an account based on careful observation unconfined by the limitations of a rigorously defined thesis can be fruitfully re-examined by successive readers using different methods of analysis, and coming to different kinds of conclusions. A justification for proposing any set of categories like the formal organization of this book (some alternative sets are outlined in Part IV below) is perhaps suggested indirectly in a remark made by I. A. Richards in his Introduction to the Pocket Books edition of Roget's *Thesaurus:* "But we need not take Roget's actual categories too seriously. To criticize them would be to bring up all the hardest problems there are. They serve their purpose—which is to remind us of all that we know about words."

A collection of cases like the present one, where each case has many facets of potential interest, has a cumulative value. Each attentive reader will find different threads of interrelationship among the cases. The cases act as a corrective severally, and even more collectively, for premature and cock-sure generalization. Cumulatively they tend to induce the kinds of attitudes which were suggested above as appropriate for the student of public administration. If an individual case helps to induce a critical and tolerant attitude in analyzing administrative problems and solutions, a collection of cases is a more effective training ground for the development of such attitudes. If the individual case suggests the need for awareness of the complexity and delicacy of the considerations that affect and underlie administrative decisions, a collection of cases drives the point home inescapably. If the individual case invites cautious generalization and provides touchstones against which to test prior speculation and hypothesis, the case collection opens up a far larger opportunity for such discipline. No one is equally at home with all the decision processes in which public administrators are involved; but it is useful for the student, whether for professional ends or as citizen, to become sufficiently immersed in the multifarious aspects of the public administrative process so that an awareness of its richness and variety becomes second nature.

III. THE TECHNIQUE OF THE CASE STUDIES

PUBLIC ADMINISTRATION CASE STUDIES—DEFINITION AND DESCRIPTION

The following definition of "public administration cases" refers specifically to the cases in this volume and to other cases prepared under the auspices of the Inter-University Case Program and its predecessor, the Committee on Public Administration Cases. In Part V of this Introduction the reader will find mention of other kinds of public administration cases to which this definition would apply only partially or not at all; and he will also note that some of the cases in this volume do not conform in all respects to the definition given here. What follows should be read with these qualifications in mind.

A public administration case (in terms of this reference) is a narrative of the events that constitute or lead to a decision or group of related decisions by a public administrator or group of public administrators.[3] Some account is given of the personal, legal, institutional, political, economic, and other factors that surrounded the process of decision, but there is no attempt to assert absolute causal relationships. Psychological speculation is avoided, though repetitive patterns of behavior are cited, and interpretations of personality by other participants in the action are quoted or summarized. The studies contain much detail and an effort is made in the composition, by a variety of rhetorical devices, to give the reader a feeling of actual participation in the action. While background and aftermath may be briefly summarized, the main detailed account is confined to a restricted time period. Emphasis throughout is on decision, whether taken as act or process, and exploration is made of rejected and hypothetical alternatives. The decision problems selected for treatment involve policy rather than technical issues.

In general, aside from a few autobiographical accounts, the cases are written from the perspective of the detached observer, but with an attempt to focus on the activities of a single person or group, or two groups in process of interaction, in each section of the narrative, even though the focus may shift several or many times during the course of the whole case. Aside from summary statements of customary administrative practice and the occasional insertion of aids to textual interpretation, formal editorializing is limited almost entirely to a pointing up of significant issues and a raising of questions about them, though of course the whole process of selection and emphasis is editorial in character.

A formal definition and description such as the one just given is addressed primarily to "what?"; it leaves vague the "how?" and the "why?" A full rationale of the methodology even of this single specialized form of applied research—the public administration case study —would be extremely complex. The following discussion treats only a few of the major elements in such a rationale, but the approach toward these is indicative of the approach toward the whole.[4]

CASE PERSPECTIVE AND FOCUS

The perspective in most of these cases, as has been noted, is that of the somewhat detached observer, viewing simultaneously and successively the actions of the chief participants, though not in all instances with equal attention to each one—the role of some, on occasion, being seen only through the eyes of other participants.

The detachment (in the sense of objectivity) is conscious, not that the author is indifferent to the actions he describes, but rather that he has made a deliberate attempt to tell the story in such fashion that the reader can be aware of the different values of the different participants and perhaps of the author as well. This is not the equivalent of a revelation of all possible types of values; but it permits the reader wide discretion in making up his mind on what "really" happened, and on the significance of the happenings.

The device of using a multiple perspective helps to secure the effect of detachment because each participant has a chance, so to speak, to have his side of the story put forward. As a by-product, the reader is likely to feel that he knows the "whole story"; but this feeling is at bottom illusory. He knows only those pieces of the "whole story" that came to the author's attention and seemed important, and he knows these only as they are reconstituted by the author's mind and only to the degree that the author's language creates in his own mind a common understanding with the author.

These are the inherent limitations of all historical writing and more generally of writ-

[3] See above, pp. x-xi, for a definition of the area of activity meant in this context by "public administration."

[4] Some of the methodological problems also raise questions for the teacher; these are discussed below in Part IV. A discussion of the methodology from the practical rather than the theoretical standpoint, and from a specialized rather than a generalized perspective will be found in an article by the author of this Introduction: "The Preparation of Case Studies; the Problem of Abundance," *APSR*, XLV (1951), pp. 479-487.

ten communication and need not be a matter of special concern. Though the cases do not represent "absolute" truth, they do supply the kind of historical material that represents a sufficiently practical re-creation of reality to make analysis and discussion useful and meaningful to practitioners as well as students.

The foregoing comments refer to the bulk of the cases in the volume. In a few, only one perspective is fully elaborated, and in two cases the treatment is autobiographical. In these two, separate comments supplied by the editor outside the historical text produce somewhat the effect of multiple perspective, for the editor's evaluation differs from the evaluation of the events that is implicit or explicit in the autobiographical account. Here too the reader is encouraged to weigh alternative choices or courses of conduct, and to consider alternative interpretations of the events.

One practical problem referred to above, arising from a multiple-perspective treatment, is the blurring that follows the recasting of the various viewpoints through the mind of the author. The problem is not soluble, but is at least reduced in importance by the practice of limiting the focus and explicitly noting each shift in focus in the successive sections of a case. Henry James preferred to see all the events in a novel through the eyes of a single observer, but even he on occasion, as he explained in the preface to *The Wings of the Dove*, resorted to different observers for different parts of the novel. Alas, historical materials, except where treated in a novelistic manner, do not permit the attainment of James' rigorous perfection—"no sacrifice of the recording consistency"; but the complexity of issues in a complex institutional environment is more manageable for the reader when the focus is made as sharp as possible, even though none of the events is seen exclusively through the eyes of a single person.

Finally, the use of the shifting perspective helps the reader to look at public administration in terms of the concept of process along the lines suggested in Part I above. Seen exclusively through the eyes of a single observer and at close range, decision tends to look like a single act of choice precipitated by a dilemma, while to the gods on high, the dilemma is merely a selected point in the perpetual flux of our world. There are, of course, decisions of high voltage and of low voltage; but any decision of either kind can be taken either from the standpoint of the ultimate choice, or from the standpoint of the total complex of which it is product and part. The device of the multiple perspective encourages awareness of the ramifying effects of administrative action, where a single focus might suggest that the process is simple and one that can be followed as a single stream over a period of time, or understood by observation of a single act.

As a result of the foregoing, there is in these cases perhaps some ambiguity in the treatment of the nature of decision. The observer's eye pauses in observing a process: the problem is analyzed momentarily as if static; there is emphasis on, and analysis of a point of decision, a choice. The eye moves on, and the emphasis shifts to the succession of events in which the point merges into the line. Under either interpretation it is not misleading to speak of decision as central to the cases, but the reader needs to be aware of the rather broad meaning given to the word and the shifting ways of looking at the action. It may be well to note that the cases, perhaps inevitably, vary in treating decision as a complex succession of events or as a single act; but a skillful reader can at least guess at the process of which the act forms a part, and can isolate points in a given process where, for the moment, decision can be looked on as act.

NORMALITY AND REPRESENTATIVENESS IN THE CASES

The terms "representative" and "normal" have many meanings. As used here, "representative" refers to the statistical frequency of occurrence of an event or phenomenon, "normal" to the common psychological reaction to an event or phenomenon. In the field of social science, in this sense, what is "representative" is what occurs frequently in a particular society, what is "normal" is what strikes most people as neither shocking nor highly surprising. To illustrate, in the United States,

polygamy is both unrepresentative and abnormal; its unrepresentativeness could be demonstrated by a count of households, its abnormality by polling the attitudes towards polygamy of a representative sample of Americans. There will presumably be some range of attitudes among citizens of this country, but the range within American society will, of course, be negligible in comparison with the difference between American attitudes and those in a tribe where polygamy is customary practice. Other types of conduct could be cited that are abnormal in a particular society, but not seriously unrepresentative, and vice versa.

In public administration, and in these cases, it is frequently easier to apply the concept of normality than of representativeness, because many of the most significant phenomena of public administration are not susceptible of statistical analysis. On the other hand, there will be little disagreement that peculation, for example, is an abnormality in public administration in this country, as is perjury, or total immersion in publicity or some other personal goal. By contrast, the form of bribery known as "squeeze," uncommon (though never totally absent) in our own Federal government, is customary, and even accepted practice, in other societies, i.e., both representative and normal.

It is the belief of the authors, the editor, and of others who have read and commented on the cases that, with one exception duly noted, they deal with normal happenings. This is the result of a deliberate policy of excluding the abnormal. It is true that a study of the abnormal has its value, occasionally indeed is invaluable, but to present the abnormal to students unacquainted with the normal has its dangers. These dangers can be avoided by adequate editorial explanation, but the ends in view for this volume seemed to be sufficiently attainable without recourse to the rather cumbersome expedient of describing the abnormal and labeling it as such.

The representativeness of the cases is a more puzzling question. The cases do not on the whole, for example, represent the kind of situations in which a junior government employee will find himself in the first few years of his career. They do, however, represent the kind of process involved in the development and execution of public policy in American government in an enormous mass of instances major and minor. For the making of a representative government decision does involve the weighing of both technical and political considerations (using both terms broadly); and decisions are commonly affected by organizational phenomena and informal relationships. In revealing these and other aspects of the complex process by which government decisions are made, the cases are representative.

The cases tend to deal with problems of policy rather than of technique; on this score there may also be some question of their representative character. But the distinction between policy and technique is subtle and variable, and is partly a matter of perspective. A recommendation based on the strategic advantages and disadvantages of a projected military campaign is a matter of high policy to the Joint Chiefs of Staff: for the President the "technical" judgment on this point may be only one of the basic considerations in his "policy" decision to go ahead. (The decision to invade North Africa in 1942 is a case in point.) It is also true that many subjects that can be treated as technical problems can also be handled from a policy standpoint: the distinction depends primarily on the degree to which the larger effects of an action are taken into account. A forced resignation may be described entirely in procedural terms; it may also be told with emphasis on non-technical factors like the prestige of the organization and general internal morale. The technical problem of dismissal merges into the policy problem of the general welfare of the agency.

This volume contains a large proportion of high-level and interagency and, above all, conflict cases. By any statistical analysis, most government activity is conducted on the lower levels and within a single agency (even a single unit); in most government activity, conflict is either absent or else so subtle, moderate, and so quickly resolved that it does not appear as conflict. The disproportion in the cases in the volume is partly a matter of deliberate choice and partly a by-product of the technique. There has been a deliberate seeking for subjects that illustrate the making of policy, and the policy content, so to speak, of decision tends to be greater at the top of the hierarchical pyramid, and where two or more agencies are involved, and where evident conflict has occurred. But it also happens that generally there are fuller records and better recollection among participants of incidents that occurred at the upper levels of the hierarchy, that involved more than one agency, and that produced conflict; such cases are therefore particularly adaptable for historical reconstruction. Whatever the basis for the selectivity, the cases may be taken, as has been suggested above, as qualitatively representative of decisions with policy involvement even though not quantitively representative of all governmental activity.

There is a final aspect of the cases concerning which the question of representativeness may be answered in still another way. This aspect relates to the portrayal of the familiar, persistent problems of administration as seen by the administrator: the jurisdictional dispute, the problem of the in-line deputy, the delays of clearance, the run around, the off-the-cuff decision, the double cross. These are some of the characteristic malaises of public administration, which lie within the ken of all bureaucrats. Indeed they tend to be characteristic of all large formal organizations, for they are created or conditioned by a complex structural environment. The cases are representative in the sense that they contain a generous sampling of these problems.

RELEVANCE IN THE CASES

In a law case, relevance is determined in large part by rules of the game, though the part played by the judge acting as umpire should not be underestimated. In a public administration "case," there are no rules of the game. Relevance for each author is what seems to bring out the issues that seem to him important in the light of his general understanding of the nature of public administration. Each author has his own sense of what is relevant. However, in the cases in this volume, the underlying premises about public administration tend to be broadly uniform, and the rather elaborate process of editorial review has tended to limit the diversity in judging what is "important."

To put the matter in very general terms, the guide for deciding what to include and what to exclude in drafting a case has been to aim at what the ideal administrator would take into account in making or reviewing a decision. The use of this concept as guide precludes the depth of legal or economic review and analysis, for example, that a lawyer or economist would seek. Contrariwise, it invites the inclusion of a multiplicity of factors such as personality, the prevailing political climate, institutional structure and habits, personal and institutional goals, and so forth, that transcend the interests of any of the administrator's specialist advisers.

The "ideal administrator" is a shadowy figure, indeed a shifting figment of the imaginations of the people who have participated in case preparation. He is no more than a personalization of the concepts of public administration outlined earlier in this Introduction, and the implied contrast between the ideal and the actual administrator is also a personalization. In analytic terms, each case includes as relevant what the administrators seem to have taken into account—consciously or unconsciously—and also the other apparent influences on the process of decision that were ignored; in both respects, of course, the qualification "as far as can be determined or judged" is to be understood.

Relevance in the cases, therefore, is to be construed in the light of the general approach to public administration outlined in this Introduction, and in the light of the general purpose of making the cases useful for teaching public administration.

IV. CASE STUDIES AND TEACHING

SOME GENERAL PROBLEMS

Few methods of teaching place a greater premium on the skill and ingenuity of the teacher than the case method; and the case studies in this book, since they are non-standardized, non-prescriptive in character, offer a peculiarly great opportunity for the deepening of insight into an area of great complexity, and for discipline in close observation and the solving of intellectual problems for which no pat solution is feasible.

These cases, as has been suggested, have some similarity to a good many of the cases prepared for use in the Harvard Graduate School of Business Administration. A case book compiled by two members of the faculty of that school, John Desmond Glover and Ralph M. Hower, *The Administrator*, includes an introduction with perspicacious comments on the case method in teaching; an illuminating and fuller discussion of the problem will be found in a pamphlet by the same authors, *Some Notes on the Use of "The Administrator."* [5] Teachers, and especially those unfamiliar with the possibilities and pitfalls of the case method, should find these discussions stimulating, even though certainly not all, perhaps not even most, teachers of public administration, will wish to adopt such a rigorous doctrine of pedagogic self-abnegation as Glover and Hower recommend.

Furthermore, there are significant differences in presentation in the two groups of cases themselves which necessarily affect classroom use. The two most important characteristics of the cases in this volume which distinguish them from most of the Business School cases are: (1) a concern with problems of values that are generally deeper and more complex than the values involved either in major business objectives or in personal relations within small working groups; and (2) a conscious effort to point editorially and otherwise to issues and questions that seem, to those concerned with the preparation of the cases, to deserve the particular (though by no means exclusive) attention of readers.

The effect of this technique is to suggest to teachers and students some of the issues and some of the avenues of analysis that may serve as a focus of classroom discussion. Whether even this limited focusing is desirable is debatable. Some of those who have been testing the cases in the classroom, or reading them for other purposes, have urgently requested further pointing up and editorial analysis; others have asked for less pointing and editorializing, and have described what is actually found in the cases as a crutch or a distraction. Whatever judgment may be made on the mid-position that has actually been adopted, the teacher can take advantage of the position in several different ways. He can, for example, guide the classroom discussion toward issues that are not pointed up in the text, leaving the students to work out for themselves what has already been called to their attention by the author; he can elicit an analysis of the text that uncovers additional alternatives or additional values in the suggested alternatives; or he can take the listed issues as starting points and have the students examine them in detail in the light of the historical account.

In one respect, the case technique may usefully be taken as a guide for classroom technique. The approach in the writing has been non-dogmatic; the same kind of approach would seem valid for teacher and student. On this assumption, students should be encouraged to think through the problems for themselves rather than accept any particular formulation on faith. Most teachers who have worked with the cases have in practice urged their students to develop their own conclusions, have pushed them into the pains of decision, have invited them to worry over the points that concern *them*. Yet the consensus of the experimenters has also been that the instructor should be more than a referee, that he need not make a fetish

[5] Richard D. Irwin, Inc., Chicago, 1949; Richard D. Irwin, Inc., Chicago, 1950. See also footnote 2, above.

of concealing his own views, and that free discussion need not be incompatible with planned consideration of various issues, especially those issues that recur to plague administrators.

One other conclusion of those who have been testing the cases in the classroom may deserve mention here: the desirability of allowing enough time for ample exploration of the issues in each assigned case, and, to the maximum extent feasible, the desirability of allowing enough flexibility in the course curriculum to permit some variation from schedule in the length of time actually devoted to the assigned cases. For almost all undergraduates, and for almost all beginning graduate students as well, these public administration cases introduce a new world. This is not the governmental world they have read about in the newspapers nor is it the world of the official speeches of administrators or of the condemnatory or laudatory statements of members of legislatures. For most students, therefore, these cases will raise perturbing and puzzling questions that may never occur to the administrator or the experienced teacher because to them the ground is so familiar. As a matter of fact, many of the questions about administration raised by the relatively inexperienced are worth raising and hard to answer, for familiarity may be an impediment as well as aid to insight. But if the educational function is to be fulfilled, the students' questions, whether wise or naïve, must not be suppressed; they may be unanswerable because they are not real questions or because our knowledge is inadequate, but the elucidation of why a question is unanswerable is in itself a useful exercise.

Another reason for allowing ample time for discussion, and for avoiding any rigid appropriation of class time to each case, is the newness of the technique to students and the baffling effect on many students of coping with classroom materials in which their chief task is to solve problems dealing with human beings. Here the situation parallels that in the law schools, where the first year students traditionally are disturbed by a kind of study for which their previous academic careers have not directly equipped them. The students' first tendencies are apt to be schizophrenic—alternatively (or in different students) to treat the cases as take-off points for conversational speculation only vaguely related to the text, or to concentrate on the details of the historical narrative without attempting to face the problems of decision. Harnessing these two opposite tendencies takes time, time in the classroom; but if the case method is one of the useful methods of teaching and learning, it is time well spent.

In suggesting the desirability of allowing extended classroom discussion and of keeping the course schedule flexible, there is no suggestion that there be no planning, no scheduling for the course. Even though it is apparent that no course in public administration, of whatever nature, can cover all the major aspects of large, formal, governmental co-operative undertakings (or even of such undertakings in, say, the national government of the United States), there are great advantages in having the students gain an appreciation of the variety of issues that public administrators face, however small the varied sample may be in relation to the whole. This deliberate exposure to different kinds of decisions and different kinds of administrative environments is difficult to ensure without scheduling, even if no hard and fast rule should or can be laid down as to the "right" amount of time for each case. No two teachers, no two classes, will respond to the same case in the same way, though by experience the teacher will learn to predict within rough limits the amount of useful discussion a given case is apt to provoke. Obviously, the longer and the more complex cases (the correlation between length and complexity is not absolute) can usefully justify much more extended discussion than the shorter ones: it might easily prove rewarding, for example, to spend several periods on the *Foreign Service* case, whereas a single period may suffice for the exploration of a group of two or three short cases like those at the beginning of the volume.

It seems unnecessary to do more here than suggest that a variety of teaching techniques can be used with the cases. Thus, for example, for obvious reasons many of the cases lend themselves rather easily to role playing, if a teacher should consider that technique desirable. Or students can be asked to write cases as term papers, using either material derived from their own governmental experience (where appropriate) or documentation from reports of investigating committees, and so forth, or, and quite fruitfully, a combination of written documentation and interviews; in the latter instance, subjects dealing with nearby governmental problems must normally be chosen. The cases can also serve as the initial focal point for research into a program area of governmental activity such as natural resources; research of this character has been tried out on both an individual and a group project basis.

These scattered notes on a few applicable teaching devices are, of course, mere suggestions and in no sense comprehensive. Nothing has been said, for example, about the use of cases as assigned reading in a formal lecture course; obviously the treatment of the material in such a course would differ from the treatment in a seminar. It is assumed that the teacher will make appropriate adjustments in such circumstances.

ORGANIZING A COURSE

In Part II of this Introduction, there has been a brief discussion of the place of categories in the analysis of public administration. It was suggested there that many different kinds of categorical analysis are useful—for different purposes—and that no system of categorical analysis possesses an absolute validity or can be, in the present state of our knowledge of public administration, completely comprehensive or logically consistent throughout. Public administration cases, treating the subject as a process in which the dynamic elements are of the utmost significance, lend themselves with particular ease to teaching under different types of categorical analysis. There are, therefore, many equally valid ways of organizing a course with the same set of cases.

The ease with which the cases can be adapted as the major substance of a course curriculum is enhanced if the course puts emphasis on an understanding of the nature of public administration in the United States rather than on comprehensive acquaintance with the formal organizational structures and procedures of national or state or local governments as such, though a few cases used as incidental illustrations can be fitted into almost any type of public administration course. Obviously, the difference between a course that points towards understanding as the chief goal, and one that points towards the acquisition of factual knowledge is a matter of degree rather than of kind. The cases in this book were not designed to "teach" the structure of the OPA, the personnel techniques of the Foreign Service, or the formal responsibilities of the Maritime Commission; yet the attentive reader of the relevant cases cannot fail to acquire information on these matters because governmental action—such as is portrayed herein—is continually affected by formal structures, procedures, and responsibilities; accordingly, the cases in this book include some of the formal material that has bulked so large in courses in the past. But since a case book presents such materials only as background to specific action, it is not the ideal tool for acquiring such information in any comprehensive fashion: it is not designed to serve as a manual. On the other hand, cases can be combined with other materials in such fashion that familiarity with major formal phenomena and the common concepts of scholars in the field is developed along with the rather different type of insights that cases can best promote. And the cases do invite the student to look for the working significance of such formal matters wherever they may be encountered.

In the organization of this volume, the headings adopted are conventional; and it would not be appropriate to treat them as categories whose formal structure carries great weight. Each case of the kind included in this book is a universe in itself. Certain teachers and scholars may wish to isolate a single element in a case for illustrative purposes; but in a general course in which the cases form the basic reading material, most teachers will find that the educational process is most effective when the students discuss all the facets in each case that interest them and the teacher, without regard to the relevance of certain of these facets to the title of any particular part of the book or course.

This procedure may seem disorderly, but there are two reasons why it has proved feasible in practice. In the first place, the products of intensive consideration are not lost overnight; the teacher will find, for example, that the insight into governmental public relations gained from a study of the *Reconversion* case will still be available when the cases gathered under the heading "Relations with the Public," are reached. Contrariwise, there will be, to take another example, an opportunity for retrospective deepening in understanding of the complex of problems discussed in the context of "Responsibility" when the *REA* case is reached. Thus, while there will be an apparent discrepancy between the categorical organization of the book and the actual content of the discussions, the values tend to be cumulative and adjustable to whatever framework may be adopted.

There is a further value for teaching, and a more significant one, in the apparent disorder created by the complexity of issues in each case, for the prime characteristic of public administration is the multiplicity of considerations that enters into all significant decisions and into an enormous mass of insignificant ones as well. One of the chief beneficial results that a successful course in public administration can achieve is a release from the intellectual bondage of over-simplification. The development of public policy is a complex affair; a sensitive awareness of this fact is a key to useful understanding, whether by student, teacher, administrator, or citizen.

The contrast between the complexity of issues in each case and the simplicity of framework suggested by any conceptual organization of the cases in a course is a normal phenomenon: the social sciences continually escape their bounds. Emphasis, selection, and order of cases will vary from teacher to teacher—even with different classes and the same teacher. Certainly the teacher need not be bound by the organization of the book itself. For two generations, law professors have been using case books and have paid just as much or as little attention to the arrangement of the book as they felt inclined. The cases in the law case book may be in pure historical sequence; the teacher may reshuffle them to follow some conceptual scheme, or he may follow a number of main themes using a historical sequence for each. A variety of considerations enters into such decisions: the teacher's interests, the focus and scope of the course, the capabilities of the class.

Any attempt to press too far the analogy of law cases and public administration "cases" would be unwise, though underlying similarities in the pedagogical process are significant. But the very lack of formally defined issues in the public administration cases opens an opportunity for the teacher to use the cases within a variety of organizational schemes, and in the context of a variety of formal subject matters.

The table of *Alternative Topical Arrangements*, pp. xxxvi-xxxvii, is designed to illustrate how the cases can be fitted within different categorical frameworks. Alternative A is taken directly from the Table of Contents of this book. The other alternatives are derived directly or indirectly from actual teaching experiments.[6]

Under each of these four suggested arrangements—as under any other—the teacher and students would presumably give some special emphasis to the interconnections among the cases listed under each topical heading, so as to develop an understanding of these larger issues. The kind of rationale that might be appropriate to each of the alternatives and developed in this fashion can be very briefly indicated.

Under Alternative A, in the analysis of the cases in Part I the teacher might bring out such matters as the significance of formal organization for specialization and the inherent dilemmas in adopting any form of organization (functional, areal, and so forth); he might take up the kinds of responsibilities that individuals have in public organizations, and that the organizations have toward the individuals. This group of cases also offers an

[6] Alternative B is adapted from a course syllabus that has been used by Professor Merle Fainsod of Harvard University, and Alternative C is similarly adapted from a course syllabus used by Professor Arthur A. Maass of the same university.

opportunity for a discussion of formal organization in relation to the pluralistic and dispersed society of the United States. The cases in Part II of Alternative A can be used to turn the attention of the student to the function of government and to highlight the significance of administrators in the development of policy and program. These cases also encourage consideration of the problems that big government intensifies by its responsibility for multifarious functions. The technique of co-ordination can be examined in relation to purpose. In Part III the teacher may find it useful to open up the larger questions of our constitutional structure and the perplexing role of the administrator in that structure. Finally the students can be asked to consider some of the questions raised by the responsibility of administrators to the general public and to specialized publics.

Alternative B is an arrangement designed to be used against a background of discussion and reading of theories of public administration. In a course so constructed, the analysis would move constantly toward the broader and more complex analyses of the nature of public administration. It would begin with the comparatively simple concepts of the pioneers like Taylor, and gradually put the study of public administration within the broader contexts of process and politics, with discussion of the theories of current writers like Herring, Appleby, Barnard, and Simon.

Alternative C is designed to introduce the student to the study of public administration from the perspective of responsibility. The scheme of the course is derived from an article by Professor Arthur A. Maass and Professor Laurence I. Radway, "Gauging Administrative Responsibility," *PAR*, IX (1949), pp. 182-193 and the cases would be subject to analysis in the conceptual terms described in the article.

Alternative D suggests an approach to public administration in terms of a series of major problem areas. The headings are designed to suggest some of the major and characteristic types of problems that the public administrator must deal with.

Under each of these alternatives, there is considerable leeway for choice in categorizing particular cases. This can be illustrated by examining the topical assignment of one case, under the four suggested alternatives. The *TVA* case is listed under "Program Co-ordination" in Alternative A, under "The Environment of Administration: the Representation of Interests" in Alternative B, under "Responsibility to the People—Pressure Groups" in Alternative C, and under "Problems of Defining Public Policy" in Alternative D. All four headings are appropriate. In practice all or some of the same chief issues in the case might be discussed in each of the courses, but there would be some shift in emphasis from one to another. The teacher and class would both be inclined to draw out particularly the connections between this case and the other cases that are included in the same group; the differences in inter-case relationships will inevitably affect the readings of the cases in the varying groups.

The foregoing illustrations of different kinds of topical organization are applicable only to general courses in public administration in which the cases form the central teaching material. Obviously in a course dealing with a specific area of public administration like personnel, or government relations with business, or executive-legislative relations, a teacher may assign two or three or a half dozen of the cases that are relevant to the particular subject matter he is developing. The present discussion, however, treats of general courses designed to open up the whole field of public administration, and the suggested alternative forms of topical organization are appropriate only to such courses.

A few additional comments on certain practical problems may be helpful. Pedagogically, it may be useful to begin with a number of the shorter and simpler cases—cases illustrating only one or two significant issues. As it happens, Alternatives A, B, and D present a number of the simpler cases under the first three or four topical headings; some teachers, wishing to make use of the general structure of Alternative C, where there is no group of simpler cases at the beginning, might prefer to begin with topics V, VI, and VII despite any consequent distortion of the logical symmetry of the suggested scheme.

ALTERNATIVE TOPICAL ARRANGEMENTS

Alternative A

I. Organization

A. Structure and Reorganization

1. *Production Planning*
2. *Children's Bureau*
3. *Education Library*

B. Responsibility

1. *Indonesian*
2. *Field Examiner*
3. *Glavis-Ballinger*

C. Federalism and Regionalism

1. *Blue Earth*
2. *Natural Cement*
3. *Gotham*

II. Program

A. Program Formation

1. *Self-Insurance*
2. *Reconversion*
3. *Defense Plant*
4. *Aluminum*

B. Program Co-ordination

1. *Search and Rescue*
2. *TVA*
3. *Tankers*
4. *Kings River*

III. Relationships

A. Relations with Legislatures

1. *City Manager*
2. *REA*
3. *Emergency Rubber*
4. *FBI*
5. *Foreign Service*

B. Relations with the Public

1. *Regional Director*
2. *Veterans' Gas*
3. *Cancellation*
4. *Cost of Living*

Alternative B

A. Theories of Formal Organization: Taylor, Fayol, Gulick, the President's Committee, the Hoover Commission

1. *Production Planning*
2. *Children's Bureau*
3. *Education Library*

B. Informal Organization and Administrative Behavior: Blue Prints vs. Informal Lines of Authority: Ideological and Personality Cleavages: the Problem of Administrative Loyalty

1. *Indonesian*
2. *Field Examiner*
3. *Glavis-Ballinger*

C. The Environment of Administration: The Representation of Interests

1. *Defense Plant*
2. *TVA*
3. *Cost of Living*

D. The Environment of Administration: Problems of Relations between Administrative Agency and Legislature

1. *City Manager*
2. *REA*
3. *Emergency Rubber*

E. The Environment of Administration: Administrators in the Legislative Process

1. *Foreign Service*
2. *FBI*

F. The Environment of Administration: Problems of Public Relations

1. *Veterans' Gas*
2. *Cancellation*
3. *Regional Director*

Alternative C

A. Responsibility to the People at Large

1. *Cancellation*
2. *Gotham*

B. Responsibility to the People—Pressure Groups

1. *TVA*
2. *Defense Plant*
3. *Veterans' Gas*

C. Responsibility to the Chief Executive Conformance to Administration Policy

1. *Blue Earth*
2. *Tankers*

D. Responsibility to the Chief Executive—Co-ordination

1. *Reconversion*
2. *Kings River*
3. *Search and Rescue*

E. Responsibility to the Chief Executive—Organization and Management

1. *Production Planning*
2. *Children's Bureau*
3. *Education Library*

F. Responsibility to the Legislature

1. *REA*
2. *Emergency Rubber*

G. Responsibility to Profession

1. *Field Examiner*
2. *Indonesian*
3. *Cost of Living*
4. *Regional Director*
5. *Glavis-Ballinger*

H. Responsibility for Formulating Policy—Legislative

1. *City Manager*
2. *Foreign Service*
3. *FBI*

Alternative D

A. Problems of Formal Organization

1. Function or Clientele —*Children's Bureau*
2. Auxiliary Services — *Education Library*

B. Problems of Co-ordination

1. The Executive Office —*FBI*
2. Interdepartmental Committees — *Search and Rescue*

C. Problems of Middle Management

1. Taylorism — *Production Planning*
2. Government by Clearance—*Self-Insurance*
3. Government by Conference — *Veterans' Gas*

D. Problems in Power

1. Grass Roots Autonomy—*Blue Earth*
2. The Commander-in-Chief—*Kings River*
3. Managerial Revolution—*City Manager*
4. Abdication of Sovereignty—*Gotham*
5. The Conditions of Survival — *Reconversion*

E. Problems of Responsibility and Ethics

1. To Congress — *REA, Emergency Rubber*
2. To Professional Standards—*Indonesian*
3. To the Press — *Regional Director*
4. To Missionary Programs — *Glavis-Ballinger, Field Examiner*

F. Problems of Defining Public Policy

1. The Shackles of Ideology—*Defense Plant*
2. Engineers and Farmers—*TVA*

ALTERNATIVE TOPICAL ARRANGEMENTS (Cont.)

Alternative A

Alternative B

G. Policy Formation in Administration
1. *Self-Insurance*
2. *Reconversion*
3. *Aluminum*

H. Problems of Co-ordination:
1. *Search and Rescue*
2. *Tankers*
3. *Kings River*

I. Problems of Federalism and Regionalism:
1. *Blue Earth*
2. *Natural Cement*
3. *Gotham*

Alternative C

I. Responsibility for Formulating Policy—Administrative
1. *Natural Cement*
2. *Self-Insurance*
3. *Aluminum*

Alternative D

3. The Limits of Commitment — *Cancellation*
4. Conflicts of National Interests—*Tankers*
5. The Equity of Exceptions — *Natural Cement*

G. Problems of Executing Public Policy
1. The Tactics of Evasion—*Cost of Living*
2. The Art of the Possible—*Aluminum*
3. Administrators Make a Law—*Foreign Service*

The teacher should also observe that the amount of reading and discussion material listed under the different topics in each alternative varies strikingly. Some topics may require discussion over several class periods, while others may be dealt with much more quickly. Reading assignments would necessarily reflect this circumstance.

There is also a more general question of reading time in relation to the assignment of cases. Each of the suggested alternatives includes all the cases in the volume. Actually, the total amount of reading matter in the cases is large, perhaps too large, for example, for a one-term undergraduate course where the students have three or four other courses to which part of their time must also be allotted. Indeed, this case book has been deliberately designed to provide the instructor with a sufficient fund of material to allow him some opportunity for choice of cases in relation to the general focus of his course and in relation to the qualifications of the students, as well as to provide variety in successive years.

There is always some rough outer limit to the total amount of reading matter that can sensibly be assigned in any course. In practice, however, except in formal lecture courses, the teacher is likely to find that reading time—especially of the more complex cases—will not tend to be the most serious limitation affecting the assignment of cases. The experimental use of these cases in teaching has led teachers in almost every instance to conclude that a surprisingly large portion of class time should be set aside for discussion of each case, especially of the longer cases. Apparently intensive rather than extensive utilization of cases has had the most effective pedagogical value, a conclusion that need not be surprising if the function of education be taken as the development of the capacity for analysis. (Obviously, intensive analysis as a general technique does not preclude somewhat cursory examination of certain cases for purposes of comparison or the illumination of specific points of interest.) The result of prolonged classroom analysis is that discussion time rather than reading time is likely to set the final limit on the number of cases that can be usefully assigned.

In view of this experience, it is also true that the instructor may well find it possible, if he is so inclined, to assign a substantial amount of specialized collateral reading without making an equivalent reduction in case assignments. Although the value of such specialized readings is fully recognized, no attempt has been made in this volume to supply a bibliography. There are many bibliographical aids in the field and the complexity of the case situations is so great that a very large part of the literature of public administration (and of the whole field of social science as well) has some relevance to the different cases. Indeed, the range of relevant material is almost indefinitely large, unless a specific frame of reference is adopted. Collateral readings relevant to the *Kings River* case might include the literature of the conservation movement, theories of formal organization, writings on the separation of powers, reports of the President's Committee and the Hoover Commission, studies of interest groups, and so forth. The bibliographical note actually appended to this particular case lists only the official documentary materials (congressional committee hearings, published reports, and so forth) that form an essential part of the documentation of the case. Much the same pattern is followed in the scattered bibliographical notes appended to some of the other cases in this volume; the titles listed are primarily source materials. It is a task of the teacher to supply the bibliographical apparatus appropriate to whatever particular frame of reference he has in mind.

V. A HISTORICAL NOTE

EARLY DEVELOPMENTS

The primary purpose of this book is to help people learn about public administration. It represents the application of an ancient technique to a field of inquiry that has only recently been identified as justifying separate study. Learning by cases, generically considered, is a kind of learning in which the student derives insights or suggestions for generalizations, or in which he is led to examine his own generalized prejudgments, from the observation of particular instances. It leads to an understanding of how people behaved in the past in given circumstances, and encourages reflection on what kinds of conditions induce what types of behavior. There is nothing new in this device: the recounting of incidents to point a moral was a living method of instruction in the days when recorded literature made its first appearance. Aesop's *Fables* and Plutarch's *Lives* had a pedagogical end in view. Such novelty as may be found in this book is, therefore, not a function of the underlying technique but of the somewhat special character of these cases, and of the use of cases of this special character in the particular field of public administration.

The case studies in this book were not written to demonstrate a new case technique as such. The intellectual impetus that led to the undertaking arose from a search for new tools to use in the study of public administration, rather than from any general concern with educational method. The study of public administration in the United States has been largely an activity of the last sixty years; in formal terms, it may be said to date from the publication of the White and Willoughby textbooks in the mid-1920's. As with any new field of inquiry, there have been wide swings in the formulation, acceptance, modification, and rejection of hypotheses and generalizations about the nature of public administration throughout these past thirty years. These changes have been reflected in the classroom and, somewhat more slowly, in the character of the materials prepared for classroom use.

Teaching materials in public administration are of two major types. Much vital material consists of the written by-products of governmental activity—laws, regulations, committee hearings and reports, press releases—which constitute an essential corpus for analysis and classroom discussion; but from their first recognition of the subject as part of an academic curriculum, teachers have also relied, especially in introductory courses, on textbooks and other writings specifically prepared for the study of public administration as such.

Official analyses of governmental processes like the Hoover Commission reports usually represent a cultural lag: they tend to summarize and apply what students have previously said and written, and what some practitioners have been doing. Textbooks and other materials prepared for the classroom are similarly more apt to be compilations of the familiar than ventures into the unknown. This lag, which is inherent in the situation and not a matter for criticism, is greatest when intellectual advance is most rapid. The search for fresh teaching materials, especially in a new field of inquiry like public administration, is thus perennial. Furthermore, the existence of useful textbooks and studies does not inhibit the search for new types of material, since there is room in teaching for many kinds of books. New approaches do not necessarily make the old obsolete; they enlarge the kit of working tools for both student and teacher.

During the past fifteen years, in which there have been such notable changes in the approach to public administration, there has also been a widespread conviction that available materials represented the state of the art inadequately, or incompletely. The newer approaches to public administration[7] seemed to require both fresh presentations within the older forms of textbook and analysis, and new kinds of materials as well. During the early years of the formal study of public administration, attention was largely concentrated on some of the technical processes of administration—fiscal controls, personnel management, and the like; later the field of interest broadened, and students turned to an examination of all phases of governmental activity. During these past fifteen years there have also been two major shifts in the way of looking at public administration, one arising from the impact of social psychology (and other closely allied studies), the other a reawakened concern with the role of values in public administration. The first of these emphasizes "*administration*"; public administration is observed as a social process, in which formal public organizations are studied as societies; the second emphasizes "*public*," and is concerned with goals and standards; public administration is observed as a part of the general political process. Both trends have led away from, although they have depended heavily on, the earlier "canons" of scientific management and the "principles" of administrative science. Both represent a further departure from an earlier conception of public administration in which the activity was largely viewed as an application of public law.

While these intellectual developments were gaining strength, the textbooks and other traditional teaching materials were useful in illuminating some, but not all, of the broadened insights. Thus, beginning in the mid-1930's, teachers found themselves using materials that were only partially relevant to what they wished to expound, or indeed to what the students wished to learn. This normal state of affairs led to a normal state of dissatisfaction and to a search for new methods of inquiry and new types of research and teaching materials, as well as for a refashioning of materials in the traditional forms.

Many people participated in the search; some were professional students of public administration or more generally of political science, some scholars in the other social sciences, and some administrators themselves. The activity was thus widely diffused; yet throughout the years from 1934 to 1945, a central role in the process was played by the Committee on Public Administration of the Social Science Research Council. Under the Committee's auspices many different research projects were carried on. Most directly relevant for present purposes was the publication of the historical and descriptive series, the "capture and record" studies, and the Case Reports. Of these, the most immediate stimulation to the present undertaking was provided by the Case Reports. It is unnecessary to attempt a summary here of the accomplishments and limitations of the Reports. This task has already been done with admirable skill and objectivity by Professor William Anderson in the Committee's report covering the years 1934-1945.[8] Three character-

[7] See, for example, the four articles, by Graham, Gaus, Ascher, and Sayre, summarizing the trends of the past decade, in the Spring, Summer, and Autumn, 1950, and Winter, 1951, issues of the *Public Administration Review.*

[8] See "Report of the Committee on Public Administration of the Social Science Research Council, 1934-1945"; this is Part I of Anderson and Gaus, *op. cit.*; the case program is discussed in Section 3, "Case Reports in Public Administration," but the whole volume should be read for an appreciation of the state of the art in 1945.

istics of the Reports should, however, be noted. In the first place almost all of them were written by administrators themselves and as such were somewhat apt to be in the nature of success stories, or otherwise cramped by their official origin; in the second place, they dealt with rather narrow and simple decision-problems; and in the third place, all or almost all were confined to problems in organization and management, personnel, and finance; program decisions were omitted.

The Reports found a ready reception. They were sold widely and were used by administrators, for whom they were particularly designed, and by teachers as well. Nevertheless, a persistent undercurrent of criticism remained, addressed partly to the self-imposed limitations of the technique, and partly to the related underlying assumptions of the project. For while the sponsors expected that the Reports would provide immediate or short-run benefits, they also hoped that in the long run the accumulation of the Reports would make an even more significant contribution. This hope rested on the theory that a corpus of recorded incidents of problems and solutions in public administration could be built up which ultimately would reveal the "principles and rules of administrative action."[9] The possibility of attaining this somewhat distant, hoped-for objective rested, of course, on the further assumption that the critical variables in human behavior in public organizations were sufficiently determinable and uniform to permit the establishment of firm generalizations with some of the quality of generalizations in the physical sciences. Obviously, this assumption rested on the still further assumption that there was some practical limit on the number of variables in situations of this character.

Today, in 1951, this long-term hope of the sponsors seems unrealizable in any proximate future; but it should be borne in mind that the area in which "principles and rules" were sought was a limited one in which the number of variables was not so patently overwhelming. For, as has been said, the Case Reports did not deal directly with decisions in the substantive fields of public activity, i.e., decisions in policy and program (as contrasted with decisions on personnel, budget, and the like). Thus, for example, a decision on the handling of an epidemic would be excluded on the ground that it would be primarily "a question of the art and science of public health and not mainly a question of public administration as such."[10] The SSRC cases should be judged within the framework suggested by this revealing comment; and it should therefore occasion no surprise that cases like those in this book, based on a broader concept of public administration —one in which administrative decisions are examined in relation to and as part of policy and program—are strikingly different in both form and content.

The SSRC Committee on Public Administration neither sought nor possessed a monopoly in administrative cases. Among subsequent ventures in the field, two must be noted: the case work carried on at the University of Kansas by Professor E. O. Stene, and at the University of Southern California by Professor Henry Reining, Jr. Professor Stene's work, a continuing project, may perhaps be described as an application of Harvard Business School case methods, especially of the cases concentrating on problems in small, intimate administrative groups, to the field of state and local public administration, while the subject matter conforms closely to the self-imposed limitations of the SSRC cases. Professor Reining's work, also a continuing project, is a compilation of personnel cases. Most of these are in the legal tradition, i.e., authoritative decisions of civil service commissions and other competent tribunals or officials; but partly because of the general lack of formal written records in this field, many of the cases represent a historical reconstruction rather than a mere reprinting of decision and auxiliary documents. Both of these instructive undertakings have been carried on by teachers as an aid to teaching, and it is a matter of regret that the products of both have not yet been made generally available.[11] A third project, similarly

[9] Anderson, *op. cit.*, p. 52.

[10] Anderson, *op. cit.*, p. 37.

[11] Professor Reining's collection, *Cases of Public Personnel Administration* (Dubuque, Iowa, 1949), was issued largely for his own use in teaching, and is still undergoing expansion and revision.

motivated and similarly limited in audience, requires a more extended discussion here because it led directly to the present undertaking.

THE HARVARD CASES

Toward the end of the war there were long faculty discussions in the Graduate School of Public Administration at Harvard about curriculum. Out of these discussions came a decision to establish two new basic introductory seminars: Economic Analysis and Public Policy, and Governmental Administration and Public Policy. The task of organizing the latter—beginning with the academic year 1944-1945—fell to Professor Pendleton Herring.

The question that immediately arose was what to teach, or, to put the question in another form, what is there about public administration that can be taught and is worth teaching. In consequence, much of the work of the seminar in its first year was devoted to an exploration of the kinds of problems that might be appropriate for analysis in the seminar; hand in hand with this went a search for the kinds of materials that could serve appropriately as pedagogic vehicles for such problems. In seeking answers to these related questions, Professor Herring, who had been a member of the SSRC Committee on Public Administration since 1940, naturally had the benefit of an intimate acquaintance with the Case Reports and the other work of the Committee; nevertheless, a more immediate inspiration for what became the seminar's chief teaching medium lay closer at hand.

As far back as 1919, the Graduate School of Business Administration at Harvard had started to "collect" cases, as the somewhat artful phrase went. In the twenty-five intervening years a tremendous mass of case material had been compiled, tested, and put to use in the training of students for careers in business.[12] Perhaps originally the teachers in the school had in mind the pattern of the case method first introduced into law teaching in this country, also at Harvard, by Professor Langdell about the year 1870, but because of the nature of the problem, "cases" in the Business School sense were strikingly different from the cases used in the Law School. In business, decisions do not have the formalized and generally authoritative character of legal decisions; there is no body of official opinions to be "collected" and set before the student. What was actually done, therefore, was not to collect cases but to write cases which were descriptive of the behavior of individuals in business organizations when faced with problems. What the individual did, what the company did, could be described as making a decision; thus the cases were cases in decision-making in private administration. For many years the teaching at the Harvard Business School had been centered on the use of these cases.

Professor Herring came to the conclusion that it was desirable to attempt something in the field of public administration that would roughly parallel what had been carried on with such success in the field of business administration. During the first year a few cases were developed by members of the seminar as part of their course work. The cases dealt with a "man in a situation having to make a decision." Seminar discussion of the papers proved fruitful: the pursuit of alternatives, the facing up to decisions in confused situations were stimulating.

During the following year, 1945-1946, seminar funds were used to make possible the preparation of a substantial number of cases. Some were developed from printed sources—records of congressional hearings and the like—others were worked up with the aid of interviews. The cases were tried out in the seminar: case preparation, teaching, and editing went hand in hand. During the same period, Professor Oliver Garceau, who did much of the general editing, carried on discussions of the program with scholars in other social science fields, and drew up some general specifications for what might be usefully attempted. Speed and simplicity were the keynotes of the operation: subjects were selected for easy availability and for simplicity and interest of chief issue rather than by some analytic system of coverage; there was little attempt at elaborate construction of background, or at detailed cross-checking; in several instances the sources of informa-

[12] See Part II of this Introduction for comment on the character of the Business School cases, and on some of the characteristics of law cases.

tion were limited to one or two participants. The problem of clearance soon arose: in some instances, names and settings were changed; for most of the cases, clearance was conditional on an assurance that they would not be circulated outside the Harvard seminar. In spite of these and other difficulties, about twenty short cases were made ready for the seminar during the course of the academic year.

During succeeding years, this same seminar has been offered regularly in the Graduate School of Public Administration; the cases have constituted the basic material for seminar discussion, although assigned supplementary readings have been used to develop a wide acquaintance with theories of public administration. From time to time new cases have been added to the series, so that enough material has become available to permit changes in assigned case readings from year to year; however, since the cases are short (averaging only twenty pages each), the total corpus of reading matter is of moderate dimensions.

The character of the cases needs no extended description, for several are included in this volume. The cases are dramatic in presentation, and illustrate generally a series of characteristic dilemmas in public administration—personal ethic vs. hierarchical responsibility, program devotion vs. hierarchy, responsibility to Congress vs. responsibility to program, and so forth; though the dilemmas are characteristic many are represented by rather violent examples. In most instances, decision appears as a sharp choice, with only a few of the underlying complexities brought to the surface. The cases are told with the spotlight largely on one person. Choice of subject and handling permit brevity in the telling.

The Harvard experiment proved extremely successful from the beginning. Both instructors and students found the cases illuminating and stimulating. Indeed the chief drawback to the accomplishment was the virtual limitation of the experience to the group at Harvard. Now at last, through the courtesy of Dr. Herring and of Professor Merle Fainsod, who carried on the seminar after Dr. Herring's departure from Harvard, we are able to include eight of the Harvard cases in the present collection; all have been revised for inclusion in this volume.

THE COMMITTEE ON PUBLIC ADMINISTRATION CASES

The Harvard experiment became known outside the university even though conditions did not then permit publication or general circulation of the cases; by the end of 1947 the time seemed ripe to establish a more organized and more adequately financed venture in the same field. It also seemed desirable to enlist the active co-operation of several universities in order to secure the benefit of varied insights and to avoid the danger that the experiment might become precious or unduly representative of a single point of view. In time, Cornell, Harvard, Princeton, and Syracuse joined together in an application to the Carnegie Corporation of New York for a grant to finance the undertaking. The application was approved, and representatives of the four universities formed the Committee on Public Administration Cases to carry on the program. In April 1948, a staff director was appointed, an office was opened in Washington, and the Committee began its work.

The application to the Carnegie Corporation contained the following summary statement of objectives:

1. To provide the basis for realistic concepts, hypotheses, and generalizations about administrative organization, behavior, and policy-making by utilizing a clinical approach and drawing on case studies of administrators in action.
2. To explore the application and possibility of integration of the various social sciences and disciplines in administrative policy-making by collecting and examining a variety of cases which illustrate the complex aspects of decision-making in the public policy area.
3. To make generally available a body of case materials which, it is hoped, will be particularly useful for teaching purposes, for scholarly inquiry, and to practitioners in the field of public administration.

The application then went on to say:

> The sponsors of this project believe that public administration should be broadly conceived as the formulation and execution of public policy and that case materials are needed which focus attention at the point where an administrator contributes to this process.

In approving the application, the Carnegie Corporation underlined the key objective: its grant was for "support of an inter-university project in preparation of teaching materials in public administration."

The operations of the Committee followed a simple pattern. General oversight of the program was entrusted to a Policy Committee composed of one or two representatives of each of the sponsors, and, from 1949 to 1951, three other scholars in the field as well. The Policy Committee was a working body: it held a total of fifteen meetings, and its members read manuscripts containing hundreds of thousands of words. It devoted a minimum amount of time to business matters, organizational problems, and the like, but instead concentrated its attention on case production. The tasks of locating usable case subjects and finding appropriate case writers were shared by Policy Committee and Staff Director, but the Policy Committee assumed most of the responsibility for final selection of case topics and, above all, reviewed and discussed at length all the cases in draft form. The value of this process of corporate review can hardly be overestimated. The complexity and vitality of the case material invite many different lines of analysis. The interplay of minds was essential in ensuring development of significant administrative issues that were submerged in the original drafts of the various cases. The corporate review also served to offset a prime difficulty in case writing—undue concentration on the historical narrative and insufficient emphasis on decisions and alternatives—and subdued excessively idiosyncratic preferences and reactions.

The Policy Committee also dealt with problems of case selection to meet predetermined priorities, i.e., cases chosen to illustrate certain kinds of issues, and review of preliminary outlines. These problems proved rather intractable. It is easy to decide that it would be desirable to have a case illuminating a particular administrative issue: but the search for a suitable illustrative subject tends to be frustrating and time-consuming. Where so many available subjects deserved development, it seemed wiser in this pioneer venture not to devote time to a search for particular topics. Similarly it was found that outlines with sufficient detail to make possible detailed examination can usually not be written until all the research has been completed. Detailed case review was therefore generally deferred until the circulation of a first draft; it may be added that second drafts were frequently, and third drafts occasionally, circulated and discussed as well.

The staff remained small. The director and two assistants (subsequently one) together wrote less than a third of the cases; staff time was largely devoted to editorial work, making arrangements with case writers and supervising their work, and a variety of special tasks. A part of the editorial burden was carried on by others on special assignment.

Except for the two cases which are autobiographical in character, all the cases in this volume are, as has been said, the products of corporate consideration; but a committee cannot write a case. Each case was, of course, written by an individual. The degree to which case preparation was supervised and case drafts subjected to editorial revision varied considerably; furthermore, the process of revision was carried on, sometimes by the author along lines suggested by Policy Committee and Staff Director, sometimes by the Committee's editorial staff, sometimes by both. However, while some of the cases have thus been substantially revised, in all instances the basic research was the work of the case writer.

The cases were published individually as they were completed and thereby made available for experimental use in teaching and otherwise. The information gained through this preliminary circulation[*] has been put to use in the preparation of this volume. All the cases have been given a final editorial revision before inclusion in the present collection, though only in a few instances (and in all the

Harvard cases) have any major changes been made in the text.

Some summary account of the case writers may be of interest. Excluding the authors of the Harvard cases, which were edited but not written under the auspices of the Committee on Public Administration Cases, and the two writers of autobiographies, the completed cases prepared for the Committee—most of which appear in this volume—were prepared by eighteen individuals. At the time, more than half the authors had had practical experience in public administration, well over half held graduate degrees in the field, and all had had some formal training in the subject; several were authors of published work as well. At the present time most of the authors are teachers of public administration; some are actively engaged in public service, while the others are pursuing further graduate or post-graduate research or editorial work.

One last aspect of the Committee's work may be mentioned. It has been noted above that one of the stated objectives of the Committee was an exploration of the possibility of "integration of the various social sciences and disciplines in administrative policy-making by collecting and examining a variety of cases which illustrate the complex aspects of decision-making in the public policy area." This statement deserves examination in two different senses.

In one sense, the statement suggests the development of case material that would be of value to different social scientists by virtue of its content. As they have turned out, the cases unquestionably "illustrate the complex aspects of decision-making in the public policy area," and perhaps for this reason they have been read and used by a wide variety of persons. The largest audience has consisted of teachers and students of public administration and political science; but various cases have also been used as teaching material, or for research purposes, by professors of law, economics, sociology, and anthropology. This is a welcome development, even though no precise or definitive evaluation of the usefulness of these cases to the various social sciences and disciplines is possible. It may be added that the cases have also proved useful or of interest in diverse ways to persons not professionally concerned with the social sciences as scholars, and notably to persons engaged in public administration.

In a second sense, the statement of objective suggests the direct participation in case work by scholars in the various social sciences (in addition to political scientists). The Policy Committee always included at least one economist in its membership, and for most of the period, three. Many cases were reviewed in draft form by various other economists and by lawyers. Informal conferences were held with other social scientists for discussion of the pros and cons of case-writing techniques and possible alternative approaches. The effect of these activities on the cases remains largely undefinable. Beyond all this, as has been pointed out, the underlying approach to public administration illustrated in the cases themselves is in large part an indirect product of the new insights of the social sciences of the past hundred years.

THE INTER-UNIVERSITY CASE PROGRAM

The original plans of the Committee on Public Administration Cases contemplated a three-year program. By the time the half-way mark had been reached there was a consensus among the members of the Policy Committee that the generally favorable acceptance of the cases in universities, among administrators, and elsewhere warranted the preparation of plans for a continuing program. A preliminary scheme was first outlined and discussed at a Case Conference attended by faculty members of some 30 universities at French Lick Springs, Indiana, in September 1950.[13] The tentative future program plans were enlarged subsequently, when at the suggestion of the Carnegie Corporation, which made a supplementary grant for the purpose, an experimental project for the preparation of three cases in international organization was undertaken. A comprehensive plan, taking advantage of ideas from these various sources, was presented at a meeting held in Washington in March 1951. At this meeting the Inter-University Case Program was organized, subject to the availability

[13] The expenses of the conference were underwritten by the Carnegie Corporation.

of funds. Shortly thereafter, a grant for a second three-year program was made by the Carnegie Corporation. Actual operations of the Inter-University Case Program, successor to the Committee on Public Administration Cases, began on July 1, 1951. Although following the same general approach to public administration and using the same case technique, the new program differs from the old program both in organization and in program emphasis.

Membership in the Inter-University Case Program is open to all institutions concerned with public administration who take out subscription-memberships; at the present time almost fifty institutions are members, and their subscription fees constitute an essential supplement to the Carnegie grant. Current operations are supervised by an Executive Board of ten members, elected by the membership and broadly representative of all areas of the United States (like the membership of ICP itself). A special effort is being made to have case preparation go hand in hand with existing university teaching and research programs.

The program of ICP is directed toward two major avenues in case development. One leads to a broadening of coverage, the other to an intensification of investigation of particular fields. Within the United States, broadening of coverage is being sought primarily by emphasis on the whole tremendous area of state and local government of which not more than a glimpse is given in the cases in this volume. Most of the recent theoretical analysis of public administration in the United States has been based on and directed toward administration in our national government. Students of state and local government have been handicapped by a lack of materials concerned with their problems but dealing with public administration in the terms in which it is conceived in this volume. It seems, therefore, peculiarly appropriate to divert some part of the energies that might otherwise go into broadening the investigation of the national government via cases to a similar exploration of the smaller governmental units.

The second comparatively untouched area for case development now being opened up is international administration. The possibilities of fruitful investigation in this area seem bright, though clearance difficulties may prove onerous.

The other chief avenue for further case development is the more intensive analysis of selected administrative problems by developing a series of cases presenting parallel or contrasting issues. Thus, for example, a whole series of cases may be prepared, over a period of time, in the general area of legislative-executive relationships. There is reason for hoping that the opportunity to examine a sizable collection of cases in such an area might lead to illuminating comparisons and might suggest new insights.

In closing this brief account of current developments in case preparation, it is perhaps desirable to add once more a word of caution. There are many other public administration activities that would yield useful results if analyzed by the case method; but there is no reason for thinking that every aspect of public administration can be best examined by this technique, nor is there reason for thinking that any given aspect of public administration, even though usefully examined by cases, should not be subjected to other types of analysis as well. As in Kipling's jingle,

> There are nine and twenty ways,
> Of making tribal lays,
> And every single one of them is right.

Washington, D. C.

HAROLD STEIN

PRODUCTION PLANNING IN THE PATENT OFFICE

CONTENTS

INTRODUCTORY COMMENT

Procedure, rather than policy or program or people is the focus of this case. It describes how a virtual breakdown in the public distribution of patent copies by the Patent Office was analyzed and remedied by application of the criteria and techniques of production planning.

During the past half century there has been a concerted effort in the United States and elsewhere to improve work processes by scientific analysis, scientific, that is, in the sense that engineering is scientific. The functions involved in "scientific management," as the movement was originally called, have themselves been subjected to analysis and classification; nowadays it is customary to refer to the general formalized activity as administrative management. Among the functions included in administrative management is what is widely known as "Organization and Methods," one of whose techniques is production planning.

The object of O & M has been defined by Leonard D. White as "securing the most complete utilization of available resources, physical and human" or, conversely, "to eliminate so far as possible waste and loss of effort." While, with the years, increasingly higher standards of technical competence have been set and achieved in administrative management, the profession has been criticized by political scientists and other students of public administration for preoccupying itself with "techniques, methods, and means" to the exclusion of social and economic trends and human values. The late Harold Smith, certainly a friendly critic, said:

> Through its resources the profession, by more or less scientific methods . . . can determine how to route or to "process" a piece of paper with the minimum number of movements and the minimum outlay of human effort. With all these analyses, however, it has no assurance that the people who do the work do it willingly or with any sense of accomplishment.[1]

The criticism is perhaps directed more at the practitioners of O & M than at the activity itself, for there is no inherent reason why O & M should not take into account as a crucial factor the fact that organization is made up of human beings. And the defenders of O & M can very properly point out that the prolonged study of the role of government in a democracy, for example, would not be in itself a sufficient background for the preparation of a detailed plan for collecting a national sales tax.

Preoccupation with procedural techniques may lead to a neglect of the political and human consequences of decision: but there are many problems in which the technical aspect is properly predominant. In the present case, the requisite decision was largely definable in technical terms, for the underlying objective—cheaper and better service for the public—was clearly a desirable political or policy goal; in fact, the institution of the procedural investigation was in itself a political response in the best sense. The case did, however, raise questions by and about the workers concerned. These are touched on only briefly in the following account. The chief stress has been laid, as it was by the responsible officials, on technical difficulties involved in solving a characteristic problem of office management—the "processing" of pieces of paper.

Until recent years relatively little was done to apply production planning and allied concepts and techniques to office management, either private or public. Production planning

[1] By permission from *The Management of Your Government*, by Harold Smith, copyright, 1945. McGraw-Hill Book Company, Inc.

in the Patent Office was an early effort to introduce mass production methods into a typical government clerical operation. This case is therefore of some historic significance.

Background

The Patent Office, since 1925 a part of the Department of Commerce, was constituted as a distinct bureau in 1802 to administer the laws passed by Congress in accordance with the portion of Article I, Section 8, of the *Constitution* instructing it to

> promote the Progress of Science and useful Arts, by securing for limited Times to Authors and Inventors the exclusive Right to their respective Writings and Discoveries. . . .

In pursuance of this purpose the Patent Office had issued, between the date of its founding, and the time of this case—summer 1945—nearly 2,500,000 patents. As a routine function connected with furnishing information on existing patents and reviewing and acting on applications for new patents the Office, through its Patent Copy Sales Branch (then called the Publications Division), supplied copies of patents to other government agencies, to inventors and their lawyers, and to the general public.

The summer of 1945 found the patent copy distribution function in a critical condition. The cumulative effect of a number of factors —particularly a rising demand for patent copies which was steadily outstripping the Branch's ability to meet it—had pushed the Branch two to three months in arrears in filling mail orders for copies of patents. The delay had passed from the stage of inconvenience and annoyance to patent applicants and their attorneys to the point where, in the opinion of some, it was threatening the nation's technological progress. This view was based on the fact that patent examiners, while considering an application, would frequently ask the applicant to add a reference to a previously issued patent. The three-month delay in securing copies of patent references had a generally retarding effect on the completion of applications and granting of patents.

The Division's problems came to the attention of the Bureau of the Budget's Division of Administrative Management (AM) sometime in the spring of 1945 when the latter, at the request of the Department of Commerce, made a staff survey of the operation of the Patent Copy Sales Branch as part of a larger exploratory study of the administration of the Patent Office. The report of this study, made early in July 1945 recommended that a "thorough analysis of work methods and procedures" be undertaken in the Branch, with the Department assuming responsibility for the study and availing itself of the services of experts familiar with mail order or similar large volume sales operations. A new Patent Commissioner, Caspar Ooms, took office later in the month. Concerned over the importance of the administrative and organizational problems that were facing his agency—of which the patent copy distribution backlog was only one—Ooms soon organized an executive staff for himself which included an executive assistant, a Management Planning Division, and a chief of personnel. He talked with Budget Bureau officials about the Copy Sales Branch's delays and shortly thereafter it was agreed that the Bureau's Division of Administrative Management would assist the Patent Office Management Planning staff in improving the patent copy distribution procedure.

This was the first time AM had had an opportunity to work with a problem in large scale office operations. During the war one of its staff members had become familiar with large scale mail supply operations during his association with an Army officer—a former mail order executive—whose task it had been to overhaul completely the supply operations of an Air Force depot. The approach taken by the expert had "contained elements, not customarily employed in traditional government procedures work" which the AM official had considered largely responsible for the success of the Air Force project, elements such as (1) undertaking the job with the broadest possible frame of reference and planning the total process without regard to existing organizational lines, (2) introducing a system of movement of work according to a definite time plan, (3)

Chart I

BUDGET BUREAU AND PATENT OFFICE UNITS CONCERNED WITH PATENT COPY SALES BRANCH REORGANIZATION

(other units omitted)

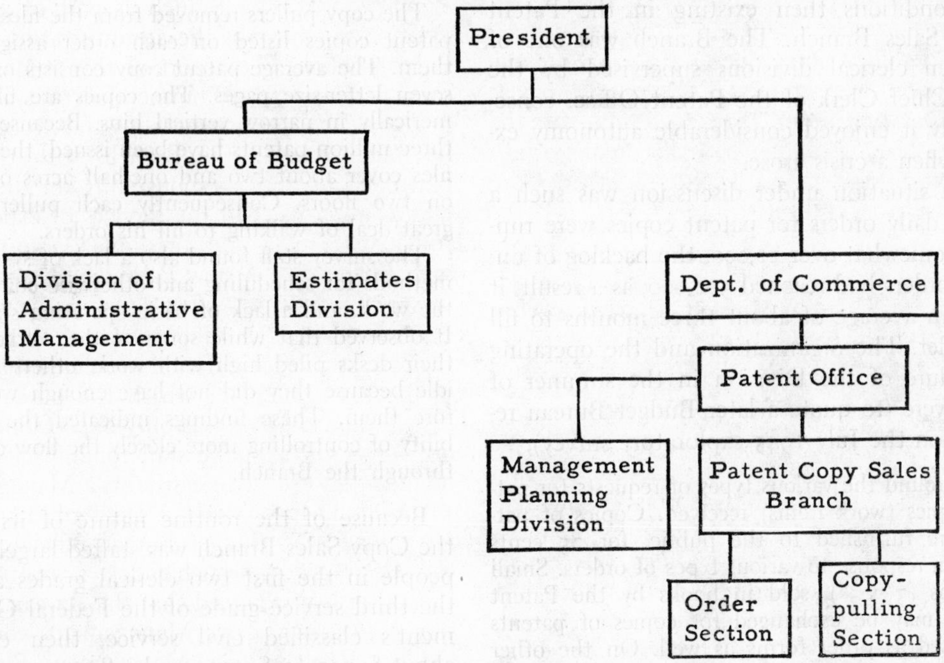

paying careful attention to the volume of operations, and (4) balancing operations to permit the smooth uninterrupted flow of work.

The AM staff member assigned to working on the Patent Copy Sales Branch's problems began his job on October 1, 1945, with a review of the AM exploratory study of the Patent Office. At first glance it seemed to him that better organization of patent copy distribution might be achieved by drawing on some of the findings of this study. At an initial meeting the AM staff member and an associate of his and Commissioner Ooms agreed to make an immediate reconnaissance of the Publications Division to determine in general whether mass operating techniques might be applicable there. In company with the Commissioner, his executive assistant, and the head of the Patent Office's new Management Planning Division, the two AM men spent half a day touring the Patent Copy Sales Branch's offices and its rows of files. At the close of the day it was agreed that Budget Bureau would make a more thorough study of the situation before reporting and recommending any changes.

The AM man's next ten working days were spent in gathering facts about the operations of Copy Sales from interviews with its employees and from detailed accounts of procedure and work load statistics furnished by the Patent Office staff, and in consulting with two mail order experts. He concluded that mass production principles were applicable to patent copy distribution and formulated recommendations for the organization of the Patent Copy Sales Branch on a mass production basis. These recommendations were presented to the Patent Commissioner's office on October 26, 1945. The various units of the Patent Office and Budget Bureau involved in the discussion, recommendation, and reorganization which followed are roughly represented in Chart I.

The Publications Division Prior to Reorganization

The recommendations made by the AM man can best be understood in the light of the conditions then existing in the Patent Copy Sales Branch. The Branch was one of the ten clerical divisions supervised by the busy Chief Clerk of the Patent Office; consequently it enjoyed considerable autonomy except when a crisis arose.

The situation under discussion was such a crisis: daily orders for patent copies were running somewhat over 20,000; the backlog of unfilled orders had reached 500,000; as a result, it took an average of about three months to fill an order. The organization and the operating procedure of the Division in the summer of 1945 were (to quote a later Budget Bureau report [2] on the July 1945 exploratory survey),

built around the various types of requests for patent copies (work items) received. Copies of patents are furnished to the public, for 25 cents each, in response to various types of orders. Small coupons (3" x 5"), sold in books by the Patent Office, may be exchanged for copies of patents and used as order forms as well. On the other hand, some customers order by letter and send cash. Others maintain open accounts. Some have standing orders for copies of all patents issued in specified classes. Orders are distinguished also by origin (e.g., lawyers who rent windows for delivery of patent copies, patent examiners, and Government agencies). In total there were then fifteen different types of orders, of which six accounted for the bulk of the business. A different group of workers handled each different type of order. The over-all flow of work was divided in parallel on that basis. Within the groups, however, there were common work steps performed serially. About 80 employees, in all, were engaged in the various steps.

The study showed that although the work items (requests for patent copies) were dissimilar, they all were processed through the common work steps of (1) coding and batching for assignment, by a batch clerk; (2) sorting and pulling copies of patents from the files, by a copy puller; and (3) assembling and mailing out the order, by an order clerk. In addition, cash and account orders were processed through two accounting work steps. [Chart II] gives a rough graphic impression of this operating plan for the six important types of requests.

The copy pullers removed from the files all the patent copies listed on each order assigned to them. The average patent copy consists of about seven letter-size pages. The copies are filed numerically in narrow vertical bins. Because nearly three million patents have been issued, the patent files cover about two and one-half acres of space on two floors. Consequently each puller did a great deal of walking to fill his orders.

The survey staff found also a lack of systematic methods for scheduling and otherwise controlling the work, and a lack of basic operating statistics. It observed that while some of the workers had their desks piled high with work, others seemed idle because they did not have enough work before them. These findings indicated the desirability of controlling more closely the flow of work through the Branch.

Because of the routine nature of its work, the Copy Sales Branch was staffed largely with people in the first two clerical grades and in the third service grade of the Federal Government's classified civil service, then earning about $1500 to $1700 yearly. Some employees had worked in the same job, with little change in salary, for as long as twenty-five years. Others were recent transfers from the war agencies who had been allowed to retain wartime classifications and salaries which were higher than those of old Branch employees performing the same work. The confusion and resentment which this contrast created had a further depressing effect on the morale of the group, already noticeably low for a number of reasons: opportunities for advancement within the Branch were very limited; there were no clearly defined agency personnel policies and procedures; the patent copy backlog was a constant nagging factor; and the physical surroundings of most of the staff were awkward. They worked at desks and tables among long rows of patent copy bins; overflow copies were inaccessibly stacked on top of some bins and also in the aisles, without regard to numerical order, while other bins remained empty be-

[2] Executive Office of the President, Bureau of the Budget. *Production Planning and Control in Office Operations.* Management Bulletin. Washington, D. C., October 1949. Pp. 21-22.

Chart II

ORIGINAL PARALLEL WORK FLOW

Patent Copy Sales Branch

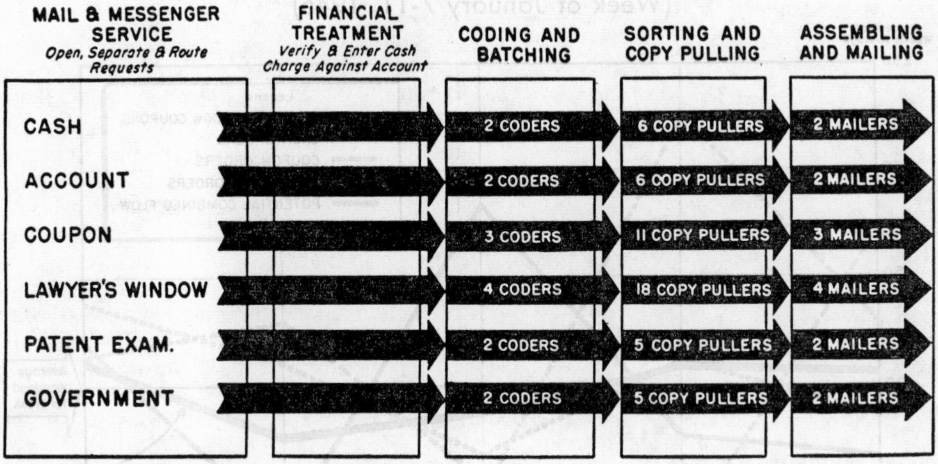

Source: Bureau of the Budget

cause their slots were not wide enough for some of the case copies and because there was no established procedure for refilling them.

A number of major defects in this set up were identified in the report and recommendations made to the Commissioner of Patents by the AM staff member in October 1945. He pointed out, among other things, the existence of fifteen separate operating channels, the extra steps taken for handling fee and account requests, the lack of basic operating statistics, and the lack of systematic methods for scheduling and controlling the flow of work.

Planning the Reorganization of Procedure

To remedy these defects in Patent Copy Sales Branch procedure the AM memorandum recommended that (1) steps be taken to combine or consolidate the several distinct channels of work ("channeling"), (2) methods of flow be changed to facilitate mass operations, (3) the proportion of orders recorded on coupons be increased, (4) a system of inventory control be installed, and (5) concerted attention be devoted to the backlog in the reproduction of copies.

The Commissioner of Patents agreed to the general plan of improvement outlined in the memorandum and directed that his staff take steps to install it with general guidance and advice from Budget Bureau staff. This was begun in mid-November 1945. One of the first effects of joint consultation was the development of arrangements to print a greater volume of patent copies so that the backlog of orders unfilled because copies were out of stock could be broken. At the same time, a five per cent sample of one week's incoming patent requests was tabulated to get a rough frequency distribution, by patent numbers, of the demand which had to be met. The entire existing office layout was also charted and estimates made of the amount of space required to organize copy pullers by sections, to centralize the storage of "overflow" copies, and to meet future expansion.

As members of both staffs worked together and analyzed Patent Copy Sales Branch procedure in great detail, viewing the job as a

Chart III

COMPARISON OF FLUCTUATIONS IN INCOMING WORKLOAD

Parallel Work Flows and One Combined Serial Flow (estimated)

(Week of January 7-11, 1946) *

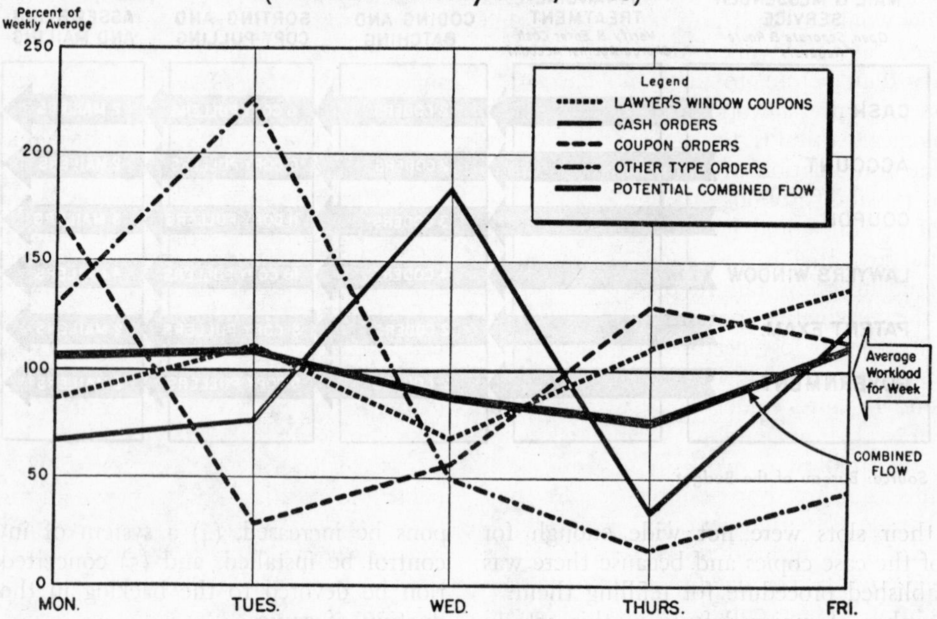

*** Daily figures for each type of order are percent of average workload for that type of order**

Source: Bureau of the Budget

whole without regard to existing organization units, the common goal of speedy service which underlay each parallel operation indicated on Chart II appeared to contrast sharply with the arbitrary nature of the existing specialization. The contrasts pointed up the possibility of channeling the procedures into a single flow and thereby gaining several distinct advantages:

1. Channeling would reduce fluctuations in work load. The overtime of some workers and the idleness of others was a reflection of the wide variations in the volume of work flowing into the separate channels graphically represented in Chart II. Although the *average* monthly volume of requests was fairly stable, there were, as the four lighter lines in the chart indicate, violent daily fluctuations for each type of order. The data on the loads indicated that if the separate flows were combined into a single procedure the individual fluctuations would tend to cancel each other and daily fluctuations for the total would be proportionately smaller than for the individual procedures. The relatively level heavy black line in Chart III shows the extent to which combining the actual flows for a particular week would have reduced daily work load fluctuations.

2. Channeling into one flow would facilitate the shift from individual sorting by each of the 51 copy pullers to mass sorting of coupons, forms, and letters containing patent orders.

3. Channeling would make possible a greater "density" in work assignments. Each clerk could be assigned full time to pull copies in a given limited area of the files because with all pulling operations combined the serial numbers of the patent orders coming in could be expected to occur in close sequence. The result: less walking per copy pulled from the files.

4. A single channel based on combined op-

erations would lead to more efficient control of work flow. With a large volume of orders moving regularly through a single channel, work could be dispatched according to a predetermined time schedule, thus establishing a rhythmic beat or tempo of work. The resulting even flow would make it possible to determine staff needs at each work station with greater certainty than before, to plan and check the progress of current work, and to provide a psychological stimulus to worker production.

5. The combination of channels, by confining the possibility of loss to one channel instead of several, could be expected to reduce fractional loss, that is, the under-utilization of staff resulting from failure of work load to equal the productive potential of the "last man." Fractional loss occurred in the Patent Copy Sales Branch (as in similar operations elsewhere) because, under the existing organization of work, it was seldom possible to equate exactly the amount of work to be done with the staff's capacity. For example, if one man could handle fifty transactions a day, his capacity was fully utilized only if volume was stabilized at fifty per day. If average volume for his unit was seventy-five, a second man was needed to handle the extra twenty-five cases. Seven such units, each caring for a different type of case, needed a total of fourteen men to handle a total work load of 525 cases, thus:

	UNIT							
	A	B	C	D	E	F	G	Total
Capacity per man	50	50	50	50	50	50	50	350
Work load	75	75	75	75	75	75	75	525
Men required	2	2	2	2	2	2	2	14

Combining the units into a single channel would eliminate the idle time of the second man and reduce the necessary total working force by three:

	COMBINED UNITS
Capacity per man	50
Work load	525
Men required	11

All the advantages which have just been enumerated led to the decision to combine work channels. For this it was necessary, first, to determine which work steps were common to all channels, and second, where further common work steps could be created. Work flow and process charts prepared by Patent Office staff revealed four steps basic to the handling of each type of order—batching and coding, sorting, copy pulling, and assembling and mailing. Channeling could be achieved by merging like steps for each type of order. But detailed procedures to be followed under a combined system had to be developed first. The following plans were evolved:

1. *Batching and coding.* Combining the processing of letter orders with that of lawyers' window forms and mail coupons meant that the former would also have to be on a 3 x 5 card. A form this size was developed for letter orders; it included space for the number of the patent requested and the identification of the requestor. This device, known as a line-item slip, was in extensive use in the mail order business where it had been found that the expense of "creating" the slip was repaid many times by the improvements in channeling and time-saving which it made possible.

2. *Sorting.* The reduction of all items ordered to the form of a 3 x 5 card made it easy to combine the sorting hitherto done separately by the fifty-one copy pullers. It was planned to assign a few women to full time sorting, using the best devices available to speed up the process. Hand-sorting into specially prepared bins proved to be the most efficient method.

3. *Copy pulling.* To eliminate the extensive walking done by copy pullers and achieve greater "density" in work assignments, it was decided to separate the copy files into a number of groups or units on the basis of the frequency distribution of patent copy demand which had been worked out earlier. Units with roughly equal demand or work loads were devised; they were not necessarily equal in area. The patent number on each order slip was to determine to which unit that slip would go. Each unit was to have its own supervisor and group of copy pullers.

4. *Assembling and mailing.* With the new line-item slip, multiple orders (those for more than one patent number) presented an opportunity for simultaneous operations. Henry

Chart IV

COMBINED SERIAL FLOW

Patent Copy Sales Branch

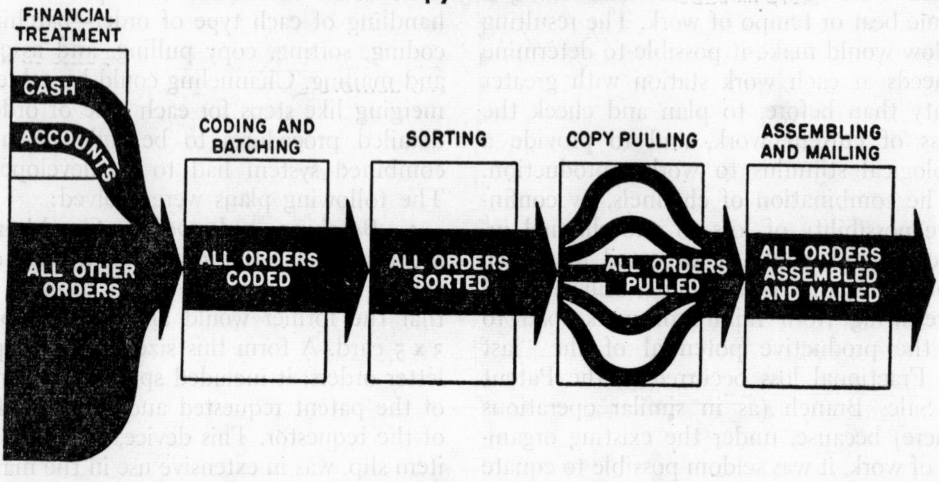

Source: Bureau of the Budget

Kaiser and others in industry had shown that a system of unit assembly or simultaneous handling would bring greater speed than the parallel plan in use in the Branch. Accordingly, under the new system an order requesting several patent numbers in different units of the files was to be broken down into several slips that could be processed simultaneously.

The assembly of multiple orders was another problem. Since line-item slips for the various patent copies requested in an order were to be routed to separate units of the copy files it appeared necessary to "code" or identify the slips so that an order could be reassembled at the end for mailing. Such a code was devised: an arbitrary number was to be given to each order, this number to be written on the letter containing the order and on each individual line-item slip. The letter would be sent on to a designated assembly-point. After the copies were pulled from the files, they too would reach the assembly-point, where the complete order would be gathered together by reference to order numbers.

These combined steps comprised a tentative channeling of procedure. Three exceptions were made from a completely standardized flow. First, cash orders and account orders had to be segregated for initial treatment by financial clerks; after financial treatment, these orders joined the mail flow. Second, only on letter orders was it necessary for the order to be transferred to line-item slips; other types of orders—made in the first place on 3 x 5 slips—would by-pass this copying step. Third, since lawyers' window cases were placed in attorneys' rented boxes in the Department of Commerce Building, the mailing step was omitted for them. Chart IV presents the revised channeling scheme.

Installing the New Procedure

A completely new procedure had been designed for the Patent Copy Sales Branch through the collaboration of the Budget Bureau and the Patent Office. By early December 1945 it was ready for installation. The first stage of the installation was the preparation of a detailed written description of the new system in the form of procedural instructions for the supervisory staff. This was done by the Patent Office Management Planning staff.

Next, the work of the copy pullers was organized. The six most efficient copy pullers were selected to serve as supervisors of the new units; the Patent Office Management Planning staff conducted a series of training sessions to explain the new system of copy pulling to them. Then, on the basis of the frequency distribution of patent copy demand, copy pullers were assigned to the various copy-pulling units, and within them to a particular segment of the files. Each copy puller was made responsible for the maintenance of her segment.

The new system was tried experimentally in one of the units of the Copy-pulling Section for a period of several days; a number of minor adjustments were made as a result. Next a temporary routing of the work of the entire Branch was designed and tested. A production record system was also developed and installed for the use of supervisors in controlling copy-pulling assignments and for the information of higher officials.

Actual installation of the new procedure later in the month was preceded by a formal meeting of the Branch's staff at which the Chief of the Branch, the Chief of Management Planning, and the Chief of Personnel explained the new system. It was then gradually put into operation.

During the first month or two under the new plan (December 1945-January 1946) Patent Office Management Planning staff found it necessary to "live with" the Branch to handle on-the-spot problems calling for interpretation or adjustment. Work assignments were adjusted, the size of work batches changed, and dispatch intervals regulated in the light of production records. It became necessary also to reorganize the storage of patent copies and to install a record keeping and copy reordering system. The reassignment and training of workers continued. Receiving and mailing procedures were reviewed and revised to improve channeling. Production records and staffing had to be reanalyzed, and shifts and changes made to promote a smoother flow of work.

Persistence of a certain fluctuation in work loads even after the channeling of the various types of orders was one of the most important problems which came up at this stage. Analysis revealed that this fluctuation was caused by a failure to distribute staff in such a way that each work station handled the same amount of work within the same time period and the work flowed evenly from one point to another. To achieve better staff distribution it was first necessary to know how many patent copies a copy puller could normally be expected to handle. Here, past experience was not a good guide, for work methods had been drastically changed. Indeed, past experience actually proved to be an obstacle to proper operation of the new procedure: it was tradition in the Copy-pulling Section that 300 copies were "a day's work." In spite of the fact that under the new system copy pullers worked in restricted areas where requests occurred at closer intervals, it appeared that custom and group opinion were restraining them from pulling more than 300 daily.

To get over this hurdle, tests or experiments with varying work loads were undertaken. Definite amounts of work were assigned to pullers, to be done before a given deadline. The size of the batches was varied until optimum capacity was determined. It was found that as many as 800 or 900 copies a day were a reasonable pulling load under the new system. Use of this method of "regulated volume" of "forced flow" made it possible to arrive at standards for the assignment of staff which, while rough at first, were superior to the previous unstandardized arrangement.

After installation of a combined work flow had been completed, Bureau staff, together with Patent Office Management Planning staff, made a check on the status of work in the Copy Sales Branch. A memorandum was prepared and discussed with the Patent Commissioner in March 1946. This report summarized the accomplishments up to that time and set forth the steps still to be taken. Of these the most important was a system of scheduling in order to control the flow of work. The channeling and balancing described above had materially increased production, but the Patent Commissioner continued to receive some complaints from people whose orders were not filled promptly. It was decided that a systematic method of controlling the flow of work would have to be inaugurated in order to ensure the prompt handling of every order.

Controlling Work Flow

In the area of controlling work flow there was much that could be learned from the experience of private industry. It was the practice of mail order houses, insurance companies, publishing firms, and other organizations handling large volumes of orders, premiums, and similar paper work to utilize a definite time-schedule system for distributing work in order to ensure the prompt handling of orders. These systems, which were naturally tailored to meet the needs of the individual firm and the operation involved, had two primary advantages. In the first place, they established control over individual pieces of work so that processing proceeded on schedule and interruptions could readily be checked and overcome. In the second place, they maintained production (a) by making certain that the work was brought to the worker when he was ready for it and (b) by establishing a rhythmic tempo to which the worker found it physically and psychologically easy to respond.

Consideration of the salient characteristics of existing time-schedule systems led to the decision that a modified form of scheduling would be most suitable to the work of the Patent Copy Sales Branch. It did not, for example, appear feasible to assign orders to the Copy-pulling Section at intervals as frequent as every ten minutes, although there were commercial firms which followed such a procedure with comfort. In the case of this Section, however, ten-minute intervals would have reduced the size of work batches to the point of impairing the increased density which had been achieved in the pulling operation after so much thought and adjustment. A four-hour interval appeared to be more appropriate to the operation, and on this basis a scheduling system was devised and installed.

Under this system, all orders, no matter what their form (coupons, line item slips, or forms) were accumulated and then sorted twice a day in a combined sorting operation. Batches were then sent to the Copy-pulling Section twice daily and subsequently reached the Mailing Section in the same two groups. Within each section, it was necessary to divide up the work still further and assign the smaller lots of orders to work units. To ensure control, however, a batch was handled as an entity. In this way there was assurance that all the orders in a batch moved ahead simultaneously and on schedule. A simple control sheet was used to check each batch in and out of each section.

Each item in a multiple order was scheduled individually so that none would be overlooked. The final assembling of multiple orders was facilitated by assigning each of them an order number and recording on a form devised for the purpose the number of copies requested in the order. After the individual items in multiple orders were pulled they reached the assembly point where all items bearing the same order number were brought together and the form recording the total number of copies requested was consulted to make certain the order was complete.

After the usual period of learning and adjustment the work flow control system proved the solution to the problem of securing continuous and accurate output.

Copy Sales Branch Staff and Production Planning

Drastic changes in operating methods in the Copy Sales Branch brought drastic changes in working conditions for the staff. Technically speaking, the new system meant improved working conditions for all and less fatigue for copy pullers. Nonetheless, when the features of the new plan were first made known to the rank and file workers at the meeting immediately prior to actual installation, the employees did not appear convinced of its merits and openly expressed a conviction that it would fail. Their attitude appeared to be governed partly by the natural human resistance to change as such (accentuated in an office where some workers had been on about the same job for as long as three or four decades) and partly by the fear that new methods would bring a reduction in staff. How much these almost instinctive reactions could have been neutralized by earlier announcement of the prospective change and a series of meetings to discuss and invite suggestions on the Branch's problems and reorganization cannot be said. Interestingly enough, it did not appear that objections to the new system were based to any significant extent on opposition to mass production methods as such.

The staff's initial negative attitude was overcome gradually through assignments and training for work under the new system, through actual experience with the increased ease of work under the new plan, and through the realization that change did not necessarily affect job security. A helpful coincidental development was the introduction of an over-all personnel program for the entire Patent Office.

The general debate over the effect of factory assembly-line techniques on worker morale has never been concluded, of course. Critics of mass production have said that the factory worker is confined to one simple physical motion, such as turning a nut, that he is chained to the speed of a mechanical assembly line, that he never turns out an end product he can see. The merits of this debate need not be considered here except to note that insofar as can be determined, once the initial installation and education period was over, the introduction of office mass production methods did not have a detrimental effect on the morale of the Patent Office Copy Sales Branch. Indeed, combined with the inauguration throughout the Office of job classification, training programs, an employee suggestion system, and a firm but well-advertised policy on absenteeism, new production methods appear to have improved morale. Production increased, absenteeism fell.

Considering the problem of morale and assembly-line techniques in the light of the change in Copy Sales Branch methods, the AM man from the Budget Bureau was led to report that production planning could be a positive stimulus to office worker morale. It overcame, he wrote, such demoralizing factors (characteristic of office work) as fatigue due to changing to and from different tasks and insecurity due to lack of clear-cut responsibility for any particular assignment. As in the Copy Sales Branch, a moderate amount of variety could be built into all office jobs, he concluded, to avoid over-routinization.

Results of Production Planning

Service to the public was improved and operating costs reduced by the introduction of mass production methods into the Copy Sales Branch. The backlog of 500,000 patent copies was eliminated. The time required to supply a copy of a patent to a purchaser was reduced from an average of about three months to an average of about three days.

Production rates showed pronounced increases. For example, the production rate for the Branch as a whole rose from 36.21 copies per man hour before installation, in August 1945, to 72.68 copies per man hour after installation, in January 1946. In the Copy-pulling Section alone, production increased from an average of 42.52 copies per man hour during the six months prior to the installation, to an average of 67.23 copies per man hour during the first six months of the installation. On a unit cost basis this meant a reduction from 2.4 cents per unit to 1.5 cents per unit.

Conservatively estimated, the net savings in copy pulling costs alone amounted to at least $45,000 per year. And, in spite of an increase in the volume of requests for patent copies from about 80,000 a week to about 100,000 a week, an actual reduction in force from fifty-four people to forty-four people was made during the first half of 1946.

THE TRANSFER OF THE CHILDREN'S BUREAU

CONTENTS

INTRODUCTION

Government agencies, or more precisely, the human beings of which they are composed, can never be indifferent to organizational proposals that will affect them. Bureau chiefs, and other officials in comparable positions, habitually desire to acquire or retain autonomy; this desire arises naturally from a feeling that they need to control means if they are to accomplish ends. Thus the achievement or maintenance of autonomy is defended as an essential element in the achievement of statutory objectives. The soundness of this view in any particular case is inevitably a matter on which disagreement can arise. Also deeply concerned are the heads of the agencies destined to acquire new bureaus or other units. Their concern usually is expressed in terms of the need for co-ordination and integration as a means for better execution of a whole group of related programs, with consequent increase in social utility. These contentions are also human and fallible.

Some problems of stress in the governmental fabric are avoidable, or at least foreseeable *ab initio;* more commonly, they are a by-product of underlying social and governmental change that can hardly be planned for on a step-by-step basis. Thus, for example, an agency is established to carry out a new and specialized function; in the course of time the government undertakes much broader responsibilities in related fields, and some of those responsibilities overlap the work of the established agency. This new intrusion raises questions: Should the now old pioneer agency absorb the new activities? should its functions be merged into a new structure? or should some other form of accommodation be sought?

It is the problem of the President and his advisors to resolve questions of this character: to balance the relative values of autonomy, with its attendant vigor, against integration, with its attendant opportunity to achieve the reinforcing effects of co-ordinated operation; to weigh the desirability of preserving a going concern against the utility of establishing a fully rationalized structure. In dealing with these questions, many factors besides theoretical managerial virtues must be taken into account, and the final decision can hardly be satisfactory to all concerned. On a smaller scale the President's problem is duplicated by the administrator's problem, when he plans a reorganization of his agency, so the recurrent tensions and difficulties can be studied on both levels. And the process of change does not have a clear-cut beginning and end. The filing of an executive order in the Federal Register does not complete the transfer process, nor indeed does the issuance of a group of orders "establishing," as they are apt to say, the organizational situs of the newly acquired unit. Adjustment is gradual.

The Children's Bureau

This study offers the reader an opportunity to observe one agency, the Children's Bureau, during a period of proposed, and later actual, transfer from the Department of Labor to the Federal Security Agency. The events are unique but not uncharacteristic; they are paralleled though never precisely duplicated by other governmental transfers. For the sake of clarity, the actions and reactions of the Children's Bureau officials are treated in more detail than the actions and reactions of the officials of the other agencies concerned. This highlighting of the Children's Bureau in the account does not mean that its officials were "right" or the others "wrong"; it is essentially an attempt to sharpen the issues. Each reader will reach his own conclusions as to where the path of true wisdom lay.

As has been suggested above, this history of a governmental reorganization reveals a familiar set of difficulties; the special characteristics of the case can be largely attributed to the special qualities of the Children's Bureau itself, the only agency in any modern democratic country organized exclusively on a population age group basis—an admirable administrative device in the eyes of the Bureau's particular friends, an anachronism (today) in the eyes of many of the groups that support a broad Federal welfare program.

Growth of the Bureau

The Children's Bureau was founded in 1912, a product of the social reform movement that also created Theodore Roosevelt's Bull Moose rebellion and Woodrow Wilson's New Freedom. Many men worked for passage of the organic legislation, but the movement was one in which women played a particularly active role; it was almost inevitable, therefore, that the chiefs of the Bureau should have all been women. From the beginning the Bureau has looked for support to women's organizations and organizations in which women play a major part. The original statute granted authority solely for research in the fields of child health, welfare, and working conditions. Action in the welfare field by the Federal government in the form of grants was improbable and regulatory action in this field was unthinkable in 1912; even research in the area was a pioneering venture for the government at that time, and politically possible only because of the special symbolic status of children. It is perhaps difficult today to appreciate the impact on opinion that the passage of the legislation had then; but the reader must remember that the political climate and the accepted interpretation of the Constitution have undergone striking changes in the intervening years.

The first notable accretion of responsibilty came to the Bureau during the 1920's, when it was authorized to administer grants-in-aid to support state maternal and child welfare programs; but this authority lapsed after a few years. Then, with the coming of the New Deal, the Bureau shared in the government's extensive new aid and regulatory activities. In 1935, with the passage of the Social Security Act, it was made responsible for the administration of certain social security grant-in-aid programs to the states, embodying technical advisory service to, and authorization of state programs in, maternal and child health, crippled children's treatment, and child welfare. With the large appropriations necessary for the Federal share in financing these state programs, and the active participation of the Bureau in their operation, these new responsibilities soon overshadowed the more traditional functions of the Bureau. But the Bureau still expended a great deal of time and energy publishing its highly popular manuals on child and infant care and development.

In 1938 the child labor enforcement duties of the newly enacted Fair Labor Standards Act were added to the Bureau's responsibilities. Actual inspection was done by the Wage and Hour Division of the Labor Department, but planning, administration and statistical reporting were handled by the Children's Bureau. War activities were highlighted by administration of the Emergency Maternal and Infant Care (EMIC) plan for wives and babies of enlisted servicemen.

Characteristics of the Bureau

Certain characteristics of the Bureau are particularly worth noting. The Bureau was originally set up in the Department of Commerce and Labor, and assigned to Labor when that Department was split off in 1913. The Bureau chief long enjoyed a close relationship with the Secretary of Labor, being directly responsible to him. This in itself is not unusual for Bureau heads in the Federal administration, but successive chiefs worked hard to develop a tradition of discretionary independence for their unit, and their success was reflected in and supported by the relationship with the Secretary. Under the administration of Secretary Frances Perkins, which began in 1933, this independence was stoutly maintained, and the chief also enjoyed the position of personal staff advisor to the Secretary on many broad social and public welfare problems. The warm friendship between Miss Perkins and the Bureau Chief, Miss Katharine Lenroot, was without doubt largely responsible for this development. It was a natural development from the identity of interests and backgrounds of the two women, both long trained in social welfare work. These close personal ties, added to Mrs. Roosevelt's interest in child welfare, made access to the White House for the Bureau Chief a relatively simple affair. There were no apparent formal changes in arrangement under Miss Perkins' successor, Judge Schwellenbach, who took office in 1945 after President Roosevelt's death. The new Secretary was content to give the Bureau a free hand within its own sphere of activity, and Miss Lenroot continued to serve as a staff advisor. Thus, though the relationship between the two was official rather than personal, the Bureau's internal solidarity was maintained. The somewhat unusual record of continuity of tenure at the head of the Bureau had done much to build up strong feelings of institutional loyalty. In 1950 the Chief was only the third person to hold that office since 1912.

The nature of the Children's Bureau's outside support has been an element of strength and, in this instance, of weakness as well. Originally it was a central focus for the attention of welfare organizations and for women's organizations like the General Federation of Women's Clubs. By the time of the New Deal in 1933, the welfare movement had broader horizons. The new relief activities of the Federal government, and later its social security program had a wider appeal and far more diversified support than the Children's Bureau. The new agencies established to carry out the new programs were now the pioneers; inter-agency tension was an inevitable development, and the organizational and functional discrepancies between the new and the old were bound to cause difficulty. The realignment of forces was clearly capable of affecting the future of the Children's Bureau.

The Emergence of Doubt

The wisdom of the independent organizational existence of the Children's Bureau and also of its location in the Department of Labor, has been questioned periodically by many Congressmen and public administrators. In 1930 the idea of consolidating its activities with the functions of other government agencies was first raised publicly at a convention of state public health and child welfare officials meeting in Washington. During the hearings on the Social Security Act in 1935 the question was raised even more insistently. The Bureau wished to share in this dramatic new action program, to go beyond its research function; but doubt was expressed in more than one quarter as to whether the grant-in-aid features of the bill should be divided among several government agencies: the Public Health Service, Office of Education, and the new Social Security Board were to administer the big security programs under the Act. In view of this decision, was there a place for separate welfare programs administered by the Children's Bureau? After the law was passed, demands began to be made in the Congress and elsewhere for the centralizing of welfare activities in one Federal agency on the grounds of logic, effective relations with the states, and administrative efficiency. When these appeals met with no success, they subsided temporarily—at least as official public utterances. However, evidence of such demands appeared in 1939, when President Roosevelt gave consideration to a proposal to transfer the Bureau to the newly established Federal Security Agency; for reasons of his own, he decided not to make the move at that time.

During the War, and with the institution of the EMIC plan, referred to above, the representatives of organized medicine began to launch an attack on the content of the new program. They embodied their criticism in the form of pointed requests to transfer the health activities of the Children's Bureau to the U. S. Public Health Service, perhaps because it was considered by the American Medical Association a more "controllable" body, though thoroughly respectable reasons for the transfer were cited. Again nothing resulted directly from this effort, but it was becoming unmistakably clear to Bureau officials that a number of forces were hostile to the continued existence of the Bureau with all its new powers intact, and at least to its retention by the Department of Labor. Perhaps the Bureau officials failed to note that the validity of a special child welfare program became debatable when the government instituted a general welfare program for all population groups.

Action Under the Reorganization Act of 1945

With the enactment, in December 1945, of the Reorganization Act of 1945, which provided that any Reorganization Plan of the President's not defeated by both houses of Congress within sixty days of its introduction would become effective immediately, rumors and speculations on Presidential plans began to circulate through the government. Aware of considerable sentiment in the Office of the Federal Security Administrator, the Budget Bureau, and the United States Public Health Service for the transfer of the Children's Bureau to the Federal Security Agency (which was fast becoming the Federal focus for health and welfare activities), Miss Lenroot and her associate chief, Dr. Martha Eliot, decided in January 1946 to discuss the matter with the Surgeon General of the Public Health Service, Dr. Thomas Parran, and with the Social Security Board chairman, Arthur Altmeyer, both of whose units were constituent members of FSA. Dr. Parran indicated a strong desire to see the Bureau's health activities committed to the Public Health Service; this was no surprise to the Children's Bureau officials, who had heard the plan proposed many times in the past. A few weeks later Mr. Altmeyer called on Miss Lenroot and told her that he had decided to urge that in the event of transfer the Bureau should come under the aegis of the Social Security Board. He maintained that this location would be best suited for preserving the organization's identity and functions intact. He expressed the view that if the Bureau came into the FSA in an independent, isolated position, its functions might be taken over by the other constituent units. Miss Lenroot objected because under Mr. Altmeyer's plan the Bureau would drop into a lower hierarchical position than it occupied in the Labor Department and she feared that the move would reduce the Bureau's effectiveness in defending the interests of children. The discussion with Altmeyer ended inconclusively.

While these preliminaries were proceeding, the Budget Bureau, vested with a continuing statutory responsibility for governmental reorganization, had been circularizing all government departments with a request for their recommendations on reorganization needs. The FSA suggested the transfer of the Children's Bureau to its authority. This proposal was well received in the Budget Bureau, which believed that all the government's welfare programs should be administered by the FSA; it also believed, as a matter of sound administrative practice, that the Federal Security Administrator should have the authority to ensure a far firmer integration of welfare activities than he had previously been granted. To the Budget Bureau, the Reorganization Act offered a greatly needed opportunity to secure a more functional and effective alignment of government activities. The Budget officials were also well aware of the demands from state welfare and health administrators to consolidate the Federal agencies with which they had to deal in connection with grant-in-aid health and welfare programs. With these matters in mind, Reorganization Plans were prepared for the President but were not disclosed to the interested agencies. This secrecy was standard operating procedure under the Reorganization Act, and approved by the President. Reorganization Plans in their nature involve the destruction of autonomy, possible degradation in the hierarchic scale, and other consequences naturally abhorrent to unit heads. Success in securing Congressional approval is therefore assumed to be largely dependent on the avoidance of any development of public opposition during the preliminary stages. Such at least is the major though not sole rationale for the operating procedure.

In late March 1946 another conference was held on the possible transfer of the Children's Bureau, this one attended by representatives of all the interested agencies. The Budget Bureau had suggested to the Office of War Mobilization and Reconversion that that agency might be interested in some of the reorganization proposals for government welfare and health activities which the Budget was considering for proposal to Congress in the event of passage of the Wagner-Murray-Dingell National Health Bill. OWMR at this time was closer to the President than was the Budget Bureau and exercised some general oversight over the President's legislative program; the two agencies worked fairly closely together, however. After this conference the Deputy Director of OWMR submitted an informal report to the President, not circulated among the participants, recommending against the transfer of the Children's Bureau to FSA. However, a change in the top personnel of OWMR occurred soon thereafter, and the report and its recommendations were forgotten. The one significant effect of the conference was its disclosure of the various agency attitudes.

By this time the lineup of forces, sentiments, and conflicting attitudes was beginning to emerge. On the one side was the Children's Bureau headed by a resolute Chief who was well known for her integrity and forthright defense of children's interests, and for her identification of those interests with the interests of her Bureau as such. The crusading vigor with which Miss Lenroot had pushed forward the children's programs for which she was responsible had ruffled a few groups in the country; and there were other organizations whose backing, for a variety of substantive or tactical reasons, was no more than lukewarm. But Miss Lenroot had managed to maintain continuing public support for the Bureau. Further, her position of relative independence in the Labor Department, plus the fact that her father had been for a long period a popular member of the Congress, strengthened her hand in dealings with that body. On learning the rumors about transfer, Miss Lenroot was not particularly displeased with the predicted separation of the Bureau from the Labor Department. She believed, however, that the loss of prestige entailed in transfer to the Federal Security Agency, which did not enjoy cabinet status, would weaken the Bureau, and therefore the Bureau's programs. Even more threatening was the possibility of loss of function and with it a breakdown of the Bureau's efforts to build up an organization equipped to handle all children's problems save education. Miss Lenroot now was taking the positive position that she would gladly take the Bureau to a Department of Health, Welfare, and Education (a creation often planned in Congress and elsewhere), if it could be assured parallel status with what would be the other major constituent agencies in such a Department; and she realized that the Federal Security Agency would become that Department, if it were established.

Those directly responsible for the preparation of the Reorganization Plan affecting the Bureau were the officials of the Budget Bureau. These officials looked on the scattering of Federal health and welfare activities as a disorderly and inefficient arrangement; to them the logic of the original creation of FSA required a full concentration of all related activities within that agency. Furthermore, they could see no justification for retention of children's health and welfare activities in the Department of Labor. Indeed, to them the Children's Bureau was somewhat of an anachronism, and its continued role in the grant programs questionable; a transfer to FSA was an essential step if rationalization of the whole structure was ever to be undertaken.

Independent support for the transfer came from state welfare and health departments which had to negotiate with a number of different Federal bureaus in connection with grant-in-aid programs which the states often administered from one central office; the organizational divisions tended to make more painful difficulties that arose in any event from a Federal program and fiscal arrangements that differed from their own. The American Public Welfare Association, of which many state officials were members, was beginning to apply heavy pressure for consolidation. Also allied with them was the U. S. Public Health Service, which favored a consolidation of the administration of programs for maternal and child health and crippled children with its other health programs; presumably it was not averse to the prestige and power advantages that would accrue, but its arguments were not necessarily unreasonable. The same attitude was true to a lesser degree of the Social Security Board in respect to the child welfare program.

Miss Lenroot consistently met these sundry arguments by pointing out (1) that any undercutting of Children's Bureau identity would be a serious mistake because children are politically powerless and need special protection; and (2) that co-operation and co-ordination of grant-in-aid administration had been improving all along, with Public Health, in perfecting joint state budget reports, and with the Bureau of Public Assistance in the Social Security Board, by synchronizing the areas and coverage of regional districts. Both the state officials and U. S. Public Health Service officers answered these points by contrasting the relative amounts of grant-in-aid moneys handled by the two bodies. Children's Bureau funds for this purpose were only a small fraction of what was dispensed by USPHS, and yet the two sets of programs had to be separately sponsored at the Federal level. The conference at OWMR had provided a sounding board for most of these conflicting views, so Miss Lenroot was well aware of them.

Reorganization Plan No. 2

A few weeks later, on May 16, the three 1946 Reorganization Plans were sent to Congress with an accompanying message. Prepared by the Bureau of the Budget in careful observance of the established procedure, the Plans had been kept a closely guarded secret until the night before transmittal, when they had been released for publication. That part of Plan No. 2 which referred to the transfer of the Children's Bureau to the FSA contained the customary broad and hence rather enigmatic language:

> . . . All *functions* of the Children's Bureau and of the Chief of the Children's Bureau except those transferred by subsection (b) of this section [the child labor responsibilities], all functions of the Secretary of Labor under Title V of the Social Security Act [the grant-in-aid programs] . . . and all other functions of the Secretary of Labor relating to the foregoing functions are transferred to the Federal Security Administrator and shall be performed by him or under his direction and control by such officers and employees of the Federal Security Agency as he shall designate, except that the functions authorized by Section 2 of the Act of April 9, 1912, [the basic investigation, research, and reporting functions] . . . , and such other functions of the Federal Security Agency as the administrator may designate, shall be administered, under his direction and control, through the Children's Bureau.

Only one thing was clear: the Administrator of the Federal Security Agency would have broad discretion to decide the whole future shape of the Bureau. He was given no specific plan of arrangement, and under the grant of power he could reduce the Bureau to a small research unit by transferring its operating functions to other units of the agency.

This paragraph was the result of a deliberate decision on the part of the Budget; it did not seek the dissolution of the Children's Bureau, but it was anxious to leave the way open for dissolution at some future date if such an action became advisable. Aside from this consideration, the vesting of the basic powers in the FSA head was based on a broad principle that the Budget applied in all such situations, even when no specific future reassignment of functions could be foreseen. It can be reasonably assumed that this section of the Plan would have been the same even if no one had ever suggested the dissolution of the Children's Bureau. Two successive presidents—Roosevelt, and now Truman—had fully subscribed to the general doctrine of vesting full discretionary authority in each agency head; and both, it may be noted, believed in the administrative wisdom of transferring the Children's Bureau to FSA, even though President Roosevelt had stayed his hand for other reasons.

The Administrator's potential power to reassign Children's Bureau functions was, of course, looked on by the Children's Bureau as an immediate peril. Dr. Eliot, in the absence of Miss Lenroot, who was attending a three-day semi-public convention on children's affairs in New York, immediately relayed the vital facts of transfer to the Bureau's officials, and a period of cautious but intense maneuvering began. Simultaneously a host of the Bureau's friends, including Edith Abbott, sister of Grace Abbott, the previous Chief, representatives of the General Federation of Women's Clubs, and labor union legislative agents began to protest against the proposed transfer. (Parenthetically it may be noted that labor's objection was probably based less on concern for the Bureau than on general opposition to any reduction in the authority of the Labor Department.)

On her return to Washington, Miss Lenroot was faced with a difficult decision. Threatened, as it seemed to her, by what might amount to a mortal blow to her organization, which was proposed by her ultimate superior, the President, she must choose a course of action which would serve the best interests of the country as a whole. If she decided to fight the transfer she had assurances of strong support. Miss Abbott, Miss Lenroot's close personal friend, was organizing an emergency committee to save the Children's Bureau. Moreover, the President was dealing with a not altogether contented Congress, and reorganizations were notoriously unpopular, since by definition they impinged on vested interests. Perhaps Miss Lenroot could win the struggle, but she feared that by so doing she would weaken a sector of the fabric of executive loyalty and responsibility, without which the Federal administration would approach impotence. In terms of the Bureau itself, for her to resign and attack from the outside would remove from the area of effective government action a veteran and successful fighter for the interests of children. Such a move might also easily dissipate a purposeful and long-nurtured *esprit de corps* within the Bureau. On the other hand, to let the Plan go through in its present form might lead to the dismemberment of the Bureau by the Federal Security Administrator, who would be fully empowered to dispose of its varied functions throughout the Agency. To Miss Lenroot this was a grim possibility, especially since the same Reorganization Plan provided for retention of the Industrial Division, charged with child labor responsibilities, by the Department of Labor. Miss Lenroot did not oppose this latter proposal as such, but feared that this divestment, together with others of a more serious nature, would leave the Bureau with little to do.

Under the circumstances the Chief felt that there was only one avenue of action open and that was to seek a solution within the general situation in which she and the Bureau had been placed—suddenly, as it seemed to her. Accordingly, about ten days after the reorganization message had been sent to Congress, Miss Lenroot arranged an interview with Watson Miller, the Federal Security Administrator. She asked him for specific assurances that the Bureau would not be broken up. He refused to commit himself except to say that he would consult her before making any definite move. Meanwhile she had been making attempts to put her case to the President through the intercession of one of the White House Assistants, Edwin A. Locke. The secrecy of the planning and the sudden shock of the presentation of the Plans without any previous consultation with the agencies involved still rankled with the Chief. She believed an interview with the President would accomplish two things: (1) get across the Children's Bureau point of view, which had not been formally presented to the Plan writers (although they were obviously cognizant of it); and (2) persuade the President to amend the wording of Plan No. 2 slightly so as to preserve the integrity of the Bureau.

There was presumably little chance for success in the latter venture because, under the Reorganization Act, Congress was authorized to accept or reject the plans in their original form. Any amendment by the President was the legal equivalent of a new submittal with a new 60-day period. The withdrawal of the Plan and submission of a new one would almost certainly have been taken by the public and the Congress as an indication of domestic difficulties within the Administration, and would have endangered the possibility of avoiding Congressional disapproval. Conceivably Miss Lenroot was not fully aware of this legal and political obstacle.

Armed with a draft of proposed amendments, Miss Lenroot finally secured an audience with the President on June 3. His office meanwhile had received many protesting letters from interested groups demanding that the Bureau be kept intact. Mr. Truman turned down Miss Lenroot's request for amendments in the Plan, but assured her that the children's interests would be safeguarded. She then asked him if he would not issue instructions to Miller to preserve the present status of the Bureau. When he refused commitment on this issue also, she asked for a letter of assurance which would mollify the women's groups clamoring for preservation of the Bureau. The conference ended with some hopeful remarks from the President on the feasibility of the last proposal.

The letter, drafted in the Budget Bureau, finally arrived on June 10. Although it restated the original refusal of the President to trespass on the ultimate discretion of the Administrator, it did contain some significant remarks:

> . . . I am asking the Federal Security Administrator to discuss with me any plans for any major reorganization affecting the basic operations of the Children's Bureau before such plans are put into effect.

and in closing:

> I am fully confident that the Bureau will have its interests well protected and that it will, indeed, be strengthened.

A copy was sent to the Administrator. Miss Lenroot immediately released the letter to the press along with a statement heartily endorsing the President's sentiments. Miss Abbott telegraphed the information to the leaders of the movement to preserve the Bureau's integrity. The following day, they, too, dropped their attacks, and the air calmed. The situation had now stabilized.

Miss Lenroot interpreted the letter as a sufficient protection of the Bureau's inviolability and existing organizational status—though it could have been read, and was presumably intended to be read, rather as an assurance that the Bureau's activities would be preserved under whatever form of organization was adopted. Relying on her optimistic interpretation, Miss Lenroot now dedicated herself to the difficult administrative tasks of actual transfer without worrying about dismemberment. Still disappointed that she would no longer be operating within a department, she was, nevertheless, able to recognize the move as a long step towards making the FSA into a department. At neither the House nor the Senate hearings on the Plan did she appear, nor did any of the groups which had been fighting the transfer, although some people testified against the proposal on other grounds.

FSA Organizational Plans

The center of activity now shifted to the deliberations going on within FSA. The Reorganization Plan had purposely given the Administrator wide authority to make flexible disposition of the units assigned to him. The Social Security Board had been abolished and its powers given to the Administrator. In addition he was supplied with two new assistant administrators who were to be used to head up large blocs of constituent units within FSA. When the Reorganization Plan was sent to Congress and the initial hostility to its intent was building up, the Budget Bureau soon sensed that many of the results it wished to see realized might be blocked if vigorous action were not taken. It seemed necessary, as a matter of protection, for the Administrator to settle his internal reorganization schemes with dispatch and finality.

In the Children's Bureau the original concern had been for retaining intact the numerous functions of the Bureau. These fears later proved to have been well founded when Budget, Public Health, and FSA memorandums written for the Administrator disclosed proposals for transfer of grant-in-aid activities to other units. The fight to forestall this originally had so occupied the Children's Bureau that the Chief assumed that her difficulties were over when she received the President's letter. In her mind (though presumably not in the

Status problems

President's) the statement that the Bureau would have its interests protected meant not only that it would preserve all its functions but also that it would be transferred into the same relative position which it had held in the Department of Labor. Furthermore, she had obtained the promise from Watson Miller that he would consult her before setting in motion any large-scale moves. In the intervening weeks she had had some brief contacts with Miller on the administrative phases of the transfer, but no discussion of the general location of the Bureau within the Agency. She was aware, of course, of Social Security Board Chairman Altmeyer's opinion on where the Bureau belonged, but in view of her long friendship and pleasant working relationships with him, it did not occur to her that he would take any major steps without informing her.

If Congress were to reject the Reorganization Plan, it had to do so by July 16, for by law the Plan went into effect on that day. On Friday the 12th, as the time limit was approaching and acceptance appeared likely, Miller finally sent for Miss Lenroot. Miller had decided to plan his reorganization of FSA without consulting Miss Lenroot, because he feared that his purposes might be defeated if the Children's Bureau had the time and opportunity once again to muster public sentiment in its behalf. He now asked her how she would like to be under Mr. Altmeyer's supervision. While she was recovering from the shock, he produced an organization chart which pictured a new Social Security Administration as one of the four principal groupings of operations within the FSA. Mr. Altmeyer was to be the Commissioner of Social Security and have under his direction the Bureaus of Old Age and Survivors' Insurance, Unemployment Compensation, and Public Assistance, and the Children's Bureau. The first three were the operating units of the old Social Security Board, and had been created by executive order to carry out the responsibilities of the Social Security Act. All power and authority had rested previously with the Board as it would now with the Commissioner, subject, of course, to the over-all supervision of the Administrator. Grouped parallel to the new Social Security Administration in the chart were the Public Health Service, Office of Education (which had fewer employees than the Children's Bureau), and a catch-all unit known as the Office of Special Services, comprising a number of smaller agencies. Thus the Children's Bureau was to occupy a lower position in the hierarchy than it had before, subordinate to a Commissioner within the Agency, and with no immediate contact with the Administrator. Even more crushing to the Chief was the realization that the Bureau would not be co-ordinate with the two other units with which she had worked for so long, Public Health Service and the Office of Education.

Mr. Miller urged his plan on Miss Lenroot with the argument that state officials were eager to have a greater measure of program coordination at their level—something which the Social Security Administration would be able to do for the states by allying the Public Assistance, Unemployment Compensation, and Children's grants under one authority. He warned that state pressure was strong and convincing. Miss Lenroot realized that her situation was delicate because of the recent public campaign against dismemberment of the Bureau, which had aroused misgivings and some resentment in both FSA and the Budget Bureau. She felt that she could not come to a decision immediately, so she asked the Administrator to give her until Monday to think it over.

Over the weekend Miss Lenroot and Dr. Eliot reviewed their position. The Bureau's bargaining strength had diminished as a result of the semi-public attack on the Reorganization Plan. They realized that White House, Budget, and FSA officials suspected that they had manipulated strong pressure forces to obtain assurances from the President. Time was now short and they had already capitalized to a great extent on their influence. Despite these considerations the two Bureau officers were convinced that this plan for their unit would mean inestimable harm to the Children's Bureau programs. They believed that their programs were dissimilar to the others under the proposed Social Security Administration because they were selective, project-type programs aimed at developing an area's resources in certain services, as opposed to the direct individual financial payments authorized by Public Assistance and Unemployment Compensation. Furthermore they looked with suspicion on the preponderance of upper bracket officers with a social insurance orientation in the Social Security hierarchy, and feared that this philosophy would be inimical to the Bureau's interests which were based on different precepts of public and social welfare. Another unattractive prospect was the simple administrative difficulty of having to clear through the Commissioner's office for all outside contacts—a procedure never hitherto necessary in the relatively independent atmosphere of the Labor Department; what would be involved as a practical matter in such clearance was, of course, still unknown. To yield to the proposal of the Administrator would undoubtedly ease the whole transfer problem, but they were sure that adoption of the plan would weaken the Bureau's program and prestige, and the morale of the Bureau's personnel.

The two chiefs drew up a memorandum summarizing their objections and suggesting instead that the Bureau be placed temporarily in a co-ordinate position with the other four branches of FSA. They further pressed for the naming of an agency committee to study the whole organizational pattern of the Agency and its relationships with the Children's Bureau, and to make recommendations that would be submitted to the President for final action. They felt justified in requesting a Presidential decision on the basis of the assurances in the President's letter of June 10.

On Monday, July 15th, Miss Lenroot and Dr. Eliot again called on the Administrator to present their memorandum, and offer oral objections to his plan. He received them in the company of Mr. Altmeyer and presented them with a *fait accompli*. The plan would stand as he had outlined it, and Altmeyer was to receive all the powers inherited by the Administrator under the Reorganization Plan—that is, all Children's Bureau responsibilities save the original functions of basic investigating and reporting. In the face of strong objections from the two chiefs the Administrator explained that he could not now change his mind because he had already shown the proposal to some Congressmen, who had wanted certain assurances before deciding to cast their vote against the resolution which would disapprove the Reorganization Plan. The Children's Bureau officials were deeply disturbed because they felt that they were being foreclosed from Presidential protection. Altmeyer scoffed at the idea of taking such a matter to the President, and Miller insisted that no changes could be made.

In desperation the two women changed their attack and demanded that all authority to administer the grant-in-aid programs be delegated to the Chief of the Bureau. Miller and Altmeyer both balked at this because they wished to retain authority in order to have a free hand with their operating units. Miss Lenroot promptly threatened to resign if she could not have decisive authority over program administration. Miller became concerned and conceded the point abruptly, and thereby something of a poor situation was salvaged. The Commissioner of Social Security would still retain the authority of ultimately approving or disapproving state plans for grant-in-aid programs, but under the compromise arrangement he would not direct day-to-day operations of the subordinate Bureaus.

Miss Lenroot's and Miss Eliot's decision to oppose the subordination of the Children's Bureau to the Social Security Administration had the subsequent effect of making more difficult the development of harmony within that organization. But at the time, of course, they did not know the strength of the proposal they were fighting. When it became evident that final Congressional acceptance of the whole Plan No. 2 might turn on the adoption of the structural form devised by the Administrator, they realized there was little point in taking their objections to the President. Under the circumstances they could only seek the maximum amount of independence possible for them within the Administrator's plan. With this in mind, Dr. Eliot asked agreement from Mr. Altmeyer that her relations with the Public Health Service be carried on without channeling through the Commissioner's office. He indicated that this arrangement would be acceptable.

The immediate results of all these adjustments were not happy. The Reorganization

Plan became effective the next day, and the Children's Bureau occupied a somewhat anomalous position. It became a subordinate unit anxious for more freedom, and suspicious, at least temporarily, of the motives of the Commissioner and the Administrator. The actual mechanics of transfer were in no way eased by these circumstances.

Later Developments

Within the next few months a series of new developments took place. The Children's Bureau found itself integrated more closely within FSA, and especially within the Social Security Administration. One of the first moves of the Administrator was to order the removal of the "U. S." before the name of the Bureau. An inconsequential act in itself, and a not unusual symbolic manifestation of the attempt to secure central direction and control (the same problem later arose with both the Public Health Service and the Office of Education), it was interpreted by Bureau officials as a psychological weapon in the battle against their institutional identity. As foreseen, the Chief was not called into any staff meetings at the Agency level, except those demanding the services of a technical expert on a specific question. This exclusion was in keeping with the Administrator's plan of administration adopted at the same time as his plan of reorganization. He equipped himself with a personal staff for policy advice and used the heads of the four constituent units as advisors on operational matters. For the most part, however, the integration efforts of the Administrator, at least as viewed by the Children's Bureau, appear to have resulted in annoyance and irritation rather than in the establishment of effective co-operation between the Bureau and the other units. They included efforts to define the channels of authority under the three-level system of administration (Administrator–Commissioner–Bureau Chief) by Agency directive; and they also included such quite different matters as car pooling, and the establishment of uniform housekeeping practices. Also required by directive was a two-level clearance before many official actions could be taken: ultimately the Commissioner's office undertook to proofread all Bureau documents (in addition to the mandatory Agency clearance) before their circulation or public release. At the same time, larger matters of substantive policy integration were discussed at frequent conferences, but, from Miss Lenroot's standpoint, with almost no substantial result.

Meanwhile, the Office of the Commissioner of Social Security was growing into what a Congressional Committee later described as an "elaborate superstructure" of bodies whose efforts were largely dedicated to co-ordinating the operations and policies of the subordinate Bureaus. In itself, this was a logical attempt by the Commissioner to make effective his new authority and responsibility. It was, however, carried out in the face of inevitable suspicion from the Children's Bureau, which had never fully accepted the thesis that all its activities could be geared in completely with other Social Security functions.

The Commissioner also tried to secure adoption of an orientation philosophy for his staff based on the idea of a "Whole Social Security Program"; under this philosophy, the operating units would be carrying on functional assignments designed to contribute to the over-all program of security covering all phases of life. This was, of course, in conflict with the old Children's Bureau theory that it should be responsible for the development of the "whole child." Logically, the concept of the "Whole Social Security Program" would seem to preclude any organization based on an age-group segment of the population.

The situation did begin to ease, however, with time and the march of events. Congress soon started a sharp curtailment of the growth of the Office of the Commissioner which greatly reduced the effective powers of that office. As the Commissioner's office lost functions, the operating bureaus gained some. With the appointment of Oscar Ewing, in August 1947, as FSA Administrator, the Office of the Administrator became more significant. An active program of integration was undertaken at the top level. Regional offices of almost all the FSA constituent units were consolidated throughout the country. The new reorganization produced much turmoil, but the Children's Bureau was left in peace. Nevertheless, in 1949, the effects of the rude original introduction to the FSA were still apparent in the over-all spirit of the Bureau. Resentment and even resignation of the higher officers had largely given way to a wary expectancy of things to come from above.

The Industrial Division

One other problem of lesser importance arose during the period of transfer which occurred simultaneously, but was not connected with the happenings in FSA. This was the separation of the Industrial Division and its retention in the Labor Department. This unit had been created some years earlier to study and advise on problems connected with child labor and youth employment. After the passage of the Fair Labor Standards Act in 1938 there was added to these research and state advisory duties the responsibility of administering the child labor provisions of the Act. As already noted, Miss Lenroot at no time actively opposed the retention of this Division by the Labor Department, because she realized that its enforcement job was a logical complement of the work of the Wage and Hour Division of the Department.

The wording of the Reorganization Plan itself was an invitation for a good deal of confused and rather heated haggling over who should go with the Bureau and who should stay with the Industrial Division. The pertinent parts read:

(a) The Children's Bureau in the Department of Labor, exclusive of its Industrial Division, is transferred to the Federal Security Agency.

(b) The functions of the Children's Bureau and of the Chief of the Children's Bureau under the Fair Labor Standards Act of 1938 . . . are transferred to the Secretary of Labor. . . .

Another portion of the Plan, however, reserved to the Bureau all its basic functions under the original 1912 statute, including the mandate: ". . . to investigate and report upon all matters pertaining to the welfare of children and child life among all classes of our people, and shall especially investigate the questions of infant mortality . . . employment. . . ." Thus, there was some conflict within the Plan. Although the Industrial Division, with its responsibilities for assisting the Wage and Hour Division in tracing down child labor law violators and persuading the public against violating the Act, was clearly to be left behind, there was considerable doubt whether the child labor research functions should be. These latter were research activities into the general problem of child labor in the United States, its prevalence, characteristics, possible dangers, and so forth, which the Bureau had carried on under its original statute; but of course they were also relevant to work performed under the Fair Labor Standards Act.

Under the Budget Bureau's original transfer scheme, the Industrial Division was to retain the research personnel assigned to it; but Miss Lenroot took the position that she could not carry out her functions under the basic Act without these persons. During the sixty-day interregnum between the transmittal of the Plan to Congress and its effective date, several conferences were called by the Secretary of Labor with Miss Lenroot and Miss McConnell, the Division Chief, to discuss where the Industrial Division should be placed within the Department. During these discussions the problem of personnel arose, and Miss McConnell tried to persuade Miss Lenroot that it would be best to leave the Division at full strength. She argued that to strip it of research personnel would so weaken its effectiveness that it could neither carry out its job adequately nor expect much sympathy from Congressional economizers. On July 3rd, the Labor Department's solicitor informed Miss Lenroot that under his interpretation of the language of the Plan, all personnel of the Division should remain in the Department.

Miss Lenroot decided to make one more effort, and shortly before the Plan became law interested Watson Miller in supporting her stand. At this point the Estimates Division of the Budget Bureau called a hearing on the various schedules of personnel and funds scheduled for transfer to FSA that had been submitted to it by the Labor Department. The

Budget officials made it quite clear that their intent had been to keep the Industrial Division at full strength in Labor. This was a difficult decision for Miss Lenroot to accept gracefully. It would mean that almost no research on child labor could be carried on by the Children's Bureau. If anything happened to the isolated Industrial Division all Children's Bureau activity in the child labor field would be at an end, because the Bureau itself had no additional research funds (though conceivably the Wage and Hour Division might carry on the work as part of its general research program). On the other hand, Miss Lenroot felt that there might be some justification for the view that a strong Industrial Division, if it must be separate from the Bureau, had a greater chance of success than one weakened at the outset. Miss Lenroot was also concerned by the opposition of Miss McConnell, who had lined up her division solidly behind her. Finally Miss Lenroot decided to acquiesce in Budget's proposals. Miller, however, sent one more letter to the Budget urging that the matter be reopened. There was no response.

The subsequent history of the Industrial Division has been painful. It has been decimated by Congressional appropriation committees. Transfers and reductions within the Labor Department have greatly reduced its effectiveness. Meanwhile, no additional research funds have been made available to the Children's Bureau itself. Consequently, while two organizations are legally authorized to carry out research in the field of child labor, both are unable to do so.

IN PERSPECTIVE

Viewed as a whole, this history of the Children's Bureau's transfer to the Federal Security Agency is not abnormal or even unusual. Concern about hierarchical position and organizational integrity is inherent in concern about program: it is a rare administrator who is both devoted to what he is trying to accomplish and able to agree that the job can be better done by someone else and in a totally different way.

Almost equally normal is the nature of the settlement: it was a compromise in which the Children's Bureau retained almost full control of its grant-in-aid programs, but subject to the good will of the Federal Security Administrator; and it lost ground hierarchically and organizationally. As with many compromises, no one was fully satisfied.

From the standpoint of the participants, the struggle was largely conceived in personal terms; almost all of them—Miss Lenroot, Mr. Altmeyer, Dr. Parran, Miss McConnell, the Budget Bureau Officials—had a sense of dedication and a feeling of moral rightness. To each of them, the opponents seemed wrong-headed, or insensitive, or ill-informed, or power-seeking. But the observer, reviewing the events, can see them in a larger perspective. The Children's Bureau had a philosophy that was a normal outgrowth of the reform wave of the second decade of the century; FSA and the Budget Bureau were impelled by beliefs that sprang naturally from the respective and allied social and administrative reform movements of the fourth decade. Organizational preference was deeply related to principle and program approach: "the whole child"; "the whole Social Security program"; "the full discretion of the agency head." The jurisdictional dispute was a perhaps inevitable outgrowth of this deeper conflict, though its form and intensity were affected by personalities and institutional loyalties; and a conviction of the rightness and importance of one's program is not unrelated to both.

relate to Weber's sociological generalizations about the bureaucracy + bureaucratic behavior.
Note the use of law as an instrument of advantage.
How many participants in the different crises and disputes
Appeals processes. To whom? when? How effective?
Congress the enigma.
Role of the Budget Bureau?
The values of the official? what were they?
What does the case show about the importance of status in the fed. hierarchy?

THE OFFICE OF EDUCATION LIBRARY

CONTENTS

INTRODUCTION

This is the story of a dispute between an agency head and a chief of a bureau of that agency in which the apparent subject was library consolidation. Although there was a valid basis for disagreement on the question in dispute, the library argument was used to precipitate a type of open warfare in which myths and slogans of administration were very much in evidence: e.g., the extent to which responsibility and authority must be linked; the concept of professionalism; and the general belief in decentralization and independence of agency units as opposed to the necessity for efficient and economical organization; centralization of agency responsibility; and the espousal of the virtues of an integrated agency working for the general welfare. These are highly respectable battle-cries.

This particular controversy was one of the first of a series that continued throughout the year and during the next year, a series which finally culminated in the resignation of the bureau chief, John Studebaker. The resignation of Studebaker brought forth the following comment from the National Education Association, which placed the various disputes in the setting of a larger question. In September 1948, the *NEA Journal* stated:

> Departure of top command from U. S. Office of Education raises again the question of the status of education in the Federal government.
>
> Should education at the federal level be accorded that independence which has been found so essential in the American pattern of life at the local and state levels? That is the question. Some educators believe the current Studebaker-Ewing controversy serves to dramatize the need for an independent educational agency headed by a national board of education which has been consistently supported for several years in resolutions of the NEA, the AASA, and the National Council of Chief State School Officers.

In light of these broader issues, the case will describe the specific library problem, and then move on to the dispute between the agency head, Oscar Ewing, and the Commissioner of Education, John Studebaker. In moving on to the dispute, this study must treat of basic relationships in large terms, since the special problem of the library dispute has real meaning only in the larger context of such questions as the logic and basis of departmentalization; professionalism within a broader hierarchy; personnel casualties of administrative reorganization; and the multi-pressure arena in which policy-making must take place.

I. History of the Federal Security Agency

The Federal Security Agency came into being on April 25, 1939, as a result of a series of reorganization proposals made over a number of years. Such an agency had been recommended by the President's Committee on Administrative Management, which had urged cutting down the President's span of control to make effective executive management possible. In 1939, Congress authorized President Roosevelt (in the Reorganization Act of 1939) to submit Reorganization Plans which would serve five definite purposes:

1. reduce expenditure
2. increase efficiency
3. consolidate agencies according to major purpose
4. reduce the number of agencies by consolidating those having similar functions and by abolishing such as may not be necessary
5. eliminate overlapping and duplication.

Among other things, Reorganization Plan No. 1 of 1939, which President Roosevelt submitted to Congress, established the Federal Security Agency, the Federal Works Agency and the Federal Loan Agency. His statement as to the purpose of the reorganization was clear: "This plan is concerned with the practical necessity of reducing the number of agencies which report directly to the President and also of giving the President assistance in dealing with the entire Executive branch by modern means of administrative management."

The Federal Security Agency brought together certain agencies already operating in various parts of the government which had been established to "promote social and economic security, educational opportunity and the health of the citizens of the nation." (Reorganization Plan No. 1, 1939) The constituent units of the FSA had all hitherto functioned with a substantial degree of autonomy. The Public Health Service had been in the Treasury Department for nearly 150 years; the Employment Service had come from the Labor Department; the Office of Education had spent its seventy years in the Department of the Interior; and the New Deal agencies, the Social Security Board, the Civilian Conservation Corps, and the National Youth Administration had reported directly to the President.

BASIS OF DEPARTMENTALIZATION

There was a general broad basis of "welfare activity" underlying the work of the units comprising the FSA, but each had been a well-recognized, distinct, and in some cases professional function with a tradition (of various durations) of independent action and responsibility. It was natural for the staff members of the units to feel that in terms of previous methods of operation, and in terms of the nature of the units, a "holding company" type of agency was almost unavoidable.

However, those in the Office of the Administrator of the Federal Security Agency, his staff who acted as his policy arms, did not regard health, education, social security, and employment as independent areas of activity. They felt that all these activities were inevitably linked in "the advancement of the general welfare," and that the services of each unit to the nation would be rendered more effectively if the overlapping program aims were directed and co-ordinated by a central administration. The division of the Administrator's staff most directly concerned with the events in this case was the Office of Administration, composed of the Budget and Finance Division, the Personnel Management Division, the Service Operations Division, and especially the Division of Administrative Planning. A memorandum from the Division of Administrative Planning upheld the theory that the activities were interrelated by stating that

> no Agency of the Federal Government has a grouping of activities as clearly related to a common cause as those of the Federal Security Agency. Nowhere is the need for integration as great. Nowhere is it so necessary to balance program activities in order to assure over-all improvements in the general welfare.

However, the heads of the constituent units could not agree that all these activities were, or should be, interrelated to advance the "general welfare." A dissenting opinion expressed in one of the units was that

> the Federal Security Administrator has the task of supervising generally a number of complex and important groups of activities. The individual activities within each group are closely related to each other. However, each group as a whole is less closely related to the other groups. Moreover, an individual activity within a given group may bear little, if any, relation to an individual activity within another group.

This difference of opinion over the basis of organization was to emerge clearly in discussions of subsequent FSA reorganization proposals. Reference back to the establishing act did not furnish final justification for either argument, since the primary purpose had been stated as reducing the President's span of control. Reference in the Plan to the internal organization of any of the agencies created at that time had been noncommittal.

The establishment of the Federal Security Agency also alleviated some of the difficulties which had arisen in connection with the administration of federal grants-in-aid to states. State agencies found that they were working with several federal administrative units in different departments in connection with grants which were being given for related activities. There were overlaps; for instance, the grants for public employment offices which were handled by the Employment Service of the Department of Labor; the grants for unemployment compensation which were administered by the Bureau of Unemployment Compensation of the Social Security Board. Thus, the Federal Security Agency was, to some extent, conceived as a convenient catchall of grants-in-aid to states.

EARLY YEARS OF THE AGENCY

The physical transfer of the component units into a central building did not take place when the FSA was established in 1939. The Federal Security Building (which had been planned originally to be the Social Security Building) had not yet been completed, and when the building was completed it was turned over in large part to the more immediately necessary wartime agencies instead of to the FSA units. So although the Administrative Offices of the FSA were centralized in the Federal Security Building, the Agency remained dismembered for the duration of the war, with its parts scattered in or around the city of Washington.

The precise role of the Federal Security Administrator had not been spelled out in the 1939 Reorganization Plan. This Plan had charged the Administrator with the "general direction and supervision over the administration of the several agencies." The scope of his legal authority was broadened by the phrase which held him "responsible for the co-ordination of their [the constituent units'] functions and activities." But "co-ordination" is an ambiguous word, subject to varying interpretations. There were many practical problems of manipulating traditions and personalities which were not solved by the mere act of charging the position with a degree of legal authority.

Paul V. McNutt, the first Federal Security Administrator, began to co-ordinate some of the operations of the Agency in the area of administrative management, such as budgeting, personnel, and fiscal functions. As events developed, the embryonic plans for administrative co-ordination of the various units had to be abandoned for the duration of the war, since McNutt soon became involved in the job of administering the War Manpower Commission as well as the FSA, and was completely immersed in the more urgent tasks of the wartime agency.

So during this period, 1939 through 1945, the "formative years" of the Federal Security Agency, the constituent units found that their way of life was affected only slightly. They remained in their former homes (though the Office of Education was ejected from the Interior Building and put into one of the temporary buildings), and they continued their familiar policy of independent action. They all now belonged officially to the Federal Security Agency, but the Agency operated as a loosely co-ordinated holding company.

After the war, however, the wartime agencies began to dissolve and move out of the Federal Security Building, making room for the rightful inhabitants of the FSA.

In 1945 there was a change of command in the FSA. Watson B. Miller became Administrator. He had been connected with the former Administrator when McNutt had been National Commander of the American Legion, and he had been Assistant Administrator of the FSA since 1941. During the years in which McNutt had been primarily concerned with the War Manpower Commission, Miller had been, in effect, in charge of the FSA.

With the prospect of physical co-ordination of the constituent units, the Administrator's staff renewed plans for effecting administrative consolidation which they had envisioned as necessary in order to strengthen the machinery which could guide the social programs of the Federal government. One advocate of reorganization wrote that "The time has come to develop the Agency along departmental lines and all employees should realize that the Federal Security Agency is to be an administrative entity, not merely a loose confederation, or a holding company."

Thus, the Administrator's staff felt it was time to develop a new organizational ethic, that consolidation was necessary in order to enable the Agency to take its place as a fully matured organization of the government "responsive to public reactions and responsible for the development of policies and programs with direction stemming from the Office of the Administrator."

This trend of thinking, leading to more closely co-ordinated agencies and departments, had been developing during the preceding years, not only in the FSA but in other departments, in Congress, and especially in the Bureau of the Budget. A drive for co-ordination probably achieved greater significance at this time because the war had brought into being many new agencies which had increased the burden placed on the Chief Executive. The reorganizations which were being planned by the President's Executive Office tended to vest more direct responsibility for over-all activity in a central administrator. The President's Reorganization Plan No. 2 of 1946, which concerned the Federal Security Agency, gave moral backing and legal impetus to the Administrator's staff to implement plans for internal consolidation.

President Truman said in the message accompanying the plan:

> To meet its full responsibilities in these fields [of education, health and welfare], the Federal Government requires efficient machinery for the administration of its social programs. Until 1939 the agencies in charge of those activities were scattered in many parts of the Government. In that year President Roosevelt took the first great step toward effective organization in this area when he submitted Reorganization Plan 1, establishing the Federal Security Agency. . . .
>
> The time has now come for further steps to strengthen the machinery of the Federal Government for leadership and service in dealing with the social problems of the country. . . . As the next step, I consider it essential to . . . strengthen its internal organization and management.

In this Plan, President Truman provided for several changes in the FSA. The most important of these, from the point of developing a rationale for further internal reorganization, was to transfer the statutory functions of several of the agencies to the Federal Security Administrator, who was made directly responsible for their direction and control.[1]

This move set the stage for the diminution of the almost complete autonomy of the units specifically mentioned, and foretold possible encroachment upon the independence of the units not mentioned specifically in this connection in the Plan, such as the Public Health Service and the Office of Education. The transfer of functions now gave the Administrator both substantive and organizational discretion in the performance of the authorized programs of his constituent units. It was now up to the leadership of the Administrator and his staff to determine the future administrative policy of the FSA. They might choose to redelegate the authority to the constituent heads and continue to function as a holding company; they might consolidate common service functions; they might co-ordinate programs. In short, the Administrator and his staff could decide what effect this Presidential directive would have on administrative organization and policy.

II. The Office of Education

All the units of the Federal Security Agency had reason to look with interest, or even with foreboding, towards the effectuation of Reorganization Plan No. 2. Quite possibly the strongest distaste for the probable future course of action was to be found in the Office of Education. The Office exists as a tight unit of about four hundred people who are fully conscious that theirs is the sole Federal agency concerned with over-all problems of educational policy and administration. The Office had been established in 1867 for the purpose of

[1] The agencies affected in this respect were the Children's Bureau, the vital statistics functions of the Census Bureau, the U. S. Employees Compensation Commission, and the Social Security Board, all of whose functions were transferred directly to the Federal Security Administrator.

> 1. Collecting such statistics and facts as shall show the condition and progress of education in the several States and Territories.
>
> 2. Of diffusing such information respecting the organization and management of schools and school systems, and methods of teaching, as shall aid the people of the United States in the establishment and maintenance of efficient school systems, and
>
> 3. Otherwise promote the cause of education throughout the country.

Its more recent operations were described to the Senate Appropriations Committee in 1947 by John Studebaker, then Commissioner of Education, as being those of a clearinghouse which collects information from the states and passes it on to those states which may not be familiar with the latest developments.

> We do that by collecting information, statistical information and other kinds of information, by research, by writing, by correspondence, and by personal contact and consultation. It is just a high-grade research and consultative service; that is what the Office is.

After operating independently for a year after its establishment, the Office of Education was transferred in 1868 to the Department of the Interior. Here little effort was made to coordinate such dissimilar units as the General Land Office (now part of the Bureau of Land Management), the Office of Indian Affairs, and the Office of Education, which were some of the agencies making up the Department at that time. As a result, for the first seventy years of its existence the Office of Education functioned within the Department of the Interior as a self-contained unit whose Commissioner was appointed directly by the President. In 1939, it was put into the newly formed Federal Security Agency, where it became officially subject to the direction and supervision of the Federal Security Administrator, although the Commissioner of Education was still appointed by the President of the United States.[2]

Thus both the Surgeon General of the Public Health Service and the Commissioner of Education remained appointees of the President, and when in 1946 the Social Security Board was abolished and the Commissioner of Social Security was established as an appointee of the Federal Security Administrator, the Surgeon General and the Commissioner of Education tended to regard their positions as being slightly more independent of administrative control than that of the Commissioner of Social Security. The Administrator, on the other hand, according to a statement by one of his staff, regarded his legal and administrative authority as being "no different in respect to the Commissioner of Education than it is with respect to the Commissioner of Social Security. There are some historical differences."[3] This somewhat ambiguous administrative condition undoubtedly contributed to later misunderstandings. The reader should understand, however, that Presidential and Senatorial confirmation of bureau chiefs is a common practice in the Federal Government; ordinarily the method of appointment is not significant in determining the relations between bureau chief and agency head.

After its transfer to the FSA in 1939, however, the Office of Education continued to function as one of the several loosely co-ordinated units of the Agency, enjoying a degree of independence which later encouraged it in persistent resistance to any attempts at supervision or control, since neither had been exercised to any great degree during the first years of the Agency.

This policy of preserving essential autonomy was supported by many of the staff of the Office of Education, since most of them tended to regard themselves as professional educators rather than as professional administrators, and thus not properly subject to any lay control. The National Education Association, the national professional organization of teachers, expressed itself frequently and clearly on this point. It felt that the Office of Education should not be in the Federal Security

[2] "The management of the Office of Education shall, subject to the direction and supervision of the Federal Security Administration, be intrusted to a Commissioner of Education, who shall be appointed by the President, by and with the advice and consent of the Senate." (U. S. Code, title 20, section 2)

[3] J. Donald Kingsley, then Assistant Administrator, Testimony before Subcommittee of the Committee on Appropriations, House of Representatives. 80th Congress, August 4, 1948, p. 9.

Agency or in any other agency or department at all, but should operate as an independent agency headed by a National Board of Education.

The attitude of the NEA and of the staff of the Office was entirely normal. Not only is education a "professional" function and hence (so goes the traditional rationale) not properly subject to interference by laymen, it is historically a function that has been kept separate from "political" control in the states and municipalities of the United States. While the place of education in the American scene is perhaps a more complex matter than this analysis would indicate, the strength of the tradition in the thinking of professional educators is a persistent and notable phenomenon. The quotation from the *NEA Journal* on page 33 reflects sentiments that have been expressed over the years in every school district in the country. Under the circumstances, the desire for autonomy on the part of the Office of Education had moral overtones that could hardly be expressed by the Office of Vocational Rehabilitation, for example, or the Social Security Board.

THE COMMISSIONER OF EDUCATION

Dr. John W. Studebaker, the Commissioner of Education, had been engaged in educational activities himself for more than twenty years before coming to the Office as Commissioner in 1934. He had spent his career as an educator working extensively in the field of auxiliary services, such as special education for handicapped children, school health programs, and especially adult education programs. He had served during this twenty year period as Assistant Superintendent and Superintendent of Schools in Des Moines, Iowa.

As Commissioner of an office rendering "specialized services" to a professional and well-defined clientele, and as custodian of a function with a tradition of independence throughout the United States, Studebaker felt it imperative that he retain the authority and responsibility not only for educational matters but for the related organizational functions and services of the Office.

This position lent itself directly to acceptance and approval of the holding company type of organization under which the Office had operated for the seventy years of its existence.

Studebaker's views coincided, more or less, with opinions expressed throughout the Office. The objections to reorganization would have tended to be the same regardless of the person actually serving as Commissioner, although the view of the Office of Education might not have found as voluble and persistent a spokesman as it did in Studebaker.

III. The Reorganization Surveys and Their Reception

Such was the agency and such the unit with which this case is concerned. The clash between the two was precipitated by the very first steps toward reorganization. In the summer and fall of 1946, in accordance with President Truman's desire to effect consolidation of the FSA and "eliminate overlapping and duplication of effort," as he had stated in the Reorganization Plan No. 2 of 1946, a series of administrative studies was undertaken by the FSA's Division of Administrative Planning. The analysts, who were recruited from different parts of the Agency, examined a wide range of functions: communications control, personnel, auditing, information, research and statistics, publications and review, library service, and others. Many of the recommendations made by the survey teams were eventually implemented; some were still being studied in 1950. This case will concentrate on the specific difficulties and arguments which arose from the recommendations of the Agency Library Service survey. Although the library question was just a small portion of the larger problem of general reorganization of the FSA, the broader area of disagreement over administrative organization in general is inherent in the disputes which arose over this more limited problem.

The library section of the survey, which in the report runs to fifty-odd pages, was made by Joseph Boyle, of the Office of Vocational Rehabilitation of the FSA, who examined the library service then available to the different units. He was interested in determining the amount of overlapping of personnel and material, the practicability of integrating the libraries under one administration, and the practicability of physically combining the existing libraries as their parent units moved into the Federal Security Building.

Two of the units, the Children's Bureau and the Food and Drug Administration, were still using the libraries of the Departments to which they had formerly been attached (Labor and Agriculture respectively). By moving into the Federal Security Building, they would no longer have convenient access to these library facilities.

The library of the Office of Education and the Social Security library, while organized to serve those particular branches and originally housed with them, were now separated from their main offices. The Social Security library was divided, with branches in several buildings, though the main collection was in the Social Security Building (now the Federal Security Building). The library of the Office of Education had been left in the South Interior Building when the Office had been transferred from the Interior Department to the FSA and its central offices moved to a temporary building. Most of the other units maintained small special collections for their immediate staffs.

Some consolidation, in any case, was essential, not only to provide library service for the member units moving into the central building without any appropriate facilities of their own, but to bring together the library and central office of both the Social Security Administration and the Office of Education.

Some idea of the comparative sizes of the libraries involved [4] can be gleaned from the following excerpt from the survey:

> Activities common to each library:
> The activities common to each library are acquiring, classifying, cataloging, shelving, and circulating library material, the answering of reference questions and to some extent the preparation of bibliographies.
>
> Of the total library staff of fifty-six employees, approximately thirty-five devote all or part time to activities common to each library. Of the thirty-five employees, twenty-eight devote full time to activities other than the preparation of bibliographies and seven devote part time.
>
> The distribution between libraries is as follows:
>
> Full-time:
> Social Security, fourteen
> Education, seven, and
> National Institute of Health, seven
>
> Part-time:
> Social Security, one
> National Institute of Health, one
> Saint Elizabeth's Hospital, two, and
> Office of Vocational Rehabilitation, two.

On the basis of these considerations of overlap and duplication found to exist between the libraries, and the lack of library facilities in some units, the recommendations presented for comment were:

> 1. That all libraries of the Agency be placed under the administration and direction of an Agency Librarian.
> 2. That the libraries of the Social Security Administration, Office of Education and Office of Vocational Rehabilitation be consolidated into an Agency library as those organizations move into the Federal Security or nearby buildings.
> 3. That an Agency Library committee be established to consist of the heads of all constituent libraries with the Chief Librarian to act as chairman.
> 4. That the Chief Librarian be the principal Agency representative on all inter-Agency library committees.

THE LIBRARIANS COMMENT

A review committee was formed of the chief librarians of the organizations affected, with

[4] Those of the Social Security Administration, the Office of Education, the National Institute of Health of the Public Health Service, St. Elizabeth's Hospital, and the Office of Vocational Rehabilitation.

representatives also present from the Office of Administration: Leonard A'Hearn, the Director of the Division of Administrative Planning, and Glenn Stahl, Deputy Director of Personnel Management, both of whom were participating in the direction of all the surveys, and Taylor McCauley of the Division of Service Operations, who was advising the committee on actual space and monetary savings.

The librarians serving on the review committee did not consider the survey particularly professional or technically comprehensive. It was, after all, the work not of a librarian but of an administrative analyst. However, the nature of the various libraries and the character of the problem were perfectly familiar to them and they were all prepared to express their judgments on the recommendations.

Margaret Doonan, Chief Librarian of the Public Health Service Library, felt that it was a "good idea to eliminate duplication and have someone in charge with over-all responsibility for a co-ordinated library."

Margaret Paulick, though not specifically a librarian, was an administrative officer on the staff of the Office of Vocational Rehabilitation and also in charge of their very small library; she also agreed that "an over-all library is a good idea."

Ellen Commons, Chief Librarian of the Social Security Administration library, said she felt that "an over-all Department Library is necessary," although she raised a question as to whether all the units of the FSA would be retained as such if the Agency were to be made into a Department of Welfare.[5]

These excerpts from the fairly uniform endorsements made by the librarians indicate that, in general, as librarians, the concept of a consolidated library seemed to make sense. On the other hand, they noted in passing that although a centralized library was felt to be an efficient way, technically, to provide more effective service to the Agency, it was possible that each individual unit might not continue to receive the same quality of specialized service under such a system. It had been made clear to them at the meeting, however, that they were being asked to comment on the recommendations of the analyst in their capacities as library technicians, and not from a viewpoint of their particular constituent organizations.

ECONOMY IN THE AGENCY THROUGH REORGANIZATION

Apparently none of the librarians considered the centralization of the libraries as a method of effecting extensive economies. Richard Logsdon, Chief Librarian of the Office of Education Library, felt that the "projected savings were of doubtful validity, and that improvement of service rather than savings should influence the decision." Since in later discussions of this reorganization it was frequently mentioned by the administrative planners that certain economies would result from reorganization, it might be well to quote the portion of the survey referring specifically to expenses and savings which could result from the administrative change.

The total cost of moving all the libraries into the Agency building was estimated by the analyst at $21,504. This cost would remain the same regardless of whether they were moved with the intention of combining them when they arrived, or whether they were moved into the building to continue as separate units. There was an additional cost of buying new equipment for the Office of Education library, estimated at nearly $60,000; but again, this cost would have occurred whether the Education library was moved into the building as a separate unit or whether it became part of an Agency library, since its shelving facilities in the Interior Building had been built-in and had to be replaced.

> The expenditure for the equipment would be amortized in a period of two years through savings resulting from the consolidation of this library [the Office of Education library] with the library of the Social Security Administration. The consolidation would result in more effective utilization of personnel through the realignment of

[5] This refers to two problems. 1. There was continual talk of the Federal Security Agency being made into an Executive Department. 2. There was pressure from the Office of Education to have the Office removed from the FSA in that event and made into a separate unit.

duties of personnel in the professional and subprofessional grades, one each in P-3 and P-2, and one in sub-professional grade SP-4. Additional savings would result through a reduction of expenditures for books. A spot check of the catalogs of these libraries shows that some duplication of books now exists because of overlapping areas of subject-matter coverage.[6]

Logsdon pointed out that "we are not dealing with a new problem when we consider consolidation of libraries. Colleges and universities have faced this problem for a number of years."

All colleges and universities that contain various types of departments have to decide (as did the multi-unit FSA) to what extent the specialized libraries should be independent and to what extent the general library should contain specialized material. Although Logsdon noted that this particular centralization might make the library remote from the users who had been accustomed to specialized service, he considered the recommendations made by the analyst "remarkably sound" and agreed that in this case the more efficient way to organize library services for the Agency as a whole would be to centralize the administration and consolidate the individual libraries.

Logsdon, who had been Chief Librarian of the Office of Education since 1945, had considerable experience in problems of library administration and organization, and his technical training was broader than that of the other library heads, though this in itself is not necessarily a measure of technical competence. (See Appendix, page 51, for more extensive background information on the librarians involved.)

Though he had endorsed the recommendations for consolidation, since the review committee was holding only this one meeting and it seemed to him that final action was about to be taken, he suggested that the recommendations be referred back to the constituent organizations for study and analysis in order to "get genuine backing of sound recommendations." This would "give them an opportunity to be assured that their operation will not be handicapped under a centralized library."

[6] The total salaries for the three civil service positions mentioned by the analyst, P-3, P-2 and SP-4 add up to a saving by the Federal Security Agency of approximately $10,000 per year.

THE COMMISSIONERS OBJECT

In accordance with the procedure which had already been agreed upon (and in line with Logsdon's suggestion) the recommendations were presently referred to the heads of the affected units for comment.

The unit heads shared the apprehension that Logsdon had anticipated. Though they spoke from diverse professional backgrounds, their objections to the plan followed a consistent pattern. They all (with the exception of the Commissioner of the Social Security Administration) objected to any such consolidation on the grounds that the professional character of the work of their office demanded specialized service to their staff, and that separate libraries could serve their needs more effectively than could a generalized Agency library.

This negative reaction from the division heads had been expected by the staff of the Office of Administration of the FSA. They were aware of the very human fact that any reorganization plan, whether sound or unnecessary, whether propounded by the President or by the chief of a division, whether sweeping or limited, inevitably treads on the toes of vested interests, which tend to resist a disturbance of routine. One memorandum from the Office of Administration which recommended adoption of the reorganization to the Administrator expressed the view that the staff considered the use of the library consolidation as a tool for weaning units away from this provincial attitude to a sense of oneness with all the Agency.

The Administrator's staff could see no reason why a consolidated library with its greater resources would not be as responsive, if not more responsive, to the needs of the individual constituents. They tended to regard the objections by the heads of the Agency divisions as opposition for the sake of opposition, a conjecture which persisted throughout the deliberations, and one which was not too well received by the heads of the several FSA units.

THE COMMISSIONER OF EDUCATION TAKES A STAND

In October 1946, the heads of the agencies of the FSA were advised by Leonard A'Hearn, the Director of the Division of Administrative Planning, that the survey concerning the advisability of a centralized Agency library had been completed and reviewed by a committee of chief librarians from each of the constituent agencies. A recommendation from the committee and from the Division of Administrative Planning to adopt the reorganization was going to be forwarded to the Administrator. In order to complete the picture of the reactions to the proposed consolidation, the heads of the units were asked to give their opinions and recommendations.

The reaction of the Commissioner of Education to the reorganization was explicit opposition to the change. Dr. Studebaker strongly urged that no steps be taken "at this time" to execute any of the recommendations. He pointed out that educators would feel it important that "the Office of Education should retain the necessary authority for operations for which it has responsibility," and that the unique interest of education would not be adequately safeguarded by a move of this type which aimed at co-ordinating what the Administrator's staff considered to be "peripheral functions" of the Office of Education.

This conclusion was reinforced by a conviction that the services of the library were not peripheral to the operations of the Office of Education, but part of its basic program. The Office of Education considered the activities of the library essential to the performance of the advisory and research functions which formed the bases for the leadership of the Office. Thus, reasoned Studebaker, if the Commissioner of Education was to be held responsible for the general performance of his Office, he would have to continue to hold both administrative and policy direction of the library activities. Any divorce of the library from the central control of the office would be considered by him a handicap to the development of the main programs of research and service. To quote Dr. Studebaker's recommendations: "The possibility of greater economy through centralized library service must be weighed against the more desirable elements of responsiveness to the library requirements of the individual constituent."

He further pointed out that any savings achieved by reducing or consolidating personnel could not be substantial, since the Office of Education library was understaffed at the time and had a huge backlog of accumulated work. Thus, any economy achieved by consolidation of libraries of other units with that of the Office of Education library would be absorbed by the needs of the staff of the Office of Education library. (For a brief period this matter of savings was in dispute, but Studebaker's conclusions on this particular issue soon gained general acceptance.)

Each of the other FSA units expressed the opinion that its own library and library staff served as part of its research staff, and that the professional character of the work of the unit required such specialized service. Although Studebaker's opposition was stated clearly and primarily in terms of whether the Office could fulfill its responsibilities without control over its library, one secondary consideration might have exerted a little more influence on Studebaker than on the other division heads. He might have had in mind the fact that Logsdon, the Office of Education chief librarian, had a higher civil service rating than did any of the other librarians involved. Studebaker may have wanted to make sure that in any event a consolidation would not result in a downgrading of the position. He was concerned that when Logsdon left (as he did before the crucial decision period, so that the position was vacant for several months) the Office of Education could continue to maintain in its library service the same quality of professional guidance Logsdon had provided. It was felt that it might be difficult to secure a successor of comparable ability if the position were to be downgraded. As it happened, although the Administrator's staff did consider the disparity in the staff, grades, and services as one of the positive arguments for the reorganization, during the discussions over this question, they upheld the Office of Education in its desire to maintain the ratings which existed in the Education library.

Although the question of primary concern in the stated objections was where the management of this service function of the Office of Education would lie, there was also always present the latent factor of Dr. Studebaker's general opposition to the impending trend of developing a more integrated Agency. The Office of Education had itself been thinking in terms of tying together all of its research and service activities into the over-all program of the Office so that it could operate more efficiently as an integrated unit under an Administrator who, up to now, had merely exercised nominal supervision.

Each of the FSA divisions shared this organizational view—that theirs was a unique, specialized program best developed by independent control. The Administrator's staff felt equally, and with just as much professional concern, that practically every program of the Agency overlapped others, some only incidentally, others to a large degree. Thus all the programs would benefit if the units worked together toward a common goal—advancement of the general welfare. Their hope was to develop, eventually, "Agency thinking," which would provide justification, in their opinion, for the existence of the Federal Security Agency as something more than a "glorified housing project" (as it was later described by Oscar Ewing). As far as the Administrator's staff was concerned, the consolidation of the libraries was a relatively harmless area in which to begin co-ordination of the administrative functions of the Agency, since the touchy problem of interference with individual programs was present only to a minimal degree. It is possible, then, that the division heads considered the question as being a first line of defense against further encroachments upon their independence, aside from the substantive importance of the particular situation.

THE RECOMMENDATIONS GO UP THE LINE

The library survey recommendations, with a summary of the objections of the several division heads of the FSA, were passed on to the Administrator, Watson Miller, by A'Hearn, who had been responsible for directing the several surveys of the different Agency functions.

A'Hearn outlined the duplication which existed in the common activities and material of each library, the space which would be saved if the libraries were consolidated as they moved into the central building, and the expansion of resources available to the Agency as a result of the consolidation. The Chief Librarians, he pointed out, had considered the proposals for consolidation reasonable and practical from a technical standpoint. Finally, he summarized the feelings of the Office of Administration by pointing out that although on some occasions one or two programs would benefit specifically by moves such as this, in the long run all would gain, since the Agency would be strengthened by co-ordination of such services.

This was one of the most difficult points on which to get common agreement, for the constituent heads had made it clear that they were perfectly willing to forego this type of "Agency thinking" in favor of continuing their long-standing policy of individual activity. For them, an "Agency" was in a sense a nonexistent creature; only the functioning constituents existed. If the Federal Security Agency were to be strengthened, the Office of Education, the Public Health Service, and the other units had to be strengthened.

One other factor is worth noting. In May 1946, a bill was passed in the Senate Committee on Education and Labor which would have made the Office of Education big business overnight. It provided for the granting of federal aid to education to the States to the tune of $225,000,000 per year, to be administered by the Office of Education (whose budget for 1947 was $19,000,000). A sum of this dimension is large even in relation to the total budget of the Federal Security Agency (which was approximately $893,000,000 in 1947). In July 1946, two months later, the surveys of the Agency were authorized and the plans for reorganization of the FSA gained impetus. However, by the fall of 1946 when the first recommendations for reorganization were presented to the Federal Security Administrator, hopes for the passage of this particular bill had died in the House Committee. This series of events should be considered in equating the simultaneous pressures which condition any decision.

THE ADMINISTRATOR'S DECISION

The problem of library consolidation did not involve compilation of technical drafts, or result in proposals which required minute sectional breakdown. The alternatives which evolved were not much more complex than: (1) the libraries should be consolidated, or (2) the libraries should not be consolidated. The whole question, however, had evoked an explicit expression of attitudes which existed about the larger area of reorganization in general, feelings which would probably be intensified when questions of more complete reorganization were advanced. This indicated a possible disruption of the relationship between the units and the Office of the Administrator which might not be balanced by the advantages resulting from the consolidation of the libraries. However, the Administrator's staff, who had been guiding the surveys, seemed to be approaching rapidly an "are we going to reorganize the Agency or not" mood. They realized that if the individual units could effectively sidetrack this minor move in the desired direction, subsequent reorganization plans would raise even stronger objections and equally substantial blockades.

The Administrator, Watson Miller, decided, however, not to take action. It is possible that he felt that the library consolidation was not a strong enough symbol to warrant overriding the strong objections presented by his constituent heads. Perhaps he felt that the benefits of consolidation would not compensate for the loss of morale which would result from the move. Like most administrators, he presumably had no concern personally with library operations in contrast with his inevitable concern with matters like budget and personnel. Thus the library consolidation may well have seemed not worth an argument. In any case, he did not appear to feel that he was personally concerned in general with the advantages or disadvantages of reorganization, laying more stress on the maintenance of harmonious relationships between units and Administrator, and among the units themselves. Therefore, when situations of this type arose, fearing that the resulting explosions might destroy Agency equilibrium, he chose to maintain the status quo.

IV. The Ewing Era

Eight months later, in August 1947, the cast of characters changed. Watson Miller became Commissioner of the Immigration and Naturalization Service in the Justice Department, and Oscar Ewing was appointed Federal Security Administrator.

Ewing had never been directly connected with government administration before. He had spent his professional career building a successful private law practice, but throughout his career he had maintained an interest in matters of public policy and national welfare, seeking as his outlet for action the Democratic Party organization. He had started as secretary of the Decatur County (Ill.) Democratic Committee at the age of 16, and had risen to the position of Assistant Chairman of the Democratic National Committee in 1940. In 1940 he had backed Paul McNutt when McNutt sought the Democratic nomination for the Presidency.

When he was appointed Federal Security Administrator there were murmurs of apprehension in the Agency, because it was felt that his extensive political activities might introduce an element of "partisan politics" and influence his policies in the Agency. His immediate staff apparently soon became assured that Ewing's political connections would not adversely influence the activities of the various divisions under his control. Dr. Studebaker and several of his staff, however, were never convinced of this. Their fears were brought out in the open when Studebaker resigned in the summer of 1948. At that time, as a result of a letter written by Studebaker shortly after his resignation, Congressional hearings on the operation of the Office of Education were held. During these hearings, many of the opinions about administrative organization held by Ewing and by Studebaker, as well as by supporters of both men, were expressed, as were some of their retrospective feelings about the library controversy.

In referring to Ewing's political activities, Studebaker had said in his letter that

> the capstone of the argument against the centralization of control which you are developing, at least as far as education is concerned, is to be found in the fact that you are admittedly a partisan politician. You work hard for your party . . . being a partisan, you secure to the extent possible as your immediate associates persons who share your partisanship. . . . But there is a deep-rooted tradition in this country, born of the harrowing experiences of the centuries, that the function of education in a democracy should be completely removed from partisanship. . . . The personnel of the United States Office of Education . . . together with their colleagues throughout the country and citizens in general, would resent any attempts to color education with partisanship and cause its policies and processes to yield advantages to a political party.

Ewing replied to this in the 1948 Congressional hearings, though perhaps without meeting the issue directly:

> Another criticism which Dr. Studebaker makes of me is the fact that I am "admittedly a partisan politician." Dr. Studebaker seeks to create the impression by this that I have attempted to inject politics into the administration of the Office of Education.
>
> I want to say as emphatically as I know how that this is absolutely false. I do not know the politics of a single person in the Office of Education. I never suggested to Dr. Studebaker the name of a living soul for appointment to a position in the Office of Education. Every appointment that has been made in that office from the time I became Administrator until Dr. Studebaker resigned was made upon his recommendation.
>
> He does not cite a thing, and he cannot, because it does not exist.

This interchange of allegation and denial is significant for an understanding of the library controversy, not because of merit or lack of merit in the charges, but because the existence of the charges could not fail to create or reflect an element of personal antagonism in the relations between the two men that was separate and apart from their differences over organizational theory.

CONGRESSIONAL ACTION

From the beginning of his term of administration in August 1947, Ewing was under more pressure than his predecessor, Miller, had been. The appropriations granted to the FSA by Congress (with a new Republican majority) for the new fiscal year, July 1, 1947, through June 30, 1948, had been cut, and the specific appropriations for the Social Security Administration of the FSA had been cut drastically. When the functions of the Social Security Board had been transferred to the Federal Security Administrator by the Reorganization Plan of 1946, it had been assumed, as the House Appropriations Committee later noted, that "the clear intention was to eliminate administrative superstructure and thereby effect considerable savings in numbers of personnel and other overhead expenses. . ." The Committee members were especially anxious that the "administrative superstructure" of the Social Security Administration be dismantled.

> The Committee is disappointed to note that in the application of such plan to the Social Security Board no economies have resulted . . . the only result to date has been the elimination of the salaries of two members of the Board inasmuch as the Board has been succeeded by a Commissioner of Social Security who apparently has by delegation of the Federal Security Administrator all the authority and power formerly invested in the Board by law. He is surrounded with all the functionaries and satellites formerly utilized by the Board.

In the report on the Appropriations Act for the fiscal year 1948, which had just been approved when Ewing entered the Agency in August 1947, the Appropriations Committee stated that "to date, no economies have resulted and the committee is convinced that no economies will be forthcoming unless the Agency is given some assistance in the form of budget reductions."

This "assistance" appeared formally as a million dollar (30%) reduction in the 1948 appropriation for the service operations of the Social Security Administration. This meant that unless funds could be transferred from other operations of the Agency, which was extremely unlikely, activities at the Social Security Board level would have to be reduced by one-third. This could be done either by shifting some of the operation down to the bureaus of the Social Security Administration, or by transferring some of the functions up to the Agency level and placing them in the Office of Administration of the Federal Security Agency. The Social Security library was affected directly and immediately since it would not have sufficient funds to purchase books and equipment until July 1948, and services such as the state legislative reference service had to be discontinued. Since very little could be gained by breaking the Social Security library into small, very specialized segments which would be attached to the various subdivisions of the Social Security Administration, the only alternative seemed to be consolidate that library with libraries of the other constituent units and form an Agency library which could then be placed in the Office of Administration of the FSA.

This budgetary crisis was occurring at the same time that the need for action in this area became particularly urgent, although the library reorganization was just a small part of the larger problems with which the Administrator was faced, and was just one of the range of recommendations resulting from the various surveys. The other FSA units were planning to move into the Federal Security building within the next few months, and the question was being raised: Were the libraries to be brought into the building as separate units, or would they be consolidated as they arrived?

Thus, when Ewing entered the Agency in August 1947, he was presented with the appropriations for the FSA for the fiscal year which had just begun. The appropriations bill had been accompanied by the rather pointed Congressional remark:

> The Committee is disappointed that these economies have not already resulted from the approval of the Reorganization Plan No. 2 [of 1946] and regrets the necessity of making reductions of this magnitude, but if the only way to secure economy in the Government's operations is to reduce budgets then the Committee on Appropriations is willing to accept the responsibility.

It was obvious that the Congressmen were prepared to swing their ax and would keep chipping away at the Agency's appropriations until they were convinced that sincere efforts at economizing were being made.

Again, it is worth noting that substantial Federal aid-to-education grants were in the background throughout this period. At this time, in August 1947, another Federal aid-to-education bill had been introduced in Congress. This bill provided for $300,000,000 yearly in grants-in-aid to States which would be administered through the Office of Education. As of July 1947 it was on the Senate calendar, having been approved by the Senate Labor and Public Welfare Committee, and was pending in the House Committee on Education and Labor. This bill might fare better than its predecessors.

RECONSIDERATION

Ewing promptly exhumed the various completed surveys to determine what steps had been contemplated in recent years.

> The studies [of the libraries] that had been made long before I got into the agencies recommended that when they were brought into that building they all be put together and under one common management. By that method, we could save money and would be a more efficient library because we would have more books. Apparently that had been discussed during the time that my predecessors were in office. Nothing had been done about it, but when I got into it, it seemed perfectly obvious that it was the thing to do.
>
> After reviewing what had taken place, I came to the conclusion that the committees were right; that there had been enough surveys; that it was time to act.[7]

[7] Ewing's testimony before Investigations Subcommittee of Senate Committee on Expenditures, August 1948.

In terms of following Congressional guidelines, Ewing was proceeding as almost any Administrator entering the Agency at this time would have had to proceed. The frequent recommendations from Congress to "exert every reasonable effort to assure against overlapping and duplication" and the pressure the Appropriations Committee had exerted through its control of funds made it quite obvious that the Committee wished to see further reorganization of the Agency and had become increasingly critical of the Agency for the slowness with which such steps were taken.

Moreover, the Administrator's staff of the FSA had placed themselves firmly on the record as favoring immediate steps to reorganize and integrate the Agency. The library consolidation was a first, relatively simple step. To disregard the FSA staff's recommendations in this matter would undoubtedly affect its usefulness to the Agency and undermine its functions.

It is difficult to evaluate the extent to which Ewing was acting on the basis of his personal administrative philosophy. Studebaker's position was both personal and historical, having been worked out throughout his career, while Ewing's was perhaps more of a corporate position. Continuity had been maintained in the administrative structure of the Federal Security Agency through the Administrator's staff, while the Administrator himself had changed twice in two years. Ewing was probably acting from personal conviction, but he was also adopting the organizational ethic of his subordinate staff officers on an issue where they were clearly on record.

In any case, time for deliberation was strictly limited since the agency units were planning momentarily to move to their new quarters.

THE ELEVENTH HOUR

Less than a month after Ewing had entered the Agency in August 1947, the machinery of reorganization was put in motion. In September 1947, two meetings were called by Leo Miller, Executive Assistant to the Administrator, at which representatives from his Office of Administration were present to discuss the year-old report on the Agency Library Service. Representatives from the divisions affected were not invited because not only had their original objections been presented in full at the time the surveys had been circulated originally but the opinion was expressed in the Office of Administration that "from experience to date, it is evident that the heads of certain constituent organizations are in general opposed to any change as such. We have found that nothing tangible is gained by requesting the comments of the heads of constituents regarding the proposed recommendations."

At the time the survey was being reconsidered, Dr. Studebaker was not in Washington and did not return until the recommendation to consolidate had been passed on to the Administrator from Leo Miller. This did not help to smooth the way for acceptance of the reorganization. The Office of Education was probably hampered by the absence of the Commissioner, and the Administrator's staff would have preferred having all the heads of the affected units present and informed, even though not present at the meetings. This series of events may have caused some members of the Office of Education to lose confidence in the purpose of the reorganization and feel that the plan was being hurried unnecessarily, since the issue had been dormant for a year.

When Studebaker returned and learned of the imminent order, he arranged a number of meetings with Ewing. According to Ewing's testimony in the 1948 hearings, every time he would go around the corner he would run into Studebaker wanting to reargue the issue. Studebaker claimed in rebuttal that he had limited his discussions to two official meetings in October. A third opinion, expressed later, was that no one was sure how many times Dr. Studebaker was up in the Administrator's office talking to Ewing, before, during, and after the decision. These retrospective opinions are interesting indications of the temperature of the situation, since even such minor points became the subject of controversy.

Studebaker's motivations in maintaining such a tenacious grip on all the activities and operations of his Office were sharply questioned by many of the people favoring the reorganization. Ewing said in the Congressional hearings, "He showed a complete lack of a sense of proportion, a complete unwillingness to co-operate, a complete unwillingness to do anything except sit in his own little bureau and tell the whole cockeyed world to go to hell."

Opinions not so strongly worded seemed to substantiate this feeling that "Studebaker just wasn't going to let *anybody* tell him how to run his Office," and that "he wanted to hang onto everything he had. If he had been in the Administrative Office, he would have been just as willing to pull the library out of Education and build up that Office."

A defense of Dr. Studebaker's opposition, although made several years later, seems representative of the opinion of the Commissioner's supporters at the time:

> Dr. Studebaker was representing a very strong and convinced segment of the educational profession in defending the necessity for separation of education. His position was based on conviction as to what was best for education, and not for reasons of personal prestige or power.

As a last compromise, at one of the meetings in October 1947, Studebaker proposed that the libraries be brought into the main FSA building but continue to operate as separate units. Although Studebaker felt at the time that the Administrator was not unsympathetic to this proposal, Ewing referred to this in the Congressional hearings the next year by saying

> It simply did not make the slightest sense to me to move the libraries into one building and have three separate organizations when, if you combined them, you could save on overhead and the people would get more efficient service, because they would have a bigger library from which to draw. [8]

On October 27, 1947, two months after Ewing entered the Agency, the directive was sent out ordering the consolidation of the libraries. Ellen Commons, who had been Chief Librarian of the Social Security Library, was appointed Agency Librarian.

V. Post-Mortem

Since a great many of the underlying feelings did not emerge until the more heated statements at the Congressional hearings held a year after the libraries were consolidated (though the hearings were not a direct outcome of that particular problem), it may be illuminating to quote from some of the pertinent passages of the public statements and testimony of Ewing and Studebaker. By the time the hearings were held in 1948, several other conflicts, equally if not more controversial, had ensued between the Commissioner of Education and the Federal Security Administrator. The temperature had risen, and the sections of the testimony concerning the library situation were, perhaps, more bitter than the actual events warranted. The statements themselves are, again, useful as indicative of the character of the situation (and of similar situations which had followed the library controversy) rather than as completely factual descriptions of the then year-old dispute.

Ewing reviewed his opinion of the relationship which had existed between Studebaker and himself:

> Here is the point of the thing and what is fundamental, I daresay: The Federal Security Agency when it was put together, represented a combination of independent agencies—and I underscore and italicize, "independent." They resented being put under any administrative control at all. This was long before I was ever in the office. And Studebaker was the one who resented it most. He was the most recalcitrant, the most unyielding, and the most unco-operative. I was warned

[8] The "three separate organizations" referred to the libraries of the Office of Education, the Public Health Service and the Social Security Administration, all of which were substantially larger than those of the other units mentioned before.

of that when I took hold, but I thought "I can work with him," and I certainly tried to. But the size of it is that the statutes that you people have adopted make me responsible, I think the words are, for the direction and supervision of the Office of Education, specifically. Now, he resents that, whereas we feel—and I not only feel but know, and I have no hesitation in saying it—that it is my legal, not merely right but duty to know what is going on in that Office and to try to exercise such reasonable direction and control as I can to make it function as efficiently as possible and to operate properly the programs that you gentlemen have appropriated money for.

Studebaker never liked that. He always conceived of the agency—he used the term "Well why cannot the agency be just sort of a loose holding company, letting each one of the units go off on its own?" I feel my job, as Administrator, is to check up on the programs of the Office of Education, Public Health Service, and every one of them, to know what they are doing, and, if I can see they are doing something, to make suggestions to improve it.

Ewing went on to state that he was proud of his record of reorganization.

It is, I think, a constructive one. We have been building an Agency—and a good one. Of course, we have had problems, problems which have been accentuated by virtue of the long delay in effecting integration of the Agency and the consequent hardening of resistance to any change.

Of course, there has been some internal resistance to certain of these moves. Old patterns are always difficult to change and many of our units had always been virtually autonomous. There is an understandable tendency on the part of the unit chiefs to see the picture only from their own somewhat narrow points of view. There is an understandable desire on their part to have exclusive control of their own affairs and to provide their own independent services; to have their own automobiles, their own libraries, their own duplicating and graphics services; to do their own independent purchasing. But such atomistic tendencies, however understandable, are precisely the reason that such units are combined in larger agencies, and precisely the reason that authority to decide which services should be common and which individual is not vested exclusively in bureau chiefs. If the public business is to be well-administered, firm stands must be taken against atomism for its own sake and in favor of the most efficient organization of common services. I have taken such stands and I believe that most of my colleagues in the Federal Security Agency recognize that they have been essential to good management. Dr. Studebaker was unusually resistant in this respect.

. . . I wish to say that in effecting these administrative changes, I have been happy to think that I was moving in a direction strongly approved by the Congress and that we have been working these matters out together. I am in entire accord with the view expressed by the Senate Committee on Expenditures in the Executive Departments when, in reporting upon S. 140 at the first session of the Eightieth Congress, it said: "It is, therefore, the opinion of this committee that the public interest, as well as the interest of the respective fields of health, education, and public welfare can best be served through the creation of a unified program comprising these three major activities!"

During the period in which I have served as Administrator, I have consistently strived to create such a unified program, and to perfect the administrative machinery necessary to its development and execution. If Dr. Studebaker regards this as "one large monolithic welfare organization," his argument is with the Congress, not with me.

This was precisely the argument Dr. Studebaker was upholding when he said that "the function of education is not a welfare function, since it necessarily represents a wide range of human interests and operates through well-defined agencies and institutions. . . ." He considered education, its programs, its services, its organization, as a professional and unique function, and could not agree with the tendency to regard education as merely one aspect of welfare activities. Standing behind this theory, he was bound to resist the attempt to draw out of the Office of Education any services or activities which were common to other "welfare functions."

Furthermore, he objected to Ewing's administrative policies as such, stating that "I am in favor of the maximum degree of decentralization of responsibility and authority. And I want to couple the two to the maximum degree." He felt that Ewing's reorganizations tended to

leave the professional people in the Office of Education responsible for achieving fruitful results in helping to improve American education while transferring to your [Ewing's] immediate staff the authority to control the means and procedures by which these professional people carry out their responsibility. This divorcement of responsibility and authority with respect to the work of the Office of Education necessarily results in the same divorcement in the divisions and sections of the Office and with all of its individuals. The result is a strange feeling of uncertainty and fear among employees. The whole scheme is well designed to devitalize and demoralize the staff.

One member of his staff, the Assistant Commissioner of Education, Dr. Norton, who had agreed with Dr. Studebaker's contention that the work of the Office of Education was being impeded by the reorganization, resigned about this time in 1948. His letter of resignation indicated that the changes in administrative organization were instrumental in his decision to leave.

I cannot look with complacency upon rapidly developing trends to subject the professional bureau that is the Office of Education to increasing controls on the part of numerous persons planted in the structural organization at levels between the Commissioner of Education and the Administrator of the Federal Security Agency, to whom the Commissioner is supposedly directly accountable.

I do not believe that it is more important to develop and support a rationale for a particular type of Federal Security Agency organization than it is to strengthen the constituent unit of the Agency responsible for professional services in education which has long been recognized as a unique function in American democracy.

Dr. Studebaker was probably referring to feelings such as these when he said in his letter to Mr. Ewing,

Your program develops frustration and a feeling of futility among the employed personnel because individuals and units of individuals in the Agency cannot control the means to the ends for which they are responsible.

The most successful private and public enterprises are those in which to the maximum practicable extent the spheres of authority and of responsibility of individuals and of units of individuals are kept identical. Your program leaves responsibility with people "down the line" in the organization, so to speak, but strips away from them the control of the essential means by which their responsibility must be executed. You vest authority in your immediate staff members, but they are not and will not be held responsible by the people for any shortcomings or failures of the operating organizations of the Agency. As frustration and futility develop, responsibility for the exercise of initiative, for the use of judgment, for securing results, also tends to move "up the line." Here we see at work what might be called "bureaucratic statism" within a government originally dedicated to the principle of individual responsibility and respect for personality. Thorough regimentation always has been and always will be destructive of individual responsibility, a quality vital to the continued progress of our country.

An outside opinion of this situation, that of the task force report on Public Welfare, prepared in 1949 for the Commission on Organization of the Executive Branch of the Government, added these remarkably ambiguous comments:

Three functions have recently been removed from the Office of Education to the central offices of the Administrator of the Federal Security Agency: Office of Education Library, auditing of educational grants to States, and the information and publications service. If the results of this removal are to improve services to the schools of the land, such a move may have much to commend it. If, however, it is for the sole purpose of amassing more power for the sake of power in the Office of the Administrator, it is to be condemned. The Office of Education library is one of the outstanding libraries in this field. Its purpose is primarily to aid in the researches of the Office and to answer requests for assistance. Its librarians have been just as much research assistants and research bibliographers as they have been librarians. Its use as a research tool should be increased rather than diminished. Any sincere attempt to make library service more effective by centralization and amalgamation should be balanced against the possibility of interference with the primary function of this library.

THE LIBRARIES REORGANIZED

By 1950, three years after the order to consolidate the libraries was given and the smoke had cleared, the gloomy predictions of the Office of Education did not seem to have been borne out. Although neither the Administrator's staff nor the Office of Education had wished to downgrade the position which had been held by Logsdon, as the Office of Education had anticipated, there was some difficulty in filling Logsdon's place. It was finally resolved by lowering the rating of the unfilled position of the Office of Education Librarian (Assistant Librarian to the Agency Librarian) one grade, and raising to this new grade one of his assistants who had been familiar with the problems and operations of the Office of Education library. The Administrator's staff of the Federal Security Agency viewed the operation as successful, with the Library serving the entire Agency competently and efficiently. The librarians felt that in the short time since consolidation had been completed (the actual move into the FSA Building was not completed until a year after the directive was issued), the effectiveness of library service to the Agency had been demonstrated, and that service to the constituent units had not been impaired. Although some of those in the Office of Education still resented the fact that the library functions were called "merely another service function," some of those in the Office who had felt most strongly about the separation of their library from the central research activities of the Office admitted that library service to their unit and staff had not deteriorated but had continued in a satisfactory manner, though perhaps its services as a research aid to the Office had not developed in the same manner as an independent education library might have.

Appendix

Ellen Commons (Social Security) studied general letters and science for two years at St. Mary's College, Notre Dame, Indiana; graduated from the Battle Creek School of Home Economics; and had a B.A. degree from the University of Wisconsin. She took a series of courses on social work at the New York School of Social Work and completed a course in classification at Catholic University Library School. In 1933 she entered the Government service as a research librarian for the Federal Emergency Relief Administration, built up the library for the Works Progress Administration, and in 1936 she was appointed librarian for the Social Security Board with a civil service rating of P-5. In 1947 she was raised a grade and made Agency Librarian.

Margaret Doonan (Public Health Service) received a certificate in library science from George Washington University. After spending several years as public library assistant in the District system and cataloger in the library of the Superintendent of Documents she entered the Department of Agriculture as librarian. She then became the Chief Librarian for the Public Health Service with a civil service rating of P-5 and has worked with that library for many years.

Richard Logsdon (Office of Education) received B.A. and B.S. degrees from the University of Wisconsin, and a Ph.D. in library sciences from the University of Chicago. He was librarian for a few years at Adams State Teachers College in Alamosa, Colorado, and was librarian and Associate Professor of Library Science at Madison College in Harrisburg, Pennsylvania. He served as Professor and head of the Library Science Department at the University of Kentucky for a short time before he entered the Navy, where he was responsible for organizing and administering a technical library for the Navy training program. He entered the Office of Education Library in 1945 as Chief Librarian with a civil service rating of P-6, left in 1947 to be the librarian at the Veterans Administration, and then became Associate Librarian of the Columbia University Library in New York City.

Bibliography

U. S. Congress. Senate. Investigations Subcommittee of the Committee on Expenditures in the Executive Department. *Operations of the United States Office of Education*, Hearings, 80th Cong., 2nd Sess., pursuant to S. Res. 189, Part 4, Sept. 27 and 28, 1948. (U. S. Gov't Printing Office, 1948.)

U. S. Congress. House. Subcommittee of the Committee on Appropriations. *Investigation of the Federal Security Agency*, Hearings, 80th Cong., 2nd Sess., on the Department of Labor-Federal Security Agency Appropriation Bill for 1949. August 4, 5, 6, 1948. (U. S. Gov't Printing Office, 1948.)

U. S. Congress. House. Committee on Appropriations. *Department of Labor-Federal Security Agency and Related Independent Offices Appropriation Bill, Fiscal Year 1948*, 80th Cong., 1st Sess., H. Report 178 (1947) to accompany H.R. 2700.

U. S. Congress. House. *Message from the President of the United States transmitting Reorganization Plan No. 2 of 1946*. 79th Cong., 2nd Sess., House Doc. 595, May 1946.

U. S. Office of Education, *Annual Report* for the fiscal year 1944.

Unpublished memoranda, Division of Administrative Planning of the Office of Administration, Federal Security Agency.

ACKNOWLEDGMENT is made to the *National Education Association Journal* for permission to quote from its article on the resignation of John Studebaker.

INDONESIAN ASSIGNMENT

CONTENTS

1. A situation not covered by policy criteria to guide action.
2. Fact-finding to provide a basis for policy decisions. Staff work.
3. Importance of indoctrinated goals + identifications.
4. Professional ideals and psychological compulsiveness. (no, only ethical compulsions) / Personal factors in the individual decision. Minimum of organizational restraints. Conscious and unconscious behavior.

What kind of orgn. behavior is called for?

5. Ideological preferences and official behavior.
6. Is this an ethical problem? why?
7. Is this a case of disobedience of authority?
8. Should this case be considered a sport? See editorial comment.
9. What does this case show about the nature of authority in an administrative situation. Note the State Dept. conflict of attitudes about the worth of his superior.
10. Kinds of orgn. behavior possible { review, discipline, delegation, consultation }

cf. Truman and the Harry Dexter White controversy. Here the superior (the Pres.) disregarding the findings of the subordinates (FBI)

I. INTRODUCTION

This case[1] involves a decision by a junior government official at the American Consulate General in Indonesia in 1946. In reading the case, the following factors might be noted as of particular importance: the uniqueness of the post and its charged political environment; the close relationship between the official and his immediate superior, the Consul General—coupled with his remoteness from the parent central organization in Washington; and finally, the clear relationship between the official's background and principles, and his decision. These factors in the case may be useful in throwing light on the intimate connections and interplay between informal and environmental influences in the process of decision-making.

At the time these events occurred, the situation presented a real and embarrassing dilemma to the official, whose responsibility it was to make the decision; yet to the reader the decision may seem obvious, easy, or perhaps both. If this is the reader's impression, the writer can only plead that perhaps it is attributable to the anatomy of retrospection and to the web of words used to describe the case. For retrospection and description can at best only partly recapture the feeling of uncertainty and discomfort confronting the individual when a decision is taken.

II. Background

INDONESIA IN 1945

On August 17, 1945, three days after the Japanese surrender, the Republic of Indonesia proclaimed its independence from the Netherlands. During the six-week hiatus between the formal surrender announcement and the arrival of British reoccupation troops to accept the Japanese surrender in Indonesia and release Allied prisoners, the Republican nationalists consolidated their forces. When the first British troops arrived, a Republican national administration was actively functioning.

The British reaction to this unexpected and unprepared for turn of events was confused and confusing. British relations with the Republic remained on an uncertain basis: the British sought to avoid antagonizing the Dutch or the Indonesians, while at the same time refraining from commitments to either. The Dutch reaction was initially one of incredulity, and later of hostility to the "Japanese-inspired" regime. After their severe deprivations both in Indonesia and Europe during the war, the Dutch longed for a return to the "good-old-days," a return which the Republic was dedicated to prevent. Even liberal Dutch elements, cognizant of the need for change, regarded the Republic as a menace to the kind of gradualism and moderation they had in mind. The Republican attitude at the time was marked by the deep-seated distrust of Dutch intentions, characteristic of the long-time nationalist movement; by uncertainty toward the British; and by a naive faith in the United States, attested to by the myriad quotations from Lincoln and Jefferson painted on signs and buildings throughout the capital city.

The interest and concern of the United States in Indonesia was economic, and strategic. Indonesia was an area of past and potential American investment, a source of critically needed raw materials (including tin, copra, rubber, and sugar), and a strategically located military and naval installation in the Pacific. As with Britain, the speed of the Japanese surrender and our inadequate intelligence sources found us totally unprepared to enunciate and execute a policy in Indonesia for the protection of American interests and aspirations. The need for on-the-spot informa-

[1] NOTE: The following account is autobiographical. The *Editorial Reflections* at the end have been supplied by the editor, not by the author of the story.

tion and analysis was critical, if such a policy were to be formulated.

For the first six months following the re-occupation, disorder in Batavia was rampant. With British, Dutch, and Indonesian forces quartered near or in the city, skirmishes were frequent. The civil administration of the capital was partly handled by the military, under British-Dutch aegis, and partly by the Republic, which ran the electric, trolley, and telephone systems and maintained a large governmental staff in the city. Living conditions for the civilian population were bad; food was scarce, and where available, unwholesome.

THE CONSUL GENERAL

The first American representative to arrive on the scene was the Consul General. He was sixty years old; he had served as Consul and Consul General in the Indies for twelve years before the war. Much of his life, his feelings, his values, and recollections, were inextricably bound up with the pre-war pattern of colonial existence. His attitude toward the plight of the Dutch was naturally one of sympathy. Years of tropical service had taken their toll on him. Those who had known him before the war found him slowed down, his speech affected by a slight stutter. For these reasons, there had been considerable controversy within the Department of State at the time of his reassignment to Batavia in mid-1945. Some felt that his age and prejudices made his reassignment to an area of political unrest and uncertainty extremely unwise, and that a younger man was preferable. Others felt that his long experience and familiarity with the area and many of its key figures were such primary assets as to outweigh any other liabilities. Within the Department itself, jurisdiction over Indonesia was shared by the Division of Southeast Asian Affairs and the Division of Northern European Affairs. The former represented the "anti" faction, while the latter supported his appointment.

The Consul General's first month in Batavia was marked by severe personal hardship. The living conditions and diet treated him harshly and enervated him acutely. He was, moreover, severely overworked. With no staff whatsoever, and only the barest equipment, he prepared cables and reports to the Department of State alone: drafting, typing, coding, and logging messages, personally taking them to the telegraph office, and repeating the reverse process on all incoming messages. The burden would have been difficult for a much younger man to bear.

Quite naturally, the Consul General addressed strong pleas to the Department for staff assistance. His most immediate need was met in the middle of December, with the arrival of a code clerk from Washington. The strain eased somewhat, but at the same time the pressure of work was increasing. Negotiations between the Dutch, the Indonesians, and the British were beginning, and political and economic conditions were becoming more and more uncertain as disorder spread from Surabaya, to Batavia, to Bandung, and to other British-held bridgeheads in the Republic. The Department's need and requests for political information increased. Besides the political negotiations, Departmental inquiries stressed the status and condition of American property, the availability of raw material stockpiles, and the outlook for new production. Concentrating on political matters, the Consul General was unable to address himself to these economic questions, and reiterated his pleas for additional staff. To meet these urgent pleas, the writer was appointed vice-consul in December 1945, and assigned to Batavia for economic analysis and reporting. A word about my own background, training, and indoctrination in the Department should be included, insofar as they are germane to the problem of decision which the case presents.

THE VICE-CONSUL

My academic training had been in economics, supplemented during 1943-1944 by an intensive program of work at Stanford in the Far Eastern Area and in the Malay and Dutch languages, in connection with the Army Specialized Training Program. My qualifications for the assignment thus were directly related to this training. After completing the course of study at Stanford, I had gone into the Office of Strategic Services, serving one year in

Europe. I received my discharge in November 1945, and, apprised of the need in Indonesia through OSS and State Department friends, I was appointed to the Foreign Service Auxiliary in December. Most of my ten weeks' indoctrination period at the State Department was spent going over material in the Division of Southeast Asian Affairs. There I learned of the earlier controversy over the Consul General's appointment to Batavia. My own hearsay-sympathies, inchoate as they were, tended to gravitate toward the Division's own stand on the matter. Moreover, my study of the pre-war pattern of colonialism in Indonesia left me with marked sympathy for the nationalist cause.

At the end of February 1946, I arrived in Batavia to begin work. My initial meeting with the Consul General was cordial and friendly, though filled with innumerable admonitions about "caution," "danger," and "the need to move slowly." By this time, the pre-war building of the Consulate General had been reoccupied, but aside from one typewriter and the Consul General's old teak desk, there was no office equipment, no stationery, not even chairs for the Chinese clerks to sit on! The Consul General informed me that all the office supplies were still down at the harbor of Tandjong Priok (where they had arrived three months ago), and requested that I undertake as my first assignment to locate the supplies and transport them to the office, so that the Consulate could begin operation. Rummaging around disordered godowns for about two weeks, I located most of the seventy-five crates which had been dispatched to Batavia. By the end of March the office was ready to handle routine Consular business, and on April 1st we opened our doors officially.

My second assignment, inevitably, was to see and talk to the scores of visitors who swarmed into the Consulate asking for information concerning visas, relatives in the United States, and others just wishing to discuss their problems; and to answer some of the correspondence which had accumulated in Consular files, mainly from American firms wishing to explore trade opportunities even before the shooting had ceased!

ECONOMIC REPORTING

With this backlog out of the way, I began my first economic reporting during May. In my economic work, I was responsible to the Consul General, who had to countersign all reports, airgrams, or cables I might draft to the Department. However, part of my indoctrination period in the Department had been spent talking to the International Resources Division and the Economic Development Division, so that I was reasonably acquainted with the type of information in which the Department was primarily interested. The decision as to subjects for reports, therefore, rested largely with me. The procedure evolved for me to discuss briefly with the Consul General a prospective project. He would make a few comments, indicate a few Dutch authorities who might help me; thereafter, the responsibility for finding, accumulating, analyzing, and interpreting the data was mine, until I presented the finished report to him for countersignature.

Initially, this procedure worked without incident. My first report dealt with agricultural prospects in the outer islands of Celebes, Moluccas, and the Lesser Sundas. These areas were already under Dutch control. The Consul General enthusiastically endorsed the subject. I proceeded to make contact with the Netherlands authorities concerned. My relations with them were friendly, and they not only gave me all their meager documentary material, but carefully answered even the most elementary questions which I addressed to them (I say "elementary," because my knowledge of tropical economy was spotty). The report was completed at the end of June. The Consul General commended me, and the Department added its approval several weeks later.

My second report proceeded along the same lines and with similar results. It dealt with the thorium content of Bangka tin ores, and while I came in contact with different Dutch personnel, their solicitousness and helpfulness duplicated that shown me in my first official contact with the Dutch.

A slight snag was struck in my next project. In response to a specific request from the International Resources people, I wanted to investigate the copra situation: the availability of stockpiles, and the condition of the coconut palms. In my preliminary discussion with the Consul General, I inquired about the need for consulting the Republican authorities in preparing the report, since a sizable part of the copra area was in Southern Sumatra, in Republican territory. His reaction was one of mild disturbance, and brought a strong restatement of the views he had expressed to me on my arrival: the need for "caution," the "ticklish political situation which you must take my word for," and the "need for waiting and moving slowly."

I took this as a clear negation of my inquiry, and therefore confined myself to talks with the Dutch Director of Economic Affairs and his staff. At the end of my report, I made a note to the effect that "it had been impossible for political reasons to consult the Republican authorities." I did this with a sense of personal discomfiture. The political implications of an inquiry concerning copra seemed to me tenuous. Moreover, I knew that through the Consul General our government was already in touch with the Republic, and my own informal acquaintance with Indonesian officials had given me a high regard for their discretion. I felt that the report clearly suffered from the exclusion of this possible source of information, and I handed it in with a feeling of dissatisfaction. The Consul General, however, read it closely and again responded enthusiastically.

Without going into details, I may add that my next project, dealing with the rubber situation, followed almost the identical pattern of the copra incident. Here again, extensive rubber areas were in Republican territory which were important to the completeness of the report. My suggestion of the need for consulting Republican authorities was, however, discounted and ruled out by the Consul General.

From my own point of view, the following was the situation when the problem of decision arose. I was, on the one hand, eminently gratified with the cordial relations built up between the Consul General and myself. Yet, I was acutely aware of the fact that the cordiality had a fragile base. The Consul General was explicitly sensitive to the great difference in our ages and perhaps implicitly to the difference in status between a career Foreign Service Officer like himself and a Foreign Service Auxiliary Officer. I had no ties with him of age or career or general attitudes that would serve to cushion any disagreement between us over an issue like contact with Indonesian officials. The possibility of a cooling in our relations was ever present, and I could not face such a cooling without considerable uneasiness. In a distant field post, friendly relations between superior and subordinate assume an even greater psychological significance than they do at home. Furthermore, the Consul General was chief of the post, and his recommendation would, of course, be important to my future in the Foreign Service. Finally, I might rationalize that any shortcomings in reporting from the field were, formally at least, his responsibility, and not mine.

On the other hand, I had a persistent feeling that the Department required full reporting from both sides to make competent policy decisions in Indonesia; that competent and complete performance of my work required building sound contacts on the Republican as well as the Netherlands side. While I had learned to feel a certain admiration for the perseverance of the Dutch, and an appreciation of the co-operation they had shown me, my ideological sympathies for the Indonesian case had been reinforced by my experiences in the field.

III. The Problem and the Alternatives

In September 1946, a confidential airgram from the Department was received at the Consulate. It requested an extensive report on "economic plans and policies in Indonesia," with almost no specificity attached to these terms. It concluded with the observation that "if possible, and with the utmost discretion, Dutch, Indonesian, and British sources should be consulted as far as feasible."

This airgram was routed by the Consul General to my desk for action on the day following its arrival. I was, at first, both enthusiastic and elated to receive it. Its importance seemed obvious in view of the prolonged silence by the United States government as to its policy, in the face of a continued complex political situation. Moreover, it clearly offered scope for originality and analysis, which was a welcome change from the relative tedium of the commodity reporting I had been doing. Further reflection made me feel that effective handling of the airgram required a basic decision. Was I to consult the Indonesian authorities in preparing my report? And if so, was this consultation to be extensive and on a high level, or simply confined to a cursory phone call to the Republic's Ministry of Economic Affairs? The airgram, from one point of view, clearly carried a mandate for consultation with the Indonesian authorities, and equally clearly the demands of a complete and useful report also pointed in this direction. Yet just as clearly, on the other side, were the qualifications which the airgram had appended to its instruction: "if possible," and "as far as feasible." For either of these reasons, consultation with the Republic could be justifiably neglected, or at least treated in summary fashion. While my own inclination was (as it had been in the copra and rubber reports) to consult the Republic, I was keenly aware that (a) such action would be likely to vitiate my position with the Consul General, and (b) that if there were any mishap in connection with my action (e.g., a "leak" to the press), I could expect to be held fully responsible by the Consul General and the Department.

I think, in retrospect, that I was more or less clearly aware that three courses were available to me. In the first place, I could approach the Consul General, as I had done on previous, though essentially different, occasions, and ask his opinion of the import of the Department's instruction, and his advice in the matter of whether to consult the Republic. I had, of course, good grounds for assuming that the response would be similar to his advice on the rubber and copra reports. But my own position would clearly be secure if there were any kick-back by the Department, both because of the loop-holes contained in the instructions, and because of the Consul General's own advice. Moreover, such a decision would clearly protect my relations with my chief.

Secondly, I could take my instructions from the airgram directly, consulting the Dutch and the British only, and relying on the vagueness of the instruction and/or the precarious political situation to explain my failure to consult the Republic, in a concluding paragraph of the report. Then, if the Department specifically desired such consultation, it could so direct in a subsequent instruction. From my own point of view, the advantages of this decision were the security of my position and the effect it would have on my already good relations with the Consul General. It would, in his eyes, clearly mark me as viewing the general situation as he did (a point on which he had expressed some concern more than once), and therefore would raise his opinion and trust of me.

Thirdly, I could consult the Republic directly, in line with my own inclinations, and could rely on the implicit mandate of the airgram for justification. This would, of course, endanger my relations with the Consul General, and leave me open to subsequent blame in case of untoward results. It would, however, acquit me of a personal consciousness of responsibility for complete and competent reporting, and for giving the Republican case at least equal treatment with that accorded the Netherlands. It might be mentioned, parenthetically, that if this were to be my decision, a further decision would have to be made: concerning the extent of my consultation with the Republic. I reached a quick decision on this point, that if I were to adopt this general position, my consultation with the Republic should not be cursory, e.g., confined to a single phone call, but should be as extensive as would appear feasible in the light of the reception I should receive upon approaching the officials concerned.

IV. The Decision

Before reaching a final decision, I spoke informally to the chief of the Republic's public relations office, whom I shall call Mr. Subandi. I had known of Subandi before coming to

Indonesia, through mutual friends at Stanford, who had held a high opinion of his reliability. This impression was confirmed by me when I met him at numerous social functions in Batavia. I secured from him, without going into details, a guarantee that any inquiries I might direct to any Indonesian government office would be treated with the utmost confidence.

I thereupon decided on the third alternative: to consult the Indonesian Ministry of Economic Affairs directly, and fully (in addition, of course, to my consultations with the Dutch and British). The results of the decision were singularly happy. I received a warm welcome from the Indonesians. My talks with the Minister were fruitful, and the Ministry staff supplemented these talks with the first documentary material on economic matters which the United States government secured from the Republic. My report was drawn up, after several redrafts, in October 1946. The Consul General made several comments which required minor editing and revision, but countersigned it at the end of the month. There was, however, a noticeable cooling in our relations,[2] and prior to countersigning the report he remarked with no little asperity, "you had better watch your step in dealing with these Indonesians in the future." Nevertheless, even this ill-feeling did not seem to be permanent. When, three months later, I received a commendation from the Department for the report, the Consul General's attitude noticeably softened, though our relations were never quite as friendly as they had originally been.

EDITORIAL REFLECTIONS

The foregoing account is, as the reader has observed, autobiographical. It may be useful for the editor to set down certain comments on the course of events that reflect considerations presumably not apparent to the participants at the time. Other conclusions will occur to the reader, but the following suggestions may at least serve as a caution against excessive generalization from a single incident and as a stimulus to further reflections and questioning.

The problem in this case was felt by the Vice Consul, and probably also by the Consul General to be an ethical problem: Was it right for the Vice Consul to consult with the Indonesians in spite of the Consul General's anticipated opposition to such action? The reader's evaluation of the Vice Consul's conduct can perhaps be made only in ethical terms. The reader may regard the conduct as insubordination, on the one hand, or as loyalty to professional and policy objectives, on the other. Whichever view the reader adopts, or whatever other judgment he comes to, he should note that the course of events clearly illustrates the truism that an ethical decision of this sort is conditioned by personality and by other external and internal factors. The Vice Consul was young, had given no hostages to fortune, had pride in his profession, was moved by sympathy for the Indonesians, and had no established ties with the Foreign Service. How different the answer might have been if the Vice Consul had been a Foreign Service Officer, a man of 45 with a family, untrained as an economist, and strongly sympathetic to the Dutch cause.

A change in other external factors might also have affected the result. The Vice Consul was operating virtually alone and in the field of his specialty, under conditions which made his presence well-nigh indispensable to the Consul General. The ethical question might never have arisen or at least might not have constituted the responsibility of one solitary person if he had been part of a sizeable staff with his report subject to review by other technicians and by a hierarchy of superiors. Decisions subject to scrutiny in this fashion tend to become corporate decisions, and as they become more impersonal they are less likely to be thought of as ethical problems. Ethical questions do arise within large hierarchical organizations, but there is greater opportunity for reaching decisions on general policy grounds instead of solely on the basis of one individual's ethical convictions. Large-scale organization, with its complex division of labor, would seem to di-

[2] The Consul General had a long-standing custom, dating back to pre-war days, of inviting some of his staff, and the top officialdom of Batavia, to his lodgings for mint juleps on Sunday mornings. After handing in my report, I did not receive another invitation to these get-togethers for five weeks!

lute the sense of immediacy and direct responsibility involved in an ethical decision. The ethical difficulty is shared, and the individual's responsibility is fulfilled by seeking to obtain appropriate group judgment.

Another external factor that was significant in creating the specific problem was the fact that Batavia was a field office, several thousand miles from Washington. The State Department officials who drafted the cables would no doubt have considered themselves foolhardy if they themselves had attempted to determine the policy issue on consulting with the Indonesians. Delegation of discretion is inherent in the field office–central office relationship, and the conditions in Indonesia made a large degree of delegation well-nigh inevitable. If the Consulate General had been vested with less discretion, the Vice Consul might have had no opportunity for painful choice: but the dangers in such a course are obvious.

The geographic isolation of the actors had another important consequence. In a large or fairly large organization, problems of this sort are frequently resolved by resort to informal channels. If, for example, the Vice Consul could have discussed the matter informally (properly or improperly) with the economists who were seeking information on the Indonesian situation, they could then have strengthened or modified their requests for reports. Alternatively, if the Consul General had had the opportunity to talk over the problem with his superiors, his opposition to consultation with the Indonesians could have been hardened to the point of a flat prohibition, or could have been withdrawn entirely. Under any of these alternatives, the ethical question would have been averted.

In the foregoing respects, the case is somewhat uncharacteristic of common governmental situations. In another respect, however, it is entirely normal. For loyalty to a profession and to one's professional colleagues inevitably comes into occasional conflict with hierarchical loyalty—loyalty to one's administrative superiors. All the professional groups in government service suffer from these difficulties at times, and the difficulties are most likely to arise when, as in this case, the professional task is performed in an atmosphere charged with political tension. There is no pat solution for such difficulties, but it is more likely that adequate solutions can be found if it is realized that the difficulties arise from the character of the organization and are not caused solely by the weakness of man.

A final comment on the behavior of the Consul General may perhaps be helpful. It would be an exaggeration to state that the conditions under which the Vice Consul and the Consul General acted are abnormal in government service, though most workers in our government are far more directly part of a large organized working group than are consular officials at small foreign posts. But even without allowing for this difference, the Consul General's failure to apply official or formal sanctions to a subordinate who had failed to follow established procedures need occasion no surprise. The use of formal sanctions is generally a last resort: the continuous process of maintaining discipline is effectuated day in and day out by modifications in informal relationships.

The Vice Consul's economic report was apparently the first action which he took overtly counter to the wishes of his chief. The Consul General could not say or feel: "his cup is full." And, finally, in noting what the Consul General did and did not do, it is well to bear in mind that official sanctions—with an open break in relations—could not fail at best to be extremely inconvenient to the Consul General. The attenuation of social relations represented a not inappropriate reaction in this situation in the light of the Consul General's problems and position.

THE NATIONAL LABOR RELATIONS BOARD FIELD EXAMINER

CONTENTS

1. Role problems - what is meant here? Person - Agency - {NLRB / Congress
2. Relation of Congress to Administration?
3. Included to give insight into informal factors and the political environment of administration.
4. Conflict between individual and authorized group goals.
5. What about administrative neutrality here? {Howard, Meacham, Nylander, Madden
6. Effort to establish some professional norm of administrative behavior. Need this as a basis for discipline as well as for direction
7. Loyalty - What does it mean for organization behavior?
   What should be the basis for relations with affected interest groups?
8. Group fictions - the examiners vs the regional director. Group norms.
9. If you were to write a code of ethics for administrators on the basis of this case, what would you include in the code?
10. Do you think the supervision of the Board was adequate, considering the dispute in the Region.

FOREWORD

The role an individual plays in his immediate working group and in the larger administrative structure of which that group is a part is determined by the interplay of many factors—his personality and previous experiences, the behavior of those both near and remote in the organization, and outside pressures—to mention only a few. Furthermore, in an administrative hierarchy, the individual's actions are necessarily a matter of organizational as well as private concern. In this case, the role that Maurice Howard, a field examiner in the Twenty-first Region of the National Labor Relations Board (NLRB), came to play over a period of about two years, from 1937 to 1939, eventually made it necessary for those at the top of the NLRB pyramid—the three Board members—to decide whether or not he should be discharged.

The Howard story is a very small fragment in the complex mosaic that constituted the pattern of public relations and personnel administration of the NLRB in its early days. The confusion and pressures which influenced that pattern were intense, for passage of the National Labor Relations Act had represented a new, big, and controversial step in labor relations, an area long marked by bitter differences of opinion. Many of the Act's opponents among employer groups never became reconciled to its existence. Labor, whom it was intended to aid, became sharply divided in 1937 with the CIO-AFL split.

The Board and its staff were caught in the three-cornered fight over unionization, jurisdiction, and the control of collective bargaining that developed. Specific criticism of the Board took the form of persistent complaints of bias in the administration of the Act, of inefficiency, of poor staffing, and the like. Combined with general anti-NLRB sentiment among certain powerful groups, these criticisms made it possible for a coalition of Republicans and conservative Democrats in the House of Representatives to secure the appointment of a Special Committee to Investigate the NLRB, under the chairmanship of Congressman Howard W. Smith, Democrat of Virginia.

Needless to say, the Smith Committee, as it was known, was not sympathetic to the NLRB. It expected to find, and sought, for example, evidence of Communist infiltration. Quite naturally it was also on the alert for charges of bias, especially of anti-employer or pro-CIO bias. And most of the allegations of bias which it took up did point to a favoring of the CIO by the Board and its staff. But in connection with its investigation of the staffing and conduct of the Los Angeles field office of the Board, the Committee found complaints of both pro-AFL and pro-CIO bias. The Howard case is a discordant part of the confused Los Angeles story.

The printed record of the proceedings of the Smith Committee covers some six thousand pages; the whole Los Angeles episode occupies perhaps no more than 200 pages of the total; and Maurice Howard's role is touched on in a relatively minor portion of the 200. This arithmetical relationship bears some reasonable resemblance to the relative significance of the Los Angeles situation and the Howard difficulties in the total complex of the Board's troubles. Indeed, investigation and action on complaints from the Twenty-first Region were permitted by the Board to drag out for a long time. The reasons for this, as Chairman J. Warren Madden described them to the Smith Committee were as follows:

Well, there were several causes. One was the ever present cause of our being short-handed and the lack of persons of importance and standing with the Board to go out on short notice to do a chore like this Los Angeles chore.

Another was that we were not as seriously disturbed by the reports from Los Angeles as it might now be made to appear. In other words, it was the impression of the Board that things were going along tolerably well at Los Angeles, and that there was not a critical situation there, and the combination of those two things postponed a final treatment of the Los Angeles situation.

Thus Maurice Howard was a pretty small factor in the problems of the NLRB; actually, in Los Angeles, as the following pages will show, Howard's difficulties were inextricably entwined in the difficulties of his superior, the Regional Director. But certain characteristic features in Howard's behavior are of general interest to students of public administration, and the whole tale is of value for the glimpse it affords of certain aspects of informal organization and leadership, group loyalty, field office—central organization relationships, discipline and morale, and "outside" pressure.

The enforcement of new and controversial legislation like the National Labor Relations Act calls for zeal and, by the same token, attracts and even develops zealots. Maurice Howard was a zealot. For some tasks zealots may be useful, even necessary; but almost inevitably they create problems. In Howard's case, his behavior led to a minor crisis in the Board: Member Leiserson recommended his dismissal, Member Smith recommended retention, Chairman Madden cast the deciding vote. The following account[1] gives in summary form the information available to Chairman Madden when he made his decision. The reader's problem is to decide what he would have done had he been in Mr. Madden's place.

Howard's Early Service in NLRB

Maurice Howard came to the Los Angeles regional office of the NLRB in the spring of 1937, and there his great struggle began. Immediately before this he had spent about two and one-half years as a $2600-a-year field examiner in the Seattle regional office. He had been an instructor at Reed College, Portland, Oregon, when he was hired, in October 1934, by Charles Hope, Seattle regional director, on recommendation of the college's president, Dexter Keezer. In a letter to the Board at the time, Hope wrote favorably about Howard:

> . . . Mr. Howard has a splendid labor background. He is familiar with collective bargaining. I believe he will be capable of handling cases in the near future. . . . I checked him through Labor and Industry in Portland. . . .
>
> A man of good habits, a student, and has a pleasing personality. . . .

Hope's expectations about Howard were not entirely fulfilled. In the fall of 1936, the Secretary of the Board, while on one of his routine tours of inspection of the regional offices, made the following report to the Board on Howard:

> Howard, according to Hope, is completely unable to settle cases. Hope sends him out to investigate them, in the first instance, and thereafter Hope finds it necessary to take over the work on cases himself.
>
> As the Board knows, Hope is not at all pleased with the type of work Howard does. He criticized Howard's tendency to go out and investigate a case in its initial stages, advise the union how to perfect its organization, advise them to further communicate with Hope and ask for his personal intervention, and then return to Seattle without having bothered to interview the employer. Hope further states that even when there is work to do around the office, Howard spends most of his time in the office reading books.
>
> I had quite a long talk with Howard and he is very frank in his attitude that the Board's chief

1 The material for this study has been derived almost exclusively from the record of the Smith Committee (Special Committee to Investigate National Labor Relations Board. Pursuant to H. Res. 258, House of Representatives, 76th Congress, Second Session). The record is composed in large part of memoranda, letters, and reports taken from the Board's files by the Committee and originally written, presumably, with little or no thought that they would eventually be used in a Congressional investigation and published. Particular reliance has been placed on a long report on conditions in the Los Angeles office prepared for the Board in the summer of 1939, by George Pratt and Gerhard P. Van Arkel, two senior NLRB staff members, under circumstances described below. All quotations, except where otherwise noted, are from the Pratt-Van Arkel report which appears on pages 233 to 300 of Volume I of the Smith Committee's hearings.

value is in actively helping labor organize, rather than just to protect their right to organize. He doesn't think the Board is doing enough for labor at the present time and believes hearings should be held even when the Board obviously has no jurisdiction, if the holding of such hearings will help labor organization.

He was unwilling to see anything done about the Boilermakers' claim for representation in the *Long View Fibre case*, because he thought any such action on the part of the Board would hurt the CIO and help the A. F. of L.

Hope is constantly fearful that Howard's actions will finally give the regional office a black eye and prejudice the employers and conservative unions to the extent of diminishing the usefulness of the office.

Whether because of this report or direct complaints from Hope, J. Warren Madden, Chairman of the Board, drafted a letter to Howard on April 6, 1937, in which he said,

The Board has a request to make of you. It is that you refrain from your close association with labor leaders and your attendance at union meetings.

The particular reason why it is necessary to ask you to do this is because of the current divisions and sub-divisions within the labor movement itself and the high feeling which quite naturally exists between the different factions. These divisions are most unfortunate as we all recognize. It would be wrong for any of us to contribute to the seriousness or duration of the current divisions of the labor movement by encouraging one faction or the other to militant action, unless that encouragement necessarily resulted from something which fell within the line of our official duties. If, outside the line of those duties, we meddle in the unhappy controversies of workers, we are only giving aid and comfort to unfair employers, and postponing the day when labor as a whole will obtain what it is entitled to.

I suppose that nearly every one connected with the staff of the Board has some preferences of his own as between the different factions in the current split in the labor movement. On many occasions our official actions necessarily operate for the moment to the disadvantage of one or the other of the factions and as a consequence we are in the disfavor of that faction for the moment. The only answer that we have to any complaint of that sort and the only justifiable answer that exists is that we were minding our own business in the action that we took and were by no means injecting ourselves into the business of others. If this answer is true, it is proved by our conduct in subsequent cases. If it is not true, and its truth is not so proved, then whatever criticism may come is justified.

I have been unduly verbose in saying a rather simple thing. My justification is that this simple thing is of very great importance to the work of the Board and to the success of the labor movement. We appreciate the excellent work that you have done in your region and feel sure that the excellence of your work will in no way be diminished by following these suggestions. . . .

When circulated to the other two Board members the draft met the following criticism from Edwin S. Smith:

. . . The . . . [letter] to Howard is pretty unfair in that it starts off abruptly by assuming the truth of the contentions that Howard is unduly mixing in union affairs. I would be willing to bet a cookie that his participation is just about one-tenth of one percent of what Hope does. I doubt if any of our directors, except, perhaps, Charlie Logan, handles his job in a more "political" manner than Hope. I am not here criticizing such tactics, but I do point out that Hope is a strange person to utter this kind of criticism. As a matter of fact, Hope's intimate contacts are with politicians and employers as well as labor leaders, so that they may be free of some of the criticism alleged to some of Howard's doings. My inclination is to believe that Hope greatly exaggerated Howard's activities and objects to them principally because they are on the side of more radical elements in the unions, with which Charlie is not sympathetic. I most strongly repudiate any censoring of Howard based on such a background. . .

I indicated yesterday that Howard was a very malleable, conscientious person. He has suffered acutely from the deprecatory attitude of Hope toward him. I certainly do not want to be a party to increasing his discomfort. The only letter which I think is warranted in sending to Howard is one that indicates that we have heard that his too close association with certain factions in the unions and particularly his attendance at union meetings had been injurious to the best interests of the Board. . .

Madden finally sent the following letter to Howard:

It has been represented to the Board that you have been rather closely identified with certain people and certain factions among organized labor; that you have attended union meetings, etc. We think that the excellent work which you have done for the Board would not be adversely affected by your refraining from doing these things. We feel sure that you will understand why we think this is necessary. . . .

It was at this time that Howard was transferred to the Los Angeles office, going as a field examiner with no change in salary. He answered Madden from Los Angeles on April 21, 1937, saying

In the rush of Board activity, I have been unable to acknowledge until now your letter of April 7, which was forwarded to me here from Seattle.

For me, a former pedagogue who has heretofore been safely sheltered from life's evil ways, to become suddenly identified as a labor factionalist is something which I cannot avoid viewing with mixed emotions. It is so reminiscent of the chaste cleric who, thrilled with the accusations of being a roué, is ashamed to confess innocence.

However, I have been for the last three weeks safely removed from temptation.

I agree with you that my work need not include the doing of the things I have been represented as doing. They will not be done. . . .

Howard Comes To Los Angeles

The transfer to Los Angeles and the gentle reprimand from Chairman Madden were not followed by a peaceful period in Howard's career; in the Los Angeles office he found himself under the supervision of a Regional Director whom he soon came to distrust. The Regional Director, who was the center of the controversy that ensued, was Towne Nylander. A former college professor, he had been in office since September 1935. At the beginning of 1937 he seemed to be on good terms with union members and labor leaders in his region, most of whom were in the AFL. He was regarded as a liberal, and his personality seems to have had an effective impact.

A favorable reaction on Howard's part might have been expected; but Howard's suspicions were soon awakened. Not long after he came to Los Angeles he asked Ralph Seward, the Regional Attorney, if Nylander was not playing both ends against the middle. Seward denied the accusation; Howard continued to suspect.

In May, Howard was given a promotion to $3,200 a year. Nylander spoke highly of him in the semi-annual salary reviews—"one of the best . . . thoroughly capable—doing an excellent piece of work"—but Howard's suspicions of Nylander seemed to increase. These suspicions became particularly acute at the time of the second *Examiner* case, shortly to be considered.

In July, the environment of the Los Angeles office underwent a change: the increasing rivalry in the national arena between craft and industrial unionism became clearly reflected on the local scene. Harry Bridges, the militant left-wing president of the International Longshoremen's Union, was appointed West Coast Director of the CIO (then still nominally within the AFL). He began an organizational drive on the West Coast and in Southern California in particular. Inter-union friction soared because, in addition to organizing groups hitherto unorganized, Bridges' staff also made strong efforts to bring into the CIO camp groups of workers who had already joined the AFL.

Soon after Bridges' appointment, Nylander made a speech in which he criticized John L. Lewis (then leader of the CIO) for appointing Bridges, saying that Bridges was not the best man for the job. This criticism of Bridges by Nylander was considered lese-majesté by many CIO members. They felt that Nylander's criticism showed beyond a question that he was either in the pay of the employers or biased in favor of the AFL or both. Howard, as a CIO sympathizer, shared this view.

Following this incident, strain began to show in the Regional Director's relations with the CIO unions, although instances were not lacking where he was sharply criticized by AFL unions as well. The major event in the development of great distrust of Nylander in CIO ranks and among members of his staff, such as Howard, was Nylander's handling of the second *Los Angeles Examiner* case.

The *Examiner* Case

In this case, the CIO Newspaper Guild filed, for the second time, charges that the *Examiner* had discriminated against some of its members in layoffs and was in collusion with a new AFL newspaper organization sponsored by the president of the local AFL Central Labor Council, named Buzzell. Stewart Meacham, the field examiner assigned to the case, described what happened in a letter written five months later at the request of the Board's Secretary.

He began by recounting that he had not been able to turn up legally sufficient evidence of discriminatory discharges but had found some suspicious occurrences pointing to *Examiner*-AFL collusion. He went on to say that one evening he overheard part of a telephone conversation between Nylander and Buzzell, in which Nylander was violently denying some sort of charge. Nylander then turned to Meacham and vigorously attacked Meacham's handling of the case (i.e., agreeing to interview witnesses at night with appointments arranged by a Guild official—a standard practice) about which Buzzell had been complaining. On the following day, according to Meacham, Nylander apologized, then asked Meacham to prepare a report and turn the case file over to him.

Meacham soon learned that Nylander, using his report, which had recommended dismissal of the discrimination charges but further investigation of the alleged collusion, had recommended a flat dismissal of all charges including collusion. Meacham was "pretty upset" over this development. He then discussed the matter, according to his own account, in general terms with the Guild organizer. The Guild appealed the Regional Director's decision to the Board, and the Board asked Nylander for a report. Nylander told Meacham to prepare a defense of the recommendation as sent, and Meacham, after talking to Howard, stalled. Eventually Nylander prepared his own defense which, according to Meacham, "contained many elements of pure fabrication."

Nylander then called a meeting of all field examiners. He told them that the Guild was attacking him for his action in the *Examiner* case, and that he had discovered that the attack had been initiated within the office. He claimed that Meacham's talk with the Guild organizer was the beginning of the trouble. Meacham then told his side of the story (not including the overheard telephone conversation). Thereupon Nylander backed down and apologized for taking the case away from Meacham. After the conference Meacham stayed behind and asked if Nylander thought him disloyal. According to Meacham, Nylander said: "No, boy, if I trusted the others the way I trust you, I wouldn't worry at all."

This incident has been told at length because it reveals characteristic patterns of action. Blocking or attempting to block Nylander by delays, and by talking sympathetically with (or even disclosing information to) CIO leaders, became normal practices; and it is to be noted that, although the *Examiner* case was Meacham's problem, Howard's advice was followed. Moreover, Nylander's behavior also was revealing. In discussing the *Examiner* case, the examiners in the Los Angeles office were sharply critical of the unexpected removal of a case from an examiner's hands, the apparent yielding to outside pressure, and the shifting of ground which they felt marked Nylander's handling of the case. In months to come they were to criticize his treatment of other cases on the same grounds.

CIO circles gradually learned of Nylander's recommendation that the collusion charges be dismissed and they branded this a "double cross." The leaders of the so-called Bridges group (the left-wing CIO) talked with Howard, who they felt was sympathetic, and Howard, in turn, became even more distrustful of Nylander. With the *Examiner* incident as a nucleus, stories of Nylander's alleged favoritism toward the AFL grew and multiplied in the months following January 1938.

By March the AFL-CIO split had become exceedingly bitter in the Los Angeles area. Nylander's long-standing friendships with AFL leaders were now regarded with deep suspicion by the CIO; but he refused to give them up. His personal invitations to CIO leaders to win their good will only antagonized them further.

During this same period, the CIO began

earnest attempts to raid some small furniture companies which the AFL had organized after a three-year struggle in 1937. In handling the numerous cases which followed, Nylander made some mistakes, as he later admitted, mistakes which mostly worked against the CIO. This increased suspicion of him. Howard, on the other hand, during this period, irritated the AFL by advising companies not to enter into any AFL contracts while petitions filed by the CIO were pending.

Development of the Clique

Turnover in the field examiner staff during the early months of 1938, resulting partly from Nylander-examiner friction, left Howard the senior member of the group. Two new examiners arrived, Pomerance in April and Muir in May. The three soon found a kinship in their similar reactions to Nylander's procedures, and their interaction seems to have widened the breach between Nylander and the examiners. It should not be forgotten, however, that the local organization drive of the CIO was posing many problems in administration, labor relations, law, public relations, and the like which would have tended to aggravate individual differences of opinion over procedure in any Labor Board office. Yet it was certain aspects of Nylander's administration of the office rather than larger questions which—over the period of the next twelve months—caused the split in the Los Angeles office.

Howard was the leader of the anti-Nylander faction in the office. The complaints he and the others made against Nylander fell into five categories:

1. They charged him with a lack of honesty in dealing with people, including the examiners themselves, by making contradictory statements to employers and unions with regard to cases.

2. They were disturbed by his practice of "short circuiting" cases—i.e., holding conferences with union and company representatives without calling in the examiner who had been handling the case. This practice would presumably have been annoying in any event to the examiners, though it was obviously within Nylander's discretion; under the particular circumstances of the Los Angeles office they regarded his behavior as darkly suspicious.

3. The examiners felt that Nylander treated them like college students. On one occasion in the spring of 1938, Nylander told the examiners that he would recommend no one for a pay increase unless he took outside study courses. This led Howard to an open outburst, in which he was supported by all the other examiners but one.

4. The examiners did not like the way they were given case assignments; some examiners were given only AFL cases, others only CIO cases. At the request of an AFL labor leader, Howard was removed from an Arizona assignment and another examiner sent there in his stead.

5. The examiners did not like Nylander's manner in dealing with them. They complained that at times he attacked them violently, and then would apologize profusely. They felt that he did not discuss the serious issues of the cases with them and that he was inaccessible.

The result of these practices (as viewed and interpreted by the examiners) was that Nylander alienated almost every one of them. Of the six employed in the office in the spring of 1939 only one, McKay, kept aloof from the developing "clique." Howard had the strongest and most persistent feeling of opposition to the regional director; Pomerance was quite critical; Muir and Davies were willing followers; and a fifth, Yager, was "on the fence."

Howard, in short, was in a position of leadership among the examiners. Zealous and aggressive in his work, he was almost fanatic in carrying it on. With his zeal went an automatic suspicion of those who disagreed with him. His sympathies lay with the left wing of the contending labor factions, though according to a later report there was no "evidence that he [was] or [had] been a member of the Communist party or fellow traveler." Nor did he appear to slight his work in cases brought by right-wing labor factions.

Howard believed that the Board and its staff had the duty to organize unions; in varying degrees, the other examiners accepted this philosophy. Nylander, on the contrary, approached his job from more of a mediatory standpoint and relied largely on personal relations. His speech was frequently violent, but his actions tended to be indecisive. And as more and more difficult cases came up, his prestige in the labor circles of the Los Angeles region declined.

From the middle of 1938 on there were an increasing number of instances where the regional director and the examiners took divergent views on the handling of a case. When the disagreement was discussed, Nylander often accepted his subordinate's views. At other times, there was no open insubordination but considerable obstruction by the examiners. They developed the habit of withholding important papers from the case files—by locking them in their desks—and of omitting information from oral reports, in order to influence Nylander's decisions and action. Accordingly, there were instances where Nylander made recommendations to the Board or took other official moves without full cognizance of the available facts of a case.

Obstructive behavior was becoming more customary among the examiners when the "Arizona incident" took place; it became notorious not so much for what had happened as because it indicated Nylander's very close friendship with Andrew Holohan, Secretary of the Arizona State Federation of Labor. The incident was a party in Holohan's Phoenix apartment. Just what happened at this party no one was ever able to determine—who attended and for how long, who got drunk, what happened to the waitress who kept racing dogs. Howard, who was accompanying Nylander to Phoenix on a case, was at the party with him and was deeply disturbed by what seemed to him excessive friendship between the Director and the AFL union chief. He brought back the story of the night and it traveled a number of grapevines, further influencing opinion of Nylander in the office. A third or fourth hand account in "garbled" form eventually reached the Board in Washington.

Appeals to Washington

On the basis of matters like the Arizona party, which seemed to indicate to Howard and Pomerance (who then had been with the office less than two months) that Nylander was at best an incompetent supervisor and at worst in collusion with employers and the AFL, the two examiners collaborated on May 19, 1938, on a letter to Nathan Witt, Secretary to the Board, in which, without being more specific, they accused Nylander of "association with discredited labor leaders" and asserted that "things have been growing steadily worse." Replying, at their request, to Howard's home, Witt wrote that R. M. Gates, one of his traveling assistants, was coming to Los Angeles in June and that the examiners could have confidence in him. It may be noted that Witt was closely associated with the left wing of the CIO, and possibly predisposed to think the worst of Nylander whose sympathies lay elsewhere.

Howard and Pomerance were aware when they wrote to Witt that Harry Bridges was in the midst of conducting his own investigation of Nylander's administration of the Los Angeles office and planning a protest to the Board. This soon took the form of a letter to Witt from a CIO official named Robertson, on behalf of the Los Angeles CIO Council (dominated by Bridges), complaining of Nylander's handling of certain CIO cases.

Gates arrived in Los Angeles in June to hear examiner and union complaints. He had been instructed by Witt to conduct his investigation in the manner of a routine check up in order to conceal its purpose from Nylander. He spoke with both the examiners and certain union representatives, behaving all the while as though there were no charges and no special investigation. Nylander did not become suspicious. On the other hand, there was no opportunity for Gates to hear the regional director's side of the story or for him to report the results of the investigation to the examiners.

Despite these limitations on his inquiry, Gates was able to make some shrewd guesses on the whole situation in his account to Witt and to the Board of the Los Angeles office's problems. He reported his suspicion that there were some "leaks" from the office to labor groups outside (presumably from the examiners) and cited some questionable points and instances of poor judgment. But there was nothing in his report that suggested or seemed to require extreme disciplinary action at the time.

No action at all was taken by the Board on any aspect of the report. Nor was Nylander informed of the charges against him, for Gates felt that life would become "unbearable" for Howard and Pomerance if Nylander were told. However, whatever the merit of this conclusion, the failure to advise Howard and Pomerance of the substance of Gates' report led them to conclude that their accusations were accepted *in toto* and that the Board would soon take drastic action, action directed solely against Nylander. Nylander, ignorant of the whole affair, took no steps to correct the unsatisfactory state of examiner morale and behavior.

Washington–Los Angeles relations were not improved by the complaints about Nylander. At least from the time of Gates' report, the Secretary's office began to distrust Nylander's judgment. By the fall, it suspected his motives. Witt corresponded with Nylander in July and August and mentioned some of the CIO charges. Nylander asked to be told of all such matters. The Secretary replied that Nylander should make an effort to re-establish the confidence of the CIO.

During the summer of 1938 both the examiners and the Bridges group were waiting for some action by the Board on the basis of Gates' report. Both became increasingly dissatisfied when nothing happened. Howard, Pomerance, and Muir had by that time come to distrust Nylander utterly, especially since, by reason of their conversations with Gates, they felt that the Board was relying on them rather than on Nylander.

In September, Muir lunched with Morgan Hull of the Newspaper Guild (CIO) and "leaked" to him what he had picked up around the office about the Arizona incident. It was through a letter from Hull that the Board learned in October, five months after the event, about the party in Holohan's apartment.

By October, Howard and Pomerance had become so anxious over the Board's silence that they chipped in to buy Pomerance a ticket for an airplane trip to Washington on his vacation. Pomerance talked with the three Board members, and with Gates and Witt about Nylander's handling of certain cases, and left them memoranda on the matter. Examiner criticism of Nylander was again brought before the Board in November when Howard went to Washington as a representative of the Examiners' Union at an annual conference.

Whatever opportunities these visits provided the Board for clearing up the situation were neglected. Nothing was done, and Nylander was told nothing. The result was merely to leave a further feeling of distrust and suspicion toward Nylander in the Washington office. During Howard's visit, however, he was told that another representative of Secretary Witt's office, Fred Krivonos, would be coming out to Los Angeles, probably some time before Christmas, and would look into the situation.

In late November, the examiner group became fully organized. All were members of the Examiners' Union (McKay subsequently quit) but opposition to Nylander appears to have been coincidental with, rather than a part of, union business. Despite the congealing of sentiment among the examiners and his own growing awareness that there was a "clique" of sorts, Nylander found reason to speak well of Howard's work in a letter to Witt on November 23, 1938, reviewing the salaries of the field examiners. He noted that Howard had the best record for adjusting the more difficult cases and recommended that he, together with one other, be given special consideration in receiving salary increases.

On December 8 Pomerance, who specialized in movie industry cases, wrote to Witt making some "serious charges" about a report Nylander had made on certain movie cases. The letter was not brought to Nylander's attention, but a subsequent memorandum from Witt to the regional director showed that Pomerance's communication had been taken into consideration. Pomerance saw the reply memorandum, which, of course, was put in the file, and this was further evidence, as far as he was concerned, that the Board was relying on him and, by inference, Howard and the other field examiners rather than Nylander. He was, of course, less inclined than ever to co-operate with Nylander for that reason.

Nylander eventually learned that Krivonos was expected at the office, and some examiners thought they saw a decided change in his behavior, lasting until March 1939.

Charge and Countercharge

Krivonos did not reach Los Angeles before Christmas. The examiners were disappointed. They met informally before the holiday and some thought they should resign, while others favored writing to the Board. Discussions on December 27 and 28 led to a decision to write. A letter was prepared by all those present (McKay was in Arizona), typed out by Muir, and mailed in. It said, in part, that the signatories would resign in a body unless action was taken on their complaints about Nylander.

The basic motive of the group, now firmly established, does not appear to have been personal or political, but rather the desire "to straighten out matters in the office," to correct what was considered "mishandling of cases." Yet opposition to Nylander reached such dimensions that morale and office administration were seriously affected. The examiners felt that the Board had accepted their estimate of Nylander but was unwilling or unable to take remedial action. Led by Howard, they concluded that they must assume responsibility themselves for preventing what they regarded as Nylander's sabotage. The three chief devices that they had come to adopt, consciously or unconsciously—aside from direct argument with Nylander—were the maintenance of a sort of united front with the CIO, "leaking" stories about Nylander to outsiders, and withholding from the files materials that they did not wish Nylander to see. Nylander knew, or suspected the existence of the united front and the calculated leaks, but he apparently did not know that the examiners, under the sway of Howard's zeal, were locking up essential materials in their desks and failing to give full oral reports on investigations.

The situation in the Los Angeles office was thus badly disturbed when the examiners' sense of virtue about their own behavior received another fillip from a blunder on Nylander's part. On February 6, 1939, Nylander, who frequently spoke publicly on labor topics, addressed the Inglewood Community Forum in the California town of that name. A newspaper account of the talk quoted him as saying: "I'll tell you frankly that when we go into a hearing, the employer hasn't got a chance. There's not a scintilla of doubt as to the employer's guilt."

Because of this account, which quickly found its way into the *Congressional Record*, the Board suspended Nylander on February 27 and ordered an investigation, by a disinterested citizen, both of the speech and the accuracy of the newspaper account. The inquiry revealed that Nylander had not been disloyal but had intended to indicate that he made as certain as possible that a case was water tight before taking action against an employer. The Board reinstated him on March 24 with a reproof for his "error in judgment" which caused "an unfounded alarm" in the minds of parties to Board proceedings and the public at large.

Krivonos arrived in Los Angeles a little before the reinstatement. He was in the midst of a routine "check up" trip to several regional offices. In Los Angeles the "check up" was awkward. Krivonos was investigating the charges against Nylander, while the latter, who had had difficulty with examiners over what Gates had allegedly told them privately about handling cases almost a year before, tried to persuade Krivonos to meet with the examiners in his presence. He did not succeed; nor was he asked to tell his side of the story.

Krivonos, who made his report to the Board late in May and in June 1939, was influenced by the feeling of distrust of Nylander which had been engendered by the incidents occurring over the previous year. Having heard only one side of the story, his report was partial. As a result, the Washington staff and the Board itself did not really understand the Los Angeles situation; all their information came from the two reports, both based on *ex parte* investigations, from two letters from left-wing CIO unions, and from the letters and visits of the examiners.

Conflicting Recommendations

Probably as a result of Krivonos' report and possibly also because Seligman, an organizer for the United Shoe Workers (CIO), while in Washington in May had suggested to Board Member Leiserson that the Los Angeles situation be looked into, Nylander and Howard were summoned to the Board in July 1939 to explain what had been going on. They remained in Washington from the 5th through the 8th. There Nylander learned for the first time of the examiners' letter and of the other ways in which his staff had criticized him to the Board. So great was the disparity between his and Howard's account of events in Los Angeles that the Board decided to assign two experienced and trusted staff members—Gerhard P. Van Arkel and George Pratt—to examine the situation thoroughly and report. Pratt and Van Arkel began the job on July 10. They reviewed records, correspondence, cases, and reports both in the Washington and Los Angeles offices, and interviewed and invited statements from staff and others in both places.

In the meanwhile, Howard and Nylander returned to Los Angeles—the regional director taking the train, the examiner going by plane. Howard arrived first, on a Monday, and discussed what had happened in Washington with the other examiners. During his four-day ride across the country, Nylander decided to tender his resignation to the Board and then wait to be cleared and reinstated. Not long after his return on Thursday, he called in AFL and CIO representatives, separately, and told them of his decision. Before the time scheduled for Nylander's own press release on the subject, two AFL officials issued a statement announcing the resignation and alleging that it was the culmination of "a long chain of intrigue" carried on by the CIO and the Communist Party to gain control of the local NLRB office. Nylander countered with another release characterizing the attempt to discredit the CIO in connection with his resignation as "ridiculous."

Nylander's letter of resignation to the National Labor Relations Board laid down two conditions under which he would accept reinstatement; first, that he not be hampered in speaking publicly on labor topics and second, that all the examiners in the Los Angeles office, except McKay, be dismissed.

Pratt and Van Arkel completed their investigation on August 23, 1939. The major conclusions contained in their report to the Board were: (1) that, although Nylander did not deliberately sabotage the work of the Board as charged, he was by temperament and personality unsuited for the job—hence should not be rehired; (2) that all the examiners except Howard be transferred to other offices (or at least Muir and Davies be transferred) and that all of them be strongly reprimanded for their insubordination; (3) that, in order to avoid such situations in the future, a new administrative division be established in the Washington office to relieve the Board's Secretary of supervision of the Regional Offices; and (4):

> . . . with respect to Howard, it is felt that his zeal for his convictions and an overly suspicious nature led him to set himself up as opposition to Nylander without any adequate evidence that Nylander was disloyal to the Board. The task of any Director who succeeds Nylander in the office will be impossible with Howard there as the center of the group of examiners. While Howard might function properly in another Regional Office under a strong Director with adequate and close supervision, it is felt that the Board should not assume such further responsibility and it is therefore recommended that he be dismissed. If not dismissed, he should be strongly reprimanded for his part in the affair and made to understand not only his subordinate position to the Regional Director but the necessity of loyalty to his superior and he should be transferred to a region on the East Coast on probationary status.

In this way the Board was left without a clear-cut recommendation for action on Howard, although Pratt and Van Arkel indicated the administrative problems which would arise from his retention.

Board Member Edwin Smith favored transferring Howard to another region. He wrote, in a letter to Chairman Madden,

> Briefly my ideas about Howard are these: I am willing to believe that he is a zealot and that this quality, unless drastically curbed, could well

result in making his work for the Board not what we would wish. However, I also believe that he is both intelligent and conscientious. My definite inclination would be to give him another chance in an office where we have confidence in the director or where he could be closely supervised from Washington. I would suggest Chicago, Philadelphia, or Baltimore.

He certainly has given devoted service to the Board under two different directors, whose own temperament and activities would be most likely to call out Howard's weaknesses. In an office more normally run, and with a good stiff lecture, I think he might still be made into an asset. I would definitely put him on a six-month probation in such a situation, and that is my recommendation. . . .

Board Member William Leiserson disagreed in a note which was attached to this letter:

I think Howard's performance in connection with the Los Angeles situation justifies his dismissal. It is important that his services be discontinued in order to establish confidence in the Los Angeles office. He should be given an opportunity to resign if he prefers that.

A summary view of the justification for dismissal was contained in another letter:

It is the function of a Field Examiner of the Board, as a public officer, to take a calm and dispassionate attitude toward the interests which the Act and the Board's work touches, doing his part to enforce the law and leaving it to the event to determine whether this means more unions or less unions, or more or less success for any particular union. It is his further duty, as a part of an organization, to do his work within the boundaries of that organization. That means that he should not disclose the information or supposed information which comes to him as a member of an organization to outside interested people, for the purpose or with the effect of impairing the interests and effectiveness of other members of the organization. It means that he should not maintain an undue intimacy with persons representing one interest in relation to the Board's work, thereby making other interests suspicious as to whether he is or can be impartial and objective in his work. It means that he should not be unduly and unjustifiably suspicious of other persons in the organization, assigning improper motives to their conduct, in some cases without reason. It most certainly means that he should not carry on official work outside the rules of the organization, withholding from the official files papers and information which belong to the Board.

With all these factors in mind, Chairman Madden cast the deciding vote. How do you think he should have voted?

THE GLAVIS-BALLINGER DISPUTE

CONTENTS

FOREWORD

The data and material with which the social scientist works are generally not amenable to precise measurement or final uncontrovertible judgment. Political scientists must work and progress in their understanding of public life in the presence of many hotly disputed facts and unsettled controversies. One of the most enduring of controversies in the American political arena has been the Glavis-Ballinger dispute, which took place during the administration of President William Howard Taft, and particularly during the years 1909-1910.

The fight arose from the belief of a rather obscure young field official in the General Land Office of the Department of the Interior that his superior officers, including Richard A. Ballinger, first, Commissioner of the General Land Office, later Secretary of the Department, were handling certain Alaskan coal land claims improperly. The land was thought to be immensely valuable, though later it turned out to be of little commercial value, but this the disputants did not know. When Glavis felt his position was not being given adequate consideration within the Department of the Interior he decided to carry his case elsewhere and appealed for support to certain highly articulate "progressive" and conservationist forces which were in opposition to the Taft administration. The outcome of the battle was not clean-cut but it is generally agreed that the furor and debate were in some measure responsible for the subsequent political eclipse of both Ballinger and President Taft.

The drama of the Glavis-Ballinger controversy and the stirring nature of the economic and political issues which it appeared to involve led many at the time and during the years that followed to look over the lengthy record and reach a verdict of their own. Harold L. Ickes, while Secretary of the Interior, was moved in 1940, by his reading of Henry F. Pringle's account of the Taft administration, to reconsider the entire matter. Whereas in 1910 he had sympathized with Glavis and his conservationist supporters, and in 1936 had restored Glavis to employment in the Department, in 1940 as the result of his reconsideration, he wrote an article "by way of confession and penance" in which he described Ballinger as an American Dreyfus and denied that the Glavis criticisms of Ballinger and his subordinates had had any validity. The affair, at bottom, was largely political, Ickes concluded, asserting, "Personal animus, devouring ambitions, conniving schemes to defeat Taft and renominate Roosevelt in 1912, all got tangled up in the Ballinger affair."

Professor Alpheus T. Mason dipped into the same record and declared, in 1941, in a volume devoted to the Glavis-Ballinger dispute and its significance, that Glavis and those who supported him were right. He said:

> The Ballinger case makes it clear that all monopoly rests on unregulated private control of natural resources and economic advantages; that no such control is possible without the help of partisan politics and a friendly press; above all, that an alliance of special interest with "the law" means the end of popular government; and, finally, that the only way government of the people can long endure is by fullest publicity in all matters vital to the public. The light must be turned on and kept on. . . .
>
> The powerful machinery of the federal government was put into action to crush . . . [Glavis], to frustrate democracy.

And there is a host of other commentators and partisans who have taken or are prepared to take one or the other of these two completely antithetical positions or a stand somewhere in between.

The present account is not a review of the record nor an effort to assess the merits of the Glavis and Ballinger arguments. Rather, it recounts some of the incidents in the dispute as illustrative of administrative behavior. The behavior that is presented for examination is Glavis', so most of the quotations are from him. They are not adequate for an informed judgment on the whole controversy; they are, it is hoped, adequate for a specialized purpose—for a consideration of questions such as these: How is individual initiative, and how much can it be, fostered or permitted within the hierarchy? Where does "zeal for the right" end and disloyalty and insubordination begin? What is the nature of "discipline" when the term refers to accepted modes of behavior in the Executive Branch of the Federal government? The Glavis case was a single spectacular episode; but questions like these are perennial.

Conservation and the Alaska Coal Lands

The word "conservation" and the public protection of natural resources which it generally implies were new and controversial ideas in the United States in the early 1900's when the events described in this case study took place. Conservation was one of the pioneer and enduring aspects of the Square Deal program of President Theodore Roosevelt (1901-1909); credit for much of the public crusading for this concept (advanced some decades earlier by natural scientists) is generally given to T.R.'s close friend and adviser, Gifford Pinchot, the first Forester of the United States. The idea that, like arable homestead sites, public lands containing forest, mineral, or similar resources should pass into private hands and be put to profitable use as quickly as possible was the older and dominant belief of the time. Under its impetus farm lands and lands rich in natural wealth had been disposed of for decades with little more than perfunctory safeguards and at a nominal price. The conservation movement was, in a sense, an emergency, last-ditch effort prompted by the fact that relatively little of the lands rich in resources remained in the public domain. Conservation met with many setbacks and battles, some of which have continued to the present day. The Glavis-Ballinger controversy was an important skirmish in the larger struggle.

The primary method by which conservationists hoped to keep the fast-dwindling forest, water, mineral, and similar resources from passing completely and forever into private hands (and becoming, they feared, the bases for large monopolies) was by securing restraining legislation or other types of governmental action, such as presidential withdrawal by executive proclamation of particular forest lands under authority of an act of 1891. Legislative enactment proved only a first step, however, for the cleavage of opinion on conservation extended throughout the national administration and, significantly, through the Department of the Interior where officials not as zealous as the conservationists were able to determine the extent of enforcement of laws limiting large scale acquisition of public lands.

The central figure in this story—Louis R. Glavis, a young admirer of T.R.'s work—joined the staff of the General Land Office when he was about 20 years of age. Of Glavis, a friendly Congressional group had this to say some years later:

> A young man, . . . with but a common-school education, a plain matter-of-fact American citizen, with very little imagination, seeing only the facts which confront him; with splendid recollection . . .

The General Land Office was the old Department of the Interior agency which had presided over the rapid private acquisition of public lands during the 1800's and which was entrusted with the execution of the numerous statutes setting the conditions under which private patents to public lands—including Alaskan coal lands—could be granted.

The coal lands owned by the federal government in Alaska amounted to about 100,000 acres. Although subsequent workings were to show that the veins were not rich enough to warrant the great expense of taking the coal out, at the time, with memories of Klondike gold still fresh, the fields were believed to contain untold wealth in "black diamonds." As with other public lands, including homestead lands, individual coal land claims of limited size were open to purchase at the nominal fee of ten dollars an acre. In an attempt to prevent appropriation by corporate groups, the laws on the sale of public lands provided that each claimant take up the land in his own interest and for his own use and specifically forbade consolidation of claims before entry. This type of provision had been designed to provide individual ranches and homesteads in the western states; so far as coal fields were concerned it was a poor rule because it was manifestly unprofitable to mine the small individual claims allowed. It led to attempts to get around the law. Two methods were prevalent: either dummy entrymen were employed who later turned their titles over to the one real purchaser, or there was secret agreement between the purchasers, previous to entry, to consolidate after the separate titles had been secured and to work the claims together. By 1906 it was known in the Pacific northwest and in Washington that these methods were being used by corporations in an attempt to acquire immense Alaskan holdings. There were rumors that the northern coal fields were eventually to pass to the Morgan-Guggenheim interests, which already had acquired copper lands, fisheries, and transportation franchises in the Territory.

President Roosevelt, therefore, in characteristically forthright manner, issued on November 12, 1906 (on the authority of the 1891 law pertaining to forest lands), an executive proclamation which withdrew the Alaskan coal lands from further purchase, but which provided that claims already filed would be considered. These were to be investigated by the General Land Office and if the claims were shown to be legal, title would be transferred; however, those found to be defective or fraudulent (especially with reference to intention to consolidate) were to be cancelled. At the time of the proclamation nine hundred claims were pending. Of these, thirty-three claims, representing some 5,000 acres of coal land in the Bering River coal field were called the "Cunningham Claims" since one man, Clarence Cunningham, had staked them out in his own name and those of his friends—all well-to-do businessmen from Spokane, Seattle, and cities in Idaho and Ohio. As early as 1905, the General Land Office had been notified by one of its special agents that the Cunningham claims appeared to be fraudulent; there was evidence of an intention to consolidate.

In March 1907, Roosevelt appointed a new Secretary of the Interior, James Garfield, a staunch believer in conservation. Garfield named a former classmate of his, a lawyer and ex-mayor of Seattle, Richard A. Ballinger, as Commissioner of the General Land Office. In June, Ballinger's Assistant Commissioner, Fred Dennett, wrote to Horace T. Jones, a Special Agent in the Portland field office, that the Cunningham claimants "were engaged in a criminal conspiracy" and ordered him to make "a thorough, complete, and energetic investigation" of the Alaska coal claims. On July 20, the Morgan-Guggenheim Syndicate received an option on the Cunningham claims. Possession of a large coal supply was of considerable importance to the Syndicate in its exploitation of Alaska resources and trade. The disposition of the claims was now obviously a matter of political moment.

Ballinger visited Seattle a number of times during July and August 1907 and spoke with Jones. Not long after July 20 the Commissioner personally told Jones to alter the nature of his inquiry to a rapid and partial investigation. On August 10 Jones reported to Washington on the claims, stating that each one should be further and strictly investigated. He was ordered transferred to Salt Lake City two days later. Not long after this, Jones made a second official report recommending that the Cunningham entries be "carefully investigated by an experienced and fearless agent" because there were strong indications that the lands were to be transferred to the Guggenheim interests.

Glavis Takes Over

In October Louis R. Glavis (then a special agent for the Land Office) was made chief of the Portland field division. Jones was still in Portland and the two men talked over the Cunningham claims. Alaskan matters were not under his jurisdiction, but Glavis encouraged Jones to make a third report which said that "few, if any, of the applicants were complying with the requirements of the law." On November 5 Glavis took his first action on the matter. He sent Jones' latest report to Ballinger, mentioning that he had had some previous experience investigating some of the claimants himself, and asking to be put in charge of the Alaska coal cases.

No reply came from Ballinger. Disturbed, Glavis arranged to visit Washington later in the month. There he discussed the matter with his personal friend, H. H. Schwartz, Chief of the Field Service, and also with the Commissioner himself. The good faith of the Cunningham claimants was discussed, and Glavis pointed out that the Department of Justice would know the facts and would investigate them if the Land Office did not. Ballinger told him that he was a friend of many of the claimants involved but authorized Glavis to go ahead and investigate all the claims no matter what the result. He also wrote a letter early in December putting Glavis in charge of the investigation. Glavis returned to Seattle on December 19 and started to gather further evidence.

In January 1908, Glavis received a letter telling him that Ballinger had directed that the claims be clear-listed and accepted for patent. Clear-listing was the last step before turning title to public land over to a claimant and, in this case, amounted to a finding that the Cunningham claims were legal and valid. It also meant that Glavis' investigation would be of no use. Behind Ballinger's apparently sudden action may have been the facts that on December 7 the Morgan-Guggenheim Syndicate had taken up its option on the Cunningham claims and on December 26 an ex-governor of Washington had visited Ballinger on behalf of the claims. The Secretary had then gone over some earlier and favorable reports on the claims and ordered them clear-listed. Within another week they had been transferred from the Investigating Bureau to the Patenting Division of the General Land Office, and not long afterwards the patents making the land private property had been completed and made ready for signature. The usual time lapse between clear-listing and patenting was from three months to three years; the Cunningham patents had been processed in a few weeks.

As Glavis wrote later describing his second independent action:

> Here was my first dilemma. I did not wish to protest to Secretary of the Interior Garfield against the action of the Commissioner, and I did not like to see 5,000 acres of coal lands go to the Cunningham group when I believed the claims fraudulent. I did protest immediately, by telegram and letter, direct to Commissioner Ballinger, against the issuance of the patents. The order clear listing the Cunningham claims to patent was almost immediately revoked.

Clear-listing and granting title to the Cunningham claims by the usual process apparently was halted for the time being by this protest. Ballinger then announced his support of legislation—the Cale Bill—which, among other things, would have had the effect of validating the Cunningham claims: it provided for the consolidation of existing entries without proof of good faith of the original entrymen. The Commissioner appeared before the Public Lands Committee of the House in support of the bill on March 3, 1908.

On March 4 Ballinger resigned to resume private practice, and Dennett, Ballinger's Assistant Commissioner, stepped up into the Commissioner's office.

Glavis, the meanwhile, was not idle. By confronting the claimants with the charge that they were involved with the Guggenheims, he was successful early in 1908 in procuring affidavits which attempted to disprove such connections but which, in doing so, proved the claimants' intention to consolidate in their own interests. Armed with such evidence he went to Cunningham himself and managed to be shown Cunningham's journal. This contained, in a memorandum of agreement to consolidate dated 1903, the irrefutable proof that the entrymen took up the land with the intention of deeding it to a company. On the same day, Cunningham had made an affidavit which showed the fraudulent nature of the claims. Glavis was able to secure this evidence from Cunningham because Cunningham believed that Glavis was sympathetic to the claims and was only carrying out a routine assignment. The young field director was put in a difficult position when, in the midst of conversation, Cunningham was informed by a friend that Glavis himself had made the charges. This information had been communicated to one of the claimants by the Commissioner's office, and to Glavis it seemed that again his superiors were interfering with his work and were assisting and warning the claimants of his actions. In spite of his considerable progress he was ordered off the Alaskan cases on May 2 by Commissioner Dennett and put on other work. The reason given was "lack of funds."

At this time the status of the Cunningham claimants was somewhat changed by an act of Congress which was an outgrowth of the government's interest in increasing the allowable acreage of Alaskan coal claims to a reasonable size while preventing large-scale acquisition and consolidation. The Cale Bill, which Ballinger had supported, had authorized an acreage increase but had also permitted agreement on consolidation among the various claimants before entry of their claims. Passage of the bill had been prevented by a report by Secretary Garfield, but another bill, the Hepburn bill, also opposed by Garfield, passed on May 28, 1908. By this measure the allowable acreage of Alaskan coal claims was increased, but agreements before entry were not validated, and a very comprehensive anti-trust clause was included. The Cunningham claimants thereupon decided to rush their patents through under the old law rather than get caught in an interpretation of the anti-trust provisions of the new law.

Ballinger, meanwhile, in his role of private attorney acted for a number of the claimants whose cases were before the Interior Department; in September he undertook to prepare an affidavit which would negate the evidence which Glavis had obtained from Cunningham. Although Commissioner Dennett was willing to approve the new affidavit, Secretary Garfield was not.

In October 1908, Glavis received an order which revoked the previous demand that he suspend the Alaskan investigations. However, the evidence in the Cunningham journal had to be corroborated in the field, and this was out of the question during the winter months. Thus, nothing could be done until spring.

Meanwhile, the political situation changed. November 1908 saw William Howard Taft, T.R.'s trusted "lieutenant," elected President. It was generally hoped but not unanimously expected by Roosevelt's supporters in the progressive wing of the Republican party that Taft—who had won the Republican nomination because of T.R.'s strong support—would continue his predecessor's policies, including that of conservation. The conservationists were not reassured and T.R. was reportedly chagrined when the new President dismissed Secretary Garfield on Inauguration Day, March 4, 1909, and appointed Ballinger as Secretary of the Interior. How much Taft was actually aware of Ballinger's personal ties with public land claimants is not clear. It is a matter of record that both Taft, a former judge, and Ballinger, a practicing lawyer, supported conservation in general, but took a conservative legalistic view of the Federal government's conservation powers in contrast to Roosevelt's aggressive approach.

In any case, Glavis had to decide in March 1909 whether to continue to insist on the invalidity of the Cunningham claims and thus oppose the new secretary of the department. With final responsibility, now, for the pending Alaskan claims, Ballinger urged that they be settled quickly and placed a time limit on the investigation. Formally, because of his previous connection with the Cunningham claims, he referred them to his First Assistant Secretary, Frank Pierce; however, it appears that he still remained interested and involved in the case. Among other things he advised the Cunningham claimants to take advantage of the new coal land law of May 1908, which he said his Department would construe "liberally."

Glavis' position and action at this time are best described in his own words:

> On March 10th (six days after Mr. Ballinger took office) I received a telegram from Mr. Dennett, then Commissioner of the General Land Office, *directing me to submit at once complete reports upon the status of my investigation of the Alaskan coal cases. On April 21, 1909, I received a telegram from the General Land Office, saying that the Alaskan coal investigation must be completed within sixty days.*
>
> The Chief of the Field Service and I had agreed that a field examination of the Alaskan coal lands in question was necessary to show whether the claims in the various groups were being developed separately or together. Thus, if a field examination should prove that all the claims of the Cunningham group were as a matter of fact being worked together, that fact would be highly indicative that the entries were made with that intent. Such a field investigation could

take place only in summer. I therefore protested repeatedly to the Land Office that the cases should be postponed until fall.

In May, 1909, I came on to Washington, and consulted as to the Alaskan coal cases with Secretary Ballinger, Land Commissioner Dennett, and the Chief of the Field Service. At the conference there came up a question of the effect of a statute of 1908, allowing consolidation of Alaskan coal entries to the amount of 2,560 acres where the original entries were made by the *"entrymen in good faith" and in their own interest.*

Schwartz (Chief of the Field Service) and Glavis contended that the act did not validate fraudulent entries. Pierce and Dennett claimed that the new act validated claims otherwise held invalid. Secretary Ballinger did not commit himself, but he did request that Glavis and Schwartz draft a letter to be sent to Attorney General Wickersham requesting an opinion. Glavis and Schwartz drafted a letter and sent it to Ballinger's office.

On May 19, 1909, the Pierce-Dennett view was upheld by an opinion signed by Pierce and prepared chiefly by Assistant Attorney General Oscar W. Lawler, who was attached to Ballinger's office. Glavis, in the light of this Pierce decision, felt that he could not prevent the patenting of the Cunningham claims, and so turned in a report favorable to them.

But when he later learned that his report to Wickersham had been detoured so as never to reach the Attorney General, he decided to take matters into his own hands for a third time. He obtained, through the aid of a friend, an interview with the Attorney General on May 24th. Glavis' account is as follows:

I was then in a very difficult position. I knew what the law was, and my superiors were against me. *If I accepted their ruling, 100,000 acres of Alaskan coal lands were slipping from the United States with no hope of recovery*—and were going to claimants many of whom were fraudulent. *The chance for the wise regulation of Alaskan coal lands urged by President Roosevelt would be gone.*

Without consulting with my superiors, I went to Attorney-General Wickersham and stated the matter to him. I understand that he asked Mr. Ballinger to refer the matter to him. *Mr. Ballinger requested me to withdraw my report, which showed that if the Pierce decision was correct, the Government had no ground to object to any of the Alaskan claims.* I withdrew that report.

On June 12, 1909, Attorney General Wickersham delivered an opinion on the question which, although it did not technically reverse the Pierce decision, did deny to the Cunningham cases the benefit of the act of May 1908.

On June 29, 1909, Glavis was advised that the Cunningham claimants were prepared to stand on the old law, and that he should present his evidence for an immediate hearing. The attitude of the Department was that this case had been hanging fire for some time while being held up by Glavis and that either he should present his evidence immediately or let the case go to decision. Glavis, however, was willing to do neither. Officials in the Department became impatient with him, and Commissioner Dennett, who was to judge the case, grew extremely critical. Writing to Schwartz, the Chief of Field Service, on July 10, 1909, he said, "He is also talking conservation very strongly. . . . All round he is ugly and he is preparing to be as unpleasant as he can. . . ." Glavis lost the friendship even of Schwartz, and with that his last support within the Department of the Interior.

Glavis Appeals Outside the Department

On July 16, 1909, in Seattle, Glavis asked Ballinger for more time to investigate so that field examinations could be made before proposed hearings before Dennett were held. Ballinger refused. To resume Glavis' account,

At that time I felt very despondent about the outcome of these cases. My conversation with Secretary Ballinger, the fact that Mr. Dennett was to be the judge in the case, and the difficulties I had had with the Land Office in my preparation of the cases, led me, without consulting my superiors, to appeal to the Department of Agriculture [Forest Service] to intervene.

Glavis thought of this expedient because most of the Cunningham claims lay within the Chugach National Forest under the Forest

Service's jurisdiction. Within a week, Secretary of Agriculture Wilson asked Ballinger that the proceedings on the Cunningham claims be adjourned until a field examination of the matter could be made. Ballinger could not easily deny this request and so an adjournment was ordered.

Immediately after Glavis' appeal to the Forest Service, the Cunningham claims were taken out of his hands and given to a young attorney unfamiliar with the matter. After looking into the claims the latter, too, reported against them and concurred in Glavis' request for an adjournment for a field investigation.

On July 22, in a note to Schwartz, Dennett wrote of Glavis,

> Glavis has these coal cases on the brain. I have told him how it looks to us and have reminded him of everything we have done for him. . . . It looks a little treacherous to me, this calling in the Forestry [Service].

On August 9, Glavis visited Gifford Pinchot, the Forester of the United States, who was then in Spokane on a speaking and official inspection tour. The two men had met in 1903 when Glavis was a Special Agent. Pinchot was in the midst of the warming-up period of the larger debate over national conservation policies. In a famous speech at Spokane (and elsewhere), he criticized the Department of the Interior under Ballinger for failing to carry on the aggresive policy of conservation of public lands begun under Roosevelt and for allowing vast stretches to fall into the hands of "unscrupulous monopolies." He disagreed with Taft and Ballinger's announced strict interpretation of the constitutional right of conservation which held that many of the land withdrawals of the Roosevelt-Pinchot program had been illegal. Pinchot queried whether Taft's legalism was not furthering the monopoly purchase of lands rich in mineral and power resources at the expense of the public interest.

Glavis told Pinchot his story and asked his advice. To the Forester the situation as Glavis described it was a specific example of all he had been decrying. He felt the Cunningham claims should be stopped. As he said many years later in his autobiography,

> It was not only bad morals to let these claims go to patent, but extremely bad politics as well. The facts were known not only to the Interior Department and the Forest Service, but also to many persons in private life. Sooner or later they were bound to come out, and when they did, the dickens would be to pay.
>
> Obviously this was a matter of the gravest importance. . . .
>
> There was only one thing to do, and that was to carry the case to the President of the United States. It was the last chance.

The President Decides

Pinchot gave this advice to Glavis, who agreed to follow it. With a letter of introduction from Pinchot and a statement of about fifty pages, composed mostly of documents in the case, Glavis saw the President in his summer home at Beverly, Massachusetts, on August 18. The President read the Glavis material and then sent it on to Ballinger in Seattle. The latter returned immediately to Washington and, with his aides, prepared answers to the Glavis charges. Then they all went up to Beverly and talked with the President about the question. The President looked their material over, discussed it with Attorney General George W. Wickersham (who felt that Glavis had not presented the story in full, or fairly), and asked Ballinger's friend and assistant, Oscar Lawler, to write his decision for him on the Glavis charges "as if he were President." Lawler had been involved in a disagreement with Glavis over a land claim many years before, but it is not clear whether the President knew this. Taft revised Lawler's draft and, when published, on September 13, the letter defended Ballinger, not only against the Glavis charges, but also against criticisms Pinchot and others had been making of the Secretary's decisions on water power sites, Indian forest lands, and other matters.

With regard to Glavis the decision, in the form of a letter to Ballinger, said,

> It is sufficient to say that the case attempted to be made by Mr. Glavis embraces only shreds of suspicions without any substantial evidence to sustain his attack.
>
> The whole record shows that Mr. Glavis was

honestly convinced of the illegal character of the claims in the Cunningham Group and that he was seeking evidence to defeat the claims.

> . . . in his zeal to convict yourself . . . he did not give me the benefit of information which he had that would have thrown light on the transactions, showing them to be consistent with an impartial attitude on your part toward the claims in question.

The letter proceeded to commend Ballinger's character highly. Of Glavis it said:

> When a subordinate in a government Bureau or Department has trustworthy evidence upon which to believe that his chief is dishonest . . . it is of course his duty to submit that evidence to higher authority than his chief. But when he makes a charge against his chief founded upon mere suspicions, and in his statement he fails to give his chief the benefit of circumstances within his knowledge that would explain his chief's action on proper grounds, he makes it impossible for him to continue in the service of the government.

Taft then authorized Ballinger "to dismiss L. R. Glavis from the service of the Government for filing a disingenuous statement, unjustly impeaching the official integrity of his superior officers."

Shortly after this, Glavis was dismissed. Immediately, on September 20, he wrote a reply to the President in which he said:

> I deemed it my duty to submit the facts to you and I cannot regret my action. Since there may be now even greater danger that the title to these coal lands will be fraudulently secured by the syndicate, it is no less my duty to my country to make public these facts in my possession, concerning which I firmly believe that you have been misled. This I shall do in the near future, with a full sense of the seriousness of my action and with a deep and abiding respect for your great office.

Of parenthetical interest is a comment made by the President in a letter to Helen Taft not long after this:

> The truth is, the whole administration under Roosevelt was demoralized by his system of dealing directly with subordinates. It was obviated in the State Department and in the War Department, under Root and me, because we simply ignored the interference and went on as we chose. . . . The subordinate gained nothing by his assuming of authority, but it was not so in other departments.

Glavis Carries On

As word of Glavis' fight spread and his fifty-page report was circulated among men like Francis J. Heney of San Francisco, known for his prosecution of the Oregon land-frauds cases, and Henry L. Stimson, former partner of Elihu Root and later Secretary of State and twice Secretary of War, more fuel was added to the heated debate over conservation and Taft's policies. Glavis was offered $3,000 for the article he was writing on the coal land claims, but he refused this and gave the piece, for nothing, to *Collier's Weekly*, run by the crusading Norman Hapgood. The article appeared in the November 13, 1909, issue; Glavis' account was straightforward and simple, but the section headings, the title, and cover—"Are the Guggenheims in Charge of the Department of Interior?"—as well as previous *Collier's* criticism of Ballinger—had a powerful effect in arousing public opinion.

Ballinger announced he would sue *Collier's* for a million dollars in a libel suit, and Congress resolved to undertake a joint investigation. It also asked President Taft to send over the documents in the case. Senator Dolliver, chairman of the Committee on Agriculture and Forestry, asked Pinchot to write him a letter on what was now being called the Ballinger-Pinchot dispute, particularly on the Glavis phase of it. Pinchot, after pondering on the administrative etiquette of the situation, did this, and the letter was read on the floor of the Senate on January 6, 1910, before Taft had responded to the Congressional request for documents. On January 7, a messenger from the White House delivered to Pinchot a letter from President Taft. Referring to Pinchot's letter to Dolliver it said, in part,

> Your letter was in effect an improper appeal to Congress and the public . . . against my decision in the Glavis case before the whole evidence on which that was based could be considered . . . if I were to pass over this matter in silence, it would be most demoralizing to the

discipline of the executive branch of the Government.

By your own conduct you have destroyed your usefulness as a helpful subordinate of the Government, and it therefore now becomes my duty to direct the Secretary of Agriculture to remove you from your office as the Forester.

The Upshot

The Joint Committee of Congress to investigate the Interior Department and the Forest Service began its public sessions on January 26, 1910. Not only the specific charges made by Glavis but some broader criticisms of the Department of the Interior under Ballinger were considered. Glavis was represented by Louis D. Brandeis, whose fee was paid by *Collier's*. Brandeis' brilliant handling of Glavis' case received a good press. The evidence on Glavis' dismissal by Taft and on the conduct of the Department of the Interior which Brandeis produced was considered sensational by the newspapers and interpreted as casting suspicion on the integrity of the Administration. Forty-six days of hearings and a large mass of testimony led to a majority report from the Committee's seven Republican members which exonerated Ballinger but proposed that in the future Alaska coal land claims cases be heard before a United States court and that the government lease rather than sell coal lands. In their minority report the four Democratic members of the Committee concluded that Ballinger had not been "true to the trust reposed in him" and should be asked to resign. The lone Insurgent Republican member of the Committee reported that the charges made by Glavis and Pinchot should be sustained.

Not many days after he dismissed Pinchot, Taft, following an earlier recommendation by Ballinger, sent a strong conservation message to Congress, proposing, among other things, that legislation be passed providing that title to lands containing minerals be given for the surface only and that the federal government merely lease rights to subsoil wealth. In the course of time, legislation along these lines was enacted. Eventually, too, the Cunningham claims were held void by the courts.

Less than a year after his exoneration by President Taft, and by the Committee majority, Ballinger resigned from the Department of the Interior. In the following Presidential election, 1912, Roosevelt campaigned on the Progressive ticket and in the three-way contest that ensued both Roosevelt and Taft lost to the Democratic candidate, Woodrow Wilson.

Bibliographical Note

The primary source for material on the Glavis-Ballinger controversy is:

U. S. Congress, Joint Congressional Committee, 61st Congress, 3rd Session, *Investigation into the Interior Department and Forestry Bureau*, Senate Document No. 719, 13 volumes, 1910-11. Volume 1 contains the Majority and Minority Reports and Volume 9 contains the arguments and briefs of counsel. The brief on behalf of L. R. Glavis is on pages 5014 to 5182.

A concise presentation of the story, based on the Congressional Committee's proceedings is:

Rose M. Stahl, *The Ballinger-Pinchot Controversy*. Smith College Studies in History, Vol. XI, January, 1926.

Glavis' own account is contained in his magazine article:

Louis R. Glavis, "The White-washing of Ballinger." *Collier's Weekly*, Vol. XLIV, No. 8. November 13, 1909. Pp. 15 ff.

Other discussions of the affair, from varying points of view, are:

Harold L. Ickes, "Not Guilty!" *The Saturday Evening Post*, Vol. 212, No. 48. May 25, 1940. Pp. 9 ff. See also the editorial on page 28.

Alpheus T. Mason, *Bureaucracy Convicts Itself*. The Viking Press, New York, 1941.

Gifford Pinchot, *Breaking New Ground*. Harcourt, Brace and Company, New York, 1947. See pp. 395 ff.

Henry F. Pringle, *The Life and Times of William Howard Taft*, 2 vols. Farrar and Rinehart, Inc., New York, 1939. See Vol. 1, Chapters XXVI-XXVII.

Acknowledgment is made to the *Saturday Evening Post*, The Viking Press, Harcourt, Brace and Company, and Rinehart and Company for permission to quote from the above books and articles.

THE BATTLE OF BLUE EARTH COUNTY

CONTENTS

PREFACE

This is a story of intergovernmental conflict and eventual peace, centering around an incident which gained no more than passing attention in the press at the time it occurred. It is the story of a dispute over the hiring of an executive secretary by a local welfare board—a dispute which was to climax and then conclude a seven years' war between officials of a Midwestern county and the state and Federal administrators with whom they had to deal. Though obscure in itself, the incident deserves telling as an example of the stresses which built up within the Federal system during the decade of the New Deal and threatened at many points to disrupt the administrative process. In this case, all the elements familiar to the intergovernmental struggle were present: "perverse localism," "aggressive centralism," and the abiding sense of compromise which serves in this country to hold local, state, and Federal governments together in a workable system of administration. It was in such a spirit of compromise that the battle of Blue Earth County was finally and successfully resolved; when it was over in 1945, all three contestants could reflect upon their respective campaigns with pride and satisfaction. For the leading board members of Blue Earth County, Minnesota, it had been a gallant struggle to preserve the birthright of local self-government against attack by insidious forces of centralization. For state and Federal administrators, the controversy had been another troublesome but rewarding episode in a joint campaign to achieve acceptance of the social security program and improvement in the methods of its administration.

The story is told from the standpoint of the local officials, with only occasional light cast on the problems of the state officials, and little more than a passing glance at the Federal officers. The policy of the Federal government—Congressional and administrative—in social security is to move toward an equalization of standards of benefits and toward a "satisfactory" level of professional competence among state and local administrative officials. With these goals in mind, Federal officials look with jaundiced eyes on local opposition to what seem—from Washington—minimal standards at best. Similarly, the state officials find themselves striving for objectives that are rather different from the ends of both the Federal and the local administrators. The differences are inherent in the different situations, which engender and in turn are affected by different attitudes. The reader will therefore bear in mind that he is looking at a series of events from only one of three significant perspectives. This limitation in perspective is deliberate: it should not be misleading if it is not overlooked.

One other aspect of the case also needs to be noted and taken into account. The study was written some five years after the incident was closed. Human memories are creative. The person who recites his recollections to an interviewer inevitably tends to order the past, and usually to order it in a way that reveals himself in a favorable light. Actions that were based on accidental pique or personal dislike, for example, are explained in terms of political theory and philosophy. Hesitations disappear, and hindsight becomes foresight. No man is immune from tendencies of this sort in his reminiscent processes; and if the reader detects this kind of ex post facto rationalization in the following account, as he undoubtedly will, he should realize that he is observing a pervasive and ineradicable human tendency.

The roots of the controversy lay deep in the history and make-up of Blue Earth County. Carved out of what was still Federal territory a hundred years ago, the county took form in the profitable interplay of two dominant factors: its rich agricultural land, which the late Harold Smith described wistfully as "God's greenest acres," and its immigrant settlers (Scotch-Irish and English from the East; Germans, Norwegians, and Swedes of the Old Immigration) who for three generations carefully cultivated the soil and constructed a prosperous and stable economy. During these years, the county remained as much insulated from the wear and tear of America's industrial and urban trends as any community could under modern conditions of interdependence. If its citizens pioneered in the adoption of new methods of agriculture and industrial science, they did so in the same tradition of progressive and energetic individualism that brought them originally to settle the West and assured them their continued prosperity. But they did not often see the less fortunate or more difficult consequences of the trends they helped to promote. By 1933 their striving city of Mankato claimed half the county's total population of 35,000 and could rightly boast of being southern Minnesota's key retail, transportation, and educational center; but it showed none of the blight which characterized urban centers to the east. And throughout the county, the more or less idyllic picture held true; a mixture of nationalities, but no critical minority problem; clubs, farm bureaus, and cliques, but no rigid class stratification; low wages and some unemployment, but few cases of abject poverty; men of influence and wealth, but no entrenched bosses or organized machines.

Jefferson would have been at ease in Blue Earth County, Minnesota, except, perhaps, that the community was preponderantly Republican—from Lincoln through Hoover, GOP presidential candidates had been able to count solidly on the county's support. True, there was an exception in 1912, when the local vote was split between regular Republicans and Progressives, and the Democrats emerged with a minority coup. This exception is worth noting, for it served to point out a progressive, sometimes radical fire which still smoldered under the surface rock of conservative opinion. In part, this was a heritage brought over by the German immigrants of 1848 and left untended during subsequent years of prosperity; for the rest, it was the native fire of the Midwestern farmer. Whatever its source, it was there to be rekindled during the years of the Populists and again during the postwar periods of agricultural depression. Conservative and Republican in prosperity, Blue Earth County went Democratic in the bleak year of 1932.

The county voted for Roosevelt again in 1936, but for the last time. In 1940 the conservative half of the county's split personality was to reassert itself. During the intervening years, the community had been a reluctant dragon; apparently ill-at-ease and conscience-stricken in the ranks of the Democratic party, local voters remained there presumably because of economic advantage, and at no election could they bring themselves to support the degree of socialism advocated by the incumbent Farmer-Labor governor. With Willkie in 1940, they had hopes of being prosperous and Republican at the same time, and returned to the GOP fold.

In this volatile combination of traits lies at least one clue to the apparent paradox in community attitudes during the years of struggle. In fighting state and Federal administrators, one might suggest that Blue Earth County was externalizing an inner conflict in which opposing sides could not be easily distinguished. On this larger stage, confusion and self-contradiction seemed to disappear, and the battle seemed to be identifiable as one of local versus central interests. Actually, it was not that. The community, it is true, continued to support emotionally and by vote the members of the board most active in the fight against state and Federal supervision—men who in a sense epitomized the community's conservatism and echoed its Republican conscience. But the community also showed that it was divided against itself, and was not of a single mind in matters of public policy nor uniformly committed to the struggle against Federal and state administrators which local officials were carrying on in the county's name. Throughout the fight, many and insistent voices were heard in local opposition to the county's campaign: some, like the needy aged and the striking teamsters, agitated for relief and to hell with political principle; others, like the editor of the local newspaper, spoke the work of non-partisan conscience in declaring for the merit system despite its implications for local autonomy; still others, board members themselves, were inclined to a more temperate view of social security requirements and gradually made their influence felt in local decisions.

Administering Relief in Blue Earth

The seven years' war broke in February of 1936, although there had been occasional border disputes and skirmishes ever since the Farmer-Laborites in Minnesota and the Democrats in Washington first launched their crusades and began administrative forays into the territory of the Blue Earth. The reasons were clear. Until 1933, the county had enjoyed sole jurisdiction in the field of public relief, and had been able to decide without interference who was to get relief and in what amounts. Administrative organization for the job was elementary: a special board had been created within recent years for the handling of child welfare, but essentially it remained for the board of commissioners to exercise final responsibility and discretion. Not that the commissioners proffered freely of public funds—more often the opposite. Their policy of assistance was the implicit belief of the community, that personal effort was the basic cure for poverty; in any event, dependence was not to be encouraged by generous grants from the public treasury. To illustrate, the choice they opened to the county's aged lay between \$6-\$15 per month pension supplemented with occasional food and medical orders, and a quiet existence at the county poor farm.

In 1933, all this was changed. The county was suddenly forced to move over and make room for state and Federal relief agencies. The ground was quickly covered with new encampments. Washington in three years of participation in general relief contributed FERA, then CWA, FERA again, and finally WPA. The state moved with equal dispatch, beginning in 1933 with a system of grants to local units, which it accompanied with a rough-hewn plan for administrative supervision.

No longer the sole functionaries, shorn of some of their discretion, and greatly perturbed at the political parentage and generosity of the newer agencies, Blue Earth County's commissioners grew increasingly hostile. Particularly "Bill" Minks and "Lou" Kraus, who for all practical purposes served during this period to personify Blue Earth County and its official attitude.

The two were fast friends, and together dominated the county board. From Minks came energy and political spark; from Kraus, conservative but more thoughtful leadership. Both were prosperous farmers; both were leaders in the local farm bureau organization; both Republican, although state requirements for non-partisan local elections kept them from flying political colors in local campaigns. Minks, in addition to his job as county commissioner, held a dazzling array of other local positions, ranging from president of the Minnesota Lake Farmers Cooperative Creamery to secretary-manager and general agent for the Minnesota Lake Farmers Mutual Insurance Company. An indomitable person, given to salty phrases and occasional malapropisms, fired with intense political ambition, he had won his way to a key position in the state association of county commissioners and established himself in that post as a person of some influence in matters of state legislation.[1] For twenty-four years he continued as county commissioner, elected every fourth year on a plank which he stated as follows and signed with a flourish:

> As I see it, government in general is *drifting to centralization of power*. I am a strong advocate of HOME RULE in retaining the grass roots of government and strengthening its powers instead of subduing them, in all rural and urban territories throughout the State and Nation, and recommend an increase in the legislative salary schedule for local governmental official units to the average community income levels, which would have a tendency to invite better official material, and which naturally would create better government with more efficiency in office. And I further believe that all federal funds should be

[1] A participant in this case has given a revealing description of Minks: "If you have ever attended a county commissioners' convention or read any of their minutes, you will understand that Mr. Minks *is* the association. In fact, I attended one of their conventions at which time he chairmanned his own election and didn't even call for an opposing vote."

handled through local governing units, in the future, instead of setting up additional federal directive office.

Lou Kraus, elected just as regularly and as often, was in basic agreement with Minks, though his own platform was more quietly spoken.

By 1935, the two men had seen enough of the new era to convince them that local government was in danger; they drew their battle lines and waited an overt act on the part of state or Federal officials to precipitate an open conflict. The occasion was not long in coming.

It began as a wrangle with state relief officials over three questions: One, the general extent to which state administrators would supervise local relief operations. Two, the amount of money which should be dedicated to relief activity. Three, the basis on which state aids were to be distributed to the counties. Blue Earth's position was clear on each point: it wanted little, if any, supervision, a low relief budget, and a straight per capita base for the distribution of state aids. State officials, on the other hand, were asking for close supervision, generous relief appropriations, and a sharing of state funds on the basis of each county's need and fiscal ability. This last was equivalent to a demand that the wealthier counties, such as Blue Earth, play the role of brother's keeper to the state's less fortunate units, notably the cut-over areas of the north.

Blue Earth did not take at all well to the state's proposals, particularly since they were put forward by administrators of known loyalty to the Farmer-Labor party, then in control of Minnesota politics. Here was an alien philosophy, as well as a direct though more familiar administrative move to "destroy" local power of the purse.

As the wrangling between county and state continued, developments were taking place in Federal policy which were soon to bring matters to a head. In August 1935, Congress and the Administration made a basic change in the character of Federal participation in relief by providing welfare grants to the states (Social Security Act), by withdrawing from the field of direct relief, and by concentrating remaining relief interests into a WPA work program for the able-bodied unemployed. This left Minnesota with the task of constructing a systematic program of its own which would provide direct relief to those not covered by Federal action, and which in other categories would meet the grant-in-aid requirements of the Social Security program.

Blue Earth Joins the Social Security Program

From August on, the months were spent in preparing the state for participation in the Old Age Assistance program, which was scheduled to go into effect on March 1 of the following year. State administrators struggled to make the necessary adjustments to Federal policy, and at the same time labored to bring each of Minnesota's eighty-seven counties into line with state plans for a permanent welfare and relief program. Almost immediately, they ran into a snag of local resistance. Blue Earth County and others like her began to balk at the prospect of state and Federal "interference" on a permanent basis; Minks and Kraus were further convinced that the new line-up was nothing less than the advance guard of the socialist movement.

Their reaction was explosive. Joined by eighteen other counties, Blue Earth seceded from the state relief system and declared its administrative independence. It then proceeded, as did its confederates, to establish an old age pension scheme of its own—administered by the individual commissioners, each within his own district, and with pensions set at the traditional $6-$15 per month.

Faced with this revolt, state relief officials soon made recourse to what they believed was their power of the purse. On February 21, 1936, a week before O.A.A. was to go into effect, they served notice on the rebel band that its members were to be cut off from further state aid; charges read that these counties had abandoned the state emergency relief program and had not provided acceptable welfare plans as per requirements of the Social Security program.

Blue Earth County's response was equally incisive. Bill Minks promptly declared the whole thing unconstitutional, and set about to prove it by political and legal means. His plans were announced in a letter written to eighteen associates in rebellion: first, a rally at the state capital, and then litigation in the courts. His objective: to recover the impounded state aids which he claimed were the counties' constitutional heritage. He considered his trump card to be a subtle device which he was to continue to use in his later contests with state administrators. It lay in his awareness that Federal funds would not be forthcoming to the state unless all its counties were participants—one county's defection might be enough to sabotage the entire old age assistance program. This was a political weapon, and Bill Minks, ensconced as he was both locally and within the state association of county commissioners, was in a position to wield it.

March 1 arrived, and on the assurance of Federal approval, plus hopes of soon achieving internal peace, Minnesota declared its old age assistance program in effect. Its relief administrators then set forth for Blue Earth County to cure if they could the local defection, and to explain the adjustments necessary for county participation in the old age assistance plan. They went armed with the announcement that during February alone Blue Earth County had sacrificed nearly a thousand dollars of state aid through its misguided policy of isolation.

Their meeting with Minks and the county board was not a success. As reported in the Mankato *Free Press* of March 12:

> The hostile attitude of the county commissioners, particularly Kraus and Minks, toward the state relief system appeared to change but little after state administrators explained the present set-up. The commissioners contend that withholding state relief money from non-participating counties is unconstitutional and that the funds should be apportioned equally to counties on a per capita basis. The board decided to take more time. . . .

While they waited, Minks went into action again, once more writing his confederates and repeating his intention to take to the courts. But on March 18, conflict was suddenly made unnecessary by a terse announcement from the state relief administrator conceding that funds could not be withheld:

> Counties not participating in the State Emergency Relief Administration program may share in relief money. There is no such thing as an "out" or an independent county. It is a misnomer. Every county is eligible if it complies with certain conditions.

No explanation was given for this sudden retreat. Presumably, the action was taken on advice from the governor and may have represented an attempt both to salvage administrative relations and to avoid political antagonisms in what was a crucial election year. Whatever counsel it was which prevailed among state officials, Minks and his fellows regarded it as an outright concession of defeat and as an encouragement to make further use of resistance tactics in their future dealings with state and Federal administrators.

The announcement, satisfying as it was to local pride, paved the way to an armistice in state-local relationships which lasted long enough to bring Blue Earth County into the Old Age Assistance plan, and into subsequent Social Security Act programs. But it was a jealous truce, inasmuch as the Farmer-Laborites continued their control of state offices, and the most basic of the three original points of controversy remained unsettled. Two had been resolved by terms of the Social Security Act and state legislation, which provided that grant-in-aid money be distributed on a straight share basis, roughly one-half Federal, one-third state, and one-sixth local. This gave assurance to the county that its part in financing the system would not be disproportionate to that of other counties, and could be largely determined through local discretion in determining the amount of individual old age assistance grants. Thus the problem of a formula for distributing state aids, as well as that of the size of the local relief budget, was largely resolved. It is significant to note that under O.A.A. the county was able to continue its rule of parsimony. Average monthly payments to individuals went up after 1936, but they were only $16 in 1937 and $24 as late as 1943. In brief, Blue Earth found little difficulty in maintaining its own philosophy of public assistance even when leagued together with the infidel.

However, the first point of original controversy remained alive to touch off later conflicts between county and state welfare officials, culminating in the dispute over the board's hiring of Herb Wagen as its executive secretary seven years later. This point, it will be remembered, concerned the extent to which the state was to supervise the local administration of relief and welfare activity. There were to be three more flare-ups before Minks and the local board reached full understanding with the state officials on this point, and a lasting peace.

The First Executive Secretary

When Blue Earth County in March of 1936 won back its right to state aid and joined the rest of Minnesota's counties in the O.A.A. program, it accepted an obligation to comply with certain administrative conditions. These included an agreement to file financial and case reports with state officials, and to comply with specified personnel, organizational, and procedural requirements. Some of these requirements Blue Earth County officials had come to appreciate as necessary from their own short-lived experience with their pension scheme of 1936, and did not protest. For example, the commissioners had discovered the need for full-time staff, having been swamped by 800 pension claims within a month of their attempting to administer the plan themselves. Quite promptly, they expanded their staff to include three full-time and two part-time employees.

Thus Minks and his board could see reason for staff assistance, and they could also, for the sake of Federal-state grants, accede to the requirements for reporting. But they had no intention of complying with growing demands for state supervision of local appointments where supervision could mean a refusal to accept candidates favored by the county board. They firmly believed that local self-government would be "destroyed" when the freedom to hire was tampered with, and Blue Earth County was in no mood in 1937, with Democrats and Farmer-Laborites still in control at the state and Federal levels, to see local self-government in any way weakened.

In 1937 Aid to Dependent Children was added to the Social Security program in Minnesota. By that time Blue Earth County was operating on a revised organizational basis, with welfare activity assigned to a special board appointed by the five commissioners. (This was a refinement in administration and not in policy. Minks and Kraus continued to dominate welfare policy at both commission and welfare board level.) Serving as staff for the new board were three case investigators and a woman clerk whose job was evolving into what was later to be classified as "executive secretary." All four were local residents, handpicked by Minks, Kraus, and the majority they commanded on the board. The set-up was a tidy one, and Minks and company saw no reason to change it to accommodate the ADC program when it appeared.

But what was tidy to Minks was not so tidy to state administrators. Their concern lay in establishing ADC on the principle of professional case work; and they saw scant evidence of professionalization in Blue Earth County. The senior member of the local staff, for example, was also chairman of the district Republican committee, and in his spare hours served as local registrar for the state motor vehicle licensing division—a concession which brought him sizable returns. Since his assignment on the welfare board was, however, a limited one, state officials turned their more immediate attention to the "executive secretary," who was now being moved into position to administer the new ADC program.

The new "executive secretary" had arrived in the welfare office a year before, transferred from the county auditor's office to help with the Old Age Assistance program. For a time she continued to serve in a double capacity, dividing her day between the auditor's office and the welfare desk; by 1937, she had become a full-time welfare employee. As far as her formal qualifications for welfare work were concerned—and particularly for the work of child care and assistance—it would be generous to describe them as slight: a high school education, a familiarity with local procedures, and the good graces of courthouse officials.

State officials lost no time in protesting her assignment; but again, as in 1936, they encountered a stone wall of local resistance. Minks, speaking for the board, refused to reconsider her assignment, and with 1936 fresh in their memory, state officials soon resorted to compromise. The board could keep its appointee, but in return it must add a qualified case worker acceptable to the state welfare department. To avoid further mischance, the state department picked its own candidate for the job—the wife of a professor at the local state teachers college and a person with several years of creditable experience in the field.[2]

This arrangement was at best an unhappy one. Herb Wagen, later recalling the situation, described it as one which could not long have continued without destroying the local welfare program. The new case worker was regarded by Minks as the personification of state control and was singled out by him for treatment as a foreign agent. The situation became progressively worse as she evoked sympathy for her efforts from board members less set in their thinking than Minks. Within a year she had become a rallying point of opposition to Minks' stand on welfare policy. At the staff level, she was accepted by at least three of her associates, and on the welfare board she could rely on three of the five members for a sympathetic hearing of her recommendations. Of these, one was a commissioner who had refused to identify himself with Kraus or Minks; a second was also a commissioner, inclined toward the course of policy set by the first; a third was a community stalwart, an elderly woman whose sense of civic responsibility had made her an eminent pioneer and contributor in the welfare field. These three voted with increasing regularity for the new case worker's recommendations, and in time were joined by a fourth—a woman (representing Kraus' commissioner district) whose early skepticism had been displaced by a distinct satisfaction with the way child welfare work was being carried on in her district. Furthermore, the new influence carried beyond official quarters into the community. The head of the Community Chest, who had long been needling Minks and Kraus for their handling of clients, became a loyal supporter of the new case worker, and soon persuaded the League of Women Voters to join in the campaign. By now Minks, regretting his bargain with the state administrators, was contemplating a means of ridding himself of this albatross.

Allied with Kraus, he proceeded to make the going as rough as possible for his unwanted help; and in early spring, the pair called for a show-down in the county commissioners' meeting, where they still retained a 3-2 majority. Their wish prevailed despite bitter opposition from the two dissenting commissioners; and the professor's wife was subsequently released in an official action that was tantamount to firing.

For Minks and Kraus, and the localism they represented, this removal marked a clear-cut triumph over the higher powers, but they were not to revel long in its celebration. Two contrary winds were astir that augured ill for the local cause. One was the board's increasing embarrassment over the behavior of the executive secretary, who was turning for diversion to extra-curricular activity. As Minks phrased it: "She began to step out and didn't pay attention to her work. Wanted to get married, and chased around quite a bit." This embarrassment was temporarily put aside in the board's concern over the threat of another developing storm: the Hatch Act and its cousin piece of legislation, an amendment to the Social Security Act calling for a merit system for state and local welfare employees paid in whole or in part with Federal funds. By the slim margin of the 25¢ per case which it contributed to local administrative costs (according to Minks: "just enough so they feel they can dictate to us"), the Federal government was wedging its

[2] Her account: "I went to Blue Earth as of September 1. The amusing part . . . was that I had been there for about three days in the spring of that year in the capacity of trouble shooter for the state, and had met the executive secretary at the time, and had apparently made enough of a favorable impression so that she plugged for me with Minks and Kraus when she knew I might mean her meal ticket (so far as the state was concerned)."

influence into the selection of Blue Earth County employees.

To Minks and Kraus, this was the arrival of the dictatorship they had long predicted, and they set about with new fire to organize a third round of local resistance. Before they had time to choose their weapons or map out their strategy, Minnesota officials called a state-wide meeting of county commissioners, intending to cut off precisely this sort of opposition by announcing a merit plan so moderate in its terms as to allay the fears of such men as Bill Minks. The meeting was held in St. Paul, and was addressed by Walter Finke, Stassen's new appointee to the reorganized and now Republicanized Division of Social Welfare. Finke appeared distinctly in the role of an appeaser; he insisted that he was not minded to displace any employee that the commissioners desired to retain. His modest proposal: construct an initial examination of three parts—a written, an evaluation of training and experience, and an oral interview. Let the commissioners score the experience record themselves and allow heavy weighting to the oral interview. Result: if any incumbent could not make the grade with these odds in his favor, he was either unwanted or admittedly not worth having. Needless to say, Minks and his fellow commissioners went home impressed with Finke and at peace with the administrative world.

But Finke had apparently spoken too soon or without enough attention to the fine print. A month later, instructions were sent out by mail which varied sharply from the first impression gained by the commissioners. They were now advised that before an incumbent could be admitted to the oral examination, he would have to pass the written. Whether Finke was guilty of misstatement or inconsistency is not clear; suffice it to say, the commissioners were outraged and turned to Minks for an adequate expression of their views. Minks wasted no time and was soon involved in sharp and personalized exchanges with the now unpopular Director. The climax, and the final break between Blue Earth and the Division, came when Minks appeared at a legislative hearing and charged Finke with "belittling him."

The battle of Blue Earth County was on again, and reports of it filled the winter of 1939-40. Then on March 29, Minks opened a new offensive, choosing once more to exploit his political advantage as Number One County Commissioner in the state. To each of his fellow members in the state association Minks addressed a letter urging that "all present staff members be qualified *without examination* when their work is satisfactory." On March 30, he was reported in the *Mankato Free Press* as being "personally opposed to the entire principle of the merit system," which is "a step backward and a blow to 'home rule' . . . a great many now doing good work will be disqualified." On April 2, he joined Kraus in convening the county board in special session, and moved adoption of a fiery resolution of protest. As carried, it read:

TO THE CONGRESS OF THE UNITED STATES:

Whereas: the Social Security Act as amended in Congress in 1939, known as Sec. 701 (a) Clause (5) of Sec. 1002 (a) provides such methods of administration relating to the establishing and maintaining of personal standards on a merit basis except that the Board shall exercise no authority with respect to the selection, tenure of office, and compensation of any individual employed in accordance with such methods as are found by the board to be necessary for the proper and efficient operation of the plan;

Whereas: the personnel of the County Welfare Office administers direct relief to which the federal government does not contribute and about 50% of all tax money levied within the county is for relief purposes;

Whereas: we believe that every local county welfare board in co-operation with the County Board, should be the SOLE JUDGES OF EFFICIENCY in setting up their own personnel in administering relief within each respective county.

Therefore be it resolved: We candidly ask your sincere reconsideration on this MERIT BASIS AMENDMENT AND ASK THAT SAID AMENDMENT BE REPEALED, for we believe it a blow to home rule and a step toward central control. The local county welfare boards and county boards pay the salaries of the welfare personnel staff and should have the full jurisdiction to determine the qualifications and efficiency of their employees in the welfare personnel.

This was to be Minks's last attack on the merit system *per se;* his subsequent efforts were devoted to making its practice innocuous. For one thing, he quickly sensed from editorials in the local press that civil service was a principle given as much honor in the community as the ideal of home rule, and that to persist in opposing it was politically dangerous. Moreover, in his pocket was the means of combining political advantage with personal strategy—a letter from Finke, asking him to serve with ten other "representative" commissioners on an advisory committee to assist with the construction and installation of Minnesota's welfare merit system.

As the number of incumbents who passed the first examination soon showed, Minks and his committee were able to use their influence with telling effect. The qualifying examinations as finally given were non-competitive and pegged at a minimum level of competence. Blue Earth County's staff experienced little difficulty with them and survived the ordeal intact.[3]

Now that they were relieved of personnel pressures from above, Minks and his board could turn gracefully to the problem of their adventuresome executive secretary. The nature of her extra-official activities and the erratic record of her administration were beyond concealing; dignity as well as accumulated work demanded that something be done. In 1942, the board devoted a meeting to her case, then announced that she had "left office."

The Second Executive Secretary

At this point, the state's wisdom in giving Minks a place in the organization of the state merit system was to make itself happily apparent. Both Minks and Kraus would have preferred appointing a local staff member to the now-vacant post of executive secretary and were agreed on a favorite candidate; but out of consideration for Minks's present membership on the state merit system advisory committee, they were willing to admit that their new candidate lacked certain prescribed qualifications for the job and were prepared to yield their choice if necessary to the requirements of the merit system. Their particular preference was Herb Wagen—a nephew of Kraus and a member of the county welfare staff for five years past. On his record Wagen was a likely candidate: an able, unassuming person who had come to be highly respected both locally and among state supervisors for his handling of welfare transactions. Wherever possible, Wagen had avoided taking part in the controversy between local and state interests, and would have preferred an early and peaceful reconciliation of the dispute. He was forty-seven years old at the time, and not a welfare worker either by training or by early choice. His education consisted of four years of high school and a single year of college—as the case develops this becomes a crucial point. His first job was with Standard Oil; out of work in 1929, he turned for a year to assessment for the city of Mankato, then to case work for the local Community Chest. In 1934, he added to his duties that of directing the local surplus commodities warehouse, and in 1936, absorbed the job of certifying workers for WPA. He was to have been hired as investigator for the county welfare board in 1936, but it turned out that Minks and Kraus were outvoted at the time in favor of another local candidate "who was out of a job." Shortly afterwards, Wagen was added to the staff in another capacity, and in 1940 qualified as Welfare Worker I by taking and passing the merit system examination.

As matters stood in 1942, it was clear to Minks and all concerned that Wagen could not meet the formal educational requirements for the job: viz., four years of college, or a minimum of two years of college and at least two years of experience. Furthermore, Wagen was somewhat reluctant to accept the job, being well aware of its political intricacies and the objections which state officials would certainly raise to his appointment. The result was that Minks and the board proceeded to look

[3] The Republican investigator, preferring politics to administration, resigned the day the Hatch Act went into effect, and did not take the qualifying examinations.

for another candidate according to orthodox civil service procedure: they consulted the state merit system supervisor, checked the register of eligibles, were given three names, and then after satisfying themselves as to his antecedents, appointed the oldest and most experienced of the three candidates.

The appointment proved a dud. The new secretary was both agreeable and sincere, but he was not in good health and was slow and "soft" in his handling of welfare clients. For once, state and local officials concurred in their judgment, and no objections were raised when the new secretary was offered the opportunity to look elsewhere for employment. That he was allowed to resign rather than be fired, as other board members preferred, seems to have been due to Minks, who prides himself on being a man of decision and principle, but not given to vindictiveness.

Still Minks shared the ire of the board insofar as it was directed at the state merit system for having produced such a "lemon." Having given state procedures a try, Minks declared that from then on the board would appoint its own secretaries, and the merit system was out of luck if it objected. This declaration became a fact on May 26, 1943, when the board returned again to its original choice, Herb Wagen, and summarily appointed him acting secretary—without so much as a glance at the state's register of eligible candidates. The decision was taken with no consideration of an alternative. Minks and the board were determined to assert their independence, and they had little reason from past experience with Federal and state administrators to fear the immediate consequences of their heresy.

With the hiring of Herb Wagen, Blue Earth County entered the concluding phase in its battle with the state. Twelve months were to pass before a decision and lasting peace were reached—twelve months of attrition, negotiation, and compromise. During this period, Herb Wagen remained as acting executive secretary, unable to move forward into permanent status without state certification, but kept from retreat by the dogged persistence of his local board.

The Fight Over Herb Wagen

I. McCURDY TRIES FOR A SETTLEMENT

The state's first response to Wagen's appointment was perfunctory: a *pro forma* word of censure spoken by the Division of Social Welfare's field representative on her regular monthly visit to the local welfare office. A mild-mannered person, she had never risked embroiling herself in state-local controversies by taking firm grasp on departmental policy; and her treatment of this problem was no exception. After saying what Blue Earth expected her to say, she discharged her remaining responsibility by reporting the matter to Division headquarters.

Before her recital of the facts could reach him through official channels, Robert McCurdy, supervisor of the state merit system, had become acquainted with the problem. On his desk lay an application from Wagen, asking permission to take the examination for his new position, then classified as Welfare Secretary I. McCurdy's response, in the theory of the merit system, should have been a simple one: reject the application, state the reasons (without the required years of education, Wagen had no standing for the position), and instruct the local board to consult the civil service register for qualified candidates. But painfully aware of the practical problems of merit administration, McCurdy saw that his decision would be a difficult one. To deny the application meant to stir up trouble with the county board, and McCurdy, in his three years of nursing the merit system in Minnesota through infancy, had had enough of such trouble to make him step warily. Also, he discovered from experience that he could rely upon few if any sanctions to make his decisions stick, particularly in controversy with a board as politically astute and as rugged in its resistance as Blue Earth County. His own part in any enforcement proceeding was limited to a post-audit of the welfare payroll, followed by a report to the Director of the Division of any exceptions he might find. Eventually, state authorities might stop the payroll and suspend grant-in-aid payments to the county; but McCurdy knew, and Bill Minks knew, that such action was more effective in its threat than in its performance.

What Bill Minks did not know was that McCurdy's orders precluded the use of any such drastic device—in fact, any device which would "unnecessarily" aggravate an already strained state-local relationship. These were not formal orders: they had filtered down as instructions from Governor Thye, who in his campaign of 1942 had become particularly sensitive to local irritations and concerned with alleviating them. His gospel had become something of a good neighbor policy; and as an evangelist in the field of welfare, he had chosen his campaign manager and now director of the Division of Social Welfare, Bernard Levander. Levander's chief task became the mending of political fences among local welfare boards.

All this meant that McCurdy, who operated within the Division, would have to employ his own devices in order to resolve the Blue Earth situation and others like it. Significantly, McCurdy's personal repertoire did not include a get-tough tactic. Sociable instincts and long exposure to the elements in public office had mellowed him to a point where he could appreciate the point of view of the opposition, particularly in cases where the opposition subscribed to such homely and unquestioned principles as that of self-government.

Still, there was enough open to question in the Blue Earth situation to cause McCurdy to reply unfavorably to Wagen's request, and to summon a meeting with the local board to inquire into the reasons for their heresy. Rumors had already reached him regarding Wagen's relationship to Commissioner Kraus; and he had reason to believe reports from his field representatives to the effect that Minks and Kraus had not always been free from political considerations in their handling of welfare clients.

His meeting with the board took place that summer, in the back basement room of the county courthouse. It began on a distinctly hostile note, with McCurdy reading from the law and Minks rattling his sword of resistance. As the meeting progressed, Minks and McCurdy found they had something in common —a personal skepticism toward the educational requirements barring Wagen from his job. McCurdy admitted that he himself had no more than a year of college training; and his deputy, also present, chipped in with the observation that he didn't have a college degree either, and saw no reason for requiring one of Wagen. By now the meeting was blossoming into a friendly affair, the more so as McCurdy grew convinced that Wagen after all was a capable person and that the local welfare board was not engaging in a purely political maneuver. This was a situation where compromise seemed justified.

But McCurdy knew that compromise could not appear either as defeat or as special treatment. Fortunately for the moment, he found the answer he needed in a recent change of policy announced by the Social Security Board —a change designed to meet the problem of manpower brought on by the war. What it called for was a "Temporary relaxation of personnel standards"; in effect, this meant that the board would not object if a state found it necessary to make a "reasonable" revision downward in its scale of job requirements. McCurdy had been contemplating action along these lines before he encountered the Blue Earth problem; now he had good reason to announce his intentions and see what could be done. By revising the specifications for Executive Secretary to scale down the educational requirement, the Wagen case might be disposed of amicably and without doing violence to civil service procedure.

With this prospect in mind, McCurdy was able to give the commissioners hope that Wagen might eventually qualify for his post; and the meeting broke up with the understanding that Wagen would be allowed to take the examination. Shortly afterward he did take the examination and managed to pass the written section with a respectable score. Unfortunately, nothing had been done in the meantime to change the requirements; and when Wagen came before the state merit system board for certification, there was no alternative but to reject him. This action, in addition to further antagonizing Minks, brought the case to the attention of John Kidneigh, regional personnel consultant for the Social Security Board. Being more in the nature of a professional civil service administrator than McCurdy, and one step removed from the immediate pressures in the case, Kidneigh regarded McCurdy's conciliatory handling of the case as "an exception to personnel standards," and began pressing for firm remedial action. His criticism became more insistent as the summer wore on and more cases of "amicable settlements" were brought to his attention in the course of an audit then being conducted of the merit system's administration in Minnesota.

Fall arrived with McCurdy wedged between the two opposing forces; Kidneigh asking for strict enforcement of the rules, Blue Earth demanding either an exception or an amendment to regulations. At this critical juncture, McCurdy resigned to accept a position as director of the new Council on Intergovernmental Relations project in Minnesota (a privately financed effort to encourage grass-roots attention to the problem of interlevel co-operation), and by so doing gave up his official connection with the case. Ironically, his new assignment took him to Blue Earth County; and he was later to return to the case in the unofficial role of devil's advocate, having become thoroughly convinced in the meantime that Wagen was the man for the job.

II. CULHANE SUCCEEDS

His place in the merit system office was taken by Tom Culhane, a young and dynamic person with a growing reputation as a civil service administrator. Almost immediately the relationship between Kidneigh's office and that of the merit system changed to one of friendly co-operation. Kidneigh had known Culhane before, during the years when the latter was employed as a member of the State Civil Service Department; in his estimation, Culhane was "one of the most able young personnel men in the field." At a meeting held shortly after Culhane's appointment, Kidneigh was gratified to learn that his new counterpart at the state level shared his critical view of the Blue Earth situation.

Somewhat later, Culhane conferred with Bob Ferderer, personnel officer for the Division of Social Welfare and inclined toward the Division's point of view. Ferderer stressed the political background of the case, and informed Culhane that the Governor's good neighbor policy was still in effect—adding that as long as it was, the Division of Social Welfare "was not too anxious to disturb the Blue Earth County Board in the matter." Culhane was still not satisfied to let the appointment stand without in some way meeting the requirements of the civil service process; and his next step was to summon Minks to the state capital for a conference with himself and Ferderer. Minks recalls only his part of the conversation, which went roughly as follows: "Boys, we've got the man we want and we're going to keep him. He's as good a man as anyone you've got on the list."

With the war manpower situation growing more acute every day, Culhane was ready to admit argument on this point. But he continued to stand firm on civil service procedure, and insisted that certification would have to be made from the register. The meeting concluded pleasantly enough, but without changing anyone's point of view—Minks was still on one side, Culhane on the other, and Ferderer somewhat to the Blue Earth side of center.

Still intent on settling the matter, Culhane arranged another meeting, this time with Levander. Again the results were inconclusive: "We went over the ground and I sensed that the Director was fair-minded on the matter but was not willing immediately to call the county board to account." Another note of discouragement was to come from Kidneigh, Culhane's next stop after Levander. Ready by this time to act if necessary on his own authority, Culhane was searching for possible sanctions to back whatever step he might take; his purpose in seeing Kidneigh was to determine whether or not he could expect help from Federal quarters. Kidneigh's reply was that all he could offer was a formal statement to the effect that the Wagen appointment "was a deviation from Federal standards, *insufficient* to preclude a finding of substantial conformity to Federal standards." The system being what it was,[4]

[4] To understand the limitations under which Kidneigh was operating at this point it is helpful to refer to his statement explaining the relationship between the Federal and state governments in a matter of this kind:

"The actual fact of the matter is that if a State

the Federal government could bark in this case, but it would not bite.

It was then that Culhane became fully aware of the limitations of his position. In his own words, the situation could be summarized as follows:

(1) no action on sanctions could be expected from the Federal Social Security Board;
(2) the State Department of Social Welfare was tolerant of the situation;
(3) the Blue Earth County Welfare Board had no reason to fear any kind of action that could be instituted by the Merit System Supervisor whose sole instruments of insuring compliance were (a) persuasion and (b) post audit of payrolls with a statement to the Director of the Division of Social Welfare of the deviation from rules, salary standards, etc.

The result was that Culhane was now drawn to the same strategy which McCurdy had hit upon six months before but had not carried through: viz., gear Wagen's case to the temporary wartime relaxation of personnel standards now allowed by the Social Security Board. Culhane, independently of the Blue Earth problem, had already launched a classification study of state welfare positions, partly to meet the criticisms directed at the system as he had inherited it, partly to meet the problem of a war manpower situation. His decision to do so had drawn enthusiastic support from the regional security board office; Kidneigh, in fact, had agreed to help out with the survey by supplying a trained analyst "to work behind scenes" and to give what assistance he could. He later found the results extremely gratifying: "A very excellent job on class specification writing was completed with the establishment of uniform minimum qualifications which were, I believe, quite reasonable."

How reasonable some of the revised specifications were, and to what elements of opinion, Kidneigh may not fully have realized. The specifications for the three grades of Executive Secretary were certainly gone over with a sharp eye to the possible solution of the Wagen case, and with a determination to satisfy each of the different interests involved. Even before the survey was begun, the Division of Social Welfare had taken renewed interest in this possibility. Earl Berg, who had replaced Levander as Director of the Division, quickly discovered what a problem he had inherited. On a courtesy visit to Blue Earth County, he had walked unforewarned into a full meeting of the local welfare board, and had been given a rather testy statement of the board's point of view.[5] Also present at the meeting by local request was Bob McCurdy, who in his first weeks on his new job had had an opportunity to become better acquainted with Wagen and was greatly impressed with the latter's work as secretary. McCurdy knew Berg, and supported the local board's position in a way which made Berg share his convictions.

Before leaving, Berg committed himself to the extent of encouraging the Board to await his help in the matter. Upon his return to the capital, he passed word along to Ferderer and also to Russell Drake, his chief of field services, to see what could be done to reach a prompt settlement. Both men were primed for action, having earlier discussed their strategy with Levander; they were agreed that the particular educational requirement which barred Wagen from office had originally been set arbitrarily to serve as a rule of thumb, and that it would not be violating merit system principles to reduce that requirement to a point where Wagen could satisfy it. It was a simple matter of rewriting specifications to allow Wagen, and all other candidates, to substitute another year of experience for another year of college;

agency has a plan of almost any rational kind, the Federal government will accept it providing it is in general conformity with the Social Security Act as properly interpreted. Of course, when the State has established a plan which includes qualifications for given classes of positions, the Federal Government will expect the State to live up to its own plan. The question therefore in the Wagen case was not would the Federal Government approve what the State did for or with Blue Earth County, but was the State administering its own plan according to the conditions of its own plan. Obviously, it was not.

"When, however [here Kidneigh refers to the later solution of the case] the State changed its plan there could be no other decision rendered than was rendered."

[5] Minks's opening remark was: "Before you get rid of Herb Wagen, you're first going to have to get rid of Lou Kraus and Bill Minks."

in other words, at least one year of college plus enough years of experience to give a total of four years of background and training was now established as the minimum requirement—and Wagen, with his one year of college and more than three years of experience, was now in a position to file for examination and office.

One question remained. Would the Social Security Board, as represented by Kidneigh, agree to this cutback in requirements? Interestingly enough, in view of Kidneigh's own feeling that he had no alternative, neither Ferderer nor Drake expected to obtain his approval; in their previous contacts with Federal consultants, Drake and Ferderer had found them "unyielding" and pledged to a rigorous interpretation of personnel standards. It was therefore to their surprise that Kidneigh offered no objection to the change, considering it a reasonable adjustment to wartime conditions and an integral part of Minnesota's reclassification project to which he had already given his wholehearted approval.[6]

Culhane added his consent;[7] the change was adopted; and Wagen suddenly found himself qualified to take the examination and be certified for his job. Everything seemed to fall neatly into place; and what had been for long months a subject of heated controversy and dramatic action changed overnight into a drab factual paragraph in a matter-of-fact letter for the records: "The minimum qualifications for appointment to the position of Executive Secretary II were modified on April 1, 1944. Mr. Wagen met the new minimum qualifications and his provisional appointment was approved on May 4, 1944. On June 10, 1944, Mr. Wagen took an examination for the position of Executive Secretary II and attained a passing grade. He was subsequently certified for appointment and made a permanent employee."

Peace at Last

Thus the controversy was concluded, and with it the whole of the seven years' war. As it turned out, Herb Wagen was a person dedicated to the principle of intergovernmental co-operation and to radically improved concepts of local welfare administration. His comment upon taking office in 1943 was to the effect that "I cannot do the job without fully qualified staff and improved relations with the state Division of Social Welfare." Since the request came from a man they had no reason to fear or distrust, Minks and Kraus accepted it and adopted it as policy. Within a matter of months, Wagen had attracted favorable reports from visiting state supervisors; and in 1949, state officials could reflect on the changes in Blue Earth attitudes and describe them as no less than miraculous.

It is an exaggeration, of course, to credit Wagen for everything that was accomplished locally after 1944. In the latter stages of the controversy and the years which followed, Minks showed the mellowing effects of his participation in the Council on Intergovernmen-

---

[6] Kidneigh was apparently not aware of the strategy involved in making this particular change. He was later to write:

"The reason . . . for the shift in minimum qualifications that occurred is not connected at all with the Wagen case but was a shift in minimum qualifications throughout the whole classification structure based upon resurvey of the total situation in all county welfare employment in the State of Minnesota."

Though unlikely that he would, even if he had known, have attempted to block the change (cf. his earlier statement, p. 103), it is significant that no one on the state level seems to have made any notable effort to inform him.

[7] Culhane lists the factors in his decision:

"I could have been stubborn and kept on taking payroll exceptions to Wagen's appointment, but nothing good would have been accomplished. Administration is the science of the possible!

"No objective studies had demonstrated that the existing minimums for the selection of Executive Secretaries (regarding college education) were any more valid than the ones proposed that would permit Wagen to compete.

"I was *not* influenced by:

"Wagen's reported competence. I had already learned that it was always the best employees who had trouble with civil service appointments.

"Minks' influential position: The most powerful men politically are the quiet ones you seldom meet.

"Blue Earth's revolt: It was no greater in our eyes than some other and more troublesome ones—but I must admit they were a persistent group.

"McCurdy's switch: We were aware of it, and it lent aid and comfort to the local group; but I don't think it influenced my decision."

These factors may well have influenced others' attitudes, however.

tal Relations and of his contacts with state and Federal officials which the Council's project afforded. More than anything else, the Council was to make him aware of the greatly expanded role open to him in the new era of co-operative intergovernmental relations. To enter these new approaches to fame and political achievement, Minks needed a means of graceful exit from his former notions of autonomy and isolationism. That exit was provided him in his apparent victory over bureaucratic compulsion.

Nor can the reasons for final peace be found entirely in Minks' belated conversion to the co-operative faith. His own change of outlook was part expression of the groundswell movement that was taking place in the community's thought. By the end of the war, the community had by and large come to accept Federal security programs as an integral part of government on the local scene.

IN RETROSPECT

In retrospect, the seven years' war between Blue Earth County and the higher powers seems in many of its respects a case study in determinism. It is difficult to see how the struggle could have been averted or any major factor changed by the calculated action of state or Federal administrators. Given the nature of the community, the personalities of its officials, and the character of the New Deal, the conflict was certain to arise; the turbulent years which followed were but a record of the stormy adjustments by which conservatism and the new philosophy were hammered into a pattern of co-operative administrative relations. The irony of it all was that insistence upon orthodox principles of administration, in this case refusal to bend civil service requirements to the exigencies of the situation, almost cost the final victory.

Perhaps the one opportunity which was presented to state administrators to settle the case on their own terms came late in the campaign and was lost to them for reasons beyond their control. This was the point in 1942 when Minks fired his executive secretary and acceded to the principles and procedures of the merit system. Had the state been able to supply an able candidate, it might have won Blue Earth officials permanently to its standards of welfare administration. As it was, the war decimated the list of eligibles on the register, and no candidate was left competent enough to make capital of the opportunity.

But if the case fails to demonstrate the possibility of heroic administrative action under such circumstances, it does provide insight into the nature of the intergovernmental administrative process and contributes toward a better understanding of its intricacies. The following are but suggestive of the morals, or conclusions, which can be drawn.

(1) There is an inescapable blending of politics and administration in the intergovernmental process, in at least two ways. One, by reason of the political role of the chief executive (in this case, the governor) and the consequent flavoring of administrative directives. Two, by virtue of the fact that what is an administrative assignment at one level is often a political duty at another. In this instance, it was a group of political personalities with whom state welfare administrators had to deal.

(2) Sanctions, even when provided by law, are seldom available and seldom used—particularly if the sanctions are weighty. The intergovernmental process, as both McCurdy and Culhane were to learn, is one of persuasion and compromise, rather than of command and compulsion.

(3) Decision-making in the intergovernmental process is a problem in simultaneous equations. A state administrator, as in this case, faces two unknowns in any decision: the policy of the Federal government and the response of the local unit. Seldom if ever do representatives of the three levels come together to take joint action; certainly, there is no formal or continuing process which enables or requires them to do so.

With these conclusions in mind, it is not difficult to appreciate the inconclusiveness of administrative action during the battle of Blue Earth County, nor the satisfaction of administrators with the final outcome.

THE NATURAL CEMENT ISSUE

CONTENTS

INTRODUCTION

Much has been written within recent years about the process of decision-making: how an administrator makes up his mind and what factors influence him in doing so. Analyses of this sort have proved extremely helpful; but in stopping short at the point where the decision is made, as they frequently do, they tell only part of the story. Administrators not only make decisions, but they also have to live with them—and living with a decision is not the easiest or the simplest part of an administrator's job. The story of the Natural Cement Issue is a striking case in point. The incident described is one of prolonged and bitter controversy resulting from a decision made in 1940 by the State Commissioner of Highways in Minnesota—a controversy so far rooted in politics and involving such an aggressive opposition as to have early cowed a less rugged administrative spirit than that of the Commissioner. It will be seen in the course of the narrative that the formal decision of 1940 was more the beginning than the end of the process. The Commissioner's antagonist did not give up easily, and after 1940 there was a whole series of decisions on both sides until the matter was finally settled—albeit perhaps only temporarily—in 1948.

There is another aspect of the study of decisions that should be noted here. In general, writers on public administration treat business actions as mere phenomena that the public administrator must take into account, while writers on business administration usually treat government actions in the same way. But frequently government action and business action are so closely linked that a whole series of events may occur in which the public official and the businessman provoke alternate successive decisions in a sort of chain reaction.

Such is the case here. As a formal matter, the Commissioner's action in 1940 may be regarded as the pivot of this tale; but in the events that led up to that decision, and in the long aftermath, the president of a small company in Minnesota was just as much a protagonist as the Commissioner.

This then is a story about two men; but like all studies of administration, the actions of the administrators did not take place in a vacuum. Affecting each, and affecting the other actors too, was an institutional environment and institutional ideals. The clash of personalities would not have occurred if the accepted objectives of the different institutions had not collided. Once the collision occurred the stage was set for a rather vivid display of personalities. No doubt other men might have behaved quite differently in this situation, yet the course of conduct on each side was directed if not determined by institutional needs. In one light, therefore, this can be read as a story of a business firm and a government agency in conflict.

There is one further element in the Cement Issue that was of significant concern to the major participants—federalism. In Minnesota, as in all other states, the highway program receives crucially important aid from the Federal government and, as under other Federal aid programs, the Federal government can therefore establish standards. In all such relationships differences arise from time to time between the Federal and state agencies. Conventionally it is assumed that the prime *casus belli* is the Federal agency's insistence on its own too rigid standards. In the Cement Issue the problem was quite different. Here the state agency was embarrassed by the failure of the Federal agency to issue officially a policy that it was known to favor, and further embarrassment was caused by the fact that the Federal agency permitted another state to retain the same policy that both it and Minnesota opposed. In spite of these embarrassments, as the reader will observe, in substance the Federal and state commissioners were united in their opposition to the demands of the businessman.

It is at least possible that Federal-state relations in technical areas are more fundamentally characterized by this community of approach on the part of engineers and other technicians than by the battles over rights and jurisdiction that are so frequently talked about. While the story narrated in the pages that follow constitutes only a single example of a kind of co-operative federalism, further research might reveal that the example is a typical one.

The story is not an easy one to unravel or relate, because of its involvement with disputed questions of motives, with personal issues, and with debate over a problem in technical research. Given such a setting, it becomes all but impossible to recapture the "truth" of what happened at each stage of the developing story. Fortunately for the telling of the story, the "truth" in any abstract sense is not always relevant or revealing. The realities of the case—"what really happened"—are what the people involved thought had happened and let govern their own actions.

It is on this premise that the following narrative is based; wherever possible, the participants are allowed to speak for themselves. It should be added, however, that most of the quotations have been taken from statements provided well after the incidents they described took place. Whether they tend to reshape the "truth" or reorder the past can be left a moot question, although it is one that must be raised and re-raised throughout the reading of the case.

The main thread of the cement story can be traced in a few words. In 1939, "Harry" Carney, president of a natural cement company in Minnesota, asked "Mike" Hoffmann, the State Highway Commissioner, to look into a recent research report of the Federal Bureau of Public Roads that indicated the desirability of specifying a blend of natural and portland (i.e., manufactured) cement for use in concrete highways in preference to the customary use of unblended portland. New York State, Carney learned, required the use of the blend, much to the advantage of a natural cement manufacturer in that state.

As time went on Carney pressed for a mandatory specification in Minnesota, as well as for a sizable mileage of experimental contracts using the blend. He argued his case partly on the conclusions of the research report, partly on the announced state policy of encouraging local industries, partly on the New York State precedent.

At about the same time the issue first arose, another (non-official) research report appeared which indicated that the same beneficial results attributed to the blend might be obtained by the use of so-called air-entrained portland cement, i.e., portland cement prepared by a special process. In 1940, Hoffmann finally decided to specify the blend and air-entrained portland as optional alternates. Hoffmann argued that both state and Federal policy required the freest competitive bidding.

The argument continued for several years. On occasion, Carney appealed to the governor, to the legislature, and to the Federal Bureau of Public Roads. Hoffmann stood his ground. The Federal Bureau, apparently awaiting the results of more conclusive research, sympathized with Hoffmann, but hesitated to give their unqualified support and did not require New York to abandon its mandatory specification of the blend.

Compromises were reached and abandoned. Each man persisted in his policy. Carney obtained temporary advantages by the use of political means, but Hoffmann's prestige was unshaken. Since 1948, all highway contracts in Minnesota have permitted the use of either air-entrained portland or the blend of natural and portland cement, and the market has been lost to Carney; but both protagonists continue to be convinced of the righteousness of their cause.

Preface to a Decision: The Background of the Cement Debate

The cement affair goes back to the late Twenties and early Thirties, when it was discovered that concrete highways in the northern states were showing a tendency to "scale"—i.e., for the top half-inch or so of pavement to crumble and slough off, leaving the surface rough and difficult to maintain. Upon investigation, it was soon learned that there was a direct relationship between scaling and the use of chlorides which had come into vogue as a method of removing snow and ice from the pavements during winter. Further causes of deterioration were found to be the alternate freezing and thawing to which the pavement was subjected, and in some areas (as, for example, the western part of New York State) the use of materials which were of borderline quality.

To combat the problems of scaling, the New York State Highway Department began a series of research projects in 1925 designed to improve the composition of concrete. The most significant of those projects was launched in 1934 and completed in 1937. Its results indicated that scaling could be minimized and the quality of concrete improved by using a blend of two different types of cement: portland cement (five parts) and natural cement (one part). Since the difference between the two types of cement is crucial to an understanding of the case, it is a difference which should be made clear from the start.

PORTLAND v. NATURAL CEMENT

Portland cement is a synthetic product, manufactured by combining certain minerals (limestone and clay, or limestone and blast furnace slag) according to a set formula. These materials are then ground, clinkered, and reground into final powderized form. There are about 150 plants in the United States which produce portland cement; nearly half of them, accounting for the major share of total output, have combined for research and promotional purposes into the Portland Cement Association. During the thirty years of its existence, the Association has proved itself a tightly organized and highly effective pressure group; under its leadership, portland cement has become "big business." The steel industry has also had a hand in this development, inasmuch as it owns a number of the larger portland cement plants and supplies them with slag used as an ingredient in production.

In contrast to portland, natural cement is produced directly from rock which already contains the necessary ingredients in the desired amounts—although it should be emphasized that neither the ingredients nor the proportions are identical with those found in portland cement. Production of natural cement depends upon an accident of nature, being feasible only where the rock is found in sufficient quantity and close enough to the market. All told, there are no more than four or five natural cement plants in the country, each of them independent and distinctly of the small business variety.

Of the two types of cement, natural cement is the older; it was known and widely used in this country well before portland cement was invented or locally manufactured.[1] Still it was unable to hold the market against its new competitor once the latter became available. One reason was that its production was limited to a certain few localities; a second was that it took longer to harden than portland cement and did not develop as high compressive and flexural strength. Particularly for the second reason, natural cement never found a

[1] Portland cement was invented in England in 1824 and first produced in this country in 1871. Natural cement was being produced commercially in this country before 1830.

place in the most extensive of all cement markets, the construction of concrete highways, where quick setting and high strength were at a premium. The producers of natural cement had to be content with sales for masonry work and other purposes—areas of use in which their product enjoyed good repute.

The overwhelming growth of the portland cement industry, particularly after 1916, with the expansion of highway and other construction, and with the founding of the Portland Cement Association, nearly drove the natural cement industry out of existence. Several plants closed, and the others continued to operate only on a bare margin. But portland, too, had its troubles, even with its lion's share of the market and its firm hand over the major part of the cement industry. In confederating its members, the Association had been obliged to set its standards for portland cement at a point within reach of all its member firms. The result was that portland cement varied considerably in quality, depending upon which plant produced it and at what level above the minimum requirements it pegged its own standards; yet portland cement was marketed as a standard product, and any failure in performance reflected on the credit of the entire industry. Another growing source of trouble after the market for highways had been developed seems to have been the increasing emphasis upon compressive and flexural strength. To meet this need, the Association concentrated on building up the strength factor in its cement, and soon encountered the criticism that it was not paying enough attention to concomitant effects on other qualities, durability in particular.

FINDINGS OF THE NEW YORK STATE HIGHWAY DEPARTMENT

This was the situation in the cement industry when "scaling" became a problem. That New York State chose to meet the problem by experimenting with a blend of portland and natural cement was not a matter of accident or sudden inspiration. Rosendale, the oldest and largest natural cement firm in the country, was located in New York State, and its principal promoter, Bert Wait, had for several years been conducting a shrewd and vigorous campaign for a share in the highway construction market. He had been eastern manager for the Portland Cement Association for eleven years; then to the surprise of most who had worked with him he resigned his remunerative post to promote the cause of natural cement—certainly, in view of developments, a risky proposition. Wait's reasons were pointed: he had watched the rise of what he referred to as "the cement trust" and the "parallel deterioration in the quality of its product"; on the other hand, he had discovered that natural cement was a "superior product which had proved its worth over one hundred years of unquestioned performance. It needed only imaginative enterprise and wide-scale promotion to give it the share in the market it deserved." He began immediately to build favor among contracting engineers by publicizing the record of natural cement, and by distributing free truckloads of the material to any contractor willing to experiment with it. He concentrated on showing the greater resistance of natural cement to the action of chlorides and its superior performance under conditions of repeated freezing and thawing. His classic proofs were the base of the Statue of Liberty and the foundation piers of the Brooklyn Bridge, built of natural cement and successfully resistant to brine and freezing temperatures.

One of those [2] who listened sympathetically to Wait's arguments was Ira Paul, Director of the New York State Highway Department's Research Laboratory. As a test, he set up the series of experiments referred to earlier, using a blend of natural and portland cements. To him the results seemed conclusive. They showed that the blend provided most of the strength and speed-of-setting peculiar to portland, and in addition, the superior resistance to chlorides and to freezing which, according to Wait, was the distinctive advantage of natural cement.

On the basis of these tests, New York State changed its specifications for concrete paving

[2] Other states attracted to the use of the blend at this time were Maine, New Hampshire, Vermont and Massachusetts.

so as to require the blended cement in all its highway construction work.

ENTER CARNEY NATURAL CEMENT AND THE MINNESOTA INCIDENT

Before New York State could commit itself finally to the use of the blend on Federal-aid roads, it needed the approval of the Federal Bureau of Public Roads. A formal request was entered; and the Bureau decided to make an investigation of its own to check the findings of the New York State laboratory. The result was the now classic Kellermann-Runner Report, published in 1938. Its conclusions were that "although the crushing and flexural strength of pavement concrete may be slightly reduced by the substitution for portland cement of 14 or 28 per cent Natural Cement G, the resistance of the surface of the pavement to alternate freezing and thawing will be materially increased." The tests also demonstrated an improved resistance to chlorides.[3]

In the course of a few months, the Kellermann-Runner Report came to the attention of the Chief Engineer for the Minnesota Department of Highways, J. T. Ellison. Ellison relayed the information to F. C. Lang, the Department's Materials and Research Engineer, and suggested that the matter be looked into. This was in February 1939. By that time the Report had also reached "Harry" Carney, president of the Carney Natural Cement Company of Mankato, Minnesota, who for some time had been in contact with developments in New York State.

Upon hearing of the Report, Carney immediately got in touch with Ellison to make certain that the Highway Department was informed and interested. His next move was to dispatch a letter to State Highway Commissioner "Mike" Hoffmann, asking for the latter's personal attention to the matter. With this letter began the case of Natural Cement and the Minnesota Highway Program.

THE MINNESOTA SCENE

Carney wrote Hoffmann on May 13, 1939. This was six months after Harold Stassen had swept Elmer Benson and his Farmer-Laborites out of state office, and just one month after he had capped a whirlwind campaign for reform by securing legislative approval of a new blueprint for state administration. Mike Hoffmann was Stassen's choice to clean up the State Highway Department, which under Benson's administration had allegedly been shot through with political appointments and manipulation. "Mike" was by all odds the logical choice for this assignment. He had risen from the ranks and was thoroughly familiar with both the organization and the work. His personal qualities were apparent: he was a rugged and determined individual, blunt, independent, and honest. He came to rule the Department of Highways by command and by respect; neither the governor nor the legislature could move him in any direction he believed wrong without pounding the table or passing a law. Many persons have disagreed with Hoffmann, but few have doubted his integrity.

Harry Carney, during the years of his dispute with the Commissioner, became one of those few; and Hoffmann was left with doubts of his own about Carney. The two men are superficially alike in their directness, but Carney is evidently by temperament much more volatile. Like Hoffmann, Carney in 1939 had just been made top man in his organization. The company he headed was a family firm, founded in 1883; Harry was the third in a line of Carneys to become its president. In his youth, he had been a disappointment to his father; and as late as 1937, he had been read out of the firm. In 1938 he was called back upon the death of his father to learn, with some surprise, that he had inherited the business.

A quick check of the company's books at that time showed Carney that his immediate task would be to expand sales if he and the

[3] American Society for Testing Materials *Proceedings,* Volume 38, Part II (1938), p. 350. Also printed in *Public Roads* (U. S. Bureau of Public Roads), Vol. 19, No. 8 (Oct. 1938). Natural Cement G, though not identified in the report, was Rosendale cement. It is important to note that a second type of natural cement tested did not give the same beneficial results.

hundred men he employed were to stay in business. He was told shortly afterwards by his chief chemist of Rosendale's latest accomplishments in New York, and he decided at once to duplicate that success in Minnesota, if at all possible. The news of the Kellermann-Runner Report, confirming the advantages of using natural cement in highway construction work, came as an apparent godsend, and Carney set about with characteristic ebullience to make the most of it.

He began his campaign convinced that he had a proper claim upon the state. His cement was good, and he could point to research findings published by the Federal government which showed what benefits would follow if his cement were used in highway construction. But even more, he was a Stassen Republican in good standing, and had already served the Governor well—once at election time, and again on the more recent occasion of Stassen's attempt to advertise the state's resources and his own administration. This attempt originated in Stassen's campaign promise to promote Minnesota industries and resources, and took form in the establishment of the Minnesota Resources Commission, designed to serve as an instrument for planning and publicity. One of the first promotional ventures consisted of a series of radio programs featuring new Minnesota enterprises; an early topic was Carney's rock-wool plant, begun as an off-shoot of his cement works and established as the first factory of its kind in the state. By co-operating with the Commission—and incidentally paying all the expenses of the broadcasts—Carney believed he was laying the basis for a continuing and harmonious relationship with state officials. As he put it:

> The new Stassen administration wanted to publicize the fact that there was a new industry in Minnesota and we naturally co-operated. The Resources Commissioner himself attended the grand opening and five radio stations in the State of Minnesota broadcast the ceremonies of the opening of this first rock-wool plant. The Carney Company, of course, had a great deal to gain publicity-wise on this new venture from such a plan. The new administration had a chance to ballyhoo a new industry. We naturally concluded that the State was interested in developing new production within its border, without necessarily discriminating against products from outside the state.

Preface to a Decision: The Issue in 1939-1940

Because of his record of co-operation and the administration's expressed interest in developing state industries, Carney was optimistic when he wrote his letter to the Commissioner. His assurance grew when his letter was answered almost immediately (May 16) by Lang, the Department's research engineer. In his reply Lang assured Carney of the Department's interest, and stated that he would be glad to discuss the matter with Carney's research chemist. However, when the summer months of 1939 passed without further action in his favor, Carney became impatient, concluded he was "getting nowhere fast," and decided to do something about it. Remembering his friends on the Resources Commission, he wrote them and was shortly afterwards invited to attend a late fall meeting of the Chemists Forum (an advisory group to the Resources Commission) where it was arranged that the topic of natural cement would be raised and discussed. Lang was also invited. When the discussion had concluded, Lang agreed to the suggestion of the Commission that he investigate the matter further on his next trip to Washington, scheduled then for December. While in Washington on that occasion, Lang consulted with the Highway Research Board (a member body of the National Research Council), and later conferred with New York State engineers, returning much impressed with the reports he had been given of the effectiveness of the new cement blend.

In January 1940, Lang wrote to Carney formally outlining a proposed research and experimental program by which he planned to test the blend in Minnesota and provide the Department with the evidence needed to make a final decision respecting its use. Following his letter, Lang paid a visit to Carney's chief chemist, the results of which apparently satisfied both parties. He then returned to the capital and, with Hoffmann's approval, proceeded with his program of research.

This much accomplished, Carney seemed to be making headway with his campaign to secure a new market for natural cement in Minnesota. Given a favorable report by Lang —and after the New York and Kellermann-Runner studies there seemed no reason to expect otherwise—the outcome would presumably be the same as in New York: a change in specifications to require use of natural cement, blended in a one-to-five ratio with portland. Time was the only problem; and time, for two important reasons, had Carney extremely worried.

In the first place, the financial fortunes of his company were at dangerously low ebb; a spurt in income was needed and needed badly. Second, and in the long run far more crucial, the Portland Cement Association was at that point publicizing a research discovery which, if true, destroyed the main talking point for the use of natural cement. Well aware of the problems of scaling and deterioration, the Association and several of its member companies had launched a series of their own laboratory studies shortly after hearing of those being conducted in New York; and the preliminary findings from these studies were made available to member companies and their sales representatives in two reports, dated October 31, 1938 and October 31, 1939. The findings showed that the benefits attached to the use of natural cement (resistance to salts, etc.) were not inherent in natural cement, but resulted from the use of certain admixtures, notably beef tallow, fish oil, or grease, to facilitate grinding.[4] Assuming this to be valid, the benefits could be incorporated into portland cement by the use of the same or similar admixtures—in other words, by a simple change in the technique of production. Once this change were made, there would be no further need for using the blended cement, which entailed the inconvenience and added expense of handling two separate types of cement from two separate firms, and of mixing the two cements on the job.

The news of this research, and its arrival at this particular juncture, were to prove deciding factors in the development of the cement episode in Minnesota. Carney's reaction to the news was a matter of no less significance; it did much to explain the cause and nature of the long controversy which was to follow. He refused from the first to accept the findings of the Association as impartial or conclusive, although it was not until later that he was able to document his criticism with countering research data of his own. As far as Carney was concerned, the Association's report was a beginning move in an ominous and all-out campaign by the "cement trust" to regain lost ground, to stamp out competition, and to stifle small business. Anyone who then or later gave full credence to the report or adopted its research point of view was regarded by Carney as having "sold out to the interests," or having been waylaid by the Association's high-powered propaganda. He continued to find support for his feelings in the cousin dissents being pointedly registered by Bert Wait and by Ira Paul in New York.

Thus haunted by the twin specters of bankruptcy and a conspiring opposition, and aware that time was running against him, Carney intensified his campaign, and began to press Hoffmann and other members of the Department for an immediate commitment favorable to his cause. His arguments at this stage were as follows:

(1) the administration was committed to a policy of aiding state industries;

(2) natural cement was a product worthy of such aid, having been endorsed by impartial research experts of both state and

[4] Grinding aids of this sort had been found necessary because of the extreme fineness of the natural cement particles. The grinding aids used are organic substances which are introduced in very minute quantities and have the effect of entraining small amounts of air in the concrete. It is this air which was found by portland chemists, and later by a number of independent researchers, to give the improved durability and resistance to salts, not the use of the natural cement itself.

Federal governments for use in the construction of concrete highways;

(3) precedent for the aid Carney was asking—a commitment by the state to the required use of blended cement in the construction of its paved highways—had already been set by New York State, acting with Federal approval.

Commissioner Hoffmann's Decision

By mid-1940, Carney had built up enough support both independently and through the Resources Commission to make it apparent to Hoffmann that a decision was in order—a decision which would have more immediate consequence than further laboratory research. The latter was now being regarded with suspicion by Carney as a mere delaying tactic, although Carney was willing to grant that the person in charge (F. C. Lang) was on the whole sympathetic to the cause of natural cement, and could be trusted to carry on "impartially."

Hoffmann regarded the situation with some distaste: as he saw it, the problem was the familiar one of a local business interest demanding preferential treatment, and he could see no good reason—legal, technical, or political—for granting Carney's request.

From the legal point of view, Hoffmann thought himself bound by Federal grant-in-aid restrictions not to respect the home-industry argument; these specifically provided that "No requirement shall be contained in any contract entered into by any State providing price differentials for, requiring the use of, or otherwise discriminatory in favor of materials produced within the State."

Further on the legal side, Hoffmann argued that he was bound by

> . . . policy actually . . . established by the state laws of Minnesota expressed by the State Legislature. This public policy specified that public work should be performed pursuant to a call for bids with free and unrestricted competition as a necessary incident to such policy. Within my own experience in the Highway Department I had observed the adverse effect of inserting in contract proposals for public lettings provisions which unduly restricted free and unlimited competitive bidding. In one instance, a former commissioner of highways had inserted in the call for bids a restrictive requirement on the part of the bidders which in effect limited the work to local contractors. Such restrictive provisions were found void by the Minnesota Supreme Court in the case of *Regan* v. *Babcock*, 188 Minn. 192, 247 N.W. 12. My reluctance to insert in any contract a requirement that would restrict or in any way limit free and competitive bidding was then and still is based in large part on the law and public policy of my state as I understand it to be.

Hoffmann's feeling that he was compelled in this instance by both Federal and state law not to grant favored treatment hinged on his growing acceptance of the theory that it was air-entrainment, and not natural cement per se, that improved the resistance and durability of concrete. Consequently, the natural cement–portland blend was to be considered as an alternate, and not an exclusive, method of accomplishing the desired results, and the rule of open competition was therefore to apply. Hoffmann felt he could not grant Carney's claims to the contrary, particularly in view of the growing consensus among cement technicians that there was much to be said for the air-entrainment theory and for the new air-entraining portland cement which had recently been placed on the market. The latter was now being widely experimented with, and the results so far seemed favorable.

Quite apart from the unresolved controversy over air-entrainment, however, there was still another technical question to be settled. As the Kellermann-Runner Report had shown, not every variety of natural cement could be counted on to give full protection against scaling; and in 1940, with Lang's research just begun, Hoffmann had no assurance other than Carney's own assertions that Minnesota natural cement was the equivalent of Rosendale (or Type G) in New York and would give the same beneficial results.

Political considerations at that time entered little into Hoffmann's thinking; but insofar as he took them into account, they were no deterrent to his refusal to grant Carney's request. From past experience with like matters Hoffmann had concluded that

(1) The position of a special interest is usually vulnerable. In this case, Carney's was not the only cement produced within the state. The Universal Atlas Company of Duluth, a portland cement firm, could with equal right press an appeal for special consideration as a home industry.[5]

(2) Pressures generated by one interest group will usually be offset by those of another. To yield to Carney in this instance would mean turning loose a counter political force of even greater magnitude. Knowing this to be true, Hoffmann had little reason to believe that the governor or the legislature would favor Carney's request, or would contradict his own refusal to do so.

Everything pointed, therefore, to a decision which was dear to Hoffmann's thinking as an engineer and well in keeping with the long tradition of highway policy: allow the two new types of cement (air-entrained portland cement, and the natural cement–portland blend) as alternate materials and settle the issue of their comparative merits by the tried and true method of open competition. In the end, relative costs and performance on the job would yield an answer; and if Carney were not in position to meet competition, it was not Hoffmann's responsibility as an administrator, nor within his authorized realm, to make what policy concessions might be necessary to equalize the situation.

To give effect to his decision—and at the same time to expand the research program already underway—Hoffmann authorized the construction of a half-mile strip of pavement, one half the length to be built with air-entrained portland, the other half, with the blend. The project was labeled as experimental, and as such was approved by the Bureau of Public Roads. Actual work on the project was begun and completed during the fall of that year (1940).

Aftermath of a Decision: The Campaign of 1940-1941

To Carney, Hoffmann's decision seemed no decision at all—it was an outright surrender to the portland cement interests. And the more he studied Hoffmann's reasons, the more certain he became of it: none of the reasons seemed to him to hold water. If it were true that state policy ruled out the possibility of restricted contracts, that could be changed at the instigation of a governor who was at all interested in fulfilling his campaign promise to aid state industry. If true that Federal regulations contained the section quoted by Hoffmann, it was also true that the State of New York, with Federal approval, had written into its specifications a requirement that the blend be used exclusively—proof enough that Hoffmann could make similar arrangements in Minnesota if he wanted. Furthermore, Carney soon found a statement of Bureau of Public

5 "Which," Hoffmann added, "it did not do, even though much of the portland cement used in the Minnesota paving program had consequently been brought in from Iowa plants. As a matter of fact, the theory of advancing the interests of home industry could have been six times as well served by applying such a policy to *all* cement as by merely applying it to natural cement. In other words, at best, only one-sixth of the cement used would have been affected by arbitrarily compelling the use of natural cement; whereas, six-sixths of the business would have been directed to home industry had the state considered itself in position to compel the use of Universal Atlas in preference to the products of other plants outside the state's boundaries."

Roads policy which seemed to him an adequate offset to that quoted by Hoffmann:

> Recognizing that in a country as large and diverse in its economic and physical conditions as the United States no fixed standard of road construction can be applied in every section, Public Roads has not attempted to promulgate absolute standards of design and construction applicable to all States. Rather it has endeavored by agreement with the individual State highway departments, to establish for each State standards compatible with the highway needs and available resources of the State.

As to the reputedly equal merits of the new air-entraining portland cement, the only substantiating research Carney could find was that which had been carried out and publicized by the Portland Cement Association. The single exception was a corroborating experiment performed at M.I.T. and reported in a letter to the editors of the *Engineering News Record* in November 1940, well after Hoffmann had designated the new portland product as an acceptable alternative to the blend. But in that same issue of the *Record* had appeared a second letter, from Ira Paul of the New York State Public Works Laboratory, taking vigorous exception to the claims and conclusions of the Portland Cement Association research staffs, and renewing the argument that there were inherent advantages in natural cement which could not be gained by the simple expedient of entraining air into portland.[6]

As a final point, Carney was willing to grant that his was not the only cement plant in the state; but he could see no further parallel between his own situation and that of Universal Atlas in Duluth. The latter was a well established concern which needed no assistance. Carney's firm, from the point of view of its potential development, was an infant industry—precisely the kind he believed the Governor and the Resources Commission were committed to help.

After several months of contemplating these arguments and of returning again and again to the conclusion that he was being systematically squeezed from the market, Carney decided to go into action. Late that year, he wrote Hoffmann and demanded an audience.

THE INCIDENT IN THE GOVERNOR'S OFFICE

Carney left for his interview in January 1941; when he arrived at the capitol, he was told that the Commissioner was in conference with the Governor. Since it was his impression (though it later developed, not the Commissioner's) that he had a scheduled appointment with Hoffmann, Carney went to the Governor's office and waited in the anteroom for the conference to conclude. The contrast in the impressions of the two men as to what followed is as significant as it is interesting. As Carney remembers it:

> Hoffmann came out of the Governor's office (an hour after our scheduled appointment) and kept walking on into the hallway. It didn't look as though he intended to stop, so I stood up and called to him. He answered in an off-hand way; then I asked him whether he and the Governor had come to any decision in the matter.
>
> Hoffmann: "We didn't have a chance to talk about it."
>
> Carney: "But you told me you'd have it settled by today."
>
> Hoffmann: "Carney, if I were to bother with every hare-brained idea, I'd never get my job done."
>
> With that, he walked out of the office. I stayed and exploded. It wasn't long before one of the Governor's secretaries had arrived to calm me down; by then, I had asked for the office phone to call my plant, and was in the middle of telling them to spend our last thousand dollars to build a thirty-foot sign on our building, reading: "Closed, by courtesy of the State Highway Department." When he heard this, the Governor's secretary said: "You can't do this to the Governor." To which I replied, "The Hell I can't," and went home. The next day I was called by my local state senator and told that the Governor would like to see me. I returned to the capi-

[6] Anyone venturesome enough to explore the literature of the technical debate which followed, with a view toward determining the merits of the case on his own, will find a listing and summary of the principal articles and research reports in the Appendix. Suffice it at this point to say that Ira Paul and the research chemists of the natural cement industry are currently almost alone in their point of view.

tol, and went with the senator to the Governor's office where a conference had been arranged. After some discussion, the Governor asked what I'd be satisfied with in the way of more mileage of pavement, to be set aside for further experiments with the blend. We finally agreed on 20 miles.

Hoffmann's version of the incident:

I do not recall having any specific appointment with Mr. Carney . . . although this is not an important matter. . . . I had gone to see the Governor about seven or eight matters which I wished to discuss with him, and had not, to my knowledge, made any agreement to meet Mr. Carney at that time. I had just gotten started discussing with the Governor the various matters which were the object to my visit when his secretary informed him of a scheduled appointment which made it necessary for us to abruptly end our conversation. As I emerged from the Governor's office, Mr. Carney was waiting, came up to me and asked about the matter in which he was interested. I told him that I had not had an opportunity to discuss it with the Governor, which was the truth. I made no reference to "hare-brained" ideas or any similar remark. If Mr. Carney at this point went into any sort of a tantrum, it was not in my presence. It is also news to me if he called the plant and engaged in the reported conversation.

After I had been unable to complete a discussion with the Governor of the various matters I had in mind, I returned directly to my office at the Highway Department. Whether Mr. Carney had an audience with the Governor at that time, I do not know. I have no recollection or knowledge of the Governor or anyone else in authority ever having specifically promised any 20 miles of this type of work. I might add that I am sure that the Governor never at any time discussed this matter or entered into any understanding directly or indirectly about it with the Portland Cement Association or any of its representatives.

Some weeks later, Carney returned to the capital to confirm the understanding he thought he had with the Governor. This time he found Governor Stassen "short." The latter now raised the point, on advice from Hoffmann, that the arrangement was not likely to be approved by the Federal Bureau of Public Roads; that to go through the motions of a request would only result in retarding the Minnesota highway program, inasmuch as construction depended upon the continuous flow of Federal grants.

Carney was not impressed by the argument, and once more gave vent to his feelings. He questioned the validity of the argument, and demanded that Hoffmann "quit talking in hypotheses and get down to submitting an actual request to the Bureau of Public Roads." Thus pressed, Stassen advised Hoffmann to do so, and Hoffmann obliged by instructing his chief engineer to forward a request to the regional office in St. Paul. A copy of the letter, and another of the reply it brought, summarize Departmental and Bureau thinking at that point:

Chief Highway Engineer Ellison to the Federal Public Roads District Engineer Palen, March 1, 1941

Dear Sir:

Re: Cement Blends

As you know, during the last construction season we used a small amount of natural cement blended with Portland cement in the construction of about one-half mile of pavement near Mankato. There is a mill located in Minnesota which manufactures natural cement and we have been very strongly importuned by them to make it a standard for use on all concrete paving and certain other structures.

We are at the present time conducting laboratory experiments in the nature of freezing and thawing in combination with salt and calcium chloride in order to determine whether concrete manufactured with a 15% blend of natural cement has any more resistance to such action than concrete manufactured with Portland cement. One of the principal arguments which has been brought forth by the manufacturers of this product is the claim that New York state uses it on all of their concrete pavements. The claim is also made that several other of the northeastern states use it on substantially all of their concrete pavements.

While we are continuing laboratory tests, we do not feel that they have progressed sufficiently far, nor have the results obtained shown sufficient definite advantage either way, to warrant any final conclusions. What I would like to know of the Bureau is whether or not they would be ready to approve a revision of our Standard Specifications to provide for use of the 15% blend of natural cement. If you would not care to approve it as a specification change, would you be willing to approve it as a special provision on a lesser amount of work, perhaps on one job.

We have not as yet satisfied ourselves as to whether or not sufficient material benefit has been obtained to warrant its inclusion in all of our concrete pavements. There is also a question as to whether or not exactly the same action occurs with the blend of this cement with all of the Portland cements now available on the market. These Portland cements such as we use in Minnesota have quite a wide range in general content, some of them being manufactured from limestone and others from slag.

There is also the question as to whether or not the natural cement as manufactured in New York or the eastern part of the United States has exactly the same characteristics as the natural cement manufactured in Minnesota. There is also the question as to the use of a grinding agent.

We would be very glad to hear from you on this subject, particularly since you may have had from time to time received similar questions from various parts of the United States. This question on account of local pressure is becoming quite acute. For your information we might state that there is only one natural cement mill within reasonable distance of projects in Minnesota and that is located at Mankato.

We would be very glad to hear from you relative to this particular subject.

[s] *J. T. Ellison*

BPR District Engineer Palen to Commissioner Hoffmann, March 13, 1941

Dear Sir:

Relative to Mr. Ellison's letter of March 1, 1941 on the use of natural cement admixtures, it would appear that until some service reports are available from the Nicollet-Mankato job on U. S. 14, together with the findings of your laboratory, that there is no basis upon which a recommendation could be made for a specification including natural cement in all paving projects in this state.

In this connection I would refer you to a copy of a letter dated March 10 from Mr. Kelley, Chief of the Division of Tests, to Mr. Lang of your department wherein the matter of the use of natural cements is discussed. Should the general use of an admixture of natural cement be permitted it appears that there could be no grounds upon which you could refuse to admit the adulteration of cement with any class of material that was claimed to have a beneficial effect on the concrete.

If in your estimation further experimental projects of this nature are necessary in this state I will be glad to consider each one individually.

[s] *A. E. Palen*

When a copy of the Department's request was shown to Carney, it produced another explosive response. It was his own impression that the letter "had been written in such a manner as to practically discourage the approval"; and he was vexed to find that no effort had been made in the letter to secure Federal approval for the *exclusive* use of the natural cement blend in Minnesota. When later told by the Governor that the Bureau of Public Roads would approve only one experimental project of eight and a fraction miles and no more ("gone was the promised twenty"), Carney was left certain that the administration and the Portland cement interests had entered into an unholy alliance against him. Remembering the more happy situation of his fellow natural cement producers in New York, he phoned them immediately to check on the Governor's statement, and to ask why it was that restrictions were being applied to Minnesota but not to New York.

The response he got made him all the more certain he was "getting the run-around." According to his informants, the Bureau of Public Roads had already approved the laying of 189 miles of blended concrete pavement in New York, and had indicated that the experimental stage could be regarded as finished. From now on, New York State was free to specify the blend *exclusively*. Furthermore, Carney was told, any request for Federal approval should have gone directly to Washington, not to the district office in St. Paul—"obviously," the routing of the letter had been a "dodge."

THE ENIGMA OF FEDERAL POLICY

The variant handling of the New York and Minnesota situations came to be a well-worn argument in Carney's favor, and a source of continuing embarrassment to Hoffmann. So long as New York continued to require exclusive use of the blend, and did so with Bureau of Public Roads approval, any attempt to invoke "Federal policy" against a similar practice in Minnesota could be met with the charge of inconsistency.

What *was* Federal policy? It was not until 1947 that a formal answer was given by the Bureau of Public Roads. Until then, Carney persisted in his belief that Federal policy could be inferred from the Bureau's approval of New York State's requirement, and that this policy could be called into effect in Minnesota whenever Hoffmann chose to do so, simply by forwarding to Washington an unequivocal request for the exclusive use of blended cement.

Hoffmann, on the other hand, believed that the crucial factor in determining Federal policy was the time that had elapsed between the emergence of the natural cement issue in New York and the appearance of the same question in Minnesota. New York State's requirement of the blend had been given Federal approval in the mid-Thirties, when there were no alternate materials available; these circumstances were unique, and the Bureau's action should not be understood as constituting a declaration of Federal policy. Now, in 1940, the situation as Hoffmann saw it was quite different. Alternate materials were available (viz., the air-entraining cements developed by Portland), and Federal policy was to be read not from the isolated instance of New York but from the regular rules and regulations governing the use of competitive products.

For its part, the Bureau of Public Roads maintained official silence, reserving judgment until it could design and complete a research program into the comparative merits of blended and air-entraining cements. As the results of this research began gradually to filter in, the Bureau was inclined more and more to support Hoffmann's decision and the policy of open competition upon which it was based; but the Bureau was not fully prepared to formalize and circulate this policy until the very late stages of the Minnesota controversy. Meanwhile, it allowed New York to continue the practice of requiring exclusive use of the blend, seeing no inconsistency in its action and perhaps finding it expedient not to rouse the resistance of New York's Ira Paul, who stubbornly held to his faith in the superior virtues of natural cement.

There was, therefore, no definitive statement of Federal policy available either in 1940 or in the years immediately following which specifically related to blended cement and to the terms of its use. As a result, the debate on this point between Carney and Hoffmann waxed highly personal. Carney pointed to the New York case as Exhibit A in his favor; and certain though he was of his own position, Hoffmann was willing to admit that continued Federal approval of New York's requirements was difficult to square with a Federal policy of open competition. The inconsistency, however, was not for him but for the Bureau of Public Roads to explain.

The Bureau finally did explain in 1950.[7] Until that time, Hoffmann could only speculate as to what the Bureau's reasons might have been for distinguishing the New York and Minnesota situations, and defend as best he could a decision that he steadily maintained was thoroughly in accord with Federal policy.

APPEAL TO THE LEGISLATURE: 1941

Following his call to New York, Carney decided there was only one way to handle the situation: smother Hoffmann with political pressure and snuff out the "completely obstructive and dilatory action of the Minnesota Highway Department." Working through the members of his county's delegation and through party leaders, Carney addressed his appeal to the 1941 state legislature, then in session. Within the short space of two weeks, he managed to have passed in both houses a resolution memorializing the State Highway Commissioner to use Minnesota natural cement. According to Carney, "the inconsistencies of the Highway Department's general dilatory and obstructive policy regarding the use of Natural Cement, even experimentally, was resented by everyone outside the Highway Department connected with the State

[7] Federal Commissioner Thomas MacDonald's letter presenting this explanation is quoted in the Appendix. That Hoffmann throughout the case was unaware of the Bureau's reasons is borne out by several of his own statements, also quoted in the Appendix.

Government who knew anything about the affair." The wording of the resolution, adopted on March 27, 1941, bears eloquent testimony to Carney's success as a lobbyist on that occasion:

A RESOLUTION MEMORIALIZING THE COMMISSIONER OF HIGHWAYS TO EXPERIMENT WITH THE USE OF MINNESOTA NATURAL CEMENT IN THE LAYING OF TRUNK HIGHWAY PAVING

WHEREAS, There are known to exist in the State of Minnesota numerous and extensive deposits of limestone rock suitable for the manufacture of natural cement;

AND WHEREAS, Some of said deposits were commercially developed more than fifty years ago and that natural cement is now being commercially produced from at least one of said deposits;

AND WHEREAS, As result of experiments, it has been demonstrated that a mixture of natural cement such as that produced in Minnesota at a ratio of 15% to 25% of natural cement to 75% to 86% of portland cement produces a more frost resistant, more plastic, more resilient and more durable highway paving slab than those constructed of portland cement alone;

AND WHEREAS, The United States Bureau of Roads, through its Materials Engineers, have heretofore made thorough study of and experiments with said blended cements for highway construction and as a result thereof have approved their use for Federal aid road projects and several states are now using said blended concrete exclusively for all highway construction;

AND WHEREAS, At all times since approval of said blended cements by said United States Bureau of Roads as aforesaid, the Federal Bureau of Roads on request of any state highway department has approved of the use of said blended materials in Federal Aid highway construction;

AND WHEREAS, The Minnesota Highway Department late in the season of 1940 did specify a blend of portland cement and Minnesota Natural Cement in the ratio of 85% portland to 15% natural cement in a strip of paving approximately one-half mile in length, which specification was approved by the United States Bureau of Roads and which said paving was laid on or about the month of October, 1940, in Nicollet County, Minnesota;

AND WHEREAS, Said test one-half mile of paving laid with blended cements has in all respects demonstrated the value of said materials as compared to straight portland cement construction;

AND WHEREAS, The state administrator, through its construction department has heretofore specified and is now using a blend of natural cement such as that produced in Minnesota as a blend with portland cement in all general state construction projects and that the materials so blended have been heretofore laid and are now in satisfactory use in the State of Minnesota;

AND WHEREAS, The State of Minnesota is officially engaged and has for several years last past been engaged, through its Resources Commission, in efforts to stimulate the use of Minnesota natural resources and in that connection is maintaining with taxpayers' money said Minnesota Resources Commission;

NOW, THEREFORE, BE IT RESOLVED . . .

1. That it is the settled policy of this state and of this body that every encouragement should be given not only by the citizens of the state but by its official bodies and government to the use of Minnesota products for public as well as for private use;
2. That it appears to the [legislature] that natural cement suitable for state highway construction is now being produced in Minnesota, using a Minnesota natural resource therefor and that by the use of this product by the State Highway Department, Minnesota payrolls and tax rolls would be increased, that the establishment of additional natural cement plants in Minnesota would be encouraged and the general welfare policy of this state be thereby advanced;
3. That the Commissioner of Highways is hereby authorized and instructed to make immediate, substantial and comprehensive experimentation in the use of blended concrete in the laying of permanent trunk highway paving in the State of Minnesota, using therein Minnesota natural cement as a blend or in combination with portland cements.
4. The Secretary of the Senate is hereby instructed to forthwith forward a copy of this resolution to the Commissioner of Highways.

APPEAL TO WASHINGTON: 1941

Now that state policy was clearly in his favor, Carney set as his next task the securing of Federal approval for whatever construction contracts might come his way. Again he chose the medium of political pressure. This time, he went to a local mogul in the Democratic Party, thinking it advisable to find partisan entree to the Washington office of the Bureau of Public Roads. His contact man, a one-time candidate for state governor and a friend of Jim Farley, agreed to do the job for a modest retainer, but neglected to inform Carney that the Bureau could have been approached without the partisan niceties.

Be that as it may, when Carney arrived in Washington, he found an appointment waiting for him with Mr. F. H. Jackson, Principal Engineer of Tests for the Bureau of Public Roads. Carney was pleased with the latter's response; according to Carney, Jackson stated that

—he had received no request from the Minnesota Highway Department for approval of the use of natural cement, nor had the request earlier submitted to the St. Paul district office been referred to Washington;

—an unusual request of this sort should have been forwarded or sent directly to the Washington Office; [8]

—the Bureau could not, obviously, give approval to Carney acting personally; but

—if the Minnesota Highway Department were to ask for approval of the use of blended concrete in "reasonable" amounts for experimental purposes, the Bureau would not feel justified in refusing such a request, in view of what it regarded as successful experience with the blend in New York, Maine, Vermont and several other states.

When it came to agreeing on what might be "reasonable," Carney had better luck than he had anticipated; Jackson quickly scaled him down from 100 to 30 miles of experimental construction, which was more than Carney had hoped for when he came.

Carney's interview with Jackson had taken place on Friday, April 18, 1941. On Monday, Hoffmann and Lang appeared at the Federal Bureau to discuss the same problem. Carney claims that it was the news of his own visit reaching St. Paul that prompted Hoffmann's trip to Washington, and he tells an intriguing story to prove his point.[9] Hoffmann categorically denies any inference that his visit was dictated by political considerations; as he describes it, "I was in Washington apparently at the same time as Mr. Carney, and although the common objective of both our visits was apparently to clear up the situation with regard to Federal approval of the natural blend projects, no act of mine, nor as far as I know of the Governor's office, was contingent in

[8] Carney's memory on this point squares with his feeling that Hoffmann had influenced the district BPR office to give him a ruling favorable to his (Hoffmann's) point of view. But it does not square with Jackson's own recollection of the interview, or with standard procedure of BPR field communications. Both Jackson and MacDonald stress the fact that requests of this sort are regularly handled by the district offices; what Jackson probably did say in his interview with Carney "was that such an unusual request would probably be referred by the St. Paul office to Washington for final decision." Hoffmann is equally insistent on this point: "Standard procedure on all such matters was to go through the regional office. Normally, only on an appeal from the decision of the regional office would a request for approval go directly to the Washington office."

[9] Carney's story: "Elated with the results of my interview with Jackson, I went back to my suite in the Mayflower Hotel to find my companion closeted with a group of friends, later identified as members of the Minnesota State Democratic Committee. All of them snapped to when I described my afternoon talk with Jackson; it seems they were looking for ammunition to use against the Republican Administration in Minnesota, and this was just the sort of thing they wanted. One of them reached for the phone and called Associated Press; when I asked what for, he said 'You're about to send the fastest message to Governor Stassen you've ever sent. This will be picked off the wires in Minnesota, relayed to Stassen, and there'll be hell to pay in the administrative family.' Sure enough, two hours later I got a phone call from my plant engineer asking what I'd been up to in Washington. The Governor's secretary had called wanting to know the story. None of this ever came out in the Minnesota papers. What did come out was a statement from the Governor's office to the effect that Commissioner Hoffmann and his staff were off to Washington to get the consent of the Bureau of Public Roads to use blended cement; if successful, they would be carrying one step farther the Governor's program of encouraging home industries."

any way upon, or influenced by, political maneuvering."

The immediate results of the two Washington conferences were summarized in a letter of instructions addressed to the St. Paul district office, and dated April 22, 1941:

Dear Mr. Palen:

Mr. Carney, of the Carney Cement Company, Mankato, Minnesota, was in the office last Friday and talked with Mr. Jackson regarding the use of natural cement in concrete pavement construction for the purpose of insuring the resistance of the concrete to the action of salt used for ice removal.

Mr. Carney was advised that, in accordance with our usual practice regarding the experimental use of nonstandard material, the Bureau of Public Roads would approve a limited number of projects containing the blend, if so requested by the State, and provided each project is set up in such a manner as to permit a true comparison of the experimental concrete with the present all-portland standard construction. This would require that on each project a reasonably comparable mileage of both types be provided and that provision be made for applying salt for ice removal in a comparable manner to selected sections of each type, so that definite information would be obtained as soon as possible regarding their comparative resistance.

Yesterday we conferred with Messrs. Hoffmann and Lang regarding the matter. It was the consensus of opinion that further experimentation with blended cement in Minnesota would be desirable and to this end it was agreed that—

(1) We would approve, if desired, a sufficient number of projects to provide for the experimental use of from 25 to 30 miles of blended concrete, with sufficient straight portland cement concrete on each project to form a basis of comparison.

(2) We would, if desired, also approve the construction of short sections about 2 miles in length on any or all of these projects using portland cement treated with Vinsol Resin as well as blended with natural cement. It was understood that on any given project cement from the same mill would be used on all three sections (that is, the straight portland, the blended portland and the Vinsol resin portland).

(3) The quality of natural cement to be used in the blend would be controlled by reference to ASTM's specifications for natural cement, supplemented by a requirement that the particular cement used must meet the approval of the Department. It was understood that, before approving a given natural cement, the State would require a showing to the effect that when blended with portland cement an improvement in quality would be obtained.

(4) Where treated portland cements are used, the strength of the concrete would be controlled through a provision requiring that, under standard testing conditions, the crushing strength of the treated cement concrete be at least 85% of the crushing strength of concrete containing the same aggregates and the untreated cement from the same mill.

The meeting discussed also the use of blended cements in bridge construction. Mr. Hoffmann was of the opinion that the increased workability which would result from the use of this type of cement as well as the possible increase in resistance to frost action would warrant an extensive trial of blended cement in bridge construction in Minnesota. I believe that we should give sympathetic consideration to the request from the State for the use of blended cement concrete in this type of work.

Very truly yours,
Division of Design
by [s] *R. E. Toms,* Chief

As a follow-up to these instructions, representatives of the State Department and the district office of the Bureau of Public Roads met in St. Paul on May 9 to map out construction plans for the current year. Faithful to the agreement specified in the letter just quoted, 30 miles of pavement were set aside for experimental use of the blend. Of the remaining 65 miles scheduled for construction that year, 7 were to be built with air-entrained portland, and 58 with straight portland. Both the 30 miles of blended construction, and the 7 of air-entrained portland were to be considered experimental.

Following the conference, Carney was invited to the capital and told by Lang that his thirty miles had been reserved and approved —Lang adding in a friendly way something to the effect that "Well, you got what you wanted, didn't you?" Carney took the remark as a tribute to his strategy and political exploits, and left the interview satisfied that he had out-maneuvered Hoffmann, as well as the Portland Cement lobby, and had won a critical victory in the campaign for natural cement.

Hoffmann, on the other hand, may have been nettled; but he had been too long exposed to similar pressure campaigns and was too much involved with the regular work of the Department to regard the incident as more than another of his many administrative headaches. He did not feel, as Carney did, that he or anyone else had just been decisively beaten in a campaign which turned on a personal cause and had seen "the interests" lined up calculatingly on either side. He maintained that his position "was never influenced by either like or dislike for any person whomsoever, including Mr. Carney, or for any organization of industrial interests." The one cause he admitted to was embodied in the policy of open competitive bidding, and in his own decision to maintain that policy in the instant case. He had tried to buck what he regarded in this instance as a threat to that policy. While he had fared rather badly at the hands of the legislature and had got slightly tangled in the web of Federal directives, he had still managed to keep both policy and decision intact. Carney's success with political pressure had maneuvered the Department into a more extensive experimental program than the Commissioner wanted or at the time felt justified; still and all, the blend was to be used only on an experimental basis, and the Department had not yet been committed to its exclusive use.

Aftermath of a Decision: The War Years

World War II brought highway construction work to a halt, and there followed a four-year lull in the cement controversy. During that time, Hoffmann's attention was for the most part absorbed by problems arising out of the war, though he did take time with his staff to note and discuss the series of research reports on cement which made their appearance during the war years. Of most immediate significance was the report submitted by the Department's research engineer, Mr. Lang, covering the study he had undertaken in 1940. His results were made available in a confidential memorandum known as Investigation #130, and filed with the Commissioner in 1943. In substance, they confirmed the earlier conclusions of the Kellermann-Runner Report of 1938, and established the fact that Carney Natural Cement was of the same quality, and produced the same results, as did New York's Type G, or Rosendale.[10] Lang's research further showed that "treated" (air-entrained) portland cement gave similar results to those afforded by the blend, although it was noted that the blend with its average of 2% entrained air showed slightly more strength than treated portland, with 5%; and that the blend was also somewhat more resistant to freezing and thawing. In neither case were the differences in performance considered significant enough to alter the Departmental view that the two products—blended cement and air-entrained portland cement—should be treated as alternate materials.

Meanwhile, the Department was also kept up to date on studies being conducted by the Highways Bureau and Research Laboratory of the Portland Cement Association, particularly on the field investigations which these two units were carrying on in co-operation with a number of state highway departments. The general conclusions emerging from these studies supported the growing impression that the feats of the natural cement blend could be duplicated by using certain admixtures with straight portland. These conclusions were summarized in a policy statement issued by the Association on March 26, 1942:

> Concrete having excellent durability as measured by its resistance to freezing and thawing and to the application of common salt or calcium chloride can be produced with

[10] This finding is in contrast with the results of subsequent Federal research which indicated that Carney natural cement is more nearly like Akron (the second, and less resistant cement studied by Kellermann and Runner in 1938) than Rosendale.

(a) portland cement ground with proper quantities of certain fatty or resinous materials;
(b) blends of portland and natural cements, when they contain the proper amounts of certain fatty or resinous materials or with petroleum oil which carries paraffin,
(c) the addition of certain air-entraining materials to the concrete batch at the time of mixing.

The increased durability secured by all of the above described methods seems to be related to the air entrained in the concrete during mixing, the beneficial results from the various methods being equivalent provided optimum air voids are attained without undue sacrifice of concrete strength.

A third analysis to come to Hoffmann's attention during the war was that published by Jackson of the Bureau of Public Roads in the June 1944 issue of the *American Concrete Institute Journal*. In his article, Jackson gave support to the view that increased resistance to chlorides and freezing was attributable to air-entrainment—which could be taken to mean that this was the view to which the Bureau of Public Roads was also committed and could be expected to use as the basis for future policy decisions.

The fourth in the war-time research series to find its way into the files of the Department was a report by C. E. Lovewell, Director of Research and Chief Engineer of the Carney Company. In his report, published in the *Engineering News Record* of July 26, 1945, Lovewell conceded that "it is now generally recognized that concrete with 3-6% entrained air is highly resistant"; but he insisted that "not all of the advantages of the blend can be secured [by air-entrainment] . . . because some of them are inherent in natural cement itself."

Inherently, natural cement is extremely plastic and workable. In its manufacture, natural cement is not fused or clinkered as is the case with portland cement. For this reason, its particle structure is less glassy and the ground product is considerably finer than that of portland cement.

This combination of characteristics of natural cement particles results in higher water-retaining capacity that contributes to the reduction in bleeding or water-gain of the blend. Natural cement also contributes elasticity or toughness to concrete as evidenced by increased fatigue resistance and plastic flow properties of hardened blend concrete. The chemical compounds of natural cement generate less heat upon hydration than those of portland cement. This is important in mass concrete. . . .

When natural cement is used as a blend, more accurate control of air content in concrete is secured than when air-entraining portland cement is used. . . .[11]

Lovewell's research efforts were an indication of the fact that the cement question still simmered in Carney's mind, despite the war. After his campaign of 1941, Carney had "stayed away" from Hoffmann, believing it wise to let the dust settle and avoid chancing any further antagonism. Actually, he had little reason to decide otherwise, since the war had cut highway construction to a bare minimum and had at the same time created so much of a demand for structural concrete for other purposes that Carney was busy enough at home.

Carney during the first years of the war remained optimistic about the future of natural cement. During 1942 and 1943, blended cement had been used to build 28.7 miles of access road to newly constructed war plants; inasmuch as these were built according to state specifications, Federally approved, Carney inferred that all was well. (For their part, neither State nor Federal officials attached any significance to this incident. During the war, they were taking any approved type cement available.) His optimism grew with the news of Lang's research findings in 1943, giving support to the claims of natural cement.

But by 1945, the progress made by the Portland Cement Association in gaining acceptance of its new product and the theory underlying it had Carney very much worried. His tension

[11] Lovewell's findings summarize very well the position taken in the research debate by the natural cement interests. They run counter, however, to the results of "a considerably expanded laboratory investigation" begun by the Bureau of Public Roads in January, 1942, and completed by the spring of 1947:

"Confirming the results of earlier studies, this investigation . . . shows that such [blended] concretes, because they entrain air, have increased resistance to freezing and thawing. . . . The investigation found no properties in the natural cements, other than their air-entraining ability, that influenced the increased resistance to freezing and thawing."

increased as the war ended and he heard nothing from the Department. Nor did it help to know that most of those he had known and dealt with earlier in the campaign were no longer about. Governor Stassen had been succeeded by Governor Thye; and the list of deceased was enough to make anyone connected with the case uncomfortable. The list included:

Chief Engineer Ellison of the Department of Highways;

F. C. Lang, the Department's research engineer;

A. E. Palen, BPR District Engineer;

R. E. Toms, Chief of the Division of Design, BPR;

Mr. Oglesby, Chief Chemist for the Carney Company.

By the time VJ Day arrived, Carney could wait no longer. He decided to make another trip to the state capital and determine the lay of the land.

Aftermath of a Decision: The Renewal of the Natural Cement Campaign

As a scouting party, Carney took with him his chief engineer, his director of research, and several construction engineers sympathetic to his cause. His first stop was the Governor's office: Thye, like Stassen, had adopted the home industries plank in his campaign platform, and Carney deemed it altogether fitting that the new governor be called upon to redeem his pledge.

The conference began and ended courteously. Hoffmann was called in to speak for the Highway Department, and both he and Thye gave Carney full opportunity to present his case. But Hoffmann, in responding, indicated that he had not changed his mind; if anything, he was more positive than before in his decision not to give preference to the blend. His reasons were basically the same, interlarded now with corroborating evidence added by research and experimentation during the war.

Carney's case was also his familiar one, buttressed this time by the more detailed claims advanced by Lovewell in his recent research report. There was also, Carney argued, a new point to consider; he was not asking now, as he had in 1940, that a specification of Carney Natural Cement—or for that matter for any Minnesota cement—be written into the Highway Department's contracts. What he was asking was merely that blended cement be required, leaving the question of which producer (portland as well as natural) open for settlement by free competitive bidding.

Hoffmann rejected the reasoning as spurious: it still meant discriminating against alternate materials (viz., the air-entrained portlands) and pledged the state to the use of a particular material which was likely to prove more costly and troublesome to handle.[12] Besides, Carney's was the only natural cement firm in the general area, and being the only one to compete, it would in effect be given preferred standing if the blend were required.

To this last point Carney replied that there were other natural cement companies in the country which would be sure to compete;[13]

[12] Carney has never accepted the argument of added cost and inconvenience, even when later Hoffmann was able to document the charge with field reports. Carney points to the fact that the blend, for the same amounts of cement, gives a 2% greater yield; and that its plasticity makes it easier to handle. He also contends that the trouble of working with two cement ingredients is more than offset by the dangers of using the highly critical admixtures which produce air-entrainment in portland.

[13] This statement had a boomerang effect upon Carney. Hoffmann wanted to know what other natural cement company would compete in Minnesota; Carney, to hold up his end of the argument, later contacted a Louisville firm and asked them to submit bids on a convincing number of Minnesota projects. But the Louisville firm, it turned out, was in a position to underbid Carney; and Carney was therefore forced to sell below cost in order to win the contracts.

even if not, Carney's preferred position would not last long. In time, as events had proved in the rock-wool business, other natural cement plants would open up in Minnesota when assured of a market. All of which, Carney was quick to point out, would fit in very nicely indeed with the Governor's policy of developing Minnesota's resources and industries.

After this exchange, the discussion turned again to the question of Federal approval. Hoffmann was well aware of the fact that as yet there had been no formal directive from Washington on the subject; but he was convinced from earlier dealings with the Bureau of Public Roads and again after reading Jackson's recent article that the policy, when formalized, would require him to decide as he had.

His choice of such apparently tenuous grounds, even for but part of his defense, served only to renew Carney's suspicions that Hoffmann was insincere and was actually promoting the cause of portland cement. Regardless of what the Commissioner said about Bureau of Public Roads policy, it was still a fact that New York was continuing to use the blend exclusively, and that the Bureau of Public Roads had not yet done anything to stop it.

The conference broke up shortly afterwards. Carney left with the understanding that the blend would be specified on four construction projects under the next year's (1946) highway program. Hoffmann had no such understanding; what he apparently had said was something to the effect: "We'll have four jobs for you," intending only to announce that there would be those four projects, at least, on which Carney could expect bids for the use of natural cement to be considered, and if low enough, approved. Carney, however, took the remark as an outright guarantee, and watched developments over the next months with that "promise" in mind. The misunderstanding was to prove critical.

THE GATHERING OF THE STORM

While Hoffmann was never to regret or question his original decision, he did feel there was some justice in Carney's contention that Federal policy was being inconsistently applied and was in that sense discriminatory. He therefore took the next opportunity that offered itself to put the question directly to Bureau of Public Roads officials:

> . . . it was in Oklahoma City at the national convention of the American Association of State Highway Officials in January 1946 that I had a meeting with Mr. Hilts, assistant commissioner of the Bureau of Public Roads and Mr. Taylor, who had succeeded Palen as district engineer, going over in detail the issues involved in this situation. I was at that time advised again that the BPR was in the process of issuing an order which would bar specifying favoritism for either type of cement. I was also advised at that time that this order would be out within approximately 60 days.

On the basis of this advice, Hoffmann returned to Minnesota and proceeded to draw up specifications for the coming year's construction program. These specifications "put the alternate products in open competition. [Nevertheless they] . . . did not in any way shut out natural cement blends but simply forced this product to compete with alternate products." Of the six paving contracts awarded that spring (1946), all on an open competitive basis, two required use of the blend, while the remaining four called for air-entrained portland. According to Hoffmann:

> It was simply a case of no successful bidder having bid a price (on the four projects not using the blend) for the use of the blend which was low enough to receive an award. In fact, it was in connection with these projects that we found definitely that a requirement for the use of natural cement entailed increasing our pavement costs from $200 to $800 per mile.

Carney's impression of these events was understandably quite different. Seeing that natural cement was to be used on only half the number of contracts he remembered as being "promised" to him, and assuming that air-entrained portland had arbitrarily been substituted on the rest, he concluded that Hoffmann had gone back on his word and was once more "playing ball" with the portland cement interests. When he asked for a reason, he was told that the Department was hewing to Federal policy, that the Bureau of

Public Roads was holding up projects which did not place the different cements on an equal footing. Carney's immediate reaction was that he was "being given the old routine." It was time again, he decided, for some old-fashioned political pressure.

This time, he aimed his barbs at the Bureau of Public Roads in Washington, relying on his Congressman, Joseph O'Hara, to direct his fire. The attack was concentrated on the failure of the Bureau to iron out the alleged inconsistency in its handling of the New York and Minnesota situations.

Not long after the attack got under way, Carney's chief engineer, C. E. Lovewell, found it necessary to visit Washington on another matter. Carney commissioned him to spend additional time at the capital, clearing up if he could the enigma of Federal policy. He then inquired of Hoffmann whether the latter would be willing to join Lovewell in a conference with Bureau officials. Hoffmann agreed, and the two men made the trip together.

In the discussions which followed, it soon became evident that both Hoffmann and Carney had been correct in their contentions regarding Federal policy. The Bureau of Public Roads had begun to tighten up its review of state highway contracts preliminary to establishing a formal policy of open competition between air-entrained portland and the natural cement blend; as yet, however, this restriction had not been applied to New York. The Bureau of Public Roads seems to have agreed on this occasion that its action with respect to the New York and Minnesota situations had been inconsistent,[14] and assured its visitors that this inconsistency would be ironed out in the near future. Hoffmann and Lovewell left with the further assurance that a formal policy statement to this effect would be issued promptly and circulated among all highway commissioners.

Months passed without further word from the Bureau as to its promised directive, and without any attempt made to bring New York State highway specifications into line.[15] Unruffled by the lapse, Hoffmann continued his own practice of designating the blend as an optional rather than as a required material, believing it in the public interest to do so, and expecting BPR at any moment to confirm his decision.

Carney judged differently. To him, the absence of any directive from BPR left Hoffmann free to specify the blend; that he did

[14] Commissioner Hoffmann makes a comment at this point which seems to corroborate the view that all present at the conference felt there was an inconsistency in BPR's actions to date:

"I am sure the Public Roads administrator realized that the New York policy was inconsistent with the policy which the BPR had assured us it was going to proclaim, but it was my understanding that this inconsistency would be corrected when the new circular was issued." (Letter of February 8, 1950.)

[15] No official reason was offered then or later for the delay. While it may partly have been due, as those critical of BPR believe it was, to the fact that BPR was chary of arousing political antagonism in New York, the subsequent appearance of two further research studies suggests a more likely explanation—in short, that BPR officials were withholding the directive pending completion of what they then knew to be confirming research.

The first report appeared in May 1946, published by the Highway Research Board of the National Research Council. The report assumed as given that it was the entrainment of air, not any inherent qualities of natural cement, that produced greater resistance to salts and freezing. It then chewed deeper into the arguments for exclusive use of the blend by ascribing other supposedly inherent virtues of natural cement (see the earlier summary of Lovewell's findings) to the simple fact of air-entrainment. The *coup de grâce* to Carney's hopes for preferred treatment came with the report's acceptance of the idea that blended cement and air-entrained portland were substantially equivalent materials and should be specified as such.

The group within the Highway Research Board immediately responsible for the foregoing report was known as the Special Committee on Air-Entraining Concrete. Chairman of the Committee was F. H. Jackson of BPR; others who took part were F. C. Lang of the Minnesota Highway Department, and W. F. Kellermann, co-author of the original BPR research study on the subject of blended cement.

The Committee's report was less a report on research than a guide to the use of available air-entraining materials; for its supporting data, it presumably relied upon the extensive investigations begun by BPR in 1942 and nearly ready for announcement in 1946. Formal presentation of results was not made until June 1947, in a paper read by BPR Engineers Timms, Grieb and Werner at the fiftieth annual meeting of the American Society for Testing Materials. Preliminary findings, however, were in Jackson's hands much earlier, and were responsible for his growing support of a policy of open competition.

not, but instead placed it in competition with air-entrained portland, gave further reason to believe that Hoffmann had aligned himself with the Portland Cement industry. Carney resolved that if this was to be a war of interests, he would open it with a grand offensive.

PRESSURES VIA GREYHOUND

Carney was never the sort to make small plans. On this occasion, he chartered a Greyhound bus and filled its 40-odd seats with every person of local influence he could find who was in any way sympathetic to his cause or obligated to support him. The final list of passengers was impressive. It included the complete legislative delegations from Carney's home and neighboring counties; the editors of the two local newspapers; the mayors of both his home and neighboring cities; the engineers of both cities; the Chamber of Commerce secretaries of both cities; the full roster of commissioners from two counties; the president of the state A F of L; Carney; his engineers; and a scattering of local businessmen. Off they rolled to the state capital, and upon arrival marched in solid phalanx to the Governor's office. The time was June 1946, ten days before the primary election in which it would be determined whether Governor Thye was to be the Republican nominee for the U. S. Senate.

Thye's first move was to call in Commissioner Hoffmann. What followed was not a peaceful nor altogether pretty scene. In presenting his case, Carney waxed profanely eloquent and lost sight of certain other of the social amenities. He and Hoffmann were soon engaged in a heated exchange. Hoffmann accused Carney of choosing the time deliberately, of having no concern for what his demands would cost the state, of using political tactics to force the Governor into a regrettable decision. Carney denied it, said it was "now or never," and added that he didn't think the Highway Commissioner was the one who should make the decision in the matter. Governor Thye broke in to caution Carney against impugning Hoffmann's character and motives; Carney replied that Hoffmann had no basis for persisting in his claim that his hands were tied by Bureau of Public Roads policy.

Members of the delegation finally intervened with a question that went to the point of the meeting: Was it true as Carney claimed that natural cement blend was being used exclusively in the State of New York, and if so, would Governor Thye be willing to do for Carney what New York officials had done for Rosendale? Thye indicated that he would. The next question became: Had New York State acted with Federal knowledge and approval, and was it continuing to do so? At that point, Hoffmann suggested that they address the question personally to Commissioner Thomas MacDonald of the Bureau of Public Roads who was due in St. Paul that same night to address members of a highway conference; the matter could be settled once and for all. All present agreed; and it was decided that the Governor, Hoffmann, and a committee from Carney's delegation would meet with MacDonald that evening at the hotel where he was to be registered.

Carney agreed with a mental reservation. He was confident that the Federal Commissioner would confirm his statement of the facts concerning the New York situation, but he was not certain of MacDonald's response to the question that would follow, particularly if Hoffmann were to reach him first with his side of the story. So Carney contacted the bellhops he knew from past occasions at the named hotel, and persuaded them to give him notice the moment MacDonald put in his appearance. Notice came at about 6 P.M.—the Bureau Commissioner had arrived, but the hotel had no accommodations for him, having been blessed with an extra day's stay of an entire convention. Notice soon followed from Hoffmann confirming the miscue; and it was then arranged that the group would form and go together to a second hotel where accommodations had been obtained. Whether or not the incident had any effect on the outcome of the meeting, it at least gave Carney and other members of his delegation visual assurance that there had been no chance for collusion between the two Commissioners.

AGREEMENT ON THE MEZZANINE FLOOR

After introductions all around, the group adjourned to the mezzanine floor. For a few tense moments after they were seated, Carney found himself in competition with the labor member of his delegation. Bob Olson, President of the Minnesota A F of L, had a complaint of his own to make, and he seized upon this chance to deliver himself of his grievance. He didn't like certain features of governmental policy respecting labor, and minced no words saying so. MacDonald was displeased, and wanted to know whether Olson was referring to Federal policy. Olson replied sharply that he was, and was about to continue his tirade when Carney, for once the moderator, intervened. The discussion was shortly brought around to the subject of cement.

With MacDonald present, Carney and Hoffmann found it easier to state their positions without show of temper—MacDonald later recalled that he sensed none of the sharp personal feeling which he had been told marked the earlier meetings of the two men. Carney went directly to his question: If New York State could require use of the blend, was there any reason to prevent Minnesota from doing so? Hoffmann wanted only to know when he could expect formal confirmation of what he had been given to believe was Federal policy.

MacDonald readily supported Hoffmann's impression that it was the sense of Federal policy not to give preferential treatment either to the blend or air-entrained portland, inasmuch as research had failed to show a significant difference in performance between them. Contracts for the construction of concrete pavements should be awarded to the lowest bidder, regardless of which type of cement he proposed to use.

At the same time, MacDonald agreed with Carney that the policy he had just outlined had not been formally issued or announced, nor had it yet been applied to the State of New York. When Carney pressed the point, asking when the policy would be formalized and uniformly applied, MacDonald replied only that it would be "soon."

At this juncture, Governor Thye broke in to observe that there had obviously been a misunderstanding somewhere along the line. With that bit of understatement, he began impromptu fashion to devise a way out of what appeared to him to be a bad situation. Accepting the lapse as creating a political obligation, the Governor advanced a rather straightforward solution: give Carney the mileage he might otherwise have secured if the State Highway Department had not regarded Bureau of Public Roads "policy" as binding.

Commissioner MacDonald (who seems not to have made any particular effort on this occasion to explain any difference that may have existed between the New York and Minnesota situations) agreed with the Governor that Carney had in a sense been discriminated against; and he promised Bureau of Public Roads approval of enough additional mileage (later set at 62) of blended cement construction to match the amount already built that year with portland cement. Both Hoffmann and Carney seemed satisfied with the bargain, and both gave evidence of thinking that the entire situation would clear up. Carney's parting remark to Hoffmann was, "We're not asking special favors in spite of what you think. When New York is brought under this policy, we'll get along with the idea of open competition."

Hoffmann, convinced that the slate had now been wiped clean, felt encouraged by Carney's apparent willingness to face competition, and expected that there would be no further trouble once Bureau policy was formally announced and uniformly applied.

THE STRUGGLE RESUMED

Since most of the construction work programed for 1946 had already been let by the time the June bargain had been struck, Hoffmann was obliged to defer action on the promised 62 miles until the following year's contracts were ready to be let. Again the passage of time was to work against Carney.

Summer wore on into fall, and there was still no formal word from the Bureau of Public Roads as to its policy. MacDonald's promised directive did not arrive, and reports from the East indicated that New York was still specifying the blend without being challenged by the Federal bureau.

Meanwhile, another situation was in the making which soon became a *cause célèbre* and broke up this happy, if somewhat delicate, truce resulting from the June bargain. About the time of the critical fall (1946) election, an irate newspaper editor in the southwestern part of the state launched a stinging attack on the state administration, directed in particular at the Highway Department. The editor in question was the son of a recently deceased state legislator who had himself been a critic of the Department and one of those responsible for passage of the 1940 resolution prodding Hoffmann into the use of natural cement. To give substance to what was by now a family allegation, the son chose a 14-mile stretch of new pavement in his area and belabored it as a signal example of poor construction.

Ironically, the 14-mile stretch was one of those laid with the blended cement; and there was apparently something to the charge that it was not the smooth and free-riding pavement it should have been.[16]

Hoffmann had heard of this problem before it became a political issue, and had already begun an investigation to determine the cause. The splurge of publicity encouraged him to press the investigation yet further; and he then found "there was a little more to the factors of uncertainty" than had first appeared:

> Two jobs on which the blend had been specified in 1946 construction had proved so rough that they were bringing severe criticism from the press and others, and not without some justification. The Department was searching into the problem to try to determine the cause of the roughness, and whether or not it could be attributable to some unanticipated result of the materials used. Consequently, a meeting was called with the Carney Company. Their chemist and general sales manager responded. Meeting was also participated in by representatives of the Highway Department, the Minnesota Attorney General's Office and others, striving to find the source of the trouble on the two jobs performed the previous year. It became obvious in these discussions that the answer was not one which could be readily determined, as it was shown that the responsibility might be that of the contractor, the finishers used on the job, the materials, or possibly a combination of adapting finishing methods to the new material. At this meeting the sales manager said they previously had applied political pressure to get their jobs and threatened to do so again. At this point I then said that if he felt that way about it, we would await his action and see what would happen. In the interim, engineers and inspectors were called in. After all the available information had been reviewed we still had not reached a final solution.

This impasse, combined with the lack of any further word from the Bureau of Public Roads, left Hoffmann in something of a quandary:

> . . . the time was approaching to call for bids on the 1947 program which was presumed to take up the remainder of the 62 [promised] miles of blended cement concrete. This naturally raised the question as to what position I would take and what responsibility I would assume in ordering a continuation of this type of work without knowing more about what results were to be anticipated.
>
> While the question was still being pondered, Mr. Lovewell of the Carney Company volunteered the information that an admixture had been substituted[17] which might be a factor in the unsatisfactory condition developing on the 1946 work. In other words, to this extent, the

[16] Carney's own feeling was that the road was not as rough as many people claimed. "If it had not been a new highway and a lot of personal feeling I doubt if anyone would have commented on the roughness of the road."

[17] The substitution remained a sore point with Carney—he credited the Department of Highways with forcing it upon the Company, and held the Department responsible for the trouble which ensued. The contrast between his and Hoffmann's statements on this point are indicative of the controversy over what might euphemistically be referred to as the "facts" in the case:

Carney: "Although some of the best concrete paving in the State of Minnesota was put down with the blend during 1940-1-2, the specifications were changed in 1946 to require high limits of air-entrainment, both in the blend and in air-entrained portland cement. The Carney Company, furnishing three jobs in 1946, was forced to change its formula from the successful one of the earlier years in order to meet the 1946 specifications."

Hoffmann: "As a matter of fact, the specifications referred to were not arbitrary but were in accordance with the recommendation and request of Lovewell of

natural cement plant had found it necessary to depart from the [stearate] specifications of grinding compound originally used in the test material.

It is true that some of the representatives of the Carney Company, one at least, accused me of "stalling," but . . . this was by no means the case. I could not justify specifying blended cement if our technical men could not satisfactorily explain the 1946 rough surface jobs. Personally, I feared likelihood of repetition.

Because of the uncertainty and his own premonitions, Hoffmann decided finally to abandon his earlier intention of earmarking certain of the 1947 contracts for use of the blend, and returned instead to his former practice of allowing the blend as no more than an alternate material. It was on the basis of open competition that he began calling for bids on paving contracts scheduled for the coming year. The "June bargain" was off.

Aftermath of a Decision: The Final Offensive

While Hoffmann wrestled with uncertainty, Carney grew increasingly bitter. He resented the delay in carrying out the terms of the June bargain, and suspected the Department of an ulterior motive in making so much of the rough pavement incident. His resentment increased as he learned that final payments on the projects in question had been held up, pending results of the Department's investigation. Though he knew this was standard practice, he was also aware that the word was getting around, and that road contractors were beginning to shy away from further use of the blend.

When January and February of 1947 passed, still without any evidence that the June bargain would be honored, and with most of the year's paving contracts already let, Carney reached his boiling point. Steaming mad, he rallied his political forces for one grand and (it was to prove) final offensive:

In the spring of 1947, I went to nearly every member of the House of Representatives and the State Senate and told the Natural Cement story of Minnesota. We pointed out that we believed in competition and that we had always had plenty of it and survived, but when we were able to pioneer in this section of the country the use of better concrete with resultant longer life over the years to come, we were entitled to some consideration. We pointed out the advantage of natural cement . . . and stated that if this Company, in the face of all the political strength mustered against it, was to fail at this time in putting over its cause, then the Legislature, the Administration and the State of Minnesota had failed in keeping faith with its citizens.

Carney had little trouble gaining the support of members from his own and surrounding districts, most of them having been passengers on the famous Greyhound bus trip of the previous summer. His most effective argument in re-enlisting their support was his charge that Hoffmann had reneged on the promise made at the hotel conference of June last. Of the 62 miles promised, only 26.8 miles had been constructed to date; and there was no sign from the Department that the remainder of the bargain would be fulfilled.

Early in his campaign, Carney scored heavily by winning to his support Senator Oscar Swenson, a powerful figure in both the legislature and the Republican Party, and more than once mentioned as gubernatorial material. Swenson was a rural senator, widely respected for his integrity and conservatism—any cause he backed politically was likely to succeed.

Because Swenson's relations with Hoffmann had always been of the best, there is some question as to why he agreed to champion Carney's crusade. Several answers have been

the Carney Company on July 2, 1945, that they be permitted to use darex in their grinding rather than the stearate that had previously been used. The portland cement on these jobs contained no air-entraining agent, the job specifications called for an air content of 2.5 to 6.0% which is the standard of our air-entraining portland cement concrete. The specifications were reviewed by Mr. Lovewell of the Carney Company and concurred in by him as far as they related to the requirements of the natural cement."

suggested. One is that Swenson viewed the request as a challenge to demonstrate his power in the Senate; another, that he did it as a personal favor to his colleague from Carney's district, who was not certain of his ability to swing it alone; still another, that the Senator was aware that local sympathy with Carney's cause had overflowed into his own (neighboring) constituency. None of these suggestions is incompatible with Swenson's own explanation. Though a friend of Hoffmann and convinced of the latter's integrity, Swenson believed that the Commissioner in this instance had acted arbitrarily. He was particularly vexed with Hoffmann's refusal to complete the construction of the promised mileage; this, to Swenson's way of thinking, seemed an inexcusable breach of faith.

Hoffmann's intransigence and Swenson's dislike of it became more pronounced as the legislative session of 1947 wore on. As a result of Carney's persistent lobbying, Hoffmann was summoned to the Speaker's Chambers for an informal conference with leading members of the legislature. Hoffmann recalled the meeting later as "definitely loaded." He was asked why he had discriminated against natural cement. He replied that he had not; and he listed his reasons, defending in particular his recent action in connection with the rough pavement incident. When asked whether he could, if he chose, specify that natural cement be used, Hoffmann replied that he guessed he could—at least on the mileage for which MacDonald had promised Federal approval.[18] Would he? Not, as he declared, of his own volition—"but pass a law and I'll have to."

Following this exchange, Swenson was more intent than before on clipping Hoffmann's wings. His own impression of Hoffmann's performance at the meeting was that "he didn't give any real explanation in full, though he had his excuses." Weighing his next step, Swenson concluded that it would be best not to spend more time with Hoffmann, and not "to go to the Governor at this time"; instead, he decided that the Commissioner would have to be forced into compliance by legislative fiat. Accordingly, he and his cohorts in the cause, drew up a bill, submitted it to the Attorney General for a legal check, and on April 3—just three weeks before the session was slated to adjourn—introduced it simultaneously into both houses of the legislature.

A BILL FOR AN ACT RELATING TO THE USE OF A BLEND OF NATURAL AND PORTLAND CEMENTS IN THE CONSTRUCTION OF CONCRETE PAVEMENT IN THE STATE OF MINNESOTA

BE IT ENACTED BY THE LEGISLATURE OF THE STATE OF MINNESOTA:

That the Commissioner of Highways of the Minnesota State Highway Department, in the preparation of specifications for concrete highways on which bids have not been requested shall, from and after the passage

[18] The promised BPR directive had finally arrived, dated January 15, 1947—too late to be of any real or immediate help to Hoffmann in holding the line against the pressure tactics of Carney. It confirmed Hoffmann's earlier assertions respecting Federal policy, and followed his lead by calling for open competition; but by the time it arrived, Carney had exploited the situation and was beyond the point where he could be reached by arguments from Federal policy. Furthermore, as Carney soon discovered, BPR's directive had no restraining effect on New York State, which continued to specify the use of the blend to the exclusion of alternate air-entraining materials. While the wording of the directive was probably of minor significance in New York's decision to continue its practice, it seemed to allow for such action: Note the use of the word "desirable" in the concluding paragraph.

GENERAL ADMINISTRATIVE MEMORANDUM No. 313

"It has been established by extensive experimental work during the past few years that the increased resistance to frost action of air-entraining concrete is, within limits, a function of the amount of entrained air . . .

"Three approved methods for obtaining air-entrainment are:

1. The use of normal portland cement . . . with improved admixture introduced at the mixture.
2. The use of an air-entraining portland cement . . .
3. The use of a blend of normal portland cement and an approved natural cement. . . .

"The [Bureau of] Public Roads believes in full and free competition between all manufactured products that meet the approved engineering specifications of the individual States. If an individual State desires to specify air-entrainment, and materials are available, it is desirable that the three methods be set up in the specifications as alternates optional with the bidder. Competition should be permitted on all work between natural cements meeting the requirements. . . ."

of this act, specify that such concrete highways shall be made of a Blend of Natural and Portland cements containing not less than 15% of Natural Cement.

Introduction of the bill was the signal for an open clash between Carney and the interest groups who opposed giving natural cement a preferred position. Spearheading the opposition movement were the representatives of the Portland Cement Association; but they did not lack support from other groups. These included the state CIO, the Hennepin County (Minneapolis) Good Roads Association, the Minnesota Society of Professional Engineers, and the Minnesota Contractors Association. Their motives in joining were immediately questioned by Carney, who regarded the opposition line-up as a calculated and unholy alliance against him. By now, he saw a sinister design in everything; the way things looked to him

—the engineers were on the spot, caught between Hoffmann's preference for open competition, and pressure from portland cement companies on the other.[19]

—the CIO was the union in control at the portland cement plant in Duluth (Universal Atlas), and "naturally" would join the opposition.

—the Good Roads Association was concerned only with the costs of highway construction, and on this point they had been misled by portland propaganda.

In a more positive vein, Carney paraded the virtues of natural and blended cement; cited performance records in Minnesota, New York, and other states; claimed that Lang's researches for the Minnesota State Highway Department had shown the blend superior to its rival, air-entrained portland; and stressed the point that recent reports of a $200-$800 differential in costs between use of the blend and use of air-entrained portland (favorable to the latter) were misleading. "In one case," he argued, "the second low bidder on the basis of total dollars actually bid the Blend Concrete at a lower figure per square yard than the low bidder, but was higher in the total dollars due to other features of the work having nothing to do with concrete—such as grading, etc."

While Carney fought on, and on one occasion struck a low blow,[20] Hoffmann claims to have scrupulously avoided any effort at deliberate politicking: "While Carney's political campaigning was going on, I did not at any time ask a single member of the State Legislature to take any position whatever in this issue." Carney's vision of a sinister massing of forces against him was nothing more than self-delusion, as far as the Commissioner was concerned; the latter's own convictions were that

—the Portland Cement Association's only concern throughout the struggle was to secure equal recognition of their own product, which research had proved at least the equivalent of the blend.

—the Portland Cement Association had at no time exerted counterpressure upon him or upon any member of his Department.

—"every member of the Legislature realized, that I have never held any animosity with any of the individuals, industries or materials involved . . . my position was not one of antagonism toward any material but simply of reluctance to specify that material to the exclusion of alternate materials, particularly alternate materials which so far in our experience had indicated they were of equal quality and lower cost to the people of the state."

—engineers took the position they did because they "were unconvinced as to there being any advantages in the use of the blend, but they recognized the extra work of mixing that its use entailed, the increased costs which were then becoming evident, and were naturally apprehensive of preferential legislation which interfered with the state's regularly established policy of open competition."

19 Carney's lobby brochure stated the point with some indirection: "It has also been pointed out that if alternate bids are insisted upon, and with the shortage of Portland cement as it has existed recently, the contractor might be obliged to bid the air-entraining Portland lower than the Blend in order to obligate himself 100% to the Portland company for assurance of delivery of the required cement."

20 The charge was circulated that the son of O. L. Kipp, Assistant Commissioner of the Highway Department, was employed by Portland and was one of the influences accounting for Hoffmann's decision. Apart from the substance of the insinuation, which no one who knew Hoffmann's character took seriously, the facts were that it was the son of the former Chief Engineer (Ellison, now deceased) who was so employed—and then only for two summer months following graduation, while he looked for a permanent job elsewhere.

Members of the opposition who were active in the lobby were equally adamant in their refusal to grant Carney's contentions. Their own main point of rebuttal continued to be that portland cement was as much a home product and a state industry as Carney's natural cement; that it was cheaper to use and easier to handle; and finally, that legislation was no way to handle a problem of this sort. Open competitive bidding was the proper method; and for that reason, Hoffmann's decision should be allowed to stand.

As a matter of fact, most members of the legislature were inclined to accept these arguments; at the time the bill was introduced, neither Carney nor his legislative friends had much hope it would carry. Neither they nor the opposition were particularly surprised when the bill passed the House by a near unanimous vote—it was agreed that the test was to come in the Senate, and it was commonly felt that Carney was fighting a lost cause. Hoffmann's standing with the legislature, and the impressive opposition lobby, were two strikes against him.

The critical point in the legislative history of the bill came at the hearings of the Senate Highway Committee. Pressed for time in the hectic last days of session, the Committee limited its hearings on the bill to a single afternoon meeting. Swenson, a member of the Committee, recounts that "the cement people were out in force" and adds that "Hoffmann was there siding in with them." Hoffmann's memory is that the "engineers were out in force," for reasons which he heartily agreed with and proceeded himself to present forcefully to the Committee assembled. He concluded his testimony by reminding the Committee that a similar bid for preferential legislation had been made some years before by manufacturers of Minnesota granite; that the measure, when passed, had quickly revealed the dangers of such favoritism. "There had been quick and harmful retaliation on the part of other states of such a serious nature that that preferential act was repealed at the first opportunity afforded the succeeding Legislature."

"For three solid hours," Swenson says, "those opposed to the bill plied the Committee with their arguments." No one spoke for Carney. Swenson's hunch was that it would be wise to omit any harangue, in view of the shortage of time. Nonetheless, when it came time for adjournment, the Senator realized that the sentiment of the Committee was clearly with Hoffmann and the opposition. "Had a vote been taken then, it would have been 11-2 against Carney."

It was at this point that Swenson displayed the political acumen for which he was so widely noted. First, he waylaid a motion to postpone consideration of the bill indefinitely —a proposal clearly intended to kill the measure. Then he spoke briefly to the Committee, mentioning that this was the first time he had heard many of the points which had been so convincingly argued that afternoon. He would like, as he was sure the rest of the Committee would also, to have additional time to consider the matter. Therefore he would move that the Committee's vote be postponed until the next day. To the disappointment of those intent on an immediate decision, his motion carried and the meeting stood adjourned.

Swenson's strategy was just begun. Early the next morning, before the opposition could rise and reassemble, the Senator had the Committee reconvened; after a forceful presentation of his views, he asked his colleagues to report the bill, even if without recommendation. This was done, and the bill now went before a Senate caught in the maelstrom of closing days. The press for time and Swenson's personal endorsement proved the clinching factors in the brief debate which followed. When the vote was taken on April 23, the bill squeezed through by the rather slender margin of three votes.

The final hurdle to be cleared lay in obtaining the signature of the new Governor, Luther Youngdahl. For a time, early in the course of the bill's passage, it had seemed likely that the Governor would not approve the measure. When he first learned of the proposal, he had called Hoffmann to his office and asked him to explain the situation. The Commissioner reminded him of an earlier conference they had held at the time of the dispute over the rough paving projects—a conference which had resulted in the Governor giving Hoffmann a vote of confidence for his handling of the entire matter. Youngdahl remembered, and reaffirmed his support.

His inclination, at this point, to veto the measure dissolved at a later luncheon meeting with two of the legislative leaders pledged to Carney's support. He was now reportedly advised that a veto would probably stir up enough resentment to make rough sledding for the anti-slot machine bill—a pending measure upon which the Governor had staked much of his political reputation. The Governor thereupon suggested that if a time limit were attached to the bill, restricting its effect to the current calendar year, he would withdraw his objection. The compromise worked; the bill was passed in the amended form, and signed.

THE LAST MILE

Carney was once more to be disappointed in success. By the time the bill became law, all except one of the paving projects scheduled for the calendar year 1947 had been let—the exception covering a stretch of 19 miles in the western part of the state.[21] This contract was later awarded on the basis of specifications set forth in the Act, and represented Carney's only gain from his victory in the legislature.

After the Act had expired, Carney called on Hoffmann once again. The Commissioner was now free to act as he chose; but Carney continued to hold him to account. The 19 miles awarded him in 1947, he argued, did not make up the difference between the 62 miles guaranteed by the June bargain, and the amount allotted to him prior to the act: over 20 miles of the promised 62 remained. Hoffmann surprised Carney by acknowledging the claim as legitimate, and by referring to his own commitment as a moral obligation. To show good faith, he arranged that year for 34 additional miles of pavement on which use of the blend should be specified. He had no qualms in doing so, having in the meantime cleared up the mystery of the rough paving incident to his own satisfaction. Nor did he have difficulty reminding the Bureau of Public Roads of its own part of the bargain, and securing that agency's approval.

Hoffmann fulfilled his promise in 1948. Since then, highway contracts in Minnesota have been let on a strictly competitive basis; and it is significant to note that all but 2.74 miles have been built with air-entrained portland. Only one contractor has submitted a successful bid based on use of the blend, and he was a friend of Carney's, pledged to the man and to the cause.

To Hoffmann, this record seems justification enough of his decision not to give preferential treatment to the blend, and of his long struggle to maintain that decision. It is his conviction that under conditions of open competition, the bids of contractors have provided a reliable index of comparative costs and performance of the two products and that the index now shows that it would have been against the better interests of the State to exclude air-entrained portlands in favor of the more costly natural cement blend.

To Carney, still disconsolate over his defeat "at the hands of the interests," the record proves only that the contractors are adjusting their estimates and choice of materials to fit Hoffmann's predilections and the pattern of dominant political strength.

Here the Case Stands

The Carney Cement Company is still in business, still doing reasonably well in its production and sale of cement for masonry and related purposes. But it is clear that Carney has lost his fight to expand his market through any such device as a change in state highway specifications to provide for exclusive use of the blend. As long as Mike Hoffmann is Commissioner of Highways in Minnesota there will

[21] Even this project was to have been let earlier. Hoffmann explains that "the delay was granted in response to a specific request of the Legislative group for Carney, to permit passage of the bill requiring use of blended cement."

be open competitive bidding; and as long as there is open competitive bidding, portland cement seems to be in a position to command the market—barring, of course, the breakdown in its long-run performance which natural cement producers are now forecasting as inevitable.

Carney will not be able to count on further help from the legislature. For one reason, Senator Swenson and those who worked with him in the 1947 campaign have gone on record as opposing further preferential legislation. "From here on in," Swenson says, "Carney's cement will have to prove itself. We were only making sure he would be given a fair chance to demonstrate its merits." The same feeling is shared by the editor of the influential daily newspaper in Carney's community [22] and by many of the local businessmen whom Carney earlier relied upon to bring pressure upon Hoffmann and the Governor. Not even the well-circulated news that New York State continues to favor natural cement in its area seems enough to revive interest in another local crusade.

A second reason seems to be that Hoffmann's position as an administrator and his reputation as a man have over the years become so secure as to be almost invulnerable against continued attacks of the sort launched by the natural cement interests in Minnesota. Senator Swenson, even when opposing Hoffmann in 1947, regarded the Commissioner "as an honorable person," and appreciated the difficulty of his position. ("Hoffmann was up against a problem. No one knew for sure the value of natural cement, and the Commissioner was right in resisting pressure if he thought he had good reasons. I just didn't think he had.") A second Carney supporter and a leader in both legislative campaigns seems to have summed up existing feeling toward Hoffmann in a post-mortem comment which he recently added to the case:

> The Commissioner didn't lose anything with the legislature—no cuts in appropriations or anything like that. Certainly he didn't lose anything with me. If he hadn't had integrity it would have been a different matter.

None of which means that Hoffmann necessarily has heard the last of his decision. The New York situation is still alive; so are the contentions of Researcher Ira Paul, upholding the virtues of natural cement; [23] so, too, the problem of scaling and deterioration, along with the need for developing a still more durable and resistant concrete; [24] not to mention the Carney Natural Cement Company of Mankato, Minnesota, which still dreams of capturing a rich new market.

[22] The editor was never very happy about the use of political tactics, but felt that under the circumstances of Hoffmann's refusal to act in 1946-47 "there was no other recourse." His mood at the time was reflected in the editorial he wrote (April 4, 1947; *Mankato Free Press*) supporting the bill: "It is a rather strange commentary that the state should have a State Resources Commission, financed and staffed with state tax money, the sole object of which is to find ways and means by which more Minnesota natural resources may be developed to increase state income and strengthen the state economically, and that still such a long fight should be necessary to have one of the state's own resources used by its highway department."

[23] But note the recent announcement that a new antidote to scaling has been developed and will be used by the New York State Department of Public Works—"A special distillate oil treatment which water proofs the new concrete and virtually eliminates the scaling conditions." (*New York Times*, Sept. 23, 1950.) Whether this indicates a change in policy or attitude as respects the use of natural cement has not been made clear. What is clear is that the U. S. Bureau of Public Roads, with the lesson of the natural cement episode still before it, has no intention of letting negotiations regarding this and other developments get out of hand. Writes Commissioner MacDonald (Sept. 8, 1950)

"I am advised that we now have some thirty-six (36) other materials of a similar nature under investigation. We hope in these investigations that the facts, as they present themselves in orderly development, will not lead to discussions as extended as were encountered in this particular case in Minnesota."

[24] "Research in Concrete and Cement," an article in the Dec. 1948 issue of *Rock Products*, records the opinions of leading cement users, production technicians, and research experts on the subject of improving concrete. Greater durability was agreed to be the most pressing need; but there was little agreement as to how it might be achieved.

Appendix A

A List of Some of the More Significant Research Reports, Articles, and References on the Subject of Natural Cement Blends and Air Entrainment

(In the order of their appearance)

1. Ira Paul, (A) "Chloride Salts—Resistant Concrete in Pavements"; in the *Proceedings* of the Association of Highway Officials of the North Atlantic States, at the 14th Annual Convention held in Atlantic City, N. J.; Feb. 16-18, 1938. (B) Letter to the editor of the *Engineering News Record;* Vol. 125; p. 598 (November 7, 1940).
2. W. F. Kellermann and D. G. Runner, "The Effect of Using a Blend of Portland and Natural Cement on the Physical Properties of Mortar and Concrete," American Society for Testing Materials *Proceedings;* Vol. 38, Part II (1938). Also printed in *Public Roads;* Vol. 19, No. 8 (October, 1938); pp. 153-166.
3. Portland Cement Association Research Laboratory, *Semi-Annual Reports* of October 31, 1938, and October 31, 1939.
4. O. L. Moore (Director of Tests and Research, Universal Atlas Cement Company of New York), "Pavement Sealing Successfully Checked." *Engineering News Record;* Vol. 125; pp. 471-476. October, 1940.
5. Wait Associates, Inc., *Rosendale Cement, 1831-1941.* Promotional pamphlet released in February, 1941, and distributed by the firm (N. Y. City).
6. M. A. Swayze, "More Durable Concrete with Treated Cement." *Engineering News Record;* Vol. 126, pp. 946-949. June 19, 1941.
7. Portland Cement Association Research Laboratory, *Report* for the period ending January 31, 1942. Salient features of this report (on field and laboratory tests made in connection with experimental road projects) discussed in a paper by A. A. Anderson published in the *Proceedings* of the 17th Annual Convention of the Association of Highway Officials of the North Atlantic States (1941).
8. Portland Cement Association, "History of Development, and Policy Regarding Use of Concrete Pavements of Treated Portland Cement, Blends of Treated Natural Cement with Portland, and Air-producing Mixtures"; (mimeographed) March 26, 1942.
9. Minnesota State Highway Department (F. C. Lang), "Effect on Physical Properties of Concrete of a Blend of Natural and Portland Cement and of Treated Portland Cement" (confidential report, filed as Investigation #130); 1943.
10. Symposium: "Concrete Containing Air-Entraining Agents," Concrete Institute *Journal;* June, 1944.
11. H. F. Connerman, "Tests of Concrete Containing Air-Entraining Portland Cements or Air-Entraining Materials Added to Batch at Mixer," *Journal of the American Concrete Institute;* Vol. 15, No. 6. June, 1944.
12. C. E. Lovewell (Carney Company), "Report on Research." *Engineering News Record;* Vol. 135, pp. 100-102. July 26, 1945.
13. Portland Cement Association, Highways and Municipal Bureau, "The Elimination of Pavement Scaling by Use of Air-Entraining Portland Cement." Release No. HB 18. First edition in 1945.
14. Portland Cement Association Research Laboratory, "A Working Hypothesis for Further Studies of Frost Resistance of Concrete." Bulletin 5; February, 1945. Bulletin 5a, containing a supplementary symposium, followed in March, 1946.
15. Special Committee on Air-Entraining Concrete of the Highway Research Board, "Use of Air-Entraining Concrete in Pavements and Bridges." No. 13, *Current Road Problems;* May, 1946.
16. W. F. Kellermann, "Effect of Blended Cements and Vinsol Resin-Treated Cements on Durability of Concrete," *Journal of the American Concrete Institute;* Vol. 17, No. 6. June, 1946.
17. B. F. Wait, "Portland-Rosendale Cement Blends Give High Frost Resistance," *Journal of the American Concrete Institute;* Vol. 17, No. 6. June, 1946.
18. B. F. Wait, "Discussion of Natural Cement Blends and Air Entrainment." Paper prepared for presentation at the New York and New England Materials Engineers Conference, Boston, Mass., October, 1946 (mimeographed).
19. F. T. Sheets (President of the Portland Cement Association), "Discussion of Problems Relating to Air-Entraining Portland Cements for Concrete Pavement Construction." Confidential report submitted January 12, 1946 (mimeographed).
20. U. S. Public Roads Administration, "Air-entrainment in Concrete on Federal-Aid Construction." General Administrative Memorandum No. 313. January 15, 1947.

21. U. S. Public Roads Administration, Division of Physical Research, "The Effect on Properties of Concrete of Natural and Portland Cement Blends," *Public Roads;* Vol. 25, No. 2. December, 1947. (Report written by P. R. A. Engineers Timms, Grieb, and Werner.)

22. Bror Nordberg, "Research in Concrete and Cement," *Rock Products;* Vol. 51, No. 12. December, 1948.

It should be noted that U. S. Public Roads Administration, cited in items 20 and 21, was previously, and is currently named Bureau of Public Roads, and is so referred to in this study.

Further data of a promotional sort may be readily obtained from the Portland Cement Association (Boston, New York or Philadelphia offices) and from Wait Associates (Rosendale), 51 East 42nd St., New York City.

Acknowledgment is made to the *Engineering News Record* for permission to quote from the above reports.

Appendix B

Statement of Federal Commissioner Thomas MacDonald Explaining the Policy of the Bureau of Public Roads

(Letter of February 16, 1950)

I should like to comment first upon the broad premise . . . that the conditions in New York which led to the use of natural cement to improve the durability of concrete are comparable to those in Minnesota. In my judgment, they are not at all comparable and this fact will explain our apparently inconsistent policy in dealing with the problem in these two States. The following statement will, I believe, make clear . . . the basic difference that I have in mind.

Natural cement was first approved for use as a blend with portland cement in New York State in 1934—several years before the discovery of the principle of air-entraining portland cements. As the result of field trials and laboratory tests, including our own, it was found that the use of a blend of Rosendale natural cement with portland cement markedly improved the durability of concrete, not only as regards increased resistance to the surface scaling of roads caused by the use of salts for ice removal, but also resistance to the action of freezing and thawing in general. It was also shown in this earlier work that the natural cement from Rosendale, New York, was more effective than the natural cement from Akron, New York, a fact that we could not explain at the time, but which we found later to be due to the probability that the Akron natural cement, as originally manufactured, did not entrain air in the concrete to the same extent as the Rosendale.

New York State was having trouble with concrete long before the practice of salting pavements to remove ice had become general. This was particularly true of that portion of the State lying west of an approximately north and south line running through Syracuse. In this region, severe weather conditions (that is, frequent and rapid changes in temperature, resulting in an unusually large number of cycles of freezing and thawing during the winter) in combination with the use of aggregates of borderline quality, had resulted in the premature failure of many concrete structures—bridges as well as roads. It is not surprising then that the Bureau should have approved the use of Rosendale natural cement when all indications pointed to the fact that a much more durable concrete would be obtained thereby. The important thing to remember is that, at that time (1934), the possibility of using air-entraining portland cements to accomplish the same purpose was not even dreamed of.

The situation in Minnesota was quite different. Their troubles were not due to a general lack of durability as in New York, but rather to the surface scaling of roads caused by the use of chloride salts for ice control. Concrete pavements which had formerly proved entirely satisfactory commenced to scale badly when chemicals were applied. Natural cement proposed in Minnesota to correct this difficulty; not to improve the general over-all durability of concrete as in New York. Furthermore, the proposal to use natural cement in Minnesota coincided almost exactly with the discovery of the principle of air-entrainment, a discovery which, in turn, resulted in the development of air-entraining portland cements. There were available to Mr. Hoffmann, therefore, two alternate methods of protecting his concrete roads, one by the use of a natural cement blend and the other by the use of an air-entraining portland cement. It seems perfectly reasonable, therefore, that he should have chosen to utilize both methods, particularly when he knew that it was the general policy of the Bureau to encourage competition between alternate acceptable ways of accomplishing the same purpose.

It is true that as our information regarding the real function of natural cement (that of entraining air in concrete) developed, and as air-entraining portland cements became available, we did not require New York to revise its specifications. There were several reasons for this. In the first place, it should be remembered that the use of Rosendale natural cement had become well established in New York State in the 6-year period following its adoption in 1934 and before the discovery of air-entraining cements around 1940. It had a head start of 6 years over air-entraining cements, and this experience record made it difficult to convince the State Highway Department that it should modify a practice which was producing good results. Furthermore, New York State has never been willing to grant that the virtues of Rosendale natural cement are due solely to its air-entraining properties. The State Highway Department has consistently maintained that the virtues of this particular product are inherent in the cement itself and are not due to the entrainment of air. This has been a highly controversial subject for years and the time and research effort necessary to obtain answers to the technical questions involved accounts for the fact that no formal policy regarding air entrainment was available until early in 1947. On January 15 of that year a memorandum setting forth three approved methods for obtaining air-entraining concrete was issued. This clarified the picture and is the policy under which we have been operating since that time.

GOTHAM IN THE AIR AGE

CONTENTS

FOREWORD

New York is the largest city in the Western Hemisphere, and the first or second largest in the world—New Yorkers hardly care which. When the 1950 census showed a population several hundred thousand less than had been estimated by that sober commercial organization, the Consolidated Edison Company, the city remained unconcerned. In all conscience, New York has enough residents, enough visitors, and enough daily commuters to create problems of such size and complexity that the citizens and officials of the city need seek no further augmentation of their population or difficulties.

The scale and scope of the social and governmental problems and activities in New York and the tremendous metropolitan area of which it is the center necessitate a great deal of advance planning. By the same token, however, problems tend to remain submerged or shunted aside until they become big enough to be noticeable on that enormous stage.

This case deals with such a problem, one that was ignored or dealt with by temporary expedients until finally—rather suddenly—it became a major political issue that required immediate and radical solution.

When World War I ushered in the Air Age—the age of practical, large-scale commercial aviation—the city fathers were not disposed to pay it any heed. Two generations earlier, they had come to grips with the rationalization of the piers which service ocean shipping, the life blood of the port. One generation before, they had begun to wrestle with the problems of rail facilities in the port area. Now, they were feeling the pressure of the traffic problem generated by a new means of travel, the automobile. They were caught up in the constant, insistent demands for service of an expanding population. No wonder they would not be concerned about the first flimsy airplanes.

In the years following World War II, they could not avoid thinking hard and long about aviation. The war had demonstrated clearly the implications of the Air Age, and it was obvious that the requirements of the new era could not be ignored, deferred, or treated perfunctorily. New York had to decide what to do and how to do it. How its officials became aware of the problem and how they reached a decision on the necessary course of action constitute the substance of the story that follows.

It might have been a shorter and simpler tale had the surrounding circumstances been somewhat different. But a great many factors tended to make the process of decision-making difficult and complicated. One of the most important of these factors was the contrast, and the conflict, between the personalities and individual aspirations of the public officers who were drawn into the process. Another was the heavy burden on the municipal government imposed by the need to construct facilities and improve services which had been deferred during the war years. Still another was the fact that the City's administrative machinery, though it may have been adequate in earlier times, had not been designed with the Air Age in mind.

Especially significant in the process of decision-making was the fact that New York City is a part of a larger whole that straddles political boundaries. Fourteen million people dwell in a great semi-circle, with a radius of about 60 miles, around the waters of upper New York Bay. Politically, they are divided into many compartments; state boundaries separate New York City's citizens from the New Jerseyites on the west, while Connecticut lies only a few miles away from the northern border of the City; and there are literally hundreds of lesser units of government, ranging from counties, and cities of the first magnitude to small towns and villages. Sociologically, however, the fourteen million constitute a single vast and complex organism; their welfare and the very fabric of their lives are bound by a thousand ties into an indivisible unit. The decision the City of New York had to make in this instance was one that vitally concerned and directly affected the entire metropolitan area and was, in turn, affected by how all the people, through their local governments, adjusted to the maturation of commercial aviation.

Equally important were the financial limitations to which the City is subject. Under the State constitution, the tax levy is limited to 2 per cent, and the borrowing capacity to 10 per cent of the average realty valuations over a five-year period. There are, to be sure, some exceptions to these ceilings, but the limits are nonetheless highly effective. In addition, though New York City has relatively broad powers under the home-rule provisions of the State constitution, the approval of the State legislature is required before it can undertake certain types of action. These are common enough restrictions, municipalities being legal creatures of the states, and they are widely regarded as expressions of governmental prudence and wisdom. At the same time, however, they add to the perplexities of city officials, especially when those officials face the needs of a metropolis like New York.

On a subject of national significance—for national defense, for interstate and foreign commerce, for the carrying of the mails—it was also requisite that the city's policies and actions be accommodated to the requirements of Federal agencies in order to claim Federal assistance.

All these things, and a great number of others that will doubtless occur to the reader in the course of the account, increased the difficulty and complexity of the decision New York's leaders had to make about how to adapt to the Air Age. Viewed broadly, that decision was the work of a great many people who participated in the process by which it was reached. In a more formal sense, however, it was made by the Mayor and the Board of Estimate.

The City of New York, as it exists today, and the general structure of its government were created by the Charter of 1897. At that time the boundaries of New York City—theretofore coextensive with Manhattan Island (which is still "New York" to the visitor)—were enormously enlarged to include contiguous counties and a host of municipalities. The four counties within the new city retained certain minor functions—since further attenuated—related to the administration of justice and the existing party structure. Local pride and, in a minor way, local patronage were served by dividing the City into five boroughs—of which more below.

Over the years there have been changes in the City's charter. The changes have strengthened those elements in the City government tending towards central control and authority and limiting the powers of the legislative body. Today the government of the City of New York is organized on the Strong Mayor—Council plan. The 25-member Council is the local legislative body, elected by districts every two years. The mayor is elected every four years; his main executive powers are the veto of local legislation and the authority to appoint and remove at pleasure the heads of 27 City departments, as well as to appoint the members of eight commissions and seven boards. But New York stands apart in government as in all else. Many of the principal administrative duties of the City are performed by the Board of Estimate, a body unique in municipal government.

The Board of Estimate (successor to the earlier Board of Estimate and Apportionment) was set up by the new Charter of 1938. It consists of eight ex officio members who have a total of 16 votes. The three officials elected by city-wide ballot have three votes apiece: the mayor (who is chairman), the comptroller (the City's chief financial officer and auditor), and the president of the City Council (who presides over the Council but casts a ballot in that body only in the event of a tie); the borough presidents of Manhattan and Brooklyn have 2 votes each, and the borough presidents of the Bronx, Queens, and Staten Island 1 vote each.

The borough presidents, elected by borough-wide ballot, each head another institution unusual in city government. The borough is a subdivision of the City with its own elected executive; the powers of the borough governments, however, are today minor indeed, and they now exercise authority only over construction of streets and certain minor public facilities. The real significance of the borough lies in the fact that it provides a modicum of geographical representation on the powerful Board of Estimate.

All the members of the Board of Estimate are elected concurrently for four-year terms, but because of the varying composition of the electorate in the different areas of the City, it is normal for one or more of the borough presidents to be of a different political party from the mayor, though the mayor and the two other city-wide officials elected on the same ticket are invariably of the same party. Since these three members of the Board of Estimate cast 9 of the 16 votes, they control it—unless they have a falling out. Nevertheless, the Board provides a useful and sometimes effective forum for a borough president of either party who feels that the needs of his section of the city are being slighted.

The Board of Estimate constitutes the board of directors of the City, determining the "policy with respect to all financial affairs, local assessments, franchises, zoning, city planning, public improvements, and real estate belonging to the City"; it also serves as a second legislative chamber with respect to a few specified—and highly important—types of local law, including the adoption of the budget. The Board is at the same time one of the chief administrative agencies of the municipal government. In fact, in it is lodged the residual power of New York, for it is authorized to exercise, subject to the charter, "all power vested in the city except as otherwise provided by law." To this group, with the mayor as leader, fell the primary and not entirely welcome responsibility for deciding how the City would meet the challenge of aviation.

I. New York City Feels the Air Age

THE FIRST REACTIONS

This is the story of New York City's governmental adjustment to the Air Age. It begins at the end of World War I, with the first inattentive responses to an infant industry by a municipal government preoccupied with more pressing problems, and covers the recognition of the problem, the grappling for a solution, the impact on the City government, the inability of that government to provide a solution within itself, and the way the governmental resources of the large metropolitan area produced a workable answer that satisfied the needs of modern aviation and at the same time saved the municipal government from curtailing its own traditional services to the people. The course of this story might have been entirely different if the early leaders had been able to foresee the extent to which aircraft would develop in a single generation; they might then have tried to make fiscal and administrative arrangements to meet the inevitable demands of the new transportation. But no one then knew what lay ahead and no special preparations were made, with the result that technology strode rapidly ahead while government practically stood still; when the time came for the discrepancy to be eliminated, the shock to the City administration was so great that it almost seemed for a time that New York might not be able to do the job.

On April 8, 1925, the chairman of the Committee on Landing Places for Commercial Air Lines of the New York Board of Trade and Transportation transmitted to the Board of Estimate and Apportionment of the City (then the upper House of the former bicameral Assembly and the predecessor of the present Board of Estimate) a resolution of his organization recommending that the City make available for commercial aviation certain facilities in its possession. This appears to be one of the earliest moves to bring the question to the attention of the City government. A month later, the Committee of the Whole of the Board of Estimate and Apportionment referred the resolution to the Board's Chief Engineer with instructions to

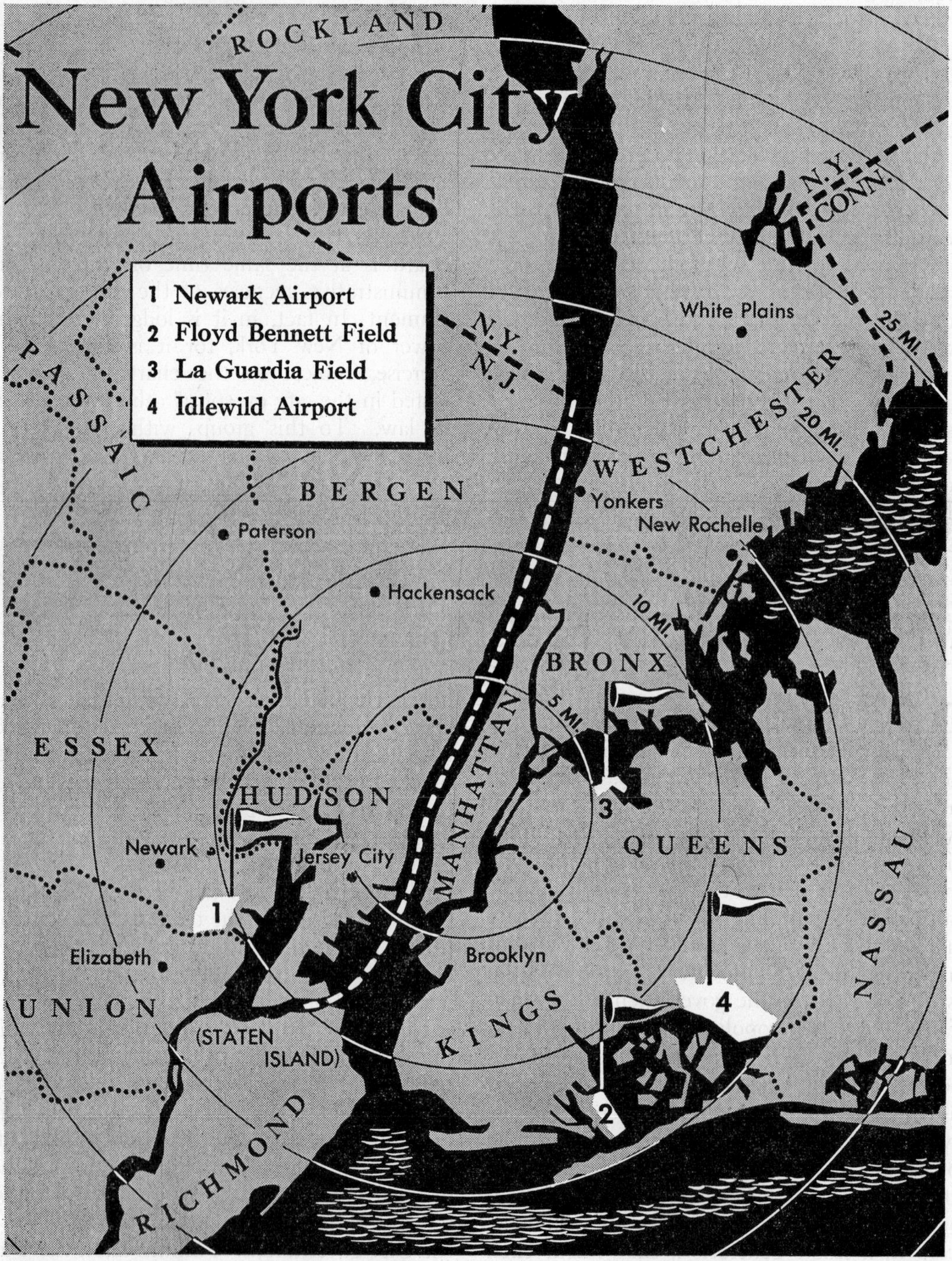
New York City Airports
1 Newark Airport
2 Floyd Bennett Field
3 La Guardia Field
4 Idlewild Airport
ROCKLAND
PASSAIC
BERGEN
ESSEX
HUDSON
UNION
RICHMOND
(STATEN ISLAND)
MANHATTAN
BRONX
WESTCHESTER
QUEENS
KINGS
NASSAU
N.Y.
N.J.
N.Y.
CONN.
White Plains
Yonkers
New Rochelle
Paterson
Hackensack
Newark
Jersey City
Elizabeth
Brooklyn
5 MI.
10 MI.
20 MI.
25 MI.
1
2
3
4

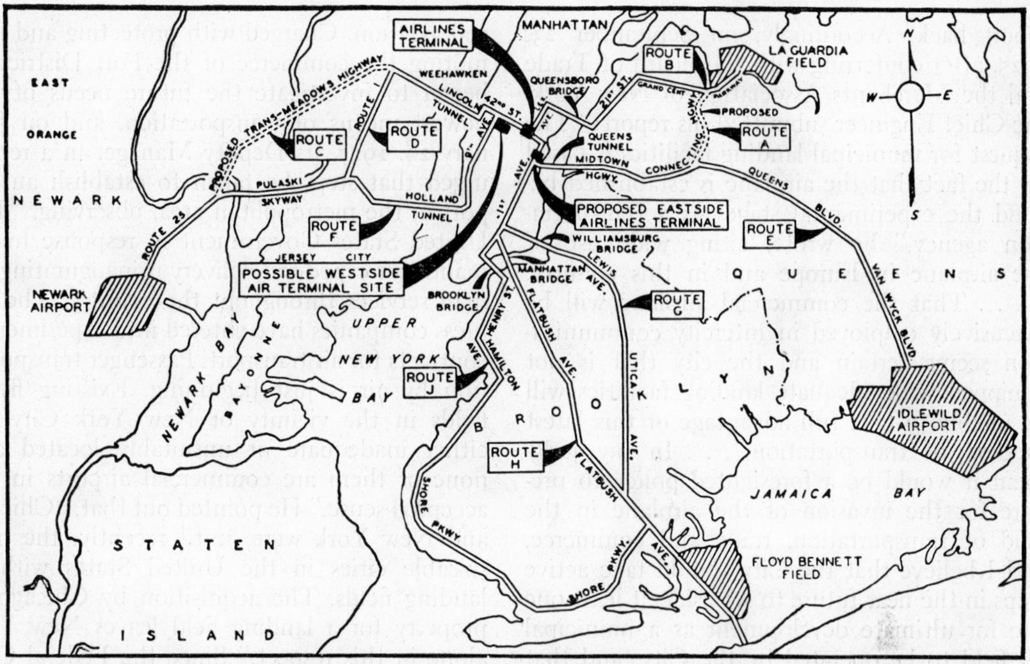

From *Airports of Tomorrow*, by the Regional Plan Association, Inc. By permission. *Source:* Test Runs by Port Authority on April 24-26, May 3, August 22-23 and September 30, 1946.

TRAVEL TIME AND DISTANCE BETWEEN MIDTOWN MANHATTAN AND NEWARK, LA GUARDIA, IDLEWILD AND FLOYD BENNETT AIRPORTS

From airlines terminal via	*To airport*	*Time minutes*	*Distance miles*
Route A	LaGuardia	20.5	8.93
Route B	LaGuardia	29.0	8.15
Route C	Newark	31.1	12.97
Route D	Newark	34.7	14.22
Route E	Idlewild	38.0	15.10
Route F	Newark	44.7	13.47
Route G	Floyd Bennett	53.5	15.03
Route H	Floyd Bennett	53.8	14.04
Route J	Floyd Bennett	54.3	22.08

From possible west side air terminal site via	*To airport*	*Time minutes*	*Distance miles*
Route C	Newark	21.9	12.10
Route D	Newark	25.5	13.35
Route A	LaGuardia	30.0	9.82
Route F	Newark	35.5	12.60
Route B	LaGuardia	38.2	9.02
Route E	Idlewild	47.2	15.97
Route G	Floyd Bennett	63.0	15.92
Route H	Floyd Bennett	63.3	14.93
Route J	Floyd Bennett	63.8	22.97

From proposed east side airlines terminal via	*To airport*	*Time minutes*	*Distance miles*
Route A	LaGuardia	14.7	8.15
Route B	LaGuardia	29.2	8.55
Route E	Idlewild	34.8	15.35
Route C	Newark	36.9	13.75
Route D	Newark	40.5	15.00
Route G	Floyd Bennett	47.7	14.25
Route H	Floyd Bennett	48.0	13.26
Route J	Floyd Bennett	48.5	21.30
Route F	Newark	50.5	14.25

report back. Accordingly, on September 23, 1925, after conferring with the Board of Trade and the Merchants Association of New York, the Chief Engineer submitted his report: "The request for municipal landing facilities is based on the fact that the airplane is established beyond the experimental stages as a transportation agency," he wrote, citing wide use of the airplane in Europe and in this country. " . . . That the commercial airplane will be extensively employed in intercity communication seems certain and the city that is not equipped with adequate landing facilities will be unable to take full advantage of this latest method of transportation. . . . In my judgment it would be a foresighted policy to prepare for the invasion of the airplane in the field of transportation, trade and commerce, and I believe that the City should take active steps in the near future to set aside at least one site for ultimate development as a municipal air field to be operated by the City, and that the day is not far distant when such a field will be self-supporting."

It is not clear whether any action was taken on these recommendations; in any event, there is no evidence of any progress toward the construction of an airport by the City for at least two years. It may be that there was some doubt about the Chief Engineer's estimate of the future of commercial aviation; one gleans an idea of the technological status of aircraft from the Engineer's observation that the field ought to be at least 100 acres square—scarcely more than the area of the terminal buildings alone in modern fields. There may well have been skepticism about the commercial prospects for the wood-and-canvas crates that abounded at that time. Furthermore, two of the four sites recommended by the Engineer were already owned by the city, and so no special action was called for in these cases. At any rate, it is worthy of note that the first impetus to provide municipal airports came from prospective beneficiaries of the airlines rather than from the City administration.

The interest of the Port of New York Authority, an agency created by an interstate compact between New York and New Jersey, about which more will be said later, was evidently stimulated by the growing concern for commercial aviation. Charged with protecting and promoting the commerce of the Port District, it began to investigate the future needs of the newest means of transportation, and on January 29, 1927, its Deputy Manager in a report urged that steps be taken to establish an airport in the metropolitan area, observing, "The United States Government in response to demands for expedited delivery is inaugurating air mail services throughout the country. The express companies have entered into experimental contracts for air transport. Passenger transportation by air is just beginning. Existing flying fields in the vicinity of New York City are either inadequate or unsuitably located and none of them are commercial airports in the accepted sense." He pointed out that, "Chicago and New York were, until recently, the only sizeable cities in the United States without landing fields. The acquisition by Chicago of property for a landing field leaves New York alone in this respect." Since the Federal Government assumed that local enterprise would provide terminal airports, he suggested that the air service companies, the states, municipalities, or other governmental agencies, or any combination of these, would have to undertake the task. The field, which would consist ideally of 120 acres and four sod runways, with an additional 80 acres for expansion, was not expected to be self-supporting for some time. Nevertheless, "The Metropolitan District of New York . . . should have one or more thoroughly modern airports or terminal flying fields."

Later that year, the Aeronautics Branch of the United States Department of Commerce grew concerned over the lack of airports in the New York area. Secretary of Commerce Hoover therefore appointed a Fact-Finding Committee on Suitable Airport Facilities for the New York District, consisting of representatives of 23 civic, commercial, industrial, and government organizations. The Committee met for the first time in August, and on November 29, 1927, wound up its work and submitted its report.

The Committee, adopting a regional point of view, suggested six general localities for fields, two of which were in New Jersey and the remainder in New York. "As a result of the studies that have been made," the report declared, "it is felt that a general plan looking toward the development of a system, or series, of airports should be recommended which may be carried out as the increasing needs of commercial aeronautics and of private flying may require." For the whole metropolitan district, the Fact-Finding Committee saw a need for an ultimate aggregate airport area, exclusive of auxiliary airports, of from 2,000 to 2,800 acres. However, despite their interstate approach to the problem, the members unequivocally declared their belief that the two States or their political subdivisions rather than any interstate agency should develop the airports, and the member representing the Port Authority joined all his colleagues in signing the report that carried this stipulation.

In 1928, the Committee on the Regional Plan of New York and its Environs, then a young, private research and civic pressure organization, later known as the Regional Plan Association, published the transit and transportation volume of its all-embracing regional survey. The book took note of the three airport studies completed previously and commented that the sites they recommended were "no more than adequate to meet the needs of the immediate future. . . . The urgent need," it went on, "is to acquire ample areas for all possible purposes in connection with air transportation." These observations were made more concrete when the overall regional plan appeared the following year. This plan advocated a regional system of 32 airports at an absolute minimum, with an optimum number of 46 spread through New York and nearby New Jersey and Connecticut as a preferable quantity to provide for future aviation requirements. "The proposed sites," the report declared, "should be obtained without delay or else the communities within the Region will be faced with either enormous costs in removing buildings, as well as increased land prices, or they will have to do without the facilities necessary to make New York an efficient center for air transportation."

Meanwhile, work was already proceeding on one of the sites in the region: the City of Newark was already at work on Newark Airport. In October, 1928, Newark Airport was opened and at once became the principal field in the New York area.

IMPROMPTU ADMINISTRATION

The New York City administration thus found itself under several types of pressure. Commercial groups were urging action. The Chief Engineer of the Board of Estimate and Apportionment himself had strongly recommended steps toward the provision of airport facilities, a recommendation he reiterated, incidentally, in a second report to the Board on May 4, 1927. In May and June of 1927, new horizons were opened by the transatlantic flights of Lindbergh, Chamberlain and Levine, and Byrd. The Port Authority and the Fact-Finding Committee had already pointed to the need for a municipal field. Newark was in the process of constructing one that promised to take over whatever air commerce might develop in the area and leave New York high and dry. Finally, the Mayor acted. In January 1928, even before Newark Airport began operations and before the Regional Plan Committee underscored the urgency of the situation, he instructed the Commissioner of Docks "to proceed with studies and plans for designing and constructing a municipal airport on property under the jurisdiction of his Department." On February 2, the Board of Estimate and Apportionment approved the development of an airport on one of the sites named jointly by the Chief Engineer, the Port Authority, the Fact-Finding Committee, and the Regional Plan Committee—a filled-in area on Jamaica Bay, in Brooklyn.

That the Department of Docks was directed to perform this function was probably nothing more than a convenient accident. The city property on which the airport was to be erected was already under administration by this agency; prior to 1928, it was to have been used for the construction of a number of long piers into Jamaica Bay Channel. The Department had been created in 1870 to repossess and develop waterfront property below 42nd Street, 90 per cent of which had been previously ceded away through city grants; by 1914, it had spent $100,000,000 on the task and had fallen heir to the City's docks generally. Thus it came about that this agency was in charge of the land upon which the municipal airport was to be built, and the New York City Department of Docks thus provided aviation with its first administrative home.

In a sense, it was as good a place to put aviation as any in the administrative branch. No other department would have been a more logical candidate for the job, and the Department of Docks did have engineers and experience with land-filling operations. But it is very likely that this disposition of the problems of the Air Age was simply a hurried expedient rather than a planned response. Aviation remained very much the junior partner in the Department, marine functions taking precedence over it. Indeed, for three years, while the first municipal airport was under construction, aviation received no organizational recognition whatsoever; no unit in the Department was created to handle the new function. In 1931, a Division of Aviation was set up, but this was simply a minor part of the Bureau of General Administration. Not until 1941 did it gain Bureau status (after a second municipal airport had been in operation for two years), and only in 1942 did aviation formally receive recognition of equality when the Department was redesignated the Department of Marine and Aviation. Even then, leases for space on the city's airports continued to be executed on dock forms and under laws applying to dock space. From an administrative point of view, aviation was a step-child, and the administrative arrangements adopted to accommodate it were for the most part impromptu.

The work of construction and study proceeded, and by 1929 the Chief Engineer of the Department of Docks was able to declare that the new field, designated Floyd Bennett Field, would be "one of the greatest in the world, with all up-to-the-minute facilities, and one whose problems of design and construction have been well thought out." Floyd Bennett Field was completed in 1931 and dedicated on May 23rd of that year. It had cost the City about $4,000,000 and covered 388 acres; it boasted two concrete runways (4,112 and 3,480 feet, respectively) and eight hangars. Its completion was an act of faith, for the downward turn of the depression had half its course still to run.

THE BEGINNING OF RIVALRY

When Newark Airport, which was on a similar scale to Floyd Bennett, had opened two and a half years before, it was an experiment. Newark had complied with Federal design, equipment, and operations specifications, and had invested in what was then the most expensive and elaborate airport in this area in the hope and probably the expectation that there would be a profit in handling the air traffic for the whole New York metropolitan district. It was built with the assurance from the Federal Government that it would be named the air mail terminus for the district, an important consideration, since the infant airlines survived on the basis of air mail subsidies and flew wherever the air mail contracts took them. Newark Airport became one of the busiest airports in the country within a short time.

There seems little doubt that New York intended to draw much, if not all, of this business to Floyd Bennett Field. The year Newark opened, the Commissioner of Docks observed bluntly, "It is our hope to induce the Federal authorities to recognize the unsurpassed facilities of the field. . . . If this tube [a pneumatic mail tube from the field to the Long Island Railroad station nearby] be constructed, the field will have a facility for dispatching mail to Manhattan possessed by no other airport." And, he added pointedly, "As a matter of fact, Floyd Bennett Field appears to be troubled less by fogs and mists than other airports in this district. On several recent occasions, transport planes have landed at Floyd Bennett Field when they were prevented by fogs from landing at their intended destination"—which was, of course, Newark. Indeed, every subsequent annual report listed in meticulous detail the number of Newark-bound planes forced to land at Floyd Bennett by poor weather conditions at the New Jersey field. During 1932, more vigorous efforts to improve service were instituted, clearly in order to make the New York field more attractive. The principal road to Floyd Bennett was widened and repaired. Bus service connecting the field with the subway was begun. Work on a seaplane base was rushed, and the City tried to persuade the backers and operators of seaplanes to designate the Brooklyn base as their terminus. There were even steps in the direction of a flying shuttle service to Manhattan designed to cut the time needed to reach Times Square to eight minutes. The Commissioner of Docks announced optimistically, "Floyd Bennett Field's future appears brighter at present than at any time since its dedication, and, with the field rapidly achieving recognition as one of this country's greatest airports, it is believed that, in the very near future, it will be the center of all aviation activity in the New York area." In 1933, New York prepared to move into action on still another front: the Commissioner of Docks reported that "Steps will be taken during the early part of 1933 to have the Federal Government designate the field as an air mail terminal." New York had set out to recoup the loss incurred by its tardy realization of the significance of air commerce.

LA GUARDIA ELECTED: THE BATTLE IN EARNEST

If the City of New York was energetic in its efforts to attract the airlines to Floyd Bennett Field before Fiorello H. LaGuardia took office as mayor on January 1, 1934, its early action seemed puny compared to the campaign on which he embarked upon coming to power. LaGuardia had been a pilot in World War I; he was interested in aviation and was an extremely air-minded person; and he had many friends among airline officials, some of whom he had first met in his Army days. With LaGuardia's election, lively municipal competition ended and acrimonious hostilities began. And the fact that LaGuardia was elected on a Republican-Fusion ticket was to prove no real bar to his efforts to secure Federal Democratic New Deal support in his airport campaign.

He fired the first shot even before he officially took over the reins of City government. After the election in November 1933, he and his wife went to Florida to recuperate from the strain of the campaign. On November 24, 1933, they flew back to New York aboard a TWA airliner. The plane landed at Newark, the terminal for New York City. But Mr. and Mrs. LaGuardia refused to disembark; their tickets, the Mayor-elect insisted, called for New York, not for Newark, and he maintained that he would not alight until delivered to his destination. So adamant was he that the plane took off again and landed him at Floyd Bennett.

Such an incident helped dramatize the situation, but it accomplished nothing in the way of bringing air traffic to the Brooklyn airfield. The first report of the Commissioner of Docks to Mayor LaGuardia observed that a more concrete measure had been adopted by the Department: "Floyd Bennett Field has been installed on the [U. S.] Department of Commerce teletype circuit. Complete up-to-the-minute weather reports from all over the country, as well as weather maps, are now available at the field for the use of pilots, thus increasing the popularity of the field with airmen. Also, Floyd Bennett Field weather is sent out hourly over this circuit, as well as being broadcast hourly from the Department of Commerce weather broadcasting station, making Floyd Bennett Field weather available at airports throughout the country, as well as to pilots in the air. We believe this will go a long way toward bringing to the attention of pilots and aviation officials the advantage Floyd Bennett Field holds over Newark Airport in the matter of weather conditions."

But the weather argument had been run ragged, and the Mayor apparently realized that it was not going to change things. No matter how the question was approached, two cold facts remained: (1) In spite of the fact that Floyd Bennett was situated within the New York city limits, it took considerably longer to go from Floyd Bennett Field than from Newark to the heart of the City. The latter distance was actually shorter, and there were the added advantages of the Holland Tunnel and the new Pulaski Skyway (an elevated, express motor highway), so that it was possible to reach Newark in from 50 to 60 per cent of the time needed to thread through the traffic of lower Manhattan and the East River bridges, through the congested business district of downtown Brooklyn, and out across the width of that whole Borough to the New

York Municipal Airport. (2) Newark Airport was much closer to main line railroad facilities; mail from Floyd Bennett Field, in poor weather, would have to be returned all the way to Manhattan before it could be put on trains.

There were only two ways to overcome these handicaps. Either the Post Office Department had to be convinced that it should designate Floyd Bennett Field as the New York District's air mail terminus, thus bringing commercial aviation to it, or New York City had to build a new air terminal closer to the center of town. The City administration embarked immediately on the first of these courses and soon began preparations for the second, meanwhile also seeking other inducements to lure the airlines to New York.

THE FIRST BATTLE OF THE POST OFFICE

In the early days of commercial aviation, from 1918 to 1927, the Post Office Department operated its own mail planes, selected the routes, and designated the airports serving the various cities. From 1927 to 1938, air mail service was operated under contracts with the Department, the location of landing fields provided by the contractors at first being subject both to the approval of the postmasters nearest those fields and then to the final approval of the Department in Washington, and later (from 1934 on) to the approval of the Washington office alone. When the Roosevelt administration came into power, the terms and manner of awarding these contracts before 1933 led to a Senatorial investigation and to wholesale contract cancellation on charges of collusion. There was a brief period of Army operation, then a whole new set of awards to commercial lines, followed by litigation and a major political controversy. Route certificates issued after 1934 by the Post Office Department in substitution for previous contracts stated that the mails would be received and delivered at fields and points therein designated on schedules prescribed by the Postmaster General. Though the terms of compensation were modified, the new contracts still provided revenues without which the airlines probably would not have been able to function, so the companies were sure to use the fields specified by the Post Office. Postmaster General Farley, no peronal friend of Mayor LaGuardia, but intimately acquainted with the angles and tangles of New York City politics, and well aware too of Mayor Hague's strength in Jersey City, took the dominant role in reshaping air mail contracts in 1934.

The first air mail terminus for the New York Metropolitan District had been located in 1918 at Mitchell Field, Mineola, Long Island; but it was early shifted to Hadley Field, New Brunswick, New Jersey. Hadley Field lay more than 30 miles from Times Square and the trip required from an hour and a half to two hours. Thus, as soon as Newark Airport opened in 1928, the transfer of operations to this much closer and more convenient base was a foregone conclusion.

Mayor LaGuardia's campaign on behalf of Floyd Bennett Field moved vigorously in the fluid context of the 1934 renegotiations of air mail contracts. Soon bitter complaints began to be heard from across the Hudson River. Said Meyer C. Ellenstein, the Mayor of Newark, on November 25:

> In opposition to the presidential program to eliminate unfair competition, in conflict with the policies in this respect of the Interstate Commerce Commission and in disregard of the comity that should exist between neighboring cities—in brief, in defiance of the first principles of competitive fairness, New York officialdom is now attempting to sacrifice the Newark Metropolitan Airport to an airport of its own at Floyd Bennett Field, on Long Island . . . Mayor Fiorello LaGuardia . . . is bringing the utmost pressure to bear on official Washington to secure the designation of that field as the eastern air mail terminus. Success in that effort would automatically force all air mail carriers operating out of the East to remove to the Long Island field.
>
> What New York has offered as inducements to the airways companies is not officially known in Newark. It can only be conjectured that those inducements exceed anything that can be construed as fair competition while they must oppose every principle of sound economic business practice. On the face of it, vain ambition and not monetary concern is the one motivating consideration. Newark has made every possible conces-

sion to the companies now operating out of Newark Airport to retain their patronage. It cannot hope to compete with New York in its financial resourcefulness. On the other hand, it cannot afford to give away an airport in which its people have invested more than $5,000,000.

Mayor Ellenstein's moral arguments do not seem to have had much effect on New York City officials, since they betrayed the fact that Newark was not financially capable of meeting New York's challenge. The New Yorkers drove ahead relentlessly and, considering the vigor of Mayor LaGuardia's leadership, his personal interest in the problem, his contacts and influence in Washington as a recent Congressman, and the undeniably greater resources New York could draw upon to induce the airlines to transfer, Newark's fears were well founded. However, this rivalry played into the hands of the airlines: in order to secure the aviation business, the cities were making drastic concessions to the companies, and there is no reason to believe that the companies did not exploit the situation to the fullest.

By late spring of 1935, New York City had persuaded the Post Office Department to undertake a survey of the situation, and its technical experts and officials made a series of studies. Mayor Ellenstein of Newark countered New York's moves by heading a citizens committee and appearing before First Assistant Postmaster General Harllee Branch to defend the Newark Airport and to present a formal brief stating Newark's side of the case. This brief was later reprinted by a Newark financial institution and some 25,000 copies distributed. Newark won the first round, for, on August 24, 1935, Mr. Branch made the following announcement:

After months of investigation by . . . the Post Office Department, and after careful consideration of all points involved, it has been determined to retain Newark Airport as the Air Mail terminus for the air mail routes serving the New York metropolitan district.

The Post Office began its survey several months ago at the request of Mayor Fiorella LaGuardia, of New York City, who urged that Floyd Bennett Field, on Long Island, be designated as the air mail terminus for the metropolitan district.

The advantages and disadvantages of both Newark Airport, which is the present terminus, and Floyd Bennett Field, as affecting both the air mail and the air passenger traffic, have been thoroughly canvassed. As a result of the study made, the Post Office Department finds that both from the standpoints of prompt handling of the air mail and facility of transporting air passengers to and from the airport, as well as the expense involved to the Post Office Department, Newark Airport offers superior advantages. . . .

The surveys and study made by the Post Office Department show that to remove the air mail terminus from Newark Airport to Floyd Bennett Field would involve an initial expense to the Post Office Department of between thirty and forty thousand dollars, and that the additional annual expense thereafter would amount to between one hundred fifteen and one hundred twenty-five thousand dollars. This additional annual expense would be incurred in increased pay to the air mail carriers for the new mileage flown, the necessity for retaining Newark Airport for certain schedules, and the added cost for handling mail to and from Floyd Bennett Field.

On the whole, no plan proposed in connection with the use of Floyd Bennett Field would offer any substantial saving in the time of handling the mails between the airport and the General Post Office in New York City. On the contrary, serious delays would be encountered at Floyd Bennett Field which could be avoided at Newark. Those railroad facilities at Newark play a very important part in the prompt handling of air mail when flights have to be cancelled or are delayed.

A change to Floyd Bennett Field would put the air mail carriers to an additional expense, as they would be required to maintain services to Newark Airport as well as to provide services and terminal facilities at Floyd Bennett Field.

THE SECOND BATTLE OF THE POST OFFICE

Mayor LaGuardia recovered quickly from this resounding defeat and remobilized his forces. In four months, he was again ready to do battle, through a Committee on Airport Development, appointed by him to prevail upon the Postmaster General to reopen the case and afford New York an opportunity to make a further statement and present further evidence to justify designating Floyd Bennett Field as air mail terminus. A hearing before Postmaster General Farley was held on December 12, 1935. Mayor Ellenstein promptly requested an opportunity to be heard further, and a hearing was held for the representatives of Newark on January 20, 1936. Meanwhile, Mr. Farley directed postal officials to review their surveys and the status of the proposed terminal change. On March 21, 1936, having heard the evidence personally and having further reviewed the stenographic record, Mr. Farley issued the following statement:

> On August 24, 1935, the Post Office Department reached a decision that it would be inadvisable to transfer the terminal from Newark to Floyd Bennett Field for the reason that to do so would result in considerable extra expense to the Post Office Department and in a delay in the handling of the air mail. . . .
>
> No proposal was made by the New York Committee as to the handling of mail from Floyd Bennett Field to the general post office in New York, other than had been made in previous hearings. . . . No proposal and no evidence was offered to show that the air mail could be better served from Floyd Bennett Field than from Newark Airport and nothing was produced which rebutted the position of the Post Office Department that the air mail could be handled more expeditiously from the Newark Airport than from Floyd Bennett Field. . . .
>
> Should some feasible plan be later evolved for use of Floyd Bennett Field, which would provide more expeditious service to the majority of the patrons of the air mail service in the New York metropolitan area, further consideration will be given to this matter.

Mr. Farley went on to point out that mail and passenger service would have been slowed by the change, and that it would have increased the expenses of the Post Office both by incurring the cost of the change and by requiring a greater annual outlay for the handling of mail. The finality of tone in this decision apparently dampened even Mayor LaGuardia's enthusiasm, and the City dropped the effort to convince the Post Office of the desirability of the change.

BUILDING A SECOND AIRPORT

Even while Mayor LaGuardia sought to win the Post Office to his point of view, he was also laying the groundwork for pursuing the second course of action open to the City—construction of another field closer to the center of Manhattan than either Floyd Bennett or Newark. At the end of 1934, the City entered into a lease with Curtiss-Wright Air Terminals, Inc., owner of the Glenn H. Curtiss Airport at North Beach, Long Island, on Flushing Bay, in the Borough of Queens and within the New York city limits. The agreement provided for active operation of the field by North Beach Air Services, Inc., until 1936, when the City was to assume full control, and granted the City an option to purchase. In February 1936, the City took over control of the field and began to draft plans for its enlargement. Thus, even at the time of the Postmaster General's ruling, the City was ready to follow its second alternative.

The Works Progress (later Projects) Administration had already assisted the City in the enlargement and improvement of Floyd Bennett, and it was anticipated that a good deal of the funds for the airport at North Beach would come from the same source. Construction proceeded during 1937, and New York exercised its option and acquired title to the property. A huge filling operation was carried on in 1938, and a field of 550 acres and four runways from 3,500 to 6,000 feet long was laid out. On October 15, 1939, the field was officially dedicated and opened to flying; the total cost was estimated at $45,000,000. "New York Municipal Airport, LaGuardia Field," was the name adopted by the City Council on November 10, 1939.

Even as late as 1939, LaGuardia Field was regarded as a tremendous undertaking by most people; it was ridiculed as fantastic in some quarters, and there was some feeling that New York's air-minded Mayor had presented the City with a white elephant that would never justify its existence.

The task of construction again fell to the Department of Docks, whose Division of Aviation was now the recognized center of the City's aviation operations. Partly perhaps because the Federal Government through WPA bore a large part of the cost of constructing LaGuardia Field, it was apparently assumed that New York City could handle its airport problems within its own governmental structure by normal administrative arrangements.

NEWARK DEFEATED

LaGuardia Field lay closer to the heart of Manhattan than Newark. Under favorable traffic conditions it could be reached via the Queens-Midtown Tunnel or over the Tri-Borough Bridge in from fifteen to twenty minutes—a considerable saving over the time needed to reach Newark Airport. Well before construction was completed, the City began to move toward securing the designation of LaGuardia Field as air mail terminus for the metropolitan district.

Meanwhile, the forum of Federal decision had changed. The Civil Aeronautics Act, passed by Congress in 1938, had created the Civil Aeronautics Authority and vested in it the power to regulate aviation and allocate routes to commercial aviation companies. The Civil Aeronautics Authority was empowered to issue certificates of convenience and necessity to air carriers, specifying the stops to be served and the airports to be used. The Post Office Department could appear before it as an interested party in any case involving the carriage of air mail, but the decision lay in the hands of the Authority.

The first official attempt, under this Federal act, to transfer operations from Newark to the new field at North Beach, like later efforts to this end, came from an airline rather than from the New York City government. There is no doubt that the airlines were encouraged in this by the City, and especially by Mayor LaGuardia, whose deep personal interest was manifest and who was on close personal terms with some of the airlines executives. But it is equally certain that the airlines themselves were anxious to commence operations at the new field. Faster service to the Times Square area would boost passenger traffic. The new facilities were greatly improved over those at Newark or even at Floyd Bennett; they had been designed by the Department of Docks in cooperation with airlines engineers and reflected every foreseeable need in the companies' expanding operations. Finally, the airlines officials were anxious to take advantage of the great concessions the City administration proposed to make to the companies in the matter of rentals in order to induce them to establish their eastern terminals and their maintenance bases in New York. With all these incentives it is not surprising that the airlines were willing to take the initiative in seeking to have LaGuardia Field designated terminus for the metropolitan district.

An early effort by American Airlines resulted in a temporary setback for the company: a Civil Aeronautics Authority examiner, ruling on the line's application for a certificate of convenience and necessity to operate into New York City, held on February 7, 1939, that a "grandfather" clause in the Civil Aeronautics Act froze the situation as it had been during the "grandfather period," May 14 to August 22, 1938, and that he was powerless to grant the new certificate. However, while this ruling for the time being kept Newark as the only airport through which the company could serve New York City, the examiner observed that airlines might apply for amendment of their original certificates.

American Airlines shortly applied for such an amendment, requesting on July 18, 1939, that LaGuardia Field instead of Newark Airport be designated the company's terminal for the metropolitan district. This case was joined a month later, with similar applications, by Transcontinental and Western Air and by United Airlines, and finally by Eastern Air Lines, which applied to have LaGuardia named co-terminal with Newark. Hearings were held before the Civil Aeronautics Authority for two full weeks, beginning on the 11th of September, and here the battle reached its climax.

The record of this case fills three thick volumes. It covers almost a thousand pages of testimony and dozens of exhibits offered by representatives of the two cities involved (the cities coming into the picture as intervenors, New York naturally supporting the airlines' petitions and Newark opposing them), by postal authorities, and by the officials of the airlines. Newark's Mayor appeared personally, leading the fight for his city. The supporters of the Newark position succeeded in mobilizing opinion in New Jersey, and the Authority received substantial quantities of mail urging rejection of the companies' applications. Mayor Ellenstein called attention once again to Newark's pioneering role in developing its airport a decade earlier. Newark's defenders assailed the favorable terms offered the airlines in the leases drawn up by New York, claiming unfair competition.

But neither sentiment nor energy could overcome the basic weakness of Newark's contentions: LaGuardia Field was indisputably larger, newer, and closer to Manhattan. Newark fought desperately, but it fought for what it must have known was a lost cause.

On November 7, 1939, the Civil Aeronautics Authority issued a decision amending the certificates of the air carriers, making LaGuardia Field a co-terminal with Newark Airport for mail, passengers, and freight in the metropolitan area. On December 2, every major airline in the district, with the exception of Eastern Airlines, transferred its major terminal to LaGuardia Field and commenced operations. Eastern followed later.

The city fathers of Newark were not willing to leave any stone unturned. They made one last attempt to salvage their airport by filing an appeal from the Civil Aeronautics Authority decision in the United States Circuit Court of Appeals. But they apparently recognized the futility of their case, and on November 29, 1940, joined the Authority in signing a stipulation for dismissal; the case was dismissed on the same day.

Newark later closed its airport, with the reported intent of renovating it and recapturing some of the lost business. However, before any such program could get under way, the Air Forces took it over for the duration of the war, and New York's victory was temporarily complete.

TOO SMALL A DREAM

Mayor LaGuardia may have seemed a starry-eyed visionary when he first presented the airfield bearing his name to the world. But the work of a man who dreamed big dreams justified itself very early; the business that came to LaGuardia Field turned his vision into a very practical plan. Indeed, hardly before Mayor LaGuardia had enjoyed the plaudits that go to the man of vision, he discovered that his great accomplishment was not enough to meet the needs of the overwhelmingly rapid expansion of air commerce. Taking into account the normal distribution of slack and rush hours, the capacity of the field was rated at about 350 plane movements a day; within two years after the opening day, the volume of traffic approached this safe maximum on many days, and it was obvious that the time was not far off when the *average* of daily movements would pass this mark. The services in the terminal buildings were sorely taxed by the flow of over two million passengers and 100,000 flights between 1939 and 1941, and hundreds of thousands of visitors added to the strain. Runways and other facilities designed in the day of the two-engined, 25,000-pound DC-3 liner threatened to become obsolete as four-engined planes of double and even triple that weight began to make their appearance and still larger ones were envisoned. And not only was there every indication that the *absolute* volume of air traffic was going up; even the *rate of growth* showed signs of swift increase. The fears of having to support a white elephant faded. Mayor LaGuardia began to think of a new airport, a *really* big field.

A VAST SCHEME FOR IDLEWILD

On December 2, 1941, at a celebration of the second anniversary of the commencement of commercial operations at LaGuardia Field, and just before the beginning of his third term, Mayor LaGuardia announced: "Now that the airport is a success it doesn't mean that we will stop there. Only a few minutes ago in the city offices here we were working on details and plans of another airport. No Mayor worth his salt can avoid looking ahead five, ten, twenty-five or fifty years in providing for the city's needs. It is due to the neglect of past administrations that we have so much patching and mending to do now. But that will not happen to my successor." These words were spoken a few days before the Pearl Harbor attack, but against the background of a year and a half of increasingly feverish military and industrial mobilization.

The new field to which he referred was one for which funds had been recommended by the City Planning Commission a month earlier, and which had been approved by the Board of Estimate in order to secure monies the Federal Government would make available for part of the basic construction costs, provided the City acquired the site and put up the administration building and other improvements. By the end of the year, title to the property, a 1,200-acre tract in the Idlewild section of Queens just across Jamaica Bay from Floyd Bennett Field, had been acquired by condemnation, and construction began shortly thereafter. Strong objections were heard from The Bronx, whose officials set up a clamor to have the field located in that Borough, but this opposition was simply overridden in one case and persuaded to yield in another. Nevertheless, the Borough President of The Bronx continued to complain for many years.

During the early part of 1941, the Navy Department completed negotiations with the City for the lease of Floyd Bennett Field. In April 1942, the Navy acquired title by condemnation; just under $10,000,000 was paid to the City for the airfield; this sum was earmarked for expenditure on the new airport at Idlewild. Work was getting under way.

This time, Mayor LaGuardia did not encounter the criticism he had met when he first advocated the large-scale project that bore his name. For one thing, his confidence in the future of aviation had been vindicated; the validity of his original arguments silenced possible critics. More immediately, the Army wanted the field built at once. This alone probably would have been argument enough at a time when serious military reverses were occurring in all theaters of war. Thus, when one City Councilman registered strenuous objections to some of the engineering fees being paid for technical services at Idlewild, Park Commissioner Robert Moses, about whom more will be said later, declared to the press, "If this war is going to be fought by crackpots like [the Councilman], God help us!" There was no really determined opposition.

The responsibility for the details of construction, and for operation when the field was completed, continued to be lodged in the Department of Docks. However, as mentioned earlier, the Department had already acknowledged the growth of its aviation activities by promoting its Division of Aviation to the status of a co-ordinate Bureau during 1941; by 1942, the increasing scale of these activities in the light of the new municipal field at Idlewild resulted in a reorganization of the whole Department into a Department of Marine and Aviation.

Administration leaders retained personal control over the broad developmental aspects of Idlewild. Spurred on by Mayor LaGuardia, they decided not only to build a 1,200-acre field as originally planned to fill the Army's requirements, but to create an airport that would meet the needs of growing traffic for years to come, an airport that would put New York in the lead in this respect all over the world. The wartime development of huge bombers and transports promised to make the runways at LaGuardia Field too fragile and short for postwar use, and the upsurge of the popularity of air travel left no doubt that the capacity of that field would be dangerously overloaded. Airlines officials doubtless encouraged LaGuardia in these views. They foresaw a tremendous postwar expansion in air commerce which they could not exploit without landing facilities on a scale beyond anything previously seen. LaGuardia's mind was fertile ground for such ideas. Municipal works that would win plaudits for his administration were a favorite field for his energies. Even more than most people, he patently enjoyed the credit that goes with being associated with big things, and he had here a chance to create a monumental public utility as a reminder of his foresight and achievement. Aviation was an especially exciting and congenial medium for his enthusiasm. And civic and personal pride would pay off in commercial advantage if he could succeed in making New York the air center of the world. It is not any wonder, therefore, that the project grew in size until, by the end of August 1945, it was approaching 4,900 acres in area—nine times the size of LaGuardia Field, which had been considered extravagant when it was opened a scant six years before. Ultimately, it was to be equipped with 12 concrete runways of from 6,000 to 11,200 feet in length. The total cost of the field, hangars and other improvements included, was expected to run to $200,000,000. The wagon was hitched to a star.

SIGNING THE LEASES

While the construction of the Idlewild airport was proceeding, Comptroller Joseph D. McGoldrick, close associate of LaGuardia as well at a key member of his administration, was conducting negotiations with the airlines to arrive at an agreement on rentals and to determine how much space each company would need. For well over two years the negotiations continued, twelve of the airlines operating international schedules out of LaGuardia Field banding together in a loose association called the New York Airports Committee and acting in concert. Early in 1944, the City sponsored State legislation at Albany authorizing the amortization of airport construction costs over 30 years instead of the usual 20 previously allowed by law, a move which made it possible to reduce the City's annual debt service for the project and thereby the rentals the airlines would have to pay (though, of course, increasing the total cost to the City of borrowing the money). By July 1945, Comptroller McGoldrick announced that agreement had been reached and made public the details of rents and fees. In another month, each of the twelve airlines had specified the amount of space it wanted at the rates agreed upon and signed a lease. A week later, the Board of Estimate, the Borough Presidents of The Bronx and Queens abstaining, voted approval.

Comptroller McGoldrick issued a report in which he analyzed the financial status of the airport based on these leases. He took the position that the financing had been so conceived that the field would become self-liquidating over the thirty-year period of the bonds. He also asserted that this meant there would be no burden on the taxpayer in the long run and that the investment in the airport would not constitute a heavy charge against the City's debt limit. This last point was particularly important: under the State Constitution, municipalities are limited in the amount of debt they can incur for projects which do not pay their own way; consequently, if the airport failed to pay its way, the debt incurred to finance it would have reduced the City's ability to provide schools, hospitals, and other vital services which produce no revenue. For both political and social purposes, the schools and hospitals were probably more important than the airport; hence, assurance on the debt limit was a major consideration.

Mayor LaGuardia paid tribute to Comptroller McGoldrick's handling of the negotiations. He was reported jubilant at having the leases signed at last, after the long period of discussion, and he expressed his thanks to the airlines for their co-operation in the huge undertaking.

As a matter of fact, however, while reasonable men differed at the time, the accumulation of evidence over the years indicates that the Mayor and Comptroller were too optimistic. The leases, as most or even all people agree today, would have brought insufficient revenues to meet both operating expenses and debt service. Shortly after they had signed them, the airlines themselves in effect admitted this by expressing their willingness to renegotiate the terms. Two independent public authorities, when called upon to submit plans later on for taking over the airport, found that they could not operate it under the terms of the existing leases because, lacking taxing power, they could not support the financial burden from the revenues. Even at the time an independent civic organization differed strongly with the Comptroller's calculations, and a disinterested attorney, privately consulted at the time of the signing of the leases, observed that "this form of lease seems to show careful draftsmanship and solicitude to protect the interest of the lessees [the airlines] and is very much less favorable from the point of view of the lessor [the City] than any lease or form of lease which has heretofore come under my observation." The City, it appears, came through the negotiations very badly; instead of becoming self-supporting, the airport was going to require City expenditures to bail it out, and all of the cost of the airport was going to have to be charged against the City's constitutional limit (though a subsequent amendment to the State constitution, which Mr. McGoldrick was instrumental in securing, made this charge applicable only to the non-self-liquidating part of the airport debt).

There are several reasons why this situation came about. In the first place, by the month of August, when the leases were approved, Mayor LaGuardia had decided not to run for re-election in 1945. He determined, therefore, to finish the Idlewild negotiations before his successor could capitalize politically on the gigantic enterprise which was in a very real sense the fruit of the labors of LaGuardia and his associates. This was especially important to LaGuardia, the vociferous foe of Tammany Hall, because of the likelihood that the Democrats would win the election. But the airlines were under no such pressure, and so their bargaining position was improved.

In the second place, the airlines held out to Comptroller McGoldrick the prospect that they would locate their maintenance bases as well as their operating terminals at Idlewild if the rates for space were attractive enough. This would have meant the creation of thousands of jobs for skilled technicians and the addition of a huge payroll to the City's resources, an enticing consideration for the municipal officials. So the City gave in on this point and granted unusually low rentals for hangar and shop space, hoping thereby to draw the companies to the field. Whether the airlines' offer would have been fulfilled had things gone as planned is a moot point, for many of them were already operating maintenance bases at former Air Forces installations in various parts of the country which they had been able to obtain (directly or by rental from local governments which had acquired them) at exceedingly low rates. At these interior locations the airlines had another bargaining weapon in dealing with municipal governments, the threat to fly over their cities unless the airline terms were met. This was a threat which could not be carried out without Civil Aeronautics Board approval, but it was nevertheless used with great effect.

Indeed, the airlines' ability to locate their maintenance bases elsewhere was considerably strengthened by the fact that Newark Airport had just been returned to the City of Newark by the Air Forces, and all the major airlines were already negotiating for space there. Newark Airport lay closer in point of time as well as distance to the Times Square area than Idlewild. If, in addition to this natural advantage, Newark made a bid to regain the business lost to New York a few years before by slashing its fees and rentals and by improving its facilities, the air carriers might very well have found it advantageous to install their principal operations over there. Obviously, this would have put New York, with its gigantic enterprise at Idlewild, in an embarrassing position. For this additional reason, New York was much more sympathetic to the airlines' arguments than it might otherwise have been. In any case, whatever were the intentions of the companies, the City was persuaded and offered them extremely favorable rentals and other terms.

In the third place, the City agreed to use 1939 cost figures as the basis for the agreements. This may have seemed logical in 1945, when price and wage controls were still in force. But the task of construction was likely to extend several years into the future, and a relaxation of government controls and a sharp rise in the costs of material and labor were probable, and in fact did occur. Thus the cost of building many of the facilities anticipated would have gone far beyond those on which the leases were predicated, and the allowances for operating and maintenance expenses on which the City based its agreement certainly would have proved inadequate. This would have meant a heavier debt than was planned and at the same time a smaller net income to pay debt service and amortization.

In the fourth place, the City doubtless used as a bargaining guide the agreements it reached with the airlines at LaGuardia Field. The new flight fees and fees for space in the administration building, for ticket offices and the like, were higher under the new contracts, but there were similarities in the over-all features. While it may have seemed to the City at the time that it had won significant concessions, it should be remembered that the LaGuardia Field leases were signed during a period when

New York was going to great lengths to secure the airlines' business from Newark and went out of its way to induce them to move across the river. Thus, it appears that the City may have used a rather distorted scale of values in its Idlewild bargaining.

The airlines leases were not the only ones to give the City trouble. Comptroller McGoldrick had begun as early as 1943 to seek to establish agreements with oil companies to supply the new airport with fuel, oil, and accessories. The amounts of money involved were not nearly so great as those in the airlines agreements, but they took almost as long to settle. After two years of negotiations, the Comptroller devised a plan to which all the oil companies agreed; on December 21, just ten days before the LaGuardia administration was to leave office, the oil leases were signed and approved by the Board of Estimate. Mayor LaGuardia had achieved his aim: opening day was near, though on a three-runway basis (which was the first stage), with most facilities still to be constructed and many services yet on a makeshift basis. But the dream was being realized.

THE SITUATION AT THE END OF MAYOR LA GUARDIA'S ADMINISTRATION

Just two decades earlier, New York City had heard for the first time the insistent clamor of the infant aviation industry. The impact of the Air Age was brought home to it by the pressure of local business interests, by planning agencies for the port district, and by the Federal Government. But most of all, the meaning of the new technology registered itself through the construction by the City of Newark of a large airfield. New York was galvanized into action and produced Floyd Bennett Field in its bid for the metropolitan area's air commerce. The bid was too small to interest the Post Office Department, which held the decisive cards at the time. With a dynamic Mayor, and aided by WPA funds, the City then built LaGuardia Field. It was a paying proposition from the beginning and established the City's dominant role in civil aviation in the metropolitan area. Its very success, coupled with Army needs in wartime and the bright prospects of postwar expansion, then encouraged the City to undertake the Idlewild project, many times as large. By the end of the war, and before the close of Mayor LaGuardia's administration, construction was well advanced and leases with the airline tenants and their suppliers were negotiated. How shaky the financial foundations of this gigantic project were, remained to be revealed.

Operation of the municipal airports by the Department of Marine and Aviation was taken for granted throughout this period. True, the demands of the Idlewild field were so heavy that the construction job was turned over to firms of consulting engineers and architects. And the negotiations with the airlines and oil companies were handled personally by the top-ranking officials of the City. But all indications pointed to assignment of the completed project to the Department for administration as a matter of course. In any event, whatever the precise organizational arrangement, the capacity of the city government to solve the airport problem was not questioned. As Mayor LaGuardia's term of office drew near its close, it looked as if Idlewild would be fitted into some normal municipal administrative pattern.

II. Administrative Readjustment

COMMISSIONER MOSES DISSENTS

The vast enterprise that Mayor LaGuardia had launched and guided through tricky political reefs appeared, after four years of planning, negotiating, arguing, and pressuring, to be in open water with clear sailing ahead. But it was not so simple. Even before LaGuardia left office, the whole direction of the project was changed. Development of the airport slowed down at once, and obstacles appeared.

The first change in course was largely the

work of Park Commissioner Robert Moses. As early as October 30, 1945 (just prior to the city elections), in his capacity as member of the City Planning Commission, Moses submitted a report to the Board of Estimate recommending that the City's capital outlay for the huge field be drastically curtailed and the task of completing and operating it be assigned to a separate airport authority so as to save City funds for schools, hospitals, housing, and so forth. It was an important and ominous sign; but Moses was then a minority of one on the Planning Commission, and Mayor LaGuardia's enthusiasm for the project was well known. In the excitement of the election the Commissioner's words had no immediately visible effect.

However, when he next appeared to press his ideas, he stood on much stronger ground. William O'Dwyer, Democrat, had been elected mayor by the largest majority ever given a candidate for that office, and he made known his firm intention to stand by a pre-election promise to retain Commissioner Moses and, indeed, to appoint him to a new post as City Construction Co-ordinator with unusually broad administrative powers over every type of construction, public and private, within the City. The Finance Committee of the City Council, which was on December 20 carefully reminded by Moses of his standing with the Mayor-elect, took heed of his words. On December 27, the City Council struck from the capital budget $45,000,000 earmarked for the construction of hangars and an arcade during the next year at Idlewild. Mayor LaGuardia, just four days from the end of his term, was bitterly disappointed and angry.

ROBERT MOSES: POWER THROUGH ADMINISTRATION

For a quarter of a century, Robert Moses has been an important figure on the political scene in New York City and in Albany. But he has never held public elective office nor is he committed to a single political party. He is neither a vote-getter nor a political boss in the general sense of the terms. The source of his power is personal, and he exercises it through administrative channels.

Moses is an exceedingly capable administrator, primarily in the general field of urban and suburban public works; he can, without question, get things done once he has decided he wants them done; very seldom is he thwarted in his purpose. This capacity, plus a notable personality and a keen intellect, first drew the attention of Governor Alfred E. Smith. Prior to 1919, Moses had served as a municipal investigator, had worked for the War Shipping Board in World War I, and had been counsel to the National Federation of Federal Employees, and, during the last period, had taken an important part in drafting a plan that was later incorporated by Congress into the first general salary classification for all Federal employees—the Classification Act of 1923. In 1919, Governor Smith appointed him chief of staff of the New York State Reconstruction Commission, a body created to prepare a plan, in advance of Smith's accession to office, providing a program of legislation. For the next nine years, Moses was closely associated with Governor Smith, participating in many activities of the State government, especially in reorganization of the State administration and in the development of parks, public works, and welfare programs. In 1927, he was appointed Secretary of State of New York, in which capacity he served as secretary of the Governor's cabinet, head of the Governor's public works committee, and generally functioned as the Governor's principal assistant for State administration. During those years he also held a number of other offices and served with a number of commissions. And after Governor Smith left office, though Moses was no longer in the cabinet of his successor, Governor Roosevelt, he was appointed to a number of temporary but influential commissions.

Moses was president of the Long Island State Park Commission, chairman of the State Council of Parks, chairman of the Jones Beach State Parkway Authority, and chairman of the Bethpage Park Authority, positions which he continues to hold to this day, when, in 1934, Mayor LaGuardia appointed him Commissioner of Parks to consolidate and administer the City's park and parkway system. By merging the powers of the five separate borough organizations into one municipal Parks Department, the Mayor greatly strengthened the Commissioner's hand. In that same year the Mayor also selected him to be chairman and chief executive officer of the Triborough Bridge Authority and head of the Henry Hudson Bridge Authority. In 1935, he became head of the Marine Parkway Authority; in 1942, the Mayor appointed him to the City Planning Commission. During 1946, the City's bridge and parkway authorities were consolidated under the Triborough Bridge Authority, to which the City Tunnel Authority was added, and Commissioner Moses was installed as head of the unified body. In the same year, Moses was made City Construction Co-ordinator in accordance with the promise, mentioned earlier, of Mayor-elect O'Dwyer. (It should be noted that only one of these City posts carries a salary, that of Parks Commissioner; Moses, however, has had the advantage of an independent income.) During these years Commissioner Moses served also on a number of commissions and performed consulting services for a number of municipalities and for a Federal agency.

More impressive than the mere list of agencies of which he has been and is an officer, are the actual achievements in which Commissioner Moses has had a significant part; in the *National Cyclopaedia of American Biography* they are described as follows:

> Under his leadership as president of the Long Island state park commission, an extensive system of state parks and parkways, including several ocean beaches, has been established along the south shore of the island extending to Montauk point. Most notable of these is Jones Beach state park, a carefully planned and splendidly equipped public recreational resort which is easily accessible from New York city over broad motor parkways entirely free from grade crossings. He supervised the plan for the unified state park system of New York covering the entire state from the Niagara frontier to Long Island which has been largely carried out in the course of his service as chairman of the state council of parks. When he assumed the post of park commissioner of New York city, he succeeded, with the support of Mayor Fiorello H. LaGuardia, in consolidating the park commission system under one head, unifying the five boroughs. Under his direction, the various parkway systems have become extended to 164 miles of modern arteries, costing more than $250,000,000, including the Southern and Northern state parkways to all points in Long Island; the Henry Hudson drive, with its new links to the George Washington Bridge, connecting the city with points west into Jersey and north and east into Westchester county and New England; the 35-mile belt parkway around Brooklyn and Queens; the Gowanus improvement connecting the belt parkway with the tunnel under construction from Brooklyn to Battery Park, Manhattan, parts of the Brooklyn-Queens connecting highway; the East river drive from 92nd street to 125th street, providing the beginning of a continuous express highway along the East river, all of which will eventually encircle four of the city's boroughs and connect with the fifth and give a continuous intercircular arterial system. He expanded the city playground system from 117 play areas in 1934 to 480 in 1942, and reclaimed the Flushing meadows for the World's fair and for a permanent park at the termination of the fair.

In none of these accomplishments did Moses serve in an elective post. His earliest direct participation in a political campaign was as the secretary of a coalition committee in the 1921 municipal election, but he did not seek an elective office at that time. In 1933, the Fusion Party offered him the nomination for Mayor of New York City, but he declined. (The nomination was then offered to Fiorello LaGuardia, who, of course, accepted and won.) He made his first and last effort to secure elective office in 1934, when he ran for governor of New York on the Republican ticket. It was a bad year for Republicans throughout the country; New York was no execption. Herbert H. Lehman defeated Moses by an 800,000 majority, one of the worst defeats ever administered a candidate of a major party in the State. Even the usually "solid" upstate areas swung out of the Republican column and returned a Democratic legislative majority. Moses did not run for office again, although he was named by Mayor LaGuardia in 1945 as one of eleven men the Mayor thought would make good leaders of the City.

Moses' relations with LaGuardia were of a rather special character. Since both men talked freely and frequently to newspaper reporters, fluctuations in cordiality were a matter of public information. Apparently, each of the two recognized that he needed the other. At the same time, both were men with emphatic ideas, and with the energy to push through projects in which they became interested. Inevitably, there were conflicts, and relations between them were frequently strained. Nevertheless, they remained together for a dozen years, even though Moses frequently threatened to resign. It was only in the last months of LaGuardia's last term that there was a split serious enough to bring to an end whatever cordiality had existed previously. Differences over the airport at Idlewild, as we shall see, lay at the heart of this disagreement.

The high status enjoyed by Moses is shown in the fact that he was a Republican who served with a Democratic administration in Albany and then was appointed by a Fusion administration that ousted the Democrats from City Hall. But the full measure of his position was brought home by the announcement of Democratic William O'Dwyer, when he was campaigning for the mayoralty in the 1945 campaign, that he was happy to be able to declare that Moses had promised to take over the work of the Co-ordinator of Construction, an office that he, O'Dwyer, would set up if elected. This state of affairs was even more remarkable because Moses had publicly supported Newbold Morris, one of O'Dwyer's opponents in the mayoralty race, and a man long connected with LaGuardia and the Fusion movement. Thus, the man who had done so poorly in his one quest for elective office and whose public support of a candidate seemed to carry so little weight with the voters proved he could establish himself so firmly in appointive office that he could outlast the officials who appointed him.

As a matter of fact, the influence of Commissioner Moses under O'Dwyer seemed to grow after the latter took office as mayor in January 1946. Warren Moscow, veteran New York *Times* political reporter and writer on New York politics, observed shortly after the new administration took office that it was an accepted fact that in matters of policy Robert Moses had emerged as "the strong man" of the O'Dwyer administration. "Mr. Moses," wrote Moscow, "nominally a Republican, is thus viewed as enjoying greater prestige in the O'Dwyer administration than he ever enjoyed in his long and varied political career."

The evidence to support such an inference was impressive: (1) Moses' right-hand man and frequent personal representative was named deputy mayor; (2) Moses was made chairman of the City Emergency Housing Committee, a key post at a time when housing was a major problem and an important political issue, and was permitted, virtually, to name almost all the other members; (3) the Mayor adopted, against a good deal of opposition, Commissioner Moses' plan to double the City sales tax in order to pay for rehabilitating the subways; (4) the Mayor moved to merge legally the Triborough Bridge and City Tunnel Authorities, with Moses to head the consolidated organization; (5) the Mayor accepted the Moses recommendations that a central market project be financed and operated by an independent authority, not by the City; (6) the Mayor also accepted a similar recommendation by Moses for the construction and operation of the Idlewild airport. Indeed, some months later, the *Christian Science Monitor*, in an interview with Moses, quoted him as describing O'Dwyer as "the big prize" in the power struggle between the political left and right in New York and as declaring he believed the conservatives, with whom he outspokenly aligned himself, had won that prize. There is no doubt that during this period Commissioner Moses wielded what was even for him extraordinary power in the new Mayor's administration, notwithstanding the fact that he was neither an elected official nor a member of the party in power. He had become the personification of the powerful administrator.

INCEPTION OF THE NEW YORK CITY AIRPORT AUTHORITY

As we have seen, it was Moses who was primarily responsible for the cut in the capital budget outlay for the Idlewild field made by the City Council on December 27, 1945. The next day, Mayor LaGuardia responded with characteristic vigor. He charged that the Council action threatened five years of his labor on the airport, jeopardized the City's air supremacy, and nullified the existing contracts with the airlines and the oil companies. Though he had only four more days in office, he offered to call a special meeting of the Board of Estimate and the City Council to restore the cuts if Mayor-elect O'Dwyer, who had announced his approval of the budget slash, would support the restoration of the funds. He reported that he had spoken to O'Dwyer on the subject and had also asked Grover Whalen, chairman of the City's official reception committee, to tell O'Dwyer that the whole airport project had been endangered. "Don't do it, Bill," pleaded LaGuardia over the air, "don't do it." The action of the City Council frustrated his long efforts, he declared, and had been taken anyway "by people who didn't know anything about it." Later, on meeting the chairman of the Council finance committee in the hall, he remarked, "You don't know what you've done to your city."

The Mayor-elect refused to take his predecessor's advice. Instead, he backed wholeheartedly the formula urged by Moses:

> The evidence shows that the city already is obligated for about $70,000,000 for basic improvements. I do not know of any reason why the rest of the financing cannot be done by a public authority, as suggested by Commissioner Moses, who has been a loyal friend and supporter of the Mayor. We simply can't put another $130,000,000 of the city's diminishing balance of capital funds into this one project in the face of all the other needs of the city.

"I am certain—in fact I know—that Mayor-elect O'Dwyer did not write that statement," LaGuardia replied. "In fact, I don't know whether he ever saw it. I recognize the . . . hand of Oberbuergermeister Moses. He is all wrong." But when LaGuardia left office, his energies taken up by other heavy duties and drained by illness, he knew the fight to have the program run as he had envisioned it was lost. From then on, he was able to do little on this score but make public statements criticizing the administration.

On assuming office, Mayor O'Dwyer at once recognized that the traditional administrative pattern had to be abandoned in favor of a new one: In his estimation, City administration, whether through the Department of Marine and Aviation or otherwise, would not suffice to meet the demands of the Air Age without involving the City in a difficult or even insoluble fiscal dilemma. He turned, therefore, to the device of the independent authority in an effort to find a financial and administrative mechanism, suited to progress in aviation, that would relieve the City of a dangerous charge on its allowable debt.

Clearly the moving force in the situation was the impact of the financial burden of the project. Former Comptroller McGoldrick insisted repeatedly that the airport would shortly have been self-supporting under the terms set down in the leases he had signed, and LaGuardia backed him on this. On the other hand, as we have seen, there was good and increasing reason to believe that the leases were excessively favorable to the lessees; consequently, there were substantial grounds for the apprehension that the self-supporting features of the airport plan might break down and throw back as a charge on the debt limit of the City the huge borrowings to finance the airfield. This would have been seriously embarrassing to the incoming Mayor, who was already faced with a tremendous construction problem with respect to streets, schools, hospitals, and other municipal functions, which were not self-liquidating and for which the uncommitted balance of the allowable debt had to be reserved. The construction of these facilities had been deferred during the war; the accumulated cost and heavy demands that they be provided quickly were necessarily uppermost in his mind. Even the *possibility* that the cost of the airfield might cut into this program was alarming; indeed, just the prospect of further City outlays for a project that might not become partially or wholly self-supporting until some time in the indefinite future was discouraging. All other things aside, this was a compelling consideration in bringing Mayor O'Dwyer behind the Moses proposal.

As for Commissioner Moses himself, later events tended to demonstrate that he was convinced the airport could not be made self-liquidating under the original leases. It is perhaps also relevant to recall that Moses over the years had become a key figure in various independent State and City authorities, and that in 1946 four City authorities were about to be consolidated in the Triborough Bridge Authority of which Moses was chairman and executive officer. Further, as the reader will observe, Moses had every reason to expect that he would have at least a hand in guiding the destinies of the City Airport Authority. In any event, for various reasons he was a long-time proponent of independent authorities for self-liquidating projects.

Consequently, before he had been in office a week, Mayor O'Dwyer took the first steps toward establishing a City Airport Authority with power to take over LaGuardia Field and to borrow money in order to finance the construction and operation of the field at Idlewild and all City airfields that might be required in the future. On January 5, 1946, he sent to State Comptroller Frank C. Moore, at Albany, a letter urging him to use his good offices to persuade the Governor and the Legislature to authorize, among other things, the creation of such an authority, as well as a consolidated Triborough Bridge and Tunnel Authority and a West Side market authority. Thomas G. Corcoran, former adviser to President Roosevelt, was named by the Mayor to represent the City in its efforts to secure passage of the necessary legislation, and Commissioner Moses spent a good deal of his time in Albany using his influence.

ENACTMENT OF ENABLING LEGISLATION

The Airport Authority bills were introduced in the Senate and Assembly at Albany on January 28, 1946. They touched off a controversy.

The Citizens Union, an independent civic organization that has for many years been engaged in municipal research in New York as an impartial, non-political organization, sent the Mayor a letter over the signature of its chairman, Richard S. Childs, attacking the City Airport Authority plan and urging that responsibility for the construction and operation of the City's airports be vested in the Port of New York Authority. Its arguments centered on the financial aspects of the problem and on the regional powers of the Port Authority. On the financial side, the Citizens Union argued that the City Airport Authority, lacking reserves, other sources of income, and taxing power, would have to pay a higher interest rate than either the City or the Port Authority for borrowing, a circumstance which would make the whole project unnecessarily costly. It also attacked what it described as giving away to the Airport Authority, without compensation, the $100,000,000 already invested by the City in its two fields. On the jurisdictional side, the Union noted that the Port Authority had power both in New York and New Jersey and was therefore in a position to develop the airports in the metropolitan area on a regional basis, building a system that might include Newark, N. J., and Westchester County (N. Y.) as well as the City proper.

Mayor O'Dwyer replied firmly a few days later that he was "astonished" at the Citizens Union's proposals. He rejected the idea of resorting to the Port of New York Authority because he doubted that the people of New York City favored "an abject surrender of the city's planning powers" to an agency subject only to the veto of the Governors of New York and New Jersey. He argued also that no regional authority was needed because the United States Civil Aeronautics Administration was available to co-ordinate the regional growth of airports; that undertaking such a huge enterprise would prevent the Port Authority from reducing its "exorbitant" tolls on bridges and tunnels because the bankers would accept Port Authority airport bonds only with the assurance that the other tolls would remain as they were; and that the City was giving nothing away because the airports and all improvements were to be returned to the City as soon as the indebtedness had been cleared up by the Airport Authority. There was no doubt that the Mayor stood firmly behind the agency whose creation he was seeking.

The legislation ran into more difficulty. The airlines were emphatically opposed to the projected agency. Their reasons were twofold: First, they feared the Airport Authority might have difficulty in financing a field on the scale they expected air commerce in the New York area to require, and they were so hard pressed at the badly overloaded LaGuardia Field that they did not want to run the risk of having construction bog down in financial mire or be reduced in size to a point where it would be inadequate to accommodate the growth of aviation. Secondly, they already had very favorable contracts with the City and they saw signs that the Airport Authority, under the influence of Moses, would insist on setting new terms.

LaGuardia also let loose another blast at the Airport Authority. He called the pending enabling legislation a "money changers' bill" and declared that LaGuardia Field and the previous investments at Idlewild by the City were to be given the new agency in order to "sweeten up" its bonds.

With strong criticism from the Citizens Union and the airlines, and the public accusations by LaGuardia, it is not surprising that opposition developed in the Legislature. The bill was subject to detailed scrutiny by the legislators; specific sections came under attack and were changed. The maximum allowable interest rate on the Airport Authority bonds was reduced from 5 per cent to 3½ per cent. The Authority was forbidden to sell bonds at below par so that not only the maximum *rate* of interest but the maximum yield could not exceed 3½ per cent. A clause that would have barred new airport construction by any public body (including the Airport Authority itself) in the City for 40 years, so as to prevent the growth of competing facilities over the life of the bonds, and thus make the bonds more attractive to investors, was stricken from the bill. In other words, the expenditure of public funds for airports in the City was authorized, provided the fields were built by the Airport Authority, or if the Authority bonds were in default for three years.

Despite all these concessions, the bill faced an uphill fight. It was not passed by the beginning of March, when the City Council adopted a resolution supporting it. It still was not passed by the middle of March, when Mayor O'Dwyer submitted a letter urging action by the legislative leaders. Even then its fate hung in the balance.

The legislative division was almost entirely among the Republican majorities in each house. Some were sufficiently impressed with the contentions of the bill's critics to want to put an outright end to it. Others, however, saw the issue as a straight home-rule problem and objected to taking the decision out of the City's hands; furthermore, they feared that killing the measure might endanger the development of the City's airports. The differences between the factions were considerable and, despite overwhelming endorsement of the bill by the Democrats, action was delayed.

In the latter part of March, activities of interested parties grew still more vigorous. Former Comptroller McGoldrick was called in by the Assembly Ways and Means Committee for consultation. The airlines retained Charles H. Tuttle, prominent New York attorney and one time Republican candidate for governor, to present their side of the matter to the Governor and legislative leaders. Commissioner Moses conferred with the chairmen of the Ways and Means Committee and the Senate Finance Committee, these being the leaders of the forces opposing passage of the measure, and succeeded in working out a compromise with them. Moses also visited Governor Dewey to urge his support for the bill, but the Governor maintained a "hands-off" policy, advising legislative leaders that he would accept whatever decision they reached. The airlines issued a joint statement to the press in which they attacked the pending legislation, criticized the City administration for failing to declare the original leases valid, and denounced the remark of a City official (clearly Commissioner Moses) who stated that the City intended to treat the leases as invalid; informally, they threatened to move to Newark if the terms of the leases were revised upwards.

The bill was reported out by the Senate Rules Committee on March 21; "this was not done," commented the New York *Times*, "with any great enthusiasm." On March 25, after Corcoran for the City and Tuttle for the airlines spent the entire day conferring with the leaders in the Senate, the bill was passed by a vote of 39 to 14. The following day, it went through the Assembly, together with a supplementary amendatory bill later approved by the Senate, by a vote of 115 to 28. All of the dissenting Senators were Republicans, the 19 Democrats in that chamber voting unanimously for it. The opposing Republicans in the Assembly numbered 25, with two Democrats and one American Laborite joining them. The division was thus confined almost entirely to the Republican side of the Legislature; it did not show any close conformity to geographical patterns, the opposition containing a number of New York City representatives, upstate urban representatives, and upstate rural representatives.

On April 1, George H. Hallett, secretary of the Citizens Union, urged the Governor to veto the Airport Authority bills because they would rule out regional development of airports in the metropolitan area, "sweeten" the Airport Authority bonds with $100,000,000 of taxpayer's bonds while depriving the City of the revenues with which to repay its bonds, and result in a boycott of the airfield by the airlines. Nevertheless, Governor Dewey signed the bill into law on April 1, basing his decision largely on the question of home rule. In a memorandum accompanying the signed bill, he explained:

> The original legislative proposals have been substantially changed. The main bill has gone through four different amendatory printings. There is still controversy concerning its terms and many of its provisions may give the City of New York new difficulties in the future.
>
> The ultimate question presented to me, by these bills, however, is whether the city shall be authorized to complete Idlewild Airport in the only way its duly elected representatives say it can be done. Obviously, the airport is essential for the growth and development of the City of New York. The city administration is entitled to the opportunity to complete the airport in the manner which it considers the only one available. Despite the well-grounded criticism of some aspects of these bills, therefore, I am constrained to approve them.

The enactment of the legislation was thus accompanied by serious doubts and misgivings. It is clear that only the insistence of Mayor O'Dwyer, or, perhaps more accurately, of Commissioner Moses, through Mayor O'Dwyer and directly as well, brought the measure through its stormy course.

THE CITY AIRPORT AUTHORITY IS ESTABLISHED

With the passage of the enabling legislation, the City Airport Authority became the focus for the airport controversies. From the beginning of April to the middle of July, all the substantive decisions about the airports were far more consequential for their impact on the Authority and its ability to take charge of the program than for their effect on the program as such. In recounting the events of these three and a half months, therefore, the actions of the Mayor and Commissioner Moses are seen in large part as they appeared to the members of the Authority, particularly to its chairman.

The New York City Airport Authority was headed by a three-man, non-salaried board appointed by the Mayor and removable by him for misconduct, inefficiency, or neglect of duties. The members were to hold office for six years, their terms overlapping so that the term of one of them would expire every two years. The Airport Authority was empowered to issue up to $250,000,000 in bonds for airport purposes, and the maximum permissible yield from those bonds was fixed at 3½ per cent. The bonds were to be free of State taxes and were to mature in not more than 40 years. The State pledged to the future bondholders not to limit or alter the rights vested in the Authority until the bonds and all other obligations to the bondholders had been fully met and discharged; however, the City and State were expressly absolved of any liability on the bonds. The Airport Authority was granted the exclusive right to build public airports in New York City as long as it had bonds outstanding and was not in default.

The purpose of the Authority was declared to be "to construct, operate and maintain one or more airports in the city." To carry out this purpose, it was given a broad grant of power, to wit:

1. To sue and be sued;
2. To have a seal and alter the same at pleasure;
3. To acquire, hold and dispose of personal property for its corporate purposes, including the power to purchase prospective or tentative awards in connection with the condemnation of real property;
4. To acquire in the name of the city by purchase or condemnation and use real property necessary or convenient for its corporate purposes. All real property acquired by the authority by condemnation shall be acquired in the manner provided in the condemnation law . . . ;
5. To make by-laws for the management and regulation of its affairs, and, subject to agreements with bondholders, for the regulation of the project;
6. With the consent of the city to use agents, employees and facilities of the city, including the corporation counsel, paying to the city its agreed proportion of the compensation or costs;
7. To appoint officers, agents and employees, to prescribe their qualifications and to fix their compensation; subject, however, to the provisions of the civil service law, as hereinafter provided [permitting transfer of city personnel to the Authority with full protection of all their civil service rights and status];
8. To make contracts and leases, and to execute all instruments necessary or convenient;
9. To construct such buildings, structures and facilities as may be necessary or convenient;
10. To reconstruct, improve, maintain and operate the projects;
11. To accept grants, loans or contributions from the United States, the state of New York, or any agency or instrumentality of either of them, or the city, and to expend the proceeds for any corporate purposes;
12. To fix and collect rentals, fees and other charges for the use of the projects subject to and in accordance with such agreements with bondholders as may be made as hereinafter provided;
13. To construct, operate or maintain in the projects landing fields, shops, passenger stations, control towers, and all facilities necessary or convenient in connection with an airport; to contract for the construction, operation or maintenance of any parts thereof or for services to be performed; to rent parts thereof, and grant concessions; all on such terms and conditions as it may determine.

The Mayor wanted members who could do the job and who would not invite, or even be vulnerable to, attack on partisan grounds. Commissioner Moses put forward the name of Laurance S. Rockefeller, who, though young and thus relatively inexperienced, had had an interest in air transportation; he was a public-spirited citizen and well respected. A second appointee, chosen by Mayor O'Dwyer, was Harry F. Guggenheim, whose reputation was excellent, whose experience in matters of high finance fitted him admirably for the financial burdens of the job, and whose interest in and activities on behalf of aviation reached back more than two decades. Guggenheim had, as a matter of fact, been one of the members of the Fact-Finding Committee selected by Secretary of Commerce Hoover to choose a site for an airport in the New York area in 1927, had for many years administered the Guggenheim Fund for the Advancement of Aviation, and had served as a Naval aviator in two World Wars.

Moses was enthusiastic about the proposed appointment and strongly urged Guggenheim to accept the offer. Guggenheim saw a chance to help the city and aviation as a whole. He therefore told the Mayor that he would take the position, but only under certain conditions. One, agreed to informally by Mayor O'Dwyer, was that General James H. Doolittle was to be the third member of the body. The choice, as a matter of fact, apparently delighted O'Dwyer, for Doolittle seemed to meet the requirements of the job in every respect, since he was a highly successful executive and well versed in aviation problems. Guggenheim was pleased to find his nominee so well received because he and Doolittle were old friends; he wanted someone on the board whose objectives and outlook were close to his own and he knew that Doolittle, in addition to his other outstanding qualifications, would fill this bill. (Moses did not oppose the Doolittle appointment, yet he showed no enthusiasm for it.) Thus the membership of the Airport Authority was established.

A second series of conditions Guggenheim insisted upon was set down in a memorandum signed by the Mayor. The most important of these in the light of subsequent developments was the agreement on the part of the Mayor to spend as much of the funds already appropriated for the Idlewild airport in the 1946 capital budget as the Airport Authority thought necessary. A first draft of the agreement, drawn up by Commissioner Moses for the Mayor, would have vested in the Board of Estimate (of which the Mayor, of course, is a member holding three votes) the discretion to reduce these funds if it so desired:

The understanding with the members of the Authority is that the Mayor will recommend to the Board of Estimate so much of the appropriation in this year's capital budget for Idlewild as will prove to be required in order that the Authority may be able to issue its own bonds to the extent needed to make the airport usable.

But Guggenheim would have none of this. If there was any power to make such reductions in appropriations, he felt it must be lodged in the Authority itself in order to protect the agency's financial position. He therefore prepared an amendment of this provision, placing the discretion in the hands of the Authority; the understanding, as signed by the Mayor, read:

The understanding with the members of the Authority is that I will recommend to the Board of Estimate so much of the appropriation in this year's capital budget for Idlewild *as the Authority will find necessary* in order to issue its own bonds to the extent needed to make the airport usable. [Italics supplied]

The stipulation was crystal clear. It did not give the Airport Authority power to require any additional outlay by the City, but it constituted a definite commitment by the chief executive to fight any reduction in the funds made available in the current capital budget without Authority concurrence. Another section called for turning LaGuardia Airport and the Idlewild field over to the Authority on or about October 1. On these terms, Guggenheim accepted the post.

On April 6, Guggenheim, Doolittle, and Rockefeller were sworn into office, the first as chairman and appointed for six years, the next as vice chairman and appointed for four years, with Rockefeller appointed for two years. So the New York City Airport Authority was launched, and it was sped on its way a few days later by a report to the Mayor from his Department of Investigation urging an end to continual changes in design that were slowing the completion of the Idlewild field.

THE APPROPRIATION IS REDUCED

Within ten days, the Authority ran afoul of Commissioner Moses. Just as Moses had earlier been the sponsor of the Airport Authority, so he now showed equal determination to guide its course—or so it seemed to Guggenheim and to a variety of interested observers. However, Guggenheim, in accepting the job, intended from the outset to manage it as he thought it should be managed. As the head of an independent agency, he would not submit to direction from any outside source. The difficulty that arose was partly one of personality, partly of overlapping authority and jurisdiction. Moses had shown, over the years, that he too was not a man to be thwarted easily; beyond that, his position as City Construction Co-ordinator imposed on him the obligation to take a hand in the airport construction question and at the same time conferred on him broad administrative powers with which to support his contentions. The post had been created in the very first local law enacted under the O'Dwyer administration in order to "expedite and accelerate the completion of plans, land acquisition, site clearance and construction for the City's official postwar program of public works so that urgently needed and desirable improvements . . . may be made available without delay and in order to provide prompt employment for discharged veterans and war workers. . . ." To accomplish these ends,

The mayor is hereby authorized and empowered to appoint and at pleasure remove a co-ordinator of the postwar construction program of the city, to be known as the city construction co-ordinator. Such co-ordinator shall schedule and, upon approval of projects by the mayor and governing bodies of the city, shall expedite the work of all agencies of the city and shall represent the city in its relations with co-operating state and federal agencies engaged in the postwar public works program. He shall investigate the prices of basic building materials, and labor and contract conditions in the local market with a view to bringing about agreements on reasonable terms and to the removal of obstacles in the way of construction. He shall have the duty and function of accelerating said program so as to create the maximum amount of local employment, and shall currently present to the mayor, the board of estimate, the city council, and other proper city officials, and also to the agencies of the state and federal governments concerned, reports on the progress of all plans and projects included in such postwar program. He shall also have such other powers and duties in relation to the postwar public works program as may be lawfully assigned to him by the mayor. . . . Such co-ordinator shall, when authorized by the mayor, have the power to use facilities and personnel of other departments and agencies under the control of the mayor to carry out the purposes of this section.

To Moses, therefore, fell a good deal of the responsibility for balancing the municipal finances among relative urgencies of schools, hospitals, highways, airports, and other construction projects needed by the City, and for getting prompt action on them. And to him, also, was granted the power to perform his broad mission, a power he used promptly and frequently.

Before the Airport Commissioners had been in office for two weeks, Moses recommended a cut of $15,000,000 from the amount the City had already appropriated for the field at Idlewild and which the Mayor had just agreed not to reduce without the concurrence of the Airport Authority. His purpose was to release those funds for other municipal construction requirements by throwing the additional burden on the Authority. Chairman Guggenheim objected strongly; he regarded the proposed action as a breach of his agreement with the Mayor, for the Authority had not had time to get any studies under way and therefore was not prepared to approve any reduction of any size. Furthermore, under the terms of the Authority's enabling legislation, all obligations of the City with respect to its airports would become obligations of the Authority when it assumed control, and Guggenheim did not want to find himself committed to build facilities for which the City had contracted but was now withdrawing its pledged support. Finally, he feared that such a move might impair the Authority's obligation under the enabling act "to maintain its [the City's] appropriate tradition of leadership in air commerce." The Mayor assured him that Moses' recommendation was nothing more than a proposal. "This represents," he wrote, "Commissioner Moses' opinion. . . . Obviously, Commissioner Moses' opinion does not change our understanding. . . ." Nevertheless, he warned:

> If you can finance a sufficient bond issue to provide for the $15,000,000 suggested by Commissioner Moses, it is your duty to do so. . . . On reflection, you and your associates will undoubtedly agree that this recommendation places no added burden upon you. It only asks that you attempt to save as much as possible of the City's Capital Budget for other essential City uses, and that you meet as much as possible of this expense through your bond issue. This is not a burden but an obligation. If you cannot function without the entire amount in the present Capital Budget, you will have to have it and I shall help you get it as previously indicated. . . . I must depend on the City Construction Co-ordinator to guide this program. . . .

Moses continued to press home his views, and by the end of May the members of the Airport Authority knew that his views had prevailed. This was confirmed on June 27, when the Board of Estimate, despite the Mayor's assurances to Guggenheim, did officially reduce the capital budget allowance for the work on the airfield by the amount recommended by the Construction Co-ordinator. The vote was unanimous, the Mayor voting for the reduction along with all the other members of the Board. Guggenheim was ready to resign after this failure to observe the terms of the agreement under which he came to office; the City, he felt, had not merely neglected to take required steps to live up to those terms but had actually taken a deliberate affirmative step to violate them. Breaking a written pledge by *failing* to do what was promised would have been irritating enough, but the breach of the agreement in this instance was infinitely more disturbing because it resulted from a *positive* action. Only Mayor

O'Dwyer's earnest pleas persuaded Guggenheim to remain.

OTHER DIFFICULTIES

Meanwhile, the Airport Authority suffered other setbacks as it tried to lay the groundwork for assuming its responsibilities. Anxious to commence operations on an independent footing as soon as possible, but lacking tangible assets on which to undertake financing, its members decided in the middle of May to ask the Mayor to turn over LaGuardia Field on July 1, three months earlier than the date set in the agreement between O'Dwyer and Guggenheim, with the field at Idlewild to follow when the City completed the basic work pledged. Concurrence by the Mayor would have been a convincing demonstration of his faith in the Authority and of his determination to make it work; and the Authority might have become a going concern. Rejection of the request, despite the fact that O'Dwyer would be entirely within his rights under the agreement, would indicate a lack of confidence and lagging support that would not help the new agency establish its position as an operating organization with an income of its own. Nevertheless, apparently accepting Moses' advice, O'Dwyer did reject the request and thereby weakened the Authority's position and struck a blow (perhaps unintentional on his part, but serious all the same) at its leaders.

In the same period, the Airport Authority prepared to make the studies it needed to draw up its program. Having no resources of its own, it submitted a request to the Mayor for a loan of just under $64,000 from the City. O'Dwyer delegated responsibility for passing on this to Moses, who then advised the members of the agency that he thought the figure too high and was recommending a loan of only $40,000. (Indeed, at one stage Moses argued that the Authority needed no staff at all because the consultants hired by the City were available.) The lesser sum was all they received. By itself, this was a minor matter; Guggenheim and Doolittle were much too upset over the cut in the capital budget to attach much weight to it, but it had symbolic significance that was not overlooked and may well have been intended.

The Authority was subject to yet another shock when, after it met with the airlines in the latter part of May to discuss problems of planning and of air traffic with respect to the airports, it found the companies concerned over the future of the leases they had signed with the City less than six months before. The Authority decided that the question of the validity of those leases would have to be passed on by the Corporation Counsel of the City, not by the Authority; the Authority, the airlines and the City were told, would assume that the leases were valid unless otherwise advised. The Mayor responded on June 26 by appointing a committee of city officials headed by Moses and comprising the Commissioner of Marine and Aviation, Frederick G. Reinicke; the City Comptroller, Lazarus Joseph; the Corporation Counsel, John J. Bennett; the Budget Director, Thomas J. Patterson; and the Deputy Transportation Commissioner, William Reid, to conduct the negotiations with the signatory air transport and oil companies. Moses called the first meeting for July 9, and the Authority members were invited to attend. General Doolittle, being an executive in one of the oil companies involved, offered in a private letter to the Mayor to step aside temporarily during these negotiations or to resign if O'Dwyer preferred. The Mayor accepted the resignation; the first Doolittle and Guggenheim knew of his action was when they read of it in the papers on July 8. In a move that came to the two men with stunning suddenness, the Mayor had taken the more drastic alternative opened by Doolittle and had released his decision to the press before he communicated it to the Airport Authority member. Commissioner Reinicke was appointed to the Authority to replace Doolittle.

In addition, during the same period, Moses proposed that the Airport Authority issue $60,000,000 in bonds to complete the airport at Idlewild and itemized how these funds should be spent. He went on to advise the Commissioner of Marine and Aviation how the Authority was going to use these bonds, and explained in detail how the money would be spent, while issuing instructions to him on how to proceed with construction using the city funds still available for basic work. Going still further, he even set up a schedule for the issuance of the bonds and for the other financial details and declared that it would govern the Authority's work. Late in June, the Mayor set the sum proposed by the Construction Coordinator as the amount the Airport Authority would seek in its first bond issue, and he adopted the Moses schedule for operations and financing. Chairman Guggenheim protested vigorously that the bond issues must be based on facts and figures, not on arbitrary decisions; the Airport Authority itself had not yet completed any surveys and even the study authorized by the Board of Estimate several months earlier was not yet complete; he thought, therefore, that there was no justification for the amount set. Nevertheless, the Mayor stood firm. Ultimately, one of the studies by the Airport Authority's technical consultants, which showed that the facilities at LaGuardia Field were in a state of disrepair, and were overcrowded and unsanitary, indicated that there were factors besides new construction at Idlewild that had to be considered in arriving at a financial decision. This indication confirmed Guggenheim's contention. But the proof came too late; Moses' figure stood.

Finally, when Guggenheim, representing the Airport Authority, sat in on the hearings between the committee appointed by the Mayor to represent the City and the committee representing the airlines as they met in the office of Commissioner Moses, a sharp disagreement arose between these two officials over what the role of the Airport Authority ought to be in such negotiations. Moses wanted Guggenheim to be an aggressive partisan on behalf of the City; in his mind, this meant denouncing the leases as invalid and insisting on beginning negotiations all over again. Guggenheim, on the other hand, felt that since the Authority did not actually have any of the airports yet, this was a matter entirely between the City and the airlines; he was willing to play the role of "honest broker," but he refused to join Moses in the repudiation of a signed agreement and in an ultimatum to the companies. It was not surprising, therefore, that the New York *Times* observed in an article shortly thereafter, "Mayor O'Dwyer's special committee headed by Mr. Moses has already in some degree superseded the functions of the Authority." Nor was it surprising, after this series of rebuffs at the hands of Moses and O'Dwyer, that Chairman Guggenheim would no longer be persuaded by the Mayor to remain in office; on July 18, as negotiations between the Moses committee and the airlines were in full swing, he tendered his resignation and advised Mayor O'Dwyer "to get the airports out of politics and turn them over to the Port of New York Authority." It was just slightly over three months since he had been appointed.

The two remaining members of the Authority were Rockefeller, Moses' nominee, and Commissioner Reinicke of the Department of Marine and Aviation, who took little part in the affairs of the new organization. Moses had disagreed with Guggenheim and Doolittle; now they were gone.

The Guggenheim resignation marked the end of a most unusual chain of events. The Chairman and Vice Chairman of the Airport Authority had demonstrated that they took seriously the responsibilities of their positions and embarked on their duties with zeal. It was clear that they were dedicated to the job to be done and equally clear that they intended to make up their own minds on what should be done. At the same time it was clear that Commissioner Moses, who had originally sponsored the Authority, favored different policies and intended to have them carried out. It was to Moses, moreover, that the Mayor looked for advice. As a result, the Authority felt that the agreement on which it had relied was not being carried out and that where it had expected help it was receiving none. Under the circumstances, Guggenheim's resignation was well-nigh inevitable. A series of decisions reached by the Mayor virtually without consultation with the Authority and obviously on the advice of Moses, thus cost the City the services of the Authority's best known and most experienced members. As will be seen, these decisions were also the beginning of a chain of events that led to the demise of the Authority; that Guggenheim and Doolittle could have averted this ultimate event is at least uncertain.

THE AIRPORT QUESTION REOPENED

Moses' opponents had disappeared from the scene, but the vehicle Moses was instrumental in creating to build and operate the Idlewild field, while now more firmly under his control than ever, had lost momentum. In gaining control, Moses had in effect discredited the Authority; and the assurance of Moses' control was coincident with the beginnings of a course of action by the Mayor in which Moses' advice was no longer accepted as definitive. Reports began to circulate that the Mayor was growing cool toward the Airport Authority; some sources insisted that he would scrap the whole thing and that the City itself would do the job if that were necessary to get the Idlewild airport open by November. O'Dwyer tended to confirm the rumors that gained currency by failing to appoint a successor to Guggenheim, whose resignation had shocked him; the Authority continued with only two members for the rest of its existence. Then, on July 22, at a meeting of the Board of Estimate, the Mayor served notice that City construction and operation, an administrative technique he had so firmly rejected when he first took office, was being reconsidered.

At the meeting the Mayor laid down a three-step procedure for completion of the field: First, the matter of size would be settled once and for all. Second, on the basis of the size decided upon, the question of whether the City or the Airport Authority should finance the work would be disposed of. Third, the contracts would be renegotiated to produce more revenue. John C. Riedel, Chief Engineer of the Board of Estimate, was appointed to make a study and report on possible reduction of the size and cost of the airport. Meanwhile, work under funds previously appropriated for the field continued under the administration of the Department of Marine and Aviation. Newspapers saw in these developments a clash between the Mayor and Commissioner Moses, but neither official would comment; it was obvious, however, that in this matter O'Dwyer was acting on his own.

The decline of Moses' influence in the administration with respect to airports was underscored a short time later. Suggestions that the Port of New York Authority be called in to complete the field at Idlewild, take over LaGuardia Field, and be empowered and required to construct and operate all additional fields in the City began to circulate persistently at the time the Port Authority prepared to submit to the City of Newark a study it had made of Newark Airport and Seaport at the request of that municipality. The Port Authority had earlier been recommended to Mayor O'Dwyer by the Citizens Union, but he had rejected it in no uncertain terms. Then Guggenheim had also advised in favor of it, to no avail. When the issue arose again, Moses made a strong statement to the press ridiculing the plan; he demanded that the Port Authority, if it had reserves large enough to undertake a venture of this kind, apply its reserves to reduction of its tolls, and that it go back to work on the original plan it had been created to carry out. This time, however, he found no support from the Mayor. On the contrary, two weeks after Guggenheim's resignation, Mayor O'Dwyer *asked* the Port Authority to make a study of New York City's airports with a view toward submitting a plan for taking them over.

THE PORT OF NEW YORK AUTHORITY

The Port of New York Authority is a corporate municipal instrumentality created in 1921 by a compact executed by the States of New York and New Jersey and approved by Congress. It was created in an effort to end useless competition, conflict, and waste fostered by two political units whose common boundary divided the single economic unit that is the Port of New York. The problem seemed especially acute with respect to railroads, each of them operating its own facilities and duplicating the operations of the others, and each of them maintaining its own piers from which to lighter and float freight across the Hudson River. The congestion grew to alarming proportions, and substantial parts of the waterfront on both sides of the river that should have been devoted to world shipping were taken up by the railroads. As early as 1911, New York and New Jersey appointed commissions to investigate the harbor, but, instead of co-operating, they joined the competitive forces of their respective states. The States made individual efforts, but they were not successful in improving the situation. In 1917, the Interstate Commerce Commission, holding that the entire port was one area and urging the parties involved to recognize that economic fact, rejected a New Jersey application asking for rates lower than New York, based on the argument that shipments destined for the west side of the Hudson should not have to pay as much as those lightered or floated over to the New York side. That year, the states again appointed commissions, and this time they worked together, even organizing as a single body. This body, the New York, New Jersey Port and Harbor Development Commission, drew up a draft of the interstate compact, submitted a monumental report on the commerce of the port area, and conceived a Comprehensive Plan to be carried out by the proposed Port Authority. The Compact was adopted in slightly amended form by both States in 1921, over the opposition of New York City, jealous of its powers in the area, and over the veto of the Governor of New Jersey, and was approved by Congress shortly afterward. In 1922, the Comprehensive Plan also became part of the agreement between those States.

One of the most conspicuous features of the Port Authority is its lack of compulsive powers. It has no power to levy taxes or assessments. It has no power to issue orders binding upon persons or property or other governmental jurisdictions. Yet, thus unarmed, it has broad responsibility for developing the "terminal, transportation and other facilities" in the Port District, an area embracing roughly all the territory lying within a twenty-mile radius of the Statue of Liberty. And the meaning of this responsibility was given the broadest possible definition.

"Transportation facility" shall include railroads steam or electric, motor truck or other street or highway vehicles, tunnels, bridges, boats, ferries, carfloats, lighters, tugs, floating elevators, barges, scows or harbor craft of any kind, air craft suitable for harbor service, and every kind of transportation facility now in use or hereafter designed for use for the transportation or carriage of persons or property. "Terminal facility" shall include wharves, piers, slips, ferries, docks, dry docks, bulkheads, dock-walls, basins, carfloats, float-bridges, grain or other storage elevators, warehouses, cold storage, tracks, yards, sheds, switches, connections, overhead appliances, and every kind of terminal facility now in use or hereafter designed for use for the handling, storage, loading or unloading of freight at steamship, railroad or freight terminals.

It is no wonder that the Port Authority struggled unsuccessfully with its program all during its early years. Erwin Wilkie Bard, in his study of the organization, described its early history as one of "repeated failures." It tested its coercive powers both by trying to force the adoption of certain improvements and by trying to stop certain undertakings—all to naught. It tried in vain to win the co-operation of the railroads in accomplishing the rationalization of the port area's transportation system, but they were strongly imbued with the idea of privileged traffic areas, closely wedded to a system of concerted negotiation that gave each railroad a veto over any plan to which all the others agreed, and apparently unimpressed by the economic advantages of the program urged by the Port Authority. Nor did it get very far in its efforts to acquire for itself the facilities that would have helped it accomplish the introduction of order into the harbor and rail system of the port. The original program that the Port of New York Authority was established to administer—achievement of union beltline rights of way; joint yards and piers, joint carfloats, lighters, and other equipment; introduction of reciprocal switching and similar co-operative practices; and freeing the waterfront area of much of the railroad activity —all this has been accomplished only in very small part.

But if the fulfillment of the Comprehensive Plan was never realized, the Port Authority met with success as it turned into new channels for the discharge of its responsibilities. It embarked on a program of construction and operation of facilities too risky or costly for private enterprise which it could handle because of its tax exemption and freedom from the need to produce profits. Two bridges between Staten Island and New Jersey were opened to traffic in 1928, and a third in 1931; the tolls on these were to pay off the bonds sold to cover the construction costs. In 1931, the Authority acquired the Holland Tunnel, between Jersey City and Manhattan, formerly managed by a separate interstate commission. In the same year, it opened the George Washington Bridge between Manhattan and Fort Lee, New Jersey. The first Union Inland Freight Terminal was opened in Manhattan in 1932; here, less-than-carload freight for eight railroads is handled at one point, relieving shippers of the chore of delivering their shipments to eight different stations, reducing the number of trucks on the streets of the congested city, and transferring the loading activities from the waterfront to an inland location. Over the Freight Terminal is the fourteen-story headquarters of the agency, the Port Authority Commerce Building, which was made self-supporting by rental of most of its space to manufacturers, distributors, and exhibitors. In 1938, the first of the Lincoln Tunnel tubes connecting New Jersey with midtown Manhattan was opened, and the second was completed after the war. In 1944, the Port Authority took over a former New York State grain terminal and its piers at Gowanus Bay in Brooklyn and turned a losing proposition into a profitable venture. The New York Truck Terminal in lower Manhattan was put into operation in 1949, and the Newark Truck Terminal was opened in 1950. A huge union bus terminal, constructed and operated by the Authority, opened in Manhattan in 1951. The Port Authority also operated that part of New York Harbor known as Port Newark under an agreement with the municipality. And, finally, the Authority is now in airport operation as a result of circumstances we shall take up shortly.

Thus, the agency that had been created principally because of the railroad and waterfront problems in the Port District made little headway toward the solution of those problems, but it did expand successfully into many other types of transportation function. It financed itself every step of the way by borrowing, each new project strengthening its credit as that project became self-supporting, as all, or almost all, did. There is no doubt that the Port Compact furnished substantial grounds to justify this branching out. Nor is there any doubt that the Authority has promoted a regional approach to the metropolitan area. At the same time, the growth of the Port Authority over the last three decades into a $670,000,000 enterprise is as remarkable an administrative and sociological development as the rise of Moses' city-state park-parkway-highway-bridge-tunnel system, although there are very considerable differences between the two.

PORT AUTHORITY *vs.* MOSES

It seems almost inevitable that two administrative forces, both expanding rapidly over the same period of time, both operating in the same geographic area, and both engaged in similar types of construction undertakings should at some point have clashed. Indeed, it is somewhat surprising that the conflict did not break out until as late as 1945, but when it did, it was a grim and bitter battle. This battle was an important factor in the background of the airport controversy.

The first smoke of battle arose when Mayor LaGuardia asked the Port Authority to undertake a study of ways of reducing the number of buses on the streets of the city. Moses was then in favor of such a study, and he took steps to help the Authority get from Albany funds for the survey and authorization to build a union bus terminal west of Eighth Avenue, outside the principal area of congestion. Things had not progressed very far, however, when the Port Authority discovered that the Commissioner had very definite ideas on what was to be done and how to do it. In particular, Moses favored letting the Greyhound Bus Lines retain and enlarge its private terminal, which was east of Eighth Avenue and close to the Pennsylvania Station. The Port Authority considered this an impossible condition, for, it contended, under that circumstance its bonds for the union terminal would become unmarketable. No other bus company would want to move west of Eighth Avenue while Greyhound was permitted to remain in a much more strategic location from the point of view of capturing traffic, and no investor would have bought bonds in a bus terminal that would not attract tenants. Besides, the problem of congestion which the Port Authority had been asked to solve would then have remained almost as great as ever. The Port Authority notified Commissioner Moses that it could not do business on that basis; the study was discontinued, and the Port Authority refunded to the State of New York the unexpended balance of funds advanced for the study. The battle was revived when Mayor O'Dwyer asked the Port Authority to build the terminal and provided a written guarantee from the Board of Estimate that no terminal would be permitted east of Eighth Avenue; again Moses entered the arena, this time as City Construction Co-ordinator, and continued the fight to exempt Greyhound from the agreement. As late as 1950, this fight was still in progress. Since 1945, when the open struggle began, informed observers have regarded the former ties between the protagonists as broken, a fact to be borne in mind as we consider the disposition of New York City's airports. And it should also be borne in mind that the Port Authority, functioning on a regional, non-partisan, completely self-supporting basis, is in a peculiarly strong position to resist local pressures that might cow less independently established organizations.

THE PORT AUTHORITY AND AVIATION

The Port Authority's interest in aviation began long before the Mayor requested the study of the City's airports. It really commenced in 1927, when the Deputy Manager issued his report on an airport for the metropolitan district. However, there was nothing in that report to indicate that the Port Authority ever contemplated operating such a field, for, while it was definitely indicated that the possibility had then crossed the Deputy Manager's mind, the idea was emphatically dismissed with the observation: "It is highly improbable that the revenues from air transportation for some time to come will be sufficient to make a local airport self-sustaining." The agency could not undertake a proposition that was admittedly not self-liquidating since it had no means of financing it. (In practice, of course, all the Port Authority's revenues and reserves stand behind any new undertaking; it can thus carry deficits incurred on individual projects, but it is not in a position to undertake anything that does not promise to pay its own way.) Later in the same year a final stamp of approval was given to the disavowal of willingness and ability to provide the airport for the City when, as noted earlier, the Port Authority representative on the Fact-Finding Committee appointed by Secretary of Commerce Hoover affixed his signature to a report that declared the task could best be performed by the states or their political subdivisions rather than any interstate agency. For almost two decades, that was the end of the matter, the only contribution of the Port Authority to aviation being through the contributions of data by its staff to agencies interested in port development. Most of its energies were absorbed by the expansion of its program in other fields.

As World War II rushed aviation from its adolescence as a limited means of transport for a few of unlimited means, to maturity as a reliable method of mass movement, independent agencies like the Port Authority came to be concerned with the impact of the new means of transportation on the traditional pattern of traffic to which they had up to that time devoted the bulk of their attention and money.

The first reaction of the Port Authority came early in the war; its report for 1942 to the Governors of New York and New Jersey observed, "We suggest . . . that the Port of New York must meet the challenge of the revolution in transportation which has been accelerated by the war. . . . The Port of New York must plan now for the development of those facilities and the acquisition of those services which will make this port the crossroads of the world's airlanes, as well as the nation's principal gateway for water-borne commerce."

In 1943, the method by which the Port Authority intended to meet the challenge was clear. It created a Department of Port Development which launched into a port planning program on an intensive basis. "Study," commented the report for 1943, "is being made of the adequacy of present and proposed airports to serve the future air-borne commerce of the district. The results of these studies are already being utilized as a basis for support of applications for new and necessary airline services from the Port of New York." That is, the Port Authority served notice that it intended to help the airlines in every way to win permission from the Civil Aeronautics Board to fly routes through New York, just as it had always performed the same function with respect to railroad and shipping routes. And, still in keeping with the services it had performed traditionally, it added, "Because of the undoubted importance of air commerce in the future, it is essential not only that the district be provided with adequate airports, but also that efficient terminal methods be provided for the swift and ready interchange of cargo and passengers between air, rail, ship and motor-truck carriers. It is in this area of terminal handling of air commerce that we believe this agency is equipped to serve the air transport needs of the district." Obviously, it had in mind the creation of centers similar to the Union Inland Freight Terminal for the railroads. Having perceived the new challenge, the Port Authority prepared to meet it in much the same way it met the problems of water-, rail-, and motor-borne traffic. From the following year on, it intervened before the Civil Aeronautics Board more and more frequently and vigorously to secure new routes and protect old ones, just as it did before the Interstate Commerce Commission, thus fulfilling its duty under the compact to "intervene in any proceeding affecting the commerce of the port."

It was also drawn into a large-scale study of the airport needs of the metropolitan area. The Regional Plan Association, now a firmly established civic group that is still devoted to trying to persuade public officials to put into effect a flexible, constantly growing plan for the whole metropolitan region (including sections of Connecticut as well as New York and New Jersey), had been growing concerned over the fact that its 1929 aviation plan, foresighted as it had been, was becoming outdated. C. McKim Norton, the executive vice president of the Association, communicated with William A. M. Burden, an Assistant Secretary of Commerce in Washington and an old friend of Norton's, under whose jurisdiction fell the Civil Aeronautics Administration. The timing of the inquiry was fortunate, for Burden was looking for a group to prepare a Regional Airport Plan for the New York area to fit into the National Airport Plan being compiled by the C.A.A. The C.A.A., in turn, needed the material to provide a basis for a request for funds from Congress for the construction and improvement of airports over the entire nation, which ultimately resulted in the Federal Airport Act of 1946. Burden came to New York and made his request at a meeting of the Regional Plan Association attended by representatives of the Port Authority. The latter had been called in because their interest in such a project was obvious and because the resources and the excellent staff of the organization could provide invaluable assistance. The work got under way during 1944 under the leadership of Paul Windels, president of the Regional Plan Association, with the active participation of the Port Authority, the regional C.A.A. headquarters, 17 counties in the metropolitan area, the New York City Planning Commission and Airport Authority, and the State Aviation Commissioners of New York, New Jersey, and Connecticut.

Thus far, it is clear, the Port of New York Authority was doing nothing that it had not done before to protect the commerce of the port. It fought for routes through the district. It investigated the interrelationship of air terminals with sea and land terminals. It studied the broad needs of the whole area. None of the evidence indicates that the officials of the agency contemplated or even considered upsetting the customary pattern of municipal airport development by moving directly into airport construction or operation.

THE PORT AUTHORITY AND THE NEWARK AIRPORT

But pressures in that direction began to build up. They first came before the public in a report to the Central Planning Board of the City of Newark, submitted in October 1945 by the consulting engineering firm of Harland

Bartholomew and Associates. The Board, faced with the return of Newark Airport from the Air Forces, and also confronted with the obsolescence of its seaport and the demands for schools, hospitals, street improvements, and similar construction jobs deferred during the war, sought the advice of the firm. The prospect of huge investment in the airfield, added to the other capital outlays, was indeed formidable and especially so in the light of the loss of air traffic to LaGuardia Field six years before.

The Bartholomew report was emphatic in its recommendation that the task of rehabilitating the airport and seaport be turned over to the Port of New York Authority if the Authority were willing to take on the task and if a satisfactory arrangement between the City and the Authority could be reached. There is no doubt that the idea suggested itself to the Bartholomew firm when it found that some of the information it needed for its study could be obtained from the staff of the Port Authority. At the same time, the energetic, positive way the firm advocated turning to the Port Authority leaves no doubt that it needed no special urging to accept the wisdom of this course. Four other possible methods of managing the rehabilitation were considered carefully and all were judged less desirable and less advantageous to the City of Newark than administration by the Port Authority. The report noted the necessity for treating the whole port as a unit, the dangers of trying to compete with New York City, and, perhaps most important of all, the existence of an agency already functioning on a regional basis and possessed of an excellent record of accomplishment upon which the City could call very conveniently. "Certainly," Bartholomew concluded, "no other agency is in so favorable a position to secure maximum returns from the seaport and the airport." The Planning Board transmitted this report to the Newark Board of Commissioners. The Commissioners, in turn, on December 27, 1945, formally asked the Port Authority to undertake a study of the two facilities and submit a proposal for taking them over. The Authority agreed and thereby took its first step toward airport administration.

When Mayor O'Dwyer took office on New Year's Day of 1946, there was thus precedent, though it had been established only a few days earlier, for looking to the Port Authority as a possible solution to the airport problems of cities in the metropolitan region. We have already noticed that the Citizens Union recommended to O'Dwyer in February 1946 that New York resort to this means instead of using a local Airport Authority, and that the Mayor rejected the recommendation flatly and firmly. The New York *Times*, while endorsing the New York City Authority plan, gingerly suggested very early that the finished airport at Idlewild and all other airport operations of the City might be turned over to the Port Authority in the future. New Jersey papers in a solid bloc lauded Newark for calling upon the Port Authority, and a stream of editorials endorsed the move.

Inevitably, some of this began to circulate in official administration circles; indeed, Harry F. Guggenheim, even before he was appointed to the New York City Airport Authority, had mentioned this possibility to the Mayor, and, as we have seen, urged its adoption after he resigned. Mayor O'Dwyer, however, during his first months in office, stood resolutely behind the Moses formula. Again, all the evidence indicates that the Port Authority made no overt, certainly no formal, move to induce New York to request a study similar to that being made for Newark; nor is there evidence of any deliberate informal steps—personal letters, conversations with city leaders, approaches through intermediaries, or the like—taken to plant the idea in the minds of the City leaders. Despite the fact that the logic of the situation moves one to believe that the Authority must have been alert to the occasion and deeply interested, all initiative seems to have been taken by the City. Inevitably, the suggestion persisted in coming before the administration even without any special effort on the part of the Port Authority.

A word ought to be said about the unanimously favorable press enjoyed by the Port of New York Authority. The underlying basis for this circumstance is the Authority's record of successful accomplishment. Its bridges and tunnels are visible and tangible, and millions of citizens derive satisfaction from their use. Businessmen throughout the area have benefited from these and other Authority facilities. And any organization of such great size and such impeccable solvency is bound to be respected by the financial community.

Thus the Port Authority had an admirable basis for friendly treatment in the press, but the matter has not been left to chance. The Authority has maintained a carefully conceived and carefully executed program of public relations. The Director of Public Relations of the Authority is a top-level officer of the agency who participates actively in the making of policy instead of learning of policy decisions second-hand. Her function is respected as no less integral a part of the organization than administrative management or finance or engineering. She is thus in a position to supply reporters and editorial writers with completely authoritative and informed information, and to furnish it promptly. Representatives of the press know where to go for data; there is no shunting from department to department, no petty official's fear of answering searching questions, no inability to furnish relevant facts. The press and its readers in the port district thus know a good deal about the Port Authority, and, being able to evaluate it for themselves, have been inclined to support it as a familiar and reliable and capable organization. In a sense, therefore, while the Authority may not actually have planted the seed of the idea of airport operation, its public relations program provided fertile soil in which that seed could germinate.

Thus, when Mayor O'Dwyer found the New York City Airport Authority running into difficulty, he also found another agency, a concern that had been going for almost thirty years and one that enjoyed an excellent reputation and credit rating, to fall back on. And he found that the idea of utilizing this organization would not die, that it had the backing of prominent persons and groups all around him, and that New Jersey papers were enthusiastic about Newark's exploration of this possible channel.

THE MAYOR'S REQUEST

Mayor O'Dwyer formally submitted his request to the Port Authority on August 2, 1946. He asked the Port Authority to institute at once a study of the field at Idlewild with a view to financing, constructing, and operating it; to consider the rehabilitation and operation of LaGuardia Field; and to submit a proposal to the City as soon as possible. This move capped the series of acts marking his growing coolness toward the New York City Airport Authority and underscored a break with Moses on the management of the airport problem. What remains to be explained are the immediate circumstances that persuaded the Mayor to move with surprising suddenness.

Two events climaxed the other forces—that is, the resignation of Guggenheim, the strong support of the Port Authority in influential circles, and a rising tide of sentiment for a Port Authority study even among some members of his official family—pulling O'Dwyer in the direction of such a request. By chance two new factors combined to precipitate the act. The first was the arrival of the capital budget season. In New York City's financial administration, the capital budget is handled separately from the expense budget, both procedurally and temporally. The former clears through the City Planning Commission and is prepared on a calendar year basis; the latter runs on a fiscal year beginning on the first of July. Thus, the work of compiling the capital budget, to be enacted by the end of each calendar year, begins as early as July, just after the expense budget has been adopted. At the end of July 1946, following quickly on the heels of Guggenheim's resignation, Mayor O'Dwyer found himself face to face with his first capital budget. He was disillusioned with the Airport Authority, for it had not relieved him of the airport problem, nor did it seem as though it could do so within any reasonable time. He was reconsidering construction and operation by the City, but the same factors that prompted him to back the Airport Authority in the first place were no weaker now than they had been six months before. The field at Idlewild, as we have noted, called for huge investment in an operation that would not become self-supporting for a substantial period of time, if ever; this meant a heavy charge against the City's constitutional debt limit and would therefore cut down the other functions—education, health, sanitation, and the like—for which there was an insistent clamor now that the war was over. The time was ripe for something to dramatize the Port of New York Authority as a possible alternative.

Something did. On July 30, the press in New York and New Jersey carried the story that the Port of New York Authority had submitted to the Board of Commissioners of Newark a proposal whereby it would take over, renovate, and operate Port Newark and Newark Airport on a scale that would bring a more representative share of the port's sea and air traffic through that City. Such a proposal, it will be recalled, had been requested by Newark in December 1945, but there is nothing to suggest that the timing of the report was deliberately calculated to catch the Mayor of New York just at the moment when he was probably most receptive to recommendations that the Port Authority be called by the City; it was, from all appearances, a pure coincidence. Nevertheless, if it had been planned, no more opportune time could have been selected.

Chance thus provided the impetus that decided the Mayor. Austin J. Tobin, Executive Director of the Port Authority, received a call from a prominent banker with whom he had worked frequently on financial matters and who was known to be closely associated with the Mayor and Comptroller as a result of having handled many financial transaction for the City. The banker declared that he was acting independently and on his own initiative, but when he inquired whether the Port Authority would be willing to undertake a study of New York's municipal airports if it were asked to do so by Mayor O'Dwyer, it became apparent that this was an unofficial trial balloon being sent up by the City administration. Tobin at once spoke to Howard S. Cullman, Chairman of the Authority's Board of Commissioners; in a hasty conference they decided that such a study would be made if requested. Tobin notified the banker and, within a few hours, the Mayor called Cullman and asked that the study be launched. The request was formally presented in the letter of August 2, and the agreement of the Chairman of the Board was officially confirmed by the Board on August 8.

THE PORT AUTHORITY'S ACCEPTANCE

There appear to be three reasons for the Port Authority's willingness to take over a venture that had staggered a government with the resources of New York City behind it. In the first place, the Authority takes seriously its duty under the Port Compact to develop all the transportation and terminal facilities in the port district, and the airports were viewed as lying within the scope of that duty. In the second place, if the Authority fails to add new functions to those it already has, it may, once its debt has been retired, ultimately become nothing more than a simple operating and toll-collecting agency for existing projects. This would scarcely enable it to fulfill its broad mission. In the third place, the returns from the completed projects had enabled the Authority to build up large financial reserves. These were a target for constant fire from groups that wanted the tolls on bridges and tunnels reduced; automobilists' associations in particular charged that the tolls were kept high to finance new undertakings. The reserves, however, served other ends besides encouraging low interest rates and supplying a working fund; another, perhaps primary, purpose was to furnish a cushion to absorb the shocks to which the agency was subjected. Severe weather, accidents that put a facility out of commission, or a catastrophe like war and gas rationing, all of which reduce traffic sharply, must be taken in stride; the Port Authority, having no taxing power, must prepare for such eventualities in advance. Hence, the officers of the Authority felt strongly that a reduction in tolls would do much more than reduce its power to expand; it might diminish its capacity to survive. The airport venture in New York clearly meant operation at a loss for a period, until the fields were on a self-supporting basis; meanwhile, the reserves would go down temporarily and relieve some of the pressure. Ultimately, when all the bonds are retired, tolls doubtless will go down. Until then, a temporary loss was to be preferred to an action which might possibly mean eventual collapse.

The distress of the municipalities was genuine. But while the Port Authority may have been motivated in part by a sympathetic desire to help, that impulse was tempered by the economic realities of the situation in which the Authority found itself. And the realities pushed it toward looking into the airport problem.

SEVEN MONTHS IN OFFICE

At the end of seven months Mayor O'Dwyer was still plagued by the same airport problem that confronted him on the day he took office. He had then attacked it vigorously, decisively, discarding as inadequate the fiscal administrative formula adopted by his predecessor, rejecting the first suggestions that he use the Port Authority, and giving his wholehearted support to the Moses-sponsored City Airport Authority. But if the LaGuardia approach was inadequate, so did the Airport Authority scheme prove to be; and the Mayor turned away from Moses' lead on this matter. Meanwhile, the forces pushing him toward the Port of New York Authority increased in number and strength, and, just as he began to reconsider City construction and operation, a chance combination of circumstances finally led him to call on the bi-State agency. The first City reaction to the Air Age had been spontaneous, but it was not wholly satisfactory as the new technology made itself felt, especially in the need for tremendous investments. The second adjustment had not been successful. O'Dwyer was exploring a third possibility, but apparently more out of a feeling of absolute necessity than from enthusiasm. Administrative adaptation to the Air Age was proving a difficult and even painful business. And the Mayor, who had begun his administration in January with apparent conviction that City Construction Coordinator Moses had the right answer, showed signs in August of wondering whether there were any right answers at all.

III. Indecision

A DELUGE OF REPORTS

The months following Mayor O'Dwyer's request to the Port of New York Authority were difficult ones for him and for the members of the City administration. For the Mayor now came to grips with the problem that he had not personally tackled during the time he had accepted the Moses formula. And he left no doubt that he intended to investigate conscientiously every possible alternative in order to arrive at a determination based on the cold facts. This inquiring approach, with its "quest for certainty," is an admirable but trying one. There was a disturbed interlude of indecision.

The administration, in the course of this period, asked for information from a number of sources, and these, together with the reports contracted for previously or volunteered by interested parties, deluged it in a flood of competing ideas and interpretations that did not make a final choice any easier. By the end of January 1947, a half dozen conflicting masses of data and suggestions lay before the Board of Estimate.

One of these—a report submitted early in the summer of 1946 by the engineering firm of Madigan-Hyland (consultants who are frequently called on by the city)—was enough to dispel any notion anyone may have had that the field of Idlewild could be abandoned. (Actually, no such notion had taken hold anywhere in official circles, but it certainly must have seemed a welcome solution to many people.) This study, requested originally by the LaGuardia administration and amended and continued under O'Dwyer, estimated that the number of domestic air passengers in the United States in 1955 would reach almost 56 million, or just under eight times the 7.4 million of 1945. About 18,750,000 of the air travelers in 1955 were expected to pass through the New York area, requiring more than 670,000 plane movements annually, or seven and a half times the 1945 total at LaGuardia Field (when almost all the commercial air traffic in the metropolitan district used this airport). Large increases were also forecast for international passenger traffic, and for freight and express. On the basis of these figures and calculations of the capacity of major airfields in the area, it was deemed absolutely necessary, under any circumstances, to have the Idlewild field in full operation by 1954, and to have it in final shape as early as 1950 if no subsidiary fields capable of handling the increasing number of privately owned itinerant craft were developed in the meantime. These figures found support among airline executives, but many joined Captain Eddie Rickenbacker of Eastern Air Lines in declaring that the estimates of New York's share of the traffic were, if anything, too low.

Under this kind of pressure to get the field in operation, the City continued to invest in construction. Regardless of the ultimate lodgment of the administrative authority, it was held essential to have the work go ahead and the field open at least on a limited basis as soon as possible.

Nevertheless, the realization that the burden might well fall on the City itself persuaded the Board of Estimate to explore ways of reducing the amount it would have to put into the airport. We saw earlier that its Chief Engineer, John C. Riedel, was instructed to study plans for reducing the program. Riedel reported informally soon afterward, but no statement of any kind was released at the time. Three weeks later, however, on August 22, 1946, the Board of Estimate took formal action by approving a contract with three architectural firms to draw up plans for smaller buildings and a more modest central area than had been contemplated originally. (The Commissioner of Marine and Aviation had already cancelled the contracts of the original architects on July 3, when it appeared that the City Airport Authority was going to take over. The architects' threats to sue were of no avail; the City went ahead in its efforts to cut down the scale of the program with new consultants.)

While the City was examining possibilities of this nature, the Citizens Budget Commission, an independent municipal research organization of long standing in the community which had first urged its scheme upon the Governor and the Legislature at Albany when the City Airport Authority legislation was being considered there in the spring of the year, but with no success, revived its pressure for solving the airport problem by the use of a terminal company similar in character to the corporation that had successfully financed and operated the union railroad terminal in Cincinnati. This plan called for completion of the field at Idlewild by the City and leasing of the finished airport to the terminal company at a rental equal to the amount of debt service on the City's total investment. In this fashion, as soon as operations were begun, the entire project would be removed from the City's debt limit. The company was to include representatives of the airlines and the City on its board of directors. A letter from the Chairman of the Citizens Budget Commission to the Mayor on July 24, 1946, called the Mayor's attention to this device, to which the Commission gave its full support. On October 7, a delegation from the Commission called on O'Dwyer to recommend once more that he study the terminal company idea, a proposition he promised to take up with the Board of Estimate but about which he was not enthusiastic because it might have meant further delay at a time when he was hopeful of getting a good offer from the Port Authority.

Another solution was proposed in October, when the Regional Plan Association released the first part of the study of airport needs of the metropolitan area begun two years earlier. This release, more fully supported by materials put out later and finally published in the form of a book, emphasized once more the tremendous effort the metropolitan area would have to make in order to accommodate itself to the explosive growth of aviation in the Air Age. It contained even higher estimates of future air traffic than the Madigan-Hyland report, and it made specific provision also for an expected increase in the number of private planes in the region to 20,000. On this basis, it recommended the fullest development of four major airports, eight supplementary major airports, 18 secondary airports, 51 local airports, and 36 seaplane bases over the length and breadth of the region. Such a plan obviously lay beyond the legal and financial powers of the City, and required action beyond the City's territorial limits; it was therefore proposed that the regional growth and co-ordination of airports be lodged in a tri-State agency, created along lines similar to the Port of New York Authority but including Connecticut as well as New York and New Jersey. The new agency would have authority only over airports; it would operate the larger ones, plan and guide the smaller ones, co-operate with the C.A.A., and supervise regional airports generally. The plan was given considerable publicity, particularly when it was accepted by the C.A.A. in Washington on December 12, 1946.

The Port of New York Authority presented its offer to the City on December 18. Calling for a $191,000,000 program for completion, rehabilitation, and operation, covering Idlewild airport, LaGuardia Field, and Floyd Bennett Field (which Mayor O'Dwyer was trying to get back from the Navy), its scope and imagination lived up to the expectations of the Port Authority's supporters who were anxious to see New York become the air capital of the world. To many municipal officials, however, some of the terms of the proposal seemed far from generous to the City. They were unhappy over the length of the suggested lease (99 years) feeling that this was too long a period for the City to give up its control over its airports. They questioned the failure of the Port Authority to guarantee payment of rental and its offer to share profits on only a fifty-fifty basis, although the City was turning over investments which had cost it about $70,000,000 already and which it would still own. They opposed the provisions that gave the Port Authority the right to cancel its lease with the City at any time if it proved unprofitable, and the option of the Port Authority to buy the airports at the original City cost at the expiration of the lease, a provision which would have made it possible for the City to lose its airports forever. They objected to the lack of any City right to conduct fiscal inspections, of enforcible legal remedies for the City, of Port Authority agreement to conform to zoning and building laws, and of any express obligation by the Port Authority as to the scheduling of airport construction to be undertaken. They were critical of the requirement that the City provide police and fire protection, and of the failure to hold the City harmless from claims based on existing leases with airlines and oil companies. Consequently, the Mayor made no immediate comment; he waited for still more comparative data, despite the fact that Harry F. Guggenheim now publicly endorsed the general outlines of the Port Authority plan and urged the City to adopt it.

Some of the additional data the Mayor was waiting for arrived December 22. It was a report from the design committee of architects, to whom other consultants had been added, which had been engaged in August to draw up a reduced plan for the Idlewild field. This discarded many of the installations contained in the plans drawn up for Mayor LaGuardia, and reduced the cost of building the field to less than $70,000,000 additional, on a six-runway basis. This scheme, which assumed the job would be done by the Department of Marine and Aviation, was a good deal less expensive than the Port Authority plan, even though the Port Authority had decided upon only seven runways for technical rather than financial reasons. An informal poll showed Board of Estimate sentiment leaning toward City construction of the design committee's proposed limited field, but no official action was taken at this time because the Airport Authority still had to submit a report.

The New York City Airport Authority, despite the setbacks it had suffered, was at that time still legally alive and was functioning under the leadership of Laurance Rockefeller, the last of the original appointees, and Commissioner Reinicke, of the Department of Marine and Aviation (the chairmanship remained vacant). Its report, requested by the Mayor, was rendered on January 13, 1947. It proposed an $80,000,000 program for the construction, improvement, and operation of the Idlewild airport, LaGuardia Field, and Floyd Bennett, when that was acquired from the Navy. With respect to its scope and cost, this report stood between the Port Authority proposal and the plan submitted by the design committee for execution by the City itself.

The Mayor now had before him a congeries of facts and ideas. He had the traffic estimates compiled by Madigan-Hyland and those worked up by the Regional Plan Association. He had proposals for the City to complete all the construction and continue to operate the municipal airports. He had suggestions that the City build the newest field and lease it, together with LaGuardia Field, to a terminal company. He had recommendations that he turn the whole job over to a City authority, a bi-State authority, a tri-State authority. He had plans ranging in cost from $70,000,000 to almost $200,000,000. And he was subject to a bewildering barrage of arguments, accusations, charges, and counter-charges by the partisans and opponents of each of the propositions. The airlines, in fact, seeking to speed City action (they supported the Port Authority), brought up the same heavy artillery that had rushed former Comptroller McGoldrick into the original contracts with them: they threatened to locate their maintenance bases elsewhere, thus depriving New York of the thousands of jobs and heavy investments such installations involved. Unable to give to this one of his many problems of municipal government the time it would require to master the financial, engineering, and aeronautical questions involved, O'Dwyer referred the whole confusing mass of data to a committee composed of the City officials immediately concerned: City Construction Co-Ordinator Moses, Budget Director Patterson, Corporation Counsel Charles E. Murphy, Chief Engineer Riedel, and Comptroller Lazarus Joseph.

PERPLEXITY AT CITY HALL

It was January 13, 1947, when the Mayor turned the airport problem over to his special committee. Two days later, the members attended an executive session of the Board of Estimate at which the Board apparently tried to take the measure of the issue it was up against. Here, two attacks on the New York City Airport Authority's plan were presented, one in a letter from the Port of New York Authority, the other from the airlines. The Port Authority called the City Airport Authority plans unrealistic, charged they were inadequate for the traffic expected, and ridiculed the idea that Airport Authority bonds, backed by nothing more than the promise of revenues from a still uncompleted airport, would sell at a reasonable rate. The letter from the airlines asserted flatly that the Airport Authority could not market its bonds. The Airport Authority was reported as insisting that it would be able to find bankers willing to take its bond issues. In any case, no action was taken, nor was the way cleared for action; the matter was thrown back into the hands of the five-man committee. Airlines officials were reluctant to submit the issue to a committee headed by Moses, presumably because of his refusal to honor the leases made by the LaGuardia administration; "Mr. Moses," observed one such official, "just doesn't like airplanes." LaGuardia himself, in a radio talk, derided the committee as a vehicle for "Moses to investigate Moses." Nevertheless, it was expected that all parties would participate and that the problem would be solved in a couple of weeks because so much of the ground had been traveled before.

Developments continued apace. The Airport Authority again wrote O'Dwyer to affirm the marketability of its bonds and to attack the "over-elaborate and expensive" Port Authority proposal. The airlines, still acting in concert, wrote the Comptroller pointing out the failure of the City Authority to accomplish anything although it had been in existence for almost a year, and reiterated their belief that the organization would be unable to finance even its limited program. Chairman Howard S. Cullman of the Port Authority sent a letter to the Mayor withdrawing two of the features of the Authority's proposal that had aroused objection: these were the clause permitting the Port Authority to cancel the lease with the City at any time and the provision granting the Authority the option to buy the airports upon expiration of the lease instead of returning them to the City. The New York *Times* now came out strongly for the Port Authority, abandoning the support of the City Airport Authority it had announced a year before. Mayor O'Dwyer stated that if the City decided to operate the airports, he would split up the Department of Marine and Aviation, separating out a new and independent Department of

Aviation to administer the City's aviation functions. The Regional Plan Association declared it would support the Port Authority proposal.

On January 29, the issue promised to come to a head at an open hearing before the Board of Estimate. The race had by then apparently narrowed down to only three alternatives: the City Airport Authority, the Port Authority, or operation by the City through its own Department. The parties had had plenty of time to appraise each other and to mobilize their own forces. This promised to be the summing up despite the fact that it was officially described solely as a means of procuring all the information about the proposals before the Board.

The Airport Authority, which Moses had so strongly advocated, and the Port Authority, a strong, independent administrative power, here tangled openly with each other. The Airport Authority, represented by Laurance S. Rockefeller, was very decidedly worsted in this contest. It produced but one banker, who was supposed to be a witness to the marketability of its securities, and even he hedged and qualified his testimony until it was obvious that it was highly questionable whether or not the bonds could be sold at all. The Port Authority, on the other hand, called five financial experts as witnesses, and all of them stated categorically that they would accept the bonds of the Port Authority under the terms and conditions it had maintained it could get. Furthermore, the Executive Director of the Port Authority read into the record letters from a dozen reputable banking houses that declared their willingness to take the agency's securities at the specified terms; these letters also made it clear that they would never accept any securities—even had they been offered by the Port Authority itself—under the conditions required by the City Airport Authority. On the engineering side, a technical witness for the Airport Authority admitted some glaring defects in its plans; the Port Authority stood on firm ground here. Administratively, the Airport Authority had argued that the C.A.A. could furnish the regional coordination of airports and aviation in the entire metropolitan area, thus obviating the necessity for the City to relinquish any of its authority to a bi-State agency; during the course of the hearing, a C.A.A. official specifically and expressly denied that his organization could perform any such function. Representatives of the Citizens Union, the Regional Plan Association, and the Aviation Section of the New York Board of Trade all appeared in support of the Port Authority; no independent witnesses backed the Airport Authority. After this clash, there was no doubt that the Airport Authority was no match for the Port Authority.

The Port Authority enjoyed especially strong support from the representative of the airlines. The airlines were behind the Port Authority plan for three reasons: First, they were clearly convinced that the City Airport Authority would not be able to finance its program, and they were desperately in need of a new field to handle the expected jump in air traffic in the spring. Secondly, they were extremely sanguine about the future of aviation and favored a program on a scale large enough to accommodate it; the City Authority proposal was far too small to suit them. Thirdly, they had in their possession a letter from the Executive Director of the Port Authority in which he promised to treat the existing City leases with the airlines as valid in principle even if subject to renegotiation in detail; against this, there was the record of controversy with Moses over this question. Later, it turned out that there was a vast discrepancy between the airlines' interpretation of the term "negotiation" and what the Port Authority thought the word meant, but this difference had not arisen at this stage and the companies stood foursquare behind the bi-State agency.

No one appeared formally to present the case for direct City operation, but Comptroller Joseph argued this position from his seat on the Board of Estimate by carefully questioning all the witnesses on relevant points. As chief fiscal officer of the City, he was concerned about whether any of the proposals would return to the City treasury sufficient revenues from the very start to meet the debt service and amortization charges on the $70,000,000 already invested in the municipal airports by the City. He made it plain that he considered anything less than this simply giving away the huge capital outlays, and it was equally clear that he would not acquiesce in any such action. Increasingly, he gave evidence of wanting the City to do the entire job itself rather than give up so much without adequate return. Beyond question, he took this stand partly because it put him in a stronger position to bargain with either of the Authorities should things come to the point where the details of the proposals were being negotiated to arrive at a final settlement. Nevertheless, he seemed to feel that bearing the burden of added investment was preferable, no matter how difficult, to making a poor bargain for the City.

None of the other possibilities received serious consideration, and none was really pressed as a serious contender. The Regional Plan Association backed the Port Authority rather than its own recommended tri-State agency, since the City could do nothing about the latter anyway. The Citizens Budget Commission's terminal company idea was not even mentioned by the organization's own representative, who gave up hope and merely criticized the plans of both Authorities and urged a new study by independent organizations; this was hastily brushed aside by the Mayor, who wanted to reach a decision as soon as possible and not to wait for the completion of still more surveys. The design committee was represented by the same technical witnesses who appeared for the Airport Authority, the two agencies having employed the same consultants anyway; its scheme was early lost to sight. By the latter part of the hearing, which lasted well into the evening, it appeared that all the possibilities but City operation and the Port Authority's plan had been virtually eliminated.

Militating in favor of City operation was the fact that the airports involved many millions of dollars in contracts. Even with provisions in the law for competitive bidding, contracts (and, to a lesser extent in cases of this kind, in spite of a merit system of civil service, patronage) still constitute an important means of holding local political parties together—and keeping them in power. Whatever other motivations moved the Mayor and Comptroller, they were doubtless cognizant of this fundamental fact of municipal political life and they must surely have had their attention drawn to this aspect of the issue by some of their political colleagues. From this point of view, City operation was tempting indeed, attractive enough to overcome even the difficulties sure to arise from the dissatisfaction of some of the Boroughs, notably The Bronx, with the location of the City's two major airports in Queens. In addition, there was the normal reluctance of a city government to relinquish control over what had become a power traditionally exercised by municipalities. Alone, these factors might have swung the decision to City operation, but, as we have seen, the issue was far more complicated than this.

The hearing had been proceeding for almost nine hours when Mayor O'Dwyer seized upon a variation of an idea that had been suggested by James J. Lyons, Borough President of The Bronx: he asked Juan T. Trippe, President of Pan American World Airways, who was representing all the interested air carriers, whether the airlines would finance and build their own hangars if the City operated and maintained the basic facilities at the airports. The idea seemed to be relatively spontaneous with the Mayor, there being no evidence that he had ever before given it any serious thought. Indeed, when Lyons a few hours earlier had thrown out his general suggestion that the airlines pay their own way with respect to terminal facilities, as railroads and bus companies did, without defining it and apparently without really having a specific plan in mind, neither the Mayor nor anyone else paid him any heed. But the idea seems to have been incubating in the mind of the chief executive, and what had been a rather casual and vague remark previously ignored was, to everyone's surprise, suddenly transformed into another possible course of action.

Trippe was not in a position to give an authoritative answer to the unexpected proposition. He was relatively sure that the financial burden was beyond the ability of the companies, but he promised to consult them on the matter. On this note, the hearing ended, having brought the City almost unwillingly to the brink of a decision, only to have the case suspended again while the airlines studied the new idea.

CONTINUED PERPLEXITY

Two days later it became known that the airlines had concluded that they could not finance the hangars themselves; the cost of financing would have been so high, it was alleged, that it would have put them in the red at the Idlewild field. Tobin and Cullman told reporters that the Port Authority could not and would not change its original plan. These declarations might have seemed enough to push the City once and for all into doing the job itself. At bottom, however, no decisive force was present; the uncertainty continued as no action was taken.

During February 1947, there were no important airport developments at City Hall. Two significant moves came from other quarters, however. The first was taken by a foreign flag airline that signed a contract to establish its main operational and maintenance base at Bradley Field, Connecticut, thus following in the path of two companies that had during the previous June taken like steps at MacArthur Field, Islip, Long Island, and one that had begun to install its principal facilities at Wilmington, Delaware, in July. Whether or not this trend was actually a result of the hesitation about New York City's airports is not at all certain, but there is no doubt that it was viewed with some concern in the City.

The second was the initiation of measures by the Port Authority to permit it to take over the airports of both New York and Newark in the event a satisfactory arrangement between the agency and the municipalities could be worked out. Legislation was introduced first in Albany, then in Trenton; by mid-April, it had passed both Houses in both States and was signed into law by both Governors. The Port Authority thus undertook very early to demolish the argument that an agreement with it would require a long wait before it could get specific power to take on the new enterprise.

Meanwhile, the Port Authority, despite its announcement at the end of January, was at work studying its original proposal to see whether there were any points on which a compromise might be reached. On March 10, 1947, amid reports of a revised proposal by the Authority much more favorable to the City than its initial offer, Mayor O'Dwyer announced that he had discussed the airport problem with his five-man special committee very recently and that he was calling a meeting at his residence to discuss the new proposal. He insisted that his mind was still open, and he denied that he was leaning toward City operation. Thus, the ball was thrown back to the committee again.

The meeting took place at Gracie Mansion, the Mayor's official residence, on the evening of March 12. Comptroller Joseph was still strongly in favor of City operation, but he agreed that the current Port Authority offer would be acceptable even though he preferred to get a still better one from the point of view of the City. Each of the other members of the committee also gave his views.

The discussion apparently produced still more confusion. It was agreed that a special three-man committee would be appointed "to co-ordinate the thinking and recommendations" of the five-man committee. This body, chaired by Corporation Counsel Charles E. Murphy, and including John C. Riedel, Chief Engineer of the Board of Estimate, and William Reid, of the Mayor's Office, was officially set up at a meeting of the Board of Estimate on March 13.

In five days the committee was ready to report, and the Board of Estimate convened to hear its findings. Most of the newspapers in the City reported that the Board of Estimate favored City operation, but the situation was so fluid that two papers still held that the City Airport Authority was preferred and three saw the Board partial to the Port Authority.

But all of them proved wrong, because the Board of Estimate deferred decision again, despite the fact that the report of the Murphy committee was unequivocally in favor of rejecting for the time the offers made by both Authorities in favor of operation of the airports by the City itself. The committee recommended that a separate Department of Aviation be set up by local law to handle the job and that the City provide funds in its capital budget to continue limited construction at Idlewild and to rehabilitate LaGuardia Field. This was conceived only as a short-range program to remain in effect pending the accumulation of sufficient data for the Board to make a decision on a long-range plan. Comparatively definite as it was, however, it did not sway the members of the Board of Estimate. Mayor O'Dwyer instead appointed a special two-man committee, consisting of Murphy and Comptroller Joseph, whose function was to confer with the Port Authority in order to seek agreement on those points in its proposal to which the Murphy-Riedel-Reid committee had raised objection.

THE PROCESS OF ELIMINATION: A SUMMARY

When Mayor O'Dwyer took office he abandoned the LaGuardia response to the challenge of the Air Age and adopted instead the Moses formula. When the Moses formula proved disappointing, he turned to the Port of New York Authority. But in turning to the Port Authority he had exhibited more a desire to get information than a firm resolve to utilize this agency. His quest for the facts that would give him a basis for arriving at his own conclusions instead of accepting someone else's ready-made answers brought him a bewildering mass of data and ideas, frequently in contradiction of each other. He had passed the whole involved problem to a committee of five City officials for clarification. Some of the alternative plans dropped quietly out of the picture, but City operation, the plan of the City Airport Authority, and the proposal of the Port Authority remained very much in the running. However, when the question was laid squarely before the Board of Estimate in January 1947, it reached no decision, but threw out instead a spontaneous proposition to the airlines suggested by the Mayor. The airlines rejected O'Dwyer's suggestion, and here the situation rested for several weeks.

The issue came to life once again when the Port Authority submitted a revised and more favorable proposal to the Mayor in March. He called together his five-man committee and heard the views of the individual members; things were still so confusing that he persuaded the Board of Estimate to appoint a three-man committee of City officials to clarify the views of the five-man committee. The three-man committee reported promptly and emphatically for City operation as a temporary solution pending a leisurely study of all the facts later on. The Board ignored the advice of the group it had itself set up only a few days before and named still another committee of two City officers to meet with representatives of the Port Authority in an effort to iron out the differences still separating the agency's proposal from the City's demand. Thus the Airport Authority, which had fared poorly at the January hearing, disappeared from the ranks of the serious contenders, and only City operation and the Port Authority plan remained in the race.

After a half-year of doubt and confusion, during which the administration found itself several times face to face with decision and each time backed away to gather, examine, and weigh the facts anew, the blurry and uncertain situation came sharply into focus. Clearly, the time for decision was at hand.

IV. A Decision Emerges

THE LAST PANGS OF UNCERTAINTY

Comptroller Joseph and Corporation Counsel Murphy met almost immediately with high-ranking Port Authority officers. The meetings, which were frequent and long and wearing, were carried on in an atmosphere of suspicion and distrust. Concessions by both sides were wrung from them only after bitter argument, each party giving ground by inches and releasing each inch grudgingly. At times, the talks threatened to break down completely as the intransigence of one of the parties would irk the other. When this happened,

Juan T. Trippe of Pan American World Airways brought his influence to bear; sitting in unofficially as representative of the airlines, and keeping in constant touch with the Mayor throughout this period, he was able to function as mediator and hold the conferees together whenever they seemed to be at the end of their patience. Meanwhile, the Regional Plan Association reiterated its support of the Port Authority plan because of its size; the alternatives were called by the Association too small for the air traffic of the future. And the Citizens Budget Commission, too, swung its weight behind the Port Authority, albeit with some reservations and qualifications.

ACTION AT LAST

On March 26, 1947, the Port Authority submitted what was described as its final and amended plan to the City officials. The proposal was discussed the same day by the Board of Estimate, which then issued an order to the Corporation Counsel to draw up a "definite agreement" with the bi-State agency. This constituted, in effect, the Board's "agreement to agree," leaving open to further negotiation the detailed terms of the final contract and even reserving the right of the City to disapprove the final contract. Some City spokesmen tried to describe this as nothing more than a "cautious step," but to everyone else it seemed that the long period of uncertainty was over at last. Cullman sent O'Dwyer a letter commending him and Joseph for driving a good bargain on behalf of the City without losing sight of the regional aviation needs of the metropolitan district, and the Board of Estimate praised the Mayor for holding out for better terms instead of accepting the Authority's first offer.

There is not much doubt that O'Dwyer himself provided the leadership within the administration that resulted in this decision, despite the fact that he had vacillated from the time he began to lose faith in the City Airport Authority. His inability to decide grew out of the complexity of the problem and from a seemingly compelling impulse to recheck the ground again and again in an effort to be sure that, when he did act, he did the right thing. Though it was apparently motivated by the Mayor's sincere desire to do the best thing for the City, the indecision did badly delay much needed new construction and repairs. At the same time, it led to a better agreement for the City than would have been possible on a faster time schedule.

The concessions won by the City were, in fact, substantial. The term of the lease, which covered all the municipal airports, was decreased from 99 to 50 years, cutting in half the time New York would have to wait before the airports return to it. The City was guaranteed an annual rental of $350,000 to 1957 and $450,000 thereafter; under the original proposal, there had been no guarantee. The City's share of the net profits was increased from 50 to 75 per cent. The Port Authority also withdrew clauses which would have granted it the right to cancel the lease if it turned out to be unprofitable and to buy the airports at the expiration of the lease for a sum equal to the City's original investment (thus making it possible for the City to lose the airports permanently). The City was given the right under the final lease agreement, not included in the original Port Authority offer, to perform fiscal inspections of the Authority's operations, to pursue (subject to bi-State approval subsequently granted) all legal, equitable, and other remedies to enforce compliance; and to approve or disapprove the construction of additional airports inside the City. The Port Authority agreed, as it had not agreed originally, to conform to zoning and building and other laws wherever possible; to submit construction plans to the City for suggestions; to spend at least $100,000,000 on the airport at Idlewild within seven years from the date of the lease (apart from hangar costs); to provide for its own police and fire protection, garbage removal and snow removal (instead of requiring the City to perform these services); to make provision for City police aircraft; and to indemnify the City and hold it harmless in the event of claims being successfully asserted against it under existing leases and contracts. All in all, while the failure to move promptly had its disadvantages, it also brought undeniable benefits.

On April 16 an executive session of the

Board of Estimate endorsed the terms arrived at. On the following day the contract was signed by the Mayor and Cullman. Almost a year and a half after the time he assumed office, O'Dwyer at last found a workable solution to the City's airport problem.

The Port Authority swung into action at once. On May 29, in accordance with the terms of the lease, Cullman delivered to the Mayor legal instruments signed by the airlines and oil companies releasing the City from any liability with respect to the leases it had previously signed with those companies for space and other facilities at Idlewild. On June 1, 1947, the Port Authority formally assumed responsibility for the fields. Finally, the Idlewild field was designated New York International Airport.

Though it was Newark that first called upon the Port Authority to propose a solution to its airport and seaport difficulties, New York was the first to reach an agreement. The Authority's original plan for Newark received an even colder reception in Newark than the New York plan did in New York, and the opposition of some of the City Commissioners in Newark who wanted to break up the airfield and subdivide it for business purposes was exceedingly energetic. However, soon after the Port Authority took over New York's fields, it also submitted a revised proposal to Newark, modeling it along the lines of the lease with New York. The Newark administration was rent by acrimonious disputes as it split up into forces for and against the Port Authority, and each mustered all the strength it could command. On October 22, the faction supporting the Port Authority won out and the City signed the lease. The way was now clear for the regional development of airports in the metropolitan area.

CONCLUDING COMMENTS

Only a couple of years more than two decades elapsed between the first petition of a committee of the New York Board of Trade to the City to set aside some of its property for a commercial landing field and the signing of the lease between New York City and the Port of New York Authority. Yet in that time, the City had felt the impact of the Air Age in full force. The drama of a great municipality at grips with the problems of a new era, discovering painfully the inadequacies of the old methods in a changing day and growing aware of the strictures of outmoded safeguards, offers an opportunity to gain insight into some aspects of the realities of public administration. But conclusions should be drawn with caution. This study can more usefully be regarded as suggestive and illustrative than as probative in character.

It would be possible to raise almost an indefinite number of questions after contemplation of the events recounted in this story, and probably any number of morals could be drawn. For example, what "principles" of administration would have helped the Mayor decide? Could the canons or techniques of "scientific management" have aided him in his task? Was the first impromptu adjustment helpful or harmful in the long run? Is there anything here to suggest that administrative forms and even governmental units hamper response to the challenges of a rapidly changing world by persisting when the forces that brought them into being disappear? What is the significance of the growth of two administrative systems (the Port Authority and Moses) each one degree removed from direct popular control, each an "efficient" organization in the sense that it gets things—big, impressive things—done quickly, each therefore enjoying the support of the people because the people see and use the things each builds, each stressing its divorce from "politics," each growing in extent from year to year? Can politics and administration be separated? And does the independent authority develop a politics and a constituency of its own?

The contrasts among the various authorities also suggest some interesting questions: Why is one "independent" authority more independent than another? How does it come about that the Port Authority's prestige is not built around a man? Is the tremendous personal impact of a single figure on an independent authority likely to have any permanent effects on the institution?

All these questions arise almost spontaneously from this text; none of them can be answered from one case study. Only as notes in various forms on more and more instances of decision-making become available will we be able to generalize with some modest degree of assurance.

A few observations about the New York City situation, on the other hand, may be ventured with less hesitation. It seems reasonably clear that the prolongation of the uncertainty that beset the City derived to a considerable extent from the personality of Mayor O'Dwyer, who on several other occasions also reversed his tack completely after wavering for a while; when the Mayor was involved, decisions somehow seemed to "get made" only by the sheer pressure of events. But we would miss something vital if we were not to push the analysis further.

One of the real sources of difficulty for the Mayor was the multiplicity of values he was trying to take into account and the incommensurability of the values to which he was sensitive. To be sure, he was interested in doing what was the best for the City, but so were all the rest—or so they said—and yet none of the chief figures seemed to agree with him or with each other. Caught as he was in the pressures of the moment, it was presumably difficult for him to articulate the shifting significance to him of the various values involved and to realize that he was trying to satisfy a variety of persons with impinging interests whose concepts of the good of the people were a conscious or unconscious projection of the more limited and specific values they were acting to preserve. Each of the values apparently seemed worthy to O'Dwyer; his problem lay in the fact that whenever he tried to realize one, several others would be lost. So he moved from one to another, endeavoring to do the right thing without perhaps ever fully having in mind what he meant by the right thing, or perhaps more accurately, without being able to satisfy himself that any one of the proposals represented a maximization of values. This situation, on the other hand, should not be permitted to obscure the fact that the Mayor doubtless realized that his uncertainty was wresting concessions from the agencies competing for the airports. He and the City stood to gain by delay and uncertainty; he could therefore indulge in hesitation with the comforting feeling—possibly only half articulate—that time was on his side.

One striking feature of the case is the fact that the decision was so little affected by the underlying economic advantages of Port Authority operation. Even the most devoted adherent to the doctrines of the Sherman Act would find difficulty in viewing with equanimity Mayor LaGuardia's competitive war with the City of Newark, with its increasing incitement to subsidy operation of the airports. And in any event, the nature of the underlying technical aviation problems makes a co-ordinated bi-State airport network desirable, perhaps even essential. Yet the responsible officials of New York City and Newark could not approach the problem on this basis. Some of the unofficial bodies placed great weight on the regional economic factors, but the elected and appointed officials were forced or seemed forced to put primary or sole emphasis on political and legal considerations.

And for New York City the decisive factor was the constitutionally created fiscal difficulty. Indeed, another striking feature of the case is the genuine financial straits in which a metropolis of the size and the resources of New York found itself. Here is a government that, with the sole exception of the Federal government, provides more services to more people than any other government in the country. Here are the greatest port in the world, a world financial center, an international commercial center. Here are located over fourteen per cent of the manufacturing establishments in the United States. Here is a city whose annual expense budget of a billion and a quarter dollars far exceeds that of any state in the union and dwarfs most of them. Here is concentrated surely the greatest accumulation of wealth in history. Here is a government with jurisdiction over land and buildings assessed at more than 18 billion dollars. Yet it could not finance its new airport.

In almost ironic contrast, the task fell to the Port of New York Authority, an organization without the city's power to tax, lacking the power to make regulations or determinations generally binding upon private citizens, not even equipped with investigatory and subpoena powers. It can raise money only by borrowing. Like the City, it is a municipal corporation, but its authority and its ultimate resources are much more limited. Yet it was able to do the job that lay beyond the City's capacity.

There are probably no easy explanations for this surprising inversion. One's attention, however, is drawn at once to the debt and tax limitations placed on the City's fiscal operations by the State constitution. The requirement that the City secure State legislative approval for certain of its functions is also prominent. It appears rather incongruous, on the surface at least, that an institution like the City of New York should be subject to controls of this nature—particularly to supervision by a legislature dominated by rural elements. To be sure, these controls in theory were enacted to protect the people of the City; in practice, they probably represented a response to a desire for protection on the part of certain groups in the City in accordance with a widely held ethic of civic virtue. Whatever their origin, there is no doubt that they restrict the capacity of the City to discharge its responsibilities, and that they sometimes tend to persuade its leaders to resort to measures that they would not otherwise consider advisable. (Indeed, with respect to borrowing power, the Port Authority is the freer of the two units.) The City's ability to take action is limited, but there is no like limitation on the additional duties, such as those created by the Air Age, that are continually imposed upon it. Clearly, there is not enough evidence in this instance to permit a final judgment of the value and wisdom of such controls, but there is enough to suggest the desirability of further study of the evils prevented as compared with the evils produced.

Another noteworthy aspect of the dilemma brought on by the airport question is the inability of the City to fulfill obligations that are essentially regional in nature. The City's jurisdiction does not extend beyond its borders; the problems with which it must grapple do. As we noted at the outset, New York is part of an economic and social unit that straddles local and state boundaries. If all its problems are like those posed by the growth of aviation, then not only must its freedom to act be reconsidered with a view to a possible broadening of its powers, but the territory of its authority may also need expanding; or alternatively, thought must be given to the creation or use of a public body with broader territorial scope. There obviously must be some agency that can operate in an integrated fashion over the entire area; and the problem cannot be solved after the fashion of Los Angeles, for example, by simple extension of territory—the State boundaries bar the way.

The Port of New York Authority suggests itself at once. It has already become the repository of many of the governmental functions that overlap political boundaries in the metropolitan area. It will, in all likelihood, continue to grow as municipalities take advantage of the existence of such an effective organization and turn over to it more of their activities which are metropolitan rather than local in character. But it is improbable that the Authority by itself can solve the problem, particularly since there may be serious doubts about the wisdom and desirability of its extension into fields other than transportation. Among the theoretical alternatives are metropolitan government—a regional city or even a city-state invested with full state sovereignty—unhampered by the obsolete lines between governmental units and by the common restrictions placed upon municipal administration. Or does the lesson of the airports suggest that somewhere between the present arrangement and full-fledged metropolitan government may be a compromise, a series of special regional authorities each carrying on a particular regional activity, which could be developed without disrupting the existing governmental framework? Whatever remedy may be adopted, indeed, one may say whatever remedies we are moving toward, the airport experience indicates gross inadequacies in the structure of local government that must be corrected.

Yet the airport problem, like so many other problems that have somehow become local burdens, is by no means of local interest alone. The Federal government is vitally concerned in the development of adequate airports in sufficient numbers to meet the Nation's commercial and security needs. The great field at Idlewild was of special national interest because the United States must have at least one airport capable of handling international air traffic, which keeps growing by leaps and bounds; and there is, of course, no more logical place for it than the World Capital, the world's first port, the world's first (or second) city. For it is here that much of that traffic is generated. Thus, though the obstacles that prevented New York City from doing the job originally stemmed from the pattern of state–local and regional relationships, the job itself was clearly of national importance.

This raises the question as to who should have borne the cost of construction. It is too simple to answer that the load should fall entirely on those who use the facility, the passengers, because, if that scheme were carried out, it would make the cost of air travel so high that few people could afford it. The field would then defeat its own purpose, which is to facilitate travel. In any case, it seems unjust to levy on the traveler alone the cost of a project that the whole country wants and needs and whose benefits accrue to all.

There would have been a certain amount of injustice, also, in placing on the local unit of government the entire financial burden, or even the greater part of it, in connection with an installation that is as much a matter of national necessity as of local advantage. To be sure, the people of New York enjoy some immediate benefits from it over and above those flowing to every American, but it is questionable indeed that they should therefore be required to provide the great bulk of the financing. The issue that presents itself here is whether it would be ethical, or even practical in the long run, to let the local taxpayer sustain such a load.

The way this issue was handled by New York is partially a matter of deflecting rather than resolving the enigma. The load was transferred from the backs of the taxpayers, to be sure. It was shifted in large part to the businessmen who rent space for concessions at the airport, for they will, under the Port Authority's plan, ultimately pay as much as seventy per cent of the operating costs; since the field creates the opportunities they will be tapping, there is no apparent ground for criticism on this score. But the fact remains that the Port Authority never could have financed the enterprise without its reserves, which made very favorable interest rates available to it. And the reserves, of course, are built out of tolls which might otherwise be reduced. To be sure, the reserves are also a provident cushion against extreme drops in traffic which would impair the agency's credit and might even put it out of business by making it unable to meet its obligations; at the same time, however, since it is the reserves that make the Authority's credit so good, it follows that those who pay the tolls on its bridges and tunnels made possible, albeit very indirectly, the airport undertaking. So, therefore, only a part of the population, and a part whose connection with the project is indirect, carries the immediate weight of an undertaking that is national in character.

The problem may become clearer if we consider what probably would have happened if, in contrast to what actually did take place in New York, no local solution had been found. It seems unbelievable that the Federal government would have taken no steps either to build the airport itself or at least to make it possible for the municipality to do so. But because the local residents (including the concessionaires and their customers, including transients) are footing the bill, the myth continues that a matter of national importance is nothing more than a problem in municipal administration. If this case is at all representative, it indicates that the role of the Federal government, particularly in its relationships with states and municipalities, will have to be re-examined and reassessed in the light of continually changing circumstances, that the myths will have to be separated from the realities.

Looking ahead, then, the case illustrates the dynamic character of administration. The settlement of one perplexing problem is often just the beginning of another; as to air transport, city, state, and nation will surely be in a continuous state of adjustment and readjustment. So, too, will the Port of New York Authority.

Indeed, the Port Authority found that its troubles with the airports only began with their acquisition; the need to complete additional construction delayed the opening of the field at Idlewild for a full year from the date the Authority took it over and, even then, another year elapsed before a dispute with the major domestic airlines was settled and these important tenants moved in. And it never did get Floyd Bennett back from the Navy. For our purposes, that is another story. Viewed broadly, however, it is just a continuation, for this is a story that never ends.

Acknowledgment is made to the National Cyclopaedia of American Biography for permission to quote from their article on Robert Moses.

Chronology

APRIL 8, 1925 Board of Trade recommends use of city facilities for aviation

SEPTEMBER 23, 1927 Chief Engineer of Board of Estimate recommends establishment of municipal airport site

NOVEMBER 1927 Fact Finding Committee recommends municipal development of airports in region

1928 Regional Plan Committee recommends acquisition of airport site

FEBRUARY 2, 1928 Board of Estimate approves development of Floyd Bennett Field by Department of Docks

OCTOBER 1928 Newark Airport opened

MAY 1931 Floyd Bennett Field opened

1931-3 Preliminary moves by Commissioner of Docks

JANUARY 1, 1934 LaGuardia takes office

1934 City leases North Beach Airport

AUGUST 24, 1935 Harlee Branch denies New York's request

DECEMBER 12, 1935 Hearing before James A. Farley begins

FEBRUARY 1936 City acquires North Beach Airport

MARCH 21, 1936 Farley denies New York's request

OCTOBER 15, 1939 LaGuardia Field opened

NOVEMBER 7, 1939 CAA makes LaGuardia coterminal

DECEMBER 2, 1941 LaGuardia announces plans for new airport

1941 Site for Idlewild acquired

1942 Department of Docks becomes Department of Marine and Aviation

1944 City-sponsored legislation permits thirty-year amortization

1945 Disagreements begin between Port Authority and Moses

JULY 1945 McGoldrick announces agreement on leases

AUGUST 1945 Idlewild planned to cover 4900 acres

AUGUST 1945 Leases approved

OCTOBER 30, 1945 Moses recommends independent Airport Authority

OCTOBER 1945 Bartholomew report recommends Port Authority operate Newark Airport

DECEMBER 27, 1945 Newark Commissioners ask Port Authority to submit proposal

DECEMBER 27, 1945 City Council strikes $45,000,000 for Idlewild from budget

DECEMBER 28, 1945 LaGuardia pleads for restoration

JANUARY 1, 1946 O'Dwyer takes office

JANUARY 5, 1946 O'Dwyer recommends enabling legislation for airport authority

JANUARY 28, 1946 Airport Authority bills introduced in legislature

FEBRUARY 1946 Citizens Union recommends Port Authority operation of Idlewild

APRIL 3, 1946 Governor Dewey signs bill

APRIL 6, 1946 Guggenheim, Doolittle and Rockefeller take office

MAY 27, 1946 Board of Estimate cuts Idlewild appropriation by $15,000,000

MAY 1946 Moses cuts planning funds for Airport Authority; O'Dwyer refuses to turn over LaGuardia Field

JUNE 1946 O'Dwyer accepts Doolittle's resignation; Moses and O'Dwyer determine amount of bond issues; Moses and Guggenheim disagree on leases

JULY 18, 1946 Guggenheim resigns

JULY 22, 1946 O'Dwyer announces reconsideration of City operation

JULY 1946 Guggenheim repeats recommendation

JULY 1946 O'Dwyer faces capital budget

JULY 30, 1946 Port Authority submits proposal to Newark

AUGUST 2, 1946 O'Dwyer requests Port Authority proposal for New York

AUGUST 8, 1946 Port Authority agrees to submit proposal

SUMMER 1946 Madigan-Hyland report on prospective airport requirements

AUGUST 22, 1946 Board of Estimate approves contract with Design Committee for limited plan

OCTOBER 7, 1946 Citizens Budget Commission recommends terminal company operation

OCTOBER 1946 Regional Plan Association recommends tri-state agency

DECEMBER 18, 1946 Port Authority submits $191,000,000 proposal

DECEMBER 22, 1946 Design Committee recommends $70,000,000 plan

JANUARY 13, 1947 City Airport Authority recommends $80,000,000 program

JANUARY 13, 1947 O'Dwyer refers problem to five-man committee

JANUARY 29, 1947 Open hearing before Board of Estimate

FEBRUARY 1947 Airlines establish bases elsewhere; enabling legislation sponsored by Port Authority introduced in legislature

MARCH 12, 1947 Meeting at Gracie Mansion

MARCH 13, 1947 Three-man committee established

MARCH 18, 1947 Two-man committee appointed

MARCH 1947 Two-man committee meets with Port Authority

MARCH 26, 1947 Port Authority submits final amended proposal: Board of Estimate agrees to agree

APRIL 1947 Port Authority enabling legislation enacted

APRIL 17, 1947 Contracts signed

MAY 29, 1947 Port Authority delivers releases from companies

JUNE 1, 1947 Port Authority takes over airports

OCTOBER 22, 1947 Newark signs contract

SELF-INSURANCE IN THE TREASURY

CONTENTS

FOREWORD

In public administration, as in literature, the situations which usually capture attention are those which involve dramatic conflict, questions of great moment, or difficult and heroic choices made under pressure. But most administrators are concerned most of the time, either alone or in co-operation with others, with solving the "low tension" problems of settled organizations, at a moderate pace, in a temperate climate. The present case deals with decisions of the latter sort made at two different periods in the Treasury Department's history, first, with regard to a special case, and then later, with regard to the same problem in general terms.

In the first instance—the switch from private insurance to self-insurance for shipments of war loan bonds and certificates by the Bureau of the Public Debt—the reader may judge that the decision was simple to make and to carry into effect. In the other, the inauguration of self-insurance for the shipment of a wide variety of valuables by a large number of Federal agencies, obstacles of various sorts appeared to combine, for many years, to make procrastination and expense easier than action and economy. The contrast between the two occasions hints at some of the reasons why reform—even on a largely procedural matter in the "housekeeping" area—can be obviously and logically necessary for a long time and still not be brought about.

Private Insurance the General Rule, 1915

It has been a long-established, though not highly articulated policy of the United States government—as of many other large governmental units and private corporations—not to carry private insurance for the risks of theft, fire, loss, or other similar disaster to its property. The government has, for the most part, been either a self-insurer or non-insurer.

Self-insurance rather loosely describes the practice of a government or governmental division of accumulating or establishing, in advance of certain statistically anticipated losses, a fund from which to pay itself when losses occur. Self-insurance is always more economical than private insurance when the losses are not expected to be great compared with the resources of the insurer; it becomes particularly desirable—in contrast to private insurance—when the risk is high (because the individual loss can be very great), and the premiums therefore high, and yet, for one reason or another, the actual losses are comparatively low.

"No insurance" is the term applied to the policy of most government units of not insuring, either by self-insurance or otherwise, their basic equipment such as buildings, furniture, ships, and planes. When losses occur, money to replace or rebuild is obtained from funds available to the governmental unit involved. Since the government itself assumes all risk in both cases, self-insurance can properly be regarded as nothing more than a bookkeeping device to remind the legislature or other competent authority that it must always be in a position to make good on possible but quantitatively undeterminable losses.

Insurance of Federal government property with private insurance companies is an anomaly, since insurance was developed, over the course of centuries, to protect, by the device of risk-spreading or pooling, those whose resources were too limited to bear catastrophic losses. The Federal government is backed by the resources of its millions of citizens, representing the largest possible aggregate of capital that could be assembled in the United States and the widest possible spreading of risk. It is able to bear the impact of a large loss because funds can always be made available for the replacement of losses. The Federal government's far-reaching police power also places it in a particularly good position to reduce, through safeguards of its own devising, the hazards to which its property is subject.

Despite the fact that the resources of the United States government have always been infinitely greater than the sum of all conceivable insurable losses, these resources have not always been legally available for replacing losses. For a considerable period of time, they could not be drawn on to provide money or precious metal to make up for an identical amount stolen or lost, nor could they back up the duplication of a bond, that is, the issuing (after certain safeguarding procedures) of a duplicate piece of paper for a lost bond and the assumption of the risk that the original, although deemed "lost," might some day be presented in a bona fide manner for redemption. Until 1937 and the events described later in this case, Federal officials responsible for shipping valuables such as coins or bonds were, under the law, personally accountable for any financial losses in the shipments they ordered made. The Federal government had the right to sue them for the full value of a stolen payroll or lost packet of securities, even if this was reckoned in thousands of dollars and even if they had taken all precautions humanly possible. In many cases, of course, special legislation by Congress ultimately relieved officials of liability for large losses over which they obviously had no control, but often—because of the cumbersomeness of this relief procedure—they agreed or were forced to pay personally for smaller amounts, although equally blameless with regard to them. In any event, replacement of the loss was painfully slow and productive of grave inconvenience and injustice. Accountable officers were therefore understandably apprehensive over their position and pressed their superior officers to develop some form of protection for them.

The Treasury Department was the government's biggest shipper of valuables. From 1889 to 1914 its shipments of money and securities were made under contract with express companies which guaranteed safe delivery and, in the case of theft or other loss, the replacement of the loss—that is, the furnishing of an identical amount of money or precious metal or, in the case of a valuable which was neither money, precious metal, nor a bond, the furnishing of its monetary equivalent. This practice was safe, from the accountable official's point of view, and superficially conformed to the basic government policy of no insurance (although doubtless the express companies were heavily insured). As long as shipments were not very large, the relatively expensive nature of express service was no deterrent to its use. But the volume of the government's currency and securities issues grew, and shipping costs in the second decade of the 1900's became very high. In 1914 the Treasury abandoned private express and arranged with the Post Office Department for the transportation of money and securities by registered parcel post. Considerable savings were immediately realized: one shipment of $50,000,000 from the Philadelphia mint to the New York Subtreasury bore the parcel post charge of $3,376.18; by express the cost would have been in the neighborhood of $25,000.

The major source of the difference was the vastly different risks assumed by the express companies and the Post Office. The latter did not guarantee to replace losses. This fact immediately created a serious hazard for the Treasury's accountable officers; it also meant that a lengthy proceeding of one sort or another would be necessary for the replacement of losses. Some step had to be taken to overcome the risk and time factors.

The situation was not fruitful with possibilities. To operate on a no-insurance basis appeared impossible, for there was no appropriation from which money could legally be drawn to make up a new payroll, for example, after one was lost or stolen. As far as the books of the accountable disbursing officer were concerned, the money had already been paid out. And government employees could not be kept waiting for their salary while a relief bill was put through Congress. As a Senate report on the subject pointed out many years later,

> . . . it is necessary for the efficient operation of the administrative machinery of the government that in case of loss there should be available a

means of prompt duplication or reimbursement, and the existing appropriation machinery has been inadequate to that end.

Self-insurance does not appear to have been considered, or perhaps it was early rejected. Insurance by private firms appeared to be the only viable alternative. The Comptroller of the Treasury, whose duty it was to settle the appropriation accounts of administrative officers, was asked to give an opinion on the matter, and in November 1914 he rendered an advance decision allowing payment of insurance premiums out of appropriations for the "transportation of moneys" and "the expenses of loans." Some months later, in August 1915, the Secretary of the Treasury ordered that currency and certain other valuables sent by the Treasury by registered mail be insured with private underwriters, the funds for premiums to be drawn from the named appropriations. Later, in April 1917, with the volume of war loans steadily increasing, Treasury officials in charge of these matters were ordered specifically to insure shipments of Liberty Bonds and Treasury Certificates of Indebtedness.

In 1921, the Comptroller General (an official appointed under the Budget and Accounting Act of 1921, who took over the functions of the Comptroller of the Treasury) ruled that competitive bids must be taken annually on government insurance contracts. Thereafter, the Treasury Department made a master contract each year with the broker whose bid was accepted, covering the entire liability of the Treasury Department's bureaus. The bids were based on an elaborate system of risk-sharing among a number of insurance companies and reinsurance by others. Other Federal departments and agencies which came to feel the need for prompt reimbursement for valuables lost in shipment asked to be taken under the coverage of the master contract from time to time. By 1936 there were some fifty named assureds, holding a volume of commercial insurance amounting to $12,000,000,000 at an annual premium of about $370,000. Each assured bore its own share of the premium from its own appropriations.

The incongruity of this situation was well described by the Senate Report already cited:

> . . . while Congress [was] . . . appropriating, indirectly, hundreds of thousands of dollars annually, to be turned over to insurance companies, it [did] . . . nothing by way of providing an adequate means within the Government to fulfill a simple intragovernmental need, but . . . hired private [insurance] corporations to perform that function.

One significant breach was, however, made in this system early in its existence. It was the result of a group of decisions to which our attention now turns.

An Exception to Private Insurance, 1919

In December 1918, Assistant Secretary of the Treasury Russell C. Leffingwell, to whom the Public Debt Service was assigned, noted that in 1917 alone the insurance premium for mail shipments of war loan bonds and certificates had reached approximately $1,000,000; he also noted that actual losses on the billions of dollars worth of securities shipped had been less than $25,000. Leffingwell communicated on the matter with the Commissioner of the Public Debt, W. L. Broughton, and with S. Parker Gilbert of the War Loan Staff. Leffingwell had brought Gilbert, his former law partner, to Washington, and Gilbert was serving as an assistant to him. Leffingwell suggested that because of the high cost of protection, the Department might well shift to carrying its own insurance.

Gilbert picked up the idea readily. In his reply, he observed that the use of private insurance had originally been justified by circumstances but was now proving too costly. Government "insurance of some sort . . . [was] . . . obviously necssary," however, in preference to the third course of no-insurance and relying on a special act of Congress to give relief in each case of loss. "Congress is not friendly to insurance of government property," he recalled, but a fairly good precedent for government insurance of shipments of valuables already existed in the public War Risk Insurance provided for ships and their cargoes in 1917. Gilbert therefore recommended to Leffingwell that a law be drafted setting up a revolving insurance fund with an initial appropriation of about $10,000,000 to be replenished annually by the amount of money which would otherwise go in premiums and by any lost or stolen amounts subsequently recovered. "The Bureau of War Risk Insurance of the Treasury should also assume the administration of the new fund," he added.

Leffingwell thereupon communicated with Assistant Secretary of the Treasury Thomas B. Love, who was in charge of the Bureau of War Risk Insurance, telling him of the proposal and asking for any assistance and suggestions he might care to give. S. R. Jacobs, like Gilbert a member of the War Loan Staff, but assigned as an assistant to Love, was given the task of drafting the proposed self-insurance scheme.

Jacobs thought he could set up the scheme of self-insurance without a new law. This was naturally a welcome development, since drafting and carrying a bill through Congress would be time-consuming; new legislation was subject to the further hazard of unwelcome changes and additions prior to enactment. In collaboration with Broughton and Gilbert, Jacobs worked out a proposal to set up an insurance fund through the establishment of what they termed a "permanent encumbrance" against the Public Debt Service's appropriation, "Expenses of Loans," equal to the value of lost or destroyed bonds. By this device a certain amount of money in the appropriation would be earmarked for replacement of losses and would be carried on the books for that purpose until used up or until the appropriation lapsed, whichever came first. No encumbrance (or "obligation," in modern fiscal parlance), could be "permanent" beyond the life of its appropriation, of course. The drafters of this self-insurance scheme were particularly fortunate because the "Expenses of Loans" appropriation was a "permanent indefinite" appropriation, that is, one from which funds for the stated purpose could be drawn without limit unless and until the appropriation was repealed. With an ordinary fixed term appropriation they probably could not have proceeded with their plan.

Gilbert, at this point in the thinking and drafting of the proposed plan, decided it would be wise to secure in advance the informal approval of the Comptroller of the Treasury. Through Leffingwell he submitted a draft of the self-insurance plan to the Comptroller, W. W. Warwick. He received Warwick's approval "in principle" on December 21, 1918, with the reservation that a trust fund rather than a "permanent encumbrance" be established. A trust fund is an amount of money received or appropriated and held in trust in accordance with an agreement or legislative act; it may be expended only in accordance with the terms of such trust or act. Like any other appropriation account, a trust fund is part of Treasury money and is appropriated to the personal credit of the officer charged with using the fund. Payments from a trust fund are made only by warrant, an official document on the basis of which money from the United States Treasury is placed to the credit of an official authorized to write checks for a purpose specified by law. In 1918, warrants had to be countersigned by the Comptroller of the Treasury.

Feeling that the trust fund approach conformed with his original idea of a revolving fund, but questioning the practicability of the formal device, Gilbert redrafted the Jacobs proposal as modified by Warwick and specified that the amounts equivalent to the estimated value of lost bonds, which would have been permanent encumbrances under Jacobs' plan, and a trust fund under Warwick's proposal, were to be paid into a special deposit account. In contrast to a trust fund, a deposit account is a sum of money withdrawn from the Treasury and then placed on deposit to the official credit of a government officer, with the Treasurer of the United States acting in the capacity of a banker. Checks may be issued against this money and payments made from it just as from a checking account, without the counter-signature of the Comptroller. Deposit accounts are used for money which must be temporarily set aside until its further disposition is made clear.

From Gilbert's point of view the chief advantage of a deposit account was that it avoided the delay of securing a warrant and the Comptroller's approval for each payment. But precisely because of these factors the proposal of a deposit account did not meet with Warwick's approval. It would not, he pointed out in a memorandum on March 20, 1919, be subject to audit by the accounting officers of the Treasury, nor to an independent check by himself. Only a trust fund would insure these necessary "exceptional safeguards" against unauthorized issues of duplicate securities in place of those which were judged "lost" or stolen.

Writing to Leffingwell after this opinion, Gilbert said, "I had hoped the Comptroller would be satisfied with the special deposit account, but in view of his insistence on a trust fund I shall, if you approve, proceed to draw the papers."

Leffingwell approved, the Securities Trust Fund was set up on paper, and on April 9, 1919 Secretary of the Treasury Carter Glass issued a memorandum inaugurating a self-insurance scheme for the registered mailing by the Public Debt Service of Liberty Bonds in coupon form and Treasury Certificates of Indebtedness when originally issued. This, as the Comptroller of the Treasury had pointed out in his March 20 memorandum, was "the nearest approach to a no-insurance basis that is possible in the absence of affirmative legislative provision for caring for the loss of securities while in the Treasury Department's custody in transit."

Thus, after a little more than three months of discussion and drafting, the use of private insurance to compensate for losses in shipment was abandoned with respect to one major group of the government's valuables.

1919-1932: Questioning and Inaction

Although the Securities Trust Fund was immediately successful as an economy measure, the device of a self-insurance fund was not carried over into the protection of other shipments of valuables during the period from 1919 to 1932. The Public Debt Service itself continued to use private insurance for its shipments of other types of valuables, and other government agencies retained and even increased their commercial insurance coverage.

This ever-widening use of ordinary insurance was not in accord with the views of the Comptroller of the Treasury or the successor to his power, the Comptroller General. The former, in a digression at the close of his March 1919 memorandum to R. C. Leffingwell, had said that

> . . . the original rulings [in 1914] authorizing insurance were fundamentally unsound as is all insurance of government property. The present plan [self-insurance] is justified as a step in the right direction . . . the elimination of the practice of insurance. Being a return to the old practice of no insurance it is justified by the evident benefits to be secured and in my opinion the appropriation is more clearly available for this purpose than it is for the payment of insurance premiums.

And later, in 1925, Comptroller General McCarl declared in a formal opinion:

> . . . the established rule is that Government officers ordinarily are not authorized to incur expenses for the insurance of public property both upon the ground that the appropriations sought to be charged with the expenses are not available and because it was held to be the policy of the Government to assume its own risks. . . .

But no action was taken during these years to try to extend self-insurance on the basis of these opinions. And, by the close of the decade the General Accounting Office (the Comptroller General's agency) showed itself unreceptive to any proposal to abandon private insurance and pay for any actual losses out of funds considered available for insurance premiums. In 1929, for example, during hearings before the Budget and Improvement Committee of the Treasury, Secretary of the Treasury Ogden Mills asked that consideration be given to the question of establishing a self-insurance fund in connection with the registered mail shipment of new currency. E. F. Bartelt, then the Chief of the Division of Bookkeeping and Warrants, drafted a scheme for self-insurance and engaged in conversations with the General Accounting Office on the subject of whether the money then going as premiums to private insurance companies could not instead be paid into a special fund for self-insurance. The GAO indicated that there was no authority in the law for such a fund to be established, thus implying (it would seem) that there *was* authority to pay insurance premiums. The matter was thereupon dropped, possibly because even among those who disagreed at this point with the General Accounting Office as to the legal *availability* of funds, there was some hesitation and doubt over the *adequacy* of existing appropriations for the repayment of losses in shipment.

The problem of adequacy, however, did not appear insurmountable to S. R. Jacobs, now Assistant Commissioner of the Public Debt, who continued to be concerned with the idea of self-insurance. In 1933 he suggested to the then Under Secretary of the Treasury, Dean Acheson, that there was no reason why private insurance should not be abandoned and losses paid from the appropriations formerly used to pay premiums, even going so far as to say, "In case the losses exceeded [the] available [amount] the matter may be presented to the Congress for a deficiency appropriation." Jacobs' proposal came to nothing, possibly because of the weight of the Comptroller General's informal opinion in 1929, as well as a general unwillingness on the part of officials to adopt a procedure which involved going to Congress for relief in cases of loss. The drafting of new legislation to place the whole matter of the protection of shipments of valuables on a definite and more regular basis does not appear to have been discussed. No doubt the problem of dealing with GAO opposition and possible lobbying by insurance firms was a deterrent to this line of action. In any event, Mr. Acheson's stay in the Treasury was brief and he was deeply concerned with other, infinitely more important matters.

The General Rule Is Changed, 1937

Elsewhere in the Treasury Department, for a number of years preceding Jacobs' note to Acheson, the insuring of government shipments of valuables had been undergoing more than ordinary scrutiny by an attorney named John Gaylord Harlan, a member of the War Loan Staff to which Jacobs and Gilbert had once belonged. That group had lingered on after the war, and under the increasing pressure of policy problems, had become a circle of advisers to the Secretary on other matters. These were years of declining status for the office of Solicitor of the Treasury Department; as a consequence, one or two of the lawyers on the War Loan Staff gained in power and occupied, in an informal manner, the posts of personal legal and policy advisers to the Secretary. Between 1929 and 1932, Harlan became, in this wise, a close adviser to Ogden Mills, Secretary of the Treasury; characteristically his title from 1931 to 1933, Senior Legal Assistant to the Under Secretary, gave no hint of his functions.

In 1929 Harlan took over the work of legal review of the annual Treasury circulars calling for competitive bids on the government's mammoth insurance contract for losses in shipment. For the first year or two he treated this as a routine matter. Then the striking statistics of the situation led him to evaluate the degree of protection the government received in return for its high premiums.[1] Shipments were guarded by the Secret Service, armed postal guards, armed convoys, and the like. When losses occurred, government agents were frequently able to effect recovery. It appeared that the government received little more from insurance than the prompt payment necessary to keep the account of a disbursing officer from showing a deficit. From observing the competitive bidding process for several years, Har-

[1] Available statistics, for a somewhat longer period than Harlan was reviewing, indicate that during the years from 1921 to 1936, insurance companies assumed approximately 70 billion dollars of liability for government valuables. They received about 3½ million dollars in premiums and paid $200,000 in losses.

lan had moreover concluded that certain procedures adopted by insurance brokers in bidding for the government insurance contract had had an undesirable effect on insurance practice in the New York-Washington area.

Harlan was apparently not familiar, at the time, with the history of the Bureau of the Public Debt's Securities Trust Fund or with previous Treasury discussions of self-insurance and no insurance. He concluded, purely on the basis of the information before him, that the Treasury should shift to self-insurance for the shipment of valuables. Some time in 1932 Harlan proposed this to Secretary Mills. The latter may then have told Harlan of the earlier history of insurance of Treasury shipments of valuables. In any case, he instructed the attorney to explore the subject further.

In the meanwhile, the environment of the entire Executive Branch changed radically. The history of the government in the years 1932-33 is part of a much larger history that has often been told. For the case in hand it is simply necessary to note a few important developments: the great depression and the impetus it gave to the drive for "economy" in public life; the shift from a Republican business-minded administration to the Roosevelt "New Deal" which was not oriented toward business; the increased flexibility of attitude and willingness to improvise administrative organizations and devices for solving old and new problems.

Specifically, for the Treasury Department, one result of the 1932 election was the appointment of Henry Morgenthau as Roosevelt's second Secretary of the Treasury on January 1, 1934, and Mr. Morgenthau's establishment of the Office of the General Counsel within the Treasury with his close adviser Herman Oliphant as its first incumbent. Oliphant completely reorganized the agency's legal establishment. The Office of the General Counsel was now established for "co-ordinating all the legal work of the department." Previously lawyers in the Department had worked in the various operating units, such as the Bureau of Internal Revenue, where they had been subordinate to the non-lawyer chief of the bureau. The reorganization lifted them out of the bureaus and gathered them all together under the General Counsel, where they continued their specialized legal work for the operating units, but under the General Counsel's and an Assistant General Counsel's supervision rather than that of a "lay" bureau chief. Structurally, a fine departmental network of attorneys, subordinate to no one but the General Counsel, was established. Since the General Counsel was a very strong figure, central control of legal matters was considerably tightened and department-wide review of general policy by the General Counsel and his staff was also made possible. While this review was naturally of a predominantly legal nature, it offered an opportunity for the systematic scrutiny of procedures. And Oliphant's prestige insured the necessary topside support for any important innovation proposed by the legal staff.

Harlan was one of the few Republican appointees retained in the new legal structure; he was made first Assistant General Counsel and served as Mr. Oliphant's chief assistant. Carrying the idea of self-insurance along in his new position, Harlan retained an insurance analyst, some time in 1934, to investigate the history of Treasury insurance of shipments and to describe the probable effects of a switch to self-insurance.

Up to this time it still was not clear whether a new law would be necessary or whether a self-insurance plan could be established under existing legislation with the addition of safeguards necessary to meet the objections of the Comptroller General. Before making a final decision on this question Harlan asked a number of responsible officials in the Department for their views. In reply, one of them summarized the chief reasons why legislation appeared to be necessary. He said, in part:

1. Without legislation, an undue burden would be cast upon accountable officers of the Government. Each loss would represent a shortage in their accounts, for which they and their sureties [private bonding companies] would be liable. This condition would result in:
   a. A reluctance to accept responsible offices in the Government.
   b. A probable increase in the cost of surety bonds.
   c. An increase in the number of private relief

bills presented to Congress, which, in turn, would result in:

(1) Greater legislative congestion.
(2) Increased work for congressional committees.
(3) Belated investigation of losses, both by congressional committees, and by the departments or agencies involved.
(4) Greater risk of injustice in certain cases.

2. The situation would be even more acute in the case of a loss which should be immediately replaced or duplicated, as for instance, a loss of a payroll or of securities which have been deposited by a taxpayer as collateral. No funds would be available for such replacement or duplication, unless the accountable officer, without statutory authority voluntarily used other funds in his hands and thereby incurred a shortage in his account. Failure to make prompt replacement or duplication might often result in hardship and justifiable criticism of the Government.
3. Federally owned corporations would be unwilling to absorb such losses as part of their ordinary expenses.

Some time later, in 1936, after reviewing this and other opinions and the report of the insurance analyst, Harlan came to the conclusion that new legislation was necessary and desirable. He turned all the material he had collected on the subject over to another attorney, Samuel Klaus, a special assistant to the General Counsel, with instructions to explore the situation and draft legislation which would substitute a fund of some type for private insurance. The decision that the mode of protection of shipments of valuables should be altered—and by legislation—was the move that broke the long stalemate between the desire of line officials to create a system of self-insurance within the existing legislative framework and the opinion of the Comptroller General that this was not possible.

Klaus picked up where Harlan had left off. He discussed the problem with the administrative officers of all the bureaus and agencies which came under the government's blanket policy, studied their suggestions and other previous proposals, and came to the conclusion that the principle of insurance "had nothing whatever to do with the problem of government losses in shipment." After outlining the general direction to be followed, he assigned the actual task of drafting a new bill to another attorney. But he was dissatisfied with the resulting draft, which provided for an insurance fund to be replenished by annual payments equivalent to the commercial premiums which would have otherwise been paid, somewhat like the proposal made by E. F. Bartelt in 1929. Klaus was convinced that a complete break should be made with the concept and form of private insurance. He accordingly wrote the first draft of a new bill himself. It provided for two complementary methods of securing repayment to the government for lost money or other valuables.

By one method, a $500,000 appropriation was authorized for use under the direction of the Secretary of the Treasury for the replacement of valuables or the payment of their value when they were lost, damaged, or destroyed in the course of shipment. A second device, a revolving fund, was set up to cover certain losses not reimbursable from this $500,000. The fund was to be established by an appropriation of $500,000 to which an additional $200,000 would be added annually until, in 10 years, the fund reached $2,500,000. Losses would be paid for out of this fund, and into it would be deposited any recoveries and repayments. Together the two funds applied to losses in shipment of all valuables in which United States government agencies or wholly-owned corporations had an interest—including coin, specie, bullion, currency, bonds, coupons, debentures, bills, notes, certificates of indebtedness, certificates of deposit, mortgages, assignments, certificates of stock, warehouse receipts, checks, trust receipts, warrants, and stamps.

By a simple but vital provision the draft also lifted from accountable officers the burden which had forced them to depend on private insurance: it said that they were relieved of further responsibility for valuables in their charge if they shipped them according to the regulations established under the act.

The bill covered one subject not originally specified by Harlan. While drafting it, Klaus happened to be assigned to substitute for Assistant General Counsel Clarence Opper, who was on vacation. Part of Opper's work was deciding on claims against the government by people who for one reason or another had never received government checks or bonds shipped to them or had received them in defaced and unredeemable condition. Klaus was impressed with the difficulty these individuals experienced in securing a duplicate bond or check, despite their bona fide claim. He decided to include some sections liberalizing the notoriously onerous conditions under which owners of lost, stolen, or defaced government checks or bonds could collect their money. The draft accordingly authorized the Secretary of the Treasury to waive, under certain circumstances, the long-standing requirement that those (including governmental subdivisions) who received duplicate bonds or checks must post a bond of indemnity to protect the Federal government in case it later turned out that the check or bond in question was improperly redeemed.

Although Klaus was given primary responsibility for preparing a draft bill (and regarded himself as its "father"), the draft could not receive the final approval of the Secretary of the Treasury for submission to the Bureau of the Budget and to Congress until every Treasury bureau or office concerned with the shipment of valuables had reviewed it and found it adequate for its own purposes. Consultation with the Post Office Department was also indicated, because that department was in charge of the actual shipment of the valuables, and with the Bureau of the Budget, since its review was essential before a bill proposed by an executive department could be submitted to Congress.

The bill met with general approval within the Treasury Department, but there were many suggestions for changes; eight months were consumed by discussion and it was November 1936 before the bill was deemed ready for submission to the Budget Bureau for its scrutiny and transmittal to Congress. There were meetings among various interested officials, circulation of alternative drafts of certain sections, and countless informal unrecorded conversations. Safeguards on the payment of lost checks and bonds had to be added or strengthened to satisfy some, distinctions between different types of bonds and securities clarified, and definitions sharpened to meet the objections of others. Debates over proper legal phraseology took up a good deal of time.

At the same time that this consultation was going on, intradepartmentally, top Treasury officials undertook to inform the important private group involved—the insurance companies and brokers—of the proposed change in government policy. Underwriters and agents were called in individually and told of the bill.

"They squawked," one attorney recalls, "and said this was contrary to the spirit of private enterprise. They would tell their congressmen!" Treasury attorneys convinced them that would have a weak case in Congress: the government would save an impressive sum of money by the change and it was not, moreover, embarking on an insurance business itself, but merely taking advantage of its own inherent ability to withstand losses. As a result of this prior consultation, insurance groups voiced no protests when the bill finally came before Congress. Perhaps the companies concluded that any poor showing they made in protesting an obviously beneficial piece of legislation would prejudice their standing with respect to whatever insurance the government or government officials still held with them, notably fidelity bonds for accountable officials.

During the drafting process, in June 1936, William H. McReynolds, Administrative Assistant to the Secretary of the Treasury, wrote to the Post Office Department telling of the contemplated change and suggesting that the Post Office might wish to undertake to promulgate the regulations for shipping valuables under self-insurance.

By November 1936 a draft bill satisfactory to all in the Treasury was ready and plans were made to send it, together with a draft letter from the Secretary of the Treasury to the Chairmen of the Senate and House Committees on Expenditures in the Executive Departments, to the Bureau of the Budget for the necessary review. Before this was done, copies of the bill and of the Secretary's letter of transmittal were sent around to the Treasury officials concerned for a last look. Sixteen officials thereupon indicated their final approval by initialing the Department's file copies of the letters of transmittal. And these carbon copies, with sixteen sets of hieroglyphics, became a concluding chapter of the Treasury's archives on the proposed bill.

This is not to say that only sixteen Treasury officials saw the Secretary's letter and the November draft—and previous drafts. More than that number undoubtedly read or penciled up some version of the bill. But these sixteen were a particular constellation for this subject; they represented the major lines of authority and areas of interest within the Treasury on the matter of legislation on losses in shipment; their signatures were necessary for final clearance. Their approval meant that there was full department support behind the proposal. Not only the large sum of money involved but the fact that the new scheme was destined to undergo full Congressional scrutiny made such prior consensus a vital matter of departmental self-protection.

For the historian, this array of officials and their titles discloses the extent to which the intelligence and experience of the organization had been mobilized behind the legislative proposal; each name, moreover, represented several others from the same office—chiefly administrative officials who would be responsible for the actual administration of the law's provisions. In order, these were the officials whose initials appeared on the file copies of the letters to Congress:[2]

W. Heffelfinger—Executive Assistant to the Commissioner, Bureau of Accounts and Deposits and *Secretary of the Department's Insurance Committee.* He would naturally have to see and approve all legislation relating to insurance.

Maurice Collins—*Assistant Commissioner, Bureau of Accounts and Deposits.* Since this Bureau kept the accounts for the payment of insurance on behalf of all the assureds and had also, before 1933, handled all Treasury legislation, its final approval was needed. As Assistant Commissioner, Collins normally saw all matters which were sent to Mr. Bartelt, the Commissioner, and both their sets of initials customarily appeared on important papers.

E. F. Bartelt—*Commissioner of Accounts and Deposits.* As chief of the Bureau of Accounts and Deposits, his consent was needed on the important changes in accounting which would result from the establishment of the two funds under the new legislation.

G. O. Barnes—*Assistant to the Treasurer of the United States.* Since the Treasurer was concerned with the safety of the currency he issued and was one of the assureds under the master policy, his office had to pass on any change in the system of safeguarding money.

Mary O'Reilly—*Assistant Director of the Mint.* Shipments of bullion between mints and assay offices had been insured under the master insurance contract, with premium payments made from an appropriation under the control of the Director of the Mint. The Mint's approval was therefore necessary for a change in the mode of protection.

W. S. Broughton—*Commissioner of the Public Debt.* Although the Bureau of the Public Debt still maintained and proposed to continue for the time being its Securities Trust Fund for the replacement of securities lost or damaged in shipment, it occasionally sent small shipments under the blanket insurance policy. For this reason, and because it was necessary that the new legislation in no way contravene or interfere with the existing Securities Trust Fund, Commissioner Broughton's approval was necessary.

S. J. Spingarn—an attorney assigned to the *Legislative Section of the General Counsel's Office.* He participated in the drafting of the law, representing the point of view of his chief, Clinton Hester, Assistant General Counsel in charge of legislation. His job was to see that the law conformed with the known policy of Congress on the subject of insurance, revolving funds, and credits, and that it was drafted in clear understandable language. Without Spingarn's approval of the law in detail, Hester would not approve it and assume the task of seeing it through Congress.

Clinton M. Hester—*Assistant General Counsel.* As the assistant in charge of legislation, Hester was the driving force behind Treasury-proposed legislation when it was before Congress. He handled the correspondence and personal contacts with the legislature. When requested, his office also wrote reports on bills for Congressional Committees—as they did later in this case. Without his approval and support, the General Counsel would not approve a bill for submission to Congress.

J. G. Harlan—*Assistant General Counsel,* occupying the post of chief assistant to the General Counsel. As the individual responsible for carrying the idea of self-insurance over from the

[2] The organizational relationship of these officials is portrayed in the chart on page 212.

previous administration and for initiating the legislation, Harlan's approval was desirable. As Oliphant's senior assistant he was approving it for the General Counsel from a general legal point of view.

S. McCaskey—an attorney assigned by the General Counsel to work with the *Bureau of Accounts and Deposits and the Office of the Treasurer of the United States*. McCaskey participated in the drafting of the law, seeing that it met the views of the Bureau of Accounts and Deposits as to any accounting procedures laid down and that it provided sufficient protection for the moneys in the Treasurer's care.

T. W. Cunningham—an attorney assigned by the General Counsel to matters of *financing and public debt*. He participated actively in the drafting of the law on behalf of the Commissioner of the Public Debt.

A. C. Aarons—an attorney who acted as *general assistant to Clarence Opper*, the Assistant General Counsel whose purview included Public Debt, Accounts and Deposits, and the Treasurer, among other matters. Aarons, together with McCaskey and Cunningham, represented Opper in the detailed drafting discussions with Spingarn of the Legislative Section, and with Klaus. Aarons was also on special assignment by the General Counsel to matters concerning registered mail insurance—the very heart of the law.

Clarence Opper—*Assistant General Counsel* assigned, as has been said, to handle legal matters for a number of bureaus, including Public Debt, Accounts and Deposits, and the Treasurer's office. He represented the combined point of view of these operating divisions and his approval of the bill as a working piece of legislation was necessary before General Counsel Oliphant would approve it.

Herman Oliphant—*General Counsel*. Both as the Secretary of the Treasury's statutory legal adviser and also as "the constant adviser of the Secretary and a regular participant in the inner departmental councils in matters of policy," Oliphant's concurrence was necessary.

W. H. McReynolds—*Administrative Assistant to the Secretary of the Treasury*. McReynolds had come over to the Treasury from the Farm Credit Administration with Henry Morgenthau. Like Oliphant, he was very close to the Secretary. As Administrative Assistant, he fell "heir to a part of the duties which previously had been those of the Under Secretary. He was the avenue for the communication of papers to the Secretary." He was also "chief adviser on all departmental questions relating to organization or procedure." His signature showed that central approval of the proposed law had been secured.

Henry Hyland—*in the office of the Secretary of the Treasury*. One of Hyland's regular duties was seeing that proposed legislation and the accompanying letters were seen by every interested party in the Treasury Department. His signature at the close of the line of initials indicated that the Secretary's office was satisfied that the file had been properly circulated.

A notable absentee from this list was Samuel Klaus. But he had drafted the Secretary's letter!

Some time elapsed while the final round of the consultative process took place, and it was not until December 10, 1936, that Administrative Assistant McReynolds sent a copy of the draft bill and the letters to Congress, to the Acting Director of the Bureau of the Budget. In an accompanying letter, McReynolds asked the Bureau to advise him whether the proposed measure was "in accord with the program of the President."

The Budget Bureau felt that the opinion of the Post Office Department was necessary before it could make any decision about the bill and accordingly it sent the draft bill to that Department. This led to a postscript, so to speak, in the drafting process. On March 16, 1937 the Post Office wrote the Budget Bureau that, subject to the inclusion of certain changes, which it set forth in detail, it was "in accord with the proposed measure." One of these proposed changes was the inclusion of a phrase stating that nothing in the bill should be

> construed as abrogating or restricting the provisions of existing law authorizing the Postmaster General to cause to be underwritten or insured with any commercial insurance companies any liability or risk assumed by the Post Office Department.

The Budget Bureau, on March 19, referred the bill and the Post Office's suggestions back to the Treasury Department. Klaus and a number of the others who had worked on the bill returned to it; they agreed with some Post Office proposals and not with others. Some Treasury–Post Office discussion on these matters ensued, leading finally, on April 14, to a version acceptable to both and to the Bureau of the Budget. The clause affirming the Post

ORGANIZATIONAL RELATIONSHIP OF MAJOR TREASURY OFFICIALS INVOLVED IN THE DRAFTING OF THE "GOVERNMENT LOSSES IN SHIPMENT ACT," 1937

(other parts of Treasury not shown)

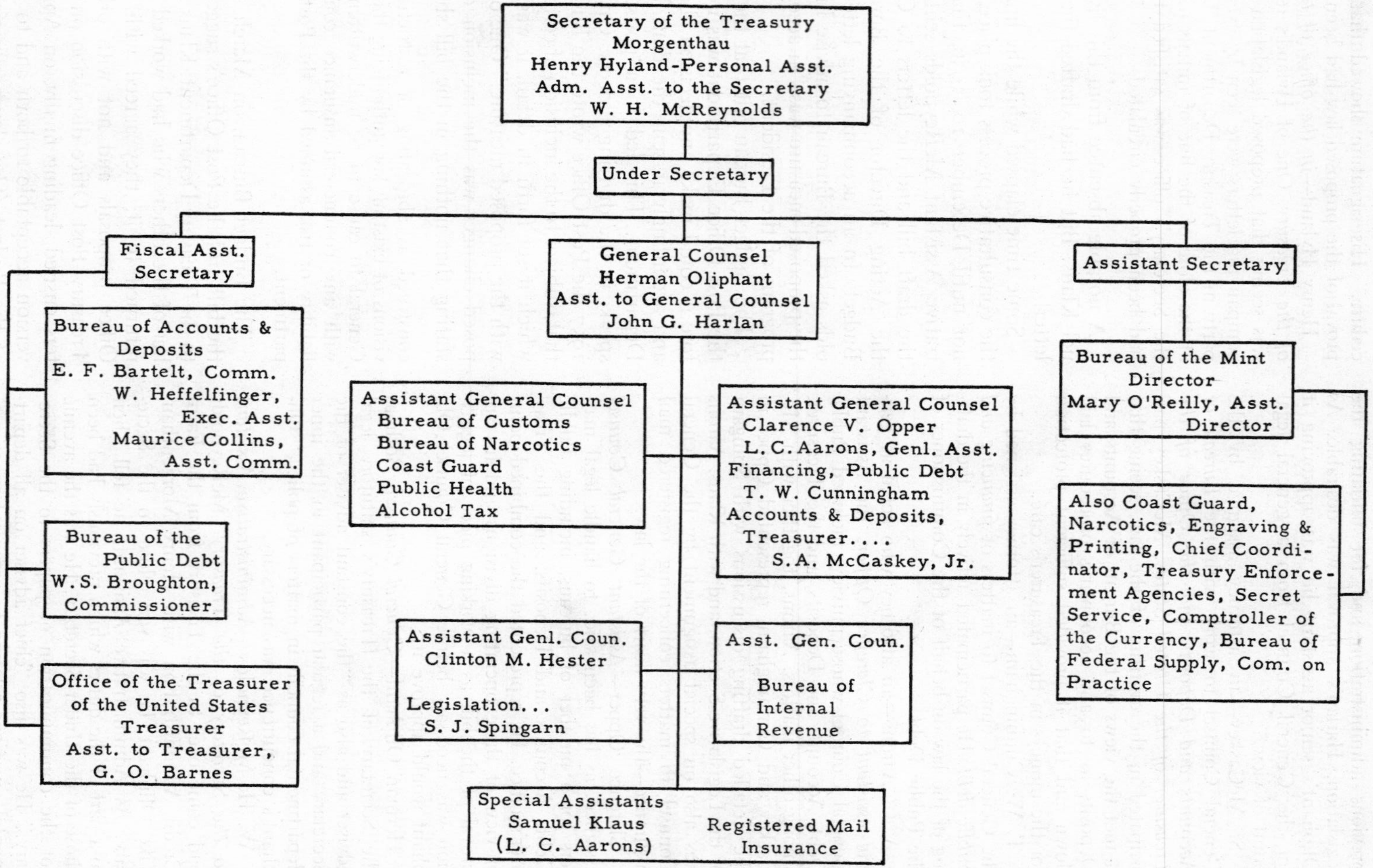

Office's right to take out private insurance was not included.

On April 23, 1937, the proposed measure, together with an explanatory letter (in the nature of a report) signed by the Acting Secretary of the Treasury (and written in the General Counsel's office) was sent to the Committees of both houses. Not all of the original sixteen initialed the carbon of the Treasury's letter this time; most of the previous ones were apparently not concerned with the subject matter of the new set of changes.

In Congress the bill received the crucial support of Congressman John J. Cochran, Chairman of the House Committee and the outstanding "economy man" in the House. After favorable reports (largely based on a memorandum prepared by Spingarn and signed by Hester) by both the Senate and House Committees on Expenditures in the Executive Departments, and some minor amendments, the bill was passed by both houses and became law on July 8, 1937.[3] Herman Oliphant, in a memorandum to the Secretary of the Treasury the day after passage of the Losses in Shipment Act, hailed this successful conclusion and called the law "a real piece of economy legislation."

POSTSCRIPT

This case contains a striking contrast.

Just two years from the time in 1917 that the Secretary of the Treasury ordered private insurance of government shipments of Liberty Bonds and Treasury Certificates of Indebtedness, the expense and anomalousness of the procedure had been noted, alternative plans canvassed, and a solution adopted for the Public Debt Service; actual negotiations and drafting took only four months.

Quite different was the progress on changing the mode of protection of other shipments of valuables. The Secretary's first general order requiring private insurance was issued in August 1915; not until July 8, 1937, did the Losses in Shipment Act become law. And active negotiations for a solution took a full year.

The reasons for the contrast are of interest to the student of public administration. No definite statement of causes is possible, but some of the more obvious conditioning factors may be noted.

There are first the technical problems: Gilbert's plan affected only one bureau, Klaus's bill was of concern to a host of Treasury offices and other agencies; Gilbert could operate within existing law, Klaus had to prepare and, as best he might, ensure the enactment of a new law.

The difference is also partially explicable in organizational terms: the Comptroller of the Treasury, while independent in his judgments, was organizationally a part of the administration; the Comptroller General was a servant of Congress. The absence of a central management organ in the Treasury was irrelevant to the solution of a problem affecting a single bureau in 1919, but highly significant in the fifteen years that followed—the organization encouraged inertia. And the establishment of the new legal structure under Morgenthau and Oliphant produced two semi-contradictory tendencies: it fostered action and a Treasury-wide viewpoint while placing a premium on elaborate and prolonged clearance and on legal perfectionism.

Finally there are numerous political factors. World War I brought new and energetic people to Washington and created an atmosphere in which innovation and improvisation were welcomed; and President Wilson's administration would not be unduly concerned with the possible antagonism of insurance companies to a procedure that was businesslike in itself. The fat years of peace and the Republican regime that ruled during that period led to government inactivity, caution, even inertia, and an acute concern for private business interests. Finally, the great depression and the New Deal reversed the movement again: there were new faces, new ideas, new organizations, and an unwillingness to equate the welfare of the nation with the welfare of private business institutions.

Lastly, there is the influence of personality. While the alertness of Leffingwell and Harlan to the need for change was, in their respective instances, the factor that initiated the move-

[3] Public No. 192, 75th Congress, 1st Session (H.R. 6635); 50 Stat. 479.

ment for reform, others carried it through. In 1919, Gilbert was the driving force in pushing to a successful conclusion the Securities Trust Fund. Klaus played the same role in 1936-37 with the Losses in Shipment Act. The significance of the personal efforts of these two energetic men does not make the end result in either instance any less an organizational product, built from the accumulated experience and ability to be found within the diversified structure; it merely emphasizes the obvious fact that some person must tap the resources of an organization if they are to be put to use.

One other aspect of the study is worthy of note. The problems to be solved in this case were all man made, and significantly they were all an outgrowth of legislation and interpretation designed to protect the government. The turn to private insurance and the need for elaborate devices to avoid the unnecessary expenditure of funds involved arose directly from the laws governing accountable officers of the government and the conditions for the payment of moneys out of the Treasury; and these direct legislative impediments to efficiency and economy were reinforced by the Comptroller General's informal ruling of 1929.

The costly effects of protective procedures of which a glimpse is given in this case are neither novel nor unrecognized: the cure (assuming cure to be desirable) is less obvious than the disease, for the disease is deeply rooted in the separation of the powers and in public attitudes of hostility toward government reinforced by Congressional hostility toward the administration.

THE RECONVERSION CONTROVERSY

CONTENTS

FOREWORD

The history of the United States mobilization for World War II may be artificially, but usefully divided into three periods: preparation for war; war; reconversion. This study is concerned with the preparation in the second period for the activities of the third. At the beginning of the first period only a few men of insight saw the necessity for an all-out effort to convert our industrial power to the job of protecting democracy. They fought hard against "business as usual" attitudes, attitudes by no means confined to businessmen. When France was conquered, this sense of urgency, previously felt only by a few, spread to others. Then came Pearl Harbor, and there was no longer confusion about the basic objective—winning the war—although government officials were still faced with enormous difficulties over ways and means. The task of mobilizing all resources at home and of securing allies or maintaining neutrals abroad absorbed their energies. Talk about the postwar world was confined to statements of broad objectives like the Atlantic Charter, or the Lend-Lease Agreements; the detailed arrangements had to wait.

When the tide of battle began to turn, postwar problems began to be anticipated. Diplomats noted that wartime agreements would create postwar *faits accomplis*. Production officials began to wonder about reconversion. Winning the war was still the prime objective, but the problems of peace began to intrude. Conflicts over what could and should be done, prior to victory, in preparation for the reconversion transition grew bitter and intense.

This case tells of such a conflict.

In the fall of 1943, the War Production Board decided that a start should be made to prepare for the third period, but only where and when resources were available. At the beginning of 1944, War Production Board Chairman Donald M. Nelson, although chief proponent of this policy, rejected—for organizational reasons—a specific plan supported by his Executive Vice-Chairman, Charles E. Wilson, for carrying it out. In June 1944, backed by the declared policies of the Office of War Mobilization and the Senate Truman Committee, Nelson announced that the War Production Board was going to issue four new regulations permitting a limited amount of reconversion activity. Opposition arose, from the Armed Services and the War Manpower Commission, but also within the WPB itself. The Director of the Office of War Mobilization, James F. Byrnes, intervened, and the issuance of the orders was postponed from July 1 to staggered dates in July and August. In August, as a result of the controversy over the orders, the long-standing friction between Wilson and Nelson came to a head. Wilson resigned, Nelson went to China, and J. A. Krug took over the duties of both. Action under the orders was gradually inhibited, and virtually complete suspension ensued in December. In April 1945, with the defeat of Germany assured, a full-scale reconversion program was instituted.

In outline, this was the episode. It was a controversy that centered primarily around Donald M. Nelson, WPB Chairman; Charles E. Wilson, WPB Executive Vice-Chairman; J. A. Krug, Nelson's successor; Robert P. Patterson, Under Secretary of War, and Brehon B. Somervell, Commanding General of the Army Service Forces. But it also involved other officials in the War and Navy Departments, the WPB, the War Manpower Commission, the Office of War Mobilization, as well as the White House, various senators, and others concerned with war production.

The controversy seemed to turn on a simple question: how much reconversion activity, if any, should American industry be allowed to undertake in 1944 while the war was still on? But the newspapers at the time construed the dissension as (a) a personal contest of Nelson against Somervell backed by Patterson; (b) a personal struggle between Nelson and Wilson; (c) a contest involving civilian vs. military control of war production; (d) an attempt by "big business" to dominate "small business." Nelson seems initially to have thought of the reconversion controversy as a matter of technical judgment about the wise management of the economy for a continuation of the war and preparation for peace, and later as an attempt by War and Navy officials to dictate WPB policy. Patterson felt strongly that Nelson's technical judgment was deficient, but he described his opposition primarily in ethical terms. To Elmer Davis, head of the Office of War Information, it called for one more fruitless attempt to persuade his colleagues in high office to settle their disputes in the conference room rather than in the newspapers. Almost all these judgments on the true nature of the fight over reconversion policy have some validity, and the list is far from complete.

The struggle had organizational aspects as well; much of the story illustrates the problems of the "in-line" deputy—the Wilson-Nelson relationship—and, in its latter stages, reveals some characteristic results of active intervention by a top policy-co-ordinating agency—the Office of War Mobilization in this case—in the affairs of operating agencies and, alternatively, of the delegation to WPB, an operating agency, of responsibility for determination of basic program and policy.

Several of the officials concerned tried with varying success to mobilize popular support for their positions. In some cases they used, or permitted their subordinates to use, methods that seemed to their opponents to overstep ethical boundaries.

It is thus apparent that the Reconversion Controversy could be written as a study in ethics, or in politics, or in psychology. The approach actually adopted is that of a study of decisions as crucial stages in the administrative process. The decisions themselves can be understood only in relation to the major institutional, psychological, economic and political factors, but the analysis of these factors is not made as an end in itself, but as an adjunct to an analysis of the decisions and how they were made.

The focal point of this study is the War Production Board because it was the agency which was acting or striving to act, the one which had the initial policy and operating responsibility for reconversion. Although material is provided to cast light on the decisions made by participants in other agencies, to treat them all with equal fullness would make the study interminably long and complex. Since this is essentially a WPB story, it would also be unnecessary. Nelson, as Chairman of the WPB, necessarily becomes the central figure; with his departure from the scene Krug takes the center of the stage.

Any historical narrative is a collection of pieces torn from a seamless web. The selection of the pieces and their fitting together are invariably and inevitably affected by a variety of factors, some of which are in the writer's control and some of which lie outside his control. The writer can be conscious in varying degrees of what he is attempting to do and of his own biases, and he can make a conscientious effort to portray the course of events "objectively." Yet one need read no more than three or four pages of Gibbon, for example, to realize how much selection and emphasis are derived from the whole psychological and social atmosphere in which men live and breathe and of which they can at best be only dimly aware.

It is hardly profitable to attempt to make articulate the whole stream of notions and assumptions that have determined the character of the following account of the Reconversion Controversy. There are, however, aspects of historical writing that lend themselves more easily to isolation and definition. Thus, as has been suggested, the arrangement and emphasis of the material in this study have been made quite consciously with an eye to the points of major decision. There has been a deliberate attempt to invite the reader to concentrate his attention on the circumstances that affect decisions in governmental organizations and on the interplay of formal and informal factors in the making of decisions.

This particular process of selection is not without its dangers. Inherent in it is a tendency to personalize decisions. The personalization of decisions is in a sense justified, for it is persons, not institutions, who make decisions.

Yet as anyone knows who has worked in large, formal, especially governmental, organizations, decisions that are part of a long drawn-out controversy inevitably are the result of corporate activity in which no single person ordinarily plays a completely decisive role. In this particular instance the key officials involved—Nelson, Wilson, Krug, Somervell, and Byrnes—were unusually active personal participants in the controversy. But certainly their thinking and their actions were greatly affected by the staff work, advice, and actions of their aides and associates. This aspect of the process receives inadequate illumination in the following account; the imaginative reader must supply for himself some understanding of the nature of the distortions involved in historical reconstruction.

Another problem inherent in the choice of any specifically limited subject is the reader's tendency, induced by the choice of materials, to assume, or at least to feel, that the participants were devoting all their energies to the particular set of decisions that are described in the text. In actual practice, the flow of work requiring some degree of attention from the leading officials was continuous and intensely demanding. Reconversion policy was only one issue among many. Nelson, apparently deliberately, chose to make it a critical issue; to various other participants it tended to be a diversion from more pressing matters. This point is of general significance in understanding the course of events. Above all, the reader must realize that the various attitudes and working relationships crucial to the Reconversion Controversy were established over a period of months, even years, in the handling of those multitudinous decisions, large and small, that were made by the war production officials. The Reconversion Controversy, however significant, is but one small part of the whole.

I. Background

A. STRATEGIC BACKGROUND

Pearl Harbor, December 7, 1941, was the first in a series of disasters. The Japanese forces spread rapidly until they were in sight of Alaska on the north, India on the west, and Australia on the south. For months the Allied Forces in the Pacific suffered a succession of defeats, finally broken in the summer of 1942 by the defensive victories of the Coral Sea and Midway. In August, with the attack on Guadalcanal, came the first striking blow in the Pacific from our side.

In the Middle East and in Russia the events of 1942 followed a similar pattern. In the summer the Germans captured Rostov and Tobruk. Finally in the fall the tide turned. In October came the advance from Egypt, in November the North African landings and the stopping of the Germans at Stalingrad.

The year 1943 was a period of slow and bloody advances in both hemispheres. Defeat no longer seemed in prospect, but, in spite of such events as the Axis collapse in Tunisia and the fall of the Italian government, the German surrender at Stalingrad, and the Allied advance in the Western Pacific, victory was still far off.

But increasingly in 1943 there was opportunity to look further ahead. By the end of the year the efforts of the United States and of the United Kingdom were pointed more and more toward the invasion of the European continent. The decision had been made, the commander chosen: the thought of victory emerged from the realm of faith to that of program and action. The possibility of a postwar future began to take tangible form. Now, for almost the first time, it seemed not unpatriotic to take heed for the days when there would be no more war.

B. ORGANIZATIONAL BACKGROUND

The War Production Board and the Army Services of Supply (later known as the Army Service Forces), established in January and March 1942 respectively, were both organizational responses to the fact of Pearl Harbor. The powers of the WPB as spelled out in the Executive Order by which it was created were extremely broad. The WPB never exercised all those powers; many were delegated and others were left in abeyance, but WPB's formal authority always remained great. It maintained general control over the allocation of scarce materials and the scheduling of production of various key items. The military supply agencies, of which the Army Service Forces was by far the largest, had actual control of the procurement of war supplies, including the determination of their own requirements, the placing of contracts, the expediting of production, and the distribution of final products.

Despite the fact that the WPB had over-all policy powers, and while it was responsible for the allocation of resources to competing claimants, it had virtually no part in the process of formulating the requirements for munitions, their procurement, and their distribution, all of which were under the control of the military agencies. In the general context of our existing governmental organization, this division of responsibilities was normal to the point of inevitability. But because WPB, on the whole, had no participation in the formulation of these decisions, it was not in a position to influence ASF (and Navy) supply policy. The converse was not true. Many of the most important areas of decision-making in the WPB were committees on which the Services were represented. To a considerable extent, however, the painful problems that form the subject of the following account were ones that lay fairly clearly within the limits of WPB's undenied jurisdiction. The difficulties over reconversion arose not over WPB's lack of powers, but over its attempts to exercise them.

The WPB had continuous relations with all the agencies dealing with military supply—Army, Navy, Army Air Forces, Maritime Commission—as well as with various agencies concerned with basic production, such as the War Food Administration and the Petroleum Administration for War. Each of the Military Supply agencies created special and difficult problems for WPB: steel plates for the Maritime Commission, aluminum and high octane gasoline for the AAF, for example. But by far the greatest problem, both in volume of production involved and in terms of difficult relationships, lay with the Army Service Forces. This agency, created as has been said, in 1942, had general responsibility for the whole enormous range of Army supply (except for most AAF materiel). The Army representatives who dealt with WPB were in ASF; for WPB, ASF *was* the Army. ASF also took the lead in all the major disputes between WPB and the procuring agencies, as they were called. In the Reconversion Controversy, as will be seen, the other interested agencies limited themselves to a supporting role: ASF carried the fight.

The WPB's relations with ASF were never entirely satisfactory, and frequently unsatisfactory. The struggle over reconversion was the culmination of a long-standing conflict and was preceded by a history of organizational squabbles and personal dislikes. Partly this condition was inherent in the situation. The ASF's major responsibility was the production of direct munitions of war; the WPB was responsible not only for munitions production, but also for maintaining the economy needed to produce the weapons of war. The Services looked only to their own needs; the WPB had to divide the Nation's productive resources among the many claimant agencies of which the Army was only one, albeit the most important. The ASF officers and the supply officers for the Army Air Forces and the Navy were naturally impatient with controls that seemed, or threatened, to interfere with their own production plans. But beyond these differences in administrative responsibilities, friction arose from personality clashes.

Donald M. Nelson, after graduating from the University of Missouri, had gone to work for Sears, Roebuck & Company where he very quickly rose to positions of major importance. When in May 1940 he went to Washington to serve in the then small defense production program, he was executive vice-president of Sears. Intending to spend only a few weeks in Washington, Nelson responded to demands upon him by the Administration and stayed on to serve successively in the National Defense Advisory Commission, the Office of Production Management, the Supply Priorities and Allocations Board, and finally in 1942 to become Chairman of the War Production Board. By his admirers Nelson was considered fair and democratic, and devoted to carrying out his job in a wise and equitable fashion; but to the Generals of the ASF, and their civilian superiors, most importantly to Robert P. Patterson, Under Secretary of War, and General Brehon B. Somervell, Commanding General, ASF, he seemed inefficient, indecisive, and overcautious. Patterson, a holder of the Distinguished Service Cross, had resigned in 1940 as a judge of the United States Circuit Court of Appeals to become Assistant Secretary of War, responsible for the entire War Department procurement program. An evaluation of Patterson was written after the war by his superior, the Secretary of War: "Probably no man in the administration was more ruthlessly determined to fulfill his assignment than Patterson; . . . he had a fierce hatred of all delay and any compromise; his only test of any measure was whether it would help to win, and for any group or individual who blinked at sacrifice he had only scorn." [1]

General Somervell, whose civilian superior was Patterson, after graduating from the United States Military Academy served with distinction as an engineering officer, rising steadily and, after 1939, rapidly, to the rank of General. In his career he had had experience in unusual assignments, such as WPA Administrator for New York City. Secretary Stimson later wrote that Somervell was "fired by the single-minded purpose of meeting the Army's needs" and "that some irritation should be caused by the driving energy of General Somervell was not surprising." [2]

Patterson and Somervell thus appeared to one partial but well-placed observer to have important qualities in common. Not surprisingly they also had many differences in character which were revealed in action. Throughout the course of events described in the following pages they were pursuing the same main objectives and operating from the same institutional base, so these differences tend to be submerged. However, since much of the Reconversion Controversy was carried on in the press, the reader will find that distinguishing personality characteristics of Patterson and Somervell, and of their chief assistant Clay, were revealed in their public relations. In any event, since this is a study in administration, the lack of psychological differentiation is not crucial, but the reader should realize that the two men were not twins in motivation or behavior pattern.

Whereas to Patterson and Somervell, Nelson seemed neither forceful nor bold, to Nelson, Patterson and Somervell seemed unimaginative, narrow-visioned, unco-operative, and unwilling to restrict themselves to their own functions. During the course of the controversy the differences became so intense that motives were freely impugned.

WPB difficulties were not all external in character. The Board itself was, officially, purely advisory in character; the formal powers were all vested in its chairman. But Nelson had troubles with his staff. By late 1942 his two chief deputies were Ferdinand Eberstadt, a prominent financier, who was Program Vice-Chairman, and Charles E. Wilson, of the General Electric Company, Production Vice-Chairman. The jurisdiction of the two was never clearly defined, and Nelson's failure to settle the inevitable disputes was not looked on with favor in the White House. Rumors of conflict between Eberstadt and Wilson began to appear in the press.

Early in 1943 the President agreed, on recommendation of former Justice Byrnes (then Director of the Office of War Mobilization) and the Secretaries of War and Navy, to supplant Nelson with Bernard M. Baruch; Eberstadt was presumably to become Baruch's deputy. At this juncture, Nelson saved himself—and incidentally Wilson—by dismissing Eberstadt. The President was pleased with Nelson's apparent vigor, and abandoned his plan.

The relations between Nelson and the Services were not improved by this incident, and it was to have further significant results. The dismissal of Eberstadt was followed by a drastic reorganization of WPB. Wilson was given charge of virtually all WPB operating func-

[1] Stimson & Bundy, *On Active Service in Peace and War*, Harper & Brothers, 1948, p. 342. By permission of the publishers.

[2] *Ibid.*, p. 493.

tions, and also of the basic planning and statistical functions as well. Charles E. Wilson, after beginning in the shipping departments, worked his way up to the presidency of General Electric. Wilson had come to WPB with considerable reluctance. One of the complaints against Nelson had been that he was not a "production man"; Wilson was to fill this gap. Nelson apparently felt that the appointment would strengthen his own position, especially vis-à-vis the Services, while his critics thought or hoped that Wilson would supply qualities of determination that they thought Nelson lacked.

Wilson was thus made Executive Vice-Chairman and given control over the basic WPB activities, in part to please the White House (which had confidence in Wilson) and, in part, to free Nelson for policy problems. The operating consequences, although perhaps predictable, were either not foreseen or underestimated.

The situation was hardly one calculated to make for satisfactory relations between the two. An effective division of responsibility between policy and operations proved illusory. The loyalties of the operating vice-chairmen quite naturally followed the line of their responsibilities, which were to Wilson, not to Nelson. Other factors increased the hazards. Wilson's staff consisted primarily of men drawn from manufacturing and finance. The few vice-chairmen still responsible directly to Nelson were drawn primarily from labor, government, or the professions. Nelson's personal staff, with significant influence over relations with Congress and the press, remained intensely loyal to him and distrustful of Wilson. Wilson's personal staff in turn were suspicious of Nelson. Wilson did not like Nelson's advisers, and Nelson was less than enthusiastic about some of Wilson's immediate staff. Between the staffs there grew up an open hostility, each building up its own chief at the expense of the other. Finally, by a curious paradox, Wilson, whose attempts to schedule production had originally been vigorously opposed by the men in the Services, developed excellent relations with them. Of the two great WPB Committees—the Requirements Committee and the Production Executive Committee (PEC)—the latter was Wilson's, and aside from himself and, for a short time, Eberstadt, its members originally all came from the Services. At the beginning such membership was appropriate, for the PEC concentrated its attention on military needs; but as Wilson's power grew, the functions of PEC expanded, and even though various WPB officials were added, it was still heavily military in composition. The appropriateness of its membership to some of its tasks that involved problems of concern to other than the military agencies was therefore diminished.

To complete this rapid sketch of the organizational background of the reconversion struggle, it is necessary to mention one other agency—the Office of War Mobilization (OWM). In the fall of 1942 the President asked Mr. Justice Byrnes to leave the Supreme Court in order to take over general supervision of the economic stabilization program and to settle disputes between the agencies involved, notably OPA, the National War Labor Board, and Agriculture. Byrnes thus became Director of the Office of Economic Stabilization. In August 1943, anxious to free himself still more completely from domestic entanglements, and to ward off congressional criticism, the President created the Office of War Mobilization, which he entrusted to Byrnes. In October 1944, with the passage of the War Mobilization and Reconversion Act of 1944, Congress expanded the functions of the OWM, changed its name to the Office of War Mobilization and Reconversion, and gave it a statutory basis. Byrnes' office had become the over-all policy agency on the war production scene and the arbiter of all agency disputes. Because of the President's preoccupation with other problems, Byrnes was usually the final arbiter.

The relations between WPB and OWM were difficult at best. Byrnes was exercising in fact many of the powers allotted on paper to Nelson. Furthermore, Byrnes had been a prime mover of the plan to bring in Baruch and was on excellent terms with the Services.

In late 1943 it seemed to many that with Wilson pushing from below, Byrnes from above, and Patterson and Somervell from the side, Nelson's terrain was being badly constricted.

Suspicion within the WPB and hostility between Nelson and the heads of the military procurement agencies did not, however, prevent the war economy from moving into high gear. As war production entered a new phase, it brought new problems—problems which soon brought personality clashes and basic differences in policy into the open.

II. The Problem and Some Solutions

A. THE PROBLEM

From the time of Pearl Harbor up to the time of the assault on Tarawa in November 1943, the cry had always been more men, more materials, more plants and other facilities. But in November 1943, looking toward 1944, it could be seen—or it was anticipated—that the nature of the problems would change, that they would be qualitative rather than quantitative in character. For in November 1943, America was producing munitions at the rate of seventy-four billion dollars a year. This was the high point of production; and the initial task of providing the capital equipment for the armed forces was being rapidly concluded. The task for 1944 would be to provide for the maintenance and replacement of munitions and to bring into production whatever new weapons might be called for. But this was not expected to require the continuation of the November rate of munitions production, and over-all production was scheduled to decline. A billion and a half dollars' worth of cutbacks *per month* was expected during the first half of 1944, and greater amounts thereafter. The 1945 program was expected to be less than sixty per cent of the 1944 program.

The expected decline in military production would be reflected in decreased needs for facilities, materials, and industrial manpower. At the same time, however, the armed forces were expected to make a significant draft on the manpower of the nation, and it was estimated that a half-million of the right kinds of workers in the right places would be required for war industries by mid-1944 to fill in the gaps caused by withdrawals and to meet the needs for new programs. Manpower was thus to become the over-all limiting factor of war production. But, according to the forecasts, this stringency would be accompanied by local pools of unemployment where production schedules were cut back.

Theoretically, a nation engaged in "total war" should be able to bring all its resources to bear, and one would expect that a decreased need for munitions workers in one area could, for example, be offset by shifting new orders to the locality, or by shifting workers to other munitions plants, or by enlarging the armed forces or the Merchant Marine. But the labor released from one war plant was not necessarily the kind needed by another war plant, nor was it necessarily the kind that could be used by the armed forces or in other essential work. The complete use of all human and material resources would also imply perfect organization—a kind of organization that perhaps can never be obtained and which certainly did not exist in the fall of 1943.

Reasonably satisfactory controls over materials had been established after many difficulties, but control over manpower was a problem of an entirely different character. Administrative machinery to insure the most effective use of manpower involves infinitely more complex and delicate problems than that for effective use of materials. There was much dissatisfaction with the voluntary and semi-mandatory controls that were gradually put into operation. But Congress shied away from compulsory manpower controls, although the Services kept insisting that they were needed, and that voluntary controls were inadequate.

This, then, was the problem. If the forecasts were right, there would be in 1944 some unused plant capacity, some unused materials like steel and copper, and some unemployed men and women available for work in certain places. Simultaneously, there would be shortages of certain kinds of workers in some war industries and in some localities, shortages that threatened to interfere with munitions production.

The way administrators react to a problem is conditioned by many factors, but by no means the least important of these is their institutional responsibility. The supply officials of the War Department and the ASF had a single and terrifying responsibility—to furnish the munitions needed to win the war in the shortest possible time. Looking at the forecasts for 1944 they could see only one problem, the one that most obviously and directly threatened war production—the shortage of workers in some war industries. The fact that there might be some unused resources and some scattered unemployment was to them unimportant, even trivial. Judged from their standpoint, the unemployed constituted a useful, perhaps essential pool from which to secure manpower still needed for the war effort at strategic production centers.

Production of munitions of war was, of course, also the basic responsibility of the War Production Board. But perhaps because of the wider range of his responsibilities, Nelson viewed the anticipated local unemployment with much more concern than did his fellow production officials in the War Department. To Nelson it presented not only a danger to the war production program, but also an opportunity, if handled properly, to solve some of the inevitable problems of reconversion. If the factual predictions were sound, it was a problem that could not be evaded; for to do nothing would in itself be a decision.

B. NELSON'S CONCLUSIONS

One of the apparent differences, though possibly more of degree than of kind, between public and private administration, is the compulsion laid upon public administrators to articulate a rationale for their major policies. The orderly rationale that is presented to the public may differ markedly from the helter-skelter reasons advanced in the give and take of staff conference, and the reasons expressed even in a confidential staff conference may omit some of the basic propulsions like hope and fear that afflict administrators as well as other human beings. To a greater or lesser extent, therefore, the expressed arguments for and against a controversial policy partake of the nature of rationalization. The following account of the opposing positions of Nelson and the Services is undoubtedly over-rationalized, but the various arguments cited were actually advanced at various times and were tenaciously held. While it is not the "whole" story, it is an essential part of it.

Nelson, anticipating idle resources in 1944, rejected the possibility of keeping munitions production at a high rate merely to take up slack: such action seemed to him wasteful of resources, dangerous in implication, and fatal to the economy. He also rejected the policy of allowing men and materials to lie idle. He did this because he was convinced that it would injure the war production program, because he did not think it would solve the manpower problem, and because he felt that it would disastrously complicate the inevitable problem of reconverting the economy from war to peace production.

Nelson's solution was based on the assumption of a long drawn-out war, in which reconversion could be carried out in three phases: a limited preparatory period after resources had been released from war production; a more general return to peacetime production after the defeat of Germany; and finally, full-scale reconversion at the end of the war.

Nelson also reached the conclusion that if the government did nothing during the first phase, when, as he assumed, war requirements did not take up all the resources, war production itself would be endangered. As early as the summer of 1943 Nelson had concluded that uncertainty as to the government's reconversion program was hindering the war effort. Nelson believed that many companies were holding inventories below efficient operating levels and that others were hesitant about taking on new war contracts. As cutbacks became a reality, the government should, thought Nelson, be able to assure industry that it was taking vigorous action to assure an orderly reconversion and that, consistent with war goals, companies without war contracts would be permitted to use idle resources for civilian production.

Most important to Nelson, the failure to provide work for even a small fraction of the prospective unemployed might have a serious effect on the morale of war workers. Many of them (e.g., women and the aged) would drift out of the labor market when dismissed from their war jobs and would not be available in the event of an increase in munitions requirements. Others, seeing unemployment around them and aware of the government's do-nothing policy, would hesitate to take war jobs, seeking industries producing goods for civilian consumption.

Furthermore, Nelson reasoned, failure to authorize the use of idle resources, manpower and material, would have especially harmful effects on small businessmen. Theirs would be the first war contracts to be canceled and, if forbidden to produce civilian items, they would be faced with failure.

Nelson was also convinced that it was unrealistic to argue that if no civilian production were authorized in those areas where manpower, materials, and facilities were available, then the unemployed could be forced into those areas and industries where they were needed. It was more likely that they would have neither the specific knowledge of the national labor situation nor the inclination or even ability to leave their homes; labor mobility, while striking, was far from complete. The solution to the manpower problem, thought Nelson, would be found only by studying each individual area, plant, or industry. The reasons for shortages, or excessive turnover, grew out of conditions in particular places. Finally, only special kinds of workers were needed; for example, foundry workers and skilled technicians: most workers, released from other jobs, could not fill these positions.

If, during phase one (the period up to the defeat of Germany), the cutbacks in war production were merely allowed to come and no civilian production was permitted to take up slack in the economy, the end of hostilities would find the nation with an economy that was slowly grinding to a halt and reconversion would be unduly delayed. During the period in which industry prepared to resume civilian production (clearing plants of war tools, liquidating war materials, preparing models, acquiring raw materials, etc.), many thousands would be unemployed. There would be a scramble for materials in short supply. This unduly complicated transition period might seriously impair the power of the United States and so fundamentally alter the nature of our economy that it would be disastrous.

On the other hand, Nelson reasoned, if civilian production were authorized in areas where surpluses of manpower, facilities, and materials appeared—if civilian production were "chinked in" as war production declined —reconversion could be a gradually accomplished fact. Thus, by cautious dovetailing, the economy would be going at full-speed as the war ended, and postwar reconversion difficulties would in large measure be avoided.

Such a program would also help ease the problem of growing shortages that threatened to impair the economy's ability to produce war munitions. The production of many items for civilian consumption had been curtailed or prohibited early in 1942. By the end of 1943 the stocks of many commodities had dwindled and shortages of refrigerators and washing machines, alarm clocks, shoes, and gloves were threatening to impair the efficiency of the workers who produced the munitions. Although increased civilian production as a reconversion measure and increased civilian production for essential war-supporting activities were separate issues, one purpose tended to serve the other as well; for in the gradual reconversion program the released resources would be devoted to needed civilian production.

And finally, Nelson was apparently influenced by the strong convictions of John Lord O'Brian, General Counsel of the WPB. O'Brian, for whom Nelson had great admiration, was convinced that the WPB was legally obligated to remove its controls as soon as they were no longer needed to insure war production.

Holding these convictions, Nelson early became an advocate of gradual reconversion. But other men who looked at the same reports on the war program came to other conclusions—

foremost among these men were Patterson and Somervell.

C. THE POSITION OF THE SERVICES

The attitudes of the Pentagon officials, although affected by personalities, were almost predictable on the basis of their responsibility. They did not object to reconversion planning, provided it was done quietly; as a matter of fact, during 1944 and early 1945, the WPB staff prepared a comprehensive and thoroughgoing post-VE Day reconversion program with the tacit or explicit approval of the Services. But they were strenuously opposed to overt action, the very thing which Nelson soon deemed an integral part of his program. The great battles of the war were still to be fought and there were many imponderables. With hindsight we may have some tendency to think that they exaggerated the risks. But at the time, for example, there was no assurance that the Russians would continue to hold the two-hundred-odd German divisions on the Eastern Front. If these divisions had been freed to meet the Allied divisions in the West, the outcome of the invasion might have been tragically different. From the early days of the war, Under Secretary Patterson had felt that civilians were being unnecessarily coddled. It was with great impatience that he heard talk about reconversion and about permitting resources released from war production to be used for civilian production. With both elections and larger cutbacks approaching in 1944, military officials feared that the WPB would be unwilling or unable to resist the pressures of labor and business and that reconversion would "snowball" out of control. They were greatly alarmed by the growing congressional pressure, the demands of labor and business, and the suggestions by various units within the WPB that civilian production be increased. To yield even slightly to these pressures, they thought, would merely increase the intensity of demand, as competitors would jockey for position to win the race for postwar markets. They were especially fearful that Nelson's gradual reconversion program would be misunderstood and would be interpreted as a sign of the war's end. They were afraid that the workers would refuse to take war jobs, and that businessmen would be reluctant to accept war contracts. Nelson's program would also interfere with their efforts to create "a sense of urgency" in order to convince Congress of the necessity of securing a national service act permitting the drafting of workers for war industries, and to impress workers with the importance of staying on the job. This strongly held belief that a "sense of urgency" could and should be "created" pervaded the whole reconversion dispute.

As has been mentioned before, to the leaders of the Services the major problem was to attract or force workers to critical areas and industries. They were positive that Nelson's program would interfere. They argued that if no civilian work was provided, the few unemployed would be forced to seek war jobs. Their opposition extended even to that civilian production which various WPB officials thought essential to keep the economy producing munitions. As long as there were any manpower shortages anywhere or as long as any munitions program was behind schedule, they were unalterably opposed to even the slightest attempt to increase civilian production.

They were convinced that more men would be needed for the Army and for the munitions factories than would be released by cutbacks. But even if some resources and manpower were left idle, they considered any attempt at new civilian production the height of folly. Any difficulties that unemployed civilian workers might incur, they felt, would be minor compared with the sacrifices others were making. In short, their program for meeting the problem of 1944 war production was first, if possible, to secure a national service law, but —failing that—to do everything possible by other methods to move workers released from one plant to where they were still needed.

Nelson saw no conflict between the two goals of recruiting needed manpower to produce munitions and of undertaking orderly reconversion; to him they complemented each other. But to the Services' production officials, no diversion, however minor, should be allowed to detract from the war effort. Any goal other than the one of producing munitions would seriously, if not fatally, interfere with this primary responsibility. As Patterson said at a later date, "We believed that issues should be decided under the guiding principle that winning the war came first, with no 'ifs' or 'buts'—winning the war, period."

The difference between Nelson and the Army and Navy officials lay largely in the area of psychological prediction. Each was trying to forecast how workers and businessmen would behave under given conditions. Both could present a logical case. Differences in temperament and even more in responsibility led conscientious men to different conclusions.

It should be noted that there was never any agreement on the basic question of just how many workers would be released by the reductions in munitions programs, and just how many would still be needed in various industries. This basic information, theoretically essential in order to deal with the problem, seems never to have been collected. Actually, because changes in the Army and Navy programs were frequent and unpredictable, an accurate forecast was probably unattainable. In the absence of any firm statement, the arguments on both sides tended to rely on hunch and guess. Whereas Nelson was convinced that the over-all manpower supply was adequate and that more workers would be released than would be needed, the military were convinced that the need for workers was much greater than the supply. Statistics were cited, but they were weapons used to buttress arguments rather than data on which to support assumptions.

Also basic to the disagreement was the fact that Patterson and Somervell felt that labor was or could be made fluid. Nelson and various others were more impressed by the impediments to labor mobility. The opposing contentions had relatively little factual background; in varying degrees they were founded on conviction rather than knowledge.

D. "THIRD FORCES"

Neither Nelson's nor the War Department's views exhausted the alternatives. For example, there was in the WPB a large group of staff members, most of them economists on leave from the universities, who sided neither with the Army nor with Nelson. These staff members remembered the difficulties in overcoming the "business as usual attitude" in the early days of the war effort, an attitude which had handicapped all efforts to curtail non-essential but highly profitable production. If this task had been difficult when patriotic urgency could be marshaled, they were greatly afraid of what would happen to hard-gained controls in the face of the divergent profit interests released by reconversion. Reasonably effective control over the use of materials had been established after a long struggle, but there was no such effective control over manpower. Since manpower was the major problem, they believed that materials controls were needed to support the manpower efforts. Furthermore, WPB controls were not so precise that the consequences of removing any single one could be accurately measured. They were so closely related to each other, and also to those of other agencies such as the OPA, that these staff members feared that if some "sticks were pulled out of the pile" the entire system might collapse. Finally they were fearful of the dissension that reconversion might engender among war and non-war workers and between various firms and their employees now in service within the WPB.

With these considerations in mind many staff members, though they did not go along with the War Department, could not warmly support Nelson's position either. And, as we shall see, Nelson soon found himself dangerously isolated.

III. The 1943 Reconversion Proposals

A. OWM OR WPB

In April 1943 the problems of reconversion were still very much in the future. Even so, Nelson, feeling that the job of reconversion would be complicated and would require advance planning, recalled Ernest Kanzler, a former WPB official, to Washington. Nelson instructed him to make a general study of the problems of reconversion, but to keep his mission confidential.

Kanzler submitted his report on June 26, 1943, and recommended among other things that a group within the WPB be designated *publicly* to prepare for the time when war production would no longer be the sole objective. He warned Nelson that unless he moved soon the military would control the demobilization process.

Nelson then had his personal staff prepare a long memorandum for the President covering four major points: the early need for a reconversion agency; basic policy in reconversion; major problems of reconversion; and organization of the reconversion agency. The memorandum and a long covering letter were ready to be sent to the President on August 21, 1943. The evidence as to whether Nelson actually sent this letter and memorandum to the President is conflicting. But the communications merit attention as significant reflections of Nelson's thinking. His letter argued that the WPB was the agency best fitted by training and experience to guide industry through reconversion, and he continued:

> The initial steps in preparing for reconversion should, in my judgment, be taken now, through the War Production Board, in order to aid war production and to insure that the reconversion problem will be fully understood, and in competent administrative hands, when the shift to peacetime production begins.
>
> . . . My personal status is not a consideration. I shall be grateful, however, for a word from you as to whether or not it will be consistent with your views for the War Production Board to continue with the development of reconversion policies, plans, and programs.

As has been indicated, the fate of Nelson's letter and memorandum are unknown. If they came to the President's attention, it can be presumed that he interposed no bar, for in September Nelson instructed the WPB Planning Division to prepare a comprehensive reconversion report and ordered the Operations Vice-Chairman to undertake a study of the hundreds of WPB orders restricting or limiting the use of materials and production of certain items with a view to determining the best way of removing them when the time came. Yet apparently the President was not prepared to exclude all other agencies from consideration of reconversion problems. On October 15, 1943, he told James F. Byrnes "to take charge of the consideration of demobilization." Presumably this proposal had been sponsored by Byrnes. On November 4 Byrnes announced that he had persuaded Bernard M. Baruch and John M. Hancock to head a Reconversion Unit within the Office of War Mobilization "to develop unified programs and policies for dealing with war and post-war adjustment problems to be pursued by the various agencies concerned." At the same time Byrnes announced that his office would not supplant the War Production Board and that Baruch and Hancock were merely to develop unified programs and general policies to be pursued by various agencies concerned in handling postwar adjustment problems. Nevertheless, many persons felt that the appointment of Baruch and Hancock indicated lack of presidential confidence in Nelson, and rumors began to circulate that the WPB would play a minor reconversion role, if any at all.

B. PRESSURES FOR ACTION

During the fall of 1943 the pressures for reconversion action were mounting. In November prominent spokesmen for business, labor, and agriculture spoke up for action. In Congress the Senate Special Committee on Postwar Economic Policy and Planning (the George Committee), the Senate Special Committee Investigating the National Defense Program (the Truman Committee), the Special Senate and House Committees on Small Business, the Senate and House Military Affairs Committees, the Senate Finance and the House Ways and Means Committees were considering various phases of the reconversion problem. Nelson, Byrnes, Patterson, and other government, business, and labor leaders were called to testify before these Committees.

On November 5 the Truman Committee issued a report on the problems of conversion from war to peace production and urged immediate reconversion preparation. On the same day Nelson outlined his reconversion thinking to the George Committee. He told the Committee that it was not within his field to prepare specific plans for the postwar world, but that any immediate readjustments in production would have an important effect on the postwar economic pattern and he felt compelled to do his utmost to see that reconversion was efficiently and quickly completed. The reconversion process, he told the Committee, was "the most important single piece of business of this Nation since the declaration of the war. . . ."

On November 18 the George Committee issued its first report and recommended, among other things, the establishment of a central office to co-ordinate reconversion programs.

Coupled with these growing pressures for action were cutbacks in the tank, airplane, escort vessel, and Army Supply programs. It seemed obvious to Nelson that materials, facilities, and some manpower would be released from war production. He became convinced that the time was fast approaching for a change in WPB policy and some limited but positive, and public, action. Accordingly he placed reconversion on the agenda of the November 30 meeting of the War Production Board.

C. NELSON'S DECISION OF NOVEMBER 30, 1943

It has been pointed out that the legal powers of the WPB were vested in the chairman. Thus Nelson could, in theory, proceed with his reconversion program without reference to his Board. But the Board had been created to serve as a consultative body for Nelson and it was Nelson's practice to discuss with the Board all major new policies and problems. The Board's titular membership included such important and interested officials as the War and Navy Secretaries, the Chairman of the War Manpower Commission, the Price Administrator, and the Secretaries of Commerce and Agriculture. Even when the top officials themselves did not appear, their agencies were represented. In general, the Board was not an "action committee"; it was a forum for discussion; but Nelson could use it to secure understanding of his programs and to gauge the reactions of other agencies. Although it lacked legal power, the Board's consensus was not to be taken lightly.

At this seventy-fourth meeting of the Board on November 30, 1943, Nelson called on Wilson to review the production trends of the past year and to outline the 1944 munitions program. Wilson gave a very encouraging report on past production and assurance that the 1944 production goals were attainable.

Nelson then took up the second item on the agenda—reconversion. For the first time at a meeting of the Board, the WPB officially turned its attention to this controversial subject, which was to strain WPB-War Department relations to the breaking point and was finally to lead to the resignation of the two top War Production Board officials. But it came on the stage without fanfare or roll of drums.

Nelson announced that the improving materials situation and cutbacks in military programs would require a full discussion of reconversion in the very near future. He asked the Board whether civilian production should be authorized if facilities and manpower became available in certain localities. Secretary of Commerce Jesse Jones stated that he was firmly convinced that resources should not be allowed to stand idle, and that he would favor approval of local reconversion even though it might throw previously established commercial relationships out of balance. Paul V. McNutt, Chairman of the War Manpower Commission, concurred, provided manpower was available. Neither the Under Secretary of War nor the Under Secretary of the Navy had anything to say. Thereupon, in the absence of objections or further comments, Nelson declared:

Hereafter as manpower, facilities, and materials become available in any given area, it shall be the policy of the War Production Board to authorize the production within that area of additional civilian goods, provided such production does not limit production for programs of higher urgency.

D. PEC, CUTBACKS AND RECONVERSION

Why the Pentagon officials did not speak during this meeting is not known; it soon became clear, however, that they were determined to oppose Nelson's proposals. Characteristically, in taking action, their action was not limited to exhortations at Board meetings by Under Secretary Patterson that the plan be dropped—though this was energetically carried on, beginning at the very next meeting of the Board on December 28. The War Department also decided to make full use of the anomalies in the WPB structure.

Clearly reconversion activities, if permitted, would come as a corollary of cutbacks in war production programs. If, therefore, both cutbacks and the reconversion program were placed under control of the same unit, and that unit one trusted by the Army, then the dangers which the Army officials feared in Nelson's plans could be kept under control, even if the plans were not revoked. This course of action had the further advantage of being entirely logical: the functional relationship between cutbacks and reconversion invited organizational unity.

The agency selected as the control device was Wilson's Production Executive Committee, and the man who assumed responsibility for making the arrangements was Major General Lucius D. Clay. At this time General Clay was not as widely known to the American people as he is now. But in 1943 when he was Director of Materiel, ASF, and General Somervell's assistant, he was a powerful figure in his own right. General Clay's first known move in the reconversion dispute—though he may well have been important in setting the policy now reflected in action—was to instruct his assistant, J. A. Panuch, to draft a plan for handling cutbacks which would permit the Production Executive Committee to determine over-all reconversion policy. Panuch proposed that a Production Executive Committee subcommittee be formed to develop cutback and reconversion policies, to evolve a reconversion program to be effective on the defeat of Germany, and to determine and direct expansion of production for non-military use.

The Production Executive Committee, known as PEC, was composed of top-ranking representatives of all the military procurement agencies, plus the War Manpower Commission and several WPB vice-chairmen. But many of the agencies concerned with more distinctively civilian problems—e.g., the Smaller War Plants Corporation, the Office of Civilian Requirements, and the offices of the two WPB Labor Vice-Chairmen—were not represented. The PEC had been established in December 1942 to give Wilson a mechanism which would enable him to exercise control over the scheduling process for items needed by the armed forces. It was thought that by sitting over the Armed Services in regular and frequent sessions he could restore order in a situation disordered by lack of co-ordinated production schedules. The War Department had strenuously opposed the reassertion by Wilson and the PEC of some of WPB's authority over scheduling. Wilson soon reached an amicable working agreement with the military officials, however, and gave great weight to their judgment. The military representatives so outnumbered the civilians on the Committee that they seemed to dominate it.

Panuch's proposals pointedly left J. A. Krug and his staff out of the reconversion organization. Krug, a government administrator with years of service in the TVA, was the only Vice-Chairman reporting to Wilson who did not come from the world of business or finance. In March 1943 he was appointed to the position of Program Vice-Chairman, but the position itself was greatly reduced in scope from what it had been under Eberstadt. The Requirements Committee of which Krug was *ex officio* chairman was responsible for the allocation of scarce materials among competing claimants, but it was gradually overshadowed by PEC; and various former program functions were transferred to the Operations Vice-Chairman. At the end of 1943 Wilson manifested no desire to upset these arrangements by assigning to Krug and his staff responsibilities that might conflict with the task of PEC and its staff.

Wilson's attitude toward the Panuch proposals was apparently not based on a philosophic divergence between himself and Krug about reconversion or civilian production, but some divergence did exist. During the winter of 1943-1944 Krug and his staff were developing plans to provide the civilian economy with essential goods. Krug was also considered a strong supporter of Nelson's reconversion approach. Thus Clay and Panuch had no motive whatever for upsetting Wilson's organizational scheme by assigning any part of the reconversion responsibility to Krug.

In December 1943 Panuch's plan was informally submitted to Byrnes, Baruch, Hancock, Nelson, Wilson, Krug, and others. Wilson favored the proposals; they maintained his position; but, also important, his attitude toward reconversion was more conservative than was Nelson's. Immersed in the job of securing maximum munitions production, he was inclined to agree with the military that it was too early to do much in the way of reconversion. He hoped, therefore, that by establishing machinery under the PEC the reconversion pressures would have a chance to let off steam without moving the reconversion engine.

At the December 15 and 22 PEC meetings the following resolutions were adopted:

> A plan for industrial reconversion for operation at PEC level should be developed. This plan should provide for the utilization of free materials, available facilities and labor without interference with the munitions program and with equity to industry.
>
> For effective co-ordination reconversion plans must be worked out at the level of the PEC and . . . cutbacks and resumption of civilian items' production must be co-ordinated by the same group.

At the December 28 meeting Wilson agreed to issue a directive to put Panuch's plan into effect, subject to Nelson's approval.

Nelson refused to approve. In his opinion, the Panuch plan would permit the military to determine reconversion policies. If PEC were expanded to include representatives of civilian interests, especially a place for Krug, Nelson had no objection to permitting it to supervise the placement of cutbacks. He did not approve, however, of giving it general supervision over the resumption of civilian production. In fact, he had already instructed one of his assistants, Bernard L. Gladieux, to prepare a plan for the handling of cutbacks in keeping with his own ideas. This plan, submitted on December 16, called for broader civilian representation on the PEC and the PEC subcommittee, and it limited the PEC's responsibilities chiefly to the determination of contracts to be terminated. Moreover, Gladieux proposed that Krug and his staff serve as the central focus of reconversion planning.

Nelson was unwilling to force this proposal on Wilson for fear of precipitating an all-out struggle; but he was equally unwilling to accept the Panuch plan. Wilson was generally expected to resign from the WPB very shortly; perhaps with this anticipation in mind, Nelson decided to postpone action on cutbacks.

E. REVERSAL OF THE NOVEMBER 30 DECISION

While General Clay was trying to bring reconversion under the control of the PEC, Patterson was trying to secure a reversal of the November 30 decision. This decision was significant chiefly as a statement of policy to be applied in the future. During the winter of 1943-44 there were very few places where production could be authorized for less essential purposes. Nevertheless, in line with this policy, at the December 28, 1943, and January

11, 1944, Board meetings, Nelson raised the question of relaxing the current restrictive facilities policy, i.e., the sharp limitations on various types of construction. These were special limitations different from the limitations on production or on use of scarce materials, but over the course of time reconversion would require new construction (or remodeling) as well as increased production. Although it might seem that the November 30 decision settled the matter and that needed facilities should be authorized whenever and wherever resources were available, Nelson apparently felt that in view of the opposition of the military and several of his own vice-chairmen, it was wise for him to reopen the subject. As far as legal powers were concerned, Nelson could have gone ahead without further discussion.

The question was raised in tentative form at the meeting of December 28. The proposed relaxation was heartily approved by Joseph B. Eastman, Director of the Office of Defense Transportation, "with respect to approvals of certain types of railroad equipment that move in that direction would increase the capacity of the railroads to perform their wartime job." Patterson expressed opposition saying that he was concerned at the volume of materials and manpower that had already gone into projects like jails, courthouses, and highway cutoffs. The subject was closed in the following way: "The Chairman replied that as the war turns increasingly in our favor the question he proposes to raise at the next meeting must be faced and that what he wishes from the Board is an expression of opinion on the matter of timing."

In accordance with this announcement, the matter was again up for discussion at the Board meeting of January 11, 1944. Nelson pointed out once again that materials such as aluminum and copper would be in excess of the needs of munitions production, that facilities were available in some areas, and that in the near future there would be unemployment in various sections of the country. Under those conditions, he suggested that it might be wise to authorize the use of those resources for production of facilities such as railroad safety and signal equipment, industrial building improvements, farm-to-market roads, schools in overcrowded war production centers, water systems, recreational facilities for war workers, etc. Nelson realized, however, that any relaxation might be interpreted to mean the war was already won, and it therefore might be best to wait until the European invasion was an established fact, although the WPB was responsible for *making plans* for the future. McNutt, Chairman of the War Manpower Commission, opposed any formal relaxation, which he feared would make it more difficult to persuade idle manpower to move to war jobs. Forrestal was also opposed because the proposal would open the way for pressure groups sponsoring local projects, and because some concerns might decline war contracts in the hope of getting back to peacetime production ahead of their competitors. Isador Lubin, Economic Advisor to the President, stated that although he was convinced that local unemployment would damage the morale of war workers, he thought the question of formal relaxation should be shelved until the war turned more decisively in favor of the United Nations. Eastman, who was already on record as favoring a more lenient policy with respect to authorization of certain railroad facilities, opposed any formal relaxation because it would invite local communities to compete to secure favorable consideration for home-town projects. Assistant Secretary of Commerce Will Clayton and Secretary of Agriculture Claude Wickard both opposed formal relaxation. Clayton expressed the view that idle manpower should be encouraged to move into other war production centers rather than remain in surplus labor areas in the hope that new construction would be authorized. Various of these speakers suggested that the existing regulations might be interpreted more liberally and thus achieve some of the objectives sought by Nelson without a wave of overoptimism.

Patterson felt that "a relaxation of the present policy would be taken as a symbol of return to civilian production. At a time when major military developments are pending, any action that might be interpreted as a relaxation on the home front would have a particularly unfortunate effect upon the morale of the fighting forces." He urged that the question of any change in the facilities policy be postponed until the military situation became clear.

The last speaker, present at Nelson's invitation, was Elmer Davis, Director of the Office of War Information. He believed that the decision against relaxation "until the course of the war is clearer" could be held to, if "all concerned would maintain a united opinion publicly and privately."

As a result of this discussion, and with Nelson's approval, the Board unanimously approved the following statement:

> The War Production Board's present policies respecting restrictions on new construction and facilities should continue in effect until the probable future course of the war makes it certain that a relaxation will not injure the war effort.

This decision referred to facilities only, but it was generally inferred that it reversed Nelson's decision of November 30, 1943, and that reconversion action was to be postponed until after the invasion of Europe. Nelson made it clear that nothing significant was to be undertaken at the time, for he told the newsmen on January 17:

> This emphatically is not the time to divert any substantial quantities of materials, labor, or facilities to less essential production. There certainly cannot be any return to volume [production] of less essential goods until the war picture is a great deal clearer.

At least in retrospect, this sharp shift in position between November 30 and January 11—without any apparent attempt on Nelson's part to salvage his announced policy—seems puzzling. It is less puzzling if the reader recalls that the excess materials, idle plants, and local pools of unemployment were still only prospective: in a practical sense action must await future developments. And this consideration is reinforced by the further consideration that the matter specifically at issue before the Board was timing. Nelson was seeking advice on that point. Furthermore, the views of the Board members, while firm on the question of a public announcement before the invasion, gave Nelson considerable scope for a more liberal application of existing policy. It should also be noted that Nelson had not pressed for any positive decision and had explained that he was aware of the divergence of views in the Board, both among the representatives of the outside agencies and among the WPB officials themselves; this was a matter of considerable importance in the tense war atmosphere, and especially to a man like Nelson, who repeatedly stressed his belief in the fundamental values of consensus and who had repeatedly in the past tried to avoid conflict by postponement of action. Finally, as recently as January 7, Nelson had received a letter (described below) from Mr. Baruch on responsibility for reconversion that seemed to him a rebuff to a friendly overture he had made somewhat earlier; Nelson was therefore uncertain of the backing he might get from Baruch and Baruch's old friend Byrnes in any argument over reconversion. There were thus a variety of circumstances that tended to induce compromise and delay.

IV. Interlude

A. THE YEAR 1944

The announcement of General Eisenhower's appointment as Supreme Commander of the Allied Expeditionary Forces at the end of December 1943 set the stage for 1944. The year 1944 would tell the tale: final victory might not, probably would not, ensue till later, but the hope of victory in the proximate future was clearly dependent on a successful invasion of Europe. Steadily through the winter and spring months the tension grew.

The production problem also changed. In 1942 the chief task of WPB had been the control of materials; by the end of the year a more effective system of materials control had been worked out and was ready to go into effect. Automatically, therefore, the major center of attention and power shifted to the scheduling of production. The techniques for this task were well established by the end of 1943. In 1944 there were many changes that required the continuing application of production controls, but the solutions of the basic scheduling problems had already been found.

The great task of 1944 was the assurance of manpower. Inevitably, painfully, and even reluctantly the center of action moved from the WPB to the War Manpower Commission (WMC), from Nelson and Wilson to McNutt. And by virtue of that fact, the need for intervention and mediation from above became more urgent: OWM became increasingly a determiner and not merely a co-ordinator of policy. The shift in attention from the physical means of production to manpower carried with it a further isolation of Nelson, of those Vice-Chairmen who still reported to him, and of the Program Vice-Chairman with his staff, from the power center of WPB. For in the fall of 1943, when manpower problems became acute, especially on the West Coast, a technique had been developed, in the absence of national service legislation, for securing the optimum use of manpower in areas of serious manpower shortage. The chief device was the establishment of two sets of committees, a pair for each area of critical shortages; one group, with WMC chairmen, were called Area Manpower Priorities Committees, the other, with WPB chairmen, were called Area Production Urgency Committees. In most cases the personnel of the two committees were identical. The Area Production Urgency Committees (APUC'S) were the principal channels through which WPB attempted to keep facility projects and supply contracts in balance with available manpower resources of various areas. Gradually these committees were extended to other areas and given more authority over administration of WPB policies in the field. Instructions to the Area Production Urgency Committees required the approval of the PEC which co-ordinated their activities. Thus Wilson maintained control of the basic link with the manpower problem.

This was the background of the renewed struggle over reconversion that had been postponed by Nelson at the beginning of the year. Appropriately enough the first significant move was made not by WPB but by OWM.

B. THE BARUCH-HANCOCK REPORT

The decision to postpone reconversion led to no improvement in the uneasy relations between Nelson and Wilson, or in the definitely unsatisfactory relations between Nelson and the Services, and Nelson and OWM.

It will be recalled that in the fall of 1943 under formal instructions from the President, Byrnes had asked Bernard M. Baruch and John M. Hancock to prepare a report and recommendations on all phases of war and postwar reconversion policy. Despite Byrnes' vague but reassuring statement at the time of Baruch's appointment, and despite Baruch's own assurances in a letter to Nelson on December 14 that he felt that the WPB had an important reconversion role, rumors continued to circulate that the Baruch-Hancock Report would recommend the creation of an entirely new agency to handle reconversion. In view of the fact that Byrnes and Baruch were not sympathetic to Nelson these rumors were given much weight. Nelson had written to Baruch on December 29 pointing out that the rumors were damaging WPB morale and interfering with his attempts to hold together his trained personnel who would be an invaluable asset in the reconversion period. Nelson also indicated his concern over "external forces . . . driving a wedge into our personal relationship. . . . Some sections of the press have spread the notion that you and I are engaged in competing for power over the reconversion administration." Nelson assured Baruch that this was not the case and that issues created between Baruch and himself were purely fictitious. Baruch had replied in a short—and, Nelson felt, curt—letter on January 7 in which he reiterated his belief in the importance of WPB in demobilization and stated that he would not permit any personal questions to interfere with the best interests of the country.

The Baruch-Hancock Report was issued on February 15 and ended the rumors that the WPB would be replaced by a new reconversion agency, but it did not settle the basic issue between Nelson and the military. For example, it stated that worthwhile projects in areas of localized unemployment should be authorized when resources were in excess of military needs, *if* this could be done without interference with war programs. That "if," of course, was the bone of contention between Nelson and the military. It did, however, reject Patterson's claim that a program of gradual reconversion would necessarily have dangerous psychological repercussions. It also called upon the WPB and the services to get together on a program to handle cutbacks and on an X-day reconversion plan to go into effect with the defeat of Germany. But because of its general, and sometimes equivocal, nature it did not help resolve the conflict between Nelson and the Army.

On February 22, 1944, Byrnes publicly stated that contract cancellations were creating problems that had to be met at once. He pointed out that 3,769 Army prime contracts had already been canceled, and that an estimated two and one-half billion dollar cutback would be ordered by the middle of the year. Therefore he was ordering the agencies concerned to implement the suggestions of the Baruch-Hancock Report.

C. PEC AND RECONVERSION

General Clay still insisted that the PEC be the agency to direct reconversion. He had formally presented Panuch's proposals to PEC in January and argued that only by centering control over reconversion in the hands of the PEC could the integrity of the military programs be maintained. Although Wilson had agreed, he refused to press for adoption of Panuch's proposals in view of Nelson's and Krug's hostility to them.

Wilson, who had long talked of resigning, visited the White House on January 21 and was persuaded to stay on in the WPB, at least until the spring. With his tenure extended, and after Baruch and Hancock had recommended the immediate establishment of interagency machinery to dispose of cutbacks, Wilson appointed a drafting committee composed of Stacy May of the WPB, Admiral C. A. Jones of the Navy, and Panuch of the Army to develop plans to implement these recommendations. On February 29 the three presented a plan which was in broad outline the one Panuch had proposed earlier and which gave control over reconversion to the PEC, the most significant change being an enlargement of civilian representation on the PEC subcommittee. Clay agreed to this change only when he became convinced of the necessity of compromise in order to secure Nelson's approval.

Nelson still refused to approve, however, despite Wilson's best efforts to convince him of the immediate necessity for establishing machinery to co-ordinate cutbacks with new military orders and civilian production. Nelson would not approve Wilson's plan nor, on the other hand, reject it flatly. To have rejected it and ordered cutback co-ordinating machinery established either under his own or under Krug's direction would, Nelson feared, lead to dissension with Wilson and Clay. Furthermore, Wilson's resignation was still scheduled for the spring. Since cutbacks were of relatively minor significance at the moment, Nelson apparently continued to feel that there was no immediate need for decision, especially if by a little delay a harmonious solution could be reached after Wilson's resignation.

D. MARKING TIME

Although no immediate reconversion action was contemplated, the early months of 1944 were marked by a continuation of the disagreement between the WPB and the Services on the question of production for non-military use, not as reconversion but as an intrinsic part of the general production program. Patterson, Somervell, and Clay were just as opposed to increased production for the supporting economy as they were to that which was proposed for reconversion purposes. They attempted, for example, to secure a limitation on civilian production to the levels of that produced during the first quarter of 1944. When Nelson stated that the WPB wished to authorize the production of certain items needed for the civilian wartime economy, but that military representatives on the various WPB subcommittees of the Requirements Committee were blocking any such action,

Patterson replied that there should be no increase in civilian production for *any* purpose. He said that the fall of the Italian government in the summer of 1943 had precipitated a wave of optimism throughout the country, and that the current victories in the Pacific would do the same; therefore no new increased civilian production should be authorized even in areas of plentiful manpower because the authorization would make it impossible to encourage workers to migrate to industries where they were needed. He followed this statement with a letter to Nelson saying:

> Civilian programs would inevitably draw manpower from essential war production. . . . Those who say that production of consumers' goods should be commenced for the sake of providing employment at any place where workers may happen to live despite the over-all need of additional workers for direct war work, place the ease and preference of particular persons above the needs of the armed forces for munitions and supplies.

At this point Nelson found new support in a report issued by the Truman Committee which sought to refute Patterson's charges. Nelson's relations with this Senate Special Committee Investigating the Defense Program were especially cordial. E. A. Locke, Jr., a member of Nelson's immediate staff, was WPB's liaison officer with the Committee and worked very closely with its staff. The Truman Committee was one of Nelson's strongest supporters and its March 3 report on "The Present Status and Future Course of the War Production Program" forcefully championed his position. The report rejected Patterson's contention that workers in surplus labor areas could be forced into areas of tight manpower supply by withholding civilian production.

> The country is too vast, our economy is too complex, and the knowledge by workers of conditions in other areas too fragmentary to support any such expectation. . . . The Committee doubts that the widespread suffering, which would result from a policy of deliberately fostering unemployment in areas separated by many miles from areas of manpower shortage, would make a contribution to the winning of the war outweighing the certain detriment involved.

The report also took issue with "high military authorities [who] have charged that there is a deterioration of morale on the home front," and called these officials to task for looking only at their individual needs and paying "less attention to the over-all effect of action which may produce small benefits to their programs at great cost to the economy as a whole."

E. BIG BUSINESS

It was also at this point that a new element was introduced into the mixture—the element that ultimately caused the explosion.

Up to the spring of 1944 the argument about reconversion (and about essential civilian production) had been waged largely on its merits. There was a definite implication in the Army's complaints, as in the Patterson letter quoted above, of a lack of patriotism on the part of Nelson and his supporters. But the question of motives was now brought to the fore.

The newspapers picked up the evidences of dissension revealed in the Truman Committee report of March 3. In following up the story they introduced a new theme: "Big Business is responsible." They reported that the representatives of big business within the Army and the WPB had forced the postponement of reconversion. Large producers, it was said, knew that they would be tied up with war contracts and therefore would be the last to reconvert. In addition, most of them were located in areas of manpower shortages. Their fear that small concerns would get the jump on the competitive market, so it was rumored, was an important cause of the reconversion delay.

The factual background of the allegations can be indicated. Several of the WPB Industry Advisory Committees had been consulted as to whether new producers should be permitted to enter a market while prewar manufacturers were still tied up with war work, and whether producers located in areas of labor surpluses should be permitted to produce unlimited amounts (consistent with war production) or should be assigned quotas on the basis of their prewar competitive position. Some of these committees advised holding off civilian production until all concerns within an industry were ready to reconvert. Also, a second alternative to Nelson's plan was put forward early in March by Arthur D. Whiteside, who had recently retired from the WPB as Vice-Chairman for Civilian Requirements. He told the American Retail Federation that it would not be wise to start up civilian production indiscriminately because it might cause a saturation of markets and result in unemployment later. Although he favored resumption of civilian production, he argued that producers should be assigned quotas on the basis of their prewar production. Some form of quota or hold-back arrangement, too, had previously been implied in the PEC resolution of December 15 in the phrase "equity to industry."

Nelson rejected these policies in a letter to Senator Murray, Chairman of the Senate Special Committee on Small Business; the letter was made public on March 7. He stated that the WPB would give manufacturers in noncritical manpower areas the materials and parts they needed to resume production of civilian goods without waiting until manufacturers in critical areas were permitted to do so. Prewar competitive patterns, stated Nelson, would not be considered. Although this policy might work hardship, Nelson felt that it would not be in the public interest to hold off reconversion until all plants were ready. This letter was reviewed and concurred in by all the Vice-Chairmen of WPB.

This is the factual background of the "big business" allegations; but the evidence of positions taken is a very different thing from proof of ulterior motives. The techniques of reconversion were a normal subject for discussion and analysis, and for difference of opinion. The economists of the Office of Civilian Supply who had worked out the original limitation orders for automobiles, refrigerators, etc., for example, had incorporated in those orders company quotas based on historical production (with some weighting in favor of the smaller companies). And these same economists, with no big business ties whatever, had had purely casual discussions at the time on the possible use of quotas in the eventual unwinding process.

The allegations related to motive. In effect the accusers were saying that WPB officials were in favor of quotas or a general hold-back plan—and were against Nelson's proposals—because they were trying to protect the interests of their own companies.

This kind of allegation is seldom susceptible of proof, and never of disproof. It may conceivably have been true of some subordinates in positions of circumscribed vision; but there are substantial reasons for believing that it unfairly misrepresented the grounds of senior officials who were responsible for the recommendations actually made.

Equally beyond the realm of proof or disproof is the question of good faith on the part of the accusers. Some of the accusers were probably originally acting in good faith; but the persistence of the allegations among others was perhaps attributable to an unwillingness to re-examine the situation, or a lack of any concern with the validity of the charges. In the latter category are possibly some of the news reporters and commentators, whose bread was buttered when they were able to garnish their stories of policy differences with the spices of personality clashes and suspected conspiracies against the public welfare.

Regardless of such unsavory speculations, the fact of the allegations of "big business" bias was important from the beginning and became crucially important, for they were used as a retort to the Army's implied claim that Nelson and the supporters of his program were unpatriotic. The bandying of these various charges led to a disastrous dissolution of the already none-too-harmonious relations between Nelson and his immediate circle, on the one hand, and Wilson and most of the rest of WPB, on the other.

Rumors beget rumor, by a variety of processes. It was said in Washington at the time that Nelson's personal staff was trying to secure for him the Democratic Vice-Presidential nomination in the coming summer of 1944; Nelson was to be built up as the defender of small business via his reconversion program.

F. THE BUILD UP

By April 1944 production officials were aware that the invasion of Europe was scheduled for spring or early summer, and talk of reconversion was again rife. At the April 4 Board meeting Wilson was more optimistic about reconversion than he had been theretofore. He told the Board that by the end of the year no less than one-half million, and perhaps as many as one million, workers would be available. He was not unmindful of the fact that raising the question of reconversion before the major military effort was accomplished involved grave risks. But the question was in fact being raised daily through program adjustments, contract cancellations and non-renewals. He enumerated the alternatives:

1. *No Reconversion*—Military production could be curtailed without expansion of non-military output by cutting two or three hours of the work week. However, experience demonstrated that this might have a greater impact on the munitions program than intended. Or military production could be curtailed by discharging workers who were not needed, in the hope that they would drift into industries needing manpower such as lumber and textiles. The objection to this method was that labor would more probably be dissipated in non-essential occupations or lost altogether.

2. *Increased Munitions Production*—If production officials were unwilling to face the charge of withholding available resources from productive use or the implications of planning for specific reconversion, they could reverse the downward trend in munitions and produce in 1944 the munitions needed for 1945. But this approach would raise the problem of excessive inventories and potential waste and would only postpone a problem that would have to be dealt with eventually.

3. *Increased Civilian Production*—The WPB could authorize the production of such volume of consumer durable goods and service equipment as could be accommodated with released resources.

Wilson reiterated that the problem was not yet pressing, but would be upon war production officials by the last quarter of 1944. He concluded: "By the end of this year reconversion must be under way on a considerable scale regardless of whether we have a one-front or two-front war on our hands."

General Clay dissented only to the extent of returning to his suggestion of December 1 that the war might take such a turn that production scheduled for 1945 should be moved ahead to 1944 and by pointing out that Japan might fall before Germany, and other uncertainties.

The discussion ended on this inconclusive note.

Nelson attempted to strengthen his own hand by appointing, on April 14, an Advisory Committee for Civilian Policy, composed of representatives of major segments of the economy. This Committee was to have a permanent staff and to play a major role in the development of reconversion policy. Nelson created it primarily to offset the influence of the military in a field which he considered of chief concern to civilians. However, Nelson's plans for the Committee proved abortive, and it never met.

Within the Board, Maury Maverick was most active in opposing the current restrictive policy. Maverick, a lawyer, former mayor of San Antonio, former Congressman, was Vice-Chairman for Smaller War Plants and he reported directly to Nelson. He opposed the military and War Manpower Commission officials at every turn and did his best to secure authorization for small amounts of production for plants that were without war work. His proposals are worth some attention because they are the immediate forerunners of the proposal that was soon to become the heart of Nelson's reconversion program.

In January 1944 Nelson had suggested that small concerns might be given a little help on critical components and be permitted to produce any article if they could make it out of surplus stock. This encouragement was all that Maverick needed; perhaps he was the one who had suggested it to Nelson. At any rate when Colonel Baxter, head of the WPB Redistribution Division, reported that small lots of various materials were increasing the "surplus input" of materials much faster than the ability of war factories to absorb them, Maverick seized upon this report to push for a relaxation of the restrictive policy on civilian production. He pointed out that many small plants had open capacity, capacity for which there was no war work. He suggested, therefore, that those plants designated by the Smaller War Plants Corporation as having open capacity should receive authorization from regional War Production Board offices to use surplus materials for civilian production, provided they had the necessary equipment and labor and would use no critical components. Maverick made little headway, however, and he was convinced that opposition came from large-scale business. When, in Nelson's absence, the PEC forbade the authorization of *any* non-military production in any area where manpower was tight, this conviction was strengthened. Although Nelson forced a modification of this policy in favor of more flexible procedures, Maverick told the Senate Special Committee on Small Business (on May 9) that this was another move on the part of big business to prevent resumption of civilian production until the end of the war.

The moment for explosion was coming closer.

G. PEC AND CUTBACKS

By May there was still no effective machinery to co-ordinate cutbacks. Wilson had continued to urge adoption of the February 29 Plan (the modified Panuch Plan). Apparently Nelson had, in the middle of March, given some sign of wavering in his opposition, because at the March 22 PEC meeting Wilson had announced that the WPB would soon be ready to adopt the February 29 Plan. Nelson, however, for reasons already mentioned, had continued to hold off his approval. Finally, on March 31, Byrnes, possibly at Clay's behest, had written to Nelson:

> It is essential that contract termination be co-ordinated with a positive program of reconversion. . . . I would like to know what progress is being made by the War Production Board in dealing with this problem. . . . I would be glad to consider any suggestions for action on my part that may be in order.

Nelson remained unmoved. He neither acted himself nor accepted Byrnes' offer to act for him.

In April, Wilson had been again persuaded by the President to remain, until July. It was no secret that the War Department production officials would have liked to see him replace Nelson as Chairman, and when it was rumored that they had been largely responsible for the President's asking Wilson to remain, it heightened the friction within WPB. It was noted that the President had not consulted Nelson before he persuaded Wilson to stay on.

Krug had resigned on April 17 to accept a commission in the Navy, and Wilson had taken over his duties, so General Clay, Panuch, and Wilson no longer objected to giving the Program Bureau and the Requirements Committee a more important reconversion role. But with Krug's resignation, Nelson was even more reluctant to permit the PEC to direct reconversion, even though the Office of Civilian Requirements finally secured its long-sought representation on that important Committee in May.

Paradoxically Nelson, the most active proponent of early reconversion, was delaying the establishment of cutback machinery, even though the co-ordination of new production with cutbacks was the key to his program of gradual reconversion. On May 12 Baruch and Hancock wrote to Byrnes censuring Nelson for his failure to act and blaming him for holding up reconversion. They wrote:

> There has been no action even though appropriate letters were sent by your office to the War Production Board, and the armed services were ready to proceed. . . .
>
> For the good of all of us, but mostly for the sake of our soldiers and sailors, let us hurry, hurry, hurry, not only in the winning of the war, but in being ready for the peace. Delays jeopardize both of these objectives.

Still no action had been taken on May 22 when the Navy publicly announced that it had made a sizable cutback in its fighter plane program and that the Long Island plants of the Brewster Corporation were to cease producing planes. The Navy had given only one day's notification to the War Production Board, three days to the Brewster officials, and less to the workers. As a result there were no plans to use the facilities and manpower thus released either for military or civilian production.

After being told for months of the importance and vital nature of their work, and then suddenly finding themselves out of a job, the men in the plants were indignant. They protested their treatment by a "stay-in-strike," announcing that they would stay in the plants until they were given additional work. This incident was a dramatic manifestation of the fears of management and labor the nation over—the fear that cutbacks in war programs would bring large-scale unemployment. The public backed up the workers, and editorials in all sections of the country heaped blame on the administration and demanded action to prevent the recurrence of such an episode. A subcommittee of the Senate Military Affairs Committee announced that it was going to investigate the affair.

Nelson still believed that the PEC should not be given authority to direct reconversion, but under the circumstances he could delay no longer. He authorized Wilson to proceed with his plans, provided that the PEC not be given over-all control of reconversion. Although Wilson's directive, issued on May 30, gave to the PEC noticeably less authority than had been contemplated in Panuch's proposals, it did not make clear just how much authority the PEC was to have in determining the amount, kind, and timing of non-military production.

On June 5 Byrnes assigned to Wilson and the PEC authority to co-ordinate contract cancellations. The precise background of this unusual procedure of by-passing the Chairman and of assigning functions to one committee instead of the entire WPB is unknown; presumably Byrnes had become convinced that Nelson would not act. Whatever its origin, it further convinced Nelson that he had to move fast or lose complete control of the situation.

Business and labor groups were growing more vocal. Several spokesmen for organized labor told various congressional committees that Nelson's gradual reconversion program was necessary to sustain the morale of the war workers. With the spread of knowledge or belief that the invasion was imminent, reconversion proposals began to crop up all through the War Production Board. On May 29 several staff members had met to consider Maverick's proposal to permit WPB regional offices to authorize production with surplus materials in areas of unemployment. On June 5 Wilson announced that he would hold a meeting to discuss various plans for resumption of civilian production.

On June 6 Fortress Europe was invaded.

V. The Battle of Reconversion

A. NELSON'S RECONVERSION PROGRAM

General Clay told the members of the PEC on June 7, 1944, that the War Department felt that the time was still not opportune for widespread publicity concerning reconversion. Nevertheless, Nelson came to the conclusion that he could no longer delay and that some positive action was needed.

On June 10 Byrnes requested Nelson to prepare a statement on his reconversion plans so that Byrnes could explain them to the Senate Military Affairs Committee. Nelson himself was scheduled to appear before the Truman Committee on June 19, so on June 12 he reviewed the entire situation with members of his staff. The military situation was good. The only bad spot in the production picture was the lagging behind schedule of certain key items as a result of suddenly increased requirements. The major hindrance to these programs was a shortage of the right kind of labor in the right places at the right times; the War Manpower Commission had announced that a new manpower program would be put into effect on July 1 to remedy this situation. But over-all production was good, and Nelson proceeded with his plans.

At the WPB meeting of June 13 McNutt charged that too many workers, misguided by unwarranted optimism, were moving out of essential war production jobs or refusing to move into necessary jobs. Therefore the WMC was extending its West Coast program to the entire nation. Among other things, war production centers were to be classified in four groups on the basis of adequacy of manpower,[3] more stringent labor controls were to be adopted in all labor shortage areas, and the inter-area recruitment program was to be intensified.

After discussion of this new and more stringent manpower program, Nelson brought up his reconversion proposals. He pointed out that if Germany should suddenly collapse, the economy could not be reconverted for several months. Up to that time the WPB had discouraged industry planning and retooling for resumption of civilian production, but the war had progressed, said Nelson, "to the stage where some reconversion machinery can safely be set in motion." He then outlined his program of permitting placement of orders on a deferred basis for developing new models and for retooling. He also expressed the feeling that WPB regional officers should be permitted to determine locally, after consultation with local War Manpower officials, whether to permit manufacture of items or use of materials no longer under blanket restrictions. "If laborers are convinced that efforts are being made to develop an orderly reconversion program, their sense of security will be enhanced and the temptation to transfer from war work to civilian type jobs will to a large extent be removed." Nelson further pointed out that some companies had already made substantial preparations for return to peacetime production—in many cases in violation of WPB orders; hence companies which observed the regulations strictly were being unfairly penalized. The necessary tooling of industry had delayed war production and would delay peace production unless the Board took steps before it was suddenly confronted with the actual necessity of reconverting. Moreover, he felt that it would be a good hedge against unemployment if machine tool and other industries could build up a backlog of orders to absorb the slack during the transition period.

[3] Group I. Acute labor shortage.
Group II. Labor shortage and those areas anticipating a shortage within six months.
Group III. Slight labor shortage that will remain after six months.
Group IV. Substantial labor reserve that will remain after six months.

Wilson supported Nelson's views. Navy representatives expressed some concern about the possible impact on the manpower program, and accepted reassurance on that point; they were even sponsoring a proposal to allow manufacturers to build and perfect experimental models.

General Clay and a representative of the Secretary of War were content to indicate that there were substantial "slippages" in critical segments of the military program and that while they did not object to planning, reconversion should therefore be approached with caution; they did not object to any of Nelson's proposals, which were generalized, except for the proposed permission to manufacturers to place deferred orders for machine tools or to build experimental models.

B. ANNOUNCEMENT OF NELSON'S PROGRAM

Nelson had not asked for an endorsement. After this cool—rather than hostile—reception he ordered his staff to continue preparations. By June 16 the beachhead in France seemed secure and Nelson was ready to release his reconversion program to the public. But when the press release was circulated among the vice-chairmen for their approval, all of them except Maverick and the two labor vice-chairmen objected. They objected to the program and to the manner in which it was to be announced. If it were to be inaugurated at all, they argued that it should be announced only after it was made clear that the production situation was still serious and that no real reconversion activity could be undertaken for some time.

Nelson was in a difficult position. To move ahead in the face of the almost unanimous opposition of the WPB vice-chairmen was not his way of doing things. On the other hand, Wilson had come to his support, at least in general terms, OWM demanded action, and the Truman Committee had to be given some assurance of progress on June 19.

Finally Nelson decided on a partial compromise. While he wanted to release the news of his reconversion program in a more positive fashion, he agreed in order to conciliate his vice-chairmen to hold up the announcement until a compromise release could be worked out. This was ready on June 18, and Nelson called the newsmen into his office. Stating that certain items were behind schedule and stressing the necessity for increased munitions production, he warned: "The next three months on the production front are of especial importance and we need 200,000 men in the war industries." Prefaced by this note of caution, he announced that the Board was going to issue four reconversion orders on or before July 1. "Studies made outside of WPB, including the Baruch Report and reports of the Truman Committee, take the view that these moves should have been made much earlier." Although they would not allow any significant increase in civilian production, they would help industry prepare for the time when the military programs would be cut back from their two-front volume. They were as follows.

First, WPB orders limiting the use of magnesium and aluminum were to be revoked so that manufacturers would be able to use these metals for essential products whenever and wherever manpower was available.

Second, manufacturers were to be authorized to acquire enough materials and components to make and test a working model of any product planned for postwar production (later known as Priorities Regulation 23).

Third, manufacturers were to be allowed to purchase machine tools and dies for civilian production out of existing surpluses, if possible, or by placing orders to be subsequently validated by WPB for production at a time and under conditions which would not interfere with war production (later known as Priorities Regulation 24).

Fourth, WPB regional offices were to be instructed to determine locally, with due consultation with the War Manpower Commission, whether or not to permit production of items on which WPB restrictions were lifted (the core of what would later be known as Priorities Regulation 25 or the "spot authorization" order).

The next day Nelson appeared before the Truman Committee and again stressed the need for critical items which had "upscheduled" as a result of experience in France (e.g., tanks and heavy trucks). He reassured the Committee that his proposed reconversion program was conservative and would be executed with caution. Though he was sure that it would not injure war production, he was equally sure that the prospect of cutbacks during the ensuing months made it imperative that this action be taken, even if there were a risk of a slight interference with the munitions program.

C. THE ARMY ATTACKS

Those who knew of the intensity of the Army opposition to Nelson's reconversion program were not startled to learn that Patterson, Clay, and Somervell did not consider the matter settled. On June 22, four days after Nelson's press conference, Patterson, emphasizing that munitions production had been slipping, wrote to Nelson:

> The War Department appreciates fully the desirability of planning for reconversion. . . . However, we are apprehensive of positive steps towards reconversion at this critical phase of the war when our troops in ever-increasing numbers are in actual contact with the enemy, and the expenditures of war material on the battlefront are amounting to huge totals.

He then reiterated the War Department's opposition to any activity which would divert the nation's manpower, materials, or concentration from the primary task of munitions production. Before Nelson could reply, he was stricken with pneumonia and forced out of the struggle.

D. WILSON TAKES CHARGE

With Nelson's enforced absence, Wilson found himself in an extremely difficult position. Though he was not enthusiastic about Nelson's scheduled reconversion program, as acting head of the War Production Board it was his responsibility to act on Nelson's convictions and to issue the orders.

Nelson had approved a draft of a reply to Patterson, but it fell to Wilson to complete and sign the letter, which, though courteous, was positive in tone. It concluded:

I would call to your attention the fact that under the mandate given to WPB by Congress and the President, restrictions which we impose on the economy must be essential to war production. When those restrictions are no longer essential for war production, we have no warrant for retaining them. Consequently, if we find that any WPB restriction can be lifted without injury to war production, we shall lift the restriction. If at any time signs appear that the lifting of restrictions by WPB is interfering with war production, you may be assured that we will move at once to eliminate the interference.

But the War Department, the Navy, and the War Manpower Commission continued to work for a reversal of Nelson's order to issue the regulations by July 1. At the PEC meeting of June 28 Admiral Robinson suggested that "the issuance of these orders be held in abeyance in view of the increased military programs and production difficulties caused by the shortage of manpower." Lawrence Appley of the War Manpower Commission stated that there was a deficiency of approximately 300,000 men for critical munitions programs, and that therefore there was no available manpower for "anything anywhere." Clay heartily agreed, but Wilson declared:

All the arguments presented . . . were previously discussed by the WPB Chairman and his staff and the substance of the proposed orders was generally agreed upon within the WPB and practically committed to the Truman Committee.

Despite this statement, Wilson agreed to accept Appley's motion that "in view of the additional requirements which have developed for munitions and manpower the WPB be requested to place the entire question of resumption of civilian and peacetime production on the agenda of the next WPB meeting." This meant that the orders would not be issued by July 1.

On June 29 the Joint Chiefs of Staff with their great prestige joined the struggle and announced—publicly:

A dangerous state of mind which cuts war production by causing people to throw up their war jobs is just as harmful as desertions on the fighting front. No effort required in the home-front battle should be diverted by any element in the production machine, whether it be ownership, management, rank and file workers, or those in the service of the Government. . . .

Thus by this date the vocal opponents of Nelson's program included not only many in the WPB itself, not only the WMC—which would obviously be directly affected—not only the military production chiefs who were regular participants in WPB's production programing; the opponents now included the Joint Chiefs whose function was to determine strategy and strategic requirements, not production.

Delay of issuance of the orders was on Wilson's conscience, and when he talked the matter over with Byrnes the latter suggested that he write and ask Nelson's approval of the postponement. He did so, but when the doctors refused to let Nelson see the letter, Wilson took over the entire responsibility. He called a special meeting of the Board for July 4.

E. THE FOURTH OF JULY

The Board meeting of July 4 took place at a moment of uncertainty in the war. The Normandy beachhead was secure, but German resistance was stiff and no breakout was in immediate prospect. It was an anxious period.

Wilson opened this meeting, one of the largest in WPB history, by saying:

The action by the Chairman before his illness has met with powerful approval, both in the Congress and in all sectors of the press. No move that I can recall in the history of the War Production Board has received more enthusiastic reception in the organs of public opinion. Response seems to bear out the Chairman's view that the country wants immediate action on reconversion preparations.

This propitiated neither the military nor the War Manpower Commission. They claimed that conditions had changed since Nelson had first announced his proposals and that therefore it would be unfair to him to proceed with his orders before he had an opportunity to reconsider. The changes on which they based this claim were reported as follows: slippages in June production, statement of the Joint Chiefs of Staff, reports of shortages from men just back from the front, the serious steel situation, and serious labor shortages.

Patterson opened the discussion by stating:

> The War Department of course is not opposed in any measure to advance planning for reconversion. In fact, we are in favor of it. We do feel that the series of orders proposed go beyond mere planning and will have the effect of interfering seriously with war production . . . there has been a very serious slippage in war production. . . . If the present trend is continued, the ability of our soldiers to pour it on in full measure to the Germans and the Japs is sure to be impaired. . . . In view of the slippage that we are now encountering and against which the Chiefs of Staff warned, at the present time we don't believe that it is any time to relax those controls right now.

He further argued that the safeguards in the orders were ineffective and would render it extremely difficult to direct manpower into basic industries under the new program of the WMC.

When Wilson replied that Nelson had realized that June production would be down, Under Secretary of the Navy Bard retorted:

> Even if he did know that the production for June was below, or May, he didn't know and he didn't have any information brought back by the heads of the Army and Navy from the fronts. . . . [Even if he knew of] . . . the seriousness of the steel situation which has developed since that time, he didn't have the report which I have had direct from the men that came back, the heads of the armed services, General Arnold and Admiral King and General Marshall. He hadn't been apprised of the hundred octane gas situation. He hadn't seen the statement of the Joint Chiefs of Staff; he hadn't had the benefit of talking with those men that are running the war. . . . I can't conceive that if he were here today that he would want a decision arrived at four weeks ago to stand regardless of the things that have transpired since. . . . The picture is changing every day, and to say that the recommendations and the needs of the Armed Forces . . . shall not be considered by the Chairman of this body . . . strikes me as something entirely out of order.

Wilson informed Bard that he had talked with Nelson within the week and that he still wanted the orders to be issued.

When the question of manpower shortages was discussed, McNutt said that the orders would endanger the success of his new program, but Wilson again reminded the Board that Nelson knew of the labor difficulties but was convinced that civilian production could be authorized in areas of unemployment without endangering the war effort. He asked Bard to cite specific items that would be held up as a result of the orders. Bard replied that the psychological effect of the orders would defeat the purpose of the War Manpower Commission's program. Patterson, basing his argument on the psychological effect of the orders, then said, "It is the opinion of the war agencies [sic] that . . . these orders will interfere with the ample supply of those men [on the Normandy Beachhead and the Island of Saipan]."

Each of the proposed orders was then considered individually. The military and the WMC opposed removal of restrictions on the use of magnesium and aluminum, but indicated that they would approve this order if it were amended to allow the use of these materials only for previously authorized end items.

Patterson objected to the order permitting the building of experimental models because the controls were inadequate to prevent interference with war production. Bard, McNutt, and Admiral Land (Chairman of the Maritime Commission) concurred.

Patterson and Bard opposed the order permitting the placing of unrated orders for machine tools and equipment, although Wilson reminded them that "if the issuance of the order is delayed, preparation for peacetime production would likewise be delayed." Patterson referred to this order as one permitting industries "to make these tools for a postwar gadget."

But their most vehement opposition was to the fourth order—PR-25—which would permit local relaxation of production restrictions where manpower and facilities were available.

McNutt offered a resolution to hold over the orders until Nelson's return; Wilson refused to permit a vote on this, but did permit a vote on the following resolution, also offered by McNutt:

Whereas, the Chairman of the War Production Board is seriously ill; and

Whereas, in the opinion of the members of this Board the issuance of the proposed orders at the present time would interfere with war production;

Now, Therefore, out of courtesy to the Chairman;

It Is Resolved that the issuance of the proposed orders be postponed until Mr. Nelson's return.

The motion carried unanimously with only the representatives of the War Food Administration and the Department of Commerce abstaining. But in spite of the resolution's strangely ambiguous sugar-coating, Wilson declared that he could not accept it as a guide to his actions. He stated that Nelson had "made it very clear to his staff that issuance of the orders was a matter of his complete responsibility and authority." He continued, "I do not believe that there is any new evidence that has been brought forward that would change his opinion." He agreed to present the Board's view to Nelson, but warned that if Nelson did not change his mind the orders would be issued after formal clearance through regular channels, a process that would take about a week. Patterson announced that he would carry the matter to Byrnes, and Admiral Robinson said that if the orders were to be issued "over the dead bodies of the War and Navy Departments" he too would appeal to higher authority.

F. THE BATTLE CONTINUES

At the July 4 meeting Elmer Davis, Director of the Office of War Information, stated emphatically that his job of explaining to the public would be made very difficult if the battle were carried to the press. His plea that the various agencies present a united front met with flat and instantaneous failure. News of the imbroglio spread rapidly through Washington. The Truman Committee heard of it within a few hours after the Board adjourned. The Committee, through its counsel, requested Wilson to issue a statement that would give the substance of the orders and would indicate his intention to proceed immediately with their issuance. Wilson replied that all statements about the orders would be held in abeyance pending his interview with Nelson. Wilson was warned, however, that if the orders were not issued promptly, a public hearing would be ordered "to obtain a public record for future action." Nelson left the hospital on the day the Board met, and members of his personal staff immediately told him what had transpired. He called Byrnes at once, apparently before Patterson was able to carry his appeal to Byrnes, and Byrnes counseled delay. Nelson agreed that, if Byrnes wished, the whole issue might be brought before him for discussion. Apparently Nelson also suggested that he would be willing to delay issuance of the fourth order (spot reconversion) until August 15. Although this was tentatively agreed to, the announcement of the postponement was delayed. Presumably Byrnes wished to consult with Patterson and McNutt and secure their approval of the compromise.

Although they had remained silent at the Board meeting, Maverick and the two Labor Vice-Chairmen, Keenan and Golden, still supported Nelson. For obvious reasons labor and small business (and, on a somewhat different basis, the Office of Civilian Requirements) were the parts of the WPB most interested in reconversion. In a memorandum circulated to all Board members on July 5, Keenan and Golden repeated the arguments for civilian production and pointed out that Nelson's program was especially designed for the current situation:

> The present and first stage of cutbacks is uneven and does not permit a program of resumed production by industries or products. But in spot situations, men, materials and facilities will be released from military production, and be unable to produce even simple items because of existing "L" and "M" [limitation] orders. The duty of the War Production Board to the military is to assure that war production requirements are met. So long as this duty is performed, the military are not in any position to oppose action by the WPB for the benefit of the civilian economy. . . .
>
> We have made sample studies of the manpower situation. There is manpower available for nonmilitary production and this manpower cannot be

utilized to fill the manpower shortages in military production.

It may be noted that Keenan and Golden took pains to point out that the military agencies were exceeding their jurisdiction—an argument that Nelson had never used.

But the Services continued to oppose the orders; the compromise that Nelson proposed, —staggering the orders and delaying issuance of the fourth order until August 15—was apparently unacceptable to them. Wilson and Sidney Weinberg (a friend of both Nelson and Wilson who had been recalled to the WPB on June 15 for the express purpose of restoring better relations between Nelson and Wilson) called on Nelson on July 7 and urged delay. Nelson refused to go beyond his suggested compromise with Byrnes for staggered issuance.

At this meeting Nelson showed Wilson a memorandum (never signed) which E. A. Locke and A. Noyes, both on Nelson's personal staff, had prepared for Nelson to send to the Vice-Chairmen. Besides restating Nelson's position, it emphasized that big business was the major pressure group behind the attempts to prevent the reconversion program from going into effect. Wilson deeply resented the implication that he and the other vice-chairmen opposed reconversion in the interests of big business. Wilson persuaded Nelson not to send the original memorandum. He and Nelson went over it and deleted the objectionable parts; but the original memorandum leaked out nonetheless. Radio commentator Fulton Lewis, Jr., the press, and Kiplinger in his *Washington News Letter*, immediately reported the big business charges. Nelson insisted that he had not given the memorandum to the press and that he had told Fulton Lewis, Jr. that the only difference between himself and the Vice-Chairmen was a question of timing. Nevertheless, Wilson and the other Vice-Chairmen were greatly aroused. Their anger was heightened by the fact that this publicity was not an isolated incident. The discussion within WPB at the Board meeting of July 4 was front-page news on July 6. The Keenan-Golden memorandum of July 5 made the headlines on July 7. The charge of big business sabotage was repeated with varying degrees of circumspection in all these stories and in editorials in the Washington papers. In general, the press took Nelson's side in the dispute.

On July 7, the same day that the Keenan-Golden memorandum (described, of course, as "secret") appeared in the newspapers, Nelson received a letter signed by Admiral Leahy for the Joint Chiefs of Staff. The letter was made officially public on July 8 under the headline, "Joint Chiefs State Nelson Program Causes Revision Strategic Plans." It read in part:

> The Joint Chiefs of Staff understand that the War Production Board is now giving consideration to the issuance of certain orders which have as their objective a relaxation in the controls now in effect over nonessential military production. . . . We are disturbed over the existing lag in war production, which if it continues may necessitate revision in strategic plans which could prolong the war.
>
> In view of the major offensive operations under way on every front it is essential at this time that there be no relaxation in war production and that deficits in deliveries be made up at the earliest possible date.

Nelson, disturbed by this letter which, he believed, exaggerated the extent of his reconversion proposals, wrote to the President on July 8 offering, if the President thought it wise, to cut short his convalescence to explain his proposals personally to the Joint Chiefs. He wrote:

> I am convinced that these measures are needed to protect both the war economy and the reconversion economy; but they have been misunderstood and misinterpreted by other war agencies, which claim to see in them a threat to war production.
>
> Yesterday, I received a letter from Admiral Leahy, for the Joint Chiefs of Staff, which makes it appear that the unwarranted fear of interference with war production as a result of these measures is now shared by high military authorities. I have answered Leahy's letter, which I attach for your consideration, together with my reply.

For some reason the reply to Leahy, referred to in the letter to the President, was not sent until July 10, two days later. In the meantime, Senators Truman and Murray, two influential administration Democrats, having learned of the pressures being placed on Nelson, came publicly to his defense. On July 8 Senator Truman called attention to the fact that the views of his Committee were in perfect agreement with those of Nelson. He said:

For months the Committee has stressed the necessity of providing for an orderly resumption of civilian production in areas where there is no manpower shortage and with materials that are not required for war production. This has become increasingly important to businesses of small and intermediate size which are completing their war contracts and which will not be given new contracts.

It has been opposed by some selfish business groups that want to see their competitors kept idle until they finish their war contracts. It also has been opposed by the Army and Navy representatives who want to create a surplus of manpower with the hope that the consequent pressure on unemployed workers would result in some of them shifting to occupations or areas in which there is still a manpower shortage. . . .

The Committee is disturbed by the delay that has already taken place in the issuance of these orders and believes they should be issued forthwith. . . . The time for discussion is past and . . . there is no satisfactory alternative for action.

Senator Murray, Chairman of the Senate Small Business Committee, endorsed Senator Truman's statement and told reporters that "chaos in the Nation's economy would result from failure in reconverting industry to peace. . . . Mr. Nelson's is the proper program . . . the one Congress would want WPB to follow." These statements seemed to provide "official" confirmation of the charges appearing in the press that the dissenting Vice-Chairmen were defending the interests of big business. The accused Vice-Chairmen were convinced that such stories had been given to the Truman Committee and "leaked" to the press by E. A. Locke, A. Noyes, and Bruce Catton (director of WPB's Information Office), all members of Nelson's immediate staff and devoted to him. As has been suggested above, one interpretation given some currency at the time was that the charges were circulated as part of a plan to secure the Democratic Vice-Presidential nomination for Nelson on a platform of business efficiency and concern for small business. The speculation about the forthcoming Democratic Convention was lively at this time; President Roosevelt's statement announcing his willingness to run was finally made on July 11, but this had been widely anticipated earlier. The Convention itself met on July 19, and the two standard bearers were chosen on the two following days. It is interesting to note that two other persons concerned with reconversion were being frequently spoken of as possible Vice-Presidential nominees during this preconvention period, Justice Byrnes and Senator Truman. As a matter of fact, practically all the chief participants in the reconversion controversy were mentioned, publicly or privately, as Vice-Presidential possibilities. Whether or not this interpretation of Nelson's conduct had any validity, it was fairly widely believed and certainly did not lessen the anger of the Vice-Chairmen, who felt that their motives were being impugned for political reasons.

In this atmosphere of congressional support and internal dissension, and with preconvention rumors in the air, Nelson sent his long reply to Admiral Leahy on the 10th; copies were sent to Byrnes and Wilson in addition to the President. He wrote:

My position is perfectly clear. War production obviously must continue to be the first responsibility of the economy . . . and no interference with war production can be allowed to result from the lifting of WPB restrictions. . . .

If I were not certain that the designated restrictions could be lifted without interference with war production, and indeed to the benefit of the overall war economy, you can be sure that I would not have initiated the present action.

It must be recognized that the War Production Board has no moral right to retain any restrictions not essential to war production; and before I decided to lift the designated restrictions, I was advised in an opinion by John Lord O'Brian, General Counsel of the War Production Board, that I have no legal authority to continue controls over materials when they are in abundant supply.

I think it is of great importance that the Joint Chiefs of Staff clearly understand the urgent need for lifting restrictions on the economy as they cease to be essential to war production. . . .

Nelson then took up point by point the various objections raised to his proposals and attempted to refute them.

I have given careful attention to representations made both within the WPB, and by the Armed Services, the War Manpower Commission and other agencies, in opposition to the lifting of restrictions at this time. Although I have over and over again opened my mind to the objections raised, I am unable to find any real substance in them.

Leahy was also assured that if the war took a turn for the worse, or if any of the orders proved harmful to the war effort, they would be rescinded immediately.

With the WMC, the Services, the Joint Chiefs, and most WPB Vice-Chairmen on one side, and Nelson, the Truman and Murray Committees, Maverick, Keenan, Golden, and labor spokesmen on the other side, the dispute was getting out of hand. On July 10 Byrnes made the following "informal statement" to the press:

The WPB is drafting reconversion orders which carry out the policies recently announced by Chairman Nelson. If any objection to the order is raised by any government department or agency the issue involved will be submitted to Director of War Mobilization Byrnes.

Byrnes also stated that although the issuance of the orders was a matter within the WPB to be settled by WPB, "if the matter is submitted to me, I will promptly decide the issue." The minatory implications of this statement could hardly be overlooked.

By this time the orders were being discussed by WPB's Order Clearance Committee, the last step prior to their issuance. When Byrnes made his public statement, he apparently told the WPB, the Services, and WMC to settle the issue in a hurry. Under the pressure, the Services accepted the compromise previously discussed by Byrnes and Nelson on July 6. On July 11 it was agreed to stagger the orders, with the fourth order delayed until August 15.

Wilson then, on July 11, called an executive session of the War Production Board to discuss the first three orders. The agreement called for the issuance of the orders as follows:

July 15. relaxation of restrictions on the use of aluminum and magnesium—revised in order to allow the use of these metals only as a substitute for others, or for the manufacture of pots and pans.
July 22. permission to make experimental models.
July 29. permission to place unrated orders for machine tools.
August 15. spot authorization, the order allowing local WPB officials to authorize manufacture of civilian items *provided* such production would not impede the munitions program.

At the Board meeting certain technical adjustments were made to meet objections raised by General Clay. It was discovered that General Jeffe, Executive Secretary of the PEC, had made a recommendation to the Inter-Agency Committee on Draft Deferment which might cause any plant producing an experimental model to lose most of its key engineers. It was finally agreed to ask General Hershey, Director of Selective Service, how he would interpret the recommendation, and to bring the order in line with his interpretation. General Clay, speaking for the ASF, said that the Army did not approve of these three orders, but if they were to be issued, the Army had no objection to their form. The fourth order was not discussed because it was not scheduled to be issued until August 15. Wilson arranged for a verbatim report of the proceedings at this meeting, as he had for the meeting of July 4; these were the only two of the one hundred meetings of the War Production Board where the minutes of the executive secretary were supplemented by a stenographic report.

The dates on which the orders would be released were then made public, with the remark that they were being staggered in order to give the War Manpower Commission an opportunity to put its program into effect. It was stated that the above conclusions had been decided by the members of the War Production Board. Wilson made the announcement and told the press that the compromise had been agreed to by Nelson.

On July 12 the Truman Committee once again threatened to hold a public hearing unless action were forthcoming within a week. On July 13 Wilson made his first public statement on reconversion when he stated that he had favored and did favor Nelson's reconversion program, and that "whatever differences of opinion existed revolved around the 'timing' of the orders rather than their objectives to be sought." He also stressed that the Vice-Chairmen were motivated only by their concern for the successful prosecution of the war. The entire WPB staff, he stated, had endorsed as early as March 7 the policy that prewar competitive patterns were not to be considered in determining the timing, place, method, or kind of reconversion.

On this day, July 13, Wilson visited the White House. As he left, he told reporters that he had agreed to stay on at WPB "a while longer." If the President was displeased over the bickerings of the past month, he obviously did not hold Wilson at fault.

Nevertheless, the tension between the Nelson and Wilson camps within the WPB was such that a slight spark could set off an explosion. David Lawrence added powder to the situation when he suggested in his syndicated column of July 15 that the President dismiss Nelson and make Wilson chairman of the War Production Board.

Nelson returned to the WPB on July 26.

G. NELSON LOSES CONTROL

Nelson's situation within WPB was now desperate. In accounting for this fact, it is difficult, or even impossible, to disentangle with precision the effects of accidental and unforeseeable factors from the general impetus arising from underlying personality characteristics and major decisions of the past. Certainly the tempo of events, if not their eventual outcome, was affected by Nelson's illness. Nelson had been overworking for years, was tired and bothered by personal problems, and not well, when his sudden attack of pneumonia sent him to the hospital on June 23. He was strained and worn during his convalescence from July 4 to July 26, and his partial participation in official affairs during this crucial period was awkward and painful for all concerned. A man who impressed all his associates as one possessed of boundless patience, he was pushed hard by loyal and, as it happened, ambitious intimates towards action that was apparently foreign to his character. Certainly all these unpredictable factors helped create the crisis atmosphere in WPB at the end of July.

Wilson's position at this point was also not totally inherent in the basic situation. Somehow he and Nelson had maintained adequate working relationships for over a year; but the distasteful responsibilities thrust on him during the month of July and the extreme awkwardness and delicacy of his position tended to make him less willing to go along with an arrangement that was never perfect. The "big business" attack, inspired as he thought by Nelson's staff, and certainly not publicly disavowed by Nelson, was becoming unbearable; early in July he had once again made known to the President his desire to resign, but he had succumbed to the President's persuasion on July 13, and had agreed to remain. Wilson, like Nelson, had advisers who urged him to take drastic measures to remedy the situation.

Yet underlying these somewhat ephemeral difficulties were others far less soluble. There were clearly fundamental personality incompatibilities between Nelson, on the one hand, and his opponents, in and out of WPB, on the other. In spite of or regardless of Nelson's efforts, the dominating role of the Army and later of OWM in the affairs of WPB had steadily increased. Nelson lacked the President's full confidence, and the organizational relationship between Nelson and Wilson was almost certainly destined to transfer power and loyalty to the subordinate. Under these circumstances, when Nelson's immediate assistants urged a drastic reorganization of WPB at the end of July, he did not move. Actually it seems likely that he could hardly have made major changes with any hope of success. Things had gone too far. The accidental difficulties had made the situation irremediable, particularly for a person with a strong distaste for open hostility.

The fundamental dilemma that now confronted Nelson had been foreseen long before. As early as August 30, 1943, W. L. Batt had written to Nelson:

The military point of view has had a large part in determining our work and the way in which we carried it out. As we go back into peace, the Military naturally has less and less interest and influence, and the social and economic considerations have more and more—Oughtn't you—make us more conscious of these broader considerations than we needed to be as we went into the war?

WPB will have to have a new approach if it is to have the public confidence in an area which will be much more controversial than the past one has been.

R. E. Johnson wrote to Nelson on June 20, 1944:

In facing the problems associated with reconversion . . . it is inevitable that our views as to what should be done will steadily diverge more and more widely from those held by the Army and Navy. They will naturally continue to think exclusively of winning the war, while we must give ever-increasing weight to factors influencing the economy as a whole, and to attaining our prime objective of maintaining total employment at the highest possible level.

One of our obvious major problems today is to make certain that we do not continue indefinitely to be ruled by the limited point of view of the Military. To escape its limitations, it will be necessary for WPB not merely to overrule the Military when their recommendations are too narrowly conceived, but also to overcome the effect of habit-forming associations between WPB personnel and the Military over the past several years. The authoritarian point of view is now so deeply ingrained in many of our people that nothing short of a basic reorganization can be expected to correct it.

What Nelson was unwilling to undertake in the summer of 1943 or the spring of 1944, he was unwilling or unable to undertake in the summer of 1944. Despite such advice from his staff, Nelson did not even make an attempt to reorganize. His full realization of the intensity of the opposition and the extent of the cleavages apparently came late. However, as soon as he returned to active duty in WPB on July 26, he called a meeting of all the key members of WPB in an effort to iron out the differences.

He opened the meeting by asking for candid discussion, insisting that he had complete confidence in the Vice-Chairmen and that he was certain that there was no basic policy difference between himself and Wilson. It was soon apparent, however, that there was a complete rift in the organization and that he was faced with a revolt of all the Vice-Chairmen except Maverick, Keenan, and Golden—none of whom was present at the meeting.

The unsigned Locke-Noyes memorandum still rankled, and the Vice-Chairmen were deeply resentful of the charges in the press that their big business bias was responsible for their opposition to Nelson's program. Although Nelson stoutly insisted that his staff had no part in inspiring the stories, the Vice-Chairmen maintained that Locke, Noyes, Catton, Maverick, and other members of Nelson's staff, irresponsible and detached from operations, had done so. When Nelson pointed out that the big business issue was first raised by the Truman Committee, Wilson responded that Locke, who was in charge of liaison with that Committee, had misrepresented WPB activities to the Committee.

Despite the fact that the Vice-Chairmen called the issue irreconcilable, Nelson still was unwilling to recognize or at least to admit the fact. Seeking for a remedy, he suggested bringing back a former WPB official for the purpose of undertaking an administrative review of the entire situation. The Vice-Chairmen dissented, insisting that the problem was primarily one of personalities and that the only solution was to fire Locke, Noyes, and Catton—i.e., to get rid of those few staff members of the WPB who remained personally loyal to the Chairman (but who were believed responsible for what the group considered a slanderous attack). Nelson did not commit himself to this course, but he did agree to a proposal which reduced his powers still further—not to sign any letter or take any official action without clearing with the appropriate Vice-Chairman.

It thus became clear that although Nelson retained public responsibility for the WPB, he had lost its control. At this time his most obvious alternatives seem to have been (1) to do nothing; (2) to fire or otherwise discipline the dissenting Vice-Chairmen; (3) to discharge his own staff; and (4) to resign and be replaced by Wilson. He chose the first alternative.

H. PSYCHOLOGICAL WARFARE

The first three orders were issued as scheduled on July 15, 22 and 29. While these were preparatory, the fourth would actually allow civilian production, and hence it bore the brunt of military opposition. "Spot" permitted WPB field offices to authorize production of items listed on an accompanying directive, though they were not to authorize any production which would use materials or labor needed for munitions or essential civilian articles. The advocates of PR-25 contended that it was particularly suited to meet the problems of the current situation because it delegated responsibility to local officials, who were best informed on the conditions in their areas. On the other hand, the military representatives argued that these local officials could not withstand the pressures which would be brought to bear on them. For example, they feared that if town A were permitted to produce pots, then business and labor in town B would force their WPB office to permit such production also, in order to protect the local industries.

Nelson thought that his compromise with Byrnes of July 4 had settled the dispute and that PR-25 was to be issued on August 15. Patterson, Somervell, and Clay interpreted this agreement to mean that it would *not* be issued *before* August 15, and that there would be a review of the military and production situation before any action was taken. As a matter of fact, Wilson had said, when making his announcement of July 11, that the order would be reviewed "in the light of the military situation existing at that time," although the formal press release contained no such proviso. The Army representatives felt deeply that PR-25 constituted a real threat to war production, especially as it led to the wrong public attitude. They were alarmed at a reported increase in labor turnover and they feared a public let-down in the war effort. All during the war they had been attempting to bring the message home that the war could be won only with the unremitting effort of the entire civilian labor force. Now they began to intensify a psychological warfare campaign which had been started against the home front on July 2. The Pentagon officials were disturbed by the absence of the "proper sense of urgency" which they thought necessary to increase production of certain vitally needed munitions by securing needed manpower and by cutting down labor turnover. For the next several months the home front was barraged with headlines and statements by War Department officials to the effect that production lags were prolonging the war and endangering the lives of American soldiers, that war workers were deserting their jobs, and that the public was too much concerned with reconversion.

On July 2 the War Department had declared that its monthly goals of war materials deliveries were not being met, and had urged the War Production Board not to relax its production controls but to exert even more vigorous efforts to increase the manufacture of weapons. Two days later Somervell announced that war production was behind schedule because of over-optimism and lack of labor. "Until we realize the war isn't over," he said, "and stop delaying production we'll just delay victory that much longer. . . . Put off that fishing trip, it can come after the war is won." The July 5 headlines declared: "Lt. Gen. Somervell Scoffs at Current Planning in View of War Needs," and the General was quoted as telling the Indiana Chamber of Commerce: "We must remember that our sons are fighting on a twenty-four-hour shift in Normandy and that there's no double pay for overtime, and no time out for their postwar planning, either!" On July 14 Patterson reported that production was off eight per cent and offered this as proof that Nelson's program was unwise; he continued: "Published reports that current schedules for the war program will be met are untrue. . . . There is a grossly mistaken feeling abroad in the country that the war is about over. . . ."

Nelson was much disturbed by these statements, which he considered misleading, but he made no public protest, and during his absence from his office apparently awaited more favorable developments. The compromise on the reconversion orders was reached on July 11; the speculation about the Democratic Vice-Presidential nomination was settled on July 21. Then, after weeks of anxiety, on July 26 came the break-through at St. Lo; this happened to be the day that Nelson returned to work. Possibly the encouraging military news provided the spur to action. In any event, on July 31 Nelson complained to Byrnes about the Patterson and Somervell statements. Byrnes promised to hold a meeting to determine the extent to which these statements exaggerated the real situation. Apparently the meeting was held on August 2, the day on which the headlines announced "Somervell Says Production Slump May Cost Many Lives." The report of Somervell's statement continued:

> Increasingly serious lags in the production of 320 vital items of equipment and supplies threaten to deprive American armies of the wherewithal to deliver that punch which will knock Germany out of the conflict . . . Somervell asserted today. . . .
>
> Manpower has been drifting away from the essential jobs in ever-increasing numbers and each month since the beginning of 1944 has seen a more drastic drop in production schedules . . . the clamor of area commanders for enough munitions and supplies to polish off the enemy, in the face of rapid dwindling of their resources in the field, may well indicate a dreary prolongation of the struggle. . . .
>
> Lacking enough of the big shells . . . the Allies must reduce their punishing assaults by substituting smaller shells and even rifle and machine gun fire, which inevitably mean closer fighting and greater loss of American lives. . . .
>
> What we have to get is a sense of the urgency of the matter. . . . Manpower is the problem, and I'd like to point out that while there are twenty-five percent more tourists right now in Michigan than there were a year ago, if you ask some of the doughboys who are battling it out on the front lines, whether the war isn't over, he'll tell you pretty quick what they think about it and how bad the situation is for them. . . . Something is going to be done about the situation.

I. BYRNES INTERVENES

While Nelson was appealing to Byrnes to tone down what he felt to be the exaggerated War Department publicity releases, the War Department was appealing to him to "do something about the situation—to help get a sense of urgency," to paraphrase General Somervell. Although Byrnes had encouraged Nelson to proceed with his program, the arguments presented by the War Department at the August 2 meeting, apparently attended by Nelson, Wilson, and Patterson, carried greater weight with him. At the conclusion of the meeting he stated that within the next forty-eight hours he was going to broadcast to the nation in order to outline the difficulties attendant on war and essential civilian production and to outline contemplated action to remedy the situation.

Almost exactly forty-eight hours later, on August 4, Byrnes announced:

> Several days ago I was advised by the procurement agencies that a shortage was developing in the production of certain vital war materials. There is a public psychology in the country that the end of the war is near at hand. No man knows when the war will end. We must produce until the last shot is fired. People want to leave their jobs in war plants in order to get back to civilian business. If the present exodus from war plants continues, it is going to interfere seriously with the possibility of an early end of the war.

To provide adequate manpower for essential war production, Byrnes directed the formation of Area Production Urgency and Manpower Priorities Committees in all Group 3 and 4 Labor Areas (they had already been established in Group 1 and 2 Areas). These committees were to determine employment ceilings in war and non-essential industries and to establish manpower priorities for the industries in their areas. The significant point of the directive for PR-25 was the following:

> The Area Production Urgency Committees . . . are charged with the responsibility of authorizing increased civilian production.
>
> No increased civilian production will be authorized in the area without the approval of this committee. It will not authorize such production until the representative of the War Manpower Commission within the area has certified in writing to the Committee that labor is available for such production without interference with local and inter-regional labor recruiting efforts therein.

In other words, the WMC and not the WPB would have the final say locally on the resumption of civilian production. Before any PR-25 applications could be approved the local WMC representative would have to take the responsibility for certifying that there would be no interference with local and interregional labor-recruiting efforts. This was the final answer to Nelson's complaint to Byrnes of July 31.

J. NELSON AND PSYCHOLOGICAL WARFARE

Although Byrnes's directive of August 4 assuaged military fears somewhat, the Service representatives continued their attempts to create "a sense of urgency." On August 5 Under Secretary of the Navy Bard told of bottlenecks in West Coast shipyards because thousands of civilian employees "are quitting to take peacetime jobs." The *Army and Navy Register* told the lower hierarchy: "Army and Navy officials attribute unhealthy [production] lag to: (1) many Americans thinking the war is over; (2) war workers in key industries quitting to seek permanent peacetime jobs; (3) industries thinking of peacetime reconversion; and (4) strikes." The Army Hour radio broadcast of August 7 featured Generals Somervell and Echols, who told of the growing demands of the war. On August 8 the War Department "publicly revealed . . . that lag in tire programs was threatening a shortage of heavy artillery movers for the invasion forces in France and thereby endangering the prospects of early victory." On August 11 Somervell was quoted as telling officials of the War Manpower Commission that battle plans had to be changed because of shortages:

> Army field generals have offered concrete evidence that shortages in supplies of bombs, trucks and other material have interfered with battle plans, Lieut. General Brehon B. Somervell . . . revealed today.
>
> One general had to call off 100 air missions because he didn't have the right type of bombs. Another commander sent word . . . that he had to abandon 3,500 heavy trucks because he could not keep them running any longer and "they had to be replaced." . . . We have to tell the general that we couldn't furnish him the trucks he wanted because we don't have them. . . . We'll have to make up what we've lost and more to meet the overseas demands. We can't debate these things for a long time. . . .

The Army also prepared a movie short "to explain its production troubles to the public." The script included condensed versions of actual requests from combat commanders for specific amounts of equipment. The *Army and Navy Journal* accused the War Production Board of fomenting strikes because its reconversion program caused workers to believe that production delays were unimportant.

In short, the impression given by these statements was that a shortage of munitions existed because of home front failures, that home front complacency and reconversion caused the production lags, and that there was a major exodus of workers from war factories.

Nelson refrained from publicly disputing the statements, but he was convinced that Patterson and Somervell in diverse ways were misrepresenting the facts. Studies of the aircraft and shipbuilding industries did not support the contention that there was a large-scale exodus from war plants on the West Coast; they pointed to the opposite conclusion. Later on the Bureau of Labor Statistics discovered that both the "quit" and "separation" rates were lower in August and September of 1944 than in the same months of 1943.

Nelson was also convinced that his reconversion program was not the cause of public optimism. It was true that the public eye viewed the state of the war through rose-colored glasses. But Nelson pointed out that cutbacks in war production preceded talk of reconversion, and at no time had any responsible civilian official made any prediction about the end of the war or encouraged any beliefs that it was about over. Nelson had always stressed the primary importance of the munitions programs. Military leaders had been more optimistic in both their accounts of success at arms and in pronouncements about the length of the war: Admiral William F. Halsey had predicted the end of the war in 1943 and General Dwight D. Eisenhower had publicly told of his hopes of ending the European War in 1944, as did Generals Arnold and Clark. Winston Churchill had also made a similar prediction.

Nelson was equally sure that there was no production breakdown. Although production had declined twenty per cent in June from its November peak, it was mainly a decline scheduled as a result of the January and February revisions of the Army supply program. It was true that certain key items were behind schedule, but specific programs had always needed special attention. Although production was eight per cent behind schedule in June, a year earlier it had been nine per cent behind schedule. Many of the schedules were unrealistic and beyond limits of physical capability. For example, General Levin H. Campbell, Chief of Ordnance, said in a private session with one of Nelson's assistants:

> The ASF [truck] requirements had been established without reference to the amount that actually could be produced. At the time the truck program was drawn up, the Tank and Automotive Center advised ASF that no schedule could be drawn until there was definite knowledge as to when and how much labor and equipment ASF could make available. Despite this advice, the delivery schedules were hurriedly established and remain as the goals against which comparisons are now being made [in the press and otherwise]. . . . Anyone can tell a man to dig a ditch in six minutes, but that does not mean that the ditch can or will be dug in that time.

General Campbell also said that except for trucks, heavy artillery, and heavy artillery ammunition, Ordnance Department production was not behind realistic schedules on any item. The report of the discussion also reveals that not all of the generals agreed with Patterson, Somervell, and Clay. The memorandum to Nelson stated that General Campbell

> was of the opinion that those steps taken by [WPB] toward reconversion were by no means precipitous nor ill-advised. They were definitely steps in the right direction; it was recognized that only small steps could be taken during the initial period. [General Campbell] expressed admiration for the lay-low policy taken by WPB in reference to the recent military statements on increasing production. Other utterances of the same general tenor may be forthcoming. It was observed that if you give some people enough rope they will ultimately hang themselves. At that time an authoritative, well-considered statement by responsible, far-seeing officials will have an added punch.

Nelson felt strongly that in those cases where production was behind schedule it was primarily because of design changes or sharp increases in demand, and not because of home front complacency or desertion by war workers. At a later date, Nelson had this to say about the War Department's publicity campaign:

> The War Department deliberately tried to make the people believe that this condition [shortage of munitions at the front] was the result of production failures at home, but the accusation was never once made directly. The Army's technique was to go into great detail about shortages at the front . . . then, in the same breath, to draw attention to the fact that war production programs at home were behind schedule. . . . Front-line shortages in the summer of 1944 were a question of logistics, and were not due to production shortages. The Army's deliberate attempt to create a contrary impression was one of the most dangerous bits of double talk I ever heard of.[4]

Nelson was especially incensed when he received, on August 10, a letter from Edward Klauber, Acting Director of the Office of War Information asking for his co-operation in a publicity campaign to emphasize the urgency of the situation. It was proposed that beginning on August 14 the psychological campaign be intensified by sixty-second announcements on sixty-five radio shows, on all four networks, with broadcasts by top generals, admirals, and war production officials. Also there were to be radio dramatizations describing "fictional military situations where the success of our arms was perhaps jeopardized for lack of materials at issue." On the same day that Nelson received this letter, he also received a request from OWI's London office that he make a statement that could be used overseas to correct the impression that the American production effort was about to break down.

[4] Nelson, *Arsenal of Democracy*, Harcourt, Brace & Company, 1946, p. 409. By permission of the publishers.

Nelson, who had up to this time remained silent, wrote an angry letter to Klauber, stating that the program outlined by OWI "seems to me to create the impression of a war production crisis which does not exist." If it were to be put into effect Nelson threatened, "I shall be obliged to take strong measures to offset its unfortunate consequences on the public mind."

Apparently Nelson's letter postponed the effective date of this intensified campaign, and Klauber responded to Nelson stating that he was delighted "to know that you and I are in precise agreement on nearly everything that is in your letter." Furthermore Klauber wrote, "on the basic question of a production crisis I know that you will be fair enough to realize that the determination does not lie with me."

K. THE MEAD COMMITTEE INVESTIGATES

On August 16 the Mead Committee (formerly Truman Committee) held executive sessions (record made public on August 24) in which Nelson and General Clay were closely questioned on the production situation. Once again Nelson defended his reconversion program, reported that the over-all production situation was good, and criticized the War Department's publicity program by saying:

Current manpower problems consist primarily of the need to maintain or increase employment in a few specific locations and in a small number of individual plants. Each of these problems calls for a carefully aimed rifle shot if it is to be licked. These problems will not be solved by letting loose a blunderbuss against the whole manpower situation or by general edicts and broad limitations on the use of labor. Each one of these is a specific case and you solve them specifically. . . . War production does not need more than 100,000 of the 700,000 already released from the munitions industry. War plants could not employ all of them, and the millions who are still needed should be given the assurance that civilian jobs will be available when war production eases up.

Clay followed Nelson before the Committee. Clay's own press releases had been carefully worded to indicate that only certain vitally needed items were behind schedule; nevertheless, he undertook to defend the War Department's publicity policies. Clay testified that the fundamental cause of the production lags was a shortage of approximately 200,000 men (Nelson had testified that only 100,000 men were needed), and that the primary purpose of the press releases was to induce 200,000 people to enter the fields in which they were needed. Said General Clay:

The job of recruiting is not our job, but the job of facilitating and helping to create the sense of urgency for the production of munitions of war is decidedly our job, and I feel if I failed to make every effort that I think will help that, I have certainly been neglectful. My judgment may be poor and the actions I take may not help to that end, but they are all directed to the end of getting munitions that I feel are vitally needed. . . .

The War Department is certainly not opposed to reconversion. Neither is reconversion primarily or basically our responsibility, and we appreciate that. We are vitally concerned with war production and with a failure to meet war schedules. We insist and urge in every way that we can that the responsible authorities meet our war schedules before doing anything that might interfere with war schedules, and that is the extent of our objection, if it could be called an objection to reconversion.

When confronted with headlines such as: "War Production Not Keeping Pace with Our Fighting Men," "Too Many People on the Home Front have Concluded War is Over, Is Charge Made by Top Place Army, Navy, and Civilian Officers," and "Production Lags Alarm War Leaders," Clay answered, "I can't answer for the headlines." The headline "American Production Fails to Keep Pace with Our Fighting Men" was, said Clay, "a plea to the American people to support war production, rather than a blast at the American people."

At the conclusion of its investigation the Committee released the following statement: "The picture presented at the closed session was not the one that had been given to the public."

L. PR-25 IS ISSUED

The day before PR-25 was to be issued the Requirements Committee met to determine the allocation of materials for spot production. To authorize production under PR-25 without making materials available would have rendered the practical effect of the order nugatory. There was no objection to providing a substantial reserve of aluminum, which was in plentiful supply. A small amount of copper was also authorized without discussion, but steel—the backbone of production—caused a real dispute.

The Program Bureau, which was the Program Vice-Chairman's staff, recommended that no steel be allotted unless substantial reductions in demand occurred due to military cutbacks or more was produced than had been estimated by the Steel Division. Representatives of the Office of Civilian Requirements, the Smaller War Plants Corporation, and of the two WPB labor offices dissented from this recommendation. OCR and SWPC, especially the latter, took exception to the Steel Division's estimate for the next quarter, and tried to prove that more steel would be available than had been allotted.

If PR-25 had to be issued, the Navy did not object to providing a steel reserve. Admiral Williams said, "I feel if the order comes through, some arrangement should be made to accomplish it," but the representatives of the Army Air Corps and the Army Service Forces felt otherwise. When Colonel Denton, the ASF representative, was asked for his opinion, he replied, "Well, Mr. Chairman, there is not much question about my vote," and the meeting burst into laughter.

S. W. Anderson, who had held the reconstituted office of Program Vice-Chairman since the end of May, and in whom the power of decision resided, refused to allocate the steel reserve after stating that Nelson had told him that it was not necessary at the time. Anderson made it clear that in the event more steel was available than had been estimated, he would make a supplementary allocation for PR-25 production.

The next day, August 15, Priorities Regulation 25 was issued.

M. EXEUNT NELSON AND WILSON

The reconversion fracas coincided with the opening of the 1944 election campaign. The Republicans pointed to this episode as proof of the charge that the Roosevelt Administration was composed of querulous old men who constantly squabbled and wrangled in public.

The President had been away from Washington during most of the controversy, but he was aware of it. As early as January 1944 he had learned of the Armed Services' confidence in Wilson and lack of confidence in Nelson. Byrnes and Patterson were increasingly dissatisfied with Nelson, and the President was disturbed by the continuance of dissension in the WPB. By the summer of 1944, however, Nelson had become the public champion of reconversion and was generally thought of as the defender of small business and labor. He had many ardent supporters including the President's running mate, Senator Truman. In the light of the reconversion controversy, if he were dismissed the President would undoubtedly be accused of backing the military and siding with "big business" in their opposition to reconversion.

A way out of the dilemma was suggested when Generalissimo Chiang Kai-shek requested, on July 13, that the President send a personal representative to China who would be qualified to speak for Roosevelt on both political and military matters. Some time between July 21 and July 26 the President proposed to the Generalissimo that General Patrick Hurley and Donald Nelson be appointed his personal representatives to the Chinese government. Since Chiang had requested a single emissary and since the primary purpose of Chiang's request was to settle matters of military command in China, it is difficult to avoid the conclusion that the primary purpose of the President's suggestion that Nelson be sent along with Hurley was to get him out of Washington. This would make it easier for the President to persuade Wilson, who had again made known his desire to resign, to stay on in the WPB. It will be recalled that Wilson's meeting with the President, at which he again agreed to stay on "a while longer," came on July 13, the date of the cable from China.

On the positive side, Nelson had already undertaken missions to help Canada, England, and Russia with their production problems, and these missions had been fruitful and productive of good will.

Apparently Chiang approved the suggestion to send Nelson and Hurley prior to August 8, for on that date Hopkins cleared the proposal with General Marshall and Acting Secretary of State Stettinius. Hopkins was anxious to get the matter settled as quickly as possible for he feared that a blowup between Nelson and Wilson, which might come at any time, would be extremely harmful to the war effort. Immediately after clearing the matter with Marshall and Stettinius he wired the President, who was then in the Aleutians, that it was his understanding that the President desired that Wilson "be offered Nelson's job with WPB" and that unless he heard from the President to the contrary, he would go ahead on that basis.

It is not clear whether the President and Hopkins planned to secure Nelson's resignation and make Wilson Chairman of the WPB or whether they intended to make Wilson merely Acting Chairman during Nelson's absence. Nor is it clear whether at this stage of the negotiations the President planned to have Nelson resume his duties as WPB Chairman after his China mission. But the weight of the evidence does point to the conclusion that Wilson was to be made Acting Chairman first, and, at an appropriate time, Chairman.

At any rate, the next day, August 9, Byrnes and Hopkins told Nelson of the President's proposal to send him to China. It seems clear that Nelson was merely told that he would be gone for a few weeks and that during his absence Wilson would be Acting Chairman. Nelson responded favorably to the suggestion. He was glad to get the opportunity for a vacation from his Washington troubles. The failure to advise Nelson of any permanent change in his assignment is not, of course, necessarily inconsistent with the conclusion suggested above.

The President returned to Washington on August 17, and on August 18 he formally appointed Nelson his personal representative to Chiang. Nelson saw the President on August 19, and at this meeting Nelson approved the suggestion that Wilson be made Acting Chairman during his absence. Apparently Nelson came away with the impression that he would be gone about five weeks.

Just when Wilson was informed of these plans is not known; conceivably the President had given some indication of his proposed course of action on July 13; somewhat later Byrnes apparently told Wilson that he would be made Chairman of the War Production Board after Nelson was safely in China. Wilson wanted to leave government service, but with Nelson away it appeared that he could "do a job," and he was more favorably disposed to remain until the defeat of Germany. Wilson saw the President on August 19, and again the President persuaded him not to resign, although precisely what the President told him is not known.

That evening the President announced that Mr. Donald Nelson, Chairman of the WPB, would be in China for several months on a confidential Presidential mission and that during his absence Mr. Charles E. Wilson would be Acting Chairman. It had not been the President's intention to announce the trip at this time, but James Y. Newton, a reporter on the Washington *Star*, published a story about the plan in his newspaper. The White House was greatly exercised by this premature announcement, but the President's hand was forced.

The announcement precipitated a wave of speculation. Up and down the long corridors of the Social Security Building, in which the WPB was located, men stopped to talk and speculate. Members of the Wilson camp appeared elated, as did those in the Services and the WMC, who apparently felt that the announcement meant the eclipse of Nelson. This seemed to be the consensus throughout Washington. Senator Ferguson, Republican member of the Mead Committee, told reporters, "I can't imagine why Nelson is going to China just now when so many important decisions remain to be made at home." Senator Wherry, Republican, announced: "The reconversion program may be stymied in his absence." The Washington *Star* featured, on August 20, a cartoon in which Vice-President

Wallace, just back from the Far East himself, was sitting idly whittling on the cornfield fence and saying to Nelson, "I see that you're going to China. What are you thinking of doing when you get back?"

Nelson, however, insisted that he wanted to go to China, that he had confidence in Wilson, that his mission was not connected with the difficulties over reconversion, and that he would return. The newspapers nevertheless reported that he was disturbed when he read the President's announcement that he would be absent for several months. Though he publicly continued to disclaim any such fears, members of his personal staff were not so sanguine. Bruce Catton, one of those loyal to Nelson, later reported that on Sunday afternoon, August 20, Sterling Green of the Associated Press called one of Nelson's WPB intimates and asked, "[Does] this trip to China actually mean that Nelson [is] being eased out of WPB and that his reconversion program [is] hereby being scuttled?" Catton writes, "The Nelson man at the other end of the wire was bitter, explicit, and slightly vulgar. 'It certainly does,' he said with feeling. 'Nelson is being kicked right square in the groin.'"[5] This is a petty incident, but it illuminates the intense personal animus that had been aroused, and the rather uninhibited relations between Nelson's staff and the press. It also helped to confirm the reporters in their guesses about the reason for Nelson's trip.

That same Sunday evening somebody put on a telephone campaign. Late that night and the next morning telegrams of protest poured into the White House. On the morning of August 21 the AP story broke that "Nelson was being kicked in the teeth." The campaign was vigorously pressed. Senators Truman and Murray sent protests to the White House, so did the Presidents of the American Federation of Labor and the Congress of Industrial Organizations. Senator Mead stated that his Committee was seriously thinking of holding hearings to determine why Nelson had been chosen for the China mission.

[5] Catton, *The War Lords of Washington*, Harcourt, Brace & Company, 1948, pp. 275-6. By permission of the publishers.

Although Nelson publicly continued to disassociate himself from these protests, the newspapers reported the rumor that he had gone to see the President and threatened to resign if not assured of continued support. Perhaps this accounts for the almost unprecedented statement by the President on August 21:

Any impression that Mr. Nelson's temporary mission to China indicates a change in the policy of the War Production Board is entirely unfounded. . . . When it is possible to tell the whole story those who charge that he is being "kicked in the teeth" will realize how wrong and unjust they have been—what a disservice they have rendered their country and Mr. Nelson personally.

But this did not stop the rumors. As the New York *Times* pointed out, observers searched the President's words to see what they did not say as well as what they did say. Why was the President "stirred to such unusual action by speculations over WPB policies and Mr. Nelson's status, since he has seldom taken similar moves to spike speculation of other officials?"

On August 23, five days after the first announcement of his trip to China, Nelson had a sixty-minute off-the-record talk with members of the Mead Committee. At the conclusion of the conference several Senators who had expressed opposition to the China trip announced that they had been reassured by Nelson. These Senators asked that their names not be used, but they told the newsmen that they got the "impression" from Nelson that he had not opposed the President's decision to send him to China. Senator Ferguson, who was not reluctant to be quoted directly, said, "I feel better about it than I did Sunday."

The Senators were scheduled to have a similar session with Wilson on the next day. But things were beginning to happen. On the same day that Nelson was reassuring the Senators, Wilson was writing to the President. He had smarted under the accusations that he had blocked reconversion in the interest of big business, and he had consented to stay on in the WPB only when convinced by the

President and Byrnes that the way was being cleared for him to run the organization. Since July 26 he had been waiting for Nelson to exonerate him and the Vice-Chairmen publicly from the accusation of big business bias. Not only had this not been done, but the charges were being renewed—renewed, Wilson was convinced, by members of Nelson's personal staff. At this point, Byrnes seems to have told Wilson that whatever plans had been made or intimations given for Wilson's formal assumption of the position of Chairman would have to be put aside or postponed: the opposition was too great. This was too much. Wilson felt that he had been betrayed. Three times he had tried to resign, and three times he had been persuaded to stay on. But this time he meant it, and on August 23 he wrote two letters of resignation to the President, one personal, the other for publication. In the published letter he pointed out that the attacks inspired by members of Nelson's staff had impaired his usefulness to the war production program. He continued:

> I need not tell you that I favor reconversion and have approved and set in operation many steps which have already affected reconversion to a large degree. I have done this without publicity because I believe publicity might interfere with war production. I have again and again expressed the view that I am opposed to any interference with war production as its necessities are presented to me by the Commander-in-Chief and by the Joint Chiefs of Staff.
>
> It is apparent to me that instead of being discontinued these attacks upon me and upon members of my staff will be increased. I cannot answer them unless I employ publicity experts. I am unwilling to do that.

Wilson's letters of resignation were received by the President on the morning of the 24th. This time it appears that the President did not talk with Wilson himself, but had Byrnes do so, apparently in a final effort to persuade Wilson to stay. The effort was unsuccessful, however, and Nelson was informed by the President of Wilson's resignation.

Wilson's conference with Byrnes and Nelson's with the President delayed a meeting of one hundred and fifty Board employees that was scheduled for that morning (August 24). The meeting finally convened around noon, when both Wilson and Nelson returned. At this point, apparently, Nelson and the President realized that Wilson would not withdraw his resignation, but they still hoped that an open break could be avoided.

Nelson spoke first. He praised Wilson's efforts and his abilities. He stated that no differences existed between Wilson and himself and that the difficulties which delayed the implementation of his reconversion orders were in no way connected with a desire to protect big business. He told of his coming trip to China, and, giving no hint of Wilson's resignation, announced that during his absence Wilson, in whom he had unqualified confidence, would run the WPB. Then, after further eulogizing Wilson, Nelson asked him to say a few words.

Wilson, convinced that Nelson had been at least indirectly responsible for the charges appearing in the press, was only further angered by Nelson's disclaimers of responsibilty and by what he considered double-talk. His "few words" turned out to be a biting speech in which he made it clear that he was convinced that the criticism against him had been inspired by persons present. A situation had been created, said Wilson, that made it impossible for him to continue within the WPB. Everything he did or said would be criticized as a knifing in the back of his absent chief. Under the circumstances he had insisted that the President accept his resignation and he was leaving the WPB pronto.

Nelson closed the meeting by again praising Wilson's contribution to the war effort.

Wilson then held a press conference at which he lashed out at Nelson, accusing him of delaying reconversion for twenty weeks during the spring, of permitting his own staff to inspire stories against the Vice-Chairmen, and of postponing the statement exonerating them from the big business charges—"always mañana—he'd do it tomorrow."

That afternoon the President released Wilson's letter of resignation and his own reply reluctantly accepting it. The President wrote: "Of course, I have been aware of some dissension within the War Production Board. I had hoped it would disappear."

On the same day, J. A. Krug, who had been in Washington for a week awaiting reassignment in the Navy, was surprised by a telephone call from the President asking him to become Acting Chairman of the WPB. Krug accepted, and the announcement was made that evening.

The next morning, August 25, the President summoned Nelson to the White House. He had before him an aide-memoire which Hopkins had prepared after learning of Wilson's resignation but before the public blow-up he had feared for so long; in it he advised the President to persuade Nelson to resign with Wilson in an atmosphere of "friendly disagreement," and thus give the President a chance to appoint a new chairman immediately. Hopkins further advised the President to tell Nelson that the WPB situation might damage his usefulness to the China mission, a mission of vital importance that would take four to six months.

Hopkins' advice came too late; there was no longer an atmosphere of friendly disagreement in which Nelson could resign. Nelson later reported that the President asked if he thought that Wilson could be persuaded to change his mind. Nelson answered that he thought not and that Krug would make an excellent replacement. The President by this time was apparently annoyed with both Wilson and Nelson and may well have been glad of the opportunity to start "fresh" with Krug. It is not known if he told Nelson at this meeting that his absence from the WPB was not merely temporary. The matter was quickly resolved, however. Nelson left immediately for China and the President held a press conference. When asked whether Nelson would return to the WPB, he replied that he was not sure, it was an "iffy" question. If there was still any doubt after this, that Nelson as well as Wilson was leaving WPB permanently, all doubt was resolved at the President's press conference of August 29. At this conference the President denied that there was any truth in a statement by Senator Ferguson that he was "reliably informed" that Nelson was slated for Byrnes's job. When the President was asked about Krug's status, he replied that Krug was head of the WPB. Although the bottom of Krug's pay check stub may say something about "Acting," stated the President, Krug runs the agency. Nelson formally resigned on September 30, 1944, after he returned from China, and Krug then was named Chairman of the War Production Board.

VI. The Decline of Reconversion

A. KRUG

Krug's appointment was hailed by the press as a victory for Nelson and a defeat for the Services. When Program Vice-Chairman, Krug had attempted to schedule increased civilian production, not in itself a reconversion move, but one equally opposed by the Services. Although only thirty-six, he had had long experience in government service in the TVA and elsewhere and was generally considered to be an able administrator.

With the appointment of Krug and the departure of Nelson and Wilson, some surcease from public bickering and internal dissension was anticipated. Krug seemed to be in a favorable position: with no great new programs anticipated for the immediate future, efficiency and harmony would suffice. But the very anticipations that greeted Krug's accession circumscribed his action. The one thing he was not supposed to do was to get into a public fight with the Army or with OWM. Yet he knew that he could not easily prevent the Army from making public any dispute that might arise. After all, it was not Byrnes or Somervell who was sent to China, but Nelson. Krug—experienced, conscientious, and orderly—showed by all his subsequent actions that he well understood the restrictions under which he must labor if he were to serve the President as the President would be served. The

1944 elections were not far away. Krug did have his disputes with the Army and his difficulties with Byrnes; but while he kept up his end, he kept his troubles from the press, and his ability to maintain his ground was limited by this circumstance.

Krug promptly undertook the reorganization of WPB. His first step was to abolish the office of Executive Vice-Chairman and to assume many of these operating responsibilities, among them the Chairmanship of the Production Executive Committee. By this means he planned to avoid the situation of divided responsibility which had existed between Nelson and Wilson.

Paris was liberated on August 26, 1944, the day after Krug's appointment was announced. Six days later Patterson returned from a tour of the battle fronts and in an unprecedented burst of optimism said that he was confident that "victory over the Germans will be won within the next four months." This was particularly striking because Patterson had been one of the severest critics of optimistic forecasts concerning the end of the war. On the same day, Secretary of the Navy Forrestal quoted General Eisenhower as saying that "if one could judge the Germans by 'normal standards,' their armies should be ready to 'roll over' now." On September 3 American troops entered Germany near Aachen. A few days later Roosevelt and Churchill met at Quebec to discuss plans for the Pacific War, and the lights went on in London.

Krug appeared before the Mead Committee on August 28. He expressed his general support of Nelson's program, including the spot authorization order, but avoided any commitment on the extent to which it might be employed. He also promised the Committee that a post-VE Day program, based on a broad relaxation of controls, would be made available to the Committee in about ten days. (This was done.) The generally optimistic climate strengthened the belief that Krug would be in a position to relax the war controls and to carry through the program of gradual reconversion, while maintaining necessary production for war, even before VE Day. During the first weeks of his chairmanship Krug pushed three programs related to reconversion: development of a post-victory-in-Europe reconversion program; plans to provide needed civilian items; and the streamlining of PR-25.

B. ATTEMPTS TO MAKE THE SPOT AUTHORIZATION EFFECTIVE

By the early weeks of September there were numerous complaints that PR-25 was not accomplishing the ends for which it had been established. For example, Keenan, Vice-Chairman for Manpower Requirements, claimed that it should signal the change in policy from "you can't do it unless it helps the war" to "you should do it unless it interferes with the war," but its procedures were too cumbersome to permit this change. On September 1 Krug appointed a task group to study PR-25 and to make recommendations for its improvement, but by November 1, when the group made its report, the situation had changed.

The attempt to secure steel for spot production was, however, successful. Maverick had continued to protest the August 14 decision which denied steel for PR-25 production and to insist that the Steel Division estimates for fourth-quarter production were too low. He pointed out that small plants were worse off than they had been before; prior to the existence of PR-25 there had been an appeals procedure for plants in distress under which small amounts of steel were allocated; this appeals procedure had been abolished when PR-25 was issued, and the distressed plants now had no recourse. Carroll Burton, second in command of the Office of Civilian Requirements, argued that because of the progress of the European war, fabricators would tend to order less steel for military purposes and thereby increase the amount available for nonmilitary purposes.

When the services turned back more than 300,000 tons of their fourth-quarter steel allotment on September 13, Anderson allotted 200,000 tons of carbon steel and 25,000 tons of alloy steel for PR-25 production. WPB regional offices were permitted to make allotments of 100 tons or less; larger allotments were to be made from Washington. Preference was first to be given to smaller war plants, then to those who were producing items on the OCR's list of preferred products, and finally to those who needed only small quantities of new materials to use large quantities of surplus materials or to provide employment for a large number of workers. This cured the steel difficulty.

The other obstacles to successful operation of PR-25 were not so easy to handle.

C. THE CHANGING WAR SITUATION

The flood tide of optimism which had been generated by the successful turn of the war began to ebb by the middle of September. The Allied Armies were driven back from their beachheads across the Rhine. Churchill, who had predicted victory by fall, announced that the European war might drag into 1945. Aachen, approached on September 3, was not captured until October 20. The month that followed showed small and bloody progress. The more urgent military programs remained behind schedule and many were revised upward once again. Krug admonished the public on September 22 to "stop thinking about next year's car," and a week later Byrnes reminded the public that the roads to Berlin and Tokyo remained "long, hard and bloody."

These pronouncements, however, followed on the heels of governmental actions on another home front sector that the public was bound to interpret as having an opposite tendency. For some months the War Food Administration and the OPA rationing chiefs, alarmed by the prospects of food surpluses and consequent losses on inventory stocks if Army purchases were suddenly cut back sharply, had been pushing a so-called "bare-shelf" policy. This meant relaxing food ration restrictions so as to move out to consumers the trade inventories of canned goods and meats before the new season's canning packs and animal slaughter replenished the food supplies again. And while Army cutbacks of munitions contracts were not generally advertised, and during 1944 had only local impacts on workers and their families, relaxations of food rationing were front-page news and immediately known to every housewife in all urban communities. The WFA policy was climaxed on September 3 when all meats except choice cuts of beef were put on the point-free list, and again on September 17 when nearly all canned goods were removed from rationing. Announcement of the latter step was made directly from Byrnes's office. In newspaper comments these moves were widely connected with the approaching Presidential and Congressional elections. Inevitably, in the eyes of the public, they belied the "sense of urgency" that Somervell and Patterson had talked about.

Nevertheless, in October munitions schedules were revised still further upward, and yet another ten per cent rise followed in November. Small arms schedules were doubled; tires and munitions schedules were greatly increased. Contrary to what might have been expected, the slow progress of the war increased interest in PR-25. Many manufacturers had hesitated to take the trouble of securing approval for spot production because they thought that the end of the war was imminent and that all WPB restrictions would be lifted. But when it began to look as if the war would be prolonged, they decided to file under PR-25.

The reconversion picture was extraordinarily confused from the middle of September to the middle of November. The effect of the uncertainties and difficulties on the European front was apparent. At the same time that the task committee and others interested in PR-25 were attempting to improve its operation, the attack on reconversion was renewed, and Patterson was working to secure suspension of the spot order. Krug's role was difficult. The war and production situation did not encourage or justify any major reconversion move. Krug continued to encourage recommendations for implementing PR-25, but he hesitated to accept them or take positive action. He was acutely aware of the skepticism with which Patterson, Somervell, and Clay had viewed Nelson, and was anxious—indeed committed—to mend relations between the War Department and the WPB. He also knew that Byrnes was generally inclined to support Patterson, and that the President was determined to avoid a repetition of the fights of the early summer. As it happened, Krug had serious disputes with the Army on other matters throughout this period; he managed to keep the arguments out of the papers; but it would have been difficult to conceal any major disagreement over reconversion, even if he had felt the time propitious for energetic action.

On September 30 Krug refused to approve a proposal by the Office of Civilian Requirements permitting manufacturers to produce parts under PR-25. On the other hand, against the opposition of the Services who insisted that the Byrnes directive of August 4 gave the authority to approve PR-25 applications to the entire Area Production Urgency Committees, a WPB field directive was issued on October 6 that made it clear that the WPB chairman of the committee had the authority to make spot authorization decisions (except as to sufficiency of manpower, which was the duty of WMC) and that the committee was merely advisory.

On October 20 Krug publicly stated that although the production program was being achieved in great part, it was lagging in a vitally important ten per cent which could delay victory in Europe for months. Four days later Elliott, Vice-Chairman for Civilian Requirements, wrote to Krug that several of the Vice-Chairmen were of the opinion that "the slower rate of military progress in Europe plus the continued failure to meet some of the more urgent production programs . . . make it unwise and even dangerous to proceed with any civilian reconversion now." It may be noted that Elliott still was seeking increased programmed essential civilian production and was inclined to believe that the dispute over PR-25 interfered with this important objective. Elliott's opposition to the reconversion activities was a further factor inducing Krug to move with extreme caution.

D. TOWARD SUSPENSION OF PR-25

The next day Patterson publicly denounced "the implication that springs so readily from necessary postwar planning that an end of the war is in sight." Patterson had been receiving reports from procurement districts that gave him the impression that strong local pressures, via Chambers of Commerce, etc., were being exerted on local production officials to permit civilian production. He also felt that there was a declining interest in the problem of securing manpower for war plants. Accordingly, he wrote to Krug suggesting that a moratorium be placed on all reconversion activities. Krug refused, but he instructed local officials to be a little more strict, and he told reporters that continued lagging programs would mean fewer spot authorizations. Byrnes, probably at Patterson's suggestion, then requested Krug to investigate these lagging programs, especially the ones caused by labor shortages, and Hiland G. Batcheller, Chief of Operations, was commissioned to make the study. At a PEC meeting on October 30, Patterson again urged suspension of PR-25.

The next day, on October 31, the various war agency heads assembled in Byrnes's office to discuss the manpower situation, especially in the foundries, in the heavy ammunition plants, and in the heavy-truck factories. Again the Service representatives asked for the suspension of PR-25. Krug opposed suspension and the issue remained undecided.

Meanwhile the task group attempting to streamline the spot order was finishing its investigation, and other interested parties were making suggestions for improvement. On November 2, twenty-three more items had been added to the list of things that could be produced under PR-25. Finally, on November 6, all interested parties met to consider the recommendations of the task group. At this meeting the WMC was asked further to decentralize authority for approval of PR-25 applications, but refused, claiming that this was a matter of internal organization and that no change could be made.

One of the major difficulties in the operation of PR-25 was the inflexible attitude of many of the military members of the Area Production Urgency Committees and their insistence on inquiring into the manpower features of applications despite WMC clearance. Both the ASF and the Navy had issued detailed and restrictive instructions to their representatives on these Committees. The military agreed to modify their instructions; but before they could do so the reaction against relaxation of PR-25 began to gain momentum. For on the same day that this task group met,

Krug (despite Maverick's most persuasive efforts and the reluctant approval of the military) refused to take action on the Smaller War Plants Corporation proposal that plants on the West Coast hiring fifty or less or those in other parts of the country hiring one hundred or less be exempt from PR-25 labor requirements.

On November 8 the movement towards streamlining PR-25 was definitely reversed when Krug decided that applications under it were to be more stringently processed. To this end he suggested that a joint statement be issued by the WPB, War and Navy Departments, and the WMC to their field representatives on the Area Production Urgency Committees. J. D. Small, Executive Officer of the WPB, drafted the statement; his version said that "for the most part" war production schedules were being met, but it outlined the nature of the manpower problem and called for increased efforts to secure the needed workers.

Patterson still insisted that PR-25 should be suspended and he refused to sign the joint statement: first, because he was holding out for suspension, and second, because he believed that it gave the wrong psychological impression. He said: "This is not the time for a statement that in effect says 'on the one hand we want war production, but on the other we want unessential production also.'" He argued that the urgency of the situation could be driven home only by a ninety-day moratorium on PR-25. Although Krug still refused to approve such a suspension, he agreed to let Somervell redraft the statement in an effort to secure Patterson's approval. Before Somervell could prepare his draft, the War Production Board met to discuss Batcheller's report and to hear Army proposals for meeting the situation.

E. BATCHELLER'S REPORT

At the Board meeting of November 14, Hiland B. Batcheller reported that although many programs were up to schedule and some even being cut back, forty per cent of war production was behind schedule. Of that forty per cent behind schedule, twenty-eight per cent was in critical programs "where schedules rise so rapidly that no amount of production for the time being would be enough." He pointed out that the munitions program had been accompanied from its inception by a series of crises in individual programs. "Today's shortages, however, are the result of actual combat operations; critical production, therefore, is not going into pipeline or strategic reserves. It is going directly into battle." His evaluation of the factors causing programs to be classified as critical was as follows:

(1) Sharp increases in demand or in requirements	40%
(2) New models or design changes	26%
(3) Labor shortages	22%
(4) Facilities shortages	12%

This, it will be noted, gave ammunition to both sides of the argument. On the one hand, sixty-six per cent of the difficulties were directly attributable to Army-ordered changes; but on the other hand, the twenty-two per cent attributable to labor shortages was too large a figure for complacency. Batcheller then discussed each program in detail, pointing out that the pressure to increase deliveries of one item interfered with the flow of supplies and components to other programs, thereby causing them to become critical. He also indicated very diplomatically that some of the difficulty arose from the failure of the military to notify WPB of coming needs in sufficient time to allow the Board to make the necessary preparations: "All too often munitions plans have been kept secret so long that critical production troubles were inevitable when requirements were made known." He concluded:

> . . . each of the critical programs should be tackled immediately on an individual basis, using practical production specialists. . . .
>
> . . . production problems in these relatively few programs are neither unusual nor new; they do not constitute a war production crisis, and they can be solved. As long as the war lasts and new tactics and products are developed, critical requirements will be inevitable.

The Army insisted that Batcheller's proposals for dealing with the critical programs were not sufficient. Howard Bruce, Director of Materiel, ASF, said:

Some action is needed to give the country a clearer understanding of the critical situation caused by the lag in military programs. To accelerate production in critical programs and to eliminate "leakage" from war production . . . some over-all slow-down of civilian production is required, in addition to the program-by-program attack on specific production difficulties. If necessary, exceptions could then be made from such a blanket retardation of civilian production.

This view was enthusiastically endorsed by Patterson, who said that although he recognized that specific production problems had to be studied and solved, he believed that more over-all pressure was also necessary. He particularly deplored what he considered the untimeliness of the trend toward resumption of civilian production under the spot authorization plan. He said:

The original theory behind the "spot" authorization plan was that war production would decline. Instead, requirements and schedules have risen to new peaks, and the continuation of "spot" authorizations is bound to detract from war production. . . . Furthermore . . . communities have not been energetic in staffing war industries until effective restrictions were placed on other industries in the same area. Accordingly . . . the "spot" authorization procedure [should] be suspended for at least 90 days in Group I and Group II labor areas.

He also stated that civilian programs proposed for 1945 were "unduly enlarged and even extravagant."

No direct answer was given to Patterson's conclusions about the inappropriateness of the spot order in a period of rising war production; one indirect answer that flourished in the rumor-ridden atmosphere of WPB was the claim by some that part of the increased military production was ordered for psychological rather than strategic purposes. But no such assertion was made at the meeting.

Isador Lubin, Economic Advisor to the President, Elliott, and Krug immediately gave Bruce and Patterson a general answer. Krug said:

. . . there has been complete agreement with the basic policy of the "spot" authorization plan; that no application will be approved if it will result in interference with war production. Since the issuance of Priorities Regulation 25 . . . not a single case has been cited where an approved application has resulted in interference with military production. . . . Indiscriminate blanket restrictions on civilian production should not be imposed; . . . Dallas, for example, should not be held back because of a special situation in Akron.

When Patterson expressed concern over the "alarming exodus of workers from the West Coast," Krug reminded him that the situation had improved and that there was no evidence to indicate that PR-25 had had any detrimental psychological effect. He further pointed out that only twenty-two per cent of the critical programs were caused by labor shortages, and that these shortages had specific rather than psychological causes, such as low wages, poor transportation, or inadequate housing.

While maintaining the position that detailed work on each critical program would provide the solution, Krug endorsed the suggestion that it would be helpful to have the President give a talk concerning the urgency of the critical programs. This speech was to be part of an organized group of talks on the seriousness of the war situation in which Krug, along with various military leaders, was also to participate. Krug was willing to co-operate in this fashion, but he refused to accept the need for suspension of PR-25.

F. PSYCHOLOGICAL WARFARE AGAIN

When it appeared that Krug was not going to follow their recommendation for suspension of PR-25, the military appealed to Byrnes for a suspension of spot authorizations in Group I and II labor areas and for a limit on the level of civilian production. Byrnes deferred action for a time in the hope that less drastic steps would suffice. He warned the public on November 16, however, that he would stop all reconversion activities unless the manpower shortages were remedied within a reasonably short time. He said:

It has been suggested that we should completely suspend the operation of the spot authorization procedure in group 1 and group 2 labor market areas and should also completely suspend resumption of the production of civilian supplies. After careful consideration I have determined to defer such drastic action for a reasonable time. If the steps herein directed do not speedily produce the necessary results, I shall not hesitate to take more drastic action.

The decision as to the issuance of spot orders will be made at the local level, but the War Production Board will issue directions to regional officials that in any locality where war production is lagging behind schedule because of lack of labor or where there is available skilled labor needed and transferable into regional recruitment, any reconversion requiring labor needed by war plants cannot be authorized. . . .

Byrnes concluded, "There is a mistaken belief on the part of some people that the war is about over."

Patterson, disturbed by Byrnes's announcement, wrote to him that it was "a disappointment." He pointed out that there was nothing new in it. Regional officials had never been permitted to authorize any reconversion requiring labor needed by the war plants.

Thus it appeared, despite Byrnes's warning, that PR-25 would not be suspended and that the WPB would be able to attack the critical programs on a program-by-program basis. But the War Department chiefs continued to work for termination of all reconversion efforts, intensifying their campaign to bring home to the public the overriding necessity of concentrating exclusively on war production.

They received support in this campaign when Henry J. Kaiser, one of the chief shipbuilders, announced that the war effort was being imperiled by workers quitting vital jobs. He said: "Workers are leaving essential war jobs in such great numbers that production of vital items for the fighting forces is being handicapped." His own West Coast shipyards, he said, were "losing men so fast that it is becoming very critical; in the Richmond yard alone, we lost about 26,000 workers as the complement dropped from 93,000 to 67,000." This report was widely circulated by the Army and the WMC, who cited it as proof of their contention that the home front was unaware of the seriousness of the situation.

On November 19 General Eisenhower stated on the Army Hour radio program that the capture of Aachen had been delayed by a shortage of ammunition, and he appealed to workers to redouble their efforts: "Expenditure of ammunition has reached ahead of our receipts from home, but I know that you do not want us to give the enemy one second's rest." Somervell then announced that the need for shells was so great that some were being flown to the front. Admiral King reported that unless some production deficiencies were remedied the tempo of Pacific operations would be slowed down. Stimson, Marshall, and Knudsen made similar statements to the press. These statements were part of the planned publicity campaign referred to above.

At the request of the war agencies, President Roosevelt said at his press conference that workers who quit critical war jobs were costing American lives on the battlefront. He urged defense plant employees not to worry about their future, asserting that he believed that the transition to peacetime production would be shorter and smoother than had been predicted.

The War Department returned twenty-seven enlisted veterans from the battlefronts "to inform workers in war plants . . . how urgently more ammunition was needed."

On the advice of the PEC Maverick agreed to discourage further plans for a discussion of smaller war plant reconversion problems. Bruce had said that it would be a bad time for announcing such a meeting, but Krug pointed out that the National Association of Manufacturers was sponsoring an American Congress of Reconversion which the Army did permit, and used as a sounding board for production pleas.

G. RESISTANCE WITHIN THE WAR PRODUCTION BOARD

Nelson's remaining supporters fought hard for his program; but in his absence it was a losing battle, as it might well have been in his presence in view of the greatly increased military production schedules and the stiffened enemy resistance. The remaining defenders of PR-25 disputed the Army's factual assertions and interpretations on every point. Clinton

Golden, Vice-Chairman for Labor Production, argued that

. . . instead of attempting to create a nation-wide fear of a war production crisis, we should endeavor to develop a popular understanding that both war production and preparation for reconversion are urgent national problems which can and must be carried forward together.

In answer to the Army's contention that suspension of PR-25 and curtailment of reconversion activities would rectify the over-optimistic attitudes which Nelson's program had created, he cited Hanson Baldwin's statements:

The causes of this over-optimism are many. Newspapers are partly to blame. . . . But fundamentally the papers and the people have taken their cues from their leaders and especially from their military leaders. . . . Admiral William F. Halsey's famous prediction about the end of the Japanese war led the list of optimistic "boners," but General H. H. Arnold has not been far behind; he has "destroyed" most of Germany's economy many times and is now engaged in doing the same thing for Japan. General Douglas MacArthur's communiques speak for themselves, they have often been premature and overly optimistic. General Dwight D. Eisenhower's hopes of ending the European War in 1944 misled many people. Even General George C. Marshall, in a recent article written some weeks ago, wrote that "before this statement is made public hostilities might have terminated in the European theatre." . . . That over-optimism should not be used as a strawman to account for potential—not actual—munitions shortages.

A check on Kaiser's widely publicized statement that his shipyards had lost 26,000 employees within sixty days revealed that those workers had been discharged over a six-month period due to reduced production schedules. Less than 900 workers had left within the sixty-day period he specified, and after July 31 employment had actually increased slightly.

Golden and Elliott argued that no evidence had been presented which showed that spot authorizations had injured the war effort. The total production authorized under PR-25 (from its inception on August 15 to November 14) amounted to only $86,000,000 (very roughly ½ of one per cent of war production for the period) and required not more than 25,000 employees, all of whom were obtained from in-plant transfers or new workers. This required only 6,276 workers in Group I labor areas over a three-month period. In each case the WMC had certified that there would be no interference with war production; the safeguards were, if anything, too strict.

Maverick wrote to Krug on November 28 that PR-25 helped rather than hindered the war effort because:

(1) it provided a way for the United States Employment Service managers to enter an applicant's plant and recruit personnel before the application was considered; this procedure made the labor in an applicant's plant available to the needs of war production;
(2) it kept plants in operating condition between war contracts; and
(3) it provided a means of calling the existence of unused facilities to the attention of the procurement agencies.

Elliott told Small that no plant operating under PR-25 had refused to accept a war contract, and the few thousand workers employed by "spot" production were "trifling evidence on which to base a reversal in WPB policy."

To the Army's claim that curtailment of spot authorization would provide war workers, Maverick said:

For some time it has been customary to accept what seems to be a simple theory that the indiscriminate and general curtailment of civilian production is the means of meeting the manpower needs of critical war programs. This is a clumsy mechanism. The situation requires more specific and effective methods. Blanket manpower measures are extremely inefficient from a standpoint of time and wasteful of labor.

He pointed out that the great bulk of the 1,067,000 workers released from work between November 1943 and August 1944 had gone into non-essential work or had left the labor field completely. He insisted that the following four steps would provide all the manpower needed:

(1) the WMC should be more active in imposing reductions in employment ceilings on non-essential enterprises;
(2) a system of wage bonuses should be devised in critical plants;
(3) greater use should be made of WPB directive powers; and

(4) the scheduling technique should be more widely used.

Finally, these proponents of reconversion pointed out that Congress and Byrnes had already determined that it was possible to prepare for reconversion without interfering with war production. The military proposals, they claimed, were not based on the experiences of war production, but on a desire

> to throw all of our possible resources into one great war production effort regardless of its effect upon other aspects of our economy. This is an emotional urge which does not yield readily to a consideration of facts. . . . An examination of the past record and our anticipated manpower needs presents no cause for alarm. The manpower attention that the critical programs need can be given them and at the same time it is possible and extremely desirable to prepare for some of the manpower problems of reconversion.

H. SUSPENSION OF PR-25

By November 26 General Somervell's draft of the WMC-Navy-Army-WPB statement to local officials on processing PR-25 was ready. As expected, this draft curtailed PR-25 by ordering any application in Group I and II labor areas referred to Washington. But Patterson still refused to sign because permission could still be given to build experimental models and to install equipment. He was holding out for complete suspension, and perhaps he had hopes that the Office of War Mobilization and Reconversion (as OWM had become in October) would force such action.

Admiral Robinson suggested that WPB issue the statement on its own responsibility, but Howard Bruce requested one more attempt at "compromise," and Krug consented. Small then redrafted the order, suspending PR-25 for ninety days in 103 areas where manpower shortages were critical or where war production was behind schedule. Authorizations could be made in unusual cases if the local Area Production Urgency Committee made a unanimous recommendation and if it was approved by the WMC area director. And provision was made for appeal to the PEC. Applications for building experimental models could be authorized under other regulations where there was clear evidence that such construction would not interfere with war production. Patterson, McNutt, and Forrestal signed this statement, Krug approved, and after a hurried meeting with Byrnes on December 1, the order was publicly announced under the headline "Reconversion Halted to Speed Arms Output."

At about this time, at a meeting in the Pentagon attended by the top WPB officials, representatives of the Services explained that the experiences of the battlefield had convinced the War Department of the need for an increased supply program for 1945. At this meeting Krug and the other WPB officials pledged their full support.

On December 7, General Program Order 5-10 was issued. This order had been under discussion since early in November and Krug had agreed to its basic premise on November 23. It limited programmed civilian production to the level already authorized for the fourth quarter of 1944 unless there was conclusive proof that additional production was essential. All production in excess of approved program levels was to take place under PR-25.

The change seriously crippled several programs being sponsored by the Office of Civilian Requirements to secure some production of certain critically needed civilian items, for by this time the spot authorization program itself was virtually abandoned. It was agreed to give the military representatives additional time to study PR-25 applications in those few places where the regulation was still in force; Patterson was still unsatisfied and requested that the field instructions be reworded to imply that applications were to be denied, and to give less emphasis to the procedure for securing approval. He also objected to the inclusion of hardship as a criterion justifying approval in unusual cases. The instructions were again revised to meet these objections.

Following suspension of PR-25 in most important centers, Somervell, Patterson, and Clay continued their campaign to create a sense of urgency about the war program. Somervell told a Boston audience on December 2:

> Today the war's end is being delayed because thousands of men have left the shipyards, the

forges and foundries, and because thousands of others have sought employment away from other war industries where production is lagging. . . . this is threatening to prolong the war, to multiply the number of young Americans who will lose their lives. . . . Aachen would have fallen sooner and with a saving of lives had there been a greater rate of fire.

In New York he said:

Workers are worrying about their post-war future when all the post-war future of many of our men, for your sons, your brothers, may be under six feet of sod in Germany. This is unthinkable.

A London *Daily Mail* dispatch, widely circulated in the United States, reported that American soldiers of the 9th Army had been unable to repulse a German tank attack because the artillery had already fired its quota of shells. Although this story was later denied, it enforced the impression given by Somervell and others that the ammunition shortages were due primarily to large-scale labor desertions.

As background of this publicity campaign, it should be recalled that all through this period the Army and the OWM were strenuously attempting to secure the enactment of national service legislation. It should also be recalled that the military position in Europe was discouraging.

I. THE MEAD COMMITTEE

Finally, the Mead Committee decided to examine the situation. On December 4, in open session, General Somervell gave a general report on production to the Committee. He reported that 331,479 men were needed for Army Service Forces programs alone. Referring to Batcheller's report, he pointed out that the deficiencies did not extend "clear across our program." His testimony and the Committee's questioning then continued:

SOMERVELL: . . . Make no mistake about it, no one so far has suffered from a lack of supplies. Our problem is to keep us from suffering from a lack of supplies.

MEAD: When you say that, General, you mean that the boys on the front . . .

SOMERVELL: (interposing). Have had everything that they could possibly move to the front . . . what we are apprehensive about is that we are not going to be able to keep on giving them everything they need. . . . I would say there is every reason for expecting a shortage at the front unless the manpower deficiencies are met.

FERGUSON: Have you had to cut down any programs at the front, any work, because of shortage of materiel—campaigns or anything of that nature?

SOMERVELL: No, sir.

FERGUSON: You have carried out the strategy outlined so that there has been no cutting of any programs at the front?

SOMERVELL: There is no production program at the front.

FERGUSON: I mean so far as the soldiers are concerned.

SOMERVELL: So far as calling off the battle is concerned, that is right.

FERGUSON: You haven't had to change in any way because of shortages at the front, so far as not making the material here? You may not have been able to transport it.

SOMERVELL: That's right.

FERGUSON: But because of lack of production, you have not had to interfere with the program of the war?

SOMERVELL: That's right.

In response to questions from Senator Harold H. Burton, Somervell pointed out that with the increased tempo of the war there had been a stepped-up demand for many items. He continued: "We haven't been able to keep up with the increased tempo. For the first time, now, our production is lagging behind the rate of expenditures." Some minutes later Senator James M. Tunnell remarked: "I was listening to the Army Hour yesterday; I heard one fellow make the statement that they fired two shots where they could have fired five because of the shortage of ammunition." And Somervell replied:

That's because of the difficulties of getting ammunition from the ships to the gun and not because of any failure of production yet. . . . But the thing that concerns us is that, knowing that, knowing that they can fire at a faster rate as soon as they get their lines in France working to maximum efficiency, we have enough to lay down in France so that they can get it up there . . . their difficulties over there so far have been difficulties of unloading and moving the ammunition, supplies, equipment, from the point of unloading to the point where they are used.

What we must do here is to be sure that as those facilities improve we lay down over there all the things that they can use. That's our problem.

Somervell then proceeded to discuss the difficulties in the manpower situation (due to losses to the Armed Forces and the drift of persons out of war industries) and describe the efforts of the Army Service Forces to secure the more efficient use of labor in co-operation with the WMC and WPB.

Somervell's testimony before the Mead Committee, although emphasizing the need to step up production and the need for more war workers, was more carefully worded than his press releases and speeches. Before the Committee he made every effort to clarify the fact that ammunition shortages were potential, that any shortages at the front had not been caused by production failures and deficiencies, but by transportation difficulties. Perhaps in his desire to leave no false impression, he even overstated the position: an actual lack of landing craft, for example, had affected strategy. But even actual supply deficiencies were apparently not the result of malingering by labor and management.

Three days later, before the National Association of Manufacturers, Somervell made a speech, a speech that Senator Mead called "very forceful." The theme of the NAM meeting was "War and Reconversion" but Somervell made it quite clear to the assembled manufacturers that War and not Reconversion was the task of American industry. He pointed out that the current production of some key items was lagging behind consumption. Nevertheless, this speech, like the testimony before the Mead Committee, was more restrained in its implications than had been his earlier statements. He told the manufacturers:

Make no mistake about our situation, they have supplies at the front right now. It's the future we must provide for. Our program is not lagging on all items. Even on the critical items many manufacturers are abreast of the schedules we have given them. Further, some of the demands are so recent that you could not be expected to have reached your maximum schedules in the time that has elapsed. . . . It is on these critical items . . . some of the new ones . . . that we must concentrate our efforts. . . . As long as the nation is at war, on one front or two, planning for war, producing for war, fighting the war is the nation's business and its only business. We must win before we can reap the fruits of victory.

As a result of the speech the NAM abandoned its discussion of reconversion problems.

On December 7 Krug appeared before the Mead Committee and explained Batcheller's report in some detail. It is interesting to note that the Mead Committee questioned Krug about some "informal information" that the Committee had received to the effect that there was an agreement between the WPB, WMC, and the War Department "not to criticize each other publicly in connection with these production programs." Krug denied this. Perhaps the Senators had in mind a decision by the war production officials to give the public the same figures on war production problems; i.e., to avoid mention by one official of a shortage of "200,000" men while another referred to the shortage of "500,000" men.

After hearing from Somervell, Krug, and others, Senator Mead told the Senate on December 16:

There has been a misconception of the problem. Insufficient production in the United States has not up to this time been the cause of the shortage of weapons and ammunition at the front. . . . Unfortunately certain news stories concerning actual shortages of ammunition in the hands of our fighting men have carried the implication that the lack of cartridges and ammunition at the front was due to some failure of production at home. These implications, we are assured, were not intended, and they are not well founded.

J. CLAY'S PROMOTION

Meanwhile, on December 11, General Clay was elevated to the Office of War Mobilization and Reconversion and made Byrnes's Deputy Director. Simultaneously with his promotion, it was made known that the OWMR would thereafter take a more active part in policy-making. This announcement tolled the death knell for the remains of Nelson's reconversion program, though the death blow is attributable to events in Luxembourg.

VII. Reconversion Dead: Reconversion Revived

A. HOME-FRONT RESISTANCE

The Army's psychological warfare campaign had reached the point of diminishing returns by the middle of December. The fact that the munitions shortages were potential did not, of course, lessen the seriousness of the situation, but the disclosures of the Mead Committee (Somervell's testimony was published in the press) aroused doubts concerning the accuracy of the Army's public statements. The cries of "crisis" had been raised so often that the public senses were becoming dulled. Labor and management resented the claim that they were responsible for delays in critical programs, when Batcheller's report, the substance of which Krug reported to the Mead Committee in open session on December 7, had clearly demonstrated that the foremost cause was the sudden rise in requirements. There was growing criticism of the manner in which the War Department was operating.

The *United States News*, a journal not unsympathetic to the Army's point of view, editorialized on December 15:

> In appraising the present outcry over military shortages, remember . . . the Army itself underestimated requirements, figured wrong on the need for ammunition, tanks, etc., and ordered cutbacks months ago. . . . The Military expected that Germany would be defeated in 1944. . . . It must be understood that at least a mild dose of salesmanship, maybe a little overemphasis, goes into the effort to convince the country that munitions must be speeded. The Military cannot afford to take chances. . . .

On December 16 Kiplinger reported that labor was tired of being blamed for the shortages and that the Army was creating new crises in order to cover up its own mistakes. On the same day a WPB Industry Advisory Committee composed of railroad manufacturers accused the War Department of canceling contracts "by resolution [sic], without giving adequate warning, and by so doing forcing inefficient use of critical manpower and supplies." Later in the month C. V. Hughes, author of the New York Sunday *Times* feature "The Merchant's Point of View," commented:

> The [Mead] Committee findings made it amply plain that some of the ordinary methods of business are ignored by the services and that out of this haphazard procedure have come these production difficulties which now result in emergency. More instead of less civilian control is the obvious remedy. . . . It is to be hoped that industry, which accomplished such an outstanding job under its own regime, is not to be made the scapegoat for military blunders. If so, the protest ought to be loud enough to bring back control to where it belongs.

B. THE BATTLE OF THE BULGE

On December 16 the German army unexpectedly broke through Allied lines to open the Battle of the Bulge. Not only did the Nazi tanks crush the Allied positions, but the Nelson program, which had also steadily been crumbling, gave way under the brunt of the German offensive. The break-through demonstrated the seriousness of the situation more than anything the production officials could say or do; but, working with Clay and Byrnes, the military reopened their psychological program with renewed vigor. On December 23 Byrnes ordered all race tracks closed, ostensibly to save manpower, prevent absenteeism, and cut down on unnecessary travel, but in great part, presumably, as a psychological measure—the race tracks being an especially good symbol of "conspicuous waste." He also ordered the draft boards to review all athletes' classifications. To save badly needed coal and to emphasize the seriousness of the situation, General Clay, through Byrnes, ordered a "brown-out" of outside electrical displays and followed it up a month later with a midnight curfew on places of amusement.

Obviously Nelson's reconversion program by now was a dead issue. In so far as these acts had a specific over-all objective in view—rather than merely being an expression of a sense of acute anxiety—the objective seems to have been to secure a national service act. Patterson had long been convinced of the necessity of a law permitting the drafting of workers for essential war jobs. Following the Battle of the Bulge, the military increased pressure on Congress to enact such a law.

On December 26 Krug announced that the War Production Board would operate on the theory that the war would go on indefinitely. Any doubt that Nelson's program was dead was dispelled by Byrnes's report to Congress and the President. This report, apparently prepared under Clay's supervision, called for by the War Mobilization and Reconversion Act of 1944, was issued on January 1, 1945; by clear implication, it placed much of the blame for production breakdowns on Nelson. This "too early start toward reconversion" of the previous summer required, wrote Byrnes, that "we had to undo what had been done . . . to hope for a change in the national psychology." Furthermore, events had demonstrated (order of paragraphs rearranged):

> we could not do two divergent things at once, that we could not pursue an all-out war production effort while simultaneously releasing materials, facilities, and manpower for civilian production. . . .
>
> Whenever workers are laid off because they are not needed in this shipyard or that aircraft plant, demands immediately spring up to provide them with peacetime employment, to permit manufacture of civilian goods. These demands are hard to resist. Yet until we get the critical programs under control, until we can assure General Eisenhower, General MacArthur, and Admiral Nimitz, of the critical supplies they need, I feel we must resist these demands, reasonable as they appear on the surface.

By the beginning of 1945 the munitions program for the year had reached sixty-two and three-tenths billion dollars, as compared with a third quarter of 1944 annual rate of sixty and six-tenths billion, and a fourth quarter of 1944 annual rate of fifty-nine and nine-tenths billion (in August 1943 dollars). The Battle of the Bulge brought new increases so that by January 15 the program was up to sixty-four and six-tenths billion dollars, and a month later another one and six-tenths billion was added. At that time the 1945 schedules called for the delivery of almost nineteen per cent more munitions than had been delivered in 1944.

The increased munitions demand coincided with calls for troop replacements, thus magnifying the manpower problem. The materials and facilities situations were also affected: materials rapidly changed from easy to tight supply, and facilities had to be expanded rapidly, with more careful distribution of components. The Army took its own warnings seriously: some of the new plants now planned for could not be brought into production for eighteen months or more. The problem was further complicated by the fact that the rise of some schedules corresponded with the decline of others: approximately fifty per cent of the programs were going up; fifteen per cent were stable; and thirty-five per cent were declining.

A fact which increased the seriousness of the situation was that some of this production seemed to be for immediate use rather than for pipelines or reserve. Somervell warned, "Some programs may have to be curtailed because of shortages. . . . The implications in operational planning of such an eventuality are so serious that this must not happen."

C. PRIORITIES REGULATION 25

Materials that had been plentiful again became scarce, and on January 13 allocations of steel and copper wire, brass, aluminum sheet, and lead were withdrawn from PR-25, a restriction that slowed down or stopped most of the spot production. Priorities Regulation 24, which allowed the placement of unrated orders for certain types of capital goods, was amended on January 20 so as to render it meaningless. At the same time requests were coming in from local Group II Area Production Urgency Committees asking that December 1 restrictions on PR-25 be extended to their areas. With only minor opposition from the Smaller War Plants Corporation and the Office of Labor Production, Krug approved an amendment requiring *unanimous* approval of Area Production Urgency Committees for

PR-25 applications in Group II labor areas. This was effective on January 18. The breakthrough had dulled the enthusiasm even of Maury Maverick, who told the Requirements Committee, after a tour of the front:

> This argument we had over reconversion, when I think of it now, I think of it as a sort of an academic discussion of scholars that was in the past. . . . Things are much more serious than anybody realizes in America and we have to do more if we really want to win the war.

Paradoxically, Maverick blamed military censorship for the unduly optimistic picture given to the home front.

When Bruce requested that Krug continue the suspension of PR-25 in Group I areas for another ninety days, the request was granted without dissent.

By the end of January all of Nelson's programs had been suspended except the orders easing controls over aluminum and magnesium and permitting the manufacture of experimental models; and the usefulness of these was limited by the stringent manpower control measures threatened by Selective Service upon any manufacturer who might venture to take advantage of them. Even the work on reconversion plans for the period following Germany's defeat was stopped. By that time Krug and the WPB seemed to the public to be operating merely to carry out the policy determined by Byrnes and the War Department. Krug, when asked by reporters to comment on reports that the generals were running the WPB, replied, "You ought to know."

D. RECONVERSION RETURNS

By the first of February the German breakthrough had been repulsed; the Russians had opened their offensive and had cut off East Prussia; the military situation was greatly improved and Germany's defeat was imminent. But the momentum of the "no-thought-about-reconversion" policy was too strong to be reversed immediately. Nevertheless Byrnes, on February 1, instructed Krug to prepare—without publicity—a reconversion program to be placed into effect on the day Germany surrendered. Krug was to have this ready by March 1. A carefully developed program adopted earlier in the fall was now unsuitable because it had been based on too optimistic estimates of the extent of military cutbacks following Germany's defeat. By March the military had revised upward their needs for the "one-front" war against Japan.

Following the Battle of the Bulge the Administration generally, and the military agencies especially, renewed their attempts to secure a national service law. In attempting to secure adoption of this law, the military spokesmen stressed—some people thought they overstressed—the need for manpower. National service legislation was opposed by all the leading business and labor organizations. As the military situation improved, growing public resentment against the military production officials again occurred. Business, writers in labor periodicals, and congressional leaders accused these officials of covering up their own mistakes by blaming the public. For example, Senate Majority Floor Leader Barkley on February 24 stated: "The military apparently set out to take advantage of the German breakthrough to horsewhip the country into a labor draft 'to make people realize there's a war on.' Everyone who had anyone in the Belgian Bulge knows there's a war on." On March 3 the editors of *Business Week* wrote a long open letter to the military leaders, reading in part as follows:

> Many of us, definitely including the Army and Navy leaders, looked for a victory in Europe last fall. Disappointment of this hope left us with a guilty feeling that we were all to blame. The Army and Navy leaders were quick to turn the situation to their advantage. They won a victory at home for the imposition of an assumption on which they knew better; that the protraction of the German war was due to a home-front failure to provide the services with adequate manpower and fire-power. In the prevailing mood of public self-accusation, this became a victory for the idea that, hereafter, the military should have a free hand. And the pen of War Dept. and Navy Dept. propaganda has been mightier than a sword in pressing that victory home. . . .
>
> And few can fashion anything at all of the make-believe that a war which didn't end last fall will now never end. Suspicion asks: "What's

behind all this?" Left groping for sound reasons it will imagine dangerous ones.

We have come into this fourth year of war with great pride in our armed forces and in the kind of military leadership that can grow out of the West Point and Annapolis traditions. This pride must not be put to the risk of the drill sergeant's bellow that "you're not supposed to think." But that is what an alert military intelligence will report that the country believes it is hearing at the present time.

This criticism was not silenced by Secretary of War Stimson's emphatic demand that the home front meet the Army's requirements without delay or discussion, nor by Assistant Secretary of the Navy Hensel's charges that there were too many "smoke screens designed solely to duck the blame for failure." He listed the smoke screens as charges of military inefficiency, and the argument that "we cannot force man to work making profits for another." The reason for many of the production breakdowns, Hensel stated, was the inordinate labor turnover.

Increasingly through February the Allied Armies in both hemispheres made progress. The atmosphere became more hospitable to a reassertion of WPB leadership in production policy. Beginning with a PEC meeting on March 5, Krug and Batcheller began to screen military requirements more critically and to evince more concern for the civilian economy, which was showing evident signs of deterioration. The remaining supporters of Nelson's buried reconversion program began to speak up for its exhumation.

In March Allied troops crossed the Rhine and encircled the Ruhr, and the Soviet forces crossed the Oder; both armies headed toward Berlin. On the 16th, O. Max Gardner, Chairman of the Office of War Mobilization and Reconversion Advisory Committee, publicly complained because Byrnes had failed to take the Advisory Committee into his confidence or ask for its advice. This Committee, established by the War Mobilization and Reconversion Act of 1944, was composed of twelve representatives of various segments of the economy. Gardner stated that the Committee was "quite aware of what was going on and some of its members were apprehensive over the continued extension of the Army's authority over the home front, but were entirely without authority to take action."

The next day, March 17, Krug announced that the WPB had been working on reconversion plans and would soon make known its program for VE Day. Reconversion returned as a respectable and patriotic subject.

On March 21 Byrnes called the members of the OWMR Advisory Committee together and asked for their advice. They advised him to drop Clay, and Byrnes answered, "He's leaving." General Eisenhower had already requested Clay's help and the President had agreed to transfer him at the end of the month.

On March 28 General Eisenhower announced that the German Army was defeated, and on March 30 General Clay left the office of War Mobilization and Reconversion to take up his onerous task in Germany.

On April 1 Byrnes sent his Second Report to Congress and the President. Unlike the First Report, its major emphasis was on the problems of reconversion.

Priorities Regulation 25 was not reinstated until April 26, by which time it was merely a small part of a much larger and more thorough-going reconversion program. It was used for a short time to authorize production of the few items still under control. As early as September 1944, Krug had adopted the policy of dropping as many controls as fast as possible after the defeat of Germany. The earlier-than-anticipated surrender of Japan in August 1945 released the entire economy for civilian production.

CONCLUDING COMMENTS

The social sciences deal with materials of tremendous complexity. It is this very complexity that forces us to isolate our subject of investigation and to center our attention on it. But we must never forget that in so doing we distort. The reader has been warned against assuming that the Reconversion Controversy can be understood as an isolated phenomenon, against the danger of over-rationalizing motives, and against the error of over-personalizing or—at the other extreme—of over-institutionalizing, the events. There are also other considerations to be borne in mind.

This study cannot be understood except in its context of the urgency of the war years and the seriousness of the decisions. We cannot and indeed should not abstain from taking advantage of hindsight; but we should remember that what is past to us was future to the actors. Our judgments should, therefore, be framed in terms of the information available to the participants and in terms of the real alternatives open to them. With these preliminary cautionary remarks, certain generalized comments may help the reader in assessing the issues in the case. The reader himself should be prepared to generalize further for himself.

First, as to the formal organizational relationship between Wilson and Nelson (administrator-to-in-line-deputy), and its interplay with the various personal and political factors that created the crisis, there is presumably some fairly specific moral to be drawn. It has been pointed out earlier that the original decision to divide authority between Nelson and Wilson by giving Wilson complete operating responsibility and the chief staff aids was in part a defensive political move and was also partially dictated by an understandable desire to give Nelson more time and opportunity for consideration of broad policy problems; but either the organizational analysis on which the decision was based was defective, or the political situation was felt to require such drastic and dire remedies that technical administrative considerations could not be given weight. The plan worked badly, and particularly so for Nelson. The policies of the War Production Board were too intimately related to the daily course of events to make feasible the kind of split in responsibility that was decided on; and the attraction of the center of executive power for the loyalties of subordinate officials had its inevitable consequences. Nor was it possible to channel WPB relations with other war agencies through the Chairman's office since the points of contact between the WPB and outside agencies occurred at all levels. Inter-agency problems were pounded out in day-to-day operations, especially through the inter-agency committees found all through the WPB. As a result of the division of responsibility, Nelson was left with an inadequate staff and was isolated from the centers of decision.

We have mentioned that the WPB really stood largely outside the process of estimating requirements, placing contracts, expediting production, and distributing military end products. There are obvious difficulties in exercising control at one point in the continuous stream that runs from needs to supplies without authority over other aspects, though the difficulty, fortunately, is one of degree rather than absolute. The top officials of the WPB also suffered from lack of information. They had no access to strategic decisions nor satisfactory information as to the supplies in the hands of the military agencies. There was no established reporting system leading up from the procuring agencies comparable to the system worked out for industry. The WPB was forced, therefore, to make decisions whose validity was always open to attack because they were not based on realistic information. WPB's partial isolation from the production process would have caused far less difficulty if the flow of information from the users of supplies had paralleled the flow of information from the producers.

The political problems (using the term "political" in its broadest sense) of the successive chairmen of WPB merit analysis. At the time, various persons in Washington, not unsympathetic to Nelson, felt that his loss of control over WPB was largely the result of his failure to heed the old political adage that one should reward one's friends and punish one's enemies. There are other ways of maintaining loyalty within an organization and undoubtedly Nelson's conviction of the desirability of securing consensus was politically as well as socially wise; but especially in the crisis atmosphere of wartime Washington and with a group of WPB officials who had positions of prominence outside the government, Nelson's particular qualities of patience and reasonableness did not suffice; decisiveness and toughness as well as patience were essential. The problem of control created or left unsolved by Nelson's personality characteristics and patterns of action was, of course, made critical by the reorganization which made Wilson the key figure in WPB. But that reorganization itself was largely determined by the political situation in WPB and with the Army, that Nelson had failed to dominate in spite of broad legal powers and an absence of any insoluble organizational problem within WPB.

The political circumstances that circumscribed Krug's actions when he took office as WPB Chairman were not of his making and offer no obvious lesson, but they may help to give a clearer understanding of the kinds of limitations that surround any administrator in government. Frequently new administrators, especially those who are unfamiliar with big government, take office with expectations of unlimited freedom in administering their particular province. They soon discover that such freedom is illusory. Their power and their ability to act are dependent on support of various kinds. In a democracy the support implies elements of personal loyalty as well as some degree of agreement on policy. Krug had no written (or, indeed, specific oral) instructions from the President other than, as he expressed it, "to get the WPB back on the track." But the lack of any formal restraint was obviously not the equivalent of a free charter. The effects of the inherent restraints are visible and therefore noteworthy to the student.

It might be suggested that the whole question of reconversion involved policy of sufficient magnitude to justify decision in the very beginning by the Office of War Mobilization, perhaps even by the President. By 1943 the War Production Board had ceased both in theory and in fact to be the over-all policy agency of the war production program. It had become merely one of many agencies, and its position was essentially that of an operating agency. Its staff of some 20,000 people at the peak were drawn chiefly from the ranks of business, and its outside operating contacts were with a clientele made up mainly of manufacturers. In the public eye it was identified mainly with business and especially with big business. Reconversion involved other agencies, like WMC, and considerations broader than those underlying munitions or essential civilian production. It is at least arguable that these considerations should have been weighed and the decisions made by an agency with broader political and administrative scope than WPB, and one free from involvement in the complexities and frictions of a large operating organization. OWM was such a high policy agency, at least in theory; but it concerned itself with reconversion policies only intermittently and largely as an appellate forum. It insisted that Nelson proceed—but took no full responsibility for his action, and later criticized Nelson by implication for the steps he had taken. In the light of the incidents described in the text, the question may well be raised as to whether the original formal attribution to WPB of the power to determine basic policies vital to the military and to the civilian economy was not unwise. But the final answer to such a question would require a consideration of political and other factors that lie outside the scope of this study.

The WPB administrative problem was also complicated by the need for securing cooperation and consensus among men from divergent backgrounds who, in many instances, had represented antagonistic interests in the past, and expected to do so again in the future. This circumstance gave rise to the suspicion, in most cases probably unfounded, that the other person thought in terms of the interest group from which he came and to which he would return, rather than in terms of the public interest. Thus the Reconversion Controversy came to be viewed by many as a struggle between big business on the one hand and small business and labor on the other.

Another question which the study does not answer but upon which it should shed light, is the extent to which an organizational conflict between a civilian and a military agency differs from an inter-civilian agency conflict. Are there any elements which made the struggle between Nelson of the WPB and Patterson and Somervell of the War Department peculiar because civilians were opposing representatives of a military branch of the government? It would certainly be wrong to interpret the Reconversion Controversy as one solely between civilians and the military. One has only to remember that the War Manpower Commission and many WPB Vice-Chairmen opposed Nelson's program as firmly as did Patterson, Somervell, or Clay. On the other hand, it would seem that there were certain elements present here not normally present in other organizational squabbles. There was the suspicion on the part of many civilians of what they termed "the military mind" and a lack of confidence in the military. The soldiers and their civilian spokesmen, on the other hand, were suspicious of "anti-service professors" and "men who play politics with their country's future"; and they were, one should add, bitterly resentful of the accusation that they themselves were "militaristic." Certainly the differences in outlook between soldier and civilian, undoubtedly exaggerated in each other's minds, created problems not present in other situations. The military had some tactical advantages in the controversy and in securing public support for their policies because in the War Department and the ASF there was greater, although incomplete, control by superior over subordinate, less need to secure general consensus, and, at least outwardly, a much greater cohesion than was found in almost any wartime civilian organization. Moreover, the military's prestige was enhanced during wartime and it was felt necessary to maintain public confidence in their leadership.

Again it is hoped that the study gives the reader a greater awareness of the types of weapons used by administrators to secure public and political support for their programs. Many different questions and problems are presented by what appears to be a normal—perhaps even necessary—tactic of democratic administration. The connection between politics and administration seems obvious. Many people felt that the anti-big-business campaign, on one side, and the production-slow-ups-are-slowing-up-the-war campaign, on the other, were both unjustifiable. Whatever the reader's own evaluation of these two forays into public relations, they merit careful consideration and analysis. Both were attempts to mobilize public opinion in support of conscientiously conceived policy objectives; but it would be difficult to describe either as public education based on objective scientific analysis. Obviously there is a danger in such intemperate approaches to the problem of securing understanding and consensus in our democracy. Unfortunately, the techniques for the institution of adequate safeguards that will not choke off education at the source remain obscure.

In this connection it is difficult to resist the conviction that the identification by some of Nelson's loyal supporters of his fortunes with those of the nation were a disservice to both Nelson and the nation. Although one would expect a "public relations sense" in these men, their essays in this field backfired. Their activities, it seems fair to say, had much to do with the failure of Nelson's program. As much as any single thing, they caused the loss of two conscientious and experienced public servants at a critical time.

There is one aspect of the great Reconversion Controversy that remains puzzling and that is probably insoluble. The various actors in the controversy took it seriously and felt that the decisions they were making would have a substantial effect on our economy both during and after the war. Yet even assuming that the war against Japan had been long drawn out and that there was to be a gradual decline in military requirements, as was the assumption in 1943-44, it is now difficult to have any strong conviction of economic significance. The course of reconversion when it finally burst forth in the spring of 1945, even without the preliminary "chinking in" of reconversion activities that Nelson had sought, was tempestuous, but there is little objective evidence to indicate that the way would have been smoothed by a previous adoption of the spot authorization program. There is also no convincing evidence (to the author) that such use as was made of the spot authorization program affected the military program at all or would have affected it if the spot authorization order had never been suspended: at its peak it involved a grand total of 25,000 workers in scattered localities! Perhaps in one sense the War Department's position had a certain validity that Nelson's position lacked. The problem of *announcing* a reconversion program (and Nelson's insistence on *announcement* was the most critical point in the dispute) was chiefly a problem in mass psychology, and Somervell was right in thinking of it almost exclusively in those terms. Nelson, on the other hand, conceived the problem as lying partly in the field of psychology and partly in the field of economics. By now, as has just been said, it seems somewhat improbable that the economic effects of action or inaction were of any great consequence. There is some evidence to indicate that Nelson's psychological appreciation of the situation with reference to workers in war industries was sound, in other words that the spot order would not lead them to desert the war industries. However, beyond that specific issue lay the larger question of the effect on our soldiers and political bodies, such as Congress, and on local governments and business organizations, who might be inclined to look at the spot authorization order as a precedent and a symbol. Vice-Chairman Elliott, for example, although constantly striving to obtain an increase in authorized civilian production, felt throughout the controversy that Nelson was misjudging the fundamental political situation, and that the spot authorization order, especially while the Battle for Germany was still pending, was unwise. On the other hand, Nelson was probably correct in his belief that the Army's exaggeration of production dangers and simplification of the cause of the difficulties had harmful effects on war production, our soldiers, and our allies, and may have had consequences beyond the war years which the Army neither intended nor realized.

Nelson relied, of course, on the support he was receiving from the Truman Committee and other congressional committees, on support from "small business" as that support was interpreted for him by Maverick and others, and on the support of organized labor as interpreted for him by Keenan and Golden. How widespread in fact that support was, and how politically articulate and effective, is hard to say. It does seem clear that the larger movements of American sentiment were not willing or could not be mobilized in effective fashion to back up Nelson, even though the Army's public relations programs gradually lost effectiveness.

The Reconversion Controversy seen in this light is an instance of an administrative program lost because of its failure on the political plane. But in closing this account it may be appropriate to suggest that the spot authorization order was not the sole conceivable administrative device for meeting the employment problem that Nelson anticipated but which never came to pass. Actually about the same results could have been achieved by a more liberal interpretation of existing appeals procedures and escape clauses. Conceivably the organizational crisis could have been avoided or postponed if this or some other alternative technique had been substituted at the right moment for the one that had become a *casus belli:* certainly there would have been less friction initially if Nelson had merely taken maximum advantage of existing regulatory loop-holes without publicity; but Nelson wanted (and the others opposed) the consequences of "reconversion" as a public symbol. Nevertheless, it must be recognized that the conflict was not merely one over techniques and that it was inextricably interwoven with the question of the personalities involved. The controversy over spot authorization was preceded, as has been noted in the introduction, by controversies over other questions. Perhaps by 1944 the situation was such that any technique planned to provide a smoother path for reconversion was doomed to failure.

Chronology

1943

JUNE 26 Kanzler submits his Report on Reconversion

AUGUST 21 Nelson writes to the President about Reconversion

OCTOBER 13 *Italy declares war on Germany*

OCTOBER 15 President instructs Byrnes to take charge of the consideration of demobilization

NOVEMBER 4 Byrnes announces that Baruch and Hancock will head Reconversion Unit within OWM

NOVEMBER 5 Truman Committee Report on "Problem of Conversion from War to Peace Production"

NOVEMBER 20 *U. S. Marines land on Tarawa*

NOVEMBER 30 WPB Board Meeting and Nelson's decision to authorize civilian production in areas with facilities available if it does not limit programs of higher urgency

DECEMBER Informal submission of Panuch's proposals to center Reconversion controls in PEC

DECEMBER 16 Gladieux's proposals limiting role of PEC in reconversion

DECEMBER 15 & 22 PEC Resolutions that Reconversion controls should be centered in PEC

DECEMBER 24 *General Eisenhower named to command Allied Invasion Armies*

DECEMBER 31 Major cutback in aluminum production

1944

JANUARY 11 WPB meeting in which decided not to relax restrictions on facilities until after invasion, generally construed as reversal of November 30 decision

FEBRUARY 15 Baruch-Hancock Report issued

FEBRUARY 22 Byrnes orders war agencies to implement Baruch-Hancock recommendations

MARCH 3 Truman Committee Report on "The Present Status and Future Course of the War Production Program" championing Nelson's program of gradual reconversion

MARCH 5 Nelson's letter to Senator Murray published, announcing that pre-war competitive pattern not to be consideration in WPB reconversion policy

MARCH 24 *Churchill promises invasion "soon"*

APRIL 4 WPB Board meeting in which Wilson announces that by end of the year there will be between one-half and one million workers available for civilian production

APRIL 14 Nelson appoints Advisory Committee for Civilian Policy

APRIL 17 Krug resigns as Program Vice-Chairman to enter Navy

MAY 12 Baruch and Hancock write to Byrnes blaming Nelson for failure to establish cut-back co-ordinating machinery

MAY 22 Brewster cut-back announced and public protest

JUNE 4 *Rome occupied by Allied troops*

JUNE 5 Byrnes assigns to Wilson and PEC the authority to co-ordinate cut-backs

JUNE 6 *Europe invaded*

JUNE 10 Byrnes requests Nelson to prepare statement on Reconversion plans

JUNE 13 WPB Meeting in which Nelson outlines his Reconversion Program and WMC outlines its manpower program

JUNE 18 Nelson releases his Reconversion Program to the public, orders to be issued by July 1

JUNE 22 Patterson writes to Nelson protesting against the Reconversion Program

JUNE 22 *Russia opens offensive on Central Front*

JUNE 23 Nelson goes to hospital

JUNE 27 *American forces occupy Cherbourg*

JUNE 28 PEC meeting in which Services and WMC representatives ask for postponement of issuance of orders

JUNE 28 Joint Chiefs of Staff publicly state opposition to Nelson's Reconversion Program

JULY 4 WPB Special Meeting in which war agencies press opposition to Nelson's program

JULY 6 Wilson and Weinberg call on Nelson to urge postponement; Nelson refuses. Unsigned memorandum discussed

JULY 8 Senators Truman and Murray come to Nelson's defense

JULY 8 Nelson writes to President

JULY 10 Nelson sends his reply to Admiral Leahy

JULY 10 Byrnes threatens to intervene

JULY 11 Announcement that orders will be issued on a staggered basis, with PR-25 to be issued on August 15

JULY 13 Wilson agrees to stay on; President receives cable from Chiang Kai-shek

JULY 15 First Reconversion order permitting use of aluminum and magnesium for production of pots and pans is issued

JULY 22 Second Reconversion order permitting limited work on experimental models is issued

JULY 26 Nelson returns to WPB and holds meeting of top WPB officials in which they ask for dismissal of Locke, Noyes, and Catton

JULY 27 *American Break-through in Normandy, beginning of German retreat from France*

JULY 29 Third Reconversion order permitting the placing of unrated orders for machine tools is issued

AUGUST 4 Byrnes issues directive giving WMC final say on PR-25 applications

AUGUST 9 Hopkins and Byrnes inform Nelson of President's proposal to send him to China

AUGUST 14 Requirements Committee Meeting in which aluminum and copper but not steel made available for PR-25 production

AUGUST 15 PR-25 is issued

AUGUST 18 Nelson accepts commission to go to China

AUGUST 19 President confers with Nelson and Wilson, Wilson induced to remain in WPB

AUGUST 20-21 Protests against Nelson's "exile" to China

AUGUST 21 President's statement refuting stories that Nelson was being "kicked" in the teeth

AUGUST 23 Nelson confers with Senators and assures them that he is not being exiled

AUGUST 23 Wilson writes letters of resignation to President

AUGUST 24 Meeting at which Wilson announces his resignation and holds press conference accusing Nelson's subordinates of being responsible for attacks against him

AUGUST 24 Release of Wilson's public letter of resignation and President's reply

AUGUST 24 Announcement that Krug made Acting Chairman

AUGUST 25 Nelson talks with the President

AUGUST 25 President implies that Nelson will not return to WPB

AUGUST 26 *Paris is liberated*

SEPTEMBER 1 Krug appoints task committee to make recommendations for "streamlining" of PR-25

SEPTEMBER 3 *American tanks cross German frontier near Aachen*

SEPTEMBER 13 Steel allotted for PR-25

SEPTEMBER 15 *Allied armies meet stiff resistance on German frontier*

SEPTEMBER 17-25 *Allied attempts to establish bridgehead across Northern Rhine fail*

SEPTEMBER 26 *Churchill warns European War may continue several months into 1945*

SEPTEMBER 30 Nelson resigns and Krug becomes Chairman of WPB

OCTOBER 1 Munitions programs revised upward

OCTOBER 3 OWM becomes OWMR under Act of Congress

OCTOBER 20 *Aachen falls after weeks of hard bitter fighting*

OCTOBER 20 Krug announces that production is lagging in "vitally" important 10 per cent

OCTOBER 25 Patterson asks Krug to suspend PR-25

NOVEMBER 1 Munitions programs revised upward another 10 per cent

NOVEMBER 6 Meeting of Task Force to discuss recommendations for "streamlining" PR-25

NOVEMBER 8 Reversal of policy to encourage use of PR-25 by Krug's orders that PR-25 applications be more stringently processed

NOVEMBER 14 WPB Board Meeting in which Batcheller presents his report on war production programs and service representatives argue for suspension of PR-25

NOVEMBER 16 Byrnes warns that new civilian production will be halted unless manpower shortages in war production are eliminated

NOVEMBER 21 General Eisenhower appeals for more ammunition

DECEMBER 1 Announcement signed by Krug, Patterson, Forrestal, and McNutt suspending PR-25 for 90 days in 103 areas where manpower shortages were critical

DECEMBER 4 General Somervell talks with Mead Committee

DECEMBER 11 General Clay elevated to become Byrnes's Deputy

DECEMBER 16 *The German Break-through of Allied Lines*

DECEMBER 28 Byrnes orders all race tracks closed

DECEMBER 28 Krug announces that WPB will operate on theory that the war will go on indefinitely

DECEMBER 28 *German Break-through halted*

1945

JANUARY 1 Byrnes issues first report under Reconversion Act of 1944 placing much of blame for production shortages on Nelson's reconversion program

JANUARY 12 War production programs further revised upward

JANUARY 13 Allocations of steel, copper wire, brass, and aluminum withdrawn from PR-25 production

JANUARY 15 Brown-out of outside electrical displays ordered

JANUARY 18 Unanimous approval of APUC's required for approval of PR-25 applications in Group II labor areas

FEBRUARY 1 Byrnes instructs Krug to prepare quietly a reconversion program to go into effect the day Germany surrenders

FEBRUARY 1 War production program further revised upward

FEBRUARY 6-7 *Soviet Armies cross Oder River; U. S. Forces penetrate Siegfried Line*

FEBRUARY 8 Aluminum plants closed in December 1943, reopened

MARCH 7 *First Rhine Bridgehead established at Remagen*

MARCH 16 O. Max Gardner, Chairman of OWMR Advisory Committee, publicly complains because Byrnes has failed to take Committee into his confidence

MARCH 17 Krug announces that WPB is working on Reconversion program

MARCH 20 OWMR Advisory Committee meets and advises dismissal of Clay

MARCH 28 *General Eisenhower announces German Army defeated*

APRIL 1 Byrnes's second report stressing Reconversion

APRIL 20 *Russian tanks enter Berlin*

APRIL 25 PR-25 reinstated

Appendix I

Bibliographical Note

The major sources used for this study were as follows:

Policy Document Files of the War Production Board.

The publications of the War Production Board and the Policy Analysis and Records Branch, Bureau of Demobilization, Civilian Production Administration, especially *Minutes of the War Production Board*, J. Carlyle Sitterson's *Development of the Reconversion Policies of the War Production Board*, and *Industrial Mobilization for War*, Volume I.

Historical Monographs, War Department, Special Staff, Historical Records Section, Washington, D. C.

Files of and interviews with many of the participants.

The New York *Times*, Washington *Star*, Washington *Post*.

Donald M. Nelson, *Arsenal of Democracy*, Harcourt, Brace and Company, 1946.

Henry L. Stimson and McGeorge Bundy, *On Active Service in Peace and War*, Harper & Brothers, 1948.

Bruce Catton, *The War Lords of Washington*, Harcourt, Brace and Company, 1948.

Herman M. Somers, *Presidential Agency*, Harvard University Press, 1950. Reports of the Chairman of the War Production Board and the Director of the Office of War Mobilization and Reconversion.

Reports of, and hearings of, the Senate Special Committee Investigating the National Defense Program, Senate Committee on Military Affairs, Senate Special Committee to Study and Survey Problems of Small Business Enterprises, Senate Special Committee on Post-war Economic Policy and Planning, House Special Committee on Post-war Economic Policy and Planning, House Committee on Appropriations.

Appendix II

Biographies (Through 1945)

A. *War Production Board Officials:*

ANDERSON, S. W. Program Vice-Chairman from 5/44-4/45; prior to that served as Deputy to Vice-Chairman for Metals and Minerals and assistant director of Aluminum and Magnesium Division. —b. La Crosse, Wisconsin, February 6, 1898. A.B., Williams, 1920; M.B.A., Harvard, 1922. Banker. Prior to war service was partner in Anderson & Allen Co. and Anderson and Conrow, investment advisers. Served as adviser to American delegation at Conference on Problems of War and Peace, Mexico City, 1945.

BATCHELLER, HILAND G. Chief of Operations from 9/44-7/45, as Operations Vice-Chairman 7/43-11/43, and Director of Steel Division, Chairman of Combined Steel Committee for U. S. and U. K., and in the Office of Production Management.—b. Brooklyn, N. Y., December 5, 1885. Ph.B., Wesleyan U., 1907. President of Allegheny-Ludlum Steel Company since 1938. Director of numerous companies.

BATT, WILLIAM L. Vice-Chairman for International Supply from 6/42-11/45. One of the earliest persons to serve in war production organizations who began his war service in middle of 1940 and became one of the most important persons in co-ordinating the production efforts of the United Kingdom, Canada, and the United States. —b. Salem, Indiana. M.E., Purdue, 1907; Dr. Engineering, 1933, Stevens Institute of Technology; Sc.D., Drexel Institute, University of Pa.; Dr. Science, Rose Poly. Institute. President of S. K. F. Industries since 1923.

CATTON, BRUCE Director of Information 1943-4/45. Served as Associate Director of Information 1942-3, and also as Director of Information for Office of Production Management.—b. Petosky, Mich., October 9, 1899. Educated at Oberlin. Special writer and Washington Correspondent for Newspaper Enterprises Association until 1942. In 1945 became Director of Information for Dept. of Commerce. Author of books and articles.

ELLIOTT, WILLIAM Y. Vice-Chairman for Civilian Requirements 5/44-8/45. Served in various war production positions since 1941.—b. Murfreesboro, Tenn., May 12, 1896. A.B., Vanderbilt, 1917; Dr. Phil., Oxford, 1923. Professor of Government at Harvard since 1931. Author of numerous books and articles. In 1945 served as adviser to House Special Committee on Postwar Economic Policy & Planning.

GLADIEUX, BERNARD Administrative Assistant to the Chairman, War Production Board 1943-44. Prior to this was Management Consultant and Chief of War Organization Section, Bureau of the Budget, Executive Office of the President.—b. Toledo, Ohio, April 12, 1907. A.B., Oberlin, 1930; Zimmern School of Internatl. Studies (Geneva, Switzerland); M.A., Syracuse University.

Served as Executive Secretary, City Manager League, Administrative Consultant, Public Administration Service. After leaving WPB served as Deputy Chief of Operations and Administration for UNRRA and since 1945 as Executive Assistant to the Secretary of Commerce.

GOLDEN, CLINTON Vice-Chairman for Labor Production 6/43-5/45.—b. Pottsville, Pa., November 16, 1888. Educated, Clinton, N. Y., Public Schools. Prior to war was Vice-President of United Steelworkers of America, CIO. Adviser to numerous agencies on labor problems. Trustee of Antioch College.

KEENAN, JOSEPH D. Vice-Chairman for Manpower Requirements 6/43-11/45. Also served as labor adviser in OPM.—b. Chicago, Ill., November 5, 1896. Educated at St. Jarloth's School, Chicago. Since 1937 has been Secretary of the Chicago Federation of Labor (AFL). Began service as labor adviser to General Clay in Berlin in 1945.

KRUG, JULIUS A. Chairman of War Production Board 9/44-12/45. Prior to becoming Chairman had served as Program Vice-Chairman, Director of Office of War Utilities, WPB, and in OPM.—b. Madison, Wisconsin, November 23, 1907. B.A., University of Wisconsin, 1929; A.M. 1930. Served with Wisconsin Public Service Commission, Federal Communications Commission, and the Kentucky Public Service Commission. In 1940, before becoming Chief Power Consultant for OPM, he was Director of Power for the TVA.

LOCKE, EDWIN ALLEN, JR. Assistant to the Chairman of the War Production Board, 1/42-9/44. Also served as Deputy Chief of Staff in the Supply Priorities and Allocation Board and served with both the OPM and the National Defense Advisory Commission.—b. Boston, Mass., June 8, 1910. A.B., Harvard, 1932. After graduation from college was associated with the Chase National Bank. After leaving the WPB served as personal and special representative of the President.

MAVERICK, MAURY Vice-Chairman of WPB and Chairman of Smaller War Plants Corporation 1/44-11/45. Served as Director of the Government Division of the WPB from 1941 to above appointment.—b. San Antonio, Texas, October 23, 1895. Educated at Virginia Military Institute, and the University of Texas. Served as a member of Congress from 1935-1939, and as Mayor of San Antonio from 1939-1941.

MAY, STACY Director of Bureau of Planning and Statistics, 9/43-9/44. Before this had directed major statistics work of the National Defense Advisory Commission, the OPM, and the WPB.—b. Philadelphia, Pa., April 18, 1896. Ph.D., Brookings Graduate School of Economics and Government, 1925. From 1932 to 1942 he was with the Rockefeller Foundation.

NELSON, DONALD M. Chairman of the War Production Board 1/42-10/44. Beginning in May 1940, he served with various war procurement and production agencies, including positions of Coordinator of National Defense Purchases, Director of Purchases, OPM, Executive Director of Supply Priorities and Allocations Board.—b. Hannibal, Missouri, November 17, 1888. B.S., University of Missouri, 1911; LL.D., University of Missouri, Harvard, Northwestern U., 1942; Dr. Business Administration, Univ. of Southern California, 1947. At the time he became Chairman of the WPB he was on leave as Executive Vice-President of Sears, Roebuck & Co. After the war he became president of the Independent Motion Picture Producers Society.

WILSON, CHARLES E. Executive Vice-Chairman of the WPB 2/43-8/44. Prior to becoming Executive Vice-Chairman served as Production Vice-Chairman.—b. New York, N. Y., November 18, 1886. Educated public schools of New York. Beginning in the shipping department worked his way up to become President of General Electric.

B. *Army Service Forces Officials:*

BRUCE, HOWARD Director of Materiel, ASF, 1944-45.—b. Richmond, Virginia, August 31, 1879. Virginia Military Institute, 1897. Chairman of Board of Baltimore National Bank and director of numerous companies such as Maryland Casualty, U. S. Lines.

CLAY, LUCIUS DUB. Major General, Assistant Chief of Staff for Materiel, Service of Supply, 1942-44; Deputy Director for War Programs, Office of War Mobilization and Reconversion, 12/44-5/45.—b. Marietta, Georgia, April 23, 1897. B.S., U. S. Military Academy, 1918. Worked through ranks of engineers to become General in 1947. Represented the United States at Permanent International Navigation Conference, Brussels, in 1934; in charge of construction of Red River Dam, Denison, Texas, and in charge of defense airport program for the Civil Aeronautics program in 1940-41. After leaving OWMR became Commander of U. S. Forces in Germany in 1945 and spearhead of resistance against Russian blockade.

PANUCH, J. A. Special and confidential assistant to Director of Materiel, 1943-45.—b. Prague, Bohemia, January 25, 1899; naturalized 1921; Fordham Prep. grad.; Fordham, A.B. 1921; Columbia, LL.B., 1925; member of bar of N. Y.; U. S. Army 1918; member of law firm 1926-38; special admiralty counsel, RFC, 1935-38; special counsel, Securities and Exchange Comm., 1938-41; chm. of policy comm., Bd. of Econ. Warfare; chief, Office of Export Requirements; member of Am. Requirements Comm., WPB, 1942-43; special adviser on military programs and reorg. to Dir. of War Mob. & Recon., 1945; app. Deputy to the Asst. Sec. of State for Admin., Nov. 15, 1945.

PATTERSON, ROBERT P. Under Secretary of War 12/40-9/45; Secretary of War 9/45-7/47.—b. Glens Falls, N. Y., February 12, 1891. A.B., Union College, 1912; LL.B., Harvard, 1915. Resigned as judge of United States Circuit Court of Appeals to become Assistant Secretary of War in 1940. Holder of Distinguished Service Cross.

SOMERVELL, BREHON B. General, Commanding General, Army Service Forces, 1942-46.—b. Little Rock, Arkansas, May 9, 1892. B.S., U. S. Military Academy, 1914. Advanced through ranks to General 1945. Did engineering work all over the world. Was administrator of WPA in New York City.

C. *Other War Production Officials:*

BARD, RALPH A. Under Secretary of Navy 6/44-7/45.—b. Cleveland, Ohio, July 29, 1884. B.S., Princeton University. President of Ralph A. Bard & Company, investments, 1934-41. Served as deputy to U. S. representative on U. N. Commission on Conventional Armaments.

BARUCH, BERNARD M. Adviser to James M. Byrnes. Head of fact-finding committee on synthetic rubber. Made report (with John Hancock) to President and Byrnes on War and Postwar Plans.—b. August 19, 1870. A.B., College of the City of New York, 1889. One of the record holders of honorary degrees. Served as chief war mobilizer in World War I and became distinguished and elder statesman consulted by President in World War II. For many years was a member of New York Stock Exchange. At end of War was U. S. representative on U. N. Atomic Energy Commission.

BYRNES, JAMES M. Director of Office of War Mobilization 5/43-10/44; Director of Office of War Mobilization and Reconversion 10/44-3/45.—b. South Carolina. Educated public schools. Member of Congress, U. S. Senate, United States Supreme Court, and Secretary of State.

DAVIS, ELMER Director of the Office of War Information, 1942-45.—b. Aurora, Indiana, January 13, 1890. A.B., Franklin College, 1910; A.M., 1911; Rhodes Scholar, Queen's College, Oxford, B.A., 1912. News reporter, analyst, radio commentator and author of many books and articles.

GARDNER, O. MAX Chairman of Advisory Committee to Director of Office of War Mobilization and Reconversion, 10/44-1/46.—b. Shelly, North Carolina, March 22, 1882. B.S., North Carolina State College Agriculture & Engineering, 1903, LL.D., Univ. of North Carolina, 1931. Governor of North Carolina, 1929-33. Active in public affairs in North Carolina and Washington.

HANCOCK, JOHN M. Author (with B. Baruch) of Report on War and Postwar Plans.—b. Emerado, North Dakota, February 2, 1883. A.B., U. of North Dakota, 1903. Industrial banker, and director of numerous corporations.

LAND, EMORY SCOTT Administrator of War Shipping Administration 1942-46, and Chairman of U. S. Maritime Commission.—b. January 9, 1879. B.S., M.A., U. of Wyoming, 1898; graduate of U. S. Naval Academy, 1907; M.S., Massachusetts Institute of Technology, 1907. Holder of numerous honorary degrees and decorations.

MC NUTT, PAUL V. Chairman of War Manpower Commission, 1942-45.—b. Franklin, Indiana, July 19, 1891; A.B., Ind. U., 1913; LL.B., Harvard, 1916. Dean of Indiana Law School, Governor of Indiana, U. S. High Commissioner to Philippines, Federal Security Administrator, National Commander of American Legion.

THE DEFENSE PLANT CORPORATION

CONTENTS

EDITOR'S INTRODUCTION

The events described in the following narrative took place in the summer and fall of 1940. The author, who had been one of the chief movers of the events at the time, originally planned to write this sketch in the fall of 1941; he was delayed and the account was not set down on paper until 1944. It is reproduced here without significant revision. There have been a few minor editorial changes for the sake of clarity and a few to correct certain unimportant technical slips, such as errors in the names of agencies; and the conclusion has been shortened. Aside from this, the story remains as it was written.

The account is autobiographical, and like any autobiographical account, it has the advantages and disadvantages arising from its perspective in personality, in space, and in time. The selection of materials, the interpretation of events, are affected by the author's own interests and sets of values. The reader will recognize, for example, that the sardonic comment on the original Wright agreement reflects the author's own characteristic attitudes: his interpretation would have been indignantly denied by other men with a different orientation. Again, as with all autobiographers, the author necessarily views the situation from the particular point of access which he enjoyed at the time. Some of the members of the National Defense Advisory Commission, for example, saw the same problems and solutions in a different context of administrative and political responsibility. If they were to write the account, their value judgments might be similar to those expressed herein, but their view of the significant events would, no doubt, be different. Furthermore, the perspective is directly affected by the point in time at which the account was written. If the story had been written in 1941, as originally planned, the criticisms would have been sharper than those actually found herein. Similarly, if the author were to revise his manuscript now—1950—the passage of time would inevitably have caused a further softening. As controversies recede, it becomes easier to perceive some virtue in one's opponents, and to be more tolerant of human frailties, even if one's basic judgments have remained unchanged. Finally, since this narrative was written mostly from memory, there may be some lack of precision in a few of the details that a historian, working from the files, might have avoided, though there is sufficient reason to believe that the general outlines are accurate.[1]

If these various limitations are understood by the reader, an autobiographical history is an extremely useful tool for analysis. In the autobiography the writer is not constrained to speculate and guess about why he did what he did. It is true that no man has perfect insight into his own springs of action. It is also true that, with a lapse of about three or four years between the events and the writing of the history, there are inevitably some distortions, some tendency to ascribe order and system to actions and decisions that were more in the nature of spontaneous reactions. Nevertheless, at least with respect to the author-actor himself, the account is apt to have a greater degree of assurance in analysis than would the product of any outside observer or historian. There is a further advantage in examining administrative problems through the eyes of one of the participants in that the matter of the administrator's understanding of his own task is in itself of importance. Administrators vary enormously in the extent to which they articulate their philosophy and rationalize their course of conduct, and the

[1] The reader may wish to compare this account with an impersonal and formal treatment of the case: see Gerald T. White: "Financing Industrial Expansion for War: The Origin of the Defense Plant Corporation Leases," *Jour. Econ. History* IX (Nov. 1949), pp. 156-183. Dr. White made use of this case study in the preparation of his article.

student has much to learn from the articulations and rationalizations of the successful administrator. In this instance, he has the opportunity of getting considerable insight into the mode of action of an unusually articulate administrator.

This account was not written for students of public administration. The author has stated why he wrote the story and his reasons were, as he makes clear, mixed. Essentially, however, he thought of it as a working document, a document that would help other administrators in performing tasks related to those which he describes. Accordingly, the student will find that the selection of the materials and emphasis are not the same as they would have been had the narrative been differently founded. As written, the decisions tend to be taken somewhat for granted. They represented successful choices among difficult alternatives, and because they were successful, the painful process of formulating the right answer is given little attention. Nevertheless, it is incumbent on the reader to understand that at each point where a new tack was taken, where another move forward was made, there was a decision which was in fact a choice among alternatives. In each instance the author had gone through painful struggle to discover a solution for each successive dilemma. In each instance he sought, and found, a best alternative among numerous alternatives. Always present was the quite feasible alternative of doing nothing. The author was under no external compulsion to draft the statute under which the Defense Plant Corporation was later authorized, to work up the contacts with the various companies for the use of the DPC facilities, and to secure broad acceptance of the DPC program within the government and outside. He felt a compelling need to do all these things, and the account reads almost as if he had no choice but to do what he did. The reader should realize that while the decisions may be regarded as inevitable, since the author was constituted as he was, certainly they might easily not have been inevitable for someone else; indeed for some people similarly situated they would have been inconceivable. The administrative analysis, the penetration into the nature of the process by which the decisions were made will, therefore, fall largely to the reader. The author provides the materials from which the analysis can be made.

The foregoing are somewhat general considerations that relate to the analytic interpretation of autobiographical material. It may also be useful to call the reader's attention to certain phases of administration that are illustrated by this case.

In general, the events described herein parallel those that occurred all over Washington during the formative days of the defense program as part of the broad conflict between "business as usual" and "get ready for war" that ran through the Government and indeed through the whole of our society. Each of the individual conflicts displayed certain generic similarities and certain specific differences. The special characteristics of the struggle over the Defense Plant Corporation were at least partly occasioned by two administrative factors—the occupational characteristics of those involved and the level at which the chief participants operated. This was an operating program set up and carried through to successful completion by lawyers; and it was likewise one which was devised below the level of the top executives and put across without solid support from any of the top executives and indeed in the face of substantial opposition from some of them.

The role of lawyers in the Federal Government has been frequently commented on and almost as frequently deplored. It is unquestionably true that at least in many New Deal agencies and in many of the war agencies, the lawyers played a part that was not determined by their particular professional accomplishments. Their role was far broader. They were deeply involved in policy. There are various explanations for this tendency. Possibly in part it came about because a number of prominent law schools for the past twenty or thirty years have had teachers who were deeply interested in large social issues. Possibly it may be partly related to the fact that the lawyer's craft is somewhat mysterious to the outsider so that by the adroit use of legal phraseology the lawyer can make the unwary non-legal administrator believe that almost any problem is legal in character. It may well derive from the fact that lawyers are trained to be articulate about all sorts of problems and to deal with general propositions as well as specific cases. Whatever the explanation, and it is undoubtedly complex rather than simple, the reader should note that of all the people who were originally most active in establishing or opposing the DPC program, only two, Jesse Jones and William S. Knudsen, were not lawyers. The way in which the lawyers used their skills for policy ends deserves careful attention, especially since the successful initiation of the DPC program was achieved primarily by the lawyers themselves.

Until fairly recently it has been rather traditional to assume that policy is made in one fixed place within a governmental structure. Policy is made "by Congress," for example, or policy is made "by the Department head." But political scientists and students of public administration are no longer content with these facile generalizations. Policy is made throughout the whole governmental structure and is intimately affected by many persons and movements outside the government. Within the Federal Government one of the levels significant as a focus for the initiation of new policies is the level immediately below that of the chief departmental executives. Persons at this level are close enough to the top so that they can seize opportunities to make suggestions or to influence their chiefs. They are in a good position to recognize major new issues as they emerge. At the same time, having less public responsibility than their chiefs, they feel somewhat freer to entertain new ideas and to push for what they believe is right in spite of the shifts of political sentiment or other obstacles. Many a department head has occasion to moan about the way in which his immediate subordinates tend to push him into situations which he later finds uncomfortable. The success with which the second level executive exercises this sort of role depends upon various factors of competence and personality. One of the chief elements in success is to be found in the subordinate's ability to guess what particular form of approach will make a proposition appealing to his chief. These homely but important aspects of policy formation are well illustrated in the events described below.

One final point may be made. It will be clear to the reader that in this dispute over public vs. private ownership of defense plants, such leaders as the author, on one side, and William S. Knudsen of the National Defense Advisory Commission, on the other, were both thoroughly patriotic and both wholehearted and conscientious in defense of opposing interpretations of public policy. Knudsen's position was certainly a natural one. A production executive himself, he was not well versed in the intricacies of corporate and governmental finance. He relied on the advice of his business friends, especially since it was his duty on the Commission to deal with the leaders of industry and to interpret their views for the Commission; he was loyal to his staff in whom he had great confidence. Others in the Commission were similarly situated. All this is normal. What is less to be expected—though hardly abnormal—is the way in which these conscientious defenders of private ownership of defense plants maintained their position after the businessmen themselves had abandoned it. On this occasion Knudsen was evidently *plus royaliste que le roi*, an interesting indication that his concern was moral rather than material. Having come to accept the principle, he was not disposed to listen to practical objections.

The author's attitudes may be interpreted in somewhat parallel terms. Like Knudsen he was prepared to persist in his position on moral grounds. He was convinced that a variety of practical considerations supported his proposed course of action, but the mainspring of his conduct appears to have been a burning conviction that his proposal was right and that it was being blocked in favor of an undesirable plan. What does not appear in the case is the rather difficult role of those who adopted an intermediate position. These officials had either no objection, or no insuperable objection, to public construction and ownership of defense plants, but equally they were also prepared to accept contractual arrangements for privately built plants that would unquestionably be highly favorable to industry. It seemed to them that insistence on a large measure of protection for the Government's financial interest was of less consequence in the summer and fall of 1940 than moving ahead with any and all possible devices to encourage prompt plant construction. Some of the actions of some of the NDAC officials that the author found incomprehensible may perhaps be understood in this light.

The author of the following account, and the chief actor therein, is Clifford J. Durr. Mr. Durr's career is summarized by *Who's Who*, 1948-49, as follows:

Durr, Clifford Judkins, lawyer; b. Montgomery, Ala., Mar. 2, 1899; s. John Wesley and Lucy (Judkins) D.; A.B., U. of Ala., 1919; B.A. in jurisprudence, Oxford Univ. (Queen's Coll.), England, 1922; m. Virginia Heard Foster, Apr. 5, 1926; children—Ann Patterson, Clifford Judkins (dec.), Lucy Judkins, Virginia Lulah. Admitted to Ala. bar, 1923, Wis. bar, 1924; asso. with Rushton, Crenshaw & Rushton, Montgomery, Ala., 1922-23, Fawsett, Smart & Shea, Milwaukee, Wis., 1923-24; mem. Martin, Thompson, Turner & McWhorter, Birmingham, Ala., 1925-33; legal div., RFC, Washington, D. C., 1933-41, asst. gen. counsel, 1936-41; v.p. and dir. Rubber Reserve Co., 1940-41; gen. counsel and dir. Defense Plant Corp., 1940-41; commr. Fed. Communications Comm. since 1941. Served in 4th O.T.C., Camp Pike, Ark., Oct.-Dec. 1918. Mem. Phi Beta Kappa, Sigma Alpha Epsilon. Democrat. Presbyterian. Home: Seminary Hill, Alexandria, Va. Office: New Post Office Bldg., Washington, D. C.

AUTHOR'S FOREWORD

When I resigned as General Counsel and a director of the Defense Plant Corporation at the end of October 1941 to become a member of the Federal Communications Commission, it was my intention to take some time off while my memory was still fresh, and set down on paper a narrative of the early operations of the Corporation as I saw them, and of some of the problems with which we were faced in preparing our industrial machine for war. I had no idea of writing for publication. However, it seemed to me that the story was one which should some day be told and which could never be adequately told by the bare files of contracts, correspondence, and official memoranda; that the story contained much useful precedent and also much that should serve as a warning.

Moreover, irrespective of whether or not we should ever become a belligerent in the war, it seemed inevitable that a program of such magnitude would some day be the object of Congressional investigation. Modern war does not allow time for leisurely deliberation or a careful selection between choices. Speed is of the essence and mistakes are inevitable. Things done in time of emergency may look entirely different when viewed in retrospect from a vantage point of safety and calm. They can be properly appraised only in the light of the circumstances under which they are done and with an understanding of the alternatives then available. This was a further reason why I felt that it would be well to set the story down in a form more permanent than mere memory.

But then came the attack upon Pearl Harbor. No account of the defense program could be written which would not contain stories of deliberate obstruction and delay, of bungling and divided loyalties, along with the stories of hard and loyal effort. Now that we were actually at war and the "defense program" had become the "war effort," I felt certain that all of the obstructions, at least those deliberately imposed, would be removed and the differences between those charged with responsibility for the program would be resolved in a common determination to place the winning of the war above all other considerations. It therefore seemed to me that it would be better for the story to remain untold than to make a record of past mistakes, and worse, which were over and done with.

Now the picture has changed again. Dunkerque and Crete, Pearl Harbor and Wake Island, have become battle cries rather than grim reminders, as we and our allies have passed through the period of desperate defense to one of confident offense. The removal of the pressure of immediate danger tends to make us forget that we have not achieved safety. With every military success, "post-war planning" becomes of relatively greater importance in our thoughts than the actual conduct of the war, and the post-war plans are as varied as the philosophies and self-interests of the individuals or groups who advocate them.

We must be on our guard lest "post-war planning" be used as an excuse for relaxation on the production front or for maneuvering among industries for post-war competitive advantages. This, however, does not mean that we should stand aside and refuse to concern ourselves with the problems of peace until military victory is won; for then events will come tumbling at us too fast to handle, and expediency instead of calm deliberation will again be the determining factor. Planning is essential, and the nearer we approach the day of military victory the more urgent it becomes.

What will we do with the enormous productive capacity we have built up to fight the war? Which plants will be retained by the Government and which plants will be sold? Which will be kept in production and which will be held as standby capacity? Will any of them have to be scrapped because they are of no further utility? In disposing of the plants, will conditions be imposed assuring that they will be kept in production and will not be used to perpetuate existing monopolies or create new ones? Will we use this enormous capacity to provide the fullest possible employment and a higher standard of living for the greatest number of people, or will we stand in the sight of our potential abundance, paralyzed by fear of its effect upon established business? Into whose hands will we place the responsibility for making these decisions about our economic future?

It now seems to me that the story of the early days in the Defense Plant Corporation should be written down after all. It may contain some of the answers to our future problems. At least we should be warned not to expect our productive capacity to be preserved by those who opposed its creation.

Looking back over the strenuous months of 1940 and 1941, it is clearer to me now than it was even then that the difficulty in getting the defense program under way did not lie solely, or even primarily, in the magnitude and complexity of the job. What was often reported as bungling and inefficiency on the part of government was more often a lack of will on the part of those in authority to do the very job they were brought in to do. Complexity was not nearly so great a problem as reluctance to do the obvious and simple things.

The decision having been made (whether wisely or not, only history can tell) that most of our military production should be sought from our existing business system, it was necessary to appeal to business motives as well as patriotism. Unfortunately, the two do not always run along parallel lines. In modern war, productive capacity is as important as soldiers. But we were then getting ready for a war that might or might not develop in so far as this country was concerned. Suppose we should not get into the war, what would happen then to all of these new plants? Would not our productive capacity be greatly "over-expanded," each new plant constituting a continuing threat to some established industry? Wasn't it safer to go a little slow and see to it that these plants should never become threats to our business economy?

Sometimes individuals found it difficult to resolve the conflict even within themselves. The plight of the conscientious business executive, torn between his sense of patriotism and his fiduciary responsibility to his stockholders, was not a simple one. Moreover, even in the case of the government official, brought in from industry to serve for the duration of the emergency, it was difficult completely to throw off old loyalties overnight. This was particularly true if his salary continued to come from his old employer and his old job was awaiting him when the job in Washington was over.

Inner conflicts, however, did not come solely from conflicting loyalties between business and government. New plants cost money—a lot of it—and the money would ultimately have to come from the taxpayers. If we should succeed in staying out of the war, then the money would appear to have been spent foolishly and those responsible would be called to an accounting. Reputations built up over years can be quickly destroyed. It is one thing in time of war, as a soldier, to risk one's life on the battlefield. If death comes, it comes with glory. The death of a reputation, however, gambled upon the mere probability of war, is likely to be ignominious.

Some of the events about which I am writing occurred nearly four years ago. Most of them happened at least three years ago. During my days with the Defense Plant Corporation, I kept few notes and wrote few memoranda; getting the day-to-day job done left little time for making records of what was done, so I will have to write for the most part from memory, relying upon a few records which I still have and upon newspaper stories of the period to refresh my recollection. However, the more important events were too clearly impressed on my mind at the time to be erased by the passage of years, and I believe that I can accurately give the outlines of the pattern, even though I may have, at times, to be general in dealing with dates and specific cases.

The Problem

On May 10, 1940, Germany invaded the Low Countries. Four days later, the New York *Times* carried the following headlines:

GERMANS GAIN IN SAVAGE ATTACK IN BELGIUM: REACH ROTTERDAM, CUTTING HOLLAND IN TWO

ROOSEVELT TO ASK INCREASE IN FUNDS FOR DEFENSE USES. . . . MAY SEEK $500,000,000

On May 15, the *Times* announced:

DUTCH RESISTANCE ENDS EXCEPT IN ZEELAND

ROOSEVELT CALLS FOR PREPAREDNESS; MAY ASK BIG FUND

Special Message is Expected to Recommend Much More than $500,000,000 Extra

By May 16, the *Times* was speculating that the President might ask for as much as a billion dollars with which to equip an army of 750,000 men, and the issue of the next day carried the President's message to Congress in which he requested an appropriation of $1,182,000,000 "to make this country's defenses impregnable to modern lightning warfare." In the same message, the President asked Congress's help in building up an aircraft industry capable of producing 50,000 planes a year.

The issues of the next few days carried stories of plans to call industrial leaders to Washington to assist in mobilizing the aviation industry, and on May 29, the *Times* carried a story announcing that the President had appointed an Advisory Commission to the Council of National Defense, consisting of:

Edward R. Stettinius, Jr., U. S. Steel Corp., industrial materials; William S. Knudsen, General Motors, industrial production; Sidney Hillman, Amalgamated Clothing Workers, labor; Chester C. Davis, Federal Reserve Board, agriculture; Ralph Budd, Chicago, Burlington & Quincy, transportation; Leon Henderson, Securities and Exchange Commission, price stabilization; Harriett Elliott, University of North Carolina, consumer protection.

Geographically, the war was still far from our shores, but World War I had shown us that the Atlantic was not so wide as we had at one time thought, and the airplane was rapidly narrowing it. Moreover, Hitler, in *Mein Kampf*, had given us full warning that his ambitions encompassed the whole world. It did not require the vision of a prophet to see that our best hope of ultimate safety lay in the destruction of the German military machine which had already crushed Poland and Norway and was meeting little resistance in Holland, Belgium, and France. All that stood between us and this machine was England. Germany had been intensively preparing for war for a decade. How long we should have to prepare depended on England, and England's policy during the period of Germany's rearmament had been to seek safety for itself in appeasement rather than in military preparation. Even if we should be fortunate enough to keep out of the war, it seemed obvious that our only chance of doing so was to make our own defense impregnable.

Our immediate problem was one of productive capacity for military supplies—particularly airplanes. The drafting of men into the military services would be a rather futile gesture without the equipment to train and arm them. The job was far too big for our existing plant capacity to handle, even if we should be willing to reduce our standard of living to the barest essentials and convert all of the rest of the capacity to military production. Moreover, the war was still too far away for us to be willing to make the sacrifice this would entail. While the United States has been justly proud of its pioneer position in the development, as well as the invention, of the airplane, the airplane industry was still in its infancy. The total number of planes produced in the United States from the time the Wright brothers made their first flight at Kittyhawk in 1903 to the invasion of Poland on the 1st of September 1939 was only a little more than thirty thousand planes of all kinds. It is not surprising, therefore, that skeptical eyebrows should have been raised at the President's announcement of a program for the production of 50,000 planes a year.

In mapping out our expansion program, the experience of the last war lay behind us. We entered that war inadequately prepared, although we had been warned by two and a half years of fighting in Europe. At the end of the war, a year and a half later, we had an army of 5,000,000 men but were still relying upon our French and British allies for field artillery and much of our other equipment and ammunition. The country which had invented the airplane had been unable to put a single fighting plane of its own manufacture into combat. We started late and then sought to bait our manufacturers into expanding their plants through offering them lucrative contracts for military supplies. As a result, much of our productive capacity got into operation after the Armistice was signed, only to be promptly scrapped to avoid taxation and "over-expansion." With the lessons of the past to guide us, there was no excuse for repeating its mistakes.

It seemed clear that the present job was too big for private industry to do alone. The $1,182,000,000 appropriation the President had asked for was obviously only a small beginning if we were to match the military strength of Germany. If the job was to be done fast enough and on an adequate scale, most of the money obviously had to come from the Government. Even the wealthier manufacturing concerns could not reasonably be expected to invest heavily in plants designed for the manufacture of military equipment for a war that might not happen. This might well be their road to financial suicide. War is not a business proposition. Only the Government could afford to take the financial risks, and it was proper that it should take them. It was also proper, however, that if the Government was to provide the money and take the risk, its investment should be safeguarded to the greatest extent commensurate with military necessities. Moreover, apart from the matter of financial protection, many, if not most, of the new plants would be capable of producing peacetime goods as well as military supplies. They would constitute an important addition to our national wealth. To leave the way open for their destruction or withdrawal from production as soon as the emergency was over would be to pave the way for the grossest kind of waste, both of physical and human resources.

STATUTORY AUTHORITY FOR DPC

Such was the atmosphere in which Defense Plant Corporation came into existence. The problem was one of bringing together in the most effective way the financial resources of the Government and the organization and production techniques of private business. The decision having been made that the Government was not to engage directly in manufacturing the munitions it needed, it seemed to me that the solution of the problem lay in Government financing and ownership of the plants and the operation of the plants by private business concerns, either under lease arrangements or management agreements.

I discussed my ideas with Mr. Hans A. Klagsbrunn, who at that time was associated with me in the Litigation Section of the Legal Division of the Reconstruction Finance Corporation. We found that we were both thinking along similar lines, and the drafting of a bill embracing our ideas (in which we had the benefit of suggestions by Mr. S. W. Livingston, who was then head of the Preferred Stock Section of the Legal Division) was a rather simple matter.

However, getting the bill adopted was an entirely different matter. Mr. Jesse Jones, the Federal Loan Administrator, had a way with Congress, and legislation carrying his recommendation seldom failed of passage. Without his support the bill was doomed to failure even if we could find someone to introduce it. His blessing was therefore essential. However, his greatest pride was in RFC's balance sheet and collection record, and plants designed for military production were hardly "sound" investments for the portfolio of an agency given to testing its operations by banking standards.

The job turned out to be somewhat less difficult than we had contemplated. Mr. Jones had an expression, "a shotgun in the corner," which he often used in referring to powers not intended for use except as a club to bring recalcitrant borrowers or banks into line; so working through Mr. Claude E. Hamilton, Jr., General Counsel of the RFC, the proposed bill was sold to Mr. Jones as "a shotgun in the corner." It was attached to a proposed bill he had already approved, which merely increased RFC's lending power and slightly relaxed existing provisions relating to security requirements. A further provision was added authorizing the stockpiling of critical and strategic materials, and the bill was introduced by Congressman Steagall on May 30, 1940. By June 14 it had passed the House of Representatives and the next day a companion bill was passed by the Senate. The differences between the House and Senate versions were reconciled by the conference committee with little difficulty and the bill was signed by the President June 25, 1940, becoming Public No. 664, 76th Cong. Getting the legislation through was merely the beginning and, as it turned out later, the least of our problems. The "shotgun" had to be taken out of the corner and put to practical use.

THE WRIGHT PROPOSAL

The first test came about the middle of June, when Mr. Knudsen asked Mr. Jones if RFC would finance Wright Aeronautical Corporation in the construction and operation of a large airplane engine plant to be located near Cincinnati, Ohio. The plant was to cost approximately $40,000,000 and the working capital requirements were expected to run into many more millions. Accompanying his request, Mr. Knudsen submitted to Mr. Jones a proposed form of financing agreement which had been prepared by his staff, suggesting that this not only be used in the Wright case but adopted as a standard procedure for the financing of all defense plants where government money was required.

The proposed agreement pointed clearly to the troubles that lay ahead. It also demonstrated that with a little imagination and a few friends placed in the right spots, war could be made to yield blessings as well as tragedies.

The proposed agreement provided, in brief, that the RFC could lend the manufacturer 100 per cent of the cost of the plant at an interest rate of 3 per cent per annum, the loan to be secured by a mortgage on the plant. The plant, however, was to constitute the sole security and it was expressly provided that there should be no recourse whatsoever against the manufacturer for the money borrowed, "it being expressly agreed and understood that the credit of the borrower shall not be deemed pledged to the payment of said indebtedness." The loan was to be without maturity and repayments were to be made solely out of an agreed portion of the sales price to the Government of the articles manufactured in the plant, this amount to be included in and added to the price paid by the Government for the articles bought. In other words, the manufacturer was to borrow from the RFC without pledging his own credit in any way, his loan would be repaid by the Army or Navy or other Government agency needing his product, and the manufacturer would end up owning the plant free and clear of all liens and encumbrances.

The agreement further provided that the RFC would lend all necessary working capital without any interest whatsoever, such loan likewise to be on a non-recourse basis and to be repaid solely from the proceeds of sales.

Mr. Jones turned the proposed agreement over to Mr. H. Mulligan, Treasurer of the RFC, Mr. Russell Snodgrass, then an Assistant General Counsel working on railroad matters, and myself, requesting that we let him have our views. We were all equally shocked by the complete disregard of the Government's interest. At that time, Public No. 664 had not yet become law but the bill had passed both Houses and there was no doubt about its ultimate approval. Neither Mr. Mulligan nor Mr. Snodgrass was familiar with this bill, but after I called it to their attention, they readily agreed with me that the method of financing which it authorized would be far preferable to that suggested by Mr. Knudsen, and we made our recommendations to Mr. Jones accordingly. The arguments I gave Mr. Jones orally at the time in favor of Government ownership or lease were later set forth in a written memorandum to him dated June 29, 1940.

Mr. Jones listened to our arguments without committing himself and then called Mr. Knudsen over the telephone, outlining the program we had suggested. While I could hear only one side of the telephone conversation, it was apparent that Mr. Knudsen was objecting vigorously. The meeting broke up without any conclusions having been reached, and a few days later Mr. Jones sent me a copy of a letter dated June 20, 1940, to Mr. M. B. Gordon, Vice-President of Wright Aeronautical Corporation, advising that the RFC would provide the necessary financing substantially in accordance with Mr. Knudsen's proposal, except that the loan would mature in eight years and bear interest at 4 per cent per annum instead of 3 per cent.

A few days later, Mr. Gordon and Mr. Harry Hotchkiss, his attorney, came to Mr. Jones' office for the purpose of working out the details of the financing, and Mr. Jones called me in. Mr. Gordon was not satisfied with the deal. It is true that the effect of the deal was to make Wright a gift of the plant, in addition to the profits it would make on the sale of airplane engines, but he wanted the gift to be tax-free. The mortgage amortization payments, which were to be loaded into the price of the airplane engines, would increase Wright's profits and its income tax would therefore be substantial unless it could offset this income by greatly accelerating the depreciation rate on the plant. The Treasury Department depreciation schedules for a plant of this kind allowed a maximum of not more than 4 per cent per annum on buildings of the type contemplated, while the allowance for standard machinery ran from 6 to 8 per cent. To accomplish Mr. Gordon's purpose, the whole works would have to be depreciated over the eight-year period. Moreover, the profit limitation imposed by the Vinson-Trammel Act was still in effect. The plant might be included in calculating the profits allowable on the contract for the manufacturers of engines. Wright wanted all the profits in cash.

I pointed out that if the Government held the title to the plant, there would be no income tax problem because the plant would not constitute income and that moreover, if the amortization payments, which were to be loaded into the price of the engines, should be paid back to the Government in the form of rent for the use of the plant, they could be deducted as expense for income tax purposes. I further suggested that if Wright thought it might need the plant after the war, we would consider the inclusion of an option provision in the lease contract which would permit Wright to buy the plant, on reasonable terms, at the end of the emergency. I further pointed out that, for flexible operations, it might be necessary quite often to shift machinery around from one plant to another, including the plants of suppliers and sub-contractors as well as Wright's own plant at Paterson, New Jersey, and that this could be very simply arranged if the RFC (or a subsidiary to be organized for the purpose) should own the machinery, for all that would be necessary for the protection of title would be to fasten on each machine a plate stating that the machine was the property of the U. S. Government, but if the money should be borrowed and a mortgage executed there would be problems of chattel mortgage releases and recordings every time a machine was moved over state lines. Mr. Hotchkiss indicated a very decided interest in my suggestions, but Mr. Gordon did not take kindly to them. He stated that he was very strongly in accord with Mr. Knudsen's policy that there should be no Government ownership of plants, even though the Government did put up all the money. I pointed out that as Congress had expressly authorized Government ownership in Public 664, it seemed to me that Mr. Knudsen's policy was in conflict with Congress's policy. Mr. Gordon raised the further objection that even if we should give Wright an option, Wright should not be placed in a position where it might have to buy a plant it did not need in order to keep its "know-how," which had gone into the construction of the plant, from passing into the hands of competitors. I asked him what he would propose doing with the plant at the end of the emergency if he found that he did not need it for normal peacetime operations. He replied, "We will pull the roof off and let the rain come in," expressing the basic philosophy of the opponents of Government title.

The solution to the tax problem was finally discovered by Mr. Hotchkiss. He produced a ruling of the Bureau of Internal Revenue holding, in effect, that where land is leased for business purposes and a building constructed on it, the building may be amortized for tax purposes over the period of the lease—a perfectly sound ruling as, at the end of the lease, title to the building reverts to the owner of the land. He outlined his proposal, which was briefly as follows:

1. RFC, pursuant to Public 664, would organize a subsidiary corporation to be known as "Defense Plant Corporation," to take title to the plant site, which was to consist of approximately 200 acres of land and to cost approximately $200,000.

2. Wright Aeronautical Corporation would organize an Ohio subsidiary with a nominal capital stock in order to insulate itself from financial liability.

3. The Wright subsidiary would lease the plant site from Defense Plant Corporation for a period of eight years at a rental equal to 4 per cent per annum of the estimated cost of the site. The subsidiary would then borrow from the RFC 100 per cent of the cost of the plant and machinery and erect the plant on the leased land.

4. $800 would be added to the price of each airplane engine manufactured and sold to the Government, and for every engine sold this amount would be applied to the repayment of RFC's loan (the $800 figure was arrived at by dividing the total amount of the RFC loan by the number of engines estimated to be produced over the eight-year period), so that the loan would be completely amortized at the end of that time.

Thus, the Army or Navy would pay off Wright's loan and Wright would be able to depreciate the plant over the period of eight years. However, at the end of the lease Wright would only own the plant and machinery, while Defense Plant Corporation would own the land on which it was located, and title to the plant would revert to Defense Plant Corporation. This should not be permitted to happen. The problem was met very simply by adding a further provision under which Wright would be given an option to buy the plant site from Defense Plant Corporation at the end of the eight-year period at its original cost of $200,000.

So for a $200,000 investment, Wright, without further risk on its part, would acquire a plant which had cost the Government $40,000,000 and at the same time would avoid paying any income tax whatsoever on the remaining $39,800,000 of value.

One problem still remained—how to eliminate the $800 per engine in determining the profit limitations under the Vinson-Trammel Act. This was solved with equal simplicity. The Wright Company would sub-lease the plant from its subsidiary. The parent company would sign the supplies contract and manufacture the engines. The $800 would be paid over to the subsidiary as rent, thus offsetting the additional income with an equal expense item.

I protested that such a deal would certainly not protect the Government's interest. However, it looked as though there was a good chance of RFC getting its money back with interest, even if payment did come by a transfer of funds from one pocket of the Government to another; so Mr. Jones instructed me to draw up the appropriate resolutions for adoption by the Board of Directors of the RFC putting the deal into effect. As one RFC director expressed it, "We have got to trade with other Government agencies just as hard as we trade with outsiders. It's up to them to look after themselves. RFC's job is to get *its* money back."

The resolution was duly drawn in accordance with Mr. Jones's instructions. However, at the request of the Wright people the maturity date of the loan was reduced from eight years to five years with a proviso that in the event Congress should not prior to December 1, 1940, adopt legislation which would permit the plant to be depreciated over a five-year period for income tax purposes, the maturity date should be extended to eight years. The amortization figure of $800 per engine was also translated to "take-off" horse power to allow for flexibility in the event the horse power of the engines should be increased or decreased from the 1500 horse power capacity originally contemplated.

A DISSENT

On August 7 I presented the resolution to the Board of Directors of the RFC, stating that it had been drawn in accordance with Mr. Jones's directions but that I was unwilling to initial it or otherwise indicate my approval. The reasons for my position were set forth in a written memorandum which is as follows:

August 7, 1940.

Memorandum Re Loan to
Wright Aeronautical Corporation of Ohio

I am unwilling to initial the resolution authorizing this loan for the following reasons:

1. The program contemplates that there will be added to the price of engines sold to the Army and Navy by Wright Aeronautical Corporation (the Parent Company) an amount estimated to be sufficient to amortize the loan, together with the interest, over the period of five years, upon an estimated production of approximately 40,000 engines. The credit of the Parent Company will not be involved directly or indirectly nor will the credit of Wright Aeronautical Corporation of Ohio (the Subsidiary) be involved, as it may discharge the loan by transferring the plant to RFC at whatever value the plant may have at the time of the transfer. In reality, therefore, the Army and Navy, rather than the borrower, will be paying off the money borrowed from RFC, and the plant will belong to the Subsidiary free and clear when the required number of engines has been produced. Notwithstanding the fact that the Parent Company will not be hazarding its credit or using its own property, it will receive net profits on the engines sold to the Government at the full rates allowed by law and will, in addition, receive the plant as a donation by reason of its ownership of the stock of the Subsidiary. It seems to me, therefore, that the plant will constitute additional profit on the engines sold over and above that permitted by law. I cannot find any statutory authority under which either the RFC or the Army or Navy may make donations of plants or equipment in connection with defense contracts.

2. The plant site is to be acquired by a subsidiary of RFC and leased to the Wright Subsidiary, and the plant will be constructed and equipped with money loaned by the RFC directly to the Wright Subsidiary, the Wright Subsidiary in turn leasing the plant to the Parent Company at a rental sufficient to amortize the loan and pay the rental for the plant site. The purpose of this procedure is to obtain concessions from the Bureau of Internal Revenue with reference to depreciation for tax purposes and allowances under the statutes limiting profits which would not be granted to the Parent Company if it acted directly. Under existing law amortization of plant facilities, to the extent included in the price paid by the Government for the engines, could not be taken into consideration as a part of the "contract price" on which the profit percentage is based. However, under existing regulations, rental is treated as an expense; and it would therefore appear that, by permitting the Parent Company to pay the amortization in the form of rent to its Subsidiary, the "contract price" may be increased, in violation of the clear legislative intent. However, the Bureau of Internal Revenue has not yet ruled on this question. The use of subsidiary corporations for the purpose of defeating legislative intent has been consistently condemned by the courts.

3. I do not think that the RFC is justified in taking the position that the price to be paid for the engines is entirely a responsibility of the Army and Navy and that the depreciation to be allowed for income tax or other purposes is entirely the responsibility of the Bureau of Internal Revenue. RFC has set up its loan in such a way as to enable these concessions to be obtained. It is further agreeing to extend the maturity of its loan from five years to eight years if this is necessary to enable the Wright Subsidiary to get the maximum depreciation allowed, although the result would

be to decrease materially the payments per engine to be applied on the loan.

[s] *C. J. Durr,*
Assistant General Counsel.

The resolution was unanimously adopted over my objections, but later in the afternoon at the request of the directors Mr. Hamilton, the General Counsel, initialed it.

WRIGHT RECONSIDERS: DPC IS ORGANIZED

About a week later Mr. Hotchkiss came by my office and stated that the deal approved on the 7th was all off. I asked him why, and he replied that some people on the "Hill," meaning members of Congress, had heard about it and had called Knudsen, "raising hell" about giving away plants paid for by the Government; that Knudsen therefore told Wright that the deal would have to be called off. I suggested to Mr. Hotchkiss that he reconsider the lease arrangement. He stated that he was inclined to believe now that the lease method would afford the most satisfactory course of procedure, as it was simple and would avoid the criticism that had been raised. However, he said that Mr. Knudsen was still firm in his position that there should be no Government title and that Knudsen's staff was attempting to work out an alternative plan.

Several days after the adoption of the resolution authorizing the loan to Wright, Mr. Emil Schram, who was then Chairman of the Board of Directors of the RFC, called me to his office and stated that he had been doing some further thinking about what I had said at the directors' meeting and was inclined to believe that I was right. He asked me to let him have a memorandum setting forth more fully my arguments in support of the lease arrangement, and I gave him a copy of my memorandum to Mr. Jones of June 29, 1940. Mr. Schram was convinced, and with his blessing we proceeded with the organization of the Defense Plant Corporation. Mr. Livingston drew the charter and it was formally approved by the directors of the RFC on August 22, 1940. The next day Mr. Schram called me over the telephone and said that he wanted to make the new corporation a "Boy Scout" organization as far as he could; that the five RFC directors and Mr. Jones and Mr. Hamilton had been appointed as directors of the new corporation, but that he had arranged to have Mr. John W. Snyder and Mr. R. L. Lindquist added to the Board, that he (Schram) was to be President, Mr. Snyder, Vice-President, A. T. Hobson, Secretary, and Harry Sullivan, Treasurer; and that I had been named as General Counsel, and that I could designate such assistant general counsels as I saw fit. Accordingly, I named Mr. Klagsbrunn and Mr. Livingston as assistant general counsels.

Mr. Snyder was Manager of the St. Louis Loan Agency of the RFC and Mr. Lindquist was Chief Auditor. Both of these men were independent of RFC's Examining Division and hence could be expected to be free of that Division's habits of thought with reference to balance sheets, earning statements, and collateral. Moreover, Mr. Snyder held a reserve commission as Colonel in the Army and retained a great interest in military affairs. He had the belief, shared by Mr. Lindquist, that the country was in danger and that airplanes were, for the moment, more important than interest collections or balance sheets. Sullivan was Assistant Treasurer of RFC, and Hobson, Assistant Secretary. Hobson, particularly, was independent in his thinking and had on numerous occasions expressed his concern that RFC's banker psychology would keep us from getting ready for war.

In the early part of September Mr. Hotchkiss was back in my office again. He said that the options which Wright had taken on the plant site were about to expire and that Wright did not have the money with which to take them up; that the Defense Commission was still working on its new plan and he did not know how long it would be before the new plan would be ready. I told Mr. Hotchkiss that as the Defense Plant Corporation had authority to buy real estate it could take up the options and agree to sell the land back to Wright, at actual cost, after the Defense Commission's new procedure was ready. He welcomed the suggestion, so a resolution authorizing the purchase of the plant site was approved by the Board of Directors of DPC on September 12, 1940, and all the options were taken up shortly thereafter. At about the same time, DPC also took up options on land near Buffalo, New York, which the Curtiss-Wright Corporation (the parent corporation of Wright Aeronautical Corporation) had selected as a site for a proposed airplane plant.

A few days later Mr. Hotchkiss and Mr. Gordon were again in my office. Mr. Gordon stated that the Defense Commission's new plan was still far from being ready and he was very much concerned about the delay in placing his orders for machinery, as it would require the machine tool manufacturers several months to make the machinery even after the orders were placed, and he was afraid that, even after his buildings were completed, he would have a long wait for the machinery before he could start operations. I pointed out that the DPC had authority to buy machinery and that if Wright would go ahead and place its machinery orders, DPC could protect Wright by agreeing to take off its hands, at cost, any machinery that was ready for delivery before the Defense Commission had worked out its plan. He said that if DPC would do this it would save Wright many months of delay. Accordingly, a very simple agreement, in letter form, was drafted and executed and Wright proceeded to place its machine tool orders.

The Packard, Barnes, and Baldwin Leases

It is necessary here to go back a few months and pick up some further threads of the story. About the same time that the Defense Commission approved the program for the manufacture of air-cooled engines by Wright Aeronautical Corporation, it also requested Packard Motor Car Company to expand its plant and equipment for the manufacture of Merlin Rolls-Royce engines, an air-cooled engine of British design. This program contemplated that the United Kingdom would purchase approximately two-thirds of the engines to be manufactured by Packard, and the United States Army about one-third, the plant facilities to be financed by the United States and the United Kingdom in a corresponding ratio, the share of the United States to be about $8,000,000.

Mr. Henry E. Bodman, attorney for Packard, came to see Mr. Jones to discuss the financing of the U. S. Government's part of the program and Mr. Jones referred him to me. I have no record of the exact date he first came to my office but my recollection is that it was the latter part of June or the early part of July. Mr. Bodman stated in effect that Packard was ready to manufacture such engines as this Government or the British might want but that Packard was in the automobile business and not in the airplane engine business and it could not afford to put up its own money for the machinery and plant expansion needed for only temporary operations. He further said, and I will quote his words as nearly as I can remember them:

> Mr. Knudsen wants us to do our financing substantially along the lines of the deal which he is proposing for Wright. However, I remember the Congressional investigations which followed the Liberty Motor deal[2] after the last war. Investigations are unpleasant and indictments are still more unpleasant whether or not there are convictions, and I do not propose to let my clients place themselves in a position where they may have to defend themselves before a Congressional committee or even possibly against an indictment. Packard expects to make a profit but it wants to make that profit above the table and not take a concealed bonus on the side in the form of a hand-out of plant or machinery. If this Government and the British will put up the money for the plant and machinery we are ready to go ahead and do the job.

I explained the proposed lease arrangement to Mr. Bodman and he stated that he was confident we could agree on a satisfactory contract along that line. Accordingly, we reported

[2] For a discussion of this deal see report of Charles Evans Hughes to the Attorney General dated October 25, 1918 (*Congressional Record*, Vol. 57, Part 1, p. 883, at p. 906). This points out that Packard made a profit of $8,000,000 on 6000 engines over a period of a year and 5 months. However, Packard was using its own plant having an estimated value of $5,500,000.

to Mr. Jones and he asked Mr. Mulligan to work with us in drawing the contract. I also asked Mr. Livingston to join in the negotiations.

Within a couple of days we had come to a substantial agreement on the contract, and Mr. Bodman left for Detroit, stating that he wanted to go over it more carefully in his office, but that, in any event, Packard would not be ready to sign it until it had completed negotiations of its supplies contracts both with the British and the United States Army. These two supplies contracts were executed by September 3, 1940, and on the same date DPC and Packard signed a contract for the plant expansion and machinery. A few days later the DPC had one of its engineers and an accountant on the job, and Packard was ordering its machinery.

Now, four years later, when we are accepting "lend-lease" with our Allies as a matter of course, it might be interesting to digress for an illustration of how our views have changed.

As I stated, Packard was to produce engines for the British as well as for the American Army, and the British were to provide their proportionate part of the money for the plant expansion. As Packard could not feasibly segregate the British production from the American production, the lease agreement provided that DPC's facilities might be used to manufacture engines for the British, and British facilities used to manufacture engines for the United States Army. Questions were immediately raised on all sides as to whether this constituted a violation of the Neutrality Act or the Johnson Act. It was my belief that neither act would be violated, and I wrote an opinion to this effect. Nevertheless, before the necessary approvals to the agreement could be obtained, all reference to the United Kingdom had to be stricken. In the agreement as finally signed, the United Kingdom was anonymous, it being merely provided that the DPC-owned facilities might be used to manufacture engines for "others."

Following the Packard negotiations, lease contracts were concluded in short order with J. F. and John Barnes Company of Rockford, Illinois, for a machine tool manufacturing plant; with Continental Motors for machinery to be used in the manufacture of tank engines; and with Baldwin Locomotive Works for machinery to be used in building tanks. Our experience with Packard, Barnes, and Continental Motors, served to give us a pretty good understanding of the manufacturers' problems, and the negotiation with Baldwin required little more than an hour after the War Department had given its final approval. The Baldwin people came to the RFC in the morning; they left on the afternoon train with an executed contract, and the next day machinery orders were being placed.

The Defense Plant Corporation procedure had proved itself as a simple and speedy method of financing plant expansion and one which reasonable manufacturers were willing to accept as fair. Mr. Knudsen raised no objection to the Packard, Continental, and Baldwin contracts because none of the plants involved constituted a "threat" to an established industry in the United States. There was no established tank industry, and Packard was making an engine of British design under a limited British license. The Barnes people were referred to us informally by an Ordnance officer who had enough imagination to see we were going to need a tremendous number of machine guns and that machine guns could not be made without machine tools. The Barnes company specialized in the manufacture of a type of machine tool that was essential for making machine guns. So far as I can recall, it was the only contract ever signed by DPC without a letter of "necessity" from the Army, Navy, Defense Commission (or its successors, the OPM and WPB) or some other agency of the Government charged with responsibility for some phase of the defense program.

The Emergency Plant Facilities Contract

While Defense Plant Corporation was taking up the options for Wright Aeronautical and Curtiss-Wright and completing the financing for Packard, Continental Motors, Barnes, and Baldwin, the Defense Commission was working on its new setup. The first draft, designated as the "Emergency Plant Facilities Contract," was completed on August 23, 1940. It was largely the work of Mr. Frederick M. Eaton, attorney for Mr. Knudsen, and Mr. Robert Proctor, legal adviser to Under Secretary of War Patterson. Proctor came from the Boston law firm of Choate, Hall, and Stewart, and had made his services available to the Government for ninety days. The plan embodied in the first and subsequent drafts of the "Emergency Plant Facilities Contract" became generally known as the "Eaton-Proctor plan."

It was clearly the intention of the proposed contract to hew as closely as possible to the original plan proposed by Mr. Knudsen, but to avoid the criticism that the Government was making a gift of plants to private industry. The way was also paved for banks to get a share in the profits of the defense program. Reimbursement for plant cost by increasing the price of the product sold to the Government was abandoned. Instead, the Government was to make a direct contract with the manufacturer to reimburse him for the cost of his plant in fixed annual installments over a period of five years, irrespective of the amount of the manufacturer's production. Title was to remain in the manufacturer, but at the end of the contract period, the manufacturer would have the election of transferring title to the Government or retaining the plant and paying the Government its "fair value," to be determined by an appraisal at the time. This sounded reasonable enough on its face. However, the contract went on further and gave the appraisers a specific formula for determining "fair value":

For the purpose of the appraisal fair value shall be deemed to be the value which the Emergency Plant Facilities have to the Contractor without regard to their original cost and considering only the prospective earning power which they will add to the Contractor's entire plant under the circumstances then existing or reasonably to be foreseen, making due allowance for the expense which the Contractor must incur if they are to be adapted or converted to the Contractor's normal peacetime activities: provided that if the appraisers find that any removable items of the Facilities, as to which an open market normally exists, have a higher value in an open market sale then under the foregoing standard, such items shall be valued at such open market value. . . .

It was further provided that land, as distinguished from plant facilities, should be valued at actual cost.

In the event the manufacturer should elect to turn any plant facilities located on his own premises over to the Government rather than pay their "fair value," the Government was given the election of (a) removing the facilities and restoring the manufacturer's property "as nearly as may be in the same general condition as existed prior to the date of this contract," or (b) leaving the facilities in place provided this would not materially impede the contractor's "normal operations" and provided further that the contractor should have the right to use the facilities without cost "to the extent that such facilities have replaced other facilities of the Contractor and are necessary to enable him to conduct his normal operations."

The Government was further to agree that, with respect to any facilities removed by it, it would not sell or lease them to any other party without giving the manufacturer an opportunity to buy or lease at an equal price or rental.

The arrangement contemplated that the manufacturer might use the Emergency Plant Facilities Contract as the basis for borrowing the necessary funds from a commercial bank, the interest paid on the loan to be loaded into the price of its product as an element of cost.

The new program was reported to the press by Mr. John D. Biggers, of the Advisory Commission, as the solution to the problem of plant expansion and the New York *Times* of August 24 carried the story in full. Mr. Biggers was quoted as saying that the plan was agreed to after consultation with the RFC as well as the War, Navy, and Treasury Departments, and the Comptroller General. I do not know what official of the RFC was consulted. Mr. Schram assured me that he was not.

Although it was not contemplated that the RFC would make any loans on the basis of

Emergency Plant Facilities Contracts except in cases where bank credit might be denied, Mr. Eaton sent me a copy of the contract for my information. A day or so later, he called me over the telephone and asked what I thought of it. I told him that I had not an opportunity to study it carefully but offhand I had two general objections: (1) that the contract was so complicated it would take longer to work out the financial and legal problems involved than would be required to build the plant, and (2) that the Government's interest was not protected. Passing over the first objection, he asked why I felt that the Government's interest was not protected. I told him that I might possibly have misunderstood the provision for determining "fair value" and also the provision for determining the value of removable items. On the latter point, I stated that the words "as to which an open market normally exists" seemed to me to require that there be a regular list price for the particular items quoted by second-hand machinery dealers. He replied that my interpretation was correct. I then gave him the following illustrations to make certain that my understanding of the provisions was correct:

Example 1. Contractor A builds a plant costing $40,000,000 in order to manufacture goods to be sold to the Government. The contract is terminated at the end of two years, at which time the Government has reimbursed him for $16,000,000 leaving a $24,000,000 balance. A has a separate plant in which he proposes to continue peacetime production but desires to keep the new plant for peak manufacturing loads which occur only for a very short period of the year, so the new plant has a use value to A of only $1,000,000. B, an independent manufacturer, desires to acquire the plant and operate it at full capacity and is willing to pay $24,000,000, the full balance due from the Government. The Government must nevertheless permit A to keep the plant and must pay him the remaining $24,000,000 less the $1,000,000 use value.

Example 2. Upon termination of the contract above-mentioned there is movable machinery in the plant of a special type for which B makes a firm offer of $10,000,000. The machinery is not of a type listed by second-hand dealers. B's offer cannot be accepted but A must be allowed to retain the machinery at its use value of say, $100,000.

Mr. Eaton answered, "That's exactly what was intended." He stated that the purpose was to meet the criticism that manufacturers would receive a "windfall"; that there would be no windfall if the manufacturer should pay the value which the plant or equipment had to him, irrespective of what it might bring on the market. I pointed out to him that this would deprive the Government of its right to salvage the maximum amount from its investment. He replied that the object was not to enable the Government to salvage its investment, but to keep the plant and equipment from falling into the hands of possible competitors and to discourage acquisition by the Government, which would be a temptation to Government operation. I told him I still felt very strongly that the Government's interest was not protected. He replied, "We must think in terms of the manufacturers' problems." I replied that I was perfectly willing to consider the manufacturers' problems but that as he and I were both working for the Government, it seemed to me we should think first in terms of the Government's interest.

OBSTACLES ARISE

As sympathetic as the draftsmen had been with the "manufacturers' problems," they had been guilty of one serious oversight. Suppose the manufacturer should elect to turn the facilities over to the Government rather than pay their "fair value" and then suppose the Government, instead of selling or leasing them to some other private manufacturer, should decide to operate them itself. The thought was shocking! If the Government wanted the manufacturers to help it get ready for war, it should assure them that it would never be guilty of any socialistic nonsense. The oversight was corrected in a draft of August 29, 1940, in which this clause was added:

The Government agrees, so far as it lawfully may, with respect to any facilities transferred to it or removed by it pursuant to this Article III that it will at no time use the same or any of them for business or commercial purposes.

The day after my conversation with Mr. Eaton, Mr. Proctor came by my office. In view of the fact that I had for several years been in charge of the Preferred Stock Section of the Legal Division of the RFC and consequently had some experience with banking problems, he wanted my opinion as to how the banks would regard the contract as a basis for loans. I told him that I had not carefully considered the contract from this standpoint, but certainly the banks would be willing to lend against a firm reimbursement agreement of the Government, as this would be the equivalent of lending against Government bonds at a much higher interest rate than the bonds themselves would carry. However, I did not think the agreement, as drawn, was airtight. For one thing, there was a law on the books that prohibited the assignment of Government contracts, so further legislation would be required. Moreover, the Constitution imposes a two-year limit on funds appropriated for the Army, and the contract contemplated reimbursement over a five-year period. I pointed out several other less serious defects. Mr. Proctor thanked me for my suggestions. I told him that it did not seem to me that the contract properly safeguarded the Government's interest, and asked if he was interested in my comments and suggestions along that line. He replied that he was not.

The income tax problem still had to be met. The difference between the "fair value" of the plant retained by the manufacturer and the cost of the plant less depreciation at normal rates would still result in pretty sizable tax. Accordingly, a provision was inserted in the Excess Profits Bill introduced on August 27, 1940 (H.R. 10413), permitting plants constructed for defense purposes to be amortized over a period of five years. A little later a bill was introduced which would permit the assignment of Government contracts of the type contemplated.

The Treasury Department, however, became annoying. It suggested to Congress that if manufacturers were to be permitted to amortize, over a period of five years, plants largely paid for by the Government either through such arrangements as Emergency Plant Facilities Contract or by increasing the cost of supplies bought by the Government, there should be some assurance that after the emergency the plants would not be destroyed but would be kept in existence against the possibility of future need. The bill was amended accordingly and the battle began. Congress was accused of being the "bottleneck" of the defense program. The Defense Commission had worked out an acceptable procedure under which manufacturers were willing to expand their plants, and the Treasury Department, with strong Congressional support, was trying to scuttle it. Congress had already evidenced its lack of co-operation by reducing the Vinson-Trammell Act profit limit on shipbuilding contracts from 12 per cent to 8 and 10 per cent.[3]

If we were to get production, all profit limitations had to be removed.[4] The National Association of Manufacturers urged adoption of the five-year amortization provisions, without restrictions on plant disposal, to "remove a serious bottleneck now holding back progress in the defense program." Mr. Knudsen testified before a joint committee of the Senate and House that defense contracts were not being signed as rapidly as desired because of uncertainty over the amortization and tax situation, and urged immediate action. Assistant Secretary of the Navy Compton testified that manufacturers were absolutely refusing to take vital Navy contracts under the maximum

[3] Mr. Eaton and Captain Sydney Krause, also of the Defense Commission, appeared before the Senate Naval Affairs Committee on June 19, 1940, in opposition to any reduction in the profit limitations. According to the New York *Times* of June 20, 1940:

"Captain Krause and Mr. Eaton replied, according to Mr. (Senator) Walsh, that there had been no direct complaints from manufacturers (against the proposed reduction of profits), but the limitations would tend to make them *'less eager'* to co-operate in the necessary production. *Their present attitude might become one of hesitancy or resistance, the witness said, if the profits problems were to be attacked too vigorously*." (Italics supplied.)

[4] The philosophy that national defense should be sought in profits, rather than patriotism, was warmly advocated by Louis Johnson, Assistant Secretary of War, in a speech to the graduating class of the Army War College, in which he expressed strong disapproval of the Walsh Bill plan to reduce profits. "We are," he said, "quite definitely approaching the moment when, through money—profits—spent by American industry, the United States Army and Navy are going to be able to reach up into the sky and reach their target." (New York *Times*, June 20, 1940.)

profit limitation of 8 per cent. He gave specific cases of aircraft engine plant expansion being held up because of uncertainty as to what rate of amortization would be applied. Secretary of War Stimson absolved the Army, the Defense Commission, and industry itself from any responsibility for delay in the program, stating that this was chiefly due to the "element of uncertainty" over taxes and over allowances for amortization of new plants built for defense purposes. Mr. Biggers and other defense officials and representatives of industry testified along similar lines.

While Congress was conducting hearings, word of the contract between Defense Plant Corporation and Packard trickled through to representatives of the aircraft industry. They began to drift into the RFC offices and ask for further information: Grumman, Beach, Consolidated, North American, Douglas, and others. They read over the Packard contract and thought it made sense. They were ready to proceed along that line. We told them that Defense Plant Corporation was ready to go ahead and all that was needed was the approval of the Defense Commission. They went to see Mr. Knudsen, Mr. Eaton, and others in the Defense Commission and returned in despair. Mr. Knudsen was not going to have any "Government title." They would have to wait until Congress had acted and the Defense Commission's plan was ready. I recall particularly the bitterness expressed by an official of Douglas. I asked him if he was worried about the idea of the Government having title. He replied in substance:

> I don't give a damn about Government title. If the Government puts up the money it seems to me it ought to have title. As I see the situation, if the country is going socialistic when the defense program is over, Douglas can't stop it by a contract. If it is not going socialistic, I figure that we can get our hands on the plant on some reasonable basis if we need it when the program is over. We would like to have an option to buy the plant on reasonable terms, but Government title doesn't bother me a bit. In fact, I would rather have it that way because it will avoid the income tax problems Congress is now arguing about. All I want is to get busy and build airplanes. The aviation industry is being accused of holding up the program because it won't expand until Congress adopts the five-year amortization provisions. As far as I am concerned, I don't give a damn what Congress does about the tax bill if the Defense Commission will only let us go ahead on a contract similar to Packard's.

Meanwhile, the Defense Commission's lawyers, with the advice and assistance of attorneys for several of our biggest banks, were rewriting the Emergency Plant Facilities Contract in an effort to make it entirely acceptable to the banks. Some slight pressure toward the protection of the Government was apparently being exerted somewhere (*my* guess is that this came from Mr. David Ginsburg, who was legal adviser to Mr. Leon Henderson). The draft of September 20 eliminated the provision giving the manufacturer the right to acquire the plant at "fair value" and substituted instead a provision fixing the price at original cost less depreciation at a rate to be agreed upon in advance and included in the contract. The problem arising out of the two-year limitation on appropriations for the Army was taken care of by providing that if, within ninety days prior to the close of any fiscal year, Congress should not have appropriated the funds necessary to meet the reimbursement installments due from the Government for subsequent years, then the entire contract would terminate, and the balance of all reimbursement payments would become immediately due and payable. This in practical effect made existing appropriations collateral for the Government's reimbursement agreements. For example, suppose the plant to be constructed should cost $20,000,000. Under the reimbursement agreement, this was to be repaid to the manufacturer at the rate of $4,000,000 per year. However, the Army or Navy would have to set aside $20,000,000 of its own appropriations against the possibility that Congress would not appropriate for the installments due in subsequent years. It could not set aside only $4,000,000 and use the remaining $16,000,000 to buy airplanes, machine guns, or other needed equipment. As has been previously stated, it was contemplated that interest paid on funds borrowed against an EPF Contract would be allowed as an item of cost in calculating the price of products sold to the Government. The net result therefore, was that the Army and Navy were being required to freeze their own appropriations and pay interest on them.

WRIGHT RETURNS

About the middle of September 1940 Mr. Burdette Wright, Vice-President of the Curtiss-Wright Corporation, called on me. He said that he was greatly worried by the delay in getting the Emergency Plant Facilities Contract ready. He stated that he was very anxious to begin construction of the airplane plant approved for his company at Buffalo, that sometimes Buffalo experienced very cold weather in October and if a cold spell should come before the foundations for the new plant were poured it might mean that all construction would have to be postponed until spring. He referred to the assistance Defense Plant Corporation had previously given Curtiss-Wright and Wright Aeronautical in taking up options on their plant sites and in placing machine tool orders, and expressed the hope that we could figure out some way of helping him out of his present difficulty. I told him I could see no solution unless he could persuade Mr. Knudsen to let him go along with a Defense Plant lease. He replied that, personally, he had never had any objection to the Defense Plant procedure, but on the contrary thought it was fair and liked its simplicity and freedom from income tax problems. I suggested that he might be able to persuade Mr. Knudsen to go along if we should draw up a Defense Plant lease substantially along the lines of the Packard contract and add a provision giving Curtiss-Wright the right to pay off the DPC and refinance under the Emergency Plant Facilities Contract at any time within nine months if the EPF Contract should be ready within that period. Mr. Wright expressed confidence that Mr. Knudsen would agree to an arrangement of this kind and immediately telephoned to Mr. Hotchkiss in New York, requesting that he join us in Washington the next morning for the purpose of drawing the contract.

That night Klagsbrunn and I worked up a draft of a contract along the lines of my discussion with Mr. Wright. The next morning Mr. Wright and Mr. Hotchkiss went over this draft, suggested a few changes, and within a couple of hours the contract was in final form and ready for signature, only Mr. Knudsen's approval being required. Mr. Wright left for Mr. Knudsen's office, taking a copy of the proposed contract with him, and expressing complete confidence that Mr. Knudsen's approval would be obtained and the contract signed before the day was over. He returned in the afternoon looking very discouraged. Mr. Knudsen had refused to give his approval, stating that the Emergency Plant Facilities Contract would soon be ready and repeating his insistence that there should be no Government title.

On September 26 the Senate and House conferees finally came to an agreement which eliminated the Treasury Department's provision for the preservation of the plants after the emergency. The New York *Times* of September 27 carried the story: "Defense Commissioners," it said, "told the Senate Finance Committee during hearings on the measure that once the amortization provisions, minus the element of Government control over disposition of new plants, were adopted, there would be no further question about private industry enlisting wholeheartedly in the defense program." The price of co-operation was being paid!

On October 1, 1940, the conference report was approved by both the Senate and the House. The Bill was signed by the President on October 8, and on October 10 the Emergency Plant Facilities Contract was ready for use. The final form followed in substance the pattern of the September 20 draft, except that the reimbursement payments from the Government, instead of being made in five annual installments, were to be made in sixty monthly installments.

Bendix and Wright

Wright Aeronautical Corporation was among the first to receive an EPF Contract signed by the Army. Mr. Gordon brought it over to the RFC and asked that RFC lend the money. He was told that RFC was not in competition with commercial banks and that he should go to the bank for his financing; that if the banks should for any reason refuse to let him have the money, he could talk to us again. He said that he did not want to go to a bank but would prefer to take his chances with the Government; that his company was comparatively in its infancy and he did not want to get in the clutches of some bank that might want to dictate the company's business policies; that he had been somewhat skeptical of the Government when he first came to Washington but in view of his experiences he was convinced that the Government was primarily interested in getting the production job done and he wanted to stick with the Government. He was told again that the RFC would not consider making a loan on an EPF Contract until the banks had turned it down. He then said that while he had opposed the idea of Government title at the beginning, he would rather get his financing through a DPC contract than go to the banks; that after further consideration he had concluded that the DPC procedure was fair after all and he liked its simplicity. We told Mr. Gordon, however, that as long as Mr. Knudsen persisted in his objection there was nothing he could do except go to the banks.

The afternoon of the same day, Mr. Palmer, Vice-President and Treasurer of Bendix Aviation Corporation, came over, accompanied by his attorney and bringing an EPF Contract on which he asked for an RFC loan. He likewise was told that he would have to go to a bank for the money. Mr. Palmer also expressed an unwillingness to borrow from a bank. He said, moreover, that he was far from happy over the EPF Contract; that under the contract offered him, the Government would reimburse Bendix 100 per cent for the cost of a plant which would be used for non-Government as well as for Government production; that from an operating standpoint all of Bendix's products had to be made on the same assembly lines and when Bendix made a panel instrument or some other type of equipment it could never be sure whether it would end up in a U. S. Army plane, a commercial airplane, or a plane owned by the British or some South American government, and that Bendix did not want to face criticism, which would inevitably come some day, that it was using Government money to build a plant which would be operated in part for its own general business purposes. He asked if there was not some other method of financing available. I mentioned the DPC setup, but told him that that was out of the question because of Mr. Knudsen's position. Nevertheless, he insisted upon seeing a specimen form of DPC contract, which I showed him. He read it very carefully and spent an hour or more in my office discussing the various provisions of the contract in detail. At the end of that time, he said that the DPC setup was the answer to his problem and that he was certain he could get Mr. Knudsen's approval.

Now that we had the support both of Wright and Bendix, I thought the time was opportune to try to persuade Mr. Jones to bring his influence to bear in favor of the DPC procedure. While Mr. Jones had approved the Packard contract he had never shown any enthusiasm for the Defense Plant Corporation procedure or, for that matter, for the defense program. At that time he could not see that what was happening in Europe could possibly menace us and had so expressed himself in my presence on several occasions. Moreover, it was not sound banking to put up money for emergency plants. He had only recently been appointed Secretary of Commerce, and we had taken advantage of his absorption in his new duties to get the Defense Plant Corporation under way and the Packard, Continental, Barnes, and Baldwin contracts signed. While Mr. Schram did see the menace of European developments and supported us, he never felt that his position in the RFC was strong enough to warrant him in "sticking his neck out" and battling for the DPC with the Defense Commission or the other Government agencies. Very early in the program, he told Snyder, Klagsbrunn, Lindquist, Livingston, and myself, in effect, "I can't stick my neck out too far. You fellows go ahead and do what you think ought to be done and if you get in trouble you can say you were acting with the approval of the Chairman of the RFC." There was no hope of beating down Mr. Knudsen's opposition unless Mr. Jones could be persuaded to help.

I asked Mr. Palmer and Mr. Gordon to go to see Mr. Jones with me and we had a lengthy session with him, Mr. Gordon arguing as strongly for the DPC setup as he had argued against it in July and August. Mr. Jones did not commit himself, but stated that he would think the matter over.

THE WAR DEPARTMENT JOINS IN

The next morning Mr. Jones called and said that he had made an appointment for me to talk with Secretary Stimson. Mr. Gordon went over to the War Department with me. Secretary Stimson was not there but one of his assistants, whose name I do not recall, took charge of the meeting. There were several other representatives of the War Department present but I do not now recall the names of any of them except Mr. Proctor. Mr. Gordon led off the discussion. He said that first of all he wanted to make entirely clear the reasons for the delay in getting the aviation expansion program under way. He outlined rather fully the history of his negotiations with the RFC and with Mr. Knudsen and others connected with the Defense Commission. He referred to the resolution of the RFC Board adopted August 7, and to the fact that the procedure provided for in that resolution had been abandoned because of Congressional criticism. "Frankly," he said, "I think now that the Congressmen who objected were right. We were getting more than we were entitled to. I am convinced now that the lease setup is fair, and it is certainly the simplest and speediest method of financing that has so far been presented, and we are ready to go ahead on that setup. I don't want to have to waste another six months negotiating with banks." I then explained the DPC procedure and outlined the basic provisions of the contracts which had been executed. Secretary Stimson's assistant, who was in charge of the meeting, expressed the view that the setup I had described sounded reasonable to him. He asked Mr. Proctor if he knew of any reasons why it would not work. Much to my surprise Mr. Proctor replied that he did not. After further general discussion, all of the War Department representatives present expressed themselves as being favorable to the lease procedure. Mr. Gordon and I were told, however, that plant expansion came under the jurisdiction of Under Secretary Patterson who was out of town but was expected back that night; that the matter would be taken up with him as soon as he returned.

The next morning, Patterson telephoned me and asked if I could come over to his office right away. I assumed that he wanted further information about the DPC procedure so I took with me copies of some contracts that had been executed. Patterson called Mr. Proctor and asked him to come in. Then, much to my amazement, instead of asking questions about the DPC he launched into a very violent and intemperate attack on me. He charged me with "holding up the defense program" and with discrediting the Emergency Plant Facilities Contract with the banks. For a moment, I was too astonished to reply, but soon found my anger mounting to a pitch that equaled his. I told him I could not understand his charge that I was holding up the program as we had had a program ready since the end of June and had actually completed the financing on four plants, notwithstanding the difficulties that had been thrown in our way at every turn; that so far as I could find out, the Defense Plant Corporation was the only agency that had a constructive program or any record of accomplishment in plant financing. Moreover, I stated that I had not discredited the EPF Contract with the banks and that I had had no opportunity to discredit it with the banks even if I had desired to do so, but at that, personally, I thought that the contract could not be justified, that it disregarded the Government's interest and moreover, that it was so complicated and cumbersome that there would be endless delay in getting the defense program under way if it had to be relied on. I told him that while I had not expressed my opinion to any banks I had expressed it to the directors of the RFC and would continue to do so. He replied that he was something of a lawyer himself and that he had gone over the contract very carefully and that it was all right and that, moreover, the lawyers for a dozen of the biggest banks in the country had gone over it and given their approval. I told him that I had the greatest respect for his legal ability but that it made no difference to me whether he or the lawyers of fifty banks thought it a good contract, my opinion about it remained the same.

There was no profit in continuing the discussion. Tempers were running too high on both sides, so I walked out. Before returning to the RFC, I went by another office in the War Department where I had another matter to take up. In a few minutes the phone rang. It was Judge Patterson. He stated that he was afraid he had been "hasty" and asked if I would come back to his office. I told him I would be glad to do so. When I entered his office, he started off by apologizing for losing his temper. He asked if I would have lunch with him so we could continue our discussion saying, "If you refuse I would not blame you. I am sorry I lost my temper but the thought of any further delay in getting the program going terrifies me. Frankly, I am not too happy about the EPF Contract but it is the only thing that the Defense Commission will approve. I am afraid I have been given some misinformation about your setup and I would like to know more about it."

We spent about two hours together at lunch and I gave him the story of the Defense Plant Corporation from the beginning, explaining in detail the provisions of the contracts which had been executed. He listened very attentively and when I had finished, said, "This is the first time I have heard that story. Your setup makes sense to me. Go ahead with Bendix and I will back you up one hundred per cent. Too many people are mixed up in the Wright matter for me to give you the go signal on that, but I will try to see if we can't arrange a joint meeting with the Defense Commission and get the whole problem threshed out."

I reported back to Mr. Jones the substance of my conversation with Judge Patterson. He said that Mr. Knudsen was coming by his office at about 6:30 to join him for dinner and asked that I come in about that time for a talk with Mr. Knudsen. Mr. Jones started the discussion by saying to me, "Cliff, you tell Mr. Knudsen what is wrong with his contract." I started out to try to tell him, but it was immediately apparent that there was little hope of making him understand the problem. His only response was "Our contract is a good contract. There is nothing wrong with it." I tried to explain the DPC lease to him, but with no more success. The conversation ended after a few minutes with Mr. Knudsen still insisting that the Emergency Plant Facilities Contract was a good contract and charging, as had Judge Patterson, that I was trying to discredit the EPF with the banks and thereby delay the program. Mr. Jones did not take part in the discussion. He merely listened.

The next morning a meeting with the representatives of the Defense Commission and the War Department was held in Mr. Jones' conference room. Mr. Biggers, Mr. Nelson, Mr. Henderson, Mr. Eaton, and Mr. Ginsburg were present from the Defense Commission. Mr. Proctor was there from the War Department, but I do not recall whether any others from the War Department were present. The meeting started off with Mr. Biggers accusing me of discrediting the Emergency Plant Facilities Contract with the banks, thereby holding up the defense program. I had considerable difficulty in keeping my temper under control but managed to do so long enough to give a fairly full story of everything that had happened since June, which clearly showed where the responsibility for the delay belonged. I also explained, as briefly as I could, how the Defense Plant Corporation operated, and described the basic provisions of its contracts. Much to my delight, Mr. Jones backed me up completely. He insisted the Government's interest was far better protected in the DPC contract than in EPF. Mr. Nelson and Mr. Henderson supported Mr. Biggers, but neither of them matched Biggers in the vehemence of his argument and Mr. Henderson's defense of EPF was far from vigorous. I was very surprised when Mr. Ginsburg spoke up and expressed agreement with me on practically every criticism I had made of the EPF. Mr. Jones held to his position in support of the DPC setup, and before the meeting broke up, an agreement was reached that any manufacturer needing financing for plant expansion could make his own choice between the EPF agreement and the DPC agreement. After the meeting, Mr. Henderson called me to one side and said, "You have got the right setup. Stick to your guns. I will tell you more later." If there is a story of disagreements within the Defense Commission, Mr. Henderson never told it to me. It was difficult to reconcile his statement with his defense of EPF in the meeting, as half-hearted as that defense was. I can only surmise he was opposed to the EPF Contract all along but felt that a semblance of unity among the members of the Commission was of vital importance at the time.

REIMBURSING RFC

That afternoon Klagsbrunn and I got busy with Mr. Hotchkiss in drafting a contract between Wright Aeronautical Corporation and DPC. Mr. Proctor came over, insisting that he sit in in order to make certain that the War Department's interest was taken care of. The War Department wanted a nominal rental of only a dollar a year instead of a substantial rental based upon the number of airplane engines manufactured and sold. He said that the War Department wanted to keep down the cost of its supplies and would see to it that all charges for the use of the plant would be eliminated from the price paid for the engines. I checked this and then found that the Defense Commission was taking a similar position.

If only nominal rent was to be collected, how could the DPC ever expect to get its money back? At the end of the program it would have nothing to show for its money except a depreciated plant which would certainly be worth far less than its original cost unless the country should run into a period of terrific inflation. Of course, the Government as a whole would have to bear the losses on all defense plants regardless of how they were financed, but for this loss to be thrown on the RFC was an entirely different matter. Mr. Jones certainly would not go along with a deal that was sure to knock RFC's balance sheet into a "cocked hat" and destroy its reputation for sound lending practices. It looked as if our victory of the morning was an empty one.

Klagsbrunn came through with the solution. In the early days of the RFC, it had been directed by Congress to make loans to states and municipalities for relief purposes. No one seriously thought at the time that these loans would ever be repaid, and they were not. They were segregated on RFC's balance sheet from its other types of loans and investments, but at the same time constituted a decidedly unsightly speck on an otherwise rosy apple. Congress finally came to the rescue and permitted these relief loans to be charged off, recognizing that they did not represent an exercise of judgment on the part of the RFC's directors and were an unfair reflection on RFC's otherwise good business record. Moreover, the EPF Contract suggested a way of providing a "cushion." In the EPF Contract the Army or Navy, as the case might be, was required to "freeze" appropriations equal to one hundred per cent of the cost of the plant. Why not require the Army or Navy to protect the Defense Plant Corporation at least in an amount equal to the first two years' reimbursement payments under the EPF Contract? This would give DPC a cushion of 40 per cent and at the same time release 60 per cent of the Army's appropriation for badly needed airplanes, machine guns, or other military supplies. Accordingly, a "take out" agreement with the War Department was drafted. Under this agreement the War Department consented, in consideration of the construction of the plant by DPC, to pay over to the DPC, on or prior to the expiration of the Army's current appropriations, an amount equal to two-fifths of the cost of the plant. It further agreed, at the end of the program, to apply to Congress for an appropriation to cover the remaining three-fifths and, if such appropriation be granted, to pay DPC the balance of the plant cost. Upon payment in full, DPC agreed to turn the plant over to the War Department. There was, of course, no legal protection in the latter provision, but it was at least equivalent to the War Department saying, "DPC put up this money because we asked it to as a matter of national defense. If there is any loss, the blame lies with us rather than with DPC."

Mr. Jones approved the "take out" agreement after adding a provision that all unpaid balances due from the War Department should bear interest at the regular four per cent per annum. The draft, with Mr. Jones' addition, was submitted to Judge Patterson who approved it but protested that four per cent was a pretty high interest rate for one department of the Government to charge another, particularly in view of the fact that RFC's money was at the time costing it more nearly one per cent. I suggested that he take up the matter with Mr. Jones. A little later, he called me back and said that he had talked to Mr. Jones, and that the interest rate would be four per cent.

THE LAST LAP

In drafting the lease agreement covering the Wright Aeronautical plant, we had little difficulty in ironing out our differences with Mr. Hotchkiss. However, Mr. Proctor raised constant objections and continually insisted upon provisions requiring detailed supervision by the War Department. Klagsbrunn and I gave in to him as far as we felt that we could without sacrificing the advantages of speed and simplicity which our type of procedure afforded. We would get one provision worked out to his satisfaction only to have him leave and return a few hours later with further suggestions. When he ran out of objections based on the alleged position of the War Department, he would turn to the Defense Commission and insist that certain provisions be inserted or eliminated to conform with the Defense Commission's policy. I insisted that he was not representing the Defense Commission and that if Defense Commission policy was involved, it should send over its own representatives. He stated that the Defense Commission consisted of a large number of members, most of whom were out of town, and that there was no one who could speak for the Commission until authorized to do so at a regular meeting. Mr. Henderson was in town, and I went over to his office and told him what we were up against. He said that the Commission had no policy with reference to the matters raised by Mr. Proctor and that he would take the responsibility of authorizing me to ignore completely Mr. Proctor's suggestions in so far as they purported to reflect Defense Commission policy. I advised Mr. Proctor of my conversation with Mr. Henderson and this stimulated him to greater imagination in raising objections on behalf of the War Department. The process continued for the better part of two days, extending until late into the night. At about 6:00 P.M. on the afternoon of Saturday, October 19, Proctor had run out of suggestions. However, he wanted the weekend to go over the contract again. He insisted that it should not be executed until the Defense Commission had formally approved it. I told him that he had had plenty of time to think of all the objections the War Department could possibly raise and that, moreover, Mr. Henderson had flatly said that the Defense Commission did not want to take part in drafting the contract; that there was no justification for any further delays and I felt strongly that we should go ahead and get the contract executed so Wright could start construction. I called Judge Patterson on the telephone and told him that the draft was completed but that I wanted to make sure that it was all right with him before it was signed. He said that he was about to leave to have dinner with Mr. Archibald MacLeish in Georgetown and asked that the contract be brought over to him at Mr. MacLeish's home. Klagsbrunn put a copy of the contract in his pocket and, insisting that Proctor accompany him, took a taxi for Mr. MacLeish's home. Judge Patterson read it over and said he thought it was an excellent job. His only criticism was that the War Department was tied in too closely. He said he thought things would move much faster if the DPC had complete charge, once the War Department had approved the project and the basic engineering designs. His criticism was directed entirely to the provisions which had been put in at Mr. Proctor's insistence.

As soon as Judge Patterson's approval was obtained, I called Mr. A. T. Hobson, Secretary of the DPC, and asked that he meet me at Mr. John Snyder's apartment. Mr. Snyder was ill at the time and confined to his bed. He got out of bed and signed the contract and Mr. Hobson attested it as Secretary, and affixed DPC's corporate seal. We then carried the contract to Mr. Gordon's room at the Carlton Hotel where he executed it on the behalf of the Wright Aeronautical Corporation. By that time, it was nearly 11:00 P.M. The last barrier was down and now we could get the airplane expansion program under way. Mr. Hobson, Klagsbrunn, and I then went to the Carlton dining-room for a supper and celebration. Mr. Hobson paid the check!

THE DISPOSAL OF THE ALUMINUM PLANTS

CONTENTS

FOREWORD

This is a study of difficulties by-passed and difficulties overcome in an attempt by government officials to carry out certain policies. It shows some facets of the behavior of these officials as members of a complex government, and some of the interactions between them and the outside world of which they were also inescapably a part. Narrowly speaking, this is an account of the disposal of the government aluminum plants. The key plants involved in these events had cost originally some $140 million; they had been built as part of the government's broad aluminum expansion program during the war, a program that cost almost $750 million in all. In the immediate post-war period, these key plants constituted about half the useful basic aluminum capacity of the country.

At the end of the war, there was one, immediately available, wealthy, and willing customer for these plants—Alcoa, the Aluminum Company of America. Disposal to others was difficult, indeed at times seemed impossible.

From 1893 to 1941, Alcoa was the sole producer of aluminum ingot in the United States. During most of that half-century the government and Alcoa were in litigation. These suits arose under the anti-trust laws, particularly the Sherman Act. In 1945, in a suit that was begun in 1937, Alcoa was adjudged to have had a monopoly in aluminum ingot; the government urged as chief remedy that Alcoa be dissolved into several smaller companies; the ultimate decision in the case (still reserving jurisdiction to the court) provided for other and less drastic remedies; this decree was made in 1950.

The Surplus Property Act of 1944, under which the disposal program was carried out, was sponsored in considerable part by persons who believed firmly in the anti-monopoly free-competition philosophy of the Sherman Act. Thus the administrators trying to dispose of the aluminum plants were under a statutory obligation to avoid strengthening monopolies. They knew of the 1945 monopoly decision in the *Aluminum* case, and they believed that they could not accept any offer from Alcoa, however favorable it might be. They endeavored to maintain this position while avoiding the accusation of being opposed to "business." It was the converging of the anti-trust tradition, the availability of the aluminum plants for disposal, the uncertainties about post-war production and employment prospects, and the increasing Congressional and public desire for friendly relations between government and business that created the problems described in this account.

But these aluminum problems and the actions of the government, of Alcoa and of others, did not occur in a vacuum. They occurred along with, and were affected by, larger happenings. When the Surplus Property Board was organized in the beginning of January 1945, the Battle of the Bulge was still being fought; cut-backs in aluminum production previously ordered had been canceled and all reconversion plans were suspended.

When the Circuit Court handed down its decision in the *Aluminum* case on March 12, 1945, the Allied armies were crossing the Rhine. On June 8, when the name of W. Stuart Symington was sent to the Senate for confirmation as Chairman of the Surplus Property Board, the war with Germany had been won and a new President was struggling with the complexities of a continuing war in the Pacific and the beginnings of reconversion at home.

The decision to cancel the Alcoa lease on August 17 was taken only three days after V-J

Day. The chief concerns of the country at that moment were speedy demobilization, housing, and the expectation of mass unemployment. Throughout the fall months, while the lease with Reynolds Metals Company was being negotiated, prospects for employment and production improved. By January 1946, when arrangements with Reynolds were confirmed, decontrol was emerging as a major political issue.

Against this background the events in aluminum took place. The government officials involved were, with few exceptions, as much or more concerned with other pressing problems. Aluminum was picked up when time permitted and dropped when other matters intervened. The disposal program for the aluminum plants was only one small, almost minute, part of the whole complex of relationships between the administrators, the Congress, and the general public. It was a primary issue only for a few specialists in the government, for officials of companies engaged or interested in the production of aluminum, and for the citizens and the national and local elected officials of the scattered areas where aluminum plants were built during the war.

This account focuses primarily on a few persons in the government whose actions seem in retrospect to have been important, and on those issues and incidents that now appear to have been most significant. But behind those who are named were many others making studies, writing memoranda, attending meetings. Without their work, the work of the officials who do emerge from anonymity would not have been possible or would have been far different in form or outcome. And all, named and unnamed, toiled at times on problems of apparently pressing importance that have since faded into obscurity. Nor should the reader overlook the fact that government problems were also business problems. The businessmen also had hard decisions to make; their conduct required courage and foresight; they too suffered from occasional divided counsels and they too formulated and reformulated policies to fit a constantly changing situation.

I. Background

THE ALUMINUM INDUSTRY

The commercial production of aluminum metal involves three steps: First is the mining of bauxite, the only economic aluminum ore. Bauxite is not an uncommon ore, but the known reserves within the United States are rather limited. Almost all the U. S. bauxite is found in Arkansas. There are, however, substantial additional quantities in the Caribbean and elsewhere in the Western Hemisphere, and large quantities in other continents.

After the bauxite is mined, it is treated in a plant which, using sizeable quantities of fuel, soda ash, and other materials, produces alumina (Al_2O_3). The third step consists of transforming the alumina into aluminum. This operation, done at plants sometimes referred to as smelters or more commonly as reduction plants, requires very large quantities of electricity. Thus the availability and cheapness of electric power constitute a critical factor in aluminum production.

Aluminum was first produced in this country in 1888 by what was then called the Pittsburgh Reduction Company. Some competition developed, but by 1893 the Pittsburgh Reduction Company (its name was later changed to the Aluminum Company of America, generally known as Alcoa) became and remained for almost fifty years the sole producer of virgin aluminum in the United States. As time went on, Alcoa built new and larger alumina and reduction plants, as well as rolling mills and other fabricating plants in which aluminum is made into various semi-fabricated and fabricated articles. Alcoa likewise acquired substantial bauxite deposits in Arkansas and abroad.

Originally, Alcoa had many foreign interests and connections, but in 1928 it sold all its foreign holdings, except for bauxite fields in Dutch Guiana and one power development in Canada that served a U. S. plant, to a Canadian holding company known as Aluminium, Ltd., which in turn controlled the Aluminum Company of Canada, its operating subsidiary in that country. In payment for these far-flung properties, Aluminium, Ltd., gave stock to Alcoa. This stock was immediately distributed to the Alcoa shareholders. Subsequently, as is explained below, it was found by the courts that Alcoa was not affiliated with Aluminium, Ltd., in violation of the anti-trust laws; however, it is of some interest to note that as recently as 1939 over fifty per cent of the stock in both companies was held by eleven stockholders, and that members of the Mellon family held over thirty per cent of the stock in each company. At the end of the war, the president of Aluminium, Ltd., was a brother of the Board Chairman of Alcoa. Even in the absence of formal corporate affiliation and in the face of denial by Alcoa, it was assumed by the interested government agencies that this community of stock ownership did or would inevitably lead to complementary rather than competitive policies on the part of the two companies. The ultimate treatment of this issue by the courts will be described below.

EXPANSION OF ALUMINUM CAPACITY FOR WAR

As the war approached, the adequacy of the existing aluminum capacity in the United States became a subject of dispute. While the needed expansion in the case of aluminum proved to be peculiarly large, this dispute was not unlike the dispute about the adequacy of steel and other industrial capacity. The most active industrial proponent of government action to increase aluminum capacity was the Reynolds Metals Company, itself a large user of aluminum; Reynolds' concern was heightened by increasing difficulty in obtaining adequate supplies from Alcoa. Alcoa initially assumed, after consultation with the government on requirements estimates, that its own capacity would be adequate for all purposes, including in its computation the anticipated results of its own large expansion program begun in 1938. Reynolds was unable to persuade the government to construct additional capacity. It finally decided to enter into the production of aluminum itself as part of the new national defense program. For this purpose it borrowed money on commercial terms from the Reconstruction Finance Corporation, pledging all its plants as security for the loan, and started to build both alumina and reduction plants in 1940. In May 1941, for the first time in half a century, virgin aluminum was produced in the United States by a company other than Alcoa.

As the government's war program developed, and particularly as the plans for airplane production were rapidly expanded, it became evident to all that there would need to be a further major expansion in the aluminum industry. By this date—1941—a variety of devices had been developed to facilitate industrial expansion for defense purposes. Among these was one generally used for the expansion of the regular peacetime industries—the construction of the facility (plant, pipeline, etc.) by a private contractor but with government funds; after construction the facility was operated by this contractor under lease from the government. During the war the government agency concerned in this particular program was the Defense Plant Corporation, a subsidiary of the Reconstruction Finance Corporation. DPC made the necessary arrangements under instructions from the appropriate sponsoring agency, usually the War Production Board in the case of iron and steel, aluminum, and similar basic materials. Thus it was the responsibility of WPB, rather than of RFC or its subsidiary, DPC, to select the site, taking into account such relevant factors as security against air attack, power, manpower, transportation, etc., and to determine production schedules for each plant. Furthermore, WPB normally selected the builder and operator, and only then did DPC enter into contractual arrangements with the persons thus selected. The various stages of planning and construction were carried forward in consultation with prospective builders and operators. Responsibility for all management details and supervision of business operations was vested in DPC.

During the course of the war the government built two alumina plants, nine reduction plants, and some twenty-five aluminum fabricating plants for the production of sheet, extrusions, forgings, castings, and other aluminum products. Whether final responsibility, in the case of aluminum, for selection of the sites and naming the operators was in fact vested, not in WPB, but in RFC or elsewhere was later the subject of argumentative discussion. Alcoa, after being consulted in the planning stage, was designated builder and operator of both alumina plants and of eight of the nine reduction plants, the ninth (the only small reduction plant) being built and operated at Tacoma, Washington, by Olin Industries, Inc. Alcoa also built and operated the bulk of the government sheet, extrusions, and forging capacity, and had some part in the production of castings as well. The assignment of so many plants to Alcoa (over the violent protests of Reynolds and of Henry J. Kaiser and others), the selection of the plant sites, and the decisions concerning the size of the plants were the subject of considerable dispute at the time. It was alleged that several plant sites were chosen so that peacetime operations would not be possible and it was also alleged that most of the plants were deliberately designed to be so large that they would not be economical for post-war operation. (All these allegations were, of course, vigorously denied.) It may be noted in this connection that one alumina plant cost $39 million, the other $26 million; and that, except for the Tacoma plant, which cost only $6 million, four reduction plants cost over $10 million each, three over $20 million, and one over $30 million; the two Alcoa-operated sheet mills cost about $45 million each. It should also be noted that the most modern Alcoa reduction plants also tended to be large.

Regardless of the allegations and denials, the construction plans were carried out without substantial modification.

The contractual arrangements between the government and Alcoa were of an unusual character, and the propriety of these arrangements was also later vigorously disputed. The Alcoa attorneys, taking careful cognizance of the government's pending anti-trust suit against Alcoa, were extremely anxious not to prejudice their case in court. They asserted their belief that the ordinary arrangements might injure their legal position. They therefore requested and received a contract under which Alcoa, in the case of the alumina and the reduction plants, did not operate on an ordinary lease from the government but acted as lessee from the government with the government retaining 85 per cent of the profits, but standing any over-all loss; the plants were built for the government by Alcoa at cost and without fee. The government attorneys did not clearly understand why the unique profit-sharing guarantee-against-loss provisions were needed to preserve Alcoa's position in the anti-trust suit. The master lease with the government, executed by Jesse Jones, chairman of RFC, and Arthur V. Davis, chairman of Alcoa, was signed on August 19, 1941. It was expanded by supplemental agreements, and in its totality constitutes a formidable document of some fifty legal-size pages. The negotiations were carried on primarily between Jones and Davis, and the Alcoa lawyers drafted the contract on the basis of instructions agreed to by the two principals. The government lawyers felt that the contemplated arrangements did not adequately secure the government's interests in the matter. As a result of their representations, certain changes were made in the contract in the course of drafting so that the final draft contained, for example, certain cancellation clauses which will be discussed below.

Aside from the possible effect of the cancellation clauses, Alcoa would have the right to retain possession of the alumina and reduction plants until various dates in 1947 and 1948; indeed most government officials assumed that the peculiar contract arrangements requested and received by Alcoa were designed to permit Alcoa to retain control of the plants into the post-war period. On the other hand, Alcoa was unable to secure purchase options on any plants.

This denial of options was based on or backed by an order from the President issued on advice of the Secretary of the Interior, who believed that the new magnesium and aluminum plants should be sold to new producers after the war. Except for the new synthetic rubber plants, the lessees of almost all other DPC plants were allowed to acquire post-war purchase options.

The master lease resulted in substantial financial benefits for both parties; when it was finally closed out in 1945, both the government and Alcoa could count up profits accruing from the enterprise taken as a whole.

LITIGATION AGAINST ALCOA

In 1912 the government obtained a consent decree against Alcoa aimed at preventing monopolistic practices in aluminum, but as time passed by the Department of Justice concluded that the monopolistic conditions persisted despite the decree. Accordingly, new litigation was begun in 1937. The government's complaint was comprehensive. It complained, *inter alia*, that Alcoa had deliberately monopolized the market for alumina and aluminum ingot in this country, that it had used unfair practices in dominating the production of certain aluminum products, and that with or through its alleged affiliate, Aluminium, Ltd., of Canada, it had entered into illegal restrictive cartel arrangements with foreign producers.

The trial was protracted. Ultimately, in a decision dictated from the bench from September 30 to October 9, 1941, Judge Caffey in District Court found in favor of Alcoa on every count. In 1942, after judgment was entered by the Court, the decision was appealed to the Supreme Court, which found itself unable to act for lack of a quorum because four of its members disqualified themselves, presumably because of their earlier participation in the case as officials of the Department of Justice. Congress then passed a law transferring final jurisdiction to a special panel of the Circuit Court of Appeals for the Second Circuit, consisting of its three senior judges. Finally, on the 12th of March 1945, Judge Learned Hand, speaking for the Circuit Court, handed down the decision. In substance he found that Alcoa had, as of 1940, a monopoly in the United States aluminum ingot market. In coming to the conclusion that Alcoa had a monopoly, he found that 90 per cent of the market for ingot was controlled by Alcoa, and in this connection he made the following comment: "That percentage [i.e., 90] is enough to constitute a monopoly; it is doubtful whether 60 or 64 would be enough; certainly 33 per cent is not."

The government's original position, presented in the government's bill of complaint filed in 1937, and maintained throughout the trial, had been that there should be a dissolution of Alcoa, as well as an injunction against various activities and practices; but when the case was argued on appeal before the Circuit Court of Appeals in January 1945, the government proposed that if it succeeded in securing a reversal of the District Court, dissolution should be postponed until the termination of the war. The court ordered the issuance of an injunction against certain practices, but this had no direct effect on the disposal of the aluminum plants. On the basic matter of dissolution, the court did not find it expedient either to grant or deny the government's plea. The relevant portions of Judge Hand's opinion read as follows:

> It is impossible to say what will be Alcoa's position in the industry after the war. The plaintiff has leased to it all its new plants and the leases do not expire until 1947 and 1948, though they may be surrendered earlier. No one can now forecast in the remotest way what will be the form of the industry after the plaintiff has disposed of these plants upon their surrender. It may be able to transfer all of them to persons who can effectively compete with Alcoa; it may be able to transfer some; conceivably it may not be able to dispose of any. The measure of its success will be at least one condition upon the propriety of dissolution, and upon the form which it should take, if there is to be any. It is as idle for the plaintiff to assume that dissolution will be proper as for Alcoa to assume that it will not be; and it would be particularly fatuous to prepare a plan now, even if we could be sure that eventually some form of dissolution will be proper. Dissolution is not a penalty, but a remedy; if the industry will not need it for its protection, it will be a disservice to break up an aggregation which has for so long demonstrated its efficiency.
>
> But there is another, and even more persuasive

reason why we should not now adjudge a dissolution of any kind. The Surplus Property Act of 1944 provides the method by which plaintiff's "surplus" properties shall be disposed of. . . . In view of these declarations of the purpose of Congress, the agency which the Board designates to dispose of the plaintiff's aluminum plants and facilities may well believe that it cannot do so without some plan or design for the industry as a whole, some comprehensive model which shall, so far as practicable, re-establish free independent private enterprise, discourage monopoly, strengthen small competitors, foster independents and not foster monopoly or restraint of trade. If it should find this method desirable, it would have to learn what purchasers were in the market, how strong they were, what units they could finance and operate, and in what position they would be to compete. In such a model or design the agency would have to assign a place to Alcoa, and that place no one of course can now anticipate. Conceivably Alcoa might be left as it was; perhaps it might have to be dissolved; if dissolved, the dissolution would depend upon how the other plants were distributed. If the agency should find it wise to proceed in this way, it may succeed in inducing Alcoa to accept the place assigned to it, particularly if the plan has not been prepared *ex parte*. If it does not succeed, then, but then only, will it be appropriate for the district court to act. We do not of course mean that in deciding whether to dissolve Alcoa, or how to do it, that court must be governed by any plan which the agency may have devised, if it does devise one. But, plan or no plan, it must wait until it learns what the agency has in fact done. Moreover, if the agency does form a plan, it will have been an attempt to realize the same objectives for which the court itself must strive; and the court may well feel that it should accord to the agency's plan that presumptive validity which courts are properly coming more and more to recognize in the decision of specialized tribunals. Nothing which we now say ought in any measure to limit the discretion of the agency to proceed in this way. Therefore we shall merely reverse the judgment, so far as it held that Alcoa was not monopolizing the ingot market, and remand the case to the district court.

The subsequent conduct of Alcoa and the government was conditioned by divergent interpretations of these portions of the decision. Alcoa interpreted them to mean that it could and should participate in the disposal program—i.e., could and should be permitted to purchase plants, and, of course, that it should be consulted with respect to the formulation of the disposal program. The government denied that the "industry plan" was the equivalent of the disposal program, and affirmed that, in general, plants could not be sold or leased to Alcoa. The government did not accept Alcoa's view that the future review of Alcoa's status by the District Court relieved the government of any concern lest the disposal of plants to Alcoa strengthen Alcoa's monopolistic position. Other differences arose over the significance of the decision with respect to Alcoa's activities other than the production of ingot upon which the monopoly decision rested.

Regardless of these lawyers' arguments, two consequences of the decision stood out. The government agencies and the Congressional committees concerned with surplus property disposal, with a statutory mandate to discourage monopoly, could not overlook the fact that Alcoa had been adjudged a monopoly—whatever the qualifications in the decision. Alcoa, on the other hand, could not overlook the existence of the finding, even though it was based on the situation in 1940; it constituted a continuing potential obstacle to Alcoa's plans and objectives. Thereafter Alcoa constantly sought to have the suit dismissed.

The decision did not end the litigation. Concurrently with the course of events described below, the lawyers on both sides were presenting arguments about the form of judgment to be entered by the District Court pursuant to the mandate of the Circuit Court. That judgment, finally entered on April 23, 1946, was itself to become, as indeed both parties anticipated, the subject of still further litigation, also described below. On each side, all the negotiations and the public relations were planned or scrutinized with an eye on the courts.

THE SURPLUS PROPERTY ACT

The Surplus Property Act, of which the court took cognizance, was a compromise of two sharply different views in the Congress. The House of Representatives favored a bill that would result in speedy disposal of surplus property with the highest possible cash return to the government. The Senate favored a bill that would emphasize other objectives, such as the fostering of independent enterprise, even if there was a smaller cash return from the disposal of the surplus property. Compromise was reached by including both sets of objectives and establishing administrative machinery and other devices to allay the fears of the Senate that the disposal of surplus property would lead to concentration of industry, speculative profits, and other undesirable consequences.

Among the objectives included in the Act were these: To re-establish free independent enterprise, to facilitate the transition from wartime to peacetime production and employment, and to discourage monopolistic practices. Among the administrative safeguards in the Act was a requirement that, for plants costing more than $5 million in specified industries, including aluminum, no sale or long-term lease be made until 30 days after the Surplus Property Board had filed with Congress a report describing the industry, the economic situation, and the proposed disposal program (Sec. 19). The Act also required each disposal agency to seek the advice of the Attorney General with respect to any possible violation of the anti-trust laws involved in a disposal, prior to the actual disposal of any plant costing more than $1 million (Sec. 20). (See Appendix I.) At the behest of the Senate, policy-making under the Act was entrusted to a three-man board rather than to the single administrator recommended by the President; disposal operations were to be carried out by government agencies to be designated by the Board as disposal agencies. In other words, the Board would issue regulations governing the sale or lease of different classes of surplus property, while each disposal agency would handle the specific sale and lease operations for the class of surplus property for which the Board made it responsible.

II. Disposal to Alcoa?

SYMINGTON AND THE SURPLUS PROPERTY BOARD

Though the Act was signed on October 3, 1944, the Board was not organized until January 1945. President Roosevelt found difficulty in getting people to serve. He finally succeeded in obtaining three members, under the chairmanship of former Senator Guy M. Gillette of Iowa. All three were unused to the administrative processes of the Federal government, however, and all three were anxious to get on with the work but equally anxious to make no serious mistakes in getting started. While the relations among the board members were courteous, even friendly, there were differences in attitude that tended to slow up action. Senator Gillette was peculiarly conscious of the need for making sure that no item of surplus property be disposed of contrary to the national interest. He was deeply suspicious of "the interests" who might seek to acquire unfair or improper advantages in connection with surplus disposal.

The Board moved forward haltingly. Its relations with the various disposal agencies were uncertain, and it found great difficulty in securing staff. President Truman decided soon after his accession to the Presidency in April that a board was an unsatisfactory administrative device, at least for this purpose, and that the Board as then constituted would never succeed. On the 25th of May, Senator Gillette announced that he wished to retire from his position, and on the 8th of June the President sent to the Senate the name of W. Stuart Symington of St. Louis as successor to Senator Gillette.

Symington was a successful businessman who was, at the time, president of Emerson Electric Co., and who had been a friend and supporter of President Truman in Missouri. As the son-in-law of a Congressman, he was familiar with the Washington scene, although he had never before been employed in an administrative capacity by the Federal government.

There was some delay in confirmation. At one point, Symington had been connected with the parking meter industry which at a subsequent date had become involved in antitrust litigation. For this reason some Senatorial doubt was voiced about Symington's suitability for the position.

Senator Joseph C. O'Mahoney was chairman of the sub-committee considering the nomination. He was a prominent member of the Senate, a loyal supporter of the Democratic administration, and noted for his continuing efforts to counteract monopolistic tendencies in business. He was extremely courteous in his conduct of the hearings. His sympathetic attitude in a situation where he could easily have been hostile was recognized by Symington. Thereafter the relations between the two men were close and friendly. During the course of his testimony, Symington affirmed his complete faith in competition and opposition to monopoly. With this assurance, on the 13th of July the Senate finally confirmed the nomination. On July 15 Senator Gillette's resignation became effective, and on the 16th Symington took office. On the following day the President sent a message to Congress recommending that the Board be abolished and that its functions be entrusted to a single administrator. This was in effect a notification to the Board that the President looked to Symington as its effective director, so to speak, as well as its chairman. The other two members realized that their tenure of office was limited and that Symington's policies would be backed by the President.

Symington's initial period of service with the Board was not without difficulties. Certain staff problems faced him immediately. He was, for instance, particularly concerned about his relations with the Board's chief administrative officer, both because of personality differences and because he himself was under a mandate to be administrator in substance forthwith, and in title as soon as Congress passed the amendatory legislation. This official soon left, however, and other members of the top staff were replaced. Symington found that most of the upper-level positions were filled by businessmen who had served in the Army and were putting in six months with the Surplus Property Board as a final act of government service; several accepted appointment because they believed that they would be released more quickly from Army service in this way. Expected and actual continuity of tenure and policy was far greater among the economists and other comparatively experienced government employees in the middle and lower grades.

CONFLICTING ADVICE ON THE ALUMINUM PROGRAM

In addition to staff and other technical but painful administrative problems, such as office space, Symington was confronted with new regulations with which to familiarize himself and a mass of policy questions that had remained undecided during the previous months. Among these problems was the disposal of the aluminum plants, a problem which contained both policy and administrative aspects within the legal framework outlined above. The aluminum problem was the most spectacular subject with which he dealt; but it should be remembered that the key plants cost only 140 million dollars, while the original cost of all domestic surpluses eventually reached about 40 billion dollars. Even during Symington's regime, aluminum was only one special segment of the whole surplus property task.

Symington soon discovered that the Board had secured the service of two experts on aluminum who were not pulling in the same direction. One adviser was Samuel Moment, an economist, previously with the Department of Agriculture and the TNEC, who had an abiding interest in aluminum deriving from the fact that his regular position was Chief of Market Analysis for Bonneville Power Administration, a division of the Department of Interior. Bonneville had power to sell; the aluminum industry was becoming its largest customer and was its best prospective customer for the years to come. In 1943, after the construction of the government aluminum plants in the Northwest, Bonneville became increasingly concerned about the future. Its large sales of power to Alcoa—especially if Alcoa eventually acquired the government's plants in the Northwest—threatened to conflict with Bonneville's statutory mandate to "prevent monopolization by limited groups." Furthermore, maximum sales of power seemed to depend on a permanent enlargement of aluminum production and consumption; in the judgment of Moment and his superiors this enlargement would be most likely of achievement if new producers entered the industry. Complete information on aluminum was essential for Bonneville; and Moment gradually acquired a mass of information on the subject. While his primary interest was in the Northwest plants, he found it necessary to take cognizance of the whole U. S. aluminum industry, and indeed, to some extent, of the world aluminum industry. In the course of his inquiries he interviewed various representatives of industry and government interested in aluminum. Thus he became familiar with the members of the staff of the Senate Small Business Committee and began what was to become a continuing exchange of ideas and information with them.

Using the materials he had assembled on power costs and other relevant data, and the suggestions received from various sources, Moment gradually developed a government program designed to insure competition in the aluminum industry. This program was first publicly announced in March 1945 by Dr. Paul J. Raver, the Administrator of Bonneville, in hearings held by the Senate Small Business Committee on the Future of Light Metals. Moment himself also testified vigorously for government support for new entrants in the aluminum industry. Basically, Dr. Raver's (and Moment's) approach was to emphasize Alcoa's powerful position, the disabilities of any new producer in the industry, and the disadvantages of the government alumina and aluminum plants. In other words, in order to insure successful entrance of new operators, Moment was anxious to have the government use every means within its power to aid them and, where necessary, to obtain additional powers to do so. He was more afraid of governmental inadequacy than of scaring off potential customers. His objective was the firm establishment of one or more integrated competitors to Alcoa; i.e., competitors operating alumina, reduction, and at least primary fabricating facilities. The key points in the Raver-Moment program can be summarized as follows:

1. Government assistance in securing bauxite for new operators via use of the government bauxite stockpile, facilitation of access to foreign bauxite, and surveys of the Arkansas deposits.
2. "Lease the Hurricane Creek alumina plant on terms that will make alumina available near cost to any operator of a government reduction plant."
3. Guarantee for a limited period the purchase by the government for stockpile of a limited portion of the aluminum output of new producers.
4. Discount uneconomic features of government plants by providing engineering guidance, by making leases conditioned upon profitable operations, and by assuming costs of plant alteration or relocation.
5. Grant reduction plant operators preference in obtaining fabricating plants.
6. Regulate the flow of government-owned surplus aluminum and aluminum scrap.

It was also proposed that a government aluminum authority be established to supervise the whole program. The program was based on the assumption that the government had one alumina plant—Hurricane Creek in Arkansas—and three reduction plants—Jones Mills, Arkansas; Troutdale, Oregon; and Spokane, Washington—that would be disposable if the various aids cited above were employed. Moment felt that there might be some opportunity for disposing of the Baton Rouge alumina plant if it were moved to the Northwest, and some possibility of disposing of the small Tacoma reduction plant. The other five reduction plants were, in effect, written off; almost all were located at sites where peacetime power would be unavailable or costly; one, the Massena, New York, plant, was apparently saleable only to Alcoa, if at all.

Moment came to Washington in April, eager to secure adoption of his action program by the Surplus Property Board. A friend obtained for him an appointment with one of the Board members, who sent him on to Col. Malcolm Smith, a partner in an investment house, who had been assigned the task of assembling a staff to prepare the industry reports required by Section 19 of the Surplus Property Act, including the aluminum report. Smith was delighted with Moment's evident qualifications and wished to hire him. Moment agreed to come, but only on loan from Bonneville. It was also agreed that he could return to Portland periodically and that he could complete some work he had in process for the Senate Small Business Committee, on aluminum and magnesium.

Moment recommended to Smith that the aluminum problem be handled "in a goldfish bowl," using a phrase popularized by Bernard M. Baruch. Smith agreed. Moment explained that under this policy copies of memoranda, etc., should be made available to other interested government agencies. He himself maintained a full file of all his own activities in the Board and of whatever other documents bearing on aluminum he could obtain. He likewise developed as close working relations as possible with staff members in the Department of Justice, in RFC, in the Office of War Mobilization and Reconversion, and in the various Congressional committees interested in the subject. Moment feared that a deal contrary to the public interest might be developed unless the progress of policies and negotiations was thus continually made known to the various interested agencies.

Moment began his work with the Board in May. His appointment was noted even before it was officially announced on April 29. Objection was raised unavailingly by the Spokane and Portland Chambers of Commerce, who asserted that Moment's testimony in favor of what they called subsidy and against Alcoa unfitted him for the post. A question about Moment's suitability was also raised by Senator McKellar on the basis of information supplied him by an Alcoa plant official.

Moment tried to secure acceptance of his program in various places, and simultaneously proceeded with the preparation of the report for Congress. Smith gradually began to worry about Moment's attitude. He felt that Moment might be biased. To remedy this, at the end of June he brought in another consultant, Gordon W. Reed. Reed was to balance Moment's idealism with practical business judgment. Reed was to review Moment's report, and to negotiate with potential plant operators. His work thus overlapped Moment's assignment, and likewise the work of RFC, the designated disposal agency for the aluminum plants. Friction developed in both directions.

For some years Reed had had an interest in the Apex Smelting Co., a large secondary aluminum smelter; i.e., a plant melting aluminum scrap along with some virgin aluminum to produce saleable aluminum; Apex was both customer and competitor of Alcoa. During the war he had been an official of the Aluminum Division of the War Production Board. While there he had many friendly contacts with Alcoa. Indeed, operating officials of WPB and other war agencies concerned with aluminum had excellent working relations with Alcoa. Where in most industries it was necessary to call an industry committee meeting to resolve differences, in aluminum a single telephone call to Alcoa usually proved to be all that was needed. Since Alcoa managed, either through ownership or through its government lease, over 90 per cent of the aluminum reduction capacity in the country, arrangements for shifts in production or diversion of shipments and similar matters could be made with the greatest of ease, and on all such matters Alcoa was extremely co-operative. The war agencies had great respect for Alcoa's efficiency and good will, and Alcoa took great pride in its war record.

Reed took the job with the Surplus Property Board on an understanding with Smith, or with Smith's immediate superior, that he could prepare a plan solely with regard to the "national welfare," as he put it, explaining that he meant by this that his plan need not conform to the theories of the Department of Justice about Alcoa.

His planning was based on four assumptions: (1) Immediate postwar annual consumption of aluminum of 800 million pounds in the U. S., a third less than post-war economical capacity; (2) Alcoa's legal power under its lease to retain control of the basic government plants until 1947 and 1948; (3) insufficient Arkansas bauxite for any operator except Alcoa to operate the Hurricane Creek plant for more than a few years; (4) inevitable imports of Canadian aluminum to fill all requirements beyond what Alcoa would supply, if the government plants shut down. In the light of these assumptions, Reed was convinced that no disposal plan could succeed unless it was agreeable to Alcoa. He also felt that the plan should conform to Judge Hand's "rule" by leaving Alcoa with rather less than 90 per cent of total aluminum capacity, but that Alcoa had every right to obtain plants at least up to 64 per cent of U. S. capacity. He believed that dissolution would be contrary to the national interest.

Bearing in mind the Court's suggestion that no plan be developed *ex parte*, and with the approval of the Board, he embarked on a series of consultations. He talked to Judge Caffey and Judge Hand. He talked without result with two or three possible purchasers or lessees. He talked with officials of Reynolds, but they regarded his plan as suggestive of a restriction on trade and broke off conversation. His discussions with Alcoa were more fruitful. On July 12 at a meeting with the top officials of Alcoa, a plan was outlined that gave some promise of being agreeable to both parties. When Symington took office on July 16, Reed's proposals were well matured.

All these preparatory moves were, of course, unknown to Symington. His first introduction to the aluminum question came at a meeting of the Board on July 24, 1945, when he had been in office only eight days. He was unfamiliar with aluminum, and equally unfamiliar with the anti-trust program and the litigation problems of the Department of Justice; indeed, on the basis of his knowledge of the parking meter case he was inclined to look on the lawyers of the Anti-Trust Division as impractical theoreticians. He knew neither Reed nor Moment.

Moment started by describing some of the difficulties in plant disposal and emphasizing the need for affirmative government action. He outlined the main points of the program he had prepared for Dr. Raver, and described his "goldfish bowl" operations.

Reed then made his proposal. He stated that he was going out on a limb—that Moment's plan had been tried and had failed—and that no disposal plan could succeed unless it recognized that Alcoa would always have a substantial monopoly.

Moment replied by saying that there seemed to him an opportunity now for the introduction of competition in the industry.

Symington expressed concern over the unemployment that would result if Moment's plan took a long time to work out. But he was cautioned by Hugh Cox, his new General Counsel—previously Assistant Solicitor General and an experienced government lawyer—that Reed's proposal involved legal questions that should be left to the Attorney General. Finally Symington asked each to outline his views in writing. Smith suggested a joint memorandum, but one of the Board members agreed with Moment that separate statements would be desirable.

In conformity with this decision, Reed sent a letter to Symington on July 26, outlining his plan. The key points in the program included the following: lease of Hurricane Creek (alumina) and sale of Jones Mills (reduction) and Baton Rouge (alumina) to Alcoa; release of Troutdale (reduction) and Spokane (reduction) by Alcoa from present lease, but sale of Troutdale to Alcoa if no other lessee or purchaser was found within 6 months; selling price of Hurricane Creek (alumina) to be set by DPC; sale of Massena (reduction) to Alcoa and simultaneous junking of near-by Alcoa plant (or retention in stand-by); sale of Tacoma (reduction) to American Smelting and Refining or Swiss Aluminum, or both; recommendation to President of reduction in tariff on bauxite and alumina; guarantee by Alcoa of same rate of production in all plants; and finally, "Suggest to Judge Caffey that the figure at which monopoly would begin in this case is 75 per cent."

In this memorandum, and in an almost identical memorandum to the Attorney General, Reed listed the concessions by Alcoa: release of Troutdale and Spokane, averaging of production, and the tariff cut. The concessions by the government were noted by Moment and others: lease of Hurricane Creek and sale of Jones Mills and Baton Rouge to Alcoa, and dismissal of the suit.

Moment's memorandum was far more extensive than Reed's. It attacked Reed's proposal as fostering monopoly, answered Reed's objection on such matters as the adequacy of the bauxite supply for a new operator of Hurricane Creek, and set forth a program substantially along the lines of Moment's and Dr. Raver's testimony before the Senate Small Business Committee in March, but with a proposal for additional responsibilities to be shouldered by the government. In accordance with procedure, Moment addressed the draft to his superior, Smith. Smith disliked its tone and its content, and was disturbed by the fact that copies were attached marked for seven officials in the Surplus Property Board and four in other government agencies. He was unsure, however, of the propriety of violating the "goldfish bowl" policy. In his uncertainty, he held the memorandum on his desk.

A few days later Moment met Senator Hugh Mitchell of Washington at a semi-social occasion. They discussed the aluminum problem, a matter of intense concern to the Senator because of the Northwest plants, and because he was a member of a subcommittee of the Mead Committee, which was preparing to hold hearings on this subject in the West. The following day an investigator for the Committee called on Moment in his office in the Interior Department. Moment spoke freely of the situation and told him of the memorandum held by Smith. The investigator then went to Smith and asked for a list of the documents in the aluminum file; some were later furnished on request to the Committee. Smith also agreed to keep the Committee informed of all meetings with prospective purchasers or lessees. In consequence of this interview, Smith released the memorandum. He also indicated to Moment some doubt about Moment's loyalty to the organization, but Moment defended himself by referring to the danger and impropriety of concealing anything from a Congressional committee.

Symington now had both plans. Moment's obviously avoided the pitfall of not fostering competition, but Symington had doubts as to its feasibility. He also was cautioned by Cox that some of the actions demanded were probably beyond the power of the Board, indeed beyond the legal authority of any government agency. But Cox also advised Symington that Reed's plan could hardly be acceptable to the Attorney General.

There, for the moment, the matter rested. Reed and Moment continued to urge the adoption of their respective programs on those who might affect the final decision. Reed worked as mediator between Symington and Alcoa, urging each to make concessions. Moment talked to government and Congressional officials and sought to gain a more solid position in the Surplus Property Board hierarchy.

As for Symington, he remained poised in uncertainty. Reed, the businessman, talked his language; Moment, the government economist, seemed strange and theoretical. He liked Reed's approach—a business-like deal with a business firm; but also, as a businessman, he was hesitant to overrule his lawyer's advice, and during that period Cox carefully limited his advice to legal questions.

Symington's reputation as an efficient salesman and executive would not be enhanced if the plants remained with the government; his reputation as a forward-looking, liberal administrator would suffer if he found himself in the position of appearing to strengthen a monopoly—so declared by the court. He was anxious to evolve some solution that might avoid the dilemma; he urged his lawyers particularly to look for an answer that would offer an effective course of action. If possible, he wished to have a plan that would promise speed, co-operation with business, and a satisfactory financial return to the government, as the Reed proposal seemed to do, and combine with this a sound fulfillment of the social objectives of the Act—the achievement of competition urged by Moment. He was unwilling to move forward with either of the two plans, and unsure that there was a third.

III. The Alcoa Lease

DISPOSAL DIFFICULTIES

On July 24, following conversations with Reed, Alcoa made an offer for two of the plants. It offered to buy Jones Mills and Hurricane Creek; or alternatively to buy Jones Mills and to lease Hurricane Creek, selling alumina from it at a price to be set by the government. Offers for other plants were being studied.

This proposal had been carefully thought out; by it Alcoa hoped to obtain plants that would be useful in business operations without jeopardizing its position in the courts. Alcoa estimated that in the post-war aluminum market it could add on at least the Jones Mills ingot production to its own without violating Judge Hand's "rule." It considered the lease proposal for Hurricane Creeek a kind of "public utility" operation—equally advantageous to itself and others; however, it was unwilling to take Jones Mills unless its Hurricane Creek offer was accepted.

The Alcoa letter raised no immediate issue with Symington because it was mislaid and neither considered nor acknowledged. However, V-E Day was past, V-J Day was approaching, and other possible operators of the aluminum plants began to make themselves known to the RFC and the Surplus Property Board, or both. In the spring, Henry J. Kaiser had indicated an interest. Columbia Metals, a new company which was building an experimental alumina-from-clay plant in the Northwest, began to negotiate for some plants. Other prospective bidders made cautious inquiries. On the 1st of August, Reynolds made a preliminary offer to Symington, dependent upon certain government actions, and had some further conversations with him, but no firm, substantially acceptable offer was in sight.

There were two stumbling blocks: One was the underlying difficulty, faced by any new entrant, in the mere existence of Alcoa's strong position and patents and know-how; and the other was Alcoa's continuing hold on the alumina and reduction plants through its lease. With respect to the first problem, on the 2nd of August a letter was sent to Symington by Sam Husbands, a director of RFC. Husbands, a businessman regarded as a shrewd negotiator with an eye for obtaining the maximum possible cash return for the government, had viewed with increasing concern his difficulties in obtaining lessees or purchasers for the big plants. He was also aware of the opposition to disposal to Alcoa. He gradually came to the conclusion that his own preference for a cash sale to the highest bidder would be inappropriate. Special techniques were in order. On August 2 he wrote to Symington and proposed that in order to induce somebody to start in on aluminum, the plants should be leased on short-term leases, the government to obtain the major share of the profits and to guarantee the operator against any loss; this was substantially the same formula that had been included in the 1941 Alcoa lease. The note to Symington enclosing the memorandum of suggestion is of interest.

August 2, 1945

Dear Stu: I am enclosing a memorandum for your personal information.

To embark on this program would be quite a departure for peacetime operations, and there might be a howl that the Government's guaranteeing an operator against loss would be construed as a subsidy.

However, the plan, under the circumstances, is common sense, if we can secure efficient and sensible operators with some background experience in metallurgy.

The facts are, the Government has the plants; knowledge of operation is restricted to Alcoa and Reynolds; the Government wants to realize on these plants; therefore, the Government will have to take the risk incident to the education of new operators.

Would like to talk with you sometime about this.

Sincerely,

[s] *Sam H. Husbands*, Director.

This letter was the outgrowth of a long period of exasperation and frustration. Husbands and his associates had been struggling with the problems of aluminum plant disposal for a year and a half. More than once he had been forced to adjust his plans to drastic changes in over-all surplus property administration and policy. He had negotiated and argued for months with prospective purchasers and with Alcoa. Moment and the staff of the Senate Small Business Committee had urged upon him the desirability of giving maximum aid to new producers. His proposal was made with these factors at least in the background of his thinking.

Symington made no immediate decision on Husbands' suggestion. Discussions continued with possible operators, Kaiser now showing renewed interest. At this point, on V-J Day, Husbands replied to a request from Kaiser for information concerning certain of the plants, but in his reply he called attention to the second great stumbling block, the fact that under the Alcoa lease it appeared that the plants would not be available until 1947 or 1948. (Actually, on all the key plants the lease ran to 1948.) This was the fact, or assumed fact, that underlay Reed's proposal.

Husbands' knowledge of the Alcoa lease was not merely legal or academic. A month earlier—on July 10—Arthur V. Davis, Chairman, and I. W. Wilson, Vice-President of Alcoa, had called on him. Davis had refused to furnish "know-how" to any new plant operators on the ground that he would not give away his stockholders' property and had asserted Alcoa's intention to maintain possession of the government plants at least until it obtained a favorable court decision on its current monopoly status.

Shortly after this discussion, the Alcoa lease was brought to the attention of Senator James E. Murray, Chairman of the Senate Small Business Committee that had held extensive hearings on light metals in the spring. Senator Murray was regarded as a strong Administration liberal and, like his colleague Senator O'Mahoney, was particularly interested in monopoly problems. On July 16 he wrote to Wilson requesting Alcoa to consent to cancellation of the lease. On July 23 Wilson replied, refusing the request. At this time, of course, there were still substantial war orders being supplied by several plants under the lease.

Soon after these occurrences Husbands put the lease question aside in the conviction or with the hope that Alcoa could be induced to vacate the lease or that the lease could somehow be canceled, if a sale or lease to someone else was actually ready for consummation. Within the Surplus Property Board, Moment was aware of the problem, but felt that Alcoa could be induced to transfer its lease to new operators because of the adverse publicity it might face if it refused. He was afraid that shutdown of the plants consequent upon cancellation might make disposal even more difficult or impossible. He thought that if Alcoa refused to transfer the lease, a further hearing before the Senate Small Business Committee, with all the facts made public, might induce a change of position, a possibility that emerged from discussions with the Committee staff.

But increasingly it seemed to Husbands, Symington, and others that a firm offer could not be obtained if the plants were not definitely available for disposal, and increasingly the Alcoa lease became the focus of attention for officials of the various government agencies interested in the aluminum plants.

Under the terms of the Surplus Property Act, the Surplus Property Board was put under the direct supervision of the Office of War Mobilization and Reconversion. Partly as a result of this, but more perhaps as a result of the fairly widespread concern about the disposal of surplus property in the reconversion program, a special adviser on surplus property problems was appointed by Judge Vinson, then Director of War Mobilization, in May 1945. This was Harold Stein,[1] a man who had spent over ten years in various positions of some responsibility in the government. He maintained close liaison with the Surplus Property Board and with members of other agencies that had an interest in the question. His contacts were at various levels including Symington, Cox, and Moment at the Board.

[1] Author of this study.

Relations between the SPB and OWMR were not confined to these staff consultations. Symington's entry into the SPB coincided fairly closely in time with the appointment of John W. Snyder as Director of War Mobilization and Reconversion. Snyder, a St. Louis banker, had spent several years as an official of RFC, and returned to Washington at President Truman's request to be Federal Loan Administrator (i.e., in effect, head of RFC), a position which he held for a brief period before coming to OWMR. He was a close personal friend of the President and of Symington. During their first months in their new positions, Symington and Snyder were in constant, perhaps daily, communication with each other.

Early in August Stein became interested in the question of the Alcoa lease. He discussed the matter with Cox, Symington's General Counsel. Both felt that any disposal program might fail completely if the plants could not be made available to new operators before 1947 or 1948. They were doubtful that any firm deal could be made, except with Alcoa, until the lease had been canceled. Neither knew the precise terms of the lease but each felt that it should be reviewed and that the problem should be brought to the attention of the policy officials without delay. Symington agreed that the subject required government-wide consideration and was anxious to have Snyder's appproval before embarking on any program of action.

Accordingly, Snyder set a meeting on aluminum for August 17. The main problem to be discussed was the Alcoa lease, although other aluminum problems and the disposal of a large steel plant were also on the agenda.

The meeting was attended by the three members of the Surplus Property Board and Cox; by Wendell Berge, Assistant Attorney General in charge of anti-trust litigation; by Husbands and John D. Goodloe, General Counsel of RFC; by the Under-Secretary of the Interior; and by various other government officials. Berge made it clear that sale to Alcoa was unacceptable to the Department of Justice. Accepting this as established, there was a long, inconclusive discussion both on whether the lease could be broken and on whether it should be broken. The Interior Department officials were afraid that if the plants closed down it would be impossible, or virtually impossible, ever to reopen them. As a result they were concerned about any cancellation action that might result in a shutdown; alternatively they wished to make sure that if the plants were closed down, the government would pay the reopening costs. Aside from this rather specific assumption, there was general anxiety about the resultant unemployment and the cost and political repercussions of a shutdown of any aluminum plants. In August 1945—the time of V-J Day—it was generally anticipated that there would be mass unemployment during the reconversion period. Accordingly, Snyder, Symington, and the others were most unwilling to be accused of causing unemployment if they could possibly avoid the accusation. Various means of securing lessees or purchasers were discussed at length, but inconclusively.

Stein suggested several times that as long as Alcoa maintained its control of the plants, it was idle to discuss any disposal program, and also pointed out that Alcoa had stated that it intended to maintain control unless it received countervailing advantages, as in the Reed plan. The question he then raised was whether the government had any legal powers to secure possession of the plants. Various possibilities were canvassed, such as requesting an order from the District Court or declaring the lease void as contrary to public policy; but all these suggested possibilities raised legal doubts, and all seemed destined for litigation and the delay attendant thereon. Finally, while it had previously been assumed that the government would not be able to invoke any of the cancellation clauses in the lease, Goodloe suggested that it would be desirable for the lawyers and economists to reexamine the lease and the status of the relevant operating statistics and see if there was, by chance, any possible escape thereunder.

The clause in the lease to which Goodloe referred provided in substance that if total production at the reduction plants fell below 40 per cent of their total rated or actual capacity, whichever was higher, during a six months' period, the whole lease covering the eight reduction plants and the two alumina plants could be canceled on sixty days' notice by either party. It was therefore decided to examine the operating statistics. Goodloe, an experienced government lawyer, sensitive to the RFC's policy of operating only under directive, was not unsympathetic to the attempt to cancel the lease, in spite of some opposition within the RFC staff; but he felt that his Board would not wish to assume full responsibility for what might result and suggested, therefore, as a measure of protection to RFC that the Attorney General assume the responsibility for reviewing the situation and, if appropriate, for approving the basis of terminaton. Snyder concurred in this suggestion, but was loath to commit himself beyond this, for he was anxious to avoid the involvement of the Administration in public controversy. But the need for decision was pressed; it was generally, though reluctantly and somewhat imprecisely, agreed in conclusion that RFC should cancel the lease if the lawyers agreed that cancellation was legally possible. It was also decided to offer Alcoa the right to continue operations at the plants on a sixty-day cancellation basis; if Alcoa accepted this offer, employment would continue, but the plants would be available for prompt delivery to a new purchaser or lessee; if Alcoa did not accept, the blame for unemployment might appropriately be attributed to Alcoa. This seemed to Symington and Snyder a hopeful escape from an otherwise unsatisfactory choice of evils. Temporarily, at least, Symington was in a position where he could hope that he might clear the plants for disposal and yet avoid the worrisome implications of lease cancellation. If no legal means of breaking the lease was available, he could so report to the Congress and shift the problem there. If the lease could be broken, no irrevocable action need be taken until he had attempted to persuade Alcoa to accept his temporary operation proposal. For the moment, the crossing of the last bridge could wait. Snyder's failure to dissent from cancellation left that hard choice still available; his failure to endorse it strongly meant that reconsideration was possible.

Actually, checking the operating statistics in the light of the legal provisions of the escape clause had begun a few days earlier under instructions from Cox. This preliminary examination seemed to show that cancellation was possible; but Goodloe's associates had questioned the figures and he had not discussed the policy implications with his Board. Because of their uncertainty, he and Cox did not mention these matters at the meeting. The work going on under their direction now had OWMR sanction and an approved goal in view.

THE SPOKANE HEARINGS

While these events were occurring in Washington, the Subcommittee on Reconversion of the Special Committee Investigating the National Defense Program, known originally as the Truman Committee and at this time as the Mead Committee, was making a trip around the country taking testimony on various reconversion problems. On the 16th of August, the Subcommittee, consisting of Senator Kilgore, Chairman, Senator Ferguson, and Senator Mitchell, met in Charleston, West Virginia. On the 18th the Subcommittee met in San Francisco, and on the 21st and 22nd it met in Spokane. The Spokane hearings were primarily devoted to aluminum and magnesium, especially aluminum. Leaving Washington soon after the meeting with Snyder, Symington and Goodloe flew out to Spokane to testify. Representatives of Reynolds, Kaiser, and Alcoa also testified, as did Dr. Raver of Bonneville, and various representatives of local organizations.

The Subcommittee was briefed with information and documents secured by its investigator from Moment and Smith. The questioning of the government witnesses was more vigorous than friendly, and contrasted in this respect with the questioning of the industry witnesses. Senator Ferguson in particular made no allowance for Symington's newness and consequent unfamiliarity with the subject matter. Symington was not clear on the demarcation between the functions of the SPB, the policy agency, and RFC, the disposal agency. He described the differences of opinion between Reed and Moment and indicated some personal preference for Reed's plan as "a more positive plan," but said that a choice between them rested on legal considerations.

He did not seem to know whether or not plants could legally be disposed of to Alcoa; but on this point, the Senators were inclined to consider the Attorney General's reputed objection as final. And, furthermore, neither government witness satisfied the interrogators on the vigor of the sales campaign, and the speed in preparing the report to Congress.

The most important part of the interrogation of the government witnesses centered around two points: first, Husbands' memo of August 2 proposing a profit-sharing lease with guarantee against loss, and secondly, the cancellation clause. With respect to Husbands' memorandum, Senator Kilgore and Senator Mitchell indicated no dissatisfaction. Senator Kilgore was apprehensive that an operator who would not have to stand a loss might tend to try "cutthroat competition"—which the Senator deplored—but aside from this, neither he nor Senator Mitchell saw any difficulty in profit sharing or in a government guarantee against loss. Senator Ferguson, on the other hand, expressed doubt as to the wisdom of the government's assuming losses and said, in effect, that the proposal smacked of subsidy. On the second day of the hearings, Mr. Marion M. Caskie, testifying on behalf of Reynolds Metals, stated that Husbands' memorandum, which had been read into the record, and with which he had not previously been familiar, provided a basis on which Reynolds might well be willing to go forward. Alcoa, in its turn, indicated great dissatisfaction with any proposal of this type and also expressed the view that it was entitled to acquire some of the plants. It felt that a co-operative program would be impossible as long as the Department of Justice remained under the sway of "an old opinion of Francis Biddle" (the former Attorney General). It asserted its intention to retain the government plants under the existing lease and stated that it was maintaining production at the required 40 per cent level. It restated its offer to buy Hurricane Creek and Jones Mills and added to that offer two Northwest reduction plants.

With reference to the cancellation clause, no answer was possible for the government witnesses at this time. Goodloe was uncomfortable; he felt that someone had "leaked" about the cancellation study and other unsettled matters to the Committee. Finally, under continued questioning about the lease, he said, "That is a matter that some very good legal minds are working on. Until they come up with a very definitive conclusion, I would rather not comment on it." Later in his testimony, Goodloe indicated that if the lease could not be broken by action of the RFC, it could legally be broken by Congressional enactment. But Senator Ferguson noted that Goodloe and Symington felt that the disposal of the plants, except to Alcoa, while they were still subject to the Alcoa lease, was not feasible. He also noted that cancellation of the lease, if Alcoa could not obtain the plants, probably meant a permanent or at least a temporary closing of the plants. He then proceeded:

SENATOR FERGUSON: Suppose you went in now and asked Congress to cancel these leases and Congress passed a statute canceling them; then you haven't even got a purchaser, then the plants would be closed down and everybody would be out of work. That would be a fine thing to do, wouldn't it?

MR. GOODLOE: That is the reason I said I wondered if the lease question at the moment is as important as some of us seem to think.

SENATOR FERGUSON: You had better get a purchaser or another lessee before you ask Congress to cancel that.

With this sharp warning and with a general injunction to file the required SPB report to Congress on aluminum promptly and to insure prompt disposal of the plants without any break in employment, the government witnesses started their return trip to Washington.

THE LEASE IS CANCELED

Symington and Goodloe reached Washington on August 24 or 25. By that time, the figures on production in the plants had been confirmed by RFC. The terms of the Alcoa lease proved somewhat difficult to apply. Paragraph 13, which was considered controlling by the RFC lawyers, provided "that if such production shall for any six (6) months' period average less than forty per cent (40%) of aggregate productive capacity, either party hereto may, at its election, terminate this agreement upon sixty (60) days' written notice to the other."

This paragraph has a deceptive appearance of clarity; in the event, the phrase "aggregate productive capacity" caused difficulty. It could be interpreted as the total capacity of the plants under lease to Alcoa; on this basis, production for the half year had been less than 40 per cent of capacity. However, (a) three pot lines (units in a reduction plant) located in two plants had been installed but never put into operation; (b) eight pot lines at one plant had been dismantled; (c) one pot line had been removed at another plant. If, in the computation, the capacity of the pot lines cited in (a), (b), and (c) were excluded, production during the six months' period was more than 40 per cent of the remaining capacity; if only the pot lines cited in (b) and (c) were excluded, production was less than 40 per cent of the remaining capacity.

The various lawyers pondered briefly. They concluded that the lease could be canceled under the terms of Paragraph 13, although they admitted that the decision was arguable and feared that Alcoa might resort to legal action in an attempt to keep the plants. They also concluded that, because two plants were being withdrawn from the master lease on August 31 by a separate unrelated prior arrangement with Alcoa, it would probably not be possible to invoke the cancellation clause at any time after that date. Alcoa's testimony in Spokane had set forth Alcoa's own belief that the cancellation clause could not be invoked and its intention to maintain production at 40 per cent. If the lease was to be canceled, Alcoa must be notified by Friday, August 31.

The RFC Board, Symington, and Snyder were advised of the situation. Symington now decided to attempt personal persuasion in an effort to get Alcoa to accept the cancellation notice (to be issued by RFC) but to continue operations on a sixty-day cancellation basis.

With this in mind, and with the approval of Snyder, Symington and Cox called on Davis of Alcoa on August 27 at his room in the Carlton Hotel; also present was Arthur P. Hall, Alcoa's Washington representative. At this meeting Symington endeavored to persuade Davis to agree to the cancellation of the contract and still continue to operate the plants. Davis apparently either did not understand that the government intended to invoke its cancellation power or doubted the existence of the power, and indicated a complete unwillingness to release any of the plants unless he was satisfied that Alcoa would obtain what he considered equitable treatment. Symington was offended by Davis' attitude, which he considered self-righteous and unco-operative; Davis was displeased with Symington's manner and approach. Symington was under fifty; Davis almost eighty.

While there was discussion of the government's need for prompt action on the cancellation notice, there was, as became clear subsequently, no real meeting of minds on an agreed course of action. Davis concluded the meeting by saying that Symington would hear from Alcoa's lawyers before the end of the month.

This meeting was a turning point for Symington. He now was convinced that Alcoa wanted to fight the government—and he was ready to fight back. From now on he was prepared to put great faith in Moment and in the Anti-Trust staff. Reed, whose mediatory activities had begun to puzzle and worry him, was no longer a man to be listened to.

Still angry at the treatment he had received, Symington waited two days. Then, though he was still painfully aware of the probable repercussions of cancellation, he was prepared to move. His thinking was strongly affected by two new considerations. First, the possibility of cancellation could not be held open, and if he missed the deadline he would undoubtedly be held accountable for his failure to act, by Congress (which could criticize quite freely after the event), by the Department of Justice, and in general by all those who believed in the urgent need for competition in the aluminum industry. Beyond this, as has been said, he was now convinced, after his meeting with Davis and in view of his failure to hear from the Alcoa attorneys, that co-operation with Alcoa was impossible.

With these compelling considerations in mind, he decided not to request reconsideration of the cancellation decision, even though there was now only a faint hope that Alcoa would accept his proposals.

On August 29th he sent two letters—one to the Attorney General requesting confirmation of his understanding that the lease could legally be canceled, the other to RFC recommending cancellation and a renewal of the offer to Alcoa of continuous operation on a sixty-day basis.

On August 30 Goodloe presented the matter to the Executive Committee of RFC. He recited the conclusions reached at the meeting of August 17 with Snyder, explained the legal position on cancellation, and read Symington's letter. The Executive Committee approved the proposed action and authorized the dispatch of a formal letter to Alcoa embodying the two points. Husbands simultaneously wrote to Snyder, reminding him of the conclusions reached on August 17, and advising him of the action now taken by RFC pursuant thereto.

After this meeting, Goodloe tried to get in touch with Davis, but found that he was in New York. Instead, Hall came to his office. Goodloe handed him the letter. Hall expressed dismay, saying that Alcoa thought Symington and Cox had agreed that no cancellation letter would be sent, but rather that there would be a standstill agreement under which the government could, if it wished, cancel on October 1 as if on September 1. He assured Goodloe that Davis would be irritated. They then spoke to Cox on the telephone; Cox said that he had not understood that there was any firm agreement at all with Davis.

Hall left and soon telephoned back. He had read the letter to Mr. Davis and Mr. Davis was in fact very angry. Goodloe then drafted the following letter:

Reconstruction Finance Corporation
Washington, D. C., August 30, 1945

Mr. Arthur V. Davis
Chairman of the Board
Aluminum Company of America
Pittsburgh, Pennsylvania

Dear Mr. Davis:

This is to confirm the following statements made orally today when I handed Mr. Arthur Hall, your Washington representative, an executed duplicate copy of the enclosed notice of termination of RFC's Agreement of Lease dated August 19, 1941, with the Aluminum Company of America covering certain aluminum reduction plants and certain alumina plants:

1. Because of the time element we are giving the notice of termination now for the purpose of protecting and preserving what we think are our legal rights under the contract.
2. We are perfectly willing and indeed are anxious to discuss the matter with you and your attorneys and if possible to adjust the whole matter on an amicable basis.
3. In the event we can arrive at a mutually satisfactory basis for adjusting the matter or should you convince us that we are wrong in our present position, we will withdraw the notice of termination.

While I am certain that Mr. Hall will convey this information to you as requested, I am taking the liberty of confirming it to you directly because we do not want you to feel that today's notice of termination is being given in a spirit of antagonism.

Very truly yours,
[s] *John D. Goodloe*
John D. Goodloe
General Counsel

Goodloe cleared this letter on the phone with Cox, who approved it, agreeing with Goodloe that every reasonable effort should be made to maintain friendly relations with Alcoa, both to avoid litigation about the cancellation, and to persuade Alcoa to keep the plants in operation. Goodloe then read the letter to Hall, who said he was sure that this would be satisfactory to Davis. Hall told Goodloe that Davis, Wilson, and the Alcoa attorneys would be in Washington on September 7th to discuss the whole matter with RFC and the Surplus Property Board in an effort to reach a friendly settlement.

On the same day, August 30, that Goodloe was serving the cancellation notice on Alcoa, Symington and Husbands started on a new sales campaign: They sent the following joint telegram to 224 companies:

With the premise that the present leasing situation on Government-owned aluminum and alumina plants can be satisfactorily resolved and an adequate supply of bauxite at a competitive price assured, please advise the Reconstruction Finance Corporation immediately whether your company would be interested in the purchase or lease of any Government-owned aluminum or alumina plants, and if so, on what basis.

The telegram, drafted by Symington, reflected his worry about Alcoa's reaction to the cancellation notice and his assumption that any new operator of Hurricane Creek would have difficulty in obtaining bauxite supplies adequate for the long run. The response was not encouraging.

ALCOA'S REACTION

No public announcement was made of the events of August 30. The interested government agencies discussed possible courses of action. There was some difference of views within the agencies on the wisdom of what had been done.

During the following week, another parallel course of action was put in train. Officials of the Anti-Trust Division of the Department of Justice, observing that Alcoa claimed a right to obtain government plants in the disposal program, felt that it might be well to have a letter from the Attorney General on record stating that, as a general matter, no plants should be disposed of to Alcoa. This idea was communicated to Cox, who immediately talked to Symington about it; both approved heartily. Even though Berge, speaking for the Department of Justice, had firmly opposed any disposal to Alcoa at the August 17 meeting, they were anxious to have such a letter, since they were ignorant of any written statement from the Attorney General subsequent to the court decision of March 12.

Actually on May 21, 1945, Biddle, the then Attorney General, had written to Gillette advising him not to dispose of any plants to Alcoa at least until the Board's over-all program was approved by Congress. Gillette, tending to act on an assumption that letters addressed to him required his personal attention and reply, did not advise the other Board members of the receipt of the letter. It remained unnoted by Gillette's successor, Symington, and by Cox. (Though Cox had been in the Department of Justice in May 1945 as Assistant Solicitor General, he had not been concerned with anti-trust affairs.) At the Spokane hearings, Goodloe, speaking as the disposal agency's legal adviser, had shown that he also had not heard of the letter.

Aside from the desirability of having a new opinion reflecting the effect of the March decision, Symington and Cox felt it highly desirable to have the position confirmed by Tom C. Clark, the new Attorney General, especially since Alcoa had already suggested and might again suggest that Justice was being guided by "an old opinion of Francis Biddle," with the implication that a different opinion might be obtained now.

A new letter was therefore drafted in the Department of Justice, and on the 6th of September a copy was made available to Cox and at least made known to Goodloe, who thought it was being signed on that day. As it happened, the letter itself was delayed. When Berge, the Assistant Attorney General, took the letter to Clark, Clark was not opposed to the position, but felt after some discussion that it would be wise not to send over to the SPB an apparently unsolicited letter. A message was therefore sent to Symington asking that a requesting letter come from Symington to Clark. The request came on Friday, the 7th of September, and Clark finally signed the opinion on Tuesday, September 11.

On September 6, at noon, while the new opinion of the Attorney General was thus awaiting formal signature, Mr. Leon E. Hickman, attorney for Alcoa, telephoned Goodloe requesting that a discussion be held that afternoon, preliminary to the meeting, requested by Hall a week earlier, that was to be held on the following day. Goodloe agreed to see him. When Hickman arrived Goodloe showed him the calculations on which the cancellation had been based and advised him that the legality of the action had been approved by counsel for the Surplus Property Board and representatives of the Department of Justice. Hickman discussed the government's purpose in suggesting continued operation on a sixty-day cancellation basis. He indicated that Alcoa was not anxious to take a final position on the termination notice unless it knew what the current official position of the government was with regard to the acquiring of surplus plants by Alcoa. Goodloe informed him that the Attorney General had newly issued an opinion precluding disposal to Alcoa, and advised him to discuss this matter with representatives of the Surplus Property Board and the Attorney General. Hickman left, telling Goodloe that he did not know if he would be accompanied at the scheduled meeting by the other Alcoa representatives.

On the following day, September 7, Hickman arrived alone at Goodloe's office. Cox and other RFC and SPB lawyers were present. Hickman had with him, and presented to Goodloe, a letter from Alcoa accepting the cancellation notice and refusing to continue operation on any temporary basis; the letter made no complaint but referred with pride to Alcoa's contribution during the war. In the discussion that followed, Hickman said that Alcoa did not consider any sort of temporary operating arrangement feasible, even on the basis of termination by either party on as much as one year's notice. He advised Goodloe and the others present that Alcoa would make every effort to remove its property by October 31, the date when the cancellation would finally become effective.

Alcoa's decision to accept the cancellation notice in this fashion was influenced by its feeling that litigation to retain the plants would adversely affect its public relations and thereby possibly also prejudice its position in the courts. Therefore, while believing that the cancellation violated the agreed meaning of the contract, it decided not to resist. It refused the temporary operation proposal because this seemed impractical when there was no prospect of retaining the plants permanently. To Alcoa, the government's action was another episode in a continuing program of unfair treatment and ingratitude for Alcoa's war-time services.

Contrariwise, the government regarded Alcoa's refusal to continue operations as uncooperative; in fact most of the officials were convinced that Alcoa could have overcome any difficulties inherent in the sixty-day cancellation clause and that the shutdown was designed to bring pressure on the government from the various plant localities to permit Alcoa to participate in the disposal program. Aside from their interpretation of Alcoa's motives, they did not believe that their own obligation to seek to attain certain statutory objectives should be influenced by Alcoa's wartime services.

With these opposing attitudes, the discussion did not prove useful to either party. During the course of the conversation a messenger delivered to Hickman a draft of a press release which he stated Alcoa was planning to release that afternoon for the morning papers. He showed it to Goodloe and Cox, who requested that it be held up for 24 hours while they discussed the matters involved with their respective Boards. Hickman telephoned to Hall, and informed Goodloe that Alcoa would hold up its release until 11:00 A.M. Saturday, September 8, provided the government gave definite assurance that there would be no government press release earlier than Monday, September 10. This counter-proposal was turned down. Hickman left; Cox and Goodloe then met with Husbands and another director of RFC, and were joined presently by Symington, as soon as they could locate him. After a discussion of the conversation with Hickman, a release was drafted and immediately issued to the press. The key paragraph reads as follows:

> The lease was terminated for the purpose of freeing the plants from the Alcoa agreement so that they could be disposed of in a manner which would create competition in the aluminum industry. The government agencies concerned have taken this course in an effort to conform to the present decision of the United States Circuit Court of Appeals for the Second Circuit and to provide additional sources of supply of this material so essential to the national security.

The release also explained why the cancellation clause had to be invoked at that particular time and described the temporary operation offer that Alcoa had declined. To the release was attached the informal letter that Goodloe had sent to Davis on August 30, quoted above.

Alcoa's press release was also issued the same afternoon. It announced the cancellation, and named the plants involved. It described briefly Alcoa's part in building and operating the plants, and its general contribution to the war effort. The cancellation was explained somewhat differently: "With the cessation of war and cancellation of war orders for airplanes and other armaments, the capacity of these plants is no longer required by the government."

The letter from the Attorney General and the breaking off of relations with Alcoa were equivalent to a final rejection of Reed's disposal plan. From that time on, with the plants freely available for disposal after October 31, one basic policy was settled; the key plants would not be sold to Alcoa. Other policy issues and many details were still to be worked out.

IV. The Subsidy Issue

The plants could now be sold or leased to operators other than Alcoa. No longer was Alcoa itself an acceptable candidate; no longer could the plants be retained by Alcoa. But there was widespread doubt that the plants would ever be competitive, and obviously the government could not force businessmen to buy or lease them. Alcoa was still, potentially or actually, a dominating figure in the industry. The next question to be settled was how far the government could, should, or must go in providing inducements to prospective operators. Were the plants sufficiently attractive in themselves, or would additional incentives be needed? What incentives could fairly be offered without gross offense to the Congress and the public? The answers to these questions were still to be learned.

THREE REPORTS

The next stage in the disposal program was characterized by the issuance of three reports. Although the three reports had independent statutory or other activating causes, and came from two quite independent agencies and one Congressional Committee, the staff members involved in the drafting overlapped, or were at least conversant with each other's progress. Their general attitudes were harmonious, and the issuance of the three reports almost simultaneously was not accidental. Alcoa, which did not appear in a favorable light in any of the reports, noted the coincidence.

The first of the reports to be issued was an Interim Report of the Surplus War Property Subcommittee of the Senate Small Business Committee, dated September 10, 1945. Senator Stewart of Tennessee was Chairman of the Subcommittee and Senators Murray of Montana and Wherry of Nebraska were members. However, the staff was primarily attached to Senator Murray as Chairman of the full Committee. As a staff report prepared to form the subject of a hearing in October, the report was not submitted to the Committee for approval, although the staff talked with Senator Murray about it. Moment, some months earlier, had done a good deal of work on the report, which was based on the spring hearings at which Raver and Moment, along with many other witnesses, had testified.

The Interim Report called for a dramatic program of government action, including but going considerably beyond the comprehensive program originally presented to the Senate Small Business Committee by Dr. Raver and Moment. It concluded with 17 major recommendations and a large number of subordinate recommendations. The sweep of the report is indicated in the following quotation:

> The Committee believes that the Surplus Property Board, which is entrusted with many responsibilities in the problem, should assume the obligation of providing the United States with a unified light-metals program, taking into consideration the national defense interests and the promotion of the industry to maximum peacetime usefulness by independent enterprise, supplemented by such government assistance as may be necessary. If the Board cannot assume this full responsibility under existing legislation, it should

come to Congress with recommendations for additional legislation.

This report had been sent to the printer before the Alcoa lease was canceled.

The second report to reach the public was the report of the Attorney General, who, under Section 205 of the War Mobilization and Reconversion Act of 1944, was directed to make surveys of, and report to Congress on, all factors tending to eliminate competition, create or strengthen monopolies, etc., in American industry. The report on aluminum under this Section had been prepared while Francis Biddle was still Attorney General, but it was not transmitted to Congress at that time. Attorney General Clark, who took office on July 1, deferred action on it. In August, he asked Symington to review it for him. Finally, at the beginning of September, some interest in the report was expressed by several Senators who had become aware of the fact that it was ready, while Clark's own position on aluminum was, of course, crystallized in the letter to Symington which he had approved on September 6. He signed the report on September 11—the same day he signed the letter to Symington—and transmitted it on September 14. A last minute revision took cognizance of the cancellation of the Alcoa lease.

The attorneys in the Anti-Trust Division of the Department of Justice were in a difficult position in preparing this report. The Department had asked the court for dissolution of Alcoa, and its request had been left in suspense. It still desired dissolution but was hardly in a position to request Congress to act on dissolution while the case was still pending in the courts. It could not openly and probably did not desire to oppose the disposal of government plants to competitors of Alcoa, but it believed that the prospects for dissolution would be decreased if the disposal program was successful. The report reflects these difficulties. Thus it deplored government subsidy for new plant operators, but feared that without subsidy, or the equivalent, no competitive operators could be obtained; and it suggested that mere subsidized competition would justify dissolution of Alcoa by the court.

The report ended with a strong call for action but no specifications as to what the action should be. In the transmittal letter of the Attorney General the following rather modest steps were spelled out:

1. In its disposal of property in this industry, the Surplus Property Board should be guided by the necessity of creating competition in the production of aluminum.
2. A complete survey ought to be made of all available bauxite reserves in this country, especially those held by Alcoa and other large companies.
3. Engineering studies should be carried on to determine power costs at various DPC producing plants and the possibilities of relocation of various plants and to determine the feasibility of cutting down the size of the larger DPC plants.

The third report was the report of the Surplus Property Board. It was filed with the Congress, on September 21, 1945, pursuant to Section 19 of the Surplus Property Act.

Symington had settled the basic policy dispute between Reed and Moment over disposal to Alcoa when he approved the cancellation of the Alcoa lease and when he requested and accepted the letter from the Attorney General advising him not to dispose of plants to Alcoa. But he did not thereby resolve all his policy questions.

Moment's draft of the SPB report had, in a sense, been in preparation since 1943. In so far as it involved a description of the property and the economic problems connected with the disposition of the property, it was largely factual in character. However, when it came to the question of the disposal program, it became involved in controversial matters.

Moment's recommended program followed closely the proposals he and Dr. Raver had made in March; it also included a statement embodying Husbands' profit-sharing lease proposal—a spelling out or perhaps further development of one of the earlier recommendations. Symington liked the brisk approach in the report, and was sympathetic with its critical attitude toward Alcoa. However, he felt that it should be given careful review by his general counsel, Cox, on whose judgment he placed great reliance.

Cox read the report himself and submitted it to two other persons for further review, these two persons being Reed and Stein. Reed, who had resigned when his plan was rejected, but who had agreed to return for this purpose, came to Washington at Symington's request and went over the report in detail with Cox. The report contained certain factual assertions that Cox corrected on Reed's advice; but Reed's objections concerned much more substantial matters than such minor questions of fact. He summarized his oral criticisms in a letter to Symington written not long afterward, as follows:

September 18, 1945

Mr. Stuart Symington
Surplus Property Board
Washington, D. C.

Dear Mr. Symington:

Last week, Thursday, in response to your request I went to Washington, read the draft of the Surplus Property Board's Aluminum Report and spent the evening going over, with Mr. Cox, the points that I believe can be improved.

I will write to you this week in detailed form on all points, but time being short I am listing my general comments. I am being truthful and frank to the edge of bluntness in this matter as this is the collision of the competitive and collectivist systems in our democracy and the naked truth contributes to clarity.

1. The highest court in the land laid the legal background for an *economic* settlement of the aluminum problem.

2. The proposed report recommends a *political* settlement, leading to a similar type of subsidized international competition as practised in the past by pre-war Nazi Germany.

3. The legal concept in back of this report is that of the Department of Justice rather than the Appellate Court's. This is dissolution as an objective instead of a compromise on ingot percentage for Alcoa.

4. I believe that a test of Department of Justice's and Alcoa's desire for a settlement would be to call a meeting of yourself, A. V. Davis and Tom Clark, attempt to agree among other things on a proper ingot percentage and see if Mr. Davis would co-operate on "know how," "patents," to set up competition. This procedure is plainly called for in appellate decision and hasn't been done. My general discussions with Mr. Davis indicates he would welcome this procedure. My discussion with Tom Clark indicated he was interested in such a procedure. My many discussions with the operating level in the Department of Justice indicate an obsession on this matter to the point of ignoring the appellate suggestion of a settlement and pushing for dissolution.

Plainly, the Surplus Property Board should address a formal request to the Department of Justice and Alcoa on this suggestion of the Appellate Court's, as the matter is officially unexplored.

5. Congress did not trust any existing Government Agency to adjudicate the controversial problems such as we now face, so Congress created the Surplus Property Board, accountable to Congress, to free these decisions from the bias Congress feared. As you said, "There are too many branches of the Government against a solution such as the Reed plan." In other words, Congress freed the Surplus Property Board of existing administrative bias and these same pressures dominate the report.

This, of course, is the good old technique of administrative interpretation overriding specific legislation.

6. Upon close scrutiny I believe you will find that the Canadian loan of 1941 did not constitute a subsidy, and I believe the phrasing should fit the facts.

Very truly yours,
[s] *Gordon W. Reed*
Special Assistant to the
Director of Plants Disposal

Symington's reply (drafted by Cox) was not sent for some time, but it may be convenient to include it at this point.

October 4, 1945

Mr. Gordon W. Reed,
420 Lexington Avenue,
New York, New York.

Dear Mr. Reed:

I have read with interest your letter dated September 18, 1945, commenting on the draft of the aluminum report. Revisions were made in the report after you read it, which may have dealt with many of your detailed comments. Although I believe that no useful purpose would be served by an extended discussion of your letter, I feel that in fairness to the Board I should comment briefly on some of the statements it contains.

In paragraph 2 you state that the proposed report "recommends a political settlement, leading to a similar type of subsidized international competition as practised in the past by pre-war Nazi Germany." The report concludes that it is desirable to establish competition in the aluminum industry and recommends that if possible the plants should be disposed of to persons who will compete with Alcoa. This recommendation was required by the standards of policy set out by Congress in the Act; certainly the recommendation has nothing in common with the economy of pre-war Nazi Germany.

In your paragraph 3 you complain that "the legal concept in back of this report is that of the Department of Justice rather than the Appellate Court's." The Board, like all other agencies in the Executive branch of the Government, is bound by the views of the Attorney General on questions of law. We would not be justified in substituting our views of the law, or those of our counsel, for the views of the Attorney General. In this connection I call your attention to the formal report on the aluminum industry submitted by the Attorney General to the Congress last week pursuant to the provisions of the War Mobilization and Reconversion Act of 1944. I believe that you will find that the Board's report is entirely consistent with the views expressed by the Attorney General.

In paragraph 4 you suggest that I should call a meeting at which Mr. A. V. Davis, the Attorney General, and I would attempt to agree "on a proper ingot percentage" for Alcoa. I had supposed that we had made it plain to you that the question of what percentage of the industry Alcoa should enjoy was not a question that Congress had committed to the Board's judgment.

It is not the Board's business to enforce the antitrust laws or to interfere in any way with antitrust litigation. If it attempted to do so, it would be ignoring the limitations on its powers fixed by Congress. If Mr. Davis wishes to discuss with the Attorney General the steps the company should take to bring its operations into conformity with the Sherman Act, he is free to do so, but this is not a matter with which it would be proper for me to interfere.

The complete answer to the suggestion in paragraph 5 of your letter that the Board has in some way indulged in "administrative interpretation overriding specific legislation" is to be found in the statute. It should be perfectly clear, even to a layman, that in the Act, Congress left the Attorney General in complete control of all antitrust problems involving the disposition of property that cost $5,000,000 or more. It is equally clear that Congress did not intend to give the Board any authority to interfere in antitrust litigation. Your complaint against the Board and me appears to be that we have not disregarded the instructions of Congress and attempted to usurp the duties of the Attorney General. If we have erred, it has been on the side of scrupulously staying within the limits of our authority.

So far as concerns your sixth point, I do not agree with you about the facts or the conclusions to be drawn therefrom. I think the report is right and that you are wrong. I call your attention to the discussion of this matter which is contained in the interim report of the Surplus War Property Committee of the Special Senate Committee to Study the Problems of American Small Business (79th Congress, 1st Session, Senate Subcommittee Print No. 5, pp. 9-10).

Yours very truly,

[s] W. *Stuart Symington*

Administrator

Stein, who was consulted on Moment's draft of the SPB report as representative of Snyder, also had reservations, but for quite different reasons. He felt it appropriate for the Surplus Property Board to propose that it expend funds to put the plants in sound operating condition; he likewise felt it appropriate for the government to sell bauxite which it owned to a new plant operator in accordance with established government policy on the use of stockpiles, acquired during the war for reconversion purposes, even though he was unable to judge the validity of the asserted need for the stockpiled bauxite. He did not believe, however, that the report should take a position on other questions which seemed to him to go beyond the Board's powers, and he had come to conclude that no long-term benefit would accrue from an attempt to maintain competitors to Alcoa by what the general public would regard as a subsidy program. He felt it wiser to face defeat in the disposal program, if necessary, and then seek Alcoa's dissolution; in this he concurred in a position taken, or implied, in the Attorney General's report. He was particularly concerned with certain proposed recommendations concerning the obtaining of bauxite in lend-lease settlement agreements, a possible increase in the tariff on aluminum, and the guaranteed purchase of aluminum by the government for stockpiling, since on each of these matters it seemed to him that the proposal contravened broad government policies in which the Office of War Mobilization and Reconversion was interested; a stockpiling bill sponsored by

OWMR, for example, was deliberately designed to serve exclusively as a support for national defense, and not as a support for the needs or desires of any particular industry or government agency. In addition to these substantive points, Stein was bothered by the form of the report: two alternative disposal programs were proposed—Reed's program, and a "limited competitive program"—only to be knocked down; then, and then only, were the Board's own recommendations revealed. To Stein this form of presentation seemed artificially dramatic and unsuitable for an official report; furthermore, he anticipated unnecessary argument as a consequence.

Cox, Stein, and Moment argued about the draft with considerable vigor. Cox was in substantial agreement with Stein. He redrafted most of the major points of disagreement so they were set forth not as policy decisions but merely as matters that Congress itself might wish to consider if the Board was unable to effectuate the disposal of the key plants; other points were entirely omitted. Neither Cox nor Stein was fully satisfied with the final draft, and both felt it might well cause recrimination or embarrassment later; for example, there remained an approval of leasing arrangements that would provide for guarantee against loss. However, Symington, to whom the matter was referred, was still convinced of Alcoa's uncooperative attitude and was quite willing to risk Alcoa's criticism. He was also anxious to obtain Congressional approval for all possible steps that might ensure the success of the disposal program. Furthermore, his faith in Moment had steadily increased and he now felt that Moment had been entirely right in his criticism of Reed's proposals, with which Symington was now thoroughly out of sympathy. He closed the discussion by saying that it was more important for him to get a report up to Congress without further delay than to secure perfection; with this Cox and Stein agreed.

On September 21, therefore, the SPB sent to Congress a report that contained in large measure the original Raver-Moment program, though considerably diluted and modified. (See Appendix II.) But in one respect the report went beyond Moment's own proposals. Symington, as is indicated above, unwilling to leave unanswered the question of further action if the disposal program failed, included a recommendation that Congress itself might wish to consider the maintenance of competition in the aluminum industry by "subsidized or direct operation of key plants in that eventuality." In contradistinction, neither he nor Moment regarded the proposed lease arrangements as "subsidy."

NEGOTIATIONS AND REACTIONS

Under the terms of the cancellation notice Alcoa was to give up possession of the plants on October 31. Immediately after the fruitless discussions with Goodloe on September 6 and 7, Alcoa started to close down the plants—a fairly elaborate operation. On September 11, at Moment's urgent request, the RFC telegraphed Alcoa requesting Alcoa to leave on hand the inventory of raw materials at the plants that were being shut down and requesting also to negotiate for the use of any of Alcoa's equipment or possessions previously used in the plants. The RFC offered to reimburse Alcoa for the actual cost of the raw materials. Alcoa agreed to leave the raw materials and spare parts and expressed its willingness to negotiate on patents, a subject that had been under intermittent negotiation since 1941.

At this point, the RFC and Surplus Property Board were anxious and hopeful that new operators might take possession of the plants immediately on the expiration of the Alcoa lease; the closing of the plants by Alcoa had caused unemployment and consequent protests. But negotiations with prospective operators proved to be protracted. Early in September, Reynolds proposed to take over the temporary operating arrangement refused by Alcoa; but this proposal was dropped when Reynolds learned that the plants would not be available until October 31. On September 25 Reynolds replied to the Husbands-Symington telegram of August 30 with a definite proposal to lease Hurricane Creek, substantially like the Husbands suggestion of August 2. Reynolds also requested a provision under which the government would guarantee to purchase a certain portion of the aluminum for stockpiling. This latter request had some support in one sentence in the SPB report: "Furthermore, the Army and Navy Munitions Board has recommended a stockpile of primary aluminum and bauxite for national defense and a portion of that stockpile can be provided by new producers, thus giving them an additional cushion for production." (Additional statements strengthening this line of argument had been included in the original draft of the report but had been removed in the process of revision; furthermore, the statement did not refer to the fact that though the ANMB wanted aluminum, it had consistently refused to spend its limited funds to purchase any aluminum whatsoever.)

Husbands immediately resumed his negotiations with Reynolds. He was not opposed to a guarantee-against-loss provision in principle, although there were particular elements that required discussion. He would not, however, agree to a government commitment to buy aluminum from Reynolds. A somewhat similar proposal was advanced by Columbia Metals with respect to the Northwest plants. Kaiser had replied to the telegram of August 30 with a renewed expression of interest. Alcoa continued intermittent discussions with the various agencies, and on October 9 informed its Washington representative of the specific terms he could offer, at the appropriate moment, for the lease of Hurricane Creek. Other potential lessees indicated interest but no conclusive results were reached.

While these abortive or inconclusive negotiations were proceeding, Symington finally overcame his immediate administrative difficulties in the Surplus Property Board. On September 18 the Act was amended and on October 2 Symington was sworn in as Administrator. But also during this same period there was editorial and other reaction to the three reports.

Alcoa was deeply disturbed by them. It felt that each contained distortions of fact and of law. It saved its comments on the Interim Report for the announced hearings. It decided to hold off similarly on the SPB report. The Attorney General's report, however, was promptly greeted with a press release issued on September 17. The release described the report as an argument for subsidy, took sharp issue with its factual assumptions, opposed dissolution, and cited Alcoa's war production record. A detailed reply to the Attorney General was prepared later and sent to him on December 3.

Other critics also appeared. The Surplus Property Board and RFC were criticized for shutting down the plants and causing unemployment. They were also criticized for proposing to guarantee operators against loss either wholly or partially. Many of these criticisms seemed to emanate from friends of Alcoa. Some came from Chambers of Commerce in towns where plants had been shut down. The aluminum industry has comparatively few employees in terms of the value of its product; but local repercussions from a shutdown of a single plant can be extremely painful.

There was also some outspoken Congressional criticism of the reports, culminating on October 11 in a bill, S. 1475, to amend the Surplus Property Act, introduced by Senator Bailey of North Carolina, a state where Alcoa had operated for many years. Senator Bailey's bill read as follows:

> Nothing contained in this Act should be deemed to authorize:
> (1) the commercial operation by any Government agency of any plant declared to be surplus property; or
> (2) the disposal of any such plant on terms which directly or indirectly obligate the United States or any Government agency to pay losses resulting from, or otherwise to subsidize, the commercial operation of such plant.

THE JOINT HEARINGS

When the Interim Report of the Senate Small Business Committee was issued, it was planned that that Committee would use it as the basis for hearings to be held in October. Subsequently, it was agreed to hold joint hearings on aluminum plant disposal of the Subcommittee on Surplus Disposal of the Committee on Military Affairs, the Surplus War Property Subcommittee of the Small Business Committee, and the Industrial Reorganization

Subcommittee of the Special Committee on Postwar Economic Policy and Planning. Senator O'Mahoney was chairman of the first and third subcommittees, and Senator Murray was a member of the second. However, various other Senators, such as Senator Revercomb of West Virginia, Senator Wherry of Nebraska, and Senator McClellan of Arkansas, whose attitudes and approach were entirely different, also attended the hearings. It was further agreed that these joint hearings, scheduled to start October 15, 1945, would take testimony not only on the Interim Report but also on the Attorney General's report and the SPB report. From a technical standpoint, therefore, opportunity was afforded to the members of the Senate to decide whether or not they wished to take adverse action on the report of the Surplus Property Board before their time for doing so expired on October 21 under the terms of Section 19 of the Surplus Property Act.

The first day of the hearings was devoted to the government witnesses and did not proceed smoothly from their standpoint. Symington and Husbands were testifying together, and each one kept shifting the questions to the other and each avoided answers on any of the legal points. The atmosphere was not improved when Senator Wherry asked Symington if he would sell the plants to Alcoa if there were no other purchasers or lessees. Symington replied, "It is our understanding, sir, that we cannot sell plants to Alcoa as the result of the decision of the Attorney General." Whereupon Senator Wherry asked, "What decision?" And Symington replied, "I will have to apply for a little legal aid on that."

Although Symington introduced the Attorney General's letter of September 11 into the record the following day, legal aid was not forthcoming at that immediate moment. The Department of Justice was represented by Assistant to the Attorney General James P. McGranery, through whose office the new Attorney General, in an attempt to obtain more effective control of his department's relations with Congress, had centralized all Congressional contacts. McGranery, perhaps not expecting to testify, was unfamiliar with the subject matter and was apparently unaware of the letter the Attorney General had sent to Symington on September 11. He quoted from Judge Hand's opinion and avoided a direct answer; finally he suggested a course of procedure that had been consistently advocated by Alcoa and opposed by the Department of Justice. Symington and Husbands continued their testimony with some description of the negotiations that had taken place, and Symington commented in detail on the Interim Report, pointing out that while he had followed some of its recommendations, to a large extent they lay beyond the powers of the Surplus Property Board.

When asked why the Surplus Property Board had canceled the Alcoa lease, Symington expressed himself as unable to answer, and the explanation was finally made by Cox. But gradually both Symington and Husbands began to make a better impression. Symington was particularly persuasive in making his own direct statement.

Most of the interest of the interrogators, especially of Senators Wherry, McClellan, and Revercomb, turned on the proposed guarantee against loss which they described as "subsidy." There was also active questioning by Senators McClellan and Revercomb on the cancellation of the Alcoa lease. The most effective defense of the past actions of the Surplus Property Board and of its recommendations to the Congress was made by Senator O'Mahoney rather than by the government witnesses.

On the second and third days of the hearings the government witnesses were much more effective. They described in detail the negotiations they had had with Alcoa, and Symington moved to the attack. He said that Alcoa was "not co-operative in maintaining the lease."

Symington's attack was in part caused by his anger at Alcoa's reply to the SPB report which he had just received. He was also affected by a futile meeting he had had with Wilson on October 13, when he had attempted to work out a co-operative understanding, and had found no basis of agreement. He also still remembered his unpleasant session with Davis.

Husbands also described in detail the various steps he had taken to interest suitable companies in leasing or purchasing the aluminum plants. It was significant, however, that both on the first day, and even more directly on the second day, Husbands himself expressed great doubt about the guarantee-against-loss provision, even though he was its author, and even though Symington had given such a provision formal approval in his report to Congress. Husbands said in answer to a question by Senator Revercomb, "I would not lease plants on this basis unless it was indicated to us by Congress that we should proceed in this way." Later when explaining his reason for this statement, he said, "Yes, for the reason the government is called upon to guarantee the losses, Senator, and it smacks of a subsidy." It will be recalled that Husbands had foreseen this "howl" when he wrote to Symington on August 2 first proposing this provision.

The power of the Surplus Property Board and of the RFC to enter into a contract containing a guarantee-against-loss provision and also to make any guarantee for the purchase of aluminum was exhaustively examined. The lawyers carefully explained that the RFC, under its existing powers, could legally enter into a contract with a guarantee-against-loss provision, but they were inclined to believe that without new legislation the power to guarantee purchase of aluminum was not vested in any government agency. It was also brought out in the course of the testimony that the acceptance or rejection of the Surplus Property Board report to Congress would not in a strict legal sense affect RFC's power to enter into the proposed lease with Reynolds because the lease was only for a five-year period and therefore exempt from the prohibitory provisions of Section 19 of the Surplus Property Act. However, the government witnesses made it clear that they had no intention of taking advantage of this technicality and that their course of action would be determined by Congressional attitudes.

It was evident at the hearings that a number of the Senators were strongly opposed to implicit approval of the report of the Surplus Property Board because of what they described as "subsidy." Senator O'Mahoney as chairman was anxious to reach some solution that would be generally acceptable. Notwithstanding the venerability of the anti-trust tradition, "subsidy" was a battle-cry that would create grave dangers for the Surplus Property Administrator and his friends in Congress. Certainly, Congressional approval of the report could not be secured without sharp conflict. For this reason O'Mahoney and the other Senators agreed on a resolution postponing for a month the date on which Congress was required to take final action on the Surplus Property Board report; the resolution was promptly passed by both houses and signed by the President.

The rest of the hearings was devoted primarily to industry witnesses, the two chief statements coming from Alcoa and Reynolds. Alcoa had prepared for the hearings an answer to the Surplus Property Board report; its oral testimony included animadversions on the report of the Attorney General and the Interim Report. Alcoa's reply to the SPB report was in the form of a letter to Symington dated October 15. The subheading on the cover sheet reads, "A letter of protest sent to the Surplus Property Administrator by the Aluminum Company of America." The second paragraph reads as follows:

> In order to meet a non-existent condition, the report proposes the following six-point subsidy program which applies to every phase of aluminum manufacture and sale—a cradle to the grave program which, once started, can never be terminated:
>
> Subsidy No. 1: Government guarantee against losses.
>
> Subsidy No. 2: Purchase options based on earnings' record under the subsidized leases.
>
> Subsidy No. 3: Government procurement of bauxite.
>
> Subsidy No. 4: The subsidized manufacture of alumina for sale at prices equal to or lower than Alcoa's cost of manufacture.
>
> Subsidy No. 5: Reduced power rates on government-owned power to operators of government plants.
>
> Subsidy No. 6: Government stock-piling of aluminum ingot purchased from operators of the government plants.

As this quotation indicates, Alcoa's reply was sharply critical; even so, the published letter was a redraft of a much more vitriolic reply that had been discarded as inappropriate.

The testimony for Alcoa was given chiefly by I. W. Wilson, Vice-President. The questioning was carried on largely by Senator O'Mahoney and by staff assistants of the Committees. Senator Wherry intervened at various times, largely to assist Alcoa in answering Senator O'Mahoney's questions. In fact, at more than one point, the witnesses were forgotten and the two Senators argued with each other. Senator O'Mahoney, anxious to secure some *modus vivendi*, asked Wilson if he would be willing to discuss a temporary arrangement with RFC. Wilson immediately agreed, and before the end of the day, an appointment was made for him with Husbands for the following morning; but during the course of the next afternoon, Wilson reported back that he had been unable to arrive at any satisfactory agreement with Husbands: Wilson was unwilling to operate the plants without an acknowledgment of Alcoa's right to participate in the disposal program; Husbands would not and could not give this assurance.

Reynolds' testimony at the hearings was in sharp contrast to Alcoa's. Caskie, testifying for Reynolds, expressed broad approval of the three government reports. He defended the Reynolds' proposal against the charge of subsidy and expressed consternation at Husbands' testimony. In this connection he said:

> Until we heard Mr. Husbands' statements here, we were under the impression that both he and Mr. Symington were considering the proposal made by Reynolds, which was submitted to them in an effort to meet what we understood to be their combined viewpoints. We did not know until Mr. Husbands so stated before you, that he had arrived at the conclusion that he could not recommend to Congress the acceptance of our proposal. Indeed, we were conferring with him right up to the time you started the present hearings last Monday morning. It is true that he asked us if we could make some modifications of our proposal that would be more favorable to the Government, and we stated that we had no changes in our proposal to suggest at the time, but that we would discuss details with him further. We were told by these gentlemen that ours was the only specific proposal they had received up to that time from interests who were qualified to operate these plants, so it came as something of a shock to us to hear Mr. Husbands' short criticism of our proposal. What Mr. Symington's attitude now is, of course, we do not know.

This expression of surprise related primarily to the guarantee-against-loss proposal; on the question of government purchase of aluminum for stockpile, Caskie recognized the existence of a legal doubt. He did not relinquish the possibility of resolving that doubt by further study, or of extinguishing it by appropriate Congressional action.

Caskie's further testimony related not only to Reynolds' proposals for leasing the government aluminum plants, but also to other existing arrangements with the government. Taking the position that Alcoa and the Aluminum Company of Canada, the probable major suppliers of the domestic market, had both received benefits that were tantamount to subsidy, he argued that the terms of Reynolds' RFC loan should be modified and that TVA should grant Reynolds a more favorable power rate. All of Caskie's requests had been included as recommendations in the Small Business Committee Interim Report.

When the hearings ended it was apparent that Reynolds' original proposal and the corresponding portions of the SPB report would not be acceptable to a majority of the members of the Committees: the Senators considered the proposed guarantee a "subsidy," and they were opposed to subsidy. On the other hand, it was also clear that they were not disposed to oppose the Attorney General's inhibition against disposal to Alcoa.

Both government and industry officials concluded that the attitude of this group of Senators was representative of general Congressional reaction. They noted also that the Congressional reaction had received favorable comment in the press. Indeed, on the last day of the hearings, President Truman at a press conference said that he thought the plants could and would be disposed of without subsidy. The issue—regardless of formal Congressional action on the SPB report—was regarded as settled.

This abandonment of a publicly announced decision was not solely the result of lively public or Congressional criticism, or of the President's announcement. It seemed to both Symington and Husbands that their senatorial friends could not sustain them against attack, especially since the subsidy accusation had persisted in Congress and press over the months, ever since it was first raised when Moment testified in March. But aside from this consideration was the fact that the plants were now actually available and the further fact that fears of a recession, so strong at the beginning of August when Husbands first made his proposal, were fast ebbing. While Symington still was not sure that the plants could be leased without a guarantee provision, he could be far more hopeful now than he had been. Husbands was convinced that the government's bargaining position was much stronger now. If the inducement was not really necessary, it could hardly be worth fighting for.

V. The Patent Issue

THE PATENTS

The Joint Hearings were concluded on October 19. The two months that followed were a period of active negotiation, particularly with Reynolds. Taking cognizance of Congressional attitudes, Reynolds withdrew its original request that any lease arrangement provide full or partial guarantee against loss and a government guarantee to purchase aluminum. Concurrent with its withdrawal from this position, it cut down the scope of its proposal so as to include only the Hurricane Creek alumina plant and the Jones Mills reduction plant. While this was less satisfactory to the government negotiators than a proposal covering more plants, Husbands and Symington now preferred a more limited proposal than a broader one that included an agreement that might be labeled "subsidy." Reynolds' willingness to negotiate for a commercial-type lease greatly simplified the problem of reaching agreement. Husbands gradually worked out with Reynolds a proposal under which Reynolds was to pay rent on a sliding scale rising from 4 per cent to 8 per cent of the fair value of the portion of plant capacity actually used during the five-year life of the lease.

The revised form of the Reynolds lease became known to Congress. It was acceptable to most of the Congressmen and Senators interested in the subject; not so, however, to members from the Northwest. Throughout 1945 the Northwest, with rich power resources and little industry, had been in the forefront of the drive for a prompt disposal program, and especially for one that would result in a competitive aluminum industry. Now, though they could claim part credit for the victory, their representatives in Congress felt that the Northwestern states were being deprived of the fruits of victory. Both Senator Mitchell and Congressman Coffey of Washington argued against the Reynolds lease because of the exclusion of the Northwest plants. They feared that these three reduction plants and the rolling mill would stay closed down. Accordingly, on November 20 (the same day that the Surplus Property Board report finally was officially accepted by virtue of Congress' failure to act adversely) Senator Mitchell introduced a bill, S. 1612, under which the RFC was authorized and directed to stockpile aluminum above current commercial demand up to 1½ billion pounds, a figure originally suggested by Moment in March. Co-sponsors of the bill included the two Republican Senators from Oregon, Morse and Cordon, and one Democratic Senator from Arkansas, Fulbright. Although Moment and other government officials favored it, especially those concerned with Bonneville, the bill did not receive administration support and was not reported out of committee. Senator Mitchell continued his attacks on the government's program with a long speech on the 7th of December in which he quoted a memorandum he had sent to the President. At that point he said that Reynolds was actually closing with RFC.

While negotiations for Hurricane Creek and Jones Mills were thus making progress, there remained one difficulty that threatened to prevent consummation. This was the question of the patents. Most of the patents for the manufacture of alumina and aluminum had long since run out. Indeed, Judge Caffey had found that there were no patent obstacles facing any prospective competitors in either alumina or aluminum. But whatever the significance of this finding in the law courts, it did not dissolve certain stubborn facts connected with patents that greatly affected the plant disposal program. Thus at Hurricane Creek Alcoa had tried out commercially for the first time, and with success, a patented process known as the combination process, which makes it possible to use on an economic basis lower grade bauxite than can be used in the standard Bayer process employed elsewhere. Since the supply of high grade Arkansas bauxite is limited, it was generally assumed that, without the use of this patent, Hurricane Creek could not be successfully operated for any significant period of time, except possibly by Alcoa itself. Two or three other lesser patents were also involved at Hurricane Creek, and still other Alcoa patents of varying degrees of significance affecting various stages of the manufacturing processes as well as certain aluminum alloys were found to be in use or useful at other plants. Availability of the patents to operators other than Alcoa thus seemed essential at Hurricane Creek and of consequence elsewhere.

The hearings had ended in a somewhat disappointing fashion for the government officials, and for Senator O'Mahoney, who still sought what he might have described as a constructive solution. After talking further with Berge, he called in Wilson of Alcoa and pressed upon him the urgency of finding a solution. In friendly fashion, he warned Wilson that if business fails to co-operate under present-day conditions, government operation or control or subsidy is almost inevitable; enlightened business and enlightened government must work together. Wilson was impressed with O'Mahoney's sincerity and said he would do his best.

Following up on this, the Senator gave a luncheon on November 11 to which he invited a large group of officials of the Surplus Property Administration, the Department of Justice, and the RFC. With them he canvassed the situation, seeking to identify those factors that still impeded the disposal program. It was agreed that Reynolds at least did seriously intend to lease Hurricane Creek and Jones Mills, and it was further agreed that the only remaining obstacle was the patent question. O'Mahoney then made two recommendations or requests: first, the three agencies must work together in complete harmony; second, there must be a genuine effort to reach a prompt and fair agreement with Alcoa. All present gave their assurances on both points. As a result, negotiations with Alcoa were pressed, and the agencies worked as a team. Symington in particular took pains to maintain close personal working relations with the lawyers and economists in RFC and Justice.

But an effective solution of the patent problem had to be acceptable not only to the three agencies and Alcoa; it also had to be acceptable to Reynolds. It promptly became a key point in the negotiations with Reynolds largely carried on by Husbands and Goodloe. In testimony at the Joint Hearings, Caskie had included as one of the points in Reynolds' proposal the furnishing by the government of whatever Alcoa patents might be necessary to operate the plants. Reynolds did not concede Alcoa's right to the patents and was unwilling to negotiate directly with Alcoa on the matter. The government was therefore forced to abandon one possible alternative solution: direct negotiations between Reynolds and Alcoa, with the government acting only as friendly mediator. Government negotiations with Alcoa were essential.

As has been indicated above, the government had begun its discussions with Alcoa on the use of Alcoa patents in government-built plants when the original lease agreement was signed in 1941, or not long thereafter. During the war Alcoa made certain patents available in government plants on a royalty-free basis. This it did not regard as a precedent. It maintained that the patents were valuable properties belonging to its stockholders and that it could not properly give away this property; i.e., it could not properly issue royalty-free licenses. On the other hand, lawyers in the Department of Justice, adopting a position developed long before in the RFC, argued that the government had been given an implied royalty-free license on patented equipment in government plants. And the Department maintained that license payments by new operators would tend to perpetuate the monopoly enjoined by the court and would therefore be contrary to public policy. But at this time—in the late months of 1945—Surplus Property and RFC lawyers and officials tended to be more interested in immediate matters, like a clear title to make plants saleable; most of them were far less concerned with the effect of establishing a precedent, however far-reaching the results, than with delay in plant disposal. They were not unwilling to pay Alcoa a reasonable royalty. The SPB report made no direct reference to the patent issue at all.

Both Alcoa and the Department of Justice had come to look on the legal dispute as a moral issue, even though there were recurrent assertions by Alcoa that the patent question would not really present any obstacle in the government's disposal program.

Alcoa's position on patents was not entirely consistent. In a statement prepared for the Senate Small Business Committee in March, referring to these production patents as distinguished from patents covering aluminum uses, Alcoa had said: "It has not been our practice to grant licenses under them." At other times it denied all significance to the patents. (In Alcoa's delayed reply to the Attorney General's Report sent on December 3, there is a sentence that reads: "The manufacturing processes involved are unpatented and well-known," thus repeating a statement made at the Joint Hearings in October.) On the other hand, in a telegram to Husbands on September 11, it had said: "We are ready any time to negotiate along lines of long outstanding offer regarding any and all equipment and processes patents." And again in Alcoa's final proposal for Hurricane Creek on December 28, Wilson said: "As you are aware, we have always taken the position and confirmed to you that we will license under these patents any future operator of Hurricane Creek plant at reasonable royalty rates." But these offers did not seem to lead to any conclusion.

Presently Reynolds amended its proposal by suggesting that the government indemnify Reynolds against any patent infringement suit. When this new proposal was first made to the RFC it was not looked on favorably by the directors because they feared that they might thereby involve the government in a large contingent loss. However, as time passed and further examination was made of the problem, the government lawyers, primarily under urging from the Department of Justice, became increasingly convinced that aside from their contention that the government had a legal right to royalty-free licenses, Alcoa's position in the public eye and before the courts would be so seriously prejudiced by initiating a patent infringement suit that the government was in fact risking nothing by offering to indemnify Reynolds. It was preferable as a matter of public relations and to avoid even a remote contingent liability to obtain an agreement on the patents before the Reynolds lease was signed, but various government officials, especially Goodloe, became satisfied that the Department of Justice lawyers were right and that this obstacle was apparent rather than real. The agreement with Reynolds could be signed even if Alcoa had not made any prior agreement on patents, if, but only if, RFC was willing to take the financial and publicity risks involved. Symington, head of the policy agency, could advise and recommend; it would be difficult for him to insist.

Negotiations with Reynolds were finally concluded on December 14. On that date the RFC sent letters to the Attorney General and to the Surplus Property Administrator outlining the proposed terms of the Reynolds lease for Hurricane Creek and Jones Mills.

In the draft that was submitted it was proposed that the government secure a free license for Reynolds and also indemnify Reynolds against any patent infringement suit. Reynolds was prepared to proceed without the licenses if the government would guarantee indemnity against suit; no final commitment on the point had been made by the RFC board.

PEACE WITH ALCOA

Negotiations with Alcoa on the patents had continued intermittently. At a conference in the late fall Attorney General Clark requested Alcoa to submit its own proposed disposal program. On December 17 Davis wrote to Clark in compliance with the request.

Davis' letter took cognizance of RFC's announcement of acceptance of the Reynolds proposal and assumed that the proposal would be approved by Symington and Clark. (Symington gave tentative approval on December 19; Berge approved for the Department of Justice on January 4.) In view of this assumption, the letter suggested that the three remaining economic reduction plants be leased on the same basis (sliding scale of rentals) and that they secure alumina from Hurricane Creek. It also suggested that the plants be held in stand-by if no prospective purchaser or lessee was found; it made no purchase or lease offer on its own behalf. (This did not constitute a withdrawal of its earlier offer; the offer was renewed on December 28, to make the record clear.) It doubted any immediate need for the Baton Rouge alumina plant. It indicated that there would be no shortage of bauxite. No mention was made of patents, but the letter ended with the following proposal:

> If such a competitor is found and he needs the benefit of Alcoa's manufacturing "know-how" in his early operations, Alcoa will supply on reasonable terms whatever "know-how" he needs.

A copy of this letter was sent to Symington by Clark. Its avoidance of the troublesome patent question was promptly noted.

As has been observed above, Alcoa had published a long letter of protest to Symington on the occasion of the Joint Hearings—a letter describing Symington's program as a cradle-to-the-grave subsidy. Symington resented the letter when it was received and published, and determined forthwith to issue a reply. A draft reply was prepared by Moment, under instructions from Symington to "make it strong." It was reviewed by Cox who found that it was unsuitable for publication. It was then revised by Symington himself and again, at his request, reviewed by Cox, who felt that this draft was also unsatisfactory. Cox then began the task of revising it himself. By now, considerable time had elapsed and the reply seemed to have lost any news value. Symington took up the matter with Senator O'Mahoney and the Committee staff, suggesting that the hearings be reopened to receive the reply; but a reopening of the hearings at this late date merely to hear Symington's reply to the Alcoa protest did not seem appropriate. It was then suggested to Symington that he might tie his reply to the difficulties he was having with Alcoa on the patent question. Symington felt that Alcoa was stalling; perhaps a sharp letter would bring matters to a head. Alcoa's letter of December 17 arrived soon after the receipt of this advice. It provided the sought-for occasion. Symington construed it as a deliberate and even insulting evasion of the patent question. He arranged for the preparation of a covering letter that would include a history of the abortive patent negotiations. The whole reply to Alcoa, thus revised and amplified in the form of a covering letter and long report, was finally sent to Senator O'Mahoney on December 28.

The covering letter summarized the reply to Alcoa and added a history of the patent problem. The general tone can be noted in the following sentences:

> Alcoa is using its patents to obstruct the Reynolds transaction despite the fact that it has hitherto publicly assured both your subcommittee and the Senate Committee on Small Business that its patents would not prevent or hinder the disposal of Government plants to competitors. Although the Government understood that the plants constructed for it by Alcoa were to be capable of independent operation, now for the first time Alcoa suggests that the Hurricane Creek plant can be sold as an effective operating unit to a competitor of Alcoa only if we accept the terms and conditions that Alcoa may dictate.

The attached report of some thirty pages was a sharp but carefully constructed point-by-point refutation of the Alcoa attack.

The letter treated warily of the conclusion of the Reynolds lease. It took the position that Alcoa was preventing or trying to prevent the consummation of the lease; it implied that the lease could not or might not be consummated without the licenses. The situation at this point was uncertain; and Cox, on the point of departure from the government, did not have the time to settle the question of the patents and the Reynolds lease with Justice and the RFC, even assuming that a definitive decision was possible or desirable at that moment.

While the letter to Senator O'Mahoney was not officially published at the time it was sent, copies were passed about and in a few days it came to the attention of Alcoa. Approximately at this same juncture—the end of December 1945—Alcoa had determined to make an overall attempt to clarify its situation. It was particularly anxious to learn if it could acquire some of the aluminum fabricating plants—a point that was still unsettled. It arranged for a series of conferences with various agencies, but primarily with the Department of Justice, to culminate in a meeting to be held with the Attorney General himself on January 8th. For various reasons Alcoa at this stage was inclined to feel that Clark and his staff would be more willing to consider new proposals with an open mind than would Symington and his associates.

These conferences represented a new departure. Hitherto the government had normally been the active party, seeking concessions from Alcoa, while Alcoa had usually been content to rely on its bargaining position and to put forward the concessions it desired as counterproposals. Now the bargaining position was weaker. The lease had been broken. Disposal of two plants to Reynolds seemed imminent. Even the patents no longer appeared to constitute an absolute trump card. On the other hand, Alcoa foresaw long-continued litigation; its position in that litigation would be weakened if the government could contend plausibly that Alcoa had tried to prevent the entry of new producers in the government plants and had refused to co-operate at all in the disposal program. Thus for Alcoa a reasonable agreement on one or more points would be advantageous, even beyond any substantive advantages in the agreement itself.

General knowledge of the letter to Senator O'Mahoney came in the middle of the round of conferences. Symington decided to publish the letter and had a summary statement prepared to which the full text was attached for release on Sunday, January 6.

Alcoa prepared a release for the same date. It consisted of a brief letter to Senator O'Mahoney denying the charges and referring to the conferences then in progress to map out "a comprehensive program of co-operation." The letter stated:

> We can only assume that Mr. Symington was unaware of these developments when he addressed his letter to you under date of December 28th. In the midst of a series of discussions which are proceeding harmoniously, it seems inappropriate for us to answer each of the many accusations made against Alcoa.

On January 8, two days after the press releases, the scheduled meeting took place in the Attorney General's office. This meeting was attended by lawyers from all the government agencies involved, by a number of other officials from government agencies and from Congressional staff, and by Davis, Wilson, and Hickman of Alcoa; Symington telegraphed Moment to fly back to Washington from Portland just for the occasion. They were all ushered into the Attorney General's large office and took chairs around the walls. Finally, the Attorney General himself emerged in his shirt sleeves from a back entrance, took a chair at a table in the center of the room and said in substance, "Well, what's up?" Alcoa began by protesting against Symington's pugnacious letter; Hickman then proceeded to present Alcoa's requests. First, if the patent question was satisfactorily resolved, Alcoa wished the Department of Justice to have the suit dismissed. The Attorney General refused this request immediately. Alcoa then requested permission, assuming a settlement on patents, to negotiate for the purchase of the government alumina and reduction plants. This request was also turned down without discussion. It then asked what the Department's position would be if it spent its own money to increase its own capacity for the manufacture of aluminum. No definitive answer was given, but Berge pointed out that Alcoa would proceed at its peril; expansion might lead the Court to decree dissolution.

The discussion then proceeded to other matters. The first point raised, and this was the chief topic of discussion, was the acquisition by Alcoa of government fabricating plants. Since the Court's monopoly finding had related only to aluminum ingot, Alcoa believed that it should be free without limit to acquire other facilities. The Justice lawyers argued, however, that increasing Alcoa's control over fabricating facilities which constituted the chief market for ingot would thereby increase Alcoa's control over ingot. (Similarly the Justice lawyers argued that to increase Alcoa's alumina production would strengthen its control of ingot, since alumina is the essential raw material for the reduction plants.) On this ground the request was denied, at least for the immediate future; any possible change of position would depend on actual market conditions, rather than on any arithmetical computation of relative capacities.

Finally, the discussion returned to the question of the patents. Alcoa expressed unwillingness to grant royalty-free licenses to competitors without some *quid pro quo*. The debate was carried on largely between Assistant Attorney General Berge, and Hickman and Davis of Alcoa, Clark assuming the role of mediator. Each side argued its position as a matter of legal and moral right. Finally Symington joined in and announced that he intended to go ahead with the Reynolds lease, with or without the licenses. The Alcoa spokesman remarked that Symington was again becoming pugnacious. Symington defended himself by saying that a patent is merely a right to sue. At this point Alcoa decided not to pursue the discussion further but said that it would take the request for royalty-free licenses under advisement and notify the government on the following day.

It may be observed that several of the decisions announced or reaffirmed at this meeting were based exclusively on the Department of Justice's technical interpretation of the antitrust laws and of the *Aluminum* decision. No special weight seems to have been attached to Symington's independent statutory responsibility "to foster the development of new independent enterprise." Indeed, throughout the whole six months' period Symington tended to place major responsibility for his policy relations with Alcoa on the Attorney General. He had been struck initially with Cox's advice to leave the question of monopoly to the Department of Justice; he had been impressed with the importance of avoiding any disunity in the government's policy while the litigation was still in process; and he was convinced that he was far more secure from public or Congressional attack if he could relate each of his moves back through the Attorney General to that indisputable fact—the monopoly decision. Finally, over the months Symington's personal relations with Clark had grown steadily closer. After Cox left the government on December 31, Symington sought from Clark much of the legal and policy advice and support that he had previously obtained from Cox and Snyder.

On the following day, January 9, Wilson, having ascertained that the government would be willing to give public recognition to any agreement that might be reached, went to Berge's office with a new proposal. Wilson proposed that Alcoa grant royalty-free licenses for Hurricane Creek until production reached a certain level; thereafter a reasonable royalty was to be paid. Berge took this under advisement. After Wilson left, Berge and his staff reviewed the offer. They agreed that it represented a substantial concession by Alcoa and that the payments involved should not prove onerous. However, acceptance meant abandonment of a basic position; and, beyond that, the terms of the offer carried the implication that the government and Alcoa would favor a small competitor, but would treat a larger and more dangerous competitor less favorably. The terms would also tend to discourage the sale of alumina by Reynolds to other operators, who might lease or buy the Northwest reduction plants.

Berge discussed these conclusions with Symington by telephone. Symington, anxious to take definitive action, was well impressed with the proposal. At his request a member of Berge's staff went to his office at three o'clock when Wilson and Hickman arrived to negotiate. Berge's objections were fully explained. Symington expressed appreciation of Alcoa's good faith in making the offer, but again used all his persuasive powers in urging them to grant royalty-free licenses. He pointed out that such action would constitute a splendid send-off for him—he was about to leave the Surplus Property Administration—and would at the same time greatly enhance Alcoa's impaired public relations. The whole conversation was friendly and hopeful, although the atmosphere was still tense. Both sides felt that the moment of decision was at hand; the opponents would make a real peace or declare open war.

Again Wilson and Hickman left, with the understanding that they would meet with Husbands later on for further discussion. As they rode back to their hotel they discussed Berge's objection—unfavorable treatment for a strong competitor. Wilson felt that it was pertinent; regardless of the merits of the case, there could be no adequate public defense against such criticism. There thus seemed to be only one solution to the problem, since Alcoa could not at this point put itself in the position of replacing this offer with one less favorable to the government; another unpleasant government press release was sure to follow. They also believed that Symington was prepared to proceed with Reynolds anyway, and they were anxious for a settlement, particularly one that would redound to their credit.

They promptly changed their plans and, after receiving Davis' approval by telephone, returned once again to Symington's office. This time Wilson told Symington that Alcoa was ready to issue royalty-free licenses for Hurricane Creek. Symington's response was immediate and enthusiastic. He said, in substance: "This is wonderful. We'll have a joint press conference tomorrow and release the exchange of letters between us. I'll get a letter from Tom Clark and I'll telegraph Senator O'Mahoney in Florida and get a statement from him."

Wilson was surprised at this development but not displeased. He was relieved that an agreement had been reached and felt that the press conference could hardly fail to place Alcoa in a favorable light.

Symington's agreement was, of course, subject to approval by the Department of Justice. In his conference with the officials of the Anti-Trust Division that followed he was enthusiastic and urged their concurrence. They were of a divided mind. The proposed agreement included a cross-licensing arrangement under which any patented improvements made by Reynolds at Hurricane Creek would be made available without royalty to Alcoa. This was objectionable on two counts: first, since it was a kind of payment for the Alcoa licenses, it compromised the government's claim that royalty-free licenses were a matter of right; second, it was not a true cross-licensing arrangement, since Alcoa improvements were not similarly covered.

Symington was eager for a decision. He felt that any attempt to secure a modification of the proposal would cause an explosion. The Justice officials were uncertain. Some were convinced that this substantial negotiated government victory over a firm identified, as they believed, in the public mind with the word "monopoly" would be highly advantageous for the Department's anti-trust program. Others, convinced that RFC could be persuaded to sign with Reynolds anyway, wanted to hold out for complete victory. Finally, Symington was told to go ahead.

On the 10th of January, therefore, all the arrangements having been made, Symington and his staff and the Alcoa representatives met the press in Symington's office and handed out copies of a press release in which the world was informed of the agreement and of the conclusion of the lease with Reynolds. Attached to the press release was a letter from Davis making the offer and ending with the following paragraph:

> Except for the public considerations which you have presented to us so effectively, we could not consider a royalty-free license under such a valuable asset. However, we are glad to accede to these considerations and, if by so doing we have contributed in any substantial way to the solution of the complex problems of surplus property disposal confronting the Congress, the Surplus Property Administration and other governmental agencies, we are well repaid.

Also attached was a letter from Symington to Davis. The last paragraph of this letter reads as follows:

If in the past I have had occasion to be critical of the Aluminum Company of America, today's action on your part demonstrates to my complete satisfaction that your company, no less than the Government agencies concerned, is moving constructively toward the solution of the problems which confront the Surplus Property Administration, the aluminum industry, and the country as a whole.

Likewise attached was a letter from Clark to Symington. The last paragraph reads as follows:

It is this teamwork of Government and business —evidenced by the public spirited action of Alcoa in granting a royalty-free license and in the cooperative spirit of the Reconstruction Finance Corporation and Surplus Property Administration —that will get the reconversion job done. My hearty congratulations to all of you.

Senator O'Mahoney's telegram, also attached, opened with the following sentence:

I learned with great pleasure from Surplus Property Administrator Symington of the action of Alcoa in making available to the Government the patents for the operation of the aluminum plant at Hurricane Creek.

The press conference went well. The only possibly discordant note came when a reporter asked Symington if he took back all the harsh things he had said about Wilson a few days before; to which Symington replied that he would take back whatever Wilson would want him to take back.

The public reception of the news was excellent. Both Symington and Alcoa were highly praised. The reaction within the government was generally but not uniformly favorable. Some of the lawyers, particularly in the Anti-Trust Division of the Department of Justice, were still disturbed. They had not been consulted on Clark's letter. They noted that Alcoa's offer did not clearly cover all the useful patents at Hurricane Creek, and that the so-called cross-licensing arrangements were actually grant-back provisions favoring Alcoa; and they believed that the agreement affected the government's legal position. They thought the publicity unnecessary. But the top officials were all delighted.

On January 31 Symington resigned to become Assistant Secretary of War for Air.

VI. Epilogue: January 1948-June 1950

THE INDUSTRY

The period of four and a half years between the announcement of the Reynolds agreement and the Communist aggression in Korea was characterized in the economy of the United States by an almost unbroken boom; aluminum was in the forefront of the beneficiaries. Reed had anticipated immediate post-war consumption of 800,000,000 pounds of new metal; the SPB report had said: "it may take 5 years after the war before this country will require anything like 1 billion pounds of its primary metal capacity." As matters turned out, consumption in the United States during the period never fell below 1,150,000,000 pounds of primary metal per annum, though there were two sharp but brief slumps in demand. Much of the time consumers' needs were met only by drawing on RFC stocks and Canadian imports, and on numerous occasions customers' orders remained unfilled. Time and again the independent fabricators complained, as Reynolds had done in 1940, that the integrated producers were using an undue share of aluminum ingot in their own profitable fabricating operations. During this period the price of aluminum rose only slightly, far less than the price of other basic metals (though the price of scrap aluminum underwent great fluctuations). The tariff on Canadian aluminum was reduced by trade agreement.

The Reynolds agreement broke the log jam. Kaiser quickly followed by leasing the Baton Rouge alumina and Mead reduction plants and by buying the small Tacoma reduction plant. Kaiser and Reynolds were given preference over other bidders in acquiring plants, and both gradually achieved fully integrated status by securing diversified fabricating plants. In the course of time their short term leases were supplanted by long term leases and then by outright purchase agreements. Capacity was enlarged by new arrangements for power and by the addition of pot lines secured from the uneconomic government plants. In all this activity (with two minor exceptions noted below) Alcoa did not share; but, using its own funds, it too proceeded to enlarge its own primary and fabricating capacity. It is worth noting that some of the additional power supplies were obtained, not from hydroelectric installations, but from thermal plants. As the situation stabilized, Alcoa held about 50 per cent of total U. S. primary capacity, Reynolds about 30 per cent, Kaiser about 20 per cent.

THE GOVERNMENT AND THE INDUSTRY

The relations of the government with the industry went through a variety of phases. During the immediate post-war reconversion period, there was a serious shortage of soda ash —needed for the manufacture of alumina; the staff of the Senate Small Business Committee was active in securing supplies for Reynolds and Kaiser.

This Committee was active in other ways as well. On December 31, 1946, in the closing days of the 79th Congress, its chairman, Senator Murray, issued a report to the members of his Committee which was published as a Senate Committee Print. The report was primarily a sharp attack on the agencies concerned with the disposal of the aluminum plants. While it recognized that the key plants had been leased (a few had been sold), it emphasized the fact that the leases were for comparatively short periods. (Subsequently, as we have seen, the leases were extended and finally converted into sales.) It also criticized the agencies involved for failing to take some of the steps outlined in the Interim Report of the Committee and the SPB report on aluminum. It blamed the RFC for having failed to cancel the Alcoa lease until it was "forced by other agencies." It sharply criticized the War Assets (i.e., Surplus Property) Administrators who succeeded Symington (one of them in particular) for certain actions that were taken during the year 1946. The only individuals who receive praise in the body of the report are Husbands and Symington.

The preface to the report speaks somewhat grudgingly of the comparative success of the aluminum disposal program; it also says:

> It is doubtful whether any such pattern of disposal resulting in the development of two major integrated competitors to the former single producer of metal would have developed had it not been for the co-operative action of the unofficial but nonetheless effective committee which worked together with the support of those who sought a sound solution of this problem in the interest of an expanding competitive economy.

The preface then names as members of this group three economists on Congressional committee staffs, and two in administrative agencies; it continues:

> The subject matter of this report was assembled by Samuel Moment, on loan to the Committee from the Bonneville Power Administration for this purpose. His high competency in this important field is attested by its merit as a document objectively appraising the work done to date to set up a sound competitive situation in light metals as a result of the Government's disposal program.

This report was prepared for the purpose of warning the War Assets Administrator to abide by the program of positive government support laid down in the original SPB aluminum report to Congress. The authors, convinced that the comparative success in plant disposal up to then was attributable to the "positive program," feared that War Assets' failure to give active support would lead Reynolds and Kaiser to cancel their leases or at least to fail to renew them.

Senator O'Mahoney's Military Affairs Subcommittee also issued a staff report on December 31, 1946. While expressing some concern over the administrative complexities of surplus property disposal, it expressed broad approval of the aluminum plant disposal program.

On February 12, 1947, Robert M. Littlejohn, a successor to Symington, submitted a supplemental report on aluminum plants and facilities to the Congress. The report is factual in character, listing the plants that had been sold and leased, and describing the current structure of the industry. While no direct reply is made to the criticisms in Senator Murray's report, the various limited steps taken under the heading of "Measures of Government Support" are listed in some detail. This report was submitted to the new 80th Congress. A direct reply to Senator Murray's report was no longer necessary. The new Congress was interested in other matters.

AN OVER-ALL SETTLEMENT WITH ALCOA

The government's problem did not disappear. Reynolds persisted in attempts to have aluminum bought for stockpile. Pointing to its own difficulties during the brief slumps in demand, and aided by the increasing concern for national security, it finally secured the enactment of legislation which permitted the government to accept payment for surplus plants in the form of aluminum to be added to the stockpile.

Alcoa, however, remained the chief problem. The patent negotiations dragged on for three years. Finally, in October 1948 a settlement was arrived at. All patents in dispute were made available to anyone in the industry: some on a royalty-free basis, some on payment of a moderate lump sum by the government, and others on a royalty basis that would not prove onerous to producers. Under the same over-all settlement, the government sold its Massena plant to Alcoa, while Alcoa agreed to withdraw from production an equivalent capacity at its own old plant at a nearby site and maintain it in a stand-by condition. The agreement also provided for the sale to Alcoa of certain equipment to expedite completion of a new plant Alcoa was building. This agreement settled all outstanding issues between Alcoa and the War Assets Administration, Alcoa having previously been permitted to acquire one aluminum extrusion plant.

In announcing the agreement on November 9, 1948, the War Assets Administrator emphasized the importance of the settlement for national defense; he noted the fact that neither Reynolds nor Kaiser had raised any objection; and pointed out that the government's aluminum disposal program had now been successfully brought to a conclusion.

What the Administrator did not mention was the position of the Department of Justice. The Attorney General had been consulted on the sale of the Massena plant, under Section 20 of the Act, and had advised the Administrator that disposition to Alcoa would be in contravention of the anti-trust laws. The Administrator considered that he was not necessarily bound by this advice, and decided to go ahead for reasons of national security. (The whole agreement had been submitted to the defense agencies and approved by them.) Ultimately, however, it was agreed all round that title to the plant would be temporarily withheld, but that the deed would be executed promptly if a pending decision in the *Aluminum* case were consistent therewith; the various individual license agreements were also made subject to any court ruling.

Thus the course of events comes back to the courts.

LEGAL DEVELOPMENTS

When the Circuit Court issued its *Aluminum* decision on March 12, 1945, it remanded the case, in accordance with established procedure, to the District Court. The District Court entered judgment on April 23, 1946, enjoining certain practices, and adjudicating the existence of a monopoly of the aluminum ingot market as of August 14, 1940, but reserving jurisdiction to determine the remedy, if any, at a later time, and also "for the purpose of enabling the Aluminum Company to apply to this court for a determination of the question whether it still has a monopoly of the aluminum ingot market in the United States." On March 31, 1947, Alcoa initiated a proceeding in the District Court under the right reserved to it in the District Court's judgment. It petitioned the District Court to adjudicate that Alcoa no longer had a monopoly of the aluminum ingot market of the United States. The government moved to dismiss this petition. Judge Caffey overruled the motion and set October 15, 1947, as the date for the trial of the issue raised by Alcoa's petition.

On September 13, 1947, the Department of Justice filed with the Circuit Court of Appeals for the Second Circuit a motion for a writ of mandamus to strike out of the judgment of April 23, 1946, the authority given to Alcoa to initiate such supplemental proceedings and to direct the District Court to dismiss Alcoa's petition and halt the trial scheduled for October 15. The Circuit Court of Appeals heard argument on the mandamus on October 14, 1947, and two weeks later dismissed the government's motion on the ground that appellate jurisdiction had reverted to the Supreme Court and that it alone could pass upon the issue raised by the motion for mandamus. The District Court suspended proceedings until its jurisdiction to proceed was determined. The Supreme Court granted certiorari to review the decision of the Circuit Court and on May 24, 1947, reversed the Circuit Court of Appeals for its refusal to take jurisdiction, remanding the case to that Court for further proceedings. Concurrently with the certiorari application, the Department had filed in the Supreme Court a petition for leave to proceed with its mandamus action in that Court, but two weeks after the decision of May 24 the Supreme Court denied the petition, thereby returning the entire issue to the Circuit Court of Appeals.

Matters then proceeded to a climax. The government filed its petition for dissolution in District Court. And the Circuit Court while denying the writ of mandamus, returned the whole matter to the District Court for trial on both petitions under a reinterpretation of its earlier decision; the critical paragraph in the Court's new opinion reads:

> Dissolution . . . will not depend on the single issue whether "Alcoa" at the time of the judgment shall have a monopoly of the ingot market. On the contrary, it will depend upon what is "Alcoa's" position in the industry at that time: i.e., whether it must be divided into competing units in order to conform with the law. The continuance of the monopoly in ingot aluminum may in the court's judgment be enough to justify dissolution; but its absence will forbid neither dissolution, nor any other remedy.

Under this interpretation of the mandate, it was clear that Judge Caffey's view that he could try the matter on the single issue of the continued existence of monopoly, in other words, by trial exclusively on the issue presented by Alcoa's petition, was untenable. In any event, before the case came up for trial Judge Caffey had retired, and the trial was held before Judge Knox. The trial began on March 28, 1949, but after it began, there was a long recess, so the record was not finally closed for proof until January 16, 1950; argument followed in February. On June 2, 1950, Judge Knox handed down his opinion. The opinion runs to some 180 pages and reveals careful adherence to the views of the Circuit Court. The court's specific conclusions are interspersed at appropriate points; later, in the formal Final Judgment issued on July 6, the conclusions were assembled in systematic form as follows (purely technical matters such as definitions are omitted):

II

> The petition of Alcoa filed on March 31, 1947 is hereby denied on the merits, and dismissed.

III

> The execution of the program approved by the Congress for disposal of certain government-owned aluminum plants and facilities, together with Alcoa's acts in aid thereof, have not wholly overcome the effects of the decree of monopolization that was entered herein on April 23, 1946. For such reason, further remedial action of an appropriate nature is required.

IV

> The evidence in this proceeding is insufficient to give the Court a well founded assurance that, in future years, competitive conditions of an effective and lawful nature will prevail in the domestic aluminum industry. Consequently, the injunctions contained in paragraph 9 of the judgment of April 23, 1946 will be continued in full force and effect.

V

> In order further to promote the establishment of the requisite competitive conditions in such manner as will give assurance that they will hereafter prevail, Alcoa and the individual defendants who own stock in both Alcoa and Aluminium Limited, . . . are directed to prepare and submit a plan or plans for carrying out the disposal of stock interest either in Aluminium Limited or in Alcoa. . . .

VI

The grant-back provisions running to Alcoa, . . . in each of the three royalty-free patent license agreements between the United States of America and Alcoa . . . are hereby decreed to be unenforcible, and Alcoa shall make no claim or assertion to the contrary.

VII

The agreement . . . between War Assets Administration . . . and Alcoa with respect to the sale to Alcoa of the government-owned aluminum smelting plant located at Massena, New York . . . shall forthwith be fully executed and carried out.

VIII

The divestiture of plants and properties of Alcoa, for which the plaintiff has petitioned, is presently denied; however, jurisdiction of this cause is retained for five years from the date of adoption by the Court of a plan, pursuant to paragraph V of this judgment, for the disposal of stock interests, within which period, if conditions so warrant, the plaintiff may petition this Court for further and more complete relief. . . .

X

Jurisdiction of this cause is retained for the purpose of enabling the plaintiff or Alcoa to apply to the Court at any time for such further orders and directions as may be necessary or appropriate for the construction or complete execution of this judgment, for the modification or termination of any of the provisions thereof, for the enforcement of compliance therewith, and for the punishment of any violations thereof. . . .

Both sides had reason to be pleased, and displeased:

Alcoa had failed in its attempt to be declared free from all monopolistic taint, to have the injunction of April 23, 1946, dissolved, and to be released from court supervision. It had lost on the minor but persistent issue of the grant-back provisions in the patent agreements. And various defendants—primarily the chief officers of Alcoa—were required to divest themselves of either Alcoa or Alted (Aluminium Limited) stock—though Judge Knox carefully explained that his ruling on this point was made purely for curative reasons and did not constitute an over-ruling of Judge Caffey's non-affiliation conclusion.

The Department of Justice had failed to secure the dissolution of Alcoa—though the possibility was still left open. It had failed to prevent the sale of the Massena plant to Alcoa. And it had not secured all it had asked for in connection with stock divestment and continuing supervision.

Appeal was thus, though tempting, risky for both sides; and the new defense program constituted a strong deterrent to continued litigation. Whatever the reasons, the decision was not appealed. The details of the plan for stock divestment were to be worked out later, and for at least another five years court modification of the decree was still possible; but June 2, 1950, can be taken as the end of an era of litigation.

The reconversion period, in which the aluminum industry of the United States was remade, also came to a clear final end on June 25, 1950, with the Communist invasion of the Republic of Korea. A new defense program was set in motion. The government and the companies faced new problems.

Afterthoughts

The success of a government program is frequently a matter of perspective. In view of what lay within the control of the Surplus Property Board and its successors, and the Congressional definition of objectives, it seems clear that the aluminum plant disposal program was a success: the chief plants were sold, the government received a moderate return in cash or kind, the nation's full economic aluminum capacity was maintained in operation. Furthermore, one entirely new aluminum producer was got off to an excellent start, and one beginner was greatly strengthened. A lawyer might argue that the dissolution of Alcoa would have been in the national interest—a dissolution that may well have been forestalled by the disposal of plants to Reynolds and Kaiser. An economist might argue that, while thirty producers would create useful competition, three producers—an oligopoly—are less desirable than one—a monopoly. But whatever view is taken of these controversial speculations, it is clear that the disposals to Reynolds and Kaiser were consistent with the law, and did constitute a successful program from the standpoint of the administrator.

The interest of the student of public administration, in any event, lies less in the economic and legal results than in the processes by which public policy is formed. Perhaps most striking in this case is the complexity of the whole. Many agencies were involved, and many Congressional committees. In the light of subsequent experience, it seems reasonably clear that the SPB, the policy agency, and RFC, in its capacity of disposal agency, could have been combined with a saving of time and temper—though the separation of the two functions did not make any critical difference to the aluminum program. But simplification of the over-all organizational structure could hardly have occurred. The reader may find it useful to contemplate the reasons for this elaborate inter-agency involvement and ways and means for improving operations under the circumstances. The multiplication of special Congressional committees, it may be noted, has been abolished; but, paradoxically enough, it is not clear that an administrator today would have fewer committees to worry about than did Symington.

Policy in this case seems to have been made neither exclusively at the top nor exclusively at the bottom, neither exclusively in the administration, nor exclusively in Congress. Symington is a decisive figure in the case; yet his freedom of decision was conditioned by the work done by the various professionals on his own staff and elsewhere. Their activity too is worthy of note: Symington in all probability would have missed his chance to cancel the Alcoa lease if Cox, Goodloe, and Stein had not pressed the point. The reader will observe that their cross-relations, so important to the case in this instance, can find no clear source in any organizational blueprint.

Certainly this significant effect of informal relationships is striking in the instance of Moment, with his web of friendships in the administration and in Congressional staff. Here other questions may be asked: What about Moment's "goldfish bowl" policy? What are the ideal relations between administrative officials and Congressional staff?

Then, too, the case provides an opportunity for exploring characteristic relations between government and business. How different the relationship between Justice and Alcoa, for example, and SPB and Alcoa, or Congressional staff and Reynolds. Under what circumstances should the government compromise the niceties of its legal position to obtain a working agreement? Obviously, no definitive answers are appropriate for such questions, but their existence can be noted and some of the conditioning factors evaluated.

Finally, it may be well to bear in mind that administrators need good fortune for success. The consummation of any agreement with Reynolds in the presence of a deep depression at the end of 1945 is hardly thinkable. Symington took bold advantage of the tide; but in applauding Symington, and comparing him with others, it is well to reserve some sympathy for the unfortunate administrator who is left on the beach by the ebb that he cannot control.

Appendix I

Sections 2, 19 and 20 of the Surplus Property Act of 1944

SEC. 2. The Congress hereby declares that the objectives of this Act are to facilitate and regulate the orderly disposal of surplus property so as—

(a) to assure the most effective use of such property for war purposes and the common defense;

(b) to give maximum aid in the reestablishment of a peacetime economy of free independent private enterprise, the development of the maximum of independent operators in trade, industry, and agriculture, and to stimulate full employment;

(c) to facilitate the transition of enterprises from wartime to peacetime production and of individuals from wartime to peacetime employment;

(d) to discourage monopolistic practices and to strengthen and preserve the competitive position of small business concerns in an economy of free enterprise;

(e) to foster and to render more secure family-type farming as the traditional and desirable pattern of American agriculture;

(f) to afford returning veterans an opportunity to establish themselves as proprietors of agricultural, business, and professional enterprises;

(g) to encourage and foster post-war employment opportunities;

(h) to assure the sale of surplus property in such quantities and on such terms as will discourage disposal to speculators or for speculative purposes;

(i) to establish and develop foreign markets and promote mutually advantageous economic relations between the United States and other countries by the orderly disposition of surplus property in other countries;

(j) to avoid dislocations of the domestic economy and of international economic relations;

(k) to foster the wide distribution of surplus commodities to consumers at fair prices;

(l) to effect broad and equitable distribution of surplus property;

(m) to achieve the prompt and full utilization of surplus property at fair prices to the consumer through disposal at home and abroad with due regard for the protection of free markets and competitive prices from dislocation resulting from uncontrolled dumping;

(n) to utilize normal channels of trade and commerce to the extent consistent with efficient and economic distribution and the promotion of the general objectives of this act (without discriminating against the establishment of new enterprises);

(o) to promote production, employment of labor, and utilization of the productive capacity and the natural and agricultural resources of the country;

(p) to foster the development of new independent enterprise;

(q) to prevent insofar as possible unusual and excessive profits being made out of surplus property;

(r) to dispose of surplus property as promptly as feasible without fostering monopoly or restraint of trade, or unduly disturbing the economy, or encouraging hoarding of such property, and to facilitate prompt redistribution of such property to consumers;

(s) to dispose of surplus Government-owned transportation facilities and equipment in such manner as to promote an adequate and economical national transportation system; and

(t) except as otherwise provided, to obtain for the Government, as nearly as possible, the fair value of surplus property upon its disposition.

SEC. 19. (a) The Board, in cooperation with the various disposal agencies, shall prepare and submit to the Congress within three months after enactment of this Act, a report as to each of the following classes of surplus property (not including any plant which cost the Government less than $5,000,000); (1) aluminum plants and facilities; (2) magnesium plants and facilities; (3) synthetic rubber plants and facilities; (4) chemical plants and facilities; (5) aviation gasoline plants and facilities; (6) iron and steel plants and facilities; (7) pipe lines and facilities used for transporting oil; (8) patents, processes, techniques, and inventions, except such as are necessary to the operation of the plants and facilities herein listed; (9) aircraft plants and facilities and aircraft and aircraft parts; (10) shipyards and facilities; (11) transportation facilities; and (12) radio and electrical equipment:

(i) Describing the amount, cost, and location of the property and setting forth other descriptive information relative to the use of the property;

(ii) Outlining the economic problems that may be created by disposition of the property;

(iii) Setting forth a plan or program for the care and handling, disposition, and use of the property consistent with the policies and objectives set forth in this Act.

(b) In the event that it is not possible within such period to prepare and submit a complete report to the Congress as to any class of property, the Board shall submit an interim report three months after the enactment of this Act, and shall submit a complete report as soon thereafter as possible. If the Board determines that it is desirable to alter or change any such plan or program or to prepare a report on any other class of property, it shall prepare in accordance with the provisions of this subsection and submit to the Congress an additional report, setting forth the altered or changed plan or program or a plan or program relating to the new class of property.

(c) Whenever the Board may deem it to be in the interest of the objectives of this Act it may authorize the disposition of any surplus property listed in classes 9 to 12, inclusive, of subsection (a) of this section. With respect to the property listed in classes 1 to 8, inclusive, no disposition shall be made or authorized until thirty days after such report (or additional report) has been made while Congress is in session, except that the

Board may authorize any disposal agency to lease any such property for a term of not more than five years.

(d) The Board may authorize any disposal agency to dispose of any materials or equipment related to any surplus plant covered by this section, if such materials and equipment are not necessary for the operation of the plant in the manner for which it is designed.

(e) This section shall not apply to any Government-owned equipment, structure, or other property operated as an integral part of a privately owned plant and not capable of economic operation as a separate and independent unit.

SEC. 20. Whenever any disposal agency shall begin negotiations for the disposition to private interests of a plant or plants or other property, which cost the Government $1,000,000 or more, or of patents, processes, techniques, or inventions, irrespective of cost, the disposal agency shall promptly notify the Attorney General of the proposed disposition and the probable terms or conditions thereof. Within a reasonable time, in no event to exceed ninety days after receiving such notification, the Attorney General shall advise the Board and the disposal agency whether, in his opinion, the proposed disposition will violate the antitrust laws. Upon the request of the Attorney General, the Board or other Government agency shall furnish or cause to be furnished such information as it may possess which the Attorney General determines to be appropriate or necessary to enable him to give the advice called for by this section or to determine whether any other disposition of surplus property violates the antitrust laws. Nothing in this Act shall impair, amend, or modify the antitrust laws or limit and prevent their application to persons who buy or otherwise acquire property under the provisions of this Act. As used in this section, the term "antitrust laws" includes the Act of July 2, 1890 (ch. 647, 26 Stat. 209), as amended; the Act of October 15, 1914 (ch. 323, 38 Stat. 730), as amended; the Federal Trade Commission Act; and the Act of August 27, 1894 (ch. 349, secs. 73, 74, 28 Stat. 570), as amended.

Appendix II

Recommendations in Report of Surplus Property Board to Congress, September 21, 1945

The Board recommends the following program which it will follow, subject to any contrary indication from Congress in accordance with Section 19 of the Act:

(a) A system of priorities on disposal will be established in the following order: (1) competitors of Alcoa; (2) Alcoa to have certain facilities, subject to approval of the Attorney General, but only on terms that confer no competitive advantage; (3) stand-by service for national defense as recommended by the War and Navy Departments; (4) private enterprise for use in other industries; and (5) export to members of the United Nations.

(b) Bidders will be given preference in accordance with competence and prospective ability to survive.

(c) A plan for disposal of individual plants or groups of plants is given in detail in this report, based on present candidates and others that may become interested, and in accordance with the priorities above.

(d) Disposal of key plants will initially either be by sale or lease with option to purchase. Other plants will be sold or leased according to individual circumstances. Rentals and prices will be fixed with due regard to earning ability and not necessarily with regard to original cost or other valuations. Terms can be offered as favorable as were given Alcoa under the original lease by which the RFC stands the risk of losses, and profits are shared with the Government, subject, however, to review and approval of RFC of (1) the price at which metal is sold; (2) top salaries; and (3) extraordinary expenses. Should operators wish a larger share of profits, terms may call for them to assume a greater amount of risk. In any event, the RFC will require that the operators assume reasonable risks of working capital and that the Government withdraw its assumption of risks after some fair period.

(e) The Board will help new producers as follows: (1) the supply of bauxite owned by the RFC will be available at Hurricane Creek, and inquiries will be made to determine whether foreign ore can be obtained under international agreements or other agreements; (2) the RFC will finance necessary changes in plants in order to improve their competitive position, where costs appear to be recoverable; and (3) control over supplies of secondary metal will be maintained as indicated.

The Board believes that this program is more likely to achieve the purposes of the statute than any other. The Board recognizes, however, that conditions beyond its control may make the program impossible of accomplishment. In that event, unless the courts dissolve or reorganize

Alcoa under the Sherman Act, Congress will have to consider whether to leave the aluminum industry under the domination of one company or whether to authorize the Government, either by subsidized or direct operation of key plants, to provide some measure of production that is independent of Alcoa's control.

Appendix III

Bibliographical Note

The basic material on the disposal of the aluminum plants from the standpoint of the administration is concentrated in three reports and three press releases (the September 7, 1945 press release of RFC (RFC-2303) is printed in the SPB report of September 21, 1945): all these are described in the text above:

Aluminum Plants and Facilities: Report of the Surplus Property Board to the Congress. September 21, 1945. Washington, 1945.

The Aluminum Industry: Letter from the Attorney General, September 14, 1945. Printed as: Senate Document No. 94, 79th Congress, 1st Session. Washington, 1945.

Aluminum Plants and Facilities: First Supplementary Report of the War Assets Administration to the Congress. February 12, 1947. Washington, 1947.

SPA-180. Surplus Property Administration. Advance Release for Sunday Papers, January 6, 1946. (Mimeo.) Washington, 1946.

SPA-193. Surplus Property Administration. For Immediate Release Thursday, January 10, 1946. (Mimeo.) Washington, 1946.

The basic Alcoa material is contained in three privately printed brochures and two press releases of September 7, 1945, and January 6, 1946; the releases apparently no longer exist in mimeographed form:

A *Reply to the Surplus Property Board's Report* of September 21, 1945, with respect to the Disposition of Government-Owned Aluminum Plants and Facilities: A letter of protest sent to the Surplus Property Administration by Aluminum Company of America. October 15, 1945. Pittsburgh, 1945.

A *Reply to the Report of the Attorney General* to the Congress, dated September 11, 1945, Advocating the Break-Up of the Aluminum Company of America into regional clusters of competing units. A Letter sent to the Attorney General of the United States by Aluminum Company of America. December 3, 1945. Pittsburgh, 1945.

Letters by Aluminum Company of America Dealing with Surplus Property Disposal.

December 17, 1945—to the Attorney General of the United States.

December 28, 1945—to the Reconstruction Finance Corporation.

Pittsburgh, 1945.

The basic materials illustrating the viewpoint of the Congressional staff advocates of a "positive" disposal program are found in two reports:

Future of Light Metals: Interim Report of the Surplus War Property Subcommittee of the Special Committee to Study Problems of American Small Business, United States Senate, September 10, 1945, 79th Congress, 1st Session. Senate Subcommittee Print No. 5. Washington, 1945.

Future of Light Metals and Government Plant Disposals: Report of the Chairman to the Members of the Committee of the Special Committee to Study Problems of American Small Business, United States Senate. December 31, 1946. 79th Congress, 2nd Session. Senate Committee Print No. 14. Washington, 1947.

The two documents best illustrating the interplay of Congressional, administration and industry attitudes are the records of two of the hearings. The printed texts undoubtedly reflect some editing but are adequate for practical purposes. (Quotations herein from the Joint Hearings are from the revised edition.)

Aviation and Light Metals Industries: Investigation of the National Defense Program. Hearings before a Special Committee Investigating the National Defense Program. 79th Congress, 1st Session. (Mead Committee) Part 31. (Spokane Hearings) August 21, 22, 1945. Pp. 15,133-15,314, 15,515-15,575. Washington, 1946.

Aluminum Plant Disposal: Joint Hearings before the . . . Committee on Military Affairs, Special Committee to Study and Survey Problems of Small Business Enterprises . . . Special Committee on Postwar Economic Policy and Planning. United States Senate, 79th Congress, 1st Session, on the Aluminum Reports . . . Parts 1-5. October 15-19, 1945. Washington, 1945.

There are two articles on the disposal program of some interest. One, by Roback, contains a useful legal analysis, but the reader should realize that its approach is strongly influenced by the writer's previous active membership in the group of Congressional staff advocates of a "positive" program; the article also cites all the significant legal references up to 1946. The *Fortune* article is a dramatic and readable account of the Peace-with-Alcoa episode described herein.

Roback, Herbert: "Monopoly or Competition through Surplus Plant Disposal? The Aluminum Case" (1946) 31 *Cornell Law Q.* p. 302 et seq.
"Aluminum Reborn," *Fortune*, May 1, 1946.

The chief interest of Judge Hand's *Aluminum* decision to students of monopoly does not lie in its treatment of the disposal program, but rather in its reliance on Section 2 of the Sherman Act, the anti-monopoly section, instead of Section 1, the section prohibiting conspiracy in restraint of trade. Viewed in this light, it is a decision of critical importance, and almost all recent articles on antitrust theory include a discussion of its implications. Two such articles out of many may be cited for the benefit of those interested in the relation of the *Aluminum* decision to the anti-trust tradition:

Levi, Edward H. "The Antitrust Laws and Monopoly" (1947) 14 *Univ. of Chicago Law R.* p. 153 et seq.
Rostow, Eugene V. "The New Sherman Act: A Positive Instrument of Progress" (1947) 14 *Univ. of Chicago Law R.* p. 567 et seq.

The two crucial legal decisions in the *Aluminum* case are, of course, Judge Hand's opinion and Judge Knox's opinion. They are not only legal documents; both contain a wealth of economic data on aluminum and its producers, including statistical materials on prices, profits, production, etc., etc. The formal citations for these opinions are:

Judge Hand's opinion:
148 F (2nd) 416.
Judge Knox's opinion:
91 Fed. Supp. 333 SDNY 1950.

THE AIR
SEARCH AND RESCUE PROGRAM

CONTENTS

FOREWORD

Questions about jurisdiction arise inevitably in any large organization—though in some the answers to jurisdictional questions may be almost automatic and may remain valid for long periods of time—and they are likely to arise most frequently and cause most difficulty when new functions and responsibilities are being fitted into a partially existing and partially new organizational structure.

Jurisdictional disputes signify the existence of jurisdictional questions. Conventionally such disputes are regarded as sinful. The participants are assumed to be grabbing for power for malevolent reasons. This conclusion may fit some cases, but all jurisdictional conflicts cannot be written off so easily: indeed many observers of the Federal government, for example, where jurisdictional squabbles have been front page news for years, are doubtful that the conventional description applies with any great frequency.

The events described in the following pages constituted a jurisdictional dispute. The dispute and its practical consequences were adjusted, at least temporarily, without damage to the public interest and indeed never assumed major significance. The significance for the reader lies in the fact that the course of events is reasonably typical of interagency feuds. The way the dispute arose, the attitudes of the participants, and the nature of the compromise settlement are normal and, in the context of Washington institutional life, natural. Thoughtful consideration of this rather simple case may therefore be helpful in suggesting ways and means for understanding, and possibly even for avoiding or alleviating more complicated jurisdictional disagreements.

The problem of securing policy consistency parallels the problem of defining jurisdiction. In very small organizations and in those whose functions are uncomplicated, it may be difficult to observe the processes by which policy consistency is obtained, or even to observe that such a process actually exists. At the other extreme, in the Federal government the organizational structure is so complicated, the policy ramifications so great, and the impacts of agency operations so widespread that analytic observation is difficult because too much material is available. It is thus hard for the outsider and frequently even for the insider to follow with intelligence the course of policy formation when various agencies are involved. This difficulty of analysis persists even when an interagency committee, which is a formal co-ordinating device, is at work. Frequently even the members of such committees are quite uncertain about the effects of committee work. The following narrative may be helpful in casting some light on this problem. For here, in fairly concrete terms, can be seen one very small portion of the operations of one interagency committee. Excessive generalization on the basis of this tiny example would be unwarranted; but the analysis of this case may suggest questions to be asked of the operations of other similar committees.

The problems of jurisdictional conflict and operating co-ordination of diversely controlled resources illustrated by the occurrences described below arose in the course of efforts to reach a decision on a specific question—the handling of search and rescue operations for aircraft in distress. Ultimately, as will be seen, a compromise decision was arrived at and put into effect by the interdepartmental committee known as the Air Co-ordinating Committee; but the reader will also observe that the final decision came about only after a whole succession of previous decisions—by individuals, by agencies and by committees. No attempt has been made to analyze the various alternatives that might have been selected in each instance in lieu of all the particular decisions that were in fact actually made. But the reader will, of course, realize that each of these decisions represented a choice among alternatives. While the alternatives are not described in detail, the reader can observe the interaction of individual and agency personalities and interests as they affected the various actions. The reader can also observe the impact of the hierarchical committee structure on the whole process by which final and preliminary decisions were made. Finally it may be noted that the last decision on the search and rescue program was not agreed to until the top committee also agreed to enlarge its membership.

The Air Co-ordinating Committee

The historical context of the following events needs little explanation. By the beginning of the war, the acceptance by the Federal government of the responsibility to aid in the development of air commerce had caused many existing departments and agencies of the government to expand existing functions and also had resulted in the assumption of new functions and the establishment of new organizational units. The necessity for finding some sort of co-ordinating mechanism to secure consistency of action in the exercise of these diverse functions became apparent and resulted initially in the establishment of some rather informal interdepartmental committees. Later, during the tremendous spurt of aviation activity in World War II, many government officials came to the view that a more formal top level co-ordinating mechanism was needed. This need received further impetus as a result of the Chicago Convention on international civil aviation, convened at Chicago in late 1944 under the sponsorship of the United States, which was now assuming leadership in the encouragement and development of international co-operation in various fields. At this convention plans were developed for an international civil aviation organization, the establishment of which would place further responsibilities upon the United States—should she join—with respect to practically all phases of our aviation policy. Such responsibilities would require continual co-ordination of interested agencies and departments in order to secure a concerted United States governmental position on the various aspects of aviation policy. After several attempts at establishing a top level aviation council or committee, a joint Interdepartmental Memorandum was drawn up on March 27, 1945, which provided for an Air Coordinating Committee (ACC). This memorandum was signed by the Acting Secretary of State and the Secretaries of Navy, War, and Commerce; within a few weeks the Civil Aeronautics Board (CAB) agreed to join the Committee. The members of the ACC at that time were the Assistant Secretary of State, the Assistant Secretary of War for Air, the Assistant Secretary of Navy for Air, the Assistant Secretary of Commerce for Air, and the Chairman of the CAB.

The Interdepartmental Memorandum also contained a list of subjects which were to be considered by the ACC. Some of these subjects were: International operating rights for American commercial and military aircraft; operating rights in United States territory for foreign commercial and military aircraft; establishment and operation of navigational aids abroad for the benefit of United States commercial and military aircraft; instructions to be issued from time to time to the United States representative on the Interim Council of the Provisional International Civil Aviation Organization (PICAO); designation and operation of Federal airways; search and rescue; communications; aviation education.

The ACC was to be concerned with the co-ordination of major policies in aviation to ensure an integrated and consistent program; the implementation of agreed-upon policy was to be left to that agency in whose area the operating responsibility for the particular program primarily lay.

In September 1946 the ACC was given more formal recognition by the issuance of an Executive Order re-creating the ACC with its original membership, plus the Post Office Department and the Bureau of the Budget, the latter agency to serve as a non-voting member. (Earlier a request for membership in the ACC by the Treasury Department, of which the Coast Guard is a bureau, had been refused by the ACC on the ground that that department did not have sufficient concern in aviation matters to warrant its membership on the Committee; in those instances in which Treasury had sufficient interest it could send a representative to the ACC meeting.) The order also provided for the establishment of procedures authorizing non-member agencies to participate and vote in the ACC or its subcommittees when appropriate. Pertinent provisions of the order stated that the ACC ". . . should examine aviation problems and developments affecting more than one participating agency; develop and recommend integrated policies to be carried out and actions to be taken by the participating agencies or by any other government agency charged with responsibility in the aviation field; and, to the extent permitted by law, co-ordinate the aviation activities of such agencies except activities relating to the exercise of quasi-judicial functions . . . and consult with the representatives of the United States to the Provisional International Civil Aviation Organization or to the permanent successor thereof and recommend to the Department of State general policy directives and instructions for the guidance of the said representatives." The ACC ". . . after obtaining the views of the head of each agency concerned, shall submit to the President, together with the said views, (a) such of the Committee's recommendations on aviation policies as require the attention of the President by reason of their character or importance, (b) those important aviation questions the disposition of which is prevented by the inability of the agencies concerned to agree. . . ."

Soon after its inception the ACC had found it convenient to assign to ad hoc subcommittees for study and recommendations many of the questions which had been referred to it and which required detailed study. The members of these subcommittees were technicians from various departments. Modification of the structure and procedures of the ACC followed shortly after the issuance of the Executive Order. There were established three divisions, Economic, Technical, and Industrial, each of which was in effect a subcommittee of the top committee, and each division had assigned to it specific permanent subcommittees. Membership in each of the three divisions consists of those ACC member agencies who have an interest in the matters of that division; the same is true with respect to the various subcommittees. Each agency on a division has one vote (as it does on a subcommittee), and where unanimous agreement prevails on any question, except those which deal with "major policies" or PICAO matters, a division may act for the ACC. This delegated authority may be redelegated to a subcommittee when agreed to by the ACC. Matters of "major policy" are referred to the ACC for final action, while PICAO (now ICAO—International Civil Aviation Organization) matters are referred to the PICAO panel, which is constituted outside the division structure but in a similar manner. The reorganization also established a legal subcommittee outside of the division structure and an industry advisory panel. The latter panel, while acting in only a consultative capacity, can present papers to the ACC, attend ACC meetings by invitation, and participate without vote in subcommittees upon matters of interest to it where no issue of security or the like is present.

A permanent full-time staff is maintained by the ACC: there is an Executive Secretary for the ACC and a secretary for each of the divisions. The Executive Secretary is authorized to appoint such assistants as appear necessary. General housekeeping functions are also performed by permanent staff personnel. Not long after the issuance of the Executive Order the permanent full-time staff numbered eighteen. Each agency designates one or more liaison representatives whose duty is to be the point of contact between his agency and the ACC hierarchy. The representative keeps his agency informed of the status of all issues in ACC of interest to his agency and refers to ACC those problems of his own agency which require attention of the ACC because of the concern of member agencies. Most of the liaison men spend full time on ACC affairs.

A question of aviation policy may be introduced at any level of the ACC hierarchy by a member agency or the industry advisory panel, and a non-member agency may make arrangements to introduce a paper into the ACC for recommendations. Completed papers carry a summary of the problem, conclusions, and recommended action. Certain subcommittees need not clear these completed papers with either the appropriate division or the ACC if the issue is a routine matter; depending upon the importance of the policy under consideration, a paper is otherwise cleared through a division or a division and the ACC itself. Often the importance of an issue is determined informally by the division secretary—over a period of time the division secretaries have been able to routinize the determination of the importance of certain types of issues which have recurred in sufficient volume to indicate a fairly fixed pattern of action. Moreover, informal discussion among the Executive Secretary, a division secretary, and a liaison representative often secures agreement on the nature and importance of an issue before it is introduced into the hierarchy for consideration.

The Search and Rescue Problem

Of the many aviation matters requiring co-ordinated activity by the U. S. Government perhaps the most prevalent are those arising out of the responsibilities of the United States as a member of ICAO. One of these responsibilities is the provision of facilities, in co-operation with other nations, for search and rescue of aircraft in distress. Article 25 of the Chicago convention (the convention on Civil Aviation drawn up at Chicago in December 1944) provides that contracting states shall ". . . provide such measures of assistance to aircraft in distress in its territory as it may find practicable . . . ," and that each ". . . contracting state, when undertaking search for missing aircraft, will collaborate in co-ordinated measures which may be recommended from time to time pursuant to this convention."

Search and rescue is the attempt to find and return to safety an aircraft in distress but still airborne or the persons from an aircraft that has crashed. In simple terms, search and rescue means locating the plane or its passengers, and guiding the plane back to safety—if possible—or, alternatively, finding the passengers and bringing them to safety. Fundamentally the problem is rather similar to forest fire control: in fighting forest fires there must be a nucleus of trained men with fixed responsibilities and procedures who can set into motion organized teams and specialized equipment, and can call on the necessary number of auxiliaries who are not themselves professional fire fighters. Permanent facilities are maintained for spotting fires in the major danger areas, and there are permanent communications facilities that are rapidly augmented when the need arises. In any specific fire, managerial responsibility must be fixed, but speedy co-operation by other agencies is essential.

So with search and rescue. There must be centers for action within range of main routes or in a network covering a whole region. Distress calls, reports on overdue planes, and information from observers must be received and acted on. Guidance of crippled planes and location of accidents involve the use of radio and radar of various types, some specialized, much of it part of the general air and sea navigation system. Searching parties—by land, sea, or air—must be organized and equipped; here again there must be great reliance on non-specialized equipment such as vessels at sea, and commercial or military planes, on regular routes or diverted from their routes, or sent out specially. The organization of each search and rescue operation is dependent on the use of standardized procedures, specialized knowledge of available facilities and physical conditions, and on prompt co-operation by various agencies public and private. As with forest fires, in each specific search and rescue operation there must be fixed managerial responsibility, established procedures, specialized equipment, and prompt co-operation by other agencies.

As a practical matter, the characteristics of air transportation are such that search and rescue in the United States and off its shores, if they are to be effective, must be the responsibility of the Federal government. Only the

Federal government can make sure that the over-all program is adequate and that requirements have been determined and facilities established—regardless of ownership—that will be available at the right place and time. The responsibility of the government has, over the years, been somewhat indeterminate; there has been some question about the propriety of the establishment of government facilities for private transport; but perhaps because of humanitarian considerations, the responsibility is now well established domestically. And in participating in PICAO, the government formally assumed responsibility for search and rescue in the international area. The problem of administrative co-ordination is a consequence of the acceptance of the function of responsibility.

There are in the United States several agencies which can claim significant interest and varying responsibility for search and rescue. By statute and tradition the Coast Guard has had a concern over safety of life at sea. In the eyes of the public the Coast Guard has been long associated with dramatic rescues of ships and personnel in maritime disasters. The gradual enlargement of its responsibilities to include air disasters at sea was hastened when, in 1944, by direction of the Joint Chiefs of Staff, there was established a Search and Rescue Agency headed by the Commandant of the Coast Guard with an advisory board consisting of representatives of the Army Air Forces, Army Service Forces, and the Navy. This agency performed no operational work in the field but was primarily concerned with conducting studies of a technical nature for the primary use of the military agencies. The appropriateness of centering this activity in the Coast Guard presumably rested on the fact that the Coast Guard was technically well equipped for the work; but it should be noted that the war was still on, and in time of war the Coast Guard is transferred from the Treasury to the Navy. And in this connection, it may be added that when the Coast Guard was transferred from the Navy back to the Treasury Department in December 1945, the Executive Order stated that the "Coast Guard shall continue, for such period as may be mutually agreeable to the Secretary of the Treasury and the Secretary of the Navy, Air-Sea Rescue functions . . . under the directional control of the Navy. . . ." The facilities and equipment required for these activities were placed under the jurisdiction of the Treasury Department. Thus during the period in which the events described in the following pages took place, the Coast Guard was regarded by some as an auxiliary or quasi-auxiliary of the Navy with respect to search and rescue operations, though the formal contacts with other agencies were in fact conducted by the Secretary of the Treasury (or his delegate) rather than the Secretary of the Navy.

The Army Air Forces (and now the Air Force) has always maintained facilities to conduct search and rescue for its own personnel and those of the Army. And during and since World War II the Air Force by reason of its far-flung bases has of necessity maintained rather extensive facilities for this activity and has utilized them to aid in search and rescue in civil air accidents.

Other agencies are also involved. The Navy participates in civil search and rescue operations when it is requested to do so or in emergencies in which Naval facilities can speedily be brought to aid; the Navy, however, maintains no specific organization or program for this purpose. The statutory responsibility of the CAB and CAA in matters of civil aviation safety necessitates their interest in aircraft failures and crashes. Moreover the CAA, through acceptance of flight plans, initiates search and rescue action in overdue flights, and through its traffic control and communications facilities can aid in reporting information in emergencies. In certain circumstances the high-frequency direction-finding network of the Federal Communications Commission (FCC) may be used to aid aircraft in emergencies.

Of all these various agencies, the Coast Guard and Army Air Force were, in 1946, the most interested in search and rescue for civil aviation. The Coast Guard's interest in its aviation activities had been greatly stimulated before the war under Secretary of the Treasury Morgenthau, and during the war while it was assigned to the Navy, and now, in 1946, it was anxious to preserve with respect to civil aviation the significant position it held in wartime with the military search and rescue agency and in peacetime with the maritime industry. The Army Air Forces, during the course of events related below, was in the process of becoming an entity in itself through proposed merger or unification plans, and in moving toward an independent role it was anxious to assert and maintain its full responsibilities in all aspects of aviation. The officers in both agencies were aviation enthusiasts and confident of great developments in the future. Because of these attitudes and the overlapping of interests and functions, it was inevitable that questions of jurisdiction would arise.

The Dublin Conference

In early 1946 PICAO arranged the first in a series of regional meetings to formulate a co-operative plan for the facilitation of international civil aviation. This was the North Atlantic Route Service Conference held in Dublin in March 1946. Position papers—i.e., agreed statements setting forth the views of our government—for the United States delegation to this conference were prepared by various subcommittees and working groups of the ACC. One such group was assigned to work out proposals with respect to search and rescue requirements. This group pointed out in its paper that at the time there were within the North Atlantic and other regions search and rescue facilities established for United States military purposes; however, it said, due to decreasing military necessity many of these facilities would be abandoned. Although the delegation to Dublin had made surveys to determine minimum requirements, the group wished some assurance that the existing facilities would be maintained until there was agreement upon plans for provision of civil air traffic needs. The working group therefore recommended that the ACC assure the continued operation of existing facilities until co-operative arrangements could be completed.

No final settlement was reached at the Dublin Conference concerning search and rescue operations. It was recommended at the conference that there be instituted a series of rescue co-ordination centers and units which would serve the North Atlantic flight area. And although considerable discussion took place among representatives of the participating countries, particularly with respect to the technical aspects of search and rescue operations, no program was established. Further study and participation by the various interested agencies of the United States government would be required to prepare for further negotiations, through PICAO, with the interested governments on this question in the future. Such study and participation were to be handled through the ACC.

Upon the return of the United States delegation from Dublin one member in particular was deeply concerned over the unsettled problem and quite anxious that this country move rapidly toward an established policy for search and rescue so that it would be prepared to act on forthcoming suggestions and requests from PICAO. This man was W. B. Scheibel, a Commander in the Coast Guard, a graduate of the Coast Guard Academy in 1929, and an aviator of considerable experience, particularly in search and rescue work. Indeed, he was an enthusiastic specialist in search and rescue. During the course of events related below, he served as the Executive Assistant to the Head, Search and Rescue Agency—that agency established by the Joint Chiefs of Staff referred to above.

The Coast Guard Proposal

Concerned as he was about the responsibilities of the United States with respect to any future program suggested through PICAO, Commander Scheibel started preparation of a recommended draft statement on search and rescue policy. It was his thought that the basic problem was one of assigning direct responsibility for such a program. Other questions, such as requirements for control stations, radio or radar nets, etc., he considered secondary and to be dealt with after the designation of an agency to carry on with the search and rescue problem. In view of the general agreements arrived at in Dublin to continue operation of existing facilities, and the expectation of more specific arrangements in the future, it seemed to him that a single agency in this country should take the lead in formulating plans to fulfill existing and expected obligations. One specific agency would therefore be accountable for the administration of the program, including the securing of funds, a responsibility which seemed to Commander Scheibel of critical importance. Commander Scheibel felt that this one agency could only be the Coast Guard—he reasoned that it had long been associated with safety of life at sea, that its commandant was chairman of the military Search and Rescue Agency, that it had personnel technically equipped in this field, and that its personnel had played a leading role at the Dublin Conference. He was convinced that the activity was important and that it could be properly managed only if Coast Guard was given general oversight of the program; he thought it wise to defer consideration of technical problems and operating proposals until the primary question was settled.

Soon Commander Scheibel with aid from some of his colleagues in the Coast Guard had prepared a paper on the subject which he wished to submit and receive clearance on from the ACC. This was an important matter to the Coast Guard, and it was decided that the paper should be presented to the top ACC Committee. Since Treasury (Coast Guard) was not a member of ACC, it had no automatic access to ACC; the Under Secretary of the Treasury was therefore requested to make arrangements for having the paper introduced at an ACC meeting. This was done.

In June 1946 the Treasury proposal was submitted to the ACC. Pertinent language of the paper reads as follows:

It can be expected that PICAO, at an early date, will forward to the United States specific recommendations concerning the provision of the facilities and services found necessary at the Dublin meeting. At such time it will be the duty and obligation of the United States to take immediate steps to implement these recommendations. Only by full integration of the services to be performed can the facilities be kept to a minimum and the needs of the using agencies retained within the limits of peacetime budgets. In addition, the organization and operation of facilities must be co-ordinated, not only within the United States, but with the organizations and facilities operated by countries in contiguous areas. For these reasons, it is believed that, in the interest of economy and efficient operation, the responsibility for implementation should be vested in one Agency of the Government.

It is believed essential that the designation of the Agency to fulfill the obligations of the United States as outlined herein should be made as soon as possible. All Agencies of the Government are now going through a difficult period of adjusting themselves to a peacetime status, and a determination of peacetime needs is necessary. In addition, immediate joint operational planning, domestic and international, is necessary to give early effect to the agreements arrived at, and full protection to the rapidly expanding international aviation service.

RECOMMENDED ACTION

That the Air Coordinating Committee, in recognition of the long-standing responsibility of the Coast Guard for the safety of life and property at sea, and in recognition of its existing Search and Rescue Organization, recommend the designation of the Coast Guard as the Agency within the United States to implement:

(1) The obligations of the United States for Search and Rescue as set forth under the Interim International Civil Aviation Agreement and the Regional Agreements as approved by the PICAO Council; and
(2) Such future Search and Rescue requirements as may be established by PICAO as obligations of the United States.

At the meeting (no Treasury official was present, for neither Treasury nor the ACC felt representation necessary at this time) both the chairman of the CAB and the Assistant Secretary of Commerce for Air expressed some doubts about the proposal. They both indicated that CAB was supposed to be the responsible agency, by ACC designation, for technical matters in this field because of CAB's statutory authority for the issuance of rules and regulations with respect to standards of civil aviation safety. Furthermore the CAB representative, although recognizing Coast Guard's responsibility with respect to search and rescue over water, questioned its responsibility for over-land activities. The War Department representative, the Assistant Secretary of War for Air, pointed out that his department would have to continue its own operation of search and rescue in some areas because of military necessity. It was then suggested by the Navy Department representative, the Assistant Secretary of Navy for Air, that the paper be referred to the Subcommittee on PICAO matters for further study. This was agreed to by the rest of the Committee and the paper was forwarded to the PICAO-Air Navigation Subcommittee with instructions that it pay particular attention to (1) requirements for search and rescue with respect to over-land flight, (2) recognition of the right of the military to continue its own search and rescue operations necessitated by military purposes, and (3) co-ordination of military and civil search and rescue techniques, facilities, and operations.

Subcommittee Action

The PICAO-Air Navigation Subcommittee undertook its assigned task under certain handicaps. Although it was composed of men competent in the field of navigational aids and techniques (it had been set up to aid the United States in its implementation of agreements established by PICAO on navigational and weather aids to international civil aviation), it was the view of Commander Scheibel and others closely connected with search and rescue activity that it did not contain technicians in search and rescue operations. For though there had been a working group established to deal with search and rescue problems for the Dublin Conference, that group was not active at this time. It was apparently the view of the ACC that the nature of its directives was such that they required more in the way of judgment about organization and allocation of responsibility than about technical knowledge of search and rescue, and that the members of the PICAO-Air Navigation Subcommittee were capable of dealing with the assigned problem.

Thus neither Commander Scheibel, nor any other representative of the Coast Guard, was invited to attend the meetings of the Subcommittee. The Subcommittee did not attempt to canvass personnel experienced and vitally interested in search and rescue. Almost inevitably, as a result, any recommendation made by the Subcommittee was bound to be subject to adverse criticism by those closely concerned with the problem.

Within two months the Subcommittee forwarded a paper on the Treasury proposal to the ACC top committee. This paper, while it did not grant responsibility for the program in toto to the Coast Guard, and while it did contain restrictive language necessitated by the directions of the ACC request, still left to the Coast Guard a considerable area of responsibility. The paper recommended that the Treasury paper be approved with the original "recommended action" section deleted and the following substituted for it:

1. The U. S. Coast Guard be designated as the co-ordinating agency for search and rescue operations, and as the agency with primary responsibility for providing search and rescue facilities and services, to meet the U. S. obligations to PICAO for the protection of international civil aviation over water areas.
2. Pending completion of a thorough study of the U. S. requirements for an overall search and rescue program, the U. S. Coast Guard be designated as the co-ordinating agency for all search and rescue policies and operations required to meet the U. S. obligations to PICAO for the protection of international civil aviation over land and water.
3. Fulfillment of the above responsibility to be carried out without prejudice to:

   (a) other rights and authority which may now be held by any department or agency of the government by virtue of existing law, or

   (b) the right of the military to organize facilities for, and conduct search and rescue operations to the extent believed necessary by the military to meet their needs.

   In addition, adequate measures to be taken by the co-ordinating agency to insure the co-ordination of civil and military facilities to the fullest extent possible.
4. The U. S.-PICAO Technical Committee on Search and Rescue to make a thorough study of the requirements of a search and rescue program to meet the needs of domestic civil aviation as well as the international obligations of the United States.

When Commander Scheibel received news of the recommendations of the ACC-PICAO Subcommittee, his reaction was unfavorable and intense. First of all, Coast Guard had not been represented at Subcommittee discussions and to him this was not only injustice but also stupidity. Secondly, the Treasury proposal which he had carefully prepared had, he thought, been badly mauled. As a matter of fact, it seemed to him that any deviation from the original Treasury proposal was an unwarranted compromise because of his and his colleagues' belief that the original proposal was the only correct way to attack the problem.

Partially as a result of this ACC Subcommittee action there was injected into and made a part of the search and rescue problem another issue, which, while in a sense only subsidiary, became of paramount importance to the Treasury Department and later required settlement by the ACC itself. Commander Scheibel, seeing what had happened to his proposal and feeling that its modification had occurred because of Coast Guard's (and Treasury's) inability to participate completely at the various levels of the ACC committee hierarchy, became convinced that without representation on the ACC his agency's proposals were not going to be given the backing they apparently needed in ACC deliberations. He therefore, recommended to his superiors that they again attempt to gain for Treasury membership on the ACC. (As mentioned earlier, Treasury had once been refused membership.) The Commander's attitude was soon to be strengthened by further ACC action on his original proposal.

AAF Intervention

Commander Scheibel was not the only one distressed by the Subcommittee recommendations. A copy of the ACC Subcommittee's recommendations with respect to the earlier Treasury proposal had been routed by AAF clearance procedures to a staff officer on search and rescue in Army Air Forces headquarters. This officer was Lt. Col. J. H. Batjer. Lt. Col. Batjer had graduated from Texas A & M in 1938 with a reserve officer commission in the artillery, had entered active duty with the Army in 1940, and had transferred to the Army Air Forces in 1944 when he became an executive officer of an AAF search and rescue group in the Southwest Pacific. Since 1944 he had remained active in search and rescue work. Upon receipt of the recommendations, he too was disturbed. He felt that the recommendations gave to one agency, the Coast Guard, too much responsibility and discretion in an area in which he felt there needed to be further study to determine how interested agencies might better co-operate to achieve a coordinated program in search and rescue activity. Furthermore, the Army Air Forces with its great number of facilities in actual use and available for use for search and rescue operations should, he thought, be given at least an equal voice in any Federal program. In the common phrase, the AAF was getting the runaround. Lt. Col. Batjer's reactions were not surprising. Though his conclusions were different, he was like Commander Scheibel in feeling that the proposals would not result in an adequate search and rescue program because of improper allocation of responsibility. Indeed, the jurisdictional question was inherent in the situation: the interest of both agencies in the problem was legitimate and substantial. The jurisdictional conflict that now began its course was perhaps not inevitable in the abstract, but at least well-nigh inevitable in the context of initially unco-ordinated proposals, sponsored by two conscientious and zealous officers, each proud of the capabilities of his own organization.

Lt. Col. Batjer moved to action. He discussed the Subcommittee recommendations with his superiors and with their approval forwarded his objections. He contended that the Coast Guard was given too much authority, particularly in the face of the fact that the Army Air Forces facilities were vast, were being utilized, and would continue to be used in PICAO programs as long as military requirements for them existed. Therefore, he reasoned, with such a stake in any United States-PICAO program for search and rescue, the AAF should necessarily have a real voice in the determination of policy; this, he felt, it was not getting—to his satisfaction—in the Subcommittee report. Furthermore, he now felt that the Coast Guard's approach to the program was a threat to AAF policy and interests. It might be noted that an activity such as search and rescue would be useful to the

AAF, as it could be an active program as opposed to its major function of preparing for war and a program of popular appeal, i.e., saving life. His objections were therefore put forth in strong fashion. They were heeded.

ACC Decision

On August 15, 1946, the ACC (top committee) had as one of its agenda items the consideration of the recommendations of the Subcommittee on PICAO matters on the search and rescue problem which had been assigned that Subcommittee earlier by the ACC when it considered the initial Treasury proposal. In the meeting the War Department representative said that any proposal by the Coast Guard with respect to search and rescue should be subject to concurrence of an ACC Subcommittee on search and rescue, and that with respect to that item of the Subcommittee proposal which designated Coast Guard as the co-ordinating agency for all search and rescue policies and operations in connection with U. S. obligations, the War Department wished to defer action until the study on U. S. requirements—suggested in the Subcommittee proposal—was completed. The representative of the Navy Department, however, said that Coast Guard budget and personnel considerations called for prompt action rather than delay. The Navy representative also said that the designation in the recommendations of Coast Guard as the co-ordinating authority was for an interim period only. No agreement was reached in that ACC meeting, and the topic was assigned for further consideration at the next ACC meeting. It was suggested that in the interim the War Department and Navy Department representatives get together and attempt to come to some sort of agreement.

A settlement was reached, and in the ACC meeting of September 5, 1946, the War and Navy Department representatives stated that the question of responsibility for co-ordination of search and rescue over land should be answered quickly and that revised wording they were suggesting for the last paragraph of the ACC-PICAO Subcommittee paper should serve to accomplish this end. The ACC then voted to adopt the recommendation of the ACC-PICAO Subcommittee with certain qualifications and exceptions. At the end of the first paragraph of the recommended action the following was added: "and the Coast Guard shall refer to the Air Co-ordinating Committee for concurrence in any policy or program developed under the responsibility described above." The entire second paragraph—that which gave the Coast Guard interim co-ordinating responsibility for search and rescue policy over land and water—was deleted. The fourth and last paragraph was expanded to include this sentence: "The US-PICAO Technical Committee on Search and Rescue is instructed to make every effort to expedite its study and to submit a report thereon as soon as possible."

The general effect of the foregoing changes was to leave to the Coast Guard responsibility—but subject to ACC clearance—for co-ordinating operations and for providing facilities and services in search and rescue activities over water. Furthermore, in carrying out this responsibility the existing authority of any other government agency or the rights of the military to conduct search and rescue for their own needs were not to be impinged upon. The determination of responsibility for overland operations was not referred to—it was apparently the thought of the ACC that this problem would be solved by the proposed study, but this was not explicitly stated in the ACC approved paper. An ACC Subcommittee on Search and Rescue was directed to prepare a "thorough study of the requirements of a search and rescue program to meet the needs of domestic civil aviation as well as the international obligations of the United States." In December 1946 this study was assigned to the newly established ACC Subcommittee on Search and Rescue.

Scheibel's Draft

Neither Commander Scheibel nor Lt. Col. Batjer was satisfied, and this was particularly true of the former. His original proposal had now been considerably changed, and the problem had been enlarged to include domestic search and rescue activity, whereas his original proposal had been focused only on the search and rescue operations with respect to obligations of this country to the Provisional International Civil Aviation Organization. While Lt. Col. Batjer was not completely satisfied, he had been instrumental in cutting down what he thought to be excess authority for the Coast Guard. Thus the ACC directive that a study be made meant that Scheibel and Batjer would each start anew in an attempt to secure adoption of his own preferred program. The lines were drawn. These two men represented divergent points of view—or perhaps, more important, they thought their points of view to be sharply opposed; their respective departments apparently were at odds over the question. Both of these men were vigorous crusaders in the field of search and rescue, and each now began to feel that the other was attempting to outmaneuver him and place his department in a disadvantageous position; but it should be noted that their maneuverings were designed, not for personal aggrandizement, but to secure acceptance of policy proposals. In spite of these vigorous differences, the two remained personally friendly, and each retained a respect for the competence and ability of the other. Representatives of other government agencies who were to participate to a degree in this search and rescue problem were for the most part disinterested spectators.

The Search and Rescue (SAR) Subcommittee was made up of representatives from Treasury (Coast Guard), War (Army Air Forces), CAB, CAA, Navy, and FCC. The Air Transport Association, representing the scheduled air lines, was allowed advisory representation. Commander Scheibel, because of his long experience and technical ability in the field, was made chairman of the Subcommittee. Lt. Col. Batjer was the principal War Department representative. The Subcommittee could spend only part time in the preparation of the study, for it had to help prepare, from time to time, United States position papers for PICAO regional meetings, and, of course, each member of the Subcommittee had his current duties to fulfill at his own agency.

The SAR Subcommittee did not meet regularly, and its first sessions were generally taken up in discussions of a technical nature. However, in early March 1947 the Coast Guard introduced into the SAR Subcommittee a draft study. This draft did not cover that part of the ACC instruction which called for a study of requirements for standard rescue over land; it proposed that the ACC approve a bill which would designate Coast Guard as the responsible agency for operation and co-ordination of search and rescue. The draft bill also included a provision for a search and rescue board, under Coast Guard chairmanship, composed of military, CAB, CAA, and Maritime Commission representatives. Commander Scheibel was thus still concentrating on the problem of responsibility. Lt. Col. Batjer's reaction was to refer back to the ACC directive concerning requirements. After reading the Coast Guard's draft study, and with aid of some of his colleagues in the Pentagon, Lt. Col. Batjer promptly prepared his own draft study.

Batjer's Draft

It was Batjer's thought that by presenting a draft containing proposals diametrically opposed to those of the Coast Guard draft the Subcommittee would have to dismiss both drafts as each represented an extreme end of the continuum and made agreement difficult. The Army Air Forces draft took the position that, under the directive from the ACC, the study should be focused on requirements, and the designation of any specific agency as the responsible authority for search and rescue operations and co-ordination should be excluded. The draft further pointed out that while the Coast Guard held certain responsibilities for safety of life at sea and on inland and coastal waters, the Army Air Forces had accepted responsibility for civil aircraft over-land and on certain international routes moving outward from the United States and traversed by Army Air Forces aircraft. Thus, the paper continued, there is considerable duplication between the Coast Guard and Air Forces with respect to both international and domestic search and rescue functions and responsibility. And while economy would result from the designation of one agency to be responsible in this situation, "agency" could mean a new one, an existing one, or a joint body. The paper therefore recommended that the SAR Subcommittee be directed to "study the problem of designating a SAR agency capable of discharging domestic and international search and rescue obligations." This designation, it was pointed out, could not be accomplished until the present study developed the relationship of requirements to present facilities.

The Air Forces draft served its purpose of clearing the table of both drafts and necessitating a new start on the study. It was then decided in the SAR Subcommittee that the antagonists get together and find areas of agreement and start from there. This was done. A master outline was developed principally by Scheibel, Batjer, and Lt. Commander Wuerker of the Coast Guard, who was also a member of the staff of the military SAR Agency.

H.R. 72 in the House

While the above events were taking place in the SAR Subcommittee, another issue arose which aggravated the already increasing tension between Commander Scheibel and Lt. Col. Batjer—and between the Coast Guard and the Army Air Forces. In January 1947, Congressman Hand introduced a bill, H.R. 72, which was referred to the House Committee on Merchant Marine and Fisheries. H.R. 72 read, in part, that for ". . . the purpose of saving life and property along the coasts of the United States and at sea contiguous thereto, and to assist in the national defense, the Secretary of the Treasury is authorized to establish, equip, and maintain aviation stations, not exceeding fifteen in number, at such points on the Atlantic and the Pacific coasts, the Gulf of Mexico, and the Great Lakes as he may deem advisable, and to detail for aviation duty in connection therewith officers and enlisted men of the United States Coast Guard." (The bill also contained language with respect to training aviation personnel and rates of pay for such personnel, but these provisions entered into the search and rescue problem herein discussed quite indirectly.) Heretofore the Coast Guard had been authorized to maintain only ten aviation stations.

In February the Treasury Department was requested for its views on H.R. 72 by the House Committee handling the bill. Treasury, the only department to be so solicited by the Committee, prepared a letter saying in part that ". . . the language of existing law and language parallel thereto in this bill is too restrictive in regard to the scope of aviation operations, and the location of aviation stations, in view of present needs of the service." These stations are needed, it continued, ". . . as the requirements for Search and Rescue operations are now such as to make it necessary that searches be conducted over land in the interior of the United States." Therefore it was suggested that the language in the bill be changed to read: "For the purpose of saving life and property along the coasts of the United States and its possessions and at sea contiguous thereto, and in the interior of the United States and its possessions . . . the Secretary of the Treasury be authorized to establish, equip, and maintain aviation stations, not exceeding fifteen in number, at such points in the United States or its possessions, or bases under the jurisdiction of the United States as he may deem advisable. . . ."

This letter was forwarded on March 7 to the Bureau of the Budget, in accordance with established procedures, for a report as to its compatibility with the program of the President. The Budget Bureau, on March 19, requested the War and Navy Departments and the ACC for comments as to their views on both the bill and Treasury's comments thereon.

In early May the letter which Treasury had forwarded to the Bureau of the Budget was sent by Treasury to the House Committee on Merchant Marine and Fisheries with the following notation: "In view of your request for expedition of this report it is being transmitted without the customary clearance from the Bureau of the Budget." This transmittal was entirely proper under existing procedures.

A few days thereafter the Budget Bureau received comments from the Acting Secretary of the Navy. He pointed out that with regard to the Treasury proposal concerning the location of the aviation stations the ACC was currently making a study in which was being determined the question of what agencies should discharge search and rescue operations within the United States. He suggested therefore that action by Congress on H.R. 72 be deferred pending completion of this ACC study. Within a week the Budget Bureau received the War Department's comments. The letter from the Secretary of War was more detailed and was stronger in its tone of objection to the Treasury proposal. The Secretary of War stressed several points. First of all, it was maintained that the proposed enactment was contrary to the policy of economy in the Executive Departments. It then went on to say that War could not agree with the Treasury contention that the original bill was too restrictive because of the fact that the normal air operations of the Coast Guard are confined to the coastal waters of this country and the Great Lakes. Moreover, it was pointed out that the Army Air Forces maintained an Air Rescue Service for the interior of the United States and this service was always available in times of emergency to civil aviation as well as military. This interior Air Rescue Service together with the coastal facilities of the Coast Guard thus furnished adequate coverage for the United States. The Air Rescue Service was essential to the Army Air Forces and was continually being developed within budget and personnel limitations. The letter then remarked, as had that from the Navy Department, that ACC was engaged in making a study, the completion of which should be awaited for the recommendation contained therein. The letter concluded with an expression of the belief that it would be a comparatively easy administrative task to provide for the joint use of existing facilities if it were found necessary to require more facilities.

When the ACC received the request from the Budget Bureau for comments, the request was sent to the Legal Subcommittee of the ACC for study and recommendations. The Legal Subcommittee's paper to the ACC (top level) contained a brief discussion of the proposed bill and a recommended draft reply to the Budget Bureau. This letter was sent to the Budget Bureau in June 1947. It pointed out that the ACC had no objection to the bill as originally drafted, provided that it was understood that pending the conclusion of the ACC study on search and rescue the additional facilities authorized would not be established for operations primarily within the United States and would not duplicate facilities operated by the Navy and Army Air Forces. However, the ACC felt that the Treasury proposal requesting the change in language would be a radical departure from the original bill and would so broaden the scope of Coast Guard operations as to authorize it to expand its duties in search and rescue operations to include inland points. To allow this expansion of operations at a time when an ACC study was being prepared covering the major phases of search and rescue did not seem advisable. The ACC therefore recommended that action relating to the proposed Treasury report be deferred until the completion of the ACC study; if deferral was not practicable, the ACC was opposed to enactment of the amendments to the bill suggested by the Treasury. The ACC letter also noted that the Treasury Department did not participate in any of the ACC discussions on H.R. 72, as Treasury's views were already known to the Budget Bureau.

With the receipt of the ACC letter, the Budget Bureau was finally in a position to formulate a policy on H.R. 72; but too much time had elapsed. The House Committee had requested Treasury's report in February, the report had gone to Budget in March, and had been forwarded by Treasury, without clearance, to the Committee in May. On June 13, three days after the ACC letter and before Budget had taken final action, the Committee itself moved: H.R. 72 was reported out with amendments. The provisions regarding aviation-training personnel and rates of pay were deleted. Language similar to that proposed by Treasury with respect to allowing additional aviation stations in the United States and its possessions for the purpose of saving life and property along the coasts of and in the interior of the United States and its possessions and at sea was included in the bill. The next day H.R. 72 passed the House of Representatives and was sent to the Senate where it was referred to the Committee on Interstate and Foreign Commerce.

H.R. 72 Enacted

Lt. Col. Batjer considered this bill a threat to Air Forces interests in the search and rescue field, for the Coast Guard would be given statutory authority implying responsibility for operations in the interior of the United States. He was, moreover, convinced that the Coast Guard had sponsored the original bill despite a steadfast denial on the part of Commander Scheibel, who stoutly declared that the Congressman introduced the bill without support or knowledge of the Coast Guard. He explained that because of lack of funds a Coast Guard aviation station had been closed down in Congressman Hand's district and that the Congressman was anxious to retrieve this activity for his district and was hopeful of accomplishing this through legislation enabling the Coast Guard to establish new and additional aviation stations. Regardless of the precise series of events that resulted in the introduction of the bill, the important fact is that Batjer, as well as some of his colleagues and certain of the ACC staff, thought that Coast Guard had deliberately sponsored the bill in order to achieve by this method what it had failed to do through the ACC earlier.

H.R. 72 came up for consideration by the Senate Committee on Interstate and Foreign Commerce on July 22. Inasmuch as the House Committee had not solicited views on the bill from the War Department (Air Forces), members of the Legislative Liaison office in AAF Headquarters, knowing Batjer's opposition to the bill as evidenced by the Secretary of War's letter, asked Batjer to accompany them in an attempt to get a hearing before the Senate Committee. In this they were successful, but only by dashing to the rear door of the Senate Committee room and asking to be heard. The members of the Senate Committee were, with one exception, unswayed by Lt. Col. Batjer's testimony. The exception was Senator Gurney, then Chairman of the Armed Services Committee, who objected when the bill was called on the consent calendar. Later he dropped his objection, and within a day H.R. 72 passed the Senate and was sent to the President.

The Bureau of the Budget in keeping with its legislative clearance functions again requested comment from interested executive departments on the enrolled enactment so that it might advise the President as to their views. In the first week of August the Budget Bureau had received comments from the Treasury, War and Navy Departments, and the ACC.

The War and Navy Departments and the ACC reiterated the position they had taken when first they were requested for comments. The Navy merely felt that this legislation was prejudging the ACC study and should therefore be vetoed. The War Department referred to the ACC study and furthermore pointed out that the Army Air Forces' Air Rescue Service provided search and rescue activity essential to the Air Forces operation and that because military cross-country flights are not restricted to specific routes this service could be furnished anywhere within the country. Furthermore, it claimed that the Service had a greater variety of specialized equipment than was available to the Coast Guard, unless the size of the latter agency were materially increased, and if the Coast Guard were increased in this respect, duplication with existing Air Forces functions would then follow. A proposed veto message was included with the comments.

The ACC letter, while reaffirming its previous stand, did however state that the Committee was not unanimous as to the appropriate course of action. The State and Commerce Departments and the CAB felt it wise not to recommend a veto of the bill. This disposition, however, was on the "express" assumption that the Budget Bureau in processing any Coast Guard request for funds would do so in conformity with administration policy with respect to responsibility for search and rescue activities. Furthermore, these agencies understood that enactment of this legislation would not prejudice a unified search and rescue program in the interior in the event that the ACC study suggested transferring this responsibility to an agency other than Coast Guard, under the authority of the Reorganization Act of 1945. These agencies did go on record as favoring a veto of the enrolled bill if the "express" assumption was not correct. The War and Navy Departments, said the ACC letter, favored veto of the bill primarily because it would prejudge the ACC study. The Treasury Department, ACC stated, favored enactment of the bill, which, while not a departmental measure, would with its amendments provide the Coast Guard with legislation sufficient to enable it to meet post-war needs of that agency. The Treasury Department, the ACC reported, did not contemplate seeking funds for the additional stations prior to completion of the ACC study.

The Treasury had sent to the Budget Bureau a letter saying it had no objection to a recommendation by the Budget Bureau that the enrolled enactment be approved by the President.

The Budget Bureau promptly forwarded to the President a letter of recommendation with the letters of the circulated departments attached. The Budget Bureau letter, after summarizing the positions taken by the departments and agencies, concurred in the position taken by the State and Commerce Departments, the CAB, and the ACC, and accordingly favored enactment of the bill. The Budget Bureau was apparently confident that it, through its budgetary control procedures, and the ACC, through its approval over subcommittee recommendations, could keep the responsibility for search and rescue within the framework of administration policy. The President signed the bill on August 6, 1947.

Presidential approval of the bill merely intensified the dispute over search and rescue. What at the time of the Dublin Conference had originally started in the ACC as an apparently simple task of determining how much in the way of search and rescue facilities the United States could guarantee a joint international program sponsored by PICAO had now generated a jurisdictional dispute between two agencies, a dispute that included a fierce personal squabble between the representatives of the agencies. And these two representatives, because of their technical competence and responsible positions, had been expected to frame a clear and concise recommendation on search and rescue policy, both to implement this country's obligations to PICAO and to facilitate an understanding of the domestic needs in the field. Partially because of their inability to come to agreement on what each considered to be the basic problem, that is, jurisdiction, they had involved their respective departments in acrimonious debate. H.R. 72, even if not sponsored by Treasury, had been so amended by Treasury request as to give to that agency a greatly strengthened hand in the growing jurisdictional dispute, and the incident left a feeling of bitterness with the Air Forces and the ACC.

The way in which the situation had developed had not only been unforeseen by Commander Scheibel but was distasteful to him. His original proposal had been a simple and sincere effort to initiate a program to meet United States obligations to PICAO. That he felt he should take the lead is not surprising. He was the Executive Assistant to the Head of the Search and Rescue (formerly Air-Sea Rescue) Agency. As such he would be expected to exercise initiative in this field, and in view of this relationship to the Services, the fact that most of the available facilities with which the United States intended to implement its obligations were under the Army and Navy justified his action. That most of these facilities were maintained by the Army Air Forces did not concern him. Or if it did concern him, he apparently did not consider that it invalidated his proposal for a grant of authority to the Coast Guard for a program which of necessity would involve considerable direction over facilities maintained by the Army Air Forces. After the submission of his original proposal, which he still considered sound, he had been by-passed by the ACC until the study was requested and the SAR Subcommittee established. In that interval the ACC had broadened the issue by directing that the study include domestic search and rescue. Furthermore, the course of events had pushed him so far back from his original position that he had begun to worry for fear that one of the main responsibilities and *raisons d'être* of the Coast Guard—safety of life and property at sea—might be either completely usurped or perilously weakened by what he thought was a grasping action on the part of the Air Forces. He therefore began to look upon this as a fight for life.

And, of course, in that same period, Lt. Col.

Batjer had become aware of the situation: With respect to obligations to PICAO, he was convinced that the Air Forces, because of its manifold facilities, had major interest in search and rescue; and with the broadening of the scope of the problem to include domestic activity, he saw the possibility of someone's forcing the Army Air Forces to give up its search and rescue activities to an auxiliary of the Navy. The possible implications of this for the over-all relations of the Air Forces with Naval Aviation were not overlooked. As he became aware of the developing situation a little late, he had the feeling that the fight had started and that he had lost the first two rounds because he had not even been in the ring. Thus it was that he felt obliged to carry the fight to the enemy whenever possible.

The Third Draft

In drawing up the master outline in an attempt to come to agreement on the assigned study, it was decided that each agency representative on the Subcommittee would prepare those parts which treated the responsibilities and facilities of his own agency in search and rescue operations. This was done because Scheibel and Batjer would not agree upon the jurisdictions claimed for each other's agencies. They also disagreed on another basic issue, in part because of this fundamental disagreement. While there was apparent agreement that those who possessed the necessary facilities for search and rescue should use them, it was Batjer's idea that co-ordination of these facilities should be done on a joint basis within a facility area and with over-all direction from some central board or agency; it was Scheibel's thought that because of Coast Guard's statutory responsibility it should act as the co-ordinating agency for all of the facility areas.

The two antagonists had agreed on the technical aspects, which represented the bulk of the study, but because of the basic disagreements they felt they had to argue out the recommendations of the study. In doing this they came closer together but were never in complete understanding on all the proposed recommendations. Mr. McCrary, Secretary of the ACC Technical Division, had now concluded that the two men were mainly opposing each other for reasons of misunderstandings and personality differences rather than because of differing fundamental attitudes about the problem. He had spasmodically pushed the Subcommittee into action and had aided in finding areas of agreement so that the study might progress. But he, like the members of the Subcommittee, had other duties to attend to and could not always keep in contact with the developments, and probably underestimated the deep personal feelings which Scheibel and Batjer attached to their views of the problem. He once more urged them to drop their differences and finish the study.

Thus in early August, before leaving on vacation, Lt. Col. Batjer suggested certain small changes in the recommendations to which Lt. Commander Wuerker, acting in Scheibel's absence, agreed. Batjer then suggested other amendments, but Wuerker thought they would injure the Coast Guard, and said so. After some bickering Wuerker suggested they give up and send in two sets of recommendations representing both points of view. Batjer said this was not necessary, and concluded the conversation. Scheibel and Wuerker discussed the suggestions and decided that they had gone as far as they could, and further they began to feel that for some reason Batjer was attempting to keep the study in the Subcommittee. Consequently at the next Subcommittee meeting they suggested that the study be forwarded to the Technical Division for approval. Batjer's alternate on the Subcommittee voiced opposition, but the study was sent on without the suggested amendments. Briefly the study recommended the following:

1. All Federal agencies utilize such facilities as they may have.
2. Coast Guard be given co-ordinating authority for search and rescue over water.
3. The Search and Rescue Agency in the Coast Guard be reconstituted as an interagency Board, and, through a permanent secretariat established in the Coast Guard, the Board be responsible for research, information, and standards in search and rescue and for assign-

ing authority to named co-ordination centers for over-land operations.
4. Coast Guard, or others recommended by the Board, to seek funds where necessary.
5. CAA to seek authority for standardizing facilities at airports.
6. ACC to approve the report and send it to the President.

Both Lt. Commander Wuerker and Commander Scheibel had thought that Lt. Col. Batjer had agreed not to insist on changes when he said two sets of recommendations were not necessary. They could not have been more wrong, according to Lt. Col. Batjer.

Having been alerted by his alternate as to what had taken place, Batjer returned to the fray in a near rage. First, he contacted his immediate superior, who was the War Department representative on the ACC Technical Division, and arranged to have the study stopped there. Next he prepared an angry letter to the Secretary of the Technical Division, accusing Commander Scheibel of having given him the "run-around."

At the next Technical Division meeting, the War Department objected to the study on the grounds that the SAR Subcommittee vote on forwarding the study had not been unanimous. The War Department representative asserted that not only had War opposed the forwarding of the study but also that the CAB member had not been present at the time of the vote. The Technical Division agreed to send the study back to the SAR Subcommittee.

Upon receipt of a copy of the letter which Batjer had addressed to the Secretary of the Technical Division, Scheibel was incensed. He considered this an uncalled-for personal attack. He therefore arranged all agenda items for the forthcoming SAR Subcommittee meeting to focus on the points of attack made in the letter; the search and rescue study was for the moment forgotten. Moreover, the Commandant of the Coast Guard was apprised of the letter, because there was some feeling that it demanded rebuttal for the sake of the name and reputation of the Coast Guard as a whole. However, the top command of the Coast Guard was inclined to take the matter less seriously and saw no good reason to make this such a serious issue as to embroil the Coast Guard in a violent fight with the newly created Air Force. No formal action was taken.

However, certain informal activity was to cause Lt. Col. Batjer some anxious moments as a result of the letter. Shortly after the letter was written, Mr. Foley, Under Secretary of the Treasury, mentioned the letter to Mr. Symington, Assistant Secretary of War for Air, during a Washington social event. Mr. Symington was rather disturbed, and thought it wise to look into the matter. Consequently, Lt. Col. Batjer was called to account by a Colonel and a Brigadier General representing Batjer's branch of Headquarters Staff. The General asked Batjer where he had obtained the information that the Air Force had a policy in search and rescue for civil aviation. Batjer explained that shortly after the Dublin Conference he had written to the Policy Division in the Army Air Forces suggesting certain policies with respect to search and rescue and had received clearance for them, ironically from the very Colonel who was now raising the issue. He had, moreover, during the preparation of the study, sought and received an audience with the Major General who was Assistant Chief of Air Staff for Operations. In the discussion with this officer, Batjer had received assurance that since Air Force facilities were being utilized in meeting United States obligations to PICAO, and since the Air Force did use its facilities in domestic search and rescue activities for civil aviation, the Air Force should play a major role in any over-all search and rescue program. Lt. Col. Batjer cited this discussion. Those questioning him remained somewhat skeptical. At that instant the Major General whom Batjer had quoted chanced to walk through the office. He was stopped and asked about search and rescue policy. He replied in effect that as the Air Force had such a stake in that activity, it should also have a major part to play in determining over-all policy for it. Batjer was saved. Furthermore, he was now confident of the course he had been pursuing and was determined to press forward and obtain an agreement on a study which would be at least as favorable to the Air Force as it would be to the Coast Guard.

Had the incident not occurred, the position of the Air Force in search and rescue might have been materially different and the study would undoubtedly have been further delayed.

As has been indicated, the agenda for the forthcoming SAR Subcommittee meeting was centered entirely on the charges made by Batjer, with no mention of the study, although in the eyes of the Secretary of the Technical Division it was now long overdue. At the meeting the agenda items were in a short time taken care of to the satisfaction of everyone present. Both Commander Scheibel and Lt. Col. Batjer had by now cooled off, and it was agreed that the letter should be buried in the files and forgotten. Amicable relations were restored—at least in so far as personal feelings were concerned; but the two antagonists were still at odds on recommendations to be included in the study.

By now both Commander Scheibel and Lt. Commander Wuerker realized that, with respect to the Subcommittee study, they were in a position in which they could not possibly force the type of compromise they considered necessary: they were unprotected, because they had no permanent voice in the top ACC committee. They could only hope that through persuasion they might retrieve some semblance of the program they desired.

After dispensing with the agenda items at the meeting, it was obvious to all that the recommendations of the study had to be drafted, and it was agreed to proceed with this action. Unable to persuade their opponents to forego amendments, Scheibel and Wuerker agreed to certain changes in the recommendations as then drafted. After several minor changes, which mostly consisted of deleting several references to the Coast Guard without affecting any major recommendation, two significant changes were made. The recommendation which had given the Coast Guard co-ordinating authority for search and rescue over water was deleted. Secondly, the recommendation which had given to the proposed interagency board the authority to assign the responsibilities for the co-ordination of search and rescue operations over land to specific co-ordination centers was changed so that the phrase "over land" was deleted. This meant, of course, that the interagency board was to assign the responsibility for co-ordination of search and rescue operations over both land and water. Lt. Col. Batjer was satisfied. The study was sent to the Technical Division where it was cleared and forwarded to the ACC with the suggestion that the study's recommendations be approved. This was in November 1947.

In January 1948 the ACC considered the SAR Subcommittee study. After cursory discussion, it was apparent that there was considerable skepticism over the proposed interagency board for search and rescue. Mr. Donald C. Stone, representing the Bureau of the Budget at the meeting, was asked to comment on the interagency board; he too said he was skeptical about this proposal and thought that it might bear looking into. It was then proposed that, because of the budgetary and organizational problems raised by the study, it be forwarded to the Bureau of the Budget for analysis. This was agreed to, and the study was transmitted.

The Bureau of the Budget Report

The task of analyzing the study was assigned to two men in the Budget Bureau, one in the Division of Administrative Management and the other in the Division of Estimates. After considerable study of the Subcommittee report and after interviewing several of the participants, particularly Commander Scheibel and Lt. Col. Batjer, the Budget Bureau analysts drafted a report. They were convinced that several basic errors had been made. First of all, the Subcommittee insisted upon viewing the problem as one of assigning responsibility when what was first required was a determination of the requirements for search and rescue programs. Secondly, the actual responsibility for the determination of requirements correctly lay with the Civil Aeronautics Administration (CAA), which has statutory authority to administer the Federal airways program and to administer civil aviation safety standards. There was no need for the establishment of a new interagency board; any interdepartmental co-ordination that needed to be done could be carried on through the existing mechanism, namely the ACC. The co-ordination of search and rescue operations needed no elaborate structure nor complex procedures but could be done through simple co-operation between the Coast Guard and the Air Force. With these thoughts in mind the analysts drafted their analysis and forwarded it in June 1948 to the Executive Secretary of the ACC, who in turn forwarded it to the Technical Division for recommendations. It will be noted that Budget Bureau took six months to prepare and submit its analysis. Pertinent excerpts from the analysis follow:

Conclusions

It would appear that the development of the course of action proposed in [the study] has been powerfully influenced by the continued identification of the problem as one of assigning responsibility instead of determining requirements. . . .

1. Even without a definitive study of requirements, it is clear that adequate facilities for the actual conduct of search and rescue operations exist and are available, with the possible exception of the operation on a full-time basis of a D/F net.
2. Until such time as available facilities are determined to be inadequate to serve the needs of the then carefully and definitively determined requirements, the acceptance of additional responsibilities, seeking of further authorization, or the appropriation of funds specifically for search and rescue, is not only unnecessary, but would serve to encourage the creation of facilities in excess of a reasonable need and of additional unco-ordinated competitive operations.
3. Should the available Federal, State, local, and private facilities ever be found to be insufficient to meet the needs of civil aviation, CAA would be the only appropriate agency to assume the responsibility for seeing that additional facilities are made available.
4. The problem of co-ordination at the operational level involves primarily operations of the Coast Guard and of the Air Force and is a relatively simple one not requiring the creation of a new Board, the conduct of joint operations, nor the assignment of responsibility to jointly manned rescue co-ordination centers.
5. Aviation search and rescue problems requiring co-ordination at the Washington level involve only normal interdepartmental matters. ACC offers such facilities as may be needed to facilitate such interdepartmental co-ordination.
6. Functions other than those involving co-ordination envisioned for the proposed new Board are the responsibility of CAB-CAA. . .

An Alternate Solution

An alternate solution to the problems discussed in [the study] would involve the following course of action:

1. Implementation by CAA (with the assistance of the SAR Subcommitee) of its responsibility for determining from time to time, the requirements for and adequacy of facilities for the conduct of search and rescue operations for civil aviation.
2. Acceptance by the Department of the Air Force of responsibility for advising from time to time, the extent to which and the geographical areas in which its facilities may be considered to be available,
   (a) within the continental United States and in any other area in which the Coast Guard advises that its facilities are insufficient, (1) to conduct search and rescue operations for civil aviation, (2) to determine what additional facilities will be called upon to co-operate in each instance, and (3) to co-ordinate the efforts of such other facilities called upon.
   (b) elsewhere, to co-operate under the co-ordinating leadership of the Coast Guard, in the conduct of search and rescue operations for civil aviation.
3. Acceptance by the Coast Guard of responsibility for advising from time to time the extent to which and the geographical areas in which its facilities may be considered to be available,
   (a) outside the continental United States and in any other area in which the Department of the Air Force advises that its facilities are insufficient, (1) to conduct search and rescue operations for civil aviation, (2) to determine what additional facilities will be called upon to co-operate in each case, and (3) to co-ordinate the efforts of such other facilities called upon.
   (b) elsewhere, to co-operate under the co-ordinating leadership of the Department of the Air Force in the conduct of search and rescue operations for civil aviation.

4. Implementation by CAB-CAA (with the assistance of the SAR Subcommittee) to any extent which a definitive examination of requirements reveals to be essential, of functions from (e) through (g) recommended in [the study] as functions of the proposed Board.

The Technical Division considered the Budget Bureau analysis, and agreed that the interagency board proposed by the Subcommittee study was unwise. This was as far, however, as the Technical Division agreed to the analysis presented to them; it regarded the Budget Bureau's comments as going beyond what it was requested to do. This was not dwelt upon in the meeting, but it was the rather general feeling among those present. The Budget Bureau examiners apparently read the ACC instructions differently from ACC Subcommittee members, who felt that "requirements" related only to one of three parts of the instructions given them, and then was only to be a relatively small phase of their study. Those closely associated with events in this case are inclined to believe that the Subcommittee members were correct and that the top ACC members did not have in mind a study focused on requirements when they forwarded their instructions. Consequently, little or no attention was paid to other aspects of the Budget Bureau analysis. The Technical Division forwarded the following recommendations to the ACC:

A. That the conclusions and recommendations set forth in [the study] be accepted as basically sound and approved.
B. That the SAR Subcommittee of the Technical Division be substituted in lieu of the Board recommended in [the study] and charged with the functions prescribed for the Board.
C. That the Search and Rescue Subcommittee be authorized a permanent secretariat, the provision of which shall be worked out between the Technical Division Secretary and the Chairman of the Search and Rescue Subcommittee.
D. That the Chairman of the Search and Rescue Subcommittee shall rotate periodically at intervals to be decided by the Subcommittee.
E. That the initial chairman be a representative of the Treasury—(U.S. Coast Guard).
F. That the Search and Rescue Subcommittee, in consonance with the foregoing, should proceed without delay to carry out the conclusions and recommendations of [the study].
G. That the ACC be requested to concur in the action being taken by the Technical Division, and that in accordance with recommendation 6 of [the study] that paper, as amended by these decisions, be brought to the attention of the President.

The Fourth Draft

When it had appeared to Scheibel and Wuerker that it was likely that the proposed interagency board recommended in the Subcommittee study would not be accepted, they were greatly alarmed. For if the duties recommended for the board were transferred to the ACC-SAR Subcommittee, as the Budget Bureau report had suggested, then the Coast Guard would be unprotected at the top level of the ACC. They had visions of the Coast Guard's search and rescue functions being usurped or at best being weakened by other agencies, particularly the Air Force, through the clearance functions of the top level of the ACC hierarchy at which the Air Force and other agencies had representation. Scheibel and Wuerker therefore grasped at their remaining weapon; they again suggested to their superiors that Treasury demand membership on the ACC. As Treasury had earlier sought membership on the ACC without success and as several of its staff still asserted its membership was needed, this now appeared a propitious time to obtain the membership. It was therefore decided to demand membership on the ACC as a condition to Coast Guard's agreement on the Subcommittee study. As a matter of fact, Coast Guard demanded that Treasury membership be considered on the agenda before it would consent to vote on the approval of the SAR study. (As provided by the Executive Order establishing ACC and by ACC procedures, Coast Guard could participate in voting at the top level of the Committee on the SAR report because of its substantial participation in the study.) Commander Scheibel made this decision known to Mr. McCrary, Secretary of the Technical Division. McCrary pointed out that the Coast

Guard's fears were mainly unfounded, for ACC practice was to allow voting participation at any level of the ACC when a nonmember agency was involved in a question up for ACC determination. He also pointed out to Scheibel that this was precisely what was being done in this particular instance. Nevertheless Scheibel and his colleagues remained convinced that membership was desirable and even necessary for the protection of the Coast Guard. McCrary did not think the matter was as serious as did the Coast Guard (and the Air Force), so he saw no good reason for standing in the way of Coast Guard persistence. He readily admitted that Treasury, through Coast Guard, was engaged in a substantial amount of aviation activity—certainly enough to warrant raising the question of ACC membership for that department. McCrary, after a brief study, had determined that Coast Guard had an interest in at least one-half of the activities that had been handled in the Technical Division and had therefore recommended to the members of that division that Coast Guard be voted in as a member; this had been done a few months prior to this time. Consequently the Technical Division memorandum which contained the seven recommendations with respect to the Budget Bureau analysis and the SAR Subcommittee study also contained the following paragraph:

> In arriving at the above decisions, the Technical Division took note of the responsibility of the Treasury Department (U. S. Coast Guard) for the provision of LORAN facilities, Ocean Weather Stations, and Search and Rescue facilities as well as its interest in other related aviation matters, and agreed to bring to the attention of the ACC for its consideration, the subject of Treasury Department membership on the Air Coordinating Committee.

McCrary's was not the only recommendation with regard to Treasury membership. The recently appointed Civil Aeronautics Administrator had been told that Treasury membership was to be a condition to be attached to approval of the search and rescue study. He felt the situation had become so unpleasant that his by-passing of formal channels was not unwise; although he was not a representative, as such, on the top ACC (CAA as part of the Commerce Department was represented on the top ACC through the Assistant Secretary of Commerce for Air), he drafted a letter to the Executive Secretary of the ACC setting forth pertinent reasons for voting on the Treasury membership at the next meeting. By this time the various ACC agency representatives had become aware of the membership issue and had time to dwell on the question prior to the ACC meeting.

ACC Action

At an ACC meeting in early July 1948 it was recommended that there be a vote on Treasury membership. However, the representative of the Air Force said he was not prepared to vote on the issue at that time. Action on the SAR Subcommittee study was therefore deferred, for, as the CAB representative pointed out, the study could not be considered until the Treasury membership issue had been decided. The next ACC meeting was held one week later. Prior to this meeting, several of the agency representatives met for lunch. At this luncheon the matter of Treasury membership was discussed. After considerable discussion, the Air Force representative, the Secretary of the Air Force, came to the view that no good reason existed for his standing in the way of the membership proposal. Consequently at the meeting that afternoon the ACC voted to recommend to the President that the Treasury Department be admitted as full member of the ACC. After this agenda item was finished, the ACC then considered the SAR Subcommittee study. Mr. James E. Webb, Director of the Bureau of the Budget, was chairman at this meeting and felt reluctant to push strenuously the recommendations forwarded by the Budget. He did, however, remind the members that the Bureau of the Budget analysis had pointed up certain significant aspects about the problem which the study failed to comprehend, and which the Technical Division had brushed aside in its recommendation concerning the study. The Assistant Secretary of Commerce for Air asserted that the Bureau's analysis had gone beyond the request made of it and was not therefore completely germane to the present discussion. It was apparently the attitude of the CAA (represented through Commerce) that it was not prepared to seek or spend funds for search and rescue activity; that agency was apparently at variance with the Budget Bureau analysis, which had stated that this activity was properly within the province of the CAA. Moreover, the CAA was of the opinion that other agencies were now involved as a result of the study and it would be better to leave well enough alone. At any rate, it was apparent that CAA was reluctant to accept responsibility for determining requirements for a search and rescue program for civil aviation.

The ACC did follow the recommendation of the Budget Bureau and the Technical Division and substitute the ACC-SAR Sub-committee for the interagency board proposed by the study. Several minor changes were made in the study's recommendations so as to place the top ACC in a stronger position with respect to review of future Subcommittee actions. Moreover, it was decided that the recommendation by the Technical Division that the decision to accept the study be brought to the attention of the President was unnecessary. The recommendations, with the exceptions noted, of the Technical Division were then accepted, and the study, with the revised language, was approved.

Briefly the recommendations of the ACC approved study were these:

a. The ACC-SAR Subcommittee, with the concurrence of the departments or agencies concerned, was to: (1) review and determine "all search and rescue agreements between various agencies at the operational level on the co-ordinated use of all search and rescue facilities for civil aviation search and rescue, in accordance with international agreements and national requirements"; (2) "assign to established rescue co-ordination centers the responsibility for the co-ordination of search and rescue operations for civil aviation over specified areas . . ."; and carry out these functions with the recognition that the military services could maintain and operate search and rescue programs for their own needs as could others who did so by virtue of existing law.

b. The ACC-SAR Subcommittee was also to conduct research and publish information concerning search and rescue and to prescribe, with the concurrence of the departments or agencies concerned, standards for rescue co-ordination centers.

c. Those agencies which were determined by the Subcommittee as having facilities which could be used for search and rescue were to be requested to so use and be responsible for seeking the necessary authorization for their operation; and the agency which was ". . . determined as having the paramount interest in any one area was to be given, with its own concurrence, responsibility for control of the rescue co-ordination center in that area."

d. Any agency designated in accordance with the above recommendation "c" was to be requested to seek funds for those facilities which the SAR Subcommittee felt were required.

AFTERTHOUGHTS

While some sort of agreement was finally reached, it was not without certain real failings. The study had failed to go into what many believed to be the essential or at least initial problem—requirements of a search and rescue program. The compromise had failed to settle to the satisfaction of the two main antagonists the problem which they conceived to be the principal one—the assignment of responsibility for a search and rescue program; both were dissatisfied, but one felt even more defeated than the other. Moreover, agreement on responsibility was somewhat nebulous and left a considerable area in which future jurisdictional disputes might easily arise. The interdepartmental committee action in the final stages was taken with only partial regard for the recommendation of the Budget Bureau examiners. The Bureau's major recommendation had been adopted, and in this respect at least there had been observance of general executive policy: the establishment of a new agency in a cluttered field had been avoided. But the CAA had not assumed responsibility for determining requirements. Perhaps the most concrete positive result of two years' discussion and debate was the admission of the Treasury Department to membership in the ACC, and that result was a by-product rather than a direct objective. Nevertheless, some settlement, however indecisive, was reached for the search and rescue problem. While the friction was considerable, the governmental wheels had turned.

At the time of this writing, fifteen months after ACC acceptance of the SAR Subcommittee report, search and rescue operations continue to be carried out with dispatch and with full co-operation among the participating agencies. Agreements continue to be made through ICAO for co-operative operations with foreign states.

The recommendations of the report are being implemented somewhat slowly, but both Commander Scheibel and Lt. Col. Batjer agree that this is due to the nature of search and rescue activity. With respect to reviewing "search and rescue agreements between various agencies at the operational level" and assigning to certain "rescue co-ordination centers the responsibility for the co-ordination of search and rescue operations," the ACC-SAR Subcommittee has taken no formal action; however, these activities were carried out in a generally satisfactory manner by informal agreement before the SAR Subcommittee report. But it is pointed out that as a result of the accepted recommendations there now exist formal structure and procedures by which formal agreements may be made in the future should dissatisfaction arise over existing or contemplated informal agreements or assignments of responsibility. The same situation prevails with respect to those recommendations giving the SAR Subcommittee authority to assign responsibility to the proper agencies for seeking authorization and funds for the operation of certain facilities; for here again the thought is that the SAR Subcommittee will act as a formal focal point for assigning such responsibility and supporting these agencies' claims when necessary. The SAR Subcommittee has undertaken and completed some technical research reports on search and rescue problems and standards, particularly in ICAO matters; thus this recommendation is being fully carried out. The note in the recommendations that the military could continue to maintain search and rescue programs for their own needs, as could other agencies who did so under existing law, has been respected. Those duties which are of concern to the military and which were handled by the military Search and Rescue Agency have remained in that agency.

In the introduction to this study the reader's attention was directed to the course of events in this case as an illustration of that characteristic governmental phenomenon, the jurisdictional dispute. It was suggested that the characteristics of the jurisdictional dispute between the Coast Guard and the Air Forces are entirely normal in our Federal government. The tortuous settlement of the dispute is also not unfamiliar, but was strongly affected by the structure of the Air Coordinating Committee. Obviously, the method of settlement might well have been different if the frame of reference had been ordinary bilateral departmental relations, with or without the mediation of the Budget Bureau or some other comparable agency. Accordingly, it becomes possible to examine these same events for such light as they may cast on the usefulness or disadvantages of an interdepartmental committee. In this instance, as will be realized, the difficulty in securing a concerted decision did not arise over technical questions of ways and means, nor over the general policy approach to search and rescue. Broadly speaking, all the agencies concerned were in agreement that we should co-operate fully with other nations in international search and rescue matters and that we should make appropriate use of our various facilities to carry out a search and rescue program both within the United States and off shore; aside from the nagging question of jurisdiction, the committee system seemed well able to handle problems of this kind. Thus the events may perhaps point toward the fairly obvious conclusion that an interdepartmental committee is most effective and most consistently useful when there is basic policy agreement among its members and when the activities of the committee are devoted to exploring in full the consequences of agreed policy and the co-operative techniques that will be most successful in carrying out that policy. Similarly, it seems not unreasonable to cite this case as an illustration of the conclusion that a multi-departmental committee on the whole can be most effective when its members devote themselves to subjects that are of interest to a number of members on the committee and not merely to two. The utility of the committee as a forum for the exchange of ideas seems to be lessened where there is merely a bi-lateral exchange or disagreement.

Effective committee action in the search and rescue case broke down over a question of jurisdiction. There was no agreement on jurisdiction and the committee technique did not lend itself to an effective clarification and adjudication of the jurisdictional differences. Perhaps jurisdictional questions can be settled more easily and more effectively if they are handled by bi-lateral negotiation, where reference to higher officials, able to settle the matter, is facilitated. Perhaps also there are considerable advantages in such a situation in seeking early mediation by an independent staff agency like the Bureau of the Budget. In this instance, the Bureau was called in late and took a good many months to file its report. If it had been called in earlier and had acted more promptly, the contesting agencies could have saved the time they wasted in blind alleys like the proposal for a new interdepartmental organization, and indeed might have worked out an agreement with the aid of the Bureau before extreme positions had been taken publicly at the various committee meetings.

It will be recalled that the Bureau examiners were not too well satisfied with the final outcome, but their semi-fortuitous intervention did prevent the establishment of a new agency and did thereby secure adherence to Presidential policy. But the fact that their intervention was needed or was helpful in this respect does suggest one possible danger inherent in the existence of permanent, formal interdepartmental committees.

Such a committee tends to become an enclave within the general organization of the Executive Branch—it is not amenable to effective policy control and it has some tendency to become another independent agency that in effect rivals its own parent departments. Thus the committee presents to the Chief Executive, or his agents, some of the same problems that he must face in dealing with independent regulatory boards and commissions, a difficulty that is certainly far less acceptable in relation to an interdepartmental committee than to a regulatory commission, since the committee is, or should be, wholly within the Executive Branch, and has no quasi-legislative or quasi-judicial functions to justify or excuse its independence.

The foregoing comments on some of the values and disadvantages of interdepartmental committees are to be taken primarily as suggestions for examination of certain aspects of the search and rescue struggle. It is hoped that the case can provide sufficient illustrative material to throw some light on suggested hypotheses of this character, and that it can suggest further questions that need to be asked if the answers are eventually to be found.

Appendix

SEARCH AND RESCUE AGENCY
1300 E Street, N. W.
Washington 25, D. C.

21 November, 1946

A REPORT ON THE GANDER RESCUE OPERATION

PROLOGUE

This report on the Gander rescue operation, involving the crash of the Belgian Sabena Airliner on the morning of September 18, 1946, presents for study and information the facilities and rescue methods used by the rescue forces.[1] However, before analyzing the operation, and in order to get a clear understanding of what this operation entailed, it is necessary to review briefly the background which made this operation possible.

Annex "A" to this report contains a brief comment on the "cycle of search and rescue operations on land and sea," together with a descriptive chart of each. It will be interesting to compare the land rescue chart with the actual chart of the Gander rescue. Annex "A" is the August-September, 1946 issue of the Air Sea Rescue

1 The survival techniques and emergency equipment employed will be the subject of a separate report.

Bulletin, and the part referred to is the insert between pages 24 and 25.

The high degree of co-operation between forces of the United States and between those forces and, in this case, the forces of Newfoundland is the culmination of effort and the outgrowth of necessity from the war. Search and rescue played a vital role in war; search and rescue has always played a vital role to merchant shipping, as indicated by the Safety of Life at Sea Convention; and now search and rescue is being recognized for its importance to commercial aviation as indicated by the standards and recommended practices for search and rescue being established by PICAO.

The co-ordination of effort required to successfully carry out a joint or combined search and rescue mission is the key to the entire problem. Co-ordination can be effective only when there are standards for communications and in rescue methods. JANP-300 established during the war these standards for the military forces of the United States. PICAO has been busy preparing such standards on an international basis for civil aviation. The philosophy of search and rescue developed by joint effort through the Search and Rescue Agency recognizes a fundamental principle employed by those establishing minimum search and rescue requirements, namely, to utilize all manner of facilities which may primarily be operating for other reasons.

RESCUE METHODS

This rescue was one which taxed all available facilities. Close co-operation between the Army, Coast Guard, Navy and the Newfoundland Government was the key to the rapid and successful culmination of the rescue efforts. Army and Coast Guard planes began searching the most probable areas when the wreckage was sighted by a TWA airliner, with the first good flying weather on the morning of the second day after the crash. After the sighting, the Commanding Officer of the Coast Guard Air Detachment flew to the scene and made an estimate of the situation. A combined council met and formulated plans of operation. It was decided to split the Army Rescue Party into two parts. One of these parties was to be landed in an uncharted pond, proceed downstream to a point abeam of the crash and then inland approximately one mile to the scene. The other party was to be landed at the entrance of the Southwest Gander River and proceed upstream to the scene. Later evaluation revised these plans and both parties proceeded from the uncharted pond. A thirty-man Newfoundland party started the difficult route upstream from the Gander River and reached the scene approximately a day after the Army parties.

The surgeon in charge of the Army ground party attended the survivors on the night of the second day and made them as comfortable as possible, and on the morning of the third day was able to pass on the information that there were eighteen survivors instead of the five originally sighted by aircraft. He also reported that the conditions of the survivors was such that it would be dangerous to try to evacuate them over land. It was at this time that the Commander Eastern Area of the Coast Guard was requested to send helicopters to Gander. Plans were made to remove the survivors to a small plateau about one mile from the scene of the crash. The helicopters were to land at this plateau, take aboard the survivors one at a time and fly them to the uncharted pond. Here they were to be placed in rubber life rafts for transfer to the waiting Catalinas. The Catalinas were to take off from the pond and transport the survivors to Gander where waiting ambulances would take them to the hospital. These plans were executed and the details are described in the annexes hereto:

Annex "B"—The narrative account contained in the report of Coast Guard Commander, North Atlantic Ocean Patrol.

Annex "C"—The "Narrative Report of Rescue Operations" by Headquarters, Fort McAndrew.

Annex "D"—The "Crash Report" by the Coast Guard Air Detachment, Newfoundland.

Annex "E"—The Chart of the Area of Operations.

FACILITIES

ARMY

Rescue party, Fort McAndrew

Medical Officer in Charge
Office in charge—Communications
Officer in charge—work details
Medical aid man
10 additional members in party

Aircraft

2 C-54 (Douglas DC-4) Transported Helicopters from Elizabeth City, North Carolina and Brooklyn, New York to Gander, Newfoundland.

1 OA-10A (Catalina Amphibian) Transported survivors between the uncharted pond and Gander.

1 B-17 and 1 DC-3

COAST GUARD

2 PBY5A (Catalina Amphibian) Transported survivors from uncharted pond to Gander.

1 PBIG (Flying Fortress) Dropped supplies to the survivors and rescue party. Acted as on scene communications center during rescue operations.

2 Helicopters transported survivors from the scene of the crash to the uncharted pond and then evacuated the Army Rescue Party. (1 from Elizabeth City, North Carolina and 1 from Brooklyn, New York)

Supplies

Communications Facilities

Facilities of Rescue Co-ordination Centers.

NAVY

Supplies

Communications facilities

NEWFOUNDLAND GOVERNMENT

Rescue party of 30 men

Hospital facilities at Gander

Gander Airport and tower facilities

OBSERVATIONS

The search and rescue attempts were handicapped in several ways, as follows:

1. The search attempts were severely handicapped the first 26 hours by very bad weather and reports of sightings which were false or proved to be old crashes. Apparently an international standard of obliterating and marking old crashes should be adopted.
2. The survivors had no means of signalling their position. Some means of radio communication could have eliminated all doubt as to the crash position almost immediately. Flares, or even a signalling mirror, could have given much needed search assistance.
3. Pre-flight indoctrination of the passengers might have enabled them to pass the information that there were more than five survivors present as first thought.
4. Present PICAO recommendations include helicopters, when sufficiently developed and available, for the Newfoundland area. In this case, the survivors could have been brought out one day earlier. The importance of the helicopter, when sufficiently available, to the search and rescue team thus has been both recognized and proven.

Prepared by:
Robert C. Gould, Lt., USCG
Chairman, Joint Liaison Committee
Search and Rescue Agency

Annexes:

A. Air Sea Rescue Bulletin, August-September, 1946
B. Narrative Account, ComNAOP
C. Narrative Account, Fort McAndrew
D. Crash Report, CG Air Detachment, Newfoundland
E. Chart of Area of Operations

[Annexes Not Reproduced Here]

THE TVA AMMONIA PLANT

CONTENTS

FOREWORD

The period between the beginning of the European war in September 1939 and the attack on Pearl Harbor in December 1941 is the period of the defense program. It was a time of reluctant preparations, of divided counsels. Many thought that we would not become involved in war; no one was sure what war might entail if it came.

Some of the sharpest disputes among the men responsible for our defense preparations concerned the expansion of basic industrial capacity: how much expansion was needed, where the new plants should be located, who should own and who should operate them; these questions arose repeatedly when sketchy estimates of future needs revealed deficiencies in existing productive capacity. By a curious paradox, one of the most disputed factors was the postwar impact of increased capacity, and this at a moment when no one could prove that we would ever be in the war, or ever have, therefore, in the strict sense a "postwar" period.

The following study traces the course of events which occurred in connection with the development of plans for expansion of our capacity to produce nitrogen. In 1940—as today—the bulk of all manufactured nitrogen was devoted to the manufacture of fertilizer. Thus the production of nitrogen was the intimate concern of the large chemical companies that manufactured it, and of the farmers who bought the nitrogenous fertilizer. But nitrogen is also a base for explosives, and enormous quantities of it are used in war. In 1940 the adequacy of nitrogen supply was naturally a matter of acute concern to both military and civilian defense planners, and their decisions on this subject would have inevitable consequences that were not regarded with indifference by the producers and consumers of nitrogen—the chemical companies and the farmers.

Although there were certain similarities in the various disputes about the enlargement of basic industrial capacity in the years 1939 to 1941, there were striking differences as well. The particular nitrate controversy described below (there were others) arose because of a proposal that the Army's nitrate program should include a new ammonia plant to be built and operated by the Tennessee Valley Authority, a government corporation. This case deals specifically with the contention over TVA's U. S. Nitrate Plant No. 2 at Muscle Shoals, Alabama.

Although various agencies, public and private, were concerned with the proposed TVA plant, the controversy came to head within the first major new agency of the defense period—NDAC, the National Defense Advisory Commission. This study is therefore written with its central emphasis on the Commission, where the final decision on the Army nitrate program was made. Because of accidental variations in the availability of documentary materials, it is possible to supply a somewhat more detailed account of the actions and attitudes of Chester Davis, one of the members of the Commission, and of his staff, than of two other members deeply concerned with the affair, E. R. Stettinius, Jr., and William S. Knudsen, and their staffs. Fortunately, however, the materials are sufficiently complete so that the reader has ample opportunity to learn the arguments and proposals of all concerned.

In brief outline the controversy was as follows: During the spring of 1940 the War Department decided that additional nitrogen capacity would be needed in case of war. It was tentatively decided that the du Pont and Allied chemical companies would each build a new ammonia plant, and that a third plant would be installed by the TVA at the site of an existing plant known as U. S. Nitrate Plant No. 2. The TVA proposed to erect a new and modern anhydrous ammonia plant in lieu of rehabilitating an obsolete plant at this site left over from World War I. This proposal, although objected to by certain of the chemical companies, was informally approved by the War Department in June 1940.

The Army's three-plant program was first referred to the NDAC in the same month, and discussions continued for some time. In September, Commissioner Knudsen, acting on the advice of his own staff and on recommendation of Commissioner Stettinius, approved the plans for the two plants to be built by du Pont and Allied, while action on the TVA proposal was to be indefinitely deferred. Commissioner Stettinius' recommendation was based on advice received from Dr. E. R. Weidlein and other staff advisers on chemicals. Commissioner Davis, who supported the TVA proposal, learned of this decision and succeeded in getting the whole program suspended pending a decision on the TVA proposal. After a month of debate the full three-plant program was approved by NDAC.

Each of the opposing parties to this controversy within NDAC asserted that its sole or primary interest in the matter was assurance of our national defense, which was, of course, the function of NDAC. By implication, if not by direct statement, each party took the position that its opponents were permitting extraneous considerations to guide their conclusions. Much of the argument turned on cost estimates and other technical factors: the disputants regarded their opponents' technical claims as ill-founded. The policy divergence on the postwar significance of the TVA plant was always in the background, and frequently an explicit subject of discussion.

The reader can decide for himself the merits of the opposing contentions. One point should be noted. Each side, after asserting that defense would be better served by approval of its proposal, also asserted that the postwar consequences of its proposal were more in accord with sound national policy. Thus the argument became deeply involved. The reader will therefore wish to consider: (1) the soundness of the technical arguments; (2) the extent to which the technical arguments were influenced by policy preferences; (3) the validity of the opposing policy considerations; and (4) whether or not the final decision should have been made by or on the recommendation of chemists and engineers, or, as it was, by the independent judgment of the laymen who composed the Commission.

Another series of questions to be answered by the reader relates to the administrative tactics employed by the protagonists. One side accused the other of proceeding covertly with plans for two ammonia plants to be operated by private companies, while unjustifiably blocking the TVA plans. On the other hand, the proponents of TVA were criticized for holding up action on two admittedly needed plants pending settlement of the TVA issue. The propriety and significance of these charges and countercharges also deserve analysis.

One final feature of this account may be mentioned. To a considerable extent the action is revealed in the memoranda written at the time by the chief participants and their various assistants. Some of the memoranda are quoted in full, more are represented by extensive extracts, some are merely summarized. The inclusion of these lengthy quotations has been deliberate, for it is believed that the reader can gain insight into the characteristic modes of operation of a top-level government agency by going through the process of reading the very words that the commissioners and their assistants read—and wrote—at the time.

The development of our present-day Federal government, that huge and complex formal organization, could never have occurred without the invention of the telephone and the typewriter. It is difficult to give more than a fleeting glimpse of government-by-telephone. But government-by-typewriter can be illustrated. The very fact that long analyses of complex data can be set down on paper rapidly, accurately, and legibly creates a necessity for the analyses. Davis and the others argued face to face—but much of their thinking was committed to paper. And we, a decade later, can follow that thinking in detail and with some assurance of proper insight, by reason of the very fact that these papers were drafted not for posterity but as part of the day's work.

I. Establishment of NDAC—Beginnings of the Nitrate Program

Late in May 1940, when the war in Europe was going badly for the Allies, President Roosevelt decided to revive the Advisory Commission to the Council of National Defense (NDAC) to aid in effecting the conversion of America's economy from a peacetime to a wartime basis.

Up to this time little serious effort had been made by the Administration to carry out plans for the mobilization of industry which had been drawn up by the Armed Forces for use in the event of war, for in spite of the fact that war had broken out in Europe in the fall of 1939, the President was faced with the necessity of balancing this nation's avowed neutrality policy and the strength of isolationist sentiment against the possibility that we might be drawn into war to preserve our security.

By the spring of 1940, however, it was becoming increasingly evident to the President and many others that the United States would seriously endanger its own security if it persisted too long in its efforts to retain a neutral position with regard to the struggles in Europe and if it failed to look to its own defenses. On April 9 Germany opened its spring offensive with an attack on Denmark and Norway. On May 10 the German armies invaded Belgium, the Netherlands, and Luxembourg. The Netherlands armies capitulated on May 13; and on May 28, the day that Belgium surrendered to Germany, the President telephoned the six men and one woman whom he had selected to be his defense advisers and explained to them that he was re-establishing the NDAC. On May 29 the British armies at Flanders, cut off from the mainland by a pincer movement of the German armies, were forced to retreat to the sea; and on May 30, while the British were evacuating their army from Dunkirk, the first meeting of the newly appointed NDAC was held in the President's office. While events in Europe in spring 1940 had made it imperative that the United States speed up its defense preparations, there were other factors which the President had to take into consideration in determining the method by which this might best be done. Some World War I leaders warned that powerful agencies set up before the situation was clearly known might make initial blunders which would be difficult to correct later on. On the other hand, it would have been virtually impossible for him to select any one civilian industrial leader to direct the defense efforts who would not only have the necessary experience in government and national affairs but who would at the same time be sufficiently above controversy to be acceptable to all groups and classes. And above all, the President had no desire to abdicate his constitutional functions—a danger that to him seemed inherent in the appointment of a single man to take charge of all defense preparations. He therefore decided upon a course which would obviate these difficulties. He set up an advisory commission comprised of a group of civilian leaders of industry and other segments of our life who would have no chairman and no legal powers but who could as individuals and in association stimulate action and provide a focus for co-ordination of the defense program.

FORMATION AND COMPOSITION OF NDAC

The Council of National Defense, made up of six Cabinet officers, was created by an Army Appropriations Act of 1916. This Council was charged, among other things, with the co-ordination of industries and resources for the national security and welfare and with the creation of relations which would render possible in time of need the immediate concentration and utilization of the resources of the nation. It was also empowered to nominate, for the President's approval, a seven-member Advisory Commission, each member of which was to have "special knowledge of some industry, public utility, or the development of some natural resource, or be otherwise specially qualified" for the performance of duties that might be assigned him. In 1940, the law was still on the books, though the Council had long since lapsed into desuetude.

On May 29, 1940, the Council of National Defense, with the President's approval and indeed under his instructions, directed that the Advisory Commission be established and also directed that each of the advisers should "be in charge of and responsible to the Council for investigation, research, and co-ordination in his designated field." On May 30, the seven newly appointed defense advisers met with the President, the Vice-President, the Cabinet, the Speaker of the House, the Army Chief of Staff, the Chief of Naval Operations, and the President's secretary and his military aide. At this meeting it was decided that the Council of National Defense would meet only at Cabinet meetings and that the "Commission would deal with the Council solely through the President himself or his Administrative Assistant, designated by the President . . . as Secretary of the Council and of the Advisory Commission." The Administrative Assistant so designated was William H. McReynolds.

The seven advisers who had been appointed by the Council with the President's approval included Chester C. Davis as Adviser on Farm Products; Edward R. Stettinius, Jr., as Adviser on Industrial Materials; William S. Knudsen as Adviser on Industrial Production; Leon Henderson as Adviser on Price Stabilization; Ralph Budd as Adviser on Transportation; Sidney Hillman as Adviser on Employment; and Miss Harriet Elliott as Adviser on Consumer Protection. The advisers so designated became known as Commissioners and their offices as Divisions. The Division of Employment was popularly called "Labor" and the Division of Farm Products was known as "Agriculture." On June 27 Donald M. Nelson was appointed to join the group as Coordinator of Purchases with a status equivalent to that of commissioner. Although the number had been fixed by statute at seven, the Commissioners agreed to regard Nelson as a member for all practical purposes.

Each of these Commissioners had had wide experience in the field which he was chosen to represent on the NDAC. Chester Davis had worked on farm publications in the Middle West and had been the Montana Commissioner of Agriculture and Labor before coming to Washington in 1933 as Director of the Production Division of the Agricultural Adjustment Administration, had been connected with the Commodity Credit Corporation and the Export-Import Bank of Washington, and was at the time of his appointment to the NDAC a member of the Board of Governors of the Federal Reserve System. Edward R. Stettinius, Jr., had been a Vice-President of General Motors and had held numerous positions with the United States Steel Corporation, including that of Chairman of the Board, which he resigned to accept the NDAC position. William S. Knudsen, after coming to the United States from Denmark, had first worked in New York shipyards. He later became general manager of a manufacturing company, President of the Chevrolet Motor Company, and finally President of General Motors Corporation. Leon Henderson, an economist, had had extensive experience in quasi-public agencies and in government, having worked as an economist with the NRA and the WPA; he was a commissioner of the Securities and Exchange Commission when he was appointed to the NDAC. Ralph Budd had worked in railroad engineering for many years and in 1940 was President of the Chicago, Burlington and Quincy Railroad. Sidney Hillman, a Lithuanian by birth, had had long experience as a labor leader, having been Vice-President of the CIO since its formation and for many years President of the Amalgamated Clothing Workers; he was on friendly terms with the President. Miss Harriet Elliott, Dean of Women at the University of North Carolina, had taught history and political science there for many years and had served on many state and national committees before her appointment to the NDAC. Donald Nelson had done general merchandising work for Sears, Roebuck before becoming Executive Vice-President and Chairman of its Executive Committee in 1939. He had occupied a prominent position in the NRA at the beginning of the New Deal. In June 1940 he was on leave from his company as Acting Director of Procurement in the U. S. Treasury.

The Commission began in June 1940 with the objective of strengthening our defense by assisting the Armed Services in superimposing the Defense Program upon the existing peacetime load of industry. By the end of the year, however, the realignment of relationships necessitated by the expansion of this program led to a decentralization of the Advisory Commission as such by merging most of its divisions with other newly created national defense units, most notably the Office of Production Management, and the Office of Price Administration and Civilian Supply. Although the existence of the Commission was not officially terminated at this time, it virtually lapsed into oblivion after the spring of 1941 as a result of the resignation of the original members upon their appointment to other posts.

THE NITRATE PROGRAM

During the half-year period from June 1940 to January 1941, when the NDAC was active, one of the jobs it was called upon to perform was that of approving the War Department's Nitrate Program—the plans for the expansion of ammonia-producing facilities in the United States. The involvement of the Commission in this procedure concerned more than its original function as a legally powerless body of individual advisers, for on June 6, 1940, Commissioner Knudsen was granted the power by the President to clear "all important contracts for purchases" by the War and Navy Departments, and on June 26 contract clearance by the NDAC was given statutory sanction in an Army Appropriations Act. Under this Act Congress authorized the Secretaries of War and Navy to expend certain funds and to "enter into contracts [only] upon the recommendation of the Council of National Defense, and the Advisory Commission thereof, and with the approval of the President." Congress reaffirmed this power of the NDAC in Appropriations Acts of September 9 and October 8, 1940.

Although the NDAC as a body was not asked to approve the War Department's Nitrate Program until the end of September 1940, several of the NDAC Divisions had been concerned with the program prior to this time. This case will follow closely the development of the Nitrate Program from June 1940, when the NDAC first became interested in it, until October 1940, when the NDAC finally took formal action approving the program under the authority granted by Congress.

The plans for increasing the production of ammonia which the War Department developed and eventually submitted as the Nitrate Program to the NDAC for its approval were an integral part of the Munitions Program the War Department had been working on for several months prior to the establishment of the NDAC at the end of May 1940. Under modern methods of technology, nitrogen in the air is "fixed" in the form of ammonia. Ammonia, subjected to further processing, is an essential raw material in the manufacture of smokeless powder, TNT, and other explosives. Therefore, as one of the first steps in its formulation of a Munitions Program, the War Department had made estimates, based on World War I figures, of the amount of ammonia which would be required for the production of explosives in time of war. It was then necessary to determine whether this amount would be available to the Army should an emergency arise. In studying the situation as it existed in the fall of 1939, however, it was found that most of the nitrogen being imported (mostly in the form of sodium nitrate) or produced in this country as ammonia was being used in fertilizers. The existing facilities for producing ammonia had been operating at only 50 per cent to 60 per cent of capacity prior to September 1939; but with the outbreak of hostilities abroad, production and demand increased rapidly and the attainment of capacity operation was imminent. It was therefore felt that additional facilities would have to be constructed if ammonia were not to be diverted from agricultural and industrial uses to meet military demands.

In the summer of 1939, the Army-Navy Munitions Board (ANMB), one of whose functions was the formulation of plans and policies for industrial mobilization in an emergency, had appointed a Chemicals Advisory Committee to study the production possibilities of many chemicals in an emergency. A Subcommittee on Ammonia and Nitric Acid had also been appointed at this time. The membership of this subcommittee, which became known as the "Nitrogen Committee," was composed largely of representatives of Allied Chemical and Dye Corp., the Hercules Powder Co., the Pennsylvania Salt Co., and the American Cyanamid Co. Its Chairman was F. A. Wardenburg, General Manager of the Ammonia Department of E. I. du Pont de Nemours and Co., Inc. This subcommittee worked with the War Department in studying the problems of ammonia production which arose under its Munitions Program.

In the fall of 1939 the War Department began investigating the possibilities of using U. S. Nitrate Plant No. 2 at TVA in connection with the Munitions Program. Although this plant had facilities for producing ammonia indirectly by the cyanamid process, the War Department at this time was not particularly interested in these facilities, for the cyanamid process had become obsolete by 1939. The Department was interested, however, in the part of this plant which had been designed to produce ammonium nitrate, the second step in the conversion of nitrogen to explosives.

U. S. Nitrate Plant No. 2, located at Muscle Shoals, Alabama, was built in 1917-1918, but it was never quite completed, and from 1919 to 1933 the War Department had guarded it and given it routine maintenance. In 1933 the plant was turned over to the newly created Tennessee Valley Authority, which was given permission to use any part or all of it for the experimental manufacture of fertilizers. Such part of the plant as was not used in the fertilizer program was to be maintained by the Authority in stand-by condition. It was stipulated in the TVA Act, however, that at any time the Secretary of War or the Secretary of the Navy might require the TVA to manufacture for and sell at cost to the United States government explosives or their nitrogenous content.

Since 1933 the TVA had used a few of the buildings in the cyanamid portion of this plant for the experimental manufacture of phosphatic fertilizers; and during this time the War Department had indicated to TVA on several occasions that it was not interested in utilizing any of the ammonia facilities at Muscle Shoals, and desired only that the ammonium nitrate plant be kept in stand-by condition. After the outbreak of war in Europe, however, the War Department became more interested in the plant, and during the fall of 1939 War Department officials visited and inspected the Muscle Shoals facilities to determine their possible usefulness in the present emergency. As a result of these investigations, the War Department decided that the site and facilities would be useful in the Munitions Program not only for the production of ammonium nitrate but also for the production of ammonia as well. Consequently, on January 10, 1940, the Secretary of War wrote a letter to the Chairman of the Board of TVA advising him that the War Department had reversed its previous policy on Muscle Shoals and requesting that the Authority make plans for the utilization of both the ammonia and the nitrate portions of Nitrate Plant No. 2 in the national defense. The TVA thereupon undertook a broad engineering and economic study of the problems of ammonia and ammonium nitrate production involved in the use of Nitrate Plant No. 2. As this study developed during the spring of 1940, frequent conferences were held with Ordnance officials to make sure that TVA's plans were co-ordinated with the plans of the War Department, and experts from private industry were called in for advice and assistance. TVA's planning proceeded without interruption, but in the course of discussion it was made clear that there was opposition within the chemical industry to the construction of a new ammonia plant by TVA unless TVA agreed that the plant would not be used "for peacetime competition" with industry. While TVA asserted that its experimental fertilizer program was not of a competitive nature, its representatives stated that they could not agree to any restrictions on future operations.

THE NITRATE PROGRAM IN NDAC

While the TVA plans were being developed, the nitrogen problem began to receive consideration from NDAC. Soon after the Advisory Commission was established, Stettinius, Adviser on Industrial Materials, had set up under him a number of subdivisions, one of which was a Chemical and Allied Products Division. This subdivision was headed by Dr. Edward R. Weidlein, a chemical engineer, who had been Director of the Mellon Institute of Industrial Research for many years in addition to being the Vice-President of its Board of Trustees. He had as his assistants in the Chemical and Allied Products Division E. W. Reid, a research chemist, who had once been associated with the Mellon Institute and more recently with the Carbide and Carbon Co., and D. P. Morgan, a chemical consultant for a New York investment counsel.

Dr. Weidlein and his associates promptly familiarized themselves with the War Department's nitrogen program and began to work with the Nitrogen Committee. As early as June 17 nitrogen, in the form of ammonium nitrate, ammonia, and nitric acid, was listed for inclusion on an export embargo schedule.

On the same day, June 17, David E. Lilienthal, one of the three directors of TVA, wrote to Stettinius to advise him that the President had approved, as a matter of policy, a program under which TVA would produce ammonium nitrate for the War Department and would continue to produce phosphatic fertilizers in the old cyanamid plant. He suggested a meeting at which NDAC could be fully informed of TVA plans. Two days later, on June 19, Weidlein, Morgan, and Reid met with J. A. Krug and A. M. Miller of TVA to discuss the TVA proposals. In brief, TVA proposed the construction of a new ammonia plant but suggested that in an acute emergency the old cyanamid plant could be temporarily rehabilitated. However, detailed plans were still in process of formulation and it was agreed that further consideration of the TVA program would be deferred until completion of the full TVA report on July 1 or thereabouts.

The TVA report was submitted to the Secretary of War on July 1, 1940. This report contained five detailed plans for the operation of Nitrate Plant No. 2, all of which contemplated the production of ammonia as well as ammonium nitrate at Muscle Shoals. In addition to rehabilitation and full use of the ammonium nitrate facilities, three of these plans provided for the operation of the cyanamid process; the fourth proposed the substitution of a modern synthetic ammonia plant for the obsolete cyanamid plant; and the fifth provided for the construction of a modern synthetic ammonia plant and in addition provided for the rehabilitation and temporary operation of the cyanamid plant, if the emergency demanded, before the completion of the new plant. The Authority recommended that the fourth of these plans be followed, and after informal discussion with the Ordnance Department on the various features of the report, the Chief and Assistant Chief of Ordnance gave their verbal approval to TVA's recommendation for the adoption of Plan No. 4. Before formally approving this plan, however, the War Department asked the Nitrogen Committee of the ANMB (Army-Navy Munitions Board) to study the TVA report and requested that the Industrial Materials Division of the NDAC participate in this study. Weidlein, Reid, and Morgan acted as Stettinius' representatives in the matter.

II. Rejection of the TVA Proposal

DAVIS IS BROUGHT IN

This study of the TVA report had scarcely begun, however, when word reached Lilienthal that Industrial Materials Division representatives who were working on the nitrate problem with the War Department were opposed to the construction of new ammonia facilities at Muscle Shoals. The TVA in submitting to the War Department the five alternative proposals for utilizing the facilities at Muscle Shoals for the production of explosives had recommended Plan No. 4, which called for rehabilitation of the ammonium nitrate plant and construction of a new synthetic ammonia plant to replace the existing obsolete cyanamid plant at Muscle Shoals. This plan had been recommended to the War Department on the basis of findings by TVA technicians that the cyanamid plant could, if rehabilitated, operate to capacity to produce the 150 tons of ammonia per day needed to supply the ammonium nitrate plant, but that the old machinery, even if repaired, would be undependable if operated to capacity for any length of time. It had also been determined by TVA engineers that in any case the cyanamid plant would require far more power for its operation than would a new plant using the synthetic process, and the ammonia produced there would be more expensive than that produced by a modern plant. The Authority in recommending Plan No. 4 had felt that this evidence in favor of the plan was convincing enough to guarantee it the War Department's approval and that further explanation of the reasons for this recommendation was unnecessary, as it seemed unquestionably to be the most practical of the five plans. Furthermore the War Department was concerned with defense and not with other aspects of TVA's proposals. No particular mention had been made, therefore, at the time the report was presented, of the positive advantages which this plan offered to agriculture or of the further objections which might be raised to the other plans which contemplated rehabilitation of the cyanamid plant.

Therefore, Lilienthal, upon hearing of newspaper reports that the proposed TVA plant was to be displaced in favor of another commercial plant, sent a wire to Stettinius on July 18 requesting that he meet with Chester Davis, the Agricultural representative on the NDAC, and Dr. Harcourt A. Morgan, Chairman of TVA, to discuss the important agricultural aspects of this plan; Dr. Morgan was spokesman for TVA's agricultural program.

While arrangements were being made for holding this meeting, Davis requested Dr. Morgan to send him information that would be helpful to him as background for the discussion. The memorandum which he received in reply, and which he sent on to Weidlein, reads, in part, as follows:

> The problem is to meet two of the major requirements of the emergency:
>
> (1) To produce ammonium nitrate for munitions as required by the War Department. This phase can be successfully met by adoption of the plant expansion program at Muscle Shoals developed by the Authority's technical staff at the request of the War Department. This program, as we understand it, is now being studied by the Advisory Commission at the recommendation of the War Department.
>
> (2) To develop these facilities with full recognition of the ultimate implications which nitrates hold for agriculture.
>
> This objective of potential dual use of nitrate production facilities for munitions in wartime and agricultural plant food production in time of peace was explicitly recognized in the National Defense Act of 1916.
>
> The science of soil protection through the use of plant food requires basic agricultural readjustments made possible first by the development and use of phosphatic concentrates. The partial use of the nitrate plant facilities at Muscle Shoals

since 1933 for the production of phosphatic concentrates was a necessary first step in the development of a national soil protection program. With this first step well under way, it is appropriate to consider the development of nitrate plant foods essential to the balancing of plant food applications consistent with varying soil, production and climatic conditions. A complete program of national soil protection must be achieved through proper co-ordination of research, experimentation, and demonstration under practical farm conditions. Completion and expansion of the present facilities at Muscle Shoals in order to accommodate an ultimate production program of phosphate concentrates and nitrate concentrates is a basic requirement to the perpetuity of agriculture's contribution to the national defense.

This ultimate plant food program finds its agricultural validity in the fact that reserves of phosphatic concentrates are basic to restoration of our soil *capital* whereas concentrates of nitrate plant foods are essential for increasing the *productive* use of that capital. Taken together, these plant foods, supplemented with other available elements, will make possible that type of farm diversification so essential to the achievement of self-containment in the one crop system areas of the nation.

In setting out these agricultural considerations it is recognized that the munitions requirements of the War Department take precedence in the present emergency. If at any future time the products of these proposed expanded facilities should not be necessary to meet the emergency requirements of the War Department, they would be available for agricultural use . . .

. . . the recommendations of the Authority were set forth to the War Department in the following paragraphs:

1. Begin at once the rehabilitation of that portion of Nitrate Plant No. 2 in which ammonia is converted to ammonium nitrate. This will involve overhauling and testing of all equipment to be used, the finishing of original incomplete construction, the possible substitution of modern ammonia oxidizers for those now only partially in place, and other changes in the plant which appear necessary. At the completion of this job, which can be accomplished in approximately four months, the plant can be put into service to produce 300 tons of ammonium nitrate per day using ammonia procured from existing producing sources. It is estimated that this rehabilitation would cost approximately $1,864,000.
2. Begin at once the design and construction of a synthetic ammonia plant having a capacity of 150-160 tons of ammonia per day and locate this plant on the grounds of Nitrate Plant No. 2 so as to utilize the facilities and building already available. The time required for the construction of this plant would be about 11 months, after which ammonia need no longer be procured from outside sources, and the Nitrate Plant would become a complete, independent and economical unit for the daily production of 300 tons of ammonium nitrate. Such an ammonia plant would cost approximately $4,153,000.
3. If before the synthetic ammonia plant is finished an emergency should arise and ammonia could not be procured from outside sources for conversion to ammonium nitrate at Nitrate Plant No. 2, it is proposed then to begin the rehabilitation of six of the carbide furnaces at the Nitrate Plant together with equivalent capacity in the balance of the cyanamid plant in the cheapest possible way for temporary and quick production of ammonia pending the completion of the synthetic ammonia plant discussed in Paragraph 2. About four months from the date of inception of this rehabilitation program ammonia would be available for conversion to ammonium nitrate in an amount of about 75 tons per day (half of the full capacity). This would be relatively expensive ammonia. This rehabilitation is estimated to cost $1,104,000.

THE FIRST MEETING AND ITS AFTERMATH

The meeting arranged in response to Lilienthal's wire was finally held on July 31 in the office of Dr. Edward R. Weidlein and was attended by Dr. Weidlein and Dr. Reid, representing the Industrial Materials Division of the NDAC; Chester Davis and his assistant, J. K. Galbraith of the Agricultural Division; Dr. Morgan, accompanied by Gordon Clapp, General Manager, and Neil Bass, Chief Conservation Engineer of TVA; Edward A. O'Neal and W. R. Ogg of the American Farm Bureau Federation; and Senator John Bankhead of Alabama. Dr. Weidlein, who conducted the meeting, presented the views of his Division, with a brief summary of the problems come up against and the methods which were being employed to deal with them. He specifically mentioned the co-operation his Division was receiving from industry committees and the desire of the executives in private industry to solve the national defense problem without government aid as far as possible. A report from the Nitrogen Committee was due within a week, which would clarify the situation. Dr. Morgan described to those present the attitude of TVA toward the nitrate program proposed by the War Department. He stated that, owing to the shortage of power, TVA was glad to be relieved of the power requirement which existed in the original Army plans for the rehabilitation of the cyanamid plant at Muscle Shoals, but added that they were most anxious to have ammonia-producing facilities there for a "long-geared" program of experimentation in soil improvement. Dr. Weidlein stressed the desirability of working out a program satisfactory to all, and suggested that at least the initial use of the TVA plant would be for ammonium nitrate made from ammonia produced elsewhere.

Davis later wrote that "although the meeting lasted for some time, we were unable to elicit any information whatever as to what the Army recommendations [on the TVA report] had been or what [other] projects were under consideration in the Chemicals Division. I asked Dr. Weidlein to keep my Division informed fully on this subject when he had anything concrete to discuss and he agreed to do so."

Throughout the period of the nitrate controversy, much of the detailed work on the problem was handled for Davis by his assistant, J. K. Galbraith. Dr. Galbraith, previously a teacher of economics, had later served as economist for the Farm Bureau Federation; he began his work with the NDAC on part-time loan from the Federation. On the following day, August 1, Galbraith prepared the following memorandum to give Davis the essential facts of the situation with which TVA and Agriculture were concerned.

There are two plants at Muscle Shoals of Great War vintage. One of these was built to produce Ammonium Nitrate, an explosive. The other was to produce Ammonia, the chief raw material of Ammonium Nitrate. Ammonia is also the raw material of nitrogenous fertilizers.

The Ammonium Nitrate plant must be modernized but the process is not obsolete. The Ammonia plant *could* be repaired and used but the process is obsolete, takes a great deal of power, and the product is costly. Part of this old Ammonia plant has been converted to produce the high test phosphatic fertilizer. The TVA has a widely distributed research and extension program designed to promote use of this fertilizer as a soil conservation measure. It is distributed to selected farmers through the land grant colleges and a considerable tonnage is used in the Soil Conservation program.

The proposal is for a new Ammonia plant and modernization of the Ammonium Nitrate (explosive) plant. The phosphorus production will continue. After the defense effort is complete the new ammonia plant will be used for fertilizer production; if there is an emergency need for ammonia, it is proposed to bring the old ammonia plant temporarily into production. Whatever happens, there appears to be a probability that the ammonium nitrate plant will be repaired and put into use. Ammonia will be shipped in from plants erected somewhere else. The nub of the question is whether an ammonia (cum fertilizer) plant should be erected in conjunction with the ammonium nitrate plant.

There are two questions upon which the policy, as it affects agriculture, turns. They are:

1. Is nitrogen development by TVA—the construction of an ammonia plant in particular—consistent with basic national defense objectives?
2. Does it serve a national agricultural interest as opposed to purely sectional advantage?

The answer to the first question must come primarily from the Army and the technical officers of the Commission. All that can be said here is that the TVA engineers *believe* that there are no technical barriers to the development, and that it has important technical advantages. Army engineers have, it appears, reported favorably. For the rest, the case must rest with those who are technically qualified. The advantage of alternative private development, it might appear, should be demonstrated affirmatively. Congress declared (National Defense Act, 1916) that these plants should be an integrated national defense and national conservation measure.

From the evidence I have been able to assemble I am satisfied that the answer to the second question is in the affirmative. It appears that there is a national agricultural interest as opposed to a specific sectional interest in this proposal. Three things may be noted as follows:

1. The TVA seeks construction of the Ammonia plant at Muscle Shoals to further its research and extension activities in fertilizer and plant nutrition under eventual peacetime conditions. The present fertilizer program is national in scope. The anticipated developments will parallel and amplify the present work.

   The present program, very briefly, consists in the manufacture and experimental distribution of high test phosphates. These high test phosphates, running to several times the strength of old commercial mixes, offer a substantial saving in the cost of this plant food. Since producers must be educated to their use and must adjust their fertilizer drills and techniques, the development must be on a non-commercial basis. This the TVA is doing through a memorandum of agreement with some thirty land-grant colleges and as a part of the soil conservation program of the AAA.

   When the Ammonia plant becomes available for peacetime use, the TVA proposes to extend its program to nitrates and to nitrogen-phosphorus mixes. This will mean that the experimental and conservation activities can be extended to row and cultivated crops (cash crops) where nitrogen rather than phosphorus tends to be the limiting factor.

2. Organized agriculture has supported the TVA program in terms of a national policy. The Farm Bureau studied and endorsed the fertilizer program of the TVA in 1936 through the medium of a fully representative committee. It expressed a similar interest in 1921 and again in 1938 in a special brief submitted to the Congressional Joint Committee which investigated TVA in that year. The national interest would also appear to be affirmed by the wide participation of the land-grant colleges in the fertilizer program. The agricultural program was specifically endorsed before the Congressional Committee by Dean T. P. Cooper in his capacity as Chairman of the Association of Land Grant Colleges in the Valley States.

3. The Congressional Joint Committee of 1938 concluded its finding with a positive endorsement of the fertilizer program and recommended "an expanding program of field tests to make such fertilizers available to farmers in increasing numbers throughout the entire United States."

The TVA, at Galbraith's request, supplemented his memorandum with some additional facts and figures on the TVA fertilizer program being carried on at Muscle Shoals, and brought out the point that this program had stimulated private producers to erect new plants and expand old ones to meet a greatly expanded farmer demand for concentrated superphosphate. It was further noted that since TVA hoped to extend its present program to include the production and testing of new and more concentrated nitrogenous fertilizers in a large-scale farm program, an ammonia plant, such as the one the Authority was suggesting for use in emergency production of ammonium nitrate for the War Department, would be suitable as to size and source of nitrogen to carry out this broad long-time program. It was also stated that TVA engineers had stressed the importance of the fact that the proposed ammonia plant could be constructed at Muscle Shoals at a relatively low investment because of the availability of a steam plant, shops, laboratories, power, water services, and other useful facilities, and that this would influence favorably the cost of ammonia produced both for emergency use in munitions and for benefit to agricultural progress in peacetime.

On August 8 Davis sent the following memorandum to Weidlein:

> Following our meeting in your office last week, I have undertaken to explore in some detail the agricultural significance of the Tennessee Valley Authority plant food program.
>
> It would appear from my study of the question that this program should have important significance for American agriculture. It would also appear that a very close relation exists between the present phosphate program and the possible development of synthetic ammonia supplies under Tennessee Valley Authority auspices. This phase of the defense program appears to have a close bearing on the conservation objectives of American agriculture.
>
> For these reasons I would greatly appreciate it if you would keep me very closely informed on plans and decisions relating in any way to the development of facilities in this area or to alternative facilities elsewhere. In the meantime please let me know if there are any details of the agricultural phases of this development which I can supply and which will be useful to you.

On August 13, Dr. Weidlein wrote in reply:

I appreciate your interest in the TVA plant food program.

I wish to assure you that I will keep you informed of our program on synthetic ammonia. This subject is being given very thorough and careful consideration. However, we feel that we have sufficient material available at the present time to meet all demands for at least one year, which does give us more time to study how to meet the larger amounts which will be needed after that date.

I appreciate your offer of co-operation, and you may rest assured that I will take advantage of your kind offer to furnish us with any details of the agricultural phases of this development.

Also at about this time, Davis talked with Stettinius and received, as he thought, Stettinius' personal assurance that the Agricultural Division would be kept fully and promptly informed of all developments. However, during the following week Davis received no further word from Weidlein to indicate that the War Department had made any progress in developing its nitrate program. He therefore assigned Dr. Harry A. Curtis, Dean of the College of Engineering, University of Missouri, who had been serving as a consultant to TVA, and who was acting as consultant for Davis on nitrate-phosphate problems, to secure information on current nitrate plans.

CURTIS FAILS TO GET INFORMATION

On September 10 Curtis met with Weidlein to discuss the nitrogen situation. In this meeting Weidlein referred Curtis to ANMB for information on the Army proposals, but added that a report on nitrogen would be ready soon and made available to Davis. Weidlein also said that the situation looked all right for the next twelve months, but supplied no other information. He explained his refusal to furnish information on two grounds, later summarized by Curtis as follows:

First, he had obtained part of his information from a confidential report in the office of the Army and Navy Munitions Board through a request from Mr. Stettinius, and he did not feel free to discuss the figures of this report, even with someone from another division of the Defense Commission; and, second, part of his information was given him confidentially by manufacturers.

During the second week in September Curtis attempted to secure the information from ANMB and on September 13 he reported these activities in the following memorandum to Davis:

I have accomplished a few things this week, but have spent a considerable amount of time in futile efforts to secure the information necessary to give you an accurate picture of the situation in respect to nitrogen supply in the current preparedness program.

Under normal peacetime conditions, the major fraction of all the ammonia produced in the United States is used in manufacturing nitrogenous fertilizers, only a small fraction being used for the production of munitions. The current national defense program certainly calls for a large amount of ammonia. The War Department may get this needed ammonia by:

(a) Taking it from its normal use in agriculture
(b) Increasing the output and perhaps the capacity of existing plants
(c) Curtailing exports
(d) Building new ammonia plants

The War Department, in co-operation with industry, no doubt has well-defined plans for securing the ammonia needed. I have proceeded on the assumption that when plans are made which affect a material as vital to agriculture as is ammonia, you are entitled to know in detail what those plans may be. Without such knowledge, I do not see how you can properly decide what steps, if any, may be necessary to insure an agricultural preparedness adequate to meet a war emergency.

It is my understanding that the War Department plans and information with respect to ammonia supply have been made available in detail to the chemical committee working under Mr. Stettinius. I have already submitted to you a memorandum detailing my futile effort to secure specific information through Dr. Weidlein.

My next effort was to secure through the War and Navy Munitions Board access to reports which might reveal the War Department's plans for securing the ammonia which the national defense plans will require. Your Executive Assistant, Mr. Paul A. Porter, secured from Mr. Leon Henderson the necessary card to interview the Munitions Board officers, together with a letter asking that I be allowed access to the War Department reports on nitrates. I was directed to the office of a Major Brown. Major Brown was out but Major Morgan was in charge of the office. He conducted me to the office of a Lieutenant-Colonel Tenney and there the two officers fell into a discussion as to the meaning of a letter of date August 29, 1940, from the Secretary of War regarding access to the confidential files. There, [these?] officers then went to consult someone else, and finally returned to inform me that interpretation of the Secretary of War's letter would have to be made by Colonel J. H. Burns who was not in his office at the time, but would be on hand the following morning. Major Morgan said that he would phone me in the morning. So ended my first attempt to get information.

Next morning Mr. Henderson received a letter from Colonel Burns giving permission for me to see certain confidential files. I then went again to Major Brown's office. A stack of seven or eight reports marked "confidential" had been laid out for me. I examined the first of these and saw that it was an amateur report, prepared about 1933, compiled from technical magazines and other public sources. I then examined the other "confidential" reports and found them to be wholly worthless. So, I laid the whole pile back on Major Brown's desk and told him this was "kid stuff." He was apologetic and agreed that these reports should be discarded from his files. I then asked him if I might examine the 1940 ammonia procurement report. He said that he could not show me this report because it contained information which the War Department had secured on the promise that it would not be revealed to anyone outside the Department without the consent of the companies which supplied the information. I asked Major Brown by what means Mr. Stettinius' Division had been able to secure access to the report in question. Major Brown then told me that Mr. Weidlein had been given the report only after the industrial folks on the Department's Chemical Advisory Committee (Mr. Warren Watson, Secretary) had notified the War Department that it would be all right to reveal the information to Mr. Weidlein.

I recite this trivial story only to show how the present situation has come about. I do not blame the War Department for keeping a pledge to industry, although I do not think that such a pledge is proper under current conditions. And I can forgive the Department officers for handing me some useless reports instead of revealing at once what the real situation was. It remains a fact, however, that because industry has been able to dictate to the War Department the terms on which information would be furnished, and has been able to dictate like terms to the Chemical Committee of Mr. Stettinius' Division of the National Defense Advisory Commission, your Division of the Commission is denied information necessary to you if you are to reach well-founded decisions in respect to certain important agricultural phases of the current defense program.

On the same day that Curtis submitted this report, Davis received a letter from Edward A. O'Neal, President of the American Farm Bureau Federation (AFBF), who for many years had resided at Florence, Alabama, a town adjacent to Muscle Shoals, and who had long fought for public or semi-public use of the Shoals. O'Neal wrote that he had informed the President of the fact that the AFBF Board of Directors had endorsed the TVA proposal and that he had learned that this proposal had already had the President's sympathetic interest. O'Neal added that he was sure Davis would take up this matter with the NDAC and would insist on its being carried out.

PROGRESS WITH DU PONT AND ALLIED

Davis had been on a trip into the Southwest during the first two weeks of September, and it was upon his return to Washington on September 16 that he first learned that the War Department had been making plans, which were now nearing completion, for use of the du Pont Company in its nitrate program. He therefore wrote Nelson on September 17: "It has come to my attention that negotiations are in progress for the construction of a new ammonia plant presumably at Morgantown, West Virginia, by the Du Pont Company.

"I would appreciate any information your office may have as to the status of these negotiations and further would like the opportunity to consider certain related problems before any proposed arrangement for increasing capacity for ammonia production is completed."

On the following day, September 18, Davis was informed by his Executive Assistant, Paul Porter, that no contract had yet been signed with du Pont but that details of the deal had been run down, a letter of intent had been sent out, and du Pont would undoubtedly do the job. A "letter of intent" is, roughly speaking, an informal contract for which a formal contract is later substituted. Davis then sent the following memorandum to Weidlein:

Reference is made to my memorandum to you dated August 8 and your response of August 13, 1940, with reference to the program on synthetic ammonia. I had requested to be informed on plans and decisions relating to the expansion of facilities.

It has come to my attention that consideration is being given to the establishment of a synthetic ammonia plant by the Government at Morgantown, West Virginia. I would appreciate any information on this proposed project which your division has, including terms of the proposed contract and cost data, as well as the schedule of defense requirements upon which the proposed increase in facilities is based.

Weidlein replied:

I tried to reach you on the telephone this afternoon in reply to your memorandum of today.

The two proposed synthetic ammonia plants, one to be located in West Virginia and the other in Kentucky, are to be Ordnance owned and agent operated. This program originated within the Army and has been developed to meet the requirements of the new munitions plants which will come into operation about the same time these two new ammonia plants will be completed.

In view of the fact that this is a construction program, the details of the proposed contract, cost data, and other schedules come under Mr. E. F. Johnson of Mr. Knudsen's Division.

It is my understanding that this new capacity will still be short approximately 150 tons of nitrogen per day when all the munitions plants are put into operation, and other means are being considered for taking care of this additional capacity.

The nitrogen program still requires further development work, and I hope on my return to Washington next week I can see you and explain the program in detail.

On September 19 Davis received a memorandum in reply to his request of the 17th for any information which Nelson's office might have on the proposed Morgantown plant. This reply was from A. C. C. Hill, Jr., Assistant to Mr. Nelson, and stated that "Major Dillon of the Ordnance Department has advised that negotiations in this connection have not as yet begun" and that General Harris, Assistant to the Chief of Ordnance, had been asked to keep Davis informed.

On the same day Galbraith called Davis's attention to the fact that the following items had appeared in a Weekly Operations Progress Report of Knudsen's Division, dated September 18:

Light Ordnance and Explosives Section
Letters of Intent

Du Pont Powder Company—Ammonia plant at Morgantown, West Virginia to produce 250 tons per day.

Allied Chemical Company—ammonia plant at site to be selected, to produce 150 tons per day. . . .

The appearance of these items in Knudsen's Report indicated that letters of intent to negotiate contracts had been sent by the War Department to the du Pont and Allied Chemical companies. Before such letters of intent could be sent, however, it was necessary for the War Department to secure Knudsen's approval, and the issuance of these letters therefore served as official notification to the two companies that the War Department intended to negotiate contracts with them and also as official indication of authorization from the NDAC to the War Department to negotiate contracts with these companies for the construction of ammonia plants to be used in the National Defense program.

DAVIS'S DILEMMA

On the same day that Davis received this report from Knudsen's Division, he addressed to Knudsen and Stettinius a memorandum entitled "Development of Synthetic Ammonia Capacity by the Tennessee Valley Authority," which he sent to each member of the NDAC as well as to Donald Nelson, Dr. Weidlein, A. C. C. Hill, Jr., Dr. Harry Curtis, and Dr. H. A. Morgan.

This memorandum, which was based on one Galbraith had prepared for Davis earlier in the day, stated:

Following conferences with Dr. Weidlein and other members of the Industrial Materials Division early last month, I have taken steps to obtain complete information on the agricultural phases of nitrate supply and development of nitrate capacity in the United States. In this matter I have had the services of Dr. Harry A. Curtis, Dean of the College of Engineering at the University of Missouri, who has been in conference with members of the Industrial Materials Division.

Two questions emerge in connection with the broad problem of nitrogen supply, as follows:

1. Since agriculture is by far the heaviest consumer of commercial nitrates, can this supply be adequately protected in face of the demands of the munitions program?
2. Can new nitrate capacity developed at this time be planned so as to promote long-time conservation programs for agriculture?

During this past week members of the Industrial Materials Division have arranged to make available to me full plans for meeting nitrogen requirements during the emergency period. For this reason, I should like to defer comment on the first question. However, I understand that these plans contemplate an increase in present synthetic ammonia capacity which immediately brings my second question to the fore. . . .

He continued:

The Tennessee Valley Authority in relating the use of its facilities to the defense program, in general accordance with the National Defense Act of 1916 and the TVA Act of 1933, has proposed that a synthetic ammonia plant be erected on the government reservation at Wilson Dam. This plant, with a suggested capacity of 150 to 160 tons of ammonia per day would provide product for the present ammonium nitrate plant which is in stand-by condition but which will require modernization.

It is my understanding that this proposal has been favorably reviewed by the President and by the War Department. Apart from the advantageous location adjacent to ammonium nitrate capacity, there appear to be other technical advantages. Land, a steam plant, shops, skilled services, personnel, power and water services are now available for the plant. The engineering staff of the Authority place the cost of producing ammonia at this site at 2.1 cents a pound. The cost of the installation, in accordance with the same estimates, will be $4,353,000 for the synthetic ammonia plant. An estimated $1,864,000 would be required for rehabilitation of the ammonium nitrate plant which latter has no agricultural significance.

However, it is not my intention to enter upon technical or cost aspects at this time. It is my understanding, however, that additional ammonia capacity developed elsewhere at this time will be for purposes of the defense emergency. I assume therefore that the cost of plant will be amortized over a relatively short period. In this case, the government, even though not called upon for an initial capital outlay or for financing, will, as a customer, be paying the purchase price of the plant during the defense period. While a careful comparison of costs as between this development and other sources is obviously necessary, the question of cost should not turn on the amount of initial outlay involved. A rational appraisal of cost requires that the Commission consider total outlay for ammonia during the defense period less the liquidation value or permanent asset value of the plant to the government at the end of the emergency. In light of my earlier analysis, it is clear that an ammonia plant in conjunction with the plant food program of the TVA will have a high asset value at the end of the emergency period.

Conclusion

In the post-emergency period this ammonia capacity—or such part of it as may be required—would complete the plant nutrient program of the TVA. This latter program, with its support and endorsement from farm people may, as noted, be extended to nitrates in any case. Therefore, while it is not the function of this Division to initiate plans for developing industrial capacity, the exceptional circumstances in the present case are clear. Before completing plans for development of synthetic ammonia capacity in other locations, it would appear clear that the TVA site should have the closest scrutiny. There may, of course, be cost factors or technical factors which have not been brought to my attention. Unless this is the case I would recommend that the agricultural phases of this location require that it be given priority over other locations.

Apparently Davis was not too hopeful that this letter alone would result in the Muscle Shoals properties being given at least equal priority with other locations for the construction of additional ammonia capacity. The TVA had submitted its proposal for the construction of a new ammonia plant some two months earlier, but the War Department had not yet acted upon it and had in the meantime gone ahead with plans for the construction of other ammonia plants by private companies. Davis knew that active opposition had developed to the TVA proposal and that consequently the War Department was postponing definite action on it, possibly pending later developments in the international picture. He therefore decided to take action himself to secure immediate and careful consideration of the TVA proposal by the War Department and NDAC.

Davis was experienced in the ways of government. But he was shocked by the fact that the letters of intent had been issued without his knowledge, especially in view of Stettinius' assurance a month earlier; a talk with Stettinius at this point proved inconclusive. Davis was, of course, quite conscious of the fact that his responsibility was directly to the President, not to the Commission. This much is clear. We do not know what his actual reflections were at this moment, but it is obvious that, even excluding all the possibilities of seeking assistance from outside the government, there were a considerable variety of ways in which he might have moved toward his goal. He might, for example, have brought the matter up at a meeting of the NDAC. He might have gone to Stettinius and asked him to take the necessary steps, since his Division had been asked by the War Department to study the TVA report and was working with the Nitrogen Committee on the formulation of plans for ammonia production. He might have asked the President to secure Stettinius' co-operation in this matter. Or he might have gone directly to the Assistant Secretary of War and explained the situation to him. Any of these steps might have helped and would have been consistent with Davis's concern; but the means which he did decide to use were more drastic than any of those suggested.

III. Presidential Intervention

On September 20 Davis sent the following letter prepared for him by Porter:

The President,
The White House

Dear Mr. President:

The Agricultural Division of the Commission two months ago requested the opportunity to consider plans for expansion of facilities for the production of ammonia. Without reference to this Division, the Production Division has authorized the War Department and that Department is proceeding to complete contracts with Du Pont and Allied Chemical for two plants for ammonia production to be built by the government.

The TVA has submitted proposals for installation of ammonia capacity for present defense purposes and for eventual use in conjunction with the Authority's plant food-phosphate program. I am convinced of the national agricultural significance of this proposal. If these contracts are completed, the TVA may lose the chance for this development.

It is requested that the War Department be directed *not* to complete these contracts until an adequate appraisal is made of the opportunity to utilize TVA resources for immediate defense needs and at the same time provide facilities for subsequent use in the Authority's long-time farm program.

Respectfully submitted,
(signed) *Chester C. Davis*
Chester C. Davis

And the following day he telegraphed Stephen Early, secretary to the President:

TODAY'S WHITE HOUSE POUCH CONTAINS LETTER FROM ME TO PRESIDENT WHICH I CONSIDER IMPORTANT. WAR DEPARTMENT HAS CLEARED WITH KNUDSEN'S DIVISION PROJECTS FOR TWO GOVERNMENT BUILT AMMONIA PLANTS TO BE OPERATED BY PRIVATE CHEMICAL COMPANIES AND NEGOTIATIONS ARE NEARING COMPLETION. STOP. AM REQUESTING THAT THESE BE STOPPED UNTIL CONSIDERATION IS GIVEN TO LOCATING AMMONIA PLANTS AT TVA IN LINE WITH THE AUTHORITY'S PEACETIME PROGRAM IN COOPERATION WITH AGRICULTURAL COLLEGES FOR SOIL CONSERVATION. WILL YOU PLEASE SEE THAT MY LETTER IS BROUGHT TO PRESIDENT'S ATTENTION AT ONCE.

The President, upon receipt of the letter, immediately issued instructions to the Secretary of War to suspend all negotiations with the du Pont and Allied Chemical companies pending consideration of the TVA location. The reader will note that Davis's request and the President's instructions did not require approval of the TVA proposal, but it was clear that an adverse decision by the War Department would require affirmative action.

IV. Background of the Rejection

STETTINIUS AND WEIDLEIN

In Section II of this study—"Rejection of the TVA Proposal"—the reader has seen the course of events from the beginning of July 1940 to September 20, 1940, primarily as they appeared to the TVA officials and Davis. However, while the omission of the TVA plant from the approved program listed in Knudsen's report of September 18 came as a shock to Davis, the decision itself was, of course, the end result of a long process. It is now necessary to summarize the events that led to this result —events that were unknown to Davis while they were occurring. In this section, therefore, the chief focus will be placed on Weidlein, and on the Nitrogen Committee and the War Department.

By July, Weidlein and his associates had already begun to devote considerable attention to the nitrogen problem. In late June, Weidlein assisted Stettinius in making arrangements with Assistant Attorney General Thurman Arnold to keep anti-trust indictments against officials of the du Pont and Allied companies sealed for the duration of the emergency because it was believed that court action would interfere with the Defense Program. On June 25 a first nitrogen supply and requirements balance sheet was ready: it showed a slight excess for the first year, and a slight deficiency for the second. A few days later Stettinius sent a summary of the first year balance sheet to the President, who had been inquiring about the nitrogen situation. Stettinius' memorandum, dated July 3, concluded as follows:

> It will be observed that no output is included for Muscle Shoals. This is because the facilities constructed there during the World War are now obsolete. Although they could be operated at a price, this is considered uneconomic. From this tabulation, it is seen that there is no shortage, at this stage of the game.

On the same day, July 3, Stettinius received a letter from Charles J. Brand, Executive Secretary and Treasurer of the National Fertilizer Association, Incorporated. This Association, organized for the purpose of promoting the progress and development of the fertilizer industry "in the interest of sound agriculture in its broadest sense" carries on such educational activities as will "increase the use of fertilizers and advance the interests of agriculture and the fertilizer industry." Among the private organizations which make up the membership of the Association are the du Pont and Allied Chemical companies. Mr. Brand's letter in behalf of the Association read as follows:

> We understand that a project has been or is to be proposed to the National Defense Commission for the TVA to erect and operate a nitrogen fixation plant at Muscle Shoals.
>
> The fertilizer industry feels that the erection and operation of plants to produce commodities that are standard articles of commerce in normal peacetime should be carried on by private enterprise. This is not to say that during a national emergency government subsidy may not be needed and warranted.
>
> It does seem appropriate for the government to erect and operate plants to produce commodities, such as explosives that are not articles of ordinary commerce in normal peacetimes, especially as private industry is unable or unwilling to assume that responsibility.
>
> Federal erection and operation of manufacturing plants in times of emergency to produce peacetime commodities is bound to result in adding to competition between government and private enterprise. It is not likely that governmental emergency production facilities will be permitted to remain idle in peacetime if there is ANY way of

forcing their operation even at the expense of the taxpayer.

Again, it is not feasible to keep such government facilities in "stand-by" condition during extensive peace period. Technical discoveries soon make production processes and equipment obsolete. Constant changes will be made in privately owned and operated plants, while similar changes will not have been made in government "stand-by" plants.

Present production of by-product ammonia from coke and gas plants, presently operating plants for the fixation of atmospheric nitrogen as ammonia, and existing plants now producing methanol, which are suitable for quick conversion to ammonia production, may have sufficient capacity to supply even emergency needs. If it is determined by the Commission that additional capacity is desirable or necessary, we are convinced that the needed facilities should be designed, erected, and operated by private enterprise.

Private enterprise has successfully operated nitrogen fixation plants on a large scale in this country for 18 years. The TVA, or for that matter any other government agency, would be without any experience in this type of production. Vital time would be lost even if the best technical men, starting without experience, were assigned to such an undertaking. Private enterprise has already available plans and designs tested by successful operation, and can furnish skeleton crews of trained operators. Successful production would be assured from the start.

Power is not a major factor in modern nitrogen fixation. Nearby hydro-electric power, therefore, is not an essential factor in plant location. Besides, the power-producing facilities of the TVA are already over-taxed.

Transportation of liquid anhydrous ammonia presents difficult problems. Transportation of nitric acid presents even greater difficulties. It is practical to oxidize the ammonia into nitric acid only at the explosives plant. Additional ammonia production above that now existent should be located adjacent to the explosives plant. If at all possible, such location should be within pipeline distance so that rail transportation of ammonia may be avoided.

Availability of raw materials is a minor factor in determining the location of a nitrogen fixation plant. Already we have concentration of vital plants in the Tennessee Valley. Sabotage affecting the water or power supply of the TVA might seriously affect the production of aluminum, phosphorus, powder and other commodities produced in that area. Decentralization and isolation seem better lines to follow than concentration.

It would seem that the public interest would be best served if any additional capacity needed for nitrogen fixation should be provided by the existing industry.

Very truly yours,
(signed) *Charles Brand*

P.S. Water shortage due to drought, such as now prevails at Norris Lake, also suggests the wisdom of decentralization. Thought could also be given, under present emergency conditions, to devoting to aluminum production the power now being used at Muscle Shoals to make concentrated superphosphate. Our superphosphate industry is the largest in the world, and it can readily supply 20 per cent superphosphate, the customarily used grade, in unlimited quantities. *CJB*

The occasion for Brand's letter was, as he indicated, the TVA proposal of July 1. As will be recalled, this proposal was referred for study and analysis to Stettinius' staff and to the Nitrogen Committee. The Committee acted promptly. On July 8 the Committee filed an adverse report with ANMB. In general terms, the Committee analyzed the problem by comparing estimated costs at TVA with estimated costs at Morgantown, assuming that the needed 150 tons of ammonia per day could be taken care of by an appropriate enlargement of the projected du Pont plant. On this assumption, the Committee concluded that ammonia and ammonium nitrate could be manufactured (and delivered to loading plants) more cheaply at Morgantown. The Committee also concluded that since TVA lacked know-how, "if a plant were built at Muscle Shoals and it were brought into capacity operation in two years, it would be a miracle." Finally, the Committee expressed its opposition to government ownership and operation of a synthetic ammonia plant in the post-emergency period.

On July 17, not long after the submission of the Committee report, Stettinius referred Brand's letter to Weidlein, saying:

> In view of the delicate relationships involved in the subject matter of the attached letter from the Executive Secretary and Treasurer of the National Fertilizer Association and your knowledge of the problem, I believe it would be advisable for you to draft for my signature a suitable reply to the letter.

The following day Stettinius received Lilienthal's telegram requesting that a meeting be held for the purpose of discussing agricultural aspects of the nitrate program, and on July 23 he replied to Mr. Brand that "this whole question of nitrogen fixation facilities is being given the most careful study."

On the same day, July 23, Weidlein sent a memorandum to Stettinius in which he set forth his views on the nitrate situation and his reaction to the TVA proposal:

We are analyzing the nitrogen problem from every point of view and from the data which has been given us with regard to the completion of explosive plants, we feel that for the first year at least we will have sufficient requirements to meet the needs. In accordance with the schedule, the completed plants on July 1, 1941 for nitrogen requirements will be 195,000 tons per year, or 651 tons per day. If we are able to continue our normal imports of sodium nitrate we will have a little surplus of available nitrogen. The ultimate consumption will be 395,100 tons per year. It will therefore be necessary to provide during the second year a larger capacity to meet this demand. It will require from twelve to fifteen months to construct a nitrogen fixation plant.

The industry is co-operating fully in the development of plans to increase the nitrogen capacity, and it is our understanding that one company is moving ahead with the construction of additional capacity. Therefore we should first find out from them their exact position and how much of this increased capacity they will be able to take care of before we consider the approval of a new nitrogen fixation plant at Muscle Shoals.

There are several factors to take into consideration in regard to the location of a plant at Muscle Shoals. If a new plant is to be constructed it would be much more advisable to have it located near the point of consumption of nitrogen. I also wish to point out that the new processes for producing nitrogen are based upon coke, petroleum, or natural gas as a raw material, and the power consumption is only one-third that of the cyanamide process. The logical source of coke supply for Muscle Shoals is Birmingham, and Birmingham is inherently a high cost coal field. It is my understanding at the present time Birmingham would not be in a position to supply this coke and we also have a bottleneck in the country's coke capacity. Even if it would be necessary to bring the coke down the Ohio River, it would involve high transportation costs so that manufacture of ammonium nitrate at Muscle Shoals can never be as economical as in a plant located in the area of low cost coking coal, for example West Virginia, Pennsylvania, or Ohio. If petroleum or natural gas are to be considered as a raw material, other locations would then offer certain advantages. The new processes for producing nitrogen depend upon cheap coal, coke, petroleum and natural gas, and that far outweighs the advantage of cheap electric power.

This problem, of course, requires the most careful study and we do not think we should be rushed into making a decision, especially in view of the fact that our requirements for the first year will not exceed the present production capacity. If an emergency should develop, we could obtain an additional supply of nitrogen by cutting down on the fertilizer requirements, and this would not be detrimental in view of the large surplus of agricultural products, particularly cotton.

On July 30th, Weidlein received from Davis the letter which Davis had received from Dr. H. A. Morgan in response to his request for background information on the TVA proposals. The meeting which Lilienthal had requested was held on the 31st.

Immediately after this meeting Weidlein sent the following memorandum to Stettinius:

I wish to advise you that I had a conference today with Senator Bankhead of Alabama, Mr. Chester Davis, Dr. H. A. Morgan, Director, TVA, and other members of the Tennessee Valley Authority organization.

They seemed rather pleased and well satisfied that we had a thorough understanding of the Muscle Shoals situation, and they expressed a willingness to co-operate in every way in the development of our nitrate requirements.

I explained to them the importance of securing the full co-operation of industry on this important problem and that to get any place it would have to be done through co-operation and thorough understanding between all parties.

I also called Senator Hill (of Alabama) on the telephone and explained to him the present position of nitrates. I plan to have a conference with him in the near future.

(signed) *Ed*

Stettinius returned this memorandum with the notation:

Ed,

Fine Business.

(signed) *Ed*

On August 8 Weidlein was asked by Davis to be kept "very closely informed on plans and decisions relating in any way to the development of facilities in this area or to alternative facilities elsewhere," and Weidlein replied on the 13th assuring Davis that he would do so and adding, "This subject is being given very thorough and careful consideration. However, we feel that we have sufficient material available at the present time to meet all demands for at least one year, which does give us more time to study how to meet the large amounts which will be needed after that date."

DEVELOPMENT OF WAR DEPARTMENT POLICY

The development of policy in NDAC and in the Nitrogen Committee was paralleled by further thinking on the problem in the War Department. As of August, the War Department had apparently made some progress on the nitrate program as it had been formulated in June 1940. Since then it had, backed by Weidlein and by the Nitrogen Committee, gone ahead on its plans for using the du Pont and Allied Chemical companies in this program. It had made little progress, however, on its plans for utilizing U. S. Nitrate Plant No. 2. The TVA report of July 1, approval of which was opposed by Weidlein and the Nitrogen Committee, was still under discussion.

In August 1940 the Chief of the Planning Section, Ammunition Division, Industrial Service, Ordnance Department of the War Department, was Major C. F. Hofstetter, a regular Army officer who had entered the service not long after his graduation from engineering college in 1914. On August 8 he sent to Colonel Booth, Chief of the Ammunition Division, a memorandum in which he recounted the development of the present situation regarding the utilization of Muscle Shoals in the National Defense scheme and concluded:

> If higher authority decides to utilize the available funds, it is recommended that Plan No. 4 be followed. It should be pointed out in this connection, that the time—11 months—is not a serious factor, since only about 4 months would be required to get into production of ammonium nitrate by the supply of ammonium nitrate solution which could be obtained from other sources, the plant thus running on ammonia or ammonia liquor shipped in during the completion of the conversion of the ammonia-producing end of the plant. At the present moment it is understood that the Allied Chemical Company from their Hopewell Plant could supply at once approximately 300 tons per day of ammonium nitrate solution for crystallization.

Just one month later, on September 9, however, Hofstetter, by now a Lieutenant Colonel, sent a second memorandum to Colonel Booth in which he reversed his previous stand on Muscle Shoals. It reads in part as follows:

> B. *The Ammonia Situation.*
>
> 1. It appears on good authority that there is no present capacity for ammonia production in this country that is not now being utilized. . . .
>
> 2. Obviously the questions to be answered are:
>
> *a.* What are the military requirements for ammonia?
> *b.* What is the present status of production?
> *c.* What is the shortage as concerns the government's needs?
> *d.* What are the best steps to meet the shortage?
>
> In answering the above, the facts will be given briefly in as far as they appear available. The Action to be taken, however, is necessarily a question of policy, and should be so determined.
>
> 3. *a. Requirements.* Requirements for anhydrous ammonia for the Ammunition Division program for the maintenance of 2,000,000-men army are . . . 640 tons/day, approximately. . . .
>
> *b. Production.* The two principal facilities now producing ammonia are the Hopewell Plant of Allied Chemical and the Belle Plant of du Pont. The former is producing about 630 tons per day, of which it is understood that 400 tons are being converted into 300 tons of nitric acid, and fertilizers. . . . The Belle plant is said to be producing 400 tons/day of ammonia, principally for fertilizer manufacture. . . .
>
> *c. Government shortage.* Of course the present capacity for production of the two above-mentioned plants, totaling 1030 tons/day of ammonia, greatly exceeds the military requirements. But, as a matter of policy, it does not seem that any appreciable diversion from their normal channels should be assumed as feasible for such production. To do so might disrupt industry seriously. As previously stated, there is not today any ammonia

capacity not being utilized, and consequently a sudden emergency would make absolutely necessary a diversion of ammonia from these plants for military use until additional facilities could be constructed. Such diversion should, it is believed, not be continued longer than absolutely necessary, as any such diversion would really result in taking it from fertilizers. A third potential source of ammonia in quantity is Nitrate Plant #2, designed to produce about 150 tons/day of ammonia finished in the form of 300 tons/day of ammonium nitrate. . . . The problem of this plant will be discussed later, but it will be assumed for the moment that Muscle Shoals will be operated. The 150 tons of ammonia produced, subtracted from the 640 tons required, leaves a balance of 490 tons still to be provided. It appears that the only practicable solution is the construction, either by or for the government, of additional ammonia capacity to the extent of not less than 400 tons/day. In considering the above, the following points should be taken into account:

(1) As stated, all available ammonia capacity is being utilized for industrial needs and fertilizer which it does not appear wise to disturb to any great extent.

(2) No account has been taken in above calculations of the probable increased requirements that planned expansion of private explosives facilities will create. Based on last war figures, use of commercial explosives is increased 30% during war periods, for mining and other industrial purposes. The present shortage will probably continue to grow more acute. . . .

(3) No account has been taken of Navy powder plant expansion understood to be under way . . . with its demand for ammonia. . . .

a. Action to Meet Shortage. In view of the situation as described, it is recommended that funds being made available for government facilities be applied to the construction of capacity for ammonia production of 540 tons/day. For both strategic and economical reasons, that such production be provided in two plants. It is suggested that one such plant be built by the Allied Chemical Company and one by the du Pont Company, one plant to be located in West Virginia and one in the Ohio Valley, preferable in Eastern Kentucky. The cost of such plants is estimated at $28,000,000. . . .

4. It will be noted that 540 tons per day of ammonia capacity in new plants, plus the potential 150 tons capacity in Nitrate Plant #2 totals 690 tons/day, as compared with military requirements for the 2,000,000-men army of 640 tons/day. This excess is very moderate in view of the time required to construct such plants, which recent information estimates at from 14 to 18 months. (The TVA estimated 11 to 12 months for construction of a synthetic ammonia plant; Major Harris states this is entirely too optimistic.) . . .

In connection with ammonia plant plans, it is believed vital to exercise some foresight, and to insure in such construction that any plants contemplated be designed for ample capacity because of the long time-factor involved. On such basis, the surplus of 50 tons in capacity indicated above as resulting from the construction of the recommended plants is considered as very conservative.

C. *Nitrate Plant #2*—Muscle Shoals.

1. In the discussion above on ammonia, it was assumed that Nitrate Plant #2 would be prepared for operation at full capacity, permitting ammonia production at the rate of 150 tons/day (or 300 tons of ammonium nitrate).

2. The War Department appears fully committed to the operation of this plant for National Defense purposes. The only valid argument for withdrawing from the position in which the Department has gone on record as placing itself would be to show that changed conditions no longer render such operation desirable from an economic standpoint. This changed condition would have to be shown to have been of recent occurrence, for as late as January 10, 1940, the Secretary of War wrote Mr. Morgan of the TVA requesting that the TVA ". . . make plans to get into production of ammonium nitrate in an emergency as rapidly as possible at the maximum capacity of the plant, including the manufacture of the necessary ammonia by the full use of the cyanamid portion of U. S. Nitrate Plant #2 at Muscle Shoals. . . ."

3. Considerable controversy has centered about the *method* of operation of Muscle Shoals—with particular reference to the *ammonia manufacturing* process. Should the synthetic process be installed or should the plant be operated as originally designed and built, employing the existing cyanamid equipment? The synthetic process, highly favorable in some respects, will first be discussed, followed by a discussion of the alternative, the operation of the cyanamid plant which, in view of present circumstances, is the method recommended.

a. The Synthetic Ammonia Process.

(1) The principal argument against the use of Muscle Shoals appears to be lack of economy in the supply of coke, and in making of ammonia by the cyanamid process. The coke situation is

one of long standing, and was just as uneconomical when the plant was built as at present. If ammonia plants are to be built for production by the economical synthetic process, such a plant can be installed for ammonia production at Muscle Shoals, where all other facilities including administrative, are available. This procedure will also overcome any objections to interference with the present use of part of the cyanamid furnace installation for TVA purposes. It also retains the cyanamid portion of the plant for getting into production quickly if a crisis occurs before completion of the synthetic ammonia plant at that location. It will also result in an ultimate reduction of power requirements for ammonium nitrate production at full capacity, at that station, to 23,000 k.w., as compared with the present estimate of 87,000 k.w. for the ammonia-from-cyanamid process.

(2) The cost of ammonia by the synthetic process would be 2.1 cents/lb. as compared with 6 to 6.5 cents/lb. by the cyanamid method. . . . The cost of the entire project . . . is estimated . . . as $6,217,000 of which $4,353,000 would be for the new ammonia plant. . . . The saving in cost of ammonia by the synthetic process would result in amortization of the plant construction in less than one year of capacity operation. The time required for construction is about 11 to 12 months. . . . The construction of an independent synthetic ammonia plant at Nitrate Plant #2 is the method indicated by the TVA as ". . . by far the most attractive of the several plans . . . for rehabilitation of Muscle Shoals to produce ammonium nitrate." This plan would avoid disturbance of the fertilizer works. It retains the potential production of about 40 tons/day of phosphorus, which might be an important item for military use by the chemical warfare service.

(3) Should a crisis arise during the year required for construction of the synthetic ammonia plant, the rehabilitation of the *ammonium nitrate facilities* can be accomplished in about 4 months, and Muscle Shoals could then turn out nitrate if ammonia were supplied from other sources. *In a crisis this could undoubtedly be done temporarily.* In such a crisis it would take 4 months to rehabilitate the cyanamid portion of the plant for ammonia production, so that (unless rehabilitation of the cyanamid plant were started simultaneously with the nitrate facilities rehabilitation) the cyanamid plant would probably be in operation but a short time before completion of the synthetic ammonia plant. Hence, it does not appear a logical proposition from an economical standpoint to spend funds on overhauling the old cyanamid plant for production of ammonia except that this appears the quickest method of obtaining ammonium nitrate from any new facility. Even though the cyanamid section of the plant has never been operated previously . . . the money expended for putting it into operation could be considered as insurance of the early production of ammonium nitrate.

b. The Cyanamid Process.

(1) The plant now has the cyanamid furnaces installed. This process is the one which the TVA was informed by the Secretary of War, January 10, 1940, that the War Department planned to use. . . . Using this process, the plant can get into operation at full capacity of 300/tons/day of ammonium nitrate in 5½ months. The cost of the rehabilitation is estimated by TVA at a total of $4,631,000. . . .

(2) This plan is considered by the TVA as not attractive for the following reasons. It calls for considerable funds to overhaul an ammonia production plant of obsolete design and uneconomical in operation. It requires large amounts of power (87,000 k.w.) which could be used for other purposes. ". . . The balance of the fertilizer works would remain idle and rapidly deteriorate. The field program in fertilizer testing and demonstration . . . would have to be abandoned. The cost of the ammonia produced would be exorbitant. . . ."

(3) However, there appears no other certain method of getting an ammonium nitrate plant into finished nitrate production at an early date, and consequently it is believed that the TVA should be requested to proceed with rehabilitation of Nitrate Plant No. 2, employing the cyanamid process. At a later date, when the new ammonia plants are completed, any surplus ammonia that may be available could be supplied to Muscle Shoals to release some of the cyanamid furnaces for TVA purposes. . . . This procedure may have to be followed in any event, as there seems to be a question as to the dependability of equipment at Muscle Shoals. *It is understood that there is apt to be rapid deterioration of the old types of equipment when under capacity operation. This is an argument in support of providing an ample ammonia supply in plant employing the modern synthetic process.* . . .

Hofstetter therefore recommended to Colonel Booth that the construction of ammonia plants by du Pont and Allied Chemical begin at once and that TVA be requested to rehabilitate the existing ammonia and ammonium nitrate facilities at Muscle Shoals, thus withdrawing his previous support of the TVA Plan No. 4 which called for construction of a new synthetic ammonia plant at Muscle Shoals rather than rehabilitation of the existing facilities.

It may be noted that in the foregoing memorandum, Hofstetter based his reversal on the importance of timing to the exclusion of all other considerations. Specifically, it should be noted that whereas he had previously recommended the construction of a new synthetic ammonia plant at Muscle Shoals saying that "the time—11 months [estimated for construction of a new plant at Muscle Shoals] is not a serious factor, since only about 4 months would be required to get into production of ammonium nitrate by the supply of ammonium nitrate solution which could be obtained from other sources . . .", he now recommended rehabilitation of the cyanamid plant stating that "there appears no other certain method of getting an ammonium nitrate plant into finished nitrate production at an early date."

Although Hofstetter's views as expressed in his latest memorandum did not receive formal approval of the War Department, this memorandum does reflect a feeling then prevalent in the Department that the proposal recommended by TVA the previous July would not be approved; and the expectation that the proposal would be rejected was inherent in the decision made by the Ordnance Department on September 11 to recommend the negotiation of contracts with du Pont and Allied even though a decision on the TVA plant was still pending.

NDAC AND THE WAR DEPARTMENT PLANS

According to the Presidential directive under which the NDAC was set up, the responsibility of the Industrial Materials Division to consult with and advise the War Department with regard to its plans for the construction of ammonia plants ceased with the development of these plans from words to actions, at which point it became the responsibility of Knudsen's Production Division to participate with the War Department in the actual negotiation of contracts. Thus the Ordnance Department's recommendation that contracts be negotiated with du Pont and Allied was made in the form of a letter concerning each plant addressed to Mr. Knudsen, requesting his approval for the negotiation of contracts; these letters were dated September 11, two days after Hofstetter's second memorandum. Knudsen gave his approval on September 12, and the War Department thereupon issued letters of intent to du Pont and Allied respecting plants at Morgantown and in Kentucky (the exact site not specified).

The events summarized in this chapter show how it came about that the du Pont and Allied proposals were approved, while the TVA proposal, informally approved by the War Department in June, was laid aside. Looked at from a formal standpoint, it was the responsibility of the War Department to submit a proposed program, of the Nitrogen Committee to give advice in the preparation of the program, of Stettinius (and then Knudsen) to approve or disapprove the program as submitted. In fact, however, Stettinius effectively delegated his authority to Weidlein, and Weidlein was expected to, and did, work with the Nitrogen Committee and the War Department in getting the program ready for submission to NDAC. From the standpoint of the working officials in Ordnance, Weidlein was properly looked upon as representing NDAC, and his views on the nitrogen program could be regarded as carrying great, and possibly conclusive weight.

One other factor may be noted. During this preliminary period there was some indication that du Pont, and possibly Allied as well, intended to construct the plants with their own money under a so-called E.P.F. contract, under which the companies would receive reimbursement from the government over a five-year period. The E.P.F. financing arrangements were being developed at this time in the NDAC and were greatly preferred, especially by Mr. Knudsen, to construction with government funds: in the former case title remained with the company, in the latter with the government.

There was confusion on this aspect of the du Pont and Allied plans in the NDAC; and later, there was argument as to whether approval of the TVA plans had forced a rejection by du Pont of the E.P.F. arrangement. The matter is mentioned here because, while the financing arrangements were of no direct concern to Weidlein, they were significant to Knudsen who was responsible for final approval of the letters of intent.

V. The TVA Proposal Reinstated

DAVIS COMMENTS

Although during the weeks immediately preceding September 23 the trend of opinion within the War Department had been moving toward rejection of the TVA proposal, the President's intervention brought immediate action from top War Department officials to comply with the President's wishes that the TVA proposal be given adequate consideration. Brig. General Westervelt, General Adviser to the Assistant Secretary of War, immediately made available to Davis full details of the War Department's then current nitrate plans, which were based on Hofstetter's recommendations of September 9. On the 24th Davis, with Galbraith's assistance, commented on these plans in the following letter addressed to General Westervelt:

I have given careful study to the report on plans for increasing Ammonia capacity which you made available to me yesterday. On the general problem of the adequacy of nitrogen supplies for agriculture, I would like to reserve judgment at this time. I do note with approval the intention to increase nitrogen capacity to take care of war needs rather than to divert nitrates from agricultural use.

I am deeply concerned, however, over the proposal [i.e., Hofstetter's] that the cyanamid portion of Nitrate Plant No. 2 be rehabilitated as an alternative to the provision of synthetic ammonia capacity at Wilson Dam. The report considers these alternatives: (a) construction of a new synthetic ammonia unit at Wilson Dam or (b) the rehabilitation of the old cyanamid process. It finds that the construction of a new ammonia unit would provide a vastly cheaper product, would require far less power, and would leave undisturbed the present plant nutrient program of the TVA. It also notes that the phosphate production of TVA would be undisturbed except as the product might be required by the Chemical Warfare Service.

Notwithstanding these advantages, the report proposes the rehabilitation of the cyanamid process and the tearing out of the TVA phosphate furnaces. The reasons for this costly step turn exclusively on the matter of time. A new synthetic plant would take a minimum of eleven months to design and construct. Rehabilitation of the cyanamid (and ammonium nitrate) plant would provide product in five and a half months and full capacity in seven months. I am not questioning the judgment of the War Department on the need for haste. Yet, use of this cyanamid plant will require sinking $2,767,000 in an obsolete plant and an added cost over synthetic ammonia operations of some $13,200 for each day of capacity operation. It involves the total disruption of a program which means many millions of dollars annually to American farmers. I do not feel that I can emphasize too strongly the importance of the present plant food phosphate program to American agriculture. A synthetic ammonia plant would make it possible to extend this program of research and field experimentation to nitrates. Rehabilitation of the cyanamid plant would, as I have said, stop the entire program. Considering the choice involved, I do not feel that the issue could be placed before American farmers.

I am informed that there are alternatives which would bridge the time between rehabilitation of the ammonium nitrate plant and completion of the synthetic ammonia unit. If the emergency is very great, half of the cyanamid plant might be rehabilitated on a very temporary basis without interfering with the phosphate operation for more than a temporary period. This would cost $1,104,-000 and the ammonia some seven cents a pound. To operate the ammonium nitrate plant at capacity supplementary supplies of ammonia might be obtained elsewhere. If this rehabilitation is not undertaken, or if an urgent demand for ammonium nitrate exists when the ammonium nitrate plant has been rehabilitated, ammonia could be shipped in temporarily from other sources as, indeed, the report proposes. Since this would involve some temporary diversion from agriculture, it would be necessary for us to have compensatory supplies of sodium nitrate from other sources—presumably these could be obtained from Chile.

Considering its post-emergency value for agriculture, I believe that under any and all circumstances a new synthetic ammonia unit should be erected by the TVA. Even if the cyanamid plant were rehabilitated for emergency reasons, this report makes clear that TVA is favorably situated for ammonia production. For its present war-time value and eventual agricultural utility, ammonia production at this site would appear fully justified. I notice, especially, that plant development by the TVA appears much more economical than at the other locations—for a 150-ton plant the Authority estimates an expenditure of $4,353,000 as against $11,000,000 ($8,000,000 each if two units are built) for equivalent tonnage at the other sites. I am unable to say whether these estimates are comparable in all respects, but the contrast is impressive.

However, I do not propose to comment now on the location of the other plants now planned for government construction. Confining my recommendation at this time to the alternative specifically considered in the War Department plans, I conclude that the feasible course is the construction of a new ammonia unit to service the ammonium nitrate plant with such interim expedients as may be appropriate. I believe this to be the only course which provides for a full alignment of national defense and agricultural objectives.

PATTERSON APPROVES THE TVA PLAN

Later the same day Robert P. Patterson, Assistant Secretary of War, sent the following

MEMORANDUM FOR MR. DONALD NELSON

Subject: Program for New Productive Capacity for Ammonia

1. Under the appropriation for "Expediting Production" the Ordnance Department has submitted a statement of its requirements for ammonia under the approved munitions program and recommended three projects for the increase of productive capacity for that material. The projects and sites recommended are outlined in the attached memorandum from the Chief of Ordnance dated September 24, 1940, and include the following:
   a. Rehabilitation of Nitrate Plant No. 2 at Muscle Shoals, including construction of a synthetic ammonia plant of 150 tons daily capacity and conversion of the same into its equivalent of 300 tons per day of ammonium nitrate. A portion of the existing plant would be reserved for phosphate production for agricultural purposes. Estimated cost approximately $6,500,000.
   b. New ammonia plant at Morgantown, West Virginia, with a capacity of 250 tons per day. This project is outlined in some detail in the attached memorandum dated September 21, 1940. Estimated cost, including land and plant, approximately $16,500,000.
   c. New ammonia plant in Kentucky, at a site to be selected, with a capacity of 150 tons per day. Estimated cost, including land and plant, approximately $13,000,000. Further detail on the site will be forwarded as soon as obtainable.
2. In connection with the program proposed by the Chief of Ordnance, attention is invited to the attached letter from Mr. Chester Davis to General Westervelt, dated September 24, 1940, reviewing an informal memorandum on the subject which had been prepared for study but had not received the approval of the Chief of Ordnance. It will be noted, however, that the program proposed by the Chief of Ordnance with respect to the Muscle Shoals development is in substantial agreement with that suggested by Mr. Davis.
3. The three projects for new ammonia capacity are now under consideration by the War Department. It is requested that the formal action of the Advisory Commission be obtained on the general program outlined and on the two specific projects mentioned, viz., Muscle Shoals and Morgantown, West Virginia.

Attached to this memorandum, in addition to Davis's letter, was a memorandum of the same date addressed to the Assistant Secretary of War from Major General Wesson, Chief of Ordnance, which is of particular interest because of its implication that the rejection or postponement of the TVA plan had come from NDAC, not from the Ordnance Department. The memorandum reads, in part, as follows:

Nitrate Plant No. 2 at Muscle Shoals was designed for the production of about 150 tons per day of ammonia, and for converting the same into its equivalent of 300 tons per day of ammonium nitrate. Plans of the Ordnance Department for an emergency have long assumed the operation of this plant at full capacity in the production of ammonium nitrate.

In line with the policy of this office, request was made on the Tennessee Valley Authority early this year for a thorough study of the Muscle Shoals situation. Such study recommended to the War Department a program of rehabilitation of Nitrate Plant No. 2, at a cost of approximately $6,500,000; including the construction of a synthetic ammonia plant of a capacity of 150 tons per day of anhydrous ammonia; and reserving a portion of the plant for agricultural purposes. The War Department accordingly recommended to the National Defense Committee approval of this program for the following reasons:

a. The cost of ammonia by the cyanamid process for which the plant is at present equipped, is more than three times the cost of production by the newer synthetic method.

b. Facilities now in use for the fertilizer experimentation and production program of the Tennessee Valley Authority are preserved.

c. The existing Technical Organization of the Tennessee Valley Authority is available for the operation of the plant for production of both ammonia and nitrate.

d. Creation of the synthetic ammonia plant will result in a great reduction in the power required to produce the same quantity of ammonia as contemplated by the old process.

In addition to the ammonia plant recommended for Muscle Shoals, recommendation was also made to the National Defense Commission for the construction of two additional plants to produce ammonia.

a. A plant at Morgantown, West Virginia of a capacity of 250 tons per day to be operated by the DuPont Company.

b. A plant in Kentucky of a capacity of 150 tons per day to be operated by the Allied Chemical Company.

It is recommended that an opportunity be afforded to present the views of the Ordnance Department to the National Defense Committee on the subject of ammonia requirements and production.

Even though Nelson had not yet sent on the Patterson memorandum to Davis for his action in the matter, Davis had been kept informed of the War Department's plans as they had developed in those busy two days after September 23. The revised plans had been checked and the basis found satisfactory to TVA, and consequently on September 25 Davis sent the following letter to the President:

On September 20 I advised you that negotiations were proceeding for the government-built synthetic ammonia plants to be operated by private chemical companies without adequate provision for the development of ammonia production at TVA which a well-rounded defense and agricultural program seems to call for.

I have learned from the War Department that on September 23 you wired the Secretary of War requesting that negotiations for the construction of the two ammonia plants be held up until you had an opportunity to look into them, and suggesting that consideration be given to the location of the plants in the Tennessee Valley area.

The War Department is now prepared to submit new recommendations which call for the immediate rehabilitation of Nitrate Plant No. 2 at Muscle Shoals, including construction of a synthetic ammonia plant of 150 tons daily capacity and conversion of the same into its equivalent of 300 tons per day of ammonium nitrate. A portion of the existing plant would be reserved for phosphate production for agricultural purposes. Estimated cost approximately $6,500,000.

This is the exact program which the Tennessee Valley Authority recommends to round out its facilities for both the defense and the agricultural programs. From the agricultural point of view it is entirely satisfactory.

Therefore I recommend that the Secretary of War be authorized to resume the negotiations for the ammonia and ammonium nitrate projects, provided that the Tennessee Valley developments described above go forward at once. The contemplated private projects appear to be necessary, in addition to the new capacity at Wilson Dam, to insure the production of enough ammonia to meet the expanded munition requirements without making inroads upon the quantity of nitrates required currently by agriculture. If this clearance can be given the Secretary of War by telegram, it will appear to complete the record satisfactorily.

VI. Objections from Stettinius and Knudsen

DAVIS DEFENDS TVA

As far as the NDAC was concerned, however, the record on nitrates was far from complete at this point, for on September 25, the same day that Davis wrote the President to say that the War Department's new nitrate program was entirely satisfactory to him, Weidlein sent Davis a two-year forecast of nitrogen supply and requirements; on the same day he wrote a memorandum entitled, "Development of Synthetic Ammonia Capacity at Muscle Shoals" in which he raised numerous objections to the construction of new facilities at this site. Upon receipt of this memorandum, whose contents are reflected in the reply quoted below, Davis began immediately to check the validity of Weidlein's objections and consequently on September 30 sent the following memorandum to Stettinius:

I have given careful study to Dr. Weidlein's memorandum of September 25 on the question of developing synthetic ammonia capacity under the auspices of the Tennessee Valley Authority. This memorandum, together with supplementary information that Dr. Weidlein has furnished me in the last few days, leads me to believe that there will be no grave shortage of agricultural nitrates during the defense emergency. However, I should like to reserve judgment on this matter at the present time.

On the question of developing synthetic ammonia capacity at Muscle Shoals there are several important points where my information is at variance with that of Dr. Weidlein's, or where his memorandum leaves me somewhat in doubt as to what is actually implied. I would make special note of the following.

1. Dr. Weidlein does not deal with the development of ammonia capacity in conjunction with the ammonium nitrate facility which is already at Muscle Shoals. While, in my judgment, a strong case exists for development of a part of the new nitrogen supply under Tennessee Valley Authority auspices, the fact that the Army intends to use the present ammonium nitrate plant is one of the important reasons for settling upon this location.
2. Dr. Weidlein makes a strong point of the shortage of coke capacity in the Alabama district and of the rail haul from Birmingham to Sheffield. The Tennessee Valley Authority has a land grant rate on coke from Birmingham to Sheffield of $1.35 a ton. The Authority now obtains its coke from Birmingham and I am informed that this freight charge is not considered unreasonable.

However, Dr. Weidlein rests his main case on the shortage of coke in the Birmingham area. I am aware that there is some possibility of a nationwide coke deficiency with present oven capacity. With this in mind, I requested the Bureau of Research and Statistics to make a study of utilization of coke capacity in all parts of the country. I am attaching a copy of their report which states that in August of this year:

"The furnace plants in Pennsylvania were operating at 100 per cent of their rated capacity, and those in West Virginia had reached 96 per cent of their rated capacity. Moreover, the furnace plants in Michigan and New York, and the merchant plants in Kentucky, New York, and West Virginia were operating close to their practical capacity. The big bulk of the unutilized capacity in August was found at merchant plants in Alabama and Michigan."

Assuming the validity of these figures, I am at a loss as to why the shortage of coking capacity should be a factor militating against location in the Birmingham area.

In further checking on this matter I am informed that actual construction of coke ovens is contemplated in connection with the Morgantown and Kentucky developments.

3. Dr. Weidlein's second objection to the Tennessee Valley Authority site is the heavy concentration of other activity in this area. The only other ordnance plant contemplated for this vicinity, so far as I am aware, is a shell machining plant at Gadsden, Alabama. While Dr. Weidlein may have reference to the considerable expansion in the TVA area in recent years, including the expansion of aluminum capacity now under way, it remains that

this area is still largely rural—more so than locations farther to the North and East.

4. I am somewhat puzzled by Dr. Weidlein's last statement, "we were naturally not consulted on the type of contract or sites" and am unable to reconcile this with his earlier statement that "careful consideration was given to the location of the synthetic ammonia plants including Muscle Shoals."
5. Finally, I should like to draw attention to the central feature of the Tennessee Valley Authority plant-nutrient program. This involves experimental manufacture and distribution of plant nutrients on a sufficient scale for nationwide testing. The research includes experimentation in the commercial process as well as in the distribution of new and improved products. For such a program, it is not a question of buying nitrogen compounds and giving them to farmers to test. It involves rather, experimentation through all the phases of manufacture and use. It is for this reason that the addition of an ammonia plant to the existing phosphate facility will have post-emergency importance to agriculture.

On September 26 Nelson's office had transmitted to Davis Patterson's request for formal NDAC approval of the War Department's nitrate program, and Davis gave his reply on September 30 in the following memorandum to Colonel Hiram S. Brown, Assistant to Nelson:

I refer to your memorandum of September 26 transmitting War Department memoranda under date of September 24 recommending rehabilitation of Nitrate Plant No. 2 and the construction of a new ammonia plant at Morgantown, West Virginia.

I am approving these two projects subject to certain assurances which have been given me informally by War Department officials. I draw attention to the fact that a modern government-owned ammonia plant at Muscle Shoals will have outstanding post-emergency value in the experimental and educational plant-nutrient program of the Tennessee Valley Authority. The post-emergency use of a government-owned plant at Morgantown is less certain. Therefore, my approval of the Morgantown project is conditional upon the development at Muscle Shoals.

I should like also to draw attention to the difference in costs as between these two facilities. The construction of a new synthetic ammonia plant at Muscle Shoals together with the rehabilitation of the old ammonium nitrate plant is estimated to cost $6,500,000. The construction of a new ammonia plant at Morgantown, West Virginia, to produce 250 tons of ammonia a day, i.e., 100 tons more than at Muscle Shoals, is estimated to cost $16,500,000. In other words, to obtain 250 tons of ammonia Morgantown will require an outlay of nearly four times as much as the 150-ton plant at Muscle Shoals, when allowance is made for the part of the cost at Muscle Shoals which is required in the rehabilitation of the ammonium nitrate plant. Because of this difference in cost, I am further concerned with seeing that the development at Morgantown is conditional upon development of the cheaper facility at Muscle Shoals.

Further, it is my understanding that the Tennessee Valley Authority estimates were submitted several months ago. If increasing costs or too narrow figuring in the original estimates should force the Authority to revise its original estimates, this will not be considered a barrier to development at this site. I observe in this connection that TVA has apparently submitted detailed estimates while the other site is estimated on a rough figure which presumably includes a substantial margin for error.

Finally, my approval is for the specific proposal outlined in this memorandum—that is, for a new modern synthetic ammonia plant at Muscle Shoals together with rehabilitation of the ammonium nitrate plant. My approval does not cover expenditure of funds for the rehabilitation of the cyanamid process of ammonia manufacture.

WEIDLEIN ELABORATES HIS OBJECTIONS

The other members of the Commission had also received copies of Patterson's request for formal NDAC approval of the nitrate program during the preceding week, and Weidlein, after studying these plans, commented on them in a long memorandum to Stettinius also dated September 30; pertinent portions read as follows:

. . . This program was recommended by the War Department for the approval of the National Defense Council for reasons of cost and economy of power consumption. It was also pointed out that, under the proposed program, facilities now in use for the fertilizer experimentation and production program of the TVA are preserved while at the same time the existing technical services of that organization would be available. . . .

In reply to these memoranda (1) we accept the military requirements of ammonia of 670 tons per day; (2) we concede the need for substantial new synthetic ammonia capacity; and (3) we agree that the cyanamid units at U. S. Nitrate Plant No. 2 should not be rehabilitated except in extreme emergency and that the portion of this plant now devoted to the TVA Plant Nutrient Program should be reserved for these purposes. But we submit that the construction of new synthetic ammonia capacity at Muscle Shoals raises questions which merit serious consideration. . . .

Weidlein then went into a detailed analysis of the comparative merits of Muscle Shoals and Morgantown as sites for plants to manufacture ammonia and ammonium nitrate based on information which had been included in the July 8 report of the Ammonia Subcommittee to ANMB. In this section he again brought up the same points on comparative costs which Davis had taken exception to in his reply to Weidlein's memorandum of September 25, and in addition cited the lack of technical "know-how" at TVA as a further argument against the construction of a synthetic ammonia plant at Muscle Shoals. He stated in this connection that

. . . of the large ammonia plants using the water gas process contemplated here, there are only two: DuPont, at Belle, West Virginia, and Allied Chemical and Dye, at Hopewell, Virginia. It took these companies years to get their plants operating at the present high rates of efficiency. Outside their employ there are comparatively few men who have the proper "know-how." To be sure, some excellent men with the right background and training are available for Muscle Shoals. Yet, this plant has not made ammonia for over twenty years, and then by an entirely different and presently obsolete process. Consequently, it will be necessary to organize an entirely new staff of highly trained men.

The experienced men in this field who were selected to advise the ANMB reported as follows in this regard: "An ammonia plant is a highly complicated technical operation on which years of experience are required properly to design, properly to build, and properly to put into operation. A plant the size of the one proposed at Muscle Shoals would require a considerable organization. It cannot possibly be done by one man. After the plant is designed, it must be built and this also requires highly skilled personnel; finally, the plant has to be put into operation, and the building of an organization for satisfactory operation is really a matter of years. If a plant were built at Muscle Shoals and it were brought into capacity operation in two years, it would be a miracle."

Following these comments the memorandum continues with a summary of the technical objections:

Based on the findings of the ANMB Subcommittee Report the comparison between Muscle Shoals and Morgantown as sites for Synthetic Ammonia plants with and without Ammonium Nitrate facilities may be summarized as follows:

1. *Ammonia, alone*

a. The investment required may be regarded as the same in each case.
b. The cost of operating at capacity favors Morgantown to the extent of $2.20 a ton of Ammonia. On the basis of an output of 51,800 tons per year this amounts to a savings of $112,000 at Morgantown.

2. *Ammonia and Ammonium Nitrate*

a. According to TVA engineers, the investment at Muscle Shoals would be less by $2,600,000 than at Morgantown. This difference is decreased to $1,600,000 by the ANMB Report on the grounds that $1,000,000 worth of the equipment must be replaced.
b. Savings per year at Morgantown, including delivery of product in 75 per cent solution to a loading plant in Northern Ohio, amount to $3.69 per ton of ammonium nitrate. On the basis of an annual output of 115,000 tons of this product there would be a saving of $425,000 by locating at Morgantown.

This difference would be somewhat less for a loading plant in Northern Illinois. Much greater differences in favor of Morgantown would be obtained if it was decided to ship solid ammonium nitrate or anhydrous ammonia. However, the advantages of shipping a 75 per cent solution of ammonium nitrate are so plain that it is assumed this procedure will be adopted.

The memorandum concludes as follows:

POST EMERGENCY SITUATION

The importance of providing for the post emergency situation of the Plant Nutrient Program at

Muscle Shoals has been stressed by Mr. Chester C. Davis. It is emphasized that it is necessary to construct synthetic ammonia capacity at Muscle Shoals now in order to insure an adequate supply of this material for the continuance of the Plant Nutrient Program after the emergency has passed.

In our opinion the need for concern in this respect is greatly overexaggerated. For, while it is true that the TVA has no synthetic ammonia plant, it is equally the case that industry is already oversupplied with such capacity, and, if the present National Defense Program is carried to completion, this situation will be greatly aggravated. In this connection, it should be recalled that, prior to the outbreak of hostilities abroad, last September, the major portion of our domestic synthetic ammonia industry was operating at only 50 to 60 per cent capacity and the industry as a whole had never operated at full capacity. Add to this the fact that the official estimates of military requirements call for an enormous increase in existing productive capacity plus the fact that Canada is rushing to completion a huge program for ammonia synthesis and it should be apparent that the markets in this country after the emergency will be glutted with nitrogenous materials.

After the emergency the farmer and the TVA should be able to acquire all the ammonia desired at cost or better. However, since Muscle Shoals, for lack of ready accessibility to important raw materials, is not the optimum site for a synthetic ammonia plant, it follows that other plants will be able to produce more economically. In fact, it is difficult to see why the farmer could not be served as well, if not better, from sites other than Muscle Shoals which have been selected for reasons of sound engineering economics. Furthermore, production at such plants would definitely not interfere with the activities now being carried on at Muscle Shoals in connection with the Plant Nutrient Program. From all appearances, at the close of the emergency private industry in the synthetic ammonia field will be in just as great need of assistance as the farmer is today. Why not plan to buy from industry and help the business man as well as the farmer?

TIMING

The possibility of a pressing need for nitrogen compounds for National Defense Purposes may become an indisputable reason for rehabilitating the old cyanamid plant in U. S. Nitrate Plant No. 2. This is because it has been reported that this plant can be put into commission in a period of four months. And, in this connection, it should be observed that the engineers now ask for five and a half and preferably seven months for this job. But, accepting the four months figure, it is a fact that several months have already gone by, and while (quite rightly in our opinion) nothing has been done to start work at Muscle Shoals, still during this interval private business has been on the job and has ordered bottleneck items, such as heavy forgings, with the result that it might not take the anticipated twelve months from now to get the initial units of their plants into operation. Just the same, if in a pinch the rehabilitation of the cyanamid plant at Muscle Shoals could be accomplished in even six or seven months, it might well serve the nation at a time and under conditions when questions of high initial investment and trebled operating expenses would be immaterial.

This memorandum signed as it was by E. W. Reid and D. P. Morgan, as well as by Weidlein, represented the stand which the IMD (Industrial Materials Division) was to take in the ensuing controversy over NDAC approval for the War Department's nitrate program, for these three men, as members of the Chemicals and Allied Products Division of the IMD, were Stettinius' advisers in all matters concerning nitrates, had participated in the discussions of earlier War Department plans for ammonia production, and were still working with the Nitrogen Committee on the formulation of further plans.

MEETING OF THE NITROGEN COMMITTEE

This Committee (Ammonia and Nitric Acid Subcommittee to the ANMB) held a meeting the following day, October 1, which was attended by its Chairman, F. A. Wardenburg, General Manager, Ammonia Department of du Pont, members E. W. Clark, President of the Barrett Co., and W. R. Ellis of the Hercules Powder Co., and the Secretary, Warren N. Watson, of the Manufacturing Chemists Association, as well as by representatives of the Division of Coordinator of Relations with South American Republics, the Treasury Department, the Army, the Navy, and other government agencies; Weidlein, Reid and Morgan represented the NDAC, but no one from Davis's or Knudsen's office was present. Military and civilian requirements for nitrates were reviewed at the meeting, during the course of which Major Myron Leedy of the Army observed that the TVA was very anxious to have 150 tons per day of modern synthetic ammonia capacity at Muscle Shoals. In the discussion which followed, it was the consensus of those present that the existence of this capacity after the emergency was over would be unfavorable since there was already an excess of capacity for above-normal consumption and that accordingly, because other new plants were being planned by the War Department, it would be necessary for much commercial capacity to shut down after the emergency if the Government was to have a plant which it could operate. It was also felt that this situation would be aggravated by the fact that new ammonia capacity which was being constructed in Canada would have no outlet except in the United States.

Although not present at the meeting, Knudsen's assistant, E. F. Johnson, had apparently been keeping in close touch with Weidlein concerning the development of nitrate plans by the War Department, and consequently, immediately following this October 1 meeting of the Nitrogen Committee, Johnson sent Knudsen the following memorandum on "Development of Synthetic Ammonia Capacity by TVA at Muscle Shoals—Reference: Mr. Davis' letter of September 19th":

> Ammonia is the base of nitric acid, which in turn is a critical and essential item in the production of smokeless powder (nitrocellulose), TNT, and all other nitrated explosives. From the beginning of the Defense activities, it has been recognized as an item which deserved most careful study and consideration. The Chemical Division of the Raw Materials Division, under Dr. Weidlein, working in conjunction with important personnel of the industry, representatives of Ordnance Department, War Munitions Board, and others, formed what has been labeled "The Nitrogen Committee" which has carried on an extensive study and investigation of this item.
>
> The following conclusions have been developed:
>
> 1. That present producing capacity by private industry is more than ample to supply all normal industrial and agricultural peacetime requirements. Previous to present anticipated military demands only about 50 per cent to 60 per cent of that capacity has been employed.
> 2. That two new plants with a combined capacity of 400 tons per day were necessary to meet increased requirements for 2,000,000-men mobilization at locations consistent with economical raw material (coke) supply.
> 3. That there will be a tremendous excess of nitrogen compounds producing capacity after the emergency for peacetime purposes which will be available to the farmers for fertilizing purposes.
> 4. That rehabilitation of the present Muscle Shoals Ammonia Plant will result in a very inefficient operation as compared with a new modern plant; in the neighborhood of 4 to 4½¢ per lb. differential in cost.
> 5. That Muscle Shoals is not a logical location for a new modern process plant. Cost of transportation and supply of coke from Birmingham District out of line with plant located near the West Virginia or Kentucky soft coal fields.
> 6. That the importation of Chile nitrates will probably tend to increase due to desire of State Department to stimulate trade and build good will in South American countries.
> 7. That Canada and other countries are likewise building several synthetic ammonia plants which will forestall any possible chance of exporting our surplus, thereby keeping prices down.
>
> No attempt has been made to make a detailed analysis of the economic factors involved—cost of plant, cost of production, etc. To do that would mean a long-drawn out, thorough engineering analysis and comparison with a similar analysis of the TVA picture.
>
> With the above general factors before us, we can safely assure Mr. Davis that: (1) Supply for agriculture will be more than adequate even in the face of demands for the munitions program, and (2) That capacity developed will protect a long-time conservation program for agriculture. A new plant in Kentucky field would without question be a more economical source of supply of ammonia for Muscle Shoals than a plant located at that point. Kentucky location would also be more economical and with less chance of delay in transportation in distribution of ammonia to munitions plants.
>
> In the face of all of the above, it is my understanding that a project for rehabilitation of Muscle Shoals (possibly including a new modern type

ammonia plant) will be submitted to the Advisory Commission for approval. Based on a cold-blooded analysis of the facts as I see them, it is hard to see how such a move could be justified. There are, however, as you know, other considerations which no doubt will have to be taken into account:

1. Long-standing feeling on the part of TVA officials and others that land, power, technical organization, overall investment by the government during many past years, etc., should be utilized in the Defense effort even at the expense of economy.
2. Commitments which apparently have been made in good faith to co-operate with TVA in rejuvenation of this operation.
3. Other political pressure.

It was my hope, previous to yesterday, that these various differences of opinion could somehow be reconciled and an agreeable compromise submitted. There seems, however, to be too wide a spread between the thinking of various people involved. It apparently must rest with the Commission as a whole, or someone in high authority, to review this situation and make a decision.

VII. Gano Dunn as Referee

DAVIS CONTINUES THE ATTACK

Davis soon received copies of Weidlein's memorandum to Stettinius of September 30 and Johnson's to Knudsen of October 1. After reviewing these materials, he concluded that industry opposition to the TVA proposal underlay the objections raised within NDAC.

Consequently, on October 3 he discussed with Leon Henderson the advisability of getting the background on private industry's connections with the Army munitions program, and Henderson offered to have Mr. Lawrence Brown in his Division look into the matter to: (1) determine how much of the munitions program authorized by the Defense Commission was under du Pont control; and (2) arrange to consult the records of all plants authorized by the Defense Commission; and (3) quietly investigate to see what the connections of Dr. Weidlein and his consultants had been.

Davis contrived to be active in other ways during the remainder of the first week in October: he had his staff prepare memoranda on the declarations of governmental policy with respect to Muscle Shoals and on statutes relating to the transfer of funds from one government agency to another; he requested and obtained from the Ordnance Department a report comparing the requirements and available productive capacity for ammonia and from the Bureau of Agricultural Economics in the Department of Agriculture, an expression of that Bureau's views on the utilization of Muscle Shoals in the defense program; he sent summaries of the background information on Muscle Shoals to W. L. Batt, deputy to Stettinius; he held consultations with H. A. Curtis and C. O. Brown, TVA consultants; and he received, through correspondence with Edward A. O'Neal, assurances that the American Farm Bureau Federation, the Land Grant Colleges, and the President were still solidly behind him in his efforts to secure NDAC approval of the plans for Muscle Shoals. O'Neal's letter, and the President's letter to O'Neal that was enclosed, were encouraging. O'Neal's letter reads as follows:

October 5, 1940

Hon. Chester C. Davis
The Advisory Commission to
the Council of National Defense
Federal Reserve Building
Washington, D. C.

My dear Chester:

Mr. Galbraith has been out [in Chicago] for a couple of days. I had about an hour with him. He tells me that you are still having difficulties with Muscle Shoals. The letter from the President, copy of which is enclosed, is encouraging. He certainly is staying by you, which is most gratifying to us all. More strength to your right arm.

Sincerely yours,
[s] *Edw. A. O'Neal*
Edw. A. O'Neal—President

(AMERICAN FARM BUREAU FEDERATION, Chicago, Illinois)

The following is the President's letter:

October 1, 1940

THE WHITE HOUSE
WASHINGTON

Dear Ed:

Mr. Chester Davis of the Defense Commission has been investigating the possibility of developing new nitrogen capacity at Muscle Shoals. He has repeated to me many of the arguments which you have raised in favor of this project. Mr. Davis reports that negotiations are proceeding satisfactorily and he hopes that they will lead to a satisfactory agreement within a short time.

Very sincerely yours,
[s] *Franklin D. Roosevelt*

Edward A. O'Neal, Esq.,
American Farm Bureau Federation
Munsey Building
Washington, D. C.

Davis was now ready to tackle both Weidlein's and Johnson's objections.

In a reply dated October 7 to Dr. Weidlein's memorandum of September 30, Davis rejected the conclusions which Weidlein had reached in his comparison of the relative advantages of Muscle Shoals and Morgantown as sites for constructing the additional ammonia capacity needed by the War Department. He noted that:

The comparison [of investment costs] made by Dr. Weidlein involves an assumption that it would be proper to add to the capacity of the Morgantown plant. This assumption is not sound and the comparison is, therefore, not a proper one. If it were desirable to create additional capacity at Morgantown as against building another ammonia plant elsewhere, as the Weidlein comparison tacitly assumes, then why build a plant in Kentucky at much greater cost? The answer is well known. At present more than half the total synthetic ammonia capacity, in the United States, is concentrated in a single plant near the Atlantic seaboard. It is obvious then, that in creating new ammonia capacity, there should be a number of medium-size plants in different locations. For this reason, among others, the Kentucky plant has been proposed. And the only proper comparison of investment costs should be between that at Wilson Dam (Muscle Shoals) and new ammonia plants elsewhere. No argument can change the basic fact that if it be desirable to have ammonia capacity at Wilson Dam, such capacity can be created there at about half what it will cost for a new plant elsewhere. Arguments to the contrary are entirely unsound.

Davis similarly rejected many of Weidlein's other comparisons which purported to show that Muscle Shoals was unfavorable as a site for constructing new ammonia facilities. Thus, for example, he asserted that Weidlein's assumptions about power costs were incorrect, that freight costs on ammonium nitrate shipments could not be based on an assumption that all the loading plants would be located in Northern Ohio and Illinois, and that the construction of the additional capacity at Morgantown would require the construction of additional utilities and would thus cost more than the plant at Muscle Shoals.

In answer to Weidlein's comment on the lack of technical "know-how" at TVA, Davis stated:

This paragraph in the Weidlein memorandum is questioned in several respects. I am advised that it is precisely the argument advanced to the Tennessee Valley Authority by the president of the only company operating relatively large phosphate smelting furnaces in the United States in 1933. His company was represented as the only one having the "know-how" for this very difficult operation. The Tennessee Valley Authority has built and operated with entire success furnaces twice the size of his.

There is nothing mysterious about a synthetic ammonia plant. In the twenty-two years since the close of the World War, the technology of this process has become well known. . . .

There is ample evidence indicating that the Tennessee Valley Authority can design and build and operate an ammonia plant, with its own engineers and with such assistance as is readily available outside the present Tennessee Valley Authority organization.

And in answer to Weidlein's concluding paragraphs, Davis wrote:

It is true that after the emergency there will be excess ammonia capacity in the hands of industry, including, in all probability, the plants to be built by industry for the Government.

This situation will only differ in degree from what it has been for several years past, for, according to Dr. Weidlein's statement, the existing ammonia plants have been operated at only 50 per cent to 60 per cent capacity. Yet the farmer has not been able to buy ammonia "at cost or better" during the past several years.

In speaking of serving the farmer with ammonia from the plants to be built by the Government for industry, Dr. Weidlein overlooks the existing phosphate plant at Wilson Dam and the extensive experimental plant food program which is centered there. Yet in order to appraise properly the arguments advanced in the two concluding paragraphs on "Post Emergency Situation" and "Timing," it is necessary to know something of what the Tennessee Valley Authority has accomplished, in co-operation with the Land Grant Colleges and the Agricultural Extension Service, with its phosphate program. Half of the State Agricultural Colleges and Experiment Stations are co-operating in a program that has brought far-reaching improvement to the soil, and great economic benefits to agriculture and the nation. The attached report by the Bureau of Agricultural Economics, and the attached statement by the American Farm Bureau Federation, which also presents a resolution adopted by the Land Grant College Association (all of which endorsed the development of nitrogen capacity by TVA) will help fill in this background.

After the emergency is over, it would not, in my opinion, be possible to develop an experimental nitrate program comparable to that which exists for phosphates, unless a modern synthetic ammonia plant is constructed and operated in conjunction with the other facilities at Muscle Shoals. That is not the immediate problem, however. The nation needs the ammonia; in terms of cost, more than half the plant is already built and paid for at Muscle Shoals. It seems obvious, therefore, that the proper course is to proceed simultaneously with completion of the Muscle Shoals plant and such private plants as are needed, first as the Department of War has recommended. This would seem to be required to carry out the mandate laid down by Congress in its original plan for use of Muscle Shoals which was re-stated and emphasized in the Tennessee Valley Authority Act of 1933. That Act dedicates the properties in the vicinity of Muscle Shoals to the interests of the National Defense and for agricultural and industrial development. In Section 5h, for example, it conjoins agricultural and defense objectives by directing the Authority: "To establish, maintain, and operate laboratories and experimental plants, and to undertake experiments for the purpose of enabling the Corporation to furnish nitrogen products for military purposes, and nitrogen and other fertilizer products for agricultural purposes in the most economical manner and at the highest standard of efficiency.

In reply to Johnson's objections to the War Department's plans for Muscle Shoals, Davis wrote Knudsen, also on October 7:

I have examined Mr. Johnson's memorandum of October 1. . . .

Mr. Johnson's estimate that 400-ton daily output is all the additional capacity required for a 2,000,000 man force does not agree with the information I have from the War Department. I am advised that they require, in addition to 150-ton daily production at Muscle Shoals, at least two additional plants, one of 250, and another of 150-ton capacity.

The nation needs this ammonia for the defense program. It has at Wilson Dam the foundation for a synthetic ammonia plant which can be completed for modern, efficient production at less than half the capital cost to the Government that a new plant of like capacity would cost in Kentucky or elsewhere.

The saving to the Government in cost of money by locating the 150-ton plant in buildings and using facilities already constructed at Wilson Dam, would in itself more than offset the disadvantage claimed by Mr. Johnson in cost of coke delivered at Wilson Dam from Birmingham.

The out-of-pocket cost to the Government for power produced at Muscle Shoals is so much less than purchased power cost in Kentucky or elsewhere that this item by itself also would offset the disadvantage claimed in the coke item.

I do not believe Mr. Johnson's point that a plant in Kentucky "would be more economical and with less chance of delay in transportation in distribution of ammonia to munitions plants," is well grounded. I understand that only two receiving plants (Ravena, Ohio, and Wilmington, Illinois) have been located as yet, and that sites in Central Tennessee quite near to Wilson Dam are now being considered by the Army for one or more of the new plants.

While, as I have indicated, several of the points stressed by Mr. Johnson cannot be accepted without qualification, paragraph 4, (p. 2), is entirely misleading. The statement that ammonia produced at the Muscle Shoals plant would cost 4¢ to 4½¢ a pound more than costs at another plant of equal size is only true if the old and obsolete cyanamid process is used at Muscle Shoals. Certainly that is the last thing in the world the agricultural groups want to see done, since it would entirely stop the nation-wide experimental and demonstration work with phosphate fertilizer now going on at Muscle Shoals. If either the difference in capital investment or power cost is taken into consideration, ammonia can be produced at Wilson Dam by modern processes just as efficiently and at just as low cost as at the other sites under consideration.

In this comment on Mr. Johnson's memorandum to you I have not attempted to cover more than a few of the points. In case you are interested in reading a more detailed discussion, I am attaching a copy of a memorandum which analyzes a statement Dr. Weidlein gave Mr. Stettinius on September 30.

There is over 25 years of history involved in this question of the use of Muscle Shoals. The law that has been established by Congress conjoins nitrogen (ammonia) production for munitions in time of war, and for a national fertilizer program in time of peace, as two objectives to be sought. . . .

It isn't a question of whether there is a peacetime shortage or surplus of ammonia production in this country. It is a question of proceeding at once with a development which the country vitally needs now, and which, after the emergency passes, will enable an experimental and demonstration project with nitrogenous fertilizers to go forward along the same lines that have been followed with concentrated phosphates. The value of that program has been too well demonstrated to require debate.

DUNN IS BROUGHT IN

On this same day, October 7, Davis and Stettinius, perhaps accompanied by certain of their assistants, met to discuss means for reconciling their differences of opinion concerning the proposed nitrate program. Although little information is available as to what took place at this meeting, it was apparently decided that Gano Dunn, president of the J. G. White Engineering Corporation and consultant to Stettinius, would study the problem with a view to finding some solution which would be acceptable to all concerned, and that the NDAC would not take final action on the War Department's request for approval of its nitrate program until Dunn had submitted his report.

There seems not to have been a true meeting of minds on the nature of Dunn's report. Dunn interpreted his role in this connection to be that of referee between the opposing factions in the NDAC; it seems probable that Stettinius leaned toward this interpretation also, but it is clear that Davis intended that Dunn's report should be only advisory; for although Davis was anxious, as were all the NDAC Commissioners, to get action on the War Department's request for formal NDAC approval of the whole Nitrate Program, his primary concern in the matter was to see that the plans for Muscle Shoals were approved. Davis did agree to co-operate with Dunn's study of the problem, since Stettinius felt that it would be helpful to the Commission; perhaps he also felt that if Dunn were supplied with full information on the Muscle Shoals situation, he would decide in favor of the Agricultural Division's position, and that if he did so those members of the NDAC who had thus far declined to approve the Muscle Shoals development would withdraw their opposition and allow the plans to go through. In any case, following the October 7 meeting Dunn began to collect material relevant to the problem of Muscle Shoals, and Davis immediately sent him copies of all the recent memoranda on this subject which had been prepared by Galbraith and himself, as well as those sent to him by the Industrial Materials Division. And the following day he addressed to Stettinius the Bureau of Agricultural Economics report endorsing the development of nitrate production by TVA, sending it to W. L. Batt, deputy to Stettinius, with a suggestion that it be turned over to Dunn.

VIII. Dunn's Compromise Proposal

On this same day, October 8, Davis mentioned in a letter to E. A. O'Neal of the American Farm Bureau Federation that "activities on the nitrate-phosphate front still continue. I am spending more time personally on that problem than any other matter before the Defense Commission." On October 9, Davis discussed with Galbraith a report dated September 30 which he had recently received from D. P. Morgan of Weidlein's section in the Industrial Materials Division on the power situation at Muscle Shoals. He also telephoned W. R. Ogg of the American Farm Bureau Federation to ask his conclusions as to the effect of the TVA phosphate program on the private fertilizer industry. Ogg replied that the TVA program, coupled with AAA distribution, was resulting in a phenomenal increase in private production. Davis said that that was the point he would like to show, since TVA now wished to do in nitrates what they had done in phosphates. Ogg replied that he could and would give figures to show that private industry could not do anything about increasing the demand for nitrogenous fertilizers until TVA had taken care of it, and expressed the view that the manufacturers were afraid they would lose the market if the farmers were to get highly concentrated nitrogen fertilizer.

DUNN INVESTIGATES

Batt of the NDAC Industrial Materials Division phoned Davis the same day to report that Dunn was going to have to go to New York and would not be able to furnish his report until the first of the week because, although Davis had already turned over to him all the necessary documents, Dunn had not yet talked to all the parties concerned and he felt that the matter was too important for him to give a snap opinion.

Earlier in the day, it had apparently been suggested to Davis that the du Pont-Morgantown plant be allowed to proceed since it was not involved in the present controversy, but Davis told Batt that the War Department was going to need all three of the plants which had been proposed and that he was not going to approve the completion of contracts with du Pont and Allied Chemical until the TVA matter was cleared up.

Dunn himself telephoned the next afternoon and left the following message for Davis:

> Wanted to come and talk to you. Have been working on the nitrate matter to the exclusion of almost everything else. Have seen a number of the parties involved and have dates with the TVA and other interests early next week. I wanted to go over with you some of the points that have already been raised but will take them up with you first of next week. Am going to New York this afternoon (4 o'clock) and am continuing the business in hand.

On Tuesday, October 15, after returning to Washington, Dunn held conferences with representatives of du Pont, Allied, and TVA. Those present at the TVA conference, the only one on which information is available, included a representative from the War Department, as well as C. O. Brown, Arthur M. Miller, and Neil Bass of TVA. Excerpts from Bass's account of this meeting follow:

> Mr. Dunn stated that the controversy centered around the Muscle Shoals plant. TVA was judged by Mr. Weidlein not to be experienced in the building and operation of a plant of such difficult character as a synthetic ammonia plant; it was further alleged that a 150-ton plant at Muscle Shoals would only represent the beginning of Government entry into a new field of private enterprise and would constitute a menace to the market of private companies after the emergency had passed when it was predicted there would be excess capacity in the ammonia field. He advised that the Chief of Ordnance and the War Department were concerned over the delay and that the total program now showed even a greater need for synthetic ammonia production capacity.
>
> Mr. Dunn stated that he had gone into the cost figure submitted by both sides and had en-

countered certain differences in points of view as to cost accounting principles which greatly affected the result. . . . As a result of his analysis, Mr. Dunn concluded that the large differences in the cost of operating in favor of Morgantown as shown by the Weidlein memorandum are offset by factors not considered. In operation cost the result is somewhat in favor of Morgantown, but in direct capital cost the result is in favor of Muscle Shoals—but the differences are not sufficient to justify a decision in favor of or against the Muscle Shoals location.

The supply of coke for both sites seems to be adequately provided for.

Mr. Dunn said that he could not bring himself to believe that TVA could assemble an organization, and design, construct, and operate the proposed Muscle Shoals plant in the time programmed by the War Department. He invited our comments, and Mr. Miller and Mr. Brown explained in detail the existence of an organization already trained in the design, construction and operation of a plant presenting problems at least as difficult as would be encountered in the ammonia plant. They indicated the advantages of a going organization. They also pointed out that the Chief of Operations in the Authority's phosphate plant was a du Pont-trained ammonia man.

Mr. Brown recounted his wide experience in the design and construction of synthetic ammonia plants. Mr. Dunn was impressed and advised us we had answered his reservation regarding the Authority's qualifications to design, build, and operate the plant. However, he still had a reservation as to whether the Authority could provide the plant and have it in operation according to the schedule fixed by the War Department. Mr. Miller called attention to the fact that the Authority had been definitely ready to go forward since July 1 and that the delay was no fault of the Authority.

Mr. Dunn stated that the industry was "bitterly opposed" to the Government's having a large nitrogen plant at Muscle Shoals. He had satisfied himself that the Authority's phosphate program was eminently necessary, and its operation in the educational program for the use of phosphates was not a detriment to the phosphate industry. Accordingly he concluded against any rehabilitation of the old cyanamid portion of the plant so as not to displace the TVA phosphate operations. He deferred to agricultural judgment that suggested a nitrogen program of the same character was needed; however, he felt that a 150-ton plant was not necessary for such a program. Therefore, he concluded that, if a smaller plant of 37½ ton capacity per day were built at the Shoals, the objection of industry would be largely overcome, especially if the Authority would agree to use the product of the plant after the emergency in an educational program and not to sell it at cost in competition with industrial nitrogen. He stated that the additional ammonia required for the operation of the ammonium nitrate portion of the plant (which he also felt should be rehabilitated and operated by the Authority) should be shipped in from plants operated by industry.

In response to his suggestion that the Authority agree to limit its use of the product after the emergency, we advised Mr. Dunn that such an agreement would abrogate the policy of Congress as written in the TVA Act, and hence would be beyond the purview of the Authority. He agreed with this interpretation and advised us that he had suggested that the Authority could not appropriately agree to this request of industry. We inquired whether a 37½ ton unit as suggested by Mr. Dunn might not be an uneconomical size (a) in relation to supplying ammonia for the ammonium nitrate needs at the Muscle Shoals plant and (b) in relation to economy of production in view of the fact that our 150-ton plant was laid out in two trains of 75 tons each, and whether economy of production in a larger size unit might not be considered as being more favorable to the Government. He advised that he was impressed that the representatives of industry would not agree to a unit any larger than 37½ tons per day.

Mr. Dunn stated that he had been advised by representatives of the industry that at least du Pont had intended to finance the construction of the Morgantown plant with its own funds. However, unless the Government refrained from building a plant larger than 37½ tons at Muscle Shoals, the industry would ask the privilege of financing the Morgantown plant with Government funds and not risk their own funds against a threatened competitive situation which would result from a Government plant at Muscle Shoals of as large a capacity as 150 tons per day. We advised Mr. Dunn that we were without authority to agree to the plan as proposed and asked if he wished us to submit the matter to our Board of Directors. He did not wish us to do so and said that he wanted to work further on the matter and, if possible, effect an agreement within the National Defense Commission.

Later that afternoon and subsequent to this conference with Mr. Dunn, Miss Marguerite Owens of the TVA Washington Office related to Mr. Miller and to me a request received from Mr. Morris L. Cooke (who was assisting Commissioner Hillman in the preparation of an answer to a memorandum which the Commissioner had received from Mr. Dunn) for factual information concerning the points raised regarding the Authority's facilities. . . .

DUNN REPORTS

The memorandum which Hillman had received from Dunn was apparently a copy of the twelve-page report which Dunn submitted to Stettinius the same day, and which reads in part as follows:

I have gone thoroly into the questions which, acting on your behalf and with the approval of Mr. Chester Davis and Dr. Weidlein, Mr. Batt on October 7 put into my hands as referee. . . .

The controversy centers around the desirability of a Muscle Shoals plant. This, it is charged, should not be relied upon for munitions in the present national emergency, because of the inexperience of those in the TVA organization who would be charged with the duty of designing, building and operating a new plant in which the engineering and construction difficulties are as great as they are in the art of producing synthetic ammonia. It is also alleged that a 150-ton plant at Muscle Shoals would not only represent the beginning of Government entry into a new field of private enterprise, but would constitute a menace to the market of the private companies after the emergency has passed, when there would be a large excess capacity in the ammonia field. . . .

The Chief of Ordnance and his associated officers are deeply concerned over the delay that has already been suffered through the holding up of these plants; and this concern has been rendered more acute by the increase in the War and Navy Departments' total program that only recently has been made, involving the production of even greater quantities of synthetic ammonia than were under consideration at the time the plants in controversy were first projected.

In response to this increased urgency, a recommendation was made on October 9th that the holdup on the 250-ton Morgantown plant be removed because of readiness to begin construction work, and because of the fact that the plant itself was not in controversy; but this recommendation was unfavorably received.

As bearing on the Muscle Shoals location, it is argued that synthetic ammonia could be produced there more cheaply than elsewhere, on account of power, site and service facilities existing there, of which advantage could be taken. . . .

I have gone into the operating cost figures submitted by both sides and have encountered certain differences in point of view as to cost-accounting principles, which greatly affect the result—which to a considerable extent depends on which set of principles is followed. . . .

On the coke situation, Dr. Morgan's study of September 30th, in my opinion, makes out a good case. I have given careful attention to the coke statistics prepared by Mr. Rogers and submitted by Dr. Galbraith, as contained in the memoranda dated September 28th and September 30th and I do not question the general validity of these figures, which cover wide areas. But I do not believe they apply to this case.

If an ammonia plant were built at Muscle Shoals, the principal coke supply would be the Alabama By-Products Corporation of Birmingham, Alabama. In a letter dated July 11th to Dr. D. P. Morgan, Mr. Porter, the President of that corporation, says that he had been approached by the TVA on a proposition to supply Muscle Shoals 10,000 tons of coke per month, doubtless for some plan of expansion they had in mind; and that it was a matter of regret that he had to point out that his company was producing all of the metallurgical coke at the moment that his present facilities would permit.

On the general question of relative cost of operation between the two sites, therefore, I am obliged to conclude that the rather large differences in favor of Morgantown shown in the memorandum of September 30th, while valid in themselves, are offset to a considerable extent by the factors not included, which I have been discussing. In respect to operating cost as distinguished from capital cost, I believe the result is nevertheless in favor of Morgantown while in respect to direct capital cost it is in favor of Muscle Shoals.

Even if, recognizing the uncertainties of all estimates, the final difference in operating cost is in favor of Morgantown the difference is not enough to be the sole deciding factor in determining for or against the Muscle Shoals location.

I have gone into the question of operation costs in order to bring conflicting points of view together as far as possible, but there are other factors that have more weight.

The design, construction and operation of a synthetic ammonia plant is one of the most difficult undertakings of mechanical and chemical engineering.

I have had personal experience with two such plants and knowledge of several others. Relative to steam pressure, the pressures at which the gases are worked are enormous, rendering piping and valve problems very difficult; and there are numerous steps in the process that are always to some extent uncertain and critical, to say nothing of being extremely complicated. A large part of the machinery and apparatus has to be especially designed and built for each case. There are wide differences in the details of the processes used by the various companies.

For all these reasons, synthetic ammonia engineering is an art by itself, which cannot be fully learned from books, nor successfully practiced from drawings only. In it there are many trade secrets learned by expensive experience, and the design and operation of such plants is an organization, rather than an individual, accomplishment.

For these reasons, notwithstanding the knowledge and skill of the experts on the TVA staff, I cannot bring myself to believe that TVA can assemble an organization and can design, construct and operate a 150-ton plant in the time programmed for the War Department to rely on it for the production of its quota of ammonia for the vital munitions needs.

I believe, however, that a synthetic plant at Muscle Shoals is desirable; and I recommend that one be located there, but of smaller capacity; so that delay or difficulty in its completion or in its functioning after completion would not disarrange the plans of the War Department to the extent that they would be disarranged if reliance were placed on a larger plant and it failed to be ready in time, or to function properly.

I recommend a quarter-size plant of a capacity of 37½ tons per day, at a cost of approximately $1,000,000. This is a quarter of the full-size plant of which the estimated cost is approximately $4,400,000.

I also recommend the rehabilitation of the ammonium nitrate part of the old cyanamid process plant, as covered by Assistant Secretary Patterson's memorandum of September 24th. This ammonium nitrate part was originally laid out to convert 150 tons of ammonia per day into ammonium nitrate, but the evidence seems to indicate it cannot be made to come fully up to that capacity. Upon rehabilitation, it can absorb the 37½ tons of ammonia per day produced by the quarter-size synthetic plant, and the difference between that and whatever capacity it can develop can be supplied by liquid ammonia bought at low cost and shipped in in the customary tank cars. . . .

On account of the recent increase in the national defense requirements over those current when the three nitrate plants under discussion were first projected, there is no question of the urgent need at the earliest possible moment of the nitrate producing capacity of all three of them, irrespective of where that capacity is located.

For this reason, additional capacity will have to be supplied to offset the deficit or reduction of 112½ tons in the capacity of the quarter-size plant which I have recommended. And I recommend that this deficit be either divided equally and half added to the Morgantown and half to the Kentucky plant or that the whole be added to the Morgantown plant.

Another reason affecting my judgment in favor of a quarter-size plant at Muscle Shoals, is that it is alleged by the private companies that if a synthetic ammonia plant with as large a capacity as 150 tons per day is now built at Muscle Shoals for munitions purposes, not only will its products cost more than that of the private companies under conditions of actual operation as compared with estimated operation, but there will be a menace to their market that will exist after the emergency has passed. They fear the entry of the Government into competition with them, particularly at a time when they are least able to meet it.

Prior to the present emergency, there was a large excess of ammonia producing capacity, only 60 per cent of the country's capacity being active.

The companies express the fear that with the Government once in the ammonia business and authorized by the TVA act to sell its product at cost without profit, a plant as large as 150 tons daily capacity will produce an effect against which they cannot contend, especially if, in response to farmer demand, the capacity might be still further increased.

For this reason, they allege that if the full-size Muscle Shoals plant be built, they fear to risk their capital and would ask the Government to put up its capital for the venture—executing management contracts with the companies to operate the plants for the Government. . . .

It is true that even if the companies put up their own capital, they will probably want to take advantage of the recently approved contract and amortize their capital cost over five years, and that this money for amortization in the long run comes out of the Government. It is, however, at the companies' risk in the meantime, and the present burden on the Government is enormously relieved—an advantage to the Government which has had weight in my recommendation of a quarter-size plant. . . .

I want to thank Mr. Davis and his associates, Dr. Weidlein and his associates, Mr. E. F. Johnson and his associates, General Wesson, General Harris and General Campbell and their associates; the representatives of the Allied Chemical and Dupont companies; the representatives of the Tennessee Valley Authority; and Mr. William H. Harrison, for the particularly willing courtesies they have extended to me in this investigation, in arriving at a judgment which I earnestly hope they all will accept.

DAVIS REPLIES

Davis, since his conversation with Leon Henderson on October 3, had been doing some investigating on his own, and he presented his findings in the matter in a memorandum to Dunn on the same day that Dunn submitted his report to Stettinius. Davis, however, apparently had not yet received a copy of Dunn's report when he wrote Stettinius on the 15th:

I told you the other day that, in my judgment, the real basis for the opposition in some quarters to establishment of a synthetic ammonia plant at TVA is fear that it would compete with and tend to displace production by commercial companies. I have given a great deal of thought to that angle, and today sent over to Mr. Gano Dunn the material, copies of which are appended here. I hope you will read the letter, at least, and glance at some of the other material, before the Commission discusses this question.

The letter to which Davis refers was his memorandum to Dunn entitled "Effect on private industry of proposed synthetic ammonia development at Muscle Shoals" in which he stated:

The point of view has been expressed that a synthetic ammonia plant of 150-ton daily capacity located at Nitrate Plant No. 2, Wilson Dam (Muscle Shoals) and operated by the Tennessee Valley Authority, would in peace-time compete with and tend to displace production by privately owned chemical companies. I have given this question a good deal of thought and I have reached the conclusion that not only would this not be the case, but that the operation of such a plant for experimental and demonstration purposes after the war emergency had passed would tend to widen the market and increase the demand for the products of the commercial manufacturers. It can be demonstrated, I believe, that the phosphate experimental and demonstration project of the Tennessee Valley Authority which uses part of the old cyanamid process furnaces and equipment, has tended to increase rather than diminish the volume of business done by the commercial companies. In this project, the Tennessee Valley Authority has pioneered in perfecting the manufacture of concentrated phosphate fertilizer and in demonstrating through farm tests all over the United States how farmers can use the product safely. This demonstration work has been followed by greatly increased demand which the commercial companies, not TVA, are depended upon to meet.

A report on experience in the phosphate program is set forth more fully in Appendix: A—"The Effect of the TVA Phosphate Program on Private Fertilizer Industry," with its related exhibits.

Part of the apprehension undoubtedly grows out of the belief that the proposed development of new ammonia capacity at Muscle Shoals, and at Morgantown, West Virginia, and at some point in Kentucky, which the War Department has proposed, would leave the country with considerable excess capacity for peacetime operations.

If our future consumption of nitrogen is limited to the amount of consumption in the past, this apprehension would seem to be well grounded. It would be unwise, however, to conclude that we are not going to apply more nitrogen to the soil in the future than we have been doing in the past. It is impossible to measure precisely the net annual loss of nitrogen from the soil of the United States (in terms of tons of ammonia) but I wish to call your attention to two estimates as they are set forth in the appended letter from Dr. P. V. Cardon, Acting Chief, Bureau of Plant Industry, U. S. Department of Agriculture (Appendix: B). The late Dr. J. G. Lipman, who was probably the foremost authority on soil fertility in the United States, estimated that our annual loss of nitrogen in terms of tons of ammonia, net after allowing for all additions, amounts to approximately 7,450,000 tons of ammonia per year. The National Resources Board presents a more conservative estimate of 4,800,000 tons.

It would require 100 plants of the size proposed by the War Department for Muscle Shoals, running practically at full capacity, to produce enough ammonia to offset the annual loss of nitrogen suggested in the more conservative estimate of the National Resources Board. I do not for a moment suggest that it would be practical to produce or economically desirable for farmers to buy anything like this amount of nitrogen. The figures are set forth merely to indicate that the country can absorb vastly more nitrogen than all of the projected plants together will produce and still be running an appalling deficit in the national soil balance sheet.

If the TVA phosphate experience is duplicated with nitrogen, then its experimental and demonstration work will lead toward more general use and consumption of nitrates and fertilizer and in consequence to a bigger demand for the product of the commercial ammonia plants.

On the question of whether the proposal of the War Department would endow this country with too much nitrogen in the form of ammonia for peacetime requirements, it may be interesting to note what Germany has done in the development of synthetic ammonia capacity. Dr. R. O. E. Davis, Acting Chief, Fertilizer Research Division, U. S. Department of Agriculture, says in a memorandum which I have in my files:

"The safety factor of Germany in regard to nitrogen supply is between 2 and 3, with a productive capacity of 1,700,000 tons of nitrogen per year. In addition, the capacity of plants in Norway, Holland and Belgium, now in possession of Germany, will probably add another 495,000 tons. No other nation in the world is so well prepared to take care of this vital supply of nitrogen, essential for both war and peacetime activities.

"It was reported by an American Consul in Germany (old Reich) that it has become necessary for Germany to restrict the consumption of fertilizer nitrogen in the year 1940-41 to 85 per cent of that consumed in 1938-39; respective quotas being 671,000 tons and 789,000 tons. This in spite of Germany's great resources and the acquirement of additional plants during the war."

In this connection you may be interested in the article on "Nitrogen Sufficiency" in Industrial and Chemical Engineering for September, 1940, by J. E. Zanetti, of Columbia University. A photostat copy is attached, marked Appendix C.

Finally, I want to call your attention to the declarations of government policy which have been made in numerous laws and in statements by Congressional committees with respect to the use of the properties at Muscle Shoals for the production of nitrogen for munitions and fertilizer. I have referred to these laws and policy declarations from time to time in various memoranda and have had them summarized in the appended "Declaration of Government Policy with Respect to Muscle Shoals Properties."

Attached to this letter as appendices were a report which Davis had obtained from W. R. Ogg of the AFBF entitled "Effect of TVA Phosphate Program on Private Fertilizer Industry," a letter dated October 11 from P. V. Cardon, Acting Chief of the Bureau of Plant Industry in the Department of Agriculture to James L. McCamy, Assistant to the Secretary of Agriculture, and the photostats of an article by J. C. Zanetti of Columbia University entitled "Nitrogen Sufficiency," which had been published the previous month in *Industrial and Engineering Chemistry*.

After sending this memorandum to Dunn and Stettinius, Davis wrote McCamy to thank him for the nitrogen information and the magazine article, and on the morning of the 16th he phoned Henderson to warn him that the TVA-nitrate problem was now coming to a head. He said that he had had a two-hour session with Dunn during which they had found that after knocking out all the economic arguments which had come up in connection with the War Department plans, the controversy over these plans came down to the fact that du Pont, Hercules, and Allied were using all their power to fight the development at Muscle Shoals. Henderson told him that the people in his Price Stabilization Division had been going over the problem, that Hamm, one of his assistants, and Galbraith had been together, and that he had spoken to Stettinius about it. Davis said he hoped they would be able to settle the matter in their own group—the sooner the better—and that he would ask Nelson to bring it up when the Commission met later in the day.

THE NDAC DELIBERATES

Davis then phoned Nelson to inquire whether Nelson would quietly call attention to the fact that the War Department's recommendation on ammonia plants had been on the agenda a long time. And Nelson replied that he would do so as he had done on each previous occasion.

The following is an excerpt from the minutes of the October 16 meeting of the NDAC:

At the request of Mr. Stettinius, Mr. Gano Dunn orally presented to the Commission the findings contained in his report of October 15, 1940 (Document 131), in connection with a memorandum dated September 24, 1940, from the Assistant Secretary of War transmitting the recommendation of the Ordnance Department for three synthetic ammonia plants: one at Muscle Shoals of 150 tons daily capacity, another at Morgantown, West Virginia, of 250 tons daily capacity, and a third in Kentucky, of 150 tons daily capacity. Mr. Dunn recommended as follows:

1. That upon the evidence that has been submitted, I am unable to conclude that a 150-ton synthetic ammonia plant can be designed, constructed and put into successful quantity operation by the existing organization at Muscle Shoals in the programmed time for the War Department to rely upon its quota in the National Defense munitions plans.
2. That the language of the original Nitrate Act of 1916 and of the Tennessee Valley Act of 1933 justifies the contention of the Department of Agriculture, the Farmer Cooperatives, President O'Neal of the American Farm Bureau Federation, and Mr. Chester Davis of the Advisory Commission to the Council of National Defense, that in respect to military purposes and in respect to post emergency conditions, there should be an ammonia plant at Muscle Shoals, to take the place of the outmoded ammonia plant now there.

   In view of Finding No. 1, I recommend that a synthetic ammonia plant of lesser size, namely 37½ tons per day (a quarter of the original proposal, to cost approximately $1,100,000) be constructed by the TVA organization at Muscle Shoals, to operate in conjunction with a rehabilitation of the ammonium nitrate part of the obsolete cyanamid plant now there; any ammonia in excess of 37½ tons per day which the rehabilitated ammonium nitrate plant can efficiently use, to be purchased and delivered in liquid form in the customary tank cars.
3. That in view of Findings No. 1 and No. 2, there would be a present capital saving to the Government of $19,753,000 or possibly more by building a ¼ size plant at Muscle Shoals.
4. That the proposed plan for rehabilitating the ammonium nitrate part of the old cyanamid plant be carried out, but that no rehabilitation of the ammonia part of it be attempted.
5. That the phosphate operations now carried on in certain of the furnaces originally constructed for the cyanamid process be not disturbed.
6. That in order to provide for the deficit of 112½ tons in production resulting from the reduction in capacity of the Muscle Shoals plant to ¼ of the originally proposed size, the amount of that deficit be divided between the Kentucky plant and the Morgantown plant, or be added to the Morgantown plant as the best engineering, economic and time considerations shall indicate.
7. That the holdup on the Morgantown and Kentucky plants be immediately removed and construction work on them and on the reduced Muscle Shoals plant be allowed to proceed; provided it is confirmed that in view of the proposed reduction in the capacity of the Muscle Shoals plant one or both of the private companies would be willing initially to advance their own capital.

Following Mr. Dunn's presentation, Mr. Davis asked him several questions pertaining to comparative costs, and the ability of TVA to get a plant in shape and in operation as recommended by the Ordnance Department. Mr. Davis stated that it was his opinion the economic thing to do and it probably should have been done long ago, is to put a synthetic ammonia plant at Muscle Shoals to match the ammonium nitrate plant located there.

Mr. Knudsen urged that action be taken immediately to clear the Morgantown plant pending the resolving of the controversy concerning the Muscle Shoals plant. However, Mr. Davis stated with Mr. Dunn's report in and distributed he would circulate certain materials he wished the Commission to consider in connection with the recommendation of the War Department and he thought a decision could be reached on the entire recommendation this week. Mr. Davis pointed out that some time ago he had approved the recommendations of the War Department as had several other Commissioners.

It was understood that this matter would be considered by the Commission for final action at the Executive Session on October 18, 1940.

DAVIS PREPARES FOR FINAL ACTION

Later the same day, October 16, Galbraith commented on Dunn's recommendation for a 37-ton Ammonia plant at Muscle Shoals in the following memorandum to Davis (attachments omitted):

I understand that a proposal has been made to reduce the size of the proposed synthetic ammonia plant at Muscle Shoals from a capacity of 150 tons a day to 37-40 tons a day. This follows a review of the situation by Mr. Gano Dunn in which he finds that the various objections advanced to this site at various stages, viz., shortage of coke in the area, heavy concentration of existing defense industry in the area, higher operating costs, heavy freight charges on outgoing product, and lack of technical "know-how" on the part of Tennessee Valley Authority engineers, are all without foundation.

While Mr. Dunn does not find the capital investment lower at Muscle Shoals than at Morgantown he does find that they are only equal by assuming that an additional 150-ton unit is added to a now non-existent 250-ton unit to be built by DuPont at Morgantown to which all overhead is charged. We have already commented on this method of cost calculation—and on the enormous concentration of ammonia producing capacity which the calculation implies. . . . It may be supposed that the army will not agree to this concentration—in fact, their disapproval is already implied by their request for an additional 150-ton plant in Kentucky.

The reason for reducing the size of the proposed plant from 150 tons to 37 tons is the opposition of private industry to the control of ammonia capacity by the Tennessee Valley Authority. Since the other reasons advanced against this site have been found by Mr. Dunn to be without substance, either there have been grave shortcomings in the technical advice which the Commission has had or the opposition of private industry has been the real reason throughout for opposition to this site. If so, this opposition is responsible for the several months delay which has already occurred in the launching of this project.

The proposal for a 37-ton plant is based not on considerations of economy or facilitating the defense effort, but on the grounds that this capacity represents no post-war threat to private industry. It will be useful to a limited extent during the war. It is hoped that it would appease the demand of this Division that consistent with speed and economy in Defense, the war-time development of nitrogen capacity should have proper regard for post-war use in general and the Tennessee Valley Authority plant-food program in particular.

In my judgment neither this Division nor the Commission can accept this proposal for the following reasons:

1. The proposal entirely overlooks the interests of national defense for which we are increasing nitrogen capacity. The 37-ton plant would provide only one-quarter of the ammonia required for capacity operation of the ammonium nitrate plant at the Shoals. The remainder would have to be shipped in from Morgantown or Hopewell, Virginia in tank cars at increased costs and in face of a conceivable tank car shortage.
2. The demand of private industry is wholly illegitimate. In the first place there is no evidence that TVA ownership of this capacity will damage private industry—the evidence from the operation of the phosphate program is entirely to the contrary. In the second place, private industry is asking abrogation by the Commission of a declared policy of the Congress with respect of the Muscle Shoals facilities and in the third place, it is quite as relevant to point out that farmers, who are also a private industry and the important users of the product, are just as insistent that nitrogen capacity be installed at Muscle Shoals. But I must repeat that type of argument is inimical to the whole national defense program and is to be deplored.
3. The construction cost of a small plant of 37 tons a day is far less economical per unit of product capacity than a larger plant. The small plant will require almost the same designing and engineering expenditure as a large plant, while condensers and other equipment are commonly designed on the basis of 80-ton operating units as a minimum. . . .
4. Unit operating costs of the smaller plant will be higher than of a larger unit. . . .
5. In the judgment of the Tennessee Valley Authority the 37-ton capacity will be insufficient for a long-time nationwide program. The TVA estimates that for an immediate research and educational program in the use of nitrates, it would require some 6,000 tons of NH_3 equivalent a year while ultimately some 36,000 tons of ammonia equivalent would be required. A 37-ton plant would serve to cover the immediate needs of the Authority but it would provide no opportunity for expansion of the program beyond the present demonstration farms. A full development of the program would require the output of a 100-ton plant. A 150-ton plant would give the Authority more capacity

than it now needs in the development of its program.

But the fact that the full capacity would not be required in the immediate period cannot be an argument for keeping down the capacity of the plant if the location is otherwise the most advantageous from the point of view of national defense. The latter is now agreed.

6. This small plant, in the event of an ammonia shortage, might easily lead to a demand that the old cyanamid process be rehabilitated for emergency purposes. Intelligent planning at this time will enable us to avoid this disastrous and costly expedient.

Should we concur in this proposal it would be apparent, I feel, that we were sacrificing the public interest and the defense program for a measure which has as its major end the appeasement of a private industry that is already profiting largely from the defense program. The reasons for installing this small plant could not be explained either to the Congress or the people of the United States. Therefore, since the economy and practicability of the army program with reference to the TVA project is now agreed, I feel that we must stand on that recommendation.

TVA COMMENTS

And Neil Bass of TVA, who had conferred with Dunn the previous day, gave Davis the following statement of his views on the Muscle Shoals dispute:

Decision concerned with Government financing of additional ammonia capacity involves two questions: first, how much capacity is required and second, where additional installation should be geographically situated.

The issue is confused if the amount to be produced at the Shoals is gauged by requirement for agricultural research and demonstration. The decision as to amount is a military one. A determination as to the place of production is likewise military up to the point at which it is shown that the Shoals location is on a parity with other localities for reasons of efficiency and economy in production and distribution.

If it appears, however, that other localities and auspices are substantially equal in desirability to the Shoals location, then, and at that time the interest of agriculture in a peacetime operation of such facilities must control the decision. In that event the issue becomes simply one as to whether the United States Government through TVA can better administer ammonia facilities (of whatever scale the National Defense may require) as an integral part of agricultural demonstration, than can private industry. If so, it necessarily follows that as much of the additional ammonia capacity as is capable of economic production and efficient distribution should be located at the Shoals.

And on October 17, Arthur M. Miller of TVA, who had also met with Dunn on the 15th, sent the following letter in compliance with a request from Morris L. Cooke of Hillman's division that he comment on the Dunn report:

It is evident from Mr. Gano Dunn's October 15 letter to Mr. Stettinius which you asked me to read, as well as from my conversations with him on October 15, that he has given very thorough consideration to the ammonia question. . . .

Mr. Dunn suggests a plant one-quarter of this size at one-fourth of this investment. Obviously, a smaller plant cannot be built at a proportionally lower capital outlay. Actually, a plant of one-fourth the size proposed would cost nearer $2,000,000 than the $1,100,000 postulated by Mr. Dunn. Furthermore, Mr. Dunn does not point out that the cost of production of ammonia in this smaller plant would increase by about 25 per cent.

Mr. Dunn quotes a July 11 letter from the President of the ABC Coke Co. to the effect that he could not supply the TVA with coke. Mr. Porter, the gentleman concerned, has more recently proposed to the Defense Commission that he would consider expanding his plant to care for TVA requirement, and would, moreover, provide the financing if the Commission would authenticate amortization of his investment on the five-year plan.

Mr. Dunn's contention that the existing ammonium nitrate plant will not develop its full-rated capacity after rehabilitation is not in agreement with the opinion of the able technical men most familiar with the plant.

Although Mr. Dunn states that difference in production cost at the three sites will not be material, he proposes to manufacture three-fourths of the ammonia (needed at MS for conversion in the existing plant to ammonium nitrate) at plants remotely located, thereby causing the War Department to pay unnecessary freight charges for transportation of ammonia. Furthermore, tank cars for such service will probably be scarce.

Despite the fact that the War Department

must finance the new ammonia capacity by direct outlay in cash, or by amortization in cost of product, Mr. Dunn proposes to increase the capital outlay for ammonia plants from $33,990,000 to $38,025,000, the difference being $4,125,000. This amount actually would be $5,025,000 if he gave effect to a reasonable cost estimate for the smaller ammonia plant which he proposes for TVA. This $5,025,000 is the penalty which the Government is asked to pay because two private industrial companies do not want the TVA to operate an ammonia plant.

The United States has a large investment at Muscle Shoals, usable economically and effectively in our national defense program. We should therefore not let hypothetical cost studies based upon theoretical cost accounting theories distort our judgment. . . .

The ammonia question resolves itself into whether the Government should take full advantage of its investment, facilities, and organization at Muscle Shoals and thereby save on capital cost for plant and on the cost of ammonia produced in the plant, or should throw away these advantages because DuPont and Allied Chemical object. Millions of dollars are involved, and the question of the public interest.

DAVIS SUMS UP

On the same day, October 17, Davis sent each of the Commissioners a copy of a memorandum which he and Galbraith had prepared, and from which the following excerpts are taken:

I am submitting herewith a statement on Mr. Dunn's review of the proposal of the Army under date of September 24 that a 150-ton synthetic ammonia plant be constructed at Muscle Shoals. I should like to say at the outset that I appreciate the care and thoroughness with which Mr. Dunn has surveyed this problem. While I cannot concur in his recommendations, I believe that he has clarified several important issues. The Commission is indebted to Mr. Dunn.

I must stress one point. This Division is not holding up the ammonia program. The proposal submitted by Assistant Secretary of War Patterson under date of September 24 received my approval in a memorandum under date of September 30. It is my understanding that it has also been approved by Commissioners Elliott, Henderson, Hillman, and Budd. The delay results from the Commission's failure to approve the proposal which the Army has made to the Commission. I do assume full responsibility for keeping the three proposals submitted by the Army linked together. It has been necessary to do this since my decision as to one plant will be vitally affected by the launching of operations for the manufacture of exactly the same product at other points.

With this clarification I should like to turn to Mr. Dunn's report. While in a document of this sort there must always be a good deal that invites discussion, I confine myself to the major points at issue which make it impossible for me to concur in his findings and in the proposal which he makes. . . .

Mr. Dunn's . . . main contention concerns technical "Know-how" and engineering organization. His conclusion is that the TVA engineering staff cannot be relied upon to bring in the 150-ton capacity in the time originally estimated. This, apparently, is a question upon which reasonable men can disagree. I draw attention to the fact that this question did not enter into discussion until a few days ago.

It does not appear in any of the Army discussions of the problem which I have seen. I would refer to a memorandum by C. F. Hofstetter entitled "Resume of the Muscle Shoals Situation" under date of August 8 in which the 150-ton plant is recommended, another memorandum entitled "The Ammonia Problem" under date of September 9, also by Hofstetter, and a memorandum from Dr. Weidlein to Mr. Batt under date of September 25 reviewing a memorandum submitted by this office. I also cite the following paragraph from a memorandum written by Dr. Harry A. Curtis, Dean of the College of Engineering at the University of Missouri and Consultant to my Division re this point, when it was first raised by Dr. Weidlein:

"(6) *Know-how*

"This paragraph in the Weidlein memorandum is amusing in several respects. It is precisely the argument advanced to the TVA by the president of the only company operating relatively large phosphate smelting furnaces in the United States in 1933. His company was the only one having the 'know-how' for this very difficult operation. He has not been heard from since the TVA built and operated with entire success furnaces twice the size of his.

"There is nothing mysterious about a synthetic ammonia plant. In the twenty-two years since the close of the World War, the technology of this process has become well known. . . .

"There is ample evidence indicating that the TVA can design and build and operate an ammonia plant, with its own engineers and with such assistance as is readily available outside the present TVA organizations."

Following the meeting of the Commission on October 16, I telephoned Mr. Charles O. Brown asking for a careful estimate of the *maximum* time required to design, build and begin operation of a synthetic ammonia plant at Muscle Shoals, allowing for contingencies of organization and recruiting of additional staff. His estimate which places the maximum time at 14 to 15 months and the basis for the estimate are in the following telegram:

"NA34 111 NT GOVT—TDWS RYE NY 16
CHESTER DAVIS, COMMISSIONER
FEDERAL RESERVE BUILDING.
21 AND CONSTITUTION AVE. WASH. D. C.

HAVE CAREFULLY REVIEWED TIME REQUIRED TO BUILD SYNTHETIC AMMONIA PLANT DESCRIBED IN REPORT BY COMPARISON WITH EXPERIENCE BUILDING JAPANESE PLANT WHICH PROJECT WAS CHARACTERIZED BY EXPERIENCED DESIGNING ORGANIZATION PROMPT MATERIAL DELIVERIES AND AMPLE SHOP FABRICATION CAPACITY AS FAVORABLE FACTORS WHILE JAPANESE ERECTION AND GREAT DISTANCE AWAY WERE UNFAVORABLE FACTORS. HARMONIZING ABOVE WITH BUILDING ALABAMA PLANT AT PRESENT TIME AIDED BY ENGINEERING FIRM AND STAFF ASSUMING NORMAL DELIVERIES MY CAREFUL JUDGMENT IS 14 TO 15 MONTHS FOR FIRST PRODUCTION FULL PRODUCTION NOT OVER 2 MONTHS LATER. TASK OF STARTING MODERN EQUIPMENT IS QUITE SURE AND DEFINITE. AFTER 20 YEARS OF DEVELOPMENT THERE IS RELATIVELY LITTLE RISK OF ANY PLANT OPERATING TROUBLES.

CHARLES O. BROWN."

However, as noted, Mr. Dunn's doubts on the question of "know-how" resolve themselves into a question of the time in which the 150-ton capacity can be brought into production at Muscle Shoals. Even if the TVA required additional time as compared with private companies, this cannot be considered a determining factor. Dr. Brown's maximum estimate is 15 months for TVA as against a minimum estimate of twelve months for the other facilities. I am informed by the Army that the ammonia requirements for explosive and propellent plants now under way or immediately planned, i.e., Redford, Charlestown, Wilmington (Tetrol and TNT) and Weldon Springs will total approximately 235 tons daily. This is at full capacity which in general will not be reached for a year and in the case of the Weldon Springs plant, for some fifteen months. If the new private plants come in according to schedule there will be 400 tons of ammonia to cover these requirements with a margin of 165 tons for ammonium nitrate manufacture. Should it require 20 months for the TVA to complete its plant, the required diversion of ammonia to meet the full Army ammonium nitrate requirements of 300 tons (150 tons of ammonia) is within the limits of the new capacity for the five months which, it is assumed, the TVA plant will be delayed. It is necessary to add, however, that it is by no means certain that the shell and bomb loading plants will be ready to absorb the full ammonium nitrate requirement fifteen months from now, and this safety factor allows for any possible increase in ammonia requirements within twenty months for new propellent or explosive capacity. Therefore, the pressure of time, properly related to requirements, is not unfavorable to Muscle Shoals even assuming the most unfavorable situation. . . .

Mr. Dunn states that a further factor affecting his judgment is the allegation by private industry that a 150-ton plant at Muscle Shoals would be inimical to their post-war position. I cannot protest too strongly against this type argument. I believe it can only be injurious to national defense. In any case the proposed post-war use is not for commercial or yardstick purposes. Should those purposes become a national policy it might quite as well apply to any government-owned plants whether in Alabama, West Virginia, or Kentucky. The TVA program is one of research and experimentation. There is no evidence that it has been damaging to private industry—in fact, the record is entirely to the contrary. I wish to draw special attention to evidence which I am appending on this point with reference to the phosphate program of the Authority.

Mr. Dunn finds that a considerable initial saving in capital outlay to the government is possible if the Muscle Shoals project is reduced or abandoned. Private companies will be willing to finance the expansion instead of proceeding with government construction and operation on an agency contract. Mr. Dunn finds, however, that this procedure will result in no net saving to the government over a five-year period.

Since no such proposal to my knowledge has hitherto been made, this must be considered a counter offer by private industry contingent upon abandonment of Muscle Shoals with its attendant advantages to the government. Since the offer holds no advantages for the government—it is an offer of installment sale rather than cash purchase

—I do not believe the offer could be seriously considered even were the question before the Commission. But since no such proposal is now before us, it must also be ruled out as irrelevant.

In my judgment Mr. Dunn does not give sufficient emphasis to the fact that there is now at Muscle Shoals an important facility for converting ammonia into ammonium nitrate. If the Army plans to use this facility, as the project now before the Commission clearly implies, then it will be necessary to supply approximately 150 tons of ammonia daily to this plant. TVA engineers estimate that upon rehabilitation the ammonium nitrate plant can convert somewhat in excess of 150 tons of NH_3. I am informed that other estimates place the capacity at less than 150 tons. I do not attempt to resolve this difference of opinion. Unless a 150-ton plant is located at Muscle Shoals, it will be necessary, if the facility is to be used at all, to ship ammonia in tank cars from other plants, convert it, and ship it on to the loading plants. Obviously in any comparison of sites the cost of shipping ammonia from outlying locations to Muscle Shoals is chargeable against operating costs at these locations. A question of availability of tank cars may possibly arise.

Since I do not find the reasons advanced against the 150-ton plant at Muscle Shoals convincing or even substantial, I cannot concur in Mr. Dunn's proposal for a 37-ton plant. However, there are some special reasons for opposing this specific proposal which must be noted as follows:

(a) The placing of a 37-ton plant at Muscle Shoals as part of the defense program would result in a serious and not unjustified interpretation of the motives of this Commission. At worst, we would be accused of gross mismanagement in placing a 37-ton plant adjacent to a 150-ton converting unit; at best, we would be accused of allowing private industry to dictate the course of the defense program in accordance with its interpretation of its eventual interest.

(b) Since the proposal has little significance for National Defense, we would be exposing the Tennessee Valley Authority to the charge that it was employing defense funds largely or solely to further its agricultural program. I am attaching a statement on this point placed in my hands by Mr. Neil Bass, Chief Conservation Engineer of the Authority, following his conversation with Mr. Dunn on Tuesday.

(c) The proposed 37-ton plant could not of itself meet the requirements of the TVA program on a long-range view. While it is true that the Authority does not at this time and will not in the near future, require 150 tons capacity, the program now contemplated would not be served by a 37-ton plant, I refer to the following interchange of telegrams with Dr. H. A. Morgan on this point.

OCTOBER 16, 1940

"H. A. MORGAN, CHAIRMAN
TENNESSEE VALLEY AUTHORITY
KNOXVILLE, TENNESSEE

PLEASE ADVISE AMOUNT OF NITROGEN ANNUALLY IN TERMS OF NH_3 EQUIVALENT WOULD BE REQUIRED FOR COMPLETE NATIONWIDE RESEARCH AND TESTING PROGRAM ALONG LINES NOW CONTEMPLATED FOR PHOSPHATE PROGRAM.

J. K. GALBRAITH
NATIONAL DEFENSE COMMISSION
2001 FEDERAL RESERVE BUILDING
WASHINGTON, D. C."

"WESTERN UNION
WK127 120 GOVT-KNOXVILLE, TENN. 16 137P
1940 OCT. 16 PM 3 11
J. K. GALBRAITH
NATIONAL DEFENSE COMMISSION—FEDERAL RESERVE BLDG.

COMPLETE NATIONWIDE TESTING AND EDUCATIONAL PROGRAM CONTEMPLATES ABOUT 200,000 PILOT FARMS. AS A MINIMUM NUMBER THESE WILL REQUIRE AT LEAST 36,000 TONS ANNUALLY OF NH_3, OR 30,000 TONS NITROGEN. IT SHOULD BE UNDERSTOOD THAT PRESENT PRACTICES RESULTING IN PROGRESSIVE DEPLETION OF SOIL FERTILITY REQUIRE VAST ADJUSTMENTS IN FARM MANAGEMENTS THROUGHOUT NATION'S MAJOR SOIL AREAS. THESE ADJUSTMENTS NECESSITATE A COMPLETE REVERSAL IN THE PRACTICES AND METHODS OF USE OF NITROGEN ANALOGOUS TO THAT OF PHOSPHORUS. CONSEQUENTLY 36,000 TON FIGURE SHOULD BE REGARDED AS MOST CONSERVATIVE AND SUBJECT TO INCREASE UPON BASIS OF CONSULTATION IN DETAIL WITH FARM GROUPS AND TECHNICIANS ASSOCIATED WITH THE GRANT COLLEGES IN ALL PARTS OF THE COUNTRY WITH WHICH THE AUTHORITY COLLABORATES—

H. A. MORGAN,
CHAIRMAN OF THE BOARD"

(d) Either for defense or for agricultural purposes this small plant would be relatively more costly than a 150-ton plant. Mr. C. O.

Brown, Consulting Engineer of the Authority, informs me as a hurried estimate, that this plant would cost approximately $2,000,000 to design and construct rather than the $1,100,000 suggested by Mr. Dunn. The ammonia cost would be in excess of $50.00 a ton as compared with $42.29 for 150-ton capacity. I am informed that the same factors operate to increase cost per unit of capacity as the size is reduced as are apparent in reducing costs when the size of the plant is increased.

IX. Final Action

DAVIS COMPLETES HIS PREPARATIONS

During the same day, October 17, Davis also sent Stettinius the following chronological summary of the nitrate dispute:

On July 31 I arranged for a conference in his office with Dr. E. R. Weidlein. Dr. H. A. Morgan, Chairman of the Board, TVA, and Dr. Reid were also present. I was accompanied at the conference by Mr. Edward A. O'Neal, President, American Farm Bureau Federation, Mr. W. R. Ogg, Director of Research, American Farm Bureau Federation, Mr. Gordon R. Clapp, General Manager, TVA, Mr. Neil Bass, Chief Conservation Engineer, TVA, and Mr. Galbraith of my office.

I asked for this conference because reports had reached me that the Chemical Section of your Division was opposed to the Army recommendation for new ammonia plant facilities including a 150-ton synthetic ammonia plant at Wilson Dam (Muscle Shoals). Although the meeting lasted for some time we were unable to elicit any information whatever as to what the Army recommendations had been or what projects were under consideration in the Chemical Division. I asked Dr. Weidlein to keep my Division informed fully on this subject when he had anything concrete to discuss and he agreed to do so.

On August 8 I confirmed my request in writing to Dr. Weidlein, again asking that he "keep me very closely informed on plans and decisions relating in any way to the development of facilities in this area or to alternative facilities elsewhere." Dr. Weidlein replied under date of August 13 repeating the assurance that he would keep us informed, in the following words: "I wish to assure you that I will keep you informed of our program on synthetic ammonia."

During late August and early September Dr. Harry A. Curtis, Dean, College of Engineering, University of Missouri, who had been appointed by me to head our section on nitrate-phosphate supply tried in numerous meetings with Dr. Weidlein to find out what specific ammonia projects were under consideration but he was unable to secure any information whatsoever.

In the meantime, as you know, I had gone into the southwest for a two weeks' trip from which I returned on September 16. I learned by grapevine that the ammonia project for Morgantown was well advanced. I believe this is the first time I had ever heard of it. I immediately wrote Dr. Weidlein (September 18) referring to my memorandum of August 8 and his assurance, calling his attention to the report I had heard about the duPont plant at Morgantown and asking him for "any information on this proposed project which your Division has, including terms of the proposed contract and cost data, as well as the schedule of defense requirements upon which the proposed increase in facilities is based." Dr. Weidlein replied under the same date, sent me a brief memorandum stating that two proposed ammonia plants, one to be located in West Virginia, and the other in Kentucky, were to be ordnance owned and agent operated and adding "in view of the fact that this is a construction program, the details of the proposed contract, cost data, and other schedules come under Mr. E. F. Johnson of Mr. Knudsen's Division."

On the same date (September 18) I learned from Mr. Knudsen's weekly progress report that his Division had issued "letters of intent" to the duPont Company and to the Allied Chemical Company. These letters of intent, as you know, were authorizations to the Chief of Ordnance of the War Department to negotiate contracts with these companies.

I immediately reported the situation to the President who issued instructions to the Secretary of War to suspend all negotiations on these contracts pending consideration of the TVA location.

I am sending you this brief chronological summary in view of the discussion we had during the Commission meeting yesterday. Incidentally in view of Mr. Batt's evident misinformation as to the part Mr. Paul A. Porter took in ammonia discussions, I can advise you that Mr. Porter has never at any time participated in any meeting in which nitrogen or ammonia were discussed.

In another memorandum Davis suggested that Stettinius ask Gano Dunn these questions:

1. What is your estimate of the cost to the Government (including the interest cost of the money invested in new plant facilities but not interest on investment in existing plant) per ton of ammonia produced at the proposed 150-ton synthetic ammonia plant at Muscle Shoals?
2. What is your estimate of the price per ton of ammonia if it is purchased by the Government from outside plants for shipment to the TVA ammonium nitrate plant?
3. On the assumption that the 150-ton plant at TVA can start production in 14 to 15 months and reach full production within 2 months thereafter, what reason would you have the Commission give for rejecting the War Department's proposal?

The same day Stettinius replied to the first:

I thank you for your memorandum of October 17th giving a chronological summary of your relation to the Muscle Shoals matter which I am calling to the attention of Messrs. Dunn and Batt.

And to the second:

I have spoken to Gano Dunn on the telephone this afternoon and passed on to him the questions you raised in your memorandum of October 17th. He said it will take several days to get the data to answer the questions but that he will do it at the earliest possible moment.

FINAL BRIEFINGS

And also on the 17th Stettinius transmitted to the other Commissioners the following letter from Dunn:

I desire to supplement my letter of October 15 with reference to a point made by Mr. Davis in the discussion that followed the reading of my report to the Commission this morning. Mr. Davis made the comment, as nearly as I recall it, in respect to Finding No. 2 of my report, that the shipping of liquid ammonia in tank cars to Muscle Shoals to make up the difference between the 37½ daily tons provided by a new synthetic ammonia plant and the 150 tons required to operate at full capacity the ammonium nitrate part of the old cyanamid plant at Muscle Shoals would be expensive and tend to clog the railroads in time of the emergency.

I think Mr. Davis was under the impression that such tank car supply of ammonia was a make-shift. I would like to point out that instead of being a make-shift and exceptional for Muscle Shoals, it is the adopted plan of the Ordnance Department in its ammonia production.

In the Morgantown and Kentucky projects there are no facilities for making ammonium nitrate and all of the ammonia produced at those two plants will be shipped as liquid ammonia in tank cars to its various destinations. These destinations will be the powder plants where the ammonia will be consumed after it is converted into ammonium nitrate in ammonium nitrate plants right at the powder plants.

There are many reasons for this, one of which is as follows: If the ammonium nitrate plants were attached to the ammonia plants, as is the case at Muscle Shoals, twice the amount of transportation cost would be necessary, because ammonium nitrate weighs twice as much as the ammonia which produces it. One hundred and fifty tons of ammonia makes 300 tons of ammonium nitrate.

If the process of transforming the ammonia into ammonium nitrate is made at the ammonia plant instead of on the delivery of the ammonia at the powder plant, the cost of transportation is doubled.

Finding No. 4 in my letter recommends the rehabilitation of the ammonium nitrate plant at Muscle Shoals, but in the text of my letter doubt is expressed that even with rehabilitation its capacity can be satisfactorily restored.

Assuming however that it can be restored, there will be involved not only a large expense between $1,000,000 and $2,000,000 but it will be necessary to ship away from Muscle Shoals to the various shell loading plants 300 tons of ammonium nitrate for every 150 tons of ammonia that is produced at or transported to Muscle Shoals.

The wisdom of rehabilitating the ammonium nitrate plant at Muscle Shoals is not at all assured and the argument that its existence justifies a 150-ton synthetic ammonia plant there to supply it as distinguished from supplying it with tank car ammonia is unsound.

On October 18, the day that the Commission was scheduled to consider the War Department's nitrate program for final action, Galbraith commented on Dunn's latest letter in the following memorandum to Davis:

Gano Dunn's Report of October 16.

The following points need to be made on Gano Dunn's statement:

1. It was not implied that shipping ammonia was a make-shift. It is clear that it would be necessary to tank car ammonia to the Shoals with the 37 ton plant and this would be unnecessary with a 150 ton plant. The 37 ton plant would require tying up some 75 tank cars for transport of the ammonia.
2. Mr. Dunn seems to have some doubts now about the rehabilitation of the ammonium nitrate plant. The intentions of the Army on this are perfectly clear. In any case, this end of the plant costs some $40,000,000. A rehabilitation cost of one to two million dollars, considering that the plant was never used, in fact never quite completed, is not a very important item. The important matter is what it would cost to duplicate these facilities elsewhere.
3. Mr. Dunn speaks of shipping ammonia rather than ammonium nitrate direct to the powder plants. He is mixed up on his chemistry. The ammonium nitrate manufactured at the Shoals will not go to the powder plants but to the loading plants to be combined with TNT for the manufacture of Amatol.

Ammonium nitrate can be shipped in two forms: as 75 per cent solution and as crystals. It is cheaper to ship it in solution but in such form it is bulky. I would expect, without being too sure of my ground, that so long as there are lots of tank cars, the solution would go to the loading and assembling plants to be crystallized there. However, there are crystallizers at the Shoals and shortage of tank car capacity would lead to use of the crystallizers at the Shoals.

Davis occupied the morning hours before the NDAC meeting at 11:00 in talking with various members of the Advisory Commission about the action that the Commission could be expected to take on the Nitrate Program at that meeting. He first discussed the matter with Stettinius, who indicated that he would like to find a way to agree with Davis and approve the original Army proposal but did not see how he could without turning down his own NDAC group, as they were unanimous in support of Gano Dunn's report. Davis then passed this information on to Henderson who, like Davis, was anxious that the Nitrate Program be approved at this meeting. But Henderson had to leave the meeting early and would be unable to make his recommendations about the Program unless the nitrate matter was placed first on the agenda. Davis next talked to William H. McReynolds, who agreed to arrange this and assured Davis that the program could be passed by a 4-3 or 5-2 vote. Davis then spoke with Miss Elliott, who said that she was confused about the ammonia problem. Davis told her that the War Department was committed to use of the Muscle Shoals facilities but said that he was sure the Industrial Materials Division was bitterly determined to prevent any substantial project going on there and that he was equally sure Stettinius would not go back on what his own staff stood for. Shortly before the meeting was to begin, Davis spoke with Henderson again about his conversation with McReynolds and told Henderson that he hoped that Stettinius might be willing to let the Nitrate Program out of the Commission if it were certified that it had been passed by a 4-3 or 5-2 vote.

While Davis was preparing for the meeting in this way, Knudsen was being briefed quite differently. On October 18 his assistant, E. F. Johnson, wrote him in part as follows: "Review of the above letters [Dunn to Stettinius and Davis to Knudsen], it appears to me that a discussion of this sort can go on indefinitely with no prospect of a definite conclusion, possibly for weeks."

Johnson continued by noting the Army requirement of 500 tons per day, and recommended immediate approval of the plans for du Pont and Allied. He then continued:

Comparison of the pros and cons of Muscle Shoals with some other location is a most complicated problem and really requires thorough technical analysis to get the real answer. Since the Raw Materials and Agricultural Sections are not willing to accept findings or point of view of the other, my suggestion is that some reliable and well equipped engineering outfit be engaged by the Commission to make a study of the situation with agreement before the fact that conclusions will be accepted as final. Concerns such as Stone & Webster; Ford, Bacon, and Davis, Day & Zimmerman, etc., are all equipped to handle a problem of this kind.

DECISION AND AFTERMATH

Finally the time came for decision. At 11:00 A.M. on Friday, October 18, the NDAC met in executive session, and during this meeting Davis penciled the following notes:

1. 3½ weeks—get it out of here.
2. No further comment on Gano Dunn memo unless specific questions.
3. Question raised yesterday as to real attitude of Army. Want 5 minutes to clear it up.
4. Finally, convinced no valid reason Commission can give public for rejection of Army proposal.

After 5 to 2 vote approving proposal of War Department's ammonia proposal, Knudsen moved, Stettinius seconding, that vote be made unanimous. Carried with no dissenting vote.

The following day, October 19, Davis sent the following letter to Knudsen:

Before you came into the meeting yesterday I presented certain quotations from official reports on file in the War Department to show that the War Department was on record as favoring the rehabilitation and use of the nitrate facilities at Muscle Shoals, including the modernization of the ammonium nitrate plant at 300-ton daily capacity, and the production of 150 tons per day of ammonia in connection with it. I call your attention to the fact that this position was taken by the War Department prior to September 23, the date on which the President wired the Secretary of War asking that negotiations for ammonia facilities elsewhere be suspended until consideration had been given to the Muscle Shoals project.

1. Quotation from memorandum "Resume of Muscle Shoals Situation" from Major Hofstetter to Colonel Booth, dated August 8, 1940: . . . .
2. Quotation from memorandum of September 9, 1940, from the Chief, Planning Section, Ammunition Division, to the Chief, Ammunition Division, Industrial Service, subject "The Ammonia Problem": . . . .
3. Quotation from memorandum for the Assistant Secretary of War from Major General C. M. Wesson, Chief of Ordnance, subject, "War Department Requirements for Ammonia, and Production at Muscle Shoals" dated September 21, 1940: . . . .

It is certainly not my wish to prolong discussion of the ammonia project, and I am sending this material to you solely because most of it was called to the attention of the other Commissioners before you joined the meeting yesterday.

On October 21, Edward A. O'Neal wrote Davis:

My dear Chester:

Mr. Ogg informed me confidentially over the telephone Saturday that you had finally put over the TVA program for the manufacture of nitrogen and it was unanimously agreed to by the Defense Commission. On behalf of the Farm Bureau people and the friends of agriculture, I want to thank you for your valiant fight. We all know from past experience how difficult it is to get for farmers the right to have their own governmental agencies to help them in their fundamental problems. For this you have our continued gratitude and thanks. I am firmly convinced that we never could have won without you. . . .

And on the 22nd Stettinius phoned Davis to ask if it would be embarrassing to have the minutes read 5 to 2 instead of the unanimous vote. Davis promptly agreed. However the vote was recorded, Davis had won his fight, and the TVA would get its new ammonia plant. Difficulties arose subsequently, but they were overcome and the policy was unshaken. The NDAC battle of words over approval of the War Department's plans for Muscle Shoals was now a matter of record, but on October 24 a parting shot was fired in Davis's direction by Knudsen when he wrote:

I feel that I owe you a reply to your letter of October 19 on the Muscle Shoals project, it being understood, of course, that in our discussions I have relied entirely on technical advice by people who are supposed to know about ammonia and the value of the different processes for the production thereof.

Quotations from the two memoranda of the War Department of August 8 and September 9 deal entirely with the present plant at Muscle Shoals—in other words, with the use of the old process which the memorandum of September 24 stamps as costing three times as much as the newer process. Consequently, the two first quotations are more or less worthless in the final instance.

The Ordnance Department in its memorandum of September 24 swings to the modern process, and I have no quarrel with that. The discussions of this project dealt not with the cost factor to any extent, but merely with the ability of the Muscle Shoals organization to produce ammonia in time by the new process, hence the suggestion by Mr. Dunn that a small installation be tried first. My main argument with your good self was your contention that regardless of the dispute regarding the ability of Muscle Shoals to handle a plant, the other two plants were to be held up until Muscle Shoals was settled, an argument which must be charged to expediency rather than to logic and to which I had to take exception.

X. Later History

Soon after the final action of NDAC on U. S. Nitrate Plant No. 2, the TVA completed its arrangements with the War Department and started on the arduous tasks involved in plant design and construction. The scheduled dates for completion of the two trains of the ammonia plant were November 15, 1941, and January 15, 1942, with full production to be reached about two months later in each instance. Actual dates of completion were August 8 and September 22, 1942, while full production in both was attained in October. In November 1942 average daily production reached 181 tons of ammonia, well above rated capacity. In its report of July 1, 1940, TVA had estimated construction cost of the ammonia plant at $4,353,000; actual cost was $7,669,000 (though the sale of salvaged equipment reduced this figure somewhat).

TVA officials attributed the construction delays exclusively to the delay in obtaining original approval and to inadequate priorities granted by the successive war production agencies, an opinion concurred in by Stone & Webster Engineering Corporation, contractors for the job. Part of the increase in construction costs was also attributed by TVA to the delays; but the bulk was caused by a somewhat larger rehabilitation program for the existing facilities than had originally been anticipated.

It was the view of TVA officials that these subsequent events demonstrated that their proposal should have been approved when it was submitted in July 1940.

The ammonium nitrate plant was ready by the time the ammonia plant was completed, but for an extended period it was operated below capacity. The need for ammonia was so acute that only part of TVA's own production was retained at Muscle Shoals for use in the nitrate plant.

It was the view of Dr. Weidlein, who retained his official connection with the chemical program throughout the war, that the later history proved the wisdom of his adverse advice to Mr. Stettinius on the TVA proposal.

THE SALE OF THE TANKERS

CONTENTS

PREFACE

This study tells how in 1947-48 the United States Government sold eighty-three government-owned ocean-going tankers to thirteen foreign nations. Such a transaction may seem simple and easy to accomplish. Actually, there were many difficulties, arising from a variety of elements in American political and administrative life, public and private. Accomplishment required action by the President himself, and his aides in the White House and in the Executive Office of the President; the problem was discussed at two cabinet meetings; it affected agencies as varied as the State Department, the Navy and the Joint Chiefs of Staff, the Maritime Commission, the Interior Department and the Department of Justice. It occupied a congressional investigating committee, and provided political advantage to Republicans in the Eightieth Congress. The CIO National Maritime Union actively opposed the sales, and the great American oil companies were embarrassed by them. Finally, and with more art perhaps than accuracy, the sales were linked with the fuel-oil shortage which afflicted New England and the Atlantic seaboard in the winter of 1947-48.

The following account reviews the attitudes and actions of the different individuals and administrative units concerned with the problem. But analysis of the past from the administrative standpoint, like other forms of history, is limited by the availability of information. Because of this uncontrollable factor, the roles of certain agencies are treated more fully than others. Hence finality of judgment on the actions of all the individual participants is hardly warranted; yet enough of the total process can be recaptured to make administrative conclusions feasible and questions inevitable.

The tanker sales can be understood only in the context of the contemporary European economic and political situation. During the spring and summer of 1947, the sales were an important symbol in our foreign policy, which was then at a juncture where the issues before it were far more clear than the policy itself. On June 30, while foreign nations waited for the tankers, the United Nations Relief and Rehabilitation Administration terminated its operations; the post-UNRRA relief program was merely a stop-gap, supported by other fiscal devices that together were admittedly inadequate to ensure European recovery. European nations, contemplating light harvests and a hard winter, wondered what the United States would do next. Although Secretary of State Marshall had made courageous promises at Harvard on European aid, these were promises only, and in the postwar devastation of Europe facts were more compelling than promises. The lag in the tanker sales was an unfortunate fact. Fifty tankers had been sold to foreign nations in 1946, but the actual transfers were not completed until a year later. Meanwhile the need for tankers grew, and the first of a new group of applications for tankers were filed by foreign nations in February 1947. All through the spring and summer not one tanker was sold in response to these new applications. Actually, it was not until eight months after the first 1947 applications were filed that the first tanker in the 1947 program was delivered abroad. The situation seemed to contradict Secretary Marshall's profession at Harvard that "any government that is willing to assist in the task of recovery will find full co-operation, I am sure, on the part of the United States Government." To the State Department particularly, the tanker delays seemed ridiculous in light of our developing foreign policy. For instance, we wished to keep the Communists out of power in Italy, and Italy had applied for tankers. Yet, while the affair dragged on, Italy obtained no tankers, and the

Communist leader, Togliatti, was sufficiently secure in position to threaten in a rally at Modena the uprising of "30,000 well-armed partisans." Soon there was a menacing, Communist-staged hunger march in Rome against the de Gasperi government.

The tankers could help Italy and other European nations by building up oil stocks which had been critically reduced by the war's destruction of transport facilities. In Italy receipt of the tankers would permit the de Gasperi government to reassure the populace against Communist forecasts of a winter of extreme suffering. There was also the grave dollar shortage. Governments like Italy depended heavily upon American bottoms to transport overseas supplies. This was costly in dollar credits and contributed measurably to the desperate fiscal situation of the summer of 1947. Italy devalued the lira; Britain stopped the free convertibility of sterling into dollars; and in September, the French Foreign Ministry predicted that the dollar resources of France would be exhausted within a month. Meanwhile the tanker decision, a potentially constructive gesture of the United States toward easing the dollar shortage, was entangled in lengthy interagency negotiations.

The delays afflicting the tanker sales were twofold in origin. Certain delaying factors existed within the Executive Branch and were shaped primarily by a lively concern for the national defense—whether wisely applied or not, the reader can judge. The purpose of the tanker sales was not opposed, nor was there substantial disagreement that some tankers could and should be sold subject to several limiting conditions. The disagreement was over the conflicting proposals put forward by various agencies.

The other source of objection to the sales lay in the Legislative Branch and was motivated by concern for national economic advantage and the interests of certain domestic groups, asserted within a highly political context. How sound this opposition was, the reader again can judge for himself. But here the objection to the sales was absolute; their potential value to our foreign policy was not expressly recognized.

The resulting events, which we are about to review, will stimulate puzzling and probably disturbing reflections. First is the circumstance, as the tanker sales illustrate, that many of our national policies must emerge as a synthesis of foreign and domestic policies. The machinery available to effect this synthesis in the tanker case was apparently incomplete in structure and haphazard in effectiveness. Even Presidential decisions that were supported by most or perhaps almost all the members of the Cabinet were long delayed or thwarted. Since the date of this episode, the creation of the National Security Council and other Executive Office agencies may have facilitated the securing of interdepartmental consensus and departmental observance of Presidential policy. Nevertheless, two basic questions still remain: does, or can, or should the Cabinet, as such, have an authoritative role, and how should a Cabinet officer reconcile his conscientious performance of a specific statutory responsibility—a significant factor in the tanker story—with his responsibility for following the instructions or wishes of his official superior, the President?

Further questions arise over the operation of the several departments and agencies, diverse in organizational nature and functional interest, which were concerned with the tanker sales. In conflict were the State Department and its responsibility for foreign policy, and the Navy Department and its responsibility for national defense. The State Department judged that Europe's plight made immediate transfer of the tankers imperative. The Navy judged that there should be definite restrictions on the size and character of the transfer. In between the two was the Maritime Commission, whose ability to act was affected by its own organizational structure. A contemplation of the conflict among these agencies and the resultant delays invites questions of various sorts.

There is, for example, the practical matter of just what part a military agency ought to have in making foreign policy. In the tanker dispute the Maritime Commission was forced by statute to consult the Navy before the tankers could be sold. The suitability of this arrangement must be judged, and the reader can decide whether something better can be devised. A host of questions can also be asked about the varied administrative devices designed to secure interagency agreement: *ad hoc* committees and working groups, and formal and informal contacts at various hierarchical levels. Involved in the effort to secure co-ordinated action were an officer specifically charged with interdepartmental liaison, a division charged with government-wide co-ordination of a functional purpose, and other officials whose departmental duties were both external and internal. Very little system governed the relations of these various persons, whose joint and harmonious action was required to effect the sale of the tankers.

To some extent, all this is a question of organizational machinery—already modified by the creation of new agencies—but perhaps more importantly it relates to the practical inability of the President, or of the Cabinet, or of any other agency, to impose policy on departments having independent statutory responsibilities. This inability in turn suggests questions about the wisdom of statutory clearance requirements, like the "consultation" requirement in this case where the "advice" of the Secretary of the Navy had to be secured before the tankers could be sold. Perhaps an acceptance of the kind of checks and balances that impeded action in the tanker case should depend on a prior judgment that the United States Government, even in the present perils of the world, can afford such haphazard progress of its interdepartmental machinery, or on the assumption that nothing better can be obtained within our general governmental structure and traditions. Others may feel that these impediments to action in themselves constitute an important safeguard and are desirable, regardless of their pragmatic consequences.

The tanker case also raises basic questions concerning the role of the independent regulatory commission. Responsibility for pivotal decisions involved in the tanker program rested in the U. S. Maritime Commission. Without action by the Commission the foreign policy of the President, supported by his Cabinet—to transfer tankers to foreign nations—could not be executed. The frustrations and effort entailed in getting the Maritime Commission to make the necessary decisions bring into focus the question of the proper role of an independent agency of this character, specifically whether the tanker affair is the kind of responsibility in which such an agency should have a more limited part or no part at all.

Finally, the tanker sales must be considered in their relation to a governmental system based upon the separation of powers. For the sales to foreign nations were substantially revised and almost stopped completely by the intervention of a congressional committee. This committee, believing that the sales violated a United States statute, requested that they be halted—notwithstanding an already established commitment in foreign policy, if not in law—pending the Attorney General's determination of the legality of the sales. All this suggests that certain inquiries be made concerning the ideal and the practical implementation of the doctrine of the separation of powers. Exactly what respective parts ought the Legislative and the Executive Branches play in the making of policy? Responses to this question in the tanker case, while governed partly by tradition, were also largely spontaneous and governed by the mere chance of personal preference. The consequent awkwardness may cast doubt upon existing arrangements and suggest the need for alternatives.

These and other significant questions, which will occur as the reader proceeds, underlie what appears to be a transaction of secondary importance. The sale of 100 tankers will hardly deserve even a footnote in the history of the cold war; but the events do happen to illuminate some of the most difficult problems in our national government.

I. Background

THE T-2 TANKERS

The Maritime Commission T2-SE-A1 Type Tankers, built during World War II, have proved to be very efficient bulk-oil carriers and are highly regarded in relative terms of speed and capacity for commercial use. They are 523 feet 6 inches in over-all length, have a molded breadth of 68 feet, and a molded depth (to the upper deck) of 39 feet 3 inches. The United States gross tonnage is 10,300 and the net tonnage 6,155. The deadweight (capacity for cargo, fuel oil, feed water and stores at 30′ 2″ summer loadline) is 16,600 tons, and the cargo oil tank volumetric-capacity "at 98 per cent full" is 138,335 barrels.

The tanker's propulsion is turbo-electric, with a single screw. Its speed is rated at 14½ knots. Wartime shortages of reduction-gearing suitable for direct turbine-drive propulsion dictated the exclusive use of turbo-electric propulsion in T2-SE-A1 Type Tankers. The electrical items of this propulsive power plant are not difficult to maintain, although its insulation deteriorates rapidly if not kept dry and clean, especially when the vessel is not in use.

Production of the tankers was concentrated in four companies, Sun, Alabama, Kaiser (Swan-Island), and Marin-Ship. Each company had its tanker propulsion-units built by other companies. Sun tankers, for instance, had propulsion-units built by Westinghouse, General Electric, or Elliott. Operating performance with ships produced by all the companies was highly satisfactory. Although various operators and government officials strongly prefer the output of particular companies, performance records show the number of tanker casualties to be slight and well distributed among all the company-builders. The basis for the preferential judgments has been said to be one of knowing the features built into the vessels by a particular shipyard for a particular contract group of vessels.

Like other ships, tankers are subject to substantial mechanical improvements, and they can become rather rapidly outmoded. In 1947 and 1948, the T2-SE-A1 Tanker was highly desirable because of its speed and capacity. By 1949, the post-World War II reduction-geared turbine propulsion high steam pressure/superheat super-tankers of over 15½ knots sea-speed came into substantial production and had a deadweight of 26 to 30,000 tons against the 16,600 tons of the T2-SE-A1 Type Tankers. These improvements were anticipated in 1947. Yet the T2-SE-A1 Type Tanker could validly promise a long and effective service-life even after the war. As a group, these tankers averaged four to five years in age. The usual service-life of a tanker ranges from thirteen to twenty years. Differences in age-expectancy depend principally upon the type of cargo carried and alternating periods of "clean" and "dirty" cargo carriage. A "clean" cargo (gasoline) shortens tanker life, since it entails rapid corrosion, particularly in the hull structure, the place of the most extensive deterioration. A "dirty" cargo (crude oil) is far less destructive of tanker life, since it is less corrosive and requires less tank-cleaning between cargoes.

The 481 war-built T2-SE-A1s, together with 19 T3-S-A1 (Turbine Reduction Gear Propulsion) Type Tankers, and several special T2 and T3 Type Tankers, comprised the most desirable part of the large tanker fleet which the Maritime Commission possessed or controlled at the end of World War II. Other T1-M (Diesel Single Screw) Tanker Types were smaller and slower. The T2-SE-A2 or "Mission Type" Tanker was designed and built for the Navy during the war. These tankers, being considerably faster than the T2-SE-A1, were retained for Navy use.

By March 8, 1946, when the Ship Sales Act (discussed below) was approved, 55 of the Maritime Commission's 481 T2-SE-A1 design tankers were owned by U. S. private citizens, 17 had been lost or scrapped, the Navy had converted 10 to Fleet Oilers, 11 were on Lend

Lease (including 4 to Russia), and 4 were in the Maritime Commission's laid-up fleet. The balance of 384 were operated for the Maritime Commission under General Agency Agreement. (Under General Agency, the Commission reimburses the agent for all expenses incurred, including repairs, insurance, and crews' wages, and in addition pays the agent a fixed fee per day, depending upon the ship's operation.) These tankers under General Agency were allocated on a voyage basis to the Navy, to U. S. industry and to foreign nationals as necessity required. With the exception of the Navy's 10 Fleet Oilers, which were subsequently turned over to the Maritime Commission for disposal and then taken back in early 1948, there were thus 399 T2-SE-A1 Tankers owned by the U. S. Government and available for sale in March 1946. During the course of the year a number of tankers were sold, and a good many were withdrawn from the active fleet and laid up. By April of 1947, when the Maritime Commission first consulted with the Navy with respect to the sale to foreign countries of the T2s involved in this story, the 399 tankers were in the following status:

Sold to U. S. citizens	45
Sold to non-citizens	25
Lend Lease to Russia	4 *
Maritime Commission-owned, operating under GAA	205
Maritime Commission Laid-Up Fleet	120
	399

* Returned to U. S. April-July 1948.

Thus, deducting those that had been sold, there were 329 tankers theoretically available for sale, but 25 of these had been promised to non-citizens, and 4 were not yet returned to U. S. control.

During May 1947 the Maritime Commission withdrew about 50 T2s from its laid-up fleet to recondition them for operation or for sale. This left 46 T2-SE-A1 Type saleable tankers in the laid-up fleet; the remaining 25 or 30 laid-up tankers were in bad condition. These 46 tankers will become the center of intense dispute in this study, and a word might be said about their condition. All of them needed some repairs, often major repairs because of war damage both from enemy action and poor maintenance by the crews. Those in the worst condition had their hulls skinned or their bottoms so badly broken that they were practically floating on the tank tops. Very little care was given to these ships by the Maritime Commission after the war, when about a dozen lay-up areas were hastily established to receive them. For the fiscal year 1947-48, Maritime had no appropriations to recondition tankers in lay-up for active service. What funds were available were limited to repairs to maintain the ships at least in the condition in which they were received into lay-up. Even in execution of this formula, Maritime's performance was sketchy. It considered itself grossly undermanned because of a 60 per cent cut in personnel in the postwar transition from the War Shipping Administration to the Maritime Commission, and, with limited manpower and funds, Maritime gave preference to the repair and maintenance of ships under General Agency operation, which required between-voyage repairs.

PETROLEUM SUPPLY AND DEMAND IN 1947

Tankers, as vehicles which transport petroleum, partake of certain characteristics of that commodity. Petroleum can be understood only in international terms. It is fluid not only physically but also in its economic influence. The efficiency and ease with which it can be transported enable it to respond to demand throughout the world. Large-diameter pipelines and large-capacity tankers make petroleum obtainable with nearly equal facility from tidewater in the three principal supply areas of the world, the United States Gulf Coast, the Caribbean, and the Persian Gulf. Only artificial and imposed limitations mar petroleum's almost perfect mobility. With the United States, these limitations are twofold. One is statutory: Congress has prohibited foreign-flag vessels, including tankers, from engaging in U. S. coast-wise trade. The other, and the cause of the first, is economic—U. S. labor costs (and possibly other factors as well) make tanker operations under the U. S. flag more costly than under any other flag. U. S. flag tankers are therefore at a continual competitive disadvantage in the international market and do not operate freely in that market. In normal times, U. S.-owned tankers tend not to operate outside the sheltered coastal trade except for those that are placed under Panamanian registry—a curious half-way status that is ambiguously U. S. or foreign in character.

In 1947, the year of the tanker story, petroleum was in short supply throughout the world. More oil was used in the United States than the entire world had consumed in 1938. U. S. per capita consumption had grown 63 per cent in ten years. Equipment for consuming petroleum products had increased faster than equipment for producing them. Oil burners, automobiles, and even diesel locomotives can be, and were, created more rapidly than oil wells, pipelines, refineries, and tankers. The phenomenal rise in the use of petroleum-consuming devices helps explain the turning-point year of 1946, when for the first time in history, oil and natural gas supplied the United States with more energy than coal.

Throughout 1946 the U. S. demands were met, but the effective reserve was scanty. The demand in 1947 was even greater. Shipments of residential oil heating units to dealers were 2⅓ times the number shipped in 1946. Diesel oil purchased by railroads was 42 per cent greater, and consumption of fuel oil by electrical utility companies in 1947 was up 24.7 per cent from 1946. All this was part of a pattern created by a record peacetime industrial activity and a record consumer demand.

The ability of U. S. supply to meet the petroleum boom was not anticipated accurately. With few exceptions the American oil industry, including the "giant" companies, did not expect in the spring of 1947 that there would be a domestic shortage in the coming winter. There was much on which to base their optimism. The industry had increased its domestic production of crude oil and associated liquids—natural gasoline and condensate from natural gas—from 5,001,800 barrels per day in 1945 to an average of 5,425,500 barrels per day in 1947, an increase of nearly 13 per cent. Yet the petroleum industry had failed to give sufficient weight to the factor that made even this increase over a supply that was adequate in the war inadequate for a peace-time year. What had happened was that while, during the war, a tremendous military demand was cared for by rationed cuts in civilian consumption, after the war the civilian consumption had risen to the equivalent of military use in war. In 1947 there was no rationing, supply had not kept pace with demand, and a shortage occurred. Apart from a few members of the industry, only the Navy Department and the Oil and Gas Division of the Interior Department foresaw the shortage which actually was only a very slight gap between demand and supply. Yet this gap was sufficient to cause considerable hardship to industry and to the thousands of space-heater users in New England and along the Atlantic Coast. Space-heater families depend upon the corner grocery store for their kerosene, a source which can operate successfully only if supply is fully in balance with demand.

Yet what shortage there was in the United States was minor, if not infinitesimal, compared with the scarcity in Europe in 1947. Testifying before the House Merchant Marine and Fisheries Committee in June 1947, William L. Clayton, Under Secretary of State for Economic Affairs, said that "an inadequate fuel supply is delaying European recovery more than any other single factor." Among all the fuels, the situation of petroleum was unique. There was a rapidly growing dependence upon its use. The grave and seemingly hopeless shortage of coal had led to an extensive movement from coal-use to petroleum-use, but there was no prospect that petroleum supply could rise to meet the new demand. In Britain, for instance, inland petroleum consumption was predicted for the first half of 1947 to be more than three times what it was in the same period of 1946. Yet against the increased demand, fuel oil stocks were decreasing from 5.7 million tons on January 1 to a predicted 4.3 million tons by mid-May. The outlook everywhere in Europe was one of drastically reduced industrial activity because of the lack of fuel.

The crux of the difficulty, however, was not that oil itself was unavailable, but that the number of tankers to transport it was completely inadequate. For Britain and Western Europe depend heavily upon outside sources of petroleum supply, up to ninety per cent, and draw from all the principal sources. In 1946, such dependence was as follows: United States 20.8 per cent, Caribbean 42.7 per cent, and the Middle East 14.8 per cent. The preponderance of withdrawals from the Western Hemisphere is largely explained by the shortage of tankers in Europe. Wartime depletions, marine losses, and the slow resumption of shipbuilding held down the capacity of tankers under foreign flag to 88 per cent of prewar. Military needs, relief requirements, and other factors had raised the shipping requirements 29 per cent higher than prewar. Altogether, it was estimated that the shortage of foreign-flag tankers was equivalent to something over 200 ships of the T-2 type (now and hereafter, unless otherwise noted, T-2 refers only to the T2-SE-A1 Tanker).

Since the run from Western Europe (except for Marseilles and points east) to the Western Hemisphere is far shorter than that to the Persian Gulf (the major center of Middle East oil), the British and others were forced by the shortage of tankers to send the bulk of their fleets to the Western Hemisphere. The choice was made despite two painful and visible consequences. First, the use of Western Hemisphere supply entailed extensive dollar commitments. In 1947 the dollar shortages of the European nations became particularly serious and led to severe fiscal measures. Second was the tantalizing sight of the neglected petroleum supply in the Middle East which was both plentiful and in some respects advantageous from the standpoint of dollars. For although Middle East sales are normally made in dollars, when the United Kingdom deals with a U. K. company, to a large extent the dollars immediately return; the French also get a portion of their dollars back, although the other purchasing European nations do not. Yet with tankers in short supply, the Middle Eastern oil was, for the most part, beyond reach. In fact, so scarce were transport facilities, that early in 1947, oil was being recycled, i.e., pumped back into the ground, and refinery production was cut back at Abadan and other Middle Eastern centers for lack of tankers to lift the oil. In the meantime, extraction of Western Hemisphere oil was rapidly reaching capacity. Thus the Europeans were paying out many dollars for less oil than they needed, while the oil of the Middle East, dollar-advantageous to the U. K. and France, was not being used.

The sight of surplus T-2 Tankers in the United States, and the urgent petroleum shortage provoked an immediate and insistent interest among the European nations for the purchase of tankers. For with these tankers they could get oil where it was most plentiful —the Middle East—and with a smaller expenditure of dollars—a matter of increasing importance.

THE MERCHANT SHIP SALES ACT OF 1946

The T-2 Tankers were a part of our tremendous postwar merchant marine which included 45 per cent of the total world tonnage of ocean-going ships, all owned by the United States Government. The Maritime Commission was responsible for the ships and also for formulating a program looking toward the development of a competitive U. S. merchant marine as a leading factor in the U. S. economy and an essential element of national defense.

Of the several statutes that affected this program, the most important was the Merchant Ship Sales Act of 1946 which established policies and procedures for the sale of much of the postwar fleet to private purchasers. The Act applied to more than 4,000 large vessels under control of the Commission, of which the T-2 Tankers were a part. Of all these vessels, up to September 30, 1947, a total of 1,555 had been sold under the Ship Sales Act—481 to United States operators, and 1,074 to governments and citizens of thirty other nations.

The sale of the T-2 Tankers to foreign nations took place under the terms of the Ship Sales Act and as part of the extensive flow of transactions under the Act. Certain provisions of the Act, reproduced in Appendix III, were crucial in the tanker sales, and require consideration here. The Act permitted sales of tankers both to U. S. citizens and non-citizens. The requirements of eligibility for each class differed in certain respects. As between eligibles of the two classes, however, the Act gave preference to U. S. citizens. Other provisions of the Act governing sales to non-citizens specified the price base, terms of payment, and repair allowances, and established the requirement of several findings by the Maritime Commission before such sales could occur.

These were:

(1) "after consultation with the Secretary of the Navy," that the tankers were not necessary "to the defense of the United States."

(2) that "for a reasonable period of time" the tankers have been available for sale to U. S. citizens, and that "no responsible offer" has been made by a U. S. citizen to purchase the vessels.

(3) "that such vessel is not necessary to the promotion and maintenance of an American merchant marine."

These determinations will play a prominent part in the tanker story.

II. Interagency Negotiations

THE OFFICE OF TRANSPORT AND COMMUNICATIONS AFFAIRS, DEPARTMENT OF STATE

On April 4, 1947, Sir John Magowen, Minister for Economic Affairs at the British Embassy in Washington, formally advised the Under Secretary of State for Economic Affairs of Britain's grave outlook on tankers and fuel oil. The picture of sharply dwindling oil stocks, reduced industrial activity, a winter of great hardship, and the plentiful petroleum supply of the Middle East put beyond reach by the shortage of tankers, was already familiar to the State Department. Sir John's report only underscored the problem.

The severities confronting Britain were duplicated in other nations of Europe, and either by representation to the State Department or to the Maritime Commission, where they were accustomed to negotiate tanker allocation arrangements, these nations repeated in their own behalf, an account of mounting shortages in oil and tankers. France, Norway, Sweden, and Italy were among the nations which took this course.

The officer of the State Department immediately concerned with the matter of tankers was Walter Radius, Director of the Office of Transport and Communications, known as TRC in State Department shorthand. Radius was an economist (Ph.D., Stanford University), thirty-seven years old, who had entered the State Department as a divisional assistant in 1942 after some business and research experience. (See Appendix I—Biographies.) In 1944 he was Special Assistant to the Director of TRC; in 1946 and until March 1947, he was Deputy Director, and thereafter Director. TRC "initiates and co-ordinates" State Department policy for transport and communications. It has three divisions: Shipping, Aviation, and Telecommunications. (See Appendix II—Organizations.) A departmental order empowers TRC and its units to negotiate on these subject matters with other U. S. agencies and with foreign governments and private enterprises.

Radius was entirely in sympathy with the Western European nations. He appreciated their shipping difficulties; he agreed with them that the tanker and petroleum problem was a world problem; he was convinced that the sale to foreign nations of United States tankers available under the Ship Sales Act of 1946 was a desirable step. Yet Radius, however sympathetic, had been unable to secure effective action. For nearly three months prior to Sir John Magowen's visit to the Under Secretary of State in April, Britain and other European nations had been prodding, with little avail, the Office of Transport and Communications to initiate action for further foreign sales of tankers under the Ship Sales Act. On February 6, 1947, the Shipping Attaché of the British Embassy had outlined to the Shipping

Division of the State Department the acute needs of the British for more tankers. In the weeks following, other European nations made similar representations to the Office of Transport and Communications. But the efforts of Radius and his colleagues had resulted in little more than forwarding the foreign requests to the Maritime Commission with expressions of hope for their approval. As late as April 2, Radius supported a French application for the purchase of tankers merely by writing an approving letter to the Maritime Commission on behalf of the Department. Radius felt himself limited to these efforts because the Ship Sales Act vested responsibility for action in the Maritime Commission, and the legislative history of the Act revealed that there was no legal basis on which the State Department might insist on a consultative role on the sale of tankers.

Sir John Magowen's visit to the State Department on April 4 was a calculated attempt to have the Department act more vigorously for foreign tanker sales. The British took the matter to the Under Secretary for Economic Affairs, who was entirely sympathetic and who informed Radius, as the British hoped, both about the scheduling of the meeting a few days before it had actually occurred, and its results.

There was advantage for Radius in the Magowen visit. Having the matter brought directly to the attention of the Under Secretary for Economic Affairs, would better enable Radius to interest the top-level officials of his Department in the tanker sales. The interest of the British government in the matter carried weight that could not fail to impress these officials and make them more readily responsive to Radius' suggestions.

Still other circumstances encouraged action. The one insuperable potential obstacle under the Ship Sales Act, applications by U. S. citizens for the surplus tankers, did not exist. As of March 31, 1947, only twelve such applications were on file in the Maritime Commission. Nor did it seem likely that citizen applications would rise. The major American oil companies, the most likely source of applications, had recently and emphatically endorsed the idea of foreign sales. Captain Bushrod B. Howard of the Standard Oil Company of New Jersey had presented to Radius a memorandum to that effect. Howard, like others in the industry, believed the sales would improve the prospective U. S. competitive position in tankers, internationally, in 1950. For the general aim of the U. S. oil industry was not to overload with old tankers—the wartime tankers—while European nations filled their fleets, depleted by the war, with tankers of more modern construction. Consequently, the giants of the U. S. oil industry—Standard Oil of New Jersey, Texas, Gulf—believed that foreign sales of U. S. tankers might desirably curtail the growing construction programs of Europe. A further, and possibly the major consideration was the desire of U. S. oil companies, whose foreign subsidiaries would actually purchase some of the tankers which might be offered for foreign sale, to encourage cheaper transportation costs for petroleum which would leave more dollars available for buying U. S. oil. (Foreign tanker operating costs are low and are paid largely in local currency.) In his memorandum, Howard justified the industry's position as beneficial for national defense and the welfare of the U. S. Merchant Marine. He recalled that after World War I, U. S. industry had acquired substantially all surplus government tankers with the result, harmful to national defense and the competitive position of the merchant marine, that the building of tankers was practically at a standstill until about 1936.

The further circumstance favorable to foreign sales was the consensus of agreement on their desirability among all of Radius' superiors and associates in the State Department. The attitude of the Petroleum Division and its chief, John Loftus, squared with Radius' and Loftus supplied helpful explanatory data which confirmed Radius' understanding of the world petroleum situation. The geographic offices of the Department, responsible for relations with the European and Latin American countries which had applied for tankers, submitted advice and supporting facts. The Assistant Secretary of State for Economic Affairs, Willard Thorp, a professional economist and Radius' temporary superior (Assistant Secretary Garrison Norton, Radius' regular superior, was attending the international aviation conference) was wholly in favor of the sales, as was the Under Secretary for Economic Affairs, Will Clayton. The Secretary himself, General Marshall was, or soon became, a strong supporter of the proposal.

NEGOTIATIONS OF THE STATE DEPARTMENT WITH THE MARITIME COMMISSION

With the way clear in the Department, and with the express approval of the major U. S. oil companies, Radius was now ready to begin negotiations with other government agencies to accomplish the transfer of tankers to foreign nations. In view of the terms of the Ship Sales Act, the Maritime Commission was the point of first approach. The Commission was empowered to authorize and administer the transfer of the ships. The matter was clearly delicate. First, there was the legislative history of the Ship Sales Act, and this decidedly was not helpful to the State Department. The legislation, as originally drafted, required the Maritime Commission to consult the Department on foreign sales of tankers. But subsequently this provision was stricken from the bill, a rather pointed indication of the Department's status—or lack of status—in this field. During 1946, amid the difficulties of the sale program under the Act, it had become clear that a considerable portion of the staff of the Maritime Commission was basically hostile to any sales whatsoever to foreign nationals. Potentially competitive types of vessels, such as tankers, particularly aroused their concern. Thus the State Department had to proceed with caution, for Maritime might easily recoil against any suspected "pressure."

In view of the foregoing, the method of approach to the Maritime Commission might be significant; as a matter of fact, the "best" method was not far to seek.

The Under Secretary for Economic Affairs, Will Clayton, now the most active exponent of the sales, was admirably suited for the task. Of the Department's ranking officers, he was the one most cordially received in the Maritime Commission. Conspicuous success in business (including the export trade) in private life and his general air of realism were qualities appealing to the personnel of Maritime who possessed what they deemed a true brand of hard-headed Americanism. Clayton was a welcome relief from Maritime's conception of the State Department official—the theoretically inclined, the falsely accented, the do-gooder for the world. Commission officers had little patience for that type. It was hoped that Clayton could overcome the Commission's general a priori reluctance about foreign sales; the Commission's prestige at this time was not great and it seemed unlikely that it would oppose Clayton, who was widely known and respected.

Thus Clayton opened the way. He had regular monthly meetings with the whole Maritime Commission, and he introduced the tanker proposal at one of these meetings. He preferred this course to use of another means, the Interdepartmental Shipping Co-ordinating Committee, of which he was chairman and on which the Maritime Commission was represented. Clayton considered the committee ineffective; it met infrequently (only six times in 1947) and did little. In any event, the Committee could not sell ships; the Commission could.

Radius and the Petroleum Division briefed Clayton thoroughly on the world-wide oil and tanker situation, and on April 3, he outlined to the Maritime Commission the need for further sales of tankers, beyond the program of fifty ships, authorized in 1946 and now in execution. Clayton urged the Commission to pursue the course set by the Ship Sales Act and consult the Navy on the national defense aspect of further transfers. He said also that State, to assist, would discuss the proposal directly with Navy. It is interesting to note that Clayton's meeting occurred the day before the call of the British minister.

This order of events was not surprising. For several months past, British applicants and their attorneys had also been busy at the Maritime Commission. During a snag which had arisen in March 1947 over the tankers sold to foreign nations in 1946, the attorney for one British company had conferred extensively with two Maritime Commissioners and convinced them that sale of U. S. tankers to Britain was desirable from a national defense standpoint. Nothing would be lost by selling to the British now, since in time of war they would require tankers for their important oil reserves in the Middle East.

Clayton's effort at Maritime was immediately fruitful. Four days later, on April 7, the Commission Chairman wrote the Secretary of the Navy that "in view of the heavy foreign demand and the admittedly critical petroleum situation, the Commission would appreciate receiving your comments as to the advisability from a national defense point of view of the sale of additional fast tankers to foreign interests." The Commission, to support its request, observed that foreign demand for tankers had increased from sixty-six applications on March 1, to eighty-four on April 7, and, if tankers were made available, the demand would rise still more.

THE STATE DEPARTMENT APPROACHES THE NAVY DEPARTMENT

Maritime having acted, the attention of Radius (made more hopeful by the support of Clayton and the British) shifted to Navy. There his expectations were those of a defeatist. Above all, there was the legislative history of the consultation provision of the Ship Sales Act which indicated that Navy did not regard its own assigned responsibility as a mere formality.

While in the drafting stage and under review in the House Merchant Marine and Fisheries Committee, the provision had been referred, along with the rest of the bill, to the Navy for report. The Acting Secretary of the Navy had asked in reply that the consultation provision be revised "to make the determination of the Secretary of the Navy as to those matters binding and final upon the Maritime Commission." The Acting Secretary argued that it was traditional for the Navy to review conclusively the national defense aspects of the merchant marine. (For example, the Merchant Marine Act of 1936 requires the Maritime Commission to submit for Navy's approval the plans and specifications of all vessels to be constructed.) Only ultimate authority, Navy also claimed, was commensurate with the magnitude of its interest in the merchant marine. Such interest it defined as one which required a merchant marine adequate (1) to afford logistic support of the fleet and bases in peace "and limited military activity," and (2) to afford "the largest possible active American merchant marine" which would provide a convincing display of our power and "otherwise serve as an instrument of national security in peace."

The Navy's request for absolute authority was unsuccessful. Legislative compromises gave the Secretary of the Navy only an advisory capacity in the final statute. How significant the distinction proved in practice can be judged by the events described below. The reader will realize that the advice of a popular and strategically placed agency (like Navy) dealing with a subject within its general competence and of national and congressional concern (like national defense) cannot be disregarded lightly, even by a politically powerful agency (which the Maritime Commission was not). The following pages may help to define how far this generalization holds. Certainly it underlay congressional use of the device.

The Navy regarded the matter as serious and, confident of the correctness and importance of its judgment in these affairs, adopted an attitude which promised to distinguish very little between "advisory" and "final" authority. In a letter to Congressman Carl Vinson, Chairman of the House Committee on Naval Affairs, March 20, 1945, Secretary of the Navy Forrestal forecast his Department's mood and approach in the actual operation of the Ship Sales Act.

"The Navy Department," wrote Mr. Forrestal, "appreciates and shares your concern that no action will be taken which will jeopardize the ready availability of a tanker fleet adequate for all eventualities. The size of such tanker fleet, both active and in reserve, cannot be determined at this time. The Navy Department is not in a position to comment independently as to our international policy and, therefore, makes no comments as to the advisability of disposal of tankers to foreign operators when such tankers may be determined at a future date to be surplus to our over-all needs." The reader will note that Mr. Forrestal regarded the retention of a certain number of tankers as deserving an absolute priority over any and all requirements of our foreign policy.

These items of legislative history were discouraging to Radius and the State Department, as was the experience gained under operation of the Ship Sales Act. In 1946, the Navy had approved the sale of fifty tankers to foreign nations, all of which had now been allocated and sold, and were in process of delivery. Navy approval had been based upon an affirmative report of the Joint Chiefs of Staff, but it was this report which provided present discomfort to the State Department. For there the Joint Chiefs had specified the minimum tonnage and the most desirable types of ships to be retained under effective U. S. control for national defense. In this respect, the report constituted a relevant and formal statement of policy and a possible though not an absolute bar to further substantial sales of tankers to foreign nations, for the Joint Chiefs would almost inevitably oppose additional foreign sales if the number sold reduced total American tanker holdings below the established number. Or, more precisely, the Joint Chiefs would probably set the maximum number available for foreign sale by deducting requirements from holdings.

Anticipation of Navy "stickiness" toward new proposals of foreign sales determined Radius' selections among the means of approach to the Department. On the whole, he abstained from informal measures to pave a way of understanding and good will preceding Navy's official action. He feared that Navy officials would resent telephone calls and informal meetings as undue interference with their statutory prerogatives and responsibility. Perhaps the only occasion where the tanker problem was discussed informally with Navy officials was at a conference in March which Radius attended. Tankers happened to come up for discussion among a number of other topics, but nothing eventful occurred. Only the staff of the Maritime Commission had the rapport with the Navy necessary for informal approaches, since the shipping requirements of national defense had often compelled the staffs of the two agencies to work jointly.

Under these circumstances, Radius chose a course of action based upon the beliefs that the primary responsibility for sale of tankers lay between Maritime and Navy, and that relations between the two agencies were substantially closer than those between State and Navy. Why not have Maritime handle the main negotiations with Navy and let State assist wherever it could? Upon this basis, Radius drafted a brief two-paragraph letter for signature of the Acting Secretary of State (Acheson), which was dispatched April 9 to the Secretary of the Navy. This letter referred to the request Maritime had directed to Navy two days earlier, and expressed the "considerable concern" of State "both from the point of view of the critical petroleum transportation situation as well as foreign policy" that additional tankers be transferred to foreign interests.

The letter also contained a suggestion designed to limit the area of Navy's possible opposition to the tanker proposal. It expressly noted that "the [Maritime] Commission in its discretion may follow a system of selectivity in approving sales to foreign applicants which would be to the best interest of the United States." Behind this expression was State's belief that Navy, if it approved further sales of tankers at all, might do so only for Britain which alone of the applicant nations controlled great sources of petroleum supply, and which, in event of war, was regarded as our most certain ally. The Navy might oppose sales to other European nations in the belief that they lay open to easy invasion by a hostile power and that the transfer of tankers to them might really be a transfer to their potential invader. Thus, rather than have the Navy assume forthwith the right to select the eligible nations, and thus restrict the sale of tankers, State emphasized the discretionary authority of Maritime where its own convictions might more readily prevail.

Maritime had already signified its agreement with this interpretation. The Commission's letter to Navy made the same point: "It is understood that the Commission can, in its discretion, follow a system of selectivity to the best interests of the United States in approving sales to foreign applicants."

ACTION WITHIN THE NAVY DEPARTMENT AND THE JOINT CHIEFS OF STAFF

The Acheson letter was routed through the Navy hierarchy to Rear Admiral William McCombe Callaghan, Assistant Chief of Naval Operations (Transportation) and to Captain W. N. Mansfield, Chief of the Merchant Vessel Section and responsible to Callaghan. (See Appendixes I and II.) Both Callaghan and Mansfield had had several decades of experience in the Navy beginning with graduation from Annapolis and including extensive service in the fleet. Mansfield had also had a period of private business experience in the Atlantic coastal trade. Callaghan was of a famous Navy family. A brother, Admiral Daniel J. Callaghan, had been killed in the Battle of Savo Island.

The tanker proposal now passed into the channels of the Navy Department. Mansfield drafted a memorandum, dated April 17, for the Secretary of the Navy addressed to the Chief of Naval Operations, Nimitz, asking that the tanker problem be referred to the Joint Chiefs of Staff for study, comment and recommendation, as a matter of urgency. Nimitz acted accordingly, and on April 22, the Joint Chiefs of Staff committed the tanker question, for report and recommendation, to its appropriate sub-committee—the Joint Chiefs ordinarily work through various "task committees," in this instance the Joint Military Transportation Committee (JMTC). Callaghan was the senior Navy member of this committee.

Referral of the tanker question to the Joint Chiefs was probably no more than routine. On this occasion it seemed obviously correct since the Joint Chiefs had previously considered the foreign sale of tankers and had adopted a policy approved by the two defense Secretaries. But however automatic was the reference, its consequences were important and, in a sense, predictable. If dissatisfaction with the Secretary's tanker policy developed, he could shield himself and it with the quasi-anonymous and irreproachable prestige of the Joint Chiefs to whom he, as merely one Secretary, could not give orders. Whereas if the policy were based merely on advice from an admiral, even one whose competence and judgment were highly regarded, the Secretary could not say that the policy was irreversible on his own motion. As for Callaghan, his membership on JMTC ensured his active and influential participation in formulating the policy.

The JMTC report was a compromise between conflicting views within Navy (Army remaining neutral), some friendly to further, but closely limited, sales of tankers to foreign nations, and others flatly opposed. The former recognized the world-wide nature of the oil transportation shortage and the need of immediate steps to improve the lot of our presumptive allies. There was also concern, in the national defense sense, with the drain Europe imposed upon Western Hemisphere oil, and the sale of tankers was a welcome means to deflect European hauls to the Middle East. Finally, in Britain, Norway, and Sweden, tanker sales might forestall new construction programs which might render the U. S. tanker fleet obsolete in a few years.

This background of approval influenced the JMTC report and its recommendation that additional foreign sales be authorized. But it failed to deter the attachment by others, less favorably disposed, of important strings to the recommendation.

To a great degree, these limitations reflected the extremely bad relations existing between the U. S. and Russia in 1947. The acrimony which had arisen in 1946 grew steadily worse in 1947. In fact, throughout the period of Navy's concern with the tanker sales, there was a persistent widespread war scare. In such an environment, and assuming, as Navy apparently did, the correctness of the intelligence reports on which the war scare was based, Navy had the paramount and indisputable duty of considering all matters of policy in terms of the immediate possibility of war. For it to have done otherwise would have been an incredible dereliction of duty. Thus the tankers were viewed according to the logistics of a possible immediate war, and probably more than any other factor this consideration determined the position of JCS and Navy on foreign sales.

Of the conditions suggested for limiting the

sales, the most important was that they be restricted to tankers in the laid-up fleet. It was felt that sales of U. S. tankers in present operation would not improve the world-wide tanker position. No additional tankers would be brought into service—the only real solution for the world petroleum shortage. The tankers already in use would merely be re-shuffled, with a possible weakening of the U. S. tanker fleet and U. S. petroleum supply. Operating tankers also were our best tankers and their sale to foreign purchasers would remove them from effective U. S. military control.

A second condition restricted the sale of tankers to nations (or nationals thereof) which satisfied several vague criteria suggested by the Joint Chiefs of Staff. The reservation apparently originated, as the State Department had expected, from fear that U. S. tankers might be distributed to countries easily susceptible to occupation by Russia. In event of war, the U. S. might find itself short of tankers and opposed by a foe strengthened by capture of the very tankers we had sold.

A final condition limited the possible new sales of tankers to thirty-five in number. This figure was founded upon a canvass of the world oil and tanker problem and the conclusion that sale of 35 tankers would bring the world deficit into balance and, at the same time, would not jeopardize the national defense which was best served by keeping the utmost number of tankers under U. S. control. But the figure, as it happened, also coincided fairly closely with the number of U. K. applications for tankers. As has been pointed out, U. K. alone had substantial oil supplies in the Middle East, and was looked on by Navy as our one solid ally in case of war.

On May 7 JMTC submitted its report and recommendations to the Joint Chiefs of Staff who advised the Secretary of the Navy accordingly on May 16. No formal communication of these recommendations was made to the Maritime Commission or the State Department at this time. In fact, it was not until May 26 that the Secretary of the Navy informed Maritime of the recommendations. Almost from the moment that JMTC had reached its conclusions, however, Maritime and State had known of them through contacts between officials of those agencies at the working level.

THE PROBLEM BEFORE THE STATE DEPARTMENT

Word of JCS recommendations was keenly disappointing to Radius and his colleagues. JCS, in their interpretation, was placing a few drops in the world's petroleum bucket, far too few for what the State Department considered a grave and extensive need. On the day that the Joint Military Transportation Committee reported, there were on file with the Maritime Commission 106 applications by governments and nationals of the United Kingdom, Panama, France, Norway, Sweden and Italy for T-2 Tankers. The 35 tankers approved by JCS fell painfully short of this demand. As if to stress the point, the British, French and Italian governments were currently complaining that the regular monthly allocations of tankers under General Agency were insufficient; their need for purchased tankers was therefore increased. The other JCS stipulations—the criteria for approving applications, and the restriction of sales to the laid-up fleet—seemed forbidding to the advocates of foreign sales. The selection of nations, or the determination of criteria for such selection, if not done by the Maritime Commission, was the function, Radius felt, of the diplomatic, not the military department. Use of laid-up ships would entail undue delay in a situation where speed was vital. On the average, three months was required to recondition a ship in lay-up, and a reconditioning program for 35 tankers seemed far beyond the severely limited appropriations available to Maritime for such purposes. State wondered if JCS had really approved the tanker proposal, or was strangling it by these tightly drawn conditions.

Radius had to reckon with another powerful force. Although the British had adroitly initiated action toward the sale of tankers, they were quite pleased with the position Navy had taken. For that position was so defined that British tanker needs would be satisfied even though the needs of the other nations would not be. Hence the British now tried to persuade Radius to abandon his efforts to arrange for a greater number of tankers than 35 in behalf of the other foreign nations. But Radius rebuffed the British, being convinced that if he accepted the decision of 35 tankers and the British obtained them, he would have no chance of securing tankers for the others. Such a course would raise delicate questions of discrimination between applicants. It would pointedly violate special understandings like the Lend Lease agreement with Norway, which was designed to rehabilitate the Norwegian fleet and which the U. S. had not honored to any appreciable extent because of Maritime's general reluctance toward making foreign sales. So Radius stood firm; the British, needless to say, were not happy over the prospect of a further struggle and the delays involved.

Radius and State, having decided their policy, had to consider the next steps. Several choices were apparent. Radius might pursue further negotiations with Callaghan and others in the Navy, though such a course was hardly promising in face of the established JCS ruling. Alternatively, Radius might bring Secretary of State Marshall and the advantage of his military associations into play through direct exchanges with Secretary Forrestal and members of the Joint Chiefs of Staff. Or,—were there other alternatives of action, and by what considerations was Radius to choose between them?

THE OIL AND GAS DIVISION, DEPARTMENT OF THE INTERIOR

Radius was not the only initiator of the tanker program. Another force was at work which paralleled, but did not touch, his efforts —the Oil and Gas Division of the Department of the Interior. The Division had been created in mid-1946 by a Presidential letter, Executive Order, and Departmental Order (see Appendix II—Organizations), to implement the President's wish that "one agency must bear the primary responsibility for providing a focal point for leadership and information for the numerous agencies of the Federal government dealing with petroleum." Nearly thirty-five agencies, ranging from Internal Revenue to the Geological Survey, were in some way concerned with petroleum affairs. The Oil and Gas Division was directed by Presidential letter and Departmental Order to "undertake the initiative in obtaining co-ordination and unification of Federal policy" of all governmental petroleum activities, to serve as channel of communication between the Federal government and the petroleum industry, and as liaison between the Federal and state governments in matters concerning oil and gas. Within the Interior Department, the Division was to co-ordinate all oil and gas activities, and keep the Secretary informed regarding "the adequacy and availability of supplies of petroleum and its products to meet the current and future needs of the nation."

After a short period under the direction of Ralph K. Davies, former Petroleum Administrator for War, the Division passed, while still in its formative stages, to the supervision of Max W. Ball. A petroleum engineer with forty years in government and private work, ranging from the Geological Survey in 1906 to the Petroleum Administration for War in 1946, Mr. Ball was an enterprising man. (See Appendix I—Biographies.) He brought definite preconceptions to his new duties. He decided to limit the powers implicit in the authority to "co-ordinate" to staff or advisory functions, as distinguished from line or command functions. Thus his Division, vis-à-vis other government units, would advise only, and not command. It would seek influence by the excellence of its work. Ball had made a deliberate choice. For the President's letter and the Departmental Order afforded an approach quite different from the one he adopted. The President had written that "Where practicable and appropriate, governmental activities relating to petroleum should be centralized" and asked that there be submitted to him "from time to time . . . proposals looking to the accomplishment of this objective." The Secretary of the Interior authorized the Oil and Gas Division to "develop" these proposals. But Ball decided not to bring all petroleum activities directly into Interior's orbit and this aspect of his authority never figures in the tanker story. His efforts remained advisory only, true to his original plans for the Oil and Gas Division.

BALL'S APPROACH TO FOREIGN SALES

Ball stumbled upon the tanker question. In March 1947, the National Petroleum Council, advisory body of the Oil and Gas Division, met in Washington. The Council consisted of eighty-five industry members, widely representative of the petroleum industry, appointed by the Secretary of the Interior. The March meeting surveyed petroleum prospects for the coming year. Ball had arranged for a representative from the Maritime Commission to address the Council and on this occasion first learned of the foreign applications then on hand for the U. S. tankers.

Ball's immediate interest in the tankers stemmed from a fundamental and far-reaching conclusion he had recently reached concerning the U. S. oil supply for 1947. As early as February he had decided that there would be an oil shortage in the U. S. in the coming winter. An analysis made by an assistant, R. E. Friedman, of information gathered by the Petroleum Council, prompted this belief. Yet, with few exceptions, the oil industry, including Standard Oil of New Jersey, disagreed with Ball and Friedman, and made their plans in the expectation that there would continue to be a sufficient supply of oil for the United States.

Ball addressed himself to the sale of tankers upon the contrary premise of a shortage. He conceived both oil and tankers as a connected world-wide problem within which it was Interior's duty to help meet U. S. needs. Tankers must be pressed into action, the more the better, in light of the threatened shortage, whether under the U. S. or a foreign flag. Since U. S. citizen interest in purchasing the tankers was minimal, the best way to assure immediate employment of tankers was by sale to foreign nations. Ball now committed himself and his organization to this project.

BALL'S NEGOTIATIONS

Despite his strong interest, the foreign sale of tankers occupied for some time a secondary place in Ball's efforts. Far more important to him in the spring of 1947, was the crisis caused by the scheduled expiration on June 30 of certain provisions of the Ship Sales Act. Chief among these was the power of the Maritime Commission to operate tankers under General Agency. The matter was critical. In April 1947, 205 Maritime Commission T2-SE-A1 Tankers were in operation under General Agency, and thus did a heavy share of the international oil haulage. Study of the question fell to the jurisdiction of a subcommittee of the House Merchant Marine and Fisheries Committee, whose chairman, Alvin F. Weichel, Republican of Ohio, was actively opposed to continuation of the General Agency provision and other policies "international" as distinguished from "American," or "governmental" as opposed to "private industry." To Ball and others, revocation of General Agency would be a catastrophic blow to both the U. S. and the international oil situation, for a great fleet of tankers would be removed from service and immobilized.

Ball kept informed through the Maritime Commission on the legislative developments, and offered to do anything necessary, even to testify before the Weichel committee, which he ultimately did. He also consulted with members of the oil industry who later testified favorably upon General Agency and impressed upon the President's Assistant, John R. Steelman, the serious nature of the legislative battle. Steelman would be immediately concerned if Presidential intervention proved necessary to save the General Agency provision. In all this activity, the foreign sale of tankers occupied an incidental, though related place; its progress, was quite unplanned and fell within the interstices of the General Agency crisis and action. Ball would mention foreign sales in conversation with Steelman and others at the White House as usefully supplemental to General Agency to cope with the forecast U. S. oil shortage. The White House aides already knew of the tanker sales project, and Ball's remarks heightened their interest.

Ball acted entirely without association with Radius. His principal contact in the State Department was with Loftus of the Petroleum Division, who supplied him with data on the world petroleum situation. (Interior's own information was limited to the U. S.) Through Loftus, Ball came upon Radius, but their meeting resulted in no collaboration on tanker sales.

Further contacts, if there were any, were by chance and made no great impression. Probably Ball heard Radius advocate the tanker sales to the Interdepartmental Petroleum Committee during its consideration of a proposed license to export steel for construction of an Arabian pipeline. But even the occurrence of this small incident is uncertain.

Thus two teams were active for foreign sales. One was the State Department, the agency of foreign policy concerned with the sale of tankers as an international transaction. The other was Interior, with government-wide jurisdiction of a function—national oil policy—which happened to have both domestic and foreign implications. Each agency drove toward the same goal in parallel effort, with minimum contact and mutual assistance.

A BACKWARD GLANCE

There is a striking contrast between the methods and substance of the positions formally asserted by the proponents and by the opponents of the foreign sales program. The Navy, for example, had recorded in the JCS report the considerations which led it to endorse only a limited sale. These, it will be recalled, were threefold. The first was that a specified number of tankers must be retained under direct U. S. control as an essential part of our defense preparations. The second was that though the Navy appreciated the world-wide shortage of tankers, yet sales of U. S. tankers already in active use to foreign nations did not seem to promise in any way to improve the world tanker situation. Improvement was possible only if tankers not in use were brought into operation. It was not clear from the letters of the State Department and the Maritime Commission whether this was contemplated. Rather, the Maritime letter seemed to imply that U. S. tankers already in service would be sold to foreign purchasers. The effect, Navy believed, would be to harm the United States already not-too-good tanker situation, without increasing the world's fleet of active tankers.

Navy's third basic anxiety was that tankers sold to foreign purchasers would, in most instances, pass to nations which might easily be overrun by a potential invader, or to nations which might remain neutral in a war, at a time when the U. S. itself would seriously need tankers.

Accordingly, Navy through JCS, approved the principle of sales only with certain important limiting conditions. The number of tankers sold must not exceed 35, a figure determined on the basis of our calculated military needs and the understood world tanker needs: possibly also by a sidelong glance at the British applications. Also, the tankers sold must be drawn from the laid-up fleet. Such a limitation would meet the objection that foreign sales would not augment the world fleet of operating tankers. Finally, sales must be limited to nations or nationals who could satisfy standards formulated by JCS. This presumably would reduce the objection that tankers might be sold to nations easily subject to invasion.

It is noteworthy that the proponents of foreign sales made no similar extensively reasoned statement of position. The letters of the Maritime Commission and the State Department did not specify, even approximately, the number of tankers required for foreign sale. Whether the tankers were to be from the active or laid-up fleet was not indicated, although by implication they were to be from the active fleet. The only position positively asserted concerned the selection of foreign nationals to purchase the tankers. Both State and Maritime argued as a matter of principle that Maritime should not be bound in making the selections. Yet the nations which might be chosen were not suggested, nor was a formula offered which would govern the choices. Thus not even the barest outline of a program of foreign sales was presented—the number of tankers to be sold, the status of the tankers, the nations to which they would be sold. Even the considerations in behalf of the sales were not indicated beyond the barely stated conclusion that the sales would provide necessary relief to the world petroleum shortage and would usefully supplement our foreign policy.

In retrospect, it would seem better for Maritime, State and Interior to have joined in preparing a thoroughgoing plan for sales and to have presented such a plan in writing to the Navy. Each agency might have contributed the knowledge in which it was expert—the Interior

Department on Western Hemisphere petroleum supply and the effects of European withdrawals, the State Department on the current objectives of our foreign policy and the setting of the tanker program within them, the Maritime Commission on the situation of our tankers from the standpoint of demand and supply and the world prospects of our large postwar tanker fleet. Each presentation could have been linked with the relevant favorable sentiments in Navy.

But this was not done. The proposal of tanker sales was sketchily made; the only concrete program was the limited one that Navy put forward. Yet there is a further question. If the steps just suggested had been taken, could State-Maritime-Interior have devised a sales program with the assurance of detail which characterized the JCS report? Or, to state the question in a different fashion, can the needs of a foreign policy, which the tankers were intended to serve, have been stated with anywhere near the exactitude with which the JCS could determine the requirements of a military policy to which the tankers were relevant?

III. Actions of the Executive Office of the President and the Cabinet

STEELMAN AND CONWAY

As already suggested, a further orbit of action was the White House and the Executive Office of the President. The officer immediately concerned was the Assistant to the President, John R. Steelman. Mr. Steelman's duties were a catch-all, as his title indicates, embracing a great variety of affairs from railroads to cost-of-living indexes. Steelman was, in effect, the President's principal personal assistant on domestic matters, although he followed certain problems into the realm of foreign affairs. Tanker sales, of course, constituted such a problem. Aiding Steelman on this matter was Captain Granville Conway, the President's Co-ordinator of Emergency Export Programs. (See Appendixes I and II—Biographies and Organizations.)

Conway was 49 years old, a member of a seafaring family; he had had wide experience in private shipping enterprises and in governmental shipping agencies, as New York District Representative of the Shipping Board (predecessor of the Maritime Commission), as Special Assistant to the Maritime Commission, as Deputy Administrator and then as Administrator of the War Shipping Administration in World War II. In 1946 he became president of the Cosmopolitan Shipping Company, primarily an operator of foreign-flag tonnage, especially Norwegian. Later in the year, President Truman appointed Conway Co-ordinator of Emergency Export Programs. He served without pay, obtaining leave from his company for the necessary period. His task was to see that our various exports, particularly grains and fuels to Europe, were maintained at sufficient speed and scope to contribute effectively to recovery. Tankers were an important interest for him, for Europe's general weakness in shipping, the result of severe wartime losses, raised a host of problems of imbalances and strains throughout her postwar economy; all of these were made worse by the European oil shortage. The powers given Conway in the Presidential letter were far-reaching, enabling him "to call on all agencies, to use their full legal powers and to take whatever steps are necessary." Nevertheless, these powers rested necessarily on prestige and persuasion. They had no clear direct legal basis of formal authority; but Conway was experienced in the securing of consent without command.

Since 1946, Conway had kept informed of the tanker situation. He had welcomed the approval of the sale in that year of fifty tankers to foreign nations, and as reports came of plans for further sales, he was immediately sympathetic. Like Radius and Ball, he regarded the oil-tanker situation from a world-wide standpoint and was convinced that Europe needed more tankers to meet its petroleum needs. He also took cognizance of the fact that the United States had on hand a large number of idle tankers of which the world was in desperate need. From several standpoints the sale of tankers would be advantageous to his general export program. The perilous condition of Europe's oil reserves had caused the diversion of numerous European dry-cargo vessels, in addition to all the available tankers, to haul oil from the Middle East. If U. S. tankers were sold to the nations of Europe, much of this non-tanker shipping committed to the Middle Eastern oil haulage could be released to serve in other commodity programs in which Conway was interested and which were vital to Europe's sustenance.

From the standpoint of the U. S. shipping industry, Conway also deemed the sale of tankers advantageous. Sales to foreign governments would tend to restrict foreign tanker-building programs already afoot and promising to rise in major proportions. The more tankers that foreign nations purchased from the United States, the less they would build themselves. In the long run, the U. S. shipping industry would gain. Having sold tankers on hand, it would have to build new ones, and these presumably would be technically and competitively superior, through scientific improvements, to the older tankers sold to the foreign nations.

Conway's rationale of the tanker question was accepted by Steelman and thus became the position of the White House and the Executive Office of the President. Technically Steelman was "in the White House," while Conway, like the Director of the Bureau of the Budget, for example, was "in the Executive Office of the President." The technical distinction has some substantive significance; the White House staff tends to represent the President more immediately and personally.

Conway's views on tankers developed independently, as the concomitant of his general responsibility for export programs. His attitudes were formed substantially before the activities of other agencies, like Interior and State, were directed to his office, and, at most, their approaches served only to reinforce impressions and decisions already established. The identity of approach made it easy for Conway to work effectively with Radius and Ball. In fact, in response to Radius' reports of the situation, Conway went to General Eisenhower and other members of the Joint Chiefs of Staff, including the President's Chief of Staff, Admiral Leahy, to discuss the tanker situation, but all stood firm on the 35 tankers.

STEELMAN'S WHITE HOUSE MEETING

We return to the State Department and the dilemma confronting it. The JCS recommendations were unsuitable for the Department's objective. The release of only thirty-five tankers seemed a niggardly response to the more than one hundred tankers requested in foreign applications. It promised a serious embarrassment—the impossible task of distributing a few tankers satisfactorily to many nation-applicants. There were further objections to the JCS action, and Radius was searching for the best means to assert them, when Steelman's office itself ended his quest.

Steelman, urged by Conway and by his own staff, was anxious to speed the foreign sales, and now proposed to have all the agencies interested meet at his office at the White House, May 14, to review the progress of affairs, the issues which obstructed, and possible further actions. It will be recalled that the JMTC report on tanker sales, filed on May 7, had not yet been approved by the Joint Chiefs and the two Defense Secretaries, although its contents were generally known. Steelman's proposal was most opportune and welcome to Radius and the State Department. Steelman's office seemed the logical place for dealing with the tanker issues. The nature of the agencies concerned and their attitudes made the sufficiency of State's own influence to compose the inter-agency differences extremely doubtful. The Navy naturally had a jurisdictional pride, reinforced by the statutory clearance provision, and Maritime was, after all, an independent agency. These circumstances sharply limited the degree and kinds of pressures that State itself could apply to the tanker situation. Steelman, speaking for the White House, and Conway, bearing his own prestige and the rather vague authority of the Executive Office, might be able to do better.

All the agencies responded favorably to Steelman's invitation. Their representatives gathered in his office on May 14—Under Secretary Sullivan and Admiral Callaghan for Navy, Admiral William Smith, Chairman, and Huntington Morse, Special Assistant, for the Maritime Commission, General Paul Yount representing Army-Transportation, Radius for the State Department, and Captain Conway. Secretary of Commerce Harriman was also present, particularly because of his Department's interest in facilitating the export of steel to build a pipeline in Saudi Arabia. The pipeline, if constructed, would reduce the need for tankers, as the use of Haifa as a loading port entails a very much shorter run than the Persian Gulf ports.

The medium on which discussion turned was a memorandum entitled "Sale Foreign by Maritime Commission of T-2 Tankers," prepared in the Steelman office, which summarized the situation and the principal arguments in behalf of the sales.

These arguments had been mustered from every possible quarter—from State and Interior and from favorably inclined persons at Navy and Maritime. Each argument was carefully selected for its ability to find wide, if not complete, acceptance among all the agencies concerned. The memorandum comprised a many-sided appeal for the foreign sales of "an adequate number of tankers" as a desirable national policy. The arguments follow, as they were stated in the memorandum.

(1) Such sales constitute a partial means of providing for ultimate withdrawal of our government operation. [This was in reference to objections like those of Congressman Weichel that continuation of the Maritime Commission in business, as it was in assigning tankers on the General Agency basis, was incongruous with the American system of free enterprise. Foreign sales would reduce the number of tankers in General Agency and to that extent would pull the Commission out of the tanker business.]

(2) Such sales will permit a more orderly development of foreign petroleum interests in planning long-range production essential as a strategic reserve for Allied emergencies.

(3) If such foreign sales are not made, the foreign countries will endeavor to expand their construction facilities.

(4) Such sales will encourage American operators to engage in an orderly building program for new and more modern type tankers for American flag operation.

(5) The T-2 tankers are turbo-electric and will deteriorate rapidly in the lay-up fleet; operated by friendly allies, they constitute a more available part of our national defense.

(6) The tankers sold can be used to supply a greater proportion of the oil requirements of the UK and Continent from the Persian Gulf instead of from USA and the Caribbean, thus reducing the drain on the latter resources to that extent.

(7) American owners have recommended that the Maritime Commission sell T-2 tankers to foreign purchasers.

The discussion based upon the memorandum proceeded with substantial but not complete consensus. Harriman and Conway strongly supported further sales of tankers to foreign nations. So, of course, did Radius. Admiral Smith concurred, though making it clear that he spoke for himself, and not for the Maritime Commission. Navy dissented. Mr. Sullivan presented at length the positions taken in the JMTC report. As discussion continued, it was evident that two of the three agencies most actively concerned with foreign sales, State and Navy, were sharply opposed on the number of tankers to be sold. Sullivan advocated 35, which JMTC had specified. Radius indicated the impossibility of allocating 35 tankers among the more than 100 foreign applications on hand. The argument proceeded inconclusively. Conway and Steelman took no position on the specific issue, though they warmly supported the principle of further sale of tankers to foreign nations. Otherwise, their contributions were limited to providing a forum for the topic, guiding the meeting to bring the issue of numbers into clear relief, and finally, in lieu of an attempt to settle it themselves, they suggested that the tanker question go to the Cabinet. All present agreed that this was the desirable course. Steelman's own concurrence in this proposed action was consistent with his general method of operation; he did not think it appropriate for him to give "orders" to members of the Cabinet. Disputes involving department heads were therefore referred elsewhere for determination, if he was unable to solve them by mediation and persuasion. The remainder, and the bulk, of the meeting was devoted to the problem of extending Maritime's statutory authority to operate tankers under General Agency. The continued hostility of the Weichel hearings was periling extension, and the group agreed that this matter too should go to the Cabinet.

The Cabinet was scheduled to meet within two days. Fast action was required on Radius' part to prepare the Secretary. Fortunately, General Marshall's sympathetic understanding of the problem and familiarity with tanker and petroleum matters simplified the task. Radius dispatched two memorandums to General Marshall, one on General Agency, and the other on the foreign sales project. They summarized the Steelman meeting and recommended two specific steps for Cabinet approval: (1) that more tankers should be sold foreign than the 35 JCS had approved; (2) that the President should intervene to win the fight on extension of Maritime's General Agency authority. General Marshall instantly and whole-heartedly agreed to press these matters.

THE CABINET DECISION

The Cabinet met on May 16. Secretary Marshall presented the State Department's recommendations and with these the Cabinet, after discussion, seemed to concur. There was agreement that the President should contact congressional leaders to help dissuade Mr. Weichel from further attacks upon General Agency. As for foreign sales, there was fairly general agreement with State's position. No specific number of tankers to be sold to foreign purchasers was mentioned at the meeting, as none had been mentioned in the State Department recommendations. But the Cabinet did seem to feel that the JCS limitation of 35 tankers was unreasonably embarrassing, from the standpoint of foreign policy, with foreign applications on hand for more than 100 tankers. Such was the mandate which State felt it had won in the Cabinet. Secretary Marshall immediately informed Radius of it by memorandum, interpreting the meeting in this sense. Whether there was actually a Cabinet "decision" or a flat ruling by the President, or whether Navy reserved its rights is unknown, and probably unknowable. The Cabinet has no secretariat, keeps no minutes, and has no written decisions. There is no reason to believe that the action in the Cabinet was formulated as an instruction in any formal or definite sense.

IV. Interagency Execution of the Cabinet Decision

PRESSURE UPON NAVY

The "decision of the Cabinet," as the State Department described the occurrence, was followed by a flurry of measures to speed and assure its observance. Secretary Marshall assumed the lead in these efforts, a duty which though not specifically determined in the Cabinet, seemed sufficiently implied. He took pains to inform Secretary of the Navy Forrestal of his desire for prompt execution of the Cabinet decision. Commerce Secretary Harriman did the same. Mr. Krug, as Secretary of the Interior, addressed a careful and extensive statement of his Department's views to Secretary Forrestal.

Shortly before the Cabinet meeting, Mr. Ball had presented the tanker question to Mr.

Krug. Ball's own developing interest in the problem and his general awareness of the dispute between State and Navy made this a natural step. Perhaps a specific catalyst was one attorney for one of the British applicants, who supplied Mr. Ball with a fund of information on the tanker question as such and on the tangled interdepartmental situation as well. He informed Ball about the British dealings with Radius and about a recent decision of the British to drop their advocacy of 35 tankers since Radius could not be shaken from his opposition to that proposal. If 35 tankers were kept as the figure, the British could not hope to get the 31 tankers they wanted, for Radius would insist that the 35 be distributed fairly among the various foreign applicants. Hence the British now switched their support to the foreign sale of 100 tankers, the approximate number applied for, as the best means for securing tankers for themselves. This plan the attorney and the British shipping attaché had discussed at length with Ball. Although in agreement with it, Ball had insisted that the British have first preference for tankers in the new batch of 100. Ball informed Mr. Krug of all these matters.

As a result, Krug had been well briefed when he went to the Cabinet meeting, and had actively favored the foreign sales and had readily concurred in Ball's anticipation of a U. S. winter oil-shortage. Krug endorsed the sales as a measure to lessen the shortage. He now followed up his action in the Cabinet by a letter (which Friedman prepared) to Forrestal, May 19, which fully stated his position. It covered many points and its most pertinent portions follow.

> I am advised that you have under consideration the matter of authorizing the Maritime Commission to sell an additional number of Government-owned tankers, surplus to United States needs, to foreign nationals. I strongly recommend your approval of this action which is of great importance in the present serious domestic and worldwide oil situation.
>
> I also strongly urge that such tankers be made available in a number fully adequate to relieve the present Eastern Hemisphere drain on Western Hemisphere petroleum resources and to enable the minimum requirements of the several foreign nations concerned to be met. The sale of too few tankers to accomplish these objectives will result in an irrecoverable loss of petroleum and petroleum products which are important to our own economy and essential to the rebuilding of the shattered economies of these other nations.
>
> While I can make no specific recommendation as to the additional number of surplus tankers which should be made available for sale to foreign nationals, it is my understanding that the agencies of the Government closest to the situation believe that between 75 and 100 tankers are needed. While I do not understand the accuracy of these figures, I am convinced that any number substantially less would not afford the relief so urgently needed.

Secretary Krug attached to his letter a memorandum (also prepared by Friedman) "giving reasons" for his recommendations. Among these reasons were the following, arranged in the sequence and groupings in which they were presented:

> If sale to foreign nationals of additional surplus tankers is necessary to conserve Caribbean and domestic oil reserves or to make increased quantities from these sources available for United States consumption, that fact has a direct relation to national defense and security.
>
> To meet a record United States petroleum demand, domestic fields are being produced at or above their maximum efficient rates, and in addition almost one-half million barrels a day (all that is available) is being imported from other Western Hemisphere sources, principally from the Caribbean. Even so, present demand is not being fully met . . . the military have been unable to cover their forward requirements and this Department is presently engaged in an intensive effort to assist them in this respect.
>
> In the face of this situation, with Western Hemisphere fields and facilities strained to the utmost, production and refining operations in the Middle East, the only area where there is excess productive capacity of any significance, are seriously curtailed. [But oil production in the Middle East is curtailed because of the tanker shortage.] The result has been that an estimated ten million barrels of petroleum products have already been lost to the world markets, while at the same time stocks in the United Kingdom and elsewhere have fallen to a critically low level. [Tankers must be made available for foreign use, as they are the key to the] world-wide supply problem.

The United Kingdom draws petroleum from the Western Hemisphere. This action has a direct and adverse effect on our own precarious supply problem. Last winter U. K. took from Curaçao one and a half million barrels a month, and even greater quantities will be withdrawn this coming winter, all of which will be lost to the Atlantic seaboard where it will be badly needed.

The United States will realize a "substantial sum" by the sales; there are many surplus tankers which cannot be disposed of under the United States flag, as the industry feels tankers are obsolescent and before long will be commercially undesirable. If this is in fact the case, it seems doubly wrong to rely upon such ships as important to the national defense, particularly since I understand that they deteriorate at an extremely rapid rate when tied up and allowed to remain idle.

Moreover, if denied these ships, both foreign nationals and we will be confronted with a continuing oil crisis over a period of several years. Eventually, however, tankers will be built in foreign yards which will be superior in performance and economy of operation to the T-2 tankers. As a result, we will have forced the tanker fleets of foreign nations into a position of superiority over our own.

Of the several differences in the supporting arguments advanced by Interior and State, one especially is to be noted. Interior, unlike State, had adopted a line of argument which endeavored to show that it was to the immediate interest of the United States itself, both from the military and the economic standpoint, to sell tankers to foreign nations.

Conspicuously absent from Secretary Krug's letter is any protest over the conditions on selected nationals and the laid-up fleet. The difference in treatment of these matters by Interior and the State Department is founded, at least in part, in their difference in attitude toward the British. Ball had drafted a letter for Krug (never sent, although Interior representatives later asserted the viewpoints contained in it), pointing out that the British should have clear-cut preference for tankers since they alone of the foreign nations had petroleum resources and hence merited top priority for tankers. Radius, somewhat resentful of British tactics in originally opposing an increase in the number of tankers from 35 to 100, regarded the selected nationals provision as a means of giving the British a possibly undue superiority of claim against the other foreign nations; the provision was also, from the standpoint of the State Department, an intrusion by Navy into the area of foreign policy. (This latter conclusion was supported by Admiral Leahy, the President's Chief of Staff and Chairman of the Joint Chiefs of Staff. In a memorandum of May 28 to the Secretary of State, he stated that the Joint Chiefs had gone beyond their area of responsibility, that their duty was limited to specifying the minimum needs of the military services for tanker tonnage in peace and war, and that they should keep clear of the responsibilities of other agencies to provide necessary tanker tonnage as needed for other purposes.)

The Navy was now under attack. There was the Cabinet decision or consensus that more tankers should be sold to foreign nations, in keeping with foreign demand, though the number was not stipulated. There was pressure from Secretaries Marshall, Harriman, and Krug, for immediate foreign sales in numbers ranging from 75 to 100. Mr. Steelman and Captain Conway, speaking for the President, wished immediate and further sales.

By this time their position had become quite precise. At Conway's request, Richard Bissell, Jr., Professor of Economics at the Massachusetts Institute of Technology, formerly Conway's assistant in the War Shipping Administration, made a thorough-going study of the tanker and petroleum problems, and his findings were incorporated in a memorandum of May 23 which Conway forwarded to Steelman. The memorandum analyzed the interlaced foreign and domestic phases of the tanker-petroleum situations, and argued the wisdom of tanker sales. U. S. purchasers had shown no interest in the tankers; keeping them might retard a U. S. tanker construction program; their use by foreign nations could not harm U. S. operators since, by statute, foreign-flag tankers could not compete in U. S. coastwise trade. Bissell discounted the defense arguments of JCS. As the tankers were turbo-electric, they were subject to rapid deterioration when not in use. They would be better preserved, and hence available for our own defense, if placed in the hands of potential allies rather than left to deteriorate through disuse. Bissell also pointed out that sale of the tankers would permit European countries to make more constructive use of their limited dollar resources. Upon canvassing the total tanker picture, Bissell concluded that the U. S. could safely sell to foreign nations 100 tankers beyond the 50 authorized in 1946. He gave no reasons for selecting the number "100" though it corresponded roughly with the number of applications on hand.

The Chairman of the Maritime Commission and members of his staff also favored the sale of additional tankers—not 100 as Conway and Bissell advocated—but, say 70, as a safer figure in face of possible rises in U. S. demand and need. But the exact number of tankers was no real item of dispute, for all the agencies were joined in the primary purpose of securing Navy's consent to the principle of a considerable increase in the sale of tankers to foreign purchasers.

NAVY'S RESPONSE

On May 26, Secretary Forrestal, himself the object of much of this pressure, replied to the letter of April 7 from Admiral Smith, Maritime Commission Chairman, which had requested the Secretary of the Navy's comments on the advisability, from the national defense standpoint, of the sale of additional tankers to foreign interests. Mr. Forrestal's response faithfully reproduced the conclusions of the Joint Chiefs of Staff set forth in their report of May 16, and exhibited no awareness of the Cabinet action of the same day. In summary, Forrestal said:

1. 35 additional tankers might be sold to foreign purchasers (this was an absolute limit; no inference seemed permissible from his letter that more than 35 tankers might be sold).
2. "The national interest as well as national defense" would be served best by the sale of these tankers "to selected foreign nationals."
3. The Secretary proposed that foreign sales should be limited to "countries which have the same political philosophy and ideology as the United States, which are politically stable and which may reasonably be expected to contribute to our tanker shipping requirements in an emergency."
4. Each of the 35 tankers to be sold must "at the time of allocation" be in the Maritime Commission's laid-up fleet.

REACTIONS TO NAVY'S STAND

Secretary Forrestal sent copies of the foregoing letter to the Secretary of War, the Secretary of State, and the Secretary of the Interior "for their information." The immediate responses of these agencies to the Navy position varied considerably. The Maritime Commission itself took no action on the letter. There was no quorum of Commissioners in Washington at this time, and with the issues so sharply drawn, no one at Maritime would dare undertake action, which by practice must come from the whole Commission. The State Department, exceedingly hopeful after the Cabinet decision, was chagrined by Navy's perseverance with the JCS report. Appeal to the Cabinet had been in vain. As the end of May came and passed Navy's position hardened, despite search by Radius for a more favorable solution in talks with Admiral Callaghan and Captain Mansfield. Indeed, their belief in the propriety of Navy's desire for the condition, say, that tanker sales must be made exclusively from the laid-up fleet was, if anything, deepened by recent developments in the U. S. tanker situation. In May, tanker allocations—U. S. and foreign—were requested for 344 Maritime Commission-operated tankers, but only 191 could be furnished. Navy's request for 17 tankers was the only application completely satisfied. "This clearly indicated," wrote a Navy officer, "that the situation could only be improved by reactivating *all* the T-2s in lay-up as soon as possible." The world was short of tankers. It was simple sense that more tankers must come into service to meet the shortage. Withdrawal of tankers from the active U. S. fleet as the Maritime Commission and the State Department desired, would serve only to aggravate the forecast U. S. oil difficulties.

Navy's position disappointed the State Department. Actually it seemed more a rejection of the tanker project than an approval. The Maritime Commission, for instance, explained that it could not abide by the laid-up fleet stipulation. The funds for reconditioning tankers were very low—indeed all available funds were committed to the normal voyage repairs of tankers under General Agency. The Government, not the private agent, bore the costs of these repairs. No funds were expressly provided in the new budget, 1947-48, soon effective, to recondition tankers in lay-up. The estimated average cost of reconditioning a tanker was $300,000 and the reconditioning of 35 tankers was judged to be a fiscal impossibility. Also, the time required to recondition tankers was exorbitantly long in view of the urgency of providing immediate relief for European tanker and oil shortages. Oil stocks in Europe had to be accumulated in the next few weeks for the coming winter. The three months' period was far beyond the point of effective aid. (Yet it might have been recalled that two years earlier, Maritime had sold dry-cargo vessels "as is," i.e., the purchaser bore the cost of repairs. In view of this, many foreign applicants actually anticipated "as is" sales of tankers, except the British who opposed them.)

Navy's other conditions were equally objectionable to State. The JCS criterion of selectivity among foreign nations seemed absurd; the ideological conditions were so unclear—"Nations whose political philosophies were like our own"—that they could easily be interpreted to exclude any nation, even Britain (which, after all, had a Socialist government) from tanker sales. The JCS action seemed to preclude the sale of tankers to Italy, which the State Department was most anxious to aid against a strong upsurge of Communist activity, for, at the moment, Italy could hardly qualify as "politically stable." This was but one diplomatic embarrassment; there were many others.

In general, Radius and his superiors seem to have acted on the belief that war was not imminent or inevitable, and that it was in our national interest to embark on a program of economic assistance, of which the tanker sales were one small portion, that could not come to full fruition for some time. Perhaps the difference in attitude of Navy and State reflected in part a difference in evaluating the intelligence reports that predicted war in the immediate future.

Fully dissatisfied, Radius resolved upon further measures. On May 29 he sent to Secretary Marshall a memorandum entitled, "Critical Tanker Situation," which recounted the difficulties: the restrictive nationalities criterion of Navy, the insufficiency of 35 tankers, and the unlikelihood that Navy would authorize more. Radius expected that Navy's selected nationals condition would actually work out to limit sales to 31 tankers to the British and 4 to the Dutch. Meantime, pressure of foreign nations upon the State Department for tankers grew. The Italian embassy wished to purchase 10 tankers in addition to those already applied for, but "JCS action," Radius wrote, "precludes favorable action on these." (In part, the Italian and other foreign applicants were indulging in tactical insurance, for they expected a cut-back when the actual allocations were made.)

Accordingly, Radius recommended that the Secretary of State request the Secretary of the Navy and the Secretary of War to reconsider JCS action in light of:

(a) Our foreign policy to assist certain countries;
(b) The drain of Western Hemisphere oil reserves for European consumption;
(c) Unwillingness of State Department to accept conclusion that "sale of only 35 tankers would adequately relieve shortage."

The companion project to tanker sales—extension of Maritime's statutory authority to allocate tankers under General Agency—was also reviewed for projected action in Radius' memorandum. This phase of the tanker problem seemed to be in growing jeopardy. Congressman Weichel still was conducting his hearings with sharp hostility. Radius reminded Secretary Marshall that, at the Cabinet meeting on May 16, the President had agreed to impress upon congressional leaders that extension of Maritime's authority was urgently needed. But the President had gone on a trip shortly thereafter, and had not acted. Meanwhile, congressional action for renewal was stalled in the Weichel subcommittee. Radius asked that Secretary Marshall raise again at Cabinet meeting "the recommendation that the President discuss with Congressional leaders extension of Maritime Commission's operating authority."

THE SITUATION EXAMINED

Before turning to the next chapter, it may be useful to pause and consider some of the arguments that were made and not made in the course of the long dispute that for the moment seemed so unsatisfactorily resolved—at least in the eyes of the Department of State. It is notable, for example, that no direct formal reply was given in any of the various memoranda to the Navy's contention that the world oil shortage would not be relieved by transferring tankers in active service from the U. S. flag to the flag of foreign nations. In fact, Navy did not make the further point, which it might have made, that there would have been some tendency for this action to increase the world stringency, since the Persian Gulf routes to which the tankers would be reassigned were longer (except for the run to Marseilles and ports in Italy and Greece) than the Western Hemisphere routes on which they were being used. This point was, however, alluded to in some of the discussions.

On the opposite side of this question, in the early days of March and April, some mention was made of what appeared to be a slight surplus in the U. S. tanker situation. The spare tankers of some of the oil companies were being held somewhat in reserve and were not being sent to the Middle East because of economic problems, so that if some of the tankers in active service were transferred to the European nations, American tankers would replace them, at least in part, from the companies' own reserve capacity.

Another technical question that was avoided rather than answered, particularly in the beginning of the debate, was the alleged practical impossibility of reconditioning the tankers in the laid-up fleet. State and Maritime took the position initially that this was for practical reasons an impossibility. Yet, later, as will be seen, the tankers were reconditioned. Obviously, the State Department's chief concern was with the delay that would ensue if the foreign nations had to wait for repairs to be made and, further, with the danger that the total foreign demand would be limited by the number of tankers in lay-up, i.e., 46. The Department was thus perhaps rather too easily impressed with Maritime's assertions about the impossibility of reconditioning the tankers. As a matter of fact, as has been noted, the "as is" method had been successfully applied to sale of other vessels previously. Indeed the "impossibility" later turned out to be really a matter of inconvenience and, of course, delay. (Parenthetically, it may be mentioned that if the 35 tankers approved by the Navy in its letter of May 26 had been put under repair immediately, they would have been sold and in service long before the first useable tankers were actually delivered—but this is hindsight.)

On the other side of the picture, it is clear that none of the other agencies directly questioned the validity of the Navy-JCS determination about the number of tankers needed by the United States in case of emergency, except in the special case of Conway's assistant, Bissell. Yet it is obvious that the figure was not regarded as sacrosanct, since the State Department proposals inevitably meant its abandonment. Nevertheless, to attack it head-on would have been to presume on a ground where JCS competence was difficult to question. The reverse of this is, of course, JCS and Naval reluctance to deny the validity of State's contention about the importance of the tanker sales for the support of our foreign policy. Perhaps at bottom most of the argument revolved about two rather different concepts of the possibility of war and the nature and situation of our allies if a war should occur. Obviously, if the Joint Chiefs had been convinced that there was no real danger of war for, say, 30 years, the whole tanker question would have been of no interest to them. All the tankers involved would have been relegated to the scrap heap long before the outbreak of hostilities. At the other extreme, it may be that State would have abandoned its attempt to bolster some of the most Eastern of the Western European countries if it had been convinced that war was imminent in a matter of weeks. These broader and more fundamental, and far more intangible considerations were hardly raised at all and never raised directly in formal correspondence. Yet they affected the jurisdictional judgments involved. If Navy had been convinced that State held the same views about the desirability of supporting secure allies and the undesirability of making tankers unwittingly available to potential enemy capture, it would have been a matter of no concern or little concern as to whether the determination of criteria for selection of the nationals was left to the hands of the Secretary of State or the Secretary of the Navy. It was because they did not see eye to eye that the problem was important to both.

In some of the discussions of the question, the Navy contention was attacked on a rather different basis. Various people concerned with the situation, such as Conway, believed that the legal registry of tankers as well as of other ships is a comparatively secondary matter in case of the outbreak of war. The important thing is the actual physical location of the ships. Thus, the British, for example, acquired various German ships at the outbreak of the last war, while the Germans at various points acquired ships of the Allied nations. This general consideration applies to all tankers and particularly to tankers operated under the flag of the great seafaring nations like the United Kingdom, Norway, the Netherlands and Sweden. A Norwegian tanker may ply for many months or even for two or three years between Abadan, for example, and Marseilles without ever returning to home port. It would be hard to conceive that a Norwegian tanker in the Mediterranean or elsewhere in the great waters of the world would fail to deliver itself to a U. S. or some other friendly port in case of war, unless it was subjected to actual physical capture. It is obvious that this argument is not absolute (especially in the case of presumed neutrals like Sweden) and is subject to certain elements of rebuttal. But it was never directly presented, at least in writing, and thus never directly answered.

One final point may be worth noting. The phrase in Secretary Forrestal's letter of May 26, "countries which have the same political philosophy and ideology as the United States, which are politically stable, and which may reasonably be expected to contribute to our tanker shipping requirements in an emergency" is a peculiarly murky one. Presumably it was meant to limit the sales to those countries that were not apt to turn Communist by internal action, that would not remain obstinately and unco-operatively neutral in case of war, and that were not in danger of being hastily overrun. But it may be that this is too precise a reading of meaning into what was probably a deliberately ambiguous statement. In any event, the interpretation of these restrictions would tend to depend not on a linguistic exercise but on the broader considerations suggested above. One chief reason for State's concern about the clause was that it would be applied in the normal course of events by Maritime officials who had previously shown themselves hostile to all foreign sales. It is also interesting to observe that later on, when faced with an actual list of countries (prepared by sympathetic officials), only one significant change was proposed by Navy and actively opposed by State, even though many, perhaps most, of the countries on the list could have been eliminated under a strict interpretation of the limiting phrases. Here and elsewhere in this episode, theoretical policy differences may have been greater than action proposals when spelled out.

V. The Second Cabinet Decision and Its Implementation

THE NEW CABINET DECISION

Radius' memorandum to Secretary Marshall of May 29 accomplished far more than its author expected. For on June 2, the Cabinet adopted, or at least seemed to agree on, measures not only to save the General Agency provisions of the Ship Sales Act, but also to improve the prospects of foreign tanker sales. The President agreed to rally party leaders of the House of Representatives to persuade Chairman Weichel, and, though Radius had not specifically requested it in his memorandum, Secretary Marshall injected the tanker sales into Cabinet discussion. The outcome was all that friends of the sales could have asked for. The Cabinet stipulated (in some fashion) that an additional 65 T-2 tankers, over and above the 35 previously authorized, were to be sold to foreign purchasers by the Maritime Commission. The further dominant opinion of the Cabinet—expressed but not formalized—was that the Navy-conceived conditions on "selected" foreign nations and the laid-up fleet entailed undue delays and complications and ought to be removed. The victory seemed complete; foreign sales of a large number of tankers might now proceed.

The Cabinet action was buttressed by a lengthy memorandum of June 3 from Steelman to the President on "The Operation of Maritime Commission Tankers." Though devoted principally to the crisis over the extension of Maritime's General Agency authority, the memorandum systematically described to the President the problems of world petroleum and petroleum transportation facilities. The conclusion that "ocean-going tanker capacity has been the principal critical limiting factor on [petroleum] supply" was one which the President took firm hold on and asserted in subsequent and critical junctures of the tanker sales project.

IMPLEMENTING THE DECISION

The events which occurred during the next nine weeks were numerous, complex, interrelated, and of concern to all the persons and organizations involved. For the convenience of the reader, these events have been grouped under the particular days on which they happened, and are presented in that manner in the pages which follow.

GETTING MARITIME TO ACT

Wednesday, June 4

Under Secretary of State Clayton met with the Maritime Commission to inform them of the new Cabinet decision. He said that the Secretary of the Navy would write to Maritime in the light of the new decision—a remark based, apparently, upon a presumed understanding between the Secretaries of State and Navy reached at the Cabinet meeting, June 2.

At this point, many in State, including the Secretary, feared that Navy would still cause difficulties, would still honor the spirit, if not the letter, of the JCS decision rather than the Cabinet decision. Navy, after all, acted under *statute*. With this premonition, Secretary of State Marshall dispatched a letter to the Secretary of the Navy, pointing out that the Maritime Commission could not act upon the Cabinet decision until it possessed the advice of Navy. Marshall was hopeful that an appropriate Navy letter would be soon forthcoming, free of the restrictive conditions of Navy's letter of May 26. Limiting tanker sales to the laid-up fleet would entail undue delay (so Marshall wrote to Forrestal) which would defeat the central purpose of foreign sales: *immediate* action to relieve the petroleum situation. The selectivity provision for foreign nationals, Marshall believed, "has little significance and greatly complicates." He suggested to Forrestal, as a course "to avoid confusion," that the May 26 letter be overridden by a new letter covering all 100 tankers, condition-free.

The Marshall letter was an unusual step. It was an attempt to secure for the second "Cabinet decision" a better fate than had befallen the first, which had been negated by Navy's action. The letter was intended to encourage Navy to abide by a formal request, presumably impending from Maritime, for unconditional approval of the foreign sale of 100 tankers. In a way, the Marshall letter betrayed a sense of uncertainty over what Navy might do, and was based upon the assumption that it is easier to affect a decision which has not been made than to undo one which has been formally taken.

A copy of the Marshall letter went to Steelman's office and was received by an assistant, who was familiar, through conversations with Radius, of the planned course of action, i.e., that Clayton would notify Maritime of Forrestal's impending letter, which in light of the Cabinet discussion, would not limit tanker sales to the laid-up fleet, and would substitute for the May 26 selectivity formula, the phrase: "friendly foreign nations approved by the Secretary of State." These understandings were noted on the copy of Marshall's letter and forwarded to Steelman.

During the course of the day, Marshall's letter was received in Navy; Forrestal referred it to Admiral Callaghan, who immediately drafted a memorandum of advice to the Secretary. Callaghan reminded Forrestal that when Navy concurrence was given in the two previous approvals of tanker sales to foreigners, the matter was referred beforehand to the Joint Chiefs of Staff "for study and recommendation." The essential reason for the first step was a JCS study made in 1945 which set forth the merchant shipping requirements which had to be satisfied for national defense.

The "current controversy," Callaghan noted, over the sale of tankers was concerned with the adequacy of the 35 recently approved and the mechanics of a revision upward of that figure if circumstances warranted. Callaghan advised the Secretary that from the standpoint of the JCS and the Secretary of the Navy, it would be appropriate for the Maritime Commission to take the initiative, as contemplated under the Ship Sales Act, and request a reconsideration. Such a recommendation, Callaghan suggested, should also be accompanied by a full statement of all facts in the case and a recommendation of exactly how many "fast tankers" were required for foreign sale to relieve the situation. Admiral Callaghan closed with a paragraph of data indicating that even with the previous foreign tanker sales authorizations —50 in 1946 and 35 in 1947—the United States would be seriously short of tankers in the event of war. Parenthetically, it may be noted that none of the agencies advocating foreign sales ever directly opposed the latter conclusion, for, strictly speaking, it was a conclusion that they were not competent to question. Nevertheless, in private various officials did question the conclusion. They thought that Navy had taken too narrow a view of the "availability" of tankers. For, as has been explained, availability is not solely a matter of registry, but also a matter of the location of the vessels when war breaks out and of the control of the sea lanes. Indeed, some U. S. tankers were operating in the same Persian Gulf-European routes as would the tankers proposed for sale to friendly foreign nations. It was widely felt that Navy's approach to the problem was unwisely legalistic.

Thursday, June 5

On this day Secretary Marshall gave his address at Harvard, which foreshadowed a great new program of aid to Europe. The Harvard speech was not directly related to the tanker problem, but further delays in disposing of the tankers would cause increasing embarrassment in the light of this public policy pronouncement.

In Washington, Forrestal made known his decision in the form of a reply to the Secretary of the Interior's letter of May 19 (which had asked for Navy approval of approximately 100 tankers to aid in solving the world petroleum crisis). The Forrestal response reflected Admiral Callaghan's thinking. Navy's earlier conditions concerning the laid-up fleet and selected nationals, Forrestal wrote, still obtained. Taking cognizance of the ceiling of

35 tankers set by JCS, Forrestal expressed only a guarded willingness to consider a request to raise the ceiling. If the tankers previously approved, the letter went on, "should prove to be inadequate for relieving a critical world-wide shortage of petroleum transportation, it is expected that the Maritime Commission will make appropriate representation in the premises."

Friday, June 6, Monday, June 9, and Tuesday, June 10

Over these days occurred numerous discussions between Radius, Callaghan and Huntington Morse, the interdepartmental liaison officer of the Maritime Commission. Radius and Morse insisted that the Navy should send a letter to Maritime approving the sale of additional tankers. From Maritime's standpoint, the whole thing would then be quite simple. Maritime did not wish to submit a request to Navy because it feared that Navy would say "no" or what would be tantamount to "no" in a condition-loaded "yes." This fear would be dispelled if Navy itself would notify Maritime of the Cabinet decision and recommend the foreign sale of additional tankers. But Callaghan would not agree; the action had to be initiated by Maritime, as the statute required, and not vice versa. As the days passed, Callaghan's firmness made the efforts seem increasingly futile.

Wednesday, June 11

The Secretary of State, in a letter drafted by Radius, wrote to the Chairman of the Maritime Commission in support of further British applications for purchase of tankers and for increased tanker allocations under General Agency.

At Navy Callaghan's position was upheld. Here and at other junctures his proposals were reviewed in discussions with the Under Secretary, the Special Assistant to the Secretary, and the Deputy Chief of Naval Operations for Logistics (Callaghan's superior). The matter of tanker sales was also considered at various points in the "Secretary's meeting" (the Secretariat and the Chief and Vice Chief of Naval Operations), and in the "Secretary's Council," a large weekly group consisting of the Secretariat, the Chief, Vice Chief, Deputy Chiefs and the more important Assistant Chiefs of Naval Operations, the Bureau and Office Chiefs, the Judge Advocate General, the General Counsel, the Fiscal Director, and other key officers and civilians. Nevertheless, Callaghan remained the principal influence upon the tanker sales in the Navy. Though others examined his proposals, few, if any, changes of importance resulted.

Thus it was on June 11. Forrestal telephoned Marshall and cited Navy's decision to stand upon the Ship Sales Act and thus consider State's letter of June 4 inappropriate. According to the Act, Maritime—not State—must take the initiative and ask Navy for its advice on the matter of further foreign sales. State's attempt to find a short-cut was thus thwarted. It had now to resort to "proper channels" and urge Maritime to make a formal request for Navy's opinion.

Thursday, June 12 and Friday, June 13

These days constituted an interlude of consultation concerning next steps made necessary by Navy's decision. Radius advised Morse of the impasse, now complete, and proposed, as the best way out, that State write Maritime, inform it of the Cabinet's action and suggest that it would now be appropriate for Maritime to write to Navy. The immediate reaction in Maritime was not sympathetic to this proposal; Morse and his associates preferred that notice of the Cabinet decision come from the President. There was more discussion with Radius about this, and also with Steelman's office. The up-shot was a consensus that the Secretary of State should write to Maritime of the Cabinet's action and request Maritime to approach Navy. Subsequently, Steelman was to write in support of State's letter. These steps were chosen with the discomfiting awareness that the Maritime Commission was an "independent" regulatory commission, as the phrase goes, and as such might claim that it had no obligations to the Cabinet or the President.

To Radius fell the task of preparing, for the Secretary's signature, State's formal request to Maritime. It was a delicate affair. Charged with the responsibility by statute of safeguarding and promoting the *American* merchant marine, the Commission typically regarded with suspicion, if not disfavor, proposals committing our shipping resources to international aid. The Commission had also been notoriously split of late. Bipartisan membership and the lack of strong leadership within (in contrast to the vigorous drive of the former chairman, Admiral Land) had made the Commission highly uncertain on various policy questions. Radius, in drafting his letter, had to be extremely discreet, attentive to niceties of phrasing and shadings of argument. A slip might provoke conflict and delay within the Commission. Radius' good working relations with Huntington Morse proved helpful in resolving his perplexities. Experienced in the Commission's ways, Morse was able to advise Radius in the drafting of State's letter on what points might be of special concern to the Commissioners. Morse was the Interdepartmental Liaison Officer of the Maritime Commission, responsible for maintaining "liaison" with other Federal departments and with foreign governments "in connection with matters of more than domestic scope." (See Appendixes I and II—Biographies and Organizations.) Morse reported "to the Commission via the Chairman." A Yale graduate, 58 years old, Morse was appointed "Assistant to the Chairman" in 1937, and during the operation of the War Shipping Administration was "Assistant to the Administrator." He had also had extensive private shipping experience. He had long had a particular interest in foreign affairs and one of his main ambitions was to reconcile successfully the sometimes conflicting objectives of an intelligent foreign policy and the maintenance of a sound American merchant marine. Over a considerable period, various foreign applicants for tankers had been pressing Morse to aid in behalf of foreign sales.

Monday, June 16

The letter of Secretary Marshall to Maritime Chairman Admiral Smith went forward in accordance with the agreement made with Steelman's office. Marshall advised Smith of the Cabinet decision of June 2 that the existing program calling for the sale of 35 tankers to foreign nations was insufficient to meet the requirements of the current world petroleum emergency and, further, that the JCS conditions, previously imposed, would "greatly complicate" and "unduly delay" foreign sales of tankers. In the light of the Cabinet action, the Secretary of State asked the Maritime Commission to consult with the Navy, as required under the Ship Sales Act, regarding the national defense aspect of the sale of an additional 65 tankers. Thus, under the State proposal, the foreign sales program would be raised to 100 T-2 Tankers, all of them free from the JCS conditions, i.e., confining sales to "selected foreign nationals" and to withdrawals from the laid-up tanker fleet. Secretary Marshall pledged the support of State to Maritime's request to Navy and offered to provide any advice and information which might be required. A copy of Marshall's letter was sent to Steelman.

Informal talks of State, Maritime and White House officials showed Maritime to be exceedingly loath to approach Navy. There were various views among Maritime Commissioners and staff on the question. Some wanted the promise of a definite unrestrictive Navy "yes" before official referral was made; another wanted a promise that the matter would not be sent again to JCS, but would be checked with the President for his approval—personally—in the light of national defense requirements for tankers. All agreed that Maritime would suffer intense embarrassment if Navy continued to insist on limitations while the other agencies continued to insist upon an expanded and unfettered program. None of the Commissioners were at all anxious to take the initiative, for obvious reasons, and none were ever enthusiastic about the sales. Radius and the others were convinced that strong persuasive efforts would be needed to secure action by the Commission.

Tuesday, June 17

These efforts began to take form promptly. Most important of all was the President's own intervention, through his Assistant, John R. Steelman. The President's personal concern with the world oil situation was considerable and was shared by Steelman, as well as by Steelman's own staff. Steelman's letter, therefore, represented the united and unreserved thinking of the White House group concerned with the problem from the President on down. Steelman's letter to Admiral Smith, Maritime Commission Chairman, reads as follows:

> General Marshall has sent me a copy of his letter of June 16 to you concerning the sale of T-2 tankers to foreign operators. I do not believe there is anything I can add at this time to General Marshall's statement of the case except perhaps to call the Commission's attention to the fact that the President is concerned about this matter. It would be extremely helpful if the Commission could give the promptest attention to General Marshall's request.

This brief letter was a determined step. Steelman's staff—who drafted the letter—were sufficiently far from the center of White House decision so that they normally avoided even an oral citation of the President's own wishes, except in unusual cases where the appropriateness of the reference was beyond question. Steelman himself, whose daily meetings with the President were officially known, was far freer to use the President's name in discussion; but even he generally avoided any direct written mention such as might implicate his superior, except in cases requiring drastic action. This was such a case.

There was also action on quite a different front. Secretary Krug held an interdepartmental meeting on the petroleum shortage at the Interior Department, attended by some 60 top government and industry officials. Krug called the meeting because of his conviction that Ball's forecast of domestic oil shortages in the coming winter was correct. The timing of the meeting had no premeditated bearing upon State's efforts with Maritime. One day Krug had phoned Ball and suggested the meeting as a device to acquaint all government agencies with the situation as Interior saw it. June 17 had been selected at random as the meeting date during the course of the conversation, as one which provided sufficient leeway for distributing notices.

Krug's letter of invitation had indicated that "The possibility of widespread shortages next fall and winter at home and abroad" required "consideration at the highest level—to weigh the facts and possibilities of the situation, to review the steps that have been and are being taken by the government and the industry, and to consider what further steps may be possible and desirable." All the agencies concerned with the tanker phase of the petroleum problem were represented. Captain Conway, Secretary Marshall, Assistant Secretary Thorp, John Loftus, and others (but not Radius) from State, Under Secretary of the Navy Sullivan, Under Secretary of War Royall, were present. Maritime had Chairman Smith, Morse and other staff members, and Under Secretary William Foster represented Commerce. The oil industry was represented by Howard Page of Standard Oil of New Jersey and John Builtright, Standard Oil of Indiana, and others. Thus the meeting included top and near-top officials. The matter of tankers was discussed extensively as part of the petroleum crisis. Sullivan of Navy asked searching questions about foreign tanker sales, which were answered chiefly by Morse of Maritime with the aid of the Interior and State Department officials. Secretary Marshall was himself active in the discussion. Though the opposing views of Navy and the other agencies were brought into focus, no attempt was made to reconcile them nor was any formal action taken on the tanker question. Krug and Ball sought to accomplish a more modest purpose: acquainting all the agencies and the industry with the petroleum shortage in order to provide a basis for future co-operation on remedial measures.

Apparently Krug and Ball did not consult Radius and Conway in calling this meeting and setting its agenda, which the latter officials resented for the moment, in view of their own considerable identification with the tanker project.

Wednesday, June 18

Krug sent his own letter (drafted by Friedman, Ball's assistant) to the Chairman of the Maritime Commission, supplementing those of Steelman and Marshall. Krug referred to the meeting in his own office the previous day as indicative of the generally serious oil situation, and the need for speedy sale of U. S. tankers to foreign nations. The letters of Marshall on June 16, of Steelman on June 17 and Krug on June 18 were linked and timed in accordance with a suggestion made by Captain Conway during talks with Ball and Radius.

THE ISSUES ARE STATED

Thursday, June 19

The device of sending the three letters seemed to work. On this day the Chairman of the Maritime Commission, in a letter drafted by Morse, requested the statutory advice of the Secretary of the Navy on the sale of the new total of 100 tankers. The most pertinent part follows:

Your reply of May 26, 1947, expressed the opinion that the sale of 35 additional T-2 tankers from the Commission's reserve fleet to selected foreign nationals, as defined by the Joint Chiefs of Staff, would not be inimical to the best interests of national defense.

As you are aware, prior and subsequent to receipt of your letter, further discussions took place at the highest level with respect to the petroleum transportation situation and the possibility of wide-spread shortages of petroleum products next fall and winter, both at home and abroad. As a result of these discussions, the Commission has received a letter from the Secretary of State dated June 16, 1947, and a letter dated June 17, 1947, from the Assistant to the President, and one of June 18, 1947, from the Secretary of the Interior concerning the critical world petroleum situation and the sale of T-2 type tankers to foreign operators.

The Maritime Commission has given careful consideration to the content of the above-mentioned letters in the light of all available information, and its estimate of the factors involved, including representation from various interests concerned, and believes that immediate action is required to relieve the petroleum situation in the United States and abroad. It is of the opinion that one of the essential remedial measures would be to make available for prompt sale to certain foreign applicants a total of 100 T-2 type tankers over and above the 50 tankers of the same type which have already been approved for sale by the Maritime Commission to non-citizens.

The Commission concurs with the views expressed in the Secretary of State's letter of June 16, that the conditions of sale established by the Joint Chiefs of Staff as cited in your letter of May 26 would unduly complicate and tend to delay action.

However, the Commission considers that it would be desirable and in the best over-all interests of the United States to consult with and obtain the advice of the State and Navy Departments in regard to the transfer to non-citizens of such T-2 tankers as may be cleared by the Navy before approving their sale.

Accordingly, in line with the provisions of section 6, sub-section 2, of the Merchant Ship Sales Act of 1946 and the specific request of the Secretary of State, the Maritime Commission desires to consult the Secretary of the Navy with respect to the transfer of 100 additional T-2 type tankers to foreign operators at this time, without the limiting definition of selected foreign nationals set forth in the letter of May 26, and without the condition that these vessels be taken from the laid-up fleet.

Copies of this letter were sent to all the members of the Maritime Commission, the General Counsel of the Commission, Steelman, Admiral Callaghan, the Secretary of State, and the Secretary of the Interior. Enclosed were the letters of Steelman, Marshall and Krug, referred to in the text.

On this same day, Secretary of the Navy Forrestal wrote to Secretary Marshall in acknowledgment of the June 4 letter from State and their phone talk on June 11—State's direct approach to Navy on the tanker sales, and Navy's rebuff on grounds of procedural propriety. In this new letter, Secretary Forrestal's comments were limited to the amenities; promises comforting to advocates of the tanker sales were noticeably absent. Though Forrestal, whose letter Callaghan drafted, acknowledged the existence of "general agreement" that "more T-2 tankers be sold foreign," there were of course "legal formalities," and they must be observed. Yet the Secretary's phrase did at least seem to indicate an awareness of the Cabinet action. Forrestal added that he understood Maritime was preparing a request for an additional 65 tankers, to which, he said, Navy would give "prompt and full consideration."

Friday, June 20

Navy did indeed give prompt consideration, for on this day the Secretary of the Navy replied to Maritime. The letter was drafted for Forrestal's signature by Callaghan on the basis of a conference attended by Under Secretary Sullivan, Admiral Nimitz, Callaghan, and a special assistant to Secretary Forrestal. The letter was discussed several times by telephone between Sullivan and Admiral Smith, the Maritime Chairman, before it was signed. Sullivan obtained from these conversations the impression that Smith agreed with the letter's contents. Its most germane parts were as follows:

Inasmuch as your letter referred to 100 additional T-2 tankers, inclusive of the 35 covered by my letter of May 26, I infer that your request that the disposal of those tankers be approved without the limiting definition of "selected foreign nationals" is intended to refer to the original 35 as well as the additional 65 covered in your letter of June 19.

Upon receipt of your letter of April 7, to which you attached requests of foreign nationals for the purchase of 84 T-2 type tankers, I referred this matter to the Joint Chiefs of Staff. As you recall, the Joint Chiefs of Staff advised me that in their opinion the national interest as well as national defense would be served best by the sale to selected foreign nationals of not exceeding 35 T-2 type tankers, which at the time of allocation for sale are in the Maritime Commission's laid-up fleet. The Joint Chiefs of Staff further expressed the opinion that the sale of these tankers should be restricted to foreign nationals of those countries which have the same political philosophy and ideology as the United States, are politically stable, and may reasonably be expected to contribute to our shipping requirements in an emergency.

Because such a short time has elapsed since my last referral of this program to the Joint Chiefs of Staff and because the only new factor since that referral has been a greater stress on the critical world economic situation, I have not again referred this matter to the Joint Chiefs of Staff. I have, however, consulted with the Chief of Naval Operations, Fleet Admiral Chester W. Nimitz, and he and I are of the opinion that there should be adherence to the two conditions recommended by the Joint Chiefs of Staff, that sale of tankers should be limited to selected foreign nationals and that insofar as is possible the tankers should come from the Maritime Commission's laid-up fleet.

We are advised by your Commission that there are now in the Maritime Commission laid-up fleet approximately 100 T-2 type tankers. Of this number, 24 are former Navy tankers, specifically equipped for naval operations with the fleet. I believe your Commission agrees with the Navy that these 24 should not be sold. Of the balance of 76, I am advised by your Commission that 46 are saleable with some repairs. I recognize the validity of the recommendations of the Joint Chiefs of Staff who are quite properly concerned with the adequacies of tanker tonnage to meet the requirements of any future emergency. I further recognize, however, that the sale foreign of additional tankers at this time will contribute materially to the betterment of world economic conditions and will thereby help to prevent the development of those factors which might lead to economic chaos and international discord.

Accordingly, I hereby advise you that I have no objection to the sale foreign of 46 T-2 type tankers from the Maritime Commission laid-up fleet and 54 T-2 type tankers from the Maritime Commission active fleet, subject to the conditions as to eligible purchasers set forth in my letter to you dated May 26, 1947.

The Secretary of the Navy did not cite a further important reason which brought Navy approval to foreign sale of increased numbers of tankers: "the depleted oil reserves in this hemisphere make it desirable to encourage oil production in other parts of the world." (Statement by Secretary Forrestal, *Hearings*, Special Committee to Study American Small Business, U. S. Senate, Part 23, Nov. 14, 1947, p. 2520.) The Navy had come to conclude that "To the extent that oil from the Middle East can be supplied to Europe, to the United States, or to both, not only by tankers, but also by pipe lines, the strain on our own reserves can be reduced." (*Ibid.*) The similarity of this line of argument to Interior's previously stated position is striking and prompts conjecture that the Krug-Ball efforts did much to bring Navy to drop its insistence on sale of no more than 35 tankers.

These two letters of Maritime and Navy provided the foundation of subsequent and extensive negotiations, and it may be useful to review, at this point, the items on which there was agreement between the agencies and the items on which there was disagreement. For notwithstanding Under Secretary Sullivan's impression that Chairman Smith of Maritime agreed with the Navy position, the Navy and

Maritime letters obviously diverged. Smith, in conversations with Sullivan, had spoken only for himself, and not for the Commission. The Maritime letter, on the other hand, was understood to have the Commission's approval. Yet between the letters lay a substantial area of agreement. Both agencies were recorded in favor of foreign sales to the extent of 100 tankers. Clearly, therefore, the number of tankers was no longer in dispute as it once had been. Whatever disagreement existed between the positions of Navy and Maritime existed within this framework of basic agreement.

But there were differences, and they were twofold—the use of tankers from the laid-up fleet and the selection of foreign nationals. Each question had arisen in the negotiations about the 35 tankers and had been carried over to the present negotiations about the 100 tankers. As to the laid-up fleet, Navy specified that of the 100 tankers intended for foreign sale, 46 had to be taken from the laid-up fleet, while the remaining 54 could come from the active fleet. Though the Navy's reasons for advocating withdrawals from lay-up were not specified in its letter, they were well known both to Maritime and the State Department.

Both these agencies felt that the Navy's terms would impose delays upon foreign sales of tankers that would defeat the objective of providing *prompt* assistance to European nations suffering from the petroleum and tanker shortages. The Maritime Commission estimated that the task of readying a tanker from the laid-up fleet would, on the average, require three months—an unreasonable period, since summer was already at hand and the European nations built their reserve stocks of petroleum during the summer in preparation for the coming winter.

From Maritime's standpoint, there was a particular reason to question the use of the laid-up fleet. This was the problem of funds; Maritime had no substantial appropriations to recondition laid-up tankers. Although the Commission was enjoying a heavy return from its tanker operations, approximately ten million dollars a month, all such revenue was covered into the miscellaneous receipts of the Treasury, and was thus unavailable to recondition tankers. The cost of reconditioning was estimated to be on the average of three hundred thousand dollars per tanker. But Maritime had no funds appropriated for that purpose in the approaching fiscal year and the funds to be carried over were negligible. The principal hope, and by no means a sure one, was that Congress might soon make available to the Commission some left-over War Shipping Administration funds which could be used, among other purposes, for reconditioning. It was also felt that while funds could probably be obtained to recondition vessels for use in General Agency assignments to U. S. shipping companies, funds to prepare vessels for sale to foreigners would not be easily forthcoming.

An even more compelling and urgent reason for Maritime's opposition to the laid-up fleet provision was the impending lapse of its statutory authority to operate tankers under General Agency Agreement. The existing statute (Public Law 6—80th Congress, approved February 26, 1947) authorized GAA operations until June 30. As has been indicated, there was no assurance that the authority would be extended; indeed, Congressman Weichel's attacks made it extremely likely that the authority would lapse, and the danger increased daily as Weichel's campaign continued. In view of this ominous prospect, Maritime had become most anxious to sell tankers from the operating fleet before July 1 when they would have to be taken out of service. The Navy condition of course blocked this. But on June 28, only two days before the GAA authority was to lapse, Congress passed Public Law 127, notwithstanding the Weichel campaign, which extended to March 1, 1948, both the GAA authority and the original termination date of the entire Ship Sales Act. The action of Congress removed an important factor in Maritime's opposition to Navy's insistence on use of the laid-up fleet.

The second basic issue, expressed in the Navy and Maritime letters, was that concerning "selected" foreign nationals. Navy desired the sales of tankers restricted to nationals of selected nations, out of the fear that otherwise tankers might pass to countries subject to easy invasion by a power potentially hostile to the U. S. Previously, the State Department had recognized the right of free selection in the Maritime Commission, and Maritime also had claimed the right for itself. Actually, Maritime had acted more upon the State Department's than its own convictions, for it was State, not Maritime, which provided the considerations on which the opposition to Navy was based. State deemed the Navy proposal that sales be limited to nations with our own "political philosophy and ideology" confused and restrictive. State was especially concerned, as has been pointed out, that minor officials in the Maritime Commission would use this language to advance their own prejudices.

Here matters stood. There were two issues and their resolution became the objective of the immediate further efforts of the agencies to advance foreign sales. None of the arguments, it will be noted, had met head-on. None was developed to any extent in the correspondence. In such an elusive state, could they be successfully resolved? The negotiations which followed were directly addressed to this question.

FURTHER NEGOTIATIONS

Monday, June 23

There was annoyance in many places, particularly in the Executive Office, over the failure of Navy and Maritime to agree and the hardening of disagreement into official letters. Steelman and Conway saw as the necessary next step an immediate meeting of the disputant agencies to iron out all differences. Both officials began to urge Chairman Smith to call a meeting. Somewhat reluctantly he concurred and directed Morse to proceed with arrangements.

Tuesday, June 24

Morse, Mansfield, Radius and others from Navy, Maritime, and State met on this date at Maritime. The group came to grips with the two harrassing questions posed in the Navy-Maritime exchange of letters: selection of nationals and laid-up fleet.

1. Selection of nationals. Here Maritime took the initiative and presented a list of foreign nations to whom or to whose nationals tankers were to be sold. The list was composed chiefly from the tanker applications then on hand, and the procedure employed at the meeting turned out to be advantageous to State. Maritime introduced the entire list of the nations at the meeting's outset and invited objections. Of the twelve countries listed, Navy objected only to Sweden. The State Department believed it would have fared much worse had the list been constructed country by country in the meeting. Nothing was decided on Sweden.

2. The laid-up fleet. There was retrogression if anything, after considerable discussion, much of it heated. Somehow the Navy representatives were asked what they understood the June 20 letter of the Secretary of the Navy to mean. They replied that none of the 54 tankers in the active fleet could be sold to foreign nationals unless 46 tankers in the laid-up fleet were sold concurrently. The Maritime and State representatives made emphatically clear that they did not subscribe to this interpretation of Navy's letter, and the session ended in deadlock on this point. Why Maritime did not proceed with its own interpretation of the Navy letter without raising the question at all is not clear.

Wednesday, June 25

There was a meeting of the Maritime Commission. Morse, who attended all meetings as Special Assistant to the Commission, reported the status of foreign sales. Extensive discussion followed concerning the report and Navy's attitude. The upshot was a decision to seek a reconciliation with Navy over the laid-up fleet perplexity. Maritime had, at this point, been heartened by the intervention of Majority Leader Halleck and other Republican party leaders which had checked Congressman Weichel's intransigence, and assured extension of Maritime's General Agency authority. The resulting optimism led the Commissioners to feel that Congress would make available the War Shipping Administration funds, now tied up, to recondition tankers. So confident had the Commission become, that it decided, as a measure to meet Navy's objections, to recondition at Maritime's expense and with the

WSA funds, all of the 46 tankers in the laid-up fleet.

Thursday, June 26

Admiral Smith and Morse conferred with Steelman, outlined the entire situation—the positions of Maritime and State, the position of Navy, and Maritime's compromise proposals adopted the day before, which, it was hoped, would satisfy Navy and avoid having the tanker matter brought back to the Cabinet or the President. Steelman expressed his approval of the Commission's proposals.

Friday, June 27

A further aftermath of the conference was a meeting convened on this day, by Captain Conway, of representatives of Army, Navy, Interior, State and Maritime, to discuss the oil and tanker situation and Maritime's compromise proposal. Encouraged by the friendly atmosphere of the meeting, Morse afterwards phoned to Admirals Ramsey and Carney (who were substituting for Callaghan then on vacation), and secured their promise to "strongly recommend these proposals to the Secretary of the Navy and Under Secretary Sullivan." The Admirals asked, however, that the proposals be put into writing for this purpose. Accordingly, Morse sat down to draft a letter for signature of Chairman Smith.

Saturday, June 28

The President signed Public Law 127, extending the Maritime Commission's operating authority for tankers from July 1, 1947, to March 1, 1948. The law also extended the termination date of the Merchant Ship Sales Act from December 31, 1947, to March 1, 1948.

Monday, June 30

The Maritime Chairman sent to the Secretary of the Navy Maritime's new proposal that up to 100 tankers be sold foreign from the active fleet, and that Maritime repair and restore to operation 46 tankers from lay-up. Maritime, in this letter, reaffirmed its opposition to the suggestion in Navy's letter of June 20 that 46 of the 100 tankers be from the laid-up fleet, though its compromise offer represented a partial adoption of Navy's viewpoint, for the arrangement would bring additional tonnage into operation. Admiral Smith also pointed out that this compromise proposal would meet one of Maritime's objections to withdrawals from the laid-up fleet. The Navy approach, Maritime had felt, would commit tankers of the more desirable makes to foreign sale. Maritime's new approach would completely avoid this danger. Only an observation to this effect was made in Maritime's letter, but in a staff memorandum, a comparison of Navy-Maritime proposals in terms of "desirable" and "undesirable" company-makes of T-2s involved in foreign sales appeared as follows:

Navy Proposal
(exclusively from active fleet)

4	"desirable" company-make A
7	"desirable" company-make B
24	"undesirable" company-make C
11	"undesirable" company-make D
46	

Maritime Proposal
(exclusively from active fleet)

0	"desirable" company-make A
0	"desirable" company-make B
64	"undesirable" company-make C
24	"undesirable" company-make D
6	"undesirable" company-make E
100	[sic]

The Maritime letter to Navy also moved the matter of "selected" foreign nations toward final determination by indicating that following "consultation with the Department of State," it now intended to sell the tankers to the following countries: Argentina, Belgium, Canada, Denmark, France, Greece, United Kingdom, Italy, Netherlands, Peru, Sweden and Turkey. Maritime asked Navy's "confirmation" of this list.

A copy of the letter went to Steelman.

Tuesday, July 1 and Wednesday, July 2

Receiving no word from Navy, Maritime officials became uneasy.

Thursday, July 3

A Navy representative called Morse to say that Navy would stand on the Secretary's letter of June 20, and thus would not approve of

Maritime's compromise proposals in its June 30 letter. Perplexed, Morse decided to do nothing further—the Fourth of July weekend had come—and to wait until work was resumed on July 7. The turn of events was painful. Morse had expected the "compromise" to work, for the Navy representatives had accepted it in their conversations before he put it formally in the Chairman's letter. Then, unexpectedly, reversal had come; apparently the Navy representatives had stepped beyond the point where the official leadership of Navy would follow. There was, indeed, one further recourse, a direct appeal to that leadership itself. Resolved to take it, Morse waited for Monday.

At this point, the differences between the Maritime Commission and the Navy seemed extremely slight. As for the laid-up fleet, which had been the most vexatious issue, both agencies were agreed that all the 46 tankers in the laid-up fleet should be repaired and brought into operation. The sole issue arose out of the relation of that action to foreign sales. Navy wished the laid-up fleet to be a source for the tankers that were to be sold. Maritime wished the use of the laid-up tankers to be completely disassociated from the sales, though it agreed to repair them. As for the second issue, the difference between the agencies had come to be of almost insignificant proportions. Only Sweden, of all the nations to which the Maritime Commission and the State Department wished to sell tankers, was disputed by Navy.

Monday, July 7

Morse reported the situation to those most immediately concerned, Admiral Smith and Captain Conway, and then talked with Admiral Callaghan, who had returned from leave. Callaghan was sympathetic and offered the suggestion that Chairman Smith and Acting Secretary Sullivan discuss the situation. Callaghan asked that Morse take no further action until the Smith-Sullivan conference was arranged. Morse then checked with Smith and Conway and both agreed on condition that the conference be held on that very day. At noon, Callaghan called Morse, and proposed that Chairman Smith phone Secretary Sullivan in the afternoon, say that he understood that Navy's reply to Maritime's proposal would be unfavorable, and suggest further discussion. Morse agreed. A few minutes later he had a call from Robert C. Turner, Steelman's Assistant. Turner said he knew things had gone amiss and asked for the facts. Morse gave him a report and both agreed that Steelman, who was anxious for progress, might await the results of the Smith-Sullivan meeting before calling Navy or doing anything else.

The meeting was held in the afternoon. Smith and Morse for Maritime met at Sullivan's office with Sullivan, Admirals Carney and Callaghan, and Captains Mansfield and Dannenberg. Sullivan strongly opposed Maritime's program. He thoroughly mistrusted Maritime's assurances about reconditioning the 46 vessels in lay-up. He feared that Congress would not permit Maritime to use funds for reconditioning. He claimed that Maritime intended to embark upon a foreign sales program detrimental to military and domestic requirements. Sullivan was abrupt throughout the meeting with Maritime's officials and was not even inclined to listen to explanations or read memoranda of Maritime's plans. The compromise had failed, at least for the time being.

Tuesday, July 8

Morse and Smith reported orally to a meeting of the Maritime Commission the proceedings at Navy. The Commission unanimously decided to take no further action on the sale of tankers until Navy made a formal reply to the Chairman's letter of June 30.

Wednesday, July 9

Morse and Callaghan conferred, but nothing eventful developed.

Thursday, July 10

Morse and Callaghan again conferred. Morse urged Navy to reply to Maritime's letter, for he was convinced that no further progress could be made until Navy's position concerning Maritime's proposed compromise was stated in clear-cut and definitive form.

Later in the day Callaghan advised Morse that he and Carney were willing to recommend to Sullivan approval of Maritime's proposals with the provisos:

(1) that the more desirable types of vessels be retained under U. S. control;

(2) that "the Navy Department will not concur in any foreign sales program which will reduce the operating tanker fleet below that required to meet United States needs." Callaghan incorporated all this, including a statement of approval of Maritime's plan into a draft of a letter for the signature of Acting Secretary Sullivan. At the same time, in anticipation of possible unwillingness of the Secretary to sign such a letter, Callaghan drafted a second letter clearly disapproving Maritime's proposal. Callaghan and Carney took both letters to Sullivan late in the day, but Sullivan refused to decide between them until he returned from the weekend and had further discussion on Monday, July 14.

Friday, July 11

A conference in Morse's office, called at Callaghan's request, reviewed the whole matter. Present were Callaghan and Mansfield for Navy, and Morse and technical officials for Maritime. Upon reflection, Callaghan had dropped his preference for the two-letter approach, and now favored a definite stand to be taken in a single letter prepared for Sullivan's signature. There was extended discussion to determine what this stand should be. Finally, Callaghan declared that he would present to the Secretary of the Navy what he termed a "compromise proposal." It was that Navy would agree to Maritime's June 30 proffer if: (1) the more desirable types of tankers were retained under U. S. control; (2) foreign sales would not reduce the operating tanker fleet below that required to meet U. S. needs; (3) foreign sales from the active fleet exceeding 54 tankers would only be in numbers corresponding to the numbers of vessels repaired and brought into operation from the 46 tankers in the laid-up fleet.

Callaghan stated frankly that the last condition was based upon Navy's fear that otherwise Maritime might not repair the 46 tankers or might be prevented from so doing by causes beyond its control, i.e., Congressional action.

Maritime representatives pointed out that, except for the last condition, Callaghan's proposal was not at odds with Maritime's proposal of June 20. With the last condition, however, Maritime could not comply. As an independent agency, Maritime had definite responsibilities under law concerning the sale of vessels and thus it was not appropriate that Navy attempt to "dictate" to the Commission how it should carry out those responsibilities. Navy's effort was particularly inappropriate, said Maritime representatives, since "the Commission had what amounted to a directive from the Cabinet conveyed to it through the Secretary of State to seek the removal of restrictions over the sale of the 100 tankers in question and in proceeding to sell these vessels would be primarily responsible for the success and effectiveness of any program of sale decided upon."

The exchange of "compromise proposals" of Maritime and Navy therefore settled nothing. The key difference between Maritime and Navy over the laid-up fleet still obtained. Navy insisted that the repair of tankers in lay-up be linked to the foreign sales program. The official departmental position, i.e., the one approved by Acting Secretary Sullivan, was still, of course, in force. Of the 100 tankers to be sold foreign, 46 were to be sold from the laid-up fleet. Also, these 46 tankers were to be sold "concurrently" with tankers sold from the operating fleet. Maritime had rejected this arrangement and in lieu of it had offered its "compromise" that 100 tankers be sold from the operating fleet on condition that Maritime ready for service the 46 tankers in the laid-up fleet. The Navy Department, speaking principally through Acting Secretary Sullivan, had rejected the proposal. Sullivan had frankly indicated his mistrust of Maritime's intention to recondition the 46 tankers. He also feared that Congress might not permit funds to be used for that purpose. Thus, the most effective means to assure Navy's basic position, that laid-up tankers be brought into service, was to keep them linked directly with foreign sales.

Maritime had consistently rejected this proposal for reasons which seemed to increase as negotiations continued. Though Maritime was now confident that Congress would make funds available to recondition tankers in lay-up, there still was objection to inclusion of laid-up tankers among the tankers sold to foreign nations. There was the problem of time; the reconditioning of tankers had not as yet begun and the average time anticipated to recondition any tanker was, as has been said, three months. In view of the speed required to provide effective aid to Europe, this period seemed unreasonable. Also, there was a new argument, just introduced, that if Maritime followed Navy's proposal, "desirable" tankers would be sold. Observance of Maritime's approach would assure that only "undesirable" tankers would pass to foreign nations.

It will be noted that none of the arguments offered by Navy and Maritime was directly met by opposing considerations. Each argument was advanced without any refutation which challenged the argument's validity. Instead new and not directly related arguments were offered in answer. There was no head-on conflict. Maritime never answered Navy's contention that the world tanker situation would improve only if tankers not in use (i.e., tankers in lay-up) were brought into service. Navy, on the other hand, did not answer the "undue delay" argument of Maritime, i.e., reliance upon the reconditioning of ships in lay-up would violate the interest in speedy assistance to Europe.

It was in recognition of this deadlock that Callaghan's version of a compromise was presented. He made clear, however, that this was only his own position and not that of his department. The Callaghan plan entailed a limited retreat from Navy's official position. Instead of the requirement that the 46 tankers in lay-up be sold "concurrently" with active tankers, Callaghan proposed that 54 tankers be immediately sold from the active fleet without reference to the laid-up fleet. Thus the idea of "concurrent" sales of active and laid-up tankers to that extent was dropped. However, the sale of active tankers exceeding 54 would only be in numbers corresponding to the numbers of vessels repaired and brought into operation from the 46 tankers in the laid-up fleet.

Callaghan's unofficial proposal—which he offered to press upon the Acting Secretary of the Navy—was immediately and vigorously rejected by Maritime officials. In strong terms, the Navy representatives were informed that they were improperly invading Maritime's prerogative to determine the disposal of its own ships. There the matter ended. There was no analytic discussion of Callaghan's plan; it was summarily rejected, much as Maritime's earlier plan had been rejected by Sullivan.

Various reasons underlay this summary rejection. Certainly the whole scheme of foreign sales was generally disliked at Maritime. Also Maritime officials had some fear that they would be subject to further criticism by the Cabinet if the proposal were accepted and then caused delay in the disposal program. Perhaps, in part, at least, the Maritime officials had become painfully sensitive to the pulling and hauling to which they had been subjected, and now finally decided to stand on their jurisdictional rights. Perhaps they were merely extremely loath to go through another difficult session with a discordant and resentful Commission.

With Navy unyielding about the laid-up fleet, Maritime seemed to have two alternatives. First, the Commission might go ahead, on its own, with foreign sales in disregard of Navy's advice. One Naval officer, in the course of an exasperatingly long conference, actually asked the Maritime representatives if this course might not well be taken. In his opinion—an opinion which most of his colleagues shared—the negotiations were becoming repetitious and the deadlock solid. A sense of futility and boredom was settling in. Second, Maritime might throw the whole matter back into the lap of the Secretary of State. Neither alternative appeared pleasing. The first involved the grave hazard of action affecting national defense taken by a civilian agency without the approval—indeed with the disapproval—of the military agency concerned. The second alternative was equally distasteful. It admitted the defeat of a mission whose performance was formally desired by both the President and the Cabinet.

Repelled by these alternatives, and in an effort to cut the Gordian knot, Morse next suggested that Navy, in replying to Maritime's letter of June 30, concur with the Commission's proposals and at the same time recommend that Maritime abide by the two conditions of Callaghan's proposal—the keeping of desirable tankers under U. S. control and adequately safeguarding U. S. domestic and military requirements. Callaghan promised to place this new suggestion before Secretary Sullivan and advise Morse.

Monday, July 14, to Wednesday, July 16

During these days numerous telephone conversations were held between Morse and Callaghan, and other Maritime and Navy officials, which sought the fulfillment and reported the progress of Morse's plan. The outcome of these efforts was reflected in the long-awaited reply, then in draft, of Navy to Maritime.

Thursday, July 17

Navy issued its official reply in the form of a letter from Secretary Forrestal to Chairman Smith. The letter reproduced the plan which Admiral Callaghan had advanced in the interagency conferences. The Morse plan was thus not approved by the Navy Secretary, though it had been presented fully to him by Callaghan and other Navy officials.

Forrestal pointed out that after consideration of the objectives of both the Navy and the Maritime Commission, he was convinced that these could best be accomplished if the following conditions were adhered to:

(1) that not more than 54 tankers were to be sold on the foreign market until numerical replacements were made ready for service from the 46 tankers in the laid-up fleet. "This condition," the Secretary noted, "is not to restrict the sale foreign of tankers directly from the laid-up fleet should the Maritime Commission determine that course to be either practicable or desirable."

(2) that foreign sales would not reduce the operating tanker fleet below that required to meet U. S. needs.

(3) that the more desirable type of tankers be retained under U. S. control.

Secretary Forrestal noted that these conditions were to be understood to supersede the conditions of sale set forth in his letter of June 20.

The present letter perpetuated another, though far less serious, issue. The Secretary noted that Navy had no objection to sales of tankers to the countries listed in Maritime's letter of June 30, except Sweden. It hardly seemed likely, at this point, that the State Department would ever agree to the exclusion of Sweden, but in any event the other sales could proceed without debate.

Friday, July 18, to Wednesday, July 23

This was an interlude of anxious consultations of Maritime officials with Steelman and Conway and Radius and Ball, in quest of a suitable position in view of Navy's insistence upon the laid-up fleet. Maritime was deep in a quandary. It could repair some ships in the laid-up fleet and had taken steps to do so. But it was not confident that it could recondition laid-up ships at the pace that the Navy's proposal required if the prime objective of foreign sales was to be realized—immediate aid to Europe. Repair of tankers in lay-up would under best conditions average three months, exclusive of the several weeks required to bring the tankers to the yards. And the best conditions did not obtain—strikes in several yards had begun and if they spread, as was likely, extensive repair plans would be prohibited.

There was also the alternative for Maritime openly to defy Navy. No one at Maritime had stomach for that choice, and so in their consultations with the other agencies and among themselves, Maritime officials sought a position that would enable the sales to proceed satisfactorily under terms which Navy would at least not oppose.

Thursday, July 24

The results of these efforts were embodied in a letter drafted by Morse for the Chairman's signature. It was approved by the Commission and sent on this date.

The letter was conciliatory, capitalizing on existing Navy-Maritime agreement, keeping differences at a minimum, though not surrendering on the laid-up fleet. The letter began by acknowledging Navy-Maritime agreement that 100 tankers should be sold to selected nations, that the best ships be kept under U. S. control, and that domestic and military requirements be properly safeguarded. Maritime also agreed that repairable tankers in the laid-up fleet should be sold or restored to operation and pointed out that it had authorized such steps. But the letter also pointed out that full observance of the Navy stipulations was impractical. The exact condition of the 46 tankers in lay-up was unknown, and the "best interests" of the U. S. and the limited funds that Congress might provide might dictate that "some or all of these vessels be not restored to operation or sold." Thus adherence to the Navy condition might entail a corresponding cut in the number of vessels over 54 which could be sold to foreign nations.

The letter then proceeded to outline in detail a sales program evolved from the consultations with the Assistant to the President and other "interested agencies" (State and Interior), which would most effectively meet the world-wide tanker and petroleum situation and safeguard U. S. requirements.

First in priority was to be the satisfaction of U. S. citizen demand, whether for U. S. or Panamanian registry. (Many U. S. purchasers resort to Panamanian registry. The attractions are avoidance of wage scales paid to U. S. crews and the U. S. income tax. And from the Navy standpoint, Panamanian registry is about the equivalent of U. S. registry.) Second in priority was to be the tanker sales program for "selected" foreign interests. For these foreign sales, Maritime reported to Navy two additional policy determinations. Sales from the operating fleet were to be made on condition that the purchaser take the tankers "as is," which, of course, avoided liability of Maritime for repairs. Also, the purchaser had to agree to make only essential operating repairs for the first voyage, a stipulation designed to assuage Navy's objection that sales from the operating fleet might actually reduce the number of tankers in operation. Last in Maritime's priority were sales from lay-up which were to proceed to the extent that Congress permitted such tankers to be repaired.

Copies of the letter went to the Secretaries of State and Interior, and to Steelman.

Friday, July 25

Though the matter of the laid-up fleet hung unresolved, Morse and Radius agreed to further the present tentative decision on allocations of tankers to foreign nations. Accordingly, Morse held a meeting with Radius, Callaghan and Friedman present. Maritime reported that at this time 269 T-2 tankers were available for sale in the active and laid-up fleets. Of these, 113 were set aside for U. S. citizens, either for charter or purchase, and 100 were tagged for sale to foreign nationals, leaving 56 available for U. S.-controlled Panamanian flag operation. As of this date, however, there were only eight applications on file from U. S. citizens for the purchase of T-2 Tankers. Thus, the Maritime Commission considered it sound to allocate 100 tankers for foreign sale. There was no substantial U. S. citizen demand which under the Ship Sales Act had to receive consideration prior to foreign applicants.

Morse then presented the list, which allocated by priority and number the 100 tankers to be released for foreign sale. The list was based upon the foreign nations previously approved, except that Sweden had been added at the insistence of the State Department. There was some discussion of Sweden, in which all the agencies present but Interior participated. Interior hewed to the line of taking no part in the conflict over the laid-up fleet and selected nationals as Ball and his aides did not conceive it to be Interior's function to do so. In any event, after discussion, it was agreed that tankers might be tentatively allocated to Sweden. Navy suggested that the allocation to Chile be similarly treated and after further discussion Uruguay and South Africa were also added to the list of tentative allocations.

There follows the allocation agreed upon by country, priority, and number of tankers for the 100 tankers proposed for foreign sale:

1. United Kingdom	31
2. Turkey	1
3. France	11
4. Italy	16
5. Canada	3
6. Netherlands	4
7. Greece	7
8. Denmark	3
9. Belgium	1
10. Peru	1
11. Norway	11
12. Argentina	3
Total	92

Eight additional tankers were tentatively allocated as follows:

1.	Uruguay	2
2.	Chile	1
3.	Sweden	1
4.	South Africa	2
5.	Undecided	2
	Total	8

The applications on hand at the Maritime Commission as of June 12, 1947, were the principal factor in the tanker allocations. From them, Maritime compiled its list and assigned roughly the number of tankers to a nation which that nation or its nationals had applied for. The priority schedule was based largely upon criteria suggested by State, i.e., a given country's need for oil, her ability to carry it from Near Eastern sources to Europe, and her general political importance in the recovery program. Navy and Maritime acquiesced in this, Navy being particularly glad to give top priority to the United Kingdom, our principal presumed ally in event of a military emergency. On this final list, State made one reservation, which the other agencies accepted, that all applications of Greek nationals be referred to the Department for "co-ordination" with the U. S. Mission at Athens and with the Greek Government.

The meeting did not attempt to decide upon the proportion of vessels in lay-up each nation was to take against those in operation, except in the case of the United Kingdom. Here the group believed that the critical petroleum situation in the United Kingdom and the ability and expressed intention of the British to move their tankers into the Persian Gulf to carry their own oil, warranted granting them the privilege of purchasing all their tankers from the operating fleet. As for the other nations, the group believed that an equitable proportioning ought to be made between the operating and laid-up fleets. It will be noted that the deduction of the tankers for the U. K. meant that the other nations would share 23 operating and 46 laid-up tankers.

On the same day Maritime also placed all the interested agencies upon official notice of the status of its affairs with Navy. The Chairman of the Commission wrote to the Secretary of State and enclosed copies of Navy's letter of July 17, and the Commission's reply of July 24, with the comment:

> These letters clearly indicate that the Navy and the Maritime Commission are in agreement that 100 additional T-2 type tankers can be sold foreign to the nations listed by the Navy or the nationals thereof. Furthermore, that the objectives of both agencies are the same.
>
> The Commission believes that the procedure and program outlined in its letter of July 24 to the Navy constitute the most effective means of carrying out the intent and purposes of the Cabinet decision. . . .

Letters to similar effect, with the same enclosures and a copy of the above letter to State, were sent to Steelman and Secretary Krug. With these gestures, Maritime apparently considered a critical chapter in the tanker story to have ended.

Monday, July 28, to Wednesday, July 30

There was a lull, in which Maritime officials were preparing papers for Commission action pursuant to the inter-agency agreements reached on Friday.

Thursday, July 31

The Maritime Commission approved the allocations list arranged at the inter-agency meeting, July 25. Morse incorporated the list into a memorandum to the Commission reporting the meeting fully, and on this memorandum the Commission's action was taken. The pertinent excerpt from the Commission's minutes follows:

> After discussion, the Commission by the unanimous yea vote of members present approved the order of priority as listed in the foregoing memorandum with the proviso that when sale is finally consummated each vessel shall be required to fly the flag of the country under which it was purchased. . . . The Commission directed that the foregoing shall be construed only as an order of priority and not an approval of sale and that separate recommendations for specific sales shall be submitted in accordance therewith with a tabulation showing the vessels by name and whether the vessel is to be taken from the reserve fleet or from the operating fleet.

The Commission's caution, in the latter sentence, was owed to an intention not to commit desirable-type vessels, by this action, to foreign sales, for the Commission did not have a list of vessels before it. The Commission also decided, in keeping with the inter-agency agreement, to meet British requirements by sales from the operating fleet and to work out for the other countries a pro-rationing between laid-up and operating tankers.

Friday, August 1

On and after this date, the various foreign nations on the priority list were informed orally by Commission representatives—there was no written notification—of the specific number of tankers available to them for sale. By the end of August, all the countries except Canada were so notified. The countries for which allocations were tentatively made, and Canada, were not notified until October 3.

Wednesday, August 6

Maritime's letter of July 24—written for the record, as the phrase goes—was answered in somewhat similar vein by the Navy.

The Secretary of the Navy noted the disagreement with Navy's condition that not more than 54 tankers be sold from the active fleet until replacements from the inactive fleet were readied for service. The Secretary recalled that the condition originated from the JCS recommendations regarding the laid-up fleet which, in turn, were prompted by a quite proper concern with the adequacy of U. S. tanker tonnage to meet possible future emergencies. On the other hand, the Secretary recognized that foreign sale of tankers at this time would contribute materially to the betterment of world economic conditions and thus help prevent the development of circumstances which might lead through economic chaos to discord.

The Secretary followed this with an expression of the Navy's great interest in the development of a tanker construction program in the U. S., and the rise of a modern fleet; the Secretary proposed that Maritime join with the Navy in preparing and presenting to Congress legislation earmarking the proceeds of all foreign tanker sales, from 1946 on, for use in the construction of new tankers.

Then followed the critical portions of the letter.

> Speaking generally, I want to point out that the Maritime Commission was well within its rights in differing with me, from time to time, on the conditions to be applied in selling tankers. The Ship Sales Act of 1946 clearly gives final responsibility to the Maritime Commission, and specifies only that there will be "consultation with the Secretary of the Navy" before final action is taken. There has been extensive consultation in connection with the sale of tankers . . . . not only through means of the correspondence and discussions referred to above, but also through numerous conversations between officials of the Maritime Commission and officials of the Navy Department.

The Secretary then recalled the nature of the military review entailed in the statutory clearance. Though the Act did not require that JCS be consulted "in any way," he had deemed it wise to do so, "especially on the strictly military considerations." Hence JCS advised on the 1946 sales and the first 1947 sales, whereas the second 1947 sales were taken up with the Chief of Naval Operations instead of JCS because of the limited novelty of the issues involved.

Then came a paragraph of great importance to Maritime.

> This is to advise you that the Navy Department does not recede from the position expressed in its letter of July 17 regarding the controls that should be exercised over tanker sales. In the event that the Maritime Commission does not adhere to the conditions set forth in the Navy Department's letter of July 17, 1947, it will be assumed that the Navy Department's views in this matter have been reviewed by the Maritime Commission and that considerations other than of national defense have influenced the Maritime Commission in departing therefrom.

THE ISSUE REMAINING

Despite the pointed nature of Navy's letter of August 6 and Maritime's of July 25, the differences between the two agencies had actually become quite narrow. There now was only one sizeable issue: Navy wished all 46 tankers in lay-up linked with the foreign sales; Maritime wished only certain of these tankers—it did not specify how many—so disposed. Maritime based its reservation upon the belief that many of the 46 tankers could not be repaired for operation. The precise condition of the laid-up tankers was unknown to Maritime, as they had not been surveyed, but many were believed badly damaged. Their repair seemed precluded under the limited funds which Congress had provided for repair purposes. Thus observance of Navy's proposal would reduce the number of tankers sold to foreign purchasers, i.e., those tankers among the 46 which could not be repaired would lower correspondingly the number of tankers beyond the 54 active tankers available for foreign sale.

The difficulty that Maritime found itself in was largely, or perhaps entirely of its own making. The fact was that the Commission had directed as far back as June that the 46 tankers be removed from the laid-up fleet and be repaired after competitive bids had been obtained for each tanker and submitted to the Commission for approval. Yet now, as late as August, presumably because of administrative laxity, not one competitive bid had been obtained, and Maritime did not even know how many of the 46 tankers would prove to be beyond repair.

Considerable fears and confusion were provoked at Maritime by these circumstances. Though the area of disagreement with Navy was limited, its nature was forbidding. Maritime, if it held to its own plan—and only thus could the foreign sales program be fully realized—must proceed in a manner which the Navy had officially and emphatically disapproved. Some within the Commission wished, nevertheless, to move ahead. To others, the hazards seemed imposing. Tankers have obvious importance in military logistics, and, to proceed with its own sales program, Maritime would be substituting its judgment for the military's in an apparently military matter. On the other hand, there were the President's known wishes and the Cabinet's decision that 100 tankers be sold to foreign interests. Navy's approach entailed the sale of fewer than 100 and the Commission was caught between two wills.

Thursday, August 7

Confused by its dilemma, the Commission showed no disposition to take further action.

Friday, August 8

The Commission was still unmoved, but pressure from another source disturbed its inertia. The President's Assistant, Steelman, wrote the Maritime Commission, inquiring what progress had been made on the sale of 100 tankers. The Steelman letter recalled Secretary Marshall's request of June 16 and Steelman's own previous advice to Maritime of the President's concern in the matter. The letter also recalled the Secretary of the Navy's approval on June 20 of the limit of 100 tankers for foreign sale. Steelman expressed the desire to know of the Commission's present situation regarding the sale and delivery of the tankers in relation to the number of applications pending. This report was to be forthcoming at the Commission's "earliest convenience" and was to be "supplemented periodically." The letter was courteous but firmly insistent and the implication was unmistakable. The President desired action, prompt action. The choice for Maritime was now distastefully clear: either it must respond to the President's wish and speed the tanker program—which also meant defiance of Navy and the risks involved; or Maritime might abide by the Navy's will and thus considerably slow up the tanker sales—and defy the President.

Monday, August 11

The Commission contemplated.

Tuesday, August 12, and Wednesday, August 13

The Commission chose. In two days of intensive meetings, the Commission arrived at a position which seemingly straddled the Presidential and Navy policies. From the President's standpoint, the Commission directed that the sale of 100 T-2 Type Tankers to foreign purchasers "as approved and directed by the President's Cabinet" be consummated and set forth procedures of sales to govern the Commission's staff.

The further decisions of Maritime approximated the Navy letter of June 20 and its interpretation by Navy officials that sales must be made concurrently from the operating and laid-up fleets. The Commission resolved to sell 53 T-2s from the active fleet and 34 from the laid-up fleet. It adopted a schedule of the number of vessels which each foreign nation was to select from the active fleet and from the laid-up fleet, with the proviso that no vessels were to be delivered from the operating fleet until purchase contracts for vessels from the laid-up fleet were signed. These steps the Commission took upon the premise that the Secretary of the Navy had given them clearance in his letter of June 20.

Repair costs for readying ships from both the active and laid-up fleets, the Commission decided, were to be borne by the foreign purchaser.

The figures 53 and 34 (which the Commission finally reached) were based upon the original list which the Commission approved July 25. The total tankers involved at that date was 90. The number had since been reduced to 87 by Denmark's withdrawal of its tanker applications. The tankers first assigned to Denmark were now added to the few held in general reserve.

Morse notified Conway, Radius and Callaghan of these decisions by telephone, and began the task of drafting a reply for signature of Admiral Smith to Steelman's inquiry.

Such evidently sudden and sweeping action by the Commission is difficult to explain. All the factors, many of them important, which governed its conduct are not known. Yet certain circumstances are apparent and from them limited inferences may be drawn. As previously noted, the stand of the Commission on the laid-up fleet, during the lengthy negotiations, was in several critical parts somewhat vague in contrast to the Navy's characteristically definite position. The uncertainty of Maritime was symptomatic of irresolution on policy within the Commission itself. Though the Commission had some time before decided that the laid-up tankers should be brought into operation, the question *how* that purpose should be accomplished provoked an insistent dispute within the agency. So long as the question remained unresolved, it was difficult, as this account has indicated, for the Commission to adjust its position in negotiations with Navy on the laid-up fleet. For, as will be seen, that position was to be vitally determined by whatever method, among several possible methods, was chosen to bring the laid-up tankers into operation. Meanwhile, the Congress, after long delay, had decided not to make the WSA funds available for tanker repairs.

The several conflicting methods, advocated both by influential staff members and Commissioners at Maritime, were as follows:

(1) The laid-up tankers should be repaired and operated under General Agency authority. (The proponents of this course had opposed Navy's early insistence that the 46 tankers in lay-up be included in the foreign sales.) The underlying consideration here was that no substantial appropriations were available to repair the tankers, but if the laid-up tankers were diverted to General Agency, there would be available $100,000,000 which could be used for "voyage repairs." Some of the Maritime officials held that these funds could properly be used to repair the laid-up ships. Others held that this action would be contrary to the intent of Congress, and that other uses to which these funds were clearly committed precluded their expenditure on the tankers in lay-up. A diversion of the funds would antagonize Congress.

(2) The tankers should be sold from lay-up at the price prescribed by the Ship Sales Act, adjusted by such allowances to the purchaser by the Commission for repairs as could be made under the statute. In doubt, again, was the intention of Congress. Some held that Congress did not envision any "costly" items of repair for which allowances could be made. Others claimed that Congress intended that the Commission grant allowances sufficient to place the tankers in reasonable operating condition. But, against this contention, it was said that "a great many" of the laid-up tankers were "in very bad condition" and thus not more than a limited number of tankers could be sold from lay-up.

(3) The sale of the tankers "as is" from the laid-up fleet. The purchaser would bear the entire cost of repairs and responsibility for making them. This was a simple method and it did not involve the use of Commission funds. For these reasons it attracted consider-

able, and eventually successful, advocacy. Yet there was the imposing objection that "many" tankers were in such bad condition that their purchase was unlikely. To the extent that they were not sold, the foreign sales program would be reduced.

For weeks these opposing policy approaches remained unresolved within the Commission. Though the Commission had decided in June to repair the tankers in lay-up, no practical step was taken, largely because of these uncertainties which persisted until Maritime made the decisions of August 12 and 13, just noted.

Through all these weeks, the other agencies interested in foreign sales waited impatiently. To most, it seemed obvious that foreign sales would have to occur in substantial numbers from the laid-up fleet. Since May, Maritime had been running far behind in meeting its General Agency allocation applications. Certainly no ships could be diverted from those assigned to agents, as all were employed in essential commerce. More tankers were plainly needed and could be had only if laid-up tankers were brought into operation. However obvious the answer, Maritime had difficulty making its choice among methods.

The other interested departments were not disposed to intervene. Ball of Interior, for instance, did not consider it the proper function of his agency to approach Maritime concerning the matter. Ball, in fact, was diverted by other pressing business and was not much concerned with the situation, despite the extraordinary delays. Neither was Radius too disturbed. His main goal had been won. Navy had approved the sale of 100 tankers, and the countries had been agreed on. The remaining details, what tankers were to be sold and the methods of sale, he considered the internal affair of Maritime. Although he kept in touch with events through Conway and others at the White House, Radius believed that the State Department's intervention would do little to solve the problem and might even impede progress. Conway, too, had much the same attitude. He and others of the Executive Office and White House staffs refrained from taking a definite stand on the laid-up tankers, although to them, as to others, the necessity that such tankers be included in the foreign sales seemed plain.

Yet Conway and Steelman were interested in seeing that the sales proceeded promptly, an attitude which prompted Steelman's inquiry of Maritime concerning the progress of foreign sales. The Steelman letter, bearing the prestige of the White House, provided invaluable aid to the group within the Commission which had always favored foreign sales and was impatient with the irresolution of other Maritime officials. Indeed the Steelman letter may have been a decisive stroke, but of this we cannot be certain. In any event, soon after its receipt, Maritime, on August 12 and 13, finally did act to bring the laid-up tankers into operation and to carry the tanker program forward. The Commission decided that 34 tankers were to be sold by the simplest means possible—"as is" from lay-up. The uncertainties over appropriations were avoided; both the "best" and the "unsaleable" tankers could be included in the 12 tankers which would remain in the laid-up fleet and not be offered for foreign sale. By this means, Maritime could proceed most expeditiously with the sales and thus be in a position to reply satisfactorily to Steelman's inquiry and the future inquiries which his letter foreshadowed.

Thursday, August 14

Chairman Smith replied to Steelman's inquiry of August 8 and ascribed the lame progress of foreign sales to uncertainties over the outcome of legislation before Congress affecting budgetary limitations and sales provisions of the Ship Sales Act. All these affected, the Chairman stated, the speed and scope of repair-work required for tankers in the laid-up fleet. Smith said the situation had become sufficiently clear to enable Maritime to adopt plans which would carry out "the intent and purposes of the Cabinet decision" and also comply "as far as it is possible to do so" with Navy's conditions from which Secretary Forrestal in his letter of August 6—a copy was now sent to Steelman—refused to recede.

Such was the Chairman's letter. Within Maritime was the hope that its compromise would suit everyone and that foreign sales would now proceed without further hindrance.

IN RETROSPECT

The intricate affairs just reviewed were extraordinary in several respects. They required nearly nine weeks to conclude in a situation where presumably speed was of the essence. They centered upon only two issues, which, as argument progressed, proved to raise merely slight differences between the contestants and were ultimately resolved.

Meantime, however, the tedious drawn-out negotiations entailed considerable bitterness and costly delay.

Of the two issues, one proved to be almost pointless, the selection of foreign nationals. As an issue, it was put as a question of principle: by what criteria ought foreign nations be selected to receive tankers? The argument over this question was sharp in the official letters and was never resolved until applied to the specific task of selecting the nations. Then, surprisingly enough, there was only a minimum of dispute between the agencies. Sweden alone was questioned; all the other nations were approved. A lengthy debate, occasioned by considerations of principle, almost instantly disappeared when examined in terms of action.

Nearly the same pattern characterized the prolonged dispute over the laid-up fleet. The numerous letters and memoranda which passed between Navy and Maritime are conspicuous for the lack of spelled-out and factually supported argument. The discussion was doctrinaire and as such served to lengthen the dispute considerably. Navy, for instance, in its earlier letters, stated that JCS had determined that sales from the laid-up fleet were a matter of military necessity. Beyond the assertion, no further arguments were presented, not even an indication of the considerations which influenced the JCS decision. Navy did not, for instance, cite in its letters its very important conclusion that the world tanker situation could be improved only if more tankers—and these could come only from the laid-up fleet—were brought into operation. The Navy position was only stated, and then only as a conclusion. It was not argued.

The Maritime Commission, however, did argue its position on the laid-up fleet. But the argument, it should be noted, was seldom factual, and rested mainly upon principle and conjecture. For Maritime at no point knew the precise condition of the 46 laid-up tankers in dispute. Yet its stand was at various points founded largely upon their conjectured condition. Maritime feared that among these tankers were some so badly damaged that they could not be sold, and that this circumstance, under Navy's proposal, would reduce the number of tankers actually available for sale. Would this, in fact, have occurred? No proof was ever introduced in the correspondence with Navy; the number of badly damaged tankers was not specified, or even estimated.

Beyond this, Maritime did little to argue its position in letters and memoranda. It seemed merely to proceed from one stated position with increasing, though slight, variations to another. Throughout, except for several minimum concessions, Navy held to the position set by the Joint Chiefs of Staff, and after nine weeks of tedious explorations of the laid-up fleet theme, Maritime came to accept substantially the Navy's stand.

It seems reasonable to infer that much of the invention and endurance which Maritime's negotiators displayed in their dealings with Navy on the laid-up fleet were evoked and determined by circumstances entirely within the Commission. As far back as June, the Commission had ordered that the laid-up ships be repaired for service. As late as August nothing of moment had been done to execute the Commission's order. Bids had not even been solicited for the repair of the tankers. Yet if the decision in June had been followed up in Maritime with reasonable effectiveness, the tankers would have been ready or almost ready in August, while the debate on the subject was still hotly proceeding. The obstructions and delays within its bureaus tended to push Maritime into the prolonged negotiations with Navy. Faced with the fact that the Commission had not repaired the tankers, its representatives had to contrive and offer to Navy formulas which detached as nearly as possible the laid-up tankers from sales foreign. Navy, on the other hand, always doubtful of Maritime's intentions to repair the tankers, found its suspicions increasingly well founded and its position, if anything, firmer.

In other respects, the attitude of Maritime toward the laid-up fleet is puzzling. The ultimate solution, not adopted until August, was to sell the laid-up ships "as is" to foreign purchasers. Why was this step not taken earlier? From Maritime's standpoint, it should have appeared a most attractive solution. Maritime would not have been troubled with the administrative difficulties of repairs; the question of ambiguous appropriations would not have had to be faced; and apparently the foreign nationals were, on the whole, just as ready to purchase the tankers "as is" in June as in August. The sooner tankers were delivered abroad, the more they would improve the winter's petroleum supply.

Actually, in the beginning some foreign buyers were hesitant to purchase tankers on an "as is" basis. Under this method, the buyer acquired the vessel at the price specified in the Ship Sales Act, without allowances for repairs, and thus faced the prospect of bearing the cost of repairs himself. In effect, a vessel might cost some $300,000 more, depending upon its condition. Some foreign buyers, therefore, in the early stages of the sales project, were somewhat reluctant to take tankers "as is," especially as long as they could hope that sales might include allowances for repairs. But as the petroleum shortage grew in acuteness, this reluctance quickly vanished.

It is also notable that the long debate over the laid-up tankers was conducted by only two active parties, Maritime and Navy. State and Interior had no part in it. The Steelman office, after the unusual step of its initial letter, never intervened with a concrete proposal to settle the laid-up fleet issue. At most, Steelman several times made known the desirability of action, but suggested no plan for achieving it. Meanwhile, the debate went on for nine weeks. Several questions seem pertinent. In view of this initial concerted action of Interior, State and the Steelman group to have Maritime approach Navy on the 100 tankers, was it both desirable and justifiable that all these agencies play such an inactive role in the long series of events which followed? Ought they not have prodded Maritime to cease its contentions over the laid-up fleet, or, alternatively, ought they not have aided Maritime against Navy to hasten a settlement? Significantly, all these agencies seemed cautious and forbearing toward Navy, though they desired results Navy was ready to give only under closely defined conditions which were not immediately acceptable to Maritime. As difficulties ensued, the agencies did not act on them. Ought they not have done so? Was not Navy's opinion, fortified by such strong elements as a statutory clearance provision and a fully defined JCS appraisal of our defense needs, likely to persist indefinitely against the opinion of a politically weak agency such as Maritime? Was not Maritime also likely to continue in indefinite disagreement with Navy in response to its own internal difficulties?

The role of Steelman in this connection deserves especial consideration. His office did not alter nor did it attempt to alter the positions of Navy and Maritime on the laid-up fleet issue. Could Steelman appropriately have taken a firm position on the issue? Relevant in this regard is the Cabinet "decision" to transfer 100 tankers, which, as events proved, left several matters unsettled, particularly the problems of the laid-up fleet and selection of nationals. Could these not have been taken up by an agency—Steelman's office—which, like the Cabinet, could reflect the authority of the President, instead of being left, as they were, to long-delayed settlement between Maritime and Navy? Each reader will provide his own answers to questions of this sort; but the answers should not be made without awareness of the fact that Steelman and his associates had a wide variety of matters to handle with all these agencies: the tankers constituted only one item out of many. And there was the imposing fact that Congress had assigned specific responsibilities for the sales to the Maritime Commission and the Navy. The statutory requirements could not be treated as negligible by Steelman's office, or by the other agencies concerned.

VI. New Crises

Easy progress seemed definitely in prospect for the tanker program. The greatest obstacle—disagreement between Maritime and Navy over conditions—seemed removed by Maritime's resolution to proceed on terms somewhere in between its own and Navy's original positions. But, unfortunately, the respite was short-lived. Hardly had Maritime come to its decision when a new danger rose to plague the tanker sales.

SUDDEN CITIZEN INTEREST IN TANKERS

Early in September, completely without warning, an avalanche of applications from U. S. citizens for T-2 Tankers began to move upon the Maritime Commission. These applications doubtless developed from the growing realization that the East Coast would suffer a winter oil shortage. The phenomenal tanker demand lasted for nearly two months, well into October, and rose to a peak of 112 applications for tankers for private use under U. S. registry. Some of the foreign applicants had anticipated this turn of events, a reason for their urgent pressure on the State Department and Maritime to complete the sales. This new development had all the atmosphere of a "boom." It appeared within a period of two weeks, extraordinarily fast for offers to purchase large objects like tankers, costing several million dollars each, and in an industry noted for legal intricacies and cumbersome procedures. Until September, U. S. citizen applications were insubstantial. As late as August 19, there were on hand only six U. S. citizen applications for ten vessels. A week later there were only seven applications for twelve vessels. Sound economic reasons underlay the lack of interest. U. S. private operators were loath to purchase tankers when they could operate them on favorable terms for the Maritime Commission under General Agency, which made the Commission responsible for upkeep, an important expense. The major U. S. oil companies, principal users of tankers, were looking toward a tanker construction program which they did not wish to jeopardize by loading up with tankers which would become obsolete. However, the oil companies contributed little directly to the unexpected rise in tanker applications. In fact, only a small proportion of the applicants showed previous experience with tankers. The greater part of the interest was plainly speculative. The relative world scarcity of tankers made them seem a good investment risk, not only to the applicants, but to banks which financed their purchase. Some applicants proceeded into fancy "kiting" gyrations, making charters for tankers they hoped to get and obtaining loans to purchase the tankers on the basis of the expected charters. An approved application was negotiable, a circumstance which stimulated speculation.

The surprise appearance of these U. S. citizen applications gravely embarrassed the Maritime Commission and the foreign sales program. Under the Ship Sales Act, eligible U. S. citizen applicants were preferred in the purchase of tankers over eligible alien applicants. This provision and the sudden presence of U. S. citizen applications confronted the Maritime Commission with an imposing question: Must foreign sales now be adjusted to this sudden U. S. demand?

THE FUEL OIL SHORTAGE

Coupled with the speculative rise of U. S. applications was the fuel oil shortage which afflicted New England and other parts of the Eastern seaboard in the fall and winter of 1947-48. The shortage produced nearly the same quality of surprise as the rush of tanker applications. It will be recalled that the Oil and Gas Division of the Interior Department and the Navy had been almost alone in anticipating in the spring and summer of 1947 a petroleum shortage during the coming winter. Nearly the entire petroleum industry, the big companies included, confidently expected to meet the year's petroleum demand. In April, Standard Oil of New York staunchly favored the foreign sale of tankers. It had enough tankers for 120 per cent of its anticipated needs, and other companies testified to the same effect before the Weichel committee: tankers must be made available by sale or General Agency to foreign purchasers whose tanker needs exceeded those of U. S. operators. This was, of course, an answer—temporarily valid—to the original Navy argument concerning the laid-up fleet: better distribution of operating tankers was still possible in April. But in the fall of 1947 these considerations were changed by the upsurge in unfilled domestic demand for petroleum. In October, a representative of Standard Oil of New Jersey reported to a Senate Committee that despite record output of Standard's refineries, demand could not be met. Shortages of tankers, tank cars, and pipeline capacity hampered ability to make petroleum products available to consumers. Particularly serious was the Gulf Coast situation where, according to Standard, shortages of tankers made impossible the meeting of its customer-demand throughout the East.

The New England fuel oil shortage was acutely felt and its political repercussions were loud and explosive. However, in actual tonnage the shortage was relatively small; it could have been averted by pressing into service a comparatively small number of additional tankers. The 46 tankers in the laid-up fleet would have been ample. Some of those concerned with the foreign sale program were convinced that the New England shortage would never have occurred if the Maritime Commission and State had accepted at the very beginning the Navy provisos concerning sales from lay-up; it might even have been averted if Maritime had really acted upon its June decision to recondition the laid-up vessels.

EFFECTS ON THE MARITIME COMMISSION

These twin currents of domestic applications and the New England shortage greatly upset the Maritime Commission, particularly the U. S. citizen applications, where its responsibility, under statute, was immediate. The Commission's meeting on September 17 showed the impact of the difficulty. Certain Commissioners took immediate and decisive stands upon the proper course for the Commission in the new turn of events. Commissioner Mellen, for instance, felt that the sudden demand for tankers was due primarily to their short supply, and thus he could not subscribe to further execution of the foreign sales program. He proposed that all foreign sales be stopped at once, and that the Commission establish a future date, until which U. S. citizens might file applications for purchase of tankers for operation under U. S. or Panamanian registry. After the cut-off date, and in light of the number of tankers remaining after satisfaction of U. S. demand, the Commission would proceed to execute whatever part of the foreign sales program it could.

No action was taken on Mr. Mellen's proposal. After some further discussion, it was suggested that Morse and Pimper (Chief of the Large Vessels Sales Division) draft for the Commission's approval a letter to the State, Navy and Interior Departments, informing them of the strong U. S. citizen demand, and indicating that "the factors relating to United States ownership were serious and should be duly considered, although the Commission was not opposed to the sale of 100 tankers foreign as approved by the President's Cabinet." (The Commission was indulging in some protective hedging. If retreat on foreign sales should prove necessary, the agencies were now on notice.)

STEELMAN-CONWAY MEASURES

The Commission continued in its uncertainty for the next few weeks. The foreign sales program made little progress in the way of contracts signed and tankers made ready for sale. Everything seemed desultory. Conway watched closely, as part of his duties as Co-ordinator. Familiar with the new developments, he was still convinced, as were the President and Steelman also, that the foreign sales should continue. It would be calamitous to Europe and the plans to aid its recovery if our projected tanker assistance were now withdrawn. But Conway was also distressed by what he now recognized as an impending oil shortage in the United States for the coming winter. His information from the industry depicted ample petroleum supplies where the refineries were located, but shortages in consumer areas, particularly along the Atlantic seaboard. The difficulty seemed definitely a scarcity of transportation facilities, especially tankers. Conway decided that the most fitting measure, in face of both a world-wide and U. S. transportation shortage, was to transfer all the tankers possible from the laid-up fleet into active operation. If this were not accomplished, the Administration would be open to severe criticism. (It was clear that Ball's early prophesy of the fuel oil shortage had not been sufficiently heeded. If it had been, interest in the laid-up fleet would have increased long ago and Navy's insistence on reactivation would have received support.) Conway thought an immediate meeting of Maritime, Commerce, Army, Navy, State and Interior desirable to review the whole tanker and petroleum situation, domestic and international, and to devise means to bring laid-up tankers into operation. For some days, Chairman Smith had sought to have these agencies meet on a matter of more limited scope—the U. S. citizen applications and their relation to foreign sales. But a meeting devoted to a broader agenda, as Conway desired, found favor among Radius, Callaghan, Ball, Steelman, and also Smith.

On October 1, Steelman, after making careful arrangements with Conway, called the agencies together at the White House. Present were those most continuously concerned with foreign sales: Chairman Smith, Vice-Chairman Raymond McKeough, Morse and others from Maritime; Assistant Secretary Norton and Radius of State; Ball and Friedman of Interior; Callaghan and Mansfield of Navy; and Assistant Secretary of Commerce David Bruce. Steelman presided initially over the meeting and opened with a statement that the President and the Cabinet still felt it of the utmost importance that the 100 T-2 Tankers be sold to foreign interests; the representatives of State and Interior joined him in urging that the program be expedited in every way possible. Steelman then explained that he had to leave the meeting, but before doing so, appointed a "Task Committee" (which had been arranged before the meeting) to follow through with measures to meet the acute oil situation, of which the tanker foreign sales program was an important part. Steelman named Conway Chairman of the Task Committee and said that the rest of its membership would be composed of officials from the agencies present.

After Steelman left, Conway presided over the meeting and a table indicating the current supply and demand of T-2 Tankers was extensively discussed. The phases considered were as follows:

(1) The 13 tankers which remained unallocated in the foreign sales program were reviewed. The consensus was that all or part of them should be definitely allocated and sold against applications from the countries previously only tentatively approved: Uruguay, Chile, South Africa, and Sweden. Also to speed up the foreign sales program, it was suggested that Maritime decide finally on the matter of an allowance for repairs to vessels to be sold out of lay-up. This was a matter of present dispute among Maritime staff. Some favored the granting of no allowance, others a very limited one. Further, Maritime was also urged to hasten the nominations from foreign countries of named vessels recommended for sale to specific applicants.

(2) The sale of T-2 Tankers was to proceed upon the assumption that the foreign sales program would be completed. It was agreed that Maritime should announce a date, say two weeks hence, as a cut-off for U. S. citizen applications to be received. It was also believed that a large portion of the applications on hand would fail to meet the eligibility requirements of the Ship Sales Act. Those which proved eligible could probably be satisfied without a cut-back of tankers allocated for foreign sale.

(3) The changing events had given the mat-

ter of reconditioning the laid-up fleet a new urgency. Steelman had emphasized how the world-wide and domestic oil and tanker situation were reaching a peak of difficulty, and that it was not unlikely that some means of curtailing petroleum consumption might have to be instituted in the U. S. All suitable tankers from the laid-up fleet must be reactivated as promptly as possible. The Navy representatives stated in response that the Navy would have $5,000,000 available to recondition 26 of the Mission-type Tankers (T2-SE-A2) then in lay-up and thus could release a corresponding number of the T2-SE-A1 type, now serving military needs, for civilian use. Maritime also agreed to recondition 24 ex-Navy oilers (14 T2-SE-A2 and 10 T2-SE-A1) in lay-up which likewise would release commercial-type tankers, now serving military needs, for civilian use. Presumably these methods of enlarging the fleet of active commercial tankers had been available all along, but they seem not to have been mentioned before.

As Chairman of the Task Committee, Conway now became a leading figure in the tanker episode. His purpose was to complete the foreign sales as expeditiously as possible and to bring all laid-up tankers into operation. (The similarity of the latter part of his objective with Navy's long-held position is to be noted.) The center of his efforts was the Maritime Commission, where nearly all action, as affairs stood, was to be forthcoming. The foreign applications had to be processed there, the tankers made ready for sale, the contracts signed and executed, and the tankers actually delivered. Whether the Maritime Commission could execute these tasks with promptness was doubtful. It was thought generally that the leadership of the Large Vessels Sales Division—the unit of Maritime now most concerned with foreign sales—was not unduly eager to execute the program.

Also, at this period, Maritime was subject to constant criticism for its alleged inefficiency. Apparently the charges were not without some foundation in fact, for in 1948 the Commission took the unusual step of requesting the Senate Expenditures Committee to study and recommend improvements in its performance. The Senate Committee's Report, *Management Survey of the U. S. Maritime Commission*, the findings of a group of private management engineers, noted these serious imperfections:

Item: The five Commissioners, one a chairman and one a vice-chairman, have equal responsibilities and authority. Each Commissioner acts as an individual administrator and each has his own sphere of interest in the operation of the Commission, some of which overlap.

Item: An analysis of the agenda for one meeting of the Commission shows that of 37 items on the docket, only 9 of them should have received the attention of the Commission. On the other 28 items, the Commission could only agree with the recommendations or overrule the technical staff supposedly qualified to make an intelligent recommendation.

Item: There is little or no correlation of activities in the bureaus and other units, and the organization is so complex and non-interrelated that some twenty-odd boards, committees and panels were formed for the sole purpose of co-ordinating the actions of the various organizational units which were concerned with the specific problems over which they have cognizance. In one bureau are such different activities as the maintenance of records on merchant seamen and the determination of repairs to be made on vessels. A transaction involving the sale of a ship might concern as many as nine different bureaus. This unduly cumbersome organization makes it virtually impossible to fix responsibility and no unit chief knows where to report on specific problems. It is not uncommon for the chiefs of lower organizational units to bypass their superiors and deal directly with the Commission, or with one or more of the Commissioners.

Item: There is no set operational policy. The Commission itself is involved in minute details concerning operation and administration, and major policies are often decided unilaterally at low organizational levels. Routine matters are handled as special problems, and thus special problems receive only routine attention.

Conway entered this labyrinth in behalf of the tanker sales. He established an office in the Commerce Department building where Maritime is housed. Since he was in Washington only one day per week (he had returned to almost full-time work with his shipping company in New York City), a full-time assistant, Captain Martin Goodman, attended to most of the details, and Robert Turner (Steelman's assistant) was in readiness when his services were required. Although there was no formal division of function between Conway and Turner on the tanker problem, one existed in fact. Because of his extensive knowledge of the shipping industry, Conway took the lead in all matters where such knowledge was required. In these he was aided by the prestige of his former leadership of the War Shipping Administration. But, because Conway was performing a part-time assignment, had private business connections, and was not a regular member of the White House staff, there was sometimes a question whether or not he spoke for Steelman and the President. It was naturally assumed, on the other hand, that Turner always did. Thus a number of actions, which Conway and Turner agreed were necessary, were taken by Turner so there would be no misunderstanding of their "White House" origin or approval.

Both Conway and Turner agreed upon policy and method. The policy was to press into service every possible tanker with the utmost speed. As to method, Conway's, and that of his associates, was one often called "setting fires." Conway held frequent meetings of the Maritime staff most immediately concerned with processing the applications of foreign nationals. He solicited and obtained reports on a weekly, and, subsequently, on a daily basis of the exact status of each vessel called for by the foreign applications. He precipitated action by telephone calls, and habitually worked by informal rather than formal means. He never met with the whole Commission, but dealt with individual Commissioners such as Smith and McKeough. He made no attempt to convince a Commissioner like Mellen who was opposed to the foreign sales program. Above all, Conway dealt with Morse and persons at the bureau level who did the real work in processing applications and preparing the tankers for service. It was there that a sense of urgency was most critically needed. He was immensely aided by his previous role as War Shipping Administrator which provided him a wide circle of acquaintances among those most concerned with the tanker question; many of the Commission's employees had been members of his staff during the war and his popularity was widespread. On the other hand, there were some in the Commission who appeared to be jealous of Conway and who resented what they deemed to be his interference. Some of them objected to the fact that Conway had business dealings with the Maritime Commission during this period when he was a part-time public servant.

In his task, Conway found many confusions, fears, and counterpurposes. The Maritime Commission, despite the assurance supposedly rendered by the Steelman meeting, was still alarmed by the sudden rise in citizen applications. The Commissioners were also faced with a confusing situation. They had difficulty in determining precisely what their prior actions on the foreign sales had been. No continuous and orderly record was kept of Commission meetings, and the details were far too numerous and complicated for accurate recollection. In this confused and disturbed atmosphere, a motion was made by Commissioner McKeough in a meeting of October 3, for instance, that official advice be obtained from Navy that the foreign sale of 100 tankers would not jeopardize the national defense. All entreaties by members of the Commission staff that the motion would be inappropriate, such assurances having previously been obtained, proved in vain. Apparently, most of the Commissioners hoped that Navy would object to the foreign sales program, or at least did not care if it did.

It was partly in this mood and partly in the belief that with one and the same measure it could please the two most insistent protagonists of the reconditioning of the laid-up fleet that Maritime came to a further important decision. The decision is embodied in a letter the Chairman dispatched to the Secretary of the Navy on October 10. In it the Navy was assured that all the conditions specified in its letter of July 17 would be observed, particularly the one that Maritime theretofore had steadfastly rejected, that not more than 54 tankers would be sold to non-citizens from the active fleet, until at least 46 tankers from the laid-up fleet were either sold or readied for service. The McKeough motion is reflected in the closing sentence of the letter, which reads: "unless the Commission is advised to the contrary, it will assume that the Navy is entirely satisfied." Navy did not reply to or acknowledge this letter and evidently was "entirely satisfied."

INVESTIGATION BY THE SENATE SMALL BUSINESS COMMITTEE

An important reason for Maritime's disturbance and back-tracking was a new and ominous challenge to the foreign sales program coming from the Senate Special Committee to Study Problems of American Small Business. This Committee, under the Chairmanship of Senator Kenneth S. Wherry, Republican of Nebraska, had for some time been investigating the petroleum situation of the United States in response to "many, many scores of small businessmen who have written to the Small Business Committee telling of their needs and the desperate condition in which they now find themselves relative to the distribution of oil." The essence of this "desperate condition" was that the small independent petroleum producer was often without transportation facilities to bring his petroleum to market. As the shortage grew, in September, and October, Senator Wherry was receiving "an increasing number of complaints . . . from independent oil distributors on the east coast that their supplies have been curtailed and that they have been warned by their suppliers of still further reductions." Thus both producers and distributors were now in trouble, and they were soon to be joined by business men and householders who lacked oil.

With these complaints at hand, the Wherry Committee gave extended attention to the proposed action of the Commerce Department of licensing for export a large quantity of steel pipe, tubular goods, and other steel to construct a pipeline across Saudi Arabia. The Wherry Committee vigorously opposed the export plan, arguing that with transportation facilities, particularly pipelines, in short supply for the American producer, steel ought not be shipped abroad. During an executive session in October on the pipeline question, Wherry happened upon the tanker foreign sales project. The exact circumstances are in dispute. It was believed in the State Department that some U. S. applicants for tankers, acting possibly through subordinate officials in an agency not altogether friendly to foreign sales, somehow brought the matter to Wherry's attention. In any event, Wherry quickly diverted his attention from the pipeline to the tankers, and took the position that the shortage of pipelines in the U. S. actually reflected the shortage of tankers for the petroleum trade of the U. S. eastern seaboard. Why then must the shortage be aggravated by the sale of U. S. tankers to foreign purchasers?

Senator Wherry, a member of the bar, but far better known for his business and political than for his legal accomplishments, with the aid of committee counsel, further determined that the foreign sales were illegal under the Ship Sales Act. There were on hand at the Maritime Commission a large number of U. S. citizen applications which were unfilled while sales to foreign purchasers were in progress. The Senator concluded that Section 7 of the Ship Sales Act, which gives preference to U. S. citizen applicants over non-citizens in the purchase of the vessels, was being violated by the continuation of foreign sales. All this had been pointed out in numerous letters Wherry received from the U. S. citizen applicants.

Wherry acted quickly. The situation was obviously advantageous to the Republican party then in majority in Congress. Wherry strongly disapproved of this apparent concern of the Administration for foreign needs at the expense of American needs and concluded that it made a good political issue. Also Wherry made clear his belief that a congressional committee is obliged to see that the laws of Congress are faithfully observed in the Executive Branch. When on occasion, as with foreign sales, the law seems disregarded, the legislator ought to intervene, ascertain the facts and somehow prevent the illegal action. Otherwise, executive agencies would be free to thwart any law they pleased. Wherry's doctrine was widely held to be sound both in Congress and among the public.

On October 28, Wherry embodied his conclusions in a letter to the President and requested that foreign sales be halted at once and that further transactions concerning the tankers be conducted "according to law." (See Appendix III.)

Also on October 28 there was a meeting of Under Secretary of the Navy Kenney, the Secretary of Commerce, the Chairman of the Maritime Commission, and the officials of Maritime, State, and Navy most prominently concerned with the tanker project. Having heard that Wherry would start an investigation, the group met to agree on a defensive position. The nature of the U. S. citizen applications was reviewed at this meeting, the Maritime Chairman believing that at least half of them would fall short of the requirements of the Ship Sales Act. The Chairman also reported an opinion of the Commission's counsel, recently rendered, that the Commission's action of June 25 constituted "a firm obligation" to sell tankers to the foreign purchasers. Discussion followed and the group agreed that the problem arising from Senator Wherry's interest in the tanker sales was essentially one of legal interpretation: The proper priority of U. S. citizen and foreign claims for tankers. It was also agreed that a ruling on these questions should be sought from the highest non-judicial legal authority—the Attorney General, by whose judgment Wherry might possibly abide. If the Attorney General concurred with Maritime's General Counsel, then, the group believed, "the Commission would be obliged to complete its commitments."

Meanwhile, Senator Wherry continued active. Two days later, October 30, he wrote to the Chairman of the Maritime Commission, enclosing a copy of his letter to the President, and requested the Commission to postpone all further foreign sales until it could be shown that they complied with the Ship Sales Act. Wherry said he would be glad to meet with the Commission and other government agencies to discuss the matter.

At the White House, Conway and Steelman were fully aware of Senator Wherry's moves and were informed of the inter-agency meeting on October 28. The Presidential assistants immediately reaffirmed their position that the sales were to continue notwithstanding the adverse pressures. Knowledge of this White House insistence spread: an article in the *New York Times* on October 29 stated that Mr. Steelman had given the Maritime Commission a "go ahead" on tanker sales to foreign interests. Maritime, Wherry learned, had concurred in this policy and was actually proceeding with the sales. Anxious to forestall further action, Wherry issued a press release on October 31, summarizing his discoveries and linking the threatened U. S. fuel oil shortage with the lack of transportation and the foreign sales of tankers. He also foreshadowed his next move. "Because of the disregard of my protest," he said, "I have no alternative but to appeal to the leaders of both the Senate and the House of Representatives to prevent this action."

The appeal followed and in response there descended upon the President and the Maritime Commission a flurry of telegrams and letters opposing the sales. Mr. Vandenberg, President *pro tempore* of the Senate, Mr. Taft, Chairman of the Senate Majority Policy Committee, Mr. White, the Republican Whip, and other key Republican figures such as Senator Wiley, Congressman Halleck, and Congresswoman Rogers joined in. Some took the position that though they had made only a superficial study of the question, whether the foreign sales were within the law and within sound policy, the doubts could not be resolved without a full exploration of the facts. Transactions of the magnitude and importance of tanker sales should be free of doubt and the sales ought to be halted until consultation between the Maritime Commission and the Wherry Committee could be completed. Another legislator proposed that since Congress (which was then not in session) was scheduled for an early return, no further sales be completed pending congressional study. Senator White, as Chairman of the Committee on Interstate and Foreign Commerce, requested that foreign sales be withheld until Congress reconvened and his Committee had an opportunity to explore the matter.

Despite this attack, foreign sales still proceeded. In the last week in October and the first week in November, the Commission sent letters of notification to various foreign purchasers advising that their applications had been "approved," indicating the terms of sale, and requesting "within five days, your acceptance—." The numerous foreign purchasers who thereupon made such an acceptance assumed they had executed a valid contract. Evidently Steelman and Conway were continuing to employ the utmost pressure to keep the foreign sales in progress.

Meanwhile, Wherry resolved upon further steps. He announced that his Small Business Committee would begin hearings on the sales on November 14. Among those to testify would be all the Maritime Commissioners, Secretary of Defense Forrestal, Navy Secretary Sullivan, Under Secretary of State Lovett, Steelman, and Conway, "who is now reported to be making a study of the tanker situation for the President."

Following Wherry's announcement of the hearing date, the Maritime Commission, in a jittery session, decided to carry the foreign sales no further. The administrative machinery which was processing the sales was completely halted. Letters which had been prepared to notify Norwegian, Greek, Argentine, Swedish, and South African purchasers were not sent (twenty-five tankers were involved), and formal contracts, based upon previous notifications by the Commission and acceptances by foreign purchasers, were not signed by the Commission. Although the foreign nations had signed, the contracts were kept in the Chairman's safe. These moves surprised everyone. They came without warning to the other executive agencies, including the State Department, and the foreign purchasers were utterly dismayed. Most disturbed of all were the British applicants who had completed the formidable paperwork with Maritime and awaited only delivery of the tankers. In this hectic interval, the counsel for one British company advised it to accept tankers without inspection to "get under the wire" before the Maritime stoppage went into effect. (There was a period of several days' warning.) As a final blow, Maritime Commission officials refused to give bills of sale to British companies to whom tankers had already been delivered. The affair had become a diplomatic nightmare at the State Department, where the foreign nations were emphatically protesting.

Much of the foregoing was disclosed at Senator Wherry's hearings, although only some of the persons originally scheduled to appear actually did testify. Not heard were Steelman, Conway, Thorp, acting for Lovett in the absence of Norton, and Maritime Commissioners Parkhurst and Carson. Indeed, the testimony on the two hearing days, November 14 and 18, was limited to the Navy and the Maritime Commission. Present, as the hearings began, were Wherry, as the sole representative of his Committee, and Senator Moore of the Interstate and Foreign Commerce Committee. Wherry earlier had found the Chairman of the latter Committee, Senator White, claiming jurisdiction of the tanker affair. But White was on vacation in Maine and Wherry had proceeded, hopeful that measures to keep White, his Committee and staff apprised might satisfy him. Invited, but not present at the hearings were Senator Wiley, Chairman of the Judiciary Committee, and Congressman Weichel.

Senator Wherry opened the hearings with an extensive statement of his position on foreign tanker sales. He depicted hardships among the American people fostered by post-war shortages and the consequent unsoundness of sale abroad of such scarce items as tankers and steel pipe. He introduced a letter of October 15 from C. A. Newland, of Standard Oil of New Jersey, describing the inability of U. S. tankers to satisfy the fuel oil requirements of the Eastern seaboard. Introduced also were bulletins of the American Petroleum Institute showing oil to be backing up on the Gulf Coast; on November 9, 1946, only 48,764,000 barrels had been on hand there, while on November 8, 1947, 50,541,000 barrels were on hand. "Certainly," said Wherry, "that is concrete evidence that it would only result from the lack of transportation facilities." Upon the premise that if American needs are not satisfied before foreign needs, the policy is unsound, Wherry proceeded to attack the foreign tanker sales.

His primary contention was that foreign sales violated Section 7 of the Ship Sales Act, which gave preference to citizens over noncitizens. Maritime witnesses responded that many sales had in fact been made to citizens, and also that most of the citizen applications on hand were ineligible. The latter contention Wherry disputed, particularly in light of the eastern U. S. petroleum difficulties. Maritime made the further defense that it was already "firmly" committed to sell 83 tankers to foreign purchasers. The commitment was based upon Maritime's belief (1) that it had made the consultation with the Navy, required under statute; (2) that it had made the statutory findings regarding national defense, the interests of the U. S. merchant marine, and the situation of U. S. citizen applicants, well before those applicants had become numerous; (3) that Maritime had taken administrative actions, e.g., giving oral notice of approved applications, signing contracts, which involved "firm commitment" on the part of the Commission, and therefore upon the part of the U. S. Government, to transfer the tankers to foreign purchasers.

All these contentions were searched in extensive cross-examination and an intensely hostile atmosphere. The facts of the tanker project were carefully reviewed from conception to current status. Representative of the somewhat acrid argument which characterized the proceedings are the following exchanges between Senator Wherry and Committee Counsel Dickey, and Chairman Smith and the General Counsel of the Maritime Commission, Wade Skinner:

WHERRY: How could you make those sales to these nonresidents of foreign countries or foreign applicants, in view of the fact that you had these applications of these citizens of the United States on file at that time. . . .

SMITH: We obtained a written opinion of the general counsel before taking the action. . . .

SKINNER: The Act requires that the Commission make a finding before it can make a sale to a noncitizen. The Commission, in my judgment, constructively made its finding and could justifiably have made it actually, if it had been the practice to do that, on June 25, or in any event when the allocations were made on August 12 and 13, and July 31. Anything taken subsequent to that date was subordinate to the position that they had taken previously. I am not contending there was a legal contract. Of course, there was not, but there was an arrangement between nations. They had conferred with these countries after July 1, and different rules apply than would be required in making a legal contract between you and me. . . .

DICKEY: You mean they made the finding as of June 25?

SKINNER: Constructively, they did. That was the practice. They never make the findings the day they approve the sale. . . .

DICKEY: Now, when did the Commission finish its consultations with the Secretary of the Navy?

SKINNER: You are referring to a letter sent the Secretary of the Navy in October. If that is what you are referring to, I can answer that that was apparently an oversight in the reply to the Secretary of the Navy, and we were complying with his request, and some of the staff also requested a formal reply so that the record would show what we were doing.

DICKEY: Now, on October 3, did not Commissioner McKeough make a motion which was unanimously adopted that an official communication be obtained from the Navy Department that the sale of 100 tankers foreign would not violate or jeopardize national defense of the Navy Department?

SKINNER: That was to have the record buttoned up.

DICKEY: Then, as of October 3, you had not finished consulting with the Secretary of the Navy; had you?

SKINNER: If you call that consulting.

DICKEY: What would you call it? Would you not call it consulting?

SKINNER: They had adopted the Navy's requirements . . .

DICKEY: This has nothing to do with the Navy. This is a further question, asking the Navy if this would interfere with or jeopardize, national defense plans in the Navy Department. You have said technically you think that is consultation and the statute says that one's findings must be made by the Commission.

SKINNER: That is right.

DICKEY: That is, a finding on the national defense aspect after consultation. The word "after" legally means after they are finished?

SKINNER: Well, to be technical, you will not deny they did not have consultation from April on through May and June.

DICKEY: But I do not think they finished the consultation and could not possibly have made the sale on June 25 that you say they made constructively.

SKINNER: I heard the Commission discuss it.

WHERRY: In fact, they consulted clear up to October 27 before they made further commitments.

SKINNER: No, I believe there were two or three countries, the British and the Turks.

WHERRY: About the middle of October?

SKINNER: I think the British signed their contracts in August through September.

WHERRY: So that any time up to the middle of October they were still consulting with the Navy. They were still going into the question of the allocation of these vessels; were they not?

SKINNER: That I cannot answer.[1]

The positions Skinner and the Commission asserted were vigorously contested at the hearings by one of the Commissioners, Mr. Mellen. In effect, Mellen agreed with the attitude of the Wherry Committee that the "incoming American citizen applications" should receive preference under the Ship Sales Act. Mellen testified that the Commission had done nothing which legally precluded the preference and that "the action of the Commission on June 25 merely dealt with a proposal of something to be done at some time in the future. There certainly was not before us at that time any specific purchaser. We never discussed any specific ships. The law requires that we do that in our procedure to meet legal approval."[2] Mellen's argument did not cover the British, whose case was easier than that of other foreign nations, because their contracts had been signed. For them, Mellen said, "there might be some stretch of the imagination."[3] As for the other nations, he deemed the Commission's letter to Navy on October 10 a refutation of the argument that their applications were "finally determined" June 25. He put no weight on the letters of notification sent by the Commission at the end of October and in early November and the claims of foreign purchasers that they constituted a valid contract.

The only other Commissioner, besides Smith and Mellen, questioned at the hearings was the Vice Chairman, Raymond McKeough. An Administration appointee, McKeough was a former member of Congress (1935-43, Democrat, Second District, Illinois). Each of the principal legislative investigations of the tanker sales program, by the Weichel and the Wherry Committees, dwelt in part upon what seemed to them the undue responsiveness of McKeough to Presidential desires and the consequent lack of "independence" suitable to an "independent commission" such as Maritime. Illustrative is an earlier exchange between Congressman Weichel and Commissioner McKeough, May 6, 1947, before the Weichel subcommittee. Under discussion was the scrapping of some ships in the Maritime Commission's reserve fleet.

WEICHEL: If Mr. Steelman cracks the whip and says you are going to scrap them . . .

MCKEOUGH: Mr. Chairman, he doesn't crack the whip. I don't think it is fair to imply that this Commission is subject to the whim or capricious judgment of Mr. Steelman or anyone else.

WEICHEL: Do you say you don't have pressures to do these things?

MCKEOUGH: . . . I wouldn't call it pressure.

WEICHEL: What do you call it?

MCKEOUGH: It is a suggestion for the benefit of the over-all national economy under current conditions. I have no objection to that. I think he is sound in that position.[4]

Senator Wherry pursued the same course on November 14, with respect to a declaration of McKeough in defense of his support of foreign sales by the Commission.

MCKEOUGH: Now, when the Cabinet asked us to make this sale, and I speak very frankly, I am on the team in the Commission. I was appointed by President Truman. I had a little trouble getting in, you may recall, but I finally made it.

WHERRY: You said you play on the team of the Cabinet, and the Cabinet is the one that said, "This is what you should do to help out the general oil supply." Is not Maritime an independent agency?

MCKEOUGH: Yes.

WHERRY: Then is not your responsibility to Congress?

MCKEOUGH: That is right.

WHERRY: Then we have a team, too.

MCKEOUGH: That is right. I agree. I do not yield to anyone in my regard of the Congress.

WHERRY: Certainly, playing on the team with

[1] *Hearings*, Special Committee to Study Problems of American Small Business, U. S. Senate, Part 23, Nov. 14, 1947, pp. 2585-2589.

[2] *Ibid.*, p. 2620.

[3] *Ibid.*, p. 2633.

[4] *Hearings, Proposed Amendments to the Merchant Ship Sales Act of 1946*, Committee on Merchant Marine and Fisheries, 80th Congress, House of Representatives, May 6, 1947, p. 278.

the Cabinet does not alter the requirements set out by the statute.

MCKEOUGH: No, not at all; but I differ as to whether or not we did violence to the statute.[5]

What testimony there was at the Wherry hearings of the other executive agencies was reasonably unified. A prepared statement by Secretary of Defense Forrestal, read by Under Secretary of the Navy Kenney (drafted by Admiral Callaghan), upheld foreign sales as warranted by the grave shortage of European petroleum stocks, the under-tapped supply of the Middle East, and the undue depletion of Western Hemisphere reserves. Wherry's questioning developed the issues which had been negotiated at length between Navy and Maritime. Sullivan, now Secretary of the Navy, who at various stages had opposed Maritime Commission proposals, resisted Senator Wherry's enticements to further hostility. Asked if the Joint Chiefs of Staff had approved the list of foreign nationals, Sullivan replied that the list had not been submitted to them, "but I strongly suspect they would approve." [6] "Upon further evidence, if it were divulged," asked Senator Wherry, "that . . . [the tankers sold foreign] are not to be used in the Middle East shipping of oil, would you withdraw your affirmation to the sale?" Sullivan remained steadfast. "We are in no position," he said, "to withdraw any affirmation to the sale. Under the statute the Maritime Commission asks the advice of the Secretary of the Navy. That advice was given. The Maritime Commission has gone ahead."

No agencies other than Navy and Maritime were brought to testify. The State Department, through Assistant Secretary Thorp, presented a prepared statement of its views upon the tanker project, but this was not incorporated into the printed record. Thorp, Radius, and others from State attended the hearings, but were not asked to testify. Steelman did not appear (his absence was in accordance with normal practice), and Conway, though present, was not called forward. Wherry, pursuing his own attack, introduced a letter from Senator Allen J. Ellender, Democrat of Louisiana, opposing the sales as harmful to farmers of the South, who, by reduced transportation facilities entailed in foreign sales of tankers, might suffer "in that shipments of urgently needed Chilean nitrates might be discontinued at a time when the farmers badly need this product." The relation between tankers and nitrates was not disclosed. The Independent Petroleum Association of America, an organization of "small" producers, objected to Navy's support of foreign sales of tankers and the threat of smaller future foreign markets for U. S. oil. Finally, there was an extensive letter from the Executive Secretary of the CIO Maritime Commission, a council of CIO unions interested in maritime problems, demanding that the sales be halted. (See Appendix III.)

THE ATTORNEY GENERAL'S OPINION

Such was the drama, publicly viewed, of the Wherry investigation. Yet, behind the scenes, negotiations were in progress which proved far more decisive than anything said in the public session. Through the din of two long days of hearings, one motif was dominant: the conflict over the legal status of foreign sales. The resolution of that conflict was the subject of a conversation at the White House between Wherry and his counsel, on the one hand, and Steelman and Conway on the other. The exact date of this discussion is not known, but it doubtless occurred in the first half of November. It produced agreement between Wherry and Steelman that the entire legal controversy should be referred for advice to the Attorney General. By his opinion all would abide.

It will be recalled that the device of securing an Attorney General's opinion had been discussed even earlier at the inter-agency meeting on October 28, when Senator Wherry's campaign was just beginning. The agencies had approved the idea, which apparently had been originally suggested by an attorney for one of the foreign applicants and had found immediate favor at the Maritime Commission. Most, perhaps all, of the Commissioners were quite willing to abide by the Attorney General's ruling, whatever it might be, since it promised to relieve them of responsibility. To the pro-

[5] *Hearings*, Senate Commitee on Small Business, p. 2592.

[6] *Ibid.*, p. 2530.

ponents of the sales, Steelman and Conway included, the idea was highly acceptable because they were convinced that the opinion would undoubtedly be favorable to the sales. An adverse ruling would tend to cast doubt on the breadth of the President's constitutional responsibility for foreign policy: it is emphatically not the function of the Attorney General to circumscribe the President's constitutional powers.

The real problem was twofold: To make sure that an opinion would be forthcoming, and to ensure that it would be respected by Senator Wherry. As has been seen, Senator Wherry's agreement was secured in due course, though what means of persuasion were employed is not known. Information is, however, available on the steps that led to the issuance of an opinion. Concern on this point had arisen because the Attorney General, as a matter of policy, is loath to issue opinions on issues that may later become the subject of litigation. Various devices are available to him in the pursuit of a policy of avoidance including, for example, the occasional invocation of a rule normally evaded that formal opinions are rendered only to Cabinet officers and the President—not to heads of other agencies. Informal opinions, however, are frequently rendered to the independent agencies where the Attorney General is willing to do so; when a formal opinion is required, and the Attorney General is willing, he requires that the agency submit its request through the President. An opinion concerning the tanker sales would probably be semi-formal in nature and difficult, and hence it seemed a wise precaution to have the President request it.

Thus at this point the assistance of the White House was invoked. Steelman had both agreed that an opinion was desirable and promised to help secure one. At the same time, he insisted that the tanker sales continue, which they did. On October 29, upon Steelman's suggestion, Matthew Connelly, Secretary to the President, had sent a memorandum to the Attorney General, with Senator Wherry's letter to the President attached. Connelly asked that the Attorney General supply the President with a "memorandum" reviewing the various objections made in Wherry's letter to the foreign sale of tankers. Some time later, as has been noted, Steelman obtained Wherry's agreement to abide by the Attorney General's forthcoming opinion.

The President's request was referred to the Office of the Assistant Solicitor General where opinions of the Attorney General are prepared. The opinion, which was soon ready, was prepared by David Reich and Abe Harris, aides to Assistant Solicitor General George T. Washington. Normally, the work of this office tends to be rather anonymous; in this instance Reich and Harris had to collect information from numerous sources, and the fact of their assignment was therefore well known. By October 29, the tanker issue had become notorious; Harris and Reich were familiar with its general outlines and had discussed it casually with interested persons. But real work did not begin until the request arrived from the White House. Before describing how the request was handled, it may be useful to analyze briefly the character of the function that was invoked on the President's behalf by Presidential Secretary Connelly.

Some requests for opinions come to the Attorney General (and thence to the Assistant Solicitor General) as legal abstractions for which an opinion is wanted, regardless of its tenor. Far more commonly the President or department head outlines a proposed or actual course of action and asks if he may legally proceed with it. In some cases, the ASG is forced, as a conscientious lawyer, to prepare a negative opinion. Sometimes a favorable opinion is obviously correct. In many cases the law is ambiguous and can be variously construed. In these instances it is the duty of the ASG to indicate a legal path by which the policy may be pursued and not to find legal reasons for opposing it. The work on the President's request for advice on the tanker sales was undertaken in this spirit, and especially so, as has been indicated above, because a negative opinion might have had an adverse effect on the President's role in the field of foreign policy.

The writing of the tanker opinion was preceded by an extensive survey by ASG of the facts and views of the agencies most closely associated with the project. There were many discussions with Commissioners and staff of

Maritime. As might be expected, it was difficult to find agreement within Maritime on the facts around which an opinion might be built. Different Maritime officials had different versions of what had happened and its significance. For ASG this was vexatious, as the opinion could not proceed with shifting facts. The eventual solution was a letter over Chairman Smith's signature which Morse prepared, in which the facts were fully summarized from Maritime's standpoint. Reich and Harris also talked with Radius of State, and Kenney and Callaghan of Navy, and examined pertinent files. There was no reference to Interior.

One other source of ASG contact which preceded drafting of the opinion deserves mention. The counsel of the Wherry Committee, Dickey, approached the Attorney General and ASG regarding the opinion. To ASG, this was most useful, for the opinion could be rendered with benefit of the fullest appreciation of Wherry's and Dickey's views and after examination of a complete transcript of the hearings (not yet available in print). Having tapped these sources, Reich and Harris proceeded to draft the opinion.

It had been decided at a Cabinet meeting that Conway, Kenney, and a Maritime representative should sit with an aide of the Justice Department to assist in working out the rationale of the memorandum. This was done and the agreed-on rationale formed the theoretical framework of ASG's efforts. The completed draft was referred, before its official release, to two places—Maritime and Steelman's office. Such referrals are not usual, and their occurrence depends largely upon the nature of the President's request. Where appropriate to the request, referral may be made. (A more common practice, which has the same substance, is to review the matter informally before the final draft is prepared.) A reading was sought from Maritime to check the facts, as the opinion is itself largely a recital of the facts of the tanker project. The referral to Steelman was made not by ASG but by the Office of the Attorney General itself. The purpose was to make sure that every question in which the President and his aides were interested, was covered. The draft opinion was dated December 6. Three days later, the final opinion was sent to the President. After recounting at length the pertinent statutes and administrative actions, and generally following the reasoning of Maritime's General Counsel Skinner, in sum the opinion sustained as legal the program of tanker sales to foreign nations. (The opinion is reproduced in Appendix III.)

The chief conclusion in the opinion was that the sale program for the 96 tankers had been properly instituted and could legally be completed, and the whole course of the opinion leads up to this one conclusion. Beyond this, however, the Attorney General warned the President that recision in the case of the 25 tankers actually delivered and the 26 for which contracts had been signed by both parties would involve "grave risk of legal liability." On legal liability with respect to the remaining 45 tankers, he cautiously remarked that that "would depend primarily on the facts involved in each transaction." As a practical matter, therefore, 51 tankers were removed from Senator Wherry's reach; 45 were still subject to a possible tug-of-war. But Maritime could, if it would, proceed with the sales. Friends of the program could breathe new hopes. The serious attack of Senator Wherry and his Committee had been successfully withstood. The Senator's prior agreement to be bound by the ruling meant that the opinion was definitive.

After consultation with the President, Steelman sent a copy of the Attorney General's memorandum to the Chairman of the Maritime Commission for his information and requested the Attorney General to send a copy to Senator Wherry for his information. The opinion was not published in the series of Opinions of the Attorney General, not that it was regarded as private, but because it was not deemed to have the qualities of general and more than temporary interest required for formal publication.

THE TANKER SALES PROCEED

Equipped with the Attorney General's opinion, the Maritime Commission promptly moved to complete its authorization of foreign sales, and on December 15 made its final determinations for 83 tankers of the original "not more than 100" tankers approved by the Cabinet for such sale. In a press release on the same day, December 15, Maritime announced, along with its action on foreign sales, the fact that it had now completed authorization of the sale of all available government-owned T-2 Tankers. Henceforth no more of these tankers were for sale either to citizens or non-citizens. Under the Ship Sales Act of 1946, Maritime disclosed, 390 T-2s had been sold: 133 had gone to foreign purchasers; of the group sold to U. S. citizens, 186 were for operation under the U. S. flag and 71 were for transfer to foreign registry (chiefly Panamanian).

VII. A Discordant Finale

AGAIN THE OIL EMERGENCY

Though the way was clear in law for completion of foreign sales, the way in politics and action was another matter. The political forces aroused by the East Coast oil shortage did not subside with the rendering of the Attorney General's opinion. The New England delegation in Congress met to consider measures to avert the threat of cold homes among their constituents during the winter, and the outcome was a long list of questions—twenty-seven in all—which ranged over the whole tanker and petroleum situation including foreign sales. These were put to the Maritime Commission by the Co-ordinator of Information of the House of Representatives. The governors of New England convened and telegraphed the Maritime Commission, urging the recommissioning of many more tankers with the utmost promptness. The House Interstate and Foreign Commerce Committee, and several other committees, launched extensive investigations of the Eastern petroleum shortage. Individual New England legislators were exceedingly active on the floor and in the committees of Congress and exerted insistent pressures upon the executive agencies to help their constituents.

Various agencies responded with measures to lessen the spreading hardship. The Navy, which had started to lay in additional reserves as early as March 1947 on the strength of its belief that an oil shortage was impending in the fall, was able to lend fuel oil to the New England states, New York, Virginia and various municipalities. (These preparations for an oil shortage were part of Navy's broad concept that the shortage, the tanker sales foreign, and the reactivation of laid-up tankers were all parts of one single whole.) In agreement with the Maritime Commission, the Navy also released one allocated commercial-type tanker for every Mission-type Tanker (T2-SE-A2) reconditioned and delivered to it by the Maritime Commission. The Department of Commerce markedly reduced the issuance of export licenses for petroleum products. The Interior Department supported a request of Senator Tobey, telegraphed to governors of 22 states, urging appointment of state emergency fuel oil co-ordinators to handle shortage problems. In January 1948, Interior convened the coordinators for exchanges of ideas. Also at Interior's suggestion, voluntary industry committees were established to help secure the most efficient use of all equipment available for the production and transportation of fuel oil. An executive order was issued directing all the departments and agencies to observe measures to conserve fuel oil and gas and gasoline, and the Secretary of the Interior on January 15 urged public observance of the same measures. The Office of Defense Transportation vigorously promoted a voluntary freight car production program, with emphasis on tank cars. The Coast Guard contributed its part by raising the permissible load-line on tankers, a step agreed on at Steelman's meeting of October 1, which resulted in providing the equivalent of nearly thirty additional cargoes per month on the East Coast alone. To increase the barge movement of petroleum products, the Mississippi River was kept open two weeks longer than usual, and the Illinois River all winter.

RETREAT AT MARITIME

It was in this atmosphere of emergency and special measures that the Maritime Commission ventured upon action which suddenly and seriously modified the foreign sales program. Legal impetus for the step was provided in the last sentence of the Attorney General's opinion: "As to vessels for which no contracts of sale have been signed, the question of whether or not there would be substantial possibility of legal liability in the event of a refusal by the Commission to deliver them would depend primarily on the facts involved in each transaction." The objective of this permissive vagueness was to assure that against the large and increasing number of citizen applications some tankers might be held back from foreign sale to help meet U. S. demand and allay the possible hostility of Congress. But the language of the opinion was broad, as the Maritime Commission perceived in a meeting on December 12. There, as at preceding meetings, the Commission was deeply concerned with the domestic fuel oil and transportation difficulties and the possible criticism of foreign tanker sales. With the opinion before it, the Commission resolved to rescind certain of its previous authorizations of sale: 3 to Uruguay, 2 to Sweden, and 2 to Argentina, and it reduced the number sold to Norway from 11 to 6. Before acting, the Commission contacted Steelman and revealed its plans. Steelman approved them, and the Commission proceeded. There was no notice to or clearance with the State Department on a measure which was bound to have serious diplomatic repercussions.

For officials of the State Department, Maritime's decision produced a storm of confusions and embarrassments. State protested angrily to Maritime, but in vain. The foreign nations affected remonstrated with State. The affair was now at a turn thoroughly incongruous with the main outlines of our foreign policy. We were, for instance, amid an interlude of trying to improve our relations with Argentina when Maritime's blow fell, and among the Argentine applicants were some with consistently good records against Nazi infiltration during the war. Comparable embarrassment arose with Norway. Of all our wartime allies, Norway was the most generous in supplying us with tankers, which we then gravely needed. Now, confronted with applications for 31 tankers from the Norwegians, Maritime granted only 6. Its action toward Norway and Sweden seemed strangely at odds with the Marshall Plan.

Through January and February of 1948, Maritime took other steps which modified the tanker program. These were partly in response to the evident mood and purpose of Congress. On February 27, 1948, Congress in Public Law 423 extended the Commission's operating authority and the termination date of the Ship Sales Act to March 1, 1949. But in the same Act, Congress, prompted by the East Coast shortage, terminated, effective March 1, 1948, the sale of "war-built" vessels to foreign purchasers. The intentions of Congress were clear: U. S. domestic needs, and those needs alone, were to be supplied by available tankers. There was to be no further diversion to foreign purchasers. Commissioners and staff members at Maritime were sympathetic with Congressional views and proceeded to make further modifications of foreign sales in progress. In no instance was the State Department consulted. The Italian Government, for example, under Maritime insistence, had to agree that the ten tankers sold to it from the laid-up fleet would be used, when ready for operation, for one voyage each to carry oil from the Caribbean to Atlantic Coast ports as a contribution to the domestic oil emergency. Repeatedly, the Italian Government pressed for delivery of six tankers purchased from the operating fleet, but Maritime kept the tankers in U. S. operation and refused delivery. "We will, consistent with our domestic oil needs," Maritime reported to Congressman Wolverton, Chairman of the Interstate and Foreign Commerce Committee, "make delivery of such tankers to the Italian government later." The stipulation concerning vessels from lay-up which governed Italy governed other foreign nations to the extent of twenty-five tankers. For tankers sold from the operating fleet, the conditions were equally restrictive: no operating tankers, except those allocated to the United Kingdom, were released from United States service before April —exactly a year after Clayton asked for action by the Maritime Commission, over ten months after the Cabinet had decided that the tankers should be sold foreign, and almost six months after the issuance of the Attorney General's opinion. The result of these circumstances was ironical: the tankers from the laid-up fleet—so long rejected by State and Maritime—went into service abroad ahead of most of the tankers sold from the operating fleet.

THE TASK ACCOMPLISHED

The immediate objective entertained at the inception of the foreign sales program in spring 1947 was thus imperfectly realized. The sales were to alleviate a winter which, as the Secretary of State foresaw, embodied "intolerable hunger and cold" for Europe "unless emergency food and fuel is sent from the United States by the end of the year." Substantial aid did come from the U. S., but the tanker program, except for the 31 tankers delivered to Britain, was not part of the winter's aid. Not until the spring and summer of 1948 did the bulk of the tankers pass to their foreign purchasers.

THE PENALTY

On March 29, 1948, a sub-committee of the Senate Appropriations Committee questioned intensively two officials of the State Department on tanker sales to foreign nations. Senator Wherry was the principal interrogator, and Radius and Assistant Secretary Norton the principal witnesses. The following is from the record of their exchanges:

SENATOR WHERRY: Mr. Chairman, there has not been a committee that has been more exhaustive in its investigations and research, nor, I think, more constructive in its recommendations, than the Small Business Committee has been to stop the sale of those 100 tankers. We did everything in our power. We even went, finally, to the Department of Justice and appealed for an interpretation of the law. We felt that they could not make the sale, and we finally had to bow to the decision of the Attorney General that because commitments had already been made by the State Department to these foreign governments, that they felt they should continue the contracts.

Senator Green, we have all sorts of letters from people in your State who had to have petroleum last winter. And please do not misunderstand me; I am only doing this constructively. It was the result, however, of taking out of the active service these boats that plied Coastwise between the Gulf ports and the Northeast. Maybe there is justification for taking them out on account of a world-wide need. But I want to tell you that that is one of the reasons we are short of fuel oil and oil for tractors. I understand the President is recommending in his new budget for construction of 40 tankers to try to replace some of those that were sold.

MR. NORTON [Department of State]: The Senator made a statement there which I do not wish the record to contain without a denial on my part.

SENATOR WHERRY: It is going to be in the record; you can take exception to it, but I am not going to withdraw it.

MR. NORTON: The Senator made the statement that these sales took place as a result of commitments that were made to foreign governments by the State Department. That statement is not correct.

SENATOR WHERRY: I want the record to show that I was informed by the Department of Justice that we should go ahead with these sales because the commitments had been made under those memorandum agreements, in which we agreed to sell the boats.

MR. RADIUS [Department of State]: I believe those were the actions of the Maritime Commission which constituted the commitment which the Department of Justice referred to.

SENATOR WHERRY: After the Cabinet meeting they had to bow to the administration. But prior to that time it is my understanding that if the Maritime Commission had been handling the matter the Commission would never have sold them.

In this tenor the hearings continued. Senator Wherry made clear his belief that the blame for the foreign sales should fall upon the State Department. He sought out one person as scapegoat for the whole transaction (and for a parallel dispute on a pending foreign aid bill), and his hand fell on Radius. There consequently occurred a drastic reduction in the appropriations for the Shipping Division of the State Department for the fiscal year 1948-49. As it happened, the House of Representatives had cut the item for general expenses of the

State Department by $4,050,000; of this amount the Senate Committee restored $3,-983,000, giving the following explanation of its failure to restore the last $67,000:

It is the intent of the committee that no more than $40,000 shall be allocated out of 1949 funds to the Shipping and Inland Transport Division of the Office of Transport and Communications. The only reduction below Department estimates which this committee favors is the reduction of $67,000 in that division. The money allowed for the Shipping and Inland Transport Division is adequate to cover the work in the seamen affairs section and to allow a minimum amount of work in international shipping affairs. The involvement of this division in domestic affairs this year has been wasteful of Government money and has had disastrous effect upon American shipping.

Actually, the admonitory action was somewhat misdirected. It was probably based on the mistaken belief that Radius was Director of the Shipping Division. His post in fact was higher—Director of the Office of Transport and Communications Affairs—an office with divisions of aviation, telecommunications and shipping.

THE REWARD

Senator Wherry to the contrary, the foreign sale of tankers appeared firmly established, before 1948 had ended, as a satisfactory merchandising transaction. The demand and supply picture for tankers at the close of 1948 had become exactly the reverse of 1947. Foreign construction of tankers was in full progress. The boom in the U. S. for the T-2 Tankers had disappeared with a rising interest in large new tankers considerably more efficient in capacity and speed than the T-2. Other powerful factors helped reduce the T-2 market. The U. S. was shifting rapidly toward a considerably smaller "normal" tanker fleet, estimated at as low as approximately 4,000,000 deadweight tons by the Postwar Planning Committee of the Maritime Commission. In 1947, for instance, the active U. S. flag tanker fleet was 9,695,000 deadweight tons; in 1948 it was down to 7,387,-000 tons and the forecast of the Association of American Ship Owners for 1953 was 5,999,000 tons. A large and increasing number of U. S. tankers in 1948 and 1949 thus were idle. Standard Oil of New York, for instance, had 190 per cent of its tanker needs for the U. S. coastwise trade in 1949.

In this setting, the foreign sale of T-2s in 1947 seems to have been good merchandising. The tankers were sold at nearly the last possible moment. They yielded a substantial revenue, averaging $1,500,000 per tanker, approximately half of the prewar construction cost. (In the long run the United States, through Marshall Plan funds and otherwise, will probably foot a large part of the bill.) Had they not been sold in 1947, they would have stood idle through 1948 and 1949, with no demand for them in view.

The sales have another aspect of success in the larger foreign policy of which they were a part. Over the long months in which the tankers were transferred, the main currents of our foreign policy ran a generally favorable course. Togliatti did not gain power in Italy. Europe somehow withstood the ravages of winter, and the Marshall Plan passed from a vague theory into an enormous practical operation which saved Western Europe from collapse and communist seizure. With these accomplishments came new and difficult problems which claimed the interest of the foreign nations and indeed of many of the same U. S. officials and agencies who had executed the sale of the tankers.

AFTERTHOUGHTS

Policy is a word fraught with ambiguity. Presumably most readers will feel as does the writer, that this account of the sale of the tankers is a study in the development of policy. Yet the contrast between policy and application is a matter of perspective. In this sense, the tanker proposal can be looked at as, primarily, a special application of the more generalized policy which reached fuller fruition in the Marshall Plan—the policy of aiding European recovery. This policy, in turn, was a specialized application of the underlying foreign policy of the United States, to seek the establishment of peace and freedom in the world. To pursue the same concept on a descending scale, the disagreements about the tanker program can be described as a dispute about the application of a sale policy which was accepted in principle. Thus the Maritime Commission raised no official objection to the wisdom or correctness of the basic State Department proposal nor did the Navy adopt the position that aid to other countries by the sale of tankers was in itself undesirable. It will be recalled that the three specific issues that prolonged the dispute among the executive agencies were the eligibility of applicants, the number of tankers to be sold, and the use of tankers from the laid-up fleet. The limitations proposed by Navy were matters of application, not principle; they were designed to prevent the tanker program from interfering with the Navy's plans for national defense. Even Senator Wherry, who considered the sales illegal, did not assert that the original tanker program was improper or unwise but rather that its execution in the fall of 1947 conflicted with other social and legal considerations that, in his view, deserved priority.

This case then is a study not in a basic policy cleavage, but rather, initially in the practical difficulties involved when the application of foreign policy was believed to be in conflict with the application of defense policy and subsequently, when the program to carry out foreign policy was found to conflict with the needs of New Englanders and the financial interests of the citizen applicants for tankers.

Dilemmas of this character are, of course, inherent in governmental action and are recurrent in all countries. Two aspects of the dilemma may be noted.

First is the fact that the controversy within the Executive Branch (prior to the incursion of Senator Wherry) was not one in which public officials seek to carry out what they deem to be national policy in spite of or in reconciliation with group or sectional interests. Here the problem was created by the conflicting requirements of accepted national policies, a situation that is peculiarly characteristic of defense and international programs, where group and sectional interests are often not very directly affected. During the years to come, our State Department and our Department of Defense may or may not work well together, but it is hardly likely that when problems arise the ideal solution for one will invariably also prove to be the ideal solution for the other, particularly if the solutions are narrowly conceived in terms of military and diplomatic considerations.

The second aspect of the dilemma that is of interest is the mode of resolution actually adopted. The dilemma itself was of a universal character—the satisfaction of conflicting national interests and later the satisfaction of a conflict between national and group and sectional interests—and recurrent in all countries. But modes of resolution vary decisively from country to country because of cultural and governmental differences. The tanker case is illuminating not perhaps so much because the problem is universal as because its handling was so peculiarly American. In it we can see the impact on the resolution of differences of two characteristic and unusual features of our government: the independent statutory authority and responsibility of the various Cabinet members and other heads of agencies; and the co-existence of an independent executive and an independent legislature with overlapping spheres of activity. The history of the tankers can appropriately be examined in this general frame of reference.

The President's inability to have his policy on the sale of the tankers put into effect promptly and fully can be attributed in part to the absence of adequate co-ordinating machinery. It seems clear that the then existing machinery of co-ordination did not make available to the President a fully reasoned analysis of the various implications of the tanker proposal. Since the date of these events, the National Security Council, a co-ordinating agency, has been established in the Executive Office of the President, with an area of jurisdiction that would cover the tanker problem. Assuming effective functioning of the Council, the President would today be in a better position to understand the nature of the conflict between the two departments. Whether a better briefing of this sort would have led to more effective action is not so clear. The Secretary of the Navy, it will be recalled, had an independent and inescapable statutory responsibility to advise the Maritime Commission on the proposed transaction. The advice to be given was the personal responsibility of the Secretary and could not, as it would be in a government with collective Cabinet responsibility, be determined by Cabinet action (even with Presidential approval). In this important sense, there is no such thing as a Cabinet decision in our government; the Cabinet members remain individually accountable in fact to Congress and the people. And in this sense the various devices for improving the effectiveness of the Cabinet—such as a Cabinet secretariat—are seen to have somewhat limited utility. This is not an argument against the establishment of a Cabinet secretariat—or of some mechanism that can serve as such—but it is a warning that, within the general structure of our written and unwritten Constitution, the Cabinet can hardly become a body capable of making and enforcing collective and binding decisions.

There is another respect in which the Cabinet is limited as a vehicle for decision. Membership in the Cabinet is governed by certain legislative and Presidential traditions. The Cabinet does not include, and probably never will include, without a major constitutional revolution, representatives of all the chief agencies of the government, nor are the agencies unrepresented in the Cabinet subject to Cabinet control or even to complete Presidential control, with or without Cabinet concurrence. This freedom from control is, of course, spectacularly true of the so-called independent commissions; in this particular case, for example, a Cabinet decision without the concurrence of the Maritime Commission would have been of little avail. This situation no longer entirely prevails with respect to shipping. Organizational changes since the tanker sales were consummated have established direct Cabinet representation for some shipping matters. In keeping with the recommendations of the Hoover Commission, the President's Reorganization Plan No. 21, and the Department of Commerce's Administrative Order No. 116 of May 23, 1950, the Maritime Commission has been abolished, the Secretary of Commerce has been granted control over the transfer of vessels, and the Commission's "purely" regulatory functions have passed to the Federal Maritime Board. But, as it happened, even before these structural changes were made, the Maritime Commission, an agency not noted for its independence of action, tended to go along with the President's wishes. But if the problem had concerned, for example, the Interstate Commerce Commission, the futility of a Cabinet or Presidential decision, not independently concurred in by the Commission, will be apparent.

The foregoing considerations are hardly novel. They all point to the fact that while the Cabinet may be made more useful as a means for determining policy and following up on execution, Cabinet government is not possible within our constitutional framework. Whether it would be desirable is another question that need not concern us here. The same considerations also suggest that there may be a greater opportunity for useful service in a White House secretariat than in a Cabinet secretariat. In the tanker situation, there was little consistency and coherence in notification of Presidential decision, ascertainment of acceptance, and follow-up on action. The existence of a White House secretariat might have enabled the President at least to keep posted on the results of the Cabinet "decisions" and might equally have served to facilitate the work of Steelman, Conway and the *ad hoc* committee.

The Cabinet is not the only device available to the President for establishing and effectuating executive policy. The President has at hand many other means to this end. Some, and among them some of the most effective, require the energetic personal action of the President himself—but obviously only a few selected issues can be handled in such fashion. The Bureau of the Budget and the National Security Resources Board can assume a continuing burden on behalf of the President; but these agencies are limited to certain areas of concern. Permanent Cabinet-level inter-agency committees, like the National Advisory Council and the National Security Council are limited both in jurisdiction (although NSC happens to have adequate jurisdiction for a problem like the tanker case) and in membership: it is difficult at best for an inter-agency committee to work effectively with non-member agencies. *Ad hoc* committees—such as the one established to handle the tanker problem—are a valuable adjunct of central executive action; but of course their effectiveness depends in part on the quality of the staff assistance, and in great part on the character and attributes of the chairman. In any event, except as the chairman can and does speak with authority, they cannot serve to settle significant differences of opinion: in the tanker situation the larger issues between Maritime and Navy were not soluble by an *ad hoc* committee, whereas the details of alleviating the New England shortage were successfully handled.

The wartime Office of War Mobilization and its successor, the Office of War Mobilization and Reconversion, provided a focus for inter-agency co-ordination and direction, and it used both *ad hoc* committees and informal meetings to secure reconciliation and to decide disputed questions. After June 30, 1947, the approximate successor of these two offices was the Office of the Assistant to the President. The Assistant to the President served as conciliator and spokesman for the President: in general, as in this case, he does not make and enforce decisions, particularly where Cabinet officers are involved, unless persuasion will suffice.

For the tanker case, this largely self-imposed limitation on action inhibited the prompt, or prompter carrying out of the President's policy; but it would be unwise to conclude that such an apparent gap in the President's staff assistance is susceptible to easy cure via organization chart or personnel assignment procedure. No one can assume the role of Justice Byrnes or Justice Vinson or Mr. Hopkins unless both he and the President possess certain qualities of character that make the uneasy relationship workable; and the viability of the role is probably more precarious in time of peace than in war, though the problems themselves may be slightly less urgent or multifarious.

So far these comments have been directed at the problems of the President. But, to take the question of statutory consultation as an example, the difficulties in the case were not limited to the White House. Although the consultation provision was desired by the Navy—and in even stronger form—it proved a source of embarrassment to the Secretary. To the Maritime Commission it was a cause of acute chagrin, especially since the Navy's formal advice could not be balanced and offset by different advice given with the same formality and weight from other agencies with different views. The Maritime Commission could not disregard the advice by pointing to any necessity it was under to consult a variety of agencies. It can be presumed that this result, which was tantamount to giving the Navy predominant weight in the Commission's decisions, was not unintended by the Congress. The Congress wanted defense considerations, as interpreted by the Secretary of the Navy, to have prime weight. The appropriateness of such a prejudgment of weight to be attributed to the various factors involved in such a mixed question seems doubtful. Eventually responsibility for execution of both our foreign and our defense policy falls to the President. To determine in advance by statute that in all sales of ships efforts devoted to the prevention of war and to the building up of allies in case of possible war should not have equal weight with efforts specifically devoted to our own defense establishment is to make the conduct of foreign policy difficult indeed. As the *Curtiss Wright* decision shows, the Supreme Court tends to grant the President the broadest possible leeway in the handling of foreign policy; the Congress, as any number of recent statutes concerned with our foreign economic policy indicate, is generally disposed to impose fairly decided restrictions on the President's freedom of action.

Another problem of large consequence, perhaps more difficult to solve than those mentioned heretofore, is to be found in the relations of the Executive and the Legislative Branches. The co-existence of an independent legislature and an independent executive, founded in our Constitution, has been under intermittent attack for many years. Most of the proponents of change have suggested some adaptation of the parliamentary system, particularly as it is found or assumed to be found in Great Britain—although American advocates of constitutional change do not ordinarily describe parliamentary government as it has recently been described by the President of the Indian Political Science Association as "the virtual dictatorship of the Cabinet usual in parliamentary governments."

The pros and cons of this continuing constitutional debate raise many questions not relevant to the issues in the tanker case. But even the most ardent supporter of our Constitution would find it difficult to deny that we do have difficulties in the relations of the two branches that are peculiar to our own system. A consideration of the tanker imbroglio may perhaps cast some light on the sources and nature of some of the inter-branch stresses especially in the strategically important area where domestic and foreign policies come in conflict.

To point to the difficulty is of course far easier than to specify the cure. In the present case, the difficulty was compounded by the fact that the events took place at one of those fortunately rare periods in our history where the President was of a different party from the majority in the two Houses of the Congress. Under such circumstances government is at best an accommodation. Nevertheless, it is clear that the operations under the present rules and customs of the Congress are not ideally designed to facilitate executive action in the field of foreign affairs. The student of these events is entitled to wonder if the whole Congress acting in formal fashion would have been willing to put the interests of New England and of the citizen applicants for tankers ahead of our foreign policy, both as a matter of policy and as a matter of law, as Senator Wherry did. On the other hand, Senator Wherry's willingness to abide by the Attorney General's advice to the President was a somewhat unusual accommodation that tended to facilitate further action on the tanker program. It may perhaps be noted in passing that Senator Wherry's acceptance of the Attorney General's opinion did not relieve the Maritime Commission of its concern with congressional and other pressures. This occurrence is merely another illustration of the peculiar and extremely deep-seated problems caused by the division of loyalties within the Executive Branch: loyalty to the President, and loyalty across to the Congress and to the interest groups that impinge on the Congress and the agencies themselves.

All the members of each of the two Houses of Congress are, of course, by law and by tradition equal and all of them have, at least in theory, an equal voice on all matters of legislative concern in every field. In fact, however, partly because of variations in interest in the various congressional and senatorial constituencies and partly because of the effects of the committee system, senators and congressmen do exhibit a fairly high degree of specialization. As a specialist, the congressman or senator has a vested interest which he must uphold or watch over. It seems highly improbable that the citizens of the State of Nebraska had any great interest in the tanker problem, either in its relation to the oil shortage or in its relation to the citizen applications for purchase of tankers. Senator Wherry's active interest in the problem was therefore presumably not motivated by specific pressures from his own state. In one sense, no doubt, he was living up to his responsibilities as a leading member of the Republican party, responsible for calling attention to defects in operations of the administrative agencies under a Democratic President, an activity that might also, incidentally of course, strengthen his prestige at home and in the Republican party. More pertinent, he was acting as chairman of a committee devoted to the interests of small business. In this connection it was almost inevitable for him to approach the tanker question, if he approached it at all, as an opponent to the sale of the tankers to foreign countries. The virtual inevitability of Senator Wherry's approach can be better appreciated by contrasting it with the probable treatment of the same problem if it had been taken up by the Foreign Relations Committee. The members of the Foreign Relations Committee might not have been totally indifferent to the pleas of the New Englanders or of the citizen applicants and particularly so if they had come from the New England states or had among their constituents some of the applicants, but their consideration of the question would at least have been tempered almost from the beginning by their abiding interest in the general conduct of our foreign affairs. Senator Wherry, with his quite different area of specialized interest, was able to disregard the impact of his proposals on foreign relations with no overt qualms or questionings.

Congressional committees seem to be an absolute necessity for the handling of the business that comes before the Congress. Inevitably the committee members tend to specialize, and indeed gain from specializing, in subjects which repeatedly require their scrutiny and thoughtful attention. But the obvious benefits of specialization must be balanced against the failure of the committee structure to ensure broad over-all political consideration of problems by representatives from all areas of the country and with a wide variety of interests. Such broader scrutiny is, of course, more feasible for matters that come up for action by the whole Senate or House or both, than for those that are handled within the committee structure itself. This short-circuiting which occurs within the committee structure is particularly apparent in Congress' exercise of its function of overseeing the Executive Branch—a function that is usually considered Constitutional in origin, though the responsibility is not set forth *tantis verbis* in the document itself. Some of the difficulties that arise in this connection are illustrated in the text. But the reader should not forget that there are important benefits to be gained where representatives of the legislature call to the attention of the administrative agencies aspects of the national interest that have been overlooked or slighted.

Another aspect of the functioning of Congress deserves attention. The operations of Congress permit and almost encourage the individual congressman or senator, and particularly if he is a senior member of either body, to carry his personal disagreement on administration policy to the point of punitive action. In an abstract sense, it is quite true that the cut in the State Department appropriations for the fiscal year 1949 was open for consideration and revision by the other members of the Senate Committee on Appropriations, by all the members of the Senate, by the managers of the two Houses in the conference, and eventually by the members of the House of Representatives as well. Nevertheless, as a practical matter, since the unit involved had no political support outside government, the action was essentially the responsibility of Senator Wherry himself and was merely allowed to slide by without consideration and review. This may be a somewhat extreme case, but the fact remains that the present functioning of Congress does permit or encourage action of this sort. If action of this character is deemed undesirable the reader must look for the cure, however difficult, to some modification of the rules and customs of the Congress rather than to anything that the President can do.

It seems possible that the same conclusions that apply to the great, perhaps even undue influence of individual members of Congress on particular subjects apply to a considerable extent also to the general problems of the relations of the executive to the Congress.

In the field of foreign affairs, during the five years after the end of the war, with the exception of policy on China, there has usually been a consensus between administration spokesmen and a majority of members of both houses of Congress on what should be done. Legislative action on a whole series of programs of momentous consequence has been in substantial conformity with administration recommendations: and, as well as can be estimated, in substantial conformity with the prevailing views of the country. The legislative achievement has been great and owes much to enlightened leadership of both parties in both branches of the government—and out of the government. Yet it has been accompanied by painful alarms and excursions, by an enormous expenditure of time and energy by busy men, and by a constant sense of strife and uncertainty that has militated against the very objectives that were being carried into law.

Throughout these years of struggle there have been constant complaints about the relations of the two branches. The recriminations about the bipartisan foreign policy, or its absence, have been in large part merely a disguised form of legislative-executive opposition. Amelioration has always been the result of merely personal adjustment. Perhaps no more is possible within our system; it seems fairly clear that no very significant change is to be looked for in any remodeling of the executive structure. Any hope for more significant alteration would seem to lie in some reconsideration by the Congress of its seniority and committee systems and its modes of action. Whether such change is possible, whether it is even desirable, may be uncertain; but it is hard to foresee any lessening of the recurring tensions between the two branches on any other basis.

In closing it may be useful to pause briefly to reflect on another ship sale case in our history of far greater importance than the tanker case. Henry Adams tells of it in his *Education* in the chapter called "The Battle of the Rams." It forms a curious mirror image of the events recounted herein. It concerned two ships—ironclads destined for the Confederate Navy; but these ships were to be delivered by a British national and the interest of the United States lay in preventing their delivery. Eventually Minister Adams won: Lord Russell finally " 'thought it necessary to direct that [the ironclads] be detained,' not, of course, under the statute, but on the ground urged by the American Minister, of international obligation above the statute." And Russell continued, in his letter to Palmerston, "The Solicitor General has been consulted and concurs in the measure as one of policy though not of strict law."

Apparently the appeal to the lawyers for what is essentially policy affirmation is not an unique aspect of our system. Our own use of the shield of our unwritten constitution is more oblique than the British. But in both situations—ironclads and tankers—the need for executive freedom of action in international relations was felt and affirmed.

Chronology

1947

APRIL 3 State informs Maritime of urgent need for additional sale of tankers to foreign nations beyond 50 approved in 1946

APRIL 4 Sir John Magowen, Minister, British Embassy, advises State of desperate U.K. fuel oil and tanker shortage

APRIL 7 Maritime requests Navy advice, under statute, concerning proposed sale of additional tankers to foreign nations

APRIL 9 State urges Navy to approve Maritime proposals, choice of foreign nations to be determined by Maritime

MAY 14 Meeting in Steelman's office to discuss tanker sales; agreement to refer matter to Cabinet

MAY 16 Joint Chiefs of Staff report back to Navy on Maritime letter of April 7. First Cabinet decision on tankers

MAY 19 Interior requests Navy to approve "75 to 100" tankers for foreign sale

MAY 26 Navy replies to Maritime letter of April 7; approves sale of 35 tankers but (a) from laid-up fleet; and (b) to politically stable nations which have "same political philosophy and ideology" as U. S.

JUNE 2 The second cabinet decision on tankers

JUNE 4 State informs Maritime of new cabinet decision. State asks Navy to approve 65 additional tankers without limiting conditions

JUNE 5 Secretary Marshall makes Marshall Plan speech at Harvard

JUNE 9-11 Navy insists that Maritime initiate request for additional tanker sales

JUNE 16 State requests Maritime to file request for additional tanker sales

JUNE 17 Steelman supports State's request. Interior holds meeting on petroleum problems, including foreign sale of tankers

JUNE 18 Interior supports State's request

JUNE 19 Maritime requests Navy concurrence in sale of 100 tankers (including 35 already approved) without limiting conditions

JUNE 20 Navy replies approving sale of 100 tankers, but requiring sale of 46 from laid-up fleet and other limiting conditions

JUNE 24 Meeting of State, Maritime, Navy: agreement on eligible purchasers, disagreement on meaning of other Navy provisos

JUNE 25 Maritime orders 46 tankers in lay-up reconditioned

JUNE 30 Maritime makes compromise proposal to Navy on sales

JULY 3-16 Informal negotiations between Maritime and Navy

JULY 17 Navy rejects Maritime compromise proposal

JULY 24 Maritime submits new proposal to Navy

JULY 25 Interagency committee approves allocation and priority list for sale of 100 tankers

JULY 31 Maritime approves interagency allocation

AUGUST 1 Maritime informs various foreign nations of tanker allocations

AUGUST 6 Navy letter notes disagreement with Maritime over conditions

AUGUST 8 Steelman asks Maritime for progress report on sales

AUGUST 13 Maritime orders sale of 53 tankers from active fleet and 34 from lay-up
AUGUST 14 Maritime reports sale decision to Steelman
SEPTEMBER 1-OCTOBER 31 U. S. citizen applications for tankers pour into Maritime
OCTOBER 1 Steelman holds interagency meeting to discuss: (1) New England fuel shortage; (2) citizen applications for tankers; (3) expediting foreign sales
OCTOBER 10 Maritime outlines new tanker sale procedure to Navy
OCTOBER 28 Senator Wherry asks President to halt "illegal" foreign sales. Interagency meeting to discuss prospective Wherry investigation
OCTOBER 29 White House asks Attorney General for opinion on legality of tanker sales
OCTOBER 30-NOVEMBER 7 Maritime notifies various foreign nations of approved applications
NOVEMBER 14-18 Wherry hearings
DECEMBER 9 Attorney General approves legality of foreign tanker sales
DECEMBER 18 Maritime makes "final determination" on sale of 83 tankers

1948

JANUARY-FEBRUARY Maritime restricts foreign sales
SPRING AND SUMMER Bulk of tankers are finally delivered to foreign purchasers

Principal Persons Concerned with the Tanker Sales

THE EXECUTIVE BRANCH

DEPARTMENT OF STATE

George C. Marshall (General of the Army, ret.), Secretary

William L. Clayton, Under Secretary for Economic Affairs

Willard L. Thorp, Assistant Secretary for Economic Affairs

Garrison Norton, Assistant Secretary for Transport and Communications Affairs

Walter A. Radius, Director, Office of Transport and Communications Affairs

John Loftus, Chief, Division of Petroleum

MARITIME COMMISSION

William H. Smith (Vice Adm., ret.), Chairman

Raymond S. McKeough, Vice Chairman

Joseph K. Carson, Commissioner

Richard Parkhurst, Commissioner

Huntington Morse, Special Asst. to Chairman and Interdepartmental Liaison Officer

Wade H. Skinner, General Counsel

J. J. Pimper, Chief, Large Vessels Sales Division

DEPARTMENT OF THE NAVY

James Forrestal, Secretary, later Secretary of Defense

John L. Sullivan, Under Secretary, frequently Acting Secretary, later Secretary

W. John Kenney, Assistant Secretary, later Under Secretary

William M. Callaghan (Rear Adm.), Asst. Chief of Naval Operations, Logistics

W. N. Mansfield (Capt.), Chief, Merchant Vessel Section

THE WHITE HOUSE AND THE EXECUTIVE OFFICE OF THE PRESIDENT

John R. Steelman, Assistant to the President

Robert C. Turner, Assistant to Steelman

Granville Conway (Capt.), Coordinator of Emergency Export Programs

Martin Goodman (Capt.), Assistant to Conway

Richard C. Bissell, Assistant to Conway

Matthew J. Connelly, Secretary to the President

DEPARTMENT OF THE INTERIOR

Julius A. Krug, Secretary

Max Ball, Director, Oil and Gas Division

R. E. Friedman, Assistant to Ball

DEPARTMENT OF JUSTICE

Tom C. Clark, Attorney General

George T. Washington, Assistant Solicitor General

Abe Harris, Assistant to Washington

David C. Reich, Assistant to Washington

DEPARTMENT OF COMMERCE

W. Averell Harriman, Secretary

William C. Foster, Under Secretary

THE JOINT CHIEFS OF STAFF

William D. Leahy (Fleet Admiral), Chief of Staff to the Commander in Chief, Chairman

Chester W. Nimitz (Fleet Admiral), Chief of Naval Operations, Member

THE CONGRESS

SENATE SPECIAL COMMITTEE TO STUDY PROBLEMS OF AMERICAN SMALL BUSINESS

Kenneth S. Wherry (Senator, R., Neb.), Chairman

Raymond Dickey, Counsel

SENATE COMMITTEE ON INTERSTATE AND FOREIGN COMMERCE

Wallace H. White, Jr. (Senator, R., Me.), Chairman

HOUSE SUBCOMMITTEE ON SHIP SALES, CHARTERS AND LAY-UPS

Alvin Weichel (M.C., R., O.), Chairman

OTHERS

Bushrod Howard (Capt.), Director, Standard Oil Co. of N. J.

John Magowen (Sir), Minister, British Embassy

Appendix I

Biographies[1]

BALL, MAX W. Born Munson Township, Henry County, Illinois, 1885; B.S., E.M., Colo. Sch. of Mines, 1906; LL.M., National Univ., Washington, D.C., 1914. With U. S. Geol. Survey, Aug. 1906-Mar. 1916, as chmn. oil bd.; mining engr. and law officer, U. S. Bur. of Mines, Apr. 1916-May 1917; chief geologist, Rocky Mountain div. Roxana Petroleum Co. of Okla., June 1917-Mar. 1918; gen. mgr. Royal Dutch Shell oil interests Rocky Mountain region, 1918-1921; pres. Western Pipe Line Co., 1921-27, Marine Oil Co. and asso. companies, 1922-28; Argo Oil Co., 1925-28; cons. practice since Nov. 1928; pres. Abasand Oils Limited, 1930-43; pres. Royal Royalties Limited, Denver, 1931-44. Special Assistant to Deputy Petroleum Administrator, Petroleum Administration for War, Oct. 1944 to 1946. Director, Oil and Gas Division, Interior Department, 1946- . Author, *This Fascinating Oil Business.*

CALLAGHAN, WILLIAM MC COMBE Rear Admiral, U. S. Navy. Born Oakland, California, 1897; attended St. Mary's College and the University of San Francisco; and the U. S. Naval Academy 1915-18; graduated 1918. Temporary promotion to Lieut. (j.g.) 1919, and commissioned to that rank, 1920. Assisted in fitting out and served aboard various destroyers until June 1923 and studied electrical engineering at Postgraduate School, Annapolis, Maryland and Columbia Univ., New York where he received M.S. degree, 1935. Served aboard U.S.S. *Concord* in Cuban waters, 1925-28; on duty in Repairs Division, Bureau of Engineering, Navy Dept., Washington 1928-30. Assistant engineer officer of U.S.S. *Saratoga*, 1931-33. Instructor, Dept. of Marine Engineering at Naval Academy, 1933-36. Commander of U.S.S. *Reuben James*, 1936-38; executive officer of U.S.S. *Henderson*, 1938-39. On duty in Ships' Movement Division, Office of the Chief of Naval Operations, 1939-41. Naval Observer at the American Embassy, London, England, 1941-42. On duty in the Office of the Chief of Naval Operations, 1941-42. Served on Staff of the Commander in Chief, Pacific Fleet, 1942-44 and received Legion of Merit. Fitted out and commanded U.S.S. *Missouri*, 1944-45, and participated in naval operations in Pacific during that period against Japan. On duty on staff of the Commander in Chief, Pacific Fleet, 1945. Following temporary duty in Bureau of Naval Personnel, Navy Dept., Washington, assigned, September 1945 to Office of the Chief of Naval Operations, to duty as Assistant Chief of Naval Operations (Transportation) and also Chief of Naval Transportation Service, 1945- .

CONWAY, GRANVILLE Born Cambridge, Maryland, 1898; educated in local schools, then went to sea; appointed master of a Shipping Board vessel in Cardiff, England; came ashore 1922 and was Fleet Captain and Fleet Manager in Reserve Fleet in Norfolk, New London and New York; became, 1935, District Manager of the same office of the Maritime Commission; 1942, Atlantic Coast Director of the War Shipping Administration; in 1943, Associate Deputy Administrator; 1944, Deputy Administrator; 1946, Administrator. During war served as associate member of Military Transport Committee of Combined Chiefs of Staff, Chairman of Combined Shipping Adjustment Board, member of Inter-Agency Committee on Exports, Foods and Raw Materials, and Chairman of subcom. on Transportation of that Committee. Was Shipping Adviser to President F. D. Roosevelt at Quebec and Yalta. Resigned from War Shipping Administration 1946 and became President of the Cosmopolitan Shipping Co., New York City. President Truman appointed him Coordinator of Emergency Export Programs, December 18, 1946, a post in which he served without pay, having obtained leave from Cosmopolitan.

MORSE, HUNTINGTON T. Born Chicago, Illinois, 1889; educated public schools in Chicago and private schools in Switzerland, France and England; attended Phillips Academy, Andover, Mass., 1908-1911, and Yale University, 1911-1915 (A.B. 1915). In 1916 and 1917, served as checker, receiving clerk, delivery clerk, dock superintendent for Mallory Steamship Lines, New York City.

[1] As of June 1, 1947.

In the first World War, was Lieutenant, Senior Grade, U.S.N.R.F. and served as Head of the Operations Dept., Naval Overseas Transportation Service, Port of New York. 1919-1922, Assistant Special Commissioner and London Representative of the United States Shipping Board Emergency Fleet Corporation; 1922-25, Director for Europe of the United States Shipping Board Merchant Fleet Corp.; 1925-32, served Munson Steamship Line as assistant chartering manager; assistant manager, passenger department; local manager, Buffalo, New York; 1932-34 had own wholesale business in coal; 1934-36, director of operations for U. S. Shipping Board Merchant Fleet Corporation; 1937-42, Assistant to the Chairman, U. S. Maritime Commission; 1942-46, Assistant to the War Shipping Administrator; 1946- , Assistant to the U. S. Maritime Commission.

RADIUS, WALTER A. Born San Francisco, California, 1910; educated Stanford University; A.B. 1932, M.B.A. 1934, Ph.D. 1942. Analyst in investment corp. 1934-37; research assoc. Institute of Pacific Relations 1938; appointed divisional asst. in State Department, June 29, 1942; special assistant to director Office of Transport and Communications Affairs, State Department, September 1, 1944 (P-7, $6500); adviser on inland transport, P-8, Nov. 18, 1945; deputy director TRC, July 14, 1946; director, March 27, 1947.

Appendix II

Organizations

The Coordinator of Emergency Export Programs

THE WHITE HOUSE
Washington

December 17, 1946

My dear Captain Conway:

Last year, when you occupied the position of War Shipping Administrator, I appointed you Chairman of the Interagency Committee on Export Transportation. In that capacity you coordinated the work of all agencies concerned with the shipment of grain, grain products, and coal. Under your leadership, these Government agencies succeeded in carrying out export programs of grain and coal of unprecedented magnitude.

Once again, we are faced with the problem of achieving large export goals in spite of serious obstacles. These obstacles are different, but no less serious than last year. This year, for example, we have a surplus of grain; but the export program will not succeed unless it is given central direction. Whatever the problems, I am determined that our shipments of these critically needed products must be at maximum capacity for the coming months.

For that reason I have asked you to return to Government service for approximately ninety days to assume the post of Coordinator of Emergency Export Programs. As such, I wish you to coordinate the work of all agencies concerned and to see that these programs are carried out successfully. To this end, you are authorized to call on all agencies, to use their full legal powers and to take whatever steps are necessary. You can count on the cooperation of all concerned, and I know that with this cooperation you will fulfill your mission completely.

Very sincerely yours,
[Sgd] *Harry S. Truman*

Captain Granville Conway
The Cosmopolitan Shipping Company
42 Broadway
New York, N. Y.

April 27, 1948

My dear Mr. President:

On December 17, 1946, you asked me to return to Government service for a brief period to act as Coordinator of Emergency Export Programs. When it became apparent that the problems in this field would extend beyond the period originally contemplated I was glad to continue in this post as you requested.

There will continue to be difficult problems in connection with transportation of the U. S. export supplies. Now that the Economic Cooperation Administration has been organized, however, I feel that a considerable portion of the work which my small staff and I have been performing can well be assumed by that Agency. With your permission, therefore, I would like to tender my resignation as Coordinator of Emergency Export Programs at this time, and to suggest that this office as such be terminated.

At Mr. Hoffman's request, I have undertaken to assist him for a short time in organizing shipping arrangements for the European Recovery Program. I will, of course, be available for any additional service you may wish.

I would like to express my sincere appreciation for the full cooperation I have received from you and your staff and all of the Government agencies concerned during the period of my service as Coordinator of Emergency Export Programs.

Respectfully yours,
[s] *Granville Conway*

THE WHITE HOUSE
Washington

April 27, 1948

Dear Captain Conway:

Your letter of April twenty-seventh tendering your resignation as Coordinator of Emergency Export Programs has been received. Although I deeply regret losing your services in this capacity, I agree that it is appropriate for the Economic Cooperation Administration to assume a major portion of the work you and your group have been doing. I am pleased to know that you are assisting Mr. Hoffman in organizing shipping arrangements for the European Recovery Program, and that you will be available for additional services as need arises. I should like to call upon you from time to time as consultant on special problems which you are so well qualified to handle.

Your work as Coordinator of Emergency Export Programs has been outstanding. By your foresight and vigorous action, in cooperation with all the U. S. Government and foreign agencies involved, you have played a major role in achieving a smooth and efficient movement of vital supplies to other countries in furtherance of our foreign policy. The contribution which these improvements in our export capabilities have made to economic recovery in Europe and elsewhere, and to the preservation and enhancement of democracy cannot be overemphasized.

The effective public service which you have rendered is greatly appreciated by me and by your fellow citizens.

Very sincerely yours,
[Sgd] *Harry S. Truman*

Captain Granville Conway
42 Broadway
New York, N. Y.

Department of State: Office of Transport and Communications Affairs

From *U. S. Government Manual—1947*, 2nd ed., p. 103.

The Office of Transport and Communications Affairs initiates and coordinates policy and action concerning the international aspects of transport and communications. The Office consists of an Aviation Division, a Telecommunications Division, and a Shipping Division.

Shipping Division.—This Division is responsible for the formulation and coordination of policy and action in matters concerning international shipping. This includes such activities as (a) analysis and study of all international aspects of shipping; (b) observation and review of developments in the maritime services and laws of other countries; (c) analysis and recommendation with regard to foreign policy aspects of subsidies and other governmental assistance to shipping and with regard to discriminatory laws or practices against American shipping; (d) initiation of policy on international aspects of inland transport matters and coordination of activities of other Federal agencies in this field; (e) formulation and execution of policy on matters involving the effect of ocean-freight and marine-insurance rates on foreign trade; (f) initiation and coordination of policy and action in connection with seamen's affairs; (g) analysis of regulatory measures and standards that affect shipping and trade, in order to determine their relationship to foreign policy; and (h) formulation and coordination of the work of the Department concerned with protection abroad of seamen and official services to ships by the Foreign Service of the United States.

Department of the Navy: The Deputy Chief of Naval Operations (Logistics)

From *The United States Navy, a Description of its Functional Organization*, prepared by the Office of the Management Engineer, Navy Department, July 1948, p. 23; and from *U. S. Government Manual—1947*, 2nd ed., pp. 216-217.

The Deputy Chief of Naval Operations (Logistics) initiates, develops, and executes logistic plans and policies and determines matériel requirements of the Naval Establishment. He has control of the distribution and disposal of all materials for logistic support including petroleum throughout the Naval Establishment, coordinates and directs the construction and maintenance of naval vessels and bases, and coordinates and directs logistics efforts of the bureaus and offices of the Navy Department. He has supervision of the Board of Inspection and Survey; coordinates naval logistics efforts with the Army and other Government agencies; and has representation on joint logistic agencies.

Department of the Interior: The Oil and Gas Division

THE WHITE HOUSE
Washington

May 3, 1946

My dear Mr. Secretary:

In keeping with the Administration's policy of winding up the affairs of war agencies as quickly as possible after their emergency responsibilities have been discharged, I have acted upon your recommendation to terminate, effective May 8, the Petroleum Administration for War, which has so successfully completed its wartime assignment.

I am in agreement with your views that steps should now be taken to assure coordination in peacetime of the Federal Government's many interests in petroleum, petroleum products and associated hydrocarbons.

To the extent possible one agency must bear the primary responsibility for providing a focal point for leadership and information for the numerous agencies of the Federal Government dealing with petroleum. I, therefore, request that you undertake the initiative in obtaining coordination and unification of Federal policy and administration with respect to the functions and activities relating to petroleum carried on by the various departments and agencies. Where practicable and appropriate governmental activities relating to petroleum should be centralized and I ask that from time to time you submit to me for consideration proposals looking to the accomplishment of this objective.

You should, through such office as you designate, serve as the channel of communication between the Federal Government and the petroleum industry, and as the liaison agency of the Federal Government in its relations with appropriate State bodies concerned with oil and gas. I have been impressed with the great contribution of government-industry co-operation to the success of the war petroleum program, and feel that the values of such close and harmonious relations between Government and industry should be continued. I, therefore, suggest that you establish an industry organization to consult and advise with you.

In this connection, I think it would be most helpful if Mr. Ralph K. Davies, Deputy Petroleum Administrator throughout the war, were to remain on for a brief period to assist in organizing and launching these activities and to supervise winding up the affairs of the Petroleum Administration. Mr. Davies possesses a broad experience in oil, and enjoys a high standing both within Government and within the petroleum industry. I believe that his participation would assure the full cooperation and support that is so essential in the initial phase.

I need not emphasize to you the importance of petroleum in the life of the Nation and the consequent necessity for assuring the adequate and continuous availability of this vital resource. You are requested to keep me informed concerning significant developments in the petroleum field, and to consider and recommend such steps as may be necessary appropriately to safeguard our petroleum future.

Copies of this letter are being sent to the Secretaries of State, War, Navy, and Commerce, for their information and guidance. I am sure you will find them ready to cooperate fully.

Very sincerely yours,
[s] *Harry S. Truman*

The Honorable
Julius A. Krug
Secretary of the Interior

UNITED STATES DEPARTMENT OF THE INTERIOR
Washington

May 6, 1946

Order No. 2193

Subject: Establishing an Oil and Gas Division.

Pursuant to the President's letter of May 3, 1946, to the Secretary of the Interior, there is hereby established in the Department of the Interior an Oil and Gas Division under the immediate charge of a Director.

The Oil and Gas Division with a view to the conservation of the oil and gas resources of the Nation and the achievement of petroleum security, shall:

1. Assist the Secretary in the execution of the President's instructions to:
   (a) Coordinate and unify policy and administration in respect to the functions and activities relative to oil and gas carried on by the several departments and agencies of the Federal Government;
   (b) Serve as the channel of communication between the Federal Government and the petroleum industry;
   (c) Serve as liaison agency of the Federal Government in its relations with the appropriate State oil and gas bodies; and
   (d) Review technological developments in the field of petroleum and synthetic hydrocarbon fuels and coordinate Federal policy with respect thereto.

2. Obtain and analyze information as to oil and gas matters in which the Federal Government has a proper interest and, in this connection, serve as the central Federal clearing house for statistics, technical data, and other information relating to oil and gas.
3. Keep the Secretary informed with respect to the adequacy and availability of supplies of petroleum and its products to meet the current and future needs of the Nation, and with respect to significant developments in the petroleum field, and make recommendations with respect thereto.
4. Develop proposals looking to the centralization of Federal functions and activities relating to oil and gas in keeping with the President's letter.
5. Coordinate all oil and gas policies and activities in the Department of the Interior.

Pursuant to the Executive Order of May 3, 1946, terminating the Petroleum Administration for War, the personnel, records, property and funds of the Administration are transferred to the Oil and Gas Division which Division shall proceed to wind up and liquidate the affairs of the Administration.

Upon the issuance of an Executive Order amending Executive Order No. 7756, dated December 1, 1937, and the regulations and amendments, approved October 27, 1942, for the administration and enforcement of the Act of February 22, 1935, as amended, to designate the Oil and Gas Division in lieu of the Petroleum Conservation Division, the Oil and Gas Division shall assume all the authority and duties of the Petroleum Conservation Division; funds, personnel, equipment and records of the Petroleum Conservation Division shall be transferred to the Oil and Gas Division, and the Petroleum Conservation Division shall cease to exist.

This Order shall be effective immediately.

[s] *J. A. Krug*
Secretary of the Interior

Executive Order No. 9732

RELATING TO THE ADMINISTRATION OF THE ACT OF FEBRUARY 22, 1935, AS AMENDED

By virtue of the authority vested in me by the Act of February 22, 1935, entitled "An Act to regulate interstate and foreign commerce in petroleum and its products by prohibiting the shipment in such commerce of petroleum and its products produced in violation of State law, and for other purposes," (49 Stat. 30), as amended, it is ordered as follows:

Executive Order No. 7756 of December 1, 1937, issued pursuant to the said Act of February 22, 1935, is hereby amended by substituting the words "Oil and Gas Division" for the words "Petroleum Conservation Division" occurring in the order and in its title.

The regulations approved October 27, 1942, as amended, governing the administration and enforcement of the said Act of February 22, 1935, as amended, are hereby amended by substituting the words "Oil and Gas Division" for the words "Petroleum Conservation Division" wherever the latter words appear in such regulations, as amended.

[s] *Harry S. Truman*

THE WHITE HOUSE,
June 3, 1946.

United States Maritime Commission: Interdepartmental Liaison Officer

From "Memorandum to All Employees Home Office and Field," by A. J. Williams, Secretary, December 21, 1946.

Effective January 1, 1947, the organization of the Maritime Commission shall be constituted as described herein.

1. The following departments, offices, and divisions shall report directly to the Commission via the Chairman and shall perform the functions detailed below:

. . 7. *Interdepartmental Liaison Officer*. The Interdepartmental Liaison Officer shall be responsible for performing upon assignment liaison duties with other Federal departments and with foreign governments in connection with matters of more than domestic scope. The Interdepartmental Liaison Officer shall be Huntington T. Morse.

Appendix III

Documents

Selections from the Merchant Ship Sales Act of 1946 (60 Stat. 41) (Public Law 321—79th Congress) (2d Session)

Sec. 2. (a) It is necessary for the national security and development and maintenance of the domestic and the export and import foreign commerce of the United States that the United States have an efficient and adequate American-owned merchant marine (1) sufficient to carry its domestic water-borne commerce and a substantial portion of its water-borne export and import foreign commerce and to provide shipping service on all routes essential for maintaining the flow of such domestic and foreign water-borne commerce at all times; (2) capable of serving as a naval and military auxiliary in time of war or national emergency; (3) owned and operated under the United States flag by citizens of the United States; (4) composed of the best-equipped, safest, and most suitable types of vessels, constructed in the United States and manned with a trained and efficient citizen personnel; and (5) supplemented by efficient American-owned facilities for shipbuilding and ship repair, marine insurance, and other auxiliary services.

(b) It is hereby declared to be the policy of this Act to foster the development and encourage the maintenance of such a merchant marine.

Sec. 3. (b) "War-built vessel" means an ocean going vessel of one thousand five hundred gross tons or more, owned by the United States and suitable for commercial use. . . .

Sec. 4. (a) Any citizen of the United States may make application to the United States Maritime Commission to purchase a war-built vessel, under the jurisdiction and control of the Commission, at the statutory sales price. If the Commission determines that the applicant possesses the ability, experience, financial resources, and other qualifications, necessary to enable him to operate and maintain the vessel under normal competitive conditions, and that such sale will aid in carrying out the policies of this Act, the Commission shall sell such vessel to the applicant. . . .

Sec. 6. (a) Any person not a citizen of the United States may make application to the Commission to purchase a war-built vessel . . . under the control of the Commission. If the Commission determines—

(1) that the applicant has the financial resources, ability, and experience necessary to enable him to fulfill all obligations with respect to payment of any deferred portion of the purchase price, and that sale of the vessel to him would not be inconsistent with any policy of the United States in permitting foreign sales under section 9 of the Shipping Act, 1916, as amended; and

(2) after consultation with the Secretary of the Navy, that such vessel is not necessary to the defense of the United States; and

(3) that such vessel is not necessary to the promotion and maintenance of an American merchant marine described in section 2; and

(4) that for a reasonable period of time, which in the case of tankers . . . shall not end before ninety days after publication of the applicable prewar domestic cost in the Federal Register . . . such vessel has been available for sale at the statutory sales price to citizens of the United States, or for charter . . . to citizens of the United States, and that no responsible offer has been made by a citizen of the United States to purchase or charter such vessel; then the Commission is authorized to approve the application. . . .

Sec. 7. (a) In exercising its powers under this Act and under other provisions of law with respect to the sale and charter of war-built vessels, the Commission shall give preference to citizen applicants over noncitizen applicants, and as between citizen applicants to purchase and citizen applicants to charter, shall, so far as practicable and consistent with the policies of this Act, give preference to citizen applicants to purchase. In determining the order of preference between citizen applicants to purchase or between citizen applicants to charter, the Commission shall consider, among other relevant factors, the extent to which losses and requisitions of the applicant's prewar tonnage have been overcome and shall in all cases, in the sale and charter of a war-built vessel, give preference in such sale or charter, as the case may be, to the former owner of such vessel, or to the person for whom the vessel was constructed but to whom delivery thereof was prevented by the United States. In determining the order of preference between noncitizen applicants to purchase, the Commission shall give preference to citizens of the Commonwealth of the Philippines, and in determining the order of preference between other noncitizen applicants to purchase shall consider the extent to which losses in prewar tonnage of the various member nations of the United Nations, incurred in the interests of the war effort, have been overcome, and the relative effects of such losses upon the national economy of such member nations.

(b) After the cessation of hostilities, operation of vessels in commercial service by the United States, either for its own account or through operating agents under agency agreements, shall, except as to the Panama Railroad Company and other services specifically authorized by law, be continued only to the extent necessary to effect orderly transfer of vessels to private operation.

Letter of Senator Kenneth S. Wherry to the President, October 28, 1947, protesting the illegality of the tanker foreign sales program

October 28, 1947

Honorable Harry S. Truman
President of the United States
The White House
Washington, D. C.

Dear Mr. President:

It was revealed in testimony before the Senate Small Business Committee yesterday that one hundred T-2 type United States fleet tankers are presently under allocation by the Maritime Commission for sale to foreign nations or nationals; and that such sales are being made in violation of the Merchant Ship Sales Act of 1946, and without regard to the national defense of this country.

The Maritime Commission has advised the Committee that as of October 24, the following tankers have been allocated for sale to foreign nations or nationals: United Kingdom, 31; France, 11; Italy, 16; Netherlands, 4; Belgium, 1; Peru, 1; Turkey, 1; Argentina, 3; Greece, 7; Norway, 11; Canada, 4; South Africa, 2; Sweden, 2; Uruguay, 3; Chile, 1. This totals 98 tankers (two have not yet been allocated by country). Of the 100 tankers, it is my understanding that only 17 have been delivered; all to nationals of the United Kingdom.

I call to your attention, Mr. President, that there are 126 applications pending from United States citizens for the purchase of tankers. The Merchant Ship Sales Act of 1946 requires, in part, under Section 7-(a) that:

> ". . . With respect to the sale and charter of war-built vessels, the Commission shall give preference to citizen applicants over non-citizen applicants . . ."

Citizen applicants, under Section (4) of the Act, are required, at the time of sale, to pay to the Commission at least twenty-five per centum of the statutory sale price. Inasmuch as there has never been any payment on any of the tankers allocated for purchase by foreign nations or nationals, except for the seventeen already delivered, and possibly fifteen additional tankers, which we have been told are "under contract," I cannot see where it could possibly be construed that these tankers have been sold or that definite contractual commitments have been entered with regard to them. Therefore, I feel that to consummate those sales in the light of the fact that 126 applications are pending from United States citizens for the purchase of these tankers would be directly contrary to Section 7-(a) of the Ship Sales Act quoted in part above, and Section 4 of that Act.

The Merchant Ship Sales Act of 1946 further requires that before these vessels may be offered to non-citizen purchasers, the Maritime Commission must determine, after consultation with the Secretary of Navy, that such vessels are not necessary to the defense of the United States (Section 6-(a)-(2)). The Commission must further determine that the vessels are not necessary to the promotion and maintenance of an American Merchant Marine described in Section 2 of the Act (Section 6-(a)-(3)).

I must also emphasize, Mr. President, that once these tankers are sold to foreign nationals operating under a foreign flag, they may not be operated, according to law, in the domestic area of the United States (46 USC 883; 46 USC 877; Sec. 27 Merchant Marine Act of 1920; Sec. 21 Merchant Marine Act of 1920); that is, they may not haul shipments of oil originating in United States ports to United States ports. Thus they are not only removed from the jurisdiction of the Maritime Commission and the Government of the United States in case of a national emergency, but they are also removed from service to our domestic economy.

I think it is also important to point out that there is nothing in the laws of the United States to prevent the resale of these ships by any foreign purchasers to any other foreign purchasers; or for that matter, back to our own nationals or our own Government.

I ask that the sale of any United States fleet tankers to foreign nations or nationals be stopped at once. Further, I strongly urge that all further transactions in connection with these vessels be conducted by the Maritime Commission according to law in giving preference to citizen applicants and with due regard for the national defense.

Respectfully submitted,
[s] *Kenneth S. Wherry*
Chairman

Letter of Hoyt S. Haddock, Secretary, CIO Maritime Commission, to Senator Wherry, November 17, 1947, protesting foreign sale of tankers

November 17, 1947

Senator Kenneth S. Wherry,
Chairman, Senate Small Business Committee

Dear Senator Wherry:

Our affiliated organizations and their memberships, comprising over 200,000 licensed officers, seamen, shipyard workers, and allied maritime workers, are watching your investigation into the proposed sale of 96 tankers to foreign nations with deep concern.

As you undoubtedly know, our present merchant marine is approximately half its wartime size. While no one expected permanent operation of the greatly expanded wartime fleet, American maritime workers were hopeful of retention of a fleet considerably expanded over prewar levels. As of several months ago maritime labor demand and maritime labor supply were in approximate balance—men who came to sea to aid in the war effort had returned to shore-side employment. Others trained during the war who found the sea to their liking remained in the industry, together with the professional seamen. The fleet had been reduced proportionately, and employment opportunities were good.

Beginning in July, for a variety of reasons, the dry-cargo fleet began to decline steadily and seriously. Within the last few months we have seen nearly 400 vessels go to the graveyards; 20,000 jobs at sea have disappeared, and employment opportunities in longshoring and other shore-side maritime industries have dried up.

Weekly reports from the various port agents of the National Maritime Union show increasing unemployment among maritime workers. For instance, during the week of November 4-11, 1,380 seamen registered for work at the New York shipping hall, while only 1,108 secured jobs. In San Francisco, 233 seamen registered for work between October 27 and November 12, and only 47 secured jobs. At the present rate of shipping, some seamen will be on the beach 8 weeks before securing a job.

The proposal to transfer 96 tankers to foreign nations, a sizable proportion coming from our active fleet, will mean another heavy blow to American merchant seamen.

In addition to the hardships forced upon our seamen and their families, the Nation will suffer a serious loss as more and more of our skilled maritime manpower resource, trained at great expense to the Nation, is dissipated.

Not only in the interest of preservation of an adequate merchant marine, but also in the interest of preservation of our maritime labor force and in the prevention of additional unemployment and suffering among maritime workers, these projected sales must be stopped.

We are at a loss to see how the transfer of registry of these 96 vessels will in any way alleviate the shortage of petroleum transportation facilities. We think this point must be stressed, since the sales received initial approval from Government sources based on the desperate world-wide need for oil. A tanker can carry just as much petroleum when flying the American flag as when flying a foreign flag.

In taking our stand against these sales, we wish to differentiate ourselves from the gigantic oil trusts which originally inspired these transfers and now oppose them. In view of the fact that the report of the President's Advisory Committee on the merchant marine reiterates again the position "that the best prospect for a strong, progressive merchant marine would be realized is one that is privately owned and privately operated," we believe the American people have a right to know what our national policy should be if private shipowners refuse to operate the fleet on reasonable terms.

We urge that you secure for the American people full details as to American ownership, control, and chartering of foreign-flag tankers, either directly or through foreign subsidiaries.

We urge that you bring to life the fact that B. B. Howard, of Standard Oil Co. of New Jersey; T. E. Buchanan, of the Texas Co.; and officials of the other large oil companies told the House Merchant Marine and Fisheries Committee less than 6 months ago that they would not buy any tankers for American-flag use and that the only way to alleviate the petroleum transportation shortage was to sell tankers to foreign nations. We urge you to bring to light that on April 16, 1947, the Assistant Secretary of the Navy telegraphed all known operators and owners of United States flag tankers as to their urgent need for chartered service in order to keep the Navy fleet operating; and, as Admiral Callaghan told the House Merchant Marine Committee: "As of May 13, only 31 replies have been received to the above telegram. In not one of these replies have the companies concerned offered any tanker tonnage or even indicated that they are in a position to bid on Navy requirements after June 30."

Both the House Merchant Marine Committee and the Senate Commerce Committee recognized that they were being blackmailed into extending Government operations of tankers after June 30, but they felt there was no alternative.

We presume this is the reason why the Navy originally supported transfers of tankers to foreign nations.

We hope your investigations will bring forth a program to prevent selfish private interests from ever being able again to bludgeon this Nation into dissipation of our resources. We hope you will take action to return the eighty-odd American-owned tankers flying the Panamanian and Honduran flags to the United States flag and their 3,200 jobs to American seamen.

We shall be glad to appear before your committee to present additional data.

Sincerely yours,
[s] *Hoyt S. Haddock*,
Executive Secretary,
CIO Maritime Commission

The Attorney General's Opinion on the legality of tanker sales foreign

December 9, 1947

Memorandum for the President

At your request I have examined the question of the legality of the sale by the Maritime Commission of T-2 type tankers to foreign nations and nationals.

I have asked the Maritime Commission for a full statement of the facts of this transaction. From its letter dated December 2, 1947, the following pertinent facts are summarized:

On March 8, 1946, the date of the enactment of the Merchant Ship Sales Act, there were available for sale some 400 T-2 tankers. On April 23, 1946, the Maritime Commission, in accordance with the requirements of that Act, posted the statutory price for these tankers in the Federal Register (11 F.R. 4459), with a specific notice that the Commission "hereby invites applications under the provisions of the Act and the following regulations." The regulations (General Order 60) state, among other particulars, the manner in which citizens and noncitizens, respectively, may apply for the purchase of war-built vessels (sec. 299.21 and 299.25) and that citizen applications will be preferred over noncitizen applications (sec. 299.2(b)).

At the outset there were a number of citizen applications for the purchase of these tankers. These were taken care of. After this initial demand had been satisfied, however, few citizen applications were filed in relation to the number of tankers available. These facts were discussed during the hearings before the House Merchant Marine and Fisheries Committee held in April, May, and June, 1947. Both Secretary of State Marshall and the then Under Secretary of State, Mr. Clayton, urged before that Committee that ships be made available for sale for use in the foreign economic program to avert a serious worldwide petroleum crisis. See Hearings before the Subcommittee on Ship Sales, Charters, and Layups of the House Committee on Merchant Marine and Fisheries (80th Cong., 1st sess., pp. 490-506, 654-670). The House Committee, in its report, instructed the Maritime Commission to remove itself from the business of operating tankers under general agency agreements [2] and to sell the tankers to private operators as soon as possible.[3]

In June of 1947, although there were few American applications for T-2 tankers, noncitizen applications were being filed in increasing numbers and applications for about 130 tankers were then pending. At that time over 250 tankers remained undisposed of.

By letter dated June 16, 1947, the Secretary of State informed the Maritime Commission that "On June 2 the Cabinet decided that in light of the critical world petroleum situation and in the interests of our foreign policy, it would be desirable to sell to foreign operators at this time a total of 100 T-2 type tankers over and above the 50 T-2 tankers which have already been sold or approved for sale to foreign operators by the Maritime Commission," and requested the Commission to take under consideration the disposition of these 100 tankers to foreign interests.

The Maritime Commission, by letter dated June 19, 1947, consulted with the Secretary of the Navy on its proposed undertaking to sell 100 tankers foreign. This was done pursuant to section 6 (a) (2) of the Merchant Ship Sales Act, which states, as one of the restrictions upon sale foreign of surplus war-built vessels, that the Maritime Commission must determine "after consultation with the Secretary of the Navy, that such vessel is not necessary to the defense of the United States." The Secretary of the Navy, by letter

[2] Section 5 of the Merchant Ship Sales Act grants the Commission the power to charter war-built dry cargo vessels. Tankers, however, are not in that class. The Commission has been operating tankers under general agency agreements pursuant to other provisions of law.

[3] In approving the bill (H.R. 3911), extending the Merchant Ship Sales Act and related acts, the Committee, in its report, stated: "Your committee has approved this extension with the understanding that in the coming months the Maritime Commission will make every effort to withdraw from the shipping business and to sell as many as possible of our war-built merchant ships.

". . . Among the measures which it is expected the Maritime Commission will take is that the number of tankers operated under general agency will be reduced to a maximum of 150 within 3 months of the effective date of this bill and that that number (150) be further reduced by the number of tankers that may in the future be *sold foreign* under the provisions of the Merchant Ship Sales Act of 1946." H.R. Rep. 725, 80th Cong., 1st sess., p. 2. (Emphasis supplied.)

dated June 20, 1947, replied that he had no objection to the sale of 46 T-2 type tankers from the Maritime Commission laid-up fleet and 54 T-2 type tankers from the Maritime Commission active fleet to selected foreign applicants.

On June 25, 1947, the Maritime Commission agreed that 100 tankers should be sold foreign and instructed the proper officers of the Commission "to take any and all actions necessary and proper to carry the action of the Commission . . . fully into effect." At that time there were only three citizen applications pending for eight tankers for operation under American registry, although there were some 254 tankers available for sale.

The program undertaken by the Maritime Commission did not contemplate the filing of new applications for noncitizens. On the date on which 100 T-2 tankers were allocated by the Commission, there were pending some 60 applications by noncitizens for a total of 132 T-2 tankers. These applications had been on file, in many instances, for a considerable period. The program of the Commission has, for the most part, been based on the processing of these pending applications, in an effort to give to each nation a total number of tankers deemed by our Government to be desirable in our national interest and the interests of world economy. The nature of this program was explained to the foreign interests involved, generally through their missions in this country.

At a subsequent meeting on July 31, 1947, the Commission approved the order of priority [4] by which the various countries were to be given preference in selecting T-2 tankers and the number allotted to each country was definitely fixed. The Commission directed that its action should be construed "only as an order of priority and not an approval of sale, and that separate recommendations for specific sales shall be submitted in accordance therewith, with a tabulation showing the vessels by name and whether the vessel is to be taken from the reserve fleet or from the operating fleet." On that date, there were only three citizen applications pending for six tankers for operation under American registry.

All the applications involved in the foreign sale program were then on file, with the exception of five Greek applications. The majority of these applications offered complete cash payment.[5] In the remaining instances, partial payment was offered in cash, the balance to be secured by a mortgage on the vessel guaranteed by the nation involved—a type of credit arrangement regarded as satisfactory by the Commission.

At subsequent meetings on August 12 and 13 the Maritime Commission determined definitely that 53 T-2 tankers should be taken from the operating fleet and 34 from the laid-up fleet. These ships were then allocated, part from the operating fleet and part from the laid-up fleet, to each of the countries to which the Commission had assigned a specific number of ships on July 31. On October 3, the Commission authorized the sale of 11 additional tankers, eight of which were assigned to countries to which the Commission had not theretofore allocated specific numbers of tankers. The minutes of the Commission of that date show the following:

> "Commissioner Mellen stated that in view of the numerous applications from American citizens to purchase T-2 type tankers for operation by American owners under the United States flag or by American owners for operation under foreign flag, such applications should be considered and action taken with respect thereto prior to any formal action covering the sale of the 100 tankers to foreign applicants. Commissioner Mellen withdrew from the meeting at 11:10 a.m. It was moved by Commissioner McKeough and seconded by Chairman Smith, and by the unanimous 'yea' vote by the members of the Commission present, it was agreed that the Commission reaffirm its prior actions of June 25, 1947, June 27, 1947, and subsequent dates, authorizing the sale of 100 T-2 type tankers to foreign nations in conformance with the allocations thereof as approved by the President's Cabinet, the State Department, the Navy Department and the Department of Interior.
>
> "The proper officers of the Commission were authorized and directed to take any and all actions necessary and proper to carry the action of the Commission as above set forth fully into effect."

[4] The order of priority had been drawn up by an Interdepartmental Committee which had been set up by the Commission for the purpose of considering and making recommendations on ways and means of working out a sales program on the 100 tankers. This Committee was composed of representatives of the Maritime Commission, State, Navy and Interior Departments.

[5] The five applications on behalf of Greek citizens were filed thereafter, in September and October. These, it may be noted, also offered payment in cash. As to these applications, cf. Public Law 75, 80th Cong., 1st sess.

On October 3, when the Commission took this action, there were 109 T-2 tankers available for sale to American citizens—exclusive of the 100 which had been approved for sale foreign.[6] On that date there were citizen applications for only 27 T-2 tankers for operation under American registry.[7]

The legality of the sale foreign of these 100 tankers was questioned at a hearing before the Senate Small Business Committee [8] on October 27 on the ground that it was in violation of section 7 of the Merchant Ship Sales Act since there were more American applications on hand for T-2 tankers than the available supply of T-2 tankers would satisfy. On the following day, the Chairman of that Committee wrote to you, setting forth his objections to this program of the Maritime Commission.

The program for the sale of the 100 T-2 tankers was undertaken by the Maritime Commission under the Merchant Ship Sales Act of 1946. This Act was passed in order "To provide for the sale of surplus war-built vessels. . . ." [9] Under the Act surplus war-built vessels are to be offered first to American citizens (sec. 4), who are to be given preference over non-citizen applicants (sec. 7). There are four restrictions applicable to the approval of noncitizen applications. They are contained in section 6(a), which reads in part as follows:

> "If the Commission determines—
>
> (1) that the applicant has the financial resources, ability and experience necessary to enable him to fulfill all obligations with respect to payment of any deferred portion of the purchase price, and that sale of the vessel to him would not be inconsistent with any policy of the United States in permitting foreign sales under section 9 of the Shipping Act, 1916, as amended; and
>
> (2) after consultation with the Secretary of the Navy, that such vessel is not necessary to the defense of the United States; and
>
> (3) that such vessel is not necessary to the promotion and maintenance of an American merchant marine described in section 2; and
>
> (4) that for a reasonable period of time, which in the case of tankers and 'C' type vessels shall not end before ninety days after publication of the applicable prewar domestic cost in the Federal Register under subsection 3(c) of this Act, such vessel has been available for sale at the statutory sales price to citizens of the United States, or for charter under section 5 to citizens of the United States, and that no responsible offer has been made by a citizen of the United States to purchase or charter such vessel;
>
> then the Commission is authorized to approve the application and sell such vessel to the applicant at not less than the statutory sales price."

On June 25, 1947, when the 100 T-2 tankers were allocated for sale foreign, there is no doubt that the Maritime Commission possessed the legal power to sell the ships to individual foreign applicants, pursuant to the four determinations required by section 6(a) of the Act, and that the facts then existing justified the making of these determinations.

Instead of handling the sale foreign on an individual applicant basis, the Commission evolved a procedure in cooperation with the State, Navy and Interior Departments, whereby the disposition of these T-2 tankers "could be made to the best advantage in relieving the world-wide oil and tanker situation, safeguarding domestic requirements and avoiding dislocation of tanker operations of the Maritime Commission." According to the Commission, it became evident at that time "that the world-wide petroleum situation and shortage of tankers was becoming increasingly serious and the economy of other friendly nations required a greater number of T-2 sales than the initial quota of 50. At that time the authority of the Commission to operate tankers, failing extension by Congress, was due to expire June 30, 1947; and the alternative to sale foreign was the laying up of all unsold tankers at a time when their operation was essential to world economy."

The Maritime Commission, therefore, approached the sale of these tankers on an overall

[6] Actually the program now covers only 96 rather than 100 T-2 tankers.

[7] There were also applications for 83 T-2 tankers by American citizens who stated that they intended to operate the vessels under foreign registry. The Commission, however, does not give these applications the same preference as citizen applications for American registry. See General Order 60, sec. 299.2(e) (11 F.R. 4461). This would appear to be an appropriate administrative interpretation since section 2(a)(3) of the Merchant Ship Sales Act declares it to be the policy of the Act to have an efficient and adequate American merchant marine "owned and operated under the United States flag by citizens of the United States."

[8] In the preparation of this memorandum careful study has been given to the evidence adduced at the hearings before that Committee.

[9] This quotation is from the title of the Act (60 Stat. 41).

basis, allotting a specific number of ships to specific nations and nationals. This was clearly within its legal powers.[10] Whether the Commission completed its approval of the sale foreign on June 25 or July 31 becomes immaterial since, in any event, its approval would seem to have been made definite for most of the foreign interests on August 13 and for the remaining ones on October 3. I am advised by the Commission that on both these dates citizen applications for American registry could have been amply satisfied from the tankers available over and above those reserved for the foreign sale program. It is to be presumed that these applications have been or will be processed by the Commission in accordance with the Merchant Ship Sales Act and the priorities therein established.[11]

It appears, therefore, on the basis of the foregoing facts, that the program undertaken by the Maritime Commission has met the legal requirements of section 6 and section 7 of the Merchant Ship Sales Act of 1946 and is within the framework of the law. Accordingly, the Commission would be within its legal powers in proceeding to carry out its program. Whether it may cancel or modify the program presents a separate question. Twenty-six of these vessels have already been transferred to foreign countries or nationals thereof, and contracts for the sale of 25 others have been signed by both parties. If any unilateral action to rescind the transactions just mentioned should be taken by the Commission, there would be grave risk of legal liability on the part of the United States. As to vessels for which no contracts of sale have been signed, the question of whether or not there would be substantial possibility of legal liability in the event of a refusal by the Commission to deliver them would depend primarily on the facts involved in each transaction.

Respectfully,
[s] *Tom C. Clark*
Attorney General

[10] Cf. Surplus Property Act of 1944 (50 U.S.C. App. 1611 et seq.), and *Phelps Dodge Corp.* v. *Labor Board*, 313 U.S. 177, 194 (1941).

[11] The information furnished by the Maritime Commission shows that the Commission sold 79 tankers to citizens for American registry between June 25 and November 12, 1947, and that 52 of this number were approved by the Commission between October 3 and November 12. Including 51 tankers sold under provisions of law prior to the Merchant Ship Sales Act, a total of 192 T-2 type tankers were sold to citizens for American registry up to December 2, 1947.

Appendix IV

Bibliographical Note

The most informative printed review of the tanker story is provided in *Hearings of the Special Committee to Study Problems of American Small Business*, U. S. Senate, 80th Congress, pursuant to S. Res. 20. See especially Part 23, November 14 and 18, 1947. The hearings of the immediately preceding days provide useful background.

The interlacing of tanker sales foreign and extension of general agency authority is best evidenced in *Hearings before the Subcommittee on Ship Sales, Charters, and Lay-Ups of the Committee on Merchant Marine and Fisheries*, 80th Cong., 1st Sess. (1947).

The history of the Merchant Ship Sales Act, 1946, can be traced in the following documents:

H.R. 4486, *Hearings* (House Committee on Merchant Marine and Fisheries), May 25-June 15, 1944, 78th Cong.
H.R. 5213, Introduced in House but not reported, June 1944, 78th Cong.
H.R. 1425, *Hearings* (House Committee on Merchant Marine and Fisheries), March 1-April 23, 1945, 79th Cong.
S. 292, *Hearings* (Senate Committee on Commerce), May 7-8, 1945, 79th Cong.
H.R. 3603, *House Rpt.* 831, June 28, 1945.
Senate Rpt. 807, Dec. 4, 1945.
Conference Rpt., House Rpt. 1526, Feb. 6, 1946.
Public Law 321, March 8, 1946.

Convenient reference to the Merchant Ship Sales Act of 1946 and other statutes applicable to the U. S. Maritime Commission can be had in Publication No. 55 (2nd Rev.), United States Government Printing Office, Washington, 1949.

Further repercussions of the Act and the tanker project are recorded in *Hearings, Subcommittee on Appropriations for Departments of State, Justice, Commerce, and the Judiciary* (Committee on Appropriations), U. S. Senate, H. R. 5607 (1949).

Concerning the Maritime Commission, a recent and thoroughgoing study is that by the Senate Committee on Expenditures in the Executive Departments, *Management Survey of the United States Maritime Commission*, December 31, 1948, Government Printing Office, Washington. Reference should also be made to the report of the Hoover Commission (Commission on Organization of the Executive Branch of the Government) on the *Regulatory Commissions* and to the report of the Hoover Commission's Task Force on that subject (1949). Further reference should be made to the Reorganization Plan affecting the Maritime Commission submitted by President Truman to Congress, under the Reorganization Act of 1949, on August 19, 1949.

Finally, an actor in the tanker story, Max W. Ball, has recorded in popular fashion his attitudes on petroleum factors and prospects in a book, *This Fascinating Oil Business* (New York, 1940).

THE KINGS RIVER PROJECT

CONTENTS

THE PROBLEM

In February 1940 Congress received two separate reports recommending construction of a multiple-purpose reservoir on the Kings River in California—one prepared by the Corps of Engineers and the other by the Bureau of Reclamation. The reports were dissimilar in several important respects. Each report had acquired proponents and opponents among the local interests, and the two Federal agencies were put in competition with one another to obtain the support of the California beneficiaries.

Why did two Federal water-development agencies plan similar multiple-purpose projects on the same river? Why were not the conflicts between the two agencies reconciled at an early stage in the planning process, and the competition between the two put to an end by the President's office? What have been the results of this unco-ordinated conflict? What has been the effect on the public interest of agency competition to win the support of local groups of water users? This case history of the Kings River project is designed to illustrate some of the causes and results of unco-ordinated water resource development.

Judgments on issues of national policy depend in part on the perspective and on the underlying premises of the observer. In this case the reader will note that the narrative is developed in large part from the viewpoint of the President and the Executive Office, although the contrasting attitudes of other agencies are indicated. To what extent the main outlines set forth would shift if conditions of perfect accessibility to information and perfect understanding of the multifarious sources of conduct of all parties were possible is hard to say. The materials for study and analysis are sufficiently inclusive, however, to warrant the assumption that differing judgments will derive more from differing values than from additional facts.

Description of Area

California is traversed lengthwise by two parallel ranges of mountains—the Sierra Nevada on the east and the Coast Range on the west—which converge at Mount Shasta on the north and are joined by the Tehachapi Mountains on the south to enclose the Central Valley Basin. The Basin is nearly 500 miles long, averages 120 miles in width, and includes more than one-third of California. The main valley floor, comprising nearly one-third of the basin area, is a gently sloping, practically unbroken, alluvial area 400 miles long and averaging 45 miles in width. Sacramento River drains the northern portion of the Basin and San Joaquin River the southern portion. The confluence of these two streams is in the Sacramento-San Joaquin Delta from which they find a common outlet to the ocean through San Francisco Bay.

The entire Basin, it should be noted, lies within a single state. This fact poses some special difficulties from the point of view of Federal development and control, which for the most part has dealt with improvement of interstate streams or of water resources on the public domain. These difficulties, of a somewhat controversial and legal nature, are stated, but will not be examined systematically in this study.

Water supply and water requirements in the Central Valley Basin are unbalanced geographically. Available water supplies decrease from north to south. Conversely, the water requirements are greater in the south by reason of larger irrigable areas, less rainfall, and greater evaporation. As a result, the total run-off into Sacramento Valley far exceeds its ultimate water requirements, while in the southern or Upper San Joaquin Valley local supplies are inadequate to meet local demands. On the east side of the Upper San Joaquin Valley irrigation has reached a stage where dependable stream flow has long since been completely used, and in many cases the draft on ground water greatly exceeds the natural replenishment. An alarming lowering of the ground water table has brought this overdraft forcibly to the attention of the water users of the area. For some time it has been realized that unless additional water is secured, pumping depths will become so great that considerable areas of land now irrigated will have to be abandoned because of excessive water costs.

One of the principal objectives of the Central Valley Project of the Bureau of Reclamation is to remedy this situation. An initial phase of the Project, now under construction and in partial operation, is designed to effect a transfer of surplus water from the northern to the southern portions of the Basin. The Delta-Mendota canal and two additional canals proposed for future authorization and construction will carry surplus Sacramento River water 120-140 miles southerly from the Delta to Mendota Pool on the San Joaquin River. Here the water will be used to meet the demands of crop lands on the west side of the San Joaquin River now irrigated by diversions from the San Joaquin.

By this exchange of water the run-off of the San Joaquin River can be stored in Millerton Lake behind Friant Dam, on the east side of the Valley near the headwaters of the San Joaquin, and from there it can be made available for diversion north and south, through the Madera and Friant-Kern canals, to irrigate lands in east side Upper San Joaquin Valley.

Friant Dam, Madera, and Friant-Kern canals are initial units of a comprehensive plan prepared by the Bureau of Reclamation for utilizing practically the entire run-off tributary to the southern Central Valley Basin. Additional features include planned reservoirs on each of the principal streams flowing west from the mountains into the Basin, south of Friant Dam and the San Joaquin River. The primary objective of the prospective reservoirs is temporary storage of surplus winter and snow-melt run-off until it can be released to existing and prospective canals for direct irrigation use or for ground water replenishment. Such water regulation will be of value not only for irrigation but also for flood control. The principal flood damage in the area results from large volumes of water which in wet years flow into the closed basin of Tulare Lake, south of the San Joaquin River. Extensive areas of agricultural land are flooded, but the water is subsequently used beneficially for irrigation. The reservoirs and canals proposed for east side Upper San Joaquin Valley would greatly reduce this damage by temporarily storing, and then diverting for irrigation use, water which would otherwise cause flood damage in the Tulare Lake area. Reservoirs are proposed for the Kings, Kaweah, Tule, and Kern Rivers, which are all tributary to Tulare Lake, except that Kings River now can be diverted in part by means of control works either north to San Joaquin River or south to Tulare Lake. It is with the project on the Kings River that we are primarily concerned in this case study.

Participants in Valley Development

Before launching into an account of the planning for development of Central Valley water resources, it appears desirable to identify the more important participants.

On the Federal side, the U. S. Army Corps of Engineers, the Bureau of Reclamation of the Department of the Interior, the National Resources Planning Board and the Bureau of the Budget (both of the Executive Office of the President), and the several legislative and appropriations committees of the Congress are the chief participants.

Few government services have a longer history than the Corps of Engineers, U. S. Army. The Continental Congress originally authorized the organization of a Corps of Engineers in 1779. This Corps was disbanded in 1783, and the present Corps of Engineers may be said to have originated in the Act of March 16, 1802, fixing the new military establishment. This Act authorized the President to organize and establish a Corps of Engineers consisting of five officers and ten cadets to be stationed at West Point, New York, and to "constitute a Military Academy." The headquarters of the

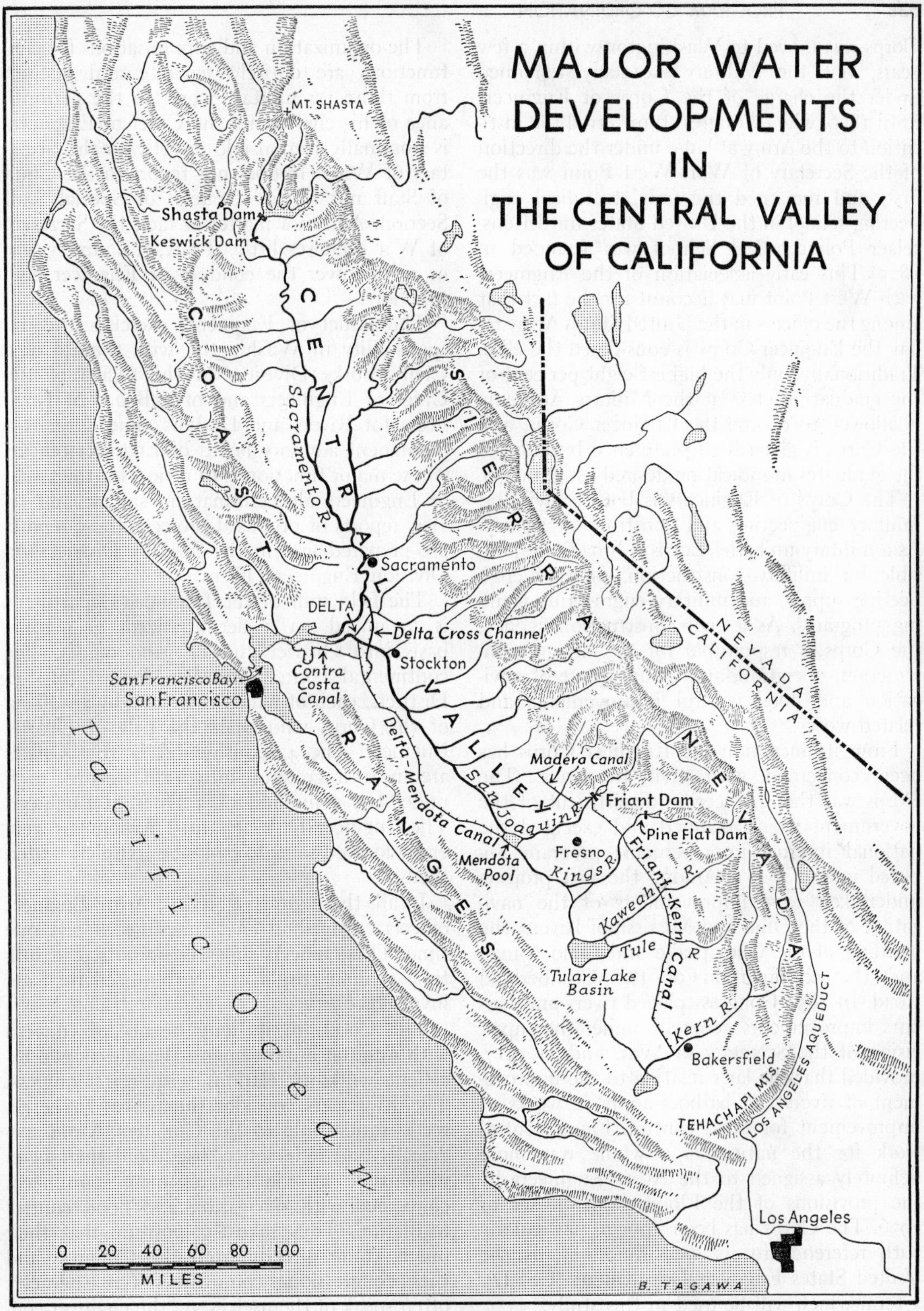
MAJOR WATER DEVELOPMENTS IN THE CENTRAL VALLEY OF CALIFORNIA
MT. SHASTA
Shasta Dam
Keswick Dam
COAST RANGES
CENTRAL VALLEY
SIERRA NEVADA
Sacramento R.
Sacramento
DELTA
Delta Cross Channel
Contra Costa Canal
Stockton
San Francisco Bay
San Francisco
Pacific Ocean
Delta-Mendota Canal
San Joaquin R.
Madera Canal
Friant Dam
Pine Flat Dam
Fresno
Mendota Pool
Kings R.
Friant-Kern Canal
Kaweah R.
Tule R.
Tulare Lake Basin
Kern R.
Bakersfield
TEHACHAPI MTS.
LOS ANGELES AQUEDUCT
Los Angeles
NEVADA
CALIFORNIA
0 20 40 60 80 100
MILES
B. TAGAWA

Corps was moved to Washington within a few years, but the Military Academy remained under the charge of the Corps of Engineers until 1866, when Congress transferred the institution to the Army at large under the direction of the Secretary of War. West Point was the first, and remained the only, technical engineering school in the United States until Rensselaer Polytechnical School was founded in 1825. This early association of the Engineers with West Point may account for the fact that among the officers in the United States Army today the Engineer Corps is considered the élite. Traditionally, only the highest eight per cent of the graduating class at the Military Academy is allowed to choose the Engineer Corps, and the Corps is given high preference by most of the graduates in indicating desired assignments.

The Corps of Engineers is both a civil and military engineering and construction agency. As a military unit, the Corps is broadly responsible for military construction, military engineering supply, and military engineering training programs. As a civil construction agency, the Corps is responsible for the design, construction, operation, and maintenance of navigation and flood control improvements and related works.

From its inception the Engineer Corps has been concerned with civil functions. The Corps was the engineering department of the government which planned and executed the national internal improvements program initiated in the 1820's. Among the first projects undertaken were improvements of the navigation of the Ohio and Mississippi Rivers, the building of the Chesapeake and Ohio Canal, and the continuation of the Cumberland Road. In 1852 Congress placed rivers and harbors improvements generally under the supervision of the Secretary of War, and in 1917, provided that the laws relating to the improvement of rivers and harbors apply to works of improvement for flood control. Flood control work for the nation as a whole was more definitely assigned to the Army Engineers by the provisions of the Flood Control Act of 1936. The Corps has been known, particularly with reference to its civil functions, as the United States Engineer Department (USED), a term which will be used in this study.

The organization and appropriations for civil functions are entirely separate and distinct from those for military work. In the performance of his civil duties the Chief of Engineers is nominally responsible directly to the Secretary of War. He does not report to the Chief of Staff nor to any General or Special Staff Section. And as a matter of fact, the Secretary of War exercises little, if any, real supervision or review over the conduct of Engineer civil functions.

The Chief of Engineers exercises this responsibility in Washington with the aid of a Civil Works Division in the Office of the Chief of Engineers and of a Board of Engineers for Rivers and Harbors. The latter is a permanent advisory board of Engineer officers whose major function is to review for the Chief of Engineers all examination, survey, and review reports of proposed projects; these reports are prepared first in the field by District and Division Engineer Offices.

The field staff of the Engineer Department is organized on a decentralized, geographic basis into District and Division offices. The continental United States is divided into 42 Districts, each of which is headed by an officer of the Corps who bears the title of District Engineer. The 42 continental District Offices are in turn grouped into 12 Divisions, each under the command of a Division Engineer. The Engineer Districts and Divisions are generally located so as to embrace complete watersheds.

In all, there are roughly 215 Army Engineer officers engaged in civil functions at any one time. These officers supervise some 40,000 full-time civilian employees. No enlisted men are involved.

The Corps, in its long history of concern with internal improvements, has developed excellent working relations with the Congress. The Engineers consider themselves to be directly responsible to the Congress. More specifically and in practice, they hold themselves responsible to the congressional committees concerned with navigation and flood control legislation. They take the position that their orders come directly from the Congress and these congressional committees. The Engineers often speak of themselves as "the engineer consultants to, and contractors for, the Congress of the United States."

This system of direct and definitive agency-legislative dealings has had inevitably an important influence on the relationship of the Engineer Department to the President. The Department, holding that, by law and tradition, it must always report directly to the Congress, has resisted most efforts by the President to require it to report to or through him and his Executive Office.

The Corps of Engineers is also distinguished by a high degree of Corps solidarity. Its members, recruited under the system described above, know each other and deal together with an internal intimacy and with an unusually solid front to the outside world when faced with opposition. While their wartime responsibilities are enormous, in peacetime their prestige as a Corps is dependent to a significant degree on their civil construction program. Corps solidarity, not unlike the group introversion characteristic of many bureaucracies, is responsible in part for the fact that the relations of the Engineers with local communities and with congressmen and congressional committees take on at times the aspect of promotion activities. Traditionally, the Engineers tend to oppose project construction by other Federal agencies where such construction might be assigned to them; other Federal construction agencies are, of course, similarly anxious to preserve their jurisdictional integrity.

As long as the Engineers were concerned largely with single-purpose navigation projects, their practice of working directly with the Congress, though resented by several Presidents (Theodore Roosevelt and Hoover, for example), did not have such serious consequences for over-all resource development programs. When, however, after 1936 the USED became involved in the planning and construction of multiple-purpose projects all over the nation, involving close relationships and possible conflicts with other agencies of government (Bureau of Reclamation for irrigation, Federal Power Commission for power, Public Health Service for pollution, etc.), the Engineer Department practice of working directly with the Congress began to create serious difficulties for the President in his efforts to develop co-ordinated resource development proposals and programs within the Executive Branch. This case study concerns one such multiple-purpose project.

The Bureau of Reclamation was established as an agency of the Federal government under the Department of the Interior following the passage of the Reclamation Act of 1902. The fundamental objectives of this Act and of the Bureau revolve around the conservation, development, and utilization of the land and water resources of the West. The primary objective is transforming dry lands into permanently productive farms through irrigation, and maintaining production on lands threatened with retrogression to desert as a result of shortage of water supplies from other systems.

Under subsequent legislation the activities of the Bureau have been expanded to include, in addition to irrigation, the construction and operation of hydroelectric power, drainage flood control, navigation, silt control, municipal water supply, and recreation facilities in order to assure more complete utilization, through multiple-purpose projects, of the water resources of the arid and semi-arid West.

The Commissioner of Reclamation, under the supervision of the Secretary of the Interior, is in administrative charge of the Bureau. He is assisted by a large Bureau staff in Washington. Headquarters of the Branch of Design and Construction, however, are located in Denver.

In the field the work of the Bureau is confined by Reclamation law to the area in the seventeen Western states lying west of the 100th meridian, though by special legislation it may be extended to other areas. The Bureau operates through seven regional field offices, whose boundaries conform generally to those of large watershed areas.

The Bureau has not developed the same almost exclusive relations to committees of Congress that characterize the Corps of Engineers. Furthermore, the congressional committees which are concerned with irrigation legislation are not the same as those which deal with navigation and flood control matters. Whereas the Corps of Engineers, in the House, has dealt with the Committees on Rivers and Harbors and on Flood Control (since the 80th Congress, Committee on Public Works), the

Bureau of Reclamation has dealt with the Committee on Irrigation and Reclamation (since the 80th Congress, Committee on Public Lands). In the Senate, the Bureau of Reclamation has dealt with the Committee on Irrigation and Reclamation (since the 80th Congress, Committee on Interior and Insular Affairs); the Corps of Engineers, with the Committee on Commerce (since the 80th Congress, Committee on Public Works). Similarly, the appropriations for the Bureau of Reclamation are considered annually by the Appropriations Subcommittees on Interior in both Houses, whereas those for the Corps of Engineers are reviewed independently by the Subcommittees on War Department Civil Functions. Finally, while the work of the Bureau is of direct concern only to senators and representatives from the seventeen Western states, the Corps of Engineers has close and cordial congressional contacts throughout the country. In individual cases the western members of Congress, sensitive to local interests, may or may not support the policies of the Bureau.

Until fairly recently, water developments in the United States were conceived generally in terms of single objectives: a levee here to protect against floods, a reservoir there for irrigation water storage. The first large-scale program for co-ordinated development of a whole river system for multiple objectives was the TVA. This new approach to water resources was reflected in the work of the National Resources Planning Board. From its early days in 1934 until its abolition by Congress in 1943, the Board (at various times known as the National Planning Board, National Resources Board, National Resources Committee) was concerned with water planning. Its Water Resources Committee, consisting of representatives of eight Federal and two state water agencies, together with two consultants of national reputation, dealt with problems of improving the collection and interpretation of basic hydrologic data, improving the techniques of water planning, developing a basic national water policy, and improving the integration of various Federal and state water programs and projects. The standing of the Board and its Water Committee, as national planning and co-ordinating authorities concerned with problems that cut across the jurisdictions of the many Federal, state, and local departments and agencies, was vastly improved in 1939 when the Board was transferred to the newly organized Executive Office of the President, along with the Bureau of the Budget and several other units. For five years prior to that time, the Board had been an independent agency of government, though it was originally established in the Federal Emergency Administration of Public Works.

In the review, evaluation, programming, and budgeting of Federal water resources development projects the Board worked closely with the Budget Bureau. Together, they were in close contact with the President who relied on them, as part of his Executive Office, to determine the relationship of various agency programs and projects to the total program of the President. Thus, when the Board was cut off in 1943, the Budget Bureau alone assumed what small part of the total co-ordination effort it was able to carry on. The Congress in fact prohibited any agencies from assuming the functions of the defunct Planning Board, and denied the Budget Bureau funds to establish an adequate public works co-ordination unit. These actions reflected the general disfavor attached to the word "planning" in anti-New Deal quarters; but, more specifically, they were presumably also related to the threat which the co-ordinated resource development outlook seemed to offer to the traditional nexus of interests operating through local groups (organized nationally in the Rivers and Harbor Congress and otherwise), the Corps of Engineers and the Public Works Committees of Congress.

The Budget Bureau, therefore, did not continue the Water Resources Committee. Instead, the Corps of Engineers proposed and sponsored a new Federal Inter-Agency River Basin Committee, consisting of representatives of the Corps, the Bureau of Reclamation, Department of Agriculture, and Federal Power Commission (the Department of Commerce was added as a participant at a later date). This Committee's functions are far less inclusive than were those of the WRC. Its major purpose is to facilitate consultation and the interchange of information among the participating agencies in the preparation of reports on multiple-purpose projects. Decisions can be made only by the unanimous vote of all participants; there is no provision for representation in any way of the Executive Office of the President; the Committee has no statutory standing and no permanent staff.

The Water Resources Committee of the National Resources Planning Board had operated in the field through 45 drainage basin committees, each consisting of representatives of state and local resources agencies and of Federal agencies operating in the area. Each committee was assisted by a water consultant on the staff of the Board. One such committee was organized for the Central Valley-San Francisco Bay-Central California Coast area. With the demise of the Planning Board the drainage basin committees ceased to operate. The Federal Inter-Agency River Basin Committee has since established subcommittees for the Missouri and Columbia basins only.

As has been noted already, the Corps of Engineers has enjoyed the warm support of the Congress, and the relationship between the two is far more cordial and intimate than is the relationship between the Corps and the President. The Secretary of the Interior and the Bureau of Reclamation, on the other hand, have received less consistent congressional support and have sought to balance the advantage of the Corps of Engineers in this respect by obtaining the support of the President and his Executive Office. In controversies between the two agencies over the development of the same watersheds, such as the one here under investigation, the general pattern of support in recent years may be expressed as follows:

Corps of Engineers + Congress
v.
Secretary of the Interior + Executive Office of the President

On the state side, water resources development looms so large in the total development program of California that a number of state agencies have been concerned with the Central Valley Project in recent years. Without differentiating the functions of each, since this case study does not deal with them in any detail, the following state organizations may be mentioned: Division of Water Resources, Department of Public Works; Water Project Authority; State Water Resources Board; Department of Natural Resources; State Reclamation Board; Districts' Securities Commission.

In addition to these, a large number of public, semi-public, and private organizations are actively concerned with water resources development in the Central Valley Basin. The programs and major interests of the large majority of these—irrigation districts, water users' associations, local chambers of commerce, etc.—may be summarized as follows: largest possible Federal contributions for construction with absolute minimum of Federal controls over operations; minimum repayment requirements for project beneficiaries; *local* control over distribution of benefits from *each individual* construction project; use of power revenues to pay costs of irrigation water—i.e., relatively high power rates for *each* project to provide cheap water at that project; primarily a program which benefits *existing*, not prospective, land owners and water users.

On the other hand, there are some interest groups—notably the State Grange and state labor organizations—which promote a wider distribution of project benefits, both water and power, and to this end urge greater Federal controls over project operations and over the distribution of, and repayment for, project benefits.

Early Planning[1]

As early as 1937 both the Corps of Engineers and the Bureau of Reclamation under-

[1] Most of the information on early planning obtained from the following:

(a) Files of the National Resources Planning Board available for public inspection at the National Archives; especially files NA-NRPB 516.22, 579.7
(b) Cong., 76/3, House, Committee on Flood Control, *Hearings on Comprehensive Flood Control Plans* (H.R. 9640), pp. 560-562
(c) The printed survey reports of the two agencies:
Corps of Engineers—Cong., 76/3, House, Doc. 630
Bureau of Reclamation—Cong., 76/3, House, Doc. 631

took investigations of the Kings River area. The investigation of the Corps of Engineers was initiated under the Flood Control Act of 1936; that of the Bureau of Reclamation, under an allotment from an appropriation under the National Industrial Recovery Act. Both investigations were requested originally by the same water users' association in the Kings River area. The association members apparently wanted to see what each agency would propose so that they would be in a position to express a preference for that plan which would afford them, as existing water users, the greatest benefits at the least cost.

The likelihood of controversy between the two Federal agencies developed soon thereafter. Although the engineers of the Corps and Bureau effected an exchange of physical data, separate field investigations were conducted and each agency developed its conclusions and recommendations independently.

Through its drainage basin committee for the Central Valley area, the Water Resources Committee of the National Resources Planning Board was made aware of the developing agency conflict before the field reports were completed. The Water Committee was very much opposed to the submission of separate reports by the two agencies; its members preferred that the survey organizations co-operate to deliver a single report reflecting the combined judgment of the water experts in the Executive Branch of the government. From experience they knew that integration of investigations is far more likely to be effective if undertaken at the initiation and field study stages of project investigations before findings are crystallized; it is largely and necessarily perfunctory if delayed until the basic conclusions have been reached independently by those concerned.

The Committee, however, was unable to stop the competition. The field reports were completed and the Valley water users, learning of the conflicting recommendations of the two agencies, began to take sides for the Bureau or for the Corps. The survey report of the District Engineer was submitted to Washington in April 1939, and soon thereafter the tentative field report of the Bureau of Reclamation was transmitted to Washington headquarters.

Either through the National Resources Planning Board, or the Secretary of the Interior, President Roosevelt was made aware of the developing conflict in the area. The President viewed the Kings River controversy with such concern, particularly as regards any precedent it might set for irrigation and flood control policy, that he instructed the two agencies to keep their reports confidential insofar as their contents had not already become known to local interests, and requested a conference in his office on the problem on July 19, 1939.

At this conference the President indicated his concern over the duplication of functions in the Central Valley and similar areas and stated his firm desire and intention to eliminate similar duplication in the future. As for the Kings River project, the President agreed to an arrangement whereby the two agencies would co-operate in preparing independent reports, but these reports should contain agreement on both design and economic features of the project. As for future areas of potential conflict, the President instructed the Departments of War, Interior, and Agriculture, in co-operation with the National Resources Planning Board, to draw up a memorandum of agreement which, by insuring consultation in the early stages of project planning, would preclude the possibility of similar conflicts.

The interagency agreement, negotiated in response to this request, and known as the Tripartite Agreement,[2] authorized free interchange of information between the three agencies in the field, in the preparation by any one, of reports on multiple purpose projects, and joint consultation in the field and in Washington on any such reports. At the time the Agreement was negotiated the National Resources Planning Board felt that it fell short of the requirements of the situation and of the desires of the President. Experience under the Agreement confirmed these fears. Although it did contribute to some improvement in field co-operation, the Agreement did not eliminate conflicts and divergencies in later reports.

[2] Copy attached as Appendix A.

The Planning Board would have preferred that the arrangement on the Kings River project provide for the submission of a joint report by the two agencies rather than of separate, but reconciled, reports. However, the President requested the agencies to submit their revised reports to him, giving them to understand that the reports would then be reviewed for the President by the Water Resources Committee before they were made public or submitted to the Congress. In this way some of the advantages of a joint report might be realized.

On January 23, 1940, the Secretary of the Interior submitted to the President, through the National Resources Planning Board, the revised report of the Bureau of Reclamation. Four days later the Director of the Board informed the Chief of Engineers that the Secretary of the Interior had forwarded his report on the project "to the President through the Board" and stated that, "When your report on the project is received, the Board will then have an opportunity to comment upon any points of difference which may exist between the two sets of recommendations. This we will do promptly."

On January 31, the Chief of Engineers acknowledged receipt of the Director's letter in writing and stated that he understood that the Reclamation report had been forwarded to the President, through the National Resources Planning Board. The Chief of Engineers, however, did not state that the report of his Department had been completed nor that it had been sent *directly* to the President on the preceding day. By the time the National Resources Planning Board heard that the Engineer Department report had been sent directly to the White House, and communicated with the President's executive clerk to catch up with it, they found that it had been allowed to pass directly to the Congress. Thus, the recommendations of the Engineer Department were made public without any opportunity for review by the Water Resources Committee and before they had been fully reconciled with those of the Bureau of Reclamation.

As for the action of the White House in allowing the War Department report to be sent to the Congress, no definite explanation is available. However, it is believed that approval for transmission of the report to Congress was the result of a clerical error, that the White House was under the impression that the report had cleared the Planning Board. As for the action of the Chief of Engineers, it may well be that the instructions of the President at the July conference had been to submit the revised and reconciled reports to him; but the Engineers knew that the reports were not fully reconciled and they knew that the Secretary of the Interior had transmitted the Reclamation report to the President through the National Resources Planning Board where it was being held, awaiting receipt of their report. Thus it seems that from the standpoint of the Engineer Department the complete by-passing of the National Resources Planning Board was merely a fortunate accident, which the Department considered to be no part of its duty to prevent. The failure to mention transmittal of the report to the President in the letter of January 31 may or may not be taken to indicate that there was no active desire on the part of the Engineers for co-ordination.

Even if the final handling of the Engineers' report was not in any way a product of the jurisdictional competition with the Bureau of Reclamation, this competition may very well have been responsible for a significant variation from the uniform procedure for the preparation of Engineer survey reports. The procedure, as prescribed by the applicable *Orders and Regulations*, requires that the District Engineer conduct the survey in the field and that the Division Engineer, the Board of Engineers for Rivers and Harbors in Washington, and the Chief of Engineers, each review the survey report and state their conclusions and recommendations in an endorsement to the District Engineer's report. In this case, however, the report of the District Engineer, which was transmitted to Washington in April 1939, never saw the light of day nor did any revision of this report which might have been made after the President's conference. Instead the Chief of Engineers used as the basis for his report a very brief interim report of the Board of Engineers which had been prepared in Washington in June 1939, before the original conference with the President, and which made no reference to the District Engineer's survey.

To this brief interim report the Chief attached his own recommendations, containing those revisions in project design which had been agreed to jointly by the Office of the Chief of Engineers and the Commissioner of Reclamation. It is difficult to understand this procedural variation unless it can be attributed to a desire on the part of the Engineers to act quickly, a desire growing from the jurisdictional competition. More important, however, the President and the Congress were thereby provided with a report which, though designed to serve as the basis for action upon a highly controversial project recommendation, was seriously lacking in basic data.

Upon learning that the Engineer report had gone to Congress, the Chairman of the National Resources Planning Board, on February 2, 1940, wrote to the President:

> We understand that the Army report has already gone to the Congress. In justice to the Secretary of the Interior and the Bureau of Reclamation, it now seems desirable that the Interior Department report should also go to the Congress even though the Army and Reclamation recommendations have not yet been completely reconciled.

And so, in February 1940, the Congress received two separate reports from two Federal agencies, each recommending construction of a reservoir at Pine Flat site on the Kings River. The reports were generally reconciled on features of engineering design but were far apart on matters of water economics. The conflicting recommendations became a matter of public record. They attracted ardent proponents and opponents. The Planning Board scheme of insuring integration prior to the crystallization of findings and recommendations had failed.

Future events were to confirm the conviction of the Board that integration which is delayed until basic conclusions have been reached and published independently by those concerned is extremely difficult, if not impossible, of effective attainment.

Basic Differences in Plans[3]

The reports of the Bureau of Reclamation and the Corps of Engineers were in agreement as to the design of the project. They both recommended construction of a multiple-purpose reservoir with a storage capacity of one million acre feet at the Pine Flat site on the Kings River and of channel improvement works to regulate the flow passing into Tulare Lake. After some differences of opinion, the agencies reached agreement on estimates of cost—$19,500,000 for the Pine Flat Reservoir, exclusive of any power development, and $200,000 for the channel improvement works.

The basic differences in the reports which remained unreconciled when they were submitted to Congress related to major questions of policy rather than to design.

Basically at difference were the water-use philosophies of the two agencies. These philosophies were partly the result of different basic statutory authorities, but the statutory differences in turn were a reflection of the use philosophies of the agencies and in varying degrees of their supporters. The Bureau of Reclamation has viewed the development of the Kings River area as part of a comprehensive plan for the development of the Central Valley Basin, with emphasis on water conservation and maximum water use. The Corps of Engineers on the other hand had little interest in any basin-wide comprehensive plan at the time and considered the development of the water resources of the Kings River almost entirely from the point of view of local flood protection. Thus, for example, the Division Engineer at San Francisco told the Central Valley drainage basin committee, during the

[3] Most of the information on basic differences obtained from the following:

(a) The agency survey reports, *op. cit.*
(b) Letter from Secretary of the Interior dated June 10, 1940, transmitting to Congress communication from President concerning Kings River project. Cong., 76/3, House, Doc. 631, Part 2
(c) Memoranda on project reports dated April 12, May 15, and May 20, 1940, in files of NRPB. NA-NRPB 579.7
(d) Report on allocation of costs of Kings River, dated January 31, 1947. Cong., 80/1, House, Doc. 136

preparation of the Kings River survey report:[4] "There seems to be a conflict as to how the water should be handled. The Army investigations have been only from the standpoint of flood control."

As has been said, the reports of the District and Division Engineers on the project were never released, and the brief reports of the Board of Engineers for Rivers and Harbors and the Chief of Engineers which were transmitted to Congress did give some consideration to water conservation. But the conflicting water-use philosophies of the two agencies, as we shall see, were bound to produce significant disagreements.

Stemming from this basic conflict, the independent recommendations of the two agencies and their later modifications have revealed the following important areas of conflict:

(1) Should the project be built in accordance with flood control law or irrigation law? The most significant differences between the two laws as they have been applied by the two agencies relate to the matters of repayment and project operation.

With respect to *repayment*, the traditional provisions of reclamation law require the repayment of irrigation costs by water users in periods up to forty years (with the addition of a developmental period not to exceed ten years), but free from interest. The water users, thereby, are charged for vendible benefits so as to repay those portions of project costs allocated to irrigation. On the other hand, where irrigation features of Engineer Department projects have been planned for development under flood control law prior to 1945, the provisions with respect to repayment have been largely indefinite and have not been dependent upon any consistent legislative standard. The amounts to be repaid by beneficiaries were the requirements for local contribution recommended by the Chief of Engineers in survey reports and approved by the Congress in authorizing the construction of projects in accordance with these reports or modifications thereof.

[4] From minutes of a meeting of the California Central Valley—Central Coast Drainage Basin Committee at Hanford, California, April 14, 1939. NA-NRPB 516.22

In the Kings River report the Bureau of Reclamation recommended that the water users repay the entire cost allocated to irrigation—$9,750,000—over a period of forty years without interest. The Corps of Engineers, on the other hand, recommended that local interests contribute a lump sum of $4,710,000 for irrigation benefits, which if borrowed by the local interests at an interest rate of 3½ per cent per annum would make their total payout roughly equal to that under the Reclamation plan.

Repayment contracts negotiated by the Bureau of Reclamation in accordance with reclamation law contain restrictions on water and land use which are wholly lacking in projects constructed entirely under flood control law prior to 1945. In general the reclamation law provides for significant Federal control over irrigation development whereas the Engineer Department policy under flood control law has provided for local autonomy. The reclamation law contains *acreage limitations* designed to protect the smaller working farmer from land monopoly, to promote communities of independent farmers who will make homes on the land. No water in excess of that required to irrigate 160 acres, or 320 acres in community property states, may be delivered to a landowner until he has contracted to sell his excess lands.

Similarly, reclamation law contains provisions designed to protect the smaller working farmer from *land speculation* at his expense. For all projects constructed under reclamation law, the owner of excess lands, if he wishes to dispose of them in order to become eligible for delivery of water, must agree to sell on terms and conditions satisfactory to the Secretary of the Interior and at prices based upon an appraisal made without reference to any increment of value due to Federal reclamation.

For the Kings River project, the Bureau of Reclamation would have applied the statutory restrictions on acreage and speculation. The Corps of Engineers, by constructing the project under flood control law, would have exempted the project beneficiaries from these restrictions.

There are notable differences in the *operation* of completed irrigation facilities as between those developed by the Bureau of Reclamation in accordance with reclamation law and those developed by the Engineer Department in accordance with flood control law. Works constructed by the Corps of Engineers are often turned over to local interests for administration, with only general control by the Corps; works constructed by the Bureau of Reclamation are ordinarily operated by it for a period of years, and some works remain under its jurisdiction indefinitely.

Most irrigation projects require a dam and reservoir to retain and store water and supplemental irrigation canals, ditches, and spreading works to distribute the water. Where landowners fail to comply with the requirements of reclamation law, it is a simple engineering matter to cut off water deliveries. In areas like the Upper San Joaquin Valley, however, additional irrigation water may be provided by the construction of dams without the necessity of supplemental Federal works. Existing privately owned canal and distribution systems are fed from the main river channels; and water in the channels and canals, not required for immediate use, can seep into the ground from which it can be pumped when needed for irrigation purposes. Any operation of the completed reservoirs will allow more water, formerly wasted to the sea, to be diverted into ground water for later use by irrigators through pumping. But multiple-purpose dams and reservoirs in this area are bound to give rise to difficult operation problems and controversies, depending on the ultimate water use and controls envisaged; and such controversies are inevitably sharpened when two Federal agencies promote different basic proposals for project operation and maintenance.

This is the case in the Kings River project. Because the project is part of its basin-wide plan for the Central Valley, the Bureau of Reclamation recommended that it be operated by the Federal government in harmony with other developments in the Valley. The Bureau reported:

> The complexities of irrigation uses, the potentially conflicting interests of irrigation and flood control, the co-ordination of power production by the Kings River and the Central Valley projects, and the prospect of sale of water from the Central Valley project to portions of Kings River service area, make it highly advisable for the government to operate the contemplated Kings River project works, leaving the operation of the canals and the distribution of water in local hands. Water releases, except in rare cases, must conform to vested irrigation rights.

The Corps of Engineers, on the other hand, recommended that the project be turned over to local interests for operation. They reported:

> It is noted that water rights in the area under consideration are complex and involved, and that local interests have expressed a willingness and desire to maintain and operate the proposed improvements in accordance with regulations to be prescribed by the Secretary of War. Such an arrangement is desirable as it would relieve the United States of the responsibilities involved in the operation of conservation storage.

Through these conflicting recommendations, the related issues of "Federal domination" and of local water rights entered into the controversy between the Bureau and Corps in the Central Valley.

With respect to water rights, local records and the report of the Bureau of Reclamation disclosed "overschedule water" or water in excess of entitlement in Kings River to which present water users, represented by their water associations, asserted a right and claim based on use and necessity. The Corps of Engineers, by turning operation of the project over to local interests—the water users' associations—would have allowed the present water users to arrange disposition of the "overschedule water" themselves. The report of the Bureau of Reclamation recognized the validity of vested irrigation rights, but proposed to retain operation of the project under Federal control, and thereby to deny to present water users the 100 per cent control over all releases from the reservoir which they sought in their own interests.

A third difference between flood control and reclamation law which bears on this case study should be mentioned—that of authorization. The rules of Congress provide that no money can be *appropriated* except for activities that have already been *authorized* by Congress. Under the reclamation law, a project is considered to be legally authorized when the Secretary of the Interior determines that it is economically and engineeringly desirable and feasible under the standards set in the statute. No additional legislative authorization is required, though the Congress must appropriate money for the specific project before construction can begin. Under flood control law, on the other hand, the Congress must authorize each separate project, on the basis of Engineer Department survey reports, before an appropriation can be provided.

Thus, with respect to the Kings River project, the report of the Secretary of the Interior submitted to Congress in February 1940 constituted in effect authorization for the project under reclamation law. The report of the Chief of Engineers constituted a recommendation that Congress authorize the project under flood control law.

(2) Should the development of power be initiated as part of the irrigation improvement, or should provision be made for future development under license by the Federal Power Commission? In its report, the Bureau of Reclamation recommended the construction of a power plant, with provision for an ultimate capacity of 45,000 kilowatts, but with an initial installation of 15,000 kilowatts, and the provision of transmission lines to connect with lines of the Central Valley project. The Bureau considered the power development to be essential to the proper and most beneficial utilization of conserved waters. The initial power installation was needed to meet the immediate local requirements of pumping and would constitute the most favorable immediate step in the full development of power on the Kings River.

The Corps of Engineers, on the other hand, did not propose the immediate development of hydroelectric power, but suggested that provision be made for the installation of penstocks for possible future development of power, under Federal Power Commission license. The Corps considered that the development of power was not an essential part of the flood control and irrigation improvement and that the public interest would be best served by development under private license from the Federal Power Commission.

The largest water users' association in the area preferred the Army scheme because it planned to file with the FPC for the license to develop the power and then to set power rates which would yield sufficient revenues to help retire the local contribution for irrigation benefits. In other words, they would use power primarily as a means of obtaining cheap water. If the Bureau of Reclamation developed the power and tied it in with the Central Valley project, power rates would be set in the light of a combination of economic, social, and other objectives rather than in the light of cheap water alone.

(3) What should be the allocation of project costs and benefits as between flood control, irrigation, and power? Flood control improvements are largely constructed at Federal expense; irrigation improvements (when constructed under reclamation law) must be paid for by project beneficiaries over a period of forty years, but without interest; power improvements must be paid for by power users with interest. Thus, where a multiple-purpose project involves these three uses, the allocation of costs is a matter of vital concern to the local interests. Where two agencies propose to construct the same multiple-purpose project and at the same time propose different cost allocations, the project beneficiaries will naturally align themselves with the agency which proposes the greater allocation to flood control (a 100 per cent Federal contribution for reservoirs) and the lesser allocation to irrigation.

The survey reports of the Corps and Bureau submitted to Congress in February 1940 were in general agreement on cost allocation. Half of the reservoir costs of $19,500,000 were to be allocated to flood control and half to irrigation. The costs of river control works—$200,000—were to be allocated to flood control, and those of the Pine Flat power plant and transmission lines, proposed in the Bureau report only, to power.

This agreement on cost allocation did not hold for long, however. As soon as construction costs began to rise and the two agencies were required to re-examine total project costs and allocations, they failed to continue any agreement and their recommendations came into sharp conflict. As we shall see, the agency which recommended the greater allocation to flood control—the Corps of Engineers—received thereby the bulk of the local support.

Turning from cost allocations to estimates of the distribution of benefits, the reports were in disagreement from the very beginning, as the following table indicates:

Annual Benefits From	*Corps of Engineers 1940 Report*	*Bureau of Reclamation 1940 Report*
Irrigation	$ 995,000	$1,255,000
Flood Control	1,185,000	1,185,000
Power	none	683,000

These differences are important not only because they are reflected in cost and repayment allocations, but because they raise a question as to the primary or dominant purpose of the project when considered alone.

(4) When should the project be built (a) in relation to other projects in the area and to the six-year construction programs of the Corps and the Bureau, and (b) in relation to the negotiation of repayment contracts? The problem of timing in terms of the year in which a project should be built is subject to a complexity of factors, among them the authorization procedure, the priority of the project in the agency's six-year construction program, the speed with which definite plans and specifications can be completed, problems relating to land acquisition and the fulfillment of requirements for local contributions, the appropriations made available by the Congress, etc. Where two agencies have planned construction of the same project, but are subject to different procedures for authorization, use different criteria for programming based on different philosophies of water use, and receive different treatment from the Congress in regard to appropriations, it is to be expected that they will differ on the exact timing of a project. The local interests will naturally support the agency which promises to build first.

The problem of timing in relation to the negotiation of repayment contracts is quite another matter. If the Kings River project were constructed as originally recommended by the Corps of Engineers under flood control law, the local interests would have to satisfy the Chief of Engineers that they had made or were prepared to make the cash contribution of $4,710,000 before construction was begun. If, on the other hand, the Kings River project were constructed as originally recommended by the Bureau of Reclamation under reclamation law, the constructing agency would have to negotiate repayment contracts with the prospective irrigation beneficiaries before the project was begun. This is true because the Kings River area is one in which the construction of a Federal water distribution system is not required in order to deliver the irrigation benefits. It would be almost impossible to secure repayment contracts or to enforce acreage limitations and speculation controls after a reservoir is in operation, for there would be no effective and economical means of denying irrigation benefits to those who failed to comply. As we shall see, this aspect of the timing of construction became the center of controversy between the two agencies six and seven years after the original reports were submitted to the Congress.

The Growing Controversy, 1940-1944[5]

Once the survey reports were published without restriction, the controversy between the two agencies and their supporters in California broke wide open. Secretary Ickes expressed concern lest a decision on the basic differences in the two reports be left entirely to the most directly interested groups. If the controversy were to be settled on the basis of which Federal agency could acquire the preponderant support

[5] Most of the information on the period 1940 to 1944 obtained from the following:
(a) NRPB file NA-NRPB 579.7
(b) Cong., 76/3, House, Committee on Flood Control, *Hearings on Comprehensive Flood Control Plans* (H.R. 9640), pp. 517-578, 950-956; and Report 2103
(c) Cong., 77/1, House, Committee on Flood Control, *Hearings on Flood Control Plans and New Projects* (H.R. 4911), pp. 93-114, 159-166, 176-195
(d) Cong., 77/1, House, Report 1174
(e) Cong., 78/2, House, Committee on Flood Control, *Hearings on Flood Control Plans and New Projects* (H.R. 4485), pp. 636-638

of local interests in the Kings River area, then such a settlement might well not be in the public interest. The Secretary therefore proposed to the President that the National Resources Planning Board review both reports with a view to recommending to the President a reconciliation in the national interest. The Secretary's letter follows:

March 7, 1940

My dear Mr. President:

With respect to the separate reports submitted by the Bureau of Reclamation and the Corps of Engineers on the Kings River project in California, I believe your attention should be called to the fact that a local controversy has developed and is growing more heated in the area. This controversy revolves around the question as to which report proposed the most attractive development judged solely by the cost of water to prospective irrigators, and without regard to the ability and responsibility of the irrigators to pay as a result of benefits to be received.

Reports from the area indicate that the plan proposed by the Army and the plan proposed by the Reclamation Service each have supporters who are organized and intend to fight.

I cannot believe that it is in the public interest to leave the decision to interested groups for a settlement on the basis indicated. I would not attempt now to guess what the eventual outcome might be if this controversy should be permitted to develop and to run its course, but I have no reason to believe that the Reclamation project would not be chosen. It seems doubtful, however, whether any decision would be made in several years, and much unnecessary bitterness might result. I do not believe that representatives of either the Corps of Engineers or of the Bureau of Reclamation are participating in the contest.

I would not want the project built by the Bureau of Reclamation if I felt that the local, interested groups had been responsible in having it so for the selfish reason that by adopting the Reclamation project they could shift an undue burden to the Federal Government. On the other hand, I would be greatly disappointed if the Reclamation plan were to be rejected solely because the irrigators of the Basin felt that the Army plan would cost them less and the United States more.

The situation described has developed largely because of the circumstances which resulted in submission of the two reports to the Congress without a review by the National Resources Planning Board and with no indication of preference by the Administration for either plan or for a division of responsibility in connection with the project.

I suggest, therefore, the advisability of a review of the two reports by the National Resources Planning Board, even though the reports already have been submitted to the Congress. The National Resources Planning Board would make such a review and would report if requested to do so by you. The report of the National Resources Planning Board, when approved by you, could be submitted to the Congress. This should be instrumental in having the questions revolving about the 2 proposals decided in the national interest.

I am submitting, therefore, for your consideration, a draft of a letter to the National Resources Planning Board requesting a review and report on the Kings River project plans.

Sincerely yours,
[s] *Harold L. Ickes*
Secretary of the Interior

Copy for National Resources Planning Board
Washington, D. C.

The Corps of Engineers did not express any similar concern over reaching a settlement within the Executive Branch. They urged their own proposals on the Congress without reference to the views of the Secretary of the Interior and the President; and they took the position that the issues could be decided properly on the basis of local support.

The President agreed to the suggestion of Secretary Ickes, and the Water Resources Committee undertook to analyze the two reports carefully and to point up the major areas of disagreement: power development, agency to construct project, method of repayment, method of operation.

Before the WRC could complete its analysis, the House Committee on Flood Control conducted hearings on the Kings River project in April 1940. The Engineers testified in favor of authorization of the project under flood control law and in accordance with their report. The Commissioner of Reclamation presented the views of his agency. The three representatives of local interests who testified all favored the Army, though there were petitions from groups on both sides. The House Committee reported out a Flood Control Bill in early May 1940, recommending among other things that the Kings River project be authorized for construction by the Corps of Engineers. However, the Bill was never considered by the House, so no final congressional action was taken in 1940.

In the meantime, the Water Resources Committee completed its analysis, and the President, on May 29, 1940, made a decision which was intended to serve as the Administration policy on the matter and to put an end to the unseemly squabbling between two executive agencies. The President wrote to the Secretary of the Interior, with a copy to the Secretary of War, as follows:

> With respect to these matters, it seems to me that the project is dominantly an irrigation undertaking and is suited to operation and maintenance under the reclamation law. It follows, therefore, that it should be constructed by the Bureau of Reclamation, and that the portion of the project cost to be charged to irrigation should be financed on the basis of the prevailing Federal policy of 40 annual payments by irrigation beneficiaries. The project should be maintained and operated by the Bureau of Reclamation, but operation for flood control should be in accordance with regulations prescribed by the Secretary of War.

So as to publicize the Administration policy, the Secretary of the Interior transmitted the President's letter to Congress, where it was printed as a House Document.[6]

The decision of the President, however, does not appear to have had any effect whatsoever on the position taken by the Corps of Engineers. As remarked above, the Engineers have traditionally held that they, as the engineer consultants to Congress, are "an agency of the Legislative Branch"; and in accordance with this traditional position, they resisted this attempt by the President to intervene in the direct relations between the Corps and the Congress.

Thus, when the House Committee on Flood Control reopened hearings on the Kings River project in April 1941, the Engineers once more testified in favor of constructing the project under flood control law. They never once mentioned the President's policy in the matter. They stated that the project was primarily for flood control and did not mention that the President had found the project "dominantly an irrigation undertaking."

At these hearings the Commissioner of Reclamation supported the President's policy which favored his agency and the Reclamation program.

As these hearings reopened the entire controversy, the President took the matter up at a Cabinet meeting. The decision reached at that meeting, representing a reaffirmation of the previously determined Administration policy, is stated in the following letter of May 5, 1941, from the President to the Secretary of War:

> Recalling the discussion at the recent Cabinet meeting, I believe it wise to record for reference the decision made with respect to the interests of the Corps of Engineers and of the Bureau of Reclamation in proposed developments on the Kings River and on the Kern River in California.
>
> The Kings River and the Kern River projects are dominantly irrigation projects and as such they should be built at the appropriate time by the Department of the Interior through its Bureau of Reclamation rather than by the War Department through the Corps of Engineers. My letter to the Secretary of the Interior of May 29, 1940, which is published in part 2 of House Document 631, Seventy-sixth Congress, third session, clearly stated my decision on the policy which should be applied to the Kings River project. This decision is applicable to the Kern River project as well. I do not consider it wise to authorize these projects, or any project dominantly for irrigation for construction by the Corps of Engineers.
>
> I am writing to Chairman Whittington of the Flood Control Committee of the House of Representatives to inform him on this matter. By thus clearing doubts which may have persisted with respect to the scope of the fields of operation of the two outstanding construction agencies of the Government it is my hope that unnecessary duplication of work will be avoided and that potential sources of friction will be eliminated.
>
> Copies of this letter are being sent to the Secretary of the Interior, to the Director of the Bureau of the Budget, and to the Chairman of the National Resources Planning Board for their information.

[6] The reader may note that the formula of project assignment by dominant purpose enunciated in the President's letter was an outcome of the Kings River controversy and constituted a new Presidential policy.

In writing to the Chairman of the House Committee on Flood Control on the same day, the President proposed, as a basis for delineating the jurisdictions of the Corps of Engineers and the Bureau of Reclamation, the dominant interest theory:

A good rule for Congress to apply in considering these water projects, in my opinion, would be that the dominant interest should determine which agency should build and which should operate the project. Projects in which flood control or navigation clearly dominate are those in which the interest of the Corps of Engineers is superior and projects in which irrigation and related conservation uses dominate fall into the legitimate field of the Bureau of Reclamation.

On this basis, the President said:

Good administration continues to demand that projects which are dominantly for irrigation should be constructed by the Bureau of Reclamation, Department of the Interior, and not by the Corps of Engineers, War Department. The Kings River project is authorized for construction by the Bureau of Reclamation at this time. . . . Neither of these projects, [the letter also concerned the Kern River project] therefore, should be authorized for construction by the Corps of Engineers, to do so would only lead to needless confusion.[7]

The project was not put in the Flood Control Bill of 1941 as reported and passed by both Houses because of the President's known opposition. However, a separate bill, authorizing the Kings River project in accordance with the Army plans, was reported favorably by the House Flood Control Committee in August 1941. The Committee report stated:

The Committee felt that inasmuch as Congress had authorized the Chief of Engineers to examine the project and inasmuch as the land owners affected and the citizens interested, after carefully considering the project as proposed by the Commissioner of Reclamation and the project proposed by the Chief of Engineers, approved the project of the Chief of Engineers, the bill should be reported to provide for construction by the Chief of Engineers.

In deference to the views of the President of the United States and the Secretary of the Interior, the project was not included in the flood control bill. . . . The Committee, however, felt that in all the circumstances, the bill should be favorably reported, and that the public interest would be promoted by the construction of the project by the Chief of Engineers of the War Department, as prayed for by the citizens' interest.

The special bill was not considered further by the Congress.

The Bureau of Reclamation, considering the Kings River project authorized under reclamation law, requested funds for the commencement of construction for fiscal year 1942 and again for fiscal year 1943; but each time the Bureau of the Budget denied the request, as the project was not considered to be of immediate value to the national defense and war programs, and all such public works projects were to be deferred for postwar construction.

During the war, however, certain control works on lower Kings River to permit the deflection of flood waters away from Tulare Lake were constructed by the Corps of Engineers. As the Kings River project had not been authorized under flood control law, the Army built this small unit of the project under the authority of a war emergency flood control appropriation for repairs and maintenance. This justification was seriously questioned by some members of the Executive Branch and of the Congress. More important, the move itself put the Corps of Engineers to work for the first time in the Kings River area, and naturally was likely to leave the impression locally that future work would be under the same auspices. Although the particular works constructed and repaired were relatively minor and were primarily for flood control, they did provide some irrigation benefits, and these benefits were made fully non-reimbursable under the emergency flood control appropriation—a welcome gift to the local beneficiaries from the Federal government.

The Showdown—1944

In 1944 the controversy between the partisans of the Corps and the Bureau was fought

[7] The reader will note that in this letter the President gave general application to the dominant interest theory first formulated in his letter of a year earlier.

out in Washington on three legislative proposals—the Interior Department Appropriation Bill, the Flood Control Bill, and the Rivers and Harbors Bill.

Interior Department Appropriation Bill for 1945[8]

Apparently to forestall authorization of the Kings River project by the Congress in the Flood Control Bill then under preparation in the House of Representatives, the President, in March 1944, transmitted to Congress a budget request of $1,000,000 for the Bureau of Reclamation to cover plan preparation, preconstruction explorations, purchase of rights-of-way, and clearing on the Kings River project. The congressman from the district and the master of the Kings River Water Association appeared before the House Appropriations Committee in opposition to the budget request. The Committee did not approve the estimate. They called attention to the local opposition and to the fact that the House Committee on Flood Control had included the project for Army construction in the pending Flood Control Bill.

The Senate Appropriations Committee restored the full estimate and reported as follows:

> The committee has reinstated the Budget estimate of $1,000,000. . . . The committee is impressed by the statement in the hearings that it is more advantageous to the government to have the Kings River project constructed by the Bureau of Reclamation because of the indefinite provisions with respect to repayment contained in the pending flood control bill, H.R. 4485, which proposes authorization of the construction of the project by the Corps of Engineers. That bill provides no legislative standard for repayment by the beneficiaries and leaves the repayment obligation of the local interests entirely at the discretion of the Secretary of War. If the Secretary of War should adopt a recommendation made by the Chief of Engineers in House Document 630, Seventy-sixth Congress, third session, the cost to the landowners would be only $4,710,000 as compared to repayments of $9,750,000 which are provided in the Reclamation Bureau plan. The landowners would gain and the reclamation fund would thus lose $5,040,000.
>
> Another effect of the proposed transfer of constructing the Kings River project from the Reclamation Service to the Corps of Engineers would be to escape from the provisions of section 46 of the Reclamation Adjustment Act of 1926. . . .
>
> Under existing law, as above quoted, reclamation project water is available to any landowner regardless of the size of his holdings provided that he agrees to sell any irrigable land in excess of 160 acres when and if an opportunity occurs at a price not in excess of its fair appraisal value. This law has been in effect for 18 years on more than 60 reclamation projects and there is excellent proof that it operates in a reasonable and equitable manner and is achieving the purpose for which it was intended. It does not require sudden or precipitate breaking up of real estate holdings but, in an orderly and gradual way, it prevents land monopoly and speculation in benefits created by the expenditure of Federal funds. Most of all, it assures that there will be opportunities for men to secure farms and make homes and livelihood for themselves and their families without incurring a ruinous debt because of the wild gambling of land speculators.

The Committee's statement that landowners would gain and the reclamation fund would lose $5 million if the project were constructed under flood control law was only half true; the reclamation fund would lose, but the landowners would not gain. Under flood control law the landowners would have to borrow money to meet their lump sum contribution, and it was estimated by the Board of Engineers that, at an interest rate of 3½ per cent, the total payout by the beneficiaries under the flood control law would be roughly the same as that under reclamation law.

[8] Most of the information on the Interior Department appropriation request obtained from the following:
(a) Cong., 78/2, House, Doc. 480
(b) Cong., 78/2, House, Committee on Appropriations, *Hearings on Interior Department Appropriation Bill for 1945*, pp. 730-735, 1138-1148; and Report 1395
(c) Cong., 78/2, Senate, Committee on Appropriations, *Hearings on Interior Department Appropriation Bill for 1945*, pp. 216-218, 335-337, 372-373, 663; and Report 899
(d) Cong., 78/2, House, Report 1678

The conference committee of the two Houses agreed to eliminate the budget request, so that the Bureau of Reclamation was denied funds to proceed with detailed plans for its project in fiscal year 1944.

Flood Control Bill of 1944[9]

The House Committee on Flood Control had commenced hearings on the Kings River project on February 9, 1944, in connection with the important Flood Control Bill of that year. In order to forestall consideration of the project for authorization under flood control law, the Secretary of the Interior had written to the Secretary of War on January 20 as follows:

My Dear Mr. Secretary:

I understand that Chairman Whittington of the House Committee on Flood Control is preparing to hold hearings on a bill to authorize the construction of the Kings River project in California by the Corps of Engineers. I know that you cannot control the actions of the congressional committee and its chairman.

It will be embarrassing to both our Departments, however, if the hearings could bring about authorization for construction of the project by the Corps of Engineers, since the project is already authorized for construction by the Bureau of Reclamation under the reclamation law.

You may want to review the history of this project. The War Department report was printed as House Document No. 630, Seventy-sixth Congress, third session, and the Interior Department report was printed as House Document No. 631, Seventy-sixth Congress, third session. You will find printed in this document a letter by the President authorizing me to submit my report.

On May 29, 1940, the President sent another letter to me assigning the project to the Department of the Interior. This letter is printed in full in House Document No. 631, part 2, Seventy-sixth Congress, third session, and the body of it reads as follows:

[letter not reproduced here]

On several occasions since this decision was made by the President and since the project was authorized under the reclamation law, the Flood Control Committee has held hearings for the purpose of considering bills to authorize the project for construction by the War Department. I believe it would be helpful if you should call the status of this project to the attention of the Chief of Engineers in order that he might be prepared to set the committee right with regard to your Department's position with respect to it.

When there is so much to be done, I can see no profit in preparing lengthy presentations to be made at hearings that serve no useful purpose. This hearing, at best, could only reopen a controversy that would be troublesome to us both and which was settled nearly 4 years ago.

Sincerely yours,
[s] *Harold L. Ickes*
Secretary of the Interior

The reply of the Secretary of War did not indicate that his Department would in any way oppose favorable consideration of the project for authorization under flood control law:

January 26, 1944

Dear Mr. Secretary:

Reference is made to your letter of January 20, 1944, regarding prospective hearings by the House Committee on Flood Control with respect to the proposed Pine Flat Dam on the Kings River, Calif. In your letter you state that the project is already authorized for construction by the Bureau of Reclamation under the reclamation law and you ask me to call the status of the project to the attention of the Chief of Engineers in order that he may be prepared to advise the committee relative to the position of this Department with respect to the project.

As you mention in your letter the Flood Control Committee has considered the Pine Flat project in public hearings on several occasions, the most recent having been in June of 1943. The record of these hearings indicates very clearly the status of the Pine Flat project both as pertains to the War Department and the Interior Department. I have requested the Chief of Engineers to present your letter of January 20 to the Flood Control Committee if he or his repre-

[9] Most of the information on the Flood Control Act of 1944 obtained from the following:

(a) Cong., 78/2, House, Committee on Flood Control, *Hearings on Flood Control Plans and New Projects* (H.R. 4485), pp. 611-652, 737-768; and Report 1369

(b) Cong., 78/2, Senate, Committee on Commerce, *Hearings on Flood Control* (H.R. 4485), pp. 11-14, 201-264, 276-340, 362-364, 449, 452-455, 459-465; and Report 1030

(c) Cong., 78/2, House, Doc. 545, pp. xi-xii

(d) 90 C.R., pp. 4119 ff., 7882-3, 8185 ff., 9264

sentatives are called upon for further testimony on the subject of the Kings River project.

Sincerely yours,
[s] *Henry L. Stimson*
Secretary of War

Two days before Representative Whittington opened hearings on the project the President wrote him in a further attempt to avert approval of the Corps' project by the Congressman's committee. The President said:

February 7, 1944

My Dear Mr. Whittington:

Over 2 years ago, on May 5, 1941, I wrote to you about the Kings River project and the Kern River project in California. Your committee was then considering the authorization of both of these projects for development by the Corps of Engineers under the jurisdiction of the Secretary of War.

The schedule of hearings on the Flood Control bill of 1944 indicates that proposals for authorizing these projects as undertakings of the Corps of Engineers will be considered again on February 9, 1944. I shall appreciate it if you will read this letter into the record at that time.

In my letter of May 5, 1941, I said, in part: "Good administration continues to demand that projects which are dominantly for irrigation should be constructed by the Bureau of Reclamation, Department of the Interior, and not by the Corps of Engineers, War Department. The Kings River project is authorized for construction by the Bureau of Reclamation at this time. The proposed project on the Kern River . . . is dominantly an irrigation project. . . . Neither of these projects, therefore, should be authorized for construction by the Corps of Engineers. To do so would only lead to needless confusion." That letter is applicable today.

These projects should be constructed by the Bureau of Reclamation and that portion of their cost to be charged to irrigation should be financed on the basis of the prevailing Federal policy of 40 annual payments by irrigation beneficiaries. These projects should be maintained and operated by the Bureau of Reclamation, but operation for flood control should be in accordance with regulations prescribed by the Secretary of War.

In my letter of May 5, 1941, I suggested that a sound policy in connection with these water projects would consist of selecting the construction agency by determining the dominant interest. Projects in which navigation or flood control clearly dominate are those in which the interest of the Corps of Engineers is superior and should be so recognized. On the other hand, projects in which irrigation and related conservation dominate are those in which the interest of the Bureau of Reclamation in the Department of the Interior is paramount and should be so recognized. No matter which agency builds a multiple-purpose structure involving in even a minor way the interests of the other, the agency with the responsibility for that particular interest should administer it in accordance with its authorizing legislation and general policies. For example, the Bureau of Reclamation in the Department of the Interior should administer, under the reclamation laws, and its general policies, those irrigation benefits and phases of projects built by the Corps of Engineers. These suggestions are, to my mind, even more pertinent today. For today we gird for peace. Confusion over jurisdiction ought not to be allowed to disrupt the great preparations now being made for post-war construction of vital public works.

Sincerely yours,
[s] *Franklin D. Roosevelt*

At the hearings, the representative of the Corps of Engineers read into the record the letters reproduced above and answered all questions asked by Committee members. At no time did he advance any support for the President's policy. The Commissioner of Reclamation presented the views of the Administration and of his agency.

After the hearings on the project had been concluded, Representative Whittington wrote to the President that the Kings River project was in fact dominantly a flood control project. The Congressman implied that the President had been misinformed in believing that the project was for the primary purpose of irrigation and that a strict application of the President's own dominant interest theory would dictate its authorization under flood control law. In the hearings, the representative of the Chief of Engineers and several members of the Committee had given emphasis to the fact that the report of the Chief of Engineers allocated the greater percentage of project benefits —54 per cent—to flood control and only 46 per cent to irrigation. It will be remembered that the Reclamation report, on the other hand, allocated the greatest benefits—40 per cent—to irrigation; 38 per cent to flood control; and 22 per cent to power. Representative Whittington's letter follows:

I gladly read your letter of February 7, 1944, into the record of hearings now being conducted by the Flood Control Committee on February 9, 1944, when the multiple purpose projects on the Kings and Kern Rivers, California, were under consideration. The committee had previously given most careful consideration to your letter of May 5, 1941.

The reports on these projects were submitted by the Chief of Engineers of the United States Army in response to the authorization in the Flood Control Act of June 22, 1936.

The Chief of Engineers and the Commissioner of Reclamation were heard by the Committee on Flood Control. I think it is a fair statement to say that aside from either the statements or reports of the Chief of Engineers or the Commissioner of Reclamation the testimony given at the hearings, including the testimony of consulting engineers of outstanding merit and reputation, shows conclusively that flood control is the dominant interest in the Kings and Kern River projects, and that these projects have no direct relation to the Central Valley project, including the Mt. Shasta and Friant Dams and related works, under construction by the Bureau of Reclamation.

I think it proper also to report to you that the testimony shows that there are no Federal Reclamation projects nor have there ever been any such projects along the Kings and Kern Rivers. The local interests have constructed and maintained through the years reclamation projects without federal aid. The testimony shows that no public lands are involved and that very little, if any, new land is to be brought under water.

The hearings also disclose that there is a definite flood problem and that the local interests without federal contribution have constructed local protective works. Recent excessive floods have demonstrated that these works are inadequate.

The local interests, seeking flood protection through the construction of the projects in question, have over many years acquired adequate water rights under California laws and, as stated, have established and operated their own irrigation systems. The citizens and the landowners with one accord object as disclosed by the hearings to being brought under the restrictions of the Reclamation Act.

I beg to assure you that the policies as outlined in your letter of February 7, 1944, will be fully considered by the Committee on Flood Control in the light of the facts developed at the hearings.

In reply, the President emphasized the importance of viewing the Kings River project as a multiple-purpose element in a basin-wide plan, rather than as an isolated project.[10] By taking this approach, the President hit at the very fundamental difference in water-use philosophies of the Corps of Engineers and the Bureau of Reclamation, and stated his conviction that the most favorable development of water resources can result only from an approach which emphasizes basin-wide planning and development. The President now interpreted his own dominant interest theory to apply to the principal objective of a closely integrated basin-wide plan, rather than to the principal objective of a single multiple-purpose project considered in vacuum. The President said:

March 7, 1944

My dear Mr. Whittington:

I have received your letter of February 17, 1944, in which you discuss the proposed Kern River, California, multiple-purpose project. It may well be, as you state in your letter, that, when the structure proposed by the Chief of Engineers is considered alone, the benefits are predominantly flood control. However, I feel that neither the Kern River project nor the Kings River project can properly be viewed without regard to the development of the Central Valley of California as a whole.

It seems to me that the multiple-purpose projects proposed by the Chief of Engineers on the Kings and Kern Rivers are only two elements in a basin-wide plan for the development and use of the water resources in the Great Central Valley of California, and that the primary and dominant objective of that plan, especially in the southern part of the valley, is the provision of water supplies for domestic, municipal, industrial and irrigation uses. It would appear that, if any such plan is to be successful, the operation of all units of the plan should be fully co-ordinated on a regional basis. Such co-ordination, insofar as the

[10] The reader will note that here again the continuing Kings River controversy led to the development and formulation of a new Presidential policy—the dominant interest theory applied to a whole river basin rather than to individual projects.

projects undertaken by the Federal Government are concerned, can best be obtained by a single agency constructing, operating and maintaining the multiple-purpose elements of the plan, particularly those projects involving water conservation. Since the Congress has already authorized the construction and operation by the Bureau of Reclamation of certain multiple-purpose elements of the Central Valley plan involving water conservation, from the standpoint of good Federal administration it would follow that the Bureau of Reclamation should also be authorized to construct and operate the other multiple-purpose elements, such as the projects proposed on the Kings and Kern Rivers by the Chief of Engineers, with appropriate care exercised, of course, to observe the existing local irrigation rights established by usage, decrees, and agreements.

I know that you will understand that my expression of views arises from my desire to obtain what I believe to be the best method of Federal participation in the over-all plan for the development of the Central Valley, and not from any intention of interfering with the proper consideration of this matter by the Congress.

Sincerely yours,
[s] *Franklin D. Roosevelt*

Despite the firm Administration policy, the Committee on Flood Control reported the Kings and Kern River projects favorably, and they were approved by the House. The Committee stated that it had adhered to the policy of reporting projects only where the dominant interest is flood control. "Differences of opinion in executive departments as to the dominant interests respecting a few of the projects included in the bill exist. All interests were heard, and only those projects where the preponderance of the testimony showed that flood control was paramount are contained in the pending bill." The Committee justification for these Central Valley projects was generally similar to that contained in Representative Whittington's letter to the President.

The President was not content to accept this verdict and apparently was no better pleased with the attitude of the Corps of Engineers, which he considered an agency of his executive establishment. Soon after the Flood Control Bill had passed the House, he wrote the following curt note to the Secretary of War.

THE WHITE HOUSE

Washington, May 16, 1944

Memorandum for the Secretary of War:

I want the Kings and Kern River projects to be built by the Bureau of Reclamation and not by the Army engineers. I also want the power generated at projects built by the Army engineers to be disposed of by the Secretary of the Interior. I hope you will see that the rivers and harbors and flood-control bills include appropriate provisions to effectuate these.

F.D.R.

The Secretary of War transmitted the President's memorandum to the Chairman of the Senate Committee on Commerce. He said in his letter of transmittal, "I accordingly recommend that your Committee give its earnest consideration to the desires expressed in that memorandum." The Secretary's letter and the President's memorandum were both inserted in the record of the Senate Committee hearings on the Flood Control Bill, along with a number of other communications. There was no discussion of the memorandum at the time. And while an examination of the record of the Committee hearings reveals no expressed opposition to the President's position, it likewise shows no single occasion on which representatives of the Corps of Engineers, in testifying on the Central Valley projects, supported the President's program in this respect. Sole executive support was provided by the President, his Executive Office, and the representatives of the Department of the Interior.

The Senate Committee on Commerce voted to leave the Kings River project in the bill. Senator Overton informed the President of this decision, and the President responded as follows on August 7, 1944:

The dam and reservoir projects in the Central Valley of California, which would be authorized by H.R. 4485 for construction by the Army engineers, should, for purposes of sound administration and co-ordinated operation, be constructed by the Bureau of Reclamation in the Department of the Interior. These projects constitute logical extensions of the existing Central Valley project of the Bureau of Reclamation. California, in common with the other Western States, has a flood-control problem and a need for water. The basic and best solution of her flood control problem lies in the maximum storage and use of water for irrigation. Every flood control project and every navigation project in the West should therefore be made, so far as practicable, to play its part in the great scheme of conservation of water for beneficial consumptive uses.

It may well be that testimony before your Committee in favor of the construction of these projects by the Corps of Engineers was a reflection of the desire of certain large land interests in California to obtain irrigation and other benefits without being subjected to the repayment requirements and to the other public safeguards that are a part of the reclamation law, but I do not believe that this should be allowed to obscure the fundamental objectives of that law.

. . . I hope, therefore, that the Congress will see fit to place in the Bureau of Reclamation the authority and the responsibility for accomplishment of the great objectives that the Federal Government should achieve in California.

Despite this strong stand, the Senate failed to strike the Kings River project from the legislation, so that the Flood Control Act of 1944 included authorization of that project and several similar ones in the Upper San Joaquin Valley.

However, this same Flood Control Act contained a general provision with respect to the irrigation features of projects built and operated by the Corps of Engineers which was designed to accomplish Administration policy at least in part. Other than the Central Valley projects, there were a number of projects in the pending Flood Control and Rivers and Harbors Bills which had potential irrigation values. The President had decided that responsible public policy dictated that irrigation features of Engineer Department projects be planned, constructed, and operated in accordance with reclamation law. If this were not done, irrigation features of Engineer Department multiple-purpose projects would be developed under conditions for repayment, delivery of water, and project operation quite different from those for irrigation features developed by the Bureau of Reclamation.

Thus, the President had written to the Chairman of the House Committee on Rivers and Harbors on February 7, 1944:

Some of the projects to be authorized by the bill, particularly those affecting the arid and semiarid areas of the West, may have substantial potential values for irrigation purposes. Obviously, where these values exist provision should be made for their eventual realization through the construction of irrigation works complementing the works constructed by the Corps of Engineers. . . . It can hardly be questioned that the best way of accomplishing this objective is under the tested procedures of the Federal reclamation laws. Accordingly, I recommend that suitable provision also be made in the bill for the undertaking by the Bureau of Reclamation, in the form and manner prescribed by these laws, of reclamation works connected with or dependent upon projects covered by the bill.

Such a provision, applicable to all navigation and flood control projects to be constructed in the future was enacted as Section 8 of the Flood Control Act of 1944.

When it became apparent that, despite Administration policy, the Congress was going to authorize the Kings River and other Central Valley projects under flood control law, Administration supporters sought to make certain that the new policy of Section 8 would apply, so that the irrigation benefits of these projects would become subject to repayment under reclamation law and to the acreage and speculation restrictions of that law. They feared that some question might arise with respect to the Central Valley projects because these projects did not require the construction of additional Federal works for the distribution of irrigation water and because of the nature of the language of the Bill relating to these specific projects.

The following interchange on the floor of the Senate between Senator Hill (Ala.), the acting Majority Leader, and Senator Overton (La.), Chairman of the Subcommittee on Flood Control of the Committee on Commerce and floor manager of the Bill, can leave no question, however, as to the intent of Congress (in the technical sense) that the reclamation law be made applicable to all Central Valley projects:

SENATOR HILL. There still seems to be confusion on the part of some Senators with reference to the application of reclamation laws in regard to some of these projects.

I heard the distinguished Senator from Louisiana, when the bill was under consideration, and I think he made it very clear. However, I wish to ask this question: Is it not a fact that section 8 of this bill, as agreed to in conference, makes some reclamation laws applicable to the handling of irrigation water of any of the projects, including California projects, where it is found that irrigation may be carried out? I ask the Senator in charge of the bill whether it is not a fact that the President wanted the California projects in this bill constructed under the Bureau of Reclamation so that the water policies would conform to reclamation laws?

SENATOR OVERTON. The Senator is correct with respect to the projects in the so-called Central Valley of California. The President wrote me and the chairman of the subcommittee in this regard. However, in view of the fact that the Senate amendment made not only the California projects but all such projects subject to irrigation laws, and in view of the fact that the House concurred in this action by agreeing to section 8 of the Senate bill, I am sure that the President will feel that we have met the problem which he raised. Section 8 of the bill clearly places reclamation uses of water from these projects under the Secretary of the Interior and under the applicable reclamation laws. No project in this bill which may include irrigation features is exempted from the reclamation laws.

SENATOR HILL. I thank the Senator.

SENATOR OVERTON. The Senate amendment made not only the California projects, but all such projects subject to the irrigation law. In view of the fact the House concurred in that action by agreeing to section 8 of the bill, I am sure the Senator from Alabama will feel that we have met the question which he has raised. As I stated a while ago, section 8 of the bill clearly places reclamation uses of waters from all projects authorized in this bill under the Secretary of the Interior and under the applicable reclamation laws.

With this assurance that the irrigation features of the Central Valley developments would be subject to reclamation law, Secretary Ickes recommended that the President sign the Flood Control Bill. He said:

. . . I recommend that the President approve H.R. 4485. . . .

Were H.R. 4485 to be approved, the situation of the California projects would be as described below. The Corps of Engineers would be authorized to build a number of projects in the Central Valley area of California, including the Kings River project and the Kern River project. However, the power generated at those projects would be disposed of by the Secretary of the Interior in accordance with the provisions of section 5 of the bill, an excellent incorporation in law of the public power policy of the President. Under section 8 of the bill, the use of water from those projects for irrigation purposes would be subject to the jurisdiction of the Secretary of the Interior and would be governed by the Federal reclamation laws. In net effect, therefore, while the Corps of Engineers would be authorized to construct the projects and to operate them for flood control purposes, their use for reclamation and power purposes would be governed by the reclamation laws and by the public power provisions of section 5, and their administration for these purposes would be vested in the Secretary of the Interior. Hence these projects can and will be integrated into the Central Valley Project. I believe that the undertaking of physical construction by the Corps of Engineers, instead of by the Bureau of Reclamation, if that ultimately becomes necessary, is a price worth paying for the sweeping defeat of the California interests who oppose the power policies and the land policies of the Administration. True the matter of construction is not without significance in the programming of further development of public power and reclamation in the Central Valley of California. However, if the California interests attempt to hinder a construction program that is in the public interest, their attempts can be dealt with when they are made.

The President signed the bill on December 23, 1944, but immediately instructed the Secretary of War to make no allocation of funds, or submit any estimate of appropriations, either for the construction or for the preparation of detailed plans for the construction of projects authorized by the Bill, until such proposed allocations of funds or estimates of appropriations had been taken up with the Bureau of the Budget for the President's approval. This instruction was designed to insure that no further work whatsoever be done on the Central Valley projects and certain others until the interests of the Departments of the Interior and War were fully reconciled.

Rivers and Harbors Act of 1945[11]

Immediately when it became apparent that the Kings River and other Central Valley projects, though authorized by flood control law, were to be made subject to the reclamation law for irrigation benefits, those interests in California which had worked hardest to obtain Engineer, rather than Reclamation, construction and operation of the projects in the Upper San Joaquin sought exemption of the Central Valley from the acreage and speculation restrictions of the reclamation law, even though reclamation law would apply in other respects. Representative Elliott of Kern, Kings, and Tulare Counties pressed hard for such an exemption in the pending Rivers and Harbors Bill. The House enacted the exemption. In the light of determined Presidential opposition to the provision and an aroused public concern over the distribution of benefits from Federal expenditures, the Senate eliminated the exemption. The Congress came to an end with the two Houses deadlocked over the so-called Elliott rider. The new Congress in 1945 hurriedly enacted the Rivers and Harbors Bill without the controversial provision. No attempt will be made in this case study to follow the history of current legislation to alter the 160-acre law in its application to the Central Valley. Suffice it to say that the Bureau of Reclamation has recognized the desirability of some modification in the application of acreage restriction to certain areas in the Central Valley, though it remains completely opposed to repeal of the limitation. What will eventually happen is uncertain; as late as 1948, the law remained unchanged.

[11] Most of the information on the Rivers and Harbors Act of 1945 obtained from the following:

(a) 90 *C.R.*, pp. 2921-4, 8875, 9478, 9493, 9745, 9787
(b) Cong., 78/2, Senate, Committee on Commerce, *Hearings on Rivers and Harbors* (H.R. 3961), Pt. 4, p. 529; Pt. 5; Pt. 6, p. 993; Report 903
(c) Cong., 79/1, Senate Report 22 and House Report 63
(d) 91 *C.R.*, p. 1381.

Appropriations for Preconstruction, 1945[12]

As of January 1, 1945, then, the Kings River project was authorized for construction by both the Bureau of Reclamation and the Corps of Engineers. The conflict between the two administrative agencies thus became one over appropriations. Whichever bureau could first obtain funds from the Congress for preconstruction and construction operations would thereby in effect be designated as constructing agency.

The President still favored construction by the Bureau of Reclamation, in spite of the action of Congress in passing the Flood Control Bill of 1944. In his budget for Fiscal Year 1946, submitted to Congress in January 1945, the President approved an item of $490,000 for the Bureau of Reclamation for preliminary work on the Kings River project; he did not submit any request for the Engineers for this project. However, before the House Committee on Appropriations had reported out the Interior Department Appropriation Bill, the Congress had added to the President's budget request for the Corps of Engineers an amount to cover the preparation of detailed plans for the Kings River project by the Engineer Department. In signing the War Department Civil Functions Appropriation Bill on April 2, 1945, President Roosevelt stated his serious objection to the provision in the Bill authorizing the Corps of Engineers to commence pre-

[12] Most of the information on the appropriations for preconstruction operations obtained from the following:

(a) Cong., 79/1, House and Senate, Hearings, reports, and debate on the War Department Civil Functions Appropriation Bill for 1946 (H.R. 2126)
(b) Cong., 79/1, House and Senate, Hearings, reports, and debate on Interior Department Appropriation Bill for 1946 (H.R. 3024)
(c) Cong., 79/1, House and Senate, Hearings, reports, and debate on First Deficiency Appropriation Bill for 1945 (H.R. 2374)
(d) Cong., 79/2, Senate, Committee on Appropriations, *Hearings on War Department Civil Functions Appropriation Bill for 1947* (H.R. 5400), pp. 521-3

construction operations on the Central Valley projects. He said:

I have approved reluctantly H.R. 2126, the War Department civil functions appropriation bill, fiscal year 1946.

Notwithstanding the fact that the bill contains appropriations for certain worthwhile purposes, I have been reluctant to sign it because of the fact that it contains also appropriations for work by the Corps of Engineers in connection with projects in the Central Valley area of California, such as the projects in the Kings and Kern Rivers and tributaries.

On a number of occasions, I have expressed the opinion that these projects, which are predominantly irrigation projects, should be constructed and administered under the Federal reclamation laws. The provision of funds now for plans for their construction by the Corps of Engineers may affect adversely existing Federal reclamation work in the Central Valley area and has a tendency, in my judgment, to undermine the established policy which seeks, through Federal reclamation projects, to create farm homes while providing, to the fullest practicable extent, for reimbursement of costs.

I am convinced that the Congress, which has sought by all appropriate means in the past to preserve and to extend the 40-year-old Federal reclamation policy, will realize, as I do, that all of these projects in the Central Valley area of California are, in fact interrelated units, comprising one scheme of Federal reclamation; that the construction and operation of some of them by the Army engineers, while others are under construction and operation by the Bureau of Reclamation, leads to conflicts of policy and jurisdiction and to operation difficulties—adding up to an administrative headache—and resulting in depriving not only California but the Nation of ultimate benefits which should be derived from vast expenditure of public funds in connection with the Central Valley reclamation plan.

Accordingly, I propose in the near future to submit to the Congress recommendations for legislation transferring jurisdiction over all of these projects in the Central Valley of California to the Bureau of Reclamation, Department of the Interior.

After considerable debate the Congress denied the appropriation requested for the Bureau of Reclamation. The Secretary of the Interior, in May 1945, submitted to the new President a draft message to Congress to effectuate President Roosevelt's proposal to transfer jurisdiction of the Central Valley projects. President Truman deferred action on this message pending further negotiations between the two Departments on the whole Central Valley matter and pending the completion by the two Departments of comprehensive basin reports on the Sacramento and San Joaquin Rivers.

Application of Section 8 to Central Valley[13]

If the Corps of Engineers were to build the Kings River project, and if the reclamation law were made to apply to the irrigation benefits to be derived therefrom, it would be essential that the Bureau of Reclamation make all required arrangements with local interests, including the negotiation of repayment contracts, *before* actual construction of the dam was undertaken. As has been seen, the Kings River area, like most of the Upper San Joaquin, is one in which the very construction of a reservoir and the release of water therefrom will yield irrigation benefits without the necessity for the construction of supplemental irrigation delivery works. Thus, it would be almost impossible to secure repayment contracts or to enforce acreage limitations and speculation controls after the reservoirs are in operation, for there would be no effective and economical means of denying irrigation benefits to those who failed to comply.

President Truman had this situation in mind when he wrote to the Secretary of War in June 1945 concerning all projects authorized

[13] Most of the information on application of Section 8 of the Flood Control Act of 1944 obtained from the following:

(a) Cong., 79/2, Senate, Committee on Appropriations, *Hearings on War Department Civil Functions Appropriation Bill for 1947* (H.R. 5400), pp. 521-3

(b) Proceedings of California Water Conference, December 6-7, 1945, State Capitol, Sacramento, California, pp. 72-75

(c) Cong., 80/1, House, Doc. 136

(d) Corps of Engineers, Supplement to Comprehensive Report, Sacramento-San Joaquin Basin Streams, California, July 1948 under flood control law but involving irrigation benefits. The President desired that (1) the Department of the Interior be given full opportunity to participate; (2) the Department of the Interior be given full opportunity and a sufficient period of time in which to negotiate repayment contracts *before* any construction was begun; and (3) the Engineer Department, in discussing any project plans with other authorities, make it perfectly plain that the water users can receive water only under reclamation law, including all requirements for repayment. The pertinent paragraph of the President's letter follows:

I recognize that in this as in other areas the conflict among Federal agencies arises in part from the different laws under which the various agencies operate. I believe, nevertheless, that the disharmony could be reduced through the conscientious effort of those engaged in the work. In this connection, in consonance with the Flood Control Act of 1944 which clearly established the intent of the Congress to support and maintain the principles of the Federal reclamation laws for all irrigation uses of water in connection with flood-control projects, I desire that, in connection with the development and construction of any flood-control projects in which irrigation features may have a direct relation, the Department of the Interior be given full opportunity to participate and that, before any construction is begun or contracts for construction advertised or awarded, that Department be given full opportunity and a sufficient period of time in which to negotiate such repayment contracts as are inherent in the plan of development. It is my desire that in discussing such plans or projects with other authorities it be made perfectly plain that the water users can receive water only under the reclamation laws, including the requirement that they make appropriate reimbursement to the Federal Government for all waters received in consequence of the construction or operation of flood-control projects.

Despite these specific instructions from the Chief Executive, the Chief of Engineers proposed to commence construction of the Kings River project as soon as labor and materials became available after the war; he did not propose to wait for the Bureau of Reclamation to negotiate. In the face of the legislative history of the provision and of the instructions of the President, the Chief of Engineers held that Section 8 of the Flood Control Law had no application to projects in which additional Federal works for distribution of irrigation water were not needed; that instead jurisdiction over payments by local interests for water conservation benefits in the San Joaquin Valley was vested in the War Department.

In the fall of 1945, General Robins, the Deputy Chief of Engineers, went to the West Coast and delivered several widely reported public addresses in which he informed California water users that Section 8 of the Flood Control Act did not apply to the lower Central Valley projects; that water users, therefore, would not be subject to the 160-acre law and other limitations of reclamation law, and that the Corps of Engineers planned to commence construction of some of the projects, including the Kings River project, as soon as funds were made available.

The Sacramento *Bee* of August 21, 1945, reported:

Major General Thomas M. Robins, deputy chief of the U. S. Corps of Army Engineers, told Sacramento civic leaders yesterday the people of the central valleys have been denied flood control by a "lot of arguments that are neither here nor there" on what should be done with the water behind proposed dams.

"If Californians would wake up and get the water first and then decide what to do with it she would be better off," General Robins declared. He added that by the time water problems are settled "we may all be dead."

The Fresno *Bee* of August 17, 1945, reported:

General Robins said . . . Section 8 does not apply to projects in the upper San Joaquin Valley and could not without jeopardizing users of water from the streams now.

The General won great favor for his organization among California water users on this field trip to the Central Valley. The promise to provide irrigation benefits with none of the restrictions of reclamation law, despite Section 8 of the Flood Control Law, was a happy one for present landowners in the area.

Similarly, the Chief of Engineers in a letter to the Governor of California of December 3, 1945, stated:

The actual agreements for such repayment will be between local interests and the War Department. It is not mandatory under the law that these agreements comply with the provisions of the Reclamation Acts. . . .

Without going into details of later developments, it should be noted that, due to constant pressure from the President, the Chief of Engineers subsequently withdrew from his position with respect to the applicability of Section 8 to the Kings River project. However, he has maintained that position with respect to other Central Valley projects. As late as July 1948, the Chief of Engineers, in a supplemental report on the Sacramento-San Joaquin River Basins, stated with reference to the Flood Control Act of 1944, "In substance, the law provides that the Secretary of the Army will make agreements for repayment to the United States for conservation storage when used. Under instructions from the President, a somewhat different procedure is actually being followed in the case of the Kings River Project in California in determining repayment under the Flood Control Act of 1944."

Furthermore, the Chief of Engineers did not change his position with respect to a number of Central Valley projects, including the Kings River project, that they should be built immediately, allowing no delay for the Bureau of Reclamation to negotiate repayment contracts.

Appropriations for Construction, 1946[14]

The President's budget requests for postwar public works did not include any funds for the beginning of construction of the Upper San Joaquin multiple-purpose projects. "In order that there may be no misunderstanding of the Bureau of the Budget action on these . . . estimates and that War Department witnesses testifying before the appropriation committees of Congress may have full knowledge thereof," the Director of the Budget informed the Secretary of War that the Engineer Department request for funds for the Kings and Kern River projects had been eliminated pending completion by the War and Interior Departments of their comprehensive reports on the Central Valley and "in advance of a decision by him [the President] as to the course to be followed on these works."

Without waiting for any further decision from the President, the representative of the Corps of Engineers nevertheless stated before the Senate Appropriations Committee, with respect to the San Joaquin River projects, that "we are ready to make a definite recommendation to undertake the construction, sir, and we included that in the estimates to the Bureau of the Budget." The Senate Committee added to the War Department Civil Functions Appropriation Bill $2 million to commence construction on both the Kings and Kern River projects with the proviso that none of the appropriation for the Kings River be used for construction of the dam "until the Secretary of War has received the reports as to the division of costs between flood control, navigation, and other water uses from the Bureau of Reclamation and local organizations and shall have made a determination as to what the allocation shall be." The reports were to be made not later than nine months from the enactment of the Appropriation Bill.

While the bill was in conference, the President on March 30, 1946, sent letters to the majority leaders of the House and Senate recommending that the $2 million appropriation be deleted, but that if it were allowed to remain, satisfactory provision be made to insure repayment under reclamation law.

The President's request for elimination of the appropriation aroused some public sympathy as the following editorials reveal:

From San Francisco *News*, April 4, 1946:

President Truman exercised wise statesmanship yesterday in asking congressional leaders to hold up final action on appropriations for dams on the Kern and Kings Rivers until settlement of the

[14] Most of the information on appropriations for construction obtained from the following:

(a) Cong., 79/1, House and Senate, Hearings, reports, and debate on First Deficiency Appropriation Bill for 1946 (H.R. 4805)
(b) Cong., 79/2, House and Senate, Hearings, reports, and debate on War Department Civil Functions Appropriation Bill for 1947 (H.R. 5400)
(c) Cong., 79/2, House and Senate, Hearings, reports, and debate on Interior Department Appropriation Bill for 1947 (H.R. 6335)

conflict between the Army Engineers and the Reclamation Bureau over development of the Central Valley project.

There is need for adjustment between the 2 Federal agencies. Conflicting statements emanating from both have confused the situation in the public mind and, we fear, also in the minds of some of the representatives of the 2 services. It was for this reason that the President called upon both to report in detail their plans for development of California's inland waters. These reports either are in his hands or soon will be. He should have a chance to study them before Congress acts upon recommendations contained therein.

The Army Engineers insist that there is no difference between them and the Reclamation Bureau. With respect to the type and size of the proposed dams on the Kern and Kings Rivers, that is true. But with respect to other features, such as repayment of the cost of the dams from use of water for irrigation and power, and the 160-acre limitation feature, the Reclamation Bureau indicates a decided difference of opinion. And it is naive to claim no controversy exists over other parts of the Central Valley Project. The Reclamation Bureau has made known its positive assumption that the undertaking is primarily concerned with reclamation—not flood control and navigation, the fields to which the Army Engineers are limited.

So long as these two Federal services are not in agreement upon principles governing the development of California's valuable inland waters the danger of improper development will continue to exist. If that danger should become reality, California's resources might suffer permanent injury.

Hence the *News* is glad to see President Truman's move to intervene and hold up construction until the differences can be adjusted.

From Washington *Post*, March 30, 1946:

. . . Similarly, it was the clear purpose of the Senate when it passed the 1944 Flood Control Act authorizing these dams, among others, to apply the reclamation laws to all flood control projects where any irrigation water would be developed. But the assistant chief of the Army Corps of Engineers, Major General Thomas M. Robins, says flatly that if his agency does the job the 160-acre provision will not apply.

We do not suppose that more than a few members of the Senate understood this or recognized its grave implications when they passed the appropriation measure adding the Kern and Kings River dams to those for which the House appropriated. The measure is now in conference. We hope that the conferees will kill this slick deal of their own accord. If they fail to do so, a Presidential veto is in order. For the whole basis of the reclamation program is threatened by this shoddy evasion of it. Whether, in the end, the Army Engineers or the Bureau of Reclamation builds these dams, the reclamation laws should be rigorously applied to the lands enriched by them.

While the Appropriation Bill was under consideration by the Senate-House conference, the Chief of Engineers, on a field trip to California, publicly urged immediate construction of the disputed dams by his organization. The San Francisco *Chronicle* of April 3, 1946, reported:

Immediate construction of flood control dams in California was urged yesterday by Lt. Gen. Raymond A. Wheeler, Chief of the Army Engineers.

"These dams should have high urgency because of their immediate need for flood control," he said.

Approximately $2,000,000 has been voted by the Senate for start of construction on low level flood control dams on the Kern and Kings rivers but has not yet been approved in the House.

The conference committee eliminated the appropriation for the Kern River but retained that for the Kings River and modified the language to insure that allocation of costs be made by the Secretary of War *with the concurrence of* the Secretary of the Interior.

In signing the appropriation measure the President issued a special statement impounding the funds appropriated for the Kings River project pending (1) determination of allocation of costs and (2) the making of necessary repayment arrangements. The President's statement follows:

The War Department civil functions appropriation bill, 1947 (H.R. 5400), which I approved on May 2, 1946, makes appropriations for a number of thoroughly worthwhile projects that will further the development of the water resources of the nation. I am also glad to note that the Congress, by the addition of certain provisos to the item for the Kings River project, California, has afforded an opportunity for assuring that the Federal reclamation policy, including repayment and the wide distribution of benefits, will apply to that project. This is in accordance with the view that I have heretofore expressed and the position repeatedly taken by the late President Roosevelt. It is consistent with the policies laid down by the Congress in the Flood Control Act of 1944.

Consistently with the action taken by the Congress on the Kings River project, I propose in the near future to send to the Congress my recommendations regarding an over-all plan for the development of the water resources of the Central Valley area in California. I am withholding action in that regard pending receipt of comments from the Governor of California. The over-all plan for the Central Valley area of California will include means for achieving comprehensive development and utilization of its water resources for all beneficial purposes, including irrigation and power, and it will provide adequately for flood protection. It will have regard for the need for integrated operation of reservoirs which is essential for complete utilization of the land and water resources of the area. It will provide for application in the Central Valley area of the Federal reclamation policy—including repayment of costs and the wide distribution of benefits. I hope that the Congress will, by the adoption of that plan, act to put an end to a situation which, in California and in Washington, has been productive of administrative confusion as well as confusion to the general public.

In the meantime, in view of the legislative history of the provisos in the Kings River item, and in view of the disadvantageous position in which the government would be placed if repayment arrangements were unduly postponed, I am asking the Director of the Budget to impound the funds appropriated for construction of the project, pending determination of the allocation of costs and the making of the necessary repayment arrangements.

Allocation of Costs and Repayment Arrangements[15]

Release of funds for construction of the Kings River project, then, was not to be made until the Corps and the Bureau had come to an agreement on the allocation of costs and until adequate repayment arrangements had been negotiated.

With respect to division of costs, the various agencies recommended as follows:

[15] Most of the information on allocation of costs and repayment arrangements obtained from Cong., 80/1, House, Doc. 136

	Irrigation	*Flood Control*
Department of the Interior	$14,250,000	$19,250,000
Corps of Engineers	13,232,000	20,268,000
State of California	10,000,000	23,500,000
Local water users	10,000,000	23,500,000

After considerable negotiation, the Secretary of War agreed to accept the Reclamation figure as the ceiling on the amount to be repaid by water users. In a letter to the President, he said:

> In arriving at his recommended allocation the Chief of Engineers has given careful consideration to views of both Federal and local irrigation interests; and in the normal case I would consider that he had arrived at a solution equitable to both of those interests. The Secretary of the Interior is firmly convinced that any repayment less than $14,250,000, which he has found to be well within the repayment ability of the water users, would adversely affect adjacent Federal reclamation programs in the Central Valley of California; and because irrigation features are involved in this project I feel that the views and requirements of the Department of the Interior must be weighed carefully. Likewise the local agencies, on the basis of actual experience with irrigation in this area, present strong support for their lower evaluation of irrigation benefits and for their offer of repayment of $10,000,000. Although differences are relatively small, there is no agreement on a specific figure. Obviously any division of cost, to be of practical value and in the public interest, must be one agreed to by water users who must pay the bill and by the Bureau of Reclamation which you have charged with making repayment arrangements. I therefore determine, in order to meet the requirements of existing law, that the division of cost to irrigation should be set at an amount not to exceed $14,250,000, the exact amount to be as agreed upon between the Bureau of Reclamation and the local agencies concerned.

By placing a ceiling on the amount to be repaid by water users rather than a fixed allocation, the report of the Secretary of War would appear to conform to neither the law nor the President's instructions. However, the Secretary of the Interior concurred in the proposal, and the President transmitted it to Congress on February 17, 1947.

No explanation has ever been offered for the acceptance by the Secretary of the Interior and the President of this allocation proposal, which was presumably not wholly satisfactory to the former and which was clearly in contravention of instructions issued by the latter. The President, to be sure, was faced with a proposal approved by two members of his Cabinet who had previously been in disagreement on the matter. If the President refused to concur, he would be reopening a dispute that had been resolved.

Behind this specific factor may have lain other influences deriving from a change in the administrative environment. Secretary Ickes had resigned in February 1946 and had been succeeded by Secretary Krug in March 1946. On taking office Secretary Krug made known his firm distaste for the jurisdictional disputes to which his predecessor had never shown the slightest aversion.

Whatever the influence of factors such as this, the acceptance of the allocation proposal remains surprising. Even more surprising, however, is the action of the President and Secretary Krug with respect to the repayment provisions of the Secretary of War's report. The necessity for the completion of repayment negotiations *before* construction of the Kings River project has been emphasized. The Chief of Engineers, however, was not willing to wait for the Bureau of Reclamation to negotiate repayment contracts before he started construction. In the report on allocation, the War Department proposed "that the Kings River project be constructed *immediately* and operated *initially* for flood control. The project will not be operated for irrigation until agreement has been reached between the Bureau of Reclamation and local water users on the division of cost and on repayment arrangements." However, due to the physiographic and hydrologic characteristics of the area, this was not physically possible. It was estimated that at least 50 per cent of the irrigation benefits would result from the very construction of the dam, whether or not its operation was limited to flood control. And once the dam was constructed it would be difficult, if not impossible, for the Army, even if it were so inclined, to resist the pressure from local interests to release water in the most economical manner from the point of view of downstream water users.

These circumstances were well known to the Secretary of the Interior and the President. Nevertheless, the Secretary finally concurred in the recommendation of the Secretary of War. The President transmitted the report to Congress and released the $1,000,000, instructing the Secretary of the Interior "to continue work in connection with repayment agreements to the end that full benefits of the project can be attained promptly upon completion of construction and that Federal reclamation policies can be carried out." Construction was commenced soon thereafter.

The Bureau of Reclamation, however, is experiencing difficulty in negotiating any repayment contracts whatsoever. The attitude of the landowners is about as follows: "Let's just wait and see how this project is operated for flood control only. Then, if there would appear to be significant advantages to our land in a change in project operation, we can consider negotiating contracts. But even then, we shall have to balance the advantages of whatever needed additional water can be provided by a change in project operation against the disadvantages to us, as present landowners, of application of the acreage restrictions and speculation controls of the reclamation law." It may well be that the Federal government will never receive a penny for a large part of the irrigation benefits provided by this project, and the benefits will accrue to the present owners of land rather than to the small independent farmer around whom the whole philosophy of Federal reclamation has been built.

A Change in the Allocation of Benefits—Why?[16]

In 1940 the Corps of Engineers informed Congress that the Kings River project was

[16] Most of the information on benefit allocations obtained from the following:

(a) NRPB file NA-NRPB 579.7
(b) Cong., 76/3, House, Doc. 630
(c) Cong., 80/1, House, Doc. 136
(d) Bureau of Reclamation, Transcript of public meeting on Kings River project, Fresno Memorial Auditorium, Fresno, Calif., July 30, 1946
(e) Corps of Engineers, Supplement to Comprehensive Flood Control Survey Report on Sacramento-San Joaquin Basin Streams, Calif., July 1948

dominantly a flood control project. The distribution of annual benefits was calculated to be $1,185,000 for flood control and $995,000 for irrigation—a ratio of 1.19 to 1 for *flood control.*

Partly on the basis of this analysis, the House Committee on Flood Control justified its conclusion that the project was properly one for authorization and construction under flood control law.

In 1948, with the project well under way, the Engineer Department recalculated prospective annual benefits as follows: for flood control, $2,126,000; for irrigation, $3,382,000—a ratio of 1.59 to 1 for *irrigation.* According to this later analysis, then, the project ceased to be primarily a flood control project, even using the Engineer Department criterion—ratio of prospective benefits allocated to different purposes for each individual project. And yet it is being built and will be operated by the Corps of Engineers.

The progressive changes in benefit allocations are illustrated in the following table:

DISTRIBUTION OF BENEFITS AS BETWEEN FLOOD CONTROL AND IRRIGATION—CORPS OF ENGINEERS REPORTS ON KINGS RIVER PROJECT

Report	*Preliminary Draft Report* 1939	*Report Submitted to Congress—* 1940	*Figures in Connection with Cost Allocation Report,* 1946	*Supplement to Comprehensive Report—*1948
Flood Control	$1,185,000	$1,185,000	$3,377,000	$2,126,000
Irrigation	430,000	995,000	2,179,000	3,382,000
Ratio: Flood Control to Irrigation	2.75:1	1.19:1	1.55:1	0.63:1

The reasons for this complete reversal in benefit calculations are not known. However, it might be pointed out that the flood control benefits from the Kings River project accrue largely to the Tulare Lake area; that three other streams on which the Corps of Engineers is authorized to build multiple-purpose projects (Kaweah, Tule, Kern Rivers) also flow into the closed basin of Tulare Lake and contribute to flood damages there; that there exists the possibility of shifting the distribution among the four projects of the total flood benefits that will result in the Tulare Lake area when all four dams are built; that there is no longer a jurisdictional advantage for the Corps in showing flood control benefits greater than irrigation benefits for the Kings River project, as the dam is already being constructed under their supervision, whereas there may be an advantage in showing a favorable ratio of flood control to irrigation benefits for certain of the other projects.

Kings River and the Central Valley[17]

For illustrative purposes this case study has been concerned with the Kings River project. The history of this project, however, is not unique. Very much the same story is true of other river developments in the Upper San Joaquin—Isabella Reservoir on the Kern River, Success Reservoir on the Tule River, and Terminus Reservoir on the Kaweah River. Large parts of the case history have application to multiple-purpose projects planned or authorized by both agencies elsewhere in the Central Valley (such as New Melones Reservoir on Stanislaus River, Folsom Reservoir on American River, Bullards Bar or Narrows Reservoir

[17] Most of the information on the Central Valley comprehensive plans obtained from the following:

(a) U. S. Department of the Interior, Comprehensive Plan for Water Resources Development, Central Valley Basin, California, Project Planning Report No. 2-4, 0-3, Nov. 1945, mimeo.

(b) State of California, Department of Public Works, Views and Recommendations on Proposed Report of Secretary of the Interior Entitled Comprehensive Plan for Water Resources Development, Central Valley, California, April 1946, mimeo.

(c) State of California, Department of Public Works, Views and Recommendations on Proposed Report of Chief of Engineers, U. S. Army, entitled Comprehensive Flood Control Survey Report on Sacramento-San Joaquin Basin Streams, California, April 1946, mimeo.

on Yuba River, Monticello Reservoir on Putah Creek, Indian Valley or Wilson Valley Reservoir on Cache Creek, Iron Canyon or Table Mountain Reservoir on Sacramento River, Black Butte Reservoir on Stony Creek), as well as to river developments in the arid and semi-arid West outside of the Central Valley of California. All the Central Valley projects are covered in the two separate comprehensive basin-wide reports prepared by the Corps and the Bureau for the Central Valley. In these reports the conflicting water-use philosophies of the two agencies are shown up in sharp contrast in their respective concepts of comprehensive planning. The stage was set for a new era of competition on a large number of multiple-purpose projects in the same area, at a time when funds were likely to become available for large-scale activity.

The two reports were submitted to the Governor of California and to the Executive Office of the President in November 1945. As they were obviously in conflict, the Executive Office (Budget Bureau) returned them to the originating agencies for reconciliation of differences —it was hoped, through the Federal Inter-Agency River Basin Committee. As of this writing (December 1948), over three years later, the reports have not been reconciled; they have not been submitted to the Congress. The Governor of California has submitted his views on each report; but the Inter-Agency Basin Committee has been unable to do its job; and the Executive Office of the President has been unable to do more than prevent the submittal of conflicting reports to the Congress. The affirmative action required to develop a co-ordinated basin-wide plan is still ahead.

CONCLUDING COMMENTS

This case has been written to illuminate the problems it poses for the President in the co-ordination of government activities. These problems need to be seen in historical perspective. During the first third of this century there was no apparent need for co-ordination between the Bureau and the Corps. They pursued different objectives, but they did not get in each other's way.

The Bureau was the child of the agrarian unrest prior to the turn of the century, and of President Theodore Roosevelt's interest in conservation. It was endowed with the intellectual baggage of the time, a Jeffersonian concept of self-reliant individualism in farming, applying the principles of the Homestead Act to the conditions of the arid Western lands with the practical assistance of Federal investments in large-scale irrigation works. Reclamation policy stressed benefits for small operator-owners to the point of excluding holders of more than 160 acres; and it obligated water users to pay, within what was believed to be a lenient estimate of their capacities, for benefits as these were realized. Its main outlines were thus congenial to deeply rooted traditions of American life, and it found a growing acceptance in part, at least, because it was applied to otherwise largely worthless public lands where the disturbance of vested local interests was at a minimum. It found official sponsorship among many Western congressmen and senators, in the Secretary of the Interior, and in the White House. It survived the argument sometimes made during the agricultural depression after World War I that less rather than more farms were needed, perhaps because of the attendant local benefits of public works spending.

The Corps, on the other hand, is much older than the Bureau. It forms a professional guild, with the added prestige of the uniform. Its technical work has commanded general respect —it was capable of building the Panama Canal. It operates in most congressional districts around the country, and its public relations have been of the best. Its procedures have been geared over the years to the political system as that operated characteristically in the United States, at least until recently—a system whereby bureau chiefs annually made their individual arrangements and commitments with the relevant congressional committees, under the surveillance of locally powerful interest groups, in this case organized nationally into the Rivers and Harbors Congress with members of the United States Congress as its nominal officers. The votes necessary to ratify these arrangements were assembled by *ad hoc* alliances and trading. This system, too, is congenial to long tradition, and to the dispersion of political power functionally and geographically; it is familiar to students of tariff history as well as of public works.

With all these differences the Bureau and the Corps went their separate ways for years. The line between them was partly geographical, partly functional. The Bureau was restricted by its organic law to the lands which now comprise the 17 Western states, where the Corps was not much concerned. The Bureau specialized in irrigation works and later added incidental power developments. The Corps began much earlier with harbor improvements and river channel-dredging. In the 1920's it moved to the maintenance and construction of levees to protect cities on the lower Mississippi River. Levees provide only partial protection from floods; so the Corps inadvertently backed upstream, so to speak, into flood control as a major activity. Its jurisdiction over this function for the entire country was established by law in 1936.

What brought the two agencies into conflict, and therefore brought the need for co-ordination, were the obvious successes of the Boulder Canyon project and more especially of the TVA. These were the first large-scale multiple-purpose natural resource developments broadly conceived to transform the life of the areas involved. They were dramatic and popular. They challenged the adequacy of the concepts by which either the Bureau or the Corps had been working; and, in addition, the TVA provided a new model of autonomous regional organization that invited copying, and that automatically excluded the older agencies from operating in its territory. The Bureau and the Corps have since been in agreement that they want no more river valley authorities established. Apart from that point of agreement, however, both agencies have been easily and naturally drawn into competition to keep their positions in water development. The Kings River case is an episode in the competition. In arid lands, irrigation works require dam-building and dam-building leads to flood control and power development. Flood control also leads to dam-building and so to irrigation works and public power. In the West, the old jurisdictional boundaries disappeared, and a race ensued.

In that race the Bureau made the mental adjustment quickly. Its horizons were broadened; it embraced the multiple-purpose and basin-wide planning concepts, and it received energetic support from Secretary Ickes. It became particularly alert to public power potentialities. The Corps, on the other hand, exhibited the cultural lag that might have been expected from its training and its operating environment; and the heavy battalions, in terms of votes in Congress, have been on its side. By pursuing its course without apparent regard for the President's wishes, but with active cultivation of the support of its clientele, it has won the congressional authorizations and appropriations it sought. The result is a typical dilemma of the constitutional separation of powers, in political terms; and in terms of organization it is the difficulty to be expected when one agency is organized on the basis of major purpose—conservation uses of water—while another is organized on the basis of a special skill or technique—engineering. The end of the competition is not in sight, but it it unseemly and wasteful that it should continue.

In the circumstances, what alternatives have been, or are, open to the President? He might, of course, abandon his support of the Bureau; but to do so would be to turn his back not only on the whole course of natural resource development policy of the past two decades, but also on the evolution of his own office as the focus of policy and management in the Executive Branch since the Budget and Accounting Act of 1921. He might, alternatively, seek a viable new line of demarcation between the agencies. President Roosevelt attempted this when he announced the "dominant purpose" formula, at first on a project basis, and then basin-wide. The formula was unsatisfactory: both sides could accept it in principle without agreeing on which way it settled a particular case, since the estimates and allocations of costs to multiple purposes are susceptible of too much variation and manipulation.

Another attempt of this kind (which had some precedent at the Bonneville and Fort Peck dams) may be read in Sections 5 and 8 of the Flood Control Act of 1944: let the

Corps construct the multiple-purpose works for which it has congressional authorization, and even operate them for flood control or power generation purposes, but turn over the disposition of the irrigation water and power so produced to the Interior Department to administer according to its policies. But this formula too promised only a limited and uneasy truce, in the prevailing climate of opinion. The Bureau is critical of the Corps' original construction plans as hampering Bureau policies in their operation afterward, and it knows that possession is nine points in administration as well as in law—the Corps, once in, may not be dislodged. Moreover, the Congress cannot be counted on not to modify the formula in favor of the Corps as particular cases come along.

Another approach is the strengthening of central organs of co-ordination in the Executive Office to the point where the President's views can be imposed on the Corps, or at least the Corps' plans blocked in so far as they impinge on projects of the Bureau that have the President's support. President Roosevelt tried that too, without success, first through the National Resources Planning Board and later through the Budget Bureau, and President Truman has continued the effort, using the latter. But the Congress, sensing the danger to its customary way of handling public works inherent in the existence of the NRPB, abolished that body; and the Budget Bureau has so far been unequal to the task—Congress has disregarded its views in this field, however strenuously pushed.

A fourth possibility is co-ordination by amalgamation; that is, to merge the Bureau and the civil works functions of the Corps by a Reorganization Plan. The Hoover Commission has since recommended this solution. But in all the reorganization acts of the past decade the Congress has taken special pains to protect the autonomous position of the Corps. During the period reviewed there has not been the slightest apparent chance of pushing the Corps out of the civil works field, and it would require an extraordinary conjunction of circumstances to effect such a possibility within the foreseeable future.

A fifth and longer term possibility remains, that of reconciling the social objectives of the two agencies to a degree that would permit a working division of labor between them without mutual recrimination and suspicions. For the Bureau this would mean, at the very least, giving up its cherished policy of acreage limitations in favor of small owners, and acquiescing in the consolidation and enhancement of vested local interests, both in water and power use, to the detriment of new settlers and prospective urban beneficiaries of its projects. This would go hard with the Bureau, and if accepted for future projects, will naturally open up the question of extending equivalent concessions to existing reclamation projects. This could involve claims running possibly to many millions of dollars. The evidence of a single case is not conclusive, but the events of this case suggest that established reclamation policy confronts major obstacles when it is sought to be applied in areas already settled and partly developed, where local interests are strong and organized. It is certainly clear that there are many such areas in the West, where plans for water developments to be financed with Federal funds are being actively pushed, and also clear that the number of remaining untouched areas susceptible of development is few.

For the Corps, such a course would involve a more fundamental and therefore slower reeducation, to take account of values it has heretofore regarded lightly, and to reduce its reliance on the forces that have been its principal source of political strength. Some signs point in this direction, the Kings River case notwithstanding. What has happened to tariff policy under the Reciprocal Trade Agreements acts may some day come to public works too. It may be doubted whether the Corps can safely disregard indefinitely the expanding role of the Presidency and the balance of forces exerted on the Executive Office; and, if it ceases to do so, whether it will not be obliged to alter its traditional strategy for securing authorizations and funds. After all, the engineer services of the Corps can be counted on, in time, to be at the disposal of whatever public policy ultimately commands dominant political support. If this is a long-run possibility, however, it should be evident that it has not been an alternative in the sense of a choice open to any recent President within the term of his office. At present, then, we must conclude that the quest for co-ordination in this field has in practical terms meant Presidential maneuvering in support of the Bureau's policies against hostile congressional sentiment; and has so far resulted in either stalemate or defeat.

We may indeed wonder whether permanent peace—or lasting jurisdictional adjustment—between the two agencies is possible so long as they continue to hold conflicting concepts of administrative responsibility, and look to competing sources of power for their support. This question, sharply raised by this case, is as old as federalism and the separation of powers; the dispute over policy feeds on the division of authority. Here it is appropriate to observe that while the Congress may ultimately ratify a settlement, it is by the very nature of its own organization and procedure precluded from the role of a co-ordinating force.

This case leaves little doubt about two subsidiary points. One is that the task of co-ordination here, whether of policy or of jurisdiction, is beyond the capacity of an interdepartmental committee. The Federal Inter-Agency River Basin Committee, in the circumstances, can hardly act otherwise than as a council of ambassadors. The other is that conflict rather than co-ordination was fostered by permitting the two agencies not only to draw up but also to publish their rival plans. This procedure played into the hands of local interests, strengthened the Corps' position, and made the President's task much more difficult. Only the naive will suppose that it promoted democratic participation in administration.

In some case studies the outcome of interagency conflict is largely affected by the personalities of the principal actors; in others, institutional attitudes and agency loyalties are so firmly set that personalities make little difference. In this case we may speculate that the outcome would not have been altered, though the same end might have been reached sooner, if a less vigorous chief of the Bureau, or a less pugnacious Secretary of the Interior, or a less determined President had been in office. It is hardly conceivable that another Chief of Engineers would have behaved very differently.

Nor is this a significant case study in civil-military relations. The heads of the FBI and of the Passport Division in the State Department rely on similar forces and tactics to achieve, within the spheres of their respective technical services, results in every way comparable to those of the Chief of Engineers. It may only be noted in passing how ironical and illusory is the notion sometimes held, that because the President is constitutionally the Commander-in-Chief of the armed services, he can command the actions of anyone in military uniform.

On three further points the case does not afford materials enough for more than speculative inquiries. Supposing that the Central Valley lay not wholly within the State of California, but instead traversed two or three states, could the Bureau have expected to muster more effective local support, or to have divided its opposition? The question here is whether, as additional senators, representatives, and governors became directly involved, a different alignment would have resulted. This might depend on whether the interests of local users in the upper reaches of the watershed were substantially different from those further downstream, as has been the case with the Colorado and Missouri rivers.

Or, suppose the electric power potentialities of the project, instead of being an incidental concern to local water users and the residents of nearby towns, had been of such magnitude as to rival the main sources of power for the San Francisco Bay metropolitan region: would a major public power controversy have put the case in a decisively different setting? On this supposition, again, the range of contending interests would have been widened. In northern California the Pacific Gas & Electric Co. has long been a dominant influence exerted on the side of private power development. (Remember the controversy over the Hetch Hetchy project.) In the Kings River case, during the period reviewed, this influence never emerged from the background; presumably it would have supported the Corps' position if that had seemed necessary. In southern California, on the other hand, where it can be dramatized to appeal to a multitude of urban consumers, public power has been a successful crusading issue; and there are public power senators and representatives in other parts of the country, as well, who might be rallied in that cause. The injection of the power issue could therefore have been expected to bring new participants to the fight on both sides, though the outcome might well have remained unaltered.

These suppositions, however, highlight another question that is only implicit in the case as it stands: What are the effective and appropriate techniques for agencies that need to organize and use the support of interested publics?

We may leave the case with a somewhat more philosophical question, which underlies all those that have been raised previously. Are there any "scientific" criteria (sufficiently measurable to be useful) of the "public interest" in the development of water resources, for multiple purposes and according to a basin-wide plan, in an area where various special interest groups are already located? Or must we conclude (for lack of alternatives, or for some positive reason) that the "public interest" lies simply in whatever compromise of contending interests will, at a given time, bring agreement—an extension of the classical economists' view that out of the private pursuit of selfish ends comes the public good? Or is there possibly a third basis for judgment and appraisal? These questions go to the goals of public administration in a democracy.

Chronology

1937 First investigations of Kings River area by Corps of Engineers and Bureau of Reclamation

July 19, 1939 President confers with agencies on conflicting field reports

August 8, 1939 Tripartite Agreement

January 23, 1940 Reclamation report submitted to NRPB

January 27, 1940 NRPB notifies Engineers of receipt of Reclamation report and anticipation of Engineer report

January 30, 1940 Engineer report submitted direct to President

February 2, 1940 Engineer report transmitted to Congress

February 10, 1940 Reclamation report transmitted to Congress after NRPB recommends release

March 7, 1940 Interior recommends review of reports by NRPB

April 1940 Hearings on Kings River project by House Committee on Flood Control

May 29, 1940 President assigns project to Interior on dominant interest theory

April 1941 Hearings on Kings River project reopened

May 5, 1941 President reaffirms dominant interest policy in letters to Secretary of War and Congressman Whittington

August 13, 1941 Favorable report of Flood Control Committee on special bill to authorize Engineer construction

January 20, 1944 Secretary of Interior requests Secretary of War to ensure observance of President's policy in coming hearings

January 26, 1944 Secretary of War's reply

February 7, 1944 President restates dominant interest policy in letter to Congressman Whittington; also requests Reclamation operation of irrigation works of Engineer projects

February 9, 1944 House Flood Control Committee begins hearings

February 17, 1944 Congressman Whittington replies to President, disagreeing

March 7, 1944 President in reply applies dominant interest theory to whole river basin

March 1944 President requests $1,000,000 for Kings River operations by Reclamation

May 9, 1944 Flood Control Bill including Kings River project passes House

May 16, 1944 President sends note of instructions to Secretary of War

May 20, 1944 Senate Committee restores full amount for Reclamation previously removed by House Committee

June 17, 1944 Conference Committee omits funds for Reclamation operation

June 22, 1944 Senate Committee on Commerce retains Kings River project in Flood Control Bill

August 7, 1944 President writes Senator Overton opposing Committee action

December 12, 1944 Senators in debate announce application of Section 8 to Kings River

December 19, 1944 Congress adjourns deadlocked on Elliott rider (Rivers and Harbors Bill)

December 23, 1944 President signs Flood Control Bill but orders withholding of funds

February 22, 1945 New Congress passes bill without rider

January 1945 President recommends $490,000 for Reclamation for Kings River

April 2, 1945 President signs Civil Functions Appropriation Bill

May 19, 1945 Interior submits draft message to President

JUNE 2, 1945 President writes to Secretary of War to ensure application of Section 8

AUGUST 1945 General Robins publicly opposes President's policy

OCTOBER 16, 1945 Director of Budget eliminates Engineers funds for Kings and Kern River projects pending completion of comprehensive reports

DECEMBER 3, 1945 Chief of Engineers writes Governor of California denying application of Section 8

MARCH 18, 1946 Senate Appropriations Committee recommends $2,000,000 for Engineers

MARCH 30, 1946 President requests deletion of $2,000,000 appropriation

APRIL 3, 1946 Chief of Engineers publicly urges immediate construction

MAY 2, 1946 President signs Appropriation Bill requiring Interior concurrence in cost allocation and impounds funds

FEBRUARY 17, 1947 President transmits Secretary of War's report to Congress without objection; releases funds

JULY 1948 Chief of Engineers still denies applicability of Section 8 outside Kings River

Appendix A

Tripartite Agreement

PROCEDURE TO INSURE CO-OPERATION IN THE PREPARATION OF REPORTS ON MULTIPLE-PURPOSE PROJECTS

To permit agencies of the Departments of War, Interior, and Agriculture to co-operate more completely in the preparation of reports on multiple-purpose projects and to correlate the results to the greatest practicable extent, the following procedure is established:

1. When investigations on multiple-purpose projects are ordered by any one of the three Departments each of the others will be advised. The National Resources Planning Board will also be advised and will maintain liaison with all agencies concerned throughout the preparation of the reports.

2. To insure that prompt contact is established by field offices, whenever the Chief of Engineers, the Commissioner of the Bureau of Reclamation, or the Chief of the Bureau of Agricultural Economics shall determine that his organization has a direct responsibility in a project to be investigated by another agency, he shall notify the latter to that effect.

3. In all co-operative projects the field offices will be instructed to communicate and to confer with each other to:

(a) Determine what pertinent data is in existence and to arrange for the interchange of such data so as to avoid duplication of effort.

(b) Determine what pertinent data each agency intends to secure for its own purposes and to arrange a schedule which will avoid duplication and facilitate the concurrent submission of reports so far as practical.

(c) Arrange for interchange of information throughout the preparation of reports.

(d) Arrange for conferences between field offices during preparation of reports and when reports are completed and ready to go forward. Each office will be authorized to submit its comments on the reports of other agencies, such comments to be forwarded with the reports.

4. A conference will be held in Washington between affected agencies when the tentative draft of the final report is prepared so as to permit discussion of it prior to its submission in final form.

5. All work done by one agency at the request of and for the use of a second agency will be paid for by the latter; all work performed by one agency for its own purposes, even though the resulting data are made available to a second agency, shall be paid for by the former.

6. Information obtained by one agency from another will be treated as confidential until released by the giving agency or until the final report is released.

[SIGNED] *J. L. Schley*
Chief of Engineers

John C. Page
Commissioner, Bureau of Reclamation

Eric Englund
Acting Chief, Bureau of Agricultural Economics

Concurred in:
[SIGNED] *Charles W. Eliot*
Director, National Resources Planning Board
August 8, 1939

THE CAMBRIDGE CITY MANAGER

CONTENTS

INTRODUCTION

This case recounts the story of a running battle, occurring over a period of years, between the city manager of Cambridge, Massachusetts, and the city council, to which he was responsible, over the issue of pay raises for city employees and especially for members of the Police and Fire Departments.

The battle, it seems, was not to be avoided, partly because of peculiarities in the state law affecting Cambridge, partly because of the political background of the council-manager plan in Cambridge, and partly because of the personality and competence of the city manager himself.

The statute defining "Plan E" (the particular form of council-manager government adopted under state law by the Cambridge voters) gave directly to the manager certain powers and responsibilities, including the powers of the mayor under the previous form of government. The earlier mayor, and the present city manager, have had the responsibility of proposing appropriations and salary levels which the council normally does not have the power to increase. As a result, the Cambridge city manager has in effect the power to establish salary ceilings for city employees; and, save perhaps in times of depression, the power to establish ceilings is tantamount to the power to establish salary scales.

Under the normal council-manager charter, in contrast to this situation, power to establish basic pay scales does not rest with the manager. Most such charters (and the Code of Ethics of the International City Managers Association) do indeed provide that the city manager should have full discretion in acting on individual personnel cases; but under normal practice, the council decides the general questions of salary schedules and general pay raises by ordinance or by its control over appropriations, without any more disagreement with the manager than over any other question of municipal policy; if there is disagreement, it is solely on policy, not on jurisdiction. Accordingly, the Cambridge battle was not caused by the general theory of the council-manager plan but by the particular circumstances surrounding the application of the council-manager charter in Cambridge; indeed, so protracted and full-scale a battle would be unlikely to occur where legal control over wage scales was clearly and fully vested in the council.

To most city managers, then, the power of the Cambridge manager with respect to salary scales might well seem odd; but for Cambridgites, it was a survival from the past, and that fact made it seem entirely natural. Indeed, accepting it as natural, the city manager assumed that the power to establish salary scales was an inherent city manager responsibility, and he so interpreted the Code of Ethics of the International City Managers Association.[1] Under the particular circumstances of Massachusetts law and the Cambridge city charter, he was prepared to defend the position he took, even though, because of different provisions in other states, most members of the City Managers Association could not, or would not, take a similar view with respect to salary scales in their own city administrations.

Two additional constitutional and statutory provisions made the situation even more unusual and, given the structure of authority noted above, helped set the stage for the Cambridge battle. Under a special act passed by the Massachusetts legislature in 1935 (before the Cambridge council-manager plan was adopted), the salaries of members of the Police and Fire Departments in Cambridge were to be established by ordinance, i.e., by decision of the city council. In Cambridge, this provision constituted a breach in the authority of the executive, even though it had the effect of providing for these two departments a procedure common to the establishment of *all* municipal

[1] See Appendix A.

salaries in council-manager cities outside Massachusetts. Furthermore, salaries of school teachers and of clerical, janitorial, and other employees of the School Department were, under the state constitution, established by neither council nor manager but by the School Committee, an elective body of citizens wholly independent of both manager and city council; here was a second breach in the manager's authority; or, from the standpoint of the council, and taking their control of police and fire salaries as the norm, a second breach in the council's effective authority over wage scales.

By this legal framework, then, the council was empowered to raise salaries for the Police and Fire Departments, and the School Committee to raise salaries of all School Department employees. However, pay raises for a part of a working force must lead to raises for all, or in time efficient administration is impaired. Clearly, unless policy control over council, manager, and School Committee were established by a group independent of them, or unless the three forces could agree together about wage policy, conflict was likely. In Cambridge, for political reasons, no early agreement or centralizing of control was possible, and the respective powers, duties, and responsibilities of the three forces have come into conflict repeatedly.

John B. Atkinson took office as city manager of Cambridge on January 7, 1942, and within one month he and the majority in council had undergone what we might call Round One of a "pay raise match" that has had many rounds and may have more.

Certainly in that first encounter there was no real meeting of minds among the contending forces. It was a time of mutual uncertainty and suspicion for the manager and those councilors who favored a pay raise for employees—uncertainty of respective responsibilities, authority, and legal standing; suspicion of individual honesty and motives. In a sense, the two opposing forces spoke different languages. Those councilors who were most squarely behind the effort to raise municipal salaries were politicians of long standing. To them a "pay raise" was conceived in terms of what it meant to those who would get it—the men and their families. Many of their best friends were among the employee group. The issue was not wholly a personalized one, but the human meaning was central in their thinking. Necessarily, the councilors' concern was not wholly for the welfare of city workers. There was potentially a kind of "dividend" to a pay raise, collectible by the councilors who gave it—the votes of these employees on election day. As elective officials, therefore, the councilors were deeply concerned with the reactions of the employees (and their families and friends) as electors.

Atkinson was an appointed, not an elected official. He too was not unaware of the human aspect of a pay increase, for the men concerned were his subordinates, members of an organization which he wanted to weld into an enthusiastic team. He needed their loyal and willing support, and was anxious to build it by considerate and fair handling of their interests. Nor could he be entirely unconcerned personally—whatever his official neutrality—with the re-election prospects of those members of the council who normally supported his views. But there were other factors demanding his consideration.

A businessman by training and disposition, he was in fact overwhelmingly concerned with some aspects of the pay raise problem which to his opponents were of only secondary interest. In the manager's view the most important and immediately compelling job he had was to bring down the astronomical tax rate, which was driving industry from the city and forcing a rapid downward spiral in the financial capacity of the city. Over and beyond this emergency task was the long-range objective of protecting and enhancing the "assets of the city." A third determinant was Atkinson's concept of his job—his responsibility to be exactly what the words "chief executive" meant to him, so that he could bring to Cambridge honesty and efficiency in government—characteristics which he believed had been almost completely absent for many years. He was convinced that "personnel policy" was part of "administration," and that wage scales were part of "personnel policy." To have others determining his personnel policy as thus defined seemed to him to violate the code of ethics he had accepted.

The manager's concern for these objectives was re-enforced by the organizations and individuals who had worked in the previous three or four years to install a council-manager form of government in Cambridge. These forces were continuing to lend him support indirectly by campaigning for council members who would commit themselves to the support of the new government. The manager's aims were underlined also by the general state of opinion in Cambridge; a little more than a year previously a majority of voters had sent the old charter to the scrap heap in favor of a new form of government which, it was widely understood, would lead to reduced taxes and rehabilitation of city equipment and services. Atkinson's friends, too, were predominantly business and professional men who were overwhelmingly supporters of the new experiment. It was far from possible for the manager to regard a pay raise exclusively from the viewpoint of the men who would so much have liked to have one.

It is clear, as we have suggested, that the councilors who were behind the pay raise efforts were fully aware of the political implications of the policies they championed. It is no derogation of the councilors' interest in city employees as human beings to say that they also had a great interest in the workers as possessors of the vote. These councilors knew that in the pay raise issue—in regard to which the state legislature had given the council so handy a weapon—they potentially had a device for eliciting the political allegiance of a citizen group which in fact was numerous enough (especially if one includes their relatives and friends) to swing the balance away from the new form of government. To some councilors such a shift was a desirable and most vital objective. At least all of those who had worked so hard for the new charter were convinced that some of the councilors wished to use the pay raise issue to regain control of local government. Beyond this, motives undoubtedly varied with individuals among the opposition councilors. The pre-1942 record seemed to attest that some of them were primarily concerned with their own welfare. To those who stood most firmly behind the new charter, then, the "pay raise gang" was a group of selfish ("cheap") politicians, out to overturn Plan E and bring the city to ruin in an orgy of patronage and graft. The proponents of Plan E were convinced that the opposition councilors were concerned with regaining power in part because most men like to see their good works written upon the face of a city, but primarily for personal gain in prestige, power, and wealth for themselves rather than the welfare of "the people of Cambridge" or certainly, of the taxpayers. To the proponents of a "decent living wage" in the council, on the other hand, Atkinson was a "businessman" who, like the organizations and individuals who stood behind him, was more worried about taxes and profits for industry than about the downtrodden and unfortunate groups in the city. Furthermore, it seemed to them that the manager sought to take away from the council—the "sovereign representatives of the people"—duties and powers which it had long exercised; he seemed to them to grasp at every means of control, and to seek to become a local dictator.

It is no wonder, then, that the battle was acrimonious, nor that it has been, through the years, sometimes quiescent, sometimes flaring up again. It will be of interest to the reader to notice the effort of the manager to resolve the conflict of objectives so as always to "put first things first" according to his own scale of values, which kept shifting in these times of rapid social, economic, and political change. Also involved in the case are interesting questions of the relationship of legislative authority to the role of the executive. The early American theory of separation of powers was generally applied to municipal as well as to state and Federal government. In the 20th Century, however, this theory was discarded for many municipalities first by the commission plan and second by the council-manager plan. The council-manager plan, by giving the council the right in its discretion to appoint and remove the city manager, and by vesting basic municipal powers in the council (in most instances) discarded the dogma of the separation of powers. At the same time, the desire of reform groups to insure orderly and integrated administration led them to write into city charters (following the Model Charter of the

National Municipal League) provisions designed to establish the city manager as the administrative head of the city; to require that the council act through him in dealing with the administrative departments; and to require the council to permit the manager discretion in the appointment and removal of his subordinates.

This is the general meaning of the following provisions in the Code of Ethics of the International City Managers Association: "In order to achieve effective, democratic government, the council-manager plan provides that municipal *policy shall be determined exclusively by a legislative body* elected by the people, and that the *administration of* policy *shall be vested in the city manager*, as administrative head of the city . . ." (italics supplied).

In some cities this general idea of a division of responsibilities, and the legal provisions which support it, has had little effect on the council. By its power of appointment and removal, a city council is generally able to determine how much or how little administrative discretion to leave to the city manager. In other cities, however, civic associations or political organizations have made the manager into a more active and conspicuous leader, and have succeeded in securing the election of council members more or less according to their attitude toward the role of the city manager, or in some cases even according to their commitment to support a certain individual as manager; and some managers, without much organized support, have achieved a position of leadership by force of personality and ability.

Thus within the apparently simple theory of the council-manager plan a great variety of practice has been possible. Some cities have had strong councils which, at the same time, left administrative control of the municipal departments to a strong city manager. Others have had strong councils and weak managers, or weak councils and strong managers—and in this last case the council-manager plan, in spite of the formal power of the council to appoint and dismiss the manager, has been converted into something very much like a plan of separation of powers.

This was the situation in Cambridge. It was so partly because of the personal leadership of the city manager, partly because the group that put the city manager plan into effect was not able to capture effective control of the council, partly because that group then turned to the city manager as a public defender of its position, and partly because the peculiar legal situation gave the city manager not only a ground of appeal to the public, but also the right of appeal to the courts against his employer, the council.

Even so, the city manager did not take on one of the most important characteristics of a political chief executive: He did not appeal directly to the people, or carry on any personal campaign for the election of his supporters and associates.

Let us turn now from a consideration of the general theory of the council-manager plan and note how the conflict looked to its local participants.

The effect of the special act conferring authority upon the council in matters of police and fire salaries (and of the similar powers of the School Committee) was to put in jeopardy the ability of the chief executive to meet responsibilities which he believed to be fundamental to his administration of the city. When under this special authority the council majority persisted in giving him directions which it regarded as legislative policy determinations but which he regarded as in conflict with other policies of the council and with his obligations under the policy dicta of the city charter, the manager had to come squarely to grips with the question of what his fundamental responsibilities to the council and the people were. When commands of the legislature are mutually contradictory and seem to conflict with those of the basic law, what should the chief executive do?

The fundamental decision of the manager was that it was his responsibility to fight for what he regarded as the correct interpretation of his duties and responsibilities under the charter, and to leave to the judiciary and to the people at the polls the ultimate decision as to the interpretation of conflicting authority. He therefore refused to give way before any temporary majority in the legislative body. He was ready to risk his job and even the council-manager plan in Cambridge in order to retain effective control of wage scales. On more than one occasion he defied his opposition in the legislative arm by going to the courts for decision on disputed issues. The manager believed that by both specific and implied written authority, he was charged with being at the helm; so long as he was, it was possible for him in fact to guide the ship; but he could not do so if another agent could, at will, give the wheel a twist.

Inevitably, in taking so resolute a stand, the manager ran the risk of seeming to deny the authority of the local legislature to lay down public policy. To the opposition councilors and that part of the public which stood behind them he seemed to be doing exactly what they had feared would occur under the new form of government: elevate executive authority over the legislative. To these citizens it seemed that the manager wanted to make himself a dictator. To himself and to those who supported council-manager government, his actions were essential if he was to carry out the fundamental policies and directives of the city charter and the council. Theories of demarcation of responsibility between executive and legislative arms of the government provided no solution of the controversy. The latent ambiguity of the terms in which the theory was stated provided ample scope for differing interpretations, and it is notable that opinion in the opposing groups crystallized over practical preferences for which, with a minimum of difficulty, they found theoretical support.

One of the strongest traditions in American political life, although not an exclusive one, has been the desire to limit the power of governments; the tradition remains strong today in spite of the vastly increased scope of governmental activity. To a considerable extent the application of the doctrine of the separation of powers was specifically designed to inhibit governmental activity by a form of mutual frustration. But the spectacle of mutual frustration is frequently distasteful to those who have helped to create the conditions that produce the result. The Cambridge experience provides an interesting illustration of this phenomenon, for there can be no doubt that there would have been an early public revulsion from the council-manager government if it had been unable to act decisively and with a considerable degree of consistency. The irony of the situation is increased when it is realized that the council-manager plan was originally devised to prevent the kind of frustration and impasse that threatened to undermine the effectiveness of city government in Cambridge.

There are other interesting aspects of this case which are more technical in nature. The developing story of administrative effort and achievement reveals a number of effective techniques that can be employed in winning employee support and in creating teamwork. Personnel matters constituted one of the areas of administration in which the Cambridge manager felt himself best-schooled, and his marked success in creating a team under his leadership argues for the reader's attention to these matters.

Granted that an ability to transform an organization into a team, to elicit "willingness to serve," is one of the attributes of the successful administrator, what constitutes this kind of leadership ability? What other qualities are needed in administration? How important are what we might call "formal" qualities, which conscious effort can create over a relatively brief period, as against "personal" qualities which are in-born or created over a longer period of time? And where in the scale of qualifications shall we place technical preparation? Again, the Cambridge experience is but one example where many would be needed for generalization, but that experience suggests that some interesting answers are possible.

Of the other points of administrative interest which will suggest themselves to the reader of this case, the last which we shall mention here concerns the importance of good legal advice to the top administrator. The case speaks for the importance of competent legal assistance, but, more subtly perhaps, it also indicates one of the most important criteria for making effective use of that advice. The position of the manager within his organization as well as outside it was greatly strengthened by his success in court, just as his position would have been undermined by failure. It is worthy of notice, therefore, that the manager's relations with his solicitor all along have been in the nature of seeking counsel before decisions are made, rather than of seeking a way to bail out the administration after things have gone wrong. Yet in considering the role of the lawyer in this case, the student should bear in mind the fact that the manager's ability (with political support) to use the tactics of litigation against his employer, the council, was made possible by the peculiarities of our governmental habits in general, and the Cambridge situation in particular, which permitted judges to decide questions of administrative jurisdiction. The judicial power to intervene in administrative disputes is not an immutable fact of governmental life, though it happens to be a common phenomenon in the United States which greatly enhances the significance of legal advice in administration.

I. Background

A. LOCAL GOVERNMENT IN MASSACHUSETTS

In order to grasp the larger setting of this case, some knowledge of state and local governmental forms and relationships in Massachusetts is necessary.

Massachusetts government is a complex of institutions and forms, some brought down from colonial days either consciously or through inheritance; some representing innovations which, in their day, have inspired development in other states throughout the country; and others the product of reforms, partial or drastic, introduced in the course of more than three hundred years of growth and development. In theory, in all states, units of local government are "mere creatures" of the state, amenable to decisions of the state legislature in respect to virtually all matters. In fact, many states have taken steps toward decentralization of authority to local units. "Home rule" is an extreme reflection of this movement, and in the constitutions of many states local autonomy is protected in a number of ways, perhaps the most common of these being the requirement of local referendums in the determination of issues which bear closely upon local interests. It would simplify an understanding of the state-local relationship in Massachusetts if we could characterize the state as clearly one of those in which power is gathered and retained in the state, or on the other hand, as one in which local units are largely set free to make their own way. But it is not surprising that in a "system" which embodies so much of old as well as new, of conscious decision as well as of inheritance, no such characterization is possible. "Home rule" is unknown to Massachusetts cities and towns; the legislature is master of them all, and by "special acts" introduced and enacted in behalf of particular local units, it can—and sometimes does—meddle in local affairs absolutely without restraint. Yet, moving from the realm of theory to that of fact, it is true that local units in Massachusetts enjoy a large element of autonomy in local affairs. The special act, while so prone to abuse that three-fourths of the states have prohibited or closely circumscribed its use, is in Massachusetts normally a means of enlarging rather than obstructing local power. When unwanted legislative interference is threatened, the cry of "threat to home rule" is heard; it frequently gains a hearing among the populace and has political effect. Perhaps the key to this situation lies in the fact that Massachusetts is predominantly an urban state; in 1945 some 46 per cent of the population lived in the 43 cities and towns of the Boston Metropolitan area alone, and only 10 per cent of the population of the state was classed as rural. While there are certain differences of interest between large and small units, the sharp controversy found in many legislatures between rural and urban representatives has not upset state-local relations in Massachusetts. This may well be the fact which makes possible a large degree of local autonomy in a system which on paper looks like one of highly centralized power.

The only local units of importance in Massachusetts are towns and cities. Towns of 12,000 or more population may petition for a city charter, but need not do so, and many have not done so. Counties exist, but are peculiarly creatures of the state, and their main functions are judicial. They operate record offices and county jails, and have other minor functions which vary from county to county; they have no legislative functions. They levy no taxes and are wholly supported by the state government. School districts as such do not exist; towns and cities constitute the districts, and the government of the public schools is vested in specially elected school committees whose authority and power in respect to school affairs is very great.

The state legislature—the "General Court" as it is called—in 1915 enacted four optional charters which cities other than Boston may adopt by vote of the people. These include Plan A—strong mayor and council; Plan B—weak mayor and council; Plan C—commission; Plan D—elected mayor and council of four elected at large, with a city manager. Plan B was similar to the form under which the great majority of cities were operating by special act or charter; Plan D, while a "city manager form," differed in important ways from the "model" propounded by the National Municipal League. Very few adoptions occurred under any of these plans, cities preferring to remain under their pre-existing forms. Finally in 1938 Plan E was enacted and signed into law. The Plan was specifically modeled upon the Cincinnati, Ohio, charter, and provided a city manager form which met the "specifications" of the model of the National Municipal League. Cambridge, in adopting Plan E at a referendum vote in 1940, became the first city in the state to adopt a manager charter.

B. CAMBRIDGE, MASSACHUSETTS

Cambridge is the fourth largest city in Massachusetts; in the Boston metropolitan area, which in 1945 comprised some 2,066,000 persons, its 111,000 people made it second only to Boston itself. With its geographic center less than five miles from the port of Boston and with a flat terrain, it has inevitably become one of the three or four foremost industrial cities in New England. Yet its land area of 6.5 square miles makes it the smallest city with a population in excess of 100,000, save one, in New England. While the city is well known as a center of industry, it is perhaps known even more widely as a university city, home of Harvard University, Radcliffe College, and the Massachusetts Institute of Technology.

Cambridge is one of the oldest cities in America. Founded in 1630, it grew slowly during its first two hundred years. In the years around the turn of the 19th century, bridges were thrown across the river from Boston, and two new villages arose east toward Boston from "Old Cambridge." With the great influx of Irish immigrants into Boston after 1840, these villages mushroomed, and rivalry with Old Cambridge at Harvard Square became a sociological factor which continues on down to the present to have pronounced effects. Feeling among these communities was such in the 19th century that on several occasions residents of the Old Village petitioned the General Court to allow them to withdraw from the city of Cambridge. The "natives" were resentful at the arrival of impoverished Irish immigrants, who themselves had to make a drastic adjustment to urban life in an unreceptive economic, social, and religious environment. It is natural that the immigrants responded with a cohesiveness which was a result of their common experience, nationality, and religion. In the course of the years they were readily aligned with the Democratic Party, which provided another powerful and continuing source of friction. The growing numbers of Irish and Irish-Americans made them increasingly important in political affairs. Political organizations were readily established on the basis of "services" which had particular attractions for a self-conscious immigrant group. Later immigrations of Italians into the area and the development of an "Italian colony" in East Cambridge facilitated continuing development of these organizations. With the strengthening of the machines, the ends of local government were consistently subverted to private rather than public weal, and in Cambridge as in Boston and other cities in the metropolitan area, municipal physical and financial well-being became more and more precarious.

Cambridge today has a highly cosmopolitan population, the largest ethnic group being the Irish, with perhaps 60 per cent of the population. Other large groups are of English and Scotch, French Canadian, and Italian backgrounds. A Negro group comprises about 4 per cent of the inhabitants. In the 1948 state election, 68 per cent of the voters cast ballots for the Democratic candidate for governor; the Democratic vote has often been more than 75 per cent of the total.

The city is one of the country's most crowded urban areas, with an average of nearly 50,000 persons per square mile of residential area. This fact, taken together with the age and industrial character of the city, make it not at all surprising that housing conditions over much of the area are poor. A WPA survey made in 1941-43 of some of the more crowded housing areas of the city—embracing some 64,000 of the city's 110,000 inhabitants at that time—found that approximately 86 per cent of those surveyed were living in dwellings classed as substandard.[2] Counting industrial and commercial as well as residential taxpayers, there are fewer than 12,000 in the city. Yet, in "Old Cambridge," centering along Brattle Street, there is an area of large old homes with spacious yards, where many of the "old families" of Cambridge have lived and live today.

In short, Cambridge is a city of sharp social differentiation. In any city there are among the citizens differences of employment, wealth, national background, religion, and politics. In Cambridge, residents have been particularly conscious of these differences, partly because of historical factors and partly because of the extremity of some of the differences. In general, the issue is drawn between the relatively wealthy in the area of Brattle Street (Ward 8—one of the two consistently Republican wards in the city) and the laboring groups who make up the great bulk of the population. In terms of community areas, the lines are drawn with North and East Cambridge and Central Square vs. "Old Cambridge" west of Harvard Square. Feeling between the areas has undoubtedly subsided since "Old Cambridge" tried to withdraw from the rest of the city, but as we shall see in later pages of this case, consciousness among the Cambridgites of differences of social, economic, and religious kinds has continuously been an important factor in local politics.

[2] This classification applied to any dwellings deficient in one or more of the following respects: in need of major repairs; unfit for use in terms of safety, welfare, and health; no installed heating system, no flush toilet, no bathing unit; or more than 1.51 persons per room.

C. EARLY CHARTERS AND THE PLAN E OPTION

When Cambridge adopted its first city charter in 1846, it chose a mayor and council government with the mayor, 6 aldermen and 20 councilors all elected by the people. In 1891, a new charter was obtained, expanding the number of aldermen to 11 and of councilors to 22. Twenty-four years later, following the provision by the General Court of the four optional forms which have been noted above, Cambridge adopted a modified Plan B form, with a "weak" mayor and council of 15, 11 of whom were elected in the city's 11 wards, and 4 at large. The mayor enjoyed a power of veto over acts of the council, but his veto on any issue could be overridden by two-thirds vote of the council. His appointments and certain other major administrative actions required council approval. Under these circumstances, a close working relationship—one might say a relationship of mutual bargaining—developed between the mayor and the council and the council recognized that it held a strong and secure position, if not a clearly superior one, vis-à-vis the chief executive.

It was in June 1938, that the Massachusetts General Court adopted as Plan E an optional charter which was in accord with the important characteristics of the city manager form as propounded by the National Municipal League. Cambridge in 1940 became the first city in the state to adopt a Plan E charter, and the new government went into office in January 1942. The major characteristics of a Plan E charter are these:

1. A city council of seven or nine, depending upon the number of city wards, is elected at large by proportional representation for a two-year concurrent term. Councilors by majority vote may establish their own salaries, up to a maximum of $4,000. In the council is vested "all the legislative powers of the city," except such powers as are reserved to the School Committee or the voters.

2. A mayor is elected by the council; he is its presiding officer, and "the official head of the city for all ceremonial purposes." He is to be "recognized by the courts for the purpose of serving civil process and by the governor for military purposes. In time of public danger or emergency, as determined by the city council, he may, with its consent, take command of the police. . . ." He is, in addition, chairman of the School Committee.

3. A city manager is appointed by a simple majority of the council; he serves at the pleasure of the council and may be removed at any time, although he may require that charges against him be in writing, and that the final vote on his discharge be preceded by a public hearing. The city manager is "the chief administrative officer of the city, and shall be responsible for the administration of departments, commissions, boards and offices of the city—except that of the city clerk, city auditor, any official appointed by the governor or any body elected by the voters of the city." He need not be a resident of the city when appointed.

4. A School Committee of seven is elected, six at large by proportional representation, at the same time and for the same term as members of the city council. The mayor is chairman, presiding officer, and seventh member of the School Committee. The Committee is given "general charge of all the public schools" —a provision of the General Laws that has consistently been interpreted broadly by the courts. By law the city council is "bound" to appropriate "an amount sufficient for the support of the public schools. . . ." The judgment of the School Committee as to what amount is "sufficient" is virtually unchallengeable.

While the course of municipal affairs was to take a turn for the worse in the years after 1938, considerable revulsion at the practical costs of machine politics was already evident at that time. The tax rate was $41 per thousand in 1938, up $1.40 from 1937; and the city's borrowings had reached a new high—a level which would undoubtedly have been exceeded in the ensuing years but for tumbling property valuation and a consequently falling debt limit. Considerable citizen interest in Plan E had been generated in Cambridge while the debates were still going on at the State House. Indeed, it was a group made up predominantly of Cambridge citizens who were working in the legislature for adoption of the Plan E optional charter. In no small part as a result of the efforts of the Honorable Christian A. Herter, Speaker of the Massachusetts House of Representatives, Plan E became law June 1, 1938. Shortly thereafter, a Cambridge resident, Mr. Chandler W. Johnson, who had sparked the original creation of a group to press for a city manager optional charter, approached the officers of the Cambridge Taxpayers Association, a civic group which for many years had tried to maintain a constructive opposition to actions of the city government which it felt to be detrimental to the interests of taxpayers. Clearly the time had come to decide whether to place a referendum vote on Plan E before the people in the state elections that fall. A delay until 1940 was required, under the law, if no effort was made in 1938. After reviewing a list of members of the Taxpayers Association, the Chamber of Commerce, and the League of Women Voters, Johnson called together a group of about seventy men and women known to be interested in civic affairs. The issue of whether to make a try for Plan E that fall was debated and many counseled delay in order to carry out an "educational campaign." The majority concluded, however, that the best possible educational technique was to make an attempt on the ballot, and a committee was appointed to undertake formation of a campaign committee.

D. THE CAMPAIGN OF 1938

Earnest efforts were made to have the "Cambridge Committee for Plan E"—the "Plan E

Committee" as it was soon labeled—as representative as possible of the people of the city. For a committee having such a genesis as this one, however, this was no easy task. The group decided, after dispelling conservative opposition, to ask Dean James M. Landis of the Harvard Law School, then well-known as a New Deal Democrat whose services were highly valued by the Roosevelt Administration, to assume the Chairmanship. The group—and the Dean—recognized the possible disadvantage of his connection with Harvard, but the group saw in his local prestige as a leading Democrat an asset which should offset this political liability. Under the vigorous leadership of Dean Landis, a campaign organization was created. Positions of leadership were filled by representatives of different religions and party affiliations and of different ethnic backgrounds. Through the tireless efforts principally of women who also were members of the League of Women Voters, the necessary signatures for a referendum petition were acquired and the petitions were filed with the city council. The temper of local political affairs is suggested by the response of the council to this action—it refused to meet to take the necessary action to forward the petitions to the Secretary of State so that the issue might be placed upon the ballot. With the deadline looming, George A. McLaughlin of the Plan E Committee found a judge of the Superior Court who was prepared to issue a mandamus to compel the council to meet and take the necessary action. This incident in itself would make an exciting short story. Suffice it here to observe that the crucial day was a Saturday and the members of the council were heading that afternoon for the Harvard Stadium to enjoy a football game, courtesy of the University. At the seat of each councilor was a deputy with a warrant, requiring the holding of a council meeting forthwith. Thus it was that, on the eve of the deadline, the council transmitted the petitions as by law it was required to do.

In the ensuing campaign a major charge against Plan E initially was that it was dictatorial and communistic—a charge which was readily enough believed by many people to whom city government is known not as a theory of politics or of organization, but as a group of individuals who to them are friends and compatriots. Many honest citizens, schooled in the tradition of a diffusion of responsibility as democracy's surest safeguard, believed earnestly that the manager would have virtually dictatorial power. In comparison with the weak mayor forms, the new form did indeed make possible, though it did not insure, a strong executive. The communist charge lost its potency, however, when the Communist Party announced its opposition to a Plan E charter. This led to an intensification of another major line of attack to the effect that Plan E was the enemy of the "ordinary people" of Cambridge. It was alleged to be the means by which the "Harvard-Brattle Street - Money - Taxpayer - Republican" forces would regain the control of the city which they enjoyed in early days and govern it exclusively in their own behalf. The battle featured a recommendation by the city council that Harvard be expelled from Cambridge and incorporated as a university city. Despite the brief period before the November election for a campaign to explain this radically new form of government, Plan E lost out in 1938 by the narrow margin of 1,767 votes out of 46,280 cast.

The challenge of Plan E did not produce in the existing city government an urge for internal reform. The incumbent mayor was reelected by a very narrow margin. This second term of his was cut short, however, by his indictment and subsequent conviction and imprisonment for requesting and accepting bribes. The city council, if more devoted than the mayor to the public well-being, was not enough so to prevent a worsening of the quality of city government and of its financial underpinning.

The mayor got off to a poor start in his second term by failing to comply with the requirements of state law in presenting a budget to the council. The budget he presented was a mere summary in lieu of the itemized document required by law, and it proposed to boost city expenditures $1.2 millions, more than ten per cent. To halt the $5 to $7 rise in the tax rate which this budget would have entailed, a group of citizens under the aegis of the Taxpayers Association took the matter to court and won their case when the Supreme Court held the budget to be illegal. Under the law, the city was obliged to operate on the budget for the prior year—a much lower budget. The mayor tried to borrow his way out of his resulting predicament of having inadequate funds to meet his expanded city payrolls. He realized full well the political impact of jeopardizing payment of the salaries of the city's 2,000 workers. This group was perhaps the most important political group in the city, for city employees influence the votes not only of their own families but also of their relatives and friends. One of the most astute leaders in the city has estimated that 20 per cent of the total votes is "controlled" by city employees. The mayor himself confided to a local newsman when the court decision invalidating his budget was handed down that this action would cost him the next election. But borrowing his way out in the summer of 1940 was a difficult thing for the mayor to do. Cambridge was so close to its debt limit that, of the 600,000 needed for the Street Department that year, the city could legally borrow only $400,000 at the time. With a land area so small that only one or two cities in its population group in the country were smaller, and with the fourth highest assessed valuation per capita of cities of any size in Massachusetts, one would have expected Cambridge to have low municipal costs and a low tax rate. Yet in 1940 a tax rate of $43.00 was established, very nearly the highest in Massachusetts. Valuations had fallen $1.2 millions in a year as industries sought less costly bases of operation. One-year tax delinquencies were more than 15 per cent. Nearly $10 of the tax rate was required for debt service alone.

The financial plight of Cambridge was, then, clear to many citizens when the campaign for the second Plan E referendum got under way, prior to the regular state elections in the fall of 1940. The mayor's mishandling of the budget earlier that year and the ensuing "budget goulash" as the city weekly called it, was a clear indication of the state of affairs at City Hall. Furthermore, many citizens knew that in August the District Attorney had begun an investigation into the hiring of trucks and other city services.

E. THE CAMPAIGN OF 1940

While the 1940 campaign was bitter, it was conducted on a somewhat higher plane than in 1938. The major focus of the attack of the opposition was on proportional representation. It was charged that "P.R." encouraged voting along group and racial lines and would elevate minorities to majorities. It was also alleged, probably because of the rather complex manner of counting ballots, that P.R. deprived a citizen of his right to have his vote counted. The Plan E Committee waged a vigorous campaign, holding rallies and meetings and organizing a corps of speakers to appear before any group in the city upon request. The organization had resident representatives in every ward, but the difficulties it faced are suggested by the fact that, in some of the most heavily Democratic wards in the city, its representatives were Republicans. Aided, certainly, by the votes of hundreds and probably thousands of citizens who were primarily voting *against* the existing state of affairs rather than *for* Plan E, the proposed new city manager charter was adopted by 25,875 votes out of 44,198, or nearly 59 per cent. Three of the city's eleven wards had majorities adverse to Plan E—wards in the east and north of the city, where "town against gown" consciousness was especially keen, wards in which registered Democrats outnumbered registered Republicans 25 to 1, 6 to 1, and 8 to 1 respectively.[3] Under the law, the new council was to be elected at the regular municipal elections in 1941, and a Plan E government was to be formed on January 5, 1942.

In a real sense, the incumbent council was now a "lame duck" with more than a year of its term remaining. Furthermore, two weeks after the voters of Cambridge had chosen a Plan E charter, the mayor's indictment was handed down. He continued, pending trial, to

[3] Wards 1, 3, and 11. See Appendix B.

discharge the duties of his office. The council, looking toward the coming elections, made uncommon efforts to please all factions, in the ensuing months. In February after the Plan E triumph, it passed a resolution in praise of Harvard for extending one of its scholarship programs to include local residents. The Cambridge weekly editorialized, "Talk about the man biting the dog . . ." Less than a month later the council unanimously passed a resolution addressed to President Roosevelt urging "all-out aid to Ireland," including arms, ammunition and food because of the "probability of invasion by Germany."

Meanwhile the mayor was encountering increasingly troubled days. In early January 1941, he was again indicted, this time on 64 additional counts of requesting and accepting bribes on various city construction and repair jobs; he now was obliged to post $2500 bail, but continued to act as mayor, pending trial. At the council meeting next following this incident, he made a pronouncement which brought him and Cambridge renown in newspapers as far away as London, England. Urged by the council to present an appropriation request for $5350 for new snow plows—of which at the time the city owned not even one—he refused, observing that as "the Almighty sends the snow, . . . He will in time remove it." The mayor and his predecessors had long found it politically wise to remove snow with the hand-shovel power of unemployed political supporters rather than with machinery, but in the winter of 1940-41 there was money neither for men nor machines. At the very next meeting of the council, the chief of police advised the council of a compelling need for new vehicles. Of nine police cars owned by the city, four were "propped up on boxes" in the police garage minus tires or other vital parts taken to keep the other five running. All nine were three years old, and had been driven at least 40,000 miles a year, he reported. "The cars are no good to chase anyone. They couldn't catch another car," he stated. Finally, in mid-March, the mayor was convicted in the County Criminal Court on 42 counts of requesting and accepting bribes, and while he took an unsuccessful appeal to the Supreme Judicial Court of Massachusetts, he now was required to give up his mayoral duties and responsibilities.

A special committee of Cambridge state legislators was appointed by the General Court to study appropriate next steps for the city of Cambridge, and the president of the city council took over such functions as he could legally perform, pending enactment of special legislation. On July 23, after three months of wrangling, the General Court approved a bill vesting certain powers in the acting mayor until the Plan E government was formed. The legislation specified that no civil service appointments could be made save with the approval of the state civil service department, and that in any case the terms of any persons appointed to any city positions would expire on January 5, 1952. Promotions and salary increases other than within-grade "step-rate" increases were prohibited outright and borrowing power was curtailed.

The municipal campaign to select the first Plan E council and School Committee was held that fall. The outcome of this first council election was of crucial importance to the forces behind Plan E, for selection of a city manager and implementation of the program of the Plan E Committee hinged upon obtaining an effective majority in the council. Interest in the election was tremendous; eighty-three persons filed nomination papers for the nine council seats, perhaps in part because one of the tasks of the council would be to establish the salaries of councilors, and these it could set as high as $4,000 per year. Dean Landis, chairman of the Plan E Committee, had announced at the time of the successful vote on the Plan E referendum that his Committee would endorse a slate pledged to carry out the Plan E program and during the summer of 1941 an interviewing committee was appointed to stimulate the candidacy of certain persons selected by the Committee and to investigate the qualifications of all candidates and interview any who might seek the Committee's endorsement and support. About a month before the elections, the Committee announced endorsement of a slate of eleven men whom it had chosen after reference to factors of personal qualification for office and to factors of race, religion, politics, and residence. The Committee's effort was to endorse a "balanced" slate. Shortly thereafter, the Republican city organization announced its endorsement of a list of candidates—three of whom were also on the Plan E list—despite the non-partisan nature of municipal elections in Massachusetts. The Democratic committee soon followed suit, its chairman charging that "it is an open secret that the new form of city government is the foster child of one of the political parties (not the Democratic Party)."

The campaign was a hard-fought one in which the Plan E candidates, seeking to exploit such personal support as they enjoyed independently of Plan E endorsement, did not always try to clarify the questions in the minds of many citizens as to the operation of the new form of government, or as to the meaning of their "endorsement" by what to many citizens looked like a new political machine maneuvered by Harvard and Brattle Street. Nonetheless, the Plan E endorsers conducted a vigorous campaign as individuals, and the Plan E Committee followed suit in their collective behalf, sponsoring rallies, undertaking door-to-door campaigning, providing speakers, arranging for publicity by newspaper, placard, and radio, and organizing a motor brigade to get voters to the polls on election day. The opposition was at least equally resolute. On election eve the Democratic organization distributed a "newspaper" printed in green ink which, by a careful choice of suggestive words and phrases, sought to link Dean Landis and one of the Plan E candidates (a labor lawyer) with Communists. In vivid terms it urged the election of "real" as against "pseudo" Democrats.

F. THE ELECTIONS OF 1941

The results of the election were terribly disappointing to the Plan E group; only four of its endorsees were successful, a fifth candidate losing out at the end of the slate by a margin of 30 votes. The following tabulation characterizes roughly the political disposition of the elected councilors:

Councilor	*Voted for Atkinson for City Manager*	*Supporter of Plan E Government*	*Endorsed by Plan E Committee*	*Endorsed by Democratic Organization*
John H. Corcoran, Mayor	X	X	X	
Edward A. Crane	X	X	X	
William M. Hogan, Jr.	X			X
John D. Lynch			X	
Thomas M. McNamara				
Marcus Morton, Jr.	X	X	X *	
Hyman Pill	X	X		X
Francis L. Sennott	X			X
Michael A. Sullivan				
Totals	6	4	4	3

* Also endorsed by Republican City Committee.

In the School Committee only two of the six persons elected were endorsees of the Plan E Committee, and the other four were known opponents of a Plan E program. On the face of it, implementation of the mandate given by the voters in 1940 might well be frustrated by the action of the voters in 1941.

The immediate problem of the new city council would be of course the appointment of a city manager and election of a mayor. The council-elect began to hold a series of informal meetings shortly after the election with a view to deciding these issues in advance so that they might be carried into effect immediately upon the formation of government.

It was at this point that a characteristic of Cambridge political forces which has continued in all the successive years to be true of the Plan E opposition in the council became evident: the "opposition," as we shall call those opposed to the Plan E program, was not a united opposition. Councilor Lynch would tip his hat to no man; as a former mayor and (until 1949) the leading vote-getter in nearly every election, he was proud of his independence of any faction. Councilor Sullivan was an almost legendary character—honest, absolutely independent, tireless in his effort to help anyone in need, loved by those who knew him as a friend; yet he was suspicious of executive power to the point of impassioned opposition, a hater of Plan E and core of the opposition to the manager. Councilor McNamara in those early days shared Sullivan's doubts about the council-manager experiment; like Lynch and Sullivan he was not aligned with a local party organization, but for several years stood with Sullivan on virtually every issue. Sennott and Hogan, endorsees of the Democratic City Committee, voted independently on numerous issues. Lynch, Sullivan, McNamara, and—on the pro-manager side—Pill, all have enjoyed large support in their own wards, support which has come to them as friends and neighbors, independently of any party organization or faction. In that first Plan E council and in subsequent councils, these men (excepting Hogan) have served many times, but undoubtedly because of their independent political strength, no force has ever been able to unite them. It is this division of the council opposition to Plan E which made possible the selection of a city manager acceptable to the Plan E group that December.

A number of applicants for the managership were considered by the new council but because he enjoyed the support of Councilors Hogan and Sennott as well as the four supporters of the Plan E program, Colonel John B. Atkinson took an early lead in the consideration. The support of Hogan and Sennott is interesting, because both had opposed a Plan E charter and Sennott in particular in the ensuing years was a consistent opponent of the manager and the Plan E group in the council. It has been alleged that a former Massachusetts governor played an important role in making possible Atkinson's election, and that appointments involving a personal friend of Sennott and a relative of Hogan were made subsequent to the formation of government in 1942. However this may be, it seems certain that no man save Atkinson could have commanded a majority vote in the council, or at least that a bitter wrangle over the selection of a city manager would have occurred.

Colonel Atkinson was a Cambridge resident "long prominent in the shoe business," according to the Cambridge Chronicle as, three weeks in advance of his election, the newspaper reported on progress reputedly being made at the informal council meetings. Atkinson was not a professional city manager. In fact, his only prior taste of public business came while, as a student at Boston College Preparatory School and Boston College, he had covered for local papers the meetings of the Cambridge Board of Aldermen. His course work at Boston College was in the classics. He had been "born and raised" in Cambridge. He was among the first ten men to enlist in the A.E.F. after war was declared in 1917. He remained in service after the war and helped reorganize the 26th Division; he retired in 1924 with the rank of Colonel. Upon returning to civilian life he entered the shoe business in Cambridge and Boston, undertaking importing as well as manufacturing and wholesaling with a good deal of success. His importing work took him to Europe and especially to Czechoslovakia frequently until 1939, when with the outbreak of war he returned permanently to Cambridge. Mr. Atkinson was also active as sales counselor to a number of firms. He could have been, and was, characterized as a "successful businessman." He was registered in the Democratic Party. At the time of his selection he was 47 years old. He was married and had one son.

At the balloting on January 5, 1942, John H. Corcoran, a Plan E endorsee, was by prior agreement elected mayor and John B. Atkinson, by a vote of 6 to 3, was appointed city manager. As he contemplated the new experience ahead of him, the manager may well have tallied somewhat as follows the probable sources of strength and weakness of the new experiment being made in Cambridge.

G. SOURCES OF STRENGTH

By law, the Plan E charter was assured a trial of at least four years. No petition proposing a different form of government could be presented for inclusion on the ballot for three years and six months.

Regardless of the lack of ability of the Plan E forces to elect a majority to the city council, there was widespread public disgust with the record of past administrations and a readiness, if not a receptiveness, in the minds of a majority of the people for a new kind of government.

The record of the administration just ended had been so bad that any improvement would probably be noticeable. Furthermore, the pyramiding of war expenditures and restriction of supplies would make for an enforced lowering of municipal expenditures, and help in attacking the unprecedented tax rate which was at the root of the city's increasing financial plight.

The new manager would enjoy the support of organized civic groups—the Plan E Committee, the Cambridge Citizens Committee, and the Taxpayers Association—and the support of individual members of the Chamber of Commerce and League of Women Voters. At the same time, he owed no direct political favors to these groups.

Indeed, in a real sense, he would enjoy a large measure of independence of any group, because of the division in the council. The absence of a Plan E majority in council was potentially a very great weakness; but because the council opposition was an opposition of individuals rather than of a machine laying down a policy line of its own, it would be necessary for him to strengthen his own position—and it would probably be possible for him to do so—by making judicious use of his opportunities. With the "hard core" of Plan E support in Councilors Corcoran, Crane, and Morton, who owed to Plan E endorsement their first term in office, and with the support of Hyman Pill upon whom by the time of his installation he knew he could count, he was likely to be able to operate satisfactorily because of the certainty that on many issues—perhaps most—he would be able to pick up an additional vote from Hogan, Sennott, or Lynch.

In any event, fortuitous personal circumstances gave Atkinson a sense of independence that results from an adequate outside source of income. He intended retaining certain of his business interests which he could attend outside of city business hours, including two shoe factories located nearby. Atkinson continued to operate these businesses through the years and himself emphasized the feeling of independence which he was able to enjoy as he tackled controversial and politically "red hot" issues which might conceivably have had different treatment from an equally honest and able executive who was without a separate income and had a family of ten.

Finally, the charter was to his liking and seemed to assure him of an opportunity to place himself in effective control of the personnel of the organization. To be sure, there was the threat represented by the right of the council to establish salaries in the Police and Fire Departments by ordinance, but he had the promise of support of the six councilors who had voted for him. These six had promised support in his effort to put the city on its feet physically and financially.

H. SOURCES OF WEAKNESS

But if Mr. Atkinson had been inclined to look at the darker side of life, most of the sources of strength could have been viewed equally well as potential liabilities. Public revulsion at the latter-day record of the Plan B government assured him of public support for the moment—but like any support which is not based on understanding of the fundamental principles involved, it was likely to shift suddenly. As a matter of fact, early opposition to Plan E and to the new manager on the part of many councilors, city employees, and citizens was in no small part an outgrowth of honest doubts about the wisdom—the safety—of concentrating so much power in one man. They forgot, or overlooked, the fact that the sizable delegation of powers to the manager under Plan E was revocable, for the council could hire and fire the manager at will, and could (except for the inability to increase the manager's proposed budget) establish policy. Opposition was, in this respect, the product of a lack of understanding of the basic principles of the new plan. To most of these people, quite in accord with American democratic theory and practice, the combined independence and interdependence of council and mayor under Plan B had appeared as an advantage. The unwanted consequences flowing from the diffusion of authority and responsibility were viewed as results of the weakness of particular men—men like the recent mayor—rather than as weaknesses of political structure. It was now foreordained that every possible step would be taken to thwart each effort of the manager to gain effective control of the organization by those councilors who, to be sure, were motivated by their own honest doubts about Plan E but who also recognized the political advantage which would be theirs if they could demonstrate that the manager was dictatorial and that Plan E was undemocratic. Under these circumstances, the only way the manager and the Plan E councilors could win affirmative support was to demonstrate in action that Plan E and its strong professional administrator did promote the public weal far more effectively than the old plan, and that the elected representatives of the people were truly the government of Cambridge. The manager was very much on the spot and would continue to be; only the record would earn continuing support.

While the manager would enjoy the aid of organized civic groups, these groups represented a segment of the population which was in the unenviable political position of having long been dominant in terms of wealth and social status and very much dominated in terms of numbers of votes. These groups, along with the Plan E councilors and above all the manager who was the focal point and symbol of Plan E, would be subjected to the incessant pounding of councilors and candidates who enjoyed support in the "lower wards." In these wards lay potential strength to overturn Plan E if the leaders who opposed it could demonstrate the truth of their charges that the new government was a device—as the Democratic committee was saying—for establishing Republican control in City Hall. The pattern was demonstrated by Councilor Sullivan on that first Monday in January 1942 when he announced that he would never give his vote to a man who had "brought scab labor into the country"—and to his way of thinking, Atkinson had done this in importing shoes from Czechoslovakia.

The division in the council might indeed make it possible for the manager and the Plan E minority to find the votes to enact most of the Plan E program; but the council could not be counted upon to take a leadership role in the formulation of policy. Even with leadership from the manager, the division in the council might well lead to inconsistency in policy decisions. Plan E forces could not be *certain* of a majority on anything.

Finally, as to the charter itself, since Cambridge was the first city in the state to try it, there were no precedents to which, either in courts of law or the court of public opinion, Plan E supporters could point in event of reverses in the early years. Litigation was certain; a case was already before the court to test the constitutionality of the proportional representation feature. Furthermore, although the manager under the charter enjoyed stronger administrative controls than the Plan B mayor whose appointment of department heads was subject to council approval, the manager's leadership of the organization was sharply challenged by the 1935 Act under which, it was widely recognized, the council would continue to establish salary schedules in the Police and Fire Departments, while the School Committee remained in control of salary scales for all employees of the Department of Education. As we have seen, under normal circumstances, a council determines all salary schedules, and a dispute between manager and council over the *right* of determination cannot arise. In Cambridge, however, the fact that the manager could in effect set salary schedules for most of the employee groups made his incapacity in respect to police and fire salaries (and School Department salaries) a breach in his authority. The serious nature of this breach probably was not foreseen at the time, either by the manager or by the Plan E support groups. Eight years later we can see that inevitably the most intense efforts would be made by the manager's political opponents, as well as by the manager himself, to attract the allegiance of city employees. The 1935 Act constituted a valuable weapon in the hands of the council—a council which the Plan E group did not control—by which a large segment of the municipal staff could be directly affected and by which the initiative in respect to salaries and working conditions for the entire working force could effectively be taken from the manager. Here was a sharp inconsistency between the manager's general power on the one hand to set a budgetary ceiling and his general responsibilities as administrative head of the organization, and on the other, the limitations on his authority under the special law and the general school laws.

It was hardly an ideal post into which Mr. Atkinson stepped.

II. Development of the Battle

A. ACTION BY THE "LAME DUCK" COUNCIL

The political proclivities of the "lame duck" Plan B city council have already been observed, but perhaps its major political move was unleashed six weeks before the new charter and administration were to come into force. Calculated to rouse the hopes of city employees and make things even hotter than they already were for the new administration, the council adopted a series of ordinances and orders, which it undoubtedly knew were illegal, providing for pay increases of about 10 per cent for all city employees and for all recipients of welfare payments out of the city treasury, effective at the beginning of the term of the new council. The council had good reason to hope that, even if its own efforts were fruitless, the new council in the ensuing melee might be forced by the weight of political considerations to validate this action. At very least, the battle could undoubtedly be counted upon to get the new manager and council off to a bad start in their working relationships.

Certain additional details about the legal framework for these and subsequent moves need to be introduced.

Under the Plan B charter and Chapter 44 of the General Laws (known as the Municipal Finance Act), the mayor was responsible for bringing before the council requests for personnel needed to man the departments of the city, and for recommending rates of compensation for all city employees, save members of the Police and Fire Departments, whose emoluments were controlled by the council. The mayor's requests and recommendations were normally embodied in his annual budget, which was required to be submitted to the council within 45 days of the annual "formation of government" on the first Monday in January. The council was empowered to cut, but not to increase, the mayor's budget. By Section 33A of the Municipal Finance Act, at any time during the financial year (the calendar year) following the mayor's presentation of the budget to the council new employees could be added or salaries increased *only* if "provision therefor has been made by means of a supplemental appropriation." Under the procedures provided by law, supplemental appropriations must be originated by the mayor and approved by the council. The council at any time could by "Council Order" *request, but not require,* the mayor to bring in supplemental appropriations for any purpose, including salary increases. Under the above provisions, therefore, the mayor had power to withstand efforts of the council to increase salaries, save in the Police and Fire Departments, or to create new positions, and the council had power to preclude similar efforts of the mayor if it was disposed to do so.

Reference has been made to the special authority granted the Cambridge city council in respect to establishing the salaries of members of the Police and Fire Departments. In 1935, at the instance of legislators from the city of Cambridge, the Massachusetts General Court had passed a special act providing as follows:

> Salaries of the members of the police and fire departments of the city of Cambridge shall be fixed by ordinance of said city, the provision of any special or general law to the contrary notwithstanding.

The effect of this law was to empower the council to increase salaries of these two departments either by ordinance enacted and made effective prior to receipt by the council of the mayor's annual budget, or enacted during the first year of its two-year term, to be effective at the beginning of the next fiscal period.[4] In either of these cases the mayor was obliged to include in his budget sums sufficient to pay such voted salaries. After submission of the budget by the mayor, the council could also undertake to induce the mayor to submit to it a supplementary appropriation in order that an increase could be granted. In this case, however, the mayor was in control; he was not required to present the requested appropriation.

All of the above provisions, including the 1935 special act, continued in force under the new charter in 1942, except that the manager was now the executive officer rather than the mayor. It should be noted, however, that while under Plan B the 1935 special act seemed no important breach in the mayor's power, under Plan E, with its rather unusual attribution of powers to the manager, it was a very disconcerting provision.

The special act of 1941 limiting the power of the incumbent Cambridge government to create new positions or grant pay increases also related directly to the situation at that time. That act read, in part:

> During the period covered by this Act [i.e., July 23, 1941, to January 5, 1942] no additional appointment, and no promotion or increase in salary except regular step-rate increases, shall be made in any appointive office, position, or employment in the service of said city.

It is and was clear then, that the effort of the "lame duck" council in November of 1941 to increase salaries of city employees was illegal, for the effect of the ordinances was to bind the successor council, and in any case the special act of 1941 specifically prohibited such pay raises. There can be no question that the council was deliberately trying to foment difficulty for the new council and administration, at the same time that it hoped to leave in the minds of city employees—who could hardly be familiar with the legal intricacies of these actions—a memory that the pre-Plan E council had been solicitous of employee interests.

[4] By judicial precedent, one council could not bind its successor, so in order to compel the mayor to include a sum for an increase in his next budget, the council would have to pass the appropriate ordinance during the first year of its two-year term.

B. GENERAL WAGE INCREASES ARE PROPOSED

At the fourth business meeting of the new council, February 2, 1942, Councilor McNamara introduced an "order," in effect a request to the manager, to raise the wages of all city employees 10 per cent up to a salary maximum of $2,500 and 5 per cent on salaries beyond that figure. The "council order" is a convenient device of Massachusetts law which permits the council to express its views but which, in regard to any matter under the cognizance of the city manager, is without legal effect. It has been a favorite device for "politick-ing" by the city council for it enables it to pass over to the manager the onus for refusing actions which are politically popular with particular groups but could hardly be said to be in the best interests of the city. (In most states, the council's order is law, and the buck cannot be passed.) The council voted unanimously in favor of McNamara's order. The Plan E councilors knew that the pay raises, if granted, would require a $4 increase in the tax rate; they knew then that the order would be absolutely opposed by the manager and the Plan E Committee. But they knew, too, that the order was without legal force, and there was no apparent reason for them to take a stand which might jeopardize their chance of attracting the support of city employees at the next election. The vote was, in a sense, the opening shot in the battle within the new government to gain the political strength which neither the opponents of Plan E nor the Plan E group itself had at that time, the strength needed to lay down a planned, integrated, consistent line of policy.

The manager was very much "put on the spot" by the order, despite its lack of legal force. His experience in public life was of exactly four weeks' duration. He had taken over an administrative organization which was at least as suspicious of him as he was of it.

There was no person to whom he could turn for advice of a policy nature. He recognized that there was some merit in the order; living costs had by this time increased 10 per cent over 1940 while salaries had remained constant.[5] For some employees this meant very real hardship; the standard rate of pay of a laborer at the time was $5 a day. It was of great importance to the manager to gain the respect and spontaneous co-operation of city employees. Yet in the days ahead it was likely that he would have to take numerous steps which would be unpopular with some employees, for many departments were overstaffed, inferior administrators having superior political ties had been elevated to positions for which they were unqualified and from which they would have to be dislodged, observance of working regulations had become intolerably careless. These considerations, added to the problem of the cost of living, argued forcefully for a raise.

The manager sought to gather all the facts bearing upon the situation. He consulted with his city solicitor to make certain of his legal standing in the matter. Atkinson's first communication to the council had been to announce his appointment as solicitor of John A. Daly, a lawyer of unimpeachable reputation and past president of the Cambridge Bar Association. Daly advised him that under the charter a decision initiating a wage increase for employees other than in the Police and Fire Departments rested exclusively in the manager's hands.

There were two elements in the situation which from the outset determined Atkinson's attitude and his final decision on this matter. During his first weeks in office, he had been engaged much of the time in preparing his budget for the current fiscal year. As required by law, the budget was an itemized document with the name and salary of every employee listed. Atkinson was appalled to find that there were for certain of the most common jobs in the city as many as three different levels of compensation for identical work. There was no system of job titles, no classification to which salaries were related. The "going rate" for a laborer was $30 a week, but one of the former mayor's relatives and a number of other men with "connections" with the past regime were paid $48 per week as laborers. An across-the-board increase of 10 per cent would exaggerate these inequalities and perpetuate them. He was determined not to perpetuate a situation which he felt grievously unfair. The second decisive element was, of course, the state of the city's finances. He felt called upon to save—quite literally—every nickel that he could. The credit of the city was shaky in the extreme, and its physical plant was in precarious condition. Plan E had been "voted into office" with the tacit understanding of its supporters that taxes would come down. The projected raise, if extended to all employees, would require an increase in the tax rate sufficient to boost it to more than $50. Whatever was happening to cost of living statistics, the fact of the matter was that Cambridge still had hundreds of men on the rolls of the WPA. He saw in the council order a plain effort to put him on the spot. Without giving a thought to a compromise on the issue, he reached his decision and informed the council of it in a formal communication at the next meeting, February 9. He stated that he would grant no wage increases to any employees until an over-all study of wages in Cambridge and in comparable communities in the state had been made and a classification system adopted, and until the financial status of the city had been appraised to determine whether a raise could be afforded at this time. He stated that in his view no person who had been receiving $48 a week for work for which the standard rate was $30 should receive an increase until such favoritism had been found and eliminated. The manager, therefore, recommended that a special council committee, appointed at the opening meeting on the motion of Councilor McNamara "to investigate and report on adjustment of salaries of city employees in proportion to the advance in the cost of living," be broadened in membership and scope, to undertake an over-all job survey and reclassification. He recommended that representatives of the two largest employee organizations and the

[5] For chart showing cost of living and index of police and fire salaries, see Appendix C.

manager be added to the McNamara committee. The council realized that many grievances resulted from present salary inequalities and voted favorably upon his recommendations. The arduous job of a personnel survey and reclassification got under way. Cambridge once again became a pioneer in the state in availing itself of authority granted all cities two years earlier.

C. INCREASED SALARIES FOR POLICEMEN AND FIREMEN

Meanwhile, Councilman McNamara had taken the lead in obtaining legal advice as to the power of the council under the new charter to continue to establish salaries in the Police and Fire Departments under the special act of 1935. The advice he received was that the special act remained in full force. Upon request, by council order, City Solicitor Daly had advised the council officially that the ordinances passed by the "lame duck" council the prior November were null and void—a decision which was no surprise to the council and one with which it had no quarrel. The council majority reacted to the solicitor's opinion with a forthright step. Early in February 1942, after one month in office and long before the special salary and reclassification committee had brought in a report, the council passed to the publication stage an ordinance granting a $200 wage increase across-the-board to members of the Police and Fire Departments; at the same meeting it referred to its Finance Committee—a committee of the whole council—an order to grant increases to all employees. Under the General Laws an ordinance is required to be published "once in full in at least one newspaper of the city, and in any additional manner that may be provided by ordinance, at least ten days before its final passage." Thus, except in the case of emergency legislation, final passage of any ordinance is delayed until the second weekly council meeting after its "passage to a second reading." Atkinson thus had two weeks to decide what move he might next make.

The manager's position on wage increases had already been made clear; so had his willingness to resist with all his power efforts by the council to interfere in matters in which he had full legal control over his organization. But an ordinance which the council clearly had legal power to adopt was a different instrument from an "order" dealing with matters squarely within the cognizance of the manager. The general course of his reasoning seems to have followed somewhat these lines:

Was he obliged to regard such an ordinance as an expression of council policy? If so, was it possible that his responsibilities in regard to such an expression of policy could conflict with broader responsibilities under the charter—responsibilities as "chief administrative officer" of the city "responsible for the administration of all departments . . ."—responsibilities that seemed to him implied in Section 104 requiring him to make recommendations concerning affairs of the city such as to him seem desirable, and to keep the council fully informed as to the city's financial condition and future needs?[6] If, as he thought, there was such a conflict, should the manager give effect to each particular policy decision of the elected representatives of the people, or should he—an appointive, professional administrator charged among other things with conserving the assets of the city—reach an independent decision and battle the council, if his decision so required, with all the powers at his command?

It is of course evident that the answer to any such question has to be sought in the light of myriad factors pertaining uniquely to the particular circumstances at hand. Not the least of these factors are the personal qualities and attitudes of the individuals concerned. Atkinson's decision to balk this latest effort of the council if he could possibly do so demonstrates his constant readiness to fight—if a fight were made necessary by refusal to compromise on his own terms—on any issue which involved his administrative leadership and control. He believed that only if he were effec-

[6] For selected excerpts from the city charter pertaining to the respective duties, responsibilities, and authority of the city council and the city manager, see Appendix D.

tively in control could he meet the responsibilities with which he was charged.

As he sized up the situation, he regarded McNamara and his supporters in council as far more interested in driving up municipal costs in order to discredit the new government than in the welfare of the employees, and his views found independent support in the weekly journal. The Cambridge *Chronicle*, commenting editorially on the police and fire ordinance, attributed it to an attempt to "put certain city councilors on the spot and to embarrass the city manager in his effort to reduce the 1942 tax rate. . . . Experienced political observers" felt that "the pay rise drive was launched for political reasons rather than as the result of a widespread organized demand by city employees."

As Atkinson saw the issue, he had two alternatives:

(1) to balk all efforts for pay increases at this time; or
(2) to cut city payrolls in order to grant an increase, firing workers at a time when the army of unemployed was still very sizeable.

He did not consider as even a remote possibility any action which would serve to increase municipal costs. One of his basic operating premises was that city costs would not be increased, and any decisions he made had to find accommodation within the area of such premises. He did consider the two alternatives, however, and made inquiries of the budget commissioner as to what men would be affected by a layoff. Layoffs in Cambridge as elsewhere would have to be made on the basis of "juniority" or reverse seniority. He discovered that among the laboring group the first man to go would be the father of eight children who was already finding it necessary to draw relief payments even while he was employed. Atkinson was hardly disposed to jeopardize the welfare of the city or of the bulk of the city employees to protect the group of men who would be affected if a layoff were necessary, but the meaning of this alternative to those men *did* weigh in the decision, and it is interesting that individual human values found a place in the balance at this moment of tension.

D. ATKINSON FIGHTS BACK

Atkinson was determined to fight the council in spite of that body's authority under the special act. He obviously needed legal advice as to how to proceed. There was no formal procedure by which he could oppose the council on the issue, Daly told him, but there was a technical device which might work. Under the provisions of law, after receipt of the budget by the council, no ordinance, vote, or appointment increasing personnel costs was valid unless "provision therefor has been made by way of a supplemental appropriation." Final balloting on the ordinance would occur at the meeting two weeks hence. Could the manager complete his budget and present it to the council before that vote was taken? Without communicating his intentions, the manager saw to it that the budget was ready for presentation. This was precisely the break he needed, for with the battle won for that year, he could in the course of the year complete the reclassification study and make such salary adjustments as he saw fit. So well did he carry out his plan that the council did not discover that the manager was giving battle until a week after final passage of the ordinance.

The line-up of the council in the vote on the salary ordinance reflects once more the weak political position of the Plan E group and the importance of the vote of city employees in the struggle for power. In the vote on the ordinance itself, the three councilors who owed their election largely if not exclusively to Plan E endorsement voted *against*. The other six included McNamara, Sullivan, Hogan, and Sennott of the outright opposition; Councilor Lynch, the North End banker who on other issues had demonstrated concern for the financial underpinning of the city; and Councilor Pill, whose views nearly always placed him with the Plan E group, but whose election could be attributed to his own political strength rather than to the Plan E group.[7]

With the ordinance passed, Councilor McNamara, who was chairman of the special salary committee, rose to say that, police and

[7] Pill had not been endorsed by the Plan E Committee in 1941.

fire employees having been given a raise, he believed all others were entitled to a similar increase. McNamara thereupon introduced a new order asking the manager to grant a raise of 10 per cent to all employees earning $2500 or less, and of 5 per cent to those earning more than $2500. In the ensuing debate, Plan E Councilor Crane spoke persuasively against the order, referring again to the complete lack of equity in present pay arrangements and stating that a comprehensive study and adjustment rather than an across-the-board increase was needed. Councilor Morton, who had also spoken in opposition to the order, asked to be excused from voting. After his request was denied, the order was passed *unanimously*. Thus the Plan E group stood behind the manager on the issue of an ordinance which it believed to have legal force, but felt that political considerations required opposing him on an order which it knew to be advisory, with the effect only of placing on the manager rather than themselves the resentment city employees would have if the increase voted to policemen and firemen were not extended to them.

The outcome of his first direct clash with the council was a complete victory for the manager. At the meeting following the enactment of the salary ordinance, Atkinson informed the council that he regarded the ordinance as illegal because it had been passed after his budget had been submitted, and that he therefore intended to ignore it. The council requested Daly to give an opinion in the matter, and in early March the solicitor advised that in his opinion the ordinance was null and void. Councilor McNamara thereupon retained an attorney and took the matter to court, seeking by mandamus to force the manager and other city officials to pay the salaries as enacted by the council. Nine months later, in mid-November, McNamara suffered his first adverse decision; an appeal was filed and in late September 1943, nearly a year later, the Appellate Court upheld the lower court. An appeal was carried to the Supreme Court, which also upheld the trial court. In the interim, during that first year, the manager was installing a classification system for Cambridge employees which subsequently became a model for many cities throughout the state. In January 1943, not long after the anniversary of the first council order to increase salaries, the council adopted by 5-3 a compromise on salaries of policemen and firemen which had the manager's approval; raises of $100 were approved for 1943 and 1944. This time the opposition was split; Councilor Hogan voted with the majority, as did Hyman Pill, who regarded this solution as politically acceptable.

III. Aftermath of Victory

A. COMPLAINTS ABOUT ATKINSON

Perhaps it is too much to suggest that, following the initial crisis in council-manager relations described above, a really cordial relationship between legislative and executive departments developed. Nonetheless it is true that the ensuing years brought steady progress toward the ideal. This is not to imply that the opposition dissolved and recrystallized as a bulwark of Plan E support, but the opposition had grown less personal in its attacks upon the manager and somewhat more constructive in its criticism.

The council did not take its defeat by the manager in 1942 "lying down." The "independents," as the councilors who were not endorsed by the Plan E Committee liked to be called, or "pols" as the Plan E Committee was wont to call some of them, continued their efforts to appear in the role of godfathers to city employees. An old favorite device was the proposal of council orders requesting or directing the manager to grant special favors of one kind or another to employees. In that first year, for example, Councilor Sullivan introduced an order asking the manager to grant vacation pay to employees entering the armed services; Pill introduced orders asking that, on one occasion, employees be released at noon on a certain day so that they might witness a parade in South Boston, and on another, urging that a special holiday be granted on Patriots Day; orders introduced by Sennott asked the manager to establish a five-day week during the summer months, and to pay employees the day before Thanksgiving; and at year's end, when the treasury appeared to be ending the fiscal period with a surplus, Lynch introduced an order asking the manager why he didn't comply with the police and fire salary ordinance passed by the council the prior February, but without legal standing, now that enough money was available to pay those salaries for two weeks of the current year. Virtually all of these orders were introduced purely for political effect; in some cases they embodied requests for actions already implemented by the manager, while others like that of Lynch were requests which the council knew full well could not for numerous good reasons be carried out. Probably it is unnecessary to add that those orders were invariably adopted by unanimous vote.

Meanwhile, in the General Court of Massachusetts, political efforts of a more serious nature were being made. Each year bills were introduced which had the aim of repealing proportional representation from the Plan E charter. Some of the support for these moves came from people who earnestly believed that P.R. deprived voters of their right to cast their vote for the candidate of their choice; or that it encouraged voting upon religious, racial, or other group lines. For the most part, however, these were points raised by professional politicians, who believed that P.R. was indispensable to the effective working of Plan E, and that the best way to attack Plan E was through the P.R. feature. Among those urging that P.R. be killed was the State Firefighters Association. Finally, in August 1949, the Legislature withdrew the P.R. provisions from Plan E, making it impossible for cities thereafter adopting a council-manager charter to elect the council and School Committee by proportional representation. The effort of the politicians then was directed to denying existing manager cities the right to elect these officials by proportional representation—an effort not yet successful. In local governmental affairs, battles must sometimes be fought not only at home but in the state capital, where political forces may contend without the close attention of citizens which deliberations in the local council usually enjoy.

At home the council opposition continued to "probe for weak spots in the enemy lines," seeking out the new lines of demarcation between legislative and executive branches. It is not surprising that this process of getting acquainted was acrimonious at first, nor that in time the bitterness of the attacks by the council opposition diminished. Councilor Sullivan's language was perhaps the most colorful; on the council floor he habitually referred to the manager as a "$15.00 a week clerk." Every possible opportunity was taken for a personal attack upon the manager. One of the favorite accusations, in which McNamara joined, was that Atkinson used his official car for trips into Boston on private matters connected with his own business enterprises. Councilor Lynch asserted, in April of that first year, that the manager was "looting the city treasury" for reimbursement of expenses for official travel outside the state; and in May he stated that the manager was "building up a political machine"—this over an appropriation for a new car for the manager's office. Lynch, McNamara, and Sullivan teamed up in June to accuse the manager of perpetrating a "land deal" in connection with the purchase of land for the city cemetery. An unspecified "connection" between the manager and a former councilman was alleged. It is interesting to note that these three councilors were that part of the opposition which was most genuinely troubled by the power of the executive in the new government. While there may have been political motives, in the narrow sense, in their charge, it is undoubtedly true that they resented the affirmative recommendation from the manager concerning the cemetery; they regarded such a recommendation as beyond the range of the kind of "administering" he had been hired to do. To these men, the manager was the "hired man" of the council. They believed their hired man was much too obstreperous, and sought every possible means of slapping him down. Yet this cemetery incident also illustrates one of the affirmative tasks of a responsible professional executive, for the fact of the matter was that unused land in the old cemetery was very nearly exhausted and the city had no prospect whatever within its heavily built-up area of finding other cemetery land which would be needed to provide for local men killed in World War II. The manager's arrangements to purchase the land in question were made with the trustees of the Mt. Auburn Cemetery, a group which manages one of the metropolitan area's loveliest burial grounds, the entire profits of which go to the Massachusetts Horticultural Society. In brief, Lynch, McNamara, and Sullivan could adduce no proof for their charges and the council subsequently approved the purchase.

Councilor McNamara seemed more genuinely concerned about the power which he saw the manager exercising than any of the other councilmen. When Atkinson established a schedule of working hours which varied from the pre-existing schedule, McNamara labeled the order by which the change was effected "one of the manager's famous war bulletins," and he requested the city solicitor to rule on the manager's authority to establish office hours. In the councilor's view, such an action pertained to the legislative powers of the council. The solicitor's opinion upheld the manager's action in forthright terms. Subsequently, when the manager ordered two police stations closed, thus giving effect to the recommendations of a survey made several years previously under the Plan B government, McNamara with the support of Councilor Sullivan, charging "encroachment of the city manager upon the powers of the council," introduced an order to remove Atkinson from office. When the order was tabled, he hired a lawyer and tried unsuccessfully by writ of mandamus to compel the reopening of the stations.

It is clear that much of this in-fighting was politically inspired—an effort to harry the new government at every turn by those councilors whose constituents were not favorably disposed toward Plan E and who felt themselves socially, economically, and politically opposed to persons who were favorably disposed toward it. Part of the struggle was, however, an outgrowth of uncertainty as to where power, authority, and responsibility truly lay, under a new form of government for which there were no precedents in the state. Over the years, in the course of contention, the loci of power and responsibility in particular issues were determined, and sources of conflict were diminished. While Councilor Sullivan's sharp mind and tongue were never dulled until his death in 1949, McNamara became progressively less bitter, his opposition more realistic and constructive. Meetings of the council became less violent, as personal political attacks upon the manager abated. The opposition remained and remains today, but with the possible exception of a single councilor it is not the suspicious, jealous, bitter opposition of 1942.

B. ATKINSON MAKES PROGRESS

The record of achievement in the fiscal and business affairs of the city being forged by the new administration, and the political strength gained by that administration and its support groups as a result, constitute the principal explanation of the change in council-manager relations. When Plan E government had come to Cambridge, as we have already observed, its political position was precarious, and it could strengthen that position only by its record in action. It was deeds, not words, which led Plan E government to the popularity which it enjoys among city employees and citizens today.

In forging that record, administrative actions initiated by the manager have played an important part. Early in his first year the manager induced the mayor to head a council committee to undertake an investigation into the administration of the Police Department. Certain personnel were shifted to new assignments. Charges of favoritism were aired, and after a period of negotiation within the department itself, the Chief of Police brought in a recommendation for measures which seemed to overcome the problems within the Department. A certified public accountant was retained to investigate the administration of the City Hospital shortly after Atkinson had replaced five of the six hospital trustees. The accountant's report, released in November

1942, explained and justified Atkinson's earlier dismissal action; "serious incompetence," inadequacy of records, "hopeless disagreement" of accounts kept at the hospital with those at the office of the city auditor, and no bills issued for services in the case of the families of three trustees—these were among the findings.

In respect to personnel administration, great strides were made. In his early months in Cambridge the manager found it necessary to take stands in regard to pay raises and the enforcement of working rules which hardly would have won him a prize for popularity. Yet, before the end of his first year, two steps had been taken which vindicated his stand on these matters and increasingly won him the respect and support of a majority of his organization. The first of these was the complete reclassification of positions throughout the city service and establishment of an equitable wage and salary plan. The second was the delineation of a forthright policy in regard to appointments and promotions. As a matter of course, appointments went to the top man on the civil service list and whenever possible, promotions were made from within the service. In case after case, the manager looked within the organization for vacancies at the level of department head and other top officials, even in those early days when considerable turnover was occurring at that level.

Another source of discontent and lack of self-respect was overcome when, in departments which had been overstaffed, "painless reductions" in numbers of employees were accomplished by a policy of transfers and not filling vacancies in unneeded positions.

In the course of the first few years of the Plan E administration another policy was in fact adopted which, although still unwritten, is acknowledged by the manager and heralded by the council—a policy of paying employees of the city of Cambridge at least as well as persons in similar jobs in any city in the state. While in particular jobs exceptions to this policy can be found, in general it has been true since the mid-forties that Cambridge has set the pace in Massachusetts in the matter of municipal salaries. In establishing this policy, the manager and Plan E councilors have had behind them the support of the Plan E Committee.

The manager made it quite clear to the council that he regarded the administration of matters pertaining to personnel as strictly his affair and none of theirs. Once again in March 1946 a council order was passed in which the city manager was "hereby ordered" to grant all employees save those of the Police and Fire Departments (who were to be dealt with separately) an increase in salary of $200 over their salaries as of December 31, 1944. In responding to the order, the manager transmitted an opinion he had obtained from the city solicitor in which the solicitor asserted that the manager could not legally substitute the wishes of the city council for his "executive judgment" in such matters. With the opinion Atkinson sent a message which stated his position succinctly:

> I wish to repeat the statement which I had previously made to your Honorable Body, namely, that I am definitely opposed to blanket raises such as the one referred to above. I consider that this would be a most unjust and inequitable proceeding and would completely disrupt the pay schedules and increment system which we have labored so long and arduously in establishing and carrying out during the past four years.

The manager reminded the council, in conclusion—as he had done the prior year "when a similar matter was brought up"—that he favored frequent reviews of pay schedules, with revision "as I see the need for it."

C. PAY RAISES AND MUNICIPAL IMPROVEMENT

In the matter of pay raises in the Police and Fire Departments, the manager was on less secure ground. He was ready to assert and fight for the right to control the personnel of these departments, as of the others, but the special act of 1935 continued to plague him, in that it gave continued authorization to the council to establish salaries in these two departments by ordinance. A compromise, reached in late 1942 at the conclusion of the initial battle over this issue, stabilized the matter during 1943 and 1944. During the war years, thanks in large part to the pervading spirit of patriotism, the manager remained in control. At the end of 1946, after a year of steeply rising living costs, Atkinson recommended and the council adopted a schedule of salary increases for all city employees amounting to approximately $400. This increase substantially restored the level of wages to the cost-of-living relationship which had existed at the end of 1945. In mid-June of 1948, the manager presented to the council a recommendation for salary increases in the aggregate of $172,000, representing permanent boosts in basic salaries of all categories of employees of about $200. Once again, the recommendation followed a thorough study by the Budget Director of the wages of Cambridge employees in relation to those paid in other municipalities and in industrial employment locally. At the same time, salary increments were adjusted so that in the case of most employees one year was added to the period required for reaching the maximum salary. In Police and Fire, for example, the top salary of privates had been $3000, reached at the beginning of the third year of employment; now the top of $3200 would be reached at the beginning of the fourth year. These increases represented for policemen and firemen—and in general for all city employees whose salaries were kept in relation to those in these two departments—an increase of about 9 per cent, bringing the index of salaries (1941 base) from 137 to 146.[8] The last prior increase on January 2, 1947 had brought the index of city salaries generally to about 9 per cent below the cost of living as of that date. Throughout 1947 and early 1948 the cost of living had been rising at the average rate of more than 1 per cent per month. Thus, just prior to the June 1948 increase, the wage index was about 25 per cent below the cost of living index and *following the increase*, it remained about 16 per cent below. Nonetheless, the manager was able to inform the council, in his message recommending the $200 increases, that:

> I have discussed these proposed increases with the heads of our two labor unions, also with the head of the Firemen's Union and the Committee from the Police Association, and they have assured me that these rates are satisfactory to them.

He added his assurance that "the working conditions in wages and hours can be considered as good as any city in the state and better than most municipalities." In his office, available to all, were elaborate studies to back up this statement.

In addition to the achievements of the manager in respect to administration, which have been enumerated above, others could be mentioned, varying from revitalizing existing departments, like Purchasing, to major reorganizations and shifts like that represented by the consolidation of six departments into a Department of Public Works. Suffice it to say that great progress was made in rationalizing organization and procedures.

The record of Plan E government in relation to matters of finance and the physical plant of the city is impressive, and constitutes one of the achievements of his administration about which the manager is most proud. Within six months of taking office, Atkinson was able to present to the city council an interim report which listed the following achievements:

1. No borrowing during the period, and adoption of a policy of avoiding all borrowing if possible. The weekly newspaper pointed out that, if continued for a year, this policy alone would save the city $185,000, amounting to about $1.00 in the tax rate.
2. Rehabilitation and cleaning up of City Hall and other city buildings and equipment.
3. Reduction of tax rate to $43.90 from the all-time high in 1941 of $46.30.

Throughout the war years the pay-as-you-go policy was adhered to and long-term borrowing was eliminated; of course restrictions on building and equipment facilitated this policy. Even tax-anticipation certificates were minimized, as the city requested and obtained the co-operation of the city's larger taxpayers in meeting their tax bills promptly. In 1946, within 72 hours of the mailing of tax bills, more than $1,100,000—18 per cent of the total levy—had been paid in. Since in 1942 the cost of borrowed funds represented nearly $10 in the tax rate, substantial reduction was possible from

[8] See Appendix C.

the new borrowing policy alone. Finally in 1948 strict pay-as-you-go was abandoned and a loan of $500,000 was obtained for rehabilitation of certain city buildings, including schools. This remains the only long-term borrowing in eight years of Plan E administration, and in 1949 the total debt of the city was down to some $2,175,000 as against a total of $12,105,000 in 1941. With the falling debt, the city's credit has become excellent.

Another fiscal achievement is the record of collections of taxes and hospital bills. In 1941, one-year delinquency of taxes was 19 per cent of the total amount levied; in 1948, the figure was 4 per cent. The improvement in collections was undoubtedly primarily the result of the general improvement in economic conditions; but the improvement here can also be partially ascribed to the 5 per cent decline in the tax rate in the face of generally rising costs.

A major effort of the manager was to bring industry and commercial development to Cambridge in order to increase the valuation base of the city. Since the low of $168.7 million of assessed valuation in 1941, a "bottom" reached after the long decline of the 1930's, $35 million had been added to the valuation base by December 1949, an increase of nearly 21 per cent. The $5.5 million increase in 1949 alone was, at the rate of the 1949 tax rate, equivalent to a tax rate increase of $1.07. At the same tax rate, the $35 million increase since 1941 represented a tax rate saving of $6.84 (based on 1949 valuation). While extensive rehabilitation of property of all sorts since the war has aided in boosting valuations and substantial upward revaluations of existing property have been made, the major contribution to the increase has resulted from the establishment of new industrial and commercial undertakings. The manager has had notable success in his efforts to bring this about.

Undoubtedly the financial achievement most heralded by the Plan E administration and its support groups is its record of reductions in the tax rate. That record is, obviously, related in a major way to the expansion of the city's valuation base. Cambridge was the only city in Massachusetts to reduce its tax rate annually from 1942 through 1947, and it has increased its rate since the war less than any other city in the state. The 1950 rate of $39.70 was $6.60 less than in 1941, despite a reduction in city working hours from 48 to 40, basic salary increases which average more than 50 per cent, and post-war cost experience generally. Cambridge was—to take note of another record—the only city in Massachusetts with a rate in 1950 lower than the rate in 1941.

Finally, municipal physical facilities have been expanded, renewed, and brought into excellent condition. Without going into extensive detail, a statement of this sort may sound like an optimistic generalization, but perhaps a few references may be sufficient to illustrate what is intended. The condition of police equipment in 1941 and the lack of any snow removal equipment at that time have been mentioned. The Police Department today owns 16 cruising cars, most of them purchased within the year; in Public Works there are 35 snow plows and 4 loaders; complete equipment for street construction has been obtained and costs of construction have plummeted from an average per mile of $51,989 in 1941, under the system of contracting out this work, to an average of $14,271 per mile in 1949; in the Fire Department, the average age of 22 pieces of motorized equipment has been cut from 13.8 to 4.7 years.

D. THE GROWTH OF PUBLIC SUPPORT

The record highlighted in the foregoing paragraphs has inevitably had political effects. To a considerable extent the city manager himself has been credited by city employees and by the populace generally with these achievements. Yet, the Plan E Committee inevitably has gained in prestige as the record has unfolded. Calculations of the number of first place votes won by Plan E-endorsed candidates shows a steady rise; 35 per cent of the first place ballots cast in 1941, 36 per cent in 1943, 45 per cent in 1945, 50 per cent in 1947. It should be recalled that a popular vote-getter, John D. Lynch, was among these Plan E candidates in 1941, 1945, and 1947. Yet it seems clear that the voting strength of Plan E candidates has increased substantially. Following both 1945 and 1947 elections, the Plan E group had a "fictitious majority" in the city council—five of the nine members, but only four of nine in fact, because of the consistent opposition to Plan E policy of Councilor Lynch, who for reasons not germane to this case was endorsed by the Plan E Committee in 1941, 1945, and 1947.[9] The scales were balanced so evenly that in both 1946 and 1948 the "formation of government" was a highly difficult matter. In 1946, it took a week of meetings and 309 ballots to elect a mayor; and in 1948 effective government in both the council and School Committee was hamstrung for three months and 18 days while 1321 ballots were taken in 35 separate sessions, as the council endeavored to select a mayor. Finally, in 1949, the Plan E group attained a true 5-4 majority in the city council and a 4-3 majority in the School Committee. Politically, the Plan E forces have not before been so firmly established.

Organization of these forces undoubtedly accounts in no small part for their growing strength. Between 1938 and 1945 the major bulwark of organized Plan E support was the Plan E Committee, the group which under the chairmanship of Dean Landis had campaigned in 1938 and 1940 for a Plan E charter. The Cambridge Taxpayers Association, the Chamber of Commerce, the League of Women Voters—these organizations which were by their constitutions prevented from taking a political stand were the source of much of the membership and active working force of the Plan E Committee. Another smaller and separate group also worked actively for Plan E government, however—the Cambridge Citizens Committee. Finally, in July 1945, all Plan E support groups came together to form the Cambridge Civic Association and a non-political affiliate, the Cambridge Research Association. The Committee for Plan E, Taxpayers Association, and Citizens Committee all now ceased to exist. The Cambridge Civic Association—the CCA—announced itself as "a political association dedicated to promoting honest and efficient local government through the support of the council-manager plan, working for and supporting competency in the office of city manager, working for and improving the school system of the city, and freeing the school system from all influences other than those which will provide the best possible education for the children of Cambridge, and seeking and supporting the candidacy of competent men and women in public office." The CCA would carry on the practice of the Plan E Committee in urging "competent persons" to run for office, in investigating the qualifications of all candidates, in interviewing candidates who wished to be interviewed, and in selecting a slate of endorsed candidates whose campaigns it would finance and support. The Research Association was to be a non-political, public service investigative agency. It is the Civic Association which has since 1945 been identified by both friend and foe as the growing force standing behind Plan E government in Cambridge. That there was in 1945 a kernel of truth lying behind the suspicions and charges of inhabitants and councilors from the "lower wards" that the CCA was a group representing "Taxpayers-Republicans-Money-Brattle Street-Harvard" is suggested by a glance at the board of directors of the organization as it stood at the time of its formation.[10] In ensuing years, steps have been taken to improve the representative character of this board.[11] Furthermore, endorsements of candidates have reflected attention to spreading support among all wards and nationality and religious groups. Indeed, the prominent role in the Plan E movement played by a number of citizens of Irish descent; the strong and almost consistent support of the CCA program given by Edward A. Crane, an Irish Democrat, son of a former city police officer, and the council's leading vote-getter; the similar support of Joseph A. DeGuglielmo who gets much of the Italian vote in the community group in Ward 1; and even the religion and national party affiliations of the city manager, have made it impossible for the opposition to make its charges stick with effective force.

The new organization of Plan E support has worked far more effectively than the old. Larger sums of money have been obtained and

[9] The endorsement of John D. Lynch by the Plan E group was always a matter of controversy within the Plan E Committee, but the issues in that controversy are not importantly related to this case.

[10] See Appendix E.

[11] *Ibid.*

spent for campaign expenditures for CCA-endorsed candidates, for periodic bulletins on civic affairs, and for other activities aimed at promoting Plan E government. Membership has grown from 880 in December 1945 to 1200 a year later and to 2200 in December 1949. The CCA stands as an organized political force ready to work for efficient government, a source of great strength for the city manager and for the councilors and school committeemen whom it endorses and who remain loyal to its objectives.

IV. The Battle of 1948-1949

A. INTRODUCTORY STATEMENT

In the late summer of 1948 the city manager and his supporters had good reason to think that all was well with Plan E in Cambridge. Achievements of the administration have been delineated above. Morale of the working force appeared to be high. The pay raises granted in June on the initiative of the administration had served to keep Cambridge salaries by and large at the top for municipal employees in Massachusetts, despite the fact that salaries of all but laborers continued to lag behind the cost of living, which was just then reaching its peak.

Suddenly that fall, within one month of November 8, 1948, the manager was faced with pay raise demands from unions and worker associations representing every group of city employees, aggregating approximately $1.3 millions, and raising the specter of a $7.00 jump in the tax rate. The prior July, a tax rate boost of $4.40 had been announced for 1948—the first increase since 1941. The further increase now threatened would, if effected, boost the tax rate to more than the 1941 figure which had, in no small degree, brought about the revulsion in which Plan E was "voted into office." In the words of the editor of the local weekly:

> Make no doubt about it, this pay raise question and its effect both on the city employees and the home owners is the most important single problem to come before the current city council.

This section will discuss the way in which this crisis arose, the manner in which the manager dealt with it, and the aftermath of the battle.

B. FORCES LYING BEHIND THE BATTLE

The city council elected in 1947 was made up as follows:

Councilor	*CCA-Endorsed*	*Consistent CCA Supporter*	*Consistent CCA Opponent*
Michael J. Neville, Mayor			
Edward A. Crane	x	x	
John D. Lynch	x		
Michael A. Sullivan			x
Hyman Pill	x	x	
Francis L. Sennott			x
W. Donnison Swan	x	x	
Joseph A. DeGuglielmo	x	x	
John J. Foley			x
Totals	5	4	3

Mayor Neville and Councilor Lynch were "independents" rather than definitely with "the opposition." On most issues the manager's requests and recommendations prevailed, more often because of the support of Mayor Neville than of Lynch.

Michael Sullivan was ailing; in early 1949 he died. Under the circumstances, the opposition leadership in the council shifted to Councilor Foley, a politician of long standing in the Democratic Party in Cambridge. As he had pointed out in a letter to the *Chronicle* when he announced his candidacy in the 1945 campaign, Foley had been an officer in the Cambridge Police Department before entering local politics. He had served two terms in the pre-1915 Common Council and two terms as councilor under Plan B. He had spent four years in the House of Representatives in the Massachusetts General Court, and two years (1944-45) on the Cambridge School Committee. He styled himself a "friend of labor," and pointed out that he had "always been interested in veterans legislation." He was elected to the council in 1945 by a narrow margin and re-elected in 1947. Foley lived in Ward II in North Cambridge, one of the wards which in the 1940 referendum had voted against adoption of a Plan E charter. He was antagonistic to Plan E and the city manager, and his personal hatred of the manager grew increasingly intense.

There is evidence to suggest that under the aegis of certain politicians in the city, among whom the last Plan B mayor was prominent, an effort was made in 1948 and 1949 to unite the opposition to Plan E in the council and in the School Committee in order to undertake a program aimed at discrediting the manager and his administration and electing an anti-Plan E council in the 1949 election. One of the first steps in the program was to be the raising of municipal costs sufficiently to bring the tax rate higher than it had been in 1941, at the time Plan E was installed.

Whether or not a well-laid plan was ever agreed upon for engineering a political coup, it seems clear that opposition councilors recognized the wasting away of their strength as the support for Plan E government among employees and local citizens continued to increase. It was essential to these men that the preponderant support of city employees be won away from the Plan E forces. The wage issue was the very issue on which the council majority had its most effective weapon for battling the manager—the special act of 1935. It was also, in the fall of 1948, an issue on which the city administration was not on completely firm ground. Throughout 1946 and 1947, the cost of living had been rising rapidly, nearly 20 per cent each year. Cities everywhere, like private businesses, were obliged to raise salaries. As we have seen, at the beginning of 1947, on the initiative of the city manager, a $400 salary increase was granted members of the Police and Fire Departments and approximately equivalent increases percentage-wise were given to other employees. In June 1948 the cost of living index had reached a peak and started downward. It was in June that the manager had introduced raises of 10 per cent or $200, whichever was less, for virtually all employees in the city. With these new rates in effect the index of salaries of policemen and firemen on a 1940 base stood at 146.1, compared with the Massachusetts cost of living index in July of 164.2. The index of wages of day laborers was 170.0, that of teachers (average) 153.8, while that of other workers in general lagged slightly behind that of policemen and firemen. But in general it was also true, as the manager had declared in recommending the June 1948 increases, that Cambridge wages and salaries were consonant with those in private industry in Cambridge and as good as or better than those in other cities throughout the state. The general, if lagging, upward trend in salaries was continuing, however, as wages in industry and other governmental units were brought into closer agreement with the now-falling cost of living index. This continuing upward trend of wages elsewhere, and the 18 per cent discrepancy between wages of policemen and firemen and the cost of living gave Plan E opponents a good issue on which to take action, calculated to win over the political support of city employees.

C. THE OPENING GUNS

The "salary battle of 1948-49," as we might call it, broke out at the meeting of the city council on October 25, 1948, when Mayor Neville, acting under the authority of the special act of 1935, introduced an ordinance to amend the salary schedules of policemen and firemen, to give them a raise of $400 effective January 1, 1949, and to remove the additional year required to progress to maximum pay, added at the time of the increase earlier that year. This projected pay increase would raise the index of salaries to 164.3, compared with a cost of living then at 162.6 and falling. The ordinance was referred to the Committee on Ordinances, a committee of the whole council.

Lying behind the mayor's action was a lot of maneuvering which cannot be fully documented. It seems probable that the initiative in seeking the pay raise lay with the Firefighters' Union and the Police Good Will Club. It is worthy of note that there are statewide police and fire organizations in Massachusetts which, in addition to employing pressure in the state legislature, are often able to take a hand in local action. The 1935 special act which applied only to Cambridge gave the Cambridge Police and Fire Departments a unique bargaining position; the state associations were always interested in the Cambridge situation because it afforded a chance for initiating statewide drives for higher wages. At the very least, we may be sure that the state associations were aware of the action being taken in Cambridge, at a time when agitation for raises was current all over the state. It seems also to be quite certain that the strategy of the pay-raise move was determined in consultation with Councilman Foley and others on the council. It was reportedly Foley who counseled a policy of no compromise, of all-or-nothing. It was he whom, along with Councilors Sullivan and Sennott, the president of the Firefighters' Local has identified as most helpful of all council members to the Union. Even if we cannot know conclusively the manner in which the pay-raise drive originated and the respective roles of the unions and of the opposition councilors, it is clear that the motives of these two groups were, as it were, cut out for each other.[12] Mayor Neville was induced by the leaders of the Firefighters' Union and Police Club to introduce the ordinance; his doing so was a signal at the outset that opposition to it was useless. The mayor's was the fifth and decisive vote; none of the four "independents" could politically afford to oppose a pay raise proposal, even if any of them was mentally disposed to do so.

Repercussions of the proposed ordinance were immediate throughout the city administration. Following introduction of the ordinance but before its final adoption, the president of the largest of the unions in the city, Local 195—Cambridge City Employees Union, had presented to the council his case for a $400 increase for all city employees. This union had never before failed to work exclusively with the manager on questions of wages and working conditions. In mid-November a small AFL affiliate, Local 602—State, County, and City Employees Union, notified the council of a vote of its membership in favor of a $400 increase for all city employees. This union also had in the past done its business with the manager on such matters. Later, in December, at the first meeting of the School Committee that month, representatives of teachers' clubs and the union of custodial employees made requests for a $500 "cost-of-living" increase. It is obvious that pressure from within the unions, if not clairvoyance on the part of the union leadership, would have compelled the city-wide labor unions to bring forward requests for increases as soon as the police and fire requests had been made. In the school system, on the contrary, a schedule of merit increases had been placed in effect in 1947 under which, given the $400 to $600 increases granted to all employees at the same time, advances in average salaries could fully equal the increase in the cost of living. To the "hard core" of three independents in the School Committee, this merit plan was obnoxious; furthermore it is fair to conclude, in view of their consistent opposition to proposals of the CCA-endorsed group, that they were quite ready to do their bit to undermine the position of the manager and of Plan E in Cambridge. The school committee in Massachusetts cities, whatever the "non-political" theory underlying it, in fact has been a stepping stone along the path of many of the state's most prominent politicians. Mayor Neville, as chairman of the School Committee, held the deciding vote between the two factions, and given his disposition toward employee pay raises, the outcome of the requests for a $500 increase was readily anticipated.

The merits of the issue of pay raises for city employees—excluding, perhaps, the members of the School Department—were mixed. The lag of salaries behind living costs has been noted, and it would appear that some increase for some categories was in order. Yet, comparative data suggested that an increase for policemen and firemen of the magnitude contemplated by the ordinance was not in order. In comparison with twelve cities in the Metropolitan area and the five largest cities in the

[12] The Fire Department employee who was president of the Firefighters' Union in 1948, when asked why the police and fire organizations approached the Council directly rather than the manager, replied that the law provided that police and fire salaries were to be established by ordinance. He paused, then added, "When you go to war, do you begin by telling the enemy all about your plans?"

state outside that area, salaries of police lieutenants, sergeants, and patrolmen and of fire captains, lieutenants and privates stood higher than *any* of the others. Comprehensive comparative data for other employees were not available. It was known, however, that wages of day laborers in comparison to the 1940 base had increased 70 per cent, or nearly 10 per cent more than living costs. The general satisfaction of other employees with wages and working conditions that fall suggests that city wages were not out of line with those paid for similar employment elsewhere in the vicinity.

As for salaries in the School Department, the issue was reasonably clear. In 1947 a three-point salary program had been adopted for teachers: (1) across-the-board pay boosts ranging from $600 for lowest paid to $400 for highest paid teachers were granted effective January 1, 1947; (2) a uniform maximum of $4500 for all teachers regardless of sex or teaching grade was established; and (3) provision was made for annual increases ranging from $100 to $300, to be awarded to teachers who passed college courses relating to their work as teachers. Although course work is the only criterion of merit for advancement under this plan, advancement to a position in which Cambridge teachers are the highest-paid in the state is possible under this schedule; and with the first round of "merit" increases on September 1, 1948, 70 per cent of the teachers had received increases of 64 per cent or more since 1941, and all teachers had had boosts of at least 55 per cent. It is hard to escape the conclusion that the proposed $500 increase was in part designed to cut the ground from under the system of merit increases. A feature of this $500 blanket increase was that it pertained to *all* employees of the School Department, including clerks, stenographers, custodial personnel, cafeteria assistants, watchmen, and others. The effects of the raise among these categories of positions would be especially startling. The boost would, for example, raise to $55 a week the salary of a junior clerk typist, a job the qualifications for which require graduation from high school and ability to type but not to take dictation—and in the city and state governments and in local industry, similar jobs were filled at $35 a week; it would bring a night watchman to a salary equal to that paid a lieutenant in the Fire Department; and it would similarly distort relationships of other salaries to those paid elsewhere, and notably to those paid elsewhere in the city service.

Viewing the issue from the manager's vantage point, the police and fire ordinance was a serious threat to his entire financial program, for it was necessarily related to the issue of raises for *all* employees. An increase of these proportions, raising all employees to a salary situation in which living cost advances had been more than offset, and to a pinnacle not approached by any other city in the state, would initially affect the tax rate in a drastic way. With such a rate, the comparative tax advantages of Cambridge, upon which the manager had been able to rely heavily in his successful efforts to attract new industry, would be substantially diminished if not completely overcome. The manager realized, furthermore, that so high a tax rate would jeopardize his standing with the very persons and groups who had been his staunchest support; so also, to have salaries of city employees higher than those paid by local industries might very likely subject those industries to demands from their own personnel, thus further undermining the popularity of the manager and of Plan E government in Cambridge. Since the strength of the manager and the strength of Plan E were and are linked in an intimate way, the fate of Plan E itself might well be at stake.

At very least, the issue of who was *de facto* head of the personnel organization of the city was in question. Atkinson was on record again and again in opposition to blanket pay increases for categories of personnel whose salary schedules were not fully integrated, and his logic in taking this position was as compelling now as it ever was. Salary advances had brought different groups into varying relation with the cost of living and other factors including comparative data needed to be appraised. Was Atkinson or was the council to establish personnel policy? Under the general theory of council-manager government, all policy—including personnel policy—is established by the council; but under Massachusetts law the manager was responsible for a broad area, though not the whole, of personnel policy: the division of authority raised the question. Equally important was the practice of city employee groups in this instance in looking to the council rather than to the manager for action. Atkinson's views on the presentation of these wage demands were well known even though he had not committed himself on the merits of a raise of some kind. If he were defeated on this issue, it is certain that his central influence in the organization would suffer a serious blow.

D. FINAL DRAWING OF THE LINES OF BATTLE

When on November 8 the police and fire salary ordinance was reported out of the Committee on Ordinances and passed without record vote to its second reading, general agreement was reached that final action at the meeting two weeks hence would be preceded by a public hearing. The disposition of the Cambridge Civic Association was made known in an advertisement in the Cambridge *Chronicle* issue which came out a few days before the hearing. The advertisement pointed out that four raises aggregating 46 per cent had been granted policemen and firemen since 1941, the last of these only five months previously; and that no police or fire department in Greater Boston was paid at higher rates. It is significant that the CCA declared that it was not opposed to an increase of some kind, but that a $400 increase would have to be duplicated for all employees, and would mean a tax rate boost of $5.00. It should be recalled that the increase for teachers had not yet been broached in the School Committee. The estimate of the required tax rate boost did not contemplate a $500 increase for all School Department employees as well.

At the hearing on the police and fire ordinance at the November 22nd meeting, the council chamber was crowded with a predominantly female audience. It would appear from the sentiments which it displayed that it was dominated by wives and other relatives of policemen and firemen. The hearing got under way with the reading by the city clerk of a report submitted by the Cambridge Research Association—sister organization of the Civic Association—in which the comparative data concerning police and fire salaries in other cities and facts concerning previous increases in Cambridge and their relation to the cost of living were summarized.[13] These data have been substantially covered in the foregoing section. The president of the CCA, Donald Spencer, then appeared in opposition to the ordinance; he was followed by Frank H. Townsend, president of the Chamber of Commerce, who opposed an increase of $400 but suggested that a compromise at $200 be reached. A considerable number of persons were then heard in favor of the ordinance. Leading off was John P. Murphy, president of the Cambridge Police Good Will Club. Murphy distributed a seven-page mimeographed statement to the council and others present (the statement had been prepared by the president of the local Firefighters' Union), in which published statements of "a so-called civic group" were called untrue, and facts to substantiate this charge were presented. The statements of the CCA which were purportedly refuted by Murphy's data had been made in a letter which CCA President Spencer had sent to all members of the Police and Fire Departments, as follows:

> The only figures we have seen so far look as though Cambridge patrolmen and fire privates are right now the highest paid in the State. They indicate also that for cities of our size and up to a quarter million, you are the fifth highest paid in the United States. . . .

The mimeographed statement presented a tabulation of 70 United States cities, varying in size from 6,406 to 7,454,995, in which salary maxima of patrolmen and fire privates were higher than the Cambridge figure of $3200. The fact is that, as Spencer had stated, only 5 cities with a population of between 100,000

[13] These data were taken for the most part from public records and reports continuously collected by the city budget director, under instructions of the city manager. The study was made for the Research Association on a reimbursable basis by four graduate students in the Harvard Graduate School of Public Administration. Actual "findings" of the Research Association were culled from the larger report submitted by the students.

and 250,000 were listed and that for cities the size of Cambridge and up to a quarter million, the Cambridge forces were fifth highest in the country. The tabulation did, of course, make it plain that *without reference to other conditions of work* or qualifications required, seventy cities in the United States had higher pay scales than Cambridge. Cost-of-living data supplied by the Massachusetts Department of Labor and Industries were presented in the statement, and the CCA was charged with having stated that the pay raises granted since 1941 had kept these salaries "abreast of the rise in the cost of living." As the CCA's sister organization, the Research Association, had pointed out in its report, police and fire salaries had not kept pace with the cost of living index; no published statements by CCA to the contrary were ever made, for the CCA had carefully maintained silence on the cost-of-living aspect of the situation which argued for some kind of a raise. The mimeographed statement also presented figures showing hourly wages paid for "the most common jobs" in local industry. It had in a prior statement calculated hourly wages of police, on the basis of a 60-hour week, at $1.03, and those of fire privates, working a 56-hour week, at $1.09. The wage rates in industry of course were higher in nearly every case.

Following Murphy's explanation of this statement, the president of the Firefighters' Union spoke; he was followed by more than a dozen persons, among them representatives of the small AFL city employees' local and of the Massachusetts Federation of Labor and the Cambridge Central Labor Union—an organization of locals in Cambridge. The city manager was not present at the meeting; in accordance with the City Charter, he comes to meetings only in response to requests of the council.

When all testimony was in, the mayor asked those present in the gallery for a show of hands; the city clerk recorded the vote as "approximately 250 persons" in favor and 4 against.

A recess was then declared. CCA President Spencer was talking with a representative of the Police Good Will Club, suggesting that if only the policemen and firemen were willing to compromise, undoubtedly a satisfactory figure could be found and agreement reached. This Club representative had understood that the CCA opposed any increase whatsoever; he appeared responsive to this suggestion, and rounded up others from the Police Association and the Firefighters' Union. It was at this point that the uncompromising nature of the stand taken by the president of the Firefighters' Union became clear. This man, serving as union president for the ninth time, had long been active in affairs of the state as well as the local union. He believed that the $400 increase could be won and he had no intention of giving up merely to avoid a fight.

Upon reconvening, the council proceeded immediately to vote on the measure, which passed by 8 to 1, only Councilor Swan—a CCA endorsee, the only councilman resident in the "Brattle Street Ward," Ward 8—in opposition. Councilors Crane, Pill, and DeGuglielmo, despite the support extended them by CCA endorsement, felt politically unable to vote against the ordinance. These councilors and Mayor Neville, far more even than the CCA and Chamber of Commerce, had hoped for a compromise to keep them out of a hot spot.

It was following this action of the council that similar demands from other employee groups were presented. While the two unions of city-wide employees filed communications with the council, they knew that the council was legally unable to grant them succor; their demands were therefore presented formally to the city manager, who had power and authority to deal with them in the first instance.

The issue of a blanket raise for teachers and other employees of the School Department came to a head at the meeting of the School Committee on December 20, 1948, a month after the council session on police and fire salaries. The meeting was so well attended that it had to be adjourned to the high school auditorium. Some 1,000 persons were present, virtually all of them favorable to the proposed increase. The manager had addressed to the School Committee a letter which was read at this meeting. The letter reviewed in considerable detail the effect of past and proposed changes in salaries and hours of work upon the tax rate, and the financial condition of the city, including rising costs of welfare and hospital activities, prospective deficit in the Metropolitan Transit Authority to be paid by the city, the prospective fall in income from state aid, the increasing difficulty of collecting taxes promptly, and the prospect of a $10 to $15 jump in the tax rate if all these unhappy developments came to pass. He observed that the cost-of-living index was now falling slowly. He urged the Committee to defer action at this time, in order to undertake a joint study with him of comparative data for other cities in the state, of the capacity of the city to pay wage increases when all data about prospective income in 1949 became available, and of the salary needs of employees not only of the School Department but of all departments of the city. Following statements by teacher representatives and debate by the Committee, the two factions split evenly, and the vote for the increase was carried when Mayor Neville voted with the CCA opposition. Perhaps in the hope of dulling the political effect of a vote against a pay raise, the three CCA-endorsed members voted "present" rather than "nay." An attempt to block reconsideration at the next meeting failed, and a subsequent motion for reconsideration assured that the issue would come up for final action at the next regular meeting of the Committee on the evening of January 3.

E. THE MANAGER ACTS

City Manager Atkinson was, as it were, surrounded by fire. But only half of this battle has been described. We need to back-track to October 25, when Mayor Neville first unveiled the police and fire pay raise ordinance. We should, furthermore, first know that in 1947 an amendment to the Municipal Finance Act had been passed which had a crucial bearing upon the city of Cambridge. This act amended Section 33A governing procedures for salary increases and for the creation of new positions after the mayor or manager had submitted his budget, and provided:

> The annual budget shall include sums sufficient to pay the salaries of officers and employees fixed by law or ordinance. Notwithstanding any contrary provision of any city charter, no ordinance providing for an increase in salaries or wages of municipal officers or employees shall be enacted except by two-thirds vote of the City Council, nor unless it is to be operative for more than three months during the financial year in which it is passed. No new position shall be created or increase in rate made by ordinance, vote or appointment during the financial year subsequent to the submission of the annual budget unless provision therefor has been made by means of a supplemental appropriation.

The purpose of the amendment was to halt the practice by which the councils of some of the cities in the state had upon occasion forced the chief executive to include in his budget for the next year funds for a pay increase voted by the council in the prior year.[14] The executive had been powerless to oppose such a move because he could withstand council pressure of this sort only in the months after his budget had been introduced into the council. The aim of the new law was to place in the executive, rather than in the council, effective control over matters of personnel. The aim of the new law was to halt precisely the kind of move made by the Cambridge city council when it adopted the $400 pay raise ordinance for the Police and Fire Departments. It seemed quite definitely to supersede the special act of 1935.

City Solicitor Daly and Mr. Atkinson became aware of the import of this new law immediately after Mayor Neville introduced the pay raise ordinance on October 25. To Daly it seemed clear that the council's authority to establish police and fire salaries was now a thing of the past. Atkinson at once undertook to speak to certain of the councilors about the new law. To his surprise, he discovered that some of them were fully aware of the law and believed that it invalidated the 1935 act. The attitude of these councilors was that if the ordinance was illegal, the place to prove that was in the courts. No single councilor could afford politically to speak out on the side of the law, for he would surely be labeled an enemy of the policemen and firemen.

In the light of this attitude in the council, the manager's best move was not entirely clear. Atkinson was not unwilling to "take the rap" for his friends on the council who, after all, were subject to an election every other Novem-

14 You may wish to turn back to pages 591-2 where the earlier provisions are set forth.

ber. He had resented bitterly the demagogic charges made against his friend Ed Crane on one occasion after Crane had spoken out in council meeting in opposition to a pay raise order; in the eyes of his critics, Crane had "betrayed the memory" of his policeman father because of his attitude. Under the circumstances, it was perfectly clear to him that an ordinance granting a raise of some sort would be passed.

A number of factors argued for a compromise, and the dead certainty that a pay raise ordinance of some kind would be passed was one of them. As we have seen, Daly had advised Atkinson this time, as he had upon other occasions, that "we can take the issue to court and have an interesting case"; and in this instance he even went so far as to say that he thought the case was a tight one. Yet, the law is never made until the appropriate supreme court says what it is. A compromise would be preferable to losing in court on the issue of $400 or nothing. Atkinson had no technical devices with which he could block the council on this occasion, for the timing of the move had been carefully chosen. Final action would be taken on November 22, weeks before his budget could possibly be ready. The merits of the case were mixed and suggested compromise also. While the cost of living was tending slightly downward, there was still a differential of some fifteen points between living costs and the salary index of most employees. A raise had been granted only six months previously, but within the next half year another raise would probably become necessary. Finally, for the CCA supporters in council, a compromise was the only happy way out of the situation. Opposition to *any* raise was unthinkable, however serious a raise of the projected magnitude might be for the city. Mayor Neville made known his reluctance to support an ordinance calling for an amount which he believed to be excessive, but explained how impossible it would be for him to argue the case before the policemen and firemen. He discussed the whole problem with the manager, and asked whether Atkinson would go along with some sort of raise.

Atkinson was unable to justify to himself under all the circumstances his opposing any salary increase whatever. This fact is apparent in that he had issued no statement of any kind since the pay ordinance was first introduced—no warnings of soaring tax rates and undermining of the city's credit.[15] Had he believed that the city could not stand a general wage increase of some size, the manager would have begun to fight at the outset and would have rallied heavy support for his views. All things considered, Atkinson replied to Neville that he was willing, somewhat reluctantly, to go along with an increase of $200. Neville was pleased and hopeful; but his hopes were crushed by the attitude of the president of the Firefighters' Union. Why should not the union hold out for the maximum when its best friends on the council advised that the entire $400 could be won, and when quite clearly the opposition held the votes to get what it wanted? The union president publicly let it be known that this was one time they were going to "show the manager where to get off."

The unyielding stand of the union made the manager's decision easier. It was out of the question to grant an increase which would elevate the salary index of all employees to a figure higher than the falling cost-of-living index, at a cost to the city which would have all the effects we have already noted. The manager had made his offer. The city solicitor had advised him that he almost certainly had the force of law on his side. He needed only to decide how he would enforce his decision.

There were two ways in which an ordinance considered to be illegal could be tested:

(1) The manager could refuse to carry out the terms of the ordinance and the injured parties would then bring suit for *mandamus* to compel its effectuation. In the ensuing trial, the issue of legality would be determined. But the manager and his administration would appear to the policemen and firemen to be fighting to block the increases given them by the council.

(2) Citizen groups under the state law could take certain action to restrain the effectuation of an ordinance which they believed to be

[15] The warnings he issued after the initial pay raise action of the School Committee, referred to on pages 608-9, came later and of course pertained to a very different issue.

illegal. Either a referendum petition could be initiated, or a group of ten or more taxpayers could bring action to enjoin performance of the act complained against.

In all debates about the proposed $400 increase for policemen and firemen, the manager had never taken a public stand for or against. It was to his advantage, in terms of his relationships with these key departments, to avoid taking a stand if he possibly could. The 1947 law afforded a chance for him permanently to avoid taking a stand, and the support extended by the Cambridge Civic Association made it possible for him to use that chance successfully.

As we have seen, the leaders of the CCA, like the leaders of the Chamber of Commerce, realized that an increase of some size—perhaps $200—was probably warranted and probably feasible for the city without undue jeopardy to the tax rate. In an issue of this sort, where its opposition was a matter of degree rather than of principle, the CCA would strongly have preferred to let someone else wage the fight against the increase as adopted, for almost inevitably, any citizen group fighting the increase under provisions of state law would be labeled "anti-labor," a "narrow-minded bunch of taxpayers," and the like, by precisely the kinds of voters whom the CCA was working to bring around to a different attitude toward its orientation and its work. The issue was at least as "hot" for the CCA as it was for the manager.

Atkinson well realized the considerations which would lead the CCA to resist taking formal action under the law to prevent the ordinance from going into effect. He respected the CCA as an organization which in general backed the projects he too was interested in, which was completely unselfish, and which never during his term had come to him to seek political favors of any kind. It was important to Atkinson to retain the support of this organization, and realizing the attitude CCA would take in the matter, he knew it might be difficult to induce that organization to take the necessary steps to block effectuation of the pay raise ordinance.

F. RESORT TO THE COURTS

The referendum procedure provided by Massachusetts law is a fairly complex one. Within twenty days of the passage of the measure objected to, petitions bearing the signatures of at least 12 per cent of the registered voters of a city must be filed with either the city council or the School Committee, as appropriate, and if the action objected to is not entirely rescinded, it must be presented to the voters of the city at a special election or at the next regular municipal election. The referendum petition is nullified if it fails to command a majority of those voting on the measure. Yet to the CCA it would be preferable to have 12 per cent of the voters of the city and a majority at an election regarded as responsible for blocking a pay raise, rather than to have a group of CCA taxpayers "take the rap." When on the initiative of the city manager the matter was first discussed, this politically easier way was suggested to President Spencer. Subsequently Spencer was informed of the possibility of accomplishing the results desired through the simple device of a suit by ten taxpayers. The political disadvantages of this course by then seemed relatively unimportant alongside the administrative difficulties of the referendum procedure. Spencer agreed to find ten taxpayers to introduce legal action. He had to telephone approximately *one hundred* taxpayers to find twelve who would consent to the use of their names. Industrial, commercial, and financial institutions were unwilling to appear to oppose the special interests of policemen and firemen.

Final approval had been given to the police and fire ordinance on November 22. On December 27, the County Superior Court issued a temporary injunction restraining the effectuation of the pay raise ordinance. The ruling was appealed to the Supreme Judicial Court of Massachusetts but meanwhile Atkinson had a preliminary ruling for a guide, the conviction of his city solicitor that the taxpayers' case was a good one, and a stay of execution on the pay raises during which he could make such further studies as he desired.

In the interim, however, the School Committee pay raise issue had arisen. The committee had voted the increases by 4-3 on December 20. Reconsideration on January 3 had been requested and because of procedural requirements, the majority behind the pay raise had been unable to stop this; but there was every reason to suppose that the motion to reconsider would fail on that occasion. The merits of the School Department increases have already been discussed; the issues were sufficiently clear so that Atkinson had not hesitated at the outset to announce his position in regard to them. His letter to the School Committee in which he had requested postponement of action had been read at the December 20 open meeting and quoted liberally in the press. Perhaps his major concern arose from the constantly increasing burden of School Department expenditures in a tax rate which, in the minds of the people of the city, was a kind of rule of thumb of the kind of job *he*, and not the School Committee, was doing. Under provisions of Massachusetts law, not only is the city government required to provide the sums which the School Committee desires, but it is required to send out to each taxpayer a bill in which there is no identification of the respective amounts for which the city government and the School Committee are responsible. In a very real sense, thus, the manager is held accountable for expenditures for which he is not responsible. Or from the standpoint of the School Committee, to some extent this body enjoys authority without responsibility.[16] In addition to the relation of the projected School Department pay raise to the tax rate, the raise had a bearing also upon Atkinson's effective control of the personnel of the city organization, for while in theory it is true that School Department employees are responsible to the School Committee and not to the manager or city council, in fact repercussions upon the morale of city employees are bound to occur when others doing similar work and paid on city payrolls are paid at very much more favorable rates.

Atkinson was determined to block the school pay raises if he could. A referendum petition on the issue was deemed impracticable because of the brief time available for getting the required signatures and the probable difficulty of sustaining the referendum at a special election. Yet in a legal battle with the School Committee he had little reason to hope for success. Controversies between executive or council and School Committee have repeatedly arisen in Massachusetts cities and towns, and a long line of precedents has been laid down by the courts. Almost without exception the courts have ruled for the School Committee, for lying behind the provisions of law is the theory that the School Committee must be kept independent of political control—that the maintenance and operation of schools should be vested exclusively in the hands of citizens chosen by the electorate for that purpose alone, and never jeopardized by the powers of a general political body or, above all, by an appointive official.

Throughout the period of the pay raise demands the manager had consulted with his city solicitor at every stage of developments. Both men realized that under the requirements of the Municipal Finance Act all departments are required to submit to the chief executive by December 1 of each year their budget estimates for the following year. The School Department, and the School Committee to which the department is responsible, had consistently ignored this provision; and for this they have enjoyed the authority of two different decisions of the Massachusetts Supreme Court holding that the law pertaining to budget submissions does not bind a school committee. It was not clear from these decisions, however, how a ruling would go if the manager's budget were *actually submitted to the council* before the School Department budget had been forwarded to him. Daly's advice was to give it a try "and we'll have an interesting court case." It was on the basis of this admittedly shaky legal framework that the manager decided to rush the preparation of his budget and present it to the council at its meeting on the afternoon of January 3.[17] This would be his first and only chance to submit his budget while final action

[16] This interesting issue has been given wide public consideration in Massachusetts, but in this case we can but invite attention to it.

[17] This action would have the further advantage of finally ruling out any effort of the council to pass a pay raise ordinance for the Police and Fire Departments early in the new year, before submission of the budget. However, budget preparation was so well advanced that such a threat could have been handled readily, if and when it arose.

on the School Committee budget was pending—for refusal by the School Committee majority to reconsider its action of December 20 was expected that very night, and that action would complete work on its 1949 budget requests and ready the budget document for submission, through the manager, to the council.

By dint of a great deal of night, week-end, and holiday work by the manager and a group of city employees, his budget was ready in accordance with his plans. Having received no budget from the School Committee as provided by law, he prepared one for them—*not* including provision for $500 pay increases. Word of his strategy had come to the School Department and just as he was leaving his office for the council meeting to explain his budget, a delegation headed by the assistant superintendent of schools presented him with a copy of the budget as voted by the School Committee on December 20, in order to prevent his submitting any other budget to the council. The manager refused to accept this document, on the grounds that it had not been finally voted upon for submission as the budget of the School Committee, and that in consequence it was no budget at all.

Upon convening of the council and opening of the meeting, a number of motions to adjourn at once were made, but Councilors Sullivan and Lynch, who normally were members of the loyal opposition, were absent and the CCA minority was *pro tem* in the majority. The manager's budget was thereupon received and referred to the Committee on Finance. Fully aware of the import of the manager's strategy, Councilor Foley asked the city clerk on what dates the manager's budget had been presented in the years 1942 to 1948. With one exception the submission had occurred in middle or late February—and in that exception, in March.

At the meeting of the School Committee that evening, Mayor Neville counseled the committee that teachers would have to bring court action if the pay raises voted by the committee were to be obtained. He indicated that, in his opinion, if the move for reconsideration failed, the vote of the committee on December 20 would stand as its final action and the budget refused by Atkinson that afternoon would be the budget which the council was bound to accept. The move for reconsideration, of course, did fail. In the ensuing weeks, after the School Committee had retained legal counsel, twenty taxpayers—Mayor Neville, Committeemen Reardon and Cassidy and Committeewoman Moughan, and 16 teachers—filed suit in the county superior court asking the court, as provided by law, to specify the additional sum which the council was to be required to appropriate to restore to the School Committee its rightful funds.

G. VICTORY FOR THE MANAGER

The manager had stopped the parade—momentarily, at the least. With the demands of the Police and Fire Departments and School Committee in the hands of the courts, he was well able to deal with the problem in respect to other city employees on his own time schedule. His hand was greatly strengthened in March when the Supreme Court ruled that, the 1935 special act having on established principle become a part of the Cambridge City Charter, under the 1947 amendment it could not stand. The ordinance granting $400 increases to policemen and firemen was therefore without legal effect. Councilor Foley, always "a friend of labor," at the next council meeting introduced an order, which the council unanimously passed, calling upon the city manager to bring in a recommendation for an appropriation sufficient to provide "an increase in salary" for all city employees; but the manager was now operating on his own terms, and chose to ignore the order.

Annual elections had meanwhile been held in the Firefighters' Union and the Police Good Will Club, and new officers were at the top. To these officers fell the task of making the most of a bad situation, and winning a pay raise via a different approach. The officers met with the manager and budget director, and each of them disassociated himself from the manner in which action had been taken the prior fall, when the associations had completely by-passed the manager and the head of the Firefighters' Union had declared that this was one time when they were going to show the manager where to head in. After a period of negotiation, during which talks with the city-wide employee unions were also held and over-all studies were completed, the manager brought in recommendations for increases of $200 for policemen and firemen, and 10 per cent up to $200 for other categories of city personnel under his direction. These increases brought the total increase in basic pay scales of the Police and Fire Departments since 1941 to 55.0 per cent and served to keep Cambridge scales at the top for all cities in the state. With the cost of living falling toward an index of 157.4 at the end of 1949, these raises very appreciably negated the cost of living as a consideration in the event further demands were forthcoming.

After nearly two years during which the school pay raise case has been before the county superior court without decision, the manager and city solicitor remain hopeful but not at all certain about the outcome. The manager's early efforts to compromise with the teachers and settle the case out of court were unsuccessful. At a conference of teacher representatives and the legal counsel of both parties in the spring of 1949, his offer to settle on a flat $200 increase for teachers was rejected. Meanwhile, current tax revenues are accumulating in an unearmarked "surplus account" at a rate sufficient to meet past and future costs of the school pay raise, if the courts rule for the School Committee.

The dire consequences for the tax rate pictured by the manager in his December letter to the School Committee have failed completely to come to pass, in part because of the rapidly expanding tax base in Cambridge and because of some rise in state aid. Rather than a $10-$15 increase for 1949, a nominal decrease of 10¢ was effected, despite the increase in employees' salaries and certain other added costs.

H. THE BATTLE IN RETROSPECT—CONCLUSION

In the fall of 1949, Plan E in Cambridge faced another political test, with the coming of the regular municipal elections. During the prior year the CCA had taken bold stands on the pay raise issue which at the time were thought to be politically precarious. It had inevitably been associated in the public mind with the taxpayers' suit which blocked the pay raise ordinance. The manager had avoided a categorical stand on pay raises except in respect to School Department employees but his association with the CCA was of course known to be close. Finally, when the time arrived for endorsement of a CCA slate for council and School Committee, preponderant sentiment in the CCA board of directors seemed to be that the disadvantages of an endorsement of the almost-consistently anti-CCA voter, John D. Lynch, outweighed the advantages of his giving CCA a fictitious majority in the council. The directors were ready to risk going into a clear minority, and were greatly concerned that, indeed, CCA might do so.[18]

The campaign that year was so quiet that the weekly paper speculated as to how and why this should be. When the results were in, however, they showed a pronounced public vindication of the Atkinson administration and the CCA program. For the first time in the history of Plan E, Cambridge citizens had elected five self-avowed CCA supporters to the council. This clear majority assured the CCA councilors of power to choose the mayor from among their number, and since three CCA-endorsed candidates had been elected to the School Committee, the Civic Association for the first time thus would also have a majority in that body. Some measure of CCA voting strength is indicated by the order in which candidates for council were declared elected:

1. Edward A. Crane (CCA—subsequently elected Mayor)
2. Hyman Pill (CCA)
3. Joseph A. DeGuglielmo (CCA)
4. John D. Lynch (Independent)
5. W. Donnison Swan (CCA)
6. Thomas M. McNamara (Independent)
7. Edward J. Sullivan (Independent)
8. John J. Foley (Independent)
9. Chester A. Higley (CCA)

Various factors contributed to this victory. Chief among them, no doubt, was the general success of the Atkinson regime. In seven years an expensive, almost bankrupt, incompetent,

[18] As it happened, Lynch did not seek CCA endorsement in 1949. It is reported that he knew he could not have it if he did.

and dishonest city government had been completely transformed. The administration in 1949 was efficiently and honestly run, and its financial structure was unassailable. The bulk of the credit for the achievement was popularly and properly given to Atkinson. As a result, his position was very strong; but now a quite different problem was in the offing.

For the CCA, while the members it had sponsored were still in the minority on the council, had been developing a program of municipal improvements that went further or faster than Atkinson thought desirable. It now remained to be seen how the relations between the council and the manager, under these circumstances, would work out; this will be a new chapter in the Cambridge story.

CONCLUDING COMMENTS

It is unwise to draw firm conclusions from individual cases. The Cambridge experience is not conclusive. But it is hardly rash to say that the experience illustrates vividly the not surprising fact that the splitting of authority over a major integral matter of policy (like wage scales for municipal employees) is likely to lead to dissension and other difficulties. In the United States, governmental salary scales are traditionally fixed by legislative bodies and it is frequently assumed that this practice is essential in a democracy. Under Massachusetts law, the situation is different: here in general, with the significant exception of school department salaries, the task is assigned to the executive. Either procedure has much to be said for it on a variety of counts. Whatever its other virtues, from the standpoint of the working executive, the split in responsibility is the least attractive of the alternatives; and whether one likes or dislikes Atkinson's moves in the long struggle with council and School Committee, the logic of his efforts to obtain power to exercise consistent action in this field was unassailable. However, each reader will have his own views on the importance of retaining independence for the School Committee and must use his own judgment on the relative advantages and disadvantages of the Massachusetts plan, with or without the separate provisions for Police and Fire Department salaries.

All these matters deserve consideration in terms of the role of municipal corporations in American government. The historical development has been complex, but the key factor (leaving aside the special complications of Federalism) is the abiding sovereignty of the state. Atkinson's jurisdictional difficulties were not directly soluble by the citizens of Cambridge, for they were derived from state statutes. Thus his recourse to the courts against the decisions of municipal legislative majorities is best understood if the agencies involved are looked on as creatures of the sovereign state; judicial intervention can then be rationalized as supporting the popular will of the whole state expressed through its legislature and interpreted by its judges. However it be rationalized, the fact that faced the elective and appointive officials of Cambridge, and the citizens themselves, was that the answers to certain questions could not be found in Cambridge; recourse was essential either to the city's representatives in the legislature, or to the state courts. Whether this state of affairs is desirable is another question. But it is clear at the very least that the state legislature would have facilitated administrative action if it had refrained from essentially inconsistent statutory prescriptions.

Statutory inconsistencies and a consistently leaderless council encouraged the assumption of leadership by Atkinson. Nor, using this case as an example, is the role of leader necessarily inappropriate in a democratic polity. Like any other manifestation of power it is subject to abuse, but the assumption that a program can emerge without someone to present it, support it, and carry it out would seem untenable. Indeed, as these events in Cambridge suggest, the fulfillment of what the people want may require leadership. Under this assumption, the problem of democratic government is not to suppress the phenomenon, but to ensure that it is subject to popular control and revocation. The role of an appointive officer in this context deserves examination.

One final matter may be mentioned. Not many years ago, one of the chief programs of government reformers in the United States was the elimination of partisan politics in municipal affairs; the reformers were widely successful and non-partisan elections to municipal office, as in Cambridge, are common today. The effect of this reform on our national parties is an interesting question, though not relevant to this case; but the effect on the municipalities themselves is also of interest and at least tangential to the issues in the case.

The assumption seems to have been that local government should be in the hands of "good men" elected on their individual merits. The question arises, however, in the light of the Cambridge experience, whether good men, subject to no group ties, can coalesce to establish policy. Alternatively, it can be asked if individuals having no common ties can be responsible. It is worth noting that the first time that there seemed to be any hope of establishing a program via the council in Cambridge came with the election of a CCA-sponsored majority. Perhaps responsible parties and party government (in the British sense) that seem so elusive on our national scene may be more practical in our smaller governmental units; but it is necessary to note that effective and consistent administration based on program choices sponsored by opposing parties and decided by the electorate is hardly possible unless both parties accept the constitutional fundamentals of the government, i.e., in Cambridge, Plan E. Without such mutual acceptance, debate over program will be perpetually confused by the efforts of one party to overturn the constitution.

There is a further problem. Before the New Deal, municipal programmatic parties were largely devoted to the somewhat aseptic and arid though worthy ideals of economy, honesty, and efficiency; perhaps for that very reason they showed little staying power; they rode into office on mass revulsion against the excesses of incumbents, but they seemed to offer not much tangible in the way of benefits for the bulk of the voters. The Plan E Committee in Cambridge was an example of this essentially negative tradition. The endurance of its more broadly based successor, CCA, may well depend on its ability to formulate and sustain a program with positive as well as negative appeal. The reader may find it useful to speculate briefly on the role of council and city manager in such a context.

Appendix A

THE INTERNATIONAL CITY MANAGERS' ASSOCIATION

THE CODE OF ETHICS

(Adopted at the 25th Annual Conference in Boston, September 29, 1938)

In order to achieve effective, democratic government, the council-manager plan provides that municipal policy shall be determined exclusively by a legislative body elected by the people and that the administration of policy shall be vested in the city manager, as administrative head of the city, who shall be appointed by and responsible to the council. The International City Managers' Association is a professional organization of city managers; its purpose is to increase the proficiency of city managers and to aid in the general improvement of municipal administration. To further these objectives, the Association believes that these ethical principles should govern the conduct of every professional city manager:

1. No member of the profession seeks or accepts a position as city manager unless he is fully in accord with the principles of council-manager government and unless he is confident that he is qualified to serve under these principles as city manager to the advantage of the community.

2. The city manager has a firm belief in the dignity and worth of the services rendered by government and a deep sense of his own social responsibility as a trusted public servant.

3. The city manager is governed by the highest ideals of honor and integrity in all his public and personal relationships in order that he may merit the respect and inspire the confidence of the administrative organization which he directs and of the public which he serves.

4. The city manager believes that personal aggrandizement or personal profit secured by confidential information or by misuse of public time is dishonest.

5. The city manager is in no sense a political leader. In order that policy may be intelligent and effective, he provides the council with information and advice, but he encourages positive decisions on policy by the council instead of passive acceptance of his recommendations.

6. The city manager realizes that it is the

council, the elected representatives of the people, which is entitled to the credit for the fulfillment of municipal policies and leaves to the council the defense of policies which may be criticized.

7. The city manager keeps the community informed on municipal affairs but keeps himself in the background by emphasizing the importance of the facts.

8. The city manager, in order to preserve his integrity as a professional administrator, resists any encroachment on his control of personnel, insists on the exercise of his own judgment in accomplishing council policies, and deals frankly with the council as a unit rather than secretly with its individual members.

9. The city manager handles all matters of personnel on the basis of merit. Political, religious, and racial considerations carry no weight in appointments, salary increases, promotions, and discipline in the municipal service.

10. The city manager curries no personal favors. He is the administrator for all the people and handles each administrative problem without discrimination on the basis of principle and justice.

Appendix B

TABULATION OF REGISTERED VOTERS (JULY 1, 1940) AND PARTY ENROLLMENT (OCTOBER 18, 1939)

CAMBRIDGE, MASSACHUSETTS

Ward	*Registered Voters*	*Democrats*	*Republicans*	*Ratio of Democrats to Republicans*
1	5,394	3,731	148	25.2
2	4,890	2,633	626	4.2
3	4,524	2,751	457	6.0
4	4,756	1,639	1,291	1.2
5	4,631	1,842	1,324	1.4
6	4,888	2,236	931	2.4
7	4,565	1,303	1,524	.9
8	4,360	1,194	1,520	.8
9	4,380	2,736	593	4.6
10	4,417	2,479	630	3.9
11	4,608	2,951	370	8.0
TOTALS	51,413	25,495	9,414	2.7

Appendix C

COST OF LIVING INDEX FOR MASSACHUSETTS AND INDEX OF SALARIES OF POLICEMEN AND FIREMEN IN CAMBRIDGE[1]

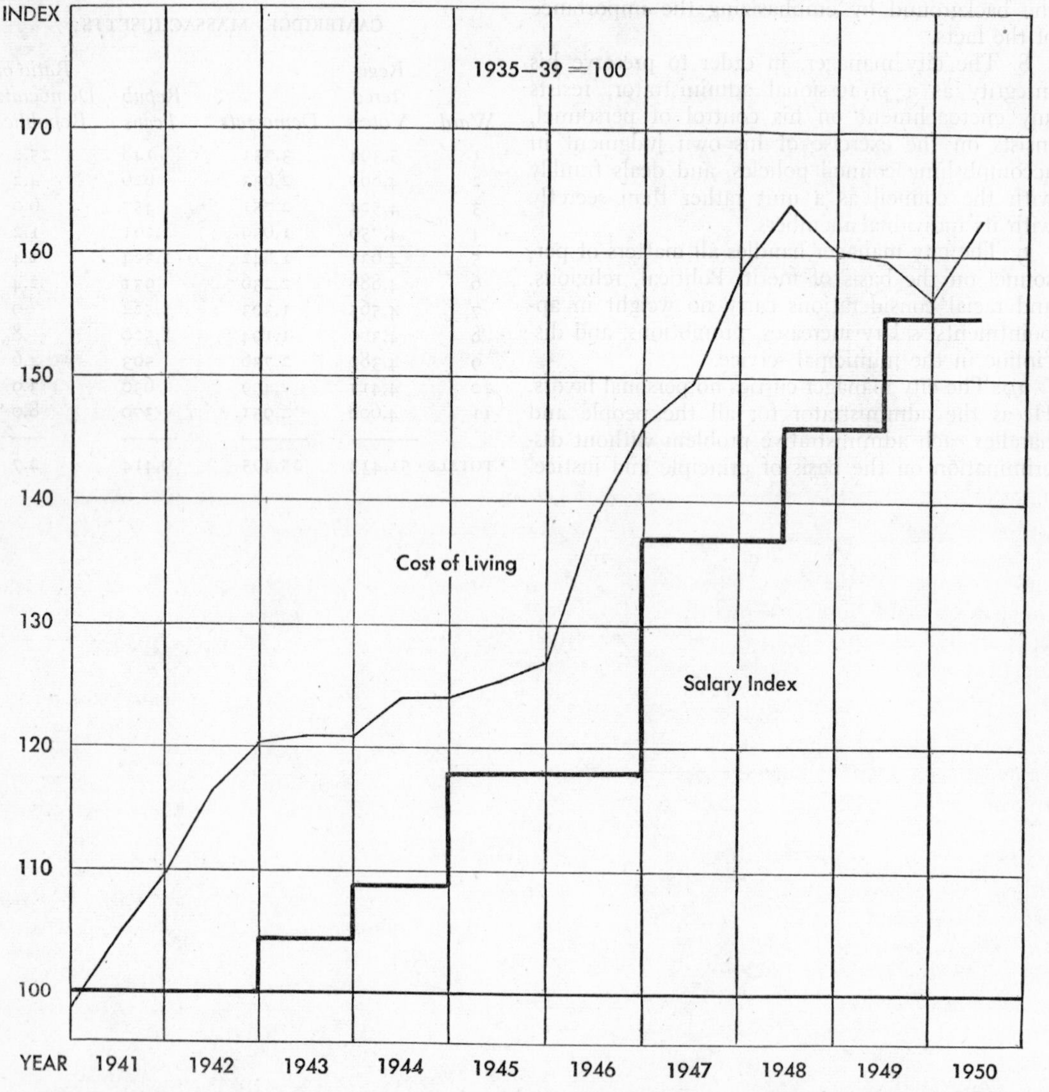

[1] Cost of living data furnished by Massachusetts Department of Labor and Industries, Boston; months of January and July are taken for reference points. Salary data pertains only to maximum salaries of patrolmen and fire privates, and was furnished by Director of Budget and Personnel, City Hall, Cambridge.

Appendix D

EXCERPTS FROM CITY CHARTER [2] PERTAINING TO RESPECTIVE DUTIES, RESPONSIBILITIES, AND AUTHORITY OF THE CITY COUNCIL AND THE CITY MANAGER

Section 96. The city council shall consist of seven or nine members, as provided in this section, all of whom shall, at each regular municipal election, be elected at large for terms of two years each by proportional representation as hereinafter provided and shall serve until their successors are qualified. . . . [Cities with seven wards or fewer at time of adoption of Plan E have seven councillors; those with more than seven wards have nine.]

Section 97. The city council shall have and exercise all the legislative powers of the city, except as such powers are reserved by this chapter to school committee and to the qualified voters of the city. . . . [No further definition is given.]

Section 98. . . . Except in the case of executive sessions, all meetings of the city council and of committees thereof shall be open to the public, and the rules of the city council shall provide that citizens and employees of the city shall have a reasonable opportunity to be heard at any such meeting in regard to any matter considered thereat.

Section 103. The city council shall appoint a city manager who shall be the chief administrative officer of the city and shall be responsible for the administration of all departments, commissions, boards and offices of the city, whether established before its adoption of this plan or thereafter, except that of the city clerk, city auditor, any official appointed by the governor or any body elected by the voters of the city. . . .

Section 104. Except as otherwise specifically provided in this chapter, it shall be the duty of the city manager to act as chief conservator of the peace within the city; to supervise the administration of the affairs of the city; to see that within the city the laws of the commonwealth and the ordinances, resolutions, and regulations of the city council are faithfully executed; and to make such recommendations to the city council concerning the affairs of the city as may to him seem desirable; to make reports to the city council from time to time upon the affairs of the city; and to keep the city council fully advised of the city's financial condition and its future needs. He shall prepare and submit to the city council budgets as required of the mayor by section thirty-two of chapter 44 [i.e., the Municipal Finance Act], and, in connection therewith, may, to the extent provided by said section thirty-two in the case of a mayor, require the submission to him, by all departments, commissions, boards, and offices of the city, of estimates of the amounts necessary for their expenses. He shall make all appointments and removals in the departments, commissions, boards, and offices of the city for whose administration he is responsible, except as otherwise provided in this chapter, and shall perform such other duties as may be prescribed by this chapter or be required of him by ordinance or resolution of the city council. The city manager shall have and possess, and shall exercise, all the powers, rights, and duties, other than legislative, had, possessed, or exercised, immediately prior to the adoption of this plan by the mayor, board of aldermen, common council, and all other boards, commissions and committees of the city and their members, severally or collectively, except such as are by this chapter conferred upon the school committee or are otherwise provided for thereby.

Section 105. Such officers and employees as the city council, with the advice of the city manager, shall determine are necessary for the proper administration of the departments, commissions, boards and offices of the city for whose administration the city manager is responsible shall be appointed, and may be removed, by the city manager. The city manager shall report every appointment and removal made by him to the city council at the next meeting thereof following such appointment or removal. The city manager may authorize the head of a department, commission, or board, or the holder of an office, for whose administration he is responsible, to appoint and remove subordinates in such department, commission, board, or office. All appointments by, or under the authority of, the city manager, if subject to chapter thirty-one (pertaining to the civil service) and the rules and regulations made under authority thereof, shall be made in accordance therewith, and all other appointments as aforesaid shall be on the basis of executive and

[2] Being Chapters 43 and 54A of the General Laws, Tercentenary Edition.

administrative ability and training and experience in the work to be performed.

Section 107. Neither the city council nor any of its committees or members shall direct or request the appointment of any person to, or his removal from, office by the city manager or any of his subordinates, or in any manner take part in the appointment or removal of officers and employees in that portion of the service of said city for whose administration the city manager is responsible. Except for the purpose of inquiry, the city council and its members shall deal with that portion of the service of the city as aforesaid solely through the city manager, and neither the city council nor any member thereof shall give orders to any subordinate of the city manager either publicly or privately. . . . [Stringent enforcement provisions follow.]

Appendix E

BOARD OF DIRECTORS

CAMBRIDGE CIVIC ASSOCIATION

1945

George A. McLaughlin, President, lawyer, former City Solicitor.

Thomas E. Ahern, realtor.

Charles Almy, officer, Dewey & Almy (local chemical manufacturers).

Stoughton Bell, lawyer, former president, Cambridge Taxpayers' Association.

Dr. William C. Brousseau, retired City Physician.

John H. Campbell, president, Superior Laundry Company.

James F. Farr, lawyer.

Charles M. Fosgate, specialist in commercial real estate.

Jesse W. Greer, president, J. W. Greer Company (manufacturers of bakery equipment).

Larkland F. Hewitt, bank examiner, State of Massachusetts.

Paul F. Hillery, president of a local trucking concern.

James M. Landis, dean, Harvard Law School.

Mrs. A. Kingsley Porter.

Alan Steinert, president, Eastern Company, RCA distributors.

Mrs. Marshall Stone, housewife.

Joseph F. White, treasurer, White Fuel Corporation, member Boston Port Authority.

BOARD OF DIRECTORS

CAMBRIDGE CIVIC ASSOCIATION

1950-1951

Residence	
7	James B. Ames, attorney.
8	Horace O. Bright, broker.
9	Miss Margaret Brine, lecturer.
5	Daniel A. Buckley, proofreader.
–	John H. Campbell, president, Superior Laundry Co.
3	John Cogan, Captain, U. S. Army.
8	Robert S. Coit, attorney.
9	Anthony Colosimo, grocery proprietor.
3	Robert G. Conley, attorney.
9	Paul R. Corcoran, owner, local department store.
5	Nicola Diodati, real estate.
9	Walter E. Doherty, Jr., attorney.
7	James F. Farr, attorney.
7	Larkland F. Hewitt, Jr., bank examiner, State of Massachusetts.
–	Edward G. Hillery, Sr., laborer.
9	Mrs. James R. Hooper, Jr., housewife.
9	John A. Lunn, management, textile company.
3	Arthur G. MacKenzie, Ford dealer.
7	James F. Mahan, attorney.
1	E. Joseph McGrath, truck driver.
4	Mrs. William J. McKinley, clerical.
9	George A. McLaughlin, attorney.
7	Miss Helen P. O'Malley, title searcher.
7	Robert Reid, architect.
10	Charles H. Riemer, supervisor, radio manufacturing.
7	Mrs. Alfred S. Romer, housewife.
9	Donald Spencer, investment counselor.
8	Alan Steinert, president, Eastern Company.
5	William Stavropoulos.
7	Miss Frances Whoriskey, proprietor, credit business.

Summary by wards:

Ward 1	— 1
2	— 0
3	— 3
4	— 1
5	— 3
6	— 0
7	— 8
8	— 3
9	— 8
10	— 1
11	— 0
Non-resident taxpayers	— 2
Total	— 30

THE RURAL ELECTRIFICATION ADMINISTRATION PERSONNEL REPORT

CONTENTS

PREFACE

In December 1939, a congressman's request for information regarding certain personnel actions of the Rural Electrification Administration precipitated a situation which required a crucial decision by the agency's Director of Management and Personnel, Mr. Kendall Foss. That decision was later the subject of acute controversy. This case study describes the considerations which Mr. Foss took into account in choosing his course of action, and the justifications for it that he gave subsequently during an official investigation.

The request was from Representative Everett M. Dirksen of the Committee on Appropriations of the House of Representatives, and related to REA promotion practices in the year ending June 30, 1939. The agency had in fact followed a policy of rapid and widespread promotion, which could be interpreted in such a way as to embarrass the Administration. Mr. Foss believed that the request was a "fishing expedition" on the part of an opponent of public power and that the information would be used to discredit the whole REA program. On the basis of this belief, Mr. Foss made certain decisions about the compilation of the statistical information requested by Congressman Dirksen that were later sharply criticized in Congress and in the Department of Agriculture. Congressman Dirksen felt that the information supplied to the committee violated "the integrity of the record."

In the following account, there will be found extensive quotations from Mr. Foss's testimony given in his own defense. The reader is thus in a position to reach an informed judgment on the justification for Mr. Foss's actions.

One word of caution is prehaps appropriate. As the reader will observe, this is an incident illustrating one of the perennial problems of Congressional-Executive relations. However, as the reader will also observe, in the course of the events, the suggestion was made that REA testimony had been given in bad faith and that there had been wilful deceit of the Congress. Argument over the quality of information given Congress by administrators is common; administrators are not infrequently accused of evasion or of a confusing presentation, or of failing to notify Congressional committees of various matters; but the tug-of-war is carried on generally under a known though uncodified set of conventions. Under those conventions the "integrity of the record" does not become a matter of dispute. Mr. Foss's actions, justified or unjustified, were unconventional, and thus are properly regarded as administratively abnormal. Mr. Foss's problem can be taken as characteristic; but his solution is one that is seldom adopted.

The case is presented here in its simplest form—the decision of an individual administrator; all consideration of the degree to which other officials such as Mr. Robert B. Craig, Deputy Administrator, may have been involved in Mr. Foss's action has been left out. The available evidence is shadowy, and in any event Mr. Foss accepted full responsibility for his actions and upheld them in the subsequent investigations. Also omitted here are the ramifications and details of the promotion schedules in question.

I. REA and the Department of Agriculture

The Rural Electrification Administration was created by Executive Order in 1935 and was given a statutory basis in 1936. It operated on direct appropriations and on funds from the Reconstruction Finance Corporation, which were used to finance the construction of electric power lines to bring electricity to farm country into which private lines did not extend. The full cost of building the rural systems was lent at the prevailing rates of interest paid by the government on its own borrowing. Corporations, co-operatives, and public bodies were encouraged to borrow money from REA. Lines were built according to government approved specifications, the cost being repaid by receipts from the sale of power. Constant conflicts with private power companies and pressure from individual farms that could not get service made REA a lively agency. The agency heads were proud of their staff, and felt that many were underpaid. From their standpoint, the close-knit organization of the agency resulted in speed of operation and dedication to public purpose.

REA functioned as an independent agency until July 1, 1939. On that date it was transferred to the Department of Agriculture by Reorganization Plan II submitted to Congress on May 9, 1939, and not disapproved under the terms of the Reorganization Act of 1939. One of the important objectives of the President in supporting the Act, and proceeding under it, was to bring various independent agencies under the regular departments.

The REA consolidation with Agriculture resulted in disputes between the Department and the REA over the extent to which REA should retain its identity as to organization and policy. The Plan had stipulated that the Administrator of REA should be responsible to the Secretary of Agriculture, but it did not specify the extent to which incorporation should be carried out, and it lacked provision for review of its intent when dispute arose.

Conflict was partly over matters of organization. For example, the Department instituted detailed control of REA's budget and personnel, although Administrator Slattery protested that this was unwarranted interference. The Department stressed the necessity of bringing the staff of REA into alignment with department policies on appointments, salaries, and promotions. This meant lower salaries for some and much slower advancement for all and, as a consequence, REA lost (or feared it would lose) some of the staff which it had built up since 1935.

Fundamentally, however, the conflict centered on policy. There were points at which REA policy unquestionably needed co-ordination with that of the Department of Agriculture. For example, REA was inclined to finance lines wherever farmers asked for help, and this crusading zeal sometimes resulted in the extension of power into areas which the department had marked, on the advice of the Soil Conservation Service, for early withdrawal from farming. An overall co-ordination point, lower than the overburdened White House, was needed in such instances.

However, in placing this co-ordination point in the Department of Agriculture, the Reorganization Plan brought into sharper conflict two divergent philosophies: that of the department was generally somewhat cautious, while REA embodied an aggressive, New Deal social program. As an example, there was controversy over REA's sponsorship of an inexpensive, electrically run flour mill which would make available to the individual farmer a constant supply of natural, vitamin-rich flour. This social-educational program was watered down by the Department for fear mention of natural vitamins might arouse the large millers—or at least so REA interpreted departmental opposition to the proposal.

There was thus constant friction between REA and various departmental officials over program, as well as over departmental supervision of publicity, budgetary, and personnel matters. The REA officials were convinced that their loss of autonomy weakened their power to defend their program not only in interdepartmental disputes, but also against attacks by anti-public power congressmen, such as they thought Representative Dirksen to be, as well as by powerful opponents in the public utilities field. This situation should be kept in mind when we come to Foss's decision, for that decision was made only six months after REA had been transferred to the Department of Agriculture, a time when the process of adjustment was still far from complete.

II. Discovering the Facts

In December 1939, in the hearings on the Department of Agriculture Appropriation Bill for the Fiscal Year 1941 (i.e., beginning July 1, 1940), various members of the House Committee on Appropriations, and notably Congressman Dirksen of Illinois, showed an acute interest in the subject of administrative promotions, i.e., pay raises within a given grade granted at the discretion (under regulations) of the agency. Congressman Dirksen requested the Department's Director of Personnel, Roy Hendrickson, to submit detailed information showing the number of employees in each bureau of the department who received such promotions during the fiscal year ending June 30, 1939, by various categories, including the number who received promotions of one step, two steps, etc., with justification for the promotion of each employee advanced three or more steps. Furthermore, concerning promotions made in units that had joined the department under the provisions of the Reorganization Act of 1939, the information supplied was to show the promotions made before, and those made after, the filing of the pertinent Reorganization Plan with Congress; REA was one of two units in the department affected by this special request.

From comments made during the course of the hearings, it was clear that in addition to a general interest in the subject of administrative promotions Congressman Dirksen expected to receive confirmation of his belief that REA had been especially liberal in granting such promotions and particularly so after the filing of the Reorganization Plan affecting REA. The significance of this filing date arose from the fact that under the law employees in transferred agencies could receive no pay increase whatever for the fiscal year that followed the date of transfer. Thus REA officials knew on May 9, 1939 (when the Plan was filed), that salaries of all REA employees would be frozen for a year beginning on July 1, 1939.

Congressman Dirksen's surmises about REA's general liberality with administrative promotions and particular liberality after May 9, 1939, were well founded. The formal justification provided somewhat later by REA Administrator Slattery for the promotion policy reads as follows:

> (1) Rural Electrification Administration personnel consists largely of persons who have had to be trained to perform specialized functions; (2) appointments had been made originally during that part of the depression when suitable people could be procured at very low salaries, and Rural Electrification Administration salaries were established on too low a base; (3) improvement in employment conditions outside Government made it difficult to retain the trained personnel without increases which had been too long delayed.

As for the sizable number of promotions made after May 9, Administrator Slattery said:

> I have ascertained that they were in accordance with administrative decisions fairly early in the fiscal year to make such promotions as soon as budgetary savings would be revealed toward the close of the year, and that they were made during the month of May in accordance with such policy adopted earlier because budgetary savings were not revealed until that month.
>
> It should be noted further that at the time the budgetary savings became revealed and the policy could be implemented, certain developments pivoted on a proposed reorganization of Government agencies, involving Rural Electrification Administration, made impossible pending reclassifications upward, as a result of which many of the individuals on the attached list were compelled to assume expanded responsibilities without the benefit of reclassification.

It may be noted that the letter containing this justification of REA's promotion practices was prepared (with slight revisions by a consultant) by the Director of Management and Personnel, Kendall Foss, whose career had been spent largely in newspaper and public relations work.

Actually, the first intimation of Congressman Dirksen's interest in administrative promotions preceded the formal request that led eventually to the reply quoted above. During the hearings on the REA portion of the Agriculture estimates for Fiscal Year 1941, on December 7, 1939, Congressman Dirksen asked the REA Deputy Administrator for certain information on administrative promotions in REA; on December 11, this specific request was in effect supplanted by the department-wide request for information on promotions addressed to Mr. Hendrickson by Mr. Dirksen in the course of the hearings on general departmental questions. The detailed specifications of what was wanted were furnished by Mr.

Dirksen in a letter to Mr. Hendrickson dated December 13; this was the formal Congressional request on which Mr. Hendrickson acted.

Following the receipt of this letter, Mr. Hendrickson advised the various bureaus of the information needed for the Department's reply. His memorandum on the subject, sent to Administrator Slattery on December 18, asked for a reply by December 22. The REA report, prepared in response under the supervision of Mr. Foss, was put together in haste and under difficulties, because of the Christmas season, by Miss Anna C. O'Connor, appointment clerk, and another girl. Part of it, dealing with civil service employees, was filed on December 28; the rest, dealing with non-civil service employees (apparently omitted by misunderstanding) was filed on January 17. This was also prepared under the supervision of Mr. Foss by Miss O'Connor; no significant questions were ever raised about this second part of the REA report.

The REA report, filed in this manner in two parts, contained numerous clerical and arithmetical errors, which later plagued persons who attempted a reconciliation of diverse sets of figures; but no serious criticism was ever leveled at Mr. Foss on this account.

When the information contained in the first part of the REA report was received by Mr. Hendrickson's office, it was rearranged but not altered, put in with the information received from the rest of the Department, and forwarded to Congressman Dirksen. Mr. Dirksen then had the REA section of the Department's report photostated, sent the photostats to Mr. Slattery, and asked him to check the figures for errors or omissions. Mr. Foss prepared a reply to Congressman Dirksen, signed by R. B. Craig, Assistant Administrator, that reads in part:

> I have had the photostats you enclosed compared with the report we submitted to Mr. Hendrickson. No discrepancies were found. I am, therefore, able to assure you that the report you have is complete and accurate to the best of my knowledge.

Mr. Dirksen did some computing, and concluded that the total annual cost of the REA promotions for the fiscal year 1939 was about $90,000 to $100,000.

At about this time, the Bureau of the Budget had occasion to submit a report on administrative promotions to the Committee on Appropriations covering the whole Executive Branch for the Fiscal Year 1939. This Budget report showed the annual cost of the REA promotions as $67,390. The Budget report was in error; this was properly the figure for the actual cost, equivalent to an annual cost not far from Mr. Dirksen's figure. (When an employee is given a promotion, for example from $3200 to $3440, the *annual* cost of the promotion is $240, but the *actual* cost for the fiscal year in which the promotion is made depends on its effective date; if made on June 1, for example, the higher salary is paid for only one month of the fiscal year and the actual cost during that year is only $20. During the following fiscal year the actual and annual costs will be the same, unless the employee's status is again changed.)

Mr. Dirksen, surprised by the discrepancy, asked the Budget to recheck. The Budget asked REA for information, and was advised in due course that the correct annual figure was $67,420. This reply seemed to confirm Budget's erroneous figure.

Mr. Dirksen was still unconvinced. On June 29, 1940, he advised the Secretary of Agriculture of the discrepancies and said that he intended to reopen the matter in the following winter, "and at that time I shall assume that your office has made the appropriate investigation."

The Director of Personnel and the Director of Finance of the Department of Agriculture proceeded to make a joint study. The substantial differences between this Department report and the REA report all occurred in the portion dealing with civil service employees, i.e., the first part of the REA report, which REA had confirmed as accurate. The Department report showed an annual cost of the REA promotions of $138,080. It showed 429 civil service employees receiving a total of 1,004 promotion steps; REA had showed only 376 such employees receiving only 678 promotion steps.

Finally, Mr. Dirksen asked the General

Accounting Office to make a report. Of employees receiving three or more promotion steps, GAO found 141; REA had listed 85, a difference of 56. Of the 85 listed by REA, GAO found that 18 had received more promotion steps than REA had indicated.

During hearings on the 1942 Appropriation Bill, in February 1941, REA officials were questioned regarding the figures in the GAO report. Mr. Foss said that he had instructed the appointment clerk to omit the 56 names in question because these promotions had been made on the "eve of reclassification." However, as the justification given in the REA report for some of the promotions actually listed was "pending anticipated reclassification," this omission was said by Mr. Dirksen to be arbitrary and unwarranted. Mr. Dirksen furnished a copy of the GAO report to the Department, which found that this report (which differed only slightly from its own) was correct. The facts were now in.

Therefore, on June 19, 1941, Mr. Dirksen requested the Secretary of Agriculture to conduct an investigation to determine whether Deputy (formerly Assistant) Administrator Robert B. Craig of REA (the official who was considered primarily responsible for the REA report) "gave testimony in good faith before the Committee on Appropriations, House of Representatives, with respect to promotions in the Rural Electrification Administration during the fiscal year 1939, or whether he willfully deceived the Committee and the Congress." In October 1941, a departmental report was presented which did not substantiate the charge that Mr. Craig had testified in bad faith, or willfully deceived the Committee and Congress; but it formed the basis for a formal reprimand addressed by the Secretary to Mr. Craig. Furthermore, the report concluded that "incomplete and inaccurate information with respect to promotions in the fiscal year 1939 was submitted to the Committee on Appropriations, to the Bureau of the Budget, and to the Department personnel office." The report indicated that Mr. Foss was primarily responsible, and he was subsequently dismissed.

As was stated above, this study does not consider the justice or injustice of departmental action with regard to Mr. Foss, nor the extent to which other officials were involved in his action, but is confined to the administrative problem which confronted Mr. Foss, and the justifications which he made for his action in the course of the departmental investigation mentioned above. The departmental investigation was painstaking and formal; witnesses testified under oath and were given (as will be seen) the fullest possible opportunity to explain their conduct.

III. Mr. Foss's Explanation

In the departmental hearing, Mr. Foss testified that, although the request to prepare the report on the 1938-39 promotions came to him through departmental channels—from the office of the Director of Personnel for the Department of Agriculture—he was aware that it came originally from Congressman Dirksen and that he believed the request "was what was known as a fishing expedition." When questioned how he came to this conclusion, he replied:

> I do not recall how we first became conscious that Mr. Dirksen was behind the request, but I feel certain that we knew it from the beginning. It may be, though my memory is vague on this point, that Mr. Dirksen had called Rural Electrification Administration once or twice and we were thus able to hook up Mr. Hendrickson's letter with Mr. Dirksen's interest. I think it is also fair to add that we knew of Mr. Dirksen as one who does not favor public power, or Government operation in the field of power, before we knew of him as one who disapproved of Rural Electrification Administration's promotion policy. Therefore, in the public power field the deduction that his request was in the nature of a fishing expedition is, I think, very natural.[1]

Mr. Foss, Mr. Craig, and Mr. Person, the consulting economist to REA, discussed the preparation of the report and a general understanding was reached as to how the matter would be handled.

Mr. Foss gave Miss O'Connor, the appoint-

[1] The investigators apparently did not know that Mr. Dirksen had made his interest in REA promotions abundantly clear at the hearings on the 1941 Agriculture Appropriation Bill; Mr. Foss apparently had forgotten this fact; hence the confusion on the point.

ment clerk, certain "guide lines" to follow, saying in effect, "We want to use every legitimate means available to keep this report from appearing unnecessarily top-heavy." It was left to Miss O'Connor to determine which promotions were to be considered as having been given pending reclassification, but the difficult cases were discussed.

There are two types of promotion: (1) within-grade promotions, given in reward for work well done; and (2) grade promotions, generally known as reclassifications, made on the assumption of new duties. Within-grade promotions are made at the discretion of the department or agency; reclassifications must be approved by the Civil Service Commission. The promotions in question in this instance were within-grade promotions to the base pay of the next highest grade, in anticipation of Civil Service Commission approval of a change in grade. They had been made on the eve of the July 1, 1939, freeze mentioned above. The employees had assumed their new duties.

To take an example from the classification system then in effect, the base pay of CAF-3 is $1620 per year. This would be appropriate for a secretary to the head of a section. Within-grade promotions run in $60 steps to $1980, and the third step is $1800. But $1800 is also the base pay for CAF-4, an appropriate grade for a division chief's secretary. Due to the burden of work on the Civil Service Commission, it often took three to six months to obtain a change in grade for a girl who moved from a section head's office to a division chief's. To avoid penalizing the girl, REA would thus on occasion award a 3-step within-grade promotion at once and pay the employee the base pay appropriate to the new duties. (When the reclassification was finally made effective, no new increase in salary would be given.)

Mr. Foss did not want to include such promotions in the list of administrative within-grade promotions, and therefore he worked out "guide lines" justifying the omission of certain of the requested promotions of three or more steps. In the testimony he explained the "philosophical reasons" which justified his guide lines.

Now, as to the philosophical explanation. In my opinion, the commonly accepted meaning of the administrative promotion is an increase in salary as a reward for work well done. When a reclassification is pending and an individual is raised in salary to the level of the pending classification because he is already performing the new duties, and this is done to avoid penalizing the individual for the slowness of a Civil Service Commission action, and there is no suggestion of work well done but rather a statement that he is now performing duties of a higher grade for which he will be paid as soon as the Commission can act—such an action does not, in my opinion, come within the accepted meaning of an administrative promotion. Therefore, to report such promotions as administrative promotions would mislead the reader in an effort to determine how many people were given more money for work well done.

The examiner then asked:

But getting down to a strict interpretation, whenever an employee receives one or more steps of promotion all within his old grade before he has actually been reclassified, it actually is an administrative, within-grade promotion, is it not?—

Mr. Foss:

There is, of course, no strictly correct way to show this difference about which I am speaking and that is why I did then and do now accept responsibility for inventing an interpretation which, in my opinion, would produce a more meaningful report and why I took it upon myself not to follow precise instructions with a mere shrug as to how close to essential truth it came. I was more interested in essential truth than literal truth.

Mr. Foss was then asked why, if 38 names were included in the report with the assigned justification that the promotions were made pending reclassification, why, then, should not the other 56 names have been included with the same justification.

ANSWER: As I recall it, at the time of the report it was my assumption that all were either in one category or the other.

QUESTION: What do you mean by one category or the other?

ANSWER: Either all included or put in with an explanation. I didn't at the time of the report know that a discrepancy had occurred. Some time later—

QUESTION: You did not know that some had been included with that justification?

ANSWER: Well, let me say this: Within the past year there was a discussion of this point at the Bureau of the Budget, at which time it developed that what apparently happened was that I instructed Miss O'Connor to omit all who received reclassification shortly thereafter and that when she brought in the report, having omitted those which, in her judgment, came under the heading of "Shortly thereafter," there were a number of others whose reclassification came reasonably shortly thereafter. Whereupon, forgetting in the haste of the moment that we had already used as a reason for exclusion the question of reclassification, I simply said, "Well, then, the best explanation for these cases is that they were pending reclassification." In other words, as I have explained to the Bureau of the Budget, in the haste and in the newspaper type of thinking, I grabbed the same reason twice and they don't jibe.

QUESTION: Could you actually have forgotten in such a short time that you had instructed her to omit the people promoted pending reclassification?

ANSWER: Oh, yes; very easily. My mind reaches for a substantial or at least a substantial-appearing reason very rapidly and, having used it and gone on to something else, reaches for another one.

QUESTION: But you admit now, then, that the 56 should have been included with the same justification that was given for the 38?

ANSWER: I admitted that before in accepting responsibility, and I do so again.

With reference to the preparation of the report, there was some discussion of Miss O'Connor's doubts about her instructions; Mr. Foss was then asked if he had made a careful examination of Miss O'Connor's work.

ANSWER: Oh, I made an administrative examination.

QUESTION: Just what did that consist of?

ANSWER: Flipping the pages over and asking her if this was correct to the best of her knowledge.

QUESTION: Not going over them item by item?

ANSWER: O Lord no! I am not now and was not then an expert in personnel matters, was not in any position to make an item by item check. The only thing I could do was say, "if this has followed the lines I suggested, for which I am ready to take responsibility," I think that is morally right, "then, of course, I will sign it."

QUESTION: Although you were not an expert on personnel matters at that time, you were not agreeable to following her idea of including all of them?

ANSWER: That is because, as I have said, I was an expert in public relation matters. Where I saw a legitimate and moral reason for omitting groups, I took responsibility for doing so, for having it done.

QUESTION: But you now admit that there was nothing in Mr. Hendrickson's memorandum which would have justified any such omission and his memorandum was so clear and specific that it doesn't appear it would have taken a personnel expert to have interpreted it.

ANSWER: I have never served in the Army and it has never been part of my make-up to follow the Charge of the Light Brigade principle. I have always, as a newspaperman, been more interested in the project of an essential truth than in letter by letter following of instructions.

Mr. Foss was then questioned regarding his free interpretation of the request he received.

QUESTION: Didn't you think it was sufficiently important when the request had come from a member of the Appropriations Committee that the instructions be followed to the letter and exactly what was requested should be furnished?

ANSWER: In my experience, many requests have come across my desk from Members of Congress. Quite frequently it is possible to determine from the language of the request what they really want. I felt it my duty to provide what they wanted, not what they asked for, if they appeared to be confused.

QUESTION: Was there anything in this request which would indicate that Mr. Hendrickson or the Appropriations Committee appeared to be confused as to what they wanted? . . .

ANSWER: They appeared to want a list of those who had received more money without regard to change of duties. I therefore eliminated from their consideration those cases where there was a change in duties and where to report that these are administrative in the sense of no change in duties would have been misleading.

QUESTION: And you took it upon yourself to interpret what the committee wanted rather than to give them what they asked for?

ANSWER: That I have said several times; it is still true.

Mr. Foss made the following statements regarding his assumption of responsibility for the report:

QUESTION: You had more responsibility in the matter than Miss O'Connor did; did you not?

ANSWER: Certainly.

QUESTION: Therefore it was your responsibility to make sure that what she did was at least in accordance with your instructions?

ANSWER: Certainly.

QUESTION. But you didn't make sure?

ANSWER: I did to the best of my ability and to the best of my judgment.

QUESTION: Now, you say to the best of your ability. Certainly you would have had the ability to have gone over each case and determined whether she was correct or not.

ANSWER: Not in the time allotted.

QUESTION: Is that the only reason why you didn't do so, there was not sufficient time?

ANSWER: No sir; it is not the only reason. It is, in fact, a controlling reason, but—

QUESTION: What other reason—

ANSWER: In addition it is not my practice to do over again the work of trusted staff members. It is my practice to ask directly whether this has been done as I requested, whether the person is satisfied that it is accurate, and then to say, "All right, I take your word for it," and put my name to it.

QUESTION: Did you ask Miss O'Connor if she considered this report as being accurate?

ANSWER: I probably asked her whether she had followed my guide lines to the best—

QUESTION: You just said it was your practice to ask the subordinate employee whether the work was accurate. Did you ask her in this instance?

ANSWER: I can foresee that you are about to distinguish between accurate and following guide lines. Therefore, I shall confine myself to saying that I probably assured myself as to following my guide lines. If I say it was accurate, we then lead to the question, "How could it be accurate if you had given false guide lines?" . . .

I would like to add in addition, at some time between the making of the report and now she has told me that she knew it was not complete, and I have again quizzed her and discussed with her what she meant by incomplete and, as I recall it, in each instance it came out that she meant by incomplete it had left off these literal cases of administrative promotions when the request from Hendrickson didn't provide authority for doing so.

QUESTION: But, Mr. Foss, you have stated that at that time and still you are not a trained personnel man, but Miss O'Connor had several years' training and personnel experience. She put you on notice that the report was not accurate, was not complete, was not what was called for, and yet you let the report go along.

ANSWER: As I recall it, I satisfied myself that what she meant by not complete and not accurate was that she saw no basis for this third category which I invented.

Regarding the names of the 18 persons who had received more promotions than had been indicated.

QUESTION: In the REA report of 85 names, 18 of the classified employees are shown as having received less steps of promotion than they actually received, did you know this?

ANSWER: Not at the time.

QUESTION. Did you know that any of them showed less steps than they had actually received?

ANSWER: Not unless you mean by "actually received" the literal interpretation of administrative increase. Clearly since I was using guide lines, I knew that some of them had received more administrative increases under a literal interpretation because I was showing, because I was openly and frankly electing to show only those which seemed to me reflected the intent to reward good work.

Mr. Foss was then asked why he had not included in the report to the Department personnel administrator, Mr. Hendrickson, an explanation of his method of making out the report.

QUESTION: If you actually believe that you are justified in omitting promotions which had been given pending reclassification, why did you not show in the letter which you drafted that such promotions had been omitted and attempt to justify them instead of wording the memorandum so that no one could tell from it that a single step of promotion had been omitted?

ANSWER: I don't know.

QUESTION: Don't you think that would have been the fair thing to have done so that Mr. Hendrickson would know when he transmitted it to the Appropriations Committee that it was not a statement of all promotions above two steps?

ANSWER: That question involves too many related matters not here under discussion for me to feel free to answer it either "yes" or "no."

QUESTION: Well, let us put it the other way around. Do you feel that it was fair to Mr. Hendrickson to prepare a letter transmitting the report and omitting any mention of the fact that certain promotions had been omitted from the report for one reason or another?

ANSWER: I don't think it sounds fair, but I don't think the question of fairness entered my mind at the time.

QUESTION: Were you not at that time still imbued with the idea of not showing any more steps than you felt under your interpretation actually had to be shown?

ANSWER: Certainly.

QUESTION: But in view of the fact that Mr. Hendrickson's letter was so specific and clear and not subject to any such interpretation, do you not think it would have been a fair thing to do to tell him, "Well, we omitted certain steps because they had been given pending reclassification," rather than to word the letter in such a way that he would have no way at all of knowing that any step had been omitted?

ANSWER: I say that it doesn't sound fair now, but at the time the question of fairness did not enter my mind.

QUESTION: Just why, then, didn't you include some such statement?

ANSWER: I am not sure, but I suspect it goes into other matters that are not here under discussion, long involved series of considerations.

QUESTION: This whole matter of the REA report, the way it was prepared, the request which was made, and instructions which were given, is all under consideration now. There must have been some reason for not telling Mr. Hendrickson that "Here is the report, but we have omitted all promotions which were given pending reclassification," when he had actually asked for all promotions in all positions held by such employees.

ANSWER: If those matters are under discussion, there were, I believe, already at that time numerous intangible, but to my mind unmistakable, evidences that Mr. Hendrickson was more concerned with pleasing an anti-public-power Congressman than with defending a new member of the Department of Agriculture. I therefore probably felt that in the larger problem of the Administration's public power program I could not count on Mr. Hendrickson as an ally, and accordingly would have to take steps which I felt I could defend, but go no further than I had to in taking other people into my confidence.

QUESTION: Just what were these intangible things that caused you to feel that way about Mr. Hendrickson?

ANSWER: I can't specify at this time what they were.

QUESTION: Isn't it a fact, though, that in connection with this matter Mr. Hendrickson only passed on to the different bureaus, including REA, the request which he had received from Mr. Dirksen and that it was Mr. Hendrickson's responsibility and duty to obtain that information when requested to do so by a member of the Appropriations Committee?

ANSWER: I have accepted responsibility and stand behind my interpretation of what we were morally obligated to show in that report.

QUESTION: But you have made a rather serious charge there with respect to the Director of Personnel of the Department, and there must be some basis for that charge, yet you say you don't know of any real basis for it, is that correct?

ANSWER: No, I did not say I do not know of any real basis. I say I can't recall which of the numerous intangible things which have produced the feeling the Department personnel office is not very well informed in the ins and outs of the power fight that came before that time and that came after that time.

QUESTION: Did the power fight enter into this particular inquiry?

ANSWER: It certainly did in my mind, because I knew that Mr. Dirksen was anti-public-power and I had no doubt of the correctness of my deductions that he was on a fishing expedition.

Mr. Foss's position is clearly set forth in his closing testimony.

QUESTION: Before we close the record, Mr. Foss, do you have any other comments or remarks that you would like to have inserted?

ANSWER: I do. From the tenor of the questioning this morning, I feel that my integrity and loyalty to the Government is not accepted as established. I want to call attention to the fact that the agency with which I was associated had at that time been experiencing some rough weather, the program was under attack, the future was far from clear. I accept responsibility for the execution of this whole incident, but I point out that there was absolutely nothing for me to gain personally, that my motives here that appear to have led me into action at variance with specific requests were wholly and entirely dictated by a desire to protect REA against any and all comers from whatever side. I have felt since that time that I was ill-advised to rely as completely as I did on Miss O'Connor's accuracy. I think perhaps it was quixotic to "stick my neck out" on behalf of such a wholly intellectual concept as public power. I have since that time made considerable progress in learning that the ethics of the light brigade will get you further in Government than any attempt to fight battles that are bigger than the individual. I somewhat resent and very considerably am saddened by the impression I appear to have created in various people's minds that I had any other intent than to protect REA. I submit there is to the best of my knowledge no possible personal gain for me in my attempt to read as painless a report as I could out of what on the face of it appears to have been an orgy of promotions. Any public relations man recognizes automatically that REA's record of salary increases throughout 1938 looks extraordinary. As I see it, I had my choice between saying, "Well, the record is Mr. Carmody's record. It is nothing to me. I will shoot the works and put it all down without any regard to what is made of it," or saying, "Whether it is Mr. Carmody's or not, it is the record of REA with which I am associated. I detect the hand of an enemy of public power behind this simple administrative request and I will be damned if I will give him anything I don't have to. I will try to be sufficiently prudent so that I can defend my actions and I will hope for the best." But the motive in all of that is absolutely simple; it is to endeavor to ward off what appeared to me to be a disguised utility attack. That is all.

Note on Sources

The information on the occurrences at the House Appropriations Committee hearings on the Department of Agriculture Appropriation Bill for Fiscal Year 1941 and for Fiscal Year 1942 is, of course, derived from the printed transcripts of those hearings. All the rest of the information in this study, and all the direct quotations, are derived from the record of the hearings before a subcommittee of the Senate Committee on Agriculture and Forestry, 78th Congress, 2nd Session, Pt. 5, May 29th, 1944. This subcommittee was established pursuant to Sen. Res. 197 to investigate the administration of the Rural Electrification Act; its investigation covered many matters concerning REA. Part 5 prints in full the findings and exhibits of the departmental investigation of the Foss report on administrative promotions. Mr. Foss's testimony before the Departmental Examiners will be found on pp. 2034-2058.

THE EMERGENCY RUBBER PROJECT

CONTENTS

PREFACE

This is a case in inter-agency relations and in executive-legislative relations. It has various facets of interest, but it is perhaps most striking as an illustration of the divergent attitudes of administrators toward the nature of their responsibility to Congress and its committees. The case, therefore, focuses on this problem.

The substantive program with which this case is concerned, the Emergency Rubber Project, 1942-45, was under the immediate supervision of the Forest Service in the Department of Agriculture. It was a very small segment of the nation's wartime rubber program and a relatively unimportant item in the Agriculture budget. In May 1945, in the face of an unanticipated natural rubber crisis, an inter-agency program to expedite the production of a kind of natural rubber known as guayule[1] was proposed to the Department of Agriculture by the Rubber Reserve Company, a wartime subsidiary of the Reconstruction Finance Corporation, and seconded by the Office of the Rubber Director in the War Production Board. Because a veteran official high in the leadership of the Department, Director of Finance William A. Jump, considered that certain aspects of this proposal were inconsistent with Congress's previous expressions of intent on guayule rubber production he would not give definite approval to the plan until after consultation with the legislature. John Caswell, a former businessman who was the liaison with Agriculture on the guayule project from the WPB Office of the Rubber Director disagreed with Jump. He watched impatiently while consultation took place and dubbed it "a lot of red tape."

This difference of opinion suggests a series of questions which includes the following: What constitutes the "legislative intent" with regard to departmental programs? How far can or should the responsible official go in "interpreting" the will of Congress? Where is the dividing line between "useless red tape" and constructive procedures calculated to maintain a top official's effectiveness and good public (in this case, legislative) relations? The history of the case will not supply answers to questions of this character, but it will provide the reader with materials that indicate some of the implications inherent in different answers.

The background of Jump's May 1945 decision contained elements that were both old and new. Pervasive in the environment of the decision was the influence of long-established custom. Jump had been Agriculture's budget officer (with increasing over-all financial responsibility) since 1922; he had entered the Department in 1907 as a messenger, at the age of fifteen. Jump was the sympathetic heir of a pattern of Agriculture Department—Congressional relations which had been developed over the many decades following the Department's establishment in 1862 and which had some counterpart, of course, in all the permanent executive agencies. It was a common observation in Washington that Jump had maintained legislative relations at a high level of co-operativeness and cordiality, notwithstanding the great changes, diversity, and complexity which characterized Agriculture's program during this period. Many shared the opinion of Macmahon and Millett who said of Jump, in 1939,

> Quietly, with unobtrusive efficiency and disciplined imagination, he had established the right to be considered one of the foremost civil servants of the time.

The more immediate backdrop to the decision was the see-saw history of the Emergency Rubber Project. Initiated in 1942, the guayule project was the fourth and smallest aspect of

[1] Guayule (commonly pronounced gwy-oo'lee) is a small gray-green bush indigenous to the dry central plateau of Northern Mexico; it is one of a number of rubber-bearing plants, including goldenrod, which have been tested as possible substitutes for the basic natural rubber plant known as *hevea*.

the U. S. wartime rubber development program. Its beginnings need to be briefly recounted as a prelude to the main theme of this study.

The Wartime Quest for New Sources of Rubber

Ninety per cent of the United States' supply of natural rubber—a basic material in both peace and war—was cut off early in 1942 when the Japanese overran the southwest Pacific. The U. S. stockpile of natural rubber at the time of Pearl Harbor amounted to some 600,000 tons, no more than one year's peacetime requirements. Despite conservation, substitution, and a continuing trickle of supplies from Ceylon and other accessible areas, the stocks on hand did not promise to be adequate to care for the anticipated requirements of a nation entering a global war of undetermined length.

As early as June 1940 the President had designated rubber as a strategic and critical material and those in charge of defense production planning began to consider how to find and quickly develop new sources of supply on the American continent. A number of measures were undertaken during 1940-42, as rubber requirements mounted and the Pacific situation deteriorated. The Rubber Reserve Company was formed by the RFC in June 1940 and was made responsible for three major aspects of the rubber program. RRC stockpiled natural rubber until reserves reached a peak of more than 600,000 tons in 1942. It entered into agreements with western hemisphere countries and Liberia to encourage their production and export of natural rubber. And it financed—with approximately $700,000,000—the development of synthetic rubber production from the test tube stage to the point where an annual production rate of more than 1,000,000 long tons was achieved at the end of 1944.

The quality of the various types of synthetic rubber and the extent to which they could satisfactorily replace *hevea* (natural) rubber—particularly in the crucial area of tire-production—were largely unknowns when the program began. Rubber experts generally agreed, however, that the synthetic product could substitute for or be combined with natural rubber for many items. As experience with rubber production and combination progressed it was the consensus of those in charge of the program that synthetic rubber could not safely be substituted for natural beyond 86 per cent of total consumption. In other words, no matter how large the synthetic rubber program, there remained an irreducible minimum of essential needs that could be satisfied only by the use of natural rubber.

The guayule program was an effort to increase the natural rubber supply through growing the product within the United States. As early as 1903, private companies had begun to extract rubber from the guayule shrub, the cells of whose branches and stems contain rubber. Guayule rubber was not as versatile as *hevea* and was considered about 70 per cent as efficient, but it could be combined with natural or synthetic rubber for many purposes and thereby lessen the drain on *hevea* supplies.

The International Rubber Company of New York (founded by Americans but controlled, in 1941, by a Dutch trust) was the primary concern in the field of guayule rubber extraction. In the years preceding World War II it had harvested from 3000 to 6000 tons of rubber annually from wild Mexican guayule. Nearly all of this was exported to the United States where it was used—in relatively small quantities combined with natural rubber—by tire producers and others. In the United States, the company maintained research facilities, a plantation, a rubber mill, and experimental plantings—concentrated for the most part at Salinas, California. The Salinas fields were over a decade old but they had not yet reached the stage of producing any regular or significant quantities of guayule rubber for the trade at a price which could compete with that of imported natural rubber.

None of the experts who had studied the guayule shrub could foretell whether it would ever be economically feasible to produce rubber from it in peacetime. Although hardy in its natural habitat, guayule required special climatic and soil conditions. Plants growing on dry land did not mature—in the sense of containing sufficient harvestable rubber—until they were about four or five years old. For harvesting they had to be pulled up whole and milled, and sometimes deresinated. New crops were started by planting the field with seedlings. The four to five year growth period in itself meant that a dry land guayule program begun in 1942 could not offer the country much immediate benefit before 1946 or 1947.

The Emergency Rubber Project, March 1942

Government interest in the production of guayule rubber started long before Pearl Harbor. In 1930 two Army officers, one of them the then Major Dwight D. Eisenhower, made an official inquiry into United States production of guayule rubber and concluded that it might provide a valuable safeguard against a wartime loss of overseas rubber sources.

In 1941 Congress began to show interest in guayule. In the spring of that year Representative Jack Z. Anderson of California (in whose district Salinas was located) introduced legislation authorizing government sponsorship of an Emergency Rubber Project for guayule rubber production. At hearings before the House Agriculture Committee early in 1942, the Department of Agriculture, the Navy, and some tire companies lent support to the bill as an emergency wartime measure. Others, particularly from the areas thought suitable for guayule cultivation—parts of Texas, California, New Mexico, and Arizona—hoped that after experimentation and research guayule might develop into a new farm crop. Both these purposes underlay the passage in March 1942—after extended debate—of the Emergency Rubber Project Act. It authorized the Secretary of Agriculture to purchase for "emergency and defense purposes," the assets of the Intercontinental Rubber Company, to establish guayule nurseries and plantations (not to exceed 75,000 acres), to lease land, to construct and operate mills, and to carry on research. The Secretary of Agriculture delegated control of the project to the Forest Service and the research bureaus of the Department co-operated with the Service on various phases of the program. The project's budget was handled, of course, through Jump's office.

Fluctuations in the Project, October 1942-March 1943

Work on the rubber project started immediately. The Intercontinental properties in California—including over five hundred acres of mature guayule bush—were purchased. Some 530 acres of land were planted with seed and some 800 acres with seedlings. In an effort to overcome the time lag inherent in the four to five year maturation period, the Forest Service decided in July 1942, to use irrigated land, whose higher moisture content was expected to hasten the bush's latex production so that harvesting and milling could take place two years after planting. This, admittedly, was expensive and somewhat risky—since the plant's development under irrigation could not be forecast with complete certainty—but to the Department of Agriculture, which regarded the rubber project purely as an emergency rather than an agricultural measure, the very critical natural rubber situation at the time appeared to justify these steps. Accordingly, arrangements were made to lease irrigated land in California and plantings were made there, too.

In August the President appointed a Rubber Survey Committee headed by Bernard Baruch. Mr. Baruch's interest in rubber was not a new one; together with a number of others, he had, in the 1930's, contributed money to the early efforts of the Intercontinental Rubber Company to extract rubber from the guayule plant. The broad and detailed "rubber program" soon proposed by the Rubber Survey affected the guayule project in two ways. First, the guayule program was expanded in October by legislation which raised the planting limitation from 75,000 to 500,000 acres; second, a WPB Rubber Director was appointed by the Chairman of the War Production Board to co-ordinate all the government's rubber producing activities—including those of RRC and the Emergency Rubber Project. The first Rubber Director, William M. Jeffers, immediately lent his support to the recommendation that guayule planting be greatly expanded; a liaison official to work with Agriculture was appointed. The Rubber Director's greatest concern, of course, lay elsewhere, in building up the synthetic rubber program.

Not long after the guayule project had begun to move into high gear, following the October 1942 legislation, the nation-wide food and manpower picture became much darker than it had previously been. Farm interests and land-leasing groups in California began to question seriously the wisdom of using, for guayule production which could not mature earlier than 1944 or 1945, fertile irrigated land and agricultural labor which could be shifted into food production of more immediate value. After considering the situation and this argument, the Rubber Director indicated to the Secretary of Agriculture in March 1943 that it was not necessary or desirable to ask that the guayule program be carried on in such a way as to divert any large quantities of land and manpower from the production of essential food crops. In his third *Progress Report*, dated May 1943, he said, "Conditions have changed. Food for 1943 has become more important to the Nation than a rubber insurance policy for 1946 and beyond." (Earlier, in his February *Progress Report*, the Rubber Director had taken note of the fact that the guayule program was expected to yield less than 1,000 tons of rubber in 1943. At the same writing, he anticipated that 1943 production of synthetic rubber would approximate 241,000 tons.)

In accordance with the Rubber Director's instructions, Agriculture ceased making leases for any more land for guayule cultivation in March 1943. The Emergency Rubber appropriation for Fiscal Year 1944 also underwent a drastic scaling down; it passed in July at $13 million, one-fourth of the original Budget estimate for the period. The guayule program thereby assumed something of a limited "stand by" status.

Nonetheless, operation of the existing plantation continued. Spring and summer 1943 saw the first guayule harvest under government auspices. Twelve-year-old shrub on 550 acres of former Intercontinental land was milled, yielding 393 long tons of rubber, somewhat less than had been anticipated. The rubber was sold to the RRC.

Abortive Effort to Increase Guayule Acreage, Fall 1943

In mid-summer of 1943 the Rubber Director's office undertook a review of the entire rubber situation. John Caswell, a former businessman and the Rubber Director's special representative and liaison with the Forest Service, inspected the guayule project in California and also the experimental plantings Agriculture had made in other selected spots; he reported favorably on the project.

Shortly afterward, in August, the Rubber Director advised the Secretary of Agriculture that he felt guayule offered a sound national rubber insurance policy. He suggested that a program be instituted which would produce, within the United States, up to 20,000 tons a year on the basis of milling 3-year-old irrigated plantings or 4-year-old plantings on dry land, using, in all cases, non-critical land. Estimates were developed in the Department of Agriculture and approved by the Budget Bureau. A recommendation for a supplemental estimate of $7,500,000 for the Fiscal Year 1944, to initiate the Rubber Director's suggested program, was transmitted to Congress by the President on September 16, 1943. The House Appropriations Committee rejected this estimate on November 4 on the grounds that

> the additional sum contemplated an extension of the present project, already under way, by planting additional acreage of guayule shrub which would not yield any rubber for use in the war effort unless the war should last beyond 1946.

On December 4 the Senate Appropriations Committee restored the Emergency Rubber item, scaling it down to $4,100,000 and recording its interest

in guayule as a source of crude rubber as a sound insurance for the future.

But this item was withdrawn in Conference Committee and the expansion program killed.

The Fiscal Year 1945—Continuation *vs.* Liquidation

In February 1944 the Fiscal Year 1945 estimates for the guayule project were being considered by the Subcommittee on Agriculture of the House Appropriations Committee. These estimates provided for carrying on the existing plantations, the Salinas mill, and essential research. The one new item proposed was the construction of a new mill at Bakersfield, California: the shrub planted on irrigated land in 1942 would be two years in the field by the end of the calendar year 1944 and if it was to be harvested in accordance with Agriculture's plans for speeding guayule production, an additional mill would be needed. The Budget estimate did not contemplate the establishment of any new plantations or the sowing of new nurseries.

At the hearings in February 1944 before the Subcommittee on Agriculture of the House Appropriations Committee, Chairman Tarver (Democrat of Georgia, and a former judge) questioned Agriculture officials searchingly on the expected wartime yield of the project, the cost of continuing, and the cost of liquidation. The skeptical attitude of Judge Tarver—who had been chairman of the Subcommittee on Agriculture for many years—carried great weight and the report of the House Appropriations Committee issued on March 21, 1944, stated that the

hearings indicated very conclusively that this project [i.e., guayule] will not achieve results in time to be of material advantage to the war effort.

The Committee recommended that a sum be appropriated and earmarked for the "progressive and final liquidation" of the rubber project during the Fiscal Year 1945. The House concurred in this recommendation.

However, the Senate Appropriations Committee, which also heard testimony on the guayule program, disagreed with House conclusions and the Senate approved the program as it had come from the Budget Bureau. The Conference Committee proved unable to reconcile these divergent positions and the matter came up again on the floor of the House. There, on June 20, 1944, Representative Anderson and other proponents of the program argued that guayule was an insurance premium, that it might be a good postwar crop for certain areas, and that it had not been cultivated long enough for its value to be accurately known. An emphatic letter from the WPB Rubber Director approving the guayule program was also read. Congressman Tarver led the opposition argument. Guayule yield had been insufficient to warrant continuation of the program, he maintained; it was extravagant in the light of the success of the synthetic rubber program. He also cited the Department of Agriculture estimate that if the project were liquidated in 1951 (after a cost of $5 million a year) a total of no more than 10,000 tons of rubber would have been produced.

Probably as much because of the Rubber Director's strongly worded letter as anything else, the House finally voted by 300 to 43, on June 20, to concur with the Senate. The guayule was continued at its existing acreage and the new Bakersfield mill was begun.

Budget Estimates for the Fiscal Year 1946

Of the many factors in the rubber problem which were doubtless in the minds of Agriculture officials as they began work on the budget for the Fiscal Year 1946 in the summer of 1944, the strongest probably were the undercurrent of Congressional opposition to the guayule project and the constantly fluctuating requirements of the rubber program. Before incorporating a guayule item in their estimates, Agriculture officials sought the recommendation of the WPB Rubber Director on what type of program his office would prefer. A letter on August 26, 1944, to the Director from the Secretary of Agriculture, outlined three possible alternative guayule programs for Fiscal Year 1946:

1. maintain the existing plantations and continue operation of the two mills, at a cost of about $5,000,000;
2. maintain existing plantations and also construct two additional mills to recover all the harvestable rubber from the existing plantations by 1950, at a cost of about $6,000,000 (this would be aimed at securing the largest quantity of guayule as soon as possible);
3. proceed with the final and complete liquidation of the project at a cost of about $4,000,000 (this would have involved plowing up most of the existing acreage without harvesting the shrub, and restoring the land to proper condition for return to its owners).

Of the three alternatives, no. 2 was the most ambitious; no. 3 was, of course, what the House Subcommittee had proposed the previous year. No. 1 was the status quo.

The Rubber Director did not reply formally to the Secretary's questions for two months, although possibly there were informal discussions of the subject during this period. The delay may have been due to the fact that the Director's office was preoccupied with a grave problem: the precarious balance between the available supply of natural rubber and the absolute minimum needed in the total rubber program was rapidly being impaired by the soaring needs of an aggressive two-front war. The year 1945 was to see further deterioration in the natural rubber situation. Concern over this was reflected in the Rubber Director's reply of November 3, 1944, to the Secretary recommending that the Department proceed with the second alternative—increased rubber production.

Agriculture thereupon sent over to the Budget Bureau a $6,000,000 budget estimate based on the second alternative. The Bureau proceeded to make several important changes in the estimates which brought them close to alternative no. 1: provision for the two additional mills was deleted and funds (about $183,000) were definitely allocated for plowing up, without harvesting, 10,000 acres which had been planted in 1944. These bore shrubs which were young and still low in rubber content. With these changes, the guayule project estimate for the fiscal year 1946 came to $5,000,000.

The Subcommittee on Agriculture of the House Appropriations Committee held hearings on the Fiscal Year 1946 budget during February 1945. Mr. C. M. Granger, Assistant Chief of the Forest Service, was asked to explain the state of the guayule project and the meaning of the estimates. In answer to a question by Judge Tarver he explained the difference between the probable liquidation dates of the three alternative guayule programs:

> If we follow the Bureau of the Budget's plan of plowing up the 10,000 acres and operating with two mills it is expected [the project will be finished] in 1952. If we have only two mills but do not plow up the 10,000 acres it is estimated that we will run to 1955. If we keep the entire acreage but construct two more mills, the estimate is 1950 . . .

Harvesting in this instance, it should be noted, would prove a quicker method of liquidation than plowing up.

Caswell of the WPB Rubber Director's office also spoke before the committee; he explained the reason for the WPB's request for additional mills:

> We consider [serious] actually anything under about 100,000 tons [of natural rubber in the government stockpile] which was [the amount] indicated in the Baruch report as being the danger point, . . . We are now in the danger zone of crude rubber very definitely. [The stockpile was expected to decline to 61,000 tons by January 1, 1946.] Therefore the [Rubber] Director . . . hopes, as he said in his letter, that the Congress might consider the construction of two additional mills as quickly as possible. . . .

Rubber Reserve Company officials also appeared before the committee in support of restoring funds for constructing additional mills to speed up harvesting; as the government's rubber purchasing agency they were interested in seeing supplies increased.

Judge Tarver reminded the group that in February 1944 he and the committee had recommended liquidation of the project and that the House had reversed this action. Since the subcommittee was only a part of the House he thought it should not recommend liquidation again. Accordingly, he proposed—and the committee accepted—the elimination of the $183,000 item for plowing under. The guayule budget (as part of the Committee on Appropriations report on the Agriculture budget) went to the House on March 20, 1945, with this change and with no recommendation for funds for the construction of additional mills.

On the floor of the House on March 23 several Congressmen tried to secure clarification of the subcommittee's views on mill construction. Congressman Poage of Texas—who had recently headed up a Subcommittee of the House Committee on Agriculture and Forestry which had reported favorably on guayule as a peacetime farm crop—offered an amendment that would have made it possible for the additional mills recommended by WPB and the Rubber Reserve Company to be constructed from other appropriated funds. He said:

Mr. Chairman, I offer an amendment: On page 44 line 1, strike out $4,250,000 and insert $4,875,000. I hope it will not be necessary to ask for the adoption of this amendment and it will not be necessary if we may have the assurance of the subcommittee that it was not their intention by the figures placed on the bill to preclude other agencies of the government using other money appropriated by other bills to carry out functions of those agencies. Specifically, I refer to the construction of guayule mills by the Defense Plant Corporation. May I enquire of the Subcommittee if it was the intention of the Subcommittee to preclude the Defense Plant Corporation, if requested by other defense agencies of the government to provide funds for the construction of additional mills, from the construction of those mills . . . ?

The following exchange then took place:

MR. TARVER: We cannot put any limitation in this bill upon the expenditures of funds carried in any other appropriation bill and manifestly we have not undertaken to do so . . . nor are we seeking to limit the expenditure of funds by other agencies of the government in any way. . . .

MR. WHITTEN: If the gentleman's worry is caused by the fact that appropriations were not made in the bill for the purpose of constructing mills to manufacture guayule rubber, may I say that so far as I am concerned, and the opinion of other members of the committee is concerned, the necessities which may face those in control of the rubber program would govern in the question of whether additional facilities should be built or not. I did not think that was a proper field for a committee on Agriculture to go into but should be controlled by those who have to do with whether or not present facilities are sufficient to meet our rubber demands . . .

MR. POAGE: I wanted to get it clear that it was the opinion of this Committee of the Whole House that if the defense agencies recommended that the Defense Plant Corporation build mills they would be at liberty to do so. I understand that is the view of the Appropriations Committee and that the failure of the Committee to include funds for the construction of the mills should not be construed as any intent to prevent the Defense Plant Corporation or any other government agency from building the mills.

Reassured by this discussion Mr. Poage withdrew his amendment. Congressman Rich (of Pennsylvania) then offered an amendment to reduce the appropriation to $4,000,000 and to hasten liquidation of the project by restoring provision for plowing under 10,000 acres. This amendment was defeated after a brief discussion, and the appropriation passed the House and Senate with no provision for the construction of additional mills or for the plowing under of the 10,000 acres.

The Proposal for Four More Mills

The program favored by the WPB rubber office was turned down by Congress at a time when the natural rubber supply was progressively worsening. On April 3, 1945, the WPB Rubber Director wrote to the Secretary of Agriculture, saying:

During the next 20 months, every available pound of natural rubber must be added to the supply of the United Nations. Steps are being taken to increase imports. I am told that it may be possible to obtain perhaps as much as 16,000 long tons of rubber between now and the end of 1946 from the shrub now being grown by the Emergency Rubber Project . . .

The Department of Agriculture Appropriation Bill for the fiscal year 1946 provides no funds for the construction of additional mills. Certain speeches recently made on the floor of the House indicate that the decision as to whether or not the rubber from domestic guayule shrub is to be made available for war production rests with the agency charged with the over-all rubber supply picture. I have asked the Rubber Reserve Co. to make a quick survey of ways and means to secure all the rubber grown by the Emergency Rubber Project . . .

The Rubber Reserve Company's survey led it to recommend that four additional mills be constructed to secure the maximum amount of rubber from the Emergency Rubber Project within the shortest period of time.

A parenthetical note on the functioning of RFC (or its subsidiaries) may be helpful. The construction and operation of plants for defense purposes constituted normal activities for RFC during the war. RFC had ample funds for the purpose and statutory powers of sufficient amplitude to permit construction and operation without any necessity for requesting specific authority for each project. In practice, RFC exercised these powers only on specific request of a sponsoring agency, like WPB, and in practice RFC as a matter of policy, usually did not begin projects of this character without some assurance of reimbursement from some source. Characteristically, for example, in plants that it managed, the price of the product, whether sold to government agencies or to industry, was set to cover amortization charges as well as expenses.

In accordance, therefore, with normal procedure, on May 7, 1945, the Chairman of the WPB wrote to the Chairman of the Board of Directors of RFC approving the recommendations of the Rubber Reserve Company. He said, in part:

. . . an investigating committee appointed by Rubber Reserve Company has confirmed estimates by the Department of Agriculture that at least 12,000 long tons of guayule rubber can be extracted from these plantations between now and April 1, 1947, provided that four additional mills are immediately constructed so as to be in operation by October of this year. . . .

In view of the critical natural rubber supply position in this country, the Special Director of Rubber Program advocates this accelerated project be started immediately, and I am taking this opportunity to inform you of my approval of this recommendation on behalf of the Board.

RFC, having received the letter from WPB, was now in a position to go ahead with the four new mills; but since their construction and operation would be an integral part of the Emergency Rubber Project which was financed by Agriculture Department funds, and operated by the Forest Service, the need for an understanding between RFC and Agriculture was evident. Agriculture's Budget Officer—William Jump—thereupon held a series of meetings in May 1945 with Rubber Reserve officials to determine how the four new mills would be financed and constructed. It is not clear what alternatives were discussed, but from the meetings there emerged tentative agreement on a RRC offer to finance initially the construction of the four new mills and to assume the operating costs of all the mills, including those at Salinas and Bakersfield, in return for an arrangement whereby it would be reimbursed through proceeds from the sale of guayule rubber. At Mr. Jump's request, Mr. S. T. Crossland, executive vice-president of the RRC, outlined the plan in a letter to Mr. Granger of the Forest Service on May 22. Referring to the responsibilities of the Agriculture Department, Mr. Crossland wrote:

. . . In the operation of the mills as well as the construction of the mills the Department will render all necessary technical consultation and other assistance to Rubber Reserve Co., or its Agent, and will make available its existing laboratory facilities for any activities found to be necessary.

The Department will continue to carry out at its own expense all cultivation, irrigation, harvesting, baling and transport activities in connection with the supplying of guayule shrub to the mills. The shrub processed by Rubber Reserve Co. in the mills operated by it will be purchased from the Department on a delivered basis at a price calculated monthly and to be equal to the current net realization by Rubber Reserve Co. from the resale of the recovered rubber content of such shrub, less the total processing costs incurred by Rubber Reserve Co. during each month, and less an amount sufficient to amortize on a monthly basis over the projected period of operations, Rubber Reserve Company's investment in the mills producing rubber . . .

Jump's Dilemma

The RRC, in short, was proposing to be repaid for constructing four new mills and operating all six mills from the proceeds of the sale of guayule rubber. The Department of Agriculture—through Jump—had to decide whether to accept this proposal.

Many questions were involved. First, and simplest, was the matter of the use of guayule rubber proceeds. The 1946 Appropriation Act for the Department of Agriculture had carried the provision that

> any proceeds from the sales of guayule, rubber processed from guayule . . . or from other sales, rentals, and fees resulting from the operations under such Act of March 5, 1942, as amended, shall be covered into the Treasury as miscellaneous receipts.

Legal counsel for the Department of Agriculture and the Rubber Reserve Company agreed that the word "proceeds" was subject to various interpretations and that the Department of Agriculture would be perfectly justified, from a legal standpoint, in interpreting it to mean the net proceeds which would be available to the Department after deducting whatever costs were necessary to make the sales. At the very least, it was clear that the intent of Congress in using this phraseology was that the costs of harvesting, baling, and processing of the shrub could be deducted from the gross proceeds from the sale of the guayule rubber, if such costs were not paid out of appropriations to the Department of Agriculture.

But Mr. Crossland's plan called for the deduction of "an amount sufficient to amortize . . . Rubber Reserve Company's investment" in the new mills. The Budget Bureau had deleted provision for two new mills and Congress had not seen fit to reverse this decision in the 1946 Appropriation Act, though discussion on the House floor had made clear that no positive prohibition against new mills was intended. The matter, as Congressman Whitten had indicated, had been left in the hands of "those in control of the rubber program," that is, WPB Rubber Director's office. Could proceeds from the Emergency Rubber Project run by Agriculture be used to repay the costs of this construction Agriculture had pointedly not been authorized to undertake?

From Mr. Jump's point of view the question was not the narrow one of legal justification through an interpretation of "proceeds" but the broader one of Congressional intent. Although granting that Congress had not left the matter of additional mills in the lap of the Department of Agriculture, Jump felt he could not automatically accept the RRC proposal because several aspects of it would entail significant changes in Agriculture's expenditures and receipts for the Fiscal Year 1946.

Thus, the RRC scheme provided not only that the proceeds from the shrub processed at the four mills be used for paying the amortized cost of the construction but also that the shrub harvested for and processed by the two existing mills be used to help cover the cost of constructing the new mills. Mr. Jump and his assistants felt there was a significant difference, from the point of view of Agriculture Department finance, between the proceeds from the two mills constructed from funds appropriated for Agriculture by Congress and the proceeds from mills to be constructed by the Rubber Reserve Company. It would not be illogical, they felt, to apply the proceeds from rubber processed in the new mills to amortize the cost of their construction; but this did not hold true for the proceeds from rubber processed in the two existing mills.

Furthermore, the RRC plan would require a reallocation of Agriculture funds so that expenditures would differ considerably from the detailed budget estimate which had been used in justifying the budget presented to Congress and which had formed the basis for the Fiscal Year 1946 appropriation. For example, the RRC plan would involve the diversion of approximately $800,000 from the item "Care of plantations" to "Harvesting and delivery of shrubs to mills" because it would be necessary to do considerably more harvesting and baling to supply shrub to six mills than to the two mills which had been involved when the budget was presented to and approved by Congress.

Naturally, none of these possible quantitative and qualitative alterations in Agriculture's pattern of expenditures had been known or anticipated by the Agriculture Subcommittee of the House Appropriations Committee when it considered the Fiscal Year 1946 budget. Jump regarded the budget as the embodiment of the legislature's will regarding departmental policy. The Department did not, in his view, have discretionary power to apportion an appropriation as it saw fit within the broad purposes established by Congress. Appropriations could or should be spent only in accordance with the detailed estimate originally submitted to Congress and used by it as a basis for an appropriation. For a department to deviate in any significant fashion from the prescription implied in its estimate was a violation of the integrity of the budget. For this reason, it had been Jump's custom, when in doubt over Congress's intent or when unforeseen conditions required that expenditures depart markedly from estimates, to consult informally with the Agriculture Subcommittee or its chairman.

The legislator with whom Jump probably had had the most contact was Judge Tarver. A Southern conservative, for many years Tarver, as chairman of the Agriculture Subcommittee of the House Appropriations Committee, had not only been concerned with and well informed on the Agriculture budget but had wielded great influence in decisions on it. Despite his personal political strength Tarver, as we have seen, bore the subordinate position of the Agriculture Subcommittee and, indeed, the House Appropriations Committee, well in mind when recommending decisions to his Committee and to the House. He was, in fact, far less willing to assume that his own views, or the views of his Subcommittee or Committee represented the views of Congress, than most Congressmen. But he was likewise convinced that the views of Congress, even when not expressed in legislation, or in a formal action like a committee report, must constitute an absolute rule for the administration.

As he considered what action to take on the RRC proposal, with its forseeable effects on Agriculture's expenditures and receipts, Jump was not unmindful that from the point of view of the final balance sheet of the United States Treasury it made no difference whether the cost of the mills was charged to the RFC—parent corporation of the RRC—or to Agriculture. The paramount consideration, of course, was the critical need for rubber.

In this connection Jump was aware of the impatience and skepticism his pondering was evoking in Caswell of the WPB Rubber Director's Office. Caswell had the businessman's traditional aversion to what he considered government "red tape"; his organization ethic was that WPB had a job to do and it was his business to get his part of it—increasing crude rubber supplies—done as efficiently and quickly as possible. He was interested in the contribution guayule rubber could make to the national stockpile and was unimpressed with the questions Jump raised; they seemed to him merely procedural and therefore unimportant. Caswell could appreciate the fact that Jump would have to "live with Tarver" for many years more, in all likelihood, and therefore would be predisposed to approach budget changes with circumspection. But this factor was not relevant to guayule, he thought, because Congress had indicated that the problem of the new mills was the responsibility of the agency concerned with the over-all rubber supply—WPB; Agriculture was merely acting as a service agency in the rubber program. Accordingly, he believed that the mills were not a concern of the Agriculture Subcommittee of the House Appropriations Committee.

Nonetheless, after considering all the arguments and factors involved, Jump was not persuaded that using proceeds from Agriculture's guayule project to amortize the RRC's cost of constructing the new mills was in conformance with Congressional intent as revealed by Agriculture's 1946 Appropriation Act. He and his staff decided to accept the RRC's proposal but to discuss it with Tarver. Accordingly RRC was told to go ahead with preliminary plans for the mills and Jump spoke with Tarver and outlined the situation briefly to him. It should be noted that so far as is known, no attempt was made to persuade or require RFC to omit a charge for amortization, a charge that RFC had full legal authority to waive.

Congressional Reaction to the RRC Plan

When Jump spoke with Tarver the latter suggested that Department of Agriculture officials discuss the RRC plan with the committee in greater detail. Jump and his assistants then came before the Subcommittee on Department of Agriculture appropriations to explain the proposed action. They had expected a handful of committee members; instead, the entire Committee was on hand and the proposal precipitated a discussion on the broad purposes of the Emergency Rubber Project. Most significant, Judge Tarver proved not greatly concerned over the problem of using guayule proceeds to pay for the mills. Instead he raised another issue: whether the accelerated harvesting would not, in effect, liquidate the rubber project more rapidly than Congress had intended. And, he asked, was not a liquidation of the project by 1947 contrary to Congressional action when it passed on Agriculture's 1945 and 1946 budgets? After some discussion by the Committee, Tarver suggested, and the Committee agreed, that the question should be taken up by the whole House. He recommended that Jump submit his request for a change in the 1946 appropriation through the usual channels so that it would come before the House.

After some discussion among themselves the Agriculture budget staff decided to follow the Committee's recommendation. Accordingly, on May 29, 1945, Jump dispatched a letter to Harold Smith, Director of the Bureau of the Budget, requesting that Budget submit a formal request to Congress to change the provisions of the 1946 appropriation to permit Agriculture to accept the proposals of the Rubber Reserve Co. The letter said in part:

If the plan proposed by the Rubber Reserve Co. is undertaken . . . the 1946 funds authorized for the Emergency Rubber Project would still be spent for the guayule project but, in view of the conditions indicated by the WPB, would be expended somewhat differently than was contemplated when the 1946 appropriation was justified and approved by Congress. While it cannot be accurately determined at this time what specific readjustment will be necessary, in general the expenses for the care of plantations and the cost of milling would be decreased while the harvesting and retrenchment expenses incident to returning the land to the owners would be increased . . .

In the administration of the Emergency Rubber Project, the Department of Agriculture has at all times endeavored to carry out the policies of the Rubber Director and the War Production Board. We believe that the current proposal by the Rubber Reserve Co. would be a means of providing urgently needed additional natural rubber and at the same time would carry on to a successful completion this emergency project which was authorized by Congress to produce natural rubber during the period of heavy war demand.

Since the proposal now under consideration contemplates much earlier completion of the Emergency Rubber Project than was contemplated when the 1946 appropriation was made, and since the proposal of the Rubber Reserve Co. provides that the amortization of the costs of construction of the additional mills be reflected in the net proceeds which would [otherwise] be returned to the miscellaneous receipts of the Treasury for the guayule shrub harvested, we deem it advisable, after informal consultation with the House Subcommittee on Agricultural Appropriations, and before the Department of Agriculture agrees to the proposal, that the Congress be asked to give further consideration to the matter in its present status. . . .

In accordance with this request, and after Jump and his staff had appeared before the Budget Bureau to explain the problem in greater detail, the Budget Bureau submitted Agriculture's request for a change in the provisions of the 1946 appropriations. Following the usual procedure, Jump and his staff were asked to appear before the Deficiency Subcommittee of the House Committee on Appropriations. (Requests for supplemental appropriations all go to this subcommittee, not to the subcommittee responsible for the original appropriation.) Congressman Cannon, Chairman of the Committee presided at the hearings which were held June 6, 1945. There the following remarks were made:

MR. CANNON: We have an estimate here transmitted by the Bureau of the Budget . . . proposing a change in language in the item for the Emergency Rubber Project contained in the 1946 Agricultural Appropriations Act.

MR. JUMP: I want to make a brief statement to get the general situation before you. . . . The situation is this, that the increasing seriousness of the need for additional rubber has brought about a situation as a result of which, following a survey requested by WPB, the Rubber Reserve Co., with the approval of the WPB, proposes to erect some additional mills in order more quickly to process guayule from the emergency rubber project.

We discussed the matter informally with the Agriculture Appropriations Subcommittee in the other room a few days ago. In view of the fact that the present proposal would greatly hasten the completion of the rubber project . . . and because we, under this plan, will turn over the raw shrub to the Rubber Reserve Co. at a price that would reflect the amortization of the cost of construction of the new mills, it was the opinion of the Subcommittee . . . that we ought to prepare a formal budget submission to have the matter clarified by Congress.

MR. TARVER: [who had been invited by Cannon to attend the hearings] We felt—and I think I express the views of the Subcommittee—that action looking toward complete liquidation of the project ought not to be undertaken upon the recommendation of our Subcommittee. We thought that if such action were taken, it should be taken by the Congress itself which had indicated, in connection with the 1945 agriculture appropriation bill, that such was not its desire. . . . I feel personally—that the guayule project has not been justified by developments. . . . I think it ought to have been abandoned in the preparation and passage of the 1945 appropriation bill; I think it ought to be abandoned now . . . but I do not think that such action should be taken without action by the Congress indicating its approval of the proposed liquidation. . . .

MR. CANNON: I notice here [indicating letter from Krug, Chairman of WPB] that it is of the utmost importance that the new mills be completed not later than October 1945. To accomplish this it is considered necessary to start construction before June 15. June 15 is very near at hand. Have you made any commitments, entered into any obligations of this character, up to this time?

MR. CROSSLAND: The Rubber Reserve Co. has made obligations to start the project, for engineering and design work.

MR. CANNON: How much is involved in that?

MR. CROSSLAND: The original letter of intent amounted to $250,000. . . .

MR. CANNON: Do you have any authority to proceed to make commitments involving expenditures of any amount of money without authorization by Congress?

MR. JOHNSON [General Counsel, Rubber Reserve Co.]: Yes, Mr. Chairman. The Rubber Reserve Co. has an appropriation, created in the RFC statute, to proceed with the project relating to necessary production.

MR. CANNON: Then why is it necessary for you to come before the Congress at this time—why not just go ahead?

MR. JOHNSON: The Rubber Reserve is not up here asking the committee for an appropriation or allocation of funds; the Rubber Reserve Company is authorized very clearly under the present statute. It is the Department of Agriculture that is appearing before your committee and not the Rubber Reserve Company.

MR. JUMP: That is correct. And that goes back to what Judge Tarver said: When we went to the Agricultural Subcommittee we did not really have in mind that it was a proposition that we would have to ask approval for, but we wanted to make sure that there would be no objection. Then we found that the Subcommittee felt that we ought not to go ahead and deliver guayule shrub to the Rubber Reserve Co. without getting clearance from Congress, because what was proposed was in effect a more rapid liquidation of the guayule project. . . . The representatives of the Rubber Reserve Co. and of WPB are here to explain the proposition or to answer any questions from the angle of their concern. . . .

MR. CANNON: . . . the matters being so directly interrelated it seems to me notable, if I may use that word instead of a word I would prefer to use, that they should go ahead and make commitments to the extent of $250,000 and take it for granted that Congress would go along with the proposal now before us.

MR. JUMP: . . . Frankly, when we consulted with the Agricultural Subcommittee it was more on the ground we would be disposing of the shrub at a price that would take into account amortization of the mills than it was a matter of the liquidation of the project . . . the point of liquidation . . . was a surprise to me. . . .

The hearings were closed with a few additional remarks. The question was placed before the House, as suggested by Judge Tarver, and subsequently approved. The proposal received formal approval from Congress by June 30, 1945—approximately seven weeks after it was first advanced by the Rubber Reserve Company.

POSTSCRIPT

Nothing, it has been said, succeeds like success. And the interest displayed by the House Subcommittee in Jump's consultation, the unforeseen question raised by Chairman Tarver, and the clear Congressional approval of the RRC scheme which finally emerged affirmed Jump's conviction that he was gauging his legislative limitations correctly in bringing the RRC plan to Tarver's attention. Caswell, from his vantage point, looked at the same series of events and the same outcome and considered that seven weeks had been spent in the "dumbest red tape."

A number of other contrasts heightened the difference in opinion between the two men. There was the divergence in viewpoint and mode of operation between the man concerned with proper procedure and the fellow who "expedites" a substantive program; this was accentuated by the fact that one was an old-timer in a peacetime agency (acting not in its own direct interest, but as a service to others), and the other a new-comer in an emergency organization.

Brief insight into the problems of inter-agency co-operation and patterns of institutional behavior are also furnished by the case. Some might draw the conclusion that an official best serves such joint ventures when he first ensures that his own agency is "in the clear." Perhaps the fact that RFC, a lending agency, was clearly avoiding any risk in the guayule venture although legally competent to assume it encouraged Jump to eliminate any element of risk on Agriculture's part. Aside from this, RFC (i.e., the majority of its officials) thought of itself as a kind of bank, wanted to avoid losses, and characteristically assumed that its activities (however important to the war effort and however fully authorized by statute) should only be brought into play on a reimbursable basis. Agriculture, on the other hand (and again to name the agency is shorthand for a description of attitudes widely shared by its employees), was so fully devoted to its program and its constituents that it characteristically refused to permit its participation in any other activity to jeopardize the harmonious relations on which its successful progress seemed to depend. The WPB, concerned (in this case) solely with the rubber shortage had sound institutional reasons for impatience.

Personalities and agency concepts of role thus blend. People like Caswell would not find the atmosphere of the Agriculture Finance Office congenial; Jump would hardly be at home in the Office of the Rubber Director. There is no pat solution to the divergences that inevitably grow from these circumstances. Two possible points of resolution suggest themselves. One is the Congress, which in this case did arrive at a definitive decision. The other is the White House, or some subordinate arm of the Presidency like the Bureau of the Budget or the Office of War Mobilization. The reader may find it useful to speculate on the various advantages and disadvantages of the two modes of co-ordination.

The reader may also wish to consider that almost mystical, yet intensely practical concept —the intent of Congress. One might imagine from a bare reading of the Constitution that the text of a statute or an appropriation contains the sum of Congressional activity; but in practice the statutory language is interpreted in the light of committee reports, debates and similar indicia of "Congressional intent"; and courts and executive agencies alike must pay heed to what is legally "Congressional intent" even though the subject may never have come actively to the attention of more than a handful of Senators or Congressmen. Nor is this all: Congress, through its various committees, or perhaps more accurately, the various committees acting in the name of, though normally without formal reference to, Congress, expand the area of legislative intent to include a whole variety of hearings, consultations, and correspondence that have no formal legal status at all.

This indeterminate zone between legislation and administration can be evaded by administrators only at their peril. Its pitfalls are numerous, not the least being divergent instructions from different committees. This study gives the reader an opportunity to observe some of the delicate and complex relationships that grow in this important area where the Constitutional separation of powers seems finally to dissolve.

Bibliographical Note

The most detailed study of the Emergency Rubber Project, particularly in its technical aspects is:

United States Department of Agriculture, Forest Service, Emergency Rubber Project. *Final Report, The Emergency Rubber Project: Report on Our War-Time Guayule Rubber Program.* Los Angeles, California, December 1946. (Mimeographed; "not for distribution to the public"; available at U. S. Department of Agriculture Library, Washington, D. C.)

A rather detailed and substantially accurate legislative history of the Emergency Rubber Project appearing at the end of this report is particularly relevant to the present case study.

Two government studies which explore the possibilities of producing guayule and other types of rubber in the United States are:

United States Tariff Commission. *Possibilities of Producing Rubber in the United States and Rubber Conservation.* Washington, D. C., September 1941.

United States Congress, House of Representatives, Committee on Agriculture. *Study of Rubber in the United States, Mexico, and Haiti.* Report No. 2098 pursuant to H. Res. 346, 78th Congress, 2nd Session. Washington, D. C., January 2, 1945.

An effort has been made throughout the case to furnish enough information on Congressional action for the reader to be able to find the relevant sources. The most detailed and informative hearings on the guayule program appear in:

United States Congress, House of Representatives, Committee on Agriculture. *Guayule Rubber.* Hearings on H.R. 6299, 77th Congress, 2nd Session. Washington, D. C., 1942.

A view of the RRC's rubber program, particularly of synthetic rubber production, is furnished by:

Rubber Reserve Company [RFC]. *Report on the Rubber Program, 1940-1945.* Washington, D. C., February 24, 1945.

Finally, for a picture of the preoccupations of the Office of the Rubber Director, WPB, the reader can consult:

War Production Board, Office of the Rubber Director. *Progress Report.* Numbers 1-6. Washington, D. C., November 30, 1942-July 25, 1944.

THE FBI RETIREMENT BILL

CONTENTS

INTRODUCTION

The legislative reference functions of the Bureau of the Budget have developed slowly over the years. Originally, in 1921, the first Director, Charles G. Dawes, required the clearance of fiscal legislation through his office, relying for this requirement on a broad interpretation of Section 206 of the Budget and Accounting Act of 1921 which forbids the departments to submit requests for appropriations or for increases in appropriations outside the President's budget, except at the request of Congress.

In 1935, clearance for non-fiscal legislation through the National Emergency Council was first required: in 1937, this function was transferred to the Bureau of the Budget, an agency which itself was transferred from the Treasury to the newly established Executive Office of the President in 1939.

The clearance of non-fiscal legislation is based less clearly on statute; it relies rather on the President's general powers under the Constitution to direct the operations of his principal officers, to advise the Congress on needed measures, and to approve or disapprove bills passed by the Congress. With the gradual development of the Bureau as a relatively well manned and rounded staff agency for the President, there has been a correlative development within the Bureau of the concept of an over-all presidential program and of the Bureau's own clearance function.

The function includes two different but closely related processes: the clearance of reports to Congressional committees on proposed or pending legislation (including legislative proposals initiated by the executive departments) and the clearance of enrolled bills. An "enrolled bill" is one which has been duly passed by both Houses and transmitted to the President for his approval or disapproval within the constitutional ten-day period, excluding Sundays. (Because enrolled bills are frequently available before formal transmittal to the White House, the working period is usually about thirteen or fourteen days.) At this stage the Bureau circulates facsimiles of the enrolled bill to all interested agencies, collects their comments, summarizes the issues and transmits the file to the White House, together with its own recommendations for signature or veto.

The clearance process for agency recommendations is governed by a deceptively simple rule. Budget Circular A-19 (edition in effect in 1947, but now obsolete) merely requires that:

> There shall be submitted to the Bureau of the Budget, before submission to the Congress, or any committee or member thereof, two copies of each recommendation or report concerning proposed or pending legislation requested from or advanced by any department or establishment or any officer thereof.
>
> 2. The submitting department or establishment will be thereafter advised by the Bureau of the Budget as to the relationship of the legislation, or of the report or recommendation thereon, to the program of the President; and when such recommendation or report is then submitted to the Congress, or to a Committee or member thereof, it shall include a statement of the advice so received from the Bureau of the Budget. (If, in any case, time will not permit the ascertainment of the advice of this character from the Bureau of the Budget, the report, or testimony shall include a statement to this effect.)

The formal requirement does not prevent any agency from sending any proposed bill or recommendation to Congress; it merely requires a notification of the Bureau's advice, or, in urgent cases, a mere notification that it has failed to secure such advice. There are, however, two fairly obvious sanctions to inhibit the transmittal of measures or recommendations opposed by the Bureau: the Director sees the President and may, if the circumstances are propitious, request the President's intervention; and secondly, the Bureau normally makes the final recommendation to the White House on enrolled bills, and all proposed bills that secure Congressional approval, by definition become enrolled bills. It may be noted in passing that effective action on the enrolled bill is largely dependent on the establishment of an adequate file during the earlier stage; and concurrence in a draft bill is almost absolute assurance of approval later on of the enrolled bill. Aside from sanctions, the relation of the Bureau to the President renders an agency head open to some suspicion of disloyalty if he disregards the Bureau's advice without obtaining the President's personal approval.

The following case study shows some of the difficulties that arise from time to time between the Bureau of the Budget and the other agencies of the government in relation to the legislative reference requirements of Budget Circular A-19. The sponsoring agency in this instance was the Federal Bureau of Investigation of the Department of Justice. The functions of the FBI are so well known that it seems unnecessary to pause for any description of that important unit of the Department of Justice or of the work of its special agents. The particular proposal sponsored by the FBI was one to grant unusual retirement privileges to its employees. As will be seen, the proposal had the firm support not only of the Director of the FBI, Mr. J. Edgar Hoover, but also of his immediate official superior, the Attorney General of the United States, Mr. Tom C. Clark. The interest of two other agencies in the matter will also be readily apparent. The Civil Service Commission, which objected to the proposal, had a general responsibility with respect to legislation affecting the status and privileges of government employees. It is, so to speak, the President's adviser on personnel policies and problems. The interest of the Treasury in the subject matter of the proposed legislation arose quite simply from the fact that within the Treasury are a number of important investigative agencies, of which the Secret Service is merely the best known. The concern of the Secretary of the Treasury with proposals which would give greater benefits to the agents of the FBI than were enjoyed by agents performing comparable or somewhat comparable duties in his Department need occasion no surprise.

No analysis is presented in the following account of the actual substantive arguments pro and con. The arguments themselves, however, are presented in sufficient detail so that the interested reader may, if he wishes, judge for himself the merits of the FBI Retirement Bill. Similarly the actions of the various participants are noted without attempt at evaluation. Again, it is believed that sufficient detail has been made available to permit the reader to make evaluations for himself; but in this process he should bear in mind two external factors of significance: first, the deep and widespread concern over the security of the United States and the correlative concern over the well-being of the FBI as an agency dedicated to the protection of our security; and second, the fact that the chief participants in this case were extremely busy men with multifarious and weighty administrative and political responsibilities. The decisions of the participants were made in this troubled atmosphere and under these difficult conditions.

I. The Pending Bill Stage

INTRODUCTION OF S. 715

S. 715 was introduced on February 26, 1947, by Senator Styles Bridges (R.-N.H.) for himself and for Senator William Langer (R.-N.D.) the Chairman of the Senate Committee on Post Office and Civil Service. The bill would amend the Civil Service Retirement Act of May 29, 1930, by adding the following new subsection:

> (i) Any special agent, special agent in charge, inspector, Assistant Director, Assistant to the Director, Associate Director, or the Director, who is at least fifty years of age and who has rendered twenty years of service or more as a special agent, or as aforesaid above, in the Federal Bureau of Investigation may, on his own application and with the consent of the Attorney General, retire from the service and such annuity of such employee shall be equal to 2 per centum of his average basic salary for the five years next preceding the date of his retirement, multiplied by the number of years of service, not exceeding thirty years.

The proposal embodied in this bill was devised in the Department of Justice. The bill itself was later described as "drawn" by Senator Langer. However, this phrase may have been intended merely as a courteous obeisance to the conventions concerning the separation of powers, for under customary practice with legislation of this character, the Department of Justice would have prepared a draft bill for Senator Langer's consideration.

LEGISLATIVE AND EXECUTIVE CONSIDERATION OF S. 715

Following the routine procedure, on February 28, Senator Langer requested the views of the FBI and the Civil Service Commission on the new bill. On March 10th, Mr. Hoover, Director of the FBI, wrote Senator Langer, in part, as follows:

> In the first place, I want to express personally and on behalf of the personnel of the FBI our very deep appreciation for your interest in sponsoring this legislation. . . .
>
> The legislation as you have drawn it seems to meet our needs in every way and I hope that it will receive favorable action.
>
> With expressions of my highest esteem and kind regards,
>
> Sincerely yours,
>
> [s] *J. Edgar Hoover*

This letter was not sent to the Bureau of the Budget for clearance before being sent to the Congress.

On the same date as the FBI letter to Senator Langer, March 10th, the Civil Service Commission transmitted its proposed report intended for Senator Langer to the Budget and stated, in the conventional formula, "It is requested that you advise whether or not the proposed legislation is in accord with the program of the President." The proposed Commission report to Senator Langer opposed the legislation; the Commission's arguments were later recapitulated in a letter reproduced below on pp. 654-5.

Mr. V. L. Almond, Acting Assisting Director of the Bureau of Budget in Charge of Legislative Reference, cleared this adverse report with the Budget's specialist in personnel matters, Mr. Joseph E. Winslow, and with other Budget officials, and on March 14th wrote to Mr. Mitchell, President of the Civil Service Commission, ". . . I am authorized by the Director of the Bureau of the Budget to advise you that there would be no objection to the submission thereof to the [Senate Civil Service] Committee."

Not long after the receipt of these letters, on March 25th, the Committee held a hearing on S. 715; the Attorney General was the only administration witness, but Senator Bridges also appeared in support of the bill. The Attorney General's arguments were later reproduced in substance in a letter quoted below on pp. 655-7. Two points deserve notice: One was the stress laid on the precedent established by the Foreign Service Act of 1946, the other was his plea for favorable action on S. 715 without amendment to extend the coverage to other groups of government employees. The Senators were well disposed toward the proposal, and their interrogation of Mr. Clark was brief and friendly and rather casual; one Senator merely desired assurance that Mr. Hoover was personally in favor of the legislation. At the conclusion of the hearing, on motion of Senator Langer, seconded by Senator Chavez (D.-N.M.) the Committee voted unanimously to report out the bill.

The Committee Report, No. 76, was issued on the following day, March 26th. In substance, it paralleled the Attorney General's testimony, whose appearance was noted. The Report also reprinted in full Mr. Hoover's letter of March 10th, but made no reference to the adverse communication from the Civil Service Commission that had been cleared by the Budget Bureau.

On April 7th, S. 715 passed the Senate without debate and without dissent. In response to a question, Senator Langer gave the following explanation of the bill:

> Mr. President, this is the so-called FBI bill. Up to the present time those who work for the FBI have not had the retirement privilege. Under the bill any one who has worked for the FBI for 20 years and has reached the age of 50 may receive a retirement pension based on 2 per cent of his average annual salary for the 5 preceding years multiplied by the number of years of service

up to 30. I might add that all civil-service employees, except those dealing with narcotics, now have the retirement privilege.

Mr. President, this is a bill suggested by the Attorney General; it has the approval of the Bureau of the Budget, and it was reported unanimously by the Committee on the Civil Service.

For those not familiar with the Civil Service Retirement System, it may be well to note that at this time, in 1947, agents and other employees of the FBI and the Bureau of Narcotics were entitled to the regular Civil Service retirement benefits; the object of S. 715 was to grant the FBI special benefits.

INTRODUCTION OF H.R. 2826

In the meantime, on March 27th, Representative Hagen (R.-Minn.) a member of the House Committee on the Post Office and Civil Service, introduced H.R. 2826, an identical bill to S. 715, and the views of the Civil Service Commission and the FBI were requested by Representative Rees (R.-Kansas), Chairman of the Committee. (Another identical bill, H.R. 2928, was introduced by Representative Smathers (D.-Fla.) on April 9th.)

LEGISLATIVE AND EXECUTIVE CONSIDERATION OF H.R. 2826

Congressional action on this legislation had been unusually prompt, and it was not until April 4th that the Treasury Department showed its interest in the measure. On that date Secretary Snyder wrote Representative Rees as follows:

The attention of this Department has been called to H.R. 2826. . . .

It is believed that investigative and law enforcement officers of the Treasury Enforcement Agencies should have the same retirement benefits as investigatory personnel of the Federal Bureau of Investigation. . . . This could be accomplished by amending the proposed new subsection (i) to read as follows . . .

In view of the fact that S. 715, the companion Senate bill, has already been favorably reported to the Senate and the possibility that your Committee may act promptly on H.R. 2826, this report is being submitted without the customary prior clearance from the Bureau of the Budget.

On April 8th, even though S. 715 had passed the Senate the day before, Mr. Joseph E. O'Connell, General Counsel of the Treasury, sent Senator Langer a copy of Secretary Snyder's letter to Representative Rees and requested that "equal treatment be accorded Treasury investigative and law enforcement personnel." Copies of both letters were sent to the Budget Bureau.

On April 9th, the Civil Service Commission replied to Congressman Rees. This reply, a copy of which was sent to the Budget, sets forth all the Commission's points of objection to the bills. The letter reads as follows:

United States Civil Service Comm.
Washington 25, D. C., April 9, 1947

Hon. Edward H. Rees,
Chairman, Committee on Post Office and Civil Service

Dear Mr. Rees:

Reference is made to your communication of March 29, 1947, relative to H.R. 2826, a bill to amend the Civil Service Retirement Act of May 29, 1930, as amended, to provide annuities for investigatory personnel of the Federal Bureau of Investigation who have rendered at least 20 years of service.

The present retirement law gives an employee who has served at least 30 years the option of retiring on full annuity at any time after attaining age 60. Further provision is made for an employee with 30 years' service to retire after attaining age 55, but the annuity in such case is proportionately reduced, being based on the present worth of the annuity allowable were the employee 60 years of age.

The proposal would amend section 1 (b) of the Civil Service Retirement Act of May 29, 1930, by adding a subsection providing that any special agent, special agent in charge, inspector, Assistant Director, Assistant to the Director, Associate Director, or Director, who is at least 50 years of age and has rendered 20 or more years of service as a special agent, or as aforesaid above, in the Federal Bureau of Investigation, may, on his own application and with the consent of the Attorney General, retire from the service. It further provides that the annuity of the employee shall be equal to 2 per cent of his average basic salary for the 5 years next preceding the date of his retirement, multiplied by the number of years of service, not exceeding 30 years.

The Commission has on several previous occasions expressed the belief that the failure to place an age limit on optional retirements would result in a substantial loss to the Government from early retirement of its more efficient servants and the delayed retirement of the less efficient. In other words, the Commission is of the opinion that the persons who would avail themselves of this option are those who believe they could better themselves in private life with the annuity as basic income, while those who would continue to retirement age will generally be less efficient. This would be particularly true with respect to the professional and scientific groups and also to the trades and skilled occupations.

The effect of the proposed amendment would be to add a new plan of computing annuities so that persons occupying any of the positions enumerated in the bill who had reached age 50 or over and had completed 30 years of service could retire with an annuity of 60 per cent of their highest five consecutive years' average salary. Under the present law, an employee coming under the plan III method of computation could retire with an annuity of 50 per cent of his highest five consecutive years' average salary only if he had completed 35 years of Federal Service.

The Civil Service Retirement Act is not limited to employees of the Federal Bureau of Investigation and includes within its provisions all employees in the executive, judicial, and legislative branches of the Government not subject to another retirement system with certain exceptions. There are numerous other employees of the Federal Government engaged in arduous and dangerous investigative work similar to that of the Federal Bureau of Investigation. These employees are found in the Secret Service of the Treasury Department, the Bureau of Internal Revenue, Treasury, involving tax and liquor violations, narcotic inspectors or agents, Treasury Department, certain post office inspectors, the Central Intelligence Group, special agents of the State Department, and probably some employees of the Immigration and Naturalization Service, the Department of the Interior, and other agencies.

The Commission feels that if Congress desires to give special recognition to employees of this type, such recognition should be extended to all such persons and not limited to those of a particular agency. The adoption of this proposal would involve a substantial increased cost to the Government per individual retiring at age 50.

For each agent retiring at age 50, the difference in value of the Government annuity beginning at age 50 and the value, at that time, of the Government annuity otherwise beginning at age 60 (assuming continuance in service until age 60), is shown in the following table:

ADDITIONAL COST TO GOVERNMENT PER AGENT RETIRING AT AGE 50

Years of service at age 50:	
20	$14,901
25	17,767
30	19,155

The above estimates are based in a level salary of $5,000 and retirement deductions of 5 per cent throughout the entire period of service. If the retirement is delayed beyond age 50, the cost is reduced.

Approval of this bill would, no doubt, result in other groups of Federal employees urging that they too receive like increased benefits.

The Bureau of the Budget advised the Commission in regard to its report on an identical bill, S. 715, that there would be no objection to the submission of such report to the Senate Civil Service Committee.

By direction of the Commission:

Very sincerely yours,
[s] *Harry B. Mitchell*, President

On April 18th, the Attorney General sent to the Budget for clearance a favorable report on H.R. 2826 prepared for Congressman Rees, with a request for advice, in the customary phrase, "as to the relationship of the proposed report to the program of the President." However, on April 21st, before the Budget had replied, Attorney General Clark and FBI Director Hoover each sent a letter directly to Representative Rees recommending the passage of H.R. 2826. The Attorney General's letter contains a full statement of his position. It reads as follows:

Office of the Attorney General
Washington, D. C., April 21, 1947

Hon. Edward H. Rees
House of Representatives, Washington, D. C.

My Dear Mr. Congressman: I wanted to write to you concerning Senate bill S. 715 and House bills H.R. 2826 and 2998, introduced to amend the Civil Service Retirement Act of May 29, 1930, to provide annuities for investigatory personnel of the Federal Bureau of Investigation who have rendered at least 20 years of service and have reached the age of 50.

It is my understanding that these bills have been referred to a subcommittee of your committee for further consideration. I feel that the passage of the Senate bill, which was unanimously approved by the Senate Civil Service Committee and approved by the United States Senate, would go a long way toward stabilizing the FBI into a career service. You will recall that the Foreign Service of the State Department has a liberalized retirement benefit at this time which will permit officers of the Foreign Service to retire after 20 years of service, providing they are 50 years of age.

I know you are thoroughly familiar with the fact that many of the State and local police agencies have granted retirement benefits to their employees which are comparable to or exceed the retirement benefits being requested for the investigatory personnel of the FBI in Senate bill S. 715 and the House bills previously referred to herein. These retirement benefits have been granted to law-enforcement officers in recognition of the type of work in which they are engaged from day to day.

The Federal Bureau of Investigation is the only general law-enforcement body of the Federal Government. Other agencies are specifically charged with the enforcement of a limited number of laws pertaining to Federal violations. The FBI has primary jurisdiction over all matters of an investigatory nature pertaining to violations of Federal statutes when such matters are not specifically assigned to other Federal investigating agencies. The investigative work performed by investigatory employees of the FBI covers a broad criminal and general field. The FBI has primary jurisdiction in the investigation of cases pertaining to kidnaping, bank robbery, extortion, and many other heinous types of crime. You will recall that the late President Roosevelt issued a directive designating the Federal Bureau of Investigation as a co-ordinating agency for internal security matters in the United States at the beginning of the war emergency. In its position as a co-ordinating agency, such internal-security matters were handled and are being handled at the present time by the Federal Bureau of Investigation. Under its broad, general powers, it continues to have jurisdiction in the investigation of crimes against the internal security of the country, such as treason, sabotage, espionage, subversivism, and other such matters.

In the performance of their duties, investigatory employees of the FBI are in contact daily with desperate criminals and their duties are such that it is impossible for them to live a reasonable, normal life. The position is such that the special agent must be available for assignment wherever and whenever the exigencies of the service demand. There are no permanent assignments in the FBI. The special agent is on call 24 hours a day, 7 days a week, and in the regular course of business the special agent is frequently called upon after the regular working hours to handle an expeditious or important investigation which cannot be held in abeyance. The work of this agency is such that it is not possible for its employees to continue on a 40-hour week. Employees at the present time are working on a 48-hour week for which reimbursement is made; however, I know that the investigative staff of the Bureau works considerably longer hours than the 48 hours for which they are paid. During the late war period, these investigators averaged 70 or more hours a week without compensation for overtime services. They are presently performing daily several hours of overtime for which no reimbursement is made. The work of the FBI during the past decade has been such that it has not been possible to grant leave benefits to a majority of the investigative staff. The employees of this agency lose annually thousands of days of accrued annual leave that cannot be taken since it exceeds the maximum allowable under existing regulations.

I know you are in agreement with me through your knowledge of the duties of the FBI that this organization is primarily a young man's organization. The day-to-day pressure, the risks taken, long hours of overtime not compensated for, and the health hazards have definitely shown that it is most difficult for a special agent to continue the pace which it has been necessary for him to undergo to carry on his work with full effectiveness subsequent to the age of 50. The special agent of the FBI realizes that he must continue to perform his duties with a maximum of efficiency and he realizes at the present time that after he reaches the age of 50, it is entirely possible that he will not be able to continue to perform his duties as efficiency demands and he fears for the future security of his family. This has resulted in a number of top-flight investigative employees of the FBI leaving the service for other positions which will afford security for their families during the latter years of their lives. If these employees have knowledge that a reasonable, financial security will be theirs in the form of a retirement benefit when they can no longer perform the duties demanded of them, they will continue in their present duties rather than leave the Government service to secure such employment in private fields. It is regrettable that the Government must lose the services of such employees after they have been thoroughly trained and are experienced investigators. Replacements, of course, can be made; however, the Government can never replace the years of experience of such employees. I personally feel that the Government would benefit tremendously through the offering of a liberalized retirement to the investigatory employees of the FBI, which will be an added incentive for them to remain in the service during their most productive years.

I am most hopeful that your committee, in the consideration of this bill, will give consideration to it on its own merits as it was considered by the Senate, since I feel that it is legislation which has the wholehearted support of the citizens of the country.

With kind regards,

Sincerely yours,
[s] *Tom Clark*,
Attorney General

On April 29th, the Acting Secretary of the Treasury wrote to Congressman Rees, suggesting certain technical changes in the Treasury's proposed amendments to H.R. 2826; a copy of this letter was sent to the Budget.

During this period, progress at the Budget was slow. On April 25th, a proposed reply to the Attorney General was prepared; to this was attached a copy of the Civil Service Commission letter of April 9th; the draft letter ended with the following paragraph:

It is the view of this office that the Civil Service Commission has taken an appropriate position with respect to the bill, H.R. 2826; and you are accordingly advised that this proposed legislation could not be considered in accord with the program of the President.

The draft letter was approved by Mr. Winslow and other Budget officials. On May 2nd it was transmitted to the Executive Assistant to the Director and to the Director by Mr. F. J. Bailey, Assistant Director in charge of Legislative Reference, with the following note:

"Hot" subject. Attorney General Clark has already recommended, and Mr. Hoover of the FBI has strongly urged, the enactment of the companion bill in the Senate (S. 715), and the Senate, on April 7, passed the bill, S. 715. Senator Langer stated on the floor of the Senate that "it has the approval of the Bureau of the Budget." This latter statement was incorrect, since, as a matter of fact, the Bureau of the Budget, on April 14, 1947 [he meant *March* 14, 1947], cleared an adverse report of the Civil Service Commission on the bill, S. 715.

Unless the President has made some commitment to the Attorney General on the bill, the attached turn-down letter is, of course, the right answer.

FJB

On May 7th, Budget Director Webb signed the letter to the Attorney General without change.

Two weeks later the Attorney General appealed the decision of the Budget Director. In a letter to Mr. Webb (May 23), after restating his arguments in favor of the bill, he said:

I will appreciate it very much if you will personally look into this matter. . . .

I understand that various agencies of the government have attempted to secure amendments to the bill. . . . While I do not wish to attempt to compare the work of the Federal Bureau of Investigation with that of other agencies of the government . . . it is my view that they should submit their claims separately and be considered on their merits. . . .

I will appreciate it very much indeed if you will personally consider the foregoing with a view to possibly indicating a different view with respect to this legislation. I personally appeared before the Senate Committee on Civil Service and urged the enactment of this legislation. . . .

If you have any questions concerning this matter I shall be very glad to have you get in touch with me as I am personally extremely interested in securing the passage of this legislation.

The matter now became urgent, because at approximately this point the Attorney General was asked to testify on H.R. 2826 (and S. 715) before the House Civil Service Committee. While the Budget Director made no written reply to the Attorney General's appeal of May 23rd, apparently there was a telephone conversation between the two; the Attorney General's later summary of this conversation is quoted below on page 658.

On May 26th, the House Committee held its hearing. Technically the hearing was supposed to cover the three identical bills—S. 715, H.R. 2826, and H.R. 2998—and also a similar bill for the Treasury investigative agencies,

H.R. 2959, and one for the Department of Justice's Immigration and Naturalization Service, H.R. 3536; as it happened, the latter two bills were not taken up for discussion at the hearing.

In addition to favorable Congressional testimony, the Committee heard the Attorney General and the Assistant Director of the FBI in support of the bill. The Attorney General's testimony followed the same lines as his testimony before the Senate Committee to which he referred in passing; he again urged that the Committee limit the bill's coverage to the FBI, but suggested that at some future date Congress might wish to extend the coverage to other employees.

After the conclusion of the testimony of the favorable witnesses, which was well received, the Committee called on a representative of the Civil Service Commission. He expressed his embarrassment, restated the Commission's views; he ventured the opinion that the other agencies would soon be in asking for similar treatment and that the measure would not solve the FBI's turn-over problem.

Apparently the Commission's objections were not considered weighty; H.R. 2826 was reported out, without delay and without dissent, on May 29th. The Report, No. 493, was quite brief, but did reprint in full the Clark and Hoover letters of April 21st, and the Civil Service Commission letter of April 9th.

Although a month was to elapse before the House of Representatives acted on H.R. 2826 (S. 715), the Attorney General evidently anticipated a favorable vote. On June 7th he sent Mr. Webb a comprehensive statement entitled "Why S. 715 should be Approved," and to this statement was attached the following handwritten note:

Dear Jim:

Here are some thoughts on the FBI Retirement Bill.

If you could agree

1. Not to oppose signing—
2. President advising Congress at time that he expects them to extend it to agencies with similar duties to perform—

it would be most helpful to me.

Your friend,

[s] *Tom*

The statement itself is primarily an amplification of the Department of Justice's previous position. It does, however, contain a list of precedents which include the Foreign Service Act of 1946, a law extending special retirement benefits to certain Secret Service employees, and various laws affecting state and municipal police forces. Two paragraphs deal with the Attorney General's personal connection with the matter. They read as follows:

> Upon my appearance before the Senate Civil Service Committee (Senator Langer, Chairman) on other matters altogether, I was asked by Senator Thye of my opinion of S. 715 which had been introduced by Senator Bridges. I was familiar with the matter in a general way but testified that I thought the bill had merit. Thereafter I was requested to appear before the House Civil Service Committee with reference to S. 715. I had called Mr. Webb, the Director of the Budget, and asked him about the matter. He stated that he thought the bill should extend to all agencies of the government and that he had no objection to my appearing before the House Committee and supporting the bill. I then appeared before the Committee and vigorously supported the bill after which the Committee reported it out and was passed by the House.
>
> While I was not asked if I represented the Administration's thinking on the matter of course the Committee assumed I had cleared my testimony and that the bill had Administration approval.

It is not known who drafted for the Attorney General the statement "Why S. 715 should be Approved" that includes these two paragraphs; a comparison with the summaries of the two hearings given on p. 653 and pp. 657-8 will show that the draftsman's historical account is imprecise.

Both earlier, and at this period, favorable publicity was given this legislation. Four editorials from different Southern papers had been introduced at the House hearing. Now Drew Pearson, in his column "Washington Merry-Go-Round," stated under the caption "Dangerous Government Jobs" the following (Washington *Post*, June 4, 1947): "The Committee approved the measure to liberalize the retirement regulations for G-men, but it is now expected that similar benefits will be voted for other Government employees."

As the month of June drew toward a close, the Budget again took up the problem. The Budget's specialist in personnel management, Mr. Joseph E. Winslow, found himself in substantial agreement with the Civil Service Commission. On June 27th, in a memorandum to the Budget Director, he listed various arguments against the bill. And in the corner of this memorandum he wrote the following note:

6/27

The Director discussed this with the President today. The President stated that he is not in favor of the proposed legislation H.R. 2826 and S. 715 for FBI 20 yr. retirement at age 50 and H.R. 3536 providing the same thing for the Immigration and Naturalization Service.

[s] *Winslow*

On the same date, Mr. Winslow prepared and cleared with the Budget staff a letter for the Director's signature to be sent to the Attorney General in reply to his appeals. This letter stated: "As requested by you, I have personally looked into this problem and have discussed it with the President, and I am authorized to inform you that the proposed legislation is not in accord with the program of the President."

The draft letter was prepared on Friday, June 27th; on Monday, June 30th, before it was signed, it had become obsolete, for on that day S. 715 passed the House of Representatives without a dissenting vote.

II. The Enrolled Bill Stage

FORMAL REPORTS TO THE BUREAU OF THE BUDGET

In accordance with the established procedure, on July 1st, after S. 715 became an enrolled bill the Budget requested the formal views of the interested agencies—the Department of Justice, the Civil Service Commission, and the Department of the Treasury—on the legislation.

On July 2nd, Secretary Snyder wrote Budget Director Webb:

The Treasury Department feels strongly that S. 715 is discriminatory legislation and that its approval by the President would affect adversely the morale of Treasury enforcement personnel. Accordingly, if the enrolled enactment should become law, the Department intends to seek legislation providing similar retirement benefits for approximately 3,000 investigative and law enforcement officers. . . .

Secretary Snyder did not recommend approval.

The Assistant to the Attorney General strongly urged that the bill be approved, citing again the reasons given earlier.

On July 3rd, the Civil Service Commission wrote the Budget Director, ". . . the Commission recommends veto of this enactment, the reasons for this recommendation appearing in the draft herewith of the proposed veto message." These reasons were the same as those already put forward.

INTERNAL BUDGET PROCESSING

Mr. Winslow, on July 3rd, in a long memorandum to the Budget Director, recommended that the President veto the bill. Five days later he prepared a lengthy rebuttal to the Attorney General's statement "Why S. 715 Should be Approved," and again recommended to the Budget Director that the President veto the bill.

On July 9th, a letter recommending disapproval and a draft veto message were prepared for the Budget Director's signature by Mr. Winslow and cleared by top Budget staff. This letter concluded, "In the interest of the Federal Service as a whole, I feel that it is my duty to recommend disapproval of the bill, and there has accordingly been prepared for the President's consideration the attached draft of a veto message, which follows the lines of the objections to the bill voiced by the Treasury Department and the Civil Service Commission."

PUBLIC OPINION

During this period press comment was expressed in favor of this legislation. The following extract from an editorial which appeared in the Washington *Star*, July 7, 1947, is typical of what was being said:

> It is hard to credit reports that President Truman may veto the bill to liberalize retirement benefits for special agents of the Federal Bureau of Investigation. This bill passed the House and Senate unanimously after its merits had been fully explored by appropriate committees.
>
> Yet there have been published rumors of an impending veto, presumably on the ground that no provision is contained in the measure for similar benefits for other Federal Investigators, including the Secret Service. While there is some merit to the contention that certain other Government agents should be similarly favored, it is too late now to amend the bill. It is to be hoped that the President will sign the FBI bill. He might as well, at the same time, suggest that consideration be given to new legislation covering any other Federal agency faced by a situation like that hampering the operation of the FBI.

BUDGET ADVICE

After the Budget had prepared, but before it had sent its letter recommending that the President veto the bill, the Attorney General personally contacted the President and the Budget Director. Thereafter, the White House informed the Budget that the President was going to sign the bill. The veto recommendation in the Budget's letter was then converted into an approval recommendation. The only reason given for this final approval recommendation is contained in the following concluding paragraph from the Budget Director's letter to the White House:

> I am inclined, under all the circumstances, and in view of the fact that the Congress has seen fit to enact the measure, without a dissenting vote, to recommend that the bill be approved.

On July 11th, the President approved S. 715, and it became Public Law 168.

III. Subsequent Events

The passage of this bill encouraged a number of additional agencies—among them the Narcotics Bureau and the Secret Service (Treasury), the Immigration and Naturalization Service (Justice), and the Civil Aeronautics Administration—to seek similar retirement benefits for their personnel in investigatory or other hazardous jobs. The Second Session of the 80th Congress responded to their requests and passed H.R. 6454, a bill which extended these increased retirement benefits to all investigative personnel. This bill was approved by the President on July 2, 1948, and became Public Law 879.

A second probable but less demonstrable result of these events also occurred in 1948. Early in the year, a bill was drafted that raised certain issues between the FBI and the Budget Bureau. On this occasion the Attorney General took pains to make sure that these issues were satisfactorily resolved before any legislative proposals were made to the Congress. There was some indication that he had in mind the history of S. 715 and wished to avoid a repetition of the situation surrounding the enactment of that bill.

THE FOREIGN SERVICE ACT OF 1946

CONTENTS

FOREWORD

This study of the Foreign Service Act of 1946 is an account of the drafting, negotiations, compromises and decisions that accompanied the preparation of a bill and the enactment of that bill into law. It focuses primarily on a critical stage in the life of the bill running from the preparation of the first complete draft in December 1945 to final Presidential approval in August 1946. It describes certain government officials in action under trying circumstances. Many of the difficulties they faced are characteristic of those widely encountered in the Federal service; to a lesser extent they are also characteristic of difficulties in other governmental organizations, or indeed in any large and complex organization. Problems of personnel management, of concurrent executive and legislative control of policy, of legislative compromise both inside and outside the halls of the legislature recur again and again elsewhere. Yet these issues take their form and have a special substance in the context of the particular circumstances and particular groups and personalities concerned.

The events described in this study were not of wide public interest. The arguments were technical in character or form. The problems were of primary interest only to four groups of active participants: a group of Foreign Service officers and their immediate associates, a group of officials in the newer branches of the State Department, a few officials in the Bureau of the Budget, and a Congressional Subcommittee; they were of real but secondary interest to a few additional groups in three or four agencies. Yet a later examination of these happenings is potentially of far wider interest.

The Foreign Service itself—its function, its nature, its composition—was, of course, the source of the key questions to be answered. There is a generic kinship among all Foreign Services; they constitute special groups, and the careers and codes of conduct of their members are strikingly similar in almost all major countries. Characteristically set apart from other government employees, they present special difficulties to every government. All governments must face the problem of recruitment for a service whose members must spend most of their lives as expatriates. All governments must concern themselves with techniques for the control of a group that operates largely in secrecy and far from the center of official control and public pressure. All Foreign Service officials must concern themselves with adequate rewards for service rendered without public acclaim. They must endeavor to fulfill their own conscientious sense of a need for participation in the life of their own country; they must seek ways of protecting themselves from the vagaries of prejudice or ignorance at distant posts. For the United States, because of our governmental structure and because we lived so long in comparative isolation, these problems are peculiarly acute and peculiarly difficult to solve. Because of our newly realized intense involvement in world affairs, these problems are also important.

A second major issue illustrated by the circumstances surrounding the preparation and passage of the Foreign Service Act of 1946 is perhaps more distinctively American in character. Admittedly the difficulty of central executive control of policy is a normal and universal phenomenon; but the problems arising from a dual executive and legislative responsibility for policy formation and the dual loyalties of an executive agency to the President by way of his staff arm, the Bureau of the Budget, and to the Congress, by way of one of its arms, a Congressional Subcommittee, are created or at least fostered in this special form by our Constitution and by the habits and traditions of our national government. To both the President and the Congress, and therefore to the people as well, this is a continuing major problem.

A third significant issue can also be discerned in the course of these events: the appropriate role of a conscious and coherent group operating within but largely apart from the larger governmental structure. Such a group is the corps of Foreign Service officers, a special small body within the whole Foreign Service. Usually called the "Professional Service" or the "Career Service" by its members, who look on themselves primarily as "political officers," it has its own distinctive entrance and tenure procedures, its own salary system, its own traditions and group attitudes, its own sensitivity and code of privacy. It constitutes as it were a guild. Other guilds, with common traditions, interests and codes of conduct, exist elsewhere in the government, the armed services constituting merely the largest and most widely recognized example. Wherever guilds exist, they and their titular—or real—superiors must find an accommodation that takes into account guild loyalties and convictions, along with broader interests and the need for political responsiveness in the widest sense. The apparent gradual disappearance of party patronage as a generally used technique in the Federal service makes particularly timely a reappraisal of guild functions, since the establishment of the institutional framework within which these groups developed was actuated in important instances by a felt need to exclude certain areas of public administration from the patronage system. The following pages afford some insight into the nature of one of the government guild groups, and some opportunity to evaluate its advantages and disadvantages.

Part I. Foreign Service Officers Prepare a New Foreign Service Bill

1. BACKGROUND

The Foreign Service of the United States has undergone many vicissitudes since Benjamin Franklin negotiated a treaty with France on behalf of the Continental Congress. Growth of a formal organization and of established procedures and traditions was slow, even into the twentieth century. The rewards and disabilities of our representatives varied widely; members of the Diplomatic Service were often forced to incur large personal outlays in the line of duty while consular posts frequently provided a handsome income from fees. Appointments were largely made as political or personal favors. The results of these arrangements were uneven, ranging from great diplomatic triumphs, like the mission of Adams to London during the Civil War, to embarrassing contretemps caused by gross incompetence or even venality. For long periods our comparative isolation was reflected in our inactivity abroad; indeed during the nineteenth century the chief value of some of our consular posts was not in the technical services performed for American citizens but rather as sinecures for eminent men of letters.

The modern Service was created by the Rogers Act of 1924. The fundamental premise underlying the Act was the creation of a special corps that would be completely safeguarded from political patronage. The Consular Corps and the Diplomatic Corps, formerly separate organizations, were consolidated into a single Foreign Service of the United States, which also included all the other employees of the State Department located abroad. Entrance into the corps of Foreign Service officers (the key group) thereafter was to be based on passage of an examination and entrance at the bottom of a hierarchy composed of one unclassified and eight classified grades, the former subsequently subdivided by administrative action into three unclassified grades. Provision was also made, however, for the exceptional entrance, without examination, and at the appropriate grade, of persons who had served in the Department for not less than five years, and at the bottom grade, without written examination, for those who had served in the field as non-career vice-consuls, etc., for the same period. The existing groups in the Consular and Diplomatic Corps were, of course, incorporated en bloc. The chiefs of mission —ministers and ambassadors—were excluded from the Service, and indeed, no Foreign Service officer could be appointed chief of mission without resigning from the Service and forfeiting his established status. Salaries were raised and retirement benefits increased; the new scales were deliberately set higher than Civil Service schedules. The first examinations were given soon after the law was enacted, and the severity of the examinations was greatly increased some years later; these examinations were particularly suited to recent college graduates who would still have freshly in mind the details of their academic courses in history, languages and related subjects. In addition to the "Career Service" thus created, the Foreign Service also included a much larger group of American "non-career" vice-consuls and clerks, and a large number of alien employees. Conditions of employment for these categories were far less favorable than for the Career officers. (See Appendix I for Note on "Career Service," "Civil Service," etc.)

The Foreign Service created by the Rogers Act was not the only Foreign Service of the United States. Other departments had representatives abroad; a law enacted in 1927 established a Foreign Commerce Service, and in 1930 a Foreign Agricultural Service was also created by statute. The Foreign Commerce Service, a sizable and active group, was engaged in commercial reporting and trade promotion functions not sharply distinguishable from some of the State Department activities abroad. In 1939, Reorganization Plan No. II under the Reorganization Act of 1939 consolidated these services into the Foreign Service of the United States and the members thereof automatically became Foreign Service Officers.

Thus, at the end of the war, twenty years after the passage of the Rogers Act, the officers of the Foreign Service had varied backgrounds. An estimate made by a reporter for the magazine *Fortune* in 1946 showed thirty persons remaining from the old pre-Rogers Act Diplomatic Service, most of whom had risen by a slow process to key positions and all, or virtually all, of whom had independent wealth. Another 175 were still left from the pre-Rogers Act Consular Service; most of these too had reached the upper ranks and a fair number were independently wealthy. About 125 had entered without examination or written examination at various levels under the 5-year rule. About 100 were former Agriculture and Commerce employees, transferred in 1939. Thus only about half of the total of 800 odd Foreign Service officers had entered via the standard examination procedure; they constituted a coherent group, all possessed of formal educational qualifications, proud of the new traditions; but much of the tone of the Service was set by the survivors of the old days.

The war found the Foreign Service not equipped to handle, with its own members, the multifarious technical tasks that arose. Most of these new functions related to our information, intelligence and economic activities abroad. Mr. Hull was anxious to preserve the Department of State as a policy rather than an operating agency and it was with his complete concurrence that OWI, OIAA, OSS, Lend-Lease, BEW, and FEA—to name only the most significant—sent individuals and whole missions abroad. Nevertheless, the Department itself, since recruitment of Foreign Service officers had stopped for the duration, found an inescapable need for expansion even for its own limited co-ordinating task; it secured the passage of enabling language in successive appropriation acts which permitted the employment of "Foreign Service Auxiliary Officers." These were temporary employees employed under the general Civil Service regulations but benefiting by the Foreign Service system of allowances. Relations between the Service and the Auxiliary and the other wartime partners varied greatly; complaints were numerous on both sides. And the mere existence of what was, for example, in effect an independent Foreign Information Service, very much larger than the whole Foreign Service, could not fail to raise troublesome questions about the functions and organization of our activities abroad. Uncertainty about the most effective way to conduct our foreign affairs in the field was intensified by both the successes and failures of the war experiments.

With the end of the war, the wartime agencies were rapidly dissolved; in the fall of 1945, the major functions of three of the largest were transferred to the State Department, where the process of liquidation, partial or complete, continued. Thus by May 1, 1946, the Office of the Foreign Service reported the composition of the Service to be as follows: 55 ambassadors and ministers, 818 Foreign Service officers (some of whom were on assignment in Washington), 640 Auxiliary Foreign Service officers, approximately 3,800 American non-career vice-consuls, clerks, etc., 3,000 alien employees; and 2,500 still undifferentiated American and alien former war-agency employees, mostly from OWI.

The impact of the war on United States representation abroad had raised, as has been said, a series of questions in the minds of many, both within and without the Foreign Service, as to its future character and function. Almost the whole government, now vigorously concerned with foreign affairs, was interested. The questions were of two sorts: Almost all Foreign Service officers and a number of other persons with a sympathetic interest in the problem were seriously concerned over the inadequacy of the laws and procedures affecting the Career officer group from the standpoint of the group itself. Salaries and allowances that had been adequate in 1924 were no longer adequate; indeed the maximum salary for ministers had not been changed since 1855, while ambassadors were limited to the maximum salary established in 1892 when the first ambassador was appointed. Assignments for temporary service in the Department in Washington, greatly prized for various reasons, were unavailable in many instances to those who might have been selected, because they could not afford the expense involved without the assistance of allowances payable only abroad. Home leave was frequently deferred for years; administrative services and training were grossly inadequate; appropriations were limited.

For the reasons just cited, the morale of the Career Service at the end of the war was low. But many or even most Career officers were disturbed by more fundamental anxieties. It was widely believed that neither Secretary Hull nor President Roosevelt had understood or supported them. Both as representatives of the United States and as employees, they suffered sporadically from the unwisdom or unfairness of some of the non-Foreign Service mission chiefs. They feared what seemed to them to be political abuses, such as favoritism for individual officers whether induced by outside pressure or by the existence of cliques within the Service. Furthermore, and more important, they were concerned about the entrance into the hitherto reserved field of foreign affairs, of groups of government employees not recruited by special examination as they themselves had been and hence, by their definition, political appointees. To many, the last crushing blow would be the blanketing in of a large number of persons—in the Auxiliary, in OWI, in OSS, in the other war agencies—who had not come up the "hard way," thus re-enacting what one Foreign Service officer described as "The Betrayal of 1939." There was some concern also over the unsatisfactory status of the non-career officers and employees; but these groups had almost no important spokesmen of their own; advocacy of their needs was largely left to the officer corps who represented somewhat ambivalently the small "Career Service" and the whole "Foreign Service."

The worries about what to do with the Foreign Service were not solely concerned with the welfare and effective opportunities of the Foreign Service officers and employees as individuals. They were likewise directed at the function and composition of the Service from the standpoint of its utility for the government and people of the United States. Thus once again the question apparently settled in 1939 was raised: Should there be a single unified Foreign Service? Should there be a separate elite corps in the modern world? was another disturbing question. The adequacy of the Service for commercial, economic, and information activities was under attack, and the appropriateness of the entrance examination system was disputed. The proper management of the new activities like cultural relations and the use of the new men who entered government service during the war was debated back and forth. The relationship between the Department and the Service itself underwent a fresh review.

Thus, in brief, as the tide of war turned in our favor, there was a resurgence of interest in the reform of the Foreign Service for differing and even occasionally conflicting reasons. This resurgence took expression in various ways. In 1943 and 1944 there was a dispute between the Department of State and the Foreign Economic Administration concerning the allocation of funds for commercial reporting in South America. As a result of this dispute, and of the consequent mediation of the Bureau of the Budget, an interdepartmental Joint Survey Group was established by the State Department on April 24, 1944, to review the techniques and procedures for such reporting. The Joint Survey Group proceeded to establish committees and subcommittees, and its activities proliferated. Perhaps inevitably, it found itself concerned with larger questions than the one for which it had been initially founded.

Similarly, the State Department, on recommendation of the Bureau of the Budget (acting under its statutory responsibilities with respect to governmental organization) began to reorganize the home base of the Foreign Service. All the administrative direction of the Service theretofore had come from two units in the Department, the Division of Foreign Service Personnel and the Division of Foreign Service Administration. On January 15, 1944, an Office of Foreign Service Administration, later called the Office of the Foreign Service, was established as one of the constituent units of the Department. On the 1st of March a Planning Staff was established within the Office of Foreign Service Administration. Now, for the first time, there was a unit, however small and informal, that had responsibility for thinking about the future organization and operation of the Foreign Service as distinguished from carrying out the daily routine of operations. In the fall, in fulfillment of one of the ideas of the Planning Staff, Mr. George T. Washington, a former professor of law and official of the Foreign Economic Administration, and Mr. Avery F. Peterson, a Foreign Service officer, filed with the Secretary a report on the Foreign Service with recommendations for its improvement.

Meanwhile, all through this year, the American Foreign Service Association had not been idle. To use its own language, "The American Foreign Service Association is an unofficial and voluntary association of the members of *The Foreign Service of the United States*. It was formed for the purpose of fostering *esprit de corps* among the members of the Foreign Service and to establish a center around which might be grouped the united efforts of its members for the improvement of the service." The Association publishes a monthly periodical, the *American Foreign Service Journal*, unofficial but authoritative; indeed, at this period the *Journal's* editorial offices were housed in the Department of State. Through the pages of this publication, the Association announced a prize essay contest, the subject to be "Suggestions for Improving the Foreign Service and Its Administration to Meet Its War and Postwar Responsibilities." Eligibility for the contest was limited to Foreign Service officers.

In addition to the essay contest (the first prize-winning essay did not actually appear until February 1945), the pages of the *Journal* throughout 1944 were replete with descriptions of steps being taken to improve the Service, with comments on pending legislation affecting the Service, and with animated correspondence concerning the problems of the Foreign Service officers and employees.

Even during this year of gestation it was generally agreed that the Rogers Act of 1924 and the various subsequent amendatory laws no longer formed an adequate basis for the operation of the Service. New and fundamental legislation was necessary. On December 1, 1944, Mr. Stettinius took oath as Secretary of State, and on December 8 General Julius C. Holmes was designated Assistant Secretary of State in charge of Administration. These new officials were receptive to the idea of new basic legislation, Mr. Stettinius because of a general desire to make constructive improvements at home and abroad, based in part on experience gained during his year of service as Under Secretary, and General Holmes on the basis of a great deal of personal knowledge. For many years he himself had served as a Foreign Service officer abroad and in the Department, and during the war, as one of the chief Civil Affairs officers of the army, he had worked constantly with our diplomatic representatives. His general plans for new legislation and for reforming the service in other ways had been approved by the Secretary even before he took office. On December 18, 1944, a Committee on Foreign Service Legislation was established. The period of active legislative preparation had begun.

2. EARLY DRAFTS

Not all the problems of the Foreign Service could be deferred for the length of time necessary to prepare basic legislation; some required prompter action. During the course of 1944, a bill, prepared in 1943, was introduced in the Congress to improve the status of American clerks and other non-career employees of the Foreign Service, to bring in, as a matter of emergency, at various levels 120 new Foreign Service officers in addition to those who would be recruited by examination at the end of the war, to authorize the detail of specialists from other government agencies, and, among other things, to remove the percentage limitations established by law. Existing legislation placed a series of limits on the number of Foreign Service officers in the various upper grades of the Service, ranging from a limit of 6 per cent of the total number of officers for Class I to 14 per cent for Class VI. As a result of these arithmetical limitations and the complete cessation of recruitment by examination during the war (thus automatically holding down the total number of officers and therefore the size of the upper classes), it became impossible for more than a handful of Foreign Service officers to progress up the promotion ladder, especially beyond Class IV. The results of the percentage limitations were therefore seriously demoralizing and regarded universally within and without the Service as unfair. These various provisions, together with others of less consequence for this study, were incorporated in the draft legislation, and in due course debated in the House. While Congress was generally sympathetic to the bill, opposition was raised to the proposal to bring in a sizable number of new Foreign Service officers at various grades and outside the regular examination procedure. This lateral entrance, as it was called, was strongly opposed by Mrs. Rogers, widow and successor of Congressman Jacob Rogers, sponsor of the Rogers Act, who believed that it would be an entering wedge for "politics." Her view was widely, though not universally, shared within the ranks of the Service itself, and the columns of the *American Foreign Service Journal* contained many arguments pro and con. On the whole, those officers who were aware of the questions being raised in Washington about the future functions of the Service were anxious to secure the enactment of legislation permitting lateral entrance. They knew how long it would take to build up the middle and upper ranks of the Service by the slow process of examination and entrance at the bottom, and they were deeply concerned that a Service too greatly understaffed would have to give up some of its functions to other agencies because of its own inability to handle the work. Some few also believed that the introduction of new blood in the middle and upper grades would have a stimulating effect on the whole Service. The policy was thus defended in the editorial columns of the *Journal*. However, in order to obtain the other improvements that were so urgently needed, it was decided to withdraw this controversial section of the legislation from immediate consideration, and to re-offer a new bill minus these provisions; on May 3, 1945, the Bloom Bill was enacted, which put into law all the other urgent reforms. The controversial lateral entrance provisions, in revised form, were put forward later in a separate bill known as the Manpower Act; this bill encountered difficulties and did not become law until July 3, 1946.

With the Bloom Bill out of the way, the Committee on Foreign Service Legislation was able to turn its primary attention to the preparation of basic legislation. The Committee was also to receive more active support from above. Assistant Secretary Holmes chose as Director of the Office of the Foreign Service Monnett B. Davis, a Foreign Service officer who previously had been Acting Director; Davis's deputy was Selden Chapin, another Foreign Service officer, a man of forty-five who had been commissioned after passing the first post-Rogers-Act examination. They took office on January 10, 1945. From this time until the final approval of the Foreign Service Act in August 1946, Chapin's chief concern was with the new Foreign Service legislation. Attached to him as head of the Planning Staff was another Foreign Service officer, Alan N. Steyne. Deeply devoted to the Service itself, Steyne had previously been chairman and the chief source of energy in the Joint Survey Group; he was full of enthusiasm and zeal for this long-sought opportunity to establish the Service and particularly the Career Service on a new and better footing.

Steyne's plans were ambitious. Taking suggestions that had been made by various persons in the Department, he developed a program for establishing a Commission of Inquiry on the Foreign Service to be composed of eminent members of the general public; an interdepartmental committee; and a departmental Steering Committee. Elaborate proposals were drawn up to govern the procedure and agenda of these bodies. Also available in due course were the reports of three teams, each composed of one Foreign Service officer, one Budget Bureau official and one representative of the general public; these teams visited various of our missions abroad and reported their findings to the Secretary.

On May 16, 1945, Chapin finally reached the peak of his professional career (under the law as it then stood) by appointment as Class I Foreign Service officer and Director of the Office of the Foreign Service. For Chapin, the appointment was not an unmixed blessing. Chapin suffered from the stresses of conflicting interests that converged on his office. His chief hope of recompense for the tribulations of the post would depend on the successful prosecution of the new legislation. His Deputy Director was Julian F. Harrington, another Foreign Service Officer; Harrington, a man of Chapin's age, had started as a clerk in the old Consular Service; he was promoted to Class II on the day he was made Chapin's deputy. (See Appendix II—Biographies.) They were chosen for these positions by Holmes, an old friend of Chapin's, to carry through the needed reform of the Foreign Service, especially via new legislation. Both Chapin and Harrington were interested in getting the job done. Neither was interested in the technical details involved in legislative drafting. With their approval the elaborate committee structure was confirmed and duly made known within the Department. General Holmes continued to manifest his interest in the enterprise and soon secured the over-all blessing of President Truman for the concept of a unified Foreign Service and for the need of basic improvements. At the beginning of June the President also approved the Committee structure and with this approval in hand a general memorandum was circulated throughout the Department requesting legislative recommendations from all and sundry.

Steyne and his associates had continued steadily at work on the substantive problems of legislation. Although the Commission of Inquiry never took form, and although the interdepartmental committee hardly met at all, the Departmental Steering Committee was active, preparing memoranda and holding meetings. A first general outline of the underlying principles to be followed was set forth by Chapin in a memorandum of May 3 in which he told Steyne that the new legislation must be solidly founded on the career principle of the Rogers Act, but that provision should be made for specialists who would be kept as a separate corps and not as an integral part of the Career Service. He opposed a consolidation of the Foreign Service with the Departmental Service, except in the event that the unified Foreign Service concept, adopted in 1939, was abandoned, with a corresponding reduction in the role of the State Department and the Foreign Service to policy co-ordinators. He directed the inclusion of a promotion-up, selection-out system somewhat like the Navy system, under which each officer would be allowed to stay in any one grade only a specified number of years; if not promoted by the end of the period, he must be retired. He suggested that the Career Service be strengthened by reserving for its members some of the Assistant Secretary positions and a guaranteed percentage of chief of mission posts, i.e., ambassadors and ministers. He proposed the establishment of a new top class of Foreign Service officers—later called the Career Minister class. He also advocated the building up of the separateness and responsibilities of the Office of the Foreign Service and its Director, and proposed some such title as Director General for the incumbent, a suggestion advanced by General Holmes. Except for the promotion-up, selection-out procedures and the hesitation over the unified Foreign Service concept, Chapin's ideas were representative of those held by most Foreign Service officers, and he looked on himself as a representative of the Service—particularly the Career Service.

Chapin's instructions, even his suggestions, had direct official weight. When Steyne received Chapin's memorandum in May 1945, he already had available the essays submitted in the prize essay competition, which were all turned over for official use, as well as a summary and analysis of all the various recommendations printed in the March 1945 issue of the *Journal*. With all this material at hand Steyne proceeded enthusiastically with his plans for a proliferation of research and the development of a great mass of information and studies from which legislation in due course would be distilled. But General Holmes and Chapin began to think rather of a timetable for action. In a discussion at the White House in the middle of June, it was agreed that an attempt should be made to send a draft bill to Congress by September and that plans for long-term studies should be abandoned. In the course of informal discussions, members of Congress had disclosed an interest in Foreign Service legislation and it was felt wise to take advantage of the favorable political climate. On June 30 this new deal, as Steyne called it, was put into effect.

Between June 21 and August 14, under Steyne's urging, a whole series of studies were prepared together with appropriate suggested drafts for implementing legislation by what was then called "An Organization to Undertake a Study of the Basic Requirements of the Foreign Service." These 12 studies and 12 substudies were in large part elaborations of a group of 29 major proposals and 18 minor proposals that had been included in a summary memorandum for the Departmental Steering Committee on June 30; but a hope Steyne expressed on June 30 that, by short-cutting some of the original procedural arrangements, a draft bill could be ready for the Assistant Secretary in six or eight weeks proved to be elusive. In any event, a new situation soon confronted Chapin and his associates.

On July 3, 1945, Mr. Byrnes succeeded Mr. Stettinius as Secretary of State. Six weeks later, General Holmes resigned and was promptly succeeded by Col. Frank J. McCarthy. In themselves, these were unsettling events. But by this time, mid-August, Steyne had already concluded that it was too late to prepare legislation in time for action in the first session of the 79th Congress. In a memorandum to Chapin, Steyne lamented the fact that the month of May had been largely wasted in attempting to establish a Commission of Inquiry, the month of June in trying to get the Steering Committee to work, and July in securing informal directives to establish various policy points. He foresaw that an ultimate review of the draft bill by the Bureau of the Budget might require additional changes too. In the light of all this, it was his recommendation that the new Assistant Secretary be advised that the attempt to rush the work should be abandoned. This recommendation was passed on to McCarthy, who agreed, and work continued at a leisurely pace. But a new difficulty then arose. When Mr. Byrnes took office, he requested the Bureau of the Budget to prepare a report on the organization of the State Department. The report was primarily concerned with the organization of the departmental service but it also included recommendations on the Foreign Service; most significantly for this study, it proposed in substance that steps be taken looking toward the consolidation of the two services. (The precise nature of this recommendation and the reasons for it are discussed below.) McCarthy decided to adopt this policy, and prepared a report for the Secretary that embodied most of the Bureau's recommendations. The Budget report and its revised version, the McCarthy report, were treated as confidential, but knowledge of their contents was acquired by some of the Foreign Service officers serving in the Department. Rumors spread and McCarthy encountered or foresaw violent opposition to his plans for reorganization.

Chapin was convinced, since the concept of a unified Foreign Service was to be retained, of the need for maintaining a Foreign Service separate from the departmental service. A decade earlier, in an article in the *Journal*, he had proposed a consolidated service with four major branches, but in 1945 he found that his colleagues were almost solidly opposed to the proposal, at least for the time being. He had dropped it, and all legislative planning had proceeded with this concept of a separate service in mind. An impasse ensued. Chapin was McCarthy's subordinate and was bound by McCarthy's directions. But he could present to McCarthy the arguments against consolidation and he could, at least temporarily, delay action.

The period between the middle of August and the middle of October 1945, when this argument was going on, was a difficult one in the Department and particularly for Chapin. He and Holmes had had only about six months in which to accomplish any of the desired reforms. He was now trying to adjust to a new Assistant Secretary. Then on August 31, by Executive Order the Department inherited over ten thousand employees, mostly in the field, from the Office of War Information, the Office of Inter-American Affairs, and the Office of Strategic Services. New top officials were brought in to direct the new programs. The machinery of the Office of the Foreign Service was badly strained. Daily problems were painful and seemed innumerable. Then finally, Steyne, who had driven himself unceasingly, had a breakdown; he left on an extended leave of absence, and on his return was assigned to other duties. The whole legislative project thereupon languished.

Insofar as Chapin could devote time to the new legislation, he was primarily concerned with an attempt to work out with the new Assistant Secretary some agreement on the problem of the single service and the related proposals for amalgamation of the management offices of the Department and the Foreign Service. He knew that any abandonment of the principle of the separate Foreign Service would cause an outcry from the whole Foreign Service officer corps. Anxious to resolve the dilemma without altercation, he had his assistants prepare a long memorandum, dated October 3, advocating the gradual consolidation of the departmental with the field service over a period of 10 years, a proposal that would be far less shocking to his colleagues than a plan involving fairly rapid amalgamation. In substance, the "Andrew Foster plan," as it came to be known from the name of its chief author, then an assistant to Chapin, proposed that there be a slow merging of the major professional groups in the Department with the Career Service somewhat along the lines of an amalgamation proposal adopted not long before by the British Foreign Office; all future appointees in these groups would be required to accept home or field service, when and as directed. In ten years or more the two services would be completely merged under Foreign Service rather than Civil Service auspices. The departmental technicians and clerical personnel would not be included in the merger. Foster himself was opposed to the plan, although he agreed that it was not entirely without merit; and some of his associates were positive advocates of it, believing in the validity of both the merger objective and the long transition period. Chapin made the proposal hesitantly because of its possible effect on the morale of the Service at that moment, although it was in line with his own thinking on the subject.

McCarthy's final judgment was never determined. Suffering from ill health, he resigned on October 11. His place was taken by Donald S. Russell, a long-time associate and former law partner of the Secretary, although a much younger man. Russell's deputy was J. Anthony Panuch, a New York lawyer who had had considerable government experience in the SEC, in various war agencies, and in the War Department. (See Appendix II—Biographies.) Immediately after Russell began the task of supervising the home and field administration of the Department of State, a task that he undertook out of personal loyalty to the Secretary, he issued a statement for the Foreign Service stating that he had read the report prepared for Secretary Byrnes by the Bureau of the Budget and that there was nothing in it that should alarm the Foreign Service officers; his statement was issued against the advice of one of the officials of the Bureau of the Budget. He also informed them, not long thereafter, that no changes affecting them would be made without prior consultation. Thus he sought to allay the suspicions and fears engendered by the rumors about the Budget and McCarthy reports; both statements were addressed to the whole Foreign Service but designed specifically for the Foreign Service officers. Russell's primary interest in his assignment as Assistant Secretary was the protection of the Secretary. These statements were part of a general policy on his part to avoid any clash between the Secretary and the corps of Foreign Service officers.

Russell then turned his attention to the problem of Foreign Service legislation. Originally he decided to stand on the policy established by McCarthy; but discussions between him and Chapin continued and in early December he reversed his position. Chapin was instructed or authorized to prepare legislation based on a continuance of the established Foreign Service separate and distinct from the departmental service. Thereafter, that conclusion, although questioned, was never threatened.

By this time, the actual work on legislation was in somewhat different hands. A Division of Foreign Service Planning had been established on April 1, 1945, within the Office of the Foreign Service. On December 1, Andrew B. Foster (principal author of the merger plan described above) was appointed Chief, and Carl W. Strom, Assistant Chief in charge of the legislative section. Edmund A. Gullion, who had been attached to the early Planning Staff was assigned to work with Strom. Also assigned were Edward T. Lampson, Lionel M. Summers, and Marion L. Neustadt. (See Appendix II—Biographies.) The first three were Foreign Service officers who had entered the Service via examination, all three during the 1930's; Foster, Class V, and Strom, Class VI, were in their middle-forties; Gullion, thirty-three, was also in Class VI; the two latter were promoted to Class V during the course of these events. (The classes indicated are those under the Rogers Act then in effect, but now obsolete.) Lampson, thirty-four, was a departmental employee in one of the middle grades who had formerly been a professor of history; Summers was a departmental lawyer in a senior grade who had spent a number of years in government work, mostly with the Rural Electrification Administration; it is perhaps not irrelevant to note that Summers was the son of a pre-Rogers Act Consular officer. Miss Neustadt, twenty-three years old, had been trained in public administration, had served as an interne in the State Department (as assistant to Alan Steyne), and had been taken on as a regular administrative analyst in a junior grade in 1945. While some aid was given by technical assistants, the main load of work was carried by these six persons.

Foster and Strom had had substantial practical experience in the administrative operations of the Foreign Service, and Summers had been serving as a legal adviser to the Office of the Foreign Service; but aside from Miss Neustadt, none of the group had had any background of formal training in the innumerable technicalities of leave, pensions, promotions, classification, and the other matters included in the proposed legislation. They were not disturbed by these possible deficiencies in training. They set to work to master those technicalities that had not already been learned by experience; for nothing could be omitted, since it had been decided by this time that the legislation should be not merely a further amendment of the existing statutory pattern, already unduly complicated by amendment, but a complete codification and revision of all legislation affecting the Foreign Service. This meant, among other things, a complete review of all the numerous relevant statutes, so that their multifarious provisions could either be revised and codified in the new law or repealed. The magnitude of the task is indicated by the fact that the Foreign Service Act of 1946, as enacted, has eleven titles and, in the slip law edition, runs to forty-seven pages; there are sixty-seven items in the repealer section that repeal previous legislation rendered obsolete or revised by the new law. As time went on the drafting group became convinced that they had more understanding of the problems involved than any of the various individuals or groups with whom they dealt from time to time; they were immersed in the task, and full of zeal.

Foster and his associates were able to make use of the work that had been done before, and in which almost all of them had been active participants at various stages. They were, as a group, genuinely concerned with the two converging forces of interest—the desire to improve the value of the Service to the government and the nation, and the desire to improve the status of the Foreign Service officers and the other employees of the Service. With Russell's second decision at the beginning of December 1945, the hard grind began. All through the Christmas season the team worked on the preparation of a complete draft of new legislation. They also prepared a long memorandum explaining and justifying each of the basic sections. On the 28th of December 1945 the first complete draft was ready, and the four-day New Year holiday was used for a first over-all revision. The first draft available for examination by the Office of the Foreign Service and its constituent divisions was dated January 3, 1946. Discussion and further revision followed immediately; new amendments were promptly proposed and drafted. Among the first amendments was one affecting the status of the Director of the Foreign Service. Picking up a suggestion originally made by Holmes that the Director be given power and prestige, the drafters planned to elevate the existing position of Assistant Secretary of State for Administration to Under Secretary (later Deputy Under Secretary) thereby allowing for the appointment of a Director General of the Foreign Service with the rank of Assistant Secretary. Russell, while not interested in the detailed provisions of the bill, decided that this proposal should be abandoned. He apparently feared that if the bill were prepared in this form he might be accused, even though unjustly, of using it as a vehicle for elevating his own status. On January 17, 1946, Chapin sent to Russell a summary of the principal features of the bill which was also circulated to the top officials of the Department for comment, but the draft bill itself was not considered ready for general circulation in the Department.

The drafting and redrafting continued and a second complete draft was ready on the 1st of February. The principal features of this draft were again summarized for Russell on February 11 and at this point Foster contemplated a considerable period of continued study and drafting. However, Chapin became concerned once again about the delay in getting the legislation finally ready. He was anxious to secure passage of a law before Congress adjourned in the summer. At a meeting in his office on February 11 he announced that all departmental clearances must be completed and an approved draft ready for the Bureau of the Budget and the Congress by March 15. Foster, aware of the number of unsolved problems, and equally aware of potential objections within the various parts of the Department, felt that compliance with this order could not fail to result in an unsatisfactory draft. He feared that errors and omissions would inevitably result; if the bill failed of passage in the 79th Congress, then in its second session, submission of a drastically revised bill in the 80th Congress would be embarrassing. But Chapin held to the new schedule.

3. BASIC ASSUMPTIONS OF THE DRAFTSMEN

The drafts dated January 3 and February 1 had received very limited circulation; successive changes in these drafts were based almost entirely on self-criticism within the Office of the Foreign Service. The underlying elements in both drafts and in the earlier studies were largely founded on a group of convictions widely held within the Service itself, especially within the Career Service, but some new points of departure became manifest as the drafting process proceeded. Thus the plan for elevating the office of Assistant Secretary for Administration to Under Secretary, or Deputy Under Secretary was dropped at Russell's request, as has been noted. Some suggestions considered politically unpalatable, such as travel allowances for maids and governesses, were omitted at the urging of the Division of Foreign Service Planning, whose members tried to be particularly sensitive to political reactions, perhaps because they were so conscious of being unversed in the ways of the government at large and the Congress. Chapin himself was perhaps solely responsible for the inclusion of the promotion-up, selection-out provisions, his abiding interest in this procedure stemming from his service years before as an officer in the Navy; though even in this instance, the proposals were at least *prima facie* acceptable because of the wide-spread belief that the Career Service had a great deal of "dead wood." The selection-out procedures had another point of appeal: Chapin and other senior Career officers were afraid that Congress might be offended by the enlarged benefits of various sorts proposed for the Career Service, and might even attack the concept itself. The promise of rigorous and continuous weeding out would tend to justify to laymen the attribution of special privileges to officers who survived the selection process by virtue of special merit. Other changes were made in response to group or individual emphasis on matters that were generally acceptable; thus, for example, much of the elaboration of the training provisions was the result of Lampson and Gullion's special interest in this subject.

The draft of March 2 represented a stage of the work at which Chapin felt that full departmental clearance was appropriate and indeed essential. It therefore merits some special consideration as constituting the last form of the legislation before the direct impact of the outside world—the Department, other government agencies, Congress—began to be felt. Suggestions had been received and accepted from these outside sources in the days of the Joint Survey Group and the Steering Committee; additional suggestions had come from the discussions concerning the Manpower Act and the treatment of the groups of newly transferred employees. The successive drafts of the statements of "Principal Features" had served as the basis for additional comment, and had indeed resulted in unsatisfied requests for copies of the bill itself. But the March 2 draft was in all essential respects the uncompromised product of a group of Foreign Service officers (with a few assistants) working, in an important sense, as representatives of the Career Service. Many dozens of changes were made subsequently; but insofar as they were made willingly, they were almost without exception technical or minor in character.

The new Foreign Service legislation, as formulated in this March 2 draft, was based on two underlying concepts, one flowing from the other. Fundamentally the draftsmen were convinced of the necessity for building around a competent and disciplined, but protected and privileged, corps composed of "generalists" who would handle our political relations with other countries. (The officers themselves normally referred to the corps as the "Professional" or "Career" Service, but the phrase "elite corps" was and is widely used; see Appendix I.) Secondly, the draftsmen believed that the legislation itself should spell out in detail all necessary safeguards.

To many Foreign Service officers, possibly to the majority, the need for a special corps was self-evident and needed no justification. The sense of dedication, of shared privilege and experience, was so strong, the feeling of participation in a profession set aside from the laity was so real, that the question of justification was frequently deemed unworthy of reply.

Such an attitude was impractical for men preparing to face interrogation outside the Service itself, and especially from Congress. Indeed Foster and his colleagues had a sense that the whole concept was made vulnerable by what some of them described as a "trade-union" attitude; Gullion, in his prize-winning essay, had said that the worst mistake would be a "concept of exclusive vested right in the foreign field." They believed that a special corps was necessary and would continue to be necessary, certainly for some years to come; but they also believed that the corps could be justified only in terms of the practical situation and the functions it served, and not because of the satisfactions it returned to its members. They wanted the corps to be less exclusive, less insensitive to values outside itself and its immediate mission, though still sufficiently entrenched to preserve its integrity. To Chapin, with a strong pragmatic bent, this approach made sense; he favored and, in a speech, went on record in support of a law that would represent a sound middle position between extremes.

The rationale for a Career Service was variously stated and indeed variously felt. In the Division of Foreign Service Planning it might have been phrased thus: "The affairs of the United States must be in the hands of competent and completely dependable servants at all posts, dull and interesting, healthful and unhealthful, and at all times. The emergency may arise only on one day a year; but when it does arise, the Foreign Service officer, however routine his normal tasks on all the other 364 days, however distasteful his surroundings, must be able to meet it intelligently and without faltering. The Service must therefore be so inviting that unusually reliable and able persons will be willing to undergo the boredom and privations of forced residence, frequent moves, and uninspiring duties. It must offer such advantages that its members will remain faithful even after the youthful glamour of foreign lands has disappeared." A less sophisticated rationale would tend to emphasize the disadvantages of the pest holes of the world, overlooking the fact that service at these posts can be, and is, specially compensated, and that many Foreign Service officers never serve in these places at all. A more sophisticated approach might lay more stress on the need to overcome the normal or common American reluctance to enter on a career that entails constant residence abroad with the disadvantages to family life that follow in its train.

Whatever the precise justification, the concept of the Career Service implies some measure of special prestige, corps solidarity, and a considerable guarantee of security and opportunity for advancement—as well as special salaries, allowances and other benefits; it implies protection for the corps, especially from domestic political influences or appointees. Those who opposed the concept—of which more later—tended to accept the premise of a need for special inducements, but felt with varying degrees of conviction that the financial inducements (and the basic satisfactions of high public service) could of themselves insure the adequate staffing of all our foreign missions. These opponents of the Career Service concept tended to doubt the need for the continuance of a special corps, or even the adequacy of such a corps in the face of the complex problems of the modern world.

The decision to write a bill containing detailed powers, responsibilities and limitations was primarily based on a desire to insure the protection of the Service, especially perhaps from political infiltration, but in other ways as well. As has been said, the draftsmen believed in a Career Service with special privileges; they feared that there would be constant pressures on the Secretary or the President to obliterate the differences between the Foreign Service and the Civil Service; to safeguard the differences, they felt it necessary or at least desirable to provide a statutory basis for all the details of salary, promotion, leave, retirement, separation, etc., that in comparable legislation for most other government employees are largely left to regulations promulgated by the President or agency head. But it should be noted that Chapin had been warned that Congress would not approve a bill for the Foreign Service that provided broad discretionary powers. The desire for detailed statutory guarantees was reinforced by a fear that, without such guarantees, the Service would not be able to attract well-qualified applicants. There was also a belief held by some that detailed legislative prescriptions are an inherent attribute of any governmental career service, the Army and Navy being cited as examples; this argument presumably rests on the assumption that corps solidarity—what might be called guild activity—can be maintained only with the assurances furnished by a precise statutory foundation. And furthermore, in March 1946 the draftsmen were painfully conscious of departmental administrative instability in the light of their service under four different Assistant Secretaries for Administration in the past sixteen months.

Finally—and this point was a matter of deep conviction to Foster and his team—highly specific statutory requirements represented an attempt to insure equitable treatment for all Foreign Service officers, and other officers and employees of the Service, to guard against what may be described as internal political pressures.

It was felt by the drafting group that many officers (and employees) had in the past suffered from arbitrary or capricious treatment by individuals or cliques; they were especially resentful of the behavior of some of the political appointees—ambassadors, etc., but they also believed that some of the Career officers had likewise been unfair. It was hoped that the political appointees and the senior Career officers, who tended to have preponderant influence in the administration of the Service, would in the future be required to follow more orderly and equitable procedures. It was also hoped that new provisions, such as the establishment of a classification system, would improve the lot of the non-career personnel, and would make the Service more efficient. Foster believed in these changes as a matter of right, but he also believed that the privileged Career Service could not be preserved unless the whole Foreign Service was administered with equity and efficiency.

Some small area of administrative discretion must be left, even in detailed legislation; and to ensure use of this discretion in a way that would deter deviation from the desired norm, Foster and his associates decided to include provisions that would ensure control by Foreign Service officers, or at least, an indefeasible opportunity for their voice to be heard.

Later opposition to this approach was vigorous; the character of the opposition will be indicated below.

This outline of the underlying rationale of the draft legislation is necessarily an oversimplification. Other factors also were at work. The very fact that this was to be in such large part a codification of existing law made detailed provisions seem almost inevitable—for most of the earlier statutes were of an extremely detailed character. Furthermore, the retention of existing provisions promised some protection against congressional attack.

As a final word—no single one of the half-dozen persons chiefly concerned with preparation of the legislation would have had precisely the approach outlined herein—no two, indeed, were in total agreement on every item and detail. To some slight extent, these variations in viewpoint are indicated below; but for the most part it is necessary to limit this sketch to a somewhat artificially articulate and composite statement of slightly varying views. Yet because of the general solidarity of the corps this composite picture represents less of a distortion than would be the case for most governmental agencies dealing with a similar problem.

4. THE DRAFT OF MARCH 2

The draft of March 2 is a long document, far too long for reproduction here, too long and too detailed even for full summary. The description at this point is limited to an account of those elements in the draft bill around which significant controversy later developed.

Direction of the Service

In the draft bill the active direction of the Service is assigned to a Director General, assisted by a Deputy Director General; appointment to these positions (the former a Presidential appointment) is limited to Foreign Service officers of Class 1 or Career Minister class. This section represents a notable enlargement and supersession of brief earlier statutory references to the Chief of the Division of Foreign Service Personnel and the Director of the Office of the Foreign Service.

General executive oversight over all personnel actions—technically primarily in the form of recommendations to the Secretary—is vested in the Board of Foreign Service Personnel, established by statute in 1931, but endowed with narrower functions than under the draft bill. Membership is partially changed so that it includes:

Assistant Secretary of State for Administration, Chairman; Director General, Vice Chairman; three other State Department officials (including at least two Assistant Secretaries); and one "acceptable" representative each of Commerce and Agriculture with sharply limited participation (as heretofore).

The setting and conduct of entrance examinations for Foreign Service officers is vested in the Board of Foreign Service Examiners, long established but hitherto non-statutory.

Newly created is an Advisory Interdepartmental Committee to be established by the

President (but with the Director General as Chairman) "to assist in planning and developing the Service."

Categories, Salaries, Appointments and Assignments

The draft bill establishes the following categories with the salary ranges indicated: ambassadors and ministers ($15,000-$25,000); Foreign Service officers ($3,000-$13,500); Foreign Service Reserve officers ($3,000-$12,000, or Civil Service salary); Foreign Service Staff officers ($3,310-$7,910); American clerks and employees ($714-$5,180); alien clerks and employees (to be fixed by the Secretary).

These salary scales represent increases over existing scales. In general the provisions covering all these groups are a refinement, simplification, and regularization of earlier statutory provisions. The sharpest departures are represented by the new top class of Career Minister for Foreign Service officers and the establishment of the Reserve.

Most of the provisions for promotion and assignment for all groups, except the Reserve, follow previous practice (Presidential appointment and Senatorial confirmation of Foreign Service officers on original appointment and subsequent promotions, diplomatic and consular commissions for Foreign Service officers, etc., etc.). Two significant exceptions are a provision for lateral entrance into the Career Service after four years in the Staff or the Reserve or the Department, and a promotion-up, selection-out system for Foreign Service officers.

Reserve Officers are limited to a four-year tour of duty with an enforced break of a year thereafter. Reserve Officers are of two types; those appointed by the Secretary from outside the government on recommendation of the Board of Foreign Service Personnel at an appropriate salary and class corresponding to one of the six numbered Foreign Service officer classes (range $3,000-$12,000); and those assigned by the Secretary from the State Department or other government agencies on recommendation of the Board at their Civil Service salary and the corresponding Foreign Service officer class, which, because of salary differentials, would normally be no higher than Class 3. Appointed Reserve officers are limited to one promotion per tour of duty; assigned Reserve officers are not eligible for promotion but must be reinstated in their original or equivalent government positions at home at the conclusion of the tour of duty.

The draft bill has elaborate provisions governing assignments, including new provisions requiring home service for Foreign Service officers for three out of the first fifteen years of duty, and also authorizing the payment of Civil Service salaries, when higher, to officers assigned to departmental duty. (These constitute the "re-Americanization program.")

The Foreign Service Institute

The draft bill includes detailed and entirely new provisions for a Foreign Service Institute. It is to be headed by a Director appointed by the President with Senatorial confirmation, who is to be in charge under the "general supervision of the Director General." The Institute is to provide in-service training and to prepare appropriate studies on foreign policy, and to co-ordinate those studies with research conducted elsewhere. The Secretary is authorized to make grants to co-operating institutions, to appoint faculty and staff on recommendation of the Director, and to assign officers and employees of the Service to the Institute or elsewhere for instruction.

The foregoing is a brief summary of certain limited portions of the bill, which also covers *in extenso* retirement, and other rights and benefits, including leave, allowances, etc., and all other aspects of personnel administration. Its provisions are extremely detailed.

5. POLICY RESPONSIBILITY FOR THE FOREIGN SERVICE BILL

As has been pointed out, the provisions of the March 2 draft selected above for summarization, are those that provoked major disagreement later on. To the drafting group these provisions and various other similar provisions were designed primarily to accomplish two objectives: to maintain and strengthen the corps of Foreign Service officers as a separate, dominant and largely self-contained group; and to improve the general flexibility and efficiency of the Service, especially by providing adequate employment opportunities for specialists in the Reserve and the Staff, so that, under the leadership of the Foreign Service officers, the Foreign Service as a whole could effectively handle any tasks assigned to it.

It will be seen that the objectives themselves, while self-evident to Foster and his associates, were subject to later attack and questioning, as were the methods chosen to attain those objectives. Those to whom the need for a special corps was axiomatic tended to find in the draft bill elements that would threaten the inviolability of the Career Service; those unsure of the necessity for or desirability of such a corps tended to foresee a Foreign Service still out of touch with the modern world and unequipped to handle its multifarious problems. In one sense, therefore, the March 2 draft represents a middle-of-the-road position; but in another and more important sense it represents a firm decision by representatives of the corps of Foreign Service officers to retain in all essentials the concept of a restricted Career Service. The major disputes that occurred subsequently arose primarily with opponents who sought either to change the fundamental basis of the proposed legislation or to change its form so that possible future amendment of the basic concept would be facilitated. Aside from the disagreement with McCarthy, there had been no major differences of viewpoint among those with direct responsibility for the preparatory work that underlay the March 2 draft; but this unanimity should not obscure the fact that alternatives did exist, and had been rejected. Much of the confusion and frustration in the debates that took place in the months that followed may well have been caused by an avoidance of the major issue and a concentration on related but secondary matters.

There is one final aspect of the choices adopted by the draftsmen that is striking: there is throughout the whole of the March 2 draft a remarkable consistency of logic even in the face of apparent deviation.

It is obvious that the new grades and salaries and other benefits were designed to reinforce the Career Service. Less obvious is the intent of the provision that gives a statutory basis to the Board of Foreign Service Examiners, or of the provision establishing the rank of Career Minister; but in the first case the examination system, with its peculiar screening character, now to be guaranteed, had been the cornerstone of the Career Service, while the second provision would provide the capstone lacking in the past. Henceforth the system itself would carry clear to the top.

The case of lateral entrance is more paradoxical; but here too Foster and his assistants were convinced that a steady, small and carefully controlled flow into the middle and upper ranks would benefit the basic system, not subvert it, and would serve as a shield against adverse criticism. And they were similarly sure that the general modernization of the Service was essential as a protection for the system, even aside from its inherent desirability.

Finally, in all the provisions for administrative direction, Foster and his associates were thinking of a self-contained Career Service run by a special group within the Career Service, but equitably and efficiently.

The draft Foreign Service Bill was thus all of a piece. It was based on simple and straightforward assumptions. Its major objectives were the objectives of the corps of Foreign Service officers. In its general approach it was a predictable guild product; objections to it from Foreign Service officers were directed at procedures or details, not at fundamental objectives. The decision to entrust the revision of the Rogers Act to an essentially undirected group of Foreign Service officers made inevitable a bill with these general characteristics. A disagreement with the results is therefore more appropriately directed at this decision than at the work of the draftsmen.

Part II. Agreement is Secured within the Department of State

6. DEPARTMENTAL PROPOSALS

The new timetable established by Chapin on February 11 called for a resolution of all intradepartmental differences and the submission of a final draft to the Secretary for his approval and transmittal to the Bureau of the Budget by March 15. This allowed two weeks, therefore, for the March 2 draft to be hammered out within the Department; but while Chapin could control the schedule of the Division of Foreign Service Planning, he could not set the pace for the rest of the Department. The process of disagreement, discussion, compromise, partial agreement, and final decision took six weeks, not two. The submission to the Budget Bureau did not take place until April 16.

The following pages are devoted to the revisions in the March 2 draft made as the result of discussions within the Department. Actually, on March 6, when copies were circulated to the various branches of the State Department, copies were also handed "informally" to the liaison officers of Agriculture and Commerce, and to the Budget examiner assigned to work with the Foreign Service; preliminary discussions ensued. But a description of these developments is deferred until a later section of this study. Similarly deferred is an account of the first contacts with the Foreign Affairs Committee of the House of Representatives, which also occurred before April 16.

There were four chief focuses within the Department for the revision of the March 2 draft: various Foreign Service officers, including those in the Office of the Foreign Service and their technical assistants; the economic offices under Assistant Secretary Clayton; the information and cultural offices under Assistant Secretary Benton; and the intelligence offices under Special Assistant McCormack. For simplicity, the following analysis tends to personalize the various positions; but it should be remembered that except in a few special instances, a phrase like "McCormack's views" is primarily a shorthand expression that covers both McCormack's own views and the views of his assistants, adjusted to accord with his general attitudes.

The changes in the draft bill made on the initiative of the Division of Foreign Service Planning were all in the nature of additional benefits for the Foreign Service personnel. To some extent they resulted from a new conviction that greater benefits—reluctantly omitted from earlier drafts—were politically feasible. Thus salary scales were increased: $15,000 rather than $13,500 for career ministers; a top of $13,500 rather than $12,000 for Class 1; a top of $10,000 rather than $7,910 for Foreign Service Staff (with which the American clerks were now consolidated); these changes roughly paralleled the increases in Civil Service salaries authorized by the Federal Employees Pay Act of 1945 and the then pending Pay Act of 1946. Retirement benefits were liberalized, especially for those "selected out." The required service abroad prior to mandatory home leave was reduced to two years for all posts. New allowances were introduced in addition to the basic allowances retained in the March 2 draft: for family maintenance away from posts where families could not be brought; for the expense of educating children in the United States (Foster regarded this as excessive); for the maintenance of establishments of ambassadors and ministers; and for medical care. These increased benefits corresponded, with the probable exception of the education allowance, to widely felt or anticipated and widely agreed needs.

More controversial, especially from the standpoint of the career officers, was the consolidation of the Foreign Service Staff and clerks, and the raising of their top salary level to $10,000, a level slightly higher than the then top Civil Service salary of $9,800, but the same as would be provided by the 1946 Pay Act, then under discussion. The motives for these changes were mixed. In part, the planning staff itself felt that the FSS was essential and could not properly perform its function without proper recognition; in part, the consolidation especially was based on a belief that the sharp distinction between FSS's and clerks was undemocratic and unnecessarily complicated. The proposal was also defended and partly motivated by a belief that an enlargement of the gap between FSO and FSS salaries would be politically unsound, and that in fact any lower ceiling for FSS than the Civil Service maximum would be unpalatable to Congress.

The reactions of the various Foreign Service officers in Washington who were asked to comment on the March 2 draft were fairly uniform. They complimented Chapin on the work that had been accomplished, but most of them evinced no extreme enthusiasm for the result. Most of the new benefits had been generally known for months and had been discounted, so to speak. Others, anticipated, were omitted —though many of these were soon included in the next series of revisions, as is indicated above. Certain provisions, like those governing the Institute and the Board of Foreign Service Personnel, tended to trespass on vested interests and were regarded at least with suspicion. But the officers were especially concerned over possible inroads on their corps; they objected above all to the "lateral entrance" provisions, and proposed, for example, that the existing five-year requirement of previous service be retained, in lieu of the new four-year requirement. Also suggested was a prohibition against entrance into Classes 1 to 3. Objection was similarly made to the moderate eligibility requirements for Foreign Service Reserve officers. One FSO proposed that at least two members of the Board of Foreign Service Personnel be Foreign Service officers; another objected to the selection-out procedure. All these Foreign Service officer recommendations ran directly counter to the whole trend of departmental criticism. They confirmed Chapin in his belief that his innovations were sufficiently drastic, and that he was in a reasonably tenable middle position. He was also supported by a general sentiment of approval obtained from the Executive Committee of the American Foreign Service Association.

More important than these selected consultations with Foreign Service officers were Chapin's discussions with the directors of the geographic offices, who were senior Foreign Service officers, and who together constituted a close-knit and extremely influential group in the Foreign Service and in the Department as well. From these discussions Chapin could gauge how far he could go in compromise without losing the support of his own corps. On the whole, this group played a larger part in determining Chapin's position than did Chapin's official superior Russell.

Turning to non-Foreign-Service objections, it can be said that McCormack's doubts about certain aspects of the bill were not in any sense decisive, though they may have been a contributory factor in helping secure changes that were made at the instance of more powerful parts of the Department.

At this period, McCormack was in the midst of a struggle that led eventually to his resignation. He was attempting to establish a central office for the intelligence work of the Department that would have on its staff all the specialists in this work. Furthermore, his own group of specialists, already at work, included almost no Foreign Service officers; it was largely composed of former OSS employees, mostly lawyers and economists, who had entered government service during the war or, in some cases, during the New Deal. These men and women constituted a diversified group strikingly different from the comparatively homogeneous career officer corps. Good working relations were not easy to achieve. But McCormack's basic thesis was in itself bound to create difficulties. In substance, he asserted that the work of the policy officials—the heads of the geographic units—of the Department should be judged in the light of information objectively analyzed and not in the light of the policy officials' own factual judgments; in other words, that the Secretary should have, as a safeguard, factual analysis by a group not concerned with the making or execution of policy. McCormack's organizational proposals were based on this thesis.

The policy officials of the Department on the geographic or political side were deeply opposed to this concept. To them political reporting and analysis were among the central functions of the Foreign Service officer. McCormack was proposing to take out of their hands in part at least a responsibility that had been traditionally their exclusive prerogative. Therefore his proposal to build a central intelligence staff was vigorously and—shortly after these events—successfully opposed by almost all the senior officials on the political side of the Department as it is called—the directors and deputy directors of the large area offices, such as the Office of European Affairs, and by their key subordinates, the chiefs of the geographic divisions, such as the Division of Eastern European Affairs (and by their subordinates, the men on the "country desks"). This group strongly urged that the central intelligence office be no more than a small co-ordinating unit and that the intelligence officials (selected by the division chiefs) be assigned to the geographic divisions as subordinates of the division chiefs. They believed that there should be no separation between factual analysis and policy formation and execution. They took the position that such a separation would lead to friction, duplication and the formulation of policy in a vacuum.

This issue between McCormack and the "political" officers of the department was not superficial. Although distinctive, it was related to the general issue of geographical vs. functional organization. Those responsible for the organization of the Department of State face the perpetual dilemma of creating a structure that will make possible the development and carrying out of broad policies, but without overlooking the special factors arising out of national characteristics and sovereignties; or, stating the same problem in its alternative form, maintaining appropriate relations with every country in the world (and with international organizations) without destroying policy consistency. The division of responsibility between functional and geographic offices is a constant source of controversy. The dilemma is inherent in the Department's function, and its horns have been made more pointed by the fact that the Department's chief representatives abroad and key officials controlling the communications to and from those representatives have been, in almost all cases, members of the corps of Foreign Service officers. Thus the inevitably delicate adjustment between the functional and the geographic offices of the Department becomes acutely difficult since it must also take into account the strong corps or guild traditions, habits and loyalties of the Foreign Service officers.

The details of McCormack's controversy lie outside the scope of this study; but its existence is relevant because in its nature, and as a controversy between departmental officials and Foreign Service officers on assignment to the Department, it tended to make McCormack question the basic assumptions underlying the March 2 draft.

There were three aspects of the bill to which objection was raised by McCormack: treatment of the Foreign Service Reserve; organization and control; and basic relationship of the Service with the Department.

While the distinction between the functions of the Reserve and the other two major groups was not clearly delineated, McCormack assumed that his representatives abroad—and the representatives of his allies, the economic and the information officials—would largely find their place in the Reserve Corps. He felt the need for easy opportunity to send staff members abroad and for full privileges for them while abroad. Therefore he objected to the requirement of recommendation by the Board of Foreign Service Personnel for appointment or assignment of FSR officers; to the mandatory application of the lower Civil Service salary scale for assigned FSR's; to the limitation of one promotion per tour of duty for appointed FSR's and, in effect, none for assigned FSR's; and to the mandatory one-year gap between tours of duty.

On organization and control, he had two objections: First, to the membership of the Board of Foreign Service Personnel which permitted only one departmental officer below the rank of Assistant Secretary and which, therefore, would probably exclude him—because his legal rank was only Special Assistant. It seemed to him that the intelligence needs of the Department would not be given proper weight in determining the personnel policies of the Foreign Service under this arrangement.

The second objection was a weighty one, and merged with the general problem of the departmental relationship with the Foreign Service. Objecting to what he considered the parochial-caste attitudes of the career group, and to its control over the geographic side of the Department, he proposed an immediate merger of the departmental and Foreign-Service administrative offices and an eventual merger of the Service and the Department (at least of the professional officials).

This proposal in substance coincided with McCarthy's rejected recommendations. To McCormack, consolidation of the two services was an essential objective because it would lead to far greater integration of economic, informational and intelligence activities and personnel with the diplomatic and political activities and personnel, and because it would lead to a far greater interchange of officials between Washington and the field. The basis of general Foreign Service opposition to this proposal has been indicated above.

The secondary merger—administration—was designed as a step toward integration and as an essential preliminary for the larger merger. For years, as has been pointed out, the Foreign Service had had its own divisions of administration and personnel. Their separateness and effectiveness had been increased by the creation of the Office of the Foreign Service. The proposed creation of the position of Director General and the proposed statutory attribution of powers to him and to the Board of Foreign Service Personnel would remove this sphere of action even further from the control of the Secretary and Assistant Secretary and would render assimilation with departmental practices even more remote.

What was a defect to McCormack, was a virtue to the draftsmen. The desire for effective insulation on the part of the Foreign Service officers has already been pointed out; but there was an additional and very practical reason for their opposition to the proposal for a merger of the administrative offices: Foster was convinced that because of the great differences in administrative practices there would inevitably be separate units for foreign service personnel, etc., etc. On this assumption, the effect of a merger would be to depress these units in the hierarchy and thereby reduce the title, rank and salary available for the unit heads—a result to be deplored both for its direct effect on those involved and for its indirect effect on the effectiveness of these units in handling the affairs of the Service. Beyond that, Foster was well aware of the significance of the administrative merger as a step toward total merger.

For reasons indicated above, McCormack's relations with the Foreign Service were none too happy. His position in the Department was insecure, and his eventual defeat was anticipated. Little or no attention seems to have been paid to his views on the Foreign Service bill.

William Benton, formerly a partner in a highly successful advertising firm, vice president of the University of Chicago, and chairman of the Board of the Encyclopaedia Britannica, now Assistant Secretary of State in charge of informational and cultural affairs, took a direct personal interest in the draft legislation. While he received detailed recommendations from one of his assistants, who also handled some of the negotiations for him, for the most part he spoke very much for himself, both orally and in writing. His initial proposals were somewhat sporadic; but as the discussions continued, both with the Foreign Service group and with Clayton's staff and other departmental officials, he developed a comprehensive and consistent program of amendments. In this task, he was also aided by discussions with Bureau of the Budget and Commerce Department officials.

Benton had been confirmed as Assistant Secretary shortly after August 31, 1945, when the foreign information functions of two war agencies were transferred to the Department. These agencies—the Office of War Information and the Office of Inter-American Affairs—were assigned to him as was the Department's own war-created Office of Cultural Affairs. At the time of transfer the three groups had over 12,000 employees, the majority in the field; all the rest of the Department and the

Foreign Service together had fewer employees than this.

To the Department and especially to the Foreign Service officers, Benton's staff constituted a dubious and unassimilable group. Its members were largely wartime recruits; it included newspaper men and women, magazine and radio writers and editors, college professors, and a large miscellaneous collection of persons with varying social and educational backgrounds chosen because of specific linguistic abilities, or intimate acquaintance with particular countries. Abroad most of them worked in separate establishments away from the diplomatic missions. Indeed when Benton took on his assignment he was pressed by some to insist on an independent Foreign Information and Cultural Service which could in large part be established forthwith as a going organization. He decided against this but he was well aware of wide-spread animosities between his field staff and the Foreign Service officers.

Benton's struggle with the Career Service did not relate solely to his personnel. Some Foreign Service officers did not like Benton's use of public relations and methods of operation. Others, and a not insubstantial number including some of the most influential, were unconvinced of the permanent need for informational and cultural activities. Their views were not concealed and were echoed in Congress, many of whose members were also deeply suspicious of Benton's program, a suspicion deepened by an equally dark suspicion of the character and antecedents of his employees.

Thus to Benton the Foreign Service bill was no academic matter. It was part of his fight for the survival of his program, in the Department and in Congress. Aside from an active and increasingly sympathetic interest in the Foreign Service in spite of his many disputes, Benton necessarily scrutinized the bill from the standpoint of its effect on his staff and their work. Since he had rejected the concept of a separate Information Service, he was eager to guard his employees and his program against discrimination and neglect within the general Foreign Service framework.

To Benton the arguments about the March 2 draft were essentially a continuation of arguments over the Manpower Act and over his daily operations that had begun with his appointment. Many of the fundamental issues were the same and on many points Benton felt that the draft represented a reversal of agreements previously secured orally with Chapin, or with Russell or Panuch.

Benton was primarily interested in two matters: a real voice in the control of the Foreign Service for his part of the Department—and adequate prestige and opportunities for his representatives abroad. These were his immediate concern, but he also had an interest in matters of general judgment, broad principles of administration, and political wisdom; furthermore, he was an enthusiastic supporter of higher salaries and larger benefits for all groups within the Foreign Service.

The question of control Benton sought to answer in two ways. He opposed the requirement of FSO status for the Director General and the Deputy Director General. He justified this proposed change on the ground that the job deserved the best possible man, no matter who he might be; but it may be noted that departmental interests might be expected to receive more attention from a neutral than from a Foreign Service officer. Even more urgently, Benton pressed for a redefinition of the role and membership of the Board of Foreign Service Personnel. He asked that the Board be given wide powers for the administration of the Service (including the power to select the Director General), with power to delegate to subcommittees, and that its membership be limited to three Assistant Secretaries of State.

This proposal was justified by the contention that a smaller board would be more effective and that its members would feel their responsibility more keenly. The analogy of a business board of directors was implied, and mention was made of the inefficiency of any large committee. Aside from these general administrative considerations, it is apparent that Benton had in mind the shift in power that would come from the exclusion of the Director General from membership, and the greater weight that the individual members would carry on a smaller board. He was at this time a member of the Board of Foreign Service Personnel.

With respect to the treatment of his representatives abroad, Benton sought three objectives: (1) easier entrance for his representatives (and others, of course) into the inner circles of the Career Service; (2) more prestige and improved benefits for FSR; and (3) more prestige and improved benefits for FSS.

Benton was uncertain about the attitude of his staff towards service as FSO's with all the privileges and compulsions attached thereto, or in the Reserve, with a flat restriction of tenure, or in the Staff without positive tenure or much prestige, but equally without compulsive character. Increasingly he came to the view that most of his personnel should fit in the Reserve, but his proposals reflect his need for anticipating all contingencies.

On acceptance as FSO's, he proposed quite simply that the prior service requirement be two years, rather than four, and that prior service in any agency transferred to the State Department be credited. This would have meant that virtually all his staff would have been immediately eligible to apply for appointment in the Career Service.

For the FSR, he proposed that its members be made eligible for diplomatic and consular commissions, that the names of FSR be included on the lists to be submitted to the President of persons recommended for appointment as career minister (if such lists were to be given statutory recognition at all, they should, he suggested, be limited to career ministers), and that the salary and promotion restrictions on FSR be removed. These changes would make the FSR more attractive to the information and cultural officers not desiring a permanent career in the government, and would, in his view, make their work more effective. Finally, again reflecting his uncertainty, Benton recommended that the enforced break between tours of duty be left to administrative discretion, or that exceptions be permitted. (Later, he was inclined to believe that limited tours of duty were desirable in his field of activity; and he conceded this point in the final negotiations.)

For the FSS, he had two proposals: make these officers eligible for diplomatic commissions and reinstate the statutory distinction between the FSS and the American clerks. These proposals had increased prestige as the object in view—the first positively, the second negatively by preventing his employees from being classed as clerks. For similar reasons, Benton had objected strenuously to an earlier proposal to consolidate the Reserve and the Staff, an acrimonious dispute that he had won.

Benton also had some general recommendations. He wished to remove a requirement that inspectors be career officers. He suggested that the functions of the Institute be clarified, that the Director not be appointed by the President, and that it avoid any attempt to rival the universities. He proposed that Foreign Service officers be eligible for reinstatement even without continuous service in the government, as required in the draft. Finally and more important, he objected to the extremely detailed character of the legislation. This objection seems to have been based partly on his belief in the general desirability of administrative flexibility, partly on a feeling that the set statutory pattern would operate to the advantage of the Foreign Service officer group and to the disadvantage of the cultural and informational activities.

For some time Chapin had been engaged in a series of running disputes with Benton and was inclined to discount the substantive weight of Benton's arguments, but Chapin—and Russell and Panuch, who espoused the Foreign Service officers' cause throughout and who also had serious disputes with Benton—did not believe that the arguments could be treated cavalierly. Benton warned them that unless certain of his proposals were accepted he would fight the bill within the Department and also in the Congress; he would even testify against it before the Congressional committees. Chapin and Russell believed that Benton, in spite of his difficulties with Congress, had enough powerful friends there so that he might well succeed in blocking the bill, if some reasonable compromise were not reached; they decided that it was necessary to meet him half way. The description of the compromise they arrived at will be set forth below in connection with the settlement made with Clayton, for the two sets of objections and the two agreements merged.

Will Clayton, in charge of the economic activities of the Department, was a man of impeccable prestige. The economic functions had come to be accepted as an integral and permanent part of the work of the Department. Economic activities had been carried on even before the war; during the war they were greatly expanded and Clayton's staff was largely newly recruited. Some of the older Foreign Service officers might lament the importance attributed to loans, and trade agreements, and aid programs, and the like; but none could deny their significance. Some "political" officers at home and in the field tended to treat the economists as junior partners, a position not greatly relished by these newcomers, but at least Clayton was not engaged in a struggle for survival. To Clayton and his staff, the Foreign Service bill was of importance and interest, but it was not of critical consequence as it was to Benton. In fact, Clayton himself was not interested in these jurisdictional and organizational problems; his own considerable energies were devoted to the substantive programs of his office. Neither he nor his deputy intervened personally in the center of the controversy.

When Clayton received the March 2 draft for comment, he turned it over to an assistant, Fisher Howe, who began a careful canvass of all the divisions of the economic side in accordance with established practice. Although Clayton's own long and successful career had been exclusively in business until he accepted a position in the Reconstruction Finance Corporation as Jesse Jones's chief assistant, his office directors and division chiefs were almost all trained economists; most of them had some background of university teaching or of service as government economists, or both; most had been in the government long enough to be experienced in public service. Furthermore, unlike almost all the other officers of the Department, Clayton's staff habitually dealt with a large number of other agencies. Problems in inter-agency relationships were a normal part of their existence. They were fully aware of the functions of the Bureau of the Budget with respect to legislative clearance and administrative management, and during this period they had some exchange of views with the Budget examiners. Benton was kept regularly informed of their views and proposals, and there was also some informal discussion of the problems with officials of the Department of Commerce, perhaps with representatives of other agencies as well. In many ways, these economists had more community of interest with their professional colleagues in other government agencies than with their official colleagues, the Foreign Service officers assigned to the Department. Furthermore, a number of Clayton's principal assistants had learned during the war that some of the objectives that could not be attained through departmental channels were attainable when proposed by the head of an outside agency like the Foreign Economic Administration or the Board of Economic Warfare.

After the views of the various economic offices and divisions had been canvassed, a long and careful memorandum was drafted by Howe and initialed by thirteen officials, discussed with Benton or one of his assistants, and sent to Russell. It praised the bill as a whole, but listed seven points to which objection was raised, setting forth the reasons in each case, and making corresponding recommendations for amendment. As will be noted, there was considerable duplication with Benton's objections, although the grounds for objection were not always identical; the analysis tended to be fuller, and the reasoning more explicit.

1. The detailed character of the bill was opposed as leading to undesirable administrative inflexibility. (Other unstated reasons may have been in the background.) It was recommended that the bill be redrafted so as to eliminate all details that could be handled by administrative regulation. It was also recommended that all regulations be subject to departmental clearance before issuance.

The other six points were based on three general objectives: the need for better integration of the Department and the Foreign Service; improved facilities for effective action by officials temporarily assigned to the Foreign Service; and better integration of the Foreign Service with other departments. (These general considerations were not newly conceived; they grew out of the experience and felt needs of the economists.) The next six specific points were as follows:

2. The Reserve Corps was objected to because its name was misleading, because there was still no easy transfer from the Department to the field on either a temporary or permanent basis, because the Reserve officers would still lack title and other prestige attributes, and because present discriminations would be perpetuated or reinforced. (To Clayton's assistants, the Reserve was significant largely for their own and other government officials on temporary assignment, and less for persons hired from the outside.) Specific objection was raised to the provision that assigned Reserve officers be placed in the class appropriate to their Civil Service salary—whereby a P-8, for example, the top of the Civil Service hierarchy, receiving $8,750 (the bottom step) would be in Class 3. Also noted as objectionable were the limitation of diplomatic commissions to FSO's, and the limitation of promotions for appointed FSR's to one per tour of duty. All these restrictions were said to conflict with the basic principle of getting the best man for the job.

The correlative recommendations were to abolish the Reserve, provide for temporary assignment of departmental officials to the Foreign Service, with eligibility for commissions after four years of departmental service, and, finally, to provide for temporary appointments in the Service from the outside, with all benefits except retirement, and with temporary or local rank.

3. The third objection was to the provisions governing appointment of the Director General and the Deputy Director General. The memorandum proposed that the appointment be made by the Secretary, not by the President. The Director General (or Deputy) probably should not be a Foreign Service officer, the memorandum said, because the FSO's are too reluctant to change existing practices, because the civil servant has objectivity, and because the change would avoid the criticism that the bill is designed to protect the Service. Alternatively, as a general principle, it was urged as desirable not to limit the choice of the best man for the job.

The recommendations on these points followed naturally: transfer the appointive power to the Secretary and either bar FSO's from the offices of Director General and Deputy Director or leave the matter open.

4. The proposed Board of Foreign Service Personnel was criticized as continuing the existing Board, which was weak and not adequately representative of real governmental interests. It was therefore recommended that a Board of the Foreign Service be established in lieu of both the BFSP, the Board of Examiners and the Advisory Interdepartmental Committee; this Board would consist of the Assistant Secretary for Administration, the Director General, three other departmental officials (including at least two Assistant Secretaries) and representatives (on a basis of full participation) of Commerce, Agriculture, Treasury, Labor, and Interior. The Board would be empowered to make recommendations to the Secretary on all matters affecting the Service, and would be authorized to establish subordinate committees.

The logical basis for this recommendation was the often announced claim that the Foreign Service serves the whole government and not merely the State Department. But the proponents of this recommendation anticipated that the representatives of the outside agencies would usually be Clayton's allies in matters in dispute with the Director General. The recommendation that the Board be limited to the status of advisor to the Secretary was the result of a conviction that the final power should be vested in the department head.

5. The re-Americanization program was heartily supported. It was recommended that at least five years out of the first fifteen and at least two out of ten thereafter be spent in departmental service. This desire to strengthen the re-Americanization program stemmed from the belief that the Foreign Service was out of touch with modern thought—and also from the concern over the inadequate integration of the departmental and field services.

6. Objection was raised to the requirement that Inspectors be career officers. The recommendation proposed that this requirement be eliminated.

7. On the sections relating to the Foreign Service Institute, the memorandum opposed

the clauses authorizing the Director to prepare appropriate studies relating to the conduct of the foreign policy of the United States, and to co-ordinate such studies with the research conducted by other branches of the government or by private institutions. It was felt that this authority would take substantial power over foreign policy away from the regular branches of the Department and lodge it in the Institute. It was recommended that the authority be limited to power to contribute to other research.

7. FINAL DEPARTMENTAL COMPROMISES

Clayton's final memorandum to Russell was sent on March 26. Some of the disputed points came up before the Secretary's Staff Committee on March 27. There was a long conference with Clayton's group on April 1 where some of the points of difference were resolved. Benton dispatched his final memorandum on April 5. On April 11 the subject again came up before the Staff Committee, apparently unannounced and at the last moment. Chapin hoped that final approval would be obtained at this time. But the inclusion of this item on the agenda became known, and objections were raised, especially by Benton; the issues still in dispute were therefore referred to a subcommittee for settlement. The subcommittee met on the same day. Chapin, aware of revived interest in Congress (described below), sensitive to the need for decision, and fearful that Benton would block the bill, made many concessions. He worked out a series of compromises that settled everything but the lateral entrance argument, and that too was quickly settled. Thus the intra-departmental clearance process came to an end. As a result of these (and other earlier meetings) the following agreements were reached.

1. On the Board of Foreign Service Personnel, (a) the name was changed to the Board of the Foreign Service, as requested by Benton and Clayton and its powers were amended to cover "policies and procedures to govern the administration and personnel management of the Service" rather than to approve or disapprove specific personnel actions; (b) full membership was limited to three Assistant Secretaries of State, but with the Director General as an alternate; and (c) the economists' recommendation for inclusion of the other agencies with full participation, and for the abolition of the Advisory Committee and the Board of Examiners was rejected; this proposal was opposed by Benton as well as by Chapin. It may be noted here that Chapin did not expect that the highly restrictive language affecting Commerce and Agriculture would prevail; but he wished to make his compromises with those departments from an extreme rather than from an already compromised position. With respect to the Board of Examiners, the creation of statutory status would tend to guarantee the perpetuation of the same kind of Career Service that then existed; opposition to the provision automatically created a suspicion that the career concept itself was under attack.

2. On the requirement that the Director General and Deputy Director General be Foreign Service officers, there was a vigorous disagreement. The attack on this requirement was unexpected and was resented. Chapin felt that he could not face his own colleagues if he gave way. A memorandum drafted for him by Foster gave the following four reasons in support of the proposal: (1) the Director General needs firsthand knowledge of the Foreign Service; (2) it is essential that there be continuity in the office (but note was not taken of the fact that until recently the Assistant Secretary dealing with administration had traditionally enjoyed long tenure, while the Director General's term was limited in the bill itself to four years); (3) the requirement is essential to maintain morale in the Service (this was the point that was decisive to Foster); and (4) the requirement is an integral element in the career principle. Chapin finally prevailed, but not without a partial compromise; the requirement was made optional for the Deputy Director General. It was also agreed that the appointment would be made by the Secretary rather than the President.

3. On the Foreign Service Reserve, Clayton's recommendation (formulated by Howe) that the Reserve, as such, be abolished (not supported by Benton) was not accepted. Appar-

ently Chapin did not fully understand Howe's proposal to substitute a simple temporary field assignment procedure, especially for government employees, for a separate corps of temporary officers; nor perhaps did Howe fully understand the technical problems involved in the integration even temporarily of classified employees in a status system (see Appendix I); but the critical factor was Chapin's conviction of the need to protect the inviolability of the Career Service by putting protective barriers around the group that was to serve as a supplement to the officer corps.

On other major points, Benton and Clayton prevailed, at least partially; Reserve officers from government agencies would be assigned to a class consistent with qualifications, age and experience rather than with Civil Service salary, and would be paid on the Foreign Service rather than the Civil Service basis. All Reserve officers would be eligible for diplomatic and consular commissions, when appropriate, and "in all other cases, suitable rank and position shall be provided." The latter point was gained perhaps primarily as the result of Benton's persuasive explanation of the possibility of bringing from the outside prominent men for short tours of duty under the proper inducement; this agreement was contingent on Benton's acceptance of the flat limitation of four years per tour of duty with an enforced break of one year between tours. This and the other compromises were worked out in an atmosphere of some confusion, engendered partly by diverging lessons drawn from the experience with the Auxiliary and more by the ambiguity in the concept of the Reserve, including as it did both tenure and functional attributes.

Benton's proposal (not supported by Clayton) that the career minister lists include the names of FSR's was rejected; the career minister class was regarded by Chapin as peculiarly the prerogative of persons in the Career Service. Also rejected were proposals to remove the limitation of one promotion per tour of duty for FSR and the requirement that Inspectors be Foreign Service officers.

4. On the Institute, the proposed changes were accepted: appointment of the Director would be made by the Secretary, not the President, and the power to "prepare" and "co-ordinate" studies was withdrawn.

5. The disagreement on lateral entrance was sharp. Chapin pointed out in a memorandum to Russell that provision for the inclusion of FSR's and FSS's among those eligible to be appointed as FSO's, and the reduction in the required period of service from five to four years constituted "a very radical step"; but eventually Chapin evolved a compromise formula. The requirement was reduced to three years for those over 31 years of age. This would sufficiently safeguard the Service from persons who might seek to use lateral entrance to evade the examination system, for these would normally be young men.

6. Benton's proposal to separate the Foreign Service staff from the American clerks, and Clayton's to increase the periods of mandatory departmental service for Foreign Service officers were rejected.

7. On the major issue of excessive detail in the legislation, Chapin made no concessions; he defended the proposal on the substantive grounds indicated above, and in effect asserted his staff's inability to redraft the bill along different lines; obviously no one else in the Department was competent to do so at that point. The validity of the substantive argument was finally accepted at least by Benton who had become increasingly sympathetic with the problems of the Foreign Service officers.

While these compromises—some determined at the Secretary's Staff Committee meetings—were greeted with complimentary memoranda expressing appreciation of the good-will and patience shown by all, there was still some uneasiness. As has been said, the final agreements were completed on April 11. Eleven days later, Benton felt impelled to present a memorandum to the Secretary's Staff Committee correcting a "misunderstanding" of his attitude. Except for the four-year lateral entrance requirement, he was entirely satisfied. He regretted the detailed character of the legislation—but understood that there were good reasons for it. The bill merited support. Benton thereafter acted on this conclusion; he urged the Bureau of the Budget to approve the bill, he testified for it, and gave it support in other ways.

The first great hurdle was out of the way; others were still to be surmounted.

On April 16, Secretary Byrnes transmitted a draft (this was a partial redraft dated March 27 with the further compromises written in) to Harold D. Smith, the Director of the Bureau of the Budget. The Secretary's letter spoke of the months of work that had gone before and stated that the bill was unanimously approved within the Department. Mr. Byrnes referred to preliminary staff conversations with the Bureau's representatives and noted that they had questioned the detailed character of the proposed legislation. Observing that he had personally reviewed the draft bill, he said "its provisions represent the irreducible minimum which we must have as a statutory basis for the efficient operation of the Service and for proper safeguards of the principles on which the Service has been maintained for the past generation." He hoped that the Bureau could act quickly.

8. SIGNIFICANCE OF THE STATE DEPARTMENT REVISIONS

The participants in the long-drawn-out clearance process in the Department of State were of varying minds concerning the significance of the changes that had been made—and rejected.

To the officers of the Career Service the retention of the career principle without substantial impairment outweighed all other matters. Some of them were disturbed at the easier terms for lateral entrance and at the reduction of differences between FSO and FSR. Others were disturbed over different matters, such as the limitation of scope of the Institute. The apparent shift in the character of the Board away from detailed operations and toward policy was somewhat incalculable in its significance. Chapin, interested in action and glad to have ended the discussion on a fairly amicable basis, was presumably better satisfied than most of his assistants; they could hardly avoid some sense of having witnessed the sacrifice of points that they had labored to establish.

Benton was also satisfied. He had gained most of what he had asked on his two major points: control by the Board of the Foreign Service, and status and adequate treatment for the Reserve. He was sufficiently impressed by what he had heard of the difficulties of the Foreign Service officers to feel that a protected Career Service was justified and that the general approach of the bill was sound. Clayton's staff were less certain of the virtues of the revised bill, but they felt that no more could be gained under the circumstances. In any event, unlike Benton on one side, and Chapin and his associates on the other, this was not a matter of vital importance to them.

Looked at in retrospect, it is difficult to escape the conclusion that none of the fundamental alternatives adopted in the March 2 draft had been altered; the control had been somewhat shifted, the Reserve had been made more attractive; but the Career Service was hardly touched. The departmental critics had had doubts about the adequacy of the Foreign Service—adequacy in terms of flexibility and responsiveness, and treatment of new programs and new men; amendments of the March 2 draft were secured that would, it was hoped, lead toward an improvement in these respects. But these amendments proceeded on the voluntary or involuntary assumption that the desired results could be obtained within the general legal and institutional framework proposed by the Foreign Service officers.

To what extent Clayton, Benton and McCormack had a real choice is open to question. McCormack alone saw fit to question the basic assumptions directly. Clayton's staff were interested in the underlying thesis, but not vitally concerned; and all of them were criticizing a bill as equals, not as superiors. Russell had chosen to sponsor the bill, the Secretary was obviously not in a position to give it extended consideration. Acheson, the Under Secretary, was not in the direct current of decision because of Russell's intimate relationship with the Secretary. The existing organization of the Department—formal and informal—and the personalities involved, operated to preclude consideration and review from a vantage point that would have transcended the more immediate interest of the parties concerned.

One more aspect of the clearance process

deserves some attention. The parties to the controversy were deeply suspicious of each other, and suspicion engendered heat. When the draftsmen wrote in the provisions concerning the Director General, they had no thought that they were creating an issue; but when the provisions were opposed, they promptly suspected a plot to destroy the career concept. Similarly, Howe and his colleagues saw in the provisions concerning the Institute a disguised threat to the policy branches of the Department, though no such end had been sought by the draftsmen. Once or twice the Secretary's Staff Committee settled disputes of this kind; for the most part they had to be bargained out in an atmosphere of courteous distrust. This too affected the bill and the particular choice of alternatives it represents. The nature of this clearance process, as well as the actual results, are worthy of some reflection.

Part III. The Bureau of the Budget and Other Agencies Propose Amendments

9. FOREIGN SERVICE ATTITUDES TOWARD THE BUREAU OF THE BUDGET

When the Foreign Service bill finally received departmental approval, its next destination before submission to Congress was the Bureau of the Budget. Here it would be reviewed on behalf of the President and here inter-agency clearance would be undertaken. If the Foreign Service bill had followed a normal course, this process would have been completed before the initiation of Congressional discussion. A normal course was not followed; but from the standpoint of the Bureau officials and the officials of other interested agencies the focus of action on the bill for the five weeks following April 16 was in the Bureau. And from Chapin's standpoint, the period began with Bureau and inter-agency review as his chief concern. Before discussing the Bureau's function and its operations in this case, it may be useful to consider first the attitude and anticipations of Chapin and his associates when the process started.

Until 1943, the Foreign Service had known the Bureau largely as an agency that looked upon its appropriation estimates with what seemed like a jaundiced eye. In 1943, active relations with the administrative management activities of the Bureau had begun in connection with the establishment of the Office of the Foreign Service. At this time, the Foreign Service officers involved were rather pleased with the technical assistance given them. Steyne's relations with the Bureau officials in the Joint Survey Group were friendly.

In 1945, there was a good deal of resentment when the Bureau demanded a functional analysis of each mission in connection with the budget estimates for the fiscal year 1947 (for inclusion in the Budget Message of January 1946). It was felt that the Bureau did not understand the needs of the Foreign Service, imposed unfair burdens on it, and was unsympathetic towards all Foreign Service officers. This feeling was intensified by disagreements about allowances early in 1946; the Foreign Service officers believed that the Bureau officials were interfering or trying to interfere in the administration of allowances and failed to understand the necessity for the rent allowance. (It need hardly be added that the Bureau officials looked on these disagreements in a quite different light.)

The latent antipathy between the two groups had also been strengthened during 1945 by the dark rumors about the reorganization proposals in the Bureau's report for Mr. Byrnes. In the same year, in connection with the Manpower Act, more difficulty arose. It will be recalled that a proposal to permit the entrance of 120 new Foreign Service officers at various grades had been included in emergency legislation presented to the Congress in 1944. Because of Congressional opposition, this provision had been withdrawn from the measure that later became the Bloom Bill, approved in May 1945. In spite of this setback, and in spite of much ill-feeling in the Service, Chapin persisted. A special Manpower Bill was prepared and ready for submission in October 1945. It proposed the entrance of not over 120 new officers in Classes III to VIII (VIII was the lowest class above the three "unclassified" classes), with eligibility limited to persons under the age of 42. When this bill was submitted to the Bureau for clearance, vigorous objection was made to all three provisions. Indeed Chapin and his associates felt that they were faced with an ultimatum. In consequence, though with great reluctance on Chapin's part, the bill was changed to permit the entrance of not over 250 new officers, with all classes open, and without any age restriction.

In the November 1945 issue of the *American Foreign Service Journal,* an editorial commenting on these changes remarked that while we "welcome the expert assistance of the Bureau of the Budget," these changes would tend to undermine the merit system and impair the morale of the Service.

This comment was significant. Chapin (whose views were, of course, reflected in the editorial) felt, and not without some reason, that his persistent support of a Manpower Bill was a bold move on his part. He and his associates were annoyed—and the annoyance persisted—because it seemed to them that the Bureau failed to appreciate the way in which he was challenging the old guard of the Foreign Service; indeed they felt that the Bureau was virtually accusing them of aiding the old guard.

The comment was significant for a second reason as well. It indicated little awareness of the Bureau's positive role in the legislative clearance process. Chapin understood that the Bureau might object to legislative provisions involving larger appropriations, and he thought that they might offer technical suggestions; he knew that in some way they insured interagency clearance; but he and all his associates assumed that this was—or ought to be—the limit of the Bureau's sphere—or legitimate sphere—of activity. His understanding of the Bureau's function was, as it happened, widely shared throughout the Department of State, and Russell, for example, had no apparent desire to urge on Chapin any thorough-going conformity with Bureau clearance procedures.

Later, in May 1946, when the intensive discussions of the Foreign Service bill were started, a request was made by Chapin or Harrington of the Legal Adviser of the Department for an opinion on the Bureau's power to inquire into all the details of the bill. Increasingly, the Office of the Foreign Service felt that it was being subjected to an unfair inquisition by people who did not understand the Service and who were interfering in matters that did not concern them. The Foreign Service officers had had no experience abroad with officials whose careers were devoted to the procedural and organizational aspects of government and they rather looked down on these activities. They felt more competent to pass judgment on what was necessary for the administration of the Foreign Service than anyone else, and they were inclined to believe that it was no one else's concern. They were sure that other career services—as they would have described them—like the Army or the Public Health Service, were not harassed by the Bureau, and they were therefore convinced that they were singled out for discriminatory treatment.

One other aspect of Chapin's attitude towards the Bureau deserves mention. Thinking of the Bureau primarily as an agency for reducing appropriation estimates, and remembering that Congress was also such an agency, Chapin was inclined to think of the Bureau as a quasi-Congressional body, whose voice would be heard with respect in the Congress. He rather anticipated that Bureau opposition to points in the draft bill would be almost automatically echoed by Congress.

A word of comment on relations at the top levels may also be useful. Mr. Smith, the Director, had dealt with the Secretary on many problems; the Secretary tended to treat him somewhat as an official of lower rank, but their relations were fairly cordial. However, the relations between Mr. Paul H. Appleby, the Assistant Director (i.e., the one statutory Assistant Director, equivalent to Deputy Director in most agencies) and the Secretary were not sympathetic; but Mr. Appleby and Mr. Dean Acheson, the Under Secretary, worked well together.

During the period from January to August 1946, Mr. Byrnes was abroad at two critical points: from June 13 to July 14, and from July 27 until after the bill became law. Mr. Smith resigned on June 19, and Mr. Webb, his successor, did not take office until July 31. But Mr. Appleby, as Acting Director, and Mr. Acheson, as Acting Secretary, were limited in various ways by their lack of full status. The possibility of a resolution of some of the difficulties by a firm agreement after face to face discussion between the agency heads was precluded by these circumstances. The use of this technique was not attempted during the period when it might have been arranged.

Finally, it is to be noted that the Department's attitude toward the Bureau may have been affected, at the top levels, by the Bureau's relations with the White House. The spirit of mutual confidence that had grown between President Roosevelt and the Bureau did not exist at this time with President Truman. President Truman and his immediate staff were not inclined to attribute much weight to the Bureau's activities or recommendations outside the technical task of budget preparation. They rather felt that the Bureau had spread into alien fields. This attitude was sensed by many department heads.

10. THE BUREAU OF THE BUDGET AND ITS LEGISLATIVE REFERENCE PROCEDURES

The legislative reference functions of the Bureau of the Budget have developed slowly over the years. Originally, in 1921, the first Director, Charles G. Dawes, required the clearance of fiscal legislation through his office, relying for this requirement on a broad interpretation of Section 206 of the Budget and Accounting Act of 1921 which forbids the departments to submit requests for appropriations or for increases in appropriations outside the President's budget, except at the request of Congress.

In 1935, clearance for non-fiscal legislation through the National Emergency Council was first required: in 1937, this function was transferred to the Bureau of the Budget, an agency which itself was transferred from the Treasury to the newly established Executive Office of the President in 1939.

The clearance of non-fiscal legislation has no very clear statutory base; it relies rather on the President's general powers under the Constitution to direct the operations of his executive officers, to advise the Congress on needed measures, and to approve or disapprove bills passed by the Congress. With the gradual development of the Bureau as a rounded and well-manned staff agency for the President, there has been a correlative development within the Bureau of the concept of an over-all Presidential program and of the Bureau's own clearance function.

The function includes two different but closely related processes: the clearance of reports to Congressional committees on proposed or pending legislation (including legislative proposals initiated by the executive departments) and the clearance of enrolled bills. An "enrolled bill" is one which has been duly passed by both Houses and transmitted to the President for his approval or disapproval within the constitutional ten-day period, excluding Sundays. (Because enrolled bills are frequently available before formal transmittal to the White House, the working period is usually about thirteen or fourteen days.) At this stage the Bureau circulates facsimiles of the enrolled bill to all interested agencies, collects their comments, summarizes the issues and transmits the file to the White House, together with its own recommendations for signature or veto.

The clearance process for agency recommendations in 1946 was governed by a deceptively simple rule. Budget Circular A-19 (edition now obsolete, but in effect in 1946) merely requires that:

1. There shall be submitted to the Bureau of the Budget, before submission to the Congress, or any committee or member thereof, two copies

of each recommendation or report concerning proposed or pending legislation requested from or advanced by any department or establishment or any officer thereof.

2. The submitting department or establishment will be thereafter advised by the Bureau of the Budget as to the relationship of the legislation, or of the report or recommendation thereon, to the program of the President; and when such recommendation or report is then submitted to the Congress, or to a Committee or member thereof, it shall include a statement of the advice so received from the Bureau of the Budget. (If, in any case, time will not permit the ascertainment of advice of this character from the Bureau of the Budget, the report or testimony shall include a statement to this effect.)

The formal requirement does not prevent any agency from sending any proposed bill or recommendation to Congress; it merely requires a notification of the Bureau's advice. There are, however, two fairly obvious sanctions to inhibit the transmittal of measures or recommendations opposed by the Bureau: the Director sees the President and may, if the circumstances are propitious, request the President's intervention; and secondly, the Bureau normally makes the final recommendation to the White House on enrolled bills, and all proposed bills that secure Congressional approval by definition become enrolled bills. It may be noted in passing that effective consideration of the enrolled bill is largely dependent on the establishment of an adequate file during the earlier stage; and concurrence in a draft bill is almost full assurance of approval later on of the enrolled bill. Aside from sanctions, the relation of the Bureau to the President renders an agency head open to some suspicion of disloyalty if he disregards the Bureau's advice without obtaining the President's personal approval.

The interest of the Bureau in the clearance process is, in simplified terms, threefold: (1) It acts as spokesman for the President's over-all policy, as it understands that policy; (2) It acts as intermediary to secure agreement among all interested agencies when proposed legislation is of interest to more than one agency; and (3) It acts to represent its own interests (which are presumably consistent with the President's, or at least general rather than special) in those areas in which it has statutory responsibilities—particularly its responsibilities for the President's budget (handled within the Bureau by the Division of Estimates) and its responsibilities for government organization (handled by the Division of Administrative Management). (In some instances, though not in this case, the other major Divisions of the Bureau—Fiscal, and Statistical Standards—are also concerned.) The clearance process itself is handled by the Division of Legislative Reference; but in 1946 the head of this Division was in considerable part concerned with the more formal aspects of clearance, and was disposed to rely rather heavily on policy views of individual examiners in the other divisions without reference to the Director or Assistant Director.

In the case of the Foreign Service Act of 1946, various Bureau officials were acting largely with an eye to their statutory responsibilities and only secondarily in their role as staff advisors to the President and leaders of inter-agency clearance; this special emphasis on the Bureau's own operating interests, in itself quite natural and normal, tended to make for a greater concern with certain secondary problems than would presumably have been evinced if the Bureau officials had not been so professionally interested in the subject matter. Substantive work on the draft bill was centered in the International Affairs Branch of the Division of Administrative Management, with some assistance from other Bureau experts on specialized problems. This branch (later abolished) was unusual though not unique in the Bureau in that it performed all the work in its field for the Estimates Division, as well as for its own; each of its members was assigned, as occasion might arise, to either activity, or of course, to legislative reference work.

In 1946, the chief of the International Activities Branch was Sherman S. Sheppard. Sheppard had held this position since 1944; before that he had been for some time Executive Director of the New Orleans Bureau of Governmental Research and had spent his whole working career in public administration. The newly designated Deputy Chief was Alvin Roseman. Roseman, who had been in the Bureau a year, had previously worked for ten years in public and private welfare and employment organizations; he had recently spent a year abroad as assistant, later deputy chief of an UNRRA mission. The examiner specifically assigned to the Foreign Service was Winthrop M. Southworth, Jr., who had spent about ten years with semipublic associations and with a firm of management consultants. He had started in the Bureau in 1942. On Southworth fell the major burden of detailed work. All three men were in their late thirties or early forties. It may be added that both Southworth and Roseman had made various trips abroad before coming to the Bureau, and that all three had considerable familiarity, as a result of their official visits, with the operations of various U. S. missions abroad.

The Assistant Director in charge of the Division of Administrative Management, Donald C. Stone, was a well-known figure in the field of public administration in and out of the government. He had been in charge of the Division since its formation in 1939. His past experience included many contacts with public officials and students of public administration in other countries. He and Southworth had also been members of two of the joint survey teams sent out in 1945. (See Appendix II—Biographies.)

In observing the background of these Bureau officials, it is to be noted that as a matter of basic approach and from experience, their sympathies lay with Civil Service rather than Career Service concepts. They preferred and perhaps had more understanding of employment systems characterized by free entrance at all levels and inter-agency movement; and they thought more easily in terms of rank according to assignment than rank in terms of status. Their questioning of the various attributes of the "Career" system aroused suspicions and antagonisms. They and the Foreign Service officers did not speak the same language. While the Bureau officials were thoroughly aware of the guild characteristics of the Career Service, they were perhaps less conscious of the fact that their own group also had, to some degree, the attributes of a professional guild—open, not closed, but nevertheless one in which the members tended to constitute a corporate body rather than a mere collection of individuals.

One other characteristic of the Bureau's organization and operating habits affected its handling of the Foreign Service bill. On the administrative side (though not on the program side), the Department of State is built like a pyramid with many layers: the Bureau is a flat pyramid. Thus an outline sketch of the formal organizations in 1946 might look like this:

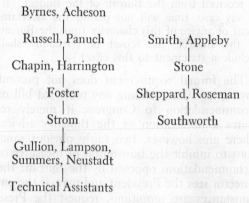

Byrnes, Acheson
Russell, Panuch
Chapin, Harrington
Foster
Strom
Gullion, Lampson, Summers, Neustadt
Technical Assistants

Smith, Appleby
Stone
Sheppard, Roseman
Southworth

In this sketch deputies have not been indicated as constituting separate levels since for the most part separate clearance with the deputy was not required. Activities in the Department in relation to the Foreign Service Act had five major focuses—since Strom and his immediate assistants acted largely as a team; and since Foster was closely associated with their work, at times it may have had only four. In the Bureau there were three focuses, with Sheppard and his assistants acting as a team. As a result of this disparity in structure, Southworth, clearly a "working staff" member, dealt directly with Chapin, who held a "prestige" position, as well as with all of Chapin's subordinates; in the later stages, Roseman and Sheppard also dealt with the same group. This circumstance increased the difficulties of all three, but especially of Southworth; the need for working side-by-side with the working team in the earlier stages made it hard to maintain a position of almost judicial aloofness during the more formal hearings.

Direct relations between the two agencies at the top levels were limited and carried on mostly by letter from Secretary (or Acting Secretary) to Director (or Acting Director), and vice versa. As will be seen, Stone did have one important meeting with the Acting Secretary, and Russell one with the Director. Benton also had a few direct contacts with Bureau officials, especially Stone.

11. REVIEW OF THE FOREIGN SERVICE BILL BY THE BUREAU OF THE BUDGET

The Bureau of the Budget was never completely out of touch with the progress of legislative planning for the Foreign Service. Bureau officials had participated actively in the early planning work in 1944 and 1945. They had served in the Joint Survey Group and in the field survey teams sent out in 1945. The imprint of some of their recommendations had carried through the planning process and could be seen in the draft bill now presented for their consideration.

In spite of this earlier background of Bureau participation, there were periods when the Bureau officials were not in close touch with Foster's activities. Thus during the first period of active statutory drafting in December 1945 and January 1946, the work went forward without consultation with the Bureau's representatives. Southworth, the Budget Examiner assigned to the Foreign Service, seems not to have seen the December 28 draft, or the so-called first draft bill of January 3 or the second draft bill of February 1. This procedure was, of course, normal from the standpoint of the draftsman. In some cases, assistance from the Budget examiners is requested by an agency before any drafting begins, but ordinarily agencies attempt to work out their own problems and secure a concerted departmental viewpoint before invoking the aid or approval of the Bureau.

Southworth's first definite information on progress and the new timetable came on February 20. On that day, Foster, the Chief of Foreign Service Planning, telephoned to advise him of Chapin's deadline decision and of their new plans to have a bill completely cleared within the Department and ready for Bureau consideration on March 15. Foster told Southworth, as he had told Chapin, of his serious doubts of the wisdom of this procedure. He also told Southworth that a copy of the draft would be made available to him on the day it went to the Secretary for final approval. A few days later, Southworth received and sent on to his superiors a copy of the February 11 draft of the "Principal Features of Foreign Service Legislation." He expressed hope that the deadline would be met and that an approved draft would be ready for consideration by the 15th of March. A day later, he gave more details of progress to his superiors. He had had a long conversation with Strom of the Division of Foreign Service Planning, who described the whole background of the current situation to pave the way for prompt clearance.

Sheppard penciled the following note on Southworth's memorandum: "How do we get in our suggestions before the situation becomes too rigid?"

Foster was better than his word. He gave Southworth two copies of the March 2 draft, even though it was not an approved version and would undoubtedly be changed as a result of departmental discussions; but he probably did not anticipate that the modifications would be as significant as those actually obtained by Clayton and Benton. When Southworth received the draft, he arranged for the preparation of a digest of its contents. On March 26, he wrote to Sheppard with Roseman's concurrence, attaching a copy of this digest and announcing that he was circulating it within the Bureau in preparation for a staff meeting that Stone was to hold during the following week. He indicated that some of the probable major issues might include administration by an interdepartmental board vs. administration by the Secretary, and the new salary scale. He also indicated that a revised edition (the March 27 draft) would be ready in a week or two. He had already been informed that in this later draft the Director General would be appointed by the Secretary rather than by the President, and that the staff officers and clerks would be consolidated into a single staff corps. He also had been told that this draft would round out the formal material of the bill by adding a statement of objectives. Roseman, reading the memorandum, set down numerous comments. He pointed out that the bill raised many issues and said, "Obviously the bill is much too detailed." He likewise raised the question of the relationship of the bill to the report on the organization of the State Department prepared by the Bureau for Secretary Byrnes in August 1945. Since this relationship was to raise a continual series of questions for the Bureau's staff, it may be useful to pause at this point to outline briefly those aspects of the report which directly concern the Foreign Service.

The recommendations affecting the Foreign Service in what the Bureau officials always referred to as the "Byrnes Report" (and the State Department as the "Budget Bureau Report") were based on two assumptions about existing defects in the Foreign Service and departmental organization. One was the assumption or conclusion that the Foreign Service was not always responsive to the Secretary of State; the second was the belief that the gap between the geographic or political offices of the Department and the functional, especially the economic offices, was too wide and that the harmful effects of this separation were aggravated by the fact that the Foreign Service officers assigned to departmental service were almost exclusively assigned to the geographic offices. With these two considerations in mind, the report made the following eight recommendations relating to the Foreign Service:

1. An immediate personnel study with the objective of removing the barriers that prevent the Secretary of State from recruiting and assigning qualified personnel wherever they are needed. In connection with this recommendation, the report described the personnel system of the Rogers Act as one in which Foreign Service officers are taken on at the bottom and are protected from "politics" by reserving all jobs for them except the chief of mission positions. The report concluded that an "elite corps" was no longer needed and that it produced unfortunate results—it tended to "foreignize" the service. The report took the position that under present-day conditions Civil Service provides adequate protection against improper political influence.

2. An immediate consolidation of the Foreign Service and departmental management offices, such as budget, personnel, etc.

3. A continuing program of recruitment at all levels. This recruitment should bring in immediately a considerable number of specialists from the Department and from other agencies, such as the Army and Navy, but the recruitment program should not be merely a "one-shot" affair. The report asserted that this proposal did not constitute "unfair competition" to the Foreign Service officers who had been recruited under the Rogers Act procedure.

4. Basic equalization of pay abroad and at home with extra allowances for service abroad and some special arrangement for Foreign Service officers serving in the Department.

5. Frequent rotation between Washington and abroad. In this connection it was proposed that there be refresher courses and a fair division of assignments of Foreign Service officers to the geographical and the functional offices, and vice versa.

6. The use of technically qualified persons for supervision and administration.

7. Systematic in-service training.

Sheppard, Roseman, and Southworth had all worked on the Byrnes Report, and Stone had had general oversight over the undertaking. Nevertheless, no clear resolution was made at this time of the fundamental disparities between the Report and the new draft bill. Stone's first reaction was just like Roseman's: the bill was far too detailed, and he asked why, if the President could be authorized to issue regulations governing Civil Service employees numbering hundreds and hundreds of thousands or even millions, he could not be entrusted to regulate the same matters for a Foreign Service group numbering only a few thousand.

During this period of March and April 1946, Southworth was in close touch with the active discussions that were proceeding within the Department of State, and assisted in the development of the various proposals for amendments. Since much of his thinking and the thinking of his superiors was paralleled (and even, as indicated, in part activated) by the criticisms made by McCormack, Benton and Clayton, no very active work was undertaken within the Bureau pending the outcome of this intradepartmental clearance process; the crystallizing issues were apparently not discussed at the top levels of the Bureau. Copies of the digest that Southworth had had prepared were made available to specialists throughout the Bureau and a memorandum was circulated indicating the differences between the provisions of the draft bill, and the recommendations of the Byrnes Report and of the 1945 field survey reports. Some of the specialists in the Bureau began to raise objections to certain technical provisions in the draft. Finally, on April 16, Secretary Byrnes made his formal submission of the bill to the Bureau of the Budget, and the time for active review had come. Since the March 27 draft did not include all the changes agreed on within the Department, the discussions with the representatives of the Foreign Service were maintained at this stage on an informal basis. Nevertheless, the period was one of active progress. Numerous changes were made, several of some consequence. Some of these arose easily out of the informal discussions between the Foreign Service officers and the Bureau officials. Thus a complicated rating list procedure for promotions, in the March 2 draft, was completely abandoned, a decision recommended by the Bureau officials, but already matured because Foster had come to the conclusion that the rating list procedure would not work satisfactorily in conjunction with the selection-out procedure. The salary scale for Foreign Service officers was amended by reducing the career-minister salary from $15,000 to $13,500, while retaining $13,500 for the top bracket of Class 1, a final salary compromise based on a judgment of Congressional tolerance. One change made specifically at the instance of the Foreign Service representatives was a prohibition against service of any person on a Promotion Review Board for more than two years; thus the prejudice of one individual could not block an officer's promotion indefinitely. Another change probably initiated by the Foreign Service group was the substitution of the Director General for the Board of Foreign Service Personnel as nominating authority for appointments or assignments to the Reserve. On the other hand, it was the Bureau officials who secured the deletion of any mention of the Board of Foreign Service Examiners from the draft; they could and did point to the fact that the system had worked successfully for twenty years without statutory authorization. But while the change was accepted, it was accepted with great reluctance. Alteration in the character of the examination system could have far-reaching effects on the Career Service.

All these and many other lesser modifications took time. More formal hearings and inter-agency clearance were deferred while a new complete draft was prepared. On May 1, the new draft was ready. On May 3, the draft was transmitted to the Bureau, and, on May 6, the Acting Assistant Director for Legislative Reference circulated copies of it to the Departments of Commerce, Agriculture, Interior, Labor, and Treasury, and to the Civil Service Commission for comment.

During the month of May preliminary conversations were held with representatives of these agencies but none of the formal replies was received until June. In the meantime, the Bureau officials proceeded with a long detailed consideration of the bill. The consideration was preceded by a discussion at a staff meeting in Stone's office on April 30. The agenda for this staff meeting consisted of a memorandum prepared by Southworth outlining some of the significant features of the bill, raising questions about them and in a number of cases suggesting answers; the questions all relate to Titles I-V, for the revised draft of Titles VI-XI was still in preparation. In summary form, the questions may be listed as follows with the recommendations, where any were given, in parentheses:

1. Should there be a career service within the Foreign Service?
2. Should all who serve abroad be included in the Foreign Service?
3. Should the Secretary be solely responsible for the direction of the Service?
4. Should there be separate legislation governing the relations of the Foreign Service with the Department of Agriculture?
5. Should the provisions of Title I be approved?
6. Should there be a Director General, and should he be a Foreign Service officer? (Eliminate.)
7. Should there be a statutory Board of the

Foreign Service? (No. Only an Advisory Interdepartmental Board.)

8. Should there be separate provisions authorizing the performance of reporting and other services for the Departments of Agriculture and Commerce or should the work for these agencies be covered by the general provision authorizing such service for any government agency? (The latter.)

9. Should there be a Foreign Service Reserve? (Yes.)

10. Should the new system of classes be approved? (Yes.)

11. Should there be a Staff Corps? (Yes, unless the bill is delayed.)

12. Should the statute specify the precise method for determining the date of entry on duty and departure from duty for salary purposes and for fixing the within-grade salary bracket of persons appointed to Class 6? (No.)

13. Should senatorial confirmation be required on the promotion of Foreign Service officers from one class to another? (No.)

14. Should there be pay differentials for hardship posts? (Yes, but this should be amended later in the light of a current government-wide study of this subject.)

15. Should the provision for four- or three-year mandatory service in the Department of State or the Foreign Service prior to lateral entrance as a Foreign Service officer be approved?

16. Should the reinstatement provisions for Foreign Service officers who leave the Service be approved? (They should be broadened.)

17. Should the detailed provisions covering appointments and assignments be approved? (They should be eliminated.)

18. Should there be provisions for custodians to be supplied by the Army as well as by the Navy?

19. Should the provisions for Foreign Service officer assignments to government agencies, etc., and for three-year mandatory service in the United States out of the first fifteen be approved? (Yes.)

20. Should the temporary payment of the higher Civil Service salary to Foreign Service officers assigned to a government agency be approved together with the use of this higher salary as the basis for computing retirement benefits?

The substance of this memorandum has been outlined in full, because it is a good introduction to what faced the Foreign Service officers during the course of their hearings before the Bureau of the Budget. The examination of the bill ranged all the way from the most searching questions on its basic premises to the most careful concern with minor details like a proposed authorization for the provision of Army as well as Navy custodians.

The results of the meeting in Stone's office were to confirm Southworth in his conclusions and in general, to approve recommendations which would tend to eliminate detail and concentrate power over the Service in the hands of the Secretary rather than in the hands of a board or subordinate official. In spite of underlying opposition, the basic issue of the continuation of an exclusive Career Service went largely by default, primarily because Stone realized that this draft bill represented a late, not an early, stage in the drafting process; to him it seemed too late to cast out the work that had been done and to start afresh—and a consolidation of the field and departmental service would have meant just this. All that could be accomplished now would be to keep the administrative structure flexible so that the difficulties of a future consolidation would be decreased. Appleby agreed with Stone's conclusions, largely because of a conviction that it would be politically unwise to attempt any fundamental revision of the Foreign Service at this time. The other officials were also opposed to the concept of a separate exclusive Career Service, but they recognized the complexities of consolidation and they too realized that any decision to require consolidation would mean a tremendous delay, if it were accepted. The issue remained as a nagging doubt throughout the negotiations on the bill and it led the Bureau officials to seek in all instances greater uniformity with Civil Service procedures and regulations whenever this seemed feasible. Nevertheless, there was an acceptance in principle of the continuation of the Rogers Act Career Service, even though a grudging one.

Meetings between representatives of the Office of the Foreign Service and various representatives of the Bureau began on Monday, May 6. The bill was gone through, title by title, section by section, page by page, line by line. On May 16, Chapin sent to Southworth six memoranda listing agreed changes in the draft bill. On May 23, a seventh memorandum was sent. Other recommendations, as has been seen, had already been reflected in the May 1 draft. By the end of the month, no further progress seemed possible. On May 29, Southworth wrote, "Although we have had very good success in making suggestions to State with respect to Foreign Service legislation, we have now gone about as far as we can on an informal basis."

The term "informal" referred, of course, to the fact that agreements and disagreements resulting from these meetings were still subject to confirmation by higher authority. The next step—moving from the "informal" to a formal basis—would be a memorandum to the Director raising the major issues still in dispute and seeking approval of the provisions of the bill, including the changes agreed to date. The preparation of a memorandum for Sheppard to send to the Director—it represented the combined thinking of Southworth, Roseman and Sheppard with careful review by Stone—was itself a substantial undertaking. The final draft dated June 11, prepared by Southworth, covered fifteen pages, exclusive of appendices. Its introduction gave a history of the legislation and listed briefly the main provisions. At the last moment, the first fruit of inter-agency clearance was received in the form of a letter from the Department of Commerce, but otherwise, as the memorandum stated, "based upon staff conferences with representatives of these agencies, we have anticipated agency positions."

After this introductory statement the memorandum was divided into three major sections: Part A consists of issues. The issues are: (1) the administration of the Service; (2) the Foreign Service Institute; (3) the appointment of Foreign Service officers at other than the bottom grade; (4) the appointment of career ministers; (5) the assignment of custodial personnel by War and Navy; and (6) leave provisions.

It will be noted that here again there is a mixture of great and small. The recommendations follow the lines that had been previously worked out with Stone. The memorandum recommends the elimination of the Board of the Foreign Service and says that "OFS (i.e., the Office of the Foreign Service) reluctantly agrees." It also recommends the elimination of the statutory provision for an Interdepartmental Advisory Board, noting in each case, however, that the Secretary would undoubtedly establish such Boards on his own authority even if they were not constituted by statute. It is noted that the Commerce Department desires a Board of the Foreign Service in order to have statutory participation in the administration of the Service and that the House Foreign Affairs Committee—of which more anon—also desires a statutory Board. The second recommendation is for the elimination of the office of the Director General and proposes instead that the Secretary be empowered to "administer the Foreign Service through such officer or officers as he may designate."

Basis for our recommendation is general Bureau policy to place full responsibility for administration in agency heads. OFS definitely opposes this recommendation. It believes the provisions essential for continuity of operations and Service morale. Presumably it also desires the provision as protection for the career system. A subcommittee of the House Foreign Affairs Committee is reportedly "belligerently" for this provision. If there must be a Director General, we recommend removal of the Class I limitation. This position should be filled with the best available person from either civil service or foreign service. OFS desires the limitation largely on the grounds of Service morale.

The memorandum recommends against the establishment of a Foreign Service Institute by statute.

Statutory establishment of an Institute with its own Director (although "under the general supervision of the Director General") would break down the principle of centralized responsibility for the Foreign Service. General plans for the Institute, moreover, are elaborate and contemplate policy studies which we believe are properly the responsibility of the research and intelligence activity of the Department. We believe that a well run training program fully supported by OFS and Department officials (which has not been the case to date) will be as effective as an Institute.

In lieu of an Institute, the memorandum proposes that the Secretary be authorized to provide for training and instruction and that certain specific additional authority be given him, such as the right to pay tuition expenses for specialized study.

The memorandum describes the restrictions on lateral entrance into the corps of Foreign Service officers, citing the three- and four-year provision as "A great step forward." It recommends that the prior service requirement be relaxed to cover service in any government agency and not only in the State Department, although pointing out that the Foreign Service believes it not feasible to evaluate performance in other government agencies. The memorandum comments, "We believe there should be no distinction between State and other agencies of government." The memorandum recommends that promotion to the class of career minister be made by the Secretary rather than by the President with Senatorial confirmation. This recommendation follows from an assumption that the Foreign Service officers had agreed to the elimination of Presidential appointment and Senatorial confirmation for promotions from Classes 6 to 1. Both recommendations are based on a desire to free the White House of the great mass of paper work involved in processing dozens or even hundreds of promotion papers each year.

The comments on the two minor recommendations are not significant.

Part B of the memorandum lists thirteen major changes agreed on at the staff level. Most of the changes are not of great consequence and most are fairly technical in character, although the recommendations are usually based on broad principles of public policy or administration. Thus, the Bureau opposed the fifteen-year-citizenship requirement for Foreign Service officers on the ground that it is improper to distinguish among American citizens; but a compromise on a ten-year requirement was agreed on in view of the Foreign Service conviction that this limitation was necessary for security reasons.

It is interesting to note that almost the only agreed changes that would tend to represent a reduction of expenditures (which the Foreign Service officers had regarded as the Bureau's chief interest) are the reduction in the proposed salary for career ministers from $15,000 to $13,500, agreed on in April, and an exclusion from participation in the Foreign Service retirement system of those comparatively few Foreign Service officers who resign to take service with the Department. The Bureau's representatives expressed no basic opposition to the rather generous salary scale and other benefits proposed for Foreign Service officers and employees.

12. INTER-AGENCY CLEARANCE AND BUDGET BUREAU PROPOSALS

The first formal request by the State Department for Budget Bureau clearance had been contained in Mr. Byrnes's letter of April 16. Full-scale review in the Bureau had begun on May 6. The conclusion of the review process and the beginning of decisions were marked by Sheppard's memorandum of June 11.

But this course of events was paralleled, and affected, by other events elsewhere. A day or two after May 6, Southworth was told by Chapin that a Subcommittee had been appointed by the Committee on Foreign Affairs of the House of Representatives to consider new Foreign Service legislation and that it wished to hold hearings. Chapin requested permission from the Bureau to proceed.

Southworth discussed this inconvenient request with Sheppard. Both feared that Congressional attitudes would become fixed before the Bureau had obtained favorable action by the Department on its own recommendations. But the Bureau obviously could not prevent a Congressional committee from holding hearings, or from requiring testimony from departmental witnesses. With Sheppard's approval, Southworth told Chapin to go ahead, but obtained, as he thought, some agreement that the discussions would merely cover general problems, and that no final commitments would be made. How realistic this agreement or assumed agreement was is open to question. The Subcommittee could insist on obtaining the text of the draft bill and an expression of the views of the Foreign Service representatives; it could make its decisions regardless of the Bureau's recommendations or progress. Chapin and his associates, in the nature of the case, would be sole spokesmen for the Service, the Department, the Bureau, and the President before the Subcommittee. But regardless of these speculations and of possible future difficulties from this source, Sheppard and Southworth had, as they saw it, a job to do. The Bureau officials proceeded on their regular course, somewhat troubled, but convinced of their obligation to carry out their assigned functions.

During the earlier hearings in May, the Foreign Service representatives apparently did not inform the Bureau officials of Subcommittee attitudes; toward the end of the month they reported the Subcommittee's views on various disputed points. A number of these reported views are reflected in the June 11 memorandum, but even at that date Southworth and his associates had no clear awareness of Subcommittee progress. Actually, as will be seen, the Subcommittee was by then farther advanced than the Bureau. For reasons also explained below, at that point Chapin and Russell decided to send to the Director a letter requesting final clearance of the draft bill. In this letter, dated June 12, Secretary Byrnes defended and asked approval of provisions respecting the Director General and the Board of the Foreign Service, but indicated his willingness to withdraw the provisions establishing the Institute.

This final attempt to reach a compromise on a semipersonal basis with Mr. Smith arrived at the Bureau of the Budget just when Sheppard's long memorandum had presented all the issues to the Director. The arrival of the letter forced a further consideration of the situation. Since the Bureau officials were unaware of the extent of progress made by the Subcommittee, they did not realize that the Byrnes letter was perhaps to be regarded more as an ultimatum than as a proposal. By this time, too, the letters from the interested agencies began to come in. The Commerce letter was dated June 10 and was amended by a second letter of June 19; the Agriculture letter, June 14; the letter from the Civil Service Commission, June 24. All these required some fresh consideration and some further resolution of the Bureau position. The subject was discussed with representatives of some of these agencies. Two weeks were spent in mulling over these problems and in trying to decide on a course of action. During these two weeks, Mr. Smith resigned, and was succeeded by Mr. Appleby who served as Acting Director from June 19 to July 31.

Of all the interested agencies, the Department of Commerce had the greatest concern with the Foreign Service and played the most active role in the events that preceded final enactment of the bill. This role requires some review. When the request for advice on the Foreign Service bill was sent out by the Bureau on May 6, it was received in the office of the Secretary of Commerce, and routed thence to the Office of International Trade, the unit in the Department most concerned with the Foreign Service and which handled most of the Department's relations with the Foreign Service. Here the issues raised by the bill were treated with the same kind of full consultation that had preceded the preparation of Clayton's memorandum to Russell on the same subject. The consultation was carried on under the supervision of Arthur Paul, a businessman who had entered the government as an official of the Board of Economic Warfare; he was assisted by one of his deputies, James L. McCamy, who had also served in BEW, and earlier as an assistant to Secretary Wallace in the Department of Agriculture. Actual drafting and checking of details were handled by Paul's general counsel, Nathan Ostroff, who had also been in the BEW and the FEA. By May 31, a draft letter was ready for submission to the Secretary.

In substance, this draft letter stated that the Department was willing to try out the Reorganization Plan of 1939; i.e., the consolidation of the Commerce Foreign Service with the State Department Foreign Service, a plan that had admittedly not been given a fair trial because of the war. It made eight recommendations for changes in the draft legislation.

(1) The Board of the Foreign Service should be given more responsibility, but the Secretary or the President should have a veto power over the Board's acts.

(2) The representatives of the Departments of Commerce and Agriculture should have full, not limited, membership on the Board, and there should also be similar representation for the De-

partment of Labor and the Treasury. The State Department should have two representatives.

(3) If the Board were to be so reconstituted, there would be no need for an Interdepartmental Advisory Committee, but a Public Advisory Committee would be necessary in any event.

(4) The statute should not require that the Director General be a Foreign Service officer.

(5) The requirements for lateral entrance into the Foreign Service should not be stated in the statute but should be left to the discretion of the Board.

(6) The re-Americanization procedures (which were approved) should be strengthened.

(7) A pool of qualified persons should be established to widen the availability of candidates for the Foreign Service.

In conclusion, the letter suggested that the Bureau might wish to establish an Interdepartmental Drafting Committee to work on the bill.

The general motivation of this letter needs no comment. There were two special factors affecting the proposals. One was the Advisory Committee on Commercial Activities in the Foreign Service established by the Secretaries of State and Commerce in the fall of 1945 at the instance of the Secretary of Commerce. This committee, composed of businessmen and representatives of business organizations interested in foreign trade, had held two all-day meetings and had filed a "First Interim Report" on March 3, 1946. Largely at the urging of Commerce officials, the committee had endorsed "the current principle of one unified Foreign Service of the United States, operating through the Department of State for a reasonable trial period." The report was temperate in tone; it recommended larger appropriations for the Foreign Service, better pay and allowances, greater emphasis on commercial and economic work, a larger voice for other departments, and improved techniques in training, in field instructions, and in commercial reporting. Paul, the Director of the Office of International Trade, had been greatly interested in this committee and felt that the new bill should have displayed some recognition of these recommendations, especially the recommendations for interdepartmental participation in administration.

The second special factor that may have affected the draft letter was some preceding informal consultation by Ostroff and other Commerce officials with the Foreign Service officers, with Clayton's staff, with Benton, and with the Bureau examiners. The letter partially paralleled the recommendations made by the latter, and the recommendation that an inter-agency drafting committee be established was perhaps not unaffected by the conviction that the Foreign Service representatives had shown a complete unwillingness to co-operate. But to Paul and McCamy, the recommendations were based on their own convictions. They thought that the bill was unsound, and that it should be completely rewritten. They were not sympathetic with the Career Service, and both felt on the basis of personal experience that the Career Service was not suited to its task.

When the draft letter was received in the Secretary's office, Bernard Gladieux, the Secretary's Executive Assistant—a former official of the Bureau of the Budget, trained in public administration and well known as a consultant in the field—turned it over to an assistant, J. Clayton Miller, also a former Budget official, for review. Miller was the Department's coordinator of international co-operation programs, i.e., primarily student exchange programs. Miller called in Robert Frase, an assistant in the Office of the Secretary, and Joel Fisher, a member of the Solicitor's Staff. Their concern was with the effect of the letter on the Secretary's relations with the Secretary of State; while they were disposed to allow the Office of International Trade to decide what would be best for its own interests, they were not sure of the Secretary's reaction to a letter that could hardly be pleasing to the Secretary of State. Gladieux discussed the question with the Secretary, who told him that he did not want to engage in a controversy with Mr. Byrnes on any issue other than the substance of foreign policy. It may be noted that Mr. Wallace's first speech, as Secretary of Commerce, proposing a new foreign policy for the United States, had been delivered on April 12; his final speech as a government official, also dealing with foreign policy, was made in September.

Miller and his associates did not repeat this

injunction to Paul and Ostroff, who were merely advised that the Secretary wished to avoid any repetition of the public controversy he had had with Jesse Jones in 1943. After some discussion, it was finally decided that the letter could safely go out, particularly since it was addressed to the Budget Bureau, not to the State Department.

On June 10, the Secretary signed the draft, but in so doing, he instructed Gladieux to take it to Appleby and discuss it with him; the Secretary wanted to be sure that the Commerce recommendations would be helpful to the Bureau in maintaining its position on the Foreign Service; obviously, also, the possibility of State-Commerce friction would be reduced if the Bureau took the lead. Gladieux was to be accompanied by McCamy; Paul and McCamy, it may be noted, were themselves close to Wallace, and had been for years, and McCamy had also worked closely with Appleby in the Department of Agriculture, where both had been assistants to Wallace. With a background of teaching in political science, McCamy had broad interests in the field of government which were shared by Appleby.

When Gladieux and McCamy brought the letter of June 10 to Appleby, they learned that it was not entirely consistent with his views. Appleby urged the desirability of vesting power in the Secretary, rather than in the Board of the Foreign Service and the Director General. McCamy and Gladieux pointed out the desirability of establishing a statutory right for Commerce to have some say in the operation of the Foreign Service. A blending of these partially conflicting viewpoints was effected. McCamy prepared a supplementary letter, signed on June 19, proposing that the office of Director General be eliminated, and that all power be vested in the Secretary of State but that the statute establish the Board as an interdepartmental body advisory to the Secretary.

A copy of this June 19 Commerce letter was sent to the Department of State by the Budget Bureau. When it reached Harrington, he sent it on to Foster with the notation: "Hold your hat."

While the Department of Commerce was thus establishing its official position, Miller and Ostroff were both independently trying to build up a united front with the other interested agencies. They consulted with the Office of Foreign Agricultural Relations in the Department of Agriculture, which was sympathetic but not greatly concerned; this department soon decided to deal independently. On June 14, the Secretary of Agriculture wrote to the Bureau, raising no objection to the bill, on the theory that the detailed arrangements between State and Agriculture governing the activities of agricultural attachés could best be handled in separate legislation; a bill to achieve this end had already been introduced.

With the Department of Labor, Commerce had partial success. That Department was in the midst of a long controversy with State over other matters, especially representation on and instructions for U. S. delegations to international agencies dealing with labor problems; it was also endeavoring to secure legislation that would provide a new Assistant Secretary of Labor who would devote himself to international labor problems. Accordingly, its representatives said that they did not wish to take an active part, but they did, in effect, agree to have Commerce act as spokesman for the Department of Labor.

In the case of Interior, Commerce found that no one had any over-all responsibility for the Department's foreign interests. Its main interest was expressed by an official in the Fish and Wildlife Service. Eventually a letter from the Secretary of the Interior was sent to the Budget Bureau on July 24, supporting the Bureau's position; but this was too late to be of any assistance.

The Department of the Treasury expressed no interest in these matters. It had its own representatives abroad and no desire for representation on the Board of the Foreign Service. Its letter, dated June 29, dealt only with technical points of tax exemption, etc., and was not received until after the Bureau's position was set.

Some support was given the Bureau (and thereby incidentally the Department of Commerce) in a letter, dated June 24, from the Civil Service Commission in response to the reference of June 6. This letter raised a series of significant questions and also proposed a number of technical amendments. The Commission suggested the possibility of delaying action on the Foreign Service legislation until a Budget Bureau—Civil Service Commission report on wage administration in the territories had been completed and also until the completion of a proposed study of wages and salaries in the Executive Branch of the government. The promotion-up, selection-out procedure was objected to on the ground that a good efficiency rating system results in constant weeding out without any such provision. In general, the letter was one of skeptical doubt rather than of specific objection. Apparently the Commission doubted that its jurisdiction justified more than an observer's comments on the bill, even though the subject matter was of such direct interest: the Foreign Service is only one of several Federal personnel systems outside the control of the Commission.

As these letters arrived, Southworth began drafting a document that would constitute appropriate action on the part of the Bureau, taking into account the Bureau's hearings, and the letters from State, Commerce and the other agencies. His first draft on June 21 was in the form of a memorandum to the President indicating a substantial agreement between the State Department and the Bureau and objecting only to the provisions concerning the Director General and the Board of the Foreign Service, thus rejecting in substance the proposals made in Mr. Byrnes's letter of June 12. In this draft, the desire of the Departments of Commerce and Agriculture for a board was cited and it was accordingly suggested that there be a non-statutory Advisory Board appointed by the Secretary. This proposal of a memorandum to the President was turned down; Stone was planning to discuss the subject with Acheson and wished to be in a position to show Acheson a draft letter; this would be difficult if the letter was addressed to the President. In any event, to bring in the President at this stage would be embarrassing. Southworth's revised drafts were all in the form of a letter to the Secretary of State, replying to the Secretary's letter of June 12.

One new possibility was considered at about this time. The Bureau officials were inclined to believe that no comprehensive Foreign Service Act would be passed during the current session of Congress and had learned that the Foreign Service officers also feared this outcome. Shortly before, Summers, the legal advisor of the Division of Foreign Service Planning, prepared a short bill as a possible stopgap measure; but this was regarded as a counsel of despair in the Office of the Foreign Service. Southworth also opposed the short bill but "on the ground that the pressure of time may help in obtaining State approval of our suggestions." This possible alternative was accordingly discarded, and Southworth prepared a fresh draft of the letter to State.

Stone and Appleby were concerned about the situation. They had heard of the hearings, referred to above and described more fully below, before the House Foreign Affairs Subcommittee, and while they had no knowledge of the precise status of these hearings, they did realize that the Foreign Service discussions with the Subcommittee would inevitably tend to compromise the Bureau's position. They realized also that Mr. Byrnes's personal support of the bill made it difficult for them to secure major changes. Desiring to move carefully, they decided that Stone, on behalf of Appleby, should discuss the question with the Acting Secretary of State, Acheson. On June 25 Stone met with Acheson and showed him Southworth's latest draft.

Acheson's position was a difficult one. He recognized an important element of validity in Stone's contention that the establishment by statute of the position of Director General and of the Board of the Foreign Service, and the statutory attribution of powers to those agencies, would impair the Secretary's power to control the Service; but he felt it difficult, indeed impossible, to support the Bureau's position since these points had been specifically approved by his superior, the Secretary. If he were to agree with the Bureau, his agreement would necessarily carry the implication that the Secretary had been unaware of the danger to his own powers involved in the draft bill. Furthermore, the Secretary and Russell were intimate friends and Russell had dealt directly with him in securing his approval of the bill; in case of disagreement, the Secretary would be predisposed to back Russell, not Acheson.

And Acheson also knew, at least in a general way, of the significant progress made by the Foreign Service representatives with the House Foreign Affairs Subcommittee; he concluded that any drastic action at this stage would only serve to complicate what was already a sufficiently complicated and delicate situation. Thus the interview was friendly but inconclusive.

When Stone returned with this news of Acheson's position, Appleby decided that the wisest thing for the Bureau to do was to go as far as it could without embarrassing Acheson on the one hand and without exposing itself to the danger of being accused of overlooking the real interests of the various departments, especially Commerce, on the other. Accordingly, Southworth was given fresh instructions on the basis of which he made a final redraft of the letter, which was then transmitted on June 26.

The letter was in form a reply to the Byrnes letters of April 16 and June 12. (The April 16 letter had never been answered because a draft reply, ready on May 1, was discarded when the new draft bill of May 1 was received.) In the letter, Appleby indicated his general approval of all the many points of agreement or assumed agreement that had been reached between the staffs of the two agencies. In spite of Mr. Byrnes's plea, he still objected to the statutory creation of the Director General and the assigned statutory responsibilities of the Board of the Foreign Service. In reference to both sections, he pointed out that difficulties had arisen elsewhere in the Federal administration from such provisions: "When rigid patterns of organization and grants of authority are located by the Congress at a level below the Secretary, his hands become tied and disunity and irresponsibility are engendered." Thus the reorganization programs of recent years had all moved in the direction of centralizing power in the agency head. He saw nothing in the nature of the Foreign Service which, he said, is merely a group of government employees with rather special terms of employment, to justify the statutory office of Director General and suggested once again that the power be vested in the Secretary. With respect to the proposed Board of the Foreign Service, a compromise position was suggested. Taking cognizance of the views of the Department of Commerce and recognizing the fact that the Foreign Service serves the rest of the government as well as the Department of State, he recommended that the elaborate provisions establishing and governing the proposed Board be eliminated and that instead there be a simple provision reading: "The Secretary shall establish a Foreign Service Board, consisting of representatives of the Departments of State, Agriculture, Commerce, Interior, Labor and Treasury and such other Departments or agencies as the Secretary of State may determine, to consider how the Foreign Service may be conducted most effectively and to advise the Secretary thereon."

A third objection centered on the requirement that the three- or four-year prior service before eligibility for lateral entrance be exclusively in the Department of State (including the Foreign Service Reserve and Staff). Appleby desired that service in other departments be given full credit, but, as a compromise, proposed that there be a probationary period of one year in the State Department. Finally, and this was an objection not previously raised in the discussions with the Foreign Service representatives, objection was made to the creation of the Reserve. Like Clayton, Appleby suggested that the Reserve be dropped and that, in lieu thereof provision be made for temporary appointments in the Service. In conclusion, Appleby referred to the letter of June 12 and stated his assumption that the Institute would be eliminated and that appropriate language (already agreed on between Strom and Southworth) empowering the Secretary to carry on training would be substituted therefor. The last paragraph of the letter reads: "If you are in agreement with the approach to the proposed legislation which I have presented above, we shall proceed with formal clearance. On the other hand, if you have reservations, I shall welcome an opportunity to discuss them with you. In view of the tentative legislative calendar, the urgency of prompt action is, of course, obvious."

The Bureau officials were not confident that the foregoing letter would accomplish its purpose. They were uneasy about the situation with the House Foreign Affairs Committee and they realized the delicacy of Acheson's position. Apparently, such hopes as they had were based on a belief that the Department would be unwilling to seek final Congressional action with these important points of difference still outstanding.

13. EFFECTS OF BUDGET REVIEW AND INTER-AGENCY CLEARANCE

Any summary of the effects of Budget Review and inter-agency clearance at this stage is necessarily somewhat incomplete; other events were occurring that tended to circumvent this whole process. Yet it may be of value to pause for some consideration of the techniques and objectives involved.

From the point of view of Stone, Sheppard, Roseman and Southworth, this was not a strange and new procedure as it tended to be for the Foreign Service officers. Review of draft bills was part of their regular work, and this particular bill, from their standpoint, while significant, was not of the very first importance.

As part of a normal process, they applied—or sought to apply—normal criteria. On the retention of the Career Service, more broadly, on the application of the recommendations of the Byrnes Report, the judgment involved hardly fell within the "broad principles" invoked by them elsewhere. They did indeed feel that principles were involved but, as has been pointed out, they decided that the time was not ripe for insistence on a move towards fundamental departmental-field service amalgamation. This choice was not made without regret—and the advantages and disadvantages of raising the basic issue sharply at this point (or perhaps earlier) bear consideration.

On the major issues that were raised—the control of the service—principles and norms were clearly involved. The Budget Bureau is and must be concerned with precedents; and it is significant that Appleby's letter of June 26 referred to the precedent for vesting control in the agency head created by the various Reorganization Plans. Each new law or Executive Order that deviates from such a precedent makes it harder to maintain the principle in the future. Therefore the preservation of the principle with respect to the Director General and the Board of the Foreign Service was of importance to the Bureau.

The arguments pro and con on organization have been set forth above in some detail. The reader can weigh the merits of the two positions.

It will be noted that Appleby eventually came to support a statutory inter-agency board with generalized advisory powers; he, or at least his associates, came to this position reluctantly, and did so either because of the substantive weight of Commerce's arguments or because Commerce seemed to have a problem for which no alternative solution was readily available, especially since the most obvious and drastic alternative—repeal of the Reorganization Plan of 1939—seemed quite impractical, whether or not it was desirable. The problem of inter-agency relations when one agency performs functions for others is recurrent. Various proposed alternative methods of treatment have been described above; others could also be suggested; but it should be observed that jurisdictional disputes—and the dispute between Commerce and the Foreign Service was partly jurisdictional in character—tend to arise when one agency feels doubt about its ability to execute its own program successfully because execution is partially dependent on performance by another agency. In one aspect, the Bureau of the Budget is a tribunal for the resolution of such disputes. The actions of the Bureau in this instance can be regarded as an attempt to fulfill this function.

The procedure adopted by the Bureau officials was conditioned, as has been suggested, by their belief that it was too late to secure passage of a bill in the current session of Congress, and by their expectation that the Foreign Service officers would not seek final Congressional action without Bureau approval. These assumptions probably had some bearing on the length of time required for Bureau consideration and probably also on the failure to obtain or permit the active participation of other agencies, especially Commerce, during the hearing process.

In hindsight it is obvious that the factual assumptions were unwarranted. But more interesting is the question as to the relation of the second assumption—action without Bureau approval—to the Bureau's somewhat tenuous authority for legislative clearance and the very gentle restrictions on agency action laid down in the Budget Circular. Obviously agencies can comply with the letter of the circular without complying with its intent. To what extent such "circumvention"—from the Bureau's standpoint—is fostered by these circumstances, to what extent more rigid requirements would be feasible, or what further educational process would make more effective the system in effect in 1946 is of interest and is perhaps illuminated by these events.

There is one further aspect of the review process that deserves mention. Bureau officials, such as Sheppard, were afraid that State Department and Congressional attitudes might crystallize before effective intervention could be had. Yet it was not until the beginning of June that the major issues were clearly brought to Smith and Appleby for consideration by Stone and the officials of the International Activities Branch, nor did the Assistant Director in charge of Legislative Reference ever raise the matter with the Director. There is always a nice question of judgment involved in such decisions: top officials can easily be overwhelmed if too many questions are brought to them too early. But, as in this case, there are dangers in complete adherence to what is sometimes referred to as the doctrine of "completed staff work."

Part IV. Congress Disposes

14. THE HOUSE FOREIGN AFFAIRS SUBCOMMITTEE

In Part III of this study the progress of the Foreign Service bill has been carried forward through the extended review in the Bureau of the Budget up to the point of Acting Director Appleby's formal proposals in his letter of June 26. But it has already been indicated that this review was conducted almost concurrently with review by a body of the Legislative Branch. To understand the circumstances under which this occurred it is necessary to turn back to an apparently unrelated event that took place in the early spring.

On the 8th of April, 1946—i.e., just before the draft Foreign Service bill was transmitted to the Budget Bureau—the Committee on Foreign Affairs of the House of Representatives held a scheduled hearing on what was known as the State Department Point-of-Order Bill. This bill was one of a group of measures prepared by the executive departments in response to instructions received during the previous session of Congress from the chairmen of the two Committees on Appropriations. For many years, the two Houses of the Congress had included items in departmental appropriation bills that had no regular statutory authorization. This practice was contrary to the rules of both Houses, and such items in the appropriation bills were technically subject to a point-of-order in either House. Such points-of-order were in fact seldom raised and many of these technically unauthorized appropriation items had been repeated in so many annual acts that they had virtually the sanctity of a permanent statutory base; in a few cases, they had even been included in the U. S. Code. Nevertheless, in view of the procedures of the Congress, the failure to provide substantive legislation for these activities was disorderly. The Appropriations Committees had growled occasionally at the requests made of them and had threatened that unless statutory enactments were sought, they would refuse to recommend appropriations for these items in the future. With a view to regularizing the situation and probably also with one eye on the possibility of cutting back expenditures, the two committees had issued the instructions described above.

Each department was therefore placed under obligation to submit to its appropriate legislative committee a statute covering all its activites for which appropriations would be sought and for which no authority outside the appropriation acts existed. The Department of State Point-of-Order Bill was thus only one of a series of such measures.

The draft Foreign Service bill was a codification of existing legislation as well as a revision and extension of such legislation. As such, the bill would automatically contain all or virtually all the Foreign Service items within the Point-of-Order Bill, although this would constitute only a portion of the whole. Nevertheless, a special Point-of-Order Bill had also been prepared and was now ready for Congressional action.

In the course of the discussion of this measure on April 8, Mrs. Bolton of Ohio, a member of the Committee, asked if the salaries of ministers and ambassadors were covered by the Point-of-Order Bill and if so, whether they were adequate under modern conditions. A State Department budget officer replied that the authorizing item was included in the Point-of-Order Bill but that the salaries thus authorized were not adequate; the necessary revision would be proposed in the course of an intensive review of all Foreign Service legislation then in progress and a new draft bill to be presented to the Committee would revise many existing practices. At this point, Foster was called on to describe the work that had been done; he explained that they had just about completed their draft legislation and that they hoped to bring it before the Committee within a few weeks. The discussion then returned to the Point-of-Order Bill itself, H.R. 5949. Mr. Vorys of Ohio was disturbed by the situation. He reminded his colleagues that it would be extremely embarrassing to pass the Point-of-Order Bill and then have many of its provisions revised by another piece of legislation coming along six or eight weeks later. As the discussion continued, there was further consideration of the need of basic Foreign Service legislation. The preparation of new legislation was an old story; various members of Congress had requested a new bill repeatedly. The members of the Committee thus knew in a general way that a comprehensive bill was in preparation; in fact, those who, like Mr. Vorys, took the trouble to read the *American Foreign Service Journal*, were informed on recent progress from an article on the subject in the February issue. The new information revealed in the testimony of the Department witnesses was that the bill was at last nearly ready for presentation to the Committee.

At this point in the discussion, Congressman Rabaut of Michigan, Chairman of the Subcommittee of the House Committee on Appropriations that handled the State Department appropriations, joined the hearing by invitation. He immediately advised the Committee to drop consideration of the Point-of-Order Bill since the appropriation for the Department was scheduled to come up on the floor of the House in two days and the Point-of-Order Bill would be too late to help them this year anyway. He urged them instead to concentrate on the new basic legislation. Mr. Vorys then suggested that the appropriation bill be delayed while the new bill was being considered; but after considerable argument, this proposal, which for obvious reasons was particularly distasteful to Assistant Secretary Russell, was dropped. Finally, the Committee decided to discontinue further consideration of the Point-of-Order Bill and to devote itself instead at the earliest possible moment to the new Foreign Service bill. It was proposed that a Subcommittee be appointed for this purpose, and it was suggested initially that Mr. Rabaut be included on the Subcommittee. Another member noted that this would be against the rules of the House, since Mr. Rabaut was not a member of the Committee on Foreign Affairs. It was therefore agreed that the Subcommittee would consult with Mr. Rabaut during its deliberations, as well as with representatives of the Department. Mr. Bloom then named the members of the Subcommittee: Judge Kee of West Virginia, Chairman; Mr. Richards of South Carolina, and Mr. Vorys of Ohio.

This Subcommittee was to play an important part in the history of the Foreign Service Act. The Chairman, Judge Kee, seventy-one years old, in Congress since 1933, came from the small city of Bluefield, West Virginia. He was born and educated in that state and except for two years in Mexico, had spent his adult life as a lawyer in Bluefield. Mr. Richards, fifty-one years old, a resident of the small town of Lancaster, South Carolina, had been born and educated in that state. A veteran of World War I, he had practiced law and served as a probate judge in Lancaster until his election to Congress in 1932. Mr. Vorys, a native of Ohio, was forty-nine years old. He had been educated at Yale, was a veteran, and had spent some time as a teacher in China and as Assistant Secretary of the American delegation at the 1922 Disarmament Conference. He had served in the Ohio State legislature and had practiced law in Columbus until he took his seat in Congress in 1939. (See Appendix II—Biographies.)

The date of this hearing and of the appointment of this Subcommittee was, as has been said, April 8, 1946. On this date, the representatives of the Foreign Service were just about to terminate their protracted and important negotiations within the Department. Not until the end of the month and the completion of the May 1 draft were they ready for the Bureau of the Budget hearings or the hearings before the Subcommittee.

The hearings that began in the Bureau of the Budget on Monday, May 6, came as a shock to the officials of the Office of the Foreign Service. They were already familiar with and disturbed by the fact that the Bureau was doubtful of the detailed character of the bill and questioned the proposed basic administrative structure. They had always anticipated some changes as a result of Bureau review, but the great difference in fundamental attitudes, and the breadth and depth of the review were disturbing, and surprising. Their earlier discussions with Southworth had not led them to expect this. Their disturbance was not allayed by the courteous atmosphere of the hearing room. As they proceeded, they soon became convinced that the Bureau deliberations would last so long and lead to so many arguments that they would never be able to transmit an agreed bill to Congress in time for action during the session. Their anticipation of painful delays was increased when they gave thought to the inter-agency clearance process that had only just begun, and that would unquestionably lead to further argument and possibly to deadlocks.

During the month of April, the Subcommittee had been anxious to start its work, but the lack of a clean revised draft inhibited action. Even after the completion of the May 1 draft, Chapin held back. He was uncertain of the proprieties in the situation, and he had an uneasy feeling that to begin hearings with the Subcommittee prior to Bureau clearance would lead to complications. However, the informal discussions with the Bureau officials in April, and even more, the first day or two of hearings in May, convinced him that strict observance of the normal procedures would lead to interminable delays and would preclude any possibility of legislation before the adjournment of Congress. At the same time, the Subcommittee was becoming increasingly anxious to begin its hearings; and Mr. Vorys advised Chapin that passage of the bill during the session was not impossible and should be attempted, and further that he would himself do all he could to push the measure. Under these conditions Chapin decided to move ahead, if he could; he informed Southworth of the Subcommittee's desires and requested permission to proceed. Southworth's approval was promptly given under the circumstances described above.

Chapin entered on the Subcommittee hearings with some trepidation. Although he was on friendly terms with Mr. Vorys, who had stayed with him for two weeks in Algiers during the war, he feared that the Subcommittee would have views similar to the Bureau's; and he was still concerned about complications with the Bureau. With this background of concern, and with the disturbance caused by the Bureau hearings vividly in mind, he and his associates attended their first hearing with the House Foreign Affairs Subcommittee on May 9. These hearings also proved surprising, but agreeably so. The Foreign Service representatives quickly learned that on all the major issues the Subcommittee supported their position and in some cases even went beyond it; and that the Subcommittee intended to take definitive action as it went along. The Subcommittee was determined that the bill contain detailed prescriptions for the administration of the Foreign Service. This conviction, shared by all three members and most forcefully presented by Mr. Vorys, was largely based on a general belief that during the New Deal,

Congress had abdicated all too much legislative power to the executive, and that it was time Congress took back into its own hands the reins of control. This general conviction was reinforced by the further consideration that where ample discretion was left to an administrator, the Committee on Appropriations would write the requirements and restrictions into law in the annual appropriation acts, and thereby, in effect, remove jurisdiction over the subject matter from the Committee on Foreign Affairs.

Other influences were also at work in persuading the members of the soundness of the draft bill. All three felt that political patronage should have no place in the appointment or promotion of Foreign Service officers; and they were not convinced that the existing immunity would be preserved if greater discretionary power were vested in the Secretary of State. The frequent changes in the direction of State Department administration—there had been four Assistant Secretaries for Administration in the past eighteen months—led them to believe that the administrative provisions of the bill were necessary to ensure continuity and consistency in the direction of the Foreign Service. Since they were also concerned about charges of Communist infiltration in the departmental service of the Department of State, they were anxious to preserve a system for the Foreign Service that apparently had guarded successfully against such infiltration in that group.

Personal factors also played some part in the Subcommittee acceptance of the basic structure and character of the draft bill. To Judge Kee it was an administration measure sponsored by a member of the President's cabinet; as such it deserved his support. To Mr. Richards it was a favored project of two fellow South Carolinians, Mr. Byrnes and Mr. Russell. As for Mr. Vorys, his interest in the Foreign Service and his conviction of the need for a non-patronage career service dated back to his work with the Disarmament Conference in 1922. At that time he had found a higher level of competence and devotion among the career diplomats and officials than among the patronage appointees on the staff of the U. S. delegation, even though he was himself a patronage appointee. To him, therefore, the Rogers Act and this proposed revision of it seemed wise.

A single example will serve to illustrate the kind of conclusion that came from these various conditioning factors. The Foreign Service representatives explained that the Bureau of the Budget was opposed to any statutory provision for the Board of Foreign Service Examiners, although it would not object to the establishment of such a Board by the Secretary himself under his general authority. Mr. Vorys asked if the Board were not the cornerstone of the whole Foreign Service personnel system, and was told that it was. On learning this, he said, "put it in the book," and the others agreed.

During the course of the eight hearings in executive session before the Subcommittee, the last of which took place on May 24, a spirit of camaraderie developed between the Foreign Service representatives and the Subcommittee members. There was some social intercourse between the Foreign Service officers, especially Chapin and Harrington, and the Congressmen. As the bill became more and more "their bill," the Subcommittee members seem to have adopted a rather paternal attitude toward the Foreign Service; the Service became for them somewhat like a constituent, whose rights and interests deserve Congressional protection. Furthermore, the Subcommittee members had a sense of participation in writing a law that was rarely open to them. The Foreign Service representatives brought to them all the changes proposed by the Bureau of the Budget and a number of other changes that they themselves wished to make. For example, at the last moment, Foster and his associates persuaded Chapin that it was unwise to specify in the statute the number of years of maximum service in each of the classes before the selection-out procedures would go into effect. They feared that this rigidity would lead to unforeseen and unforeseeable results since there was no clear policy on how drastic a selection-out was to be desired. Chapin conceded the point and this became one of the numerous departmentally sponsored changes adopted by the Subcommittee. All told as many as a hundred different amendments were considered and approved by the Subcommittee; and unlike the Bureau process, these approvals were actions —subject to change, of course, but authoritative unless changed.

Most of the amendments adopted by the Subcommittee were based on recommendations made by the Bureau of the Budget or inspired by the hearings at the Bureau; but these were technical in character or of minor importance. The Subcommittee was adamant against any of the basic Bureau proposals, such as the elimination of the statutory boards and the statutory office of the Director General. The members were not well acquainted or sympathetic with the Bureau's clearance function. They did not know the Bureau officials personally, and they had some feeling that the Bureau was trying to do their job. They rejected the major Bureau proposals with some sense of satisfaction.

The Subcommittee itself made a number of changes: aside from the reinstatement of the Board of Foreign Service Examiners in the text, the most significant of these was a provision permitting Foreign Service officers to accept a Presidential appointment in the Department (Assistant Secretary, etc.) without losing their status in the Service, a provision heartily approved by the Foreign Service representatives and perhaps originally suggested by Strom. The bulk of the Subcommittee's own changes were necessarily minor in character and were largely the result of Mr. Vorys' conscientious review of the text; all were, of course, immediately incorporated. By the end of May, therefore, the Department's master copy showed a bill fundamentally along the lines of the May 1 draft, but criss-crossed with amendments.

It has already been noted that the Foreign Service officers brought to the attention of the Subcommittee the assigned reasons for the Bureau's views; but they did not conceal their own position when it differed from the Bureau's. But the very fact of their success with the Subcommittee made the Foreign Service officials more and more concerned about the delicacy of their position with the Bureau. Their handling of this problem requires separate consideration.

15. FOREIGN SERVICE DEALINGS WITH THE BUREAU OF THE BUDGET

Chapin and Harrington were in some difficulty as to their relations with the Bureau of the Budget at this juncture. The Subcommittee made no bones of the fact that it was making decisions, and not discussing abstractions or general considerations, but the bearer of such tidings to the Bureau could hardly expect a warm welcome. Harrington did inform the Bureau officials toward the end of May, as has been pointed out, of Subcommittee views on important issues, but he failed to convey any clear realization of the fact that the Subcommittee members were planning to take conclusive action and were not awaiting final Bureau clearance before making up their own minds on what should and should not be done in the legislation. This increasing sense of embarrassment seems to have affected some of the later hearings in the Bureau. As the Foreign Service officers gained confidence from the growing intimacy of their relations with the Subcommittee, they came to feel that the decisions made by the Bureau were academic. In consequence, they became less insistent on their points of disagreement with the Bureau. There was an increasing tendency for the Foreign Service representatives, and particularly their chief representative, Harrington, to indicate merely a doubt, when in fact they were in complete disagreement, but when they knew that the Subcommittee had already made up its mind to accept their recommendation. In the outcome, as has been indicated above, on a number of points the Bureau staff was led to assume that agreement had been secured, when actually there had been merely a failure to object.

On May 14, at the Subcommittee's third hearing, the Foreign Service representatives had been informed of what would be necessary for the Subcommittee's use. The Subcommittee already had a copy of the May 1 draft and of certain explanatory materials that had been proferred by the Foreign Service representatives. The Subcommittee would need, when the hearings were completed, a clean draft of the bill as revised, and another clean draft showing the text of the new legislation in one column and alongside a column showing the text of the relevant superseded legislation, together with an introduction, explanations, and commentaries. The straight draft was completed on June 8, the double column draft on June 12. At this point, Panuch and Russell in consultation with Chapin, decided that a last attempt should be made to secure an agreement with the Bureau of the Budget that would approve a bill sufficiently similar to the bill that had just been approved by the Subcommittee so that the publication of a Committee print of the revised draft and the introduction of a bill into the House, although they might come as a surprise, would not create any basic difficulties with the Bureau. In pursuance of this conclusion, Panuch drafted a letter for the Secretary's signature which was signed on the following day, June 12. In this letter, whose receipt in the Bureau has been referred to above, the Secretary, who was leaving for Paris the next day, bespoke the cooperation of the Director of the Bureau of the Budget, Mr. Smith, in expediting clearance of the proposed legislation. He described what seemed to him to be the three outstanding points of difference between staff members of the two agencies (he assumed that the problem of the generally detailed character of the legislation had already been settled by his transmittal letter of April 16). The three points he mentioned were the statutory provisions covering the Board of Foreign Service Personnel, the Director General of the Foreign Service, and the Foreign Service Institute. He defended the Board of Foreign Service Personnel by pointing out that Congress had determined the statutory base as a matter of policy in 1924. (Strictly speaking, the Board was not accorded statutory recognition until 1931; and in the draft bill it had by now been renamed the Board of the Foreign Service.) He remarked that the House Foreign Affairs Subcommittee was strongly in favor of this statutory provision and would insist on it in any event. As for the Director General, he referred to the need for continuity in leadership and policy and suggested that this could be accomplished only by the creation of a statutory office. (There seems to have some confusion at this point between the creation of the statutory office and the additional requirement that the Director General be a Foreign Service officer; presumably both points were ambiguously in mind.) He expressed his preference for the Foreign Service Institute—a proposal strongly recommended by the Council on Foreign Relations, but indicated that he did not feel as strongly about this as about the other two points and left the impression that he was willing to sacrifice the Institute if he could get Bureau approval of the other two and more important provisions. In conclusion, he asked for Mr. Smith's personal intervention in the matter and expressed the hope that the bill would be ready for Congressional consideration by June 15. The letter was carefully drafted to convey the impression of a plea for personal agreement removed from the atmosphere of staff disputes.

It is doubtful that Mr. Byrnes himself, with many other pressing burdens on him, had any opportunity for unhurried and thoughtful consideration of the complex terms of this long complicated bill. He was strongly urged by his trusted Assistant Secretary to give the bill his support. Furthermore, this draft was the result of long-drawn-out and thoroughgoing intradepartmental clearance and represented agreed compromises. Under the circumstances, it would have been difficult for him to have refused to take the responsibility for supporting the major provisions of a proposed law that was the outcome of so much work and was so deeply desired by an essential group of employees of his Department. Russell and Panuch, who had long since decided to stand by the basic features of the legislation, had devised this particular proposal for Mr. Byrnes in the light of their knowledge of the status of affairs with the Bureau on the one hand, and the House Foreign Affairs Subcommittee on the other. The time for reaching a compromise with the Bureau, which would lead to a measure substantially like the Subcommittee bill, was drawing short. The Subcommittee had completed its work, the clean drafts were almost ready for use, and the Subcommittee report could not be indefinitely delayed, particularly if the passage of legislation during that session was to be secured.

This attempt at a negotiated settlement, and a similar negotiation later, were handled by

Russell and Panuch, in consultation with Chapin and Harrington, and were not the result of staff work by the Division of Foreign Service Planning. As a result of this lack of integration, the proposed compromise offer concerning the Institute was never carried out. On the 12th of June, Judge Kee, the Chairman of the Subcommittee, asked Russell to send him completed copies of the clean draft, and discussed the bill with him. The request was transmitted to Foster by Harrington. On June 13 Foster called Judge Kee on the telephone, and advised him that the straight and double column drafts were now ready and said he would take six copies of each to Judge Kee on the following day. Kee replied that there might be a little delay in securing formal approval of the double column draft as the Subcommittee report, because the other members were out of town. As the conversation continued, Kee explained that it was his understanding that the Institute had been stricken from the bill; this was a conclusion based on his talk with Russell. But Foster, who did not then know of the Secretary's letter (although it had been dictated on June 11), and its proposed compromise, expressed disagreement. He had understood that the Subcommittee wanted no major changes and he himself was anxious, if possible, to keep the Institute in the bill. If the Subcommittee wished to remove it, all that would be necessary would be to eliminate Title VII and renumber the remaining titles. Judge Kee explained that he himself liked the provision and would be glad to have it retained if there was nothing wrong with it.

Foster informed Harrington of this conversation and Harrington asked him to tell Judge Kee that there had merely been some difficulty with the Bureau about the Institute and that this had been in Russell's mind during the telephone conversation. Foster pointed out that the Chairman of the Subcommittee had "more or less instructed" him to make no changes and concluded, "surely, the Bureau of the Budget cannot complain that we have gone around them." In Foster's conversation with Kee, Kee also mentioned the provision of allowances for the education of children of Foreign Service officers, a section that had been strongly objected to by Congressman Vorys. Foster himself was also opposed to it, but Judge Kee suggested that it stay in the bill; the full Committee could strike it out if it so desired. (As it turned out, Mr. Vorys gained his point in the Subcommittee after securing Russell's agreement.)

The Byrnes letter of June 12—discussed in this oblique fashion by Judge Kee and Foster—remained unanswered for two weeks. As has been seen, the officials of the Bureau were gradually deciding on the proposals finally embodied in the Appleby reply of June 26. Meanwhile the members of the Subcommittee, who were not involved in this interchange (except perhaps as Judge Kee was inclined to seek an accommodation for Russell's attempt to avoid an outright break with the Bureau), moved ahead. Foster had delivered the double column draft to Judge Kee on June 14; this draft was to constitute the Subcommittee report to the full Committee. A delay followed, as Judge Kee had predicted, but on June 25 the draft was sent to the Government Printing Office. On June 27th the printed copies were ready, and on June 28, Chapin wrote to Sheppard attaching a copy of this print. He suggested that Southworth might have told Sheppard that the Office of the Foreign Service had "learned" that the House Foreign Affairs Committee had printed its own version of the Act based on the discussions between the Subcommittee and OFS "which discussions, you will recall, were authorized by the Bureau of the Budget." He wished to make it clear that the views of the Bureau had been made known to the Subcommittee. He had "told Win [Southworth] that the Subcommittee had different views." Specifically, the Subcommittee wanted the statutory boards strengthened and wholeheartedly approved of the Director General. The Subcommittee wanted legislation passed now and took the matter into its own hands. On June 14, it had asked for a draft including all the changes. "The Department will bring to the attention of the Subcommittee" Appleby's letter of June 26 which would also be brought to the attention of Russell, who was in Europe at the moment. "As soon as agreement is reached with the Bureau with respect to the bill submitted to it, a copy will be submitted to the Congress in the established manner." If a bill is introduced, the Committee will be told "frankly" of the points at issue between the bill now before the Bureau and the Committee print. The letter had been dictated by Harrington, who had been in general charge of most of the negotiations with the Bureau.

The request of June 14 for the clean draft referred to by Chapin was probably a reference to Judge Kee's telephone request on June 12, but, of course, this was merely a follow-up—the original request having been made at the hearing on May 14. It may also be noted that Chapin's suggestion of sending a new version to the Subcommittee after that body had completed its work on the bill could hardly serve any very practical purpose. But Chapin and Harrington presumably were not seeking practical results from this letter; they were "making a record," to use the bureaucrat's phrase, and they were endeavoring to retain some standing with an agency with which they would have dealings in the future. But the fate of their bill no longer seemed to rest with the Budget Bureau; their attention was turned toward the Congress.

16. H.R. 6967

Once the Subcommittee report came back from the printer on June 27, events moved fast. On July 2, the full House Foreign Affairs Committee held an open hearing at which Acheson testified in support of the bill and the Committee indicated its general approval. The hearing was brief and cordial. The members of the Subcommittee were congratulated on their labors and Mrs. Bolton remarked that the close relations of the Subcommittee with the Department of State constituted a milestone. Chapin pointed out the objections of the Bureau of the Budget to the legislation and the Subcommittee members defended what the Subcommittee had done. Judge Kee observed that the Subcommittee had had no contact with the Bureau but had heard via the State Department of the Bureau's objections and took full responsibility for the text. Mr. Richards explained that the bill had two great virtues: it would improve the Foreign Service, and it would preserve the jurisdictional integrity of the Foreign Affairs Committee, previously weakened by the intrusions of the Appropriations Committee. Congressman Bloom, the Chairman of the full Committee, announced that the full Committee would go through the whole bill. Mr. Vorys referred to a discussion he had had with a "distinguished former Under Secretary," and Mr. Bloom said that an attempt had been made to get a copy in the hands of every living former Under and Assistant Secretary. Arrangements were also made for transmittal to the Committee of copies of the letters from the Bureau of the Budget and lists of all the various changes made by the Subcommittee in the original May 1 draft. The hearing ended with a long discussion of a proposal made by Mr. Wadsworth of New York that the bill be introduced by Mr. Kee in honor of the work done by his Subcommittee. The Chairman, Mr. Bloom, pointed out with vigor that this proposal was "irregular," for custom required that the bill, as an administration measure, be introduced by the Chairman of the full Committee. But the Committee finally decided that Judge Kee should be the bill's sponsor; they were glad to compliment him, and some felt that his sponsorship would be better received by the House than Mr. Bloom's.

On July 1, the day before this, Chapin—carrying out the promise in the letter to Sheppard of June 28—had sent Judge Kee a note drafted by Foster, transmitting copies of the Byrnes letter of June 12 and Appleby's reply of June 26; in his note Chapin had reviewed very briefly the circumstances under which the Subcommittee had proceeded, noting particularly that he had kept the Subcommittee advised of the status of Bureau review and of the informal views of the Bureau on various points in the measure. On July 2, after the public hearing, Chapin prepared for the Committee members a document containing the May 1 draft, the three memoranda listing Subcommittee changes, the seven memoranda of Budget Bureau changes, and the letters of June 12 and June 26, together with a brief covering memorandum describing and explaining the enclosures.

On July 3 the full Committee considered the bill in executive session. On July 8, the bill as approved by the Subcommittee was introduced by Judge Kee as H.R. 6967. The Committee now had an official bill to work on. It completed its deliberations at a second executive session on July 8, approving, along with one fairly substantial change, a few minor and technical changes, and voting to report out H.R. 6967 as thus amended. The fairly substantial change was a requirement that Foreign Service members of the Board of Examiners be less than a majority.

On July 12, H.R. 6967 was reported out with the full Committee's amendments. The accompanying Committee report was the Subcommittee report to the full Committee, merely revised to conform to the few amendments that had been made.

The next step in the House was to obtain a "rule," i.e., in effect a formal decision by the Committee on Rules fixing a time on the calendar and establishing the terms and limits of amendment and debate. (Technically, the "rule" is a House resolution which is submitted to a vote when the bill it refers to comes up in the House; but a rule is rarely defeated.)

At this moment, the Foreign Service planners were eagerly hopeful, but far from sure of success. On July 15, Foster wrote to a Foreign Service officer in the field that it would be "a miracle" if the bill passed. But the Rules Committee voted unanimously that the bill be taken up under suspension of the rules and set debate for July 20. All seemed well.

17. LAST-MINUTE CHANGES

The critical week that was to reach its climax with House consideration of H.R. 6967 on Saturday, July 20 began under favorable auspices, but serious difficulties soon arose.

The Subcommittee report was transmitted by Chapin to the Agriculture, Commerce, Labor and Interior liaison officers on July 3; this notified the agencies of what might happen; more definite notice was given by the introduction of H.R. 6967 on July 8, when the bill became a public document. This warning to all and sundry of what was likely to be actually enacted was reinforced when H.R. 6967 was reported out on July 12.

These events had repercussions, the most notable in the Department of Commerce. McCamy, in the course of a conversation with Appleby on other matters, fell into a discussion of the Foreign Service bill, then still in Committee. Appleby told him that the Bureau of the Budget was in no position to secure amendments and agreed that Commerce should take whatever steps it could to effect improvements; Appleby knew or anticipated that the bill would be reported out soon. McCamy passed this information on to the Secretary. Shortly thereafter the bill was reported out, McCamy and Ostroff heard about it, secured a copy and saw that H.R. 6967 was in all essential respects the same as the draft bill circulated by the Bureau. Miller and his two associates, Fisher and Frase, also studied the bill. They discussed the problem and decided that their best hope of rectifying the situation lay in the Senate, rather than in the House, and thought that Senator Pepper of Florida, with whom the Secretary had a close and friendly relationship, might help; he could either insist on an opportunity for Commerce and the other departments to be heard, or, better still, he could demand that the bill be amended. The Congressional session was almost at a close and it was obvious that consideration of the bill in the Senate could occur only on the Consent Calendar, where a single objection would defeat it. Thus a threatened objection by Senator Pepper would have compelling force.

Gladieux carried these suggestions to the Secretary, who telephoned Senator Pepper forthwith. The Senator replied that he would take care of the problem. The Senate Committee on Foreign Relations considered the draft bill very briefly during an executive session on July 10. At this meeting, or possibly a little later, Senator Pepper explained the need for fair treatment for the other departments. Other Committee members agreed with him. Chapin assured them that he would work out amendments with the Department of Commerce and the other agencies that would remove the objection.

Chapin then called Paul of the Office of International Trade, and invited him to the State Department to discuss changes in the bill. Paul, McCamy and Ostroff went to

Chapin's office. They argued with Chapin and Panuch for some time. Chapin was extremely anxious to reach an agreement. Panuch insisted that the agreement should be a business-like deal. The views of Foster and his associates, who were planners, and of the lawyers (meaning Ostroff) were to be disregarded. In fact, Panuch told Chapin in effect that he would handle the interests of the Foreign Service because none of the Foreign Service officers was capable of negotiating successfully with Paul.

The deal—as Panuch described it—agreed to by Paul provided for six amendments as follows:

(1) Composition of the Board of the Foreign Service. The Departments of Agriculture, Commerce and Labor were given full representation on the Board with full right to choose their own representatives "of similar rank." The Director General was also made a full member of the board (instead of an alternate).

(2) Duties of the Board of the Foreign Service. In H.R. 6967, the Board was to make recommendations concerning "the policies and procedures to govern the administration and personnel management of the Service"; in the agreement this was enlarged to include: "the functions of the Service, the policies and procedures to govern the administration and personnel management of the Service, including appointments, assignments, promotions, and efficiency ratings."

(3) The provisions establishing an Interdepartmental Advisory Committee were removed.

(4) In the provisions governing lateral entrance, the clause in H.R. 6967 reading, "unless he has passed such written, oral, physical and other examinations," was changed to read, "unless he has passed such examinations."

(5) In the provisions governing the status of Foreign Service Reserve officers, the sentence in H.R. 6967 reading: "In all other cases, suitable rank and position shall be provided to permit Reserve officers to carry out their duties effectively" was changed to read: "In all other cases, appropriate rank and status analogous to that of Foreign Service officers engaged in work of comparable importance, shall be provided to permit Reserve officers to carry out their duties effectively."

(6) Responsibility for recommending the appointment of Foreign Service Reserve officers was assigned to the Board of the Foreign Service, instead of jointly to the Board and the Director General, as in H.R. 6967.

In reaching this agreement Paul, taking cognizance of McCamy's conversation with Appleby, concerned himself primarily with the protection of Commerce's direct interests, first by ensuring full-fledged participation for Commerce (and other agencies) in the administration of the Foreign Service; and second by strengthening the status of designees or representatives of Commerce (and other agencies) serving in the Foreign Service Reserve. He was less interested in general questions like the creation of the statutory office of Director General.

From Panuch and Chapin's standpoint the agreement was an enforced concession. In two instances, however, the changes were sponsored by them: Full membership on the Board for the Director General was necessary to retain for the State Department a majority of the revised membership; while the addition of the three agencies to the Board made the Advisory Committee unnecessary.

Foster and his staff were disturbed by the agreement. They thought that Panuch had forced their hands and they felt that some of the detailed executive responsibilities given the Board in about a dozen different sections of the bill were inappropriate for an interdepartmental body, and should have been changed when the Board's membership was changed.

The agreement was reported to the Senate Committee on July 17. A day earlier, partly at least at Benton's suggestion, Secretary Byrnes, just back from Paris, had written Senator Connally urging prompt action by the Senate, and had telephoned various other Senators requesting their co-operation. On July 17, with the agreed amendments in hand, the Senate Committee met briefly in executive session, approved the text as revised, and voted to introduce and simultaneously report out S. 2451. During the executive session, Benton was the only member of the upper hierarchy of the

State Department present to testify in favor of the bill.

The Committee members were not entirely satisfied with the way S. 2451 had been handled. They had been rushed. Their own staff had had no opportunity to prepare an analysis of the bill for them, and they themselves had had no chance to study or discuss it. However, it would have been distressing to assume responsibility for blocking a bill earnestly desired by their respected former colleague, Secretary Byrnes. They were also pushed by earnest pleas from interested House members who had been appealed to by various Foreign Service Officers. Commerce and Agriculture also now desired enactment of the legislation.

In the rush of reporting out the bill, there was no time to prepare a fresh report; the Committee's report was merely a reprint of the introduction of the House Committee Report and did not reflect the changes in S. 2451 approved by the Senate Committee itself.

After the Paul-Panuch agreement was made, Miller and his associates discussed it. They were dissatisfied, and with the Secretary's approval, it was decided to reopen the matter with State. The dissatisfaction arose from the fact that the agreement, subscribed to by Paul, was inconsistent with the Secretary's letter of June 19 to the Director of the Bureau of the Budget. In that letter, it will be recalled, the Secretary had proposed the abolition of the office of Director General, the vesting of all powers in the Secretary of State, and the assignment to the Board of the Foreign Service of the function of general advice to the Secretary. These issues seemed important to Gladieux and Miller, partly because the Secretary had already taken a stand on them, partly because (not knowing of McCamy's recent conversation with Appleby) they thought it wise not to withdraw their support from the Bureau of the Budget, and partly because they believed that more effective control by the Secretary of State over the Foreign Service might well prove beneficial to the Department of Commerce.

The assignment of approaching State was given to Miller and Fisher. They invited Paul and Ostroff to accompany them in their proposed meeting with Panuch, but Paul suggested that Ostroff go alone with them. Ostroff accompanied them, but did not feel that their dissatisfaction with the Paul-Panuch agreement was warranted.

The meeting with Panuch was unpleasant. Panuch asserted emphatically that he understood that Paul's agreement represented the final Commerce position, while Ostroff insisted that Paul had explained the need for clearance with the Secretary of Commerce. (As it happened, Paul, feeling perhaps that because of his close relationship with Secretary Wallace, he could properly speak for the Secretary on this subject, had not checked with Mr. Wallace before opening his conversations with Chapin and Panuch.) Panuch then stated that it would be unwise to make any further change since it would undermine his position with Chapin and the other Foreign Service officers; he assured his listeners with vehemence that he had been the only guardian of the interests of the other departments throughout, and that their proposals would make it impossible for him to protect their interests in the future.

In the outcome, after this heated discussion, Panuch agreed to "try to sell" to the Foreign Service representatives a new amendment of the section dealing with the functions of the Board. The clause reading "the policies and procedures to govern the administration and personnel management of the Service, including appointments, assignments, promotions, and efficiency ratings" would now read: "the policies and procedures to govern the selection, assignment, rating, and promotion of Foreign Service officers; and the policies and procedures to govern the administration and personnel management of the Service."

Panuch said that he would undertake to secure Chapin's agreement, but that he must do this privately. He left the office and returned almost immediately with Chapin and Harrington. The new agreement was ratified without objection.

The whole agreement as revised now required the concurrence of the Congressional Committees and of the other agencies. It has been noted above that the Senate Committee included the changes originally agreed to in its bill as reported out on July 17, but the final supplementary agreement, which was not made until July 18, had to be inserted later. The House Committee was also willing to accept the changes, except for the proposed relaxation of the provisions covering examinations for lateral entrance into the Foreign Service officer corps; Congressman Vorys was adamant on this point, and it was dropped. Agriculture and Labor, which were consulted, were pleased; they had received more than they had asked for. The Secretaries of Agriculture and Commerce sent notes indicating complete concurrence in the amended bill to the Secretary of State; these were transmitted to the Bureau of the Budget on July 22 by Russell. (The Secretary of Labor sent a personal note of thanks to the Secretary of Commerce after the bill finally passed.)

The negotiations with Commerce resulted in the most important last-minute changes before the House debate on July 20. Other changes were still being made by the Foreign Service representatives, including some last-minute technical corrections resulting from a careful check of the repealer section by the Legislative Reference Service of the Library of Congress; a technical amendment proposed by the Civil Service Commission was also incorporated.

But there were also still further arguments. On Tuesday, July 16, Acting Comptroller General Yates, having learned of H.R. 6967, called Congressman Bloom to protest against three provisions. This information was passed on to Foster, who immediately called the Acting Comptroller General. A meeting was agreed to, and held on Wednesday. At this meeting, which lasted for several hours, Foster and three associates argued with three representatives of the General Accounting Office over the disputed points.

The GAO objected to the provisions safeguarding the confidential character of Foreign Service personnel records. While Foster assured them that their fears were unfounded, he agreed to an amendment excluding "records pertaining to the receipt, disbursement, and accounting for public funds."

The other two controversial sections related to the Secretary's power to issue a certificate "binding upon all officers of the Government" for expenditures for allowances, and for expenditures for commissary service. The power with respect to allowances was merely a carry-over from the Moses-Linthicum Act of 1931; it was agreed that the power had never been abused; in fact, there was doubt that it had ever been used. But Foster felt that it must be retained because of possible contingencies, even though its use was rare. He urged the GAO representatives to agree to retention of the clauses with the understanding that satisfactory operating arrangements would be worked out.

At the end of the meeting it was Foster's understanding that the GAO representatives would convey this suggestion to the Acting Comptroller General and that they would then again communicate with him.

On the following day, Mr. Yates wrote to Congressman Bloom without notifying the State Department, reiterating all three of his objections. Foster was called down to Mr. Bloom's office and the members of the Subcommittee were summoned. The Congressmen sympathized with Foster, who felt that he had been treated with utter bad faith, but persuaded him not to object to the amendments, lest passage of the bill be jeopardized.

But there were also difficulties with members of the House of Representatives. It will be recalled that, at the hearing on the Point-of-Order Bill on April 8, Congressman Rabaut, Chairman of the State Department Subcommittee of the Appropriations Committee, had been told that he would be kept advised of progress on the Foreign Service bill. In the rush of events this understanding was forgotten. When Congressman Rabaut saw that H.R. 6967 had been introduced and then reported out, he made clear his disapproval of the procedure. Judge Kee discussed the matter with him and agreed to an amendment of the commissary section, ensuring, in substance, the control of the Appropriations Committees over commissary operations.

Judge Kee also discussed the bill with Congressman Taber of New York, ranking minority member of the Appropriations Committee, and Chairman presumptive of that Committee if, as was generally expected, the Republicans secured control of the House in the fall elections. In any event, Congressman Taber was a figure to be reckoned with, even as a member of the minority party.

Congressman Taber desired an amendment. In the conventional section authorizing appropriations for the Foreign Service appeared the following language: "Not to exceed 10 per centum of any of the appropriations for the Department of State under the caption 'Foreign Service' may be transferred with the approval of the Director of the Bureau of the Budget to any other appropriation or appropriations under such caption in the same fiscal year, but no appropriation shall be increased more than 10 per centum thereby." This language was taken over substantially intact from language in the State Department Appropriation Act for the Fiscal Year 1947 that had been enacted a few weeks earlier. But the inclusion of this provision in a permanent statute meant that it would no longer be available to the Appropriations Committees to award annually, so to speak, for meritorious conduct. At Mr. Taber's request, Judge Kee agreed to the deletion of the sentence.

18. PASSAGE OF H.R. 6967

All these final negotiations and changes occurred after H.R. 6967 was reported out on July 12, and the last changes were not completed until after S. 2451 was introduced and reported out on July 17. Two days later, the House Foreign Affairs Committee gave its blessing to all the amendments (with the single exception noted above), and the bill up for House debate on the following day was revised accordingly.

The Rules Committee had provided for action on H.R. 6967 under suspension of the rules. Under this arrangement, a bill cannot be amended, and only forty minutes of debate is permitted, after which the House votes on a motion to suspend the rules and pass the bill; passage requires a two-thirds vote.

When the time for debate began on July 20, Mr. Bloom made the original motion. Mr. Taber promptly asked if his amendment was included. Mr. Bloom replied that the Committee had taken care of everyone—Mr. Taber, Mr. Rabaut, the General Accounting Office, the Budget Bureau.

Judge Kee then described the bill's history: He mentioned the receipt of the draft, the long sessions with the State Department representatives (accidentally referring to these as occurring in April, rather than May), the many changes made by the Subcommittee—all approved by the State Department—the reporting out and unanimous approval by the full Committee. He referred to the fact that Senator Connally had introduced a companion bill in the Senate that had been unanimously reported out by the Senate Committee. He praised the State Department for its splendid co-operation. After H.R. 6967 was introduced, he said, it was cleared with all the interested Committee chairmen and departments, and changes were agreed on. "To the best of my knowledge I believe everyone is satisfied with the bill as it is now presented."

The Chairman of the Rules Committee praised the bill and said that the rule had been voted unanimously. Congressman Rabaut and others congratulated Judge Kee on his handling of the bill. This concluded the twenty minutes allotted to the majority. Mrs. Rogers, managing the time for the minority, led off for them with a speech praising the bill, but expressing the belief that salaries and allowances were still inadequate. She was followed by Mr. Stefan of Nebraska, ranking minority member of the State Department Subcommittee of the Appropriations Committee. Mr. Stefan had not been consulted while the bill was under consideration and was somewhat suspicious of the way in which it had been handled; apparently he was afraid that the Foreign Affairs Committee had succumbed to Foreign Service blandishments. He pointed out first that the bill would involve increased expenditures and hence increased appropriations, but his chief objection lay rather to the procedure that had been adopted; in his opinion, an important and complex bill like H.R. 6967 should have been open for full debate and amendment.

Mr. Stefan was followed by Mr. Jonkman of Michigan, a member of the Committee on Foreign Affairs. During the hearing on July 2 he had discussed with Mr. Acheson the Committee's complaints about the presence of Communists in the State Department. Shortly thereafter he had been appointed a subcommittee of one to investigate the matter. He had now completed his investigation and was not satisfied with the personnel security procedures in force in the Department. He had written Mr. Byrnes about this on July 18. Mr. Byrnes, who was out of town, had telephoned him in reply on July 19, explaining that he would look into the question on his return and take whatever steps were necessary. All this Mr. Jonkman now reported to the House, explaining that it was collateral to H.R. 6967; but he took pains to add: "I found no evidence of any suspicion against personnel in the Foreign Service." The substance of Mr. Jonkman's speech was known to the Subcommittee members in advance, and they regarded his statement of approval of the Foreign Service personnel as important in ensuring passage of the bill. The deep concern of the House over Communism at this time can perhaps be more fully appreciated when it is realized that earlier on the same day, July 20, before taking up H.R. 6967, the House had passed the Atomic Energy Act of 1946 after lengthy debate on its security provisions.

After Mr. Stefan concluded his statement, Mr. Vorys spoke at some length. He spoke particularly of the Budget Bureau objections, remarking that the Subcommittee had begun hearings prior to Budget clearance. Of the Bureau, he said:

> They wanted a streamlined bill with broad powers given the Secretary to do things by regulations. In general we insisted on a detailed bill spelling out precisely who was to do what, and when. The bill is drafted our way. That is one reason why it is so long—106 pages. We felt the bill should not be introduced at all until we could have practically a clean bill. That is why it was introduced so late. Additional last minute changes account for the other amendments we are proposing. . . . It is not perfect; time and experience will dictate changes; it still contains discretionary powers than can be abused. . . .

Mr. Bloom added a final word. He said that he had appointed Mr. Vorys to the Subcommittee because he had been the principal objector to various proposals to amend the Rogers Act; he added that Judge Kee had handled clearance with the various House Committees.

After the conclusion of Mr. Bloom's remarks, the motion to suspend the rules and pass H.R. 6967 was carried unanimously.

Chapin was now within sight of the goal; but his path was narrow. It has been explained above that the only chance for completing Senate action before the end of the session—scheduled for approximately July 31—was to pass the bill by unanimous consent on the reading of the Consent Calendar. The first, and last, opportunity for this after the House action of July 20 came on July 29.

On that day, the clerk of the Senate called the calendar and the successive bills were either unanimously approved or passed over. Finally he reached the calendar number of S. 2451; to the surprise of all and to the dismay of the bill's supporters (including Chapin and Harrington who were in attendance), Senator Revercomb of West Virginia objected. Rather like Congressman Stefan, he had no objection to the bill but objected to the summary procedure; S. 2451 was not suitable for passage without debate. Senator Connally defended the bill briefly, and asked permission to substitute H.R. 6967, which by now was also on the Senate calendar; passage of the substitute would avoid the necessity of a second action by the House or a conference between the two Houses on the slight differences between the two bills. But Senator Revercomb persisted. Senator Austin of Vermont explained that the length of the bill was caused by the fact that it was a codification of existing law. Senator Connally admitted that the Senate Committee hearings had been brief, but pointed out that the House Committee had held extensive hearings; the bill was, he said, supported by the Secretary, and by the Assistant Secretary and others who had appeared before his Committee. Senator Fulbright of Arkansas, who had been in touch with Foster for months, tried to persuade Senator Revercomb to agree. Senator Taft asked a brief question about the Institute. And Senator Revercomb still objected, "temporarily," as he said. The clerk resumed the call of the calendar.

Chapin and Harrington left the Senate chamber, all hope gone. But just as they were leaving the Capitol, they met the State Department Congressional liaison officer; he told them that something might still happen. They returned.

On went the call of the calendar. Finally it reached the number assigned to H.R. 6967. Senator Vandenberg arose and announced that Senator Revercomb was prepared to withdraw his objection. When it was noted that Senator Revercomb was not on the floor, Senator Vandenberg reported: "I am authorized to speak for him." Without objection, the bill was passed.

A few minutes later, Senator Revercomb reappeared; he explained that while he still disliked the idea of passage without debate, several members of the Foreign Relations Committee had told him how important the bill was, and, at their request, he had withdrawn his objection.

19. SOME INTERRELATIONS OF THE LEGISLATIVE AND EXECUTIVE BRANCHES

The Constitution of the United States is based, as we all know, on a separation of powers and, *pro tanto,* on the attribution of powers to the Executive and the Legislative that can, if pushed to logical extremes, result in mutual impotence. But the tremendous significance of the separation of the powers should not lead us to overlook the complex and important web of relationships that do exist between the two arms of the government. Those relationships shift and vary all up and down the Executive hierarchy, and back and forth through the subtle committee and personal structure of Congress. The preceding pages may cast some light on the importance and difficulty of the relationships.

Congress is under no specific legal or constitutional mandate to respect the devices used by the Chief Executive or by agency heads to secure policy conformity within the Executive Branch in relation to legislative proposals. Indeed, with respect to the Budget Bureau's legislative reference activities, there is some tendency for members of the Congress to feel that the Bureau is a usurper, and that it is their own exclusive function to supply an over-all independent policy review of legislative proposals. However, the committee structure of both Houses is such that the actions of the different committees, which have, after all, certain vested interests, do not always satisfy the other members that committee consideration does constitute an over-all independent policy review; such apparently was Mr. Stefan's doubt in this instance.

Whatever the theoretical considerations, in fact Congressional committees vary widely in their procedures: some normally insist on Bureau of the Budget clearance (not, of course, approval) before initiating their own consideration of legislative proposals; others ignore the Bureau's existence. One recurrent factor that creates subvariations in procedure—an important factor in this case—is the pressure of time and the legislators' sense of obligation to legislate, where legislation is needed. These variations are not derived from, but equally are not totally unrelated to party considerations: Judge Kee, an Administration Congressman, in his speech on the floor of the House showed a desire to minimize differences with the Bureau; Mr. Vorys, a member of the opposition, emphasized the points at issue.

The treatment by Congress of the Bureau of the Budget is but one facet of the perpetual problem of divided loyalties and responsibilities. Where did Chapin's responsibility lie? or Judge Kee's? And it is of interest to contemplate Mrs. Bolton's praise of the intimate relations of the Department and the Committee in the light of the possible effect of such cross-loyalties on the President's Constitutional responsibilities for foreign policy. Can the State Department serve two masters—and how can the Congress carry out its own Constitutional obligations if it relies on Executive agencies? Problems created by the doctrine of the separation of the powers are not solely those arising from its observance.

The last-minute changes in the bill are of some interest because they were so largely the result of compromise outside the Congress. The legislative process is cumbersome and many bills, although unopposed or not seriously opposed, die in the closing days of a session. The specific vulnerability of the Foreign Service Bill arose from its timing. The use of Congressional spokesmen, taking advantage of the time factor, to protect agency interests against the plans of other agencies raises questions. The willingness of the Foreign Affairs Committee of the House to accept the bill without inter-agency clearance contrasts sharply with the Senate Committee's insistence —under duress, but apparently not unwillingly —on inter-agency agreement.

More striking, perhaps, is the phenomenon of passage of a long and complex bill virtually without debate, a bill sponsored and supported almost exclusively by Foreign Service officers —a group distrusted by many members of Congress, and more frequently attacked than defended in the newspapers. The defense of the bill was ingenious—for example, the common allegation that our Foreign Service officers are half-foreign was used as a raison d'être for the re-Americanization program and thus for new legislation—but passage was not the result of intellectual ingenuity. The reasons are to be sought rather in Congressional live-and-let-live attitudes, in the persistent influence of a well-liked former Senator like Mr. Byrnes, in some residual power in the phrase "an administration measure," above all, perhaps, in the potential effectiveness of one small energetic group within the Congress sponsoring a measure that lay outside the area of major public interest and conflict.

Part V. The President Decides

20. FINAL BUDGET BUREAU RECOMMENDATIONS

It is now necessary to turn back to activities in the Bureau of the Budget. On June 26 Appleby signed the letter setting forth the Bureau's formal position on the Foreign Service bill. Two days later—on June 28—came Chapin's letter to Sheppard, transmitting the Subcommittee print. This was not in form a reply to Appleby's letter; but it made any reply academic. Sheppard's reactions can be easily imagined.

Southworth was away on vacation at the time and Sheppard was able to have only one final conversation with Stone before he too left on a trip. He also talked briefly with Southworth on the telephone. Under the circumstances he was not able to describe with complete precision all the details of the negotiations with the State Department, since they had been handled so largely by Southworth. Nevertheless, with what information he could find, he addressed a memorandum to the Director on July 5 in which he reviewed the whole history of the affair. He referred to the hearing before the Foreign Affairs Committee on the Point-of-Order Bill and the appointment of the Subcommittee on Foreign Service legislation. He said that the Foreign Service officers had told Southworth of this and had asked permission to proceed, assuring Southworth that their discussions with the Subcommittee "would not jeopardize the final and cleared proposal." Southworth, with Sheppard's approval, had agreed, and Sheppard in retrospect now remarked, "We should have had a more clearcut arrangement." Certainly in his view the approval he intended had not been designed to cover the submission of a complete draft with accompanying explanatory materials and justifications. "Acting Secretary Acheson was right in terming the current situation badly complicated by these developments." His conclusions were as follows:

(1) Appleby's letter of July 26 has been turned over to the Office of the Foreign Service with no certainty of a follow-up.

(2) The Subcommittee draft does not represent inter-agency clearance. The other agencies "will suspect a double-cross" by the Bureau of the Budget.

(3) As a matter of strategy, it is the Foreign Service that will benefit by delay. Each passing day will give impetus to the Subcommittee draft.

In Sheppard's view there was not much chance of legislation during the current session but he thought it wise to get the bill in the best possible shape. In closing Sheppard expressed the view that the Foreign Service officers had played "fast and loose" with the top State Department and Budget Bureau officials, "although this is not easily demonstrated in black and white." He recommended that an attached letter that he had drafted be sent to the Department and that the points in the last paragraph be raised with Chapin who should be warned that if the bill as introduced should be the same as the Subcommittee's, the other agencies would be free to "oppose the bill." Finally he recommended that the Foreign Service officers be required to support the "official" position.

Appleby was unwilling to send this letter. He felt that it could not fail to embarrass Acheson and that it would produce a conflict with the Secretary; obviously the Bureau could not require subordinate officials to take a position at variance with the views of their department head.

When this attempt to remedy the situation was rejected, Sheppard tried again. He drafted a letter to be sent to Senator Connally; but the Senate Committee reported out S. 2451 on July 17, the day the letter was ready; obviously it was too late to catch the bill in Committee. In any event, it seems improbable that the Acting Director would have consented to send the letter, for transmittal would have been tantamount to a request for Congressional aid in maintaining discipline in the Executive Branch. The possibility of discussing the problem informally with the staff of the Senate Committee apparently had not been considered; if considered, it was not carried out. And it should be noted that there had been no violation of the technical rules of the game: in 1946, Circular A-19 did not forbid the transmittal of any legislative proposal, it merely required that the views of the Bureau be made known to the Congress. And this was done.

Relations between the Office of the Foreign Service and the Bureau were suspended. Chapin's negotiations with Commerce and the other interested parties passed the Bureau by. Foster waited about three weeks before drafting a reply to the Appleby letter of June 26. His draft, prepared on July 17 or 18 for the Secretary's signature, was a purely formal note, ending with the statement: "I will communicate with you further," which, in view of the fact that the bill had already been reported out in both Houses, could hardly be calculated to receive a warm welcome. When the letter reached Under Secretary Acheson on July 18 or 19 for initialing, he changed the last sentence to read: "Our staff is now working with the Department of Commerce and other departments concerned on appropriate amendments." This revision, referring to the negotiations just being concluded, at least had the value of indicating to the Bureau some concern with inter-agency clearance responsibilities.

With this letter and with Russell's letter of July 22 transmitting the concurrences of Agriculture and Commerce, relations again ceased temporarily. On July 30, Strom somewhat belatedly sent Southworth a copy of Chapin's submittal of July 2 to the Foreign Affairs Committee, pointing out once more that the Subcommittee had previously had all these matters explained in detail. But the passage of the bill inevitably brought the problem back to the Bureau; the Bureau stands inescapably astride the path of every enrolled bill.

The official copy of the enrolled bill was not received from the Executive Clerk until August 2, and on that day the President's constitutional ten days, excluding Sunday, began. The Bureau, however, did not wait for the official copy; on July 30, it sent out facsimiles of the enrolled bill for comment to the Departments of State, Commerce, Interior, Agriculture, Labor, Treasury, the Civil Service Commission, and the General Accounting Office.

The replies to the request for advice came in promptly. Agriculture approved, but again referred to the need for a separate bill defining its relations with the Foreign Service, even though it had concurred in the Commerce-Foreign Service agreement. Interior expressed distinct annoyance, especially because of its exclusion from membership on the Board of the Foreign Service, and requested amendatory legislation at the next session, but waived objection. The Civil Service Commission referred to its earlier doubts but also abstained from formal objection. Comments from the other agencies were favorable. All told, the incoming letters were not illuminating.

Southworth—now back from his vacation—took up the burden once again within the Bureau. Ou July 31, he drafted a long memorandum for Stone to send to the Director. Based on work done earlier, it outlined the history of the bill, criticizing the actions of the Foreign Service officers and pointing to the bill's defective character, but ended with a recommendation that the bill be approved. Attached was a draft statement for issuance by the President, following the familiar pattern of reluctant approval with a call for future improvement. But the recommendation to the White House was not to be decided so easily.

On the same day, July 31, Mr. James E. Webb took office as Director of the Bureau of the Budget. Mr. Webb, with a background of varied experience largely spent in business, had passed the last few months as Executive Assistant to the Under Secretary of the Treasury. (See Appendix II.) While there, he had noted the deterioration in the position of the Bureau since President Truman's accession to office. He felt it essential to establish without delay his responsibility for presenting all the facts to the President and for bringing forcefully to the President his considered recommendations on those facts. Obviously the President might take into account other factors outside the Bureau's ken, and might reach other conclusions; but Webb wished the whole government to know that the Bureau could not be intimidated and would be heard.

The Foreign Service Bill was one of the first important measures to be taken up with him by his staff. He listened attentively to the account of the past negotiations with the Foreign Service, and made up his mind that their representatives had not acted in good faith. The points of agreement and disagreement were reviewed with him and he came to the tentative conclusion that the bill was a bad bill and should be vetoed. He was particularly impressed by the seriousness of one basic point: the insulation of the Foreign Service from direct control by the Secretary. At this stage, he had a preliminary talk with the President who indicated some measure of agreement with Webb's views.

The staff of the Bureau had discussed the possibility of a veto but did not feel that they should advise Mr. Webb to make such a recommendation. It was obvious that Mr. Byrnes, who was again in Paris, might accuse Mr. Acheson of negligence if the bill were vetoed. More important, a veto would clearly cause Mr. Byrnes acute embarrassment, since he had urged Congressional approval of the measure, firmly and publicly: a veto could hardly fail to be construed as a slap at him. The time was extremely impropitious for any rupture in the President's relations with Secretary of State, for the Secretary was in the midst of delicate and difficult negotiations for which his continued prestige would be essential. And undesirable international consequences could hardly fail to be accompanied by undesirable domestic consequences; both Congress and the general public would tend to magnify any apparent breach between the two men, with benefit to neither, certainly not to the President.

The inevitability of these serious difficulties convinced Appleby, Stone and the others that the Bureau should not recommend disapproval; Stone had also been assured by Benton that the bill was needed and that a better bill could not be obtained. Stone was aware of the first point and inclined to agree with the second. Webb finally decided that his associates were right, and work proceeded with the understanding that a favorable recommendation would be filed.

On August 6, a week after the first draft was completed, Southworth set to work again. He prepared a memorandum to the Director for Stone's signature to which was attached a draft memorandum for the White House and a proposed letter from the President to the Secretary of State, calling attention to defects in the bill and requesting the Secretary to seek amendatory legislation in the new Congress; the proposed letter to the Secretary was a substitute for the original proposal of a public statement by the President. The file was transmitted to Appleby; he returned it with instructions to omit the proposed letter to the Secretary and to make corresponding changes in the memorandum for the White House. Stone, noting the decision to omit the letter to the Secretary, wrote on the file that while there may have been reasons for this change of which he was unaware, "it suggests we go through a lot of idle and purposeless motions on this clearance process." It is hardly possible for an outside observer to reconstruct with assurance in 1948 reasons of which Stone professed ignorance in 1946; but there is ground for the belief that Appleby wished to avoid an impairment of relations between Mr. Byrnes and the White House, and also between Mr. Byrnes and the new Budget Director—especially so since the President was faced with a *fait accompli* that would not be changed with or without a letter of reprimand.

On August 7, Southworth took up the task once more. The new memorandum for the White House incorporated Appleby's changes and was revised in other minor respects. However, although it now was not to serve as the basis for any semi-adverse action, it still preserved its original structure: two pages of adverse strictures, and two paragraphs of favorable comment ending up with a flat recommendation for Presidential approval. Stone was not entirely happy about the form of the memorandum, but a complete revision, requiring fresh clearance, seemed impractical.

The memorandum recited the history of the bill, noting the submission of a draft to the Bureau on May 3, and the Bureau's letter of June 26; it said that H.R. 6967 was passed in a form developed by Foreign Service representatives working directly with a Subcommittee of the Foreign Affairs Committee: "The bill as passed was therefore never cleared by the Bureau of the Budget." Proceeding, the memorandum outlined briefly some of the important new features of the bill—the reduction in the number of classes, the establishment of the Reserve and Staff corps, the lateral entrance provisions, the salary and allowance systems, the retirement and disability benefits, and the selection-out and other retirement procedures.

The following five major objections to H.R. 6967 were then cited:

1. The statutory creation of a Director General and the requirement that he be a Foreign Service officer of Class 1 or a career minister; this would prevent the Secretary from determining the type of administrative arrangement he desired, and would limit his freedom of choice.

2. The statutory creation of a Board of the Foreign Service with specific defined functions, rather than a simple authorization for the Secretary to create an Advisory Board representative of the whole government; this also would limit the Secretary's power to adapt the Service to new conditions.

3. The statutory establishment of the Board of Examiners; this would legislate a detail of personnel management normally left to the agency head.

4. The mandatory establishment of the Institute, whose Director and employees would be exempt from Civil Service laws; this was a further dilution of the Secretary's power to direct the Service.

5. The establishment of the Reserve Corps; this was likely to perpetuate existing discriminations between the "career" and "non-career" officers.

The memorandum referred to other minor objections; it remarked that greater flexibility would be desirable, as would be a greater degree of comparability between the Foreign Service and the Civil Service. In general, H.R. 6967 was said to be objectionable because of its tendency to set up the Foreign Service as a quasi-independent organization for foreign affairs, when the need was for greater integration.

In a few concluding sentences, the memorandum referred to the desirability of certain features of the bill, notably the replacement of the Auxiliary, the salary increases, and the establishment of the Staff corps, on the basis of which "I feel obliged to recommend approval." The hope was expressed that later on the President would lend his support for modification.

While this final expression of the Bureau's views follows established lines, certain features of the memorandum justify comment: (1) As has been noted, the major thrust of the argument would lead to veto rather than approval; (2) the major premise, i.e., the effect of a veto on Mr. Byrnes, on which the recommendation for approval was actually based was left unstated; presumably the omission, which follows normal practice, was dictated by the inarticulate premise that the formal document should cite only the formal considerations; (3) some of the secondary problems were given prominence in such fashion as to obscure the major issues; thus the Foreign Service officer eligibility requirement for the Director General is mixed in with the objection to the statutory creation of the office, and the mention of the technical exemption allowed the Institute from Civil Service rules makes less forceful the underlying objection to the mandatory establishment of an Institute; (4) the historical account is perhaps not entirely objective, especially in its complete omission of any reference to the substantial inter-agency agreement that preceded passage of the bill.

On August 8 the memorandum was signed. A suggestion that the whole file be handed to one of the President's assistants, who was interested in the subject, for transmittal was rejected. It was sent to the office of the Executive Clerk in the usual fashion.

The 79th Congress had departed, and the President was now working against time with the usual last-minute rush of bills that had to be considered before the expiration of the constitutional time limit. He looked over the Foreign Service Bill file without delay. Presumably he still had in mind his conversation with Webb, when Webb was thinking of a veto recommendation; perhaps he also had in mind a conversation with the administrative assistant referred to above, who did not believe that the bill was sound; he was probably more impressed by the force of Webb's arguments than by the approval recommendation. Other factors may also have played a part. In any event, whatever the precise reasons, he sent the file on to his Special Counsel with a handwritten note saying that he was inclined to veto the bill.

The President's Special Counsel conceived of his function, in connection with enrolled bills, as a review of the problem presented by each bill from the personal standpoint of the President, in contrast with the necessarily somewhat institutional viewpoint of the Budget Bureau. He reviewed the file and noted Webb's statement that the bill had never received clearance from the Bureau. Taking this as his point of departure for investigation, he called the State Department.

21. STATE DEPARTMENT PLEADINGS

The White House call came on the afternoon of Friday, August 9. Russell and Chapin were both about to leave town for the week-end. They assumed that the delay of over a week had been merely a part of the normal routine, and had expected approval by the President on the 8th or 9th. The possibility of a veto had never occurred to them.

The news from the White House came as a stunning and unhappy surprise. Week-end plans were canceled, for time was running out; if the President remained unconvinced, his mere failure to sign would automatically result in a pocket veto, as it is called. Russell now took charge of affairs personally. His first step, on the same day, August 9, was to dictate and send to the Special Counsel an extensive memorandum giving his version of the clearance process and defending thereby the actions of the Foreign Service officers. In summary, the contents of the memorandum are as follows:

1. The formal submission occurred on April 16.
2. Early in May, at the insistence of the Foreign Affairs Committee, which thought the Department dilatory, and with the knowledge and informal approval of the Bureau of the Budget, the Department informally gave a copy of the draft bill to the Committee.
3. A Subcommittee was appointed early in May to review the proposed bill.
4. On June 11, having received informal advice of the Bureau's views, the Secretary wrote to the Director.
5. During May and June, eight meetings were held at which the Subcommittee prepared its own bill.
6. On June 26 the Bureau's formal views were received, and these were transmitted to the Subcommittee by Chapin on July 1.
7. On July 3, the Subcommittee submitted its bill and a report thereon to the full Committee.
8. On July 10, the Bureau's letter and all agreed changes were reported to the full Committee.
9. After two hearings, the full Committee, having considered the draft and the objections to it, approved the revised Subcommittee version.
10. On July 16, the Secretary wrote Senator Connally, soliciting his support. On July 18, State and Commerce agreed on changes.

11. The Budget Bureau was advised of negotiations, as is shown by the letter to Appleby.

12. On July 19 the House Committee accepted the modifications and reported to the House.

13. On July 19, Commerce and Agriculture wrote to State giving their approval.

14. On July 20, the House passed the bill.

15. On July 29, after Senator Connally referred to Mr. Byrnes's "very insistent request," the Senate Committee reported, and the Senate passed the bill.

16. The bill was well received in the press.

17. The bill as passed was approved by State, Commerce and Agriculture. It was emphatically advocated by the Secretary, in its present form, with the congressional leaders.

18. The objections of the Budget Bureau were fully considered and rejected. Unqualified approval is requested.

This memorandum is written with style and emphasis. Although Russell dictated it in the presence of the Foreign Service group, he was impatient with detailed suggestions and interested only in the total effect. Minor errors of fact are frequent (see, e.g., (3), (5)); and the document is frankly partisan. In notable contrast to Webb's memorandum, it does refer by implication at least to a major reason for signature—the danger of embarrassing the Secretary.

About the same time as the dictation of this document, Russell had a meeting with Webb. Russell accused Webb of trying to sabotage the bill; Webb defended his memorandum by reference to his responsibility for putting the President in possession of all the facts. The meeting had no specific outcome. Webb refused to withdraw or amend what had been said.

On Saturday, August 10, having obtained a copy of Webb's memorandum, Russell dictated and sent to the Special Counsel a memorandum of reply, citing the Bureau's general objection to the "quasi-autonomous" status of the Foreign Service, and making the following specific points:

1. *The Director General.* These provisions requiring the Director General to be a Foreign Service officer of Class 1 or the career minister class, follow "existing law," and the Director General is appointed by and holds office at the sufferance of the Secretary. Subject only to the Board of Examiners, the Secretary can recommend anyone outside the Service as a Class 1 Foreign Service officer. It would have been simpler to have omitted this requirement, but the Congress refused to accept the Bureau's recommendations. Why forsake the entire legislation for this "perfecting provision," when the same result can be obtained anyway?

2. *The Board of Examiners.* The Bureau says it should not be statutory; but what difference does the statutory requirement make? The only limitation on the Secretary's powers with respect to the Board is that he must consult with the Board of the Foreign Service with respect to the personnel of the Board of Examiners; since the BFS, with seven members, includes three Assistant Secretaries of State and the Director General, it is entirely within the Secretary's control. The vesting of advisory status in the representatives of the other three departments was not the desire of the Department or the Foreign Service, but "a gracious gesture," and a "concession" to those departments.

3. *The Board of the Foreign Service.* The Bureau says that this should be established by departmental order, but it has been statutory for over twenty years; Congress would object to the removal of this provision. In any event, the Secretary controls the personnel of the Board and argument against the statutory base is captious. Its powers are so broad that they will need to be defined by regulation, and Commerce and Agriculture would not have agreed to the bill without the Board.

4. *The Foreign Service Institute.* The Bureau says that this "dilutes" the Secretary's authority; but how can the exemption of the Director and staff from Civil Service "dilute" the Secretary's authority?

5. *The Reserve.* The Bureau objects without specification. But the Reserve officers all have the same diplomatic status as the Foreign Service officers, and are eligible for transfer at the end of their term of service.

This document was also the product of impatience and anger, but written with force and persuasiveness. It may be useful to comment on some of its rather hasty conclusions. In (1), Russell adopted the advocate's technique of seizing on the secondary objection (the required Foreign Service status), and answering that, while omitting any answer to the basic objection (the statutory creation of the office). Beyond this, it is at least misleading to say that the Secretary can recommend anyone for appointment as a Class 1 Foreign Service officer, subject only to the Board of Examiners. The Board of Examiners is specifically designed to prevent appointments on the basis of personal choice by others, and in any event the three- or four-year prior service requirement cannot be waived. It may also be noted that while Russell disavows the Foreign Service officer requirement, except as a political necessity, it had been supported by the Secretary and strongly urged by the Foreign Service.

In (2), Russell (who accepted no advice in preparation of the memorandum) was under a plain misapprehension: the statute does not require BFS consultation prior to appointment by the Secretary of the members of the Board of Examiners. The later comments on the BFS are perhaps best described as subjective; the inclusion of the other departments was indeed a "concession," but from the standpoint of the Foreign Service, it was not a "gracious gesture," but rather a concession made under duress. It will be noted that no direct answer is made to the Bureau's objection to the statutory creation of the Board, except to ask the pertinent but not necessarily conclusive question: "What difference does it make?" Russell avoided any answer to the point about the Board's specific defined statutory powers, a point which was perhaps more basic than the statutory establishment.

In (4), Russell again adopted the technique of ridiculing the major objection (dilution of the Secretary's powers in the mandatory creation of the Institute) by taking it as applicable to the secondary objection (the Civil Service exemption).

In (5), Russell was on firmer ground in stating that the Bureau's objection to the Reserve was "without specification"; at least it was without detailed specification. But Russell's statement in defense that Reserve officers have "the same diplomatic status" as Foreign Service officers is less than precise. Under the Act, the Secretary "may recommend to the President that such [i.e., Reserve] officer be commissioned as a diplomatic or consular officer, or both." In all other cases, "analogous" status is to be provided.

What importance was attributed by the President's Special Counsel to this memorandum is indeterminable; but Russell did not rest with this. He followed up with a discussion with the Special Counsel. In his discussion, he emphasized "political" points not cited in the written text of the two documents. He also followed up by a teletype conversation with the Secretary in Paris—a step that had been earnestly desired from the beginning by the Foreign Service group. The Secretary responded as had been hoped, agreeing to communicate with the President. He did so, basing his appeal on the embarrassment he would suffer from a veto, and discarding a suggested draft cable relying on more formal considerations that had been prepared for him by Russell.

How the President might have decided in the absence of Mr. Byrnes's appeal is unknown —probably unknowable. Certainly the appeal carried great weight.

On Monday, August 12, Russell sent the Special Counsel a draft statement to be issued if the President approved H.R. 6967. On August 13, the President signed the bill, and on August 15 released the statement, in which he spoke of the importance of the Service and the need for strengthening it, and listed certain major improvements that would be brought about by the Act—referring particularly but in general terms to the increased salaries, the more rigid requirements for promotion and training, the re-Americanization program, and the Reserve Corps.

22. AFTERMATH

Signature of the bill and issuance of the statement did not clear away all the clouds. Chapin and his colleagues were immensely relieved, but still deeply disturbed. Most of them were convinced that the Bureau had almost caused a veto by sending a memorandum which, notwithstanding its formal recommendation, laid all its emphasis on defects in the bill. They felt that their own motives had been misunderstood and that they had been subjected to a needless and improper inquisition. Indeed it seemed to them that they had been unfairly singled out for destructive criticism, while other similar groups like the Army and the Navy were never questioned. They also felt that Commerce had secured, by dubious means, an unsatisfactory and possible unworkable amendment.

Commerce was also not entirely mollified. Officially the Secretary had given his complete approval to the Act, but there was disagreement within his Department on the value of the last-minute amendments and a strong feeling (on the part of some) that the Budget Bureau had not protected the interests of Commerce and the other agencies. Shortly after the Act became law, Southworth had a meeting with a number of the Commerce officials. He objected to the deal they had made and told them that they should have cleared with the Bureau. They retorted in kind, saying that the Bureau had been greatly at fault in not bringing in the other agencies while the Bureau's hearings were still in progress, especially since the Foreign Service should represent the whole government. They also stated that when the Bureau lost control of the situation, the other agencies had no responsibility for further clearance. No mention was made of McCamy's conversation with Appleby. The subject was left in dispute.

The group probably most pleased by final approval of the bill were its Congressional advocates. Most members of the Congress had no interest in the subject, a great many were suspicious of all Foreign Service officers, and there was at least one persistent objector who felt that the diffusion of authority in the Act made it impossible for Congress to fix responsibility. But the members of the House Foreign Affairs Committee and particularly the members of the Subcommittee were delighted. They believed in the Act, and were proud of their contribution to it. They had enjoyed their work with the Foreign Service representatives and they felt that this was an example of how Congress should handle legislation.

In the Bureau of the Budget, attitudes were naturally quite different. A sense of frustration, of ill treatment was pervasive. It was almost an adding of insult to injury when they were accused of having tried to get the President to veto the bill. After all, the decision to recommend approval had been made reluctantly, and only with the conscientious conviction that it was their responsibility to do so. A veto recommendation would have been far more pleasant. And, as a final straw for Stone and his assistants, there was the President's approving statement. In spite of all their efforts, the record no longer promised them an opportunity to insist on the submission of amendatory legislation in the 80th Congress.

AFTERTHOUGHTS

History does not answer its own questions. Historians, consciously or unconsciously, do provide or suggest answers. And the observant reader will seek to formulate his own solutions.

A case study like this can be most useful as a guide to questions. Our theories of government, our sense of right conduct for public administrators, grow out of the climate of opinion in which we live and our individual personalities, and out of whatever knowledge we have of governmental operations. One of the limiting factors on our adoption of useful hypotheses is the prior necessity of directing our search for answers to real rather than unreal problems, and to problems of significance rather than of detail. Whatever utility this account of the development and enactment of the Foreign Service Act may have will arise primarily from its evocation of the inquiring spirit, and from its suggestion of questions that deserve answers.

In the foreword, an indication has been given of three major problem areas illustrated by this study.

The first is the appropriate character of the Foreign Service itself. The dilemma faced by the administrator is a balancing of the values of independence and security against the values of responsiveness and constant invigoration. It was largely a conflict of these values that led to the arguments about lateral entrance into the corps of Foreign Service officers and the disputes about the functions of the Director General. As in most long-drawn-out discussions, the proponents on each side tended to throw in arguments of varying degrees of validity; but each reader can appraise the arguments, and can reach his own conclusions.

What is perhaps more surprising than this heterogeneity in the debate is the failure of the debaters to probe more deeply into some of the antecedent or auxiliary questions. The role of the Director General is debated, but only as a question of statutory inclusion or exclusion; the fundamental problem of control vs. independence is equally posed by the maintenance of separate personnel, budget, and other administrative offices. Lateral entrance is discussed but the upward extension of the Career Service through the creation of the career minister class also involves the Career Service principle. These questions were hardly mentioned.

The reason for the selection of items that were actively argued is largely found in the terms of the bill under discussion. By the very act of inclusion or exclusion, the draftsmen controlled the agenda. The battle was fought on ground of their choosing, though of course this particular effect was obviously not the result of a deliberate plan.

A second primary question that is implicit or explicit in the recital of most of these events is the appropriate role of the agency, of the President and his Bureau of the Budget, and of the Congress in the formulation of policy, particularly legislative policy.

The development of the Foreign Service Act is peculiar in one respect. It is at least rare for an employee group acting not as an outside organization but in its official capacity to be the chief determinant of legislation for its own benefit. When new Civil Service legislation undergoes gestation, the various unions of Federal employees play a vocal and frequently important part; but the directing force in the Executive Branch, the Civil Service Commission, does not act as a direct representative of the prospective beneficiaries. Not so with Chapin and his associates. The fact that the procedure was unusual deserves some consideration in itself.

There is a secondary respect in which the procedure in this case is unusual: not only did a guild group in the government act as official representative of its own interests, it also acted as sole and, in effect, self-appointed representative for a much larger group of associates—the 8,000-odd non-career officers and employees of the Foreign Service.

In other respects, the problems of legislative clearance—to use a catch-all phrase for a complex process—that were met during the preparation and enactment of the law are in essence not uncommon. To what extent the President or the Bureau of the Budget (acting for him, or perhaps in fulfillment of independent statutory responsibilities) should control the legislative proposals of the departments is a question that is asked daily, and never answered finally.

Presidential control vs. agency independence in connection with legislation, when viewed as a problem of inter-agency relationships is at least a subject that finds constant thoughtful articulation in the government. Less thought is given to the questions that center on the relation of the Congress to the maintenance of discipline and policy consistency within the Executive Branch. What weight should Judge Kee and the members of his Committee have given to the Budget's responsibility for the President's program? How should Chapin have handled the Subcommittee's request for hearings? What should Sheppard have done when Chapin asked permission to start hearings? Should Commerce have concluded its agreement with Panuch? Or, should the House Committee have insisted, as the Senate Committee did, on inter-agency agreement before final action?

It is by beginning with these limited and very practical puzzles that the larger questions of Executive-Congressional relationships can take form and find solutions.

The third major problem illustrated in this study is the nature and role of a guild group within the government. The corps of Foreign Service officers constitutes such a guild. Its centripetal forces are strong, and its protective coat is thick, so that it constitutes a somewhat unassimilable element in the Department of State and in the government as a whole. As such, it is readily identifiable and its characteristics can be observed.

The Career Service can be differentiated from most other guilds in the government in that—while its members often refer to it as a Professional Service—its members are not bound together primarily or initially by a common professional academic background like the doctors, or the foresters, or the public administrators (in the special sense of the word) or the officers of the Navy. But in most other respects it is similar in its formal attributes to other easily recognizable guilds. Most of the groups that are obviously guilds—like the corps of Foreign Service officers—do have all or some of the following attributes:

Entrance: limited and primarily at the lowest grade
Conditions of Service: privileged but subject to various compulsions
Tenure: quasi-permanent and inherent in the person
Statutory basis: detailed requirements and restrictions
Functions: similar responsibilities for all members and exclusion of non-members from these areas of responsibility.

Guilds can and do exist without one or more of these characteristics, but Congressional recognition of a guild as such tends to follow these lines; and it is perhaps not without significance that many Foreign Service officers describe guilds possessed of this kind of legal structure as "career services." It may be asserted that these are but the outer trappings; but the guild codes of conduct develop within this administrative environment.

Thus the corps of Foreign Service officers fits into a larger pattern; but it is of course conditioned by the specific character of its functions, by its selection procedures, and by the fact that the locale of its operations is situated in other countries. It is also distinguishable (though not unique) in the fact that it is a Field Service that also fills the key positions in a Departmental Service.

A common formulation suggests that the President establishes foreign policy, the Secretary of State is its spokesman and the Foreign Service officers merely carry it out. The inadequacy of this formulation is apparent when thought is given to the enormous complexity of the factors that, taken together, are described as our "foreign policy." A Presidential speech can execute policy, a cable from Cairo can create it.

Under these circumstances the effects of assigning to a somewhat isolated group many of the major positions at home as well as abroad in the conduct of our foreign relations are not without significance. The arguments pro and con have been detailed at some length above and can be reviewed and evaluated. Perhaps the broader question is reflected in the fact that the representatives of the corps themselves chose to set up a Reserve without undue restrictions, to relax lateral entrance requirements, to improve the status of the Staff; for the question is the suitability of the whole Foreign Service for its tasks, when the dominant and reserved role in the development and execution of foreign policy is still assigned to a relatively closed group of employees, rather removed from public scrutiny, and specially obligated and privileged.

These suggestions about three significant areas of inquiry for which some materials are provided herein are not exclusive. Others will come to mind, many of which are far from negligible. Thus—should the Bureau of the Budget's authority over legislative clearance be left indefinite or made precise? Should the function of policy clearance be assigned to a sizable staff agency like the Bureau? Should the Secretary of State spend months abroad every year? Should inter-agency interests be guarded by vesting power in inter-agency boards? Should Congress delegate the power to establish various aspects of personnel policy? The first step towards the development of theory is the isolation of the problem. Insofar as this study is useful in indicating the existence and nature of certain problems of importance, it will have served its purpose.

Appendix I

NOTE ON CERTAIN TERMS

Merit System–Career Service–Professional Service –Civil Service–Classified Service–Civil Service Status

The term "merit system" in its special application to the Foreign Service means appointment solely on the basis of meeting certain statutory standards, and promotion from one class or grade to another on a uniform basis regardless of specific assignments and responsibilities. In practice, for most persons appointment is largely dependent on the successful passing of written examinations. Also as a practical matter, the largest factor in promotions under the Foreign Service merit system in the first twenty years after the passage of the Rogers Act of 1924 was seniority. Negatively, the "merit system" implies a complete freedom from influence on initial appointments or promotions by "political officials," i.e., Senators, Congressmen, the President, the Secretary of State, the Assistant Secretaries, etc. To all or almost all Foreign Service officers, the term also includes the concept of entrance exclusively or primarily at the lowest grade by competitive examination—this notwithstanding the fact that about half of all Foreign Service officers in service in 1946 had entered the Service in other ways. From the standpoint of the Foreign Service, the term "merit system" is applicable to the practices affecting the Foreign Service officer group—a group established as such by the Rogers Act; in their thinking the term does not apply to the rules for other Federal employee groups—the classified Civil Service, the Post Office, etc.

The term "Career Service" is also a term of art used by Foreign Service officers. The word "career" in this connection originated as a translation of a French diplomatic term—"de carrière"—and refers in substance to persons who have diplomatic or consular accreditation and who are part of the permanent bureaucracy of diplomacy. Under the Rogers Act only the Foreign Service officer group meets these qualifications; indeed under that Act Foreign Service officers who received appointments as minister or ambassador, lost their "career" status. Thus the Foreign Service officers, and only they, constitute a "career service" under the "merit system." But by extension, some officers refer to other groups with similar attributes, such as the Army or the Public Health Service as "career services."

The term "Professional Service" is used synonymously by Foreign Service officers with "Career Service." In this sense, "professional" is an antonym to "political." The thought presumably is of persons who take up the task of being a Foreign Service officer, or diplomat, for life, i.e., as a profession, as contrasted with those for whom it is a passing occupation.

In this study, the term "civil service" is used loosely, much as it is ordinarily used by Foreign Service officers. Essentially it refers to that large body of Federal civilian employees, who are, under the law and largely under the general supervision of the Civil Service Commission, promoted for merit, and who cannot be discharged except for cause or consequent upon abolition of the position occupied by the employee. The term is also used here, and generally, though imprecisely, to cover the salary scales and position classification system established by the Classification Act of 1923, as amended. Actually there are thousands of Federal civilian employees with Civil Service status in positions not covered by the Classification Act, and other thousands in Classification Act positions but without Civil Service status. These niceties have been ignored. The term is also used to describe the retirement system that covers all Federal civilian employees except those benefitting by some special retirement system or otherwise specifically exempted. Similarly the term applies to leave and other beneficial or restrictive regulations generally applicable to the civilian employees of the government other than those excluded by specific statutory provisions. It will be noted that the significant aspects of the Civil Service that differentiate it from the Career Service are: (1) entrance freely at all grades by varying types of examination or qualification procedures; (2) absence of special perquisites such as higher salaries, higher retirement benefits, etc.; and (3) tenure and promotion by work actually performed, i.e., employment under the Classification System.

The term "Classified Service" means those employees of the government serving in positions covered by the Classification Act of 1923 as amended. For all these employees status is determined essentially by the official rating given the work performed—i.e., the classification of the job. Within fairly broad limits, promotion to a higher status with a higher salary can come at any time of the employee is transferred to a job with a higher classification (or if his job is "reclassified"). Promotion is not directly related to seniority (except for so-called in-grade promotions that occur under both Civil and Foreign Service). Thus in the Classified Service, status inheres in the job not the man, and when the job is terminated, the tenure terminates as well. By contrast, in the Career Service, status inheres in the man, and is unaffected by the particular duties performed at any one time; tenure is not affected by the abolition of the job, and the responsibility for finding a new position rests with the Service, not with the individual.

"Civil Service status" means (1) that an employee who has such status cannot be discharged arbitrarily, and (2) that such an employee, whose job is abolished, is automatically eligible for appointment to any suitable position under Civil Service without examination; but such reinstatement is not guaranteed either in theory or in practice.

Appendix II

Biographies

(A) Department of State
(as of December 1, 1946)

CHAPIN, SELDEN—b. Erie, Pa., Sept. 19, 1899; St. Paul's Sch.; U.S.N.A. grad. 1919; Navy 1919-25, Lt. (jg); app. For. Ser. officer unclass. Mar. 20, 1925; also v.c. of career and v.c. at Hankow Sept. 2, 1925; app. sec. in the Diplo. Ser. Jan. 6, 1927; 3d sec. at Peking Jan. 25, 1927; at Rome June 27, 1929; class eight and cons. Dec. 19, 1929; 3d sec. at Quito Nov. 3, 1932; at San Salvador Aug. 4, 1934 (canceled); at Port-au-Prince Nov. 2, 1934; class seven July 1, 1934; 2d sec. at Port-au-Prince Jan. 31, 1935; class six Apr. 1, 1936; to the Dept. May 22, 1936; class five Jan. 3, 1938; asst. chief, Div. of the Am. Republics, Nov. 21, 1938; liaison officer with War and Navy Depts. Nov. 3, 1939; class four Mar. 1, 1940; cons. and 1st sec. at Montevideo Aug. 30, 1940; to the Dept. Dec. 27, 1941; asst. chief, Div. of the Am. Republics, Jan. 20, 1942; class three June 1, 1942; liaison officer, Emergency Advisory Comm. for Pol. Defense, 1942-43; exec. sec., Comm. on Political Planning, Nov. 2, 1942-Jan. 15, 1944; 1st sec. of emb. for duty with U. S. representative to the Politico-Mil. Commn. at Algiers Oct. 5, 1943; couns. of mission at Algiers Nov. 29, 1943; class two July 16, 1944; couns. of mission at Paris Sept. 1, 1944; to the Dept. Jan. 2, 1945; deputy dir., Office of the For. Ser., Jan. 10, 1945; class one May 16, 1945; dir., Office of the For. Ser., May 16, 1945; dir. gen. of the For. Ser., Nov. 13, 1946; mem., Bod. of the For. Ser., Nov. 13, 1946; For. Ser. officer of class one Nov. 13, 1946; class of career minister Nov. 25, 1946; married—OFS.

FOSTER, ANDREW BRISBIN—b. Philadelphia, Pa., Jan. 3, 1903; Episcopal Acad. grad.; Dartmouth, B.S. 1925; St. John's Coll., Cambridge U., England, B.A. 1929, M.A. 1933; studied in Switzerland and Danzig 1933-34; deputy dist. insp., Saar Plebiscite Commn., 1934-35; app. For. Ser. officer unclass., v.c. of career, and sec. in the Diplo. Ser. Oct. 1, 1935; v.c. at Montreal Oct. 5, 1935; For. Ser. Sch. Dec. 7, 1936; v.c. at Athens Apr. 7, 1937; at Salonika, temp., June 17, 1937; at Athens Oct. 1, 1937; also for Italian Islands of the Aegean Oct. 28, 1938; also 3d sec. at Athens Nov. 10, 1938; to the Dept. Aug. 28, 1939; class eight May 1, 1941; class seven July 16, 1943; 2d sec. and v.c. near Govt. of Greece established in Egypt Sept. 28, 1943; cons. Nov. 12, 1943; cons. near Govt. of Greece in addition to duties as 2d sec. Nov. 17, 1943; also 2d sec. near the Govt. of Yugoslavia established in Egypt Dec. 21, 1943; to the Dept. July 14, 1944; exec. asst. to asst. sec. of state Sept. 1, 1944; special asst. to asst. sec. of state Dec. 20, 1944-Aug. 17, 1945; class five May 16, 1945; chief, Div. of For. Ser. Planning, Dec. 4, 1945; For. Ser. officer of class four Nov. 13, 1946; married—FSP.

GULLION, EDMUND ASBURY—b. Lexington, Ky., Mar. 2, 1913; Western High Sch. (D. C.) grad.; Emerson Inst.; Princeton, A.B. 1935; teacher in prep. sch. 1936-37; app. For. Ser. officer unclass., v.c. of career, and sec. in the Diplo. Ser. July 2, 1937; v.c. at Marseille July 8, 1937; For. Ser. Sch. Oct. 24, 1938; v.c. at Salonika Apr. 21, 1939; at Calcutta Sept. 4, 1941 (canceled); 3d sec. and v.c. at London Jan. 13, 1942; class eight Oct. 20, 1942; For. Ser. officer, temp., at Algiers Dec. 11, 1942; 3d sec. and v.c. at London Mar. 20, 1943; 3d sec. at Helsinki Dec. 13, 1943-June 30, 1944; 3d sec. and v.c. at Stockholm July 15, 1944; class seven July 16, 1944; 2d sec. at Stockholm in addition to duties as v.c. Aug. 21, 1944; to the Dept. Mar. 6, 1945; class six Aug. 13, 1945; class five May 19, 1946; For. Ser. officer of class four Nov. 13, 1946.

HARRINGTON, JULIAN FISKE—b. Framingham, Mass., Apr. 11, 1901; Framingham High Sch. grad.; Columbia U. 1920-21; clk. 1 yr.; app. clk. in Am. Consulate at Malaga Mar. 1921; v.c. at Malaga July 5, 1922; at Antwerp May 17, 1923; For. Ser. officer unclass., v.c. of career, and assigned as v.c. at Antwerp Aug. 3, 1925; at Dublin, Mar. 9, 1926; at Ottawa July 29, 1929; class eight and cons. Dec. 31, 1929; cons. at Ottawa Jan. 22, 1930; class seven July 1, 1934; at Mexico City, Mar. 20, 1935; class six Apr. 1, 1936; sec. in the Diplo. Ser. Dec. 1, 1937; to the Dept. Feb. 1, 1938; class five June 16, 1938; on detail to the Dominican Govt. Aug. 4, 1938; to the Dept. Dec. 13, 1938; asst. chief, Visa. Div., May 29, 1940; class four May 1, 1941; 1st sec. and cons. at Madrid Mar. 5, 1942; class three July 16, 1943; 1st sec. at Lisbon in addition to duties as 1st sec. at Madrid May 30, 1944; to the Dept. Apr. 17, 1945; class two May 16, 1945; deputy dir., Office of the For. Ser., May 16, 1945; also asst. security officer June 18, 1945; class one Dec. 17, 1945; deputy dir. gen. of For. Ser., and dir., Office of the For. Ser., and For. Ser. officer of class one Nov. 13, 1946; married—OFS.

LAMPSON, EDWARD TUDOR—b. Hartford, Conn., Jan. 8, 1912; Kingswood Sch. grad.; Amherst, A.B. 1933; Harvard, Ph.D. 1939; asst. in hist., Harvard U., 1937-8; instr., Trinity Coll., 1939-41; asst. prof., Southwestern Coll., 1941-42; app. divisional asst. at $3,200 in the Dept. of State Mar. 27, 1942; at $3,300 Oct. 1, 1943; furlough for mil. ser. (U. S. Army, 2d lt.) Jan. 31, 1944-July 4, 1945; at $3,800 Feb. 16, 1944; at $4,300 (CAF-11) July 1, 1945; admin. analyst July 4, 1945; CAF-12 Jan. 7, 1946; married—FSP.

NEUSTADT, MARION L.—b. Apr. 12, 1923; app. admin. analyst in the Dept. of State, CAF-5, Mar. 6, 1945; CAF-7 Oct. 22, 1945; CAF-9 Nov. 17, 1946.

PANUCH, JOSEPH ANTHONY—b. Prague, Austria-Hungary, Jan. 25, 1899; naturalized 1921; Fordham Prep. grad.; Fordham, A.B. 1921; Columbia, LL.B. 1925; mem. of bar of N. Y.; U. S. Army 1918; mem. of law firm 1926-38; special admiralty counsel, Reconstruction Finance Corp., 1935-38; special counsel, Securities and Exchange Comm., 1938-41; chm. of policy comm., Bd. of Econ. Warfare; chief, Office of Export Requirements; mem. of Am. Requirements Comm., War Production Bd., 1942-43; special and confidential asst. to dir. of materiel, War Dept., 1943-45; special adviser on military programs and reorganization to dir. of war mobilization and reconversion 1945; app. deputy to the asst. sec. of state for admin., CAF-15, Nov. 15, 1945; chm., Comm. on Occupational Deferments, June 1, 1946—A-R/P.

RUSSELL, DONALD STUART—b. Lafayette Springs, Miss., Feb. 22, 1906; U. of S. C., A.B. 1922, LL.B. 1928; U. of Mich., grad. work 1929; law practice 1930-42; mem. of price adjustment bd., War Dept., May-Oct. 1942; asst. to dir., Office of Econ. Stabilization, 1942-43, Office of War Mobilization, 1943-44; U. S. Army, 1944, maj., overseas service; deputy dir., Office of War Mobilization and Reconversion, 1945; app. special asst. to the sec. of state at $9,800 (CAF-15) July 3, 1945; accompanied President Truman to Berlin Conf. 1945; asst. sec. of state Sept. 14, 1945; chm. Bd. of For. Ser. Personnel and Bd. of Examiners for the For. Ser., 1945-46; chm., Bd. of the For. Ser., 1946- ; married—A-R.

STROM, CARL WALTHER—b. Albert Lea, Minn., Dec. 22, 1899; Watson High Sch.; Luther Coll., A.B. 1919; U. of Iowa, A.M. 1924; Oxford U., B.A. 1927; U. of Ill., Ph.D. 1931; U. S. Army 1918, 2d Lt.; asst. instr. of mathematics U. of Iowa 1923-4, U. of Ill. 1929-30; instr. in mathematics 1919-23, 1927-29, prof. of mathematics 1930-35, registrar 1927-29, 1930-35, and dir. of placements 1930-35, Luther Coll.; app. For. Ser. officer unclass., v.c. of career, and sec. in the Diplo. Ser. Oct. 1, 1935; v.c. at Vancouver Oct. 5, 1935; For. Ser. Sch. Aug. 4, 1936; v.c. at Zurich Dec. 18, 1936; class eight May 1, 1941; to the Dept. May 16, 1941; 3d sec. and v.c. at Mexico City Jan. 6, 1943; class seven July 16, 1943; 2d sec. at Mexico City in addition to duties as v.c. Aug. 23, 1943; v.c. at Acapulco de Juarez, temp., Aug. 12, 1944; class six May 16, 1945; cons. June 15, 1945; cons. at Mexico City in addition to duties as 2d sec. June 26, 1945; to the Dept. Nov. 6, 1945; asst. chief, Div. of For. Ser. Planning, Dec. 1, 1945; class five May 19, 1946; For. Ser. officer of class four Nov. 13, 1946; married—FSP.

SUMMERS, LIONEL MORGAN—b. Madrid, Spain, of Am. parents, Nov. 20, 1905; Western High Sch. (D. C.) grad.; Princeton U., B.S. 1927; George Washington U., LL.B. 1930; Academie de Droit International, The Hague, 1930; Institut des Hautes Etudes Internationales, Paris, 1930-31; mem. of bar of D. C.; asst. on law staff, Library of Cong., 1931-33, clk. in law firm, 1933-34; atty., U. S. Agency, Gen. Claims Arbitration, U. S. and Mexico, 1934-36; asst. counsel and chief of right-of-way and title section, Rural Electrification Admin., 1936-43; app. divisional asst. at $5,600 (P-6) in the Dept. of State Dec. 17, 1943; legal specialist July 1, 1944; asst. to the legal adviser Aug. 16, 1944; P-7 Dec. 1, 1946; married—Le.

Key to Symbols:

A-R—Assistant Secretary for Administration, Mr. Russell

A-R/P—Deputy to the Assistant Secretary for Administration, Mr. Panuch

FSP—Division of Foreign Service Planning

Le—Office of the Legal Adviser

OFS—Office of the Foreign Service

(B) Bureau of Budget
(as of September 15, 1946)

APPLEBY, PAUL H.—D Grinnell, A.B., 1913; LL.D., 1942. Publisher, weekly newspaper, Mont., Minn. and Iowa, 1914-20; editor, Iowa magazine, Waterloo, Iowa, 1920-24; editorial writer, Des Moines *Register* and *Tribune*, 1924-28; publisher, weekly newspapers in Va., 1928-33; executive asst. to Secretary of Agriculture, 1933-40; Under Secretary of Agriculture, 1940-44; special adviser, Lend-Lease Administration, 1942-43; chairman, International Wheat Conference, 1941; chairman, International Wheat Council since 1942; chief,

Food Mission to Great Britain, 1941-42; member American delegation to F.A.O. conference (Hot Springs, Va.) 1943; D, 1944, Asst. Director. Vice-president, general manager, Queen City, Broadcasting Co., Seattle, Wash., 1944-45. D, 1945, Asst. Director, Member, Committee on Contributions, U.N., 1946.

ROSEMAN, ALVIN—AM and E Western Reserve U., A.B., 1931; LL.B., 1933; U. of Chicago, M.A., 1935. Various posts in public and private welfare and employment agencies, 1929-33; staff consultant, Am. Pub. Welfare Assn., 1933-35; executive asst., Soc. Sec. Bd., 1935-40; asst. to administrator, FSA, 1940-42; asst. executive director, WMC, 1942-44; asst. chief of mission, later acting director of personnel and administration, and later deputy chief of mission for finance and administration, UNRRA, 1944-45. AM and E, 1945, asst. chief, international branch of AM, and head of unit A, international group, E; 1946, Deputy chief, international Branch of AM.

SHEPPARD, SHERMAN S.—AM and E Colo. C., A.B. 1938; Syracuse U., M.S. in pub. adm., 1930. Executive secretary, Boston Govt. Assn., 1930-32; asst. executive director, Boston Municipal Research Bureau, 1932-37; executive director, New Orleans Bureau of Governmental Research, 1937-42; lecturer in local and State finance, Tulane U., 1937-42. AM, 1942, Munit. Assignmt. Bd., combined boards, organization of WFA; 1943, chief of International Section; 1944, also head of Group XI, E; 1945, also asst. division chief, AM.

SOUTHWORTH, WINTHROP M., JR.—E Brown U., A.B. 1930. Field and executive secretary, Amer. Unitarian Assn., 1930-35; consultant, Mass. League of Nations Assn., 1936; associate, Raymond Rich Associates (detailed to Amer. Council on Education 1940-42), 1936-42. AM, 1942, organization of Federal war administration; 1942, E, Group XI, Latin Amer. affairs, State Dept., and foreign field organization.

STONE, DONALD C.—AM Colgate U., A.B. 1925; Syracuse U., M.S. in pub. adm., 1926; grad. stud., U. of Cincinnati and Columbia U. Apprentice to city manager, Cincinnati, 1926; staff member, Cincinnati Bureau of Governmental Research, 1927-28; asst. director, Comm. on Uniform Crime Records, International Assn. of Chiefs of Police, 1928-29; staff member, Institute of Pub. Adm., 1929-30; director of research, International City Mgrs. Assn., director, Natl. Comm. on Municipal Standards, research associate, U. of Chicago, 1930-33; executive director, Pub. Adm. Service, 1933-39; executive director, International Assn. of Public Works officials, Amer. Soc. of Munic. Eng., 1934-35; special asst. to Administrator, WPA, 1935; consultant to TVA, SSB, USPHA, PWA, FERA, REA and CWA. AM, 1939, asst. director in charge of AM. Adjunct professor on pub. adm., Amer. U.

WEBB, JAMES E.—D U. of N. C., A.B., 1928; law courses at George Wash. U., Member, D. C. Bar, Secretary, Bureau of Educational Research, U. of N. C., 1928-29; law clerk and stenographer, Parham and Lassiter, Attys., 1929-30; Naval aviation student and aviator, 1930-32; secretary to Member of Congress, 1932-34; asst. in law office of Hon. O. Max Gardner, Atty., 1934-36; practiced law in D. C., 1936; personnel director and asst. to president, Sperry Gyroscope Corp., 1936-41; secretary and treasurer, Sperry Gyroscope Corp., 1941-43; vice president and secretary, Sperry Gyroscope Corp., asst. secretary and asst. treasurer, the Sperry Corp., 1943-44; Commanding Officer, First Marine Air Warning Group, U. S. Marine Corps, 1944-45; attorney, Gardner, Morrison and Rogers, 1945-46; executive asst. to the Under Secretary of the Treasury, 1946; D, 1946, Director.

Key to Symbols:

AM—Division of Administrative Management
D—Director's office
E—Division of Estimates

(C) Congress
(as of January 1948)

KEE, JOHN—Democrat, of Bluefield, W. Va., was born at Glenville, Gilmer County, W. Va., Aug. 22, 1874, the son of Jasper N. and Louisa Campbell Kee; educated at Glenville State Normal School and at the law school of the West Virginia University; lawyer; assistant counsel of the Virginian Railway, 1902-10; in professional practice at Bluefield, 1910-16; special legal work in Mexico, 1916-18; engaged since in practice of profession at Bluefield; member of the State senate, 1923-27; married; one son, James Kee, and one daughter, Frances Kee; nominated for Congress on the Democratic ticket in May 1932, and elected to the Seventy-third Congress at the ensuing general election; renominated and reelected to each succeeding Congress, including the Seventy-ninth; member of Christ Episcopal Church, Bluefield; honorary member, Veterans of Foreign Wars; Member of Knights of Pythias, Phi Sigma Kappa college fraternity, and life member, Moose and Elks; member, the Kiwanis Club; member of Committee on Foreign Affairs.

RICHARDS, JAMES PRIOLEAU—Democrat, of Lancaster, S. C.; born at Liberty Hill, Kershaw County, S. C., August 31, 1894, the son of Norman Smith Richards and the late Phoebe Gibbes Richards; worked on a farm and attended county schools of Kershaw County until 17 years of age; attended Clemson College; graduate of the University of South Carolina; began the practice of law in Lancaster, S. C., September 1921 and has practiced there since that date; elected judge of probate of Lancaster County in 1922, and re-elected in 1926 and 1930; while serving third term was elected to the Seventy-third Congress; re-elected to Seventy-fourth, Seventy-fifth, Seventy-sixth, Seventy-seventh, Seventy-eighth and Seventy-ninth Congresses; volunteered as private at Camp Styx, S. C., in 1917, a few days after war was declared, and served throughout war in this country and France with Trench Mortar Battery, Headquarters Company, One Hundred and Eighteenth Regiment Infantry, Thirtieth Division, as private, corporal, and sergeant, and was commissioned as Reserve second lieutenant in February 1919, being discharged March 31, 1919; married on November 4, 1925, to Katharine Hawthorne Wylie, of Lancaster County; they have two sons—Richard Evans and Norman Smith—and one daughter—Jane; member of the Masons, American Legion, and Junior Order United American Mechanics, Veterans of Foreign Wars, and other fraternal organizations.

VORYS, JOHN M.—Republican, of Columbus, Ohio; lawyer; born in Lancaster, Ohio, June 16, 1896; attended public schools in Lancaster and Columbus, Ohio; graduated from Columbus East High School, Yale University (B.A.), Ohio State University (juris doctor); naval aviator No. 73 in World War I, served overseas, retiring to inactive service in 1919 with rank of lieutenant, senior grade; teacher in the College of Yale in China, Changsha, China, 1919-20; assistant secretary, American delegation, Conference on Limitation of Armaments and Pacific and Far East Affairs, Washington, 1921-22; representative from Franklin County in Ohio General Assembly, 1923-24; senator from tenth district in Ohio General Assembly, 1925-26; first director of aeronautics of Ohio, 1929-30; member of the law firm of Vorys, Sater, Seymour & Pease, 1926-39; president, Columbus Bar Association, 1938; married Lois West, of Lucknow, India, in 1927; three children—Martin, Jeanny Esther, and Mary; elected to Seventy-sixth Congress in 1938; re-elected to each succeeding Congress.

Appendix III

BIBLIOGRAPHICAL NOTE

A popular description of the modern Foreign Service is provided by

J. Rives Childs: *The Foreign Service*, New York, Henry Holt & Co., 1947.

Mr. Childs is a Foreign Service officer and the book has a semi-official stamp. In a communication to the *American Foreign Service Journal* Mr. Childs explained that certain portions of the work do not represent his own convictions.

A great deal of incidental but penetrating insight into the habits and ways of various groups in the Foreign Service is furnished by a romantic novel:

Pat Frank: *An Affair of State*, New York, J. B. Lippincott & Co., 1948.

A readable and useful article on the post-war Foreign Service just prior to the Act is:

"The United States Foreign Service," *Fortune*, July, 1946.

Over the years there is probably no better guide to the attitudes of Foreign Service officers than their own monthly magazine published by the American Foreign Service Association:

The American Foreign Service Journal, Washington, monthly.

Issues of particular interest in the development of the Act of 1946 have been cited in the text.

The legal development of modern Foreign Service legislation is traced in:

Elton Atwater, "The American Foreign Service Since 1939," *American Journal of International Law*, 41 (1947), pp. 73 ff.

Many of the recurrent problems of State Department and Foreign Service organization are discussed in the report of the Hoover Commission on Foreign Affairs (Commission on Organization of the Executive Branch of the Government) and the related Task Force Report (Appendix H). 1949.

There is one official document of paramount importance in any study of the Foreign Service Act of 1946:

Reorganization of the Foreign Service: Report of the Committee on Foreign Affairs, House of Representatives, to accompany H.R. 6967,

House Report No. 2508, 79th Congress. Washington, 1946.

This report, prepared by Foster and his staff, gives the text of all superseded legislation and furnishes a full and thoughtful explanation and justification of the new bill. It is the Foreign Service officers' own statement of what they were doing and why. The reader should note that the report does not reflect the amendments incorporated in H.R. 6967 after the bill was reported out; in these particular sections its text and commentaries are partially obsolete.

The record of the only public hearing on the Foreign Service Bill before the House Committee on Foreign Affairs on July 2, 1946 and the record of the public hearing on the Point-of-Order Bill on April 8, 1946 before the same committee are available for inspection at the Committee office, but have never been printed. The debates on the bill in the House and Senate, on July 20 and July 29 respectively, are to be found, of course, in the *Congressional Record* for 1946 (79th Congress, 2nd Session) at pp. 9585 ff. and 9609 ff. respectively. (Bound volume edition.)

The Act itself can be obtained in slip law form:

Foreign Service Act of 1946: P.L. 724, 79th Congress, Chapter 957—2nd Session.

The reference in the U. S. Code is:

U. S. C. Title 22, Sec. 801-1203.

THE REGIONAL DIRECTOR AND THE PRESS

CONTENTS

PREFACE

Investigations of government agencies by committees of the Congress of the United States are rationalized in diverse ways by Constitutional lawyers, political theorists, and others concerned with governmental operations. Whatever rationalization be favored, such investigations as goal or as by-product are in fact used to affect modifications in agency policy, personnel and practice; to exhibit agency officials to the public as worthy of applause or condemnation and to hold them accountable. The records of such hearings are thus replete with descriptions of actions that committee members (or some of them) consider reprehensible and with the justifications offered by officials for their conduct.

Congressional hearings are not infrequently dramatic in character because of the clash in personalities and values between Congressmen and administrative officials. There is thus much drama in the hearings of the Special Committee to Investigate the National Labor Relations Board (known as the Smith Committee) established by House Resolution, in July 1939. The Resolution was sponsored by critics of NLRB, and the Committee majority, consisting of Howard W. Smith, Dem., Va.; Charles A. Halleck, Rep., Ind.; and Harry N. Routzohn, Rep., Ohio, were hostile to NLRB; two members of the committee were generally sympathetic—Arthur D. Healey, Dem., Mass. and Abe Murdock, Dem., Utah.

The National Labor Relations Act embodied a missionary program, and NLRB was a missionary agency. The contrast between Judge Smith (the committee chairman)—lawyer, farmer, judge, banker, who had graduated from law school in 1903—and the generally young, generally urban, lawyers and examiners of the NLRB who appeared before him was striking.

The Smith Committee concerned itself, under the Resolution, in large part with allegations of partiality exhibited by NLRB staff—or board-members.

This case deals with alleged partiality on the part of the NLRB Regional Director for the ninth region, a partiality that in the view of the Committee's investigator had led the Regional Director to suppress or tamper with the free flow of news at its source. This is a serious allegation in a democracy. Each reader will reach his own conclusion on the validity of the allegation in this instance; what should be noted particularly is the subtlety and complexity of the factors that entered into the Regional Director's questioned decisions and the delicacy of judgment required for an intelligent evaluation of his actions.

The materials here presented are entirely derived from the Smith Committee hearings, which were subsequently printed.[1] It will be observed that the Committee investigators had had access to the Board's files; in consequence much of the questioning turned around informal and frequently hastily prepared agency memoranda that the Regional Director had written and received.

The Case

The scene of the hearing was a room in the Old House Office Building occupied by the Special Committee. The time was December 18, 1939. In the room were the five Committee Members, with Chairman Smith presiding. Also present were Edmund M. Toland, the vigorous General Counsel of the Committee, and Charles Fahy, General Counsel of NLRB. The regional director appearing before the

[1] United States Congress, House of Representatives, Special Committee to Investigate National Labor Relations Board. *National Labor Relations Act.* Hearings pursuant to H. Res. 258. Seventy-sixth Congress, Third Session, Washington 1939-1940. See particularly vol. 4, pp. 809-817.

Committee was Philip G. Phillips, director of the ninth region of the NLRB, with offices in Cincinnati, Ohio. Reporters and the general public were also present.

Mr. Phillips was a lawyer who had received both his undergraduate and professional training at Harvard. He had practiced law at several periods after graduation in 1927, had taught law and had also been general counsel for an industry group during the National Recovery Administration code days. He had been on the staff of the NLRB about four years when he testified and had been Cincinnati regional director for about two. Counsel for the Committee questioned Mr. Phillips rather closely about the manner in which his office or he, personally, had handled a number of NLRB cases and implied that Phillips had at times acted to suppress news about cases. Phillips denied ever having done this.

The second of the instances cited by Toland was the *American Rolling Mill Company* case. Toland offered as evidence a "Personal and confidential" letter from Mr. Phillips to Nathan Witt, Secretary of NLRB, in Washington, dated January 25, 1939 which read as follows:

To: Mr. Nathan Witt
From: Philip G. Phillips, 9th Region
Subject: American Rolling Mill Company

I saw a copy of the proposed article the Cincinnati *Enquirer* was going to run against the Board. Part of it was extremely derogatory to the Board, especially speaking about the incompetency of our attorneys and intimating that they might like to use their per diems to make more money.

The editor got worried about it and sent it to the company counsel for examination as a possible libel. The counsel replied, and I saw the memorandum, that it was not libelous, but the difficulty was that he felt it presented too favorably the side of the Labor Board, and might seriously embarrass the company. The City Editor, who is a swell guy and a dear friend of mine, killed the story. The interesting thing is that the counsel for the newspaper, Mr. Carl Jacobs, is also fighting the case for the Armco. Really we ought to send this to Seldes to publish in his next edition of "Lords of the Press."

I am also informed that Mr. Jacobs is now writing his own articles for submission to the *Enquirer* on the same subject, which will be published simply as an ordinary dispatch by a "special correspondent." But the City Editor and my Guild friends will doubtless be able to take care of it without too much difficulty.

In explanation of this letter Phillips had this to say:

MR. PHILLIPS: . . . I might say that if you call a story which is made out of whole cloth news, I don't. That story was vicious, full of lies, and I pointed out to the city editor exactly why it was vicious and full of lies. And it was killed.

MR. HALLECK: Without regard to what may or may not have been the justification for your intervention, if this was an alleged or purported news story, you did in effect interest yourself in trying to have something to do with the determination by the newspaper as to whether or not it should be printed?

MR. PHILLIPS: No; simply that the truth should be printed, and I don't think that says I killed it, and I don't pride myself on having power enough to do it. But I am interested, sirs, in seeing that the truth about the Labor Board gets in print.

. . .

THE CHAIRMAN: The last sentence of this memorandum that was just read says, "The city editor and my Guild friends will doubtless be able to take care of it without too much difficulty." To whom did you refer as your Guild friends?

MR. PHILLIPS: I know a lot of boys on the newspaper, members of the Guild who have made efforts to see that the truth is printed about the Board.

THE CHAIRMAN: Are your Guild friends any different from your other friends in the newspaper world?

MR. PHILLIPS: On that particular paper I don't think there is a single Guild man.

THE CHAIRMAN: Then, why did you refer to your Guild friends?

MR. PHILLIPS: It might be printed somewhere else. I felt for a company attorney to write a story might be a bit unfair.

THE CHAIRMAN: Then pursuant to your suggestion to the Board, did you take the matter up with your Guild friends?

MR. PHILLIPS: It never arose. I don't know that the article was printed, it was vicious, too vicious, I think, to print. Nothing ever happened, as far as I know.

THE CHAIRMAN: You didn't answer my question.

MR. PHILLIPS: I don't recall ever having done anything about it, sir.

At this point Mr. Toland took over the questioning of Mr. Phillips, referring to a document entitled "Comments on Labor Situation, Region IX, June, 1938" which had been sent to Witt by Phillips. He read a portion of it as follows:

The *American Rolling Mills Company* case has been our big problem for the month. The company is going in for trying it in the newspapers in a big way. My friends at the Associated Press have shown me hundreds of words the company releases each night, and the editors of the newspapers throughout the Region tell us they are flooded with telegrams of criticism every time an article appears in a fashion which does not please the steel tycoons. The special correspondents covering the case are treated royally by the company —in fact, automobiles are placed at their disposal, and the amber or darker fluid is gratuitously dispensed, depending on their needs or wants. In such a situation it is not too hard to explain why the Press accounts of what has gone on in this case have been colored, and why we are so handicapped in getting our views across. One is inclined to give three cheers for the Newspaper Guild for at least putting us wise to what goes on behind the scenes.

MR. TOLAND: Now, do you want to change your testimony in answer to the question of the chairman? [i.e., Phillips' testimony that he had never acted to suppress news.]

MR. PHILLIPS: I most emphatically don't.

Mr. Toland then read into the record another confidential memorandum from Phillips to Witt:

Personal and confidential to Mr. Nathan Witt, January 17, 1939.
From Philip G. Phillips, Ninth Region.
Subject: *American Rolling Mill Company*, IX C530.

The Cincinnati *Enquirer* is planning in the next few days on running the story about the length of time that Armco [the American Rolling Mill Company] is taking. They have been down and the company has given them a great deal of dope. Mr. Jacobs, the attorney for the company, is also attorney for the *Enquirer*, so I have no doubt as to the source of the inspiration for the article. My friends on the desk will do their best to kill it, and, judging from my past experience with the papers here in that connection, I don't think anything derogatory will come out.

Hook [President of Armco] may be a very high-minded eleemosynary individual, but they are not stopping at anything in their efforts to spill mud. For instance, the reporter who was assigned the smelly job tells me the company attorneys are going to assign (and try to get published in the *Enquirer*) as a reason for the delay the fact that Gordon and Grossman [NLRB Field Examiners] can make extra money personally by being away in Catlettsburg. The article will state, and it is true, that the boys, when they went down there, rented a house and gave up their apartments in Cincinnati, and they are living there with their wives and still drawing the $5 per diem for being out of town. I talked to Herb Glaser about it, and he assures me that the practice is perfectly regular, but it is just another darn fool thing and another dirty thing we have to contend with. I think the boys would pay $5 a day not to have to live in Catlettsburg!

(Signed) *Philip G. Phillips*, Regional Director

Then Toland said:

Now, Mr. Phillips, do you want to make any explanation as to your previous answers that you did not take any active part or attempt to kill any story that appeared or was to appear in any papers in Cincinnati?

MR. PHILLIPS: Any time a story appeared that had any basis in fact, it appeared; but when somebody deliberately showed me a story that contained lies and falsehoods, I pointed them out to him.

MR. HALLECK: Did you think, though, Mr. Phillips, as a member of this Board, or rather an employee of the Board, that you were clothed with some authority to determine just what news should be run in the papers and what should not be run accordingly as you might think for yourself whether or not it was correct; and that thereupon, after you decided that it was not correct, you felt that you had the authority to undertake to try to stop the newspapers from publishing the story?

MR. PHILLIPS: I never have tried to stop the newspapers from publishing, but when I saw something that was not based on fact, I called it to their attention.

MR. HALLECK: What did you mean by this sentence, then, in the letter—and it is obvious and in fairness from the letter that you thought they were going to print something that wasn't correct. But what did you mean by this: "My friends on the desk will do their best to kill it; and judging from my past experience with the papers here in that connection, I don't think anything derogatory will come out."

MR. PHILLIPS: I think the papers in Cincinnati have been unusually fair to the Labor Board. I have even been called up by the editors of the papers there and asked whether so-called company hand-outs were based on fact, and I point out to them what was what, and I think the boys on the desk would, if I pointed out an obvious untruth, see that it wasn't published, sir.

MR. HALLECK: Now, let's get down to the specific parts of this sentence, because—I don't know how important it is to this inquiry here, but it is important to the matter under consideration at the moment. Did you have some friends on the desk of the Cincinnati *Enquirer?*

MR. PHILLIPS: One.

MR. HALLECK: You had one friend?

MR. PHILLIPS: One friend.

MR. HALLECK: Of course, you used the plural here in the sentence.

MR. PHILLIPS: If I did, I am wrong. I know all the labor reporters who come up every day to see me.

MR. HALLECK: You knew one man on the desk?

MR. PHILLIPS: I think I knew one man on the desk.

MR. HALLECK: You say there, "will do their best to kill it." Do you mean by that that you had some kind of agreement or understanding with your friends that they would do their best to kill the story?

MR. PHILLIPS: No; they would do their best to see that falsehoods were eliminated, not kill any story.

MR. HALLECK: Is that what you meant by killing the story?

MR. PHILLIPS: That is what I meant.

MR. HALLECK: Had you personally conferred with your friends on the desk with respect to killing the story?

MR. PHILLIPS: No; it wasn't so much killing the story as getting at what the facts were. I let them see my records.

MR. HALLECK: As a matter of fairness you wrote this in the calm consideration of the moment, and you uttered the words, "will do their best to kill the story," and you didn't use the words, "will do their best to take out of the story the parts that are untrue."

MR. PHILLIPS: I don't think there is any calm consideration of the moment in a regional office. We go pretty much at high speed. That letter, as you know, was personal and confidential, and my language may have been very ill-chosen, but I am not killing stories in the sense that I saw that news was suppressed.

MR. HALLECK: Of course, if the story was killed, if it was a news story, it would have been suppressed.

MR. PHILLIPS: And if I killed a news story based on fact, I was wrong.

MR. HALLECK: There have been some suggestions about argumentative questions [by the Committee], and I think some of them were, and I don't want too many argumentative answers, although I want you to have, as far as I am concerned, every opportunity to make every explanation you may deem necessary in connection with anything you may have written, but when you say that your friends on the desk will do their best to kill the story, that doesn't include, necessarily, any limitation to those parts of the story that were untrue. It was the story as a whole.

MR. PHILLIPS: My language was ill-chosen, and I should think it would be absolutely wrong for me to try to suppress news. To suppress lies, I am all for it.

MR. HALLECK: And you said in the final part of the sentence these words: "I don't think anything derogatory will come out." What did you mean particularly by that?

MR. PHILLIPS: Well, there was a story that my boys were drawing a per diem of $5 a day, and for that reason had been extending the hearing. I felt it was untrue. I didn't think that would come out, because I pointed out to the newsmen—I even took the newsmen in my office and showed them the expense accounts I had. I showed them letters from Grossman and Gordon saying, "For goodness' sake, can't we get this thing over? I want to get out." That is what I meant, that the untruth of the story would not appear.

MR. HALLECK: That had to do with the men who were going to write the story, didn't it?

MR. PHILLIPS: I don't know whether they were the newsmen who were going to write it, or the newsmen who showed it to me.

MR. HALLECK: In any event, you were talking to them about the compilation of this story that was to be printed.

MR. PHILLIPS: I was talking to them about the facts of the story that was to be printed.

MR. HALLECK: And you undertook to point out to them an explanation of the matter of the $5 per diem charge that is referred to?

MR. PHILLIPS: That is correct.

MR. HALLECK: In order that they get the true facts of the case.

MR. PHILLIPS: That is correct.

MR. HALLECK: But that didn't go quite as far as to say that your friends on the desk will do their best to kill it.

MR. PHILLIPS: That is all I meant by it. I am certainly not in power to kill stories in the newspapers.

MR. HALLECK: What did you mean, then, by saying that "judging from my past experience with the papers here in that connection, I don't think anything derogatory will come out"?

MR. PHILLIPS: I think the newspapers in Cincinnati have been fair in their columns toward the Labor Board. Instead of printing untruths and innuendoes, for example, as the Chicago *Tribune* will do, they print the facts and nothing else, and let the readers draw their own conclusions. By the way, their editorials may not be so friendly to the Board. For example, Bob Taft's paper has never come out in glowing terms about us.

Everything is based on fact, because when they get a handout from the employer, they come to the Labor Board and say, "Let's see what your files show," and we show the boys what our files show, and they can do anything they want after they have got the facts.

MR. HALLECK: I don't want to engage in any controversy with you as to the relative merits of the Cincinnati papers, because I read the *Tribune*.

MR. PHILLIPS: Try the Cincinnati *Post* and *Enquirer*.

MR. MURDOCK: At least one story was so bad that the editor himself got worried about it and sent it to the company counsel for examination as to possible libel.

MR. PHILLIPS: That is correct.

MR. MURDOCK: And it also appears that the same attorney was representing a company involved and also a newspaper.

MR. PHILLIPS: That is also correct, about when the story was written, incidentally.

POSTSCRIPT

This concluded the discussion of the *American Rolling Mill Company* case. Testimony was also taken on an alleged suppression of a news story about a Circuit Court decision by Mr. Phillips; but this allegation seems to have been based entirely on a misunderstanding. The questions about Mr. Phillips, Armco and the newspapers were not based on misunderstanding. They arose from sharply different interpretations of Mr. Phillips' actions, and from different evaluations arising from different codes of conduct.

These are, as has been suggested above, delicate questions: administrators should clearly keep the newspapers informed; but is there a point at which information becomes propaganda? Administrators may properly cultivate friendly relations with the press, but can friendly relations degenerate into favoritism? Administrators should be concerned with the publication of the truth about their agency, but may zeal for the truth, as administrators see it, turn into tampering with the news?

For the student of administration, as for the administrator, these are not easy questions: intelligent answers can hardly be categorical, and should take into account the complexities of actual experience. They deserve consideration because they relate to the function of government and the function of a free press in a democracy.

THE VETERANS' GAS RATION

CONTENTS

OPA and the Gasoline Rationing Program

The general purpose of the rationing programs operated by the Office of Price Administration during World War II was to ensure that the limited supplies of commodities made scarce for civilian use by the needs of war were distributed in accordance with principles consistent with the public good and the effective prosecution of the war. Various principles were involved and invoked, but the two of most general applicability were equity and essentiality. Under the first of these two principles, for example, every resident of the United States was entitled to receive a ration coupon permitting the purchase (at one period) of five pounds of sugar. Under the second principle, for example, ration tickets permitting the purchase of rubber boots were issued only as needed and only to workers in essential industries like mining and chemicals.

All OPA rationing programs had a rationale or set of rationales that included a blend of these two principles. The gasoline program was no exception. Group eligibility for special gasoline rations was determined by a Gasoline Eligibility Committee (described below); the actual program was administered by the Gasoline Branch of the Automotive Division of the Rationing Department of OPA. The branch was responsible for equating the limited supply of gasoline with demand by adjusting the value and distribution of ration coupons to the changes of gasoline supply allotted to civilian use by the Petroleum Administration for War. It maintained current statistical information on civilian use of gasoline; under the guidance of the Eligibility Committee, it determined the eligibility of various classes of civilian users for gasoline rations and the amounts to be allotted to eligible users; and it endeavored to maintain adherence to the eligibility rules by instruction and supervision of the local boards responsible for the actual issuance of rations.

The relations between PAW and OPA, it should be noted, were in theory simple, in fact both complex and usually strained. In theory PAW, which controlled the production of gasoline, fixed the amount for civilian use and certified that amount to OPA each quarter; OPA had complete charge of the distribution of gasoline to civilian consumers. In fact, OPA was frequently involved in the supply problem, PAW in distribution. Mutual recriminations and vexations were common. These frictions increased the burdens that the Gasoline Branch of OPA had to bear in any event.

One of the major functions of the Eligibility Committee was the determination of what categories of car-owners were to be eligible for gasoline so that uses vital to the war and essential civilian functions would not be excessively curtailed. The broad system of eligibility worked out to express this purpose consisted chiefly of three general types of priorities by which the local boards were to be guided in gasoline distribution: "C" rations for those car-owners whose driving was essential to the war or to public health and safety, "B" rations for those whose driving was essential as a means of getting to work or important in certain other ways, and "A" rations for all car-owners regardless of need. "C" rations were, of course, the largest and "A" rations the smallest; both "B" and "C" were individually adjusted in accordance with need (though there was a top limit on "B" rations but not on "C"), while the "A" ration was the same for all. The assigned value of the coupons was changed with variations in allotments of supply by PAW.

Inasmuch as the two major types of priorities for extra gasoline ("B" and "C" rations) were, while broad in coverage, still rigid in definition, a number of other special categories were established to cover cases of special need. They took the form of amendments to the general eligibility rules and were regarded as specific and limited directions for extensions of an

"A" ration to be used by the local rationing boards as a guide to and in lieu of personal judgment; they covered such contingencies as travel for medical care, transport of automobiles upon change of residence, demonstration of cars by dealers, and so on through about twenty-five special cases. Over and above these special amendments, the local boards were granted fixed quotas of "hardship" rations which they could use in individual cases not covered by the rules so that uncommon cases of need for gasoline could be taken care of.

Among the people on the Gasoline Eligibility Committee responsible for making these rules, a number of professional attitudes or habitual ways of thinking were developed which aided in the translation of the general purpose of gasoline conservation and the distribution of the limited supply into specific rules for the local boards. For example, a more elaborately rationalized explanation of the three broad categories of priorities was developed. In this rationalization, the central concept was "essentiality," meaning essentiality to the war effort or the home front. It was said that first call on and the largest amounts of gasoline were given to the most essential users and that all exceptions which were granted over and above the "A" ration should be explainable in terms of relative essentiality. The "C" ration was directly essential for the prosecution of the war and preservation of the economy; the "B" ration was indirectly essential for these ends, although to the general public and even to many local ration boards the only distinction was one of quantity of gasoline permitted. Even the "A" ration itself, which could perhaps have been most easily rationalized as equitable distribution to all car operators after the essential uses were taken care of, was also poured into the essentiality mold. It was not generally regarded as a political necessity arising because car-owners without special claim could not, need not, or should not be altogether deprived of gasoline, while there was gasoline to be had; nor was it usually viewed as an administrative necessity obviating the need for issuance of millions of individual specialized rations for persons whose needs were "essential" but no larger than the amount provided by the "A" ration: rather the "A" ration tended to be rationalized by the officials concerned as a method of administering the distribution of gasoline for essential personal uses or, alternatively, to relieve the strain on essential public transportation facilities by use of private cars and for the essential conservation of 23 million autos for the indefinite duration of the war.

Special ration amendments were also rationalized with the idea of essentiality. Each special extension included in the eligibility rules was described as essential to some war-related activity or essential civilian need. The officials maintained this tight logic in spite of the fact that one or two of the special amendments, instituted over the opposition of the Eligibility Committee, seemed to be the result of political pressures. Such, for example, was the grant of gasoline for representatives of the Farmers Union or the amendment issued to cover the case of one man whose usage of gasoline was by no means essential as the OPA understood the word but who was a friend of one of OPA's essential supporters in the Congress. The latter case was unique; the former was opposed by the Eligibility Committee, but debatable; in any event, there were at most no more than four or five special amendments which were in any sense forced on the Committee and the Branch by the OPA hierarchy or other agencies, so that in general the special amendments, like the basic regulations, were reasonably explicable in terms of the essentiality rationale.

Another habit of thinking which developed from the consciousness of the gasoline shortage and the transportation bottleneck (on which subjects OPA personnel received frequent lectures by representatives of the PAW and the Office of Defense Transportation) was a kind of economy-mindedness. In some degree the goal of saving gasoline for its own sake became intermingled with the more publicized principles of equity and essentiality. The spirit of economy was emphasized also by a belief that special amendments were likely to destroy the equity of the system of priorities already established. Gradually, the people in the branch came to look upon themselves as partners with the Petroleum Administration for War in the conservation of an increasingly scarce war material. The attitude had a sound legal base, for the rationing power was derived from the allocation power, granted by Congress with the conservation of scarce materials in mind. In any event, the branch continually had to struggle with the difficulties of making supply and demand come out even: if special amendments were granted too freely, ration coupons would come to have no value and the system would break down.

Thus the idea of essentiality and the consciousness of a need for conserving gasoline joined together to encourage a preservation of the existing relationships in the priority system and to discourage the establishment of new priority categories.

For a variety of reasons, the rationale formulated by the Gasoline Eligibility Committee and used by the staff of the Gasoline Branch developed into a kind of religion. The Committee operated with a good deal of freedom, and regarded the OPA hierarchy to which it was subordinate with constant suspicion. The protection of the rationale was thus protection of the Committee. Furthermore, to a considerable extent, the leading people in the gasoline rationing program were imbued with a sense of dedication: inconsistencies in the logical structure were felt as moral flaws. And this attitude was reinforced by a sense of the desirability, in the face of possible litigation, of consistency that would stand up in the courtroom. The Branch and its guiding Committee thus had a sense of mission and a coherence that acted as a counterpoise to any impulsiveness or over-sensitivity to public or partisan political pressures on the part of the hierarchy. The members of the hierarchy respected the Branch and the Committee, though at times their patience was tried by the rigidity they encountered.

Emergence of the Veterans' Gasoline Ration Issue

The veterans' gasoline ration problem arose first as part of a general consideration of veterans' problems by the top OPA management in the summer of 1944, long before the veterans' gasoline ration question became a hot issue. A special committee was established by the Rationing Department to consider three different rationing problems in which special provision for veterans had been suggested; the committee formulated a policy statement (modified in practice in two respects later) which rejected preferential treatment for veterans as such. Presently, the Administrator referred to the Gasoline Eligibility Committee the specific question of whether veterans should receive a special gasoline ration at the time of discharge from military service. On August 26 this Committee decided that veterans as such should not receive preferred treatment, but that the problem of veterans seeking employment deserved consideration. Subsequently, veterans and also discharged war workers referred to specific jobs by the United States Employment Service were made eligible for special rations. During the months that followed, the Eligibility Committee first denied and then granted special rations for entertainers visiting veterans' hospitals. A year or two earlier, it may be noted, the Committee had first denied and then granted a special ration for members of the Armed Services on furlough: this request had been made by the Army and Navy as a morale measure; the grant was rationalized on the grounds of essential business and social needs.

But with the approach of victory in Europe, in the spring of 1945, agitation for a veterans' ration arose quite suddenly. After V-E Day, the discharge rate increased, and so did the agitation for the ration. It continued at a high rate for several months until it became for a time the most important issue in the Gasoline Branch and Eligibility Committee.

During this same period other veterans' problems and promises began to be a major concern of the bureaucracy and the Congress. The Veterans' Administration was being reorganized; the Civil Service Commission was publicizing its program for veterans' employment; criticism in the press and in the Congress of laws relating to veterans had risen to a new high; and agencies such as the Farm Security Administration, the United States Employment Service, even the Selective Service were advertising what they could do for veterans. Elsewhere in the OPA new food businesses, largely run by veterans, were being allowed extra sugar rations. Within this context it is understandable that a campaign for a special veterans' gas ration developed in a very short time.

The most important pressure on the Washington office came from the local ration boards. They were the ones who frequently wanted to be able to do something to help their neighbor-veterans, who wanted to be able to show at once their sympathy and their gratitude, and who found themselves stymied by the lack of proper authorization. When they, contrary to their own emotions, had to turn down veterans' requests, they complained of their unpleasant position to district and regional gasoline representatives, and in many cases wrote letters directly to Washington to avoid the field hierarchy. The reports of the regional offices to Washington began to devote more space to this particular problem than to any other. The reports described the personal distress which the local board members felt when they had to turn down veterans to whom they had previously given furlough rations; they pointed out that many boards were using the "hardship" ration to give what was in effect a discharge ration and that this caused considerable antagonistic publicity for neighboring boards which were unable to make similar grants from their "hardship" quotas.

Supplementing these written reports, field men visiting the Washington office often urged with considerable energy that something be done about this particular matter. They argued that the Branch had better issue an amendment to legalize rations that were being given anyway and that otherwise the Branch would lose the respect and obedience of the local boards.

While the pressure from the field was great —greater perhaps than it had ever before been on any single issue connected with gasoline— and while the most important of the pressures on this issue were from the field men, still there were a number of other significant sources of agitation. There was considerable Congressional interest in the matter, although, of course, not as much as on many other phases of the OPA operation. But at least a dozen Congressmen felt impelled to write to Administrator Bowles and a number of others made telephone calls on the subject; naturally, Congressional complaints were treated by OPA with respect. There was also some comment in the press on the fact that veterans received no special ration. Newspapers in many cities carried what the OPA people were accustomed to call "horror stories" on this particular lacuna. Very little of the pressure from the local boards or from the Congress seemed to be veteran-inspired.

Crystallization of Attitudes

Within the Washington office, the outside agitation and comment created several points of view: the legalistic, the fatalistic, and the benevolent.

Much has been said and written about the OPA lawyers, about how they supposedly sabotaged programs with an unduly legalistic approach to administration, and about how they seemed unaware of administrative considerations. Various explanations have been given of this point of view. Some merely say in effect that lawyers have a different way of thinking from other folk; others point out that lawyers very understandably fought for the maintenance of an internally consistent system because such a system would be easier to defend in court; while still others claim that lawyers as a class in OPA spent most of their time throughout its history fighting to retain and trying to regain the position of abnormal power which they had held in the beginning because of the intimate relationship of the first chief counsel with Leon Henderson, a position which they lost in part with the resignation of both men. Whatever may be the explanation of the phenomenon, and while its extent has been exaggerated, it is undoubtedly true that as a group, the OPA lawyers were strict constructionists, and *a priori* opposed to exceptions and deviations. On the veterans' ration issue, it was the lawyers who were most inclined to hold the line regardless of outside pressures, and least willing to see any substantive merit in the proposal.

The lawyer assigned to the Gasoline Branch and hence the lawyer most immediately concerned with the separation ration, James C. Hyne, was regarded as particularly critical—even for an OPA lawyer—over the gasoline "leakages" sanctioned, for the various reasons which have been described, by OPA administrators. Hyne had come from private practice to OPA at its inception and had been for some months previous to the spring of 1945 publicly contemplating resignation. The reasons he gave for this proposed action (and these were accepted at their face value by the rest of the office) were that he could not properly perform his own function of aiding in conservation because OPA administrators from the top down were too political. He felt that an administrator should make a rational program (as he thought the Gasoline Branch had done in the beginning) and then should stick to it regardless of the pressures from Congress or the public—he spoke of them as "pressure groups." He complained that in a number of recent instances in which he had advised that the OPA stick to the "rational, logical program," his opinions had been summarily dismissed by administrators at various levels in the hierarchy. What had seemed to him the final straw was a meeting of all higher professional and administrative personnel of the OPA at which Administrator Bowles had spoken; it was Hyne's understanding that Bowles had urged the staff to go out of their way to listen to the advice of Congress and the public, to give in on the minor parts of the OPA program, so that the major parts of the program could be saved: but this interpretation of Bowles's speech should be construed in the light of its source.

When the issue of the veterans' ration came up soon thereafter, Hyne was violently opposed to it. To him it seemed another prospective break in the concept of essentiality, another "loss of intellectual integrity." He argued that if rewards were to be given to veterans they should be financial and not involve the dissipation of a precious war material; and he compared the gasoline situation to food rationing. Why not give veterans an extra ration of meat points, he asked.

In this he was strongly supported by his superior, Aaron Lewittes, chief counsel for the Automotive Rationing Division and recently appointed advisor on veterans' affairs to the Deputy Administrator for Rationing. Lewittes, like Hyne, had been with OPA from the beginning; he too was a purist, and disgusted with the "politicking" by administrators, and he complained about the disregard of legal advice on substantive issues of policy. He did not talk publicly of quitting, and indeed the general policy of the Gasoline Eligibility Committee was largely of his making. As advisor on veterans' affairs to the Deputy Administrator he was, of course, strategically placed for opposition to the veterans' ration.

The party which might be called the "fatalists" included most of the administrators responsible at some point in the hierarchy for gasoline rationing. Because of the gasoline situation (or rather because of their estimates of actual and prospective gasoline supply and demand), they were reluctant to use any gasoline for what they thought was a non-essential purpose; but, at the same time, they had respect for the pressures which were now being applied to them, and they were inclined to believe that OPA must make some concessions on minor matters; so they expected that they would give in somewhat to the pressure for veterans' gasoline before very long.

The gasoline situation as they saw it was this: They believed that the gasoline shortage in the spring of 1945 was quite critical. It was admittedly not as serious as in the previous fall (which had been the worst period during the war) when usage was far in excess of quota every day. By hammering at the local boards and by fighting any efforts to broaden the eligibility for extra gas, the daily excess had been cut to half of what it had been at the worst point in the fall of 1944. Shortly before V-E Day (which was May 8, 1945), the Petroleum Administrator announced that the "A" ration could be increased 50 per cent after V-E Day; this was not within his jurisdiction, but it had the psychological effect of a government promise that OPA was quite unable to over-ride. Later the Petroleum Administrator insisted, over the objections of OPA, that some 80,000 barrels per day out of some 130,000 extra being allocated to OPA after V-E

Day go to the "A" rations. This upset the logical balance of the gasoline ration structure and precluded any major improvement in the over-quota situation.

The OPA, particularly the immediately responsible planners in the Gasoline Branch, continued to regard the gasoline excess usage as so serious that, even after the reluctant increase in the value of the "A" coupons after V-E Day, they directed a campaign at the local boards to review "B" and "C" coupons to cut out all not really essential uses. The Gasoline Branch was in the ambiguous position of simultaneously acceding to an increase in what it termed non-essential use and attempting to curtail essential use on the ground that supply was short. This apparent inconsistency in the rationing program worried them. They believed that any further "waste" of gasoline at a time when they were trying to make the local boards tighten up on issuance would seem so inconsistent to the local boards that the latter would come to disregard the instructions of the Washington office completely.

At the same time they were in the difficult position of having no idea of how much gasoline would be involved in a veterans' ration. Arguably (though probably no one believed this), no extra gasoline would be used. Many local boards were giving separation rations under the guise of hardship rations, and many of them were giving in excess of thirty gallons for each veteran. It was possible that a veterans' ration would merely legalize usage of gasoline which was already a fact; but this was an extreme view. The best estimates of the probable cost of a separation ration varied (according to whether the estimator was in favor of the veterans' ration or not) from 2000 barrels a day to 6000 barrels (OPA was running over quota about 40,000 barrels a day). Thus, the separation ration probably was in itself of minor significance. Although any extra use seemed undesirable, what mostly worried the Gasoline Branch was the effect that an extra ration would have on their program of cutbacks on other types of coupons. They felt that the public misunderstood the state of gasoline rationing after the rise in the value of the "A" coupons and that the whole rationing program would be endangered by any further significant or publicized relaxation of eligibility regulations; the public might, they feared, become convinced that rationing was really unnecessary.

The two men most concerned at higher levels with policy-making for gasoline rationing, Max McCullough, the deputy administrator in charge of the Rationing Department, and Richard E. Youngblood, the chief of the Gasoline Branch, were impressed with the consideration of short supply and public reaction. But as the men who had to bear most of the public and internal OPA pressure, they were even more impressed with the way that the veterans' ration had become a popular and significant issue in a very few weeks. Both of them had been in responsible positions in the OPA long enough to be highly sensitive to public reaction about all phases of the program. They both thought that a major part of their job was the responsibility to make an unpleasant and unpopular program as palatable as possible without weakening its general effectiveness. Hence, they expected that they would have to give in on the veterans' ration and in effect they resigned themselves to a reluctant acceptance of what they felt was inevitable. They certainly did not think the veterans' ration was important enough to justify a public fight, even though they felt that it probably violated the concept of essentiality.

Lower in the OPA hierarchy, there was not nearly the concern with pressures which Youngblood and McCullough felt. This was particularly true in the Gasoline Eligibility Committee. The Committee was composed of a representative of each branch in the Automotive Rationing Division, several lawyers attached to the Division, and the chief of the Eligibility Section (which was one of Youngblood's sections), Thomas P. Shelburne, who served as secretary. With the exception of Youngblood and Shelburne, the Committee members were more impressed with the gasoline shortage and the probable effects on the public of what they regarded as "obvious waste" than with the recommendations coming in. For most of them there was a mental conflict between the philosophy which had been built up in the gasoline rationing program and the proposal for a veterans' discharge ration. They adhered to the concept of essentiality as the basis for gasoline allotments and looked upon this use as non-essential. While they were thus predisposed to hold out longer than Youngblood and McCullough, they too became fatalists as the pressure increased. However, Lewittes, a key member of the Committee, never wavered in his opposition.

One member of the Committee came to adopt a point of view different from that of the legalistic and fatalistic parties. This was Shelburne, the chief of the Eligibility Section of the Gasoline Branch, who, like everyone else, regarded the ration as non-essential and had originally opposed it; but he came to believe that the amendment should be made as a benevolent gesture. Shelburne was a man of forty or so, a former high school teacher and principal. He had embraced the philosophy of conservation and essentiality in the highest degree; once he had even threatened to resign over what seemed to him a wholly political eligibility rule which was ordered from the top of the agency. Consequently, he was at first opposed to the veterans' ration because he considered it wasteful. But he, like no one else concerned with policy-making on the subject, referred to veterans as "the boys." He wanted to do something for them. Once he was able to overcome his scruples about the waste of gasoline, he became the only enthusiastic supporter which the proposal for a discharge ration had. Some members of McCullough's staff became tolerant or sympathetic toward the proposal, but only Shelburne was enthusiastic.

In closing this schematic account of the attitudes toward the veterans' ration proposal, note should be taken of an omitted alternative. Some people felt that a fight on this issue would be bad for the general gasoline rationing program; Shelburne thought the proposal desirable as a benevolent exception to the rules. Apparently no one felt that the veterans should somehow qualify under the general rationale, or that the rationale should be broad enough as a matter of principle to cover the veterans. Obviously, the attitudes of this group of OPA officials were rather different from the attitudes of the general public, and of the local boards. The Gasoline Branch and Eligibility Committee included no veterans; but it is doubtful that the presence of veterans would have changed matters. As rationers of a scarce commodity, the staff looked on all new demands for gasoline as automatically suspect; after all, petitions for many exceptions were granted even though none of the officials was a representative of the petitioning group while the much larger volume of denials included some requests from occupational groups that were represented.

Crystallization of Policy

During April and May, 1945, letters from local boards and reports and letters from regional and district offices brought the issue of the veterans' ration to a point where some sort of action seemed to be required. Toward the end of May, McCullough polled his immediate staff on the subject in a meeting largely devoted to other matters. They all saw the problem in terms of the local board and Congressional suggestions and demands and it was finally agreed at that meeting that eventually some sort of token ration of, say, ten gallons be provided when the pressure became too strong to withstand. McCullough then talked this over with Youngblood, the chief of the Gasoline Branch, and they then decided that an amendment must presently be issued to provide for a veterans' ration. Youngblood felt that a ten-gallon ration would be worse than none at all and that the ration would need to be as large as the one customarily given on the largest furlough rations, that is, thirty gallons. McCullough definitely preferred the smaller amount, but he left the matter up to Youngblood to decide.

The matter thus seemed to be settled by the responsible officials—the Deputy Administrator and the Branch Chief; but at this point an anomaly in the structure caused a delay of two months.

A long time before, a procedure had been established under which all proposals for amendments changing eligibility for gasoline rations were referred to the Gasoline Eligibility Committee whose membership has been described above. In effect, the responsibility for such decision by the top officials of OPA, the Branch Chief or by the Chief of the Eligibility Section was delegated to this Committee. In practice the primary function of the Committee was, of course, to guard against hasty pressures from above or from the outside world.

Youngblood, after reaching the decision with McCullough, proceeded to handle the matter through the established routines. Several days after his conversation with McCullough, he received a letter from a representative of the Veterans of Foreign Wars in which it was proposed that veterans in rural areas be granted a sixty-gallon ration and veterans in urban areas be granted a thirty-gallon ration. This was the first and only suggestion made by a veterans' organization that came to him, and in fact about the only suggestion received in the Washington office during this period from either a veteran or a veterans' representative which touched on the issue at all. The letter was moderate in its tone and surprisingly enough it was never followed up, even though it indicated that further calls would be made on the matter. But Youngblood did not know this at the time. All he knew was that veterans' organizations had the reputation of being most persistent and effective pressure groups. The letter worried him because he did not at all want to get entangled in a fight with them.

Therefore, at the next weekly meeting of the Eligibility Committee (in the second week of June), he proposed a discharge ration amendment for consideration. It was discussed at some length. But the Committee finally voted it down with Youngblood's vote as the only "yea." The next week Youngblood brought the subject up again and this time also it was turned down by the same majority.

Shortly after the second failure of the amendment, a letter from a Congressman strongly advocating a discharge ration was passed on to Youngblood and Shelburne from Administrator Bowles's office. In reply to it, Shelburne (still unconverted to the idea) attempted to draft a letter which would explain the opposition of the office to the idea in sufficiently persuasive arguments to satisfy the Congressman. This letter which summarizes the Branch's rationale reads in part as follows:

> As you know, the Office of Price Administration is given each quarter a specific quota of gasoline which is available for civilian rationing. We may not disregard this allocation without endangering the war effort and essential civilian activities. At the present time we are completely consuming the allocation granted to us and all indications point to the fact that our present consumption is running over our allocation. We understand that between a million and a half and two million persons are to be discharged from the armed forces in the coming months. Obviously, an automatic discharge or bonus ration would cause a very substantial amount of gasoline to be consumed over and above our present consumption. . . .
>
> We have made every effort under limited allocations to make gasoline available for necessary travel. A number of provisions which are already in effect are designed to meet the particular needs of members of the armed forces and veterans. Included among these are special rations for transporting members of the armed forces or veterans from Army or Navy hospitals, recuperation centers or Veterans' facilities to places of recreation as a means of assisting in their recovery; special rations for transportation to interview a prospective employer when referred by a recognized referral agency; special rations for disabled veterans with additional rations for occupational travel. The "A" ration has been increased to provide as far as possible for personal necessity driving.
>
> We are daily receiving numerous complaints that the limitation on amounts made available for distribution seriously interferes with the activities of persons who need cars in order to carry on their occupations and make a livelihood. In many instances these occupations make substantial contributions to the war effort. I believe that it would be extremely hard to justify using a large amount of gasoline as a bonus or discharge ration where the necessity for such a ration is highly conjectural and, at the same time, to deny gasoline which is very badly needed for necessary occupational travel. This, of course, would apply likewise to veterans themselves who will need transportation for business purposes in automobiles when they re-enter civilian occupations.

This letter was never sent. Shelburne talked it over with Youngblood and Youngblood persuaded him that it was not a very good case or at least not good enough to persuade the Congressman.

But the chief effect of the Congressman's letter was to make Youngblood bring the proposal up before the Eligibility Committee again for a third week. By now the fact of increasing Congressional interest and the fact of an increasing volume of complaints from local boards were sufficient to swing several of the members of the Committee over to Youngblood's side. Nevertheless, Shelburne, two lawyers, and two administrators from other branches of the Automotive Division still opposed the idea so that the proposal again failed.

After this meeting, the Branch received a letter from a discharged officer complaining about OPA discrimination against officers. Since officers, unlike enlisted men, were discharged while finishing out their accumulated leave, they were technically eligible for a furlough ration at the time of discharge. Enlisted men, who remained on active duty until discharge, were not. Ration boards had been accustomed to give one gallon of gasoline per day of leave or of furlough and, since this ex-officer had ten days of leave to finish, he had received ten gallons of gasoline. He then wrote an irate letter to the Branch in Washington complaining about the discrimination against officers because he had received only ten gallons of gasoline while many enlisted men he knew had received thirty gallons of "discharge ration." Shelburne, as chief of the Eligibility Section, wrote back to explain that the writer had confused the ration given to many enlisted men who had received a month furlough after overseas duty with a discharge ration, and that, in fact, such discrimination as existed was accidentally in favor of officers rather than enlisted men. This correspondence brought to the attention of the Gasoline Branch a sore spot which it had not known about. The possibility of what was in effect discrimination against enlisted men was not only repugnant in itself, but was also potentially the basis for a lot of condemnation such as the United States Employment Service was then receiving for a similar type of accidental discrimination.

Within a few days of the receipt of this letter, the Branch also received a request for legal interpretation of the furlough ration to determine if terminal leave was properly a furlough and if it made an officer eligible for a furlough ration at the time of discharge. The legal staff, specifically Hyne, considered the problem and concluded that terminal leave was a furlough within the meaning of the regulation.

This interpretation and the letter erroneously charging discrimination, coming as they did at the same time and at the time the discharge ration was under consideration, impressed Shelburne tremendously. He was already torn between his loyalty to the idea of essentiality and his benevolent impulses. Since officers were already entitled to what was in effect a discharge ration and since the Branch followed a general rule that it was impossible to repeal a specific type of eligibility already existing, he decided that the best thing to do would be to provide for a discharge ration which would equalize the status of discharged officers and enlisted men. Thereafter he became the most ardent supporter of the discharge ration. In spite of Shelburne's shift, the Committee, meeting on June 28, while agreeing that the accidental discrimination was improper, still felt that, in the light of the supply situation, no discharge ration should be given to either group; the matter was left pending.

A little later, in Washington, the *Times Herald* (which was the Patterson newspaper) described on the front page the difficulties of a veteran who was job-hunting. This man, so the story ran, was unable to use public transportation because of combat-incurred disabilities. Since he had had some trouble finding a job for which he was suited or which suited him and since the job-hunting ration was given by OPA regulation only for a specific referral from the War Manpower Commission, this veteran had to go back to the ration board several times to get gasoline. To the *Times Herald* this was just another example of OPA red-tape and inefficiency. In spite of (or perhaps because of) a long history of antagonistic comment in the press, the OPA generally and the Gasoline Branch in particular were sensitive to newspaper publicity. Consequently, these stories carried more than a little weight with the people responsible for eligibility rules.

The story was passed about the Rationing Department and impressed the administrators from other branches on the Eligibility Committee so that they became favorably disposed to the idea of a veterans' ration.

At the next meeting of the Eligibility Committee on July 5, Shelburne brought up the proposal for a discharge ration. Youngblood, who had become disgusted by his three failures in sponsoring the proposal, had declared that he would not bring the matter up again and that he would wait until the pressure became so heavy that other people on the Committee were enough interested to raise the question. He had expected that it would be several weeks or months before the matter arose. But now that Shelburne had changed his mind, Youngblood was glad to support the proposal once more. This time, the Committee voted unanimously to approve a discharge ration; Lewittes, the chief legal representative on the Committee, was notably absent.

Even the action of the Committee was not enough to settle the matter, however, for it was customary to submit important changes in the eligibility rules to the regional representatives of the Gasoline Branch for consideration and advice before final promulgation. Sometimes they were polled by mail; but since a meeting of regional men was scheduled for the week after the Committee approved the proposal, they were consulted on it at that time.

At the meeting of regional representatives, there was heated discussion of the subject. Most of the twelve men were strongly in favor of the proposal because they believed that the misuse of the "hardship" ration should be legalized so that the gasoline allotted for hardship cases could be again used for its intended purpose rather than for a quasi-discharge ration and so that the local boards would not lose respect for Washington rules. But at least one of them, who was imbued with the philosophy of essentiality, protested long and stoutly. He lashed out against the action which he interpreted as a spineless submission to pressure. Some of the rest of the group resented this description and in consequence a very violent discussion developed around the issue. But the regional men finally voted for approval of a discharge-ration amendment.

This vote was the culmination of the morning session of their meeting. In the afternoon session, they were addressed by a representative of the Petroleum Administration for War, who emphasized the rather grave gasoline shortage and urged that every possible saving of gasoline be made. After this speech, one of the regional men proposed a reconsideration of the veterans' ration proposal. A second vote resulted in unanimous disapproval of the proposal. Shelburne, who was both surprised and baffled by the turn which events had taken, told them that he would do what he could to consider their recommendation but that, since the Eligibility Committee and the Deputy Administrator had already approved the ration, it was highly likely that it would not be possible to abide by the vote of the regional officials.

No real effort was made to follow the final recommendation of the regional men. Two weeks were consumed in preparing a procedure for the local boards to follow, in ironing out procedural problems and in getting clearance of responsible officials and staff officers in OPA. The only hitch in the process of getting clearance of the amendment was a long discussion between McCullough and Lewittes, when Lewittes refused to sign. Because of this incident, Lewittes resigned as McCullough's advisor on veterans' affairs.

Complete clearance was obtained, the amendment was printed, and finally issued on August 3, 1945. Two weeks later the war with Japan came to an end and gasoline rationing was abandoned.

Some Questions

The rationing of scarce supplies is a type of regulatory activity in which the penalty for weakness is likely to be death. If rations are issued substantially in excess of supply, or even moderately in excess for any long continuing period, the system will break down completely. In view of this perpetual danger, enlargement of the eligibility classifications on the basis of sympathy for individual problems is a treacherous path to follow. The rationer's best protection against his own generosity is adherence to a rationale, to a set of criteria that will serve to reject most applications.

But regulation, perhaps especially in a democracy, can come to a disastrous end if it becomes too logic-bound. The OPA recognized this truth by its allowance of quotas for hardship rations to be issued by the local boards. The question raised by the veterans' ration problem was whether this general release mechanism was adequate. In more general terms, the question is whether and how to accommodate exceptions that receive a high degree of public support to a tight rationale. Specifically, for example—had the Gasoline Branch permitted its rationale to harden into dogma? had the OPA hierarchy permitted its integrity to be infringed? Conversely, was the Gasoline Branch properly adhering to principle? was the hierarchy being properly and democratically responsive to the public will?

The same generic problem has an organizational facet as well. The device used in the gasoline rationing program is a standard one—the delegation to a committee of responsibility for decisions on applications for exceptions. Such committees prevent impulsive action and guard consistency. Normally, as a result, they serve as protective devices—they prevent undue embarrassment to the administrator in denying requests; but to serve this purpose, the committees must have a fairly free hand. Obviously, if an administrator over-rules his committee frequently (or even on just one or two very crucial matters), he can no longer hide behind it. By the same token, if the committee does operate freely, and with considerable finality, it is apt to achieve an independent life of its own; it becomes an enclave in the hierarchy, and its responsiveness to general policy is diminished.

This was the situation in this case, and the reader may well ask himself whether he is satisfied with the way the Gasoline Eligibility Committee operated, if Youngblood was right in accepting its decision, or if McCullough should have been bound by it. In considering this problem, it is well to remember that it is part of a larger problem. One of the things we presumably mean by phrases like "a government of laws, not men" is that the members of the bureaucracy respect their own procedures. Certainly, quite aside from the specific hazards to the gasoline rationing program involved in by-passing the Eligibility Committee, a willingness on the part of officials to disregard the established rules of OPA could eventually lead to generally unfortunate results. Whether this consideration in itself justified McCullough in waiting patiently for so long while the Committee struggled with the Veterans' Gasoline issue is another matter, and one on which opinions will differ. The answers to all such questions, as to the questions suggested above on the use of logical doctrine, are not easy. Different readers will vary greatly in their evaluations and their conclusions. There is no absolute right answer; various sensible and defensible answers are possible. The only general guide that can be suggested is the desirability of weighing the manifold considerations rather than coming to a conclusion on the basis of one or two isolated factors or principles.

Bibliographical Note

The story of the veterans' gasoline ration is told in somewhat abbreviated form in Victor A. Thompson, *The Regulatory Process in OPA Rationing,* New York, King's Crown Press, 1950, pp. 242-250; elsewhere in the same volume, Professor Thompson analyzes the functioning of the Gasoline Eligibility Committee and other matters germane to this particular problem. The basic draft of this present study was prepared in 1945 or 1946 but some use has been made of Professor Thompson's work during the course of final revision in 1951.

CANCELLATION OF THE RATION STAMPS

CONTENTS

Development of the OPA Food Rationing Program

The attack on Pearl Harbor came on December 7, 1941. Within a month, OPA—the Office of Price Administration—had started its first rationing program—tires. Other rationing programs followed with astonishing rapidity. By the end of March 1942, OPA's three major food rationing programs were already in operation.

Underlying the systems employed in these major food rationing programs was the theory that every person in the United States should be entitled to an equal amount of the rationed foodstuffs. There were minor variations on this theme, as in the granting of extra meat rations for miners and other heavy workers; but in general, differences in personal consumption habits or needs were not catered to directly.

Two different rationing systems were used in the three major food programs. For sugar, books of ration stamps were issued which contained numbered stamps. Periodically OPA would announce that a particular numbered sugar stamp would be valid for a stated period of time (the first two weeks in April, for example) and for a stated number of pounds of sugar.

For the other two major programs, processed foods, and meats and fats and oils, the underlying mechanics were more complicated. Within the processed foods category there were a host of different rationed items—canned mixed vegetables, canned grapefruit, canned tomato juice and so forth; the meat program included such diverse rationed commodities as lamb chops, butter, pork shoulders, lard, etc. For all the rationed items in the meat category, the consumer used red stamps, for the processed foods blue stamps. Each stamp was given a fixed value in "points," and periodically announcements were made of the period of validity for each batch of designated stamps, and of the "point" value of each item in each program. When pork was plentiful, its point value was reduced; when canned grapefruit was scarce, its point value was increased. The consumer was free to exercise his choice in spending his red ration stamps for any combination of meats and fats and oils that added up to the right number of points, over the ration period, and his blue stamps similarly for processed foods. OPA, by changing the period of validity for stamps, and by changing the point values of different items, kept supply and demand roughly in line.

The validity periods soon caused an unexpected difficulty. The difficulty arose most dramatically in the case of a non-food program —shoes; just before the expiration of the first shoe ration stamp, there were tremendous lines of customers in the shoe stores: people did not want to "waste" their shoe ration stamps. The situation was disorderly, worse than that, the system was obviously encouraging people to buy shoes who otherwise were ready to wait for a day, or a week, or a month, or a year. After a few months' trial, in September 1942, shoe ration stamps were made valid for an indefinite period; the rush to the shoe stores and the hoarding of shoes ceased. New stamps continued to be made valid periodically; families with growing children generally used all their shoe stamps, many others merely retained possession of their stamps, feeling that they were there and could be used if needed.

The situation in food, in varying degrees, was similar. Some food items could be hoarded easily, others not. But there was in the early days at least some rush of buying at the end of each period of validity; the ration system appeared to encourage consumption or hoarding. It also encouraged irregularities in the handling of stamps by retailers. The cure adopted, for a variety of reasons, was a compromise: new stamps were made valid some time (say a month) before the expiration of the previous batch of stamps. This device avoided the problem of the rush of customers—but it merely concealed the encouragement to over-buying caused by the fixed expiration dates. The rationing authorities did, however, retain fairly tight control over potential demands for rationed foods under this system.

1944 Food Prospects and Indefinite Validity

Anticipations of a good food supply at the beginning of 1944 were bright and there were stirrings of hope about an early end of the war.

These happy anticipations had important effects for food programing in three different agencies—the War Food Administration (WFA), the OPA, and the Office of War Mobilization, which with its satellite, the Office of Economic Stabilization, served as the President's central co-ordinating agency; Justice Byrnes was director of the former, Judge Vinson of the latter.

In all the rationing programs, in theory the supply agency (WFA in this case) determined (1) the need for rationing of a particular item; (2) periodically (usually quarterly) the amount available for rationing to consumers after allowance for military and other needs; and (3) the time for ending a rationing program. As one might expect, this neat formulation was subject to innumerable modifications on both sides. In the eyes of the public, OPA was responsible for any rationing difficulties, and the fact that the supplies on which a ration allowance was based were not forthcoming even though certified as available for the period by the supply agency, was not something that OPA could use as a shield. Experiences of this sort led OPA to make its own estimates of supplies, to seek controls over supply and to take other measures: such actions were not welcomed by the supply agencies. They, for their part, were painfully aware that OPA's administration of rationing had repercussions on price and supply and on their relations with industry; they sought, with varying success, to direct or control actual rationing operations. Justice Byrnes or Judge Vinson, appealed to by one side or the other in such controversies, frequently acted as arbiter.

In the early months of 1944, there was substantial harmony on food policy in the upper levels of WFA and OPA. WFA, counting on good supplies and hopeful of an early end of the war in Europe, was determined that a prospective abrupt cessation of military procurement should not be aggravated by the dumping of large government stocks of food, with disastrous effects for farmers. In spite of some opposition voices, in March, WFA decided on a "bare shelf" policy, with the corollaries of increased consumption and decreased stocks. Mr. Byrnes approved this policy.

In OPA, Administrator Chester Bowles of OPA was still fairly new at the job. He regarded food rationing as a temporary unpleasant necessity that should be dispensed with at the earliest possible moment; he therefore favored progressive derationing. He had brought to OPA new people from the business world who shared his views and who were temperamentally inclined to agree with WFA's statistical forecasts and policy. Grumblers remained, but the policy was set.

The chief effects of the new policy were an intermittent but notable easing of food rationing. Many items were derationed, point values on most of the rest were decreased. From early spring to late fall, the rigors of food rationing were abated, and consumption of food increased. Thus, for a considerable period, the only meats under ration were the better grades of roast beef and steak. Prices on these items were relatively very high, people bought cheaper meats, so even here the ration restrictions had little effect. Ration stamps were unneeded and unused.

In this atmosphere (though "beefsteak rationing," as it was called, came later) it was natural that hesitations about an indefinite extension of stamp validity were quickly overcome. Sugar was first: on March 15, sugar stamps were given indefinite validity.

The problem in processed foods, and meats and fats and oils was more complicated. For a long time housewives had had difficulty in counting up their blue (processed foods) and red (meat, etc.) points when making purchases;

the stamps were issued in denominations of 8, 5, 2, and 1 points; the whole process of buying groceries was slowed up by the toils of arithmetical computation. The retailers also had a problem; they were responsible for sorting out the stamps by denominations, a very real clerical burden to which they objected strenuously. To overcome these irritations, a new system had been worked out over the months which was finally put into effect on February 27, 1944.

Under the new system, all red and blue stamps had a value of 10 points. Red and blue tokens with a value of 1 point were provided for change-making purposes. Adding the points on stamps was easy, and sorting was no longer needed.

The system was immediately popular but it contained an inherent contradiction that caused almost instantaneous—and very dangerous—repercussions. The tokens, naturally, had no expiration date, and consumers promptly began to use up all stamps for the period and hoard their unused ration points in the form of tokens which would remain valid. The national supply of tokens was promptly threatened. There was, presumably, only one quick cure: indefinite validity for the stamps, and this was quickly adopted. As a matter of fact the cure had been recommended by some rationing officials before the new system was put into effect.

This amendment was made effective on March 27, just a month after the new token and point system had gone into effect.

In order to make doubly sure that neither food nor tokens would be hoarded, Chester Bowles, OPA Administrator, issued a statement when the amendment was issued, indicating that if at any time it became necessary to cancel the stamps, he would publicly notify the people of his intention to do so. The release issued to the press for March 27, 1944, said in part:

> Major relief for the nation's 600,000 retailers from the burdens of food rationing was announced today by Chester Bowles, Administrator of the Office of Price Administration, in directing the removal of expiration dates from red and blue stamps used for buying meats, fats, oils and processed fruits and vegetables.
>
> . . . . .
>
> From now on the red and blue stamps in War Ration Book Four will be good indefinitely, just as shoe and sugar stamps are. Advance notice will be given if it is found necessary to retire any food stamps.

Before turning to the events of the fall of 1944, one final minor change in system may be noted. In September, during another spurt of derationing, so few processed food items were left under ration that it seemed feasible to give all those remaining a value of ten points each, and this was done. Change was no longer needed, so the blue tokens were withdrawn.

The Fall Crisis

The summer of 1944 was a time of high hopes; the landings in France, the breakthrough, the sweep across France; by mid-September, however, hopes for an immediate victory in Europe faded. The war was going on. Even before this time, in the late summer, the doubters in OPA began to get increasingly concerned, partly because of worries about future food supplies, partly because of a technical problem in the two point-ration systems. The systems were, as OPA had learned, effectively operable only if each included a substantial number of rationed items. OPA operating officials, whatever their views on future supplies, objected to WFA's orders for derationing of most covered items: they felt that more items had to be left on each ration list—or none. Bowles, however, and his deputy administrator, and his director of the Food Rationing Division went along with WFA, and Justice Byrnes insisted that WFA's interpretation of the bare shelf policy be maintained.

In September, there were major derationing moves in spite of the opposition of the chiefs of the Meat and the Processed Foods Rationing Branches; the higher officials in OPA agreed with WFA. Thereafter, the red and blue ration systems did not work well because so few items were still rationed. One significant and inevitable result of this situation was an increasing backlog of unspent stamps in the hands of consumers. There was always a sizable backlog, but derationing made the situation much worse.

With a continuing war, with serious doubts about the food supply, the OPA rationing officials decided to tackle the problem. Their first step was to obtain information. Working at top speed, officials of the Food Rationing Division and the Deputy Administrator for Rationing prepared a questionnaire form which could be used to find out the facts on unspent food ration stamps. Various other parts of the OPA co-operated, the questionnaire was amplified to cover some other rationing problems, and the necessary complex governmental clearances were quickly obtained. The survey was conducted by the Census Bureau during the week of October 2. Preliminary tabulations were rushed through and the general character of the results was known by the third week in October.

The results of the survey were disturbing. On the average (there were great variations between rural and urban families, and among other categories), people held a 2.8 months' supply of red and blue stamps and about a two months' supply of sugar stamps—and these figures did not include the stamps in all three programs that became valid in October.[1] If the war had been about to end, if prospective food supplies had been ample for a continuation of a light rationing program, the unused stamp backlog would have made no great difference. That was not the situation.

Clearly the war was not going to end in the immediate future. As for processed foods, Curtis Rogers, the Branch Chief, saw trouble ahead. Rogers was a young executive from the food trade who had lived with the rationing program from the beginning. He knew that the new pack of canned goods, the statistics on which were now available, would not support a continuation of the then current generous rationing program. Leon Bosch, chief of the meat branch, a former instructor of marketing, reached similar conclusions on his program.

[1] See Appendixes I and II.

Both men feared that with the announcement of tighter rationing that they were sure would have to be made, consumers would use their previously unused stamps to clean out the stores. To make matters worse, inventories were low, and badly distributed.

The real crisis, however, was in sugar.

Throughout 1944 the sugar rationing system (including rations for industrial consumers like bakers and bottlers, and for home canning) had not been held under tight enough control: a total allocation of about six million tons made by WFA was being steadily exceeded and by the end of the year the excess consumption would total about a million tons. By November (with the survey results in hand), Ed Pickett, chief of the sugar rationing branch, was keenly aware of the excess rationing and he knew that dealers' stocks were dangerously low in consequence.

The situation was thus bad, but two additional factors made it critical. One was the prospect for the coming year. The total amount of sugar available for rationing of all types—home and industrial—was clearly going to be smaller, not only smaller than the amount actually used in 1944, but considerably smaller than the amount allotted for 1944—and exceeded. The second factor was, of course, the backlog of unspent stamps which assumed importance because of the supply situation.

During November these gloomy facts were discussed and debated. WFA remained firm in its faith in a "bare shelf" policy and made no move to tighten up the rationing programs.

Sugar remained the prime worry, not only to Pickett, but also to Max McCullough, Deputy Administrator for Rationing, an experienced public official who had come to the national OPA office, after service in the field. Pickett presently concluded that there was just not enough sugar in stock or becoming available to validate outstanding currency plus that which had to be issued. In fact, he asserted that if the outstanding home canning stamps were presented for redemption, there would not be enough sugar to cover the stamps which had been issued in November for the day to day sugar needs of the public; the stamps in the hands of industrial and home users would have become mere hunting licenses because of the disappearance of sugar from retailers' shelves.

The December Crisis

FOOD SITUATION IN DECEMBER

The threatening situation which OPA had perceived during October and November reached a state in December where the officials became convinced that action was necessary. The sharply reduced sugar allocation promised to bankrupt the entire sugar rationing system. OPA knew from experience that rationing collapses if ration stamps cannot be honored. While WFA now belatedly was coming to agree with the OPA officials on the general food situation, it still issued no directive placing various processed vegetables back on the ration list or restoring various types of meat to rationing. OPA continued to press WFA for tighter rationing. WFA, however, was apparently still standing by its "bare shelf" program in spite of the facts and was reluctant to alter that policy or to return to the rationing program in processed foods which had prevailed prior to September 17.

All doubts about a stricter policy were suddenly swept away by the Battle of the Bulge. After the German breakthrough on December 17, excessive optimism about an early end of the war in Europe was replaced by excess pessimism.

McCullough and Bowles (who had gradually changed his views on food rationing) no longer met active opposition from WFA. Judge Vinson, Director of Economic Stabilization, agreed with Bowles's position. WFA then directed the rerationing of many processed foods and of various meats and a tightening of the butter ration. The 1945 sugar allocation was certified to OPA—about a million tons less than the 1944 allocation, about two million tons less than 1944 use!

ALTERNATIVE COURSES OF ACTION

The need for drastic action on sugar was early apparent to McCullough; but in considering this problem, McCullough soon realized that the other two food rationing programs were also headed for trouble, and for similar reasons. Though some officials thought that drastic action might be avoided for these, since they were sure that the sugar problem had to be faced anyway, these programs were considered along with sugar and, as it turned out, were the subject of much more debate.

There was a continuing series of conferences in McCullough's office where possible courses of action were weighed. The conferences were attended by McCullough and his assistants Redford and French; by Burdick, Director of the Food Rationing Division and his assistant, Dice. The Deputy Administrator for Information, Stanford, and the Director of Information Planning, Bennet, were also called in as was Clark, the attorney attached to McCullough's office.

There was no real dispute about sugar. A reduction in sugar rations was inevitable and a further reduction adequate to permit the unused stamps to be used was far too drastic to deserve consideration. Everyone agreed that, with the announcement of the ration reduction, people would start to use their unspent stamps. The whole system would then break down. Since sugar was not part of a point system, the strain on sugar supplies could not be eased by increasing ration values of other commodities. Cancellation of the unused sugar stamps seemed the only solution, and cancellation without advance notice, for advance notice would cause a run on sugar that would be disastrous. As will be seen, some of the arguments used in the debate on meats and processed foods also applied in the case of sugar. But the sugar program was different in three important ways: (1) the supply situation was worse; (2) sugar was not part of a point system; and (3) OPA had not promised to give advance notice of the cancellation of sugar stamps.

The situation in the red and blue point programs was more complicated. By the same reasoning that applied to sugar, it was generally felt that if rationing were tightened, i.e., if consumers had to spend stamps for more food items and to pay more points for various items, unused stamps which had not been used in previous months would come into the market. Accordingly, the most urgent problem was how to blot up this reservoir of stamps which threatened to flood the market and wash away existing stocks of sugar (as has been noted) and other rationed foods. On previous occasions when it had been necessary for OPA to take up the slack in the red or blue rationing program, i.e. when reduced supplies of those foods were anticipated, OPA had merely increased the point values for the respective products. It was at first suggested that this method be adopted in the present instance. By increasing the point value of each item, it was obvious that OPA would cause people to use up many previously unused stamps. People who had not found it necessary to use all their points before would be likely to do so under a program of higher point values on a larger group of foods. However, it was also recognized that this method would work a hardship on a majority of the people. As has been pointed out, the surplus of stamps was not evenly scattered among the people but clustered in the hands of certain groups of people and in certain areas. The majority of people did not possess several months' supply of unused stamps. If point values on foods were raised and more foods were placed on the rationed list, the people who had little or no holdings in unused stamps, would find themselves hard pressed to obtain enough food for their day to day needs. The fact that they had apparently found it necessary to spend most of their previous stamps in the normal course of their living during the months when rationing was not tight seemed to indicate that they would not have enough if points were raised to any considerable extent. But unless points were raised substantially, the unused stamps in the hands of a good minority of the people would be enough to clean the shelves. The backlog of unused stamps had to be reckoned with in computing the new point system. Thus this proposal did not seem to present an equitable solution to the problem.

A second alternative was that which claimed the support of most of the OPA officials in the operating branches. This proposal was to invalidate the backlog of stamps and thereby to begin 1945 with a clean slate. OPA would then become solvent by refusing to honor outstanding currency. Burdick was favorably disposed toward the proposal as a way out of the dilemma, but continued to hesitate during the conferences. Dice was more consistently for it. Dice had come over from Agriculture when the food rationing program was first begun, and had earlier been Chief of the Sugar Branch; his argument ran approximately along the following lines: The unspent ration stamps represented a potential threat to effective rationing; while not all of these consumers would spend all their ration currency, the fact that rationing had to be made tighter would probably bring a large part of the unused stamps onto the market. Accordingly, these stamps had to be taken into account in reckoning the new point values. Yet if this two months' supply of surplus stamps were figured into the rationing program, the majority of people would suffer; it would be necessary to set a considerably higher point value on all subsequent purchases of rationed goods. This would mean that only those who had a surplus of stamps would be able to obtain adequate amounts of rationed food while all other people would be hard pressed to pay ration points for the food they needed. People with a surplus of stamps had shown that they did not need them. If they had needed them, they would have spent them. Therefore, OPA could not be charged with taking food from their mouths. It was fairer to the majority of people to wipe out the stamps unused in the hands of some of the people. This was fairer than the alternative of raising the point value on rationed foods to such a level that it would absorb the surplus points in the hands of some of the people. For this would have made it possible for these people—the very ones who apparently were not dependent upon rationed foods—to go into the market and obtain not only their fair share of the 1945 food supply but also an increase to the extent that they had a surplus of 1944 stamps.

This was substantially the view taken by McCullough. However, McCullough was concerned about the possible repercussions of such action on the public and it was for this reason that he had brought the public relations men, Stanford and Bennet, into the conferences.

McCullough wrestled with the problem of working out a solution which would on the one hand effectively remove the threat of the unused stamps in the hands of the consumer, and establish rationing on a sound and solvent basis with the new year and which would at the same time be palatable to the public. On the issue of invalidating the unused stamps, the point was raised by Stanford that Bowles had promised the people when ration stamps had first been issued with an indefinite time for their use that should conditions require that stamps would have to be invalidated, he would notify the people in advance. At the time the change was made from monthly validity to indeterminate validity, it was generally assumed that the stamps might be canceled every six months by prior notice. This method had been proved successful in the shoe rationing program. However, the seriousness of the food situation which confronted OPA in December 1944 had not been anticipated nine months earlier. Thus when the suggestion was made that a ten day or thirty day notice should be given of intent to cancel 1944 stamps, there were grave doubts of the wisdom of such prior notice. McCullough felt that to give people notice of intent as Bowles had promised, would precipitate a run on the stores which would wipe out the small stocks in the hands of dealers and wholesalers. Furthermore, notice would precipitate a great increase in the trading or giving away of stamps thus adding to the total demand on food stocks and adding to the unequal distribution of foods.

Thus the issue became simply one of invalidating the stamps without giving the people prior notice or of not going through with the proposal to invalidate the stamps. Stanford and Bennet both were inclined to forego invalidation. Bennet was a young executive who had been in advertising before going with OPA as assistant to Bowles in rationing tires in Connecticut. When Bowles had been appointed OPA Administrator, he had taken Bennet along to act as Director of the Information Planning Division. (Stanford was the top man.) Bennet was extremely concerned over what the public's reaction would be to the proposal to invalidate the stamps and over the difficult job of public relations involved. Bennet felt that since Bowles had made a promise to the public that they would be notified before their points would be declared invalid, invalidation without notice would be wrong. Ration points had become in fact what they were called in OPA: "currency." Indeed, during the war when money was more plentiful than certain foods, the ration currency had come to have more real value than money vis à vis rationed foods. Accordingly, people would actually feel as if they had been robbed. To Stanford, Deputy Administrator for Information, the problem of maintaining public faith in OPA was the principal disadvantage. Stanford had been an advertising agency man who had come down to work with OPA during the war. He stressed the public trust inherent in administration. Should OPA invalidate the stamps, people would lose confidence in future declarations by OPA and thus OPA would add to its own difficulties in rationing foods. But above and beyond its effect on the agency's public relations, was the broader issue of the people's faith in the statements of the government. OPA had secured the people's trust, slowly and arduously. This faith which had been built with considerable effort, was nevertheless fragile. The proposed action would undo much of the results they had thus far attained.

But the operating division officials remained unconvinced. They were sure that breaking a promise to the people was better than giving people who did not need the food a priority upon remaining stocks while depriving the people who really needed it. However, Bennet and Stanford had a further objection to cancellation: it would lead to improper use of the canceled stamps. Under the rationing system, dealers were required to deposit their receipts of ration stamps in their ration bank or with their wholesaler each month. The banks and wholesalers were allowed ten days to two weeks after the period, to deliver the used stamps into the hands of the OPA officials; the majority of retailers, who did not have ration bank accounts, had even more time. This period would now make it possible for dealers to accept the canceled stamps and simply add them to those which had been used for purchases during the pre-Christmas buying period.

It would be difficult to control this. Consumers could be told that they were not to give the canceled stamps to dealers because the dealer could not honor them. However, because of this very suggestion (to both dealers and consumers) or because many would not understand, it was likely that when a dealer's customer asked him to accept the stamps he would be likely to do so—especially when he could do so with little likelihood of being apprehended. Furthermore, many housewives were in the habit of giving their books to the dealer to tear the required stamps for their purchase from the ration book. A dealer could thus readily avail himself of these canceled stamps and add them to his Christmas period returns and sell an equivalent amount of rationed goods point-free.

A final argument advanced by Bennet and Stanford (originally suggested by French who had formerly been with the shoe rationing division) was that cancellation without notice would have an adverse effect upon other rationing programs, principally shoes. The situation in shoes was becoming as critical as that in foods, stocks were dangerously low and a run on shoe stores would have been very serious. Bennet and Stanford argued that a cancellation of the food stamps would foster apprehension over the continued validity of the shoe stamps and would be likely to precipitate a run on the stores to obtain shoes before the coupon would be voided. The coupons had been issued without an expiration date but notice of future invalidation was issued periodically. Thus people knew that their stamps would not remain good; but they had counted theretofore on ample warning. The failure to give advance notice in food rationing might suggest the possibility of similar action in the shoe program.

Decision Taken

ACTION WITHOUT NOTICE INESCAPABLE

Despite the arguments advanced by Stanford and Bennet and the hesitancy and reluctance of Burdick, McCullough came to the conclusion that cancellation of stamps was inescapable. During the long and arduous conferences which were held during the weeks before Christmas, he cast around for some other method of accomplishing the ends sought. But every other alternative seemed to offer less effective results while some action had to be taken—and that at once. The only way to assure equitable distribution during 1945 was to make equal shares of food available to all. This could not be done by saying to some: "you can have your 1945 share plus your balance of 1944 stamps' worth." It was McCullough's belief that the public interest would best be served by violating OPA's pledge to the people and giving all the people a fair shot at the food; OPA's greatest obligation was to secure equitable distribution. Accordingly, though he felt the action would incur public wrath, McCullough recommended the action to Bowles, who agreed with him that it was the best of bad alternatives.

IMPLEMENTING THE DECISION

It was decided that the cancellation of stamps would go into effect on December 31, a Sunday, at a time when dealers were normally required to reckon up their point balances for the preceding period. The announcement was scheduled for Saturday night since there could hardly then be a serious run over the week end when most stores would be closed. However, some ten days before the order was scheduled to be released, a leak developed. OPA had acquired the voluntary censorship of the press on stories of runs or stories which might precipitate runs. Nevertheless, one newspaper man learned of the cancellation story and made it clear that he intended to print it. Accordingly, McCullough and the others decided to move up the date and went into action to have the releases out during the Christmas period. Christmas was on Monday, the story was released to the press and radio as confidential until December 24 with the cancellation of sugar and processed food stamps taking effect December 26 at 12:01 A.M. It was announced that meats would go back on the rationed list on December 31. The information department sent an urgent message to the press explaining the circumstances of the decision and asking their help in making the people understand the necessity which prompted the action. (See Appendix III.) "Fact Sheets" giving the statistics regarding each of the rationed foods which had led up to the action were supplied the press and radio also; these Fact Sheets were prepared by further use of the information collected in the October survey. Civic and trade groups were urged to co-operate in bringing the facts home to the people. The attempt by the Information Department to take some of the heat off OPA was not entirely successful. As can readily be understood, it was a difficult job of public relations

Aftermath of the Decision

IMMEDIATE PUBLIC REACTION

While some newspapers co-operated with OPA by explaining the how and why of the action, it was too complicated a problem to be made clear to the masses of people. There had been no time to break the news gradually; to condition the people; to build up a proper frame of reference. Some newspapers and commentators were not unhappy at the opportunity for calling attention to this "latest" evidence of OPA's incompetence. Some people were prone to gripe about "bureaucrats" in general and OPA in particular. But besides these, there were some people who had been hurt by the sudden action. Individuals who had denied themselves the use of all their points because they felt it was patriotic to buy only what they could not do without; others who had been saving their points to have a little something extra when a son came home on furlough, and so forth. Whatever their personal reasons, OPA's mailbag quickly assumed gigantic proportions; Congressmen (who also had been hearing from their constituents) were also perturbed about the action. Eventually, the continuing efforts by OPA to explain the causes which led to the cancellation and to point out its unquestionable fairness to the majority of people began to take effect. Surveys which OPA conducted shortly thereafter, indicated that the majority of people had not really been hurt and that in fact the majority were not angry with OPA as might have been expected by a perusal of the OPA and Congressional mail on the subject. (See Appendix IV.) As in similar cases, those who take the trouble to write are those who feel especially strongly on the matter.

THE SPRING SUPPLY SITUATION

As had been expected, the supply of sugar for civilian use during the spring of 1945 was smaller than in any comparable period during the war. The situation in meat was even more critical during the spring of 1945; many areas were without meat for days. It was generally agreed among OPA officials that if they had not taken drastic action on the meat rationing program in December, there would have been a meat famine in many areas of the country. The situation in butter was equally critical. Processed foods, while less critically short than the other rationed foods, were nonetheless scarce during the early months of 1945. Thus there is evidence that drastic action had been necessary when OPA canceled the stamps.

Appendix I

CONCLUSIONS ON BLUE STAMPS AND TOKENS

(Processed Foods Program)

I. TOTAL OUTSTANDING STAMPS EQUAL TO 2.8 MONTHS' SUPPLY

(a) No. of unused stamps reported by survey — 206,506

(b) Estimated no. of unused stamps in U. S. — 1,673,000,000 (Value 16,730,000,000 points)

(c) No. of months' supply — 2.8

(d) These outstanding blue points are sufficient:

(1) If distributed among all institutional users, to supply them with their normal allotments for 14 months.

(2) If spent for canned fruits in #2½ cans,

at the average value of 65 points prevailing in October, to buy 10½ million cases, or 18% of the 1944 pack.

(3) If spent for fruit juices in #2½ cans at the average value of 40 points prevailing in October, to buy 17½ million cases, or 68% of the 1944 pack of rationed juices. (Grape, pineapple, tomato and vegetable combinations.)

II. 45% of Outstanding Stamps Are in the 8-Series, All of Which Became Valid Before August 1, 1944

Estimated unused stamps in U. S.:

Total 8-series stamps	756,000,000
Total 5-series stamps	917,000,000
Total of both series stamps	1,673,000,000

III. 26% of 8-Series and 70% of 5-Series Still Unused

Per cent of total stamps validated:

	Used	*Unused*
8-series	73.7	26.3
5-series	30.4	69.6
Both series combined	60.1	39.9

Appendix II

Conclusions on Sugar

14,777 Ration Book holders were "sampled" in an October survey. We wanted to get significant information on unused ration currency, opinions and attitudes about sugar. While this survey may obviously not be projected accurately into a National picture, it is an important indication of conditions generally. After analysis, these are our conclusions:

(1) 71% of the people doubt the need for sugar rationing after V-E Day; or have no opinion, or say, "it depends."

(2) 42% do not believe sugar rationing is necessary.

(3) 60% say they get all they need; 10% more than they need.

(4) 50% of farm families say they do not get enough; but only 25% of city people get less than they need.

(5) There is, therefore, an extremely important over-all job of information needed to acquaint the public with the vital need for continuing sugar rationing through at least one more year.

(6) On October 1, 27% of home canning stamps No. 40 were unused. (33% of city dwellers and 15% of farm dwellers.)

(7) 7% of regular sugar stamps are unused (twice as many in cities as in rural areas).

(8) 86% of farm families, 73% of rural families, but only 51% of city families received home canning coupons.

(9) Including all sugar stamps issued and valid (Nos. 30, 31, 32 and 40 and home canning coupons), the average consumer has unused ration evidence worth 4 pounds of sugar and equal to about two months' regular ration. Outstanding Stamps 30, 31, and 32 would buy 65,000 tons of sugar. Outstanding Stamps #40 would buy 80,000 tons. Outstanding home canning coupons would buy 103,000 tons. All together, they would buy about 250,000 tons. Of course, a great number of consumers still have Stamp No. 33 which was validated on September 1st.

Appendix III

Letter to Editors

OFFICE OF PRICE ADMINISTRATION

Washington 25, D. C.

Office of the Administrator

Personal and Confidential Until December 27th [1]

Dear Mr. Editor:

I want to enlist your help in a group of major problems which confront me today and which affect the daily lives of all of us.

I don't know of any time while I have been Administrator of OPA when we were faced with so many situations that required so many decisions that were bound to be unpleasant and that so urgently required understanding and co-operation from the public.

To create that understanding I feel I must rely to a great degree on the editors of the country to

[1] This date was moved up to December 24 at the last minute.

explain the facts which had to be faced in deciding our rationing program for 1945.

Here are the facts:

Present estimates from the supply agencies indicate we will have less meat, less butter, less sugar, and less processed food for civilian consumption in the first quarter of 1945 than in any 3 months of the war. An end of the German war in 1945 will not significantly alter these shortages.

OPA will announce a two-fold action to meet this situation for release in morning papers, December 27th. The first part of its action is an expanded list of rationed foods—adding processed foods—including most canned and bottled vegetables—raising the point value of butter, placing about 85 per cent of the meats under rationing control and tightening sugar rationing.

The second action will take out of circulation a very large number of unused ration stamps and coupons by cancellation.

Here are the jobs I especially seek your help on!

1. *To bring home to the people the facts about the food supply situation.*

2. To emphasize that *rationing works not on the principle of taking things away from people, but to make it possible to share them.*

Appendix IV

Opinion Briefs January 27, 1945

PUBLIC REACTIONS TO RERATIONING AND STAMP INVALIDATION

The recent rationing changes elicited a tremendous volume of discussion within a very short time, but the comment tapered off very quickly.

The Twohey Analysis of Newspaper Opinion reported that for the two weeks ending January 6, 1945, the general topic of shortages and rationing led all issues, both domestic and foreign, in the amount of editorial space it received. For the week ending December 30, 60% of the comment dealt with the tightening of the rationing program. During the following week, only 35% of the editorials discussed the changes in the rationing program. And for the week ending January 13, the changes in rationing are not even mentioned as one of the major topics of interest.

A telegraphic poll on January 3 of 21 members of OWI's editorial panel located in 19 widely distributed localities indicated that the criticism of the changes was already subsiding.

According to reports from DIEs on January 3, 70% of the grocers in 87 cities scattered throughout the country thought that criticism was definitely subsiding.

In general, the stamp invalidation aroused the bulk of the unfavorable comment. OWI's Analysis of Editorial Opinion reported 314 editorials dealing with the rerationing and stamp invalidation between December 26, 1944 and January 4, 1945.

Comment on the rerationing ran about six to one in favor of that change; most of the editorials pointed out the relation between rerationing and the military situation. Most of those opposed either expressed or implied the idea that political considerations had prompted the earlier relaxation of rationing and that tighter rationing was being resumed now that politics were no longer a factor.

Comment about the stamp invalidation was about four to three against the action. Some of the unfavorable editorials spoke quite bitterly about "repudiated government obligations," and "breaking faith with the public." About a fourth complained that the thrifty and patriotic housewife had been penalized in favor of the extravagant ones. Most considered the move unfortunate and unwise, felt that public confidence in OPA had been seriously impaired, and that this would lead to hoarding and over-buying. Some of those favorable to the action also expressed the fear that there would be hoarding as a result. Those editorials in favor of the change in general related it to military considerations, pointed out that the stamps probably had not been needed if they were still unused, and regarded it as the best solution to a difficult situation.

Bibliographical Note

Certain aspects of the cancellation story are described in

Joseph A. Kershaw, *A History of Ration Banking*, G.P.O., Washington, 1947.

The whole story is told as part of the general history of OPA, in

Harvey C. Mansfield and others, *A Short History of OPA*, G.P.O., Washington, 1949.

Mr. Kershaw drafted Chapter 5 of this volume which covers the cancellation episode; but this particular incident takes on more meaning if it is read in the light of the general development of OPA from 1941 to 1945.

The episode is treated separately as a problem

in the use of research in administration with emphasis on the use of the October unused-stamp survey in an article by

Joseph Kershaw and Harry Alpert, *Journal of Social Issues,* Vol. III, No. 4 (1947), pp. 40-48.

The episode is also told in abbreviated form in

Victor A. Thompson, *The Regulatory Process in OPA Rationing,* King's Crown Press, New York, 1950.

Professor Thompson uses the cancellation history as a case study in his analysis of the problem of values in administration; it will be found on pp. 250-254. It may be noted that Professor Thompson concludes that the decision was based on the principle of equality of sacrifice in spite of objections based on competing principles (e.g., numerical equality) and technical prophecies (e.g., runs on other commodities). He does not, in his conclusion, cite the technical prophecies about the effects of alternative decisions that supported cancellation.

The present study was originally drafted on the basis of interviews before any of the foregoing appeared in print, but use has been made of these accounts in the process of final revision in 1951.

THE ATTACK ON THE COST OF LIVING INDEX

CONTENTS

The Attack on the Cost of Living Index

I. PREFACE

THE FEDERAL STATISTICAL AGENCIES

About forty administrative, regulatory, and research agencies in the Federal government are charged—among other things—with making periodic public statistical reports and analyses of physical or social phenomena. They include organizations as diverse as the National Bureau of Standards and the Bureau of Labor Statistics, the Weather Bureau and the Securities and Exchange Commission. The collecting and reporting done by these offices has become a basic function of government. Their statistical reports—whether published daily or decennially—furnish the raw and intermediate data for a wide variety of users in and out of the government and are the generally accepted bases of many important policy decisions in both private and public affairs. A *sine qua non* of this acceptance, of course, is "client" confidence in the reliability and impartiality of the data, even if the clients are gamblers betting on the last digits of the Treasury daily statement. For their part, government statisticians are commonly proud of their technical competence and disinterestedness.

Normally, statistical agencies depend in some degree on pressure groups among their clients for political support. In a passive sense they need the confidence of the general public too, but the man in the street knows little or nothing about most statistical series.

The present case is concerned with the dilemma faced by the officials of a statistical agency, the Bureau of Labor Statistics of the Department of Labor, and a wartime policy-making agency, the National War Labor Board, when, during 1942-1944, a group of labor unions who had often been "clients" of the Bureau and who were represented on the tripartite Board, publicly attacked the accuracy and adequacy of the cost of living index. This index was the Bureau's most widely used statistical series and it was with its use in connection with wartime wage stabilization policy that these unions took issue. Union criticisms were voiced through many channels and came to the attention of a vast union periodical and general newspaper reading public which, before the advent of wartime price control, had seldom heard of the index and generally had no idea of its real nature and purpose.

While the economic and political setting of the dispute which ensued makes it necessary to refer to offstage developments, the story is focused chiefly on the manner in which, first the Bureau of Labor Statistics and then a special committee of the War Labor Board—the President's Committee on the Cost of Living—met the attacks on the index. The Bureau's reactions form the theme of Part III, and the Committee's activities the theme of Part IV of this study. Detailed concentration on the events in these particular areas necessitates cursory treatment of others.

THE COST OF LIVING INDEX AT THE TIME OF THE ATTACK

The Bureau of Labor Statistics cost of living index at the time of the controversy was a weighted nation-wide average of the periodic changes in the prices of about 200 commodities and services purchased by moderate income families in 34 large cities. (Appendix A contains a fuller description of the index.) The weights used for its compilation were the average amounts of each of these goods and services consumed by a sample of such families during the period 1934-36, as disclosed by a study made at that time. The index, together with separate indexes of its six major components—food; rent; clothing; house furnishings; fuel, electricity, and ice; and miscellaneous—was published at quarterly intervals until the defense program of 1940-1941 made more frequent computation necessary and possible.

The nation-wide cost of living index had been an important statistical tool for economists, statisticians, and administrators in the United States since its initial publication in February 1921. Widely used by business analysts, social scientists, government agencies, and labor unions throughout the country, the index served not only as a major indicator of the effect of fiscal and other government policies upon retail prices and the cost of living of the moderate income urban family, but also as a criterion in wage negotiations and in the adjustment of salaries.

Like the official cost of living indexes in other countries, as well as many which were privately compiled, the BLS index was a retail price index rather than a gauge of change in total family expenditures on living. In fact, to statisticians the world over the expression "cost of living index" meant an index of changes in the unit retail prices of a more or less rigidly fixed group of carefully specified consumer goods and services. More briefly put, it was a consumers' price index, as indeed it is now (1951) officially named. But the layman usually tended to think of the "cost of living" in more general and vague terms—as the total cost of everything he bought for family consumption, without reference to whether changes in the total were due to alterations in his standard of living, voluntary or forced, or to movements in prices, or to changes in the kind and quality of the various available objects of consumption.

WARTIME USE OF THE INDEX

Cost of living indexes had been developed and designed, during the second and third decades of this century, as general indicators of retail price movements and not especially for use in wartime wage negotiation or price control. Statisticians in the United States and elsewhere agreed that unless index base-period weightings and components were periodically brought up to date, the indexes could not fully reflect the gradual peacetime changes in real prices which resulted from quality appreciation or deterioration and from shifts in the objects of spending, say from ice boxes to electric refrigerators. Wartime's swift changes led a few very critical observers to assert that since consumer tastes, activities, and environment were becoming radically different from those prevailing during the BLS index's base period, 1934-36, the index's validity was greatly diminished. A basic revision of weights, sample, and the like to take account of all relevant changes would have been a time-consuming, complicated, technical task of major proportions, requiring new and expensive nation-wide surveys. It was impracticable during the war. Officials in the Department of Labor and other government agencies were inclined to think that, provided some obvious interim modifications were made—such as dropping electric appliances when they became unavailable—the index would continue to be a reasonably satisfactory indicator of what it was supposed to measure.

Abroad, in Great Britain, Canada, Australia, New Zealand, Sweden, and elsewhere retail price or "living cost" indexes similar to the BLS series were used in various ways as guides to peace and wartime economic policy formation. Whatever the qualms of professional statisticians over the effect of wartime dislocations on the accuracy and validity of the various indexes, in a technical sense, officials in charge of price and wage control in each country showed little or no hesitation in using the national index, together with other factors, in reaching decisions.

When retail prices began to rise in the United States in 1941 and early in 1942, under the impetus of government expenditures for defense and war, and when the Office of Price Administration established a system of price control, the index took on a new function—that of measuring the effectiveness of the OPA's retail price controls. Early and continued reference to the index by the price agency perhaps made more of the public at large conscious of the index than had ever heard of it before.

As World War II progressed, the index was

still more widely referred to in private and public policy making. With the development of the wage stabilization program it came to serve as a measure of the pinch of wage rate controls. In Congress, in union offices, in the White House, the OPA, the WLB, and elsewhere, the trend in wage rates was constantly compared with the movement of the index for an indication of whether labor's real wages or purchasing power was rising or falling. These comparisons multiplied after the WLB's Little Steel decision in the summer of 1942. Yet, paradoxically, it was in this decision that the WLB broke the link between the index and wages which had been developed by the "escalator" clauses in wartime wage agreements, by general use of the index as a measure of inflation, and (to some extent) by the Board's own early wage decisions. In the Little Steel decision the WLB placed a limit on general wage rate increases and, for convenience, phrased the limit in terms of the rise in the cost of living index between two dates historically significant to wage stabilization. It was over the use of the index in this connection—more fully discussed in the next chapter—that the controversy about the index developed.

THE BLS INDEX DISPUTE AS A CASE IN PUBLIC ADMINISTRATION

The public attack by a group of unions on the cost of living index, and, at times, on the Bureau of Labor Statistics, was incidental to a larger labor campaign against the Little Steel formula. The index attack began later and was of shorter duration; nonetheless it reached moments of great intensity. It drew on but was in no sense part of an older and more academic stream of "customer" criticism and comments which was a normal by-product of the index's extensive use.

There is a rich mixture of political, economic, and statistical issues in the dispute over the BLS index. Worked in one way it could provide material for a brief chapter in American trade union history. Examined from another viewpoint, it could be shaped into a study of the impact of war on the reliability of a peacetime statistical tool and of the differences in concept and policy use between a consumers' price index like the BLS index and other possible measures of change in prices or total family expenditures. The processes of wartime economic mobilization might provide another focal point for analysis of the stream of events here recounted.

The approach in the present study is from the standpoint of public administration. Economic trends and statistical problems *per se* have accordingly been given only such treatment as the logic and continuity of the main story necessitate.

One group of public officials involved in the attack—the career staff in the BLS—look back on their roles in this case as those of actors in a sort of Greek tragedy: given a political attack from a quarter in which they normally looked for support, and given their professional backgrounds and official responsibilities, they saw no alternatives to the course they took. That course, standing alone, proved insufficient to defeat the attack. The situation of a political attack on an agency whose cardinal virtues are technical expertise and neutrality is a recurring phenomenon of public administration. The reader may ponder whether alternatives in fact were open; whether, more generally, technical experts can or should be expected to take political roles also; and if not, how they may be shielded from situations they cannot cope with. He will in any event note the contrast in this case in the handling of a political problem by experts and by political officials.

This contrast raises a related question of continuing importance: What are the specifications for bureau leadership? Doctors want doctors in charge of hospitals, teachers want teachers in charge of schools, and statisticians want statisticians in charge of statistical bureaus. There is general lay sympathy for this feeling, and in the Federal government over the past generation the trend has been definitely in the direction of making the position of bureau chief a career post for a man of proved technical competence. But at some stage in the administrative (and political) process lay viewpoints must usually be controlling. Whether or not a bureau can "take care of itself" politically depends frequently on the personality and associations of its chief. In the Department of Labor, in this case, the formal line between technical and lay viewpoints was drawn somewhere between the bureau chief and the Secretary. The qualities and tactics of leadership which were displayed in both positions are therefore relevant objects of the reader's attention.

Along the same general line, it will be observed that during the period covered here the Acting Commissioner of Labor Statistics was in some sense a "pinch-hitter," the Secretary did not enjoy the full confidence of top union leaders, and the Department itself, as an old-line agency, was more or less pushed to one side as new emergency agencies dealt with the more urgent labor issues related to the war effort. In these circumstances a dispute of the kind here related was sure to become of concern to the President. It must have seemed a small problem to him, but it was also "hot." The reader will observe how he moved it characteristically from one level of the governmental hierarchy to another.

Two other aspects of the case may be worth reflection. Wartime pressures distorted the usual agency-client relations existing between the Department and the Bureau, on the one hand, and the labor organizations on the other; those relations were in a state of flux for reasons unconnected with the war but growing out of changes during the previous decade in the labor movement and in the functions of the Department. This case therefore raises the question of norms and standards in these relations.

The index dispute was finally disposed of by the War Labor Board, acting through a tripartite committee (of labor, industry, and public representatives). The case accordingly affords some basis for appraising the operations and utility of that kind of organization, and especially for observing the role of one of the Board's public members, the chairman.

II. Wage Stabilization Solves and Creates Problems

The argument over the cost of living index was part of the larger argument over wage stabilization and its administration by the War Labor Board. As background to the index dispute it will be useful to recount here the principal steps by which the wage control program was constructed.

THEORY UNDERLYING WAGE STABILIZATION

Wage stabilization was a system of control over wage rates (not total earnings) designed to minimize fluctuations or, more specifically, rises in money wage rates. It served two anti-inflationary purposes, supplementing other measures such as direct credit and price controls and taxation. It aimed, first, to reduce employer pressure for higher prices to offset increased wages and second, to keep down the amount of workers' purchasing power available to bid up the prices of the limited supply of consumer goods during the war.

There was more than one school of thought on the fiscal and monetary management of the war economy. "Pay-as-you-go" was an extreme view; a more practical approach was taken by the "inflationary gap" school, which had the largest number of adherents among government economists and policy makers, and most articulately on the staffs of the Office of Price Administration and the War Labor Board. Adherents of this school believed that when Federal government "purchases of goods and services for war" were soaring as they did between 1940 and 1944, from 2 per cent of the gross national product to about 40 per cent (faster than any possible expansion in the output of goods and services for civilian consumption), then any increases in consumer purchasing power, through wage boosts or otherwise, would create an "inflationary gap." The size of the gap would be the excess of purchasing power over the current value of the available consumers' goods (less any increases in personal taxes and savings). Like a vacuum, this gap would pull or suck up consumer prices, forcing workers to demand more wages to pay the higher prices. Wage increases which were granted in response to labor's demands would in turn force further price rises, generating further wage increases. This was the "inflationary spiral" caused by excess money competing for a diminishing stock of goods. Since individuals and groups were helpless to restrain the trend themselves, this school thought government controls were necessary to keep both wages and prices down. In retrospect, they were mistaken in underestimating the amount of civilian goods that actually proved to be available—the aggregate physical volume did not decline—but they also underestimated war expenditures, hence personal income, so the relative pressures remained and the trend of events confirmed their analysis.

THE DISPUTE OVER WAGE CONTROL

Wage control was more than a debated question in economics. It was also a thorny political issue. Widespread national control of wages had never before been essayed in the United States or any other democratic country although concurrently it was being undertaken by various means in a number of the allied countries; in Germany it had been in effect since 1936. Despite the admitted military emergency, moreover, management and labor were loath to modify collective bargaining and surrender to the Federal government their traditional control over the determination of wage rates and other conditions of work. Labor in particular found it difficult to accede to public control over wage rates because wartime manpower shortages had pushed to a zenith the workingman's potential bargaining power for higher wages. Recalling the grim days of the depression, barely past, and anticipating a slump and unemployment after the war boom, union leaders frankly aimed to get hourly wage rates up to a level that would compensate as much as possible for the expected postwar loss of overtime payments, shift differentials, and other premium rates which were increasing wartime "take home" pay.

Labor rejected the inflationary gap analysis, arguing that increased wages would not automatically inflate prices because workers would generally spend their money only on necessities and put the rest into war bonds. The labor leaders also asserted that industry could absorb wage increases without increasing prices and they were vigorous in demanding firm government control of the prices of all commodities and services because they did not feel that voluntary agreements among businessmen to keep prices down would be effective.

Industry groups, such as the United States Chamber of Commerce, generally accepted the inflationary gap analysis but with reservations about the vigor with which prices and profits were to be curbed. Many business spokesmen held the view that if prices were controlled, then wages (which they considered the price of labor) should also be controlled. The farm bloc felt this way even more strongly and urged legislative action.

Within the Federal government the control of prices, wages, and other forms of income became the subject of a contest between the Executive and Legislative Branches. Not only the President, but his entire wartime supporting staff including the OPA and WLB, were influenced in their actions at one or another point in the gradual development of the anti-inflation program through executive order and administrative regulation, by knowledge of Congress's desire to "pass a law" to impose rigid controls on wages.

CREATION OF THE WAR LABOR BOARD AND INITIATION OF OVER-ALL PRICE CONTROL, JANUARY 1942

The administrative machinery and policies for stabilization developed and extended slowly, almost jerkily, with each step seemingly taken only when forced by economic trends or when aided by a national will to mobilize, engendered by military crises. The first significant move by the Executive toward wage stabilization did not come until after Pearl Harbor, with the establishment of the 12-man tripartite National War Labor Board (WLB) by Executive Order 9017 on January 12, 1942. This order made all major labor disputes, including their wage aspects, subject to final determination by the new agency and gave the Board responsibility for the formulation of criteria and rules of procedure. The Board's establishment was a *quid pro quo* for the labor-management pledge (made three weeks earlier) that strikes and lockouts would be abandoned for the duration. At the time of the pledge labor leaders felt they had an understanding with the Administration that wage controls would not be adopted, although no time limit was given to the understanding.

While machinery for the settlement of labor disputes was being established, the Administration, aided by the general alarm following Pearl Harbor, was finally able to secure Congressional passage of a bill putting a statutory foundation under the existing "price schedules" (which rested on an executive order of dubious authority) and authorizing general price ceilings as well as selective controls on individual commodities. In view of the persistent price rise (see Chart A) which began soon after the initiation of the defense program, Administration leaders, particularly Price Administrator Leon Henderson, were insistent that stronger government price control was needed to prevent "ruinous" inflation. On January 30, 1942, little more than two weeks after the establishment of the WLB, the Emergency Price Control Act (56 Stat. 23) became law. To administer controls "whenever prices rise or threaten to rise" it continued the independent Office of Price Administration (OPA) which had been created by executive order a few months before. But because the Administration fought off statutory wage controls, farm interests succeeded in virtually excluding farm prices from control. As soon as its statute was passed, the OPA began active steps toward instituting over-all ceilings.

Chart A

CONSUMERS' PRICE INDEX (COST OF LIVING INDEX)—WORLD WARS I & II

For Moderate Income Families in Large Cities

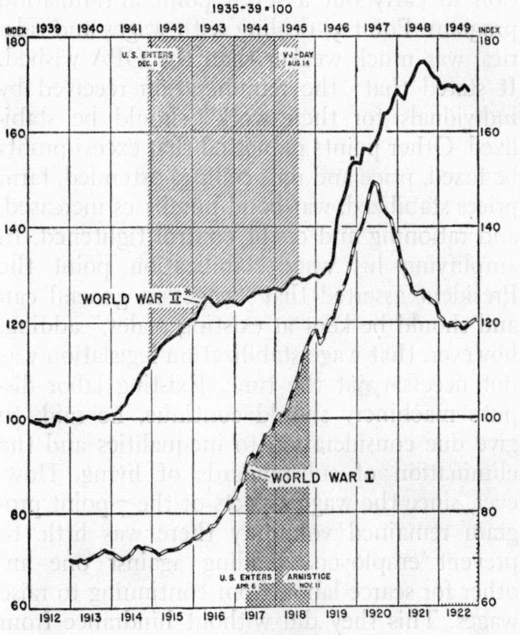

* Estimates of World War II and Postwar Understatement by the Index Were Not Included. See Monthly Labor Review for March 1947.

Source: United States Department of Labor

Bureau of Labor Statistics

The production of war goods stimulated employment and boosted payrolls early in 1942 while the output of consumer goods was halted in some cases and reduced in others. Reflecting the shortages and bloated demand in the area of consumer goods, the cost of living index in May 1942 stood about 10 per cent above the level of June 1941, in contrast to the 4 per cent rise it had shown for the preceding twelve months (June 1940-May 1941). The 10 per cent general rise led to increasingly vigorous demands for higher wages, and average hourly earnings in manufacturing rose by 15 per cent from mid-1941 to mid-1942, the period under discussion.

SEVEN-POINT STABILIZATION PROGRAM

Fighting inflation was a manifold task requiring action on several fronts. Following a series of inter-agency meetings, the President, on April 27, 1942, asked Congress and the nation to carry out a seven point anti-inflation program. Point 3, dealing with wages and salaries, was much weaker than the OPA wished. It stated that "the remuneration received by individuals for their work" should be stabilized. Other points requested that excess profits be taxed, price and rent ceilings extended, farm prices stabilized, war bond purchases increased, and rationing and credit control tightened. In amplifying his wage stabilization point the President asserted that "wages in general can and should be kept at existing scales," adding, however, that wage stabilization legislation was not necessary at the time. Existing labor dispute machinery should continue, he said, to give due consideration to inequalities and the elimination of substandards of living. However, since the wage aspects of the 7-point program remained voluntary there was little to prevent employers, bidding against one another for scarce labor, from continuing to raise wages. This they did without hindrance from WLB, which could intervene only when there was a dispute.

The day after the announcement of the 7-point program, the OPA issued the General Maximum Price Regulation setting ceiling prices on all commodities and services not already covered by price orders except agricultural products, such as poultry, eggs, meat, wheat, and flour, and most war goods and many parts and subassemblies thereof. The first rent ceilings were also announced for twenty cities not long after.

THE LITTLE STEEL CASE, JULY 1942 [1]

The War Labor Board was mainly responsible for the administration of Point 3—wage stabilization. That responsibility forced the issue of finding standards to be applied in a major case which had been on the Board's docket since February, the Little Steel wage dispute. The decision in that case, when it finally came on July 16, 1942, was a milestone in the evolution of wage stabilization policy. The United Steelworkers of America (USA-CIO) and four large steel corporations generally called "Little Steel" only because they were smaller than "Big Steel"—the United States Steel Corporation—were at odds over the union's request for $1 a day general wage increase to compensate for the 13 per cent rise in the cost of living index since the last general Little Steel wage boost of about 11 per cent in April 1941. The widespread acknowledgement that steel wage movements set patterns elsewhere in the nation meant that despite the Board's announced case-by-case approach, its decision here would be crucial: it would necessarily establish a criterion for the application of the President's principle that "wages in general . . . should be kept at existing scales."

What were "existing scales"? In order to find out, the Board reviewed the vast number of changes in hourly earnings in various segments of industry since January 1, 1941, the close of a period of relative stability in wage-price relationships, and found that in the race to maintain real earnings at their peacetime level, some groups of workers had gained more than others. Although nearly two-thirds of the workers in manufacturing had received increases of 15 per cent or more there had been no uniform or prevalent percentage rise above January 1941 which could be used to describe the "existing" wage level in, say, May 1942. It appeared equitable to the Board that before wages could "in general" be stabilized the positions of various groups of workers needed to be equalized so that the minority who, because of poorer bargaining power or special circumstances, had received the smallest raises would not be unduly penalized by a stabilization "freeze."

Some criterion was needed for judging whether or not a group had received as much wage increase as it was entitled to, and the Board turned, not unnaturally, to the BLS cost

[1] *In re Bethlehem Steel Corp., Republic Steel Corp., Youngstown Sheet and Tube Co., Inland Steel Co., and United Steelworkers of America* (CIO). July 16, 1942. (1 *WLR* 325) National War Labor Board Cases No. 2148-D *et al.*

of living index. The index had risen 15 per cent between January 15, 1941, and May 15, 1942, the first date for which the index had been computed after President Roosevelt announced the 7-point program. The public members of the Board then proposed and the industry members agreed that 15 per cent be used as an equalizing limit on further wage movements of various groups of workers who had received differential treatment since 1940. Cost of living wage rate adjustments would be authorized for Little Steel and for any group of workers up to 15 per cent above their hourly wage rate on January 1, 1941. The increase was called a "stabilization factor." The application of this factor meant that the steel workers, who had received an average wage rate increase of 11.8 per cent above January 1, 1941, on April 1, 1941, could not receive the 13 per cent additional raise they demanded, but instead an average of 2.8 per cent over April 1941 levels.[2]

One corollary of this decision was that those who had already received increases of 15 per cent or more since January 1, 1941, could keep what they had gained but could not receive any more. Another corollary was that the steel workers would not necessarily maintain their peacetime standard of living (as of January 1, 1941) if prices rose. Price control was OPA's business and the Board was assuming OPA would take care of it. There was not to be any further direct connection between wage and price movements.

In his summary of the majority opinion Chairman William H. Davis wrote that the yardsticks applied to wage stabilization in the case were

> fair and equitable and at the same time sufficient to prevent the cost of living from spiraling upward because of wage adjustments. We think they lead to a terminal for the tragic race between wages and prices.

On this basis, he continued,

> Labor will have made its move of self-restraint in the 7-point program. If all other groups likewise do their part we may expect to get and hold for the duration of the war stability of standards, and the freedom from apprehension, that goes with such stability.

The majority decision was received with outspoken disapproval and dissent by the labor members of the War Labor Board; their criticisms were echoed by unions throughout the country. The minority opinion termed the denial of the union's full wage increase demand a "grave error." It would reduce labor's relative share of the national income, and so negate the President's basic idea in the 7-point program that all groups should share equally in wartime sacrifices. They said,

> The conclusion is inescapable that the majority carried on its deliberations with a fixed intention not to grant more than a token adjustment, selecting those facts which would fit that pattern and rejecting a multitude of facts and cogent arguments which call for a more substantial adjustment.

The dissent touched critically on the Board's consciousness of general principles in this decision when it said in its conclusion,

> The National War Labor Board has a very strict responsibility to the people of this nation. This responsibility cannot be discharged by substituting theoretical discourses on putative dangers for consideration of the justice of specific demands of the workers. . . .

The Little Steel decision was most severely criticized by labor as an opening effort by the Administration to remove wages from the sphere of free collective bargaining—which, of course, had to be done if the 7-point program was to mean anything. The Office of Price Administration and its director, Leon Henderson, were given a substantial share of the blame for the War Labor Board decision.

In the light of later developments, it should be noted that the labor dissent did not include any criticism of the cost of living index or its use in developing the stabilization factor given the steelworkers. The union brief had presented clippings of newspaper advertisements to show that food prices in steel towns had risen more than the national index; but the WLB's tripartite panel which heard the case initially and which found unanimously for

[2] Computed by dividing 3.2 per cent (the difference between the Little Steel formula level of 115.0 per cent and the April 1, 1941, level of 111.8 per cent) by the April 1, 1942, level, 111.8 per cent.

the union (only to be reversed by the Board) did not give the clippings any weight.

Nor did the Board majority feel it necessary to explain or justify their almost casual use of the index. The public and industry members based their decision avowedly on the President's request in the 7-point program that wages be "kept at existing scales" with due consideration to "inequalities." They used the rise in the index unquestioningly as a handy instrument for measuring the extent of the "inequalities" they were prepared to relieve in the course of defining "existing scales" by reference to a base period.

The term "formula" did not appear in the decision. Rather, there was a reference to the "yardsticks" and "principles" leading to a "pattern" of wage adjustment involving a "stabilization factor." But less than two weeks later, public member Wayne Morse (former dean of the University of Oregon Law School), in a wage opinion in the *Remington Rand* case, called the standards of the Little Steel decision a "formula" and followed it. The 15 per cent limit was subsequently applied by the Board as a general rule to all wage disputes involving the question of "inequalities."

How firm was the formula? The Board had been groping for months for a standard of action. Now it had devised one and presumably it was good until changed. The Board could not measure in advance the extent of the stresses that might later compel a change; it could not anticipate and provide for all possible consequences. That was left to future cases. In writing the majority opinion on the wage issue, George W. Taylor, Professor of Economics at the University of Pennsylvania, contented himself with a denial that the Board was "establishing an inflexible pattern to be rigidly followed if that would unnecessarily lead to injustice." And Wayne Morse some weeks later in the *Remington Rand* opinion echoed that "Such adjustments in the [Little Steel] formula as need to be made in the light of future events and trends in the war economy of the country will be made by the Board."

In the Board's view, then, the Little Steel formula was left pragmatic.

Outside the Board, as prices and the cost of living index continued to rise late in 1942 and early in 1943, groups which found the formula uncomfortably rigid asked whether there was to be a reconsideration and revision in the event of a substantial increase in the BLS index, and if so, what would constitute a "substantial" increase. If the Board weighed the alternatives open to it during these months, it evidently preferred to keep whatever freedom of action the vagueness of the Little Steel decision permitted. How it met these questions when they were at length definitely posed to it will be described in later sections of this study.

STABILIZATION EXTENDED TO VOLUNTARY WAGE INCREASES

The Board's power to make the formula stick was seriously handicapped in the summer of 1942 by the fact that its jurisdiction was limited to dispute cases and did not cover the vast area of unrestrained voluntary wage increases. With the excess profits tax and the growing labor shortages, and with the government as their principal customer committed to pay all costs in any case, many employers lost their normal incentives to control costs. Voluntary wage increases became a cheap and frequent means of bidding for labor; the effects of this practice on the trend of urban wage rates can be seen in Chart B, page 787. Clearly, dispute cases could not long be held to the Little Steel formula if voluntary increases remained free to rise beyond it; and price stability depended on wage stability.

The crisis in the economic stabilization program was apparent during the six weeks following the Little Steel decision. As the result of a very strong demand by the President for greater price control power, on October 2, 1942, the Stabilization Act (56 Stat. 765, actually an amendment to the Emergency Price Control Act) was passed, directing the President to stabilize wages, salaries, and prices at the levels of September 15, 1942.

The following day, the President issued Executive Order 9250 which delegated to the War Labor Board his powers over wages by giving the Board control over all voluntary increases and decreases in wage rates. The

Chart B

TREND OF EARNINGS AND WAGE RATES IN MANUFACTURING INDUSTRY

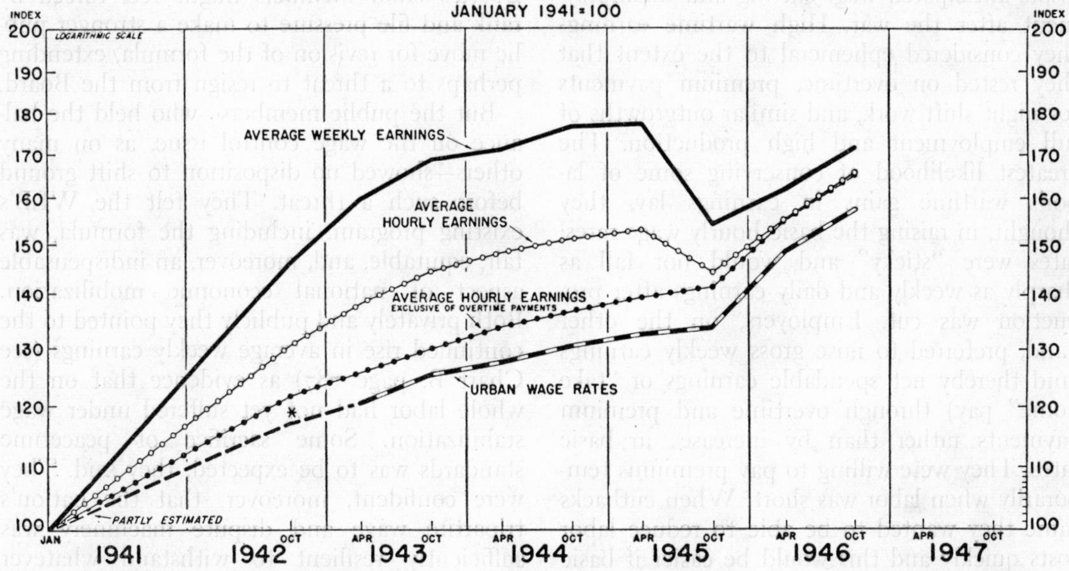

* October 1942 Beginning of Wage Stabilization

Source: United States Department of Labor
Bureau of Labor Statistics

Board's area of discretion in carrying out wage stabilization was given its first definition in the clause forbidding approval of any increase in wage rates prevailing on September 15, 1942, unless

> such increase is necessary to correct maladjustments or inequalities, to eliminate substandards of living, to correct gross inequities, or to aid in the effective prosecution of the war.

In a Policy Statement on November 6, the Board defined these four circumstances under which wage rates could be increased; the Little Steel formula was specifically adopted as the criterion for correcting "maladjustments" in straight-time wage rates.

There was "scarcely a ripple of protest" from labor over the stabilization moves of October and November 1942. Labor had escaped statutory controls; it was too soon to tell how the new price control moves would work; and the President had shown again his ability to summon the loyalty and confidence of people whose immediate goals were in conflict with his.

HOLD-THE-LINE ORDER, APRIL 1943

Within five months a new crisis developed in the anti-inflation program. In March 1943 price control faced the stiffening resistance of two key groups—the farm bloc which was unreconciled to the extension of OPA control over food prices, and the business community, many segments of which felt "squeezed" by price ceilings and considered the detail and paper work involved in complying with OPA regulations a nuisance. Similarly, although wage rates as well as earnings were still rising, union opposition to wage stabilization was gathering. (Simultaneously the labor demand for more stringent price control continued.)

The Stabilization Act of October 1942 had already, as Chart B indicates, had the effect of slowing down the rate of wage rate increase, as raises permissible under the WLB Policy Statement were used up. Union leaders in the spring of 1943 could foresee the time when all the remaining slack would be taken up and they would have no more grounds under existing policies for securing general wage increases for a rank and file which was increasingly restive. They and their advisors anticipated wage-cutting and unemployment after the war. High wartime earnings they considered ephemeral to the extent that they rested on overtime, premium payments for night shift work, and similar outgrowths of full employment and high production. The greatest likelihood of conserving some of labor's wartime gains in earnings lay, they thought, in raising the basic hourly wage rates; rates were "sticky" and would not fall as sharply as weekly and daily earnings after production was cut. Employers, on the other hand, preferred to raise gross weekly earnings (and thereby net spendable earnings or "take home" pay) through overtime and premium payments rather than by increases in basic rates. They were willing to pay premiums temporarily when labor was short. When cutbacks came they wanted to be able to reduce labor costs quickly and this would be easier if basic rates were kept stable. Thus the Little Steel formula thwarted labor's major long range goal without, from the Administration's viewpoint, preventing immediate inflationary rises in purchasing power.

The earliest labor moves to undermine the Little Steel formula came from unions which had not been able to secure much, if anything, under it because they had already received at least a 15 per cent wage boost since January 1, 1941. The United Mine Workers of America (UMW) was one of these; its president, John L. Lewis, regarded the 15 per cent rule as the product of a "biased tribunal" and early in February 1943 announced that he would demand a $2 a day wage increase in negotiating contract renewals with mine operators in March. He pointedly ignored the War Labor Board.

A bid for such a dramatically high increase made outside the framework of the wage stabilization program created great strain on the AFL and CIO leaders who were continuing officially to support the War Labor Board and who, pushed from below, were feeling the pressure of inter-federation competition as well. This situation, combined with the growing vigor with which the union press was attacking the 15 per cent rule, led to talk in the newspapers about an imminent "union drive" on the formula. The prospect grew that the Board's labor members might feel forced by rank and file pressure to make a stronger public move for revision of the formula, extending perhaps to a threat to resign from the Board.

But the public members—who held the balance on the wage control issue, as on many others—showed no disposition to shift ground before such a threat. They felt the WLB's existing program, including the formula, was fair, equitable, and, moreover, an indispensable aspect of national economic mobilization. Both privately and publicly they pointed to the continued rise in average weekly earnings (see Chart B, page 787) as evidence that on the whole labor had not yet suffered under wage stabilization. Some sacrifice of peacetime standards was to be expected, they said. They were confident, moreover, that the nation's tripartite wage and dispute machinery was sufficiently resilient to withstand whatever wage pressure lay ahead.

There appears to have been less disposition to take such a long-run view in the office of James F. Byrnes, Economic Stabilization Director. There, late in March and early in April 1943, alarm over the growing pressure on wages and prices was deepened by an awareness of the increasing stress and strain within the WLB and a realization that the public members—who were in a sense members of the Administration—were hampered in their ability to preserve firm restraints on wage rates by the debating and jockeying for position inherent in the tripartite structure. The political necessity to ensure the success of Executive control of inflation in the face of continued Congressional criticism was evident. A decision was therefore made to issue an executive order which would halt the rising crest of inflation and, incidentally, relieve the WLB of responsibility for the very "hot" Little Steel formula. On April 8, 1943, the "Hold-the-Line" Order (Executive Order 9328) was issued,

> to prevent increases in wages, salaries, prices and profits, which, however justifiable if viewed apart from their effect upon the economy, tend to undermine the basis of stabilization, and to pro-

vide such regulations with respect to the control of price, wage and salary increases as are necessary to maintain stabilization . . .

Under the order, new and more enforceable ceilings were to be placed on the prices of food and other commodities affecting the cost of living by the Price Administrator and Food Administrator and further price increases were forbidden without the Stabilization Director's approval. Concerning wages the order directed the War Labor Board to authorize

> no further increase in wages or salaries except such as are clearly necessary to correct substandards of living, provided that nothing herein shall be construed to prevent such agencies from making such wage or salary readjustments as may be deemed appropriate, in accordance with the Little Steel formula as heretofore defined by the National War Labor Board for the rise in the cost of living between January 1, 1941, and May 1, 1942.

The order further excepted reasonable adjustments of wages and salaries in case of promotions, reclassifications, merit increases, incentive wages or the like, provided such adjustments did not increase the level of production costs appreciably or furnish the basis either to increase prices or to resist otherwise justifiable reductions in prices.

The most significant effects of the Hold-the-Line Order on wage stabilization were first, to take out of the area of the Board's discretion the authority to change the Little Steel formula and second, to curtail the Board's power to grant wage increases because of inequalities and gross inequities. These latter had threatened, during the early months of 1943, to offer a basis for many further general wage changes beyond those of the Little Steel rule.

Immediately after the issuance of the Hold-the-Line Order the War Labor Board felt impelled to assert officially that it had had no hand in the order's formulation and had not known of it until it was issued. This was essentially true.

After a series of WLB discussions with Byrnes's office the Board's power to correct interplant inequities in wage rates was partially restored through the establishment of a system of wage "brackets." These were ranges of "sound and tested going rates" for each occupation in a given labor market area. But the removal of the Little Steel formula from the Board's purview was not altered.

Official union reaction to Executive Order 9328 was one of high approval of its price control features and bitter denunciation of the wage control section. In fact, it appeared for a short period after April 8 that the labor members might leave the WLB, and their attack on the public members for their supposed consultations with Economic Stabilization Director Byrnes reached an extreme of bitterness. The bracket system, although obtained as a concession from Byrnes, was highly unpopular with labor.

After April 1943, the wage stabilization program continued unchanged by statute or executive order until the close of hostilities with Japan. Since allowances under the Little Steel formula had been practically exhausted in April 1943, most wage increases made after that were under the bracket approach. Other adjustments—the so-called fringe adjustments (job reclassification, shift differentials, paid vacations, sick leave, and the like)—also served somewhat to alleviate workers' discontent over wartime price rises and shortages, although the WLB took the position that fringe adjustments should not develop into disguised wage increases. The trend of urban wage rates and other measures of worker income during the period from January 1, 1941, through 1945 can be judged from Chart B, page 787, while a comparison between the trend of prices (the cost of living index) and earnings (average straight time hourly earnings) appears on Chart C, page 790.

WAGE STABILIZATION, COLLECTIVE BARGAINING, AND UNION LEADERS

The Hold-the-Line Order completed the 15-month-long process, begun with the founding of the WLB, by which control over wages was withdrawn from labor unions and employers negotiating together privately. Top union leaders like Philip Murray, president of the United Steelworkers of America and of the Congress

Chart C
CHANGES IN EARNINGS IN MANUFACTURING AND IN THE COST OF LIVING INDEX *

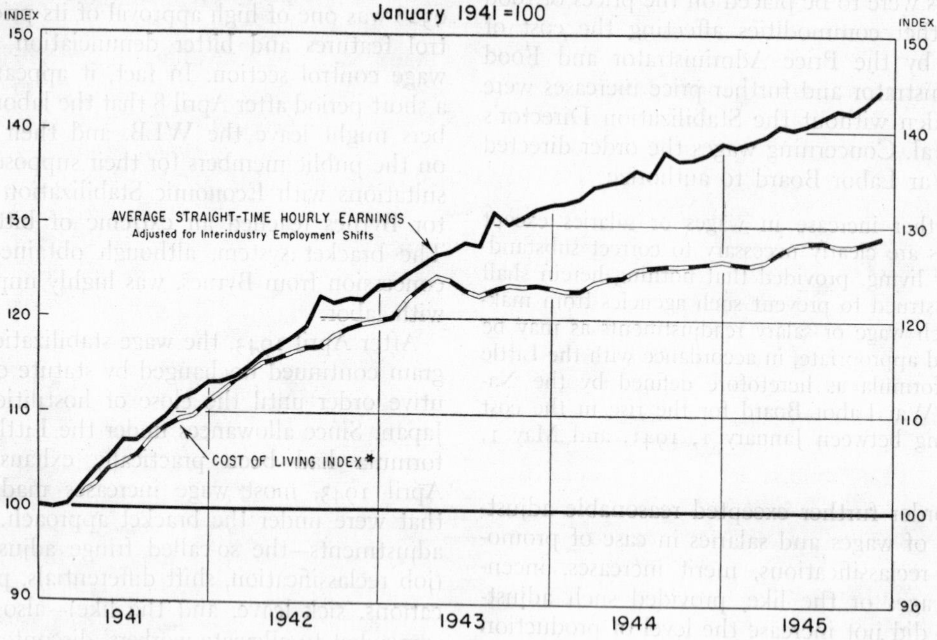

* Now called the Consumers' Price Index
Source: United States Department of Labor
Bureau of Labor Statistics

of Industrial Organizations, and George Meany, secretary-treasurer of the American Federation of Labor, knew that there was hardly any alternative to an increase in government control over labor relations under an all-encompassing war effort like that of the United States. They voiced and wrote dissents but went along with the WLB majority views which contributed to the development of Administration wage policy.

They were not unaware, of course, of labor's wartime gains—union representation on the Board on an equal footing with management, the WLB's maintenance-of-membership policy by which the membership rolls of a union which had signed a contract with management were kept intact for the duration of the contract, the Board's acceptance of the principle of equal pay for equal work, and the Board's frank recognition of the need for seniority rules, grievance and arbitration procedure, and the like.

But the narrowing of the area of possible immediate and evident achievement open to union chiefs intensified the conflict between their role as recognized "national leaders" and their more immediate and pressing task of furthering labor's cause and remaining in office. During the war years when union officials could achieve so little as union officials, hordes of new members—older marginal workers, untrained youngsters, married women, rural folk, Negroes—were pouring into the airframe, steel construction, and other unions. To them the connection between wage stabilization and winning the war was generally obscure and the great political progress represented by labor's membership on the War Labor Board not important. They could see and feel for themselves their enormous potential bargaining power. They experienced higher rents and prices in crowded boom towns and cities than they had seen "at home." And they wanted their share of what looked like a great big war pie, regardless of top labor's commitment to wage stabilization.

Union officials in locals which had experienced tremendous wartime expansion felt they had to show these newcomers some benefits of unionization or they would lose office and union membership would dwindle. The lower officers exerted pressure on the more secure leaders above for "results" in terms of wage increases. The constant upward push of the rank and file, coupled with top leadership's belief that prices and profits were "soaring" while wages were unjustly "frozen," led to moves which often contrasted sharply with the general support which the AFL and CIO gave to wage stabilization and the Administration's war program. The attack on the cost of living index can be considered one of these moves.

A by-product of the wage stabilization program was the introduction of a whole new jargon, particularly at the national level, into the vocabulary of wage dealings. It became necessary to think and speak in terms of "inequities," "Little Steel formula," and "inequalities" while the force behind the drive for wage increases remained what it had always been—a desire to increase the worker's real income. This dichotomy of drive and language explains why, when the union attack on the index was made as a political move, the articulation of the union argument was assigned to a small group of research directors who drew heavily on the statistical language common to discussions of the index.

During the period under discussion in this case, the labor situation was further complicated by AFL–CIO rivalries and by John L. Lewis's outspoken criticism of the WLB and his vigorous efforts to secure wage raises, an action frankly and deliberately inconsistent with established stabilization policy. To what extent his behavior and success influenced the thinking and actions of AFL and CIO leaders cannot be said. There is no question that the gains achieved by Lewis outside the framework of tripartite wartime wage policy made it more difficult for union leaders remaining within the emergency labor framework to keep their membership "in line."

III. Experts Cope with Political Criticism

A. INTRODUCTION

War's Two-fold Effect on the Environment of the Index

The dispute over the cost of living index developed against the backdrop of the events which have just been recounted—the economic changes and pressures of wartime, the stabilization program undertaken by the Administration to prevent these inflationary pressures from impairing either the war effort or the Nation's economic health, organized labor's growing dissatisfaction over the wage and price aspects of the stabilization program, and rivalries among the various segments of organized labor.

These developments had two kinds of consequences for the cost of living index: beginning with the defense program in 1940 there were changes in the relatively stable patterns of consumer purchases and behavior on which the index was based and, second, somewhat later, following the Little Steel decision, came changes in the political environment in which the index was used. From the first arose questions as to the reliability of the index as a statistical series. From the second arose the occasion and the incentive for the public attack by the unions on the index as a criterion for economic policy. The attack forms the climax of the present case study.

Neither of these developments which were radically to affect its work on the index and its relations with labor was set in motion by forces within the control of the Bureau of Labor Statistics. Yet, until the President, in

October 1943, took notice of the "controversy and dispute" and asked that a committee of the War Labor Board "look into the question" of the index, the Bureau of Labor Statistics and the Secretary's office in the Department of Labor were the only government agencies officially cognizant of the problems arising from growing criticism of the index.

What the BLS did to avert, answer, and allay criticisms of the index during the earlier period, from mid-1940 to July 1942, when technical questions were paramount, and in the later period, from late in 1942 to October 1943, when labor's increasing dissatisfaction with the Administration's economic stabilization policy gradually converted the issue into a political one, forms the subject of the present Part. In these months a small group of government technicians dealt with what was at first a familiar problem in agency-client relations but which, with the introduction of Administration-labor "politics," became insoluble at the Bureau level. The resolution of the conflict over the index in an arena closer to the White House is the theme of Part IV which follows.

The Bureau of Labor Statistics

The government dramatis personae of the present Part were officials of the Bureau of Labor Statistics of the United States Department of Labor. Both the Department and Bureau had been formed through the efforts of organized labor but their statutory functions differed significantly. The Bureau's duties (25 Stat. 182) were informational, factual:

> . . . to acquire and diffuse among the people of the United States useful information on subjects connected with labor, in the most general and comprehensive sense of that word, and especially upon its relation to capital, the hours of labor, the earnings of laboring men and women, and the means of promoting their material, social, intellectual and moral prosperity.

Hewing to these purposes, Carroll D. Wright, Commissioner of Labor from 1885 to 1905, was immediately successful in developing the Bureau into a fact-finding agency in the field of labor economics with an international reputation for usefulness and objectivity. In molding the Bureau's relations with the public Wright appears to have accepted the ideas of the eminent economist, Francis Amasa Walker, who once advised him to:

> . . . so distinctively and decisively disconnect the . . . Bureau of Labor Statistics from politics—from dependence on organizations, whether of working men or of employers, or from the support of economic theories, individual views or class interests—as to command the moral support of the whole body of citizens.

In contrast to the Bureau, which antedated the Department, the duties assigned to the Department of Labor by its organic act (37 Stat. 736), sponsored largely by the American Federation of Labor, were policy-making and promotional, in a sense parallel to those of a labor union. It was instructed:

> . . . to foster, promote, and develop the welfare of the wage earners of the United States, to improve their working conditions, and to advance their opportunities for profitable employment.

No misgivings were aroused in 1913 when the Bureau, which kept itself free of particularist support, was incorporated into the Department which, at least in origin, was linked to a special clientele. It was largely taken for granted that the Bureau could and would adhere to the course already set for it no matter what commitments the Department entered upon.

As the years went on, differences of opinion developed inside and outside the government over whether the Department of Labor was a representative of labor in the government or the representative of the public interest in labor problems. Throughout, the BLS managed to maintain its impartial character, adhering to the philosophy Wright had enunciated. The spirit of "loyalty to the facts" endured and flourished so strongly in the BLS that it came to be recognized as one of the agency's distinctive characteristics. Positive expression of it could be found in the development and refinement of a wide variety of statistical procedures and techniques for measuring as accurately and objectively as possible phenomena related to the field of labor economics in its broadest aspect. Some negative results were the Bureau's marked reluctance to generalize when data were considered inadequate and its desire to let "policy" conclusions emerge from Bureau materials rather than to state them explicitly.

In an era when facts unquestionably were weapons, the Bureau's pursuit of scientific objectivity and independence was as much a practical course of action as an ideal. A reputation for nonpartisanship was essential for its survival in the face of the conflicting contentions and goals of labor and management, divergences within labor itself, and the regular scrutiny of Congressional Appropriations Committees who generally showed little enthusiasm over the Department of Labor's financial needs.

In organization, the BLS resembled many other large Federal bureaus. It was headed by a Commissioner of Labor Statistics appointed by the President "by and with the advice and consent of the Senate" for a term of four years. Traditionally, Commissioners were men not only of accepted statistical competence but of sufficient personal stature to be asked on occasion to participate in the solution of some of the nation's major economic problems beyond the purview of the Bureau and the Department of Labor. Although administratively subordinate to the Secretary of Labor, a Commissioner enjoyed considerable freedom to carry on such activities without channeling them through the Secretary's office and without affecting the BLS's name for objectivity. Secretaries of Labor, for their part, took this role of the BLS chief for granted.

The Bureau's internal structure changed somewhat during the period covered by this case but in general its work on the cost of living index, labor information, retail prices, productivity, wage analysis, and in other areas was distributed among fifteen divisions organized as Chart D, page 794 indicates, into four branches. The Retail Price and the Cost of Living Divisions, which were responsible respectively for gathering retail price statistics and developing the cost of living index on the basis of these statistics, each had its own chief. Together with three other price divisions they made up the Prices and Cost of Living Branch headed by a chief who, together with several other Branch heads, had status approaching but not equaling that of an Assistant Commissioner of Labor Statistics.

Isador Lubin, Commissioner, and A. Ford Hinrichs, Acting Commissioner, during the period covered by this case, 1940-1944, were respectively the sixth and seventh men to head the Bureau. Formally speaking, Lubin was the chief throughout virtually all of Hinrichs' period of tenure. Lubin, who was appointed by Franklin D. Roosevelt in July 1933, had been a member of the research staff on labor economics of the Brookings Institution in Washington, D. C., in the 1920's and had also served as economic advisor to two Senatorial committees during this period. His versatility and experience in judging economic conditions and political forces made him one of the group of men on whom Roosevelt depended, almost from the start of his term in office, for advice on economic trends and policies. When the National Defense Advisory Commission was reactivated in May 1940 Lubin became assistant to Sidney Hillman who was Director of the NDAC's Labor Division, and later, in 1941, he became a special assistant to President Roosevelt.

Hinrichs, who had been "acting" for Lubin since mid-1940, formally became Acting Commissioner in November 1941. It was then generally assumed that Lubin would return to head up the Bureau after the war. Hinrichs had been an associate professor of statistics at Brown University, serving also as Director of the Brown University Bureau of Business Research. In 1934, he was appointed chief economist at the BLS. During the years that followed he often served as Acting Commissioner when Lubin was out of town and also as the Commissioner's alternate and deputy on interdepartmental committees.

Hinrichs's work as a teacher, practicing statistician, and BLS official had earned him a high reputation as a scholar but he had had only a limited opportunity before 1940 to take full responsibility for the direction of the Bureau. When Lubin's preoccupations left Hinrichs in charge in 1940-1941 the latter had to start from an undefined position as Bureau chief, both with regard to his staff and the public. His task was made more difficult by factors

Chart D

THE BUREAU OF LABOR STATISTICS, 1942

(Only Those Officials Concerned with Attack on Cost-of-Living Index Named)

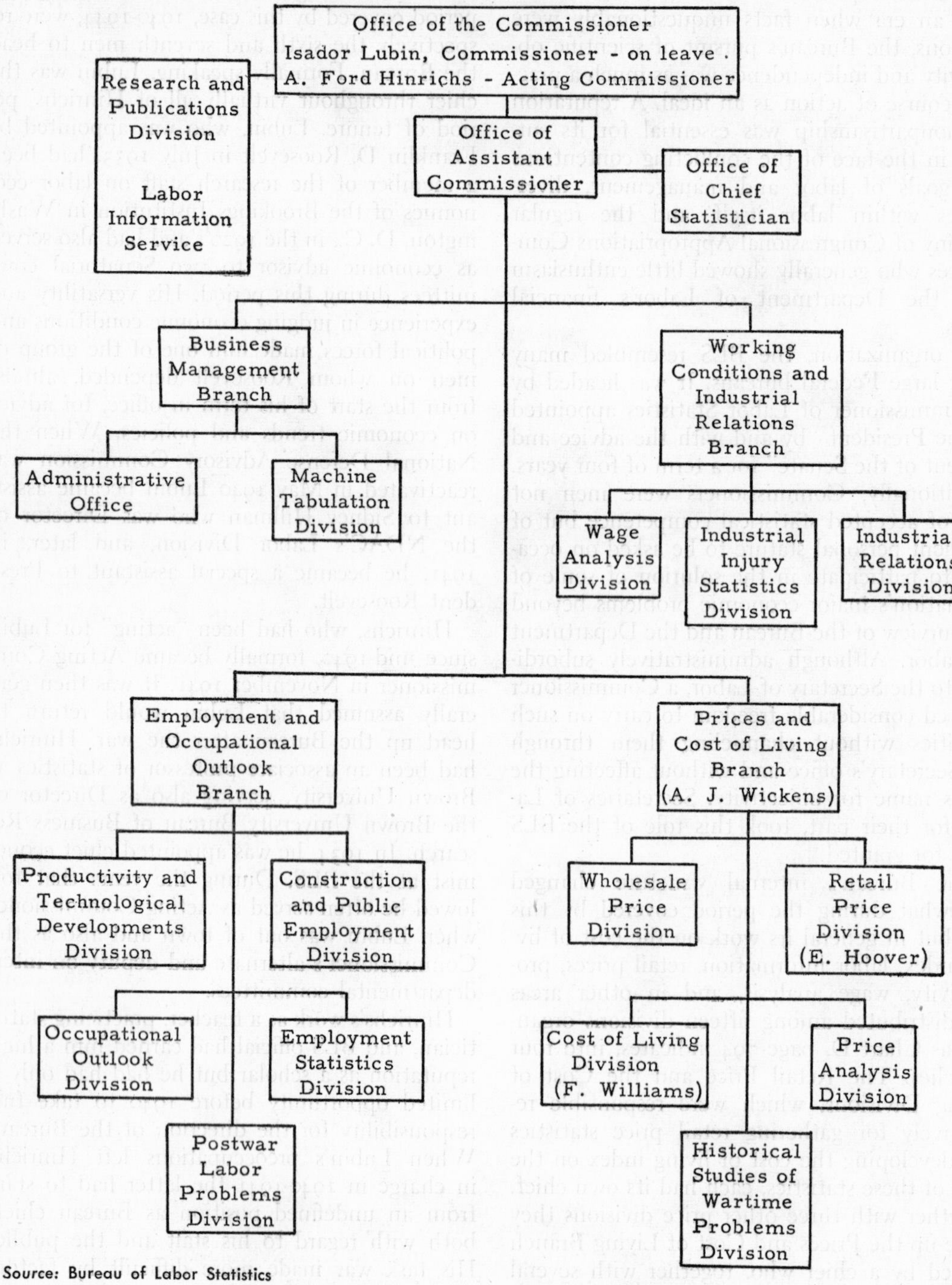

Source: Bureau of Labor Statistics

which had not been present when Lubin took the helm of the Bureau in 1933—the division and conflict in the labor movement, the controversies and unpopular controls of a period of mobilization, the reduction in the Bureau's resources at the service of non-government groups, and the fact that he remained an "Acting" Commissioner for the entire five-year period of his incumbency.

Below the Commissioner, the Bureau was staffed—in the divisions related to this controversy—by women. This practice was in accord with a tradition in the Department of Labor, which then had Miss Perkins as its Secretary and from the beginning had had a woman as chief of its Children's Bureau, but it was uncommon elsewhere in the Federal government at that level of responsibility. The Bureau's cost of living work, together with other price research, was under the general direction of Aryness Joy Wickens, Chief of the Prices and Cost of Living Branch. Faith Williams, Chief of the Branch's Cost of Living Division was in direct charge of compiling the index on the basis of data collected by the Retail Price Division under Ethel Hoover. Mrs. Wickens had been in the Federal government since 1928, after a period of teaching economics and statistics at Mount Holyoke College. Following work in the Division of Research and Statistics of the Federal Reserve Board where she was responsible for the Board's monthly summary of business conditions, she became chief statistician in the Office of the Economic Advisor to the National Emergency Council and then chief statistician at the Central Statistical Board. She came to the BLS as an assistant to the Commissioner and became chief of the Prices and Cost of Living Branch in 1940.

Miss Williams's academic training and experience were in the fields of labor economics, statistics, and consumption economics. She initiated courses in consumption economics at Cornell University and in 1929 became chief of the Section on Costs and Standards of Living of the Bureau of Home Economics in the Department of Agriculture. In 1934 she joined the staff of the BLS as chief of the Cost of Living Division. Miss Williams had been vice-president of the Consumer-Retailer Council, founded to achieve improved quality standards and labeling of consumer goods, and had worked in an advisory capacity with the American Standards Association. After she took on the direction of the Cost of Living Division, she co-operated with the Retail Price Division then under Stella Stewart, in the long and expensive job of improving and developing the specifications used for the consumer goods priced in the index. They were considered the most detailed of any in the world for that purpose.

Hinrichs, Mrs. Wickens, and Miss Williams were the three individuals in the BLS most immediately involved in the dispute over the accuracy of the index. Hinrichs was concerned with the policy aspects of the argument as they affected Bureau relations with labor, with the general public, but primarily with the wartime Administration. Miss Williams was responsible for the technical area. Mrs. Wickens operated in the region where the two merged and had shown an adaptability and willingness to deal with policy problems. Before coming to the BLS none of the three had had direct experience in dealing with labor unions. Everyday contacts and correspondence on the job, as well as the interpretations of union needs and point of view presented by the chief of the Bureau's Industrial Relations Division, Boris Stern, had developed to a considerable although varying degree their familiarity with union methods, attitudes, and requirements.

In addition to these officials in the BLS who were intimately involved in the index controversy, Secretary of Labor Frances Perkins played a role at a higher level. Miss Perkins had been in office as Secretary of Labor since 1933—crucial years that saw the growth in power and importance of organized labor during the New Deal as well as the development of industrial unionism and the subsequent split in 1937 between the AFL and the CIO. As the unionization and independent strength of labor grew, workers turned to the unions rather than to the Department of Labor for the fostering, promotion, and development of their welfare. As one observer has pointed out, ". . . the Department of Labor has been widely looked upon as the advocate of organized labor in the government—except perhaps by organized labor."

As the Federal government's role in labor relations increased and became more controversial Miss Perkins was often criticized by both labor and industry spokesmen. Much of the criticism was in a sense part of the unconcluded debate over the proper function of the Department of Labor, with Miss Perkins taking, by implication, the stand that the Department represented the public interest rather than labor alone.

B. THE BUREAU MEETS EARLY WARTIME TECHNICAL PROBLEMS, 1940-1942

The Bureau as Part of the Defense Administration

The period of defense and war brought increased activity for the BLS as a whole and for the Prices and Cost of Living Branch. The Bureau became an important research center for both military and civilian war agencies, intensifying rather than changing the character of its work. The official BLS report on Bureau activities during World War II said:

> Almost without exception, the Bureau's tasks during the war were designed to yield results for immediate administrative use.
>
> The Bureau became the special fact-finding agency for the Office of Price Administration, the War Labor Board, the War Production Board, the Army Air Forces, the War and Navy Departments, and Maritime Commission. It also served the War Manpower Commission, the National Housing Administration, the Veterans Administration, and others, though less extensively. The data collected and analyzed for these agencies concerned wages, prices, employment, factors affecting production with emphasis on wage stabilization, price control, rationing, manpower, labor turnover, accident prevention, maximum hours of labor, extent and causes of strikes, productivity of labor, and labor conditions in the United States and other countries (especially countries that were or might be occupied by Allied forces).

The Prices and Cost of Living Branch bore an appropriate share of this burden. Less than a week after the National Defense Advisory Commission (NDAC) was appointed in May 1940, Commissioner Leon Henderson ruled that price officials could not make any price indexes of their own, but were to rely on the BLS for such measures and related material. Very soon, the Price Branch embarked on a "comprehensive program of auxiliary work" for the NDAC which included, in the cost of living area, the extension of coverage to a group of "defense" cities and 20 small cities and a speed-up in the issuance of the Bureau's food price and index reports. To finance the staff expansion necessary for these and other services funds were at first obtained from the defense and later war agencies but as soon as practicable direct appropriations for extension and improvement of the regular Bureau and Branch programs were sought from Congress.

Wartime Economic Trends and the Index

While the Prices and Cost of Living Branch was thus engrossed, it was also increasingly preoccupied with maintaining the accuracy of the cost of living index under new conditions. The index was naturally affected by the economic trends set in motion by the country's mobilization, although it did not move as sensitively as, for instance, the wholesale price index also compiled in the same Branch. Price changes in themselves presented no special problem; the function of an index is to represent change. And in peacetime the usual statistical techniques are adequate to take account of gradual changes in the samples on which the index is based.

But now changes came more swiftly and they were more far-reaching and the index's factual environment was altered in four distinct although interrelated ways. First, the growth in demand gradually pushed up the unit prices of most of the commodities and services included in the cost of living index. Second, rising employment and higher wages increased the total amount of money earned and spent by most American families, including many in the income brackets previously sampled for the index weightings. In these two ways the cost of living was obviously rising both in the technical statistical sense of unit price changes and in the lay sense of total family expenditures. From the standpoint of real income the two trends somewhat offset each other, but they also altered consumption patterns: people ate more meals in restaurants, went oftener to the movies, and bought better clothes and more meat.

Third, in addition to direct rises in civilian prices, income, and expenditure, and to voluntary changes in spending habits, the diversion of materials and production to military uses cut down, cut out, or altered in other ways the normal distribution and nature of many items of civilian consumption covered in the index. Consumer durables and building materials, especially metal appliances and lumber products, were notable early casualties; gasoline, tires and cigarettes, and later, clothing and textile and paper products, meats and fats, among other things, were on the shortage lists. Shortages led producers to abandon low-end price lines (i.e., to make sport shirts instead of work shirts), to push substitutes where possible (plastic for metal toys), and generally to tolerate poorer quality in their output. Shortages led consumers, in turn, to accept substitutes when available, often "uptrading" to buy more expensive items; to make black and "gray" market purchases; to divert expenditures to new channels or to savings; and to move from their accustomed retail stores to others in search of supplies. Shortages, finally, led the government and the trade into various forms of rationing to control the distribution of scarce commodities.

Quality deterioration, which was emphasized in the BLS-union debate later, was a particularly exasperating form of indirect price increase for consumers. Often it resulted from a scarcity of the usual raw materials for manufacturing a product. At other times it was simply a consequence of the wartime sellers' market which tempted some producers and distributors to substitute inferior wares for those previously sold at the same price. Changes in durability and serviceability were sometimes obvious at first glance, but often were undetectable either by the consumer or by BLS pricing agents at the time of sale.

Fourth, war production and the disruptions of the draft brought about large scale migrations of the population and shifts in its geographic distribution, affecting many in the income groups to which the index was directly relevant. They lived in different places and in different ways than previously.

The index was based on a relatively fixed "market basket" of goods and services dating from prewar years. The last three types of changes just listed affected the contents and proportions of the market basket, and the numbers, status, and distribution of the consumers, as well as the unit prices of the items in the original basket represented in the first category. The questions facing the BLS cost of living staff as these shifts and alterations became increasingly apparent were: Which changes should be reflected in the index? Can they be measured accurately? If so, how can they be incorporated without altering the basic nature or existing uses of the index, including its comparability with past and future figures? If they cannot be measured accurately or at all, what should be done about them?

These questions were partly technical, partly matters for policy judgment. Answers could be reached only gradually, as the nature of trends and the limitations of available data became clear and as funds could be secured for extra work necessary to obtain more reliable data, to test existing data, or explore techniques of making wartime adjustments.

Maintaining the Index's Accuracy

The Retail Price and Cost of Living Divisions devoted an increasing amount of time to these matters from 1941 on. They were naturally conscious of the upward movement in family expenditures, but for purposes of maintaining a retail price index their interests lay chiefly in changes in the unit prices of the commodities and services on which the index was based and in shifts in their relative importance in the worker's pattern of consumption. Insofar as these commodities and services continued to be available, no special problems in the theory of index construction arose. A rise for example, in the price of a model of boys' shoes included in the market basket for the index, whether due to an increase in leather or labor or transportation costs, or to higher wholesale or retail markup, was reflected in the index. The BLS needed only to be sure of getting accurate, representative, and up-to-date price quotations, whether at the OPA ceiling or above.

Special problems came to the fore in mid-1941, when it became obvious that in a few months certain commodities and services included in the peacetime market basket would become very scarce or disappear completely. The prices and cost of living staffs had the alternatives of simply adhering to the original market basket, using perhaps the last quoted price and the usual weight for unavailable items (as was done for the wholesale price index), or of undertaking the complex and expensive task of constantly modifying the contents of the sample in an effort to represent wartime changes. For the latter, criteria would be required. Late in 1941 it was decided that the market basket would be modified as needed to take account only of "involuntary" changes —those which were forced on consumers by the physical unavailability of base period items. Changes which merely represented "voluntary" improvement in the workers' standard of living arising from increased income and spending would not be reflected in the index because they were deemed irrelevant to the concept underlying the index. The distinction between forced and voluntary changes was, of course, novel: the 1934-36 sample was simply a description of consumers' behavior which did not probe their motives in purchasing.

This decision, which appeared to be the only practicable one in view of the government's need for a current retail price index, led to a host of technical problems: what items to drop and when; what new items, if any, to incorporate and how soon; how to "link" in substitutes; what alterations to make in weightings; what additional retail outlets to visit; how to define specifications for substitutes; how to distinguish quality deterioration from style change; and how to measure the extent to which consumers, were being "forced" (and not merely choosing) to shift to higher priced merchandise and more expensive stores. None of these problems could be solved by routine price collecting procedures of peacetime or by arbitrary statistical adjustments; each demanded the development and testing of alternative techniques.

At intervals, beginning with the figures for January 1942 the cost of living staff revised the index in a variety of particulars. Obvious matters like the halt in passenger automobile production, the introduction of gas rationing, and the lapse in production of most consumer durable goods could be reflected quickly and with considerable precision. More subtle trends like shifts in patronage from chain to independent grocery stores were often impossible to measure with the information immediately available to the Bureau; funds and time were required for special "spot" surveys to appraise them.

In the area of quality change—where deterioration meant a hidden price rise—there were no generally accepted methods of measuring changes in style and serviceability and translating them into price changes to be incorporated in the index. Commodity specifications were redefined at least twice as frequently as in peacetime. Careful editing rules were introduced to facilitate consistent handling of quality changes in goods priced. Yet in a significant number of cases no acceptable way of representing quality change could be devised. The BLS staff was at first disposed to regard these instances as only reversing the trend of quality appreciation which took place during the 1920's and 1930's and for which no special downward price corrections had at that time been made in the index.

Because of the difficulties of finding or adopting ready solutions for some of these problems there was frequently a "lag" in the adjustment of the index for recognized changes; and because of the impossibility of measuring other factors a certain amount of "understatement" came to characterize the index. Indeed, as the Bureau staff was free to admit to those who raised the question directly with them, there was no completely satisfactory solution to the problem of maintaining an accurate retail price index when the character of consumption was changing rapidly and in many ways. To the statistically uninformed, of course, lags and understatements could appear to be errors.

The fourth group of changes mentioned above—that is, the geographic shifts in the working population—created a demand for retail price information for areas not specifically covered by the existing group of city indexes. Lay commentators and amateur statisticians began publishing their own price surveys and making their own crude comparisons between the BLS nation-wide index or the BLS index for a nearby city and prices they found in some of the new war centers. Patently erroneous conclusions were drawn, giving rise to unfounded local opinions that the BLS index was inaccurate when actually it was not meant to be representative of such mushrooming communities.

The BLS staff became concerned: should the index be revised to make it also representative of communities to which it did not apply in peacetime and probably would not apply after the war? Or should special indexes be made up for them? The second path of action was chosen for 20 "smaller cities" and a group of "defense" cities for which the OPA had requested indexes. These were not incorporated in the regular nation-wide all-items index.

All the adjustments so far described were temporary expedients and by no means as extensive as the cost of living staff wished to make them. Its members were deeply concerned over the chronic shortage of funds that prevented them from going further. They wished particularly to bring up to date the index's basic weightings, now nearly a decade old, and to extend its coverage to cities which merited inclusion on a long term basis. A start was made in 1941 on research into changing habits of consumption and saving in connection with the study of *Spending and Saving in Wartime* (an important study in its own right), but lack of funds stopped further progress early in 1942. Throughout the war and despite the transfer of some funds from the war agencies for specific projects, the Bureau never was able to secure enough money for all the adjustments it wished to make. If the money had been available it is doubtful whether the manpower could have been found. Revisions of a far-reaching nature were out of the question.

Bureau-Client Discussion of Index Limitations

These internal technical problems and the remedial efforts they evoked were matched during 1940-42 by others which might be called external and political. They arose from growing public interest in the trends of retail prices, in the shortcomings of early price controls, and in the relative movement of wages and prices. In public debate, comment, and speculation on these and related topics, the cost of living index figured prominently. Users of the index were generally laymen uninterested in its derivation and unfamiliar with its proper interpretation.

Bureau staff did not have the time, opportunity, or directive to approach users of the index—particularly those high in policy councils—and point out its wartime limitations and statistical complexities. However, by means of occasional articles in the *Monthly Labor Review* and the explanatory material included in the monthly releases of the index, and through an ever-growing volume of correspondence and personal conversation, Prices and Cost of Living Branch officials attempted in a general way to keep many users in the government, the labor movement, and industry abreast of their difficulties with the index. With respect to one group of users or "customers," union research directors, the Bureau found it possible during 1940-44 to develop and utilize a special forum for consultation—the annual union Research Directors' Conference and its standing committee and subcommittees.

The research function and the staff which carried it on began to develop in most unions four to five decades after labor research was undertaken by the Federal government. It came as a result of the vast expansion in the government's role in labor relations and the great extension of collective bargaining and arbitration, chiefly in the 1930's. Management and labor then felt increasingly the need for professional talent and technical materials, such as the BLS developed, at the bargaining table, in National Labor Relations Board hearings, Congressional committee hearings, and the like.

In addition to BLS materials, management was able to finance private research organizations like the National Industrial Conference Board (NICB). Unions did not have the resources needed for compiling data like national averages of hours and earnings, absenteeism rates, and occupational trends. They came to rely almost exclusively on governmental statistics in these areas and union leaders gradually began hiring people trained for economic and allied research to assemble and interpret data for them and to present the union's case in the special form or vocabulary demanded by the occasion. The emergence of separate professional research staffs in unions was slow for, as "intellectuals," union research people (as well as lawyers, engineers, and other union employees who had never been part of the rank and file) were at first regarded as outsiders whose academic training and knowledge were a bar rather than an aid in the comprehension of labor problems.

Like the BLS, union research departments were fact-finding in nature and not policy-making. Unlike the BLS, however, they were not old and semi-autonomous but a relatively new part of very dynamic and fluid organizations headed by labor politicians concerned not only with winning better working conditions for their membership but also, in varying degrees, with consolidating their own positions and increasing labor's voice in national affairs. A union research program could be as broad as the research director felt his resources permitted but it had to be geared primarily to the shifting needs of the top officials. American labor's first research director, Miss Florence Thorne of the AFL, once put it this way,

> As union research workers our function is that of service. The union defines policies. The union executive holds us responsible for our work to his union convention and his union organization.

Although they were the "academicians" of the unions, research directors varied widely in their understanding of the problems and philosophy of the BLS. Some discounted the Bureau's descriptions of its perennial budgetary crises and statistical hurdles as "bureaucratic excuses." Others considered the BLS staff a "fine hard-working group of people" and sympathized with their difficulties. Nonetheless a latent skepticism over what they deemed the inherent "ivory tower" and "cold and unfeeling" quality of government research kept even the second group from approving the BLS's work too loudly or often. Criticism, it was felt, was always necessary; it would keep the Bureau "on its toes."

Research directors' notions of the Bureau's proper role depended on their concept of the Department of Labor's purpose. Some, particularly those in the older AFL unions, held that the Bureau served labor best when it preserved its reputation for impartiality and simply made useful statistical and educational materials available to the unions. Others, notably in the CIO, cast envious eyes on the farmer and the Department of Agriculture, and reasoned that the Labor Department was "labor's department" and that the Bureau, as part of the Department, should service labor primarily and provide unions with information which would strengthen their arguments in collective bargaining. A minority of this group was inclined to feel that if BLS material was or could be used by employer or government spokesmen to support a viewpoint opposed by unions, then the BLS was not objective but anti-labor.

The establishment of a formal BLS-union liaison did not come until 1940; in the early 1930's labor research staffs were too new and amorphous to sustain organized contact and in the late 1930's the two camps, AFL and CIO, officially refused to work together. But in the spring of 1940 Boris Stern reported to Hinrichs and Lubin that, at the local level, he had been observing an increase in union co-operation. A research directors' conference was thereupon organized and about thirty organizations were represented at a 2-day session in June. Four annual conferences followed the initial one, through June 1944. The press was excluded from all in an effort to further the "frank exchange of information."

The conferences were designed to promote mutual understanding and to foster discussion of technical problems of common concern. The agenda were based on developments in the Bureau's program related to the work of the research directors. For their part, regardless of the agenda, the research directors introduced and re-introduced certain themes at all the meetings. First, they asked for more specific statistical aids to support labor's position before the price control authorities, in Congress, in collective bargaining, and by 1942, before the War Labor Board. Second, they wanted a larger voice in the planning of BLS surveys so that the results would more directly serve their needs. Those who supported these requests plainly felt that the BLS should orient its program more specifically to the needs of labor. (However, in the conferences from 1940 to 1942 no formal or recorded discussion of the Bureau or Department's traditional role took place.)

Union representatives also asked that the cost of living index reflect more fully the wartime worsening they saw in the consumer's position. Labor leaders in these years were pressing for stronger price control and for wage increases to compensate for price rises. Research directors were impatient over the time it took for the index to show what they considered only part of the existing quality depreciation and price rise. Price Branch officials replied by describing what had been done to overcome the technical hurdles in maintaining the index; by emphasizing that the index was a gauge of unit changes in retail prices, not a measure of total family expenditures; and by indicating the nature of budgetary limitations on BLS staff and time.

Most, if not all, the research directors were aware of the distinction between the BLS index and an index of total family expenditures for living (which did not exist) although the technical details of index compilation were of interest only to a few who possessed advanced statistical training. They showed greater interest in securing evidence, for public use, of their (and their chiefs') belief that the actual and hidden price rises experienced by the average working class family were greater in the aggregate than the Administration would recognize on the basis of the BLS index. Some asked that the Bureau develop as a substitute or supplement for the index a measure of the changes in dollars and cents in what it cost, from city to city and for the nation as a whole, to maintain a working class family in adequate "health and decency." The regular pricing of such a "family budget" could naturally be expected to be more directly useful for collective bargaining on wage matters than the existing index; the two approaches were conceptually different, of course, and not mutually exclusive.

BLS policy was against such a suggestion, although in the past it had occasionally been obliged to make budget studies. Bureau participation in the erection or pricing of any norm or standard for working class living would imply Department of Labor support of that level as adequate or minimum, and raise knotty problems of geographic and other differentials. Selecting a norm or level was a political commitment the Bureau did not feel it could or should make for the Department; it involved "welfare" judgments uncongenial to professional statisticians and outside the range of their expertise. And by the time of the June 1942 research directors' meeting, almost five months after the establishment of the War Labor Board, the Bureau was sensitive to the implications of its acts for the Board as well as the Department. This, together with a renewal of requests, at the meeting, for a budget series made Hinrichs decide to turn down the requests in as many words. He said,

> . . . it is probably true that the argument as to what is or is not an appropriate level of living is an argument which, in the present setup, would have to be made before the War Labor Board. I am quite sure that it would not be appropriate in that connection for the Bureau of Labor Statistics to attempt in advance to determine what that level is, but the Bureau is in a position to furnish you with cost of living materials with which you are probably all familiar.

The research directors also asked the BLS to make a public statement that the index did not reflect the full extent of existing quality depreciation and that it had other limitations. Solomon Barkin, research director of the Textile Workers Union of America (CIO), on one occasion suggested a BLS booklet of questions and answers about the index, its derivation, what it could and could not show, and the like. The Bureau in the fall of 1941 prepared a draft for that purpose and circulated it to a number of research directors. Changes were made on the basis of some of their comments, particularly those of Barkin and of Lazare Teper, research director of the International Ladies' Garment Workers' Union (AFL).

A letter of December 6, 1941, from Teper to Hinrichs about the draft of the booklet bears quoting because it clearly expressed the viewpoint of the research directors interested in the technical limitations of the index. He wrote that the questions and answers which had been drafted were not "adequate for labor organizations," because they

> tend to leave the reader with the impression that, despite the problems involved, the index takes into account, and reflects accurately changes in the cost of living resulting from quality changes. In my opinion, this claims for the index a greater degree of accuracy than is warranted by the facts.

Referring to recent *Monthly Labor Review* articles by two BLS staff members on understatement in the index Teper continued,

> The fact that such understatement is present in the index should be made known to those employers and labor organizations who are using the index as the basis for changes in nominal wage rates designed to maintain the level of real wages. Without such knowledge they will tend to place greater reliance on the accuracy of the index than is justified, and, by so doing, will deceive themselves into believing that they have maintained real wages, when in reality they have not. On the other hand, if they were aware of the shortcomings of the index, they would frequently be able to agree on some adjustment factor, which, while not necessarily conforming to the facts, would permit them to feel that they had done the best job possible in maintaining real wages.
>
> . . . Since it is the weaknesses of the index with which unions are most concerned, I feel that the [draft] statement will not be useful to labor organizations without some discussion of what the index cannot and does not take into account.

It will be seen later that Teper's suggestion of a pragmatic "adjustment factor" for the index and request for greater stress on its acknowledged limitations were far more moderate than the demands later made in the course of the political attack on the index in 1943-44, a move with which neither he nor Barkin was associated.

The pamphlet, *Questions and Answers on the Bureau of Labor Statistics Cost of Living Index*, as finally published in April 1942, did not reflect Teper's emphasis. It took a more general approach:

> A cost of living index can only measure the general change in the particular city of the goods and services *customarily* purchased by workers. It obviously cannot cover every conceivable increased cost which families experience. Among the costs which by their very nature cannot be covered in any measure of *average* living cost are the following:
>
> cost of commuting to jobs . . . higher costs in the defense cities than in the smaller cities and country towns from which many workers have come . . . the inconvenience caused by the more limited choice of certain goods as the war proceeds and the complete disappearance of others from the market.

Bureau Position on Publicizing Limitations

In the winter of 1941-42 this statement was as far as the Bureau felt it could or was obliged by the facts to go in publicly describing the shortcomings of the index, although in private conversations with research directors and other index users Branch staff freely acknowledged that some understatement was creeping into the index. Hinrichs was restrained from publicly acknowledging this partly by his belief that the extent of the understatement could not be measured or reliably estimated by known techniques or with available data. Therefore no numerical statement about it was scientifically possible. Sheer guesswork was, of course, out of the question.

Of more weight than this technical factor in the decision not to emphasize the limitations of the index was the obvious fact that despite its limitations, it was serving usefully in a broad variety of connections, including the formation of Administration anti-inflation policy, and bade fair to continue thus. It was, moreover, being more accurately maintained than the retail price index of any other country. A Bureau statement increasing the significance attributed to the index's defects would quickly be exaggerated for the purposes of special interests. The Bureau feared that this would be a long step toward saying that the index was "no good"; its usefulness for a host of important purposes would be psychologically and needlessly undermined. If, this reasoning concluded, Federal agencies were finding the index helpful in their work, the Bureau, as part of the wartime Administration, should not set in motion forces which would diminish or destroy that helpfulness. Hinrichs had received no directive on the index policy from any war agency but he felt that such a course of action was clearly dictated to the Bureau by the circumstances. His regular conversations with Secretary Perkins assured him that she shared this view.

C. POLITICAL CLOUDS GATHER OVER THE INDEX, 1942-1943

The Little Steel Formula and the Index

The Little Steel decision was announced on July 16, 1942. While some reference, in the decision, to the rise in the index might have been anticipated, neither Hinrichs nor his staff knew in advance that the BLS statistic would actually enter into a wage "formula." They were not consulted by the Board. Yet this use of the index formula was to have important consequences for the BLS.

First, the index became an indirect support of a highly controversial wage stabilization program. Its accuracy took on political, in addition to statistical, interest because existing wage policy depended on the index's rising at a very slow rate—if at all. In the months ahead, labor groups, restive under the Little Steel formula, trained their sights on the index, its movement, its usefulness for WLB purposes, and its accuracy.

Second, the popular misunderstanding that the index had something to do with total family expenditures was compounded by the widespread impression that wage increases were *tied* to the index by the Little Steel formula. The indirect, one-time nature of the relationship between the index and the formula was quickly obscured (if, indeed, it ever was clear) by most of the reporting and commentary the case received. The New York *Times*, for instance, announced the decision under this headline:

NWLB TIES WAGES TO PRICES
JAN. '41 TO MAY '42 THE BASIS

The pace at which these two consequences would materialize was not clear in the summer of 1942. Price and rent controls of great political and economic importance, hinging on the index, had been in existence for some time. Political protests about the index from opponents of price control, which some Bureau officials had expected, had not materialized to any significant extent. In any case, the direction of future events was as much beyond the control of the BLS as had been the Administration's anti-inflation policy.

The BLS's first reactions to the Little Steel formula were of a technical nature. They felt the WLB would experience difficulties in maintaining a formula resting only on the nation-wide index. The average trend in retail prices (as reflected by the index) was at most only one of the factors to be considered in determining wage rates. Hours of work, the extent of bonus and premium payments, labor mobility, the geographic and industrial concentration of war contracts, and trends in the supply of consumer goods were also relevant. Although the cost of living staff felt their index was a good statistical tool, they had always considered that any weight given, in wage decisions, to these other elements in the labor picture would compensate for the index's inherent limitations. The Little Steel decision, as a single national formula resting exclusively on a past rise in the index, would be likely, the Bureau foresaw, to focus the attention of critics of wage stabilization on the index and its limitations.

The Bureau was also conscious of a second set of problems it might face as a result of the Little Steel decision. The nation-wide index did not describe conditions in any particular community, especially in those not surveyed; its behavior was not characteristic of conditions in communities such as the rural or semi-rural areas where the coal and textile industries were centered; and it did not describe fully the price changes experienced by workers whose average annual income in 1934-36 was below $1500, particularly those in the very low income groups.

How much importance the omission of all these factors from the Little Steel formula would eventually assume could not be told in July 1942 but the President's delegation of full wage stabilization powers to the War

Labor Board on October 3, 1942, made it fairly certain that they would gain rather than lose significance.

Union Collection of Retail Price Data

One early reaction to the Little Steel formula that worked a change in the environment of the BLS index was private competition from some unions in the collection of retail price data, to "check up" on the BLS. In the fall and spring of 1941-1942, union research officials here and there throughout the country had begun to compile price lists from newspaper ads, store price tags, and interviews with union members on the prices of food, clothing, household goods, and housing, with the general purpose of proving that price control was ineffective and that real wages were, as a consequence, declining. This proof had a double purpose: to show that stronger price controls were necessary and that wage controls would reduce labor's real income.

Most union officers and bargaining representatives, however, showed little interest in material of this kind until the Little Steel formula narrowed opportunities for wage rate increases. Then, their need to present demands for wage boosts in terms of the formula led them to welcome any price data that would show that the prices paid by their particular union membership had not only risen by more than the 15 per cent of the formula but were soaring even higher than the rising BLS index itself. This dawning of interest in the index in the political offices of some unions presaged later events, although no direct developmental line can be drawn between them.

Not every union took this course, however. Some research directors, Lazare Teper of the ILGWU (AFL) and Solomon Barkin of the Textile Workers' Union (CIO) among them, held that labor was better served if it did not "set up a competing agency" to the BLS but acted simply as an informed critic of the Bureau. They considered that labor's need for nonpartisan statistics in arbitration, collective bargaining, and elsewhere made it preferable for cost of living data to originate with an agency like the BLS. Accordingly, they did no cost of living research on their own but continued to offer technical criticism of the official index.

By late 1942 and early 1943 union price surveys, particularly on food, were frequent, usually well publicized, and receiving increasing attention. Hastily assembled for the most part, they could not pretend to the sampling, weighting, and other techniques necessary to make them technically sound. They usually showed greater price rises than the BLS index or its food component. Thus, in Milwaukee in March 1943 the AFL Central Labor Union claimed, on the basis of its own investigation, that the cost of certain foods had risen 66.8 per cent between January 1941 and March 1943 compared with the BLS figure of 44.2 per cent for the same items in Milwaukee for the same period. This study was shown to Hinrichs privately, before its scheduled publication, by a union research man connected with the project. The BLS chief pointed out the numerous instances in which the survey violated accepted statistical procedures but the research director, referring to a topside union decision to publish it, replied "I can't interfere."

Top AFL and CIO leaders liked the new union material on price rises well enough to present a price tabulation made by a local of the AFL Truck Drivers' Union in Canton, Ohio to the President when he saw them early in 1943. (In their periodic meetings with the President the group was referred to as the Combined Labor War Board.) And, appearing before the Truman Committee, the Special (Senate) Committee Investigating the National Defense Program, at the end of March 1943, William Green of the AFL declared that

> prices are running away . . . official statistics fail to tell the truth . . . workers and their families do not eat statistics . . .

Dealing with Union Price Studies

Criticism was not new to the cost of living staff nor to the BLS as a whole; in fact, Bureau "customers" were regularly privately invited to offer criticism of Bureau material. But the widespread and public quest by a group of clients for alternate living cost data was a novelty which demanded some reconsideration of existing Bureau and Branch lines of communication with the unions.

Traditional Bureau procedure had often been to consult in private with critics in order to answer their comments without stirring up public controversy. Regular mimeographed press releases and staff articles in the *Monthly Labor Review* had been the usual general means of informing clients of changes and developments in the index and other BLS series or areas of work. During the second half of 1942 those formulating Bureau policy came to the conclusion that these procedures were not enough, that an unchecked accumulation of contradictory union data (generally derived by methods which the Bureau regarded as unscientific) eventually might put the Bureau "on the spot" because of the public's lack of accurate knowledge about the index. While they were by no means alarmed over the nature of the union findings, it seemed advisable to these officials that a stronger effort now be made to demonstrate to labor research people engaged in such surveys—and through them to their bosses—that BLS premises and procedures on the cost of living index were scientific and that, given these premises and procedures, the BLS index was the most accurate one possible under wartime conditions.

Miss Williams and her staff were too pressed for time on the basic job of keeping up the index to undertake checks of all the union data which came to their attention. Instead, it was decided that Hinrichs, Mrs. Wickens, and Miss Williams should try to devote an increasing amount of time to individual conversations with union research officers. This was begun and BLS price collecting and weighting procedures and standards were described to research people and compared with union methods. Material to supplement the index and answer union questions which the index could not meet was organized and supplied to a growing number of union correspondents.

Union price work and criticism were also jointly discussed at the December 1942 meeting of the Standing Committee of union research directors at which Hinrichs, Mrs. Wickens, Miss Williams, and Boris Stern were present. The meeting concluded with the decision that the unions should appoint a committee of two research directors to work with the Bureau in devising ways and means of keeping the unions and public at large regularly and accurately informed as to the real value and usage of the index as well as its limitations. The research officials also agreed to help the Bureau develop and promote studies of wartime changes in the expenditures of wage earners' families.

These conversations were natural extensions of existing BLS-union relationships. Early in 1943 a further step was taken as the Bureau recognized the need to talk directly with public groups and with the officers and members of unions in cities where union price surveys had been made without following proper statistical procedure. Both Mrs. Wickens and Miss Williams accordingly undertook trips early in 1943 to a number of cities—including Detroit, Milwaukee, Dallas, and Seattle. These swings around the country were for the purpose of indicating to the unions what materials on changes in food prices the BLS had; to explain the concept underlying the index and how retail price data were gathered and compiled; and to invite comments on these subjects. In the case of cities not covered by the Bureau, Mrs. Wickens and Miss Williams showed unions how to collect prices which would be comparable with cost of living figures. This was also done in Detroit where union figures had shown the greatest divergence from BLS data. There, a new union survey, following BLS procedure, showed no statistically significant difference between BLS and union data. Since Detroit was an important war production center, suffering from the shortages and problems characterizing such areas, and the Auto Workers a growing and highly vocal CIO union, the pricing project was regarded by the Bureau as a successful piece of educational work in Bureau procedure.

Other points of public contact were also given increased attention during the period beginning with late fall 1942. *Monthly Labor Review* articles on the index mentioned its limitations more explicitly but not quantitatively.

Mention should be made, too, of the informal conferences on the index between BLS staff and members of the Bureau of the Budget's Division of Statistical Standards which were going on, at this time, as part of the Budget Bureau's usual statistical review work under the Federal Reports Act. These increased in number when divergent union price data became more numerous. The difference in concept between the union and BLS approach to cost of living changes was already clear enough to lead the Budget Bureau staff to suggest to BLS personnel that there would be advantages in changing the name of the index so that it would not be taken for and criticized as a measure of change in family expenditures. An informal recommendation to this effect was made to the BLS sometime in 1943 but the Bureau indicated that a change was not feasible. In November of that year, Dr. Margaret Reid, a statistician from Iowa State College, joined the staff of the Division of Statistical Standards of the Budget Bureau to work in the general area of cost of living statistics, without specific reference to the index dispute. As will be seen, she was definitely assigned to the controversy in March 1944 when she became a member of the Mitchell Committee appraising the index for Chairman Davis of the President's Committee on the Cost of Living.

Further BLS Efforts to Improve the Index's Accuracy

Throughout this period the Bureau continued to feel that an important step to improve the index's public position technically and enable it to meet traditional Bureau standards of accuracy and representativeness would be a spot survey of family expenditures to check the accuracy of the consumption weights given to the various prices in the index. But three Bureau requests for funds for this purpose, made between July 1942 and June 1943 and backed each time by the Bureau of the Budget and, once, by the Treasury Department, were refused by Congress. Nevertheless, the Bureau, with such funds as it had, made a number of private tests of the particular aspects of the index which had encountered criticism. The results of all these fortified the Prices and Cost of Living Branch in its belief that although customary peacetime standards for accuracy were not being met, in the light of the existing staff and budget all that was possible was being done to incorporate wartime changes relevant to the index. This feeling was later reflected in an article by Miss Williams (in the July 1943 *Monthly Labor Review*) in which she said, referring to the Bureau's ability to discover quality changes:

> The degree of proficiency which the Bureau's field agents have developed in detecting changes in the quality of the goods they price, . . . has assured the users of the index of a considerable degree of accuracy in the comparison of prices on identical articles from month to month. Where changes in quality are such that the agents cannot detect them, it is obviously impossible to make allowances for them in computing the cost of living index.
>
> Today the problem [of reflecting quality deterioration] is more acute than ever before.

Up through March 1943 it was possible for the Prices and Cost of Living Branch to make adjustments in the index and its components for wartime market changes from time to time without delaying publication. By that month the cumulative changes, particularly in the food index (food rationing began that month), had become so great that the necessary revisions in weighting, commodity specifications, etc., demanded additional time. A delay in the publication of the March food index was announced by the Bureau on April 5 in a release which concluded

> . . . these changes will not affect the level of the index. The index is really a price thermometer; that is, it measures the changes from month to month in the prices of foods and other items being purchased by wage earners. It is not a measure of the change in the standard of living, which occurs when people are no longer able to buy automobiles or as much butter as they want.

The changes which were to be made in the food component as well as other phases of the index represented the first major wartime shift in the index but they were along the same lines as the adjustments which had been going on since January 1942. The close yet uninformed nature of the public attention the index was receiving was demonstrated when some observers interpreted the adjustments as a revision made in deference to critics. The

New York *Times* for April 3, 1943, printed an unsigned article which began

> The Bureau of Labor Statistics index which has been widely criticized inside as well as outside of the Bureau as not accurately reflecting the pattern of individual consumption in the emergency period, is going to be corrected, it was learned today. . . .

When Miss Williams later summarized the revisions (in the July 1943 *Monthly Labor Review* article already referred to) she put the matter quite differently and more accurately, repeating the distinction between the index and a measure of changes in the plane of living:

> With this revision, the Bureau continues its policy of making its cost of living index represent each month changes in the costs of the goods and services which wage earners and clerical workers can actually buy in the war years. The Bureau's living cost index has always taken account of changes in the purchasing habits of city families at the income levels to which the index applies. . . .
>
> In the last 19 months the goods and services produced for civilians in the United States have undergone more drastic changes than occurred in the entire period from 1919 to 1935. The level of living of the people of the country rose sharply in 1941 and was lowered in 1942. However, changes in the plane of living are quite different from changes in the cost of living, and it is the cost of living which the Bureau's index measures.

Revisions, publication of more detailed information on changes in the index, and the attempted education of labor critics, were all moves which might be normally made to further public—and union—understanding of the index. But, just before the Hold-the-Line Order was issued at the close of March 1943, Acting Commissioner Hinrichs was ready to conclude that these steps, although necessary, would not halt labor attacks on the index. He had hoped, late in 1942 and the first two months of 1943, that research directors to whom BLS staff explained and demonstrated the technical difficulties of index compilation would carry new understanding back to their political chiefs. But the continued emphasis by certain unions on price data contradicting the BLS led Hinrichs to revise such expectations; he finally abandoned them completely when the Milwaukee AFL Central Labor Union research official refused to tell his superiors about the statistical and conceptual errors which Hinrichs had pointed out in the union's price study.

It was now clear, he felt, that the argument over the index could not be settled through consultations and discussions with research directors. The union price surveys and criticism which were receiving publicity and being cited to President Roosevelt, the OPA, the WLB, and members of Congress were, he saw, quite apart from and unlike the older and continuing stream of independent technical union criticism—by such research directors as Teper and Barkin—to which the Bureau was accustomed and for which it had great respect. The research officers involved in the new rush of criticism could not influence official union decisions or correct topside misapprehensions about the index partly because they agreed with them, partly because these ideas were an outgrowth of rank and file dissatisfaction with price and wage controls, and partly because research directors did not generally possess the power to affect such decisions.

This conclusion virtually reduced to zero the value which Hinrichs could attribute to future "educational" work by the BLS among union research people. It led him to feel that if possible the Bureau should now approach union officers directly and point out that the index, despite wartime limitations, was accurate enough to withstand close technical scrutiny and that inaccurate criticism of it would, in the Bureau's opinion, lead to a dead end. He made an attempt to follow up this conclusion with action but soon found that the BLS channels of communication with union political leaders—both nationally and at the local level—were too irregular and slight to be of value. Three years of dealing with unions largely through the Research Directors' Conference, its Standing Committee, and subcommittees had all but cut off any contacts the Bureau previously had with trade union leaders. Whether or not the BLS chief considered going to the Secretary of Labor and asking her to take up the cudgel on the Bureau's behalf with respect to high union officials is not known.

In any case, as Hinrichs saw it, late in March 1943, the Bureau could not do much more than persist in keeping the index as accurate as possible and educate all its users in its proper interpretation. Despite his pessimism over the effectiveness of conversations with research directors he personally, when speaking with them, began to stress more than before the ways in which BLS material other than the living cost index—wage surveys, data on shortages, information on population shifts, and the like—could be used to support labor's case before the OPA and WLB.

The Hold-the-Line Order and the Argument over the Index

April 1943 brought the Hold-the-Line Order (E. O. 9328) embodying the Administration's answer to the wage and price rises of the winter of 1942-43 (see Chart A, page 783 and Chart B, page 787) and to the sharpening opposition of industry, labor, and farm groups to different aspects of inflation control. These had been increasingly in evidence during the course of events within the BLS's purview, which have just been described. The relation between the Hold-the-Line Order and labor resistance to wage stabilization has already been recounted in the preceding chapter. E. O. 9328 provided new impetus to forces which were pushing the BLS index into the political limelight and marked in a sense the beginning of another episode in BLS efforts to maintain the accuracy and public reputation of the index while remaining aloof and apart from the controversy over wage stabilization.

A new phase begins with the Hold-the-Line Order because, to restate what has already been said, it led, over the course of the ensuing six months, to a reshaping of the union attack on the War Labor Board's administration of wage stabilization. The prospect that union protests would lead Justice Byrnes to change the Little Steel formula was considered very remote—even by the unions—in the light of the Economic Stabilization Director's known belief in very firm controls. There remained several other possible approaches to securing a modification of the formula: an appeal to the public opinion and sympathy of the country as a whole through newspaper releases and radio addresses presenting the union contention that price increases had so far outstripped wage adjustments permissible under the Little Steel formula that labor was being unfairly deprived of its prewar standard of living; pressure on the President, OPA, and Congress; and a persistent bombardment of the War Labor Board with wage requests which involved, if approved, a revision of the formula. All these were tried with varying force at different times during the next year and a half.

But a less direct approach, previously visible though not fully explored—that of attacking public and official acceptance of the cost of living index—gradually found support in some unions as an oblique means of breaking the Little Steel formula. The widespread popular misconceptions about the index, already referred to, made it appear that such a campaign might be successful. A direct attack on the index had another tactical advantage. Underlying the adoption of the Little Steel formula had been the assumption that there would be no further substantial rise in the cost of living. Regardless of Mr. Byrnes's position in March 1943, if the index itself showed a very drastic rise compared with wage trends some modification of the formula could conceivably be insisted upon eventually; the same result might be achieved sooner if a greater rise in the cost of living than the index admitted were demonstrated in other ways. Thus a successful attack on the index could prove (a) that the Little Steel formula was unfair *ab initio*, and (b) that it was, in any event, now obsolete.

Appointment of the Mills Committee, May 1943

If the BLS could not head off such an attack it could perhaps fortify its position by securing the verdict of independent experts on the index. The Hold-the-Line Order precipitated such a move—a request that the index be evaluated by a special committee of the American Statistical Association (ASA). This step stemmed from broader considerations than the necessity to meet future union criticism. It had its origin in Mrs. Wickens's long-standing expectation that groups opposed to price control or to OPA's method of administering it might attack the index and demand an investigation by a Congressional committee. This type of criticism had appeared but had not proved as formidable as the Price Branch chief had feared. She now anticipated that it would be greatly stimulated by the Hold-the-Line Order. Opponents of strengthened price control would scrutinize the index and call its every rise a sign of inaccuracy; labor groups, *per contra,* would characterize any stability in the index as a failure to reflect the "full" extent of price rises. An unbiased outside assessment of the index by recognized technical authorities might therefore be timely as well as helpful.

Mrs. Wickens's proposal to this effect, not long after April 8, 1943, won immediate approval from her staff; Hinrichs also welcomed the idea. At his request Secretary Perkins asked the American Statistical Association "to review and appraise the cost of living index with reference both to its construction and its uses." Dr. Emmanuel Goldenweiser, president of the Association, thereupon appointed a committee of statisticians headed by Dr. Frederick Mills of Columbia University to do so.

This move was congenial to Bureau tradition. Close and friendly relations had long existed between it and professional statisticians and economists outside the government. Social scientists—in contrast to physical scientists—depend very largely on government agencies such as the BLS, Bureau of Agricultural Economics, and Census Bureau for their basic data. Over the years, the habit of consulting and seeking the advice of technicians in the field who used government data had grown up in various bureaus. Matters of common professional interest were discussed at the annual sessions of the American Statistical Association. The ASA, on more than one occasion in the past, had been asked to appoint an advisory committee to help some government statistical agency with a statistical problem or program.

The work facing the Mills Committee in May 1943, however, was not exactly analogous to ASA precedents. Committee members could not fail to know that their report, whatever its nature, would figure in subsequent public explanations by the Bureau of the wartime problems of the index. As individuals, they and other economists in and out of the government had been concerned over what they characterized as a "loss of confidence in a basic and generally accepted statistical measure" due to widely publicized accusations of error. They undertook the evaluation of the index both as a public service and as a scholarly opportunity to see for themselves how sound the wartime index was.

The major issues before the Mills Committee were partly technical and partly of a general policy nature. To avoid repetition they will be considered later in connection with the Committee's conclusions in its report released on October 10, 1943 (see pages 812 and following).

The Mills Committee was completely free to pursue its inquiry as it chose. It canvassed interested labor organizations, employer associations, and consumer groups. It held open hearings in Washington and elsewhere. It took evidence on changes in living costs from these sources and from government agencies. It made special field studies and tests of various Bureau procedures. For these the Bureau furnished the funds and the staff but planning and supervision came from the Committee.

The Mills Committee received little attention from the labor press. In late June 1943, while it was hearing testimony in Washington, the fourth Research Directors' Conference was held. Some of these officials had already appeared before the Committee and others were invited to do so at that time. Speaking before the conference, Russell Nixon of the United Electrical Radio and Machine Workers of America (then in the CIO, later expelled) applauded the appointment of the Mills Committee and characterized the opportunity for trade union representatives to meet with it as an "extraordinary opportunity." Said he,

> . . . we have to acknowledge the good faith and sincerity of the Bureau in arranging that type of approach to this particular problem . . . we have to be conscious of the co-operative attitude that has been taken by the Bureau. . . .

1943 Research Directors' Conference

The 1943 research directors' meeting heard open discussion of a number of issues which events of the year 1942-43 had brought into greater relief. Mr. Hinrichs led off with a reminder that the BLS had nothing to do with policy formation:

. . . I do want to emphasize however, that the Bureau of Labor Statistics is not an administrative agency of the Government. It has no policy-making functions to perform. Therefore, a question that might be of vital importance to you in a discussion with the WLB, or with the OPA, or with the WPB, or with the WMC is likely to result in a discussion here about which we in the BLS can do comparatively little. On the other hand, if in connection with your work with these agencies, you have found that the statistics of the Bureau are inadequate, or are inadequately presented by the Bureau, we want to know about it, so that we can correct our methods and make our work more useful.

Discussion of the index at the Conference centered around a critique that had been submitted to the Mills Committee by Teper of the ILGWU.[3] In presenting a summary of this technical paper, Teper questioned, among other things, whether quality changes were adequately reflected in the index and whether the Bureau's sample was sufficient for wartime purposes. He also stressed what he considered the Bureau's failure to take the public, and especially its "clients," fully into its confidence:

Much of the adverse comment on the Bureau's index may be laid at its own doorstep. The Bureau shows too much eagerness to defend its product. . . . The Bureau falls down in another respect. It does not, in its discussions of the cost of living index, fully explore the difficulties which exist in securing price quotations at different pricing periods for identical commodities. . . . A certain amount of misunderstanding arises between the Bureau and the users of its figures from the fact that while it is known that the Bureau must frequently makes changes and substitutions in the individual commodities it prices, little information exists, other than in terms of broad generalities, as to the why and wherefore and how of these adjustments. . . . The Bureau does not adequately describe its index and the way the various problems are actually handled in the process of constructing the index. In my opinion, the Bureau could usefully publish, even if for a limited circulation, a technical bulletin which would show monthly what adjustments had to be made in the index construction and otherwise discuss the technical problems in connection with the compilation of the cost of living figures. Such a bulletin, periodically released, would be welcomed both by professional statisticians and by representatives of unions, for it would clarify the Bureau's thinking on many of the problems it must solve.

In the discussion of Teper's paper the research directors repeated a number of familiar union requests—particularly that the index be expanded to take in more stores and commodities and cover larger areas in each city sampled. Mrs. Wickens acknowledged the criticisms of the index in a brief comment at the close of the meeting.

May I say first how very much the Cost of Living Branch appreciates the full bill of particulars this conference has given us about the cost of living index. It is very much easier to deal with a bill of particulars, however particular, than it is to deal with vague opinions that the cost of living index is simply wrong. Most of the objections which Mr. Teper raised in his paper have been anticipated by us. Some of what Mr. Teper said came up previously and some of it we were aware of. Some activities were not undertaken because of lack of funds, but I am happy to report that we have had under way for two months a comprehensive set of tests on the adequacy of our basic prices laid out in part under the direction of the Committee of the American Statistical Association headed by Dr. Mills, with whom many of you have talked today. I would like to tell you a bit about those tests off the record. I can't give you the results of all of them because some of them are still in process.

Another theme that ran clearly through the discussion was the union contention that the cost of living index was being improperly used by the war agencies and was not clearly understood by those in charge of policy formation in the government. In contrast to Teper's suggestion that there be greater and more regular publicity on the technical aspects of the index for the benefit of a small group—technicians and union representatives—Nixon of the Electrical Workers (CIO) asserted

[3] Subsequently published as "Observations on the Cost of Living Index of the Bureau of Labor Statistics" in the *Journal of the American Statistical Association* for September 1943.

> . . . the BLS should make clear to the public what the limitations of the index are—for instance, that there exists now an area of increase in the cost of living which possibly is not covered by the index. . . .
>
> The Bureau has a problem of making clear to the Government agencies—the War Labor Board particularly—just what the status of the Bureau of Labor Statistics cost of living index is. This is the one serious criticism that I have—that since May 1942, for more than a year now, we have had the national wage policy predicated on the Bureau of Labor Statistics cost of living index, without reference of any kind as to its limitations. In this connection, it seems to me, it would have been desirable, and would still be desirable, to tell the War Labor Board that the index does not exactly and adequately reflect the real increase in the cost of living, that there are certain other aspects of the picture which it cannot properly and truthfully reflect. This, I think has been generally accepted inside the Bureau of Labor Statistics, but I am suggesting that as a matter of government policy this should be made clear in a formal statement to the War Labor Board so that at least the labor members of the Board in their very important decisions relative to wage matters and relative to cost of living adjustment in relationship to wages, would have a straightforward, factual evaluation of the situation.

This challenge was taken up by Hinrichs in his closing address. He said:

> I should like to put the proposition in a slightly different fashion. There must be an index of prices and the cost of living that can be used with confidence by people who are making policy. If our index carries within it such serious shortcomings as to invalidate the policy conclusions based on it, then the thing to do is not to announce the shortcomings of the index, but to scrap it altogether or make it better. Our job is to make it better so that nobody else will scrap it.
>
> When Mr. Nixon says, "Will we tell the labor members of the War Labor Board exactly what our cost of living index is and what it looks like," the answer is we haven't been invited to do so. No, I haven't been invited to appear before the War Labor Board to tell them what our index is and what its limitations are. If asked, I am not going to avoid the question of any of the shortcomings. I have, of course, discussed our index with members of the staff of the War Labor Board, but it is not our function to ask for a formal discussion with the Board.

Hinrichs turned down the contrasting requests of both Teper and Nixon because he felt that any detailed BLS statement about the index would be a grave political error. He was aware that some of his staff were willing to issue a general statement on the statistical concepts involved in the index and the difficulties of measuring all the elements of wartime price rises. Although they agreed with him that a quantitative estimate of understatement was politically and technically out of the question, they felt that a frank admission of some unmeasurable error might disarm critics and win confidence.

But Hinrichs felt that as chief of the BLS he must judge these demands for an announcement of the index's shortcomings in the light of the Bureau's wartime role in the government as a whole. He was sure that the degree of inaccuracy in the index was essentially irrelevant to the policy uses being made of it. On the other hand, he felt there was good reason to fear that a detailed statement about the index and the problems it presented would only become grist for the mills of critics of Administration policy. A technical statement on the index might be exaggerated and twisted by unfriendly critics and so only compound the Bureau's difficulties. He thought he could best protect the government's interest in the index as a tool of the wartime administration by going no further in publicizing its technical problems than the ground covered in previous statements.

Later in the same address Hinrichs coupled a compliment to his audience with a note of warning. Said he,

> From my point of view, this has been the best of the four annual conferences which we have held. . . . This conference . . . has been tops. . . . . . But I wish to indicate one caution to you: For heaven's sake, don't put all your eggs in the cost of living basket.

This was not unfriendly or unrealistic advice, but those union research workers who were expected to supply economic arguments for blasting at the "wage freeze" of the Hold-the-Line Order considered it "defensive." And union representatives who did not take for granted the good faith of the BLS concluded that the Bureau was "meddling in politics," that it was shielding the index in order to protect the Little Steel formula.

Summer, 1943

The succeeding summer months saw the Administration and labor hammering away at opposite sides of the stabilization program. In June, the War Labor Board was faced with a cumulative rise of 24 per cent in the index since January 1, 1941, as against the 15 per cent wage rate increase it had allowed. There was violent Congressional opposition, too, to the food price subsidy program just then being introduced. The Board felt impelled to answer published speculation as to whether, in view of the gap between the formula and the index, it would propose a specific adjustment in what some labor leaders termed the "useless and oppressive" formula. The Board showed how far it was from such a move in a unanimous decision directing Chairman Davis to make a statement which in effect shifted the burden to the OPA and OES. Davis, on June 30, emphasized that the Board intended to continue with the Little Steel formula as it was and that a successful wage stabilization program called for keeping down prices, particularly food prices. He left no doubt of the Board's support of food subsidies and "all appropriate measures to control food prices." The statement did point out, however, that a continued rise in living costs might make it necessary to change the application of the Little Steel formula to wage adjustments.

This proviso—whether intended as a concession to labor or warning to the OPA—had the effect of further focusing labor's attention on the cost of living index. When the index for mid-July was announced in August, the first substantial decline since Pearl Harbor was revealed—a fall of 0.7 per cent (not index points) from the mid-June position. Largely the result of a drop of 2.0 per cent in the food component during the same period—in turn the outcome of food price "rollbacks" instituted by the OPA and made possible by the hotly disputed food subsidies—the dip strengthened the conviction of certain labor leaders that the BLS was not measuring the full extent of the price rise experienced by their membership. The comparative trend of the all-items index and its components for 1941-44 can be seen in Chart E, page 813.

At this time union chiefs were up against the very much more important and uncomfortable fact that the Little Steel formula, stiffened by the Hold-the-Line Order, was finally acting as an effective anti-inflation tool. No longer could any significant wage rate increases be secured for an impatient rank and file on the grounds of a cost of living "maladjustment." In certain quarters pressure from the membership, in other quarters a feeling of rivalry with newly expanded unions made an assault on the index and the BLS now appear necessary and possible; such a course of action might have been vetoed a year or six months before.

It probably was no shot aimed at random by the AFL when its *Weekly News Service* for September 21, 1943, called BLS price reports "a mockery of the facts" and declared

> Above all, we object to having wage rates stabilized or frozen in relation to cost of living figures which are so obviously phoney. If the cost of living increase isn't five times as great as the BLS says it is, we'll eat our hat. We'll probably have to anyway before long.

Some weeks after this, on October 10, the ASA Committee to appraise the index made public its report.

Report of the Mills Committee

Fully vindicating the BLS position, the principal conclusions of the ASA's Special Committee were:

> First, that within the limitations established for it, the cost-of-living index provides a trustworthy measure of changes in the prices paid by consumers for goods and services; second, that many of the difficulties and doubts which have arisen concerning the index have their origins in attempts to use it uncritically for purposes to which it is not adapted.

The phrase "cost of living" was ambiguous, the Committee granted, and some of the difficulties attendant on the use of the index grew out of this fact. The Committee pointed to the different factors causing family expenditures to change—a rise or fall in the unit prices of

Chart E

CHANGES IN THE BUREAU OF LABOR STATISTICS COST OF LIVING INDEX

Based on Retail Prices and Rents Charged Wage Earners and Clerical Workers in Large Cities

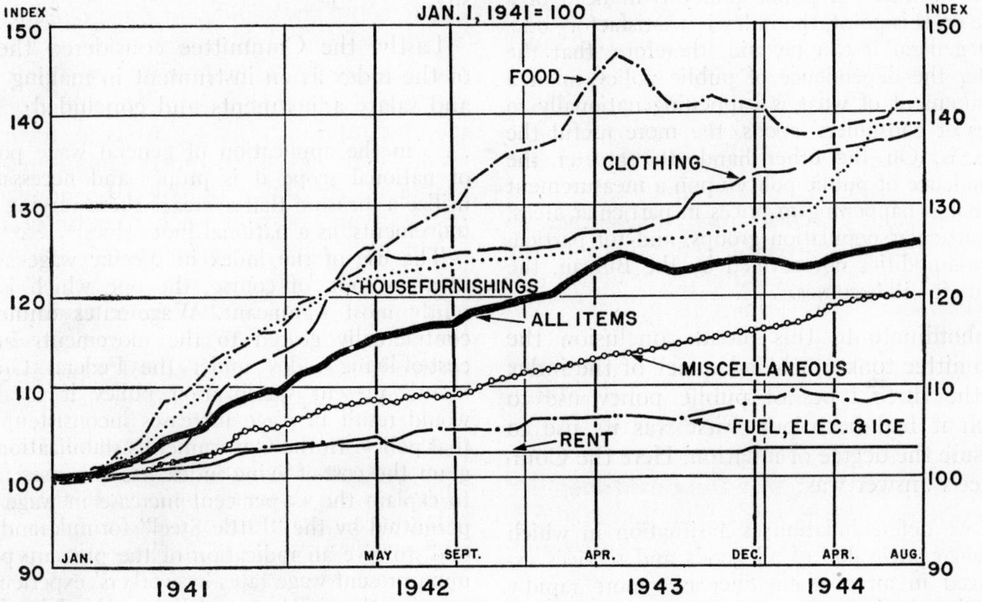

Source: United States Department of Labor
Bureau of Labor Statistics

goods and services, a forced change in the manner of living due, say, to the exigencies of war, or an increase in income leading to a rise in the standard of living. But it insisted that the term "cost of living" in "technical statistical parlance" had always applied only to the first of these—that is to unit prices. A general summary of the Committee's conclusions wound up with the paragraphs:

> After a careful investigation of the relevant evidence we believe that the index records with a satisfactory degree of accuracy what has happened to unit prices paid for consumers' goods by city families of moderate income.
>
> We have been much impressed during our investigation by the integrity, alertness, intelligence, and technical competence of the Bureau's staff. We feel that, on the whole, working under very trying circumstances, they are doing an excellent job of carrying out the task assigned to them.

The Committee phrased the major issues before it in terms of eleven questions and its conclusions on the technical and policy aspects of the index's use were incorporated in answers to them. The first ten questions were in the technical area; their answers were based on field tests made under the Committee's supervision, on statistical checks of Bureau data, and on a review of the Bureau's procedures. In general, the Committee rejected some of the technical criticisms which had been made of the index, made a number of suggestions on others, and estimated some extents of error. It made no over-all estimate of error. Excerpts from these questions and answers appear in Appendix B.

The more general policy issues generated by the Administration's use of the index were summarized by the Committee in its eleventh and final question: *Is the index an adequate instrument for users in matters of public policy?* The general answer to this said, in part:

> We have indicated our conviction that the index is a satisfactory instrument for measuring what it attempts to measure—average movements in the retail prices of goods and services purchased by city workers. If public policy is in need of a guide on this point, the index is a satisfactory one.
>
> In general it can be said, therefore, that the greater the dependence of public policy upon a measurement of what is happening nationally to prices of consumers' goods, the more useful the index is. On the other hand, the greater the dependence of public policy upon a measurement of what is happening to prices in particular areas, for particular population groups, and for particular commodities not covered by the Bureau, the less useful it becomes. . . .

Subordinate to this broad conclusion the Committee took up the adequacy of the index for the three types of public policy use to which it had been put. First was its use to measure the degree of inflation. Here the Committee's answer was:

> If we define inflation as a situation in which the aggregate value of all goods and services exchanged in an economy increases more rapidly than the physical volume of these goods and services, a cost-of-living index is an obviously relevant measuring tool. The Bureau of Labor Statistics index, however, does not cover all consuming groups in our economy. It relates only to the retail prices of consumer's goods purchased by families of moderate income in large cities. Prices in primary markets and in various wholesale markets are also important indicators of inflation. For this reason we do not believe that the Bureau's cost-of-living index should be used by itself as a measure of the extent of inflation. It has great value as one among a group of measurements available to administrators of an anti-inflation program.

Second, the Committee took up the use of the index in the control of retail prices; its judgment in this area was:

> The index is a useful instrument in retail price control. Its use would be greater if coverage were broadened to include prices of more commodities. However, it should be remembered that the commodities selected for measurement are chosen not only because they are important in the customary purchases of consumers, but also because their price movements are like those of related commodities. If the present national and city averages were supplemented by regional measures and by more detailed index numbers for commodity groups, their usefulness would be greatly increased. Effective price control cannot be based solely upon averages comprehending great diversity.

Lastly, the Committee considered the use of the index as an instrument in making wage and salary adjustments and concluded:

> . . . in the application of general wage policies of national scope it is proper and necessary to utilize a measure that averages these varying price movements, as a national index does. . . .
>
> The use of the index in specific wage adjustments is not, of course, the one which is currently most significant. Wage rates cannot be contractually geared to the movements in the cost-of-living index under the Federal Government's present stabilization policy if to do so would result in wage increases inconsistent with that policy. In the Government's stabilization program the cost-of-living index has two uses: First, to explain the 15-per cent increase in wage rates permitted by the "Little Steel" formula and, second, to give an indication of the pressure placed upon present wage rates by workers' experience in meeting the rising cost of living. We have found no evidence that would invalidate the index for the first purpose. For the second purpose, however, that of estimating the pressure on present wage rates and the present wage adjustment formula by workers' experience with living costs, a national average of living costs is not satisfactory. The reason for this does not arise from any inaccuracy, but from the fact that it is an average. The experience from which dissatisfaction comes is not that of the statistical average man. It is the experience of the individual worker or group of workers involved.
>
> The fact that the index is one of prices and not of consumers' actual expenditures should provide further warning. The difference between the movements of prices and changes in actual expenditures is significant in times of great mobility, changes in the pattern of living, commodity and housing shortages, quality deterioration, and increased taxes and bond purchases. Since a price index cannot reflect completely these facts of consumers' experience, it cannot fully measure what workers mean by changes in their cost of living. The dissatisfaction or satisfaction of work-

ers arises from their own and not the statistician's conception of the "cost of living" in relation to their own and not the average income.

One further point needs emphasis. A decline in the plane of living cannot be prevented in an economy that absorbs a large part of the country's products for military purposes. When the total available supply of consumers' goods declines, the real income and the plane of living of the average citizen must decline. . . .

Eleven recommendations were made by the Committee to help render the national index and component indexes more effective during the war and the period of postwar reconstruction. They were subject to considerations of cost as well as the needs of Congressional committees and administrators for the information the recommended studies would yield. The first five added up to the general proposal that the Bureau expand its system of cost of living indexes to provide regional living cost indicators, more representative small city indexes, a nonfarm community index, indexes for communities of different sizes and for certain specialized industrial areas such as those in which coal mining and textiles were concentrated, and measures of geographic differences in the cost of living. All these, the Committee recognized, would necessitate an expansion in samples of large and small cities and collection of additional data to derive additional weights.

The sixth recommendation had considerable significance for the controversy over the index, for it recognized something the prices and cost of living staff knew well but had rarely found the occasion to say—that the index could not be kept representative of current trends unless regular checks were made on the consumption patterns which were used as its weights. The Committee recommended:

That frequent *small-sample studies of family expenditures and incomes* be conducted, and that once in 5 years a comprehensive study be made to provide data on local differences in income and consumption habits among occupational groups in the United States. Furthermore, that adequate analyses and integration of these studies and existing data be planned and regularly provided for. Since these kinds of studies provide the weights which reflect the changes in consumption habits and are important in keeping the cost-of-living indexes in line with current economic development, it is essential that they be made periodically.

It must be noted that such regular re-surveys of consumption patterns were a rare luxury for the government bureaus responsible for the various national cost of living indexes throughout the world because of the expense involved. Legislatures were characteristically unwilling to commit themselves in advance to any periodic or automatic granting of the necessary funds.

None of the remaining recommendations of the Mills Committee touched on two questions raised often by the unions—the "deceptive" nature of the index's name and the representation of quality changes in the price index. The Committee had recognized the difference between the statistician's and layman's concept of the "cost of living" and indicated that it considered it impossible to put a dollar value on some "intangible and immeasurable" wartime quality declines. That was all.

The final Mills recommendation was in the nature of some public relations counsel. The Bureau, said the Committee, should

prepare for publication an historical summary of the development of the concept of the cost-of-living index and of the purposes for which that index is used. . . . the report . . . should, in addition, describe the expansion of uses to which the index has been put, and provide an explanation of the ideal form of index which would serve these several purposes.

The Mills Report and the BLS

The Bureau naturally was well satisfied, though not surprised, with the contents of the Mills Committee report. Technical questions about the index had been answered as well as the limits of time and funds permitted; the Bureau's reputation for professional competence had been supported. The Committee's suggestions for improving the index were good, too, the staff thought.

Hinrichs' own satisfaction went further than this. He viewed the report as a political weapon: as a disinterested evaluation of the index he thought it would go far toward reinforcing confidence in the Bureau and its work in important quarters quite apart from the labor unions: in Congress, in the Executive

Branch, in the press, in academic and business circles. Its language and contents were such, he felt, that they could not easily be used to support the exaggeration of the index's limitations which he was anxious to prevent. This conclusion appeared to be borne out by the silence with which the Mills report was met by the labor press, although presumably the document was scrutinized carefully in union research departments and summarized for top officials.

In brief, with the Mills report in hand, Hinrichs, in the second week of October 1943, felt better fortified than ever before to defend the index. He was, at the time, engaged in conversations with a number of CIO officials in an effort to persuade them that in their drive on the Little Steel formula they should avoid a head-on collision with the Bureau over the accuracy of the index. From the trend of CIO decision and action it was clear that some key wage stabilization case or cases would soon be brought before the WLB. But it was not certain, even after CIO wage cases began to be certified to the WLB on October 16, 1943, which industry—steel, automobiles, textiles—would furnish the real proving ground for the test of strength.

Hinrichs apprehended that the CIO would choose steel. Measured by the usual wage statistics the steel workers were a moderate-income-city-worker group; the cost of living index fitted their situation much more closely than say, that of the textile workers whose income and mode of living, as a group, were generally considered substandard. Since the United Steelworkers of America (USA) had long since gone on record as asserting that the rise in the index since January 1941 was too low measured by steel-worker experience, Hinrichs saw that any attack the USA made on the Little Steel formula would necessarily focus on an assumption and attempt to prove that the BLS index was *inaccurate* and inadequate rather than *inapplicable* to the steel industry. And to make good their claim union spokesmen could be expected to try to prove the index egregiously in error.

Concerned over this possibility, Hinrichs told CIO research staff members that the ASA report contained material which would nullify any union assertions that the index was statistically unsound. He pointed out that it was to labor's advantage to maintain public confidence in official data, like the cost of living index, so that the use of facts—as opposed to unverified assumptions or prejudices—would become more prevalent in the settlement of controversies over policy. There were, moreover, he said, BLS materials available on the disappearance of low-priced clothing, the maldistribution of food supplies, and other wartime changes, and a good case might on those bases be made for wage increases for certain groups, for strengthening price control, and tightening rationing without touching on the matter of the index's accuracy. He hoped, by these arguments, to persuade union leadership to abandon for the duration the drive to raise wages and to work instead for other political and social objectives.

At the same time, in an effort to be statistically prepared for the wage cases which were headed for the Board, Hinrichs talked with WLB officials and suggested that they give the Bureau funds to provide indexes on the cost of living in such "trouble" industries as coal and textiles—as the Mills Committee had suggested. The request was refused. Perhaps WLB members saw that to the extent that they helped "take the heat off" the index dispute in that manner, they only invited greater difficulties for themselves in maintaining the general applicability of the Little Steel formula. The Board was hardly in a position to add other people's troubles to its own.

D. THE PRESIDENT STEPS IN

Appointment of the Cost of Living Committee

On October 21, before CIO intentions were clarified, the President took his first official cognizance of the dispute over the index. He had long since been aware that union criticism of the index was a growing by-product of union dissatisfaction with the Little Steel formula. It was scarcely in the forefront of his thoughts, but rather something incidental which William Davis of WLB or his own assistant Isador Lubin might call to his attention now and then. Even on more serious problems it was not unusual for him—or other top officials—to delay and wait and watch for further developments and possible resolutions before taking steps himself to achieve a solution. He and his advisors may have hoped that the unions would desist in the face of WLB and OES determination to retain the Little Steel formula. He may have hoped that the Mills Committee report might dispose of the issue over the index. His opportunities for periodic discussion with William Green, George Meany, and Philip Murray, moreover, enabled him to give them personal assurances of his interest in their problems and so to avert precipitous action on their part.

But by October 21, 1943, the cumulative effect of several developments made this topside policy of drift—or benign non-intervention—with regard to the index dispute no longer expedient. First, the Mills Committee Report, with whose conclusions Lubin had familiarized the President, did not appear likely to turn or stem the tide of union criticism. It might reassure statisticians and economists; it did not persuade union leaders. At the same time it fortified the Administration in its belief that the BLS index was fundamentally sound and could stand up under close scrutiny. Secondly, the CIO was reported to be headed for a decision at its annual convention, within a week or so, to devote a major portion of its energy to a steel industry case to "crack the Little Steel formula." The level and volume of labor criticism of the index bade fair to rise very soon from the local and intermittent to the national and persistent. And the implications of this had undoubtedly been brought to the President's attention.

Mr. Roosevelt may also have had in mind the general political situation, and the necessity, for a government which depends on consent, of retaining for the administration the ultimate support of such an important segment of the voters as organized labor. His overall economic strategy for winning the war on the home front prevented him from completely satisfying the unions on the larger matters of wage and price stabilization but he still could take a step with regard to the cost of living index which would assure them of his interest in getting at the truth of the matter.

And so, when George Meany of the AFL told the President, at a meeting of the Combined Labor War Board at the White House, that the index was inaccurate, Mr. Roosevelt was in a frame of mind and position to propose that the BLS index might be investigated by a special committee of the War Labor Board. The device of an investigating committee was one to which the President was particularly sympathetic. The logic of the situation argued a tripartite committee, and one from the War Labor Board. The Board had used the index in the first place, and its conclusions would settle the question of continued reliance on it; the labor members would have to make their case to their colleagues or abandon it; the Board could dispose of the matter as the ASA could not.

The day after the union leaders saw Mr. Roosevelt, October 22, his suggestion reached Chairman William H. Davis of the WLB in the form of a memorandum from the White House. It said:

Dear Will,

There is so much controversy and dispute as to what the cost of living is that I told the labor leaders yesterday I thought it might be a good thing for the War Labor Board to appoint three of its members (labor, business, and Government) to look into the question and try to answer and make clear how the index figure is arrived at, whether any changes should be made in its component parts, or other improvements. If such a committee could agree in a statement, I think it would have a salutary effect all over the country, because today all kinds of exaggerated statements are made.

Can you do it?

F. D. R.

The President's Committee on the Cost of Living—enlarged with his consent to five so as to represent both the AFL and CIO—was immediately appointed from the War Labor Board by Mr. Davis.

BLS Reaction to Cost of Living Committee

At the Bureau of Labor Statistics the appointment of the Committee on the Cost of Living was generally regarded as a move to take the heat off the Little Steel formula and perhaps prolong its life for some months. There was no feeling that the Committee's creation implied an official rebuke to the Bureau for failure in its efforts to answer union criticism, for the Bureau knew that those concerned with the index as a policy tool were well satisfied with the Mills conclusions.

At the technical level BLS staff members were perhaps inclined to think that the attacks of the index's critics had already been answered as well as possible. But Hinrichs, by no means finished with his political task of buttressing the index and Bureau with the help of the Mills report, felt deprived of the opportunity for leadership he had so recently secured. Certainly, he decided, the President's move gave him no support. For, in the face of the general expectation that the new Committee would "do something" about the index and the formula, the Mills report could not command much attention.

On November 7, 1943, the CIO annual convention passed a resolution which stated that it had become necessary to "eliminate the so-called 'Little Steel' formula." The Steelworkers Union was virtually instructed to start action before the War Labor Board along these lines. At a Steelworkers' National Wage and Policy Conference, held in Pittsburgh on December 1 and 2, the Steelworkers adopted a program of demands for "wage adjustments and other improvements" which was topped by a plank calling for a general wage adjustment of 17 cents an hour for all steel employees. The implications of this move for the cost of living index were clear. Now uncertainty and conflict lay ahead for the BLS.

IV. A Presidential Agency Liquidates the Problem

A. INTRODUCTION

The Cost of Living Committee's Purpose—Conflicting Views

The War Labor Board, together with the OPA and OES, had been initially responsible for using the index as a policy criterion and thereby for making its accuracy a political issue. Up to this point the Board had not, however, taken any share of the burden of defending the index from the labor attacks, which fell on the BLS. Now, by his intervention, the President lifted the argument from the Bureau, out of the Department of Labor altogether, and up to the Board's level. But he did it in a manner which kept the question —at least until it was decided—on an investigatory siding apart from the main track of WLB case decision and policy determination. By the device of a President's Committee, rather than a regular WLB Committee, Chairman Davis could maintain throughout the investigation that the Cost of Living Committee had nothing to do with the Little Steel formula. It was, he could and did assert, solely a fact-finding body to examine the index; the wage policy of the Board was not within its province.

Over the next few weeks there was much popular conjecture about the purpose of the Committee, since its creation followed so closely on the Mills Committee's verdict and virtually coincided with the CIO convention's barrage against the Little Steel formula. Davis was quick to deny that the Committee's creation meant wage increases might soon be granted. On November 11 he reiterated the WLB's position that instead of giving wage increases the Administration should push back prices. In any case, he added, the Little Steel formula was now pegged by the Hold-the-Line Order, which the War Labor Board could not change. He thought it obvious that the President's Committee was not the mechanism for making wage or formula changes. Moreover, and in his view this was conclusive, changes or inaccuracies in the index were irrelevant to the formula because the relationship between the two ceased when the formula was announced. The index had been a means of arriving at the figure in the formula, but the formula was a ceiling, not an escalator.

Removed by at least two stages from the Little Steel formula, therefore, the deliberations of the Cost of Living Committee never took on major policy significance for its members. There were some lively sessions and sharp differences of opinion at the fifteen meetings held over a period of twelve months. The outcome was vital to the BLS. It was important to other Administration officials who used the index, and to industry and labor. But for the Committee members the question of the index's nature and accuracy was outranked by the major issues in many areas raised by cases which were coming before the full War Labor Board.

Union Attack on the Little Steel Formula Before the WLB

The attack on the Little Steel formula was in progress before the Board while the statistical dispute was being explored in the President's Committee. The CIO steel wage action, which had its origin at the Steelworkers' Wage and Policy Conference in Pittsburgh, reached the WLB on January 27, 1944, as the so-called *Basic Steel*[4] Case, a combination of a number of the 500 identical steel disputes then pending. It was the most important of more than ten wage cases in key industries brought before the Board by CIO unions between October 1943 and June 1944. The Steelworkers' list of demands was headed by a request for a general wage adjustment of 17 cents an hour and included a guaranteed annual wage, sick leave, dismissal pay, and a number of other "fringe" benefits (so-called because they were supplemental to rather than a part of wages).

At a WLB hearing early in February the union's representatives explicitly conceded that the 17-cent wage rate increase could not be granted under the Little Steel formula. They announced that since the USA felt the increase was justified by the rise in living costs it would ask the Board to recommend to the President that he empower it (the Board) to revise the formula. Panel hearings on the *Basic Steel* case took four months; the board's decision was not handed down until November 1944.

With the same goal of breaking the Little Steel formula but by a characteristically less dramatic method the AFL members of the board on February 9 submitted a petition asking that the WLB request the President to adjust the Little Steel formula in the light of the increased cost of living. Labor dissenting, the Board, on March 15, voted to table the petition without prejudice to its reconsideration at a later date.

The Membership of the Cost of Living Committee

The tripartite structure of the Cost of Living Committee, paralleling that of the WLB, meant that at least three sides of the argument over the index—the Administration's, industry's and the national AFL's and CIO's—would be represented in the group itself. There was no spokesman on the Committee for those unions which made no public attack on the index.

Chairman Davis was the lone public member of the Committee. A lawyer with extensive experience in government policy formation and one of the country's foremost practicing labor relations experts, he had been National Compliance Director of the NRA, Chairman of the New York State Mediation Board, and Chairman of the WLB's predecessor, the National Defense Mediation Board. Withal, labor relations were his avocation; he was a senior partner in a prominent firm of patent attorneys.

Davis was inclined, with his fellow public members on the Board, to accept the conclusions of the Mills Committee report. He was frankly convinced that the BLS index was the best possible under the circumstances. But this belief did not alter his conviction that labor's views on the index should be given a full and complete hearing in the Committee. He was accustomed to union methods of applying pres-

[4] *In re Carnegie-Illinois Steel Corp. et al., and United Steelworkers of America* (CIO), National War Labor Board Case No. 111-6230-D (14-1), et al. November 25, 1944. (19 *WLR* 568.)

sure and keenly aware of labor's problems and needs, especially as these affected top leadership. One of his favorite expressions was, "The democratic principle is rooted in persuasion." He liked to allow sufficient time and opportunity for persuasion to operate.

George Meany, AFL secretary-treasurer, took the lead in presenting labor's case against the index to the Committee, though the CIO was the more vigorous of the two federations in attacking the Little Steel formula before the full War Labor Board. Brought up in the hard school of the building trades and often spoken of as William Green's probable successor in the AFL presidency, Meany impressed his associates as an aggressive and dynamic leader. He was among those who believed the Department of Labor and the Bureau of Labor Statistics should represent labor in government councils and stand ready to aid whatever policies labor organizations decided to adopt.

The other labor member, R. J. Thomas, president of the United Auto Workers of America and a vice-president of the CIO, had less interest than Meany in the questions raised by argument over the index. Thomas' responsibilities as vice-president of the auto workers' union often called him away to Detroit; in his absences Harold Ruttenberg, research director of the Steelworkers usually served as substitute. Often Mr. Ruttenberg came when Mr. Thomas was present. Other union research officials, among them, J. Raymond Walsh, chief of CIO research, Lincoln Fairley of the national CIO, Donald Montgomery of the UAW (CIO), and Margaret Scattergood of the national AFL, occasionally attended committee meetings as observers.

Of the two industry members, George Batt, vice-president and treasurer of the Dugan Brothers Companies of Newark, New Jersey, was the more active on the Committee. Although, like Davis, he was inclined to accept the conclusions of the Mills Committee, he was tolerant of the union attack on the index. It was a healthy thing, a milestone in labor relations, he thought, that the debate over the Little Steel formula should be waged so largely in statistical terms rather than through "bluff." He regarded the attack on the index as one of those things some union leaders felt they *had* to do to satisfy their membership; he regretted that they could not be freer from such compulsions. The other industry member, Horace B. Horton, treasurer of the Chicago Bridge and Iron Corporation, was not able to attend Committee meetings regularly but kept in touch with Batt by letter and telephone. They were generally in agreement on what position to take in Committee deliberations.

Batt considered the defense of the index vital because he saw it as the cornerstone of the Little Steel formula and therefore of wage stabilization. Neither he nor Horton nor most other industrial leaders at the time participated in the public debate over the formula and index, preferring to let industry's rebuttal to the union attacks be presented privately before the Cost of Living Committee and in major WLB actions, like the *Steel* case.

Each of the three sectors of the President's Committee eventually had its own staff drawn from outside the War Labor Board, although a WLB economist, John Dunlop, was assigned to the Committee and William Waldron, Davis's assistant, acted as secretary to the Committee. The industry representatives consulted the National Industrial Conference Board, which published a cost of living index of its own, and engaged the services of Dr. Jules Backman, business consultant and professor of economics at New York University, to evaluate union and BLS statements for them. Backman was also economic advisor to the steel industry in the *Basic Steel* case. Mr. Davis appointed his own Technical Committee, headed by Dr. Wesley Clair Mitchell of Columbia University, to render an independent report on the issues raised by the controversy over the index.

Labor's active committee member was from the AFL but its research staff was CIO. The staff—numbering forty at the height of its activity—was drawn from the research departments of the national CIO, the United Steelworkers, the United Electrical Workers (CIO at the time, later expelled), and the United Auto Workers. It was headed by the Steelworkers' research director, Harold Ruttenberg, a graduate of the University of Pittsburgh, who although scarcely 30 years old, had already made a name for himself as co-author, with Clinton Golden, of *Dynamics of Industrial Democracy*, and as one of the "bright young men" in the camp of industrial unionism. He had been on leave from the Steelworkers since December 1942 to serve, in a dollar-a-year capacity, as Assistant Director for Manpower in the Steel Division of the War Production Board. In April 1944, before the index controversy was over, he left this position but continued to work for the labor members of the Committee. Rather apart from this CIO research staff was Margaret Scattergood, AFL statistician. She did not participate in the formulation of the labor research staff's conclusions.

Davis as Chairman

Those who felt the Little Steel formula was endangered by criticism of the index and who saw the Cost of Living Committee as a delaying device were swift to remark that the longer the Committee deliberated the longer would be formula be secure. But Chairman Davis, confident of strong administration support for the formula in any real crisis, never supposed it was seriously threatened by criticism of the index. There is no evidence that he acted in any way to delay the action of the Cost of Living Committee.

Yet he did not hurry it. From previous experience with fact-finding committees he knew that their work was time consuming; he did not expect this one to be an exception. None of the Committee members, including himself, were personally equipped to examine and judge the BLS's sampling procedure, quality specifications, and the like. Experts would obviously have to be taken on at some point in the project. In fact, from the start, members of the WLB staff urged Davis to secure experts for his own benefit. He delayed until an opportune moment, preferring first to see how far (if at all) toward consensus the Committee could move by itself.

The first order of Committee business, for Davis, was affording labor ample opportunity to put on record the complaints which had led to the formation of the Committee. He sat back, during the first month or two of meetings, retaining his formal control, speaking his mind occasionally, but giving Meany and Thomas full rein to propose paths of action for the Committee and to present statistics and evidence in support of their point of view.

B. LABOR RECEIVES A HEARING AND DELIVERS A PUNCH

Meany's Questions on the Index

Labor took—or was given—the lead at the first meeting of the President's Committee on the Cost of Living, held on November 8, 1943. The group unanimously accepted for consideration a list of questions which AFL member George Meany proposed for investigation. They were:

1. What is the cost of living (October 1943) compared to (a) January 1, 1941, (b) May 15, 1942, (c) September 15, 1942? *
2. How is the index figure arrived at?
3. Should there be any changes made in the present method of securing or computing the figures? This is to include method of collecting data and choice of component parts of index.
4. What, if any, concrete suggestions have we for improving the method of securing figures?

* (a) and (b) were the initial and terminal dates of the period used for the Little Steel formula; (c) was the stabilization date mentioned in the Stabilization Act of October 2, 1942.

Two weeks were set aside during which Committee members, if they wished, were to refer the questions for study and comment to experts not connected with the staff of the War Labor Board. A press release including the questions was then issued.

Two days later, the Committee met with Secretary of Labor Frances Perkins, Assistant Secretary Daniel W. Tracy, and Acting Commissioner of Labor Statistics A. Ford Hinrichs, to talk over the work before the Committee and the form which BLS participation should take. It was agreed that the Bureau should prepare and submit a statement on the derivation of the index, in answer to the second question on Meany's list. Hinrichs was asked to meet with the Committee on November 23 to discuss any issues raised by the statement.

This procedure, however, did not fully satisfy the Labor Department officials. On November 20 Miss Perkins wrote Davis, suggesting two further steps. Public hearings should be held on the index and Hinrichs should testify at them she said, explaining, "If the problem is one of illumination of the public, this would be the best way to do it." Second, a BLS representative should be present at all Committee meetings at which the index was discussed and Bureau staff should have access to transcripts of the meetings and to any exhibits filed. In this way they could keep informed of questions raised and get an opportunity, as the Secretary said, "to clarify our procedure before fixed prejudices are established."

These requests may have been prompted by Hinrichs' conclusion that the Committee's existence made impossible any BLS campaign of public enlightenment. The presence on the Cost of Living Committee of two labor leaders of a rank hitherto inaccessible to the BLS appears also to have been a consideration to the Department. If it could become an active party to publicly staged proceedings, even though cast in the role of a defendant in litigation, as it were, the BLS might hope to present its side of the story once again and, in any event, reach a wider audience than heretofore.

Davis saved his answer to Miss Perkins until the Committee's meeting on November 23. He, as a matter of fact, did not feel that public hearings would lead to more understanding on a matter about which newspaper reports had usually echoed and exaggerated disagreement. Public hearings would conflict, moreover, with his aim of securing a free interchange of ideas —particularly labor's—on the Committee. The presence of a BLS official at meetings might also inhibit this.

The Bureau's written statement on the nature of the index reached the Committee and was discussed at length—with four CIO research directors present—the day before Hinrichs was scheduled to appear. Meany opened with the comment that since the BLS statement, as well as the Mills Committee Report, said the index did not purport to measure the cost of living in the popular sense of the phrase, he no longer had any particular interest in its past behavior. His intention now, he said, was to propose a partnership between the Committee and the Labor Department "to make the index do the things it has not done." To that end he was prepared with a tentative memorandum entitled *Practices which could come about as a result of co-operation between this committee and the BLS*. It listed areas of price change in which more detailed data were needed and where studies could be made by the Bureau to check labor's view that prices had risen more than the index indicated.

A less conciliatory attitude was reflected in the questions which the CIO member proposed to put to Hinrichs the following day. Directed entirely to the omissions or limitations of the index, they asked, first, to what extent the index failed to reflect increased expenditures required of workers and their families because of ten specified types of abnormal wartime conditions; and second, whether the index, "even as an average," reflected the overall trend among special permanent types of "communities" such as textiles and low income groups.

To the second query, of course, the answer had always been "No." To the first, the reply might be "Yes," "No," or "Only to some extent," depending on whether the abnormality affected the sampling, the weighting, or the price quotations used by the Bureau. Both questions indicated clearly that the concept of the index as a measure of average change in unit retail prices was either not understood or else ignored by those who had prepared the memorandum.

After some discussion of Thomas's list the Committee agreed that talk with Hinrichs the next day would center on two questions: Does the BLS index today reflect changes in the cost of living to the same extent that it did prior to Pearl Harbor? If not, can it be adjusted to do so?

The BLS Before the President's Committee

Hinrichs and Mrs. Wickens appeared before the full Cost of Living Committee on November 23. Miss Perkins's letter to Davis was discussed first. Davis assured Hinrichs of his desire to obtain all the facts in the case and to have the BLS sit in on all the factual discussions. He left BLS participation on an invitation basis and rejected public hearings as premature, saying

. . . I surely think that in this sort of an inquiry where one bureau is really dealing with another, we ought to have a common understanding about what the public hearing is for, and what the scope is going to be when we have it.

Hinrichs accepted this statement, saying that his Department's major goal in requesting a public hearing had been to enable him to speak with Meany; this had now been accomplished since the latter was present at the Committee meeting.

Meany immediately set a contrapuntal theme, asking Hinrichs,

You say . . . [the cost of living index] is designed to measure changes in the prices paid for goods and services by city families with moderate incomes. It is a price index—not a measure of changes in the total amount spent for family living.

The point is, can we, in co-operation with you, or can you, in co-operation with us, make it a measure of changes in the amount spent for family living?

No simple answer to this question—except perhaps a blunt "No"—was possible. A retail price index could not be changed into a measure of family expenditures without losing its former identity completely. A retail price index was needed and used for many purposes besides the one now in controversy, and the BLS had no authorization or desire to give it up. Funds for the development of an index of family expenditures were not available or even dimly in sight. Finally, most economists and statisticians in and out of government—as well as stabilization policy officials—agreed that only an index of unit price changes was the proper measure for comparisons with wage rate changes. An index of family expenditures had to be matched against a measure of family income, not wage rates.

With these and probably other factors in mind Hinrichs and Mrs. Wickens made no direct reply to Meany's questions. They tried instead to point out how far the index went in describing wartime conditions for families whose consumption habits had not changed. Meany found their response evasive. A fruitless interchange of union criticism and BLS explanations was concluded when he said:

. . . I have no desire to criticize the figures of the index . . .

I would like to explore the possibility of adding things to the index that the index does not do. Of course, Mr. Hinrichs takes the position that the index does everything that we need to find the total amount spent for family living.

To this, Hinrichs and Mrs. Wickens replied, "No, no!"

R. J. Thomas's questions came next. The BLS officials explained that to alter the index so that it would reflect more fully some of the abnormal wartime conditions enumerated by Thomas would require an extensive and expensive revision beyond the Bureau's financial ability. Such a revision would also change the basic nature of the index because some of the changes which the unions wished included were not unit price increases as defined by the Bureau but were associated with increased worker income and standards of living.

"No"—said Meany,

. . . You see, you come right back to one thing which has been predetermined in your mind, that the rise in the cost of living is due to the fact that the workers get more money . . .

We are entering this thing with the hope in mind and with a spirit of co-operation, and you are saying you can't do what we want to do. You haven't advanced one real reason except that it would cost money. I think that is something for future consideration.

I think we should try to determine whether these things should be done or not, not on the basis of what they cost but on the basis of whether they are necessary to do the very thing you claim that you intended to do in this index but which you are not doing, by your own admission.

Now, if it costs money and Congress tells us they won't give you the money, that is just too bad, that is not your fault or our fault. However, we should meet that at the proper time.

Meany, for his part, refused for a while to discuss the questions which Hinrichs and Mrs. Wickens kept urging as primary: to what use would a new or revised index be put and would it not be more advisable to develop a supplementary measure to reflect the types of price changes the unions wished to see included? The BLS, asserted the AFL leader, should revise the index without asking how it would be used. Finally, toward the close of the meeting he answered the question and revealed that he shared the prevailing misconception of the relationship between the Little Steel formula and the index. In this connection the following interchange then took place:

MEANY: You ask us why we want this. I will tell you why we want it. The President's letter to us said why we want it. The people of the country, first, want to know what the cost of living is. Why do they want to know what the cost of living is? Because the War Labor Board has tied the cost of living to wages.

HINRICHS: No. You have tied the cost of living in May 1942 to wages.

MEANY: That is right, and it is still tied to wages.

HINRICHS: Our index . . .

MEANY: Your index is eight points above our cost of living because the WLB has said, "While we still tie the cost of living to wages, we will not move the wages up to the exact figure of the cost of living because the spread is not great enough . . ."

The WLB said that the spread is not great enough and that this sacrifice must be made by the workers, they must allow the cost of living to rise a certain number of percentage points above their actual income. But they indicated that if it continued to rise they would have to do something about it.

Now, we are hearing protests from all over the country that this index does not truly reflect the cost of living. We don't say that this index doesn't truly reflect prices, we haven't said that officially, although I privately think that is so. I think you could do a much better job than what you are doing in your method of getting information. I don't agree with the limited cities that you take; I don't agree with your method of getting prices. . . .

I don't think the ASA Mills Committee has done such a good job when they took 200 stores out of God knows how many millions in this country in order to measure what you had done with regard to prices.

However, I am not talking about any of those things; I am not talking about any criticism of what you have done within the limitations that you have established for yourselves. What I am saying is that you should remove some of these limitations and try to take in some of these things that are annoying our people, that we say do not reflect themselves in this [index]. I think you are under an obligation to either tell us that you will do this, or give us some definite reason why it can't be done, because if you don't do it, I don't know who is going to do it . . .

Now, all we are asking for is your co-operation to find out these things. . . .

HINRICHS: But, you see, I can't determine, in the Bureau of Labor Statistics, how you are going to use that material. It makes a world of difference how you are going to use it as to how I put it together. . . .

May I point out something to you, Mr. Meany?

If you try to tie wages to the cost of living in that fashion you may be precipitating a rather dangerous situation in the event of a deflation of wages and prices. You had a terrific fall at the end of the last war.

MEANY: Mr. Hinrichs, we are not trying to tie it at all; it is already tied. We didn't do it, we voted against it. We are accepting that condition as we find it . . .

WALDRON: What you are discussing, now it seems to me, is wage policy and that is a question for the War Labor Board.

HINRICHS: Certainly. All I need to know is enough about wage policy to know what kind of statistics will help answer the questions as to wage policy . . . I need to have some concern with the way in which the index is compiled and the way in which it is going to behave in both good times and in bad. That is, it is rather a dangerous policy to . . .

MEANY: But you see, Mr. Hinrichs, we are only concerned at the present time with just one portion of . . . [time], from January 1941 up to the present moment.

HINRICHS: I quite understand that, and yet my interest has got to run far enough so that I can produce a consistent kind of story. I can't construct an index which will go up when prices are going up and won't go down.

MEANY: You are saying what you can do and you are thinking of long terms. Unfortunately, we are dealing with a specific set of months, from January 1941 up to the present time.

Now, couldn't you just reconstruct your thinking a little bit and help us on that particular line and forget about the long pull?

When the war is over we won't object in the slightest if you go back to what you are doing now. (Laughter)

HINRICHS: But that is something I can't do.

BATT: He wants his cake and eat it too. (Laughter)

. . . .

WICKENS: I think the story is one of supplementary information. I do think for your own purposes you want to put it in another package. Don't graft it on to this thing; you don't need to.

. . . .

WICKENS: You see, this thing [the BLS index] has its uses. They are limited, they may not be what you want for this purpose, but for the OPA and for like purposes, for example, they are very good.

. . . .

THOMAS: For our purposes, up until the time the War Labor Board started, I didn't care what report you put out for the cost of living, it didn't make any difference; and I am not going to care when this war is over. I will get along all right.

Disagreement on Emphasis of the Committee's Report

Following this meeting, the research efforts of the two labor members were merged. They appeared at the Committee's fifth meeting on December 10, 1944, with a joint report entitled *Costs and expenditures not now reflected in the BLS index and recommended for investigation and report*. The two sources of such expenditures were listed as "altered merchandising practices" and "wartime living conditions." The former covered hidden price increases meriting inclusion if not already included in the index; the latter was likelier to embrace changes conceptually unrelated to the existing index. The joint statement ended with a preliminary report, based on past union discussions with BLS staff, on the possibility of obtaining through surveys and special BLS studies data necessary to supplement the existing index for union wage policy purposes. This was in line with Hinrichs's suggestions to unions, for the past ten or eleven months, that other material beside the index be used. The report recognized that the BLS would need to obtain additional funds for such studies. Close collaboration between the BLS and the unions was urged. The memorandum noted that its contents had not been reviewed by the BLS.

Chairman Davis, in his turn, was ready with an outline of what he thought the Committee's report to the President might say. It began with the assertion that in peacetime the index satisfactorily reflected the changes in the price of certain basic items purchased by "thrifty families" and that in wartime the index "no doubt" reflected "pretty well" the changes in the pressure on the budget of a wage earner with a stable income who had been able to carry on his normal mode of living with only such adjustments of living costs as were necessary to accommodate himself to average changes in the prices of staple goods and of necessary substitutes. The Committee report, Davis went on, should include a careful statement of what the index was, how it was compiled, and the adjustments that had been made to keep up with the wartime changes in buying habits, in quality, in availability, and the like. The extent to which the index "reflected the squeeze," since January 1, 1941, on the normal budget of the average consumer at the income levels to which the index was relevant, should also be indicated, but Davis continued

> In doing this there should be frank recognition of the limitations of the index. The ways in which a wage earner's cost of living may have been affected by the war, but which effects are not reflected in the index, should be clearly pointed out (including here the items brought forward by the Labor members which have not been or cannot be reflected in the index).

Finally, the Committee report should conclude with consideration of the possibility of a new BLS survey of purchasing habits. On the basis of such a survey a supplementary wartime index intended to reflect extraordinary changes in what a thrifty wage earner had to spend to get along under war conditions might be set up if such a measure could "effectively supplement" the BLS index.

Apart perhaps from the implied proposal that the Committee estimate the margin of error in the index by indicating to what extent it "reflected" the wartime "squeeze," this outline was one to which the BLS could take little exception. The industry member present pronounced the statement "very fair." Meany argued for the emphasis of the joint labor proposal, saying that the Committee's report should give more space to the failures of the index than to the extent to which it had met the wartime situation. Davis replied that there was a "great deal of danger of unfavorable repercussions" if the report was not "pretty objective" about the index. He did not want the country to think that the average working man was asking for or that the Committee wanted to give him protection from all of the hardships of the war. He did not think that the Committee could come to any definite conclusion on the validity of labor allegations about the index.

Meany then indicated his tentative agreement with Davis's report as a crystallization of the job of the Committee and a practical method of approach. He wanted a day or so to look it over, however, in order to come back with some possible revisions. After that, he felt Mrs. Wickens and Hinrichs should be called in to give their reaction to the outlined report.

> Maybe at this point they will have some ideas or will not like what we are going to do. . . .
>
> They may tell us they can't do it . . . I still think we have got an obligation to call attention to those things, things which they can measure, which are not now measured.
>
> If they need money, this Committee should say, "You should have the money."

Superficially, the outlook on December 10, 1943, seemed promising for a Committee report of the nature Davis desired. But when the Committee reconvened for its sixth meeting, on December 13, the prospect had changed. Meany was no longer "inclined to agree" with Davis' proposal. He gave no reason, simply saying that he had thought the matter over. Factors which may well have influenced his thinking were the gathering force of the CIO attack on the Little Steel formula in wage cases before the WLB and the findings and conclusions on the index being reached by the labor members' research staff under Harold Ruttenberg. The latter—who was also working on part of the USA brief for the *Basic Steel* case—spent the better part of a week in December at Faith Williams's office at the BLS going over with her the work sheets on which the consumption weights for the index's 200 or so items had been computed. Although not a statistician, Ruttenberg left Miss Williams with the impression that he had grasped her explanations and was sympathetic with the Bureau's statistical problems.

Whatever the relative weight of these and other factors in Meany's thinking, he had reverted to his previous negative approach. The Committee, he said, should say the index did not measure changes in the cost of living adequately and should explore these "failures" in great detail. Davis soon ceased pressing his own proposed report and Meany finally said, "It looks like the labor side has more or less got to carry the ball on this." He volunteered to prepare a joint labor report on union reasons for feeling the index did not adequately reflect actual wartime conditions. The group agreed to await such a tentative labor report; it would provide industry and public members with something to "shoot at." Hinrichs would not be recalled until after this, when there was something definite for him to see. Batt proposed to speak with the research people of several national trade associations about "the story from the supply side."

Labor Prepares a Report on the Index

When the Committee reconvened on January 6, 1944, a letter from Thomas to Davis was circulated stating that labor's report would not be ready for two weeks because the CIO share would take some time longer. Davis announced he was being pressured by reporters for news of the Committee's decisions. He tried to secure unanimous consent for a statement indicating that assembling the information for a Committee report was taking longer than the expected sixty days because the labor side was asking for more time to turn in its report. Any statement like that, Meany replied, would mean the end of the Committee and a solo report by labor. No agreement could be reached and no statement was made.

Indications of the nature of the labor members' report were given by such comments of Meany's and Thomas' as

> . . . the research people of our unions . . . have carried forward their studies to the point where they are convinced that the rise in the cost of

living, unreflected by the Bureau of Labor Statistics index, is very large and susceptible of unanswerable proof. . . . The more we have dug into this thing, the more my research people feel there have been some hellish discrepancies in the Department of Labor figures. . . . I am going to attempt to prove . . . that when the Little Steel formula was set up it was set up on a fallacy, and we think we can prove it. . . .

Neither Davis nor the industry members appeared likely to have reports ready when the Meany-Thomas report came in and Thomas found this difficult to accept. He protested to Meany,

THOMAS: But, George, the thing I had in mind, it don't look quite fair to me for you and I to bring in a report and lay it on the table for rebuttal if we don't have a chance to look at something too.

. . . . . .

MEANY: The point is this, Tommy, I don't look at it as if they are going to tear it apart. Perhaps they won't agree with everything that is in it, but perhaps we can reach a report on which we are substantially in agreement that will make a contribution to this problem. . . . If we can't, then there are going to be two reports, a minority report and a majority report and we want to avoid that.

. . . . . .

THOMAS: The point is, in the report I am bringing in, George, I am getting the facts so damn clear that I don't think anybody can take those facts and tear them apart. I just don't think it can be done.

DAVIS: Why should you worry, then, about it?

THOMAS: I want a chance to tear some of yours apart.

MEANY: I don't think the approach is bad. . . .

. . . . . .

DAVIS: All right. Tommy says I am neglecting my opportunity on the Committee. I am interested and I would like to do something, but there is nothing that I can think of that I can do on . . . [errors in the index]. If you fellows have found out that these figures are wrong, there is no use of my nosing around and trying to find out what you have found out when you are going to tell me in a couple of weeks. . . .

Davis indicated that he would try to work up an outline or draft of those sections of the final Committee report concerned with the method by which the index was compiled and the extent to which it reflected changes due to the war. The index, he reminded the labor members, was not a thermometer but more like a barometer. But, retorted Thomas,

This thermometer is broke down. It ain't indicating the pressure.

DAVIS: That is the second point. You say this thermometer has got a hole; it leaks.

THOMAS: It has a hole that you and I can walk through.

DAVIS: Side by side. If we go through side by side it will be all right with me.

Most of the important discussions of Committee procedure had previously been off the record. At this meeting Davis's assistant, Waldron, attempted to clarify whatever agreement there was on future procedure with regard to the BLS. He understood, he said, that there would be no Committee report after the labor material was submitted until there had really been a discussion between the labor men and the BLS. Meany agreed, with one modification. He said:

The steps were that the labor men were to bring in a proposed report for the Committee in full. The Committee was to discuss that report and see if it could agree on a tentative report. If the Committee could agree on a tentative report, then before that report was made finally, we were to call Mr. Hinrichs in and discuss it with him, but the labor report was not to be discussed with Mr. Hinrichs until this Committee either said to the labor boys, "We can't go along with you" or, "We can," because at that point we will have to decide for ourselves what we are going to do, and that will depend on the action of this Committee. Then we bring in Mr. Hinrichs and discuss it with him.

WALDRON: . . . the main point is that there is no doubt that before the thing is issued there will be another meeting with Hinrichs.

DAVIS: I think we all have the same understanding.

This understanding actually differed from Meany's suggestion a month earlier, on December 10, 1943, that the BLS be called in to talk over Davis's outline of a proposed Committee report. It should be noted, too, that there was no more talk of compiling an alternative or supplementary index to the cost of living series.

During the next three weeks the CIO research staff continued to work on the material it had collected, combining it with a small amount of material accumulated by the AFL research staff into one joint report. As time drew close to the eighth meeting of the Committee, scheduled for the afternoon of January 25, 1944, Davis heard that the union report would definitely go beyond discussing what the index did not measure into an attack on the way in which it measured the items covered. Consequently, he did no work on his own area of the Committee's report; the next step for the public and industry members would be to take a thorough look at labor's contentions.

Labor Estimates the Error in the Index—the Meany-Thomas Report

The labor members' joint report was presented to the President's Committee by R. J. Thomas on the afternoon of January 25, 1944. Meany was vacationing in Florida at the time. The impact of the report on the other members of the Committee, and a degree removed, on the BLS, was somewhat broken by the action of the Steelworkers' president and CIO chief, Philip Murray, on the morning of the 25th, in dramatically announcing that the CIO had found that prices had gone up twice as high as the BLS index indicated.

Murray did this in the course of testifying before the so-called Senate "White Collar" Committee.[5] Hinrichs was also present and scheduled to testify immediately following the CIO president. Although astonished by the nature of the CIO statistical conclusions and by the importance Murray was giving them in his attack on the Little Steel formula, the BLS chief made no reply to Murray when he rose to present the material on living costs and white collar groups which he had prepared for the subcommittee. As a technician he could not say anything—even when the union estimate was obviously in error—without a review of the computations underlying it. And as an officer of the Department of Labor he did not wish to enter into a public debate with a labor leader.

That afternoon, at the eighth meeting of the Cost of Living Committee, R. J. Thomas, accompanied by Harold Ruttenberg, submitted a mimeographed preliminary draft, without tables or charts, of the joint labor report. It was, as indicated by its title—*Recommended Report for the Presidential Committee on the Cost of Living*—a labor bid to write the Committee's report. On the basis of a rather detailed estimate of the rise in prices of some cost of living items in some areas the report's major conclusion was that the cost of living had risen by 43.5 per cent between January 1, 1941, and December 1943, a period for which the comparable BLS figure was 23.4 per cent.

Davis gave no indication of his reaction to this estimate. He immediately proposed that copies of the report be given to industry and the BLS to give them "a chance to pick it to pieces if it is vulnerable." Thomas balked, saying that "this is it" as far as labor was concerned and that labor could not wait for intensive consideration by the other two parties because the report was going to be used in the *General Motors, Basic Steel*, and other WLB cases then pending. The material could be submitted to the General Motors panel as it was, Davis replied, reminding Thomas and Ruttenberg that in any event the War Labor Board no longer had power to change the Little Steel formula. If the labor estimate of the rise in living costs proved correct and was accepted it would certainly change the whole complexion of the discussion of wages, he continued, but the essential step now was public discussion of the estimates according to "the good old-fashioned American system of making decisions."

Thomas wanted the public and industry members to take their positions on the labor report within the week so that he could feel free to release it publicly, use it in WLB cases, and send a copy to the President. He "did not care" what the final report of the Committee

[5] This was the Subcommittee on Wartime Health and Education of the Senate Committee on Education and Labor. It was headed by Senator Claude Pepper (Democrat) of Florida.

as a whole was if it was not the AFL-CIO report.

There was some discussion of the propriety of labor's plan to send a copy of its *Recommended Report* to the President. Batt, conscious that the industry members had as yet submitted no material, felt the public would misinterpret this move and think the report was the Committee's. Davis was unconcerned over submission to the President; he said,

> The President will turn it over [to us] and say, "Get this thing thrashed out; tell me what it is."

Immediately after the meeting Davis sent copies of the Meany-Thomas report to Hinrichs and the Mills Committee for their reactions. Public opinion and discussion of it were bound to be heated. He personally was awaiting its evaluation by the BLS before taking any further steps.

The Meany-Thomas (AFL-CIO) report presented the results of a study of the BLS index procedure and of the trend of certain retail prices in certain localities made by the research staff of the labor members. Its most dramatic feature was the conclusion

> that the cost of living has actually risen by at least 43.5 per cent since January 1941 . . . that the BLS Cost of Living index is not an adequate instrument for making wage adjustments . . . [that] sole reliance upon it will result in continued serious injustice to wage earners and lower-salaried workers.

The proof offered for this assertion consisted of statistical and arithmetical procedures of several kinds, together with data from a multiplicity of sources—union food price surveys in 10 cities; interviews with housewives and officials; newspaper statements; publications and unpublished memorandums of the Departments of Agriculture and Commerce, the Office of Price Administration and the Federal Reserve Board; the *Wall Street Journal*; and old and new Montgomery Ward and Sears, Roebuck catalogues. For three of the component indexes—clothing, rent, and housefurnishings—the union research people, as Table 1 indicates, found that prices had gone up more than twice as fast as the BLS data showed.

Table 1. PERCENTAGE PRICE INCREASES, JANUARY 1941-DECEMBER 1943, BLS LIVING COST COMPONENT INDEXES AND MEANY-THOMAS REPORT

	Percentage price increase	
Commodity group	*BLS index*	*Meany-Thomas estimate*
Food	40.2	74.2
Clothing	33.7	72.2
Rent	3.0	15.0
Fuel, etc.	8.6	8.6
House furnishings	27.8	62.0
Miscellaneous	15.9	15.9
ALL ITEMS	23.4	43.5

The labor report's observations and conclusions were by no means confined to technical matters. Basically, but not always explicitly, its concept of the "cost of living" was at variance with that of the BLS. It held to the assumption that the BLS index, or any cost of living index, should reflect some if not all wartime changes in the manner of living and in types of family expenditures. This was apparent in the logic of its chief argument which can be summarized briefly in two steps.

First, the argument ran, the index failed to include important items in the worker's cost of living such as extra expenses incurred when wives went to work, or the cost of moving to war centers. Although emphasizing these factors the Meany-Thomas report did not undertake to measure them.

Second, the report asserted, the index did not measure accurately even the price changes it claimed to measure because: (1) the prices collected by the Bureau's field agents were often not those actually paid by workers' families; (2) the prices of items included in the index market basket had risen less than the prices of those not included but also purchased in significant quantities by workers' families (the so-called imputed [6] items); (3) BLS prices understated the increase in the cost of living because the quality of available goods had deteriorated and because lower grade items (the low-end lines) formerly purchased were no longer available; and (4) prices had risen faster in small cities which the Bureau did not cover than in the large cities which it did cover.

[6] Imputation is discussed in Appendix A.

The price rise estimates in the labor report were interwoven with a series of charges (both outright and implied) of "politics," poor faith, inaccuracy, and dishonesty on the part of the BLS. The OPA, said the report, concentrated for political reasons on controlling and subsidizing the items priced in the BLS index (watching the index "like a hawk"); conversely, the BLS did not price items which were not controlled. It continued:

> Whether all this is the result of design or accident has not been reviewed in this report, although . . . examples, which repeatedly come to the fore, are mentioned for possible further inquiry.

With respect to remedying what it called the index's "deficiencies" it was the Meany-Thomas contention that the Bureau had had a choice in these matters and could have reduced the "deficiencies" *if* it had chosen to. It had not so chosen, the report implied, because it wished, with the Administration, to keep the index down.

Along this line, too, was the accusation that the Bureau was giving too much weight to increased worker earnings in distinguishing between voluntary and forced up-trading, that is, that the BLS was attributing to increased income and a consequent rise in the standard of living (irrelevant to the index) the higher prices paid by workers which Meany and Thomas felt should have been classified as forced price rises and included in the index. Voluntary uptrading, they conceded, should not be reflected in the index, but it was held of very much less importance than forced uptrading. This charge was important because it implied that the Bureau was not objective but was deliberately lending support to the "wage stabilization camp"—the OPA, the United States Chamber of Commerce, and others—at a time when the unions contended, on the basis of their interpretation of the trend of hourly wage rates, that real income was declining and wage stabilization was an unjust freeze. Here the labor members' staff was talking loosely and interchangeably about different concepts of an index and criticizing the normal exercise of judgment by the cost of living staff.

BLS Reaction to the Meany-Thomas Report

At the BLS the main argument of the union report evoked no great surprise. Various portions of it had been presented in varying forms often before, although never so elaborately. The large quantitative estimate of error in the index and the charges of political subservience were, however, new and astonishing. Harold Ruttenberg's close and apparently sympathetic attention to Faith Williams's explanations about the index early in December 1943 had prepared Miss Williams and her associates for a union document which invited a professional exchange of views. They were confronted instead with an elaborately supported political attack.

An organization traditionally devoted to the impartial collection of facts and to the reduction of error to the smallest possible magnitude, and unaccustomed to the rhetoric and vehemence of union briefs, could not but find the union statistics and charges appalling. A number of BLS staff members in responsible positions felt deeply outraged, personally and professionally, by the data and contentions of the labor report. This was "hitting below the belt." And they became apprehensive over possible repercussions on their own reputations and on the good name of the Bureau and index throughout the economic and statistical world. Yet they could not immediately undertake an appraisal and public refutation of the union material because the appendix containing the union's price data and other related source material was not ready for distribution and scrutiny. BLS officials held tight, waiting for the Meany-Thomas statistical tables to arrive and hoping the labor report would not reach the press before they could reply to it. But this was not to be.

Release of the Meany-Thomas Report—and Aftermath

Meany and Thomas released their report to the newspapers on January 30, 1944. The union statistics and assertions were generally given front page space together with statements by Davis, Batt, and Horton that the labor report was "not in any sense a report of the [President's] Committee" but was merely part of all the relevant data to be considered before the Committee made its final report to the President. A statement by Hinrichs in support of the index was quoted at some length on a back page of the New York *Times*.

These publicity moves led to widespread debate among the various groups interested in the accuracy of the cost of living index—government officials, businessmen, unions, professional economists and statisticians, and newspaper commentators. Although the statistical accuracy of the Meany-Thomas estimate of error was an open question in the minds of many responsible persons during the weeks before any statistical rejoinder could be made by the BLS, the report became, in the view of some commentators, a formidable "big gun" and a convincing "rationale" in the union campaign to break existing wage rate ceilings. It was one of the five documents making up the USA brief in the *Basic Steel* case certified to the WLB by the Secretary of Labor on January 24, 1944. Another one of the five—ironically—was a study of steel workers' income and expenditure on which Miss Williams and other BLS staff members had been authorized by Hinrichs to give the USA's Pittsburgh office considerable personal assistance in November 1943.

When the Cost of Living Committee met again on February 2, 1944, its members were faced by the questions: where do we stand, and where do we go? Very soon after they were all seated around the conference table, Davis rejected Meany's oft-repeated and much quoted statement that the labor report was a *proposed* report for the entire Committee. It was simply material submitted for the Committee's fact-finding operation, he said. Labor's action in publicly releasing the report, instead of waiting for all viewpoints to be submitted, appeared to have deprived the Committee of the opportunity to be regarded as impartial and to turn out a unanimous report, as he had hoped it would. Now, he remarked, he was "on the spot"—in the position of an umpire between two partial groups. He felt that the Committee needed a professional staff to review the material which was presented to it and he asked for suggestions.

Why not appoint a tripartite research staff and "preserve the belligerent status of the Committee," asked Meany. Davis ruled out this half-facetious suggestion. It would be "vamoosing and leaving it to three experts . . . passing the buck." In his view, one or two economists acceptable to all, heading up an advisory staff would be best. The economist group would not submit any report but simply facts. *Prima facie*, he felt the BLS index still was right. If it was wrong he wanted evidence of it. He and Batt also showed concern that the BLS receive adequate opportunity to answer the Meany-Thomas criticisms before any further steps were taken by the Committee and he went on to say (using the word "Board" absent-mindedly in the place of "Committee"),

> I am going to take anything that the Labor Department has to say, and I am going to take anything you fellows submit, and bring it into a five-man Board, and I am going to say, "Here is the first fact."
>
> I am going to repeat my well-known dogma and say let's see if we can't agree on it. If we can't agree on it we must be ignorant. We will continue our research till we enlighten ourselves.
>
> I have no hallucinations that you can possibly convince the country of a non-partisan attitude of this Board in any way except by a unanimous report of the Board. Now I am an idealist, as you fellows know. I am getting pretty old to be an idealist, but I still think if we have the meetings and really get down to it I think we could come to a unanimous report, because it is a factual thing that's put up to us.

Meany and Ruttenberg (representing R. J. Thomas), were pointedly uninterested in Committee research for more facts. The AFL-CIO report contained the facts, they said. In any case, only an "open-minded" research group would be acceptable to them and they forthwith ruled out statisticians from the Federal government, the National Industrial Conference Board, and the American Statistical Association.

The appointment of a research staff to consider the Meany-Thomas report was an "extraordinary proceeding," said Ruttenberg. Of a tripartite group, he pointed out, only one section had submitted a study and now the chairman was going to appoint a committee of experts to consider this study. Replied Davis,

> I am considerably disturbed by the evidence of reluctance on your part to have these facts examined.
>
> It certainly doesn't add to their conviction to me.

Ruttenberg for the first time furnished copies of the statistical tables and exhibits for the union report at this meeting. Davis immediately sent a set over to Hinrichs; he also asked the industry representatives to examine and report on the union material.

By the time the group met again on February 9, to appoint a Committee research staff, the labor members had decided to abstain entirely from such action. Davis soliloquized that he found himself closer to being an umpire at each succeeding meeting of what had begun as a factual inquiry. This was an unenviable position, he thought, and contrary to the purpose for which the President had appointed the Committee. Under the circumstances he proposed to consider and subsequently report to the Committee what next step the group should take. In the meanwhile, he suggested that the individual members of the Committee continue to study the labor members' report. Apparently, at this time, Davis was considering the submission of an *ad hoc* report to the President on the stalemate in the Committee. To that end, he asked Waldron to prepare a summary of the events of the first ten Committee meetings. This reached his desk on February 16.

On February 17, Meany and Thomas publicly transmitted their report on the index to President Roosevelt. They had been displeased over the fact that their document had been before the Committee almost three weeks without a formal presentation to the President. Nothing in the President's instructions to Davis or in the Committee's few decisions on procedure provided for such a unilateral presentation, but other considerations governed the union chiefs. They foresaw that a report by the whole Committee was unlikely to be ready until after the WLB decision in the *Basic Steel* case. This obviously would not be for many months. But panel hearings on the case were scheduled to begin soon and the Meany-Thomas report was a major portion of the steel union's argument. The publicity which would result from the submittal to the White House could no longer be foregone.

In a transmitting letter to the President the labor members pointed out that as far as they knew none of the other members of the President's Committee had as yet prepared any material on the index. They were convinced that nothing further could be expected of the Committee "for some months to come" and they concluded,

> We do not feel that we would be meeting our obligation as members of the Committee or as representatives of employee organizations, if we were not to transmit this report to you at this time. . . .
>
> Our report reveals that the Bureau of Labor Statistics, with full understanding, has permitted its index to be used as a basis for measuring the rise in the cost of living. The Bureau of Labor Statistics is aware of the fact that such use of its index reflects the gravest type of injustice that could possibly be perpetrated by it upon the American people. The very failure of the Bureau of Labor Statistics to make clear that its index does not adequately reflect the realistic and actual rise in the cost of living subjects the Bureau to very serious charges. . . .
>
> In all fairness to the American people, we urgently request that there be an intensive investigation of the part that has been played by the Bureau of Labor Statistics in the publication of an index which distorts the basic facts of our wartime living costs.

Davis, the industry members of the President's Committee, and the BLS staff had been aware that Meany and Thomas were likely to send their report to the President. Still, the labor members' gesture was annoying. Davis, Secretary Perkins, and Hinrichs all issued statements in reply. Davis called the transmittal a "surprising procedure," particularly in view of the fact that the Committee's inquiry was following the procedural steps which up till then had been proposed by the labor members and approved by the entire group. He outlined the stages that had been agreed upon; Meany and Thomas, he noted, had been given adequate time for completing their material but they were not allowing the BLS any time to analyze the union findings. It seemed, Davis concluded,

> that the report submitted by the labor members would be of no possible use until it is subjected to critical examinaiton, since it is clearly a partisan report.

Hinrichs, according to the New York *Times*, stated that the BLS had been unable to move until it received the union statistical material but that its reply to the union findings would be forthcoming shortly. Secretary Perkins issued a statement defending the integrity of the Bureau and the cost of living figures, asserting that they were the most accurately prepared of any country, and adding that,

> in the long run, labor had gained from the existence of such an index because it gave a base line for collective bargaining agreements which otherwise might be drawn out indefinitely through arguments about price levels.

Allowing that Meany and Thomas had every right to argue for wage increases the Secretary concluded that

> they should not, by misrepresentation, seek to discredit the impartial work of a Government fact-finding agency.

The President, as Davis had once predicted, turned labor's report back to the Chairman, asking him to draft an answer to Meany and Thomas's letter. Davis drafted two alternative replies for the President's signature; both said that it was not in accord with the purpose for which the Cost of Living Committee was appointed for the President to give consideration at the time to the labor members' material. The more censorious draft added that the President would await the "considered findings" of the full Committee after the labor report had been subjected to analysis in the light of all the factual material put before the Committee by the industry members, the BLS, or the chairman. In an accompanying letter to the President Davis re-emphasized what he had said about Committee procedure in his newspaper statement and concluded,

> I see nothing to be gained by a piecemeal consideration of this material until the Committee is able to make available to you its final considered report.

Roosevelt did not use either of Davis's drafts when he replied to Meany and Thomas on February 23. He simply said that he would look forward to the report of the full Committee which, he was sure, would give "due consideration" to the findings of labor and other groups.

Disagreement over the "facts" was so sharpened and publicized by the writing and release of the Meany-Thomas report that by the last week of February 1944 the Cost of Living Committee appeared split and ineffective. Actually, it was on the threshold of a new phase in its inquiry, with Davis prepared to act on his own behalf now that a Committee-wide expert group to probe the facts was an impossibility. He outlined his "personal plans" for proceeding with the inquiry before the Committee on February 25, and proposed in view of the "wide discrepancy" between the BLS and Meany-Thomas figures, to appoint a Technical Committee of three authoritative experts to give him an independent opinion on the merits of both sides of the argument. There were no labor objections to this.

The industry members were also ready to undertake independent research and indicated they would do so. They soon submitted the Meany-Thomas report to the National Industrial Conference Board for a critique and retained the services of Dr. Jules Backman of New York University for analysis of the statistical and economic matters at issue.

Davis announced at the meeting that Hinrichs, two days before, had notified him of the completion of the BLS Review and Appraisal of the Meany-Thomas report; copies of this would soon be in the hands of Committee members. Hinrichs had also asked that the President's Committee, rather than the Department of Labor, release the BLS appraisal. The Committee decided that insofar as possible it would henceforth make public after each meeting all the material it had received at that meeting. In accordance with this new procedure, the BLS report was released to the newspapers as soon as copies of it became available a day later. Davis also had a copy sent to the Mills Committee.

The BLS Review and Appraisal of the Meany-Thomas Report

In the main, the BLS Review and Appraisal was a technical examination of the procedure and conclusions of the CIO-AFL research staff. It had been written under great pressure and far into the night. Summarizing the report, Hinrichs said in a public letter to Davis that the Meany-Thomas claim that the cost of living had risen 43.5 per cent between January 1941 and December 1943 was not supported even by the union data; there was conclusive evidence that the labor members were "absolutely wrong." The union report, he continued, contained many errors of fact and made use of unrepresentative data to support its general conclusions. It did not "meet the high technical standards which usually have characterized trade-union research." Meany and Thomas would not have subscribed to the report had they been fully aware of the nature of the evidence submitted, he continued. Referring to the hospitality with which Miss Williams had received union research personnel in the late fall of 1943 the letter asserted,

> Every facility of the Bureau of Labor Statistics was placed at the disposal of the trade-union research staff delegated to undertake the work by Mr. Thomas and Mr. Meany. The members of the Bureau's staff conferred at great length with them. They were invited to check their findings with the Bureau. They did not do so.

The labor research group had dismissed "too lightly" the findings of the Mills Committee, said Hinrichs, and he pointed out that both the BLS and Mills Committee had not been unaware of the limitations of the index.

The main body of the Review and Appraisal analyzed Meany-Thomas conclusions in the light of available information, considered trustworthy, on food and clothing, prices, rent, and other categories. In general, the BLS rebuttal could be summarized in three steps.

First, the cost of living index was an adequate guide to general policy and an acceptable test of the degree of price stabilization attained during the war. It was an approximation of average change in the prices of the essentials of family living, not a micrometer nor a measure of changes in the standard of living. The index did reflect inadequacies of price control and the unavailability of cheap clothing and other low-cost merchandise. Other BLS studies which revealed these conditions more fully were used by the appropriate policy-making agencies. The Meany-Thomas suggestions for changes in coverage would not have affected the over-all figure significantly.

The index's nature had to be considered when policy use was made of it. As an average it could not show the wartime experience of certain groups; it had to be used with especial care with reference to groups whose income was lower than that of the moderate income class to which the index was particularly applicable. Simply because it was a price change index, the BLS index could not show certain things, notably the effect of migration, quality changes, and voluntary trading-up in family spending. Other techniques and other data had to be used to determine the impact of such developments.

Second, a distinction had to be made between the statistical maintenance and development of the index by the BLS and the application of the index to national policy by other agencies. The latter were responsible for its policy uses.

Third, changing the index as the Meany-Thomas report proposed would not solve the administrative problems of price control, rationing and the like, which the labor members felt had not been properly handled. These were beyond the province of the BLS; their solution should be a "major aim of governmental policy."

While disagreeing with the Meany-Thomas estimate of error the cost of living staff readily admitted in the Review and Appraisal that the index did not measure price changes exactly. In keeping with BLS policy, no estimate was made of the possible range of error.

The noticeable difference in tone between the rebuttal itself and Hinrichs' transmitting letter was due to the BLS chief's decision, while writing the letter late at night on February 25th, to make a bid for the support of those union leaders whose moderation and competent technical assistance would make them likely to understand the errors in the Meany-Thomas argument. He half hoped this might stimulate a public or private refutation or disavowal of the union claims by such people. This did not happen.

Meany and Thomas quickly countered. In a strongly worded press release, they claimed that the BLS had "distorted" their findings as it had "continuously distorted" the rise in wartime living costs and that it had not answered the basic data and major conclusions of the union report. The labor chiefs then went on,

> No group of government bureaucrats have ever before had the audacity to insult America's millions of housewives, by telling them that their experiences are all wrong and that they should try to live on BLS statistics.

The subject, continued Meany and Thomas, should be submitted to a public opinion poll of American housewives in the form of the following question:

> The AFL-CIO report found living costs rose 43.5 per cent since January 1941. The BLS reports that they rose only 23 per cent. Which report is most closely confirmed by your own experiences?

Promising the public a full analysis of the BLS "confessions and laments" the labor members wound up with a blast at the BLS report as "the most insulting document that has emanated from the Department of Labor since its creation more than three decades ago."

No reply to the polling contest challenge came from the BLS. Leaving the initiative to the President's Committee, the Bureau and Department returned to official silence after Davis released the Review and Appraisal.

C. THE COMMITTEE RECESSES FOR TECHNICAL INQUIRY

Appointment of Davis's Technical Committee

With the division of the Cost of Living Committee into its component parts for research purposes came a virtual recess lasting from March until the next Committee meeting on June 22, 1944. Davis's committee was appointed on March 1. Headed by Dr. Wesley Clair Mitchell, professor of economics at Columbia University and Director of the National Bureau of Economic Research, it included two other eminent statisticians—Dr. Simon N. Kuznets, professor of economics and statistics at the University of Pennsylvania, then serving as Director of the WPB Bureau of Planning and Statistics, and Dr. Margaret G. Reid, professor of economics at Iowa State College, on leave to work with the Bureau of the Budget, Division of Statistical Standards. Miss Reid had also been a member of the Mills Committee. All three, of course, were American Statistical Association members, and Mitchell was a past president.

The Mitchell Committee had more funds and staff than the Mills Committee and was able to appoint a small assisting group of five skilled statisticians. No field studies were made but the BLS index, the AFL-CIO contentions, and other relevant documents were examined during the next few months in great detail in the light of the knowledge of these experts. Meanwhile Davis conferred with Harold Ruttenberg to ask him to explain the wide discrepancy between the BLS and Meany-Thomas figures. In the course of the conversation, Ruttenberg readily agreed that many of the items stressed in the labor report were not priced for the BLS index; he argued that they should be. Davis was critical of this disregard of conceptual differences. He considered that it begged the question of the index's accuracy and asked Ruttenberg to represent the union argument in terms of the BLS approach. The CIO economist refused.

Word from the disbanded Mills Committee on the Meany-Thomas report was received on March 22. It said that the central criticisms contained in the labor report had been considered during the ASA Committee's investigations in 1943 and that study of the AFL-CIO document led the Mills Committee's members to reaffirm the major conclusions they had reported out on October 10, 1943.

In April, the BLS sent word to the President's Committee of a plan to print the Review and Appraisal and other documents on the index that had been submitted to the Committee. Davis halted this when Meany protested that such publication should not take place before the appearance of labor's next report, which was to be in part a rebuttal to the BLS appraisal.

WLB Action on Little Steel Formula Attacks

While action in the Cost of Living Committee was thus temporarily in abeyance, labor's direct attack on the Little Steel formula came before the War Labor Board. On March 22, with industry dissenting, the Board decided to provide a public forum for the debate over the formula which the AFL members' petition and the Steelworkers' 17-cent an hour wage demand had formally begun. If complaints against the formula proved to have merit, the Board would bring the matter to the President's attention. The procedure adopted called, first, for the panel in the *Steel* case to receive evidence on the 17-cent demand, second, for the designation of a panel to receive evidence on the AFL petition recently tabled, and third, for the Board, after considering the evidence so presented, to determine whether or not modification of wage stabilization should be further investigated. In that event all interested parties were to be given full opportunity to appear and submit data publicly before the Board.

Industry's dissent from these steps urged that revision of the Little Steel formula was of interest not only to labor but to all segments of the economy. Congress rather than the Board should therefore consider any revision of the formula. It may be noted here that the Senate Banking Committee hearings on the renewal of the Price Control Act, then in progress, covered the Stabilization Act powers of the President too. At these hearings, which lasted from March 15 to April 28, labor spokesmen reiterated the cost of living findings of the Meany-Thomas report but supported renewal of controls without any relaxing amendment on wages.

Industry joined the public and labor members of WLB in a fourth point, however, a safeguarding clause stating that the Board's willingness to consider evidence on demands whose granting would involve modification of the Little Steel formula should not be construed as "any present decision" by the Board as to whether it would eventually seek a change in the formula.

The *Basic Steel* case panel hearings on the Steelworkers' fourteen demands began March 23, 1944, and lasted until July 25. Over four thousand pages of testimony and 150 supplementary briefs and exhibits were received. The panel rendered its report on September 13. A panel to hear evidence on the AFL petition that the Little Steel formula be "realistically" modified began work on April 4. Thirty-two AFL representatives appeared, and the panel report summarizing their testimony was submitted to the Board on September 13, too.

Meany's Personal Attack on the BLS, June 1944

Controversy over the index itself flared up again at the annual Research Directors' Conference on June 8 and 9. Anticipating that the Conference's cost of living session would center largely around the Meany-Thomas findings, the prices and cost of living staff had planned to devote part of the program to the BLS Review and Appraisal. But the schedule was disrupted at the start by the unexpected appearance of George Meany, supported by Ruttenberg and one or two other CIO research directors.

These representatives of labor immediately attacked the index, repeating all previous arguments with increased vigor. The BLS Review and Appraisal was criticized for "minimizing" the importance of items omitted from the index and for generally "discrediting" the Meany-Thomas report. A strong detailed exposition of the defects of the index was made; it met no contradiction by the BLS staff or by any other union economist present.

Ruttenberg sharply rapped the Bureau over the index's name. Since, he said, it was not a cost of living index, why not appoint a joint union-BLS committee immediately to report back to the conference the following day with an accurate name? Hinrichs, who was presiding, did not feel free to debate this point. The BLS had admitted the ambiguity of the index's name, but a decision on any major change in the index—including its name—would have to be made in the offices of the Director of Economic Stabilization and the Secretary of Labor; both these officials, he knew, were then opposed to changing the name. Unable to discuss the matter openly with Meany, Hinrichs simply denied the request for a joint committee with, as one observer reported "obvious embarrassment."

The statistical attack was secondary in interest, however, to Meany's main speech, which was released to the press while he was addressing the group. As reported in the New York *Times,* he said:

> The Secretary of Labor does not represent the views of labor in the Cabinet. . . . The so-called Acting Commissioner of Labor Statistics has by his actions assumed the appearance of a bureaucratic monkey on a stick who moves up and down in conformity with the dictates of administrative wage policy. . . .
>
> There are sharp indications that the price-control policy of the Government having failed to keep living costs down, the Administration decided the next best thing to do was to keep down the cost of living index. In this policy the BLS obsequiously acquiesced. We are led to the inescapable conclusion that the bureau has become identified with an effort to freeze wages, to the extent that it is no longer a free agency of statistical research. . . .

This attack found Hinrichs without defensive weapons. Like most of the BLS staff he was not trained to discount rhetoric or inclined to dispense it. He was painfully conscious that a failure to reply to these charges would damage his standing in some eyes and leave his angry and shocked staff without a champion. He was certain that a number, if not all, of his subordinates wanted him to "lay Meany out." But he felt that Meany had now overreached himself politically and, indeed, had gone so far beyond the bounds of propriety—even for labor polemics—that he had undermined rather than aided the union cause. A strong BLS reply at this point might, Hinrichs feared, force into Meany's camp those union leaders and research officials who privately disagreed with the Meany-Thomas findings and approach and whose silence had been a tacit token of support for the BLS. Hinrichs doubted, moreover, whether he or anyone qualified to head the BLS was capable of successfully engaging Meany in a verbal slugging match. And so he remained silent.

Meany walked out immediately following his speech. Over the noon recess Mrs. Wickens, conscious of Hinrichs's hesitations, but not loath herself to take up the Bureau's defense, sought permission from her superiors to reply, in part at least, to the morning's blasts. Under strict orders to be moderate, she hastily drafted some answers to the AFL-CIO contentions. When the group reconvened—without Meany—she rose to defend the index.

It was true, she said, that not enough price data were available for the Bureau to make the full range of comparisons between 1941 and 1943 and 1944 prices which labor wanted and had attempted itself in the Meany-Thomas report. This was because in 1941 the necessary price information had not been collected. This in turn was due to the fact that at that time organized labor did not give "a tinker's damn" about the index and the appropriation for all the work of the Bureau's Cost of Living Division went through at $225,000, a sum inadequate for the purpose. A really accurate name for the index would be long and mouth-filling, she continued, and likely to be improperly shortened by the press. She called the meeting's attention to the fact that elsewhere in the world the term "cost of living index" was generally applied to similar statistical measures.

Apart from the additional publicity for the Meany-Thomas contentions, the most important result of Meany's outburst was a semiofficial rupture between the BLS and research directors as organized in the Research Directors' Conference. Angry over the attack on the Department and Bureau, Miss Perkins ordered the Conferences discontinued. The Standing Committee of research directors continued to meet, however; in fact it held a meeting with Mrs. Wickens and Miss Williams on the subject of the index and its name almost immediately after the Conference.

Shortly after the Conference adjourned, the index release for the month of April appeared, bearing a brief explanatory statement which had been considered and written by the cost of living staff earlier in the spring. It said:

> The BLS Index indicates average changes in retail prices of selected goods, rents, and services bought by families of wage earners and lower-salaried workers in large cities. The items covered represented 70 per cent of the expenditures of

families who had incomes ranging from $1,250 to $2,000 in 1934-36.

The index does not show the full wartime effect on the cost of living of such factors as lowered quality, disappearance of low-priced goods, and forced changes in housing and eating away from home.

It does not measure changes in total "living costs"—that is, in the total amount families spend for living. Income taxes and bond subscriptions are not included.

Most of the basic misunderstandings about the index were tackled in this brief statement. They had already been considered in the Mills Committee Report and the BLS Review and Appraisal. Some in the Bureau feared that nonetheless the statement would be greeted by critics as an official confession of error. It was. The AFL clip sheet called it a

> confession of the truth . . . that the BLS index no longer can be considered a yardstick for the restriction of wage rates.

and said it was written as a result of the Meany-Thomas report. "Now BLS Admits It Doesn't Measure Cost of Living" was the headline in *Steel Labor* announcing the BLS statement. But one or two research directors, more quietly, wrote the Bureau to applaud the statement.

The Mitchell Committee's "Guess" on the Error in the Index

The report of the Mitchell Committee was presented to the members of the President's Committee on June 22, 1944, two weeks after the Research Directors' Conference. Greeted as the "broadest and most distinguished contribution" which had been made to the discussion of the index, the Mitchell Committee report prefaced its findings with a sketch of wartime economic trends in which it gave support to Administration fears of an inflationary gap and concluded with the statement that, on the average, American wage earners and low-salaried workers "had improved their financial position notably since 1941." The report found that the BLS had done a competent job under very difficult market conditions in providing a measure of price changes for goods customarily purchased by families of wage earners and lower-salaried workers living in large cities.

But the outstanding and dramatic feature of the Mitchell report was that it made a specific estimate of the possible error in the index. Calling it a "guess" partly "informed" and partly "crude," the Mitchell Committee nevertheless ventured to do what the BLS and Mills had avoided. It reckoned that because of imperfectly measured or virtually immeasurable wartime developments the index was between three and four index points too low, rather than the 20 points estimated by Meany's and Thomas's staff. This broke the deadlock of assertions and counter-assertions about the accuracy of the index. Made frankly because "certain other guesses have greatly exaggerated the shortcomings of the index" the guess was described as "more considered and therefore better" than those made previously.

The Committee added, however,

> Even if we are right in thinking that the index does not represent the full increase in the price of a list of customary supplies, kept as constant as wartime conditions allow, it may not follow that the Bureau of Labor Statistics could, or should, take account of the rather intangible factors we have stressed. An official fact-finding agency is properly reluctant to state conclusions it cannot support by evidence that any fair-minded critic must accept.

Demonstrating that the three to four points were not simply pulled out of a hat, the Technical Committee furnished an estimated distribution of the possible error among the major sources of inaccuracy in the index. Table 2 compares this breakdown with that in the Meany-Thomas report in terms of the point increase—or under statement—assigned to each category of error.

This public estimate of quantitive error was accompanied by a useful reminder that most social scientists take for granted:

> Few measurements are perfect even in the physical sciences, and the range of tolerance for the index should be related to the nature of the phenomena being measured.

Consequently, said the Committee, the index should be very carefully used in formulating public policy. Where it was important to

Table 2.* ANALYSIS OF DIFFERENCE BETWEEN MEANY-THOMAS AND MITCHELL COMMITTEE REPORTS IN TERMS OF POINTS TO BE ADDED TO THE BLS INDEX FOR THE 4TH QUARTER OF 1943, STANDING AT 124

	Point increase estimated by—	
Reason given for increase	*Meany-Thomas Report*	*Mitchell Report*
Methods of pricing (greater increases in food not priced for index than in foods priced, and in rents of dwellings not priced than in rents of dwellings priced)	7.22	0.30
Disappearance of cheaper consumption items	3.62	0.06-0.11
Decline in special sales	1.35	0.44
Increase in under-reporting of prices actually charged	0.98	0.24-0.48
Quality deterioration	6.93	1.46-2.69
TOTAL INCREASE	20.10	2.50-4.02

* This table is based, with some changes, on a table in the January 1945 *Monthly Labor Review*, page 170.

isolate the price factor alone, an index confined as nearly as possible to that factor in the living costs of moderate income families was the proper measure to use. The BLS index had approximated this rather closely in peacetime; in wartime, the Bureau "had striven amidst many difficulties" to hew to the same line. But the index was only one of the necessary factual bases for public policy decisions, and could not be properly understood or applied

without thoughtful attention to the great complex of changes in the manner of living that has been forced upon the American people.

The more important the uses to which the index was put the more widely could one expect it to be criticized, the Committee pointed out, adding, "That is natural and proper." Referring to the rank and file criticisms to which the index was subjected the Committee said these often arose from a misunderstanding and ignorance of what the index tried to measure. The fact that the index was a general average was commonly overlooked, the report continued; both among the cities and items represented in it there was a great variation in the rate of price change. Extreme price increases were in the index but were submerged in "a great mass of less spectacular changes." This situation, concluded the writers of the report,

illustrates how untrustworthy an impression one may get of a complex whole from a few incidents vividly impressed on the mind of the one who experiences them. Memory of such incidents remains fresh since consumers naturally tend strongly to resent increases in prices.

Four other features of the Mitchell Committee report are worth noting. There was little doubt, it said, that the BLS index understated "considerably" the rise in prices encountered by families at the bottom of the income scale because, since the qualities bought by this group were generally not priced by the index, the extensive forced up-trading this group had experienced was not reflected. This was an important factor to be kept in mind, said the Technical Committee, by those who used the index. Second, the Committee suggested that the index be given a "less misleading name."

Third, it presented a somewhat general listing of things the Bureau might do to improve the index, but recognized very clearly that additional appropriations would be needed for these purposes:

A more extensive sample of small cities would give greater assurance that price was being measured for wage earners and lower-salaried workers in general. The pricing of a somewhat wider range of qualities for some items might make it possible to get a better measure of average price change for those groups of families, within the limitations of the fact that as the number of qualities priced increases so does the difficulty in identifying the quality. Occasional checks might be made of the importance of sales at markdowns and special discounts not included in the pricing. An expenditure survey would be valuable in bringing expenditure weights in line with present spending patterns.

These suggestions, it was noted, had all been considered by the BLS before:

Recommendations bearing on them appear in the report of the A.S.A. Committee and the BLS has testified before Congressional Committees concerning the need for and possible ways of providing more adequate data. The controversy which has given rise to the present report indicates their significance.

A fourth important feature of the Mitchell report was its detailed examination of the compilation and criticisms of each commodity index entering into the all-items index.

BLS Reaction to the Report

At the BLS, the Prices and Cost of Living staff considered that Mitchell Committee members had taken quite a bold step in publicly "sticking their necks out" to estimate an error in the index, a step which neither the BLS nor Mills Committee had felt in a position to make. The technical staff regarded the report, in general, as good support of the BLS position. (Subsequently, in October 1945, a footnote was added to regular cost of living releases suggesting that the index might be too low to the extent of some 4 points or less because of wartime conditions. This footnote was dropped in March 1947 with release of the January 1947 index.)

Hinrichs considered the Mitchell estimate more a reflection on the Meany-Thomas cost of living figure than on the index. Scrutinizing the Mitchell Committee report with the political buttressing of the Bureau and the index in mind, he was somewhat less satisfied than his staff. The unequivocal manner in which the Mitchell Committee had treated the semantic and conceptual confusion over the meaning of "cost of living" disturbed him. Now it appeared politically impossible to continue the existing index name. Yet, a change while wage stabilization was still in full force would require the approval of the Office of Economic Stabilization, the White House, and the Secretary of Labor; it might, he feared, affect the work of the WLB. Reluctantly, the BLS chief proposed to Miss Perkins that the index name be changed. The Secretary refused to accept the recommendation. A change would serve no useful purpose, she told Hinrichs, particularly since "cost of living index" was a name commonly used all over the world.

Another disquieting feature of the Mitchell report, for Hinrichs, was its length and the detail with which it went into index composition, procedure, and problems. Unfriendly and irresponsible critics of the index were only being handed more material for that distortion of facts which Hinrichs felt must be constantly guarded against. He did not agree that the full disclosure of facts might tend to lessen rather than increase political attack.

Effect of the Mitchell Report on the Index Controversy

Like the Mills report, the Mitchell report failed to get the wide and colorful publicity accorded the Meany-Thomas document. Yet the prestige of its authors, the straightforward meeting of labor's contentions, and the specific estimate of index error combined to bring about the gradual abandonment of the union attack on the index. As the report reached a widening circle of readers the force of the Meany-Thomas claims was blunted. An acceptable alternative was now available to many—Congressmen, newspapermen, government officials, business groups, labor officials, technicians—who had felt that some criticism of the index might be warranted but who distrusted both the AFL-CIO estimate of error and the attack on the Bureau and its personnel. The public and industry members of the *Basic Steel* panel found this new source of information on living cost data very useful; their report later revealed their debt to the Mitchell calculations.

For Davis, the Mitchell Committee report brought to a close the statistical debate. It provided him with material to form his own judgment. It answered his question—to what extent does the index "reflect the squeeze" in the normal budget of the average consumer since January 1, 1941? Over four months elapsed, however, before his report as Chairman of the Cost of Living Committee was submitted to President Roosevelt. Some of this time was occupied with the writing and consideration of the report. Most of it was consumed by Harold Ruttenberg's quest for a statistical compromise.

D. STATISTICAL COMPROMISE PROVES IMPOSSIBLE

Labor Requests a Statistical Reconciliation

Davis opened the twelfth meeting of the Committee on the Cost of Living, on June 22, 1944, by distributing the Mitchell report. The second union report on the index, written by Thomas' (CIO) staff, was then in nearly final shape (a copy had been given to Professor Mitchell over a week before), but it had not yet been released. Perhaps Thomas and Ruttenberg were waiting to see the Mitchell document first.

In any case, Meany, Thomas, and Ruttenberg, glanced over the Technical Committee's report and asked for a meeting between Mitchell and a committee of labor and industry statistical experts to

> determine the differences, if any, between them with respect to the Bureau of Labor Statistics index and to report to the Committee.

The rest of the Committee approved, and Davis was asked to make the necessary arrangements.

The prospect of agreement at such a meeting was very poor, of course, for the difference between the Technical Committee's approach and that of the Meany-Thomas report was irreconcilable. Ruttenberg claimed to base his hope for a successful discussion of the differences, "if any," on the fact that the Mitchell Committee granted the BLS index was not an expenditure index, and the union had actually estimated an expenditure index. This thought was again expressed four days later in the release accompanying the second union report on the index issued by Philip Murray, president of the CIO, and R. J. Thomas. Possibly Ruttenberg, accustomed to operating in the give-and-take atmosphere of collective bargaining and never completely convinced of the unshakable objectivity of government and academic statisticians, felt that the Mitchell Committee estimate of error, coming after the Meany-Thomas estimate, invited negotiation to reach a mutually acceptable figure or general statement.

Murray-Thomas Report, June 26, 1944

The second labor report was released exclusively by the CIO. Meany had withdrawn his support of the CIO staff's statistical operations sometime after the release of the Meany-Thomas report in January. He continued to direct his fire at the Bureau and the Department of Labor and his failure to sponsor further statistical research should probably be ascribed to a feeling that the previous report had accomplished all that could be hoped for and to a reluctance further to underwrite statistical operations which were subject to grave question.

In substance, the Murray-Thomas report was a reaffirmation and reiteration of the tone and conclusions of the Meany-Thomas report and a rebuttal to the BLS appraisal of the earlier document. Again there was emphasis on the CIO view that the index should be extended to cover more types of price changes if it was to be used for wage adjustment purposes:

> It is monstrous to suppose that wage adjustment should be made by reference to an index confined to the measurement of changes in retail prices. The point is too obvious to require discussion.

CIO Quest for a Statistical Agreement

Davis, understanding the vast difference between the two views of the index which had been propounded was nevertheless unwilling to ignore a labor gesture toward agreement, whatever its prospect of success. He instructed Waldron to proceed to arrange the proposed meeting between Dr. Mitchell and labor and industry experts. But Waldron found Dr. Mitchell about to leave for his summer home in Vermont and reluctant to participate. The statistician doubted that much more could be accomplished in the direction of defining differences than he had done in a recent letter to Ruttenberg in which he had pointed out the conceptual difference between the BLS and Murray-Thomas approach. Ruttenberg in turn told Waldron that without Mitchell a meeting would be a failure but that with him the technicians could develop a clear statement of the differences between them.

Waldron reported these conversations to Davis, who, in view of the poor prospects for statistical agreement, was anxious to avoid imposing on Mitchell. He accordingly asked Dr. Margaret Reid of the Mitchell Committee if she would act in Mitchell's stead. She was at first inclined to accept, with some reservations, but subsequently withdrew after discussing the matter with other members of the Technical Committee. They felt that the Technical Committee should not alter its role; that it should be prepared to elucidate any of its findings, examine new evidence, and offer technical advice on request; but that neither it nor any of its members should, as Waldron conveyed Dr. Reid's thought to Davis, "enter into negotiations" of a bargaining nature.

Davis therefore immediately reported to the members of his Committee Dr. Reid's strong feelings about the role of the Technical Committee and indicated his desire to respect this position. He did not shut the door to any possible ironing out or articulation of differences but suggested, as an alternative to Ruttenberg's plan, that the technical experts of labor and industry meet together as planned and

> work out and present a summary statement of the controversy which we must seek to solve. Perhaps they would do well to take the report of the Technical Committee and enumerate the respects in which it is acceptable to them and the respects in which it is unacceptable to them.

This proposal was rejected by both groups. A reply (dated July 6, 1944) from Meany and Thomas said in part,

> We note with interest your sympathy with the position taken by Miss Reed [sic], of your group of experts . . .
>
> In the first place, may we say that we have no interest in the position taken by *your* experts. Their refusal or reluctance to co-operate with the research experts representing Labor and Industry is your concern. . .
>
> It is to be regretted that the agreement unanimously reached by the President's Cost of Living Committee at its meeting on June 22nd cannot be carried out. In view of your evident decision to withdraw from the agreement you made at this meeting, we now feel that the Committee, as a whole, should be convened at an early date to consider all evidence that has been presented to it from the date of its formation to the present time, and, on the basis of this evidence, prepare its report to the President.

The industry reply to Davis, written by Batt, said the industry members now knew where they stood and believed the labor members did too. More experts, following all the publicity the Committee had already received, would cause more confusion than good, and Batt proposed that the Committee make an early report to clear up "once and for all" the question of the accuracy of the index.

Three weeks passed in inaction and stalemate. Davis made no more efforts to arrange for a meeting of experts. At the Committee's thirteenth meeting on August 9, he opened by saying it was desirable to get the Committee's report out as soon as possible. The crux of the matter was the question: which of the two widely discrepant estimates of the quantitative importance of the unmeasurable effects of the war on the index was right? He was frank to say his examination of it led him very definitely to agree with the Mitchell report:

> . . . in a quantitative sense the Meany-Thomas report and the CIO report just don't stand up. They do not withstand critical analysis.

He noted that the disagreement turned on what constituted the cost of living and illustrated the cleavage by an analogy:

> If I said to two engineers, what is the probable tensile strength of steel and rayon, I would expect them possibly to come back with slightly different figures in the fifth or sixth decimal place, perhaps, but I wouldn't expect them to come back and say, "What is tensile strength?"

Personally, however, Davis did not believe that there was "any such confusion" about the cost of living "as had been made out." Rather, confusion was due to a lack of understanding that an index was a standard that included some things and not others. Bringing the meeting back to the immediate question before it, he said he did not see how the President's Committee could resolve the difference between the two reports on the amount of the index error. It would have to accept one report or the other.

Ruttenberg replied that this could not be taken for granted unless the experts had met, and asked Davis again to persuade Mitchell to come in from Vermont. Davis suggested trying to secure Margaret Reid or Solomon Fabricant to talk with Ruttenberg and Dr. Jules Backman, advisor to the industry members. Horton, representing industry, saw no need for such a step. He thought the Mitchell report answered all criticisms of the index, and nothing more was to be gained by discussing "the use of words." In the end it was left to Davis to explore the matter further.

Davis was still not ready to say a unanimous report was impossible. Before leaving for his vacation later in the month he talked twice with Margaret Reid and she agreed to make herself available for a discussion with Ruttenberg, Miss Scattergood of the AFL, or any other CIO or AFL representatives

as to the possibility of reconsidering or narrowing the quantitative differences between the estimates of the Technical Committee report and that of the Meany-Thomas or the CIO reports.

While Davis was on vacation, Miss Reid met with Ruttenberg and two other union research officials on August 19. She reported in a letter to Professor Mitchell that the meeting went no farther than a restatement of the views of the Technical Committee and the Murray-Thomas report. Ruttenberg continued to press Miss Reid and Mitchell for further consideration of the union and Mitchell documents in view of what he characterized as the "area of substantial agreement" among the BLS, Mitchell Committee, and union staff. On August 23, Ruttenberg distributed a 20-page CIO document entitled *Comments on the June 15, 1944, Report of the Mitchell Committee*. Designed, in all likelihood, to evoke a reply from the Technical Committee, the *Comments* went in greater detail into Ruttenberg's argument that agreement was possible and should be sought because the BLS and Mitchell Committee agreed that the index did not measure certain "costs to workers" while the CIO study "properly" attempted to include them in its measurement of "wartime living costs." Ruttenberg sent a letter to this effect, together with a copy of the *Comments*, to Davis's office where it awaited his return.

Mitchell replied immediately to the *Comments*, saying in a letter to Ruttenberg that the CIO and Technical Committee were measuring different things. In subsequent correspondence between themselves Miss Reid and Mitchell agreed that in view of the basic conceptual difference between the Mitchell and CIO reports a unanimous report by the President's Committee was "highly improbable."

Davis returned early in September and found copies of all this correspondence and material on his desk. He concluded that his best course now was to complete his own draft of the Committee's report and submit it to the other members as a basis for discussion. He proceeded to work on the report.

WLB Action on Requests to Modify Little Steel Formula

There had been a recess, during the summer, in the larger union action to secure revision of the Little Steel formula while the *Basic Steel* panel and the panel on the AFL petition considered the materials before them and drew up their findings.

Average weekly hours worked in industry were beginning to fall off at this time as cutbacks occurred in war production. Earnings, consequently, showed signs of dropping. The obvious remedy in the eyes of labor spokesmen was an increase in the hourly wage rate. The spotlight turned therefore to the *Basic Steel* panel's report, submitted on September 13, 1944. This report gave detailed consideration to the six documents which had been written in the course of the index controvery and remarked that:

> Rarely does a panel have the benefit of so many comprehensive analyses and studies of an issue before it as this panel has had on the question of the cost of living and what has happened to it since January 1941.

On the union's contention that the cost of living had risen by at least 43.5 per cent the panel avoided any definite statement, but showed an inclination to accept the Mitchell report. The panel also found that in fact "the wage rates of steel workers have been stabilized." It found, too, that the average weekly earnings of steel workers had risen 66.6 per cent from 1939 through 1943 and that average weekly earnings for employees in all manufacturing had increased during the same period by 80.8 per cent; it forecast some decline in these.

After the *Basic Steel* and AFL panel reports were received, hearings were scheduled before the full Board for September 26. Labor leaders from both camps made vigorous representations at the hearings that action was long overdue to remedy the injustice of the Little Steel formula. Following the hearings there was public speculation on what the Board would recommend to the President and whether it would present its proposals before or after Election Day, November 7. Union periodicals expressed confidence that the Board would urge relaxation of the formula and that the President would authorize such action within the next few weeks.

But the War Labor Board, by an 8 to 4 vote, with labor dissenting, declined on October 11, 1944, to recommend to the President that the Little Steel formula be changed. The Board held that it was not

> sufficiently well informed as to possible effects of a modification of the Little Steel formula on the price structure and on the national economy generally to warrant assurance that any modification could be made consistent with the stabilization needs of the country.

"An inexcusable dereliction of duty" was the labor members' description of this statement. They found small consolation in the Board's companion decision to present to the President a report setting forth pertinent data regarding the relationship of wages to the cost of living and "an appraisal of the nature and extent of alleged inequities created by the changes which had occurred."

Nothing was said in the Board's statement of October 11 about the merits of the CIO attack on the cost of living index. But the main union campaign against the Little Steel formula—which the index maneuver was intended to support—had been rebuffed.

E. THE PRESIDENT'S COMMITTEE REPORTS IN THREE PARTS, NOVEMBER 1944

Davis's Report on the Cost of Living Index

Davis's draft of a report to the President on the index was in the hands of the other Committee members by October 20. Batt and Horton immediately wrote back that the draft was "a perfectly fair statement" and "an excellent summary." A reply from R. J. Thomas stated that he could accept neither its premises nor its conclusions.

Davis's draft gave full support to the findings of the Mills and Mitchell Committees, asserting that the statistical analysis of the Meany-Thomas report by the Mitchell Committee was "utterly convincing." It drew on the Mitchell Committee report for a description of the index and of BLS methods of correcting for wartime changes, and also for a refutation of the Meany-Thomas charges. Davis's conclusions were:

> 1. The accuracy of the BLS index figures for what they are intended to measure is confirmed. They are entitled to the good reputation they have long enjoyed. They constitute a competent measure of price changes for goods customarily purchased by families of wage earners and lower-salaried workers living in large cities. They provide from month to month an acceptable approximation to changes in the cost of living for urban workers. They are good basic figures for use in the formulation of fiscal and other policies and for observing the effects of such policies.
>
> 2. Under the exceptional market conditions which exist in wartime, and so long as we have a seller's market, allowance should be made for a hidden increase in the cost of living of probably as much as 3 and certainly not more than 4 percentage points, due to quality deterioration, disappearance of cheaper goods, decrease of special sales, and increases in under-reporting of prices actually charged. Unlike the price changes recorded by the BLS, these items of temporary disadvantage of the buyer in a seller's market are not directly measurable but they have been soundly estimated by the Mitchell Committee.
>
> 3. If the index is to be used to represent changes in the cost of living of urban workers in small as well as large cities there should be an upward adjustment of the index figures by not more than one-half of a percentage point. . . .

Relating this estimate of understatement to the cost of living index which stood on September 15, 1944, at 25.5 per cent above January 15, 1941, Davis estimated that

> the final figure for the over-all increase in the cost of living from January 1941 to September 1944 would thus be found to be 29 to 30 per cent.

The chairman was inclined to go along with the Mitchell Committee's suggestion that the index be given a new name

particularly if the new name could emphasize that the BLS index measures changes in the total cost of a fixed standard of living, not changes in total family expenditures due to changed standards of living.

In a section in which he considered what the BLS index did *not* do Davis felt impelled to answer directly the basic CIO contention that the index should measure family expenditures, not unit prices. He said,

. . . it seems to me highly important, particularly from the standpoint of those who have to battle for better standards of living in America, that it should be generally understood that the thing measured by the BLS index is the change from time to time in the aggregate cost of a *fixed typical family market basket*, so that urban workers may know whether their wage dollar has kept its real value in the market. . . . If the BLS permitted changes in income to change its index these people would have no way to measure either the gains or the losses in the value of the dollars for which they work. With a great falling off of real income, and the inevitable reduction of total family expenditure, they might be asked to believe that the "cost of living" had declined as their incomes fell off and that they were really as well off as before.

There was much else in the report in refutation of the Meany-Thomas criticisms of the index, but no reference either to wage issues in general or to the Little Steel formula. The President's Committee on the Cost of Living had not been appointed to look into those matters.

The next meeting of the Cost of Living Committee was held on October 30 and devoted to discussing Davis's report and the procedure to be followed in issuing it. Was it to be Davis's own report as Chairman or the Committee's report and how were major or minor objections by industry and labor to be presented? No decision was reached on these matters and after some changes in the draft had been suggested it was agreed that Davis would circulate it again and that a vote on it would be taken at the next meeting, to be held November 9.

Davis circulated a re-worked draft to the Committee members, to the BLS for a check of its statistical accuracy, and to Commissioner of Labor Statistics Lubin, still on leave in the White House. Lubin replied that the report was "an excellent digest of unusually difficult materials" and that it would greatly help to clarify the situation. From the point of view of "re-establishing the BLS as an impartial fact-finding agency" he felt that coverage was needed on two other points. It would be desirable first for Davis to indicate that his 3 to 4 point allowance for understatement by the index was in harmony with the BLS appraisal of the Meany-Thomas report, and second, to state in as many words that the BLS had shown itself to be an impartial fact-finding agency. Lubin attached some suggested draft paragraphs to this effect but they did not appear in Davis's final report which followed closely the draft which has been quoted.

The second circulation of Davis's draft led to further correspondence from the CIO containing suggestions for changes and emphasizing the union point that the index was not suitable for use in wartime wage stabilization policy. The final meeting of the President's Committee, held on November 9, saw further talk on a number of statistical points and on Davis's estimate of understatement by the index. Davis read the letter from the CIO aloud and discussed it point by point, rejecting the union suggestion that he include a discussion of whether or not the index was suitable for use in wartime wage adjustment. That, he said, had been "deliberately left out."

At this time a vote was finally taken on the report. Batt approved it "in the main" for industry. Meany dissented and Ruttenberg withheld his vote until he could confer with Thomas, who was not present. Both industry and labor announced that they would send Davis a copy of their comments on his report for him to submit to the President together with the report.

Batt and Horton's Summary and Conclusions, based on the NICB's critique of the Meany-Thomas report and Dr. Backman's investigation of the cost of living index, were received November 11 and the dissenting letters and comments of Meany and Thomas on

November 13. The industry communication had been written before Davis's second draft was circulated on October 20. It was supplemented by a detailed statistical analysis of the Meany-Thomas and Murray-Thomas reports, and of other labor material on the cost of living. It revealed that Batt and Horton were inclined to give numerical weight to certain references to over-statement by the index which had been made in the Mitchell report but for which no allowance had been made in the report's final estimate of error. Thus, the fourth item in their list of points on which they were in "essential agreement with the cumulative judgment" of the Mills Committee, the NICB, and the Mitchell Committee was that

> because of the disappearance and reduced supply of various items, if the BLS index were treated as an expenditures' index it would be "5 per cent below what it now is," according to the Mitchell Committee. *This 5 per cent is greater than the entire understatement reported by the Mitchell Committee and provides a cushion* against it. . . .

Thomas stated in a letter that he was in "hearty agreement" with much of Davis's report but repeated his disagreement on the basic matters in dispute. A cost of living index, he said, should be more than an index of price change; it should include changes in the "manner of living" which the Mitchell Committee and Davis excluded. Viewing living costs in this broader sense, Thomas repeated the CIO estimate that they had risen by 44.4 per cent since January 1, 1941, and concluded that the BLS index was not a satisfactory measure of living costs for use in adjusting wage rates. The necessary and just action required on wages was clear, he reiterated.

Meany's letter on behalf of the AFL repeated "labor's persistent and determined objections" to the use of the BLS index as a guide to wartime wage policy. The AFL had never agreed to the principle of basing wages on cost of living or on price inflation (the CIO's proposed basis) but on increasing productivity, he said. Meany's solution to the "serious decline in workers' real wages" was a return to free collective bargaining between employers and employees on wage increases up to 30 per cent over January 1941. This was Davis's figure on the extent to which the cost of living had increased. The end of the President's Committee's investigation, in short, found the AFL member quietly agreeing with the Chairman on statistics although not on their implication.

Davis's report was transmitted to the President on November 17, 1944, together with the labor and industry documents as well as the other major documents considered by the Committee, but not including the Meany-Thomas or Murray-Thomas reports. After twelve months and fifteen Committee meetings a three-sided view still proved necessary. It did not differ basically from the stands each of the five men would have taken a year before. The difference was that the Committee's existence had made possible a thorough culling and investigation of the facts and a hearing and evaluation of labor's criticisms.

Neither the President nor Davis had expected that the Committee's report would stop the drive for a change in the Little Steel formula but it did have the intended effect of stopping attacks on the index. Both the AFL and CIO abandoned this line thereafter. Once the elections were over and won, the union attack on the Little Steel formula was resumed with vigor.

WLB Decision in *Basic Steel* Case

The WLB decision in the *Basic Steel* case was announced on November 25, 1944. The union demand for general wage increases of 17 cents had already been ruled out by the Board's decision not to recommend a revision of the Little Steel formula to the President. The Board decided on the other hand that, on a number of the fringe issues, the union was entitled to its requests or should be allowed to bargain collectively for them with employers. Other Board decisions allowing fringe increases, coupled with a statement by Byrnes, now War Mobilization Director, that the bracket system of adjustments would be liberally applied, had the net effect, during the ensuing months, of "easing the pressure" and permitting a moderate rise in average wage rates and average hourly earnings exclusive of overtime payments. This, as Chart B on page

787 indicates, remained the wage picture, in general terms, until the close of the war.

POSTSCRIPT

There is a temptation, looking back and reconstructing the history of any series of interrelated happenings, to ponder over the relative roles of "events" and "men" in shaping the story. The BLS, both while living through the dispute over the index and in looking back on it, saw it as inevitable, as part of an inexorable sweep of events generated by the war production effort. Next to this overwhelming force they regarded the power of any individual to alter events as puny.

In a sense the index dispute was inevitable. Given the long term shift in the emphasis of the government statistician's work, noted by the Task Force on Statistical Agencies in the Federal Government, from "enumeration for purposes of historical study" to the collection and analysis of statistics

> with reference to decisions that must be made, controls that must be exercised, judgments that entail action,

the OPA's and WLB's use of the cost of living index in the shaping of price and wage stabilization policy was unavoidable, natural, common sense. The inevitability of the decision was assured by the high reputation for skill and objectivity enjoyed by the BLS and the broad acceptance accorded its data. Wage stabilization soon touched the pocketbooks of an economic group of which large segments were highly organized and habitually articulate. In their vigorous quest for vulnerable points of attack in the Administration's stabilization armor they picked on many things, including the cost of living index. Until they became convinced that attacking the index and the BLS would yield no results politically, they were not likely to abandon the attack.

Accustomed to regarding themselves as technicians working apart from politics and administration, BLS personnel could not see how they might have altered the foregoing procession of causes and effects. They could only ride out the storm.

Nonetheless some questions on possible alternatives and choices are raised by events in the story. What is the relationship between the technician and the policy-maker he serves? Should those on top undertake to protect experts who are likely to be caught in a storm of attack on policy they did not shape but for which they furnished the factual support? In this case, the OPA and WLB remained carefully aloof from the storm of union protest their price and wage policies were raising around the Bureau. It was the President who finally took note of the BLS's political dilemma and asked WLB Chairman Davis to look into it.

The Hoover Commission Task Force came no closer to this problem than to recommend:

> That, in view of the necessity for objectivity in the collection, organization, and presentation of the facts of national life, the functions of fact finding be clearly distinguished from activities involving the setting of social goals or the promotion of special-aid programs. Statistical agencies should be clearly recognized as representatives of the public, not regarded as agents of special groups nor as advocates of special interests.

Hinrichs was led much further by his wartime experience. He concluded that, at least in times of social and political strain, fact finding agencies whose work was of importance in policy determination should be accorded the "highest order" of political protection available, even perhaps, of a judicial nature. Only when soundly insulated from partisan attack could they, in his view, serve policy-makers effectively.

Looking back over the index controversy, some years later, a WLB member was inclined to take a contrary position. Public life, even that of the expert, inevitably involved some mud-slinging, he averred. It was dramatic, flattering, albeit painful proof of the BLS's usefulness that the index underwent attack, for "nobody whips a dead horse." The pleasure or privilege or duty of furnishing policy-makers with facts, he implied, carried with it responsibility for riding out public storms over top decisions.

Perhaps a more fruitful approach to the problem of protecting technical bureaus whose work is linked to policy formation can be made through the development of formal devices at the bureau level for dealing with pressures from various publics likely to be affected. In 1947 the BLS adopted this approach with the formation of a Joint Labor Research Advisory Committee and a Business Research Advisory Committee to consider, with BLS staff members, the planning and development of the Bureau's program.

It is an administrative truism that the level in the hierarchy from which a problem is sized up and handled influences the nature and success of the solution. With this in mind, and shifting our viewpoint somewhat, what answer can we give to the reader's inevitable question whether the BLS could have met the union attack on the index more successfully or whether topside treatment was definitely indicated? The Bureau's limitations, upon examination, appear to have stemmed not only from its technical frame of reference and oblique relationship to the wartime policy-making agencies, but also from the caution and lack of a clear mandate in labor affairs which characterized the Department of Labor during this period.

By contrast, William H. Davis, chairman and public member of the War Labor Board and chairman of the President's Committee on the Cost of Living, was able over a period of twelve months (given the basic soundness of the index as affirmed by his own judgment and that of the Mills and Mitchell Committees), to bring to an end the concerted AFL-CIO attack on the BLS index. He did this by doing what the BLS chief, seconded by the Secretary of Labor, had felt restrained from doing: Davis let—nay, encouraged—union spokesmen to voice and document their criticisms of the index as they wished and for almost as long as they wished. While he presided over the statistical controversy, the labor assault reached its loudest, most public, and most violent stage. Varied experience in the settlement of labor disputes had led Davis to decide that the first and most important way to meet this or any labor grievance was to hear it—in full. The BLS and Department of Labor shrank from public statements or discussion.

Being convinced—where Hinrichs doubted—that the index could not really be undermined and that Administration use of it would not be endangered, Davis did not hesitate to support a technical report which estimated a margin of error, described problems of compilation the BLS felt it wisest to discuss only with a limited group of technicians, and enlightened the public in general. As a layman who had often entered technical arcana and emerged unscathed, Davis, unlike Hinrichs, was undisturbed by public disclosure and discussion of technical problems. Indeed, like all successful labor mediators, Davis was a great believer in the therapeutic virtues of prolonged discussion. From his vantage point in the formation of Administration economic policy, he could afford the time and the public wrangling necessary to expose the fallacy of the AFL-CIO statistical position and to restore the acceptability of the cost of living index in the eyes of those who had become doubtful.

CHRONOLOGY

1942

JANUARY 12 Executive Order 9017 establishes a tripartite National War Labor Board with final jurisdiction over all disputes

JANUARY 30 Emergency Price Control Act continues Office of Price Administration to administer statutory price controls

APRIL 27 President proclaims 7-point anti-inflation program

APRIL 28 General Maximum Price Regulation issued by OPA

JULY 16 Little Steel Case decision by NWLB initiates wage stabilization (Little Steel formula)

OCTOBER 3 E. O. 9250 delegates full wage stabilization powers to NWLB

1943

APRIL 8 Hold-the-Line Order (E. O. 9328) removes Little Steel formula from NWLB's jurisdiction

MAY Mills Committee to appraise index appointed at request of Department of Labor

OCTOBER 10 Mills Committee pronounces index "a trustworthy measure"

OCTOBER 22 President Roosevelt asks Chairman Davis of NWLB to appoint a Committee on the Cost of Living to investigate index

1944

JANUARY 25 Meany-Thomas (AFL-CIO) report estimates 20-point index error

JANUARY 27 *Basic Steel* cases certified to NWLB by Secretary of Labor

FEBRUARY 25 BLS replies to Meany-Thomas report in a Review and Appraisal

MARCH 1 Mitchell Committee on index appointed by Chairman Davis

JUNE 8 Meany attacks BLS at Research Directors' Conference

JUNE 22 Mitchell Committee estimates index error of 3-4 points

JUNE 26 Murray-Thomas report criticizing index released by CIO

OCTOBER 11 NWLB, labor dissenting, declines to recommend to the President that the Little Steel formula be changed

NOVEMBER 17 Chairman Davis, in Report of President's Committee on the Cost of Living, confirms index's accuracy

NOVEMBER 25 *Basic Steel* decision released by NWLB

Appendix A

Description of the Cost of Living Index (Consumers' Price Index) [1]

The Consumers' Price Index [formerly the cost of living index] has always been the most popular series of the Bureau of Labor Statistics. Each month it is received by a mailing list of nearly 14,000 names. Countless thousands are apprised of its release through the daily newspapers and important business and news magazines. In any given month, in excess of 3,000 special requests for consumers' price information are received. Hence the index was a going concern enjoying a hardy popularity even before the General Motors-United Automobile Workers agreement recently made it almost a household byword. . . .

The Structure of the Index

The general purpose of the index is to represent the changes in the prices of a specific, fixed market basket, or shopping list, of goods and services bought by moderate-income urban (large city) consumers. Thus, the market basket remains constant for a considerable period of time, while the index reflects the changes in the prices of the articles included.

Public understanding of the index has been confused by the use of the term "cost of living" index to describe it. Among the factors which enter into changes in the "cost of living," this index measures only one: price. The index has been judged to provide "an acceptable approximation" of change in "the cost of living for urban workers" over short periods of time. The most precise and most accurate title for the consumers' price index is that which was applied to it more than 10 years ago: "Changes in the Cost of Goods and Services Purchased by Wage Earners and Lower-Salaried Clerical Workers in 1934-36." This has since been shortened [in September 1945] to "Consumers Price Index for Moderate-Income Families in Large Cities."

How do we know what goods and services in what quantities are bought by moderate-income families? The answer is that the Bureau obtains such information from the families themselves. In 1934-36 a comprehensive study of some 14,500 families was made. Records were made of the kinds, qualities, amount, and prices of foods, shoes, suits, furniture, and all categories of family expenditures.

The index is based on the experience of families in the middle income groups, excluding those at the lowest and highest extremes of the income scale.

[Selecting Index Items—Imputation]

American families buy more than 1,400 different articles and services, and each of the 1,400 may appear on the market in at least several different qualities. But it is not necessary for the Bureau to face the stupendous task of pricing all of them each month. The Bureau selects about 200 items whose price movements are representative of all 1,400 items. For example, the price movements of fresh milk can be used to typify those of buttermilk and various other milk products; those of round, chuck, rib roast and hamburger can be used to represent all beef products; doctors' fees for appendix and tonsil operations can represent changes in the fees for all surgical operations.

Objection may be made that some of the missing 1,200 items may change in price differently from the 200 included. Of course they may, especially over short periods of time. But it has been our experience that average prices of commodities within a class tend to move together, so that a few well selected articles can safely be used to represent the class. Furthermore, if several articles

[1] Excerpts from "The CPI—A Summary of its Essential Features" by Ewan Clague, Commissioner of Labor Statistics, in the *Monthly Labor Review* for July 1948, pp. 8-11.

in a group are of outstanding importance in family purchases, like round steak and chuck roast, these important articles are all included even though statistically price changes for one are similar to price changes for the others. As a result, the index for the 200 commodities and the major components (food, apparel, housefurnishings, etc.) represent the price changes of all articles purchased by moderate-income consumers.

[*Quality Changes*]

Another problem in the collection of prices is the matter of quality. The price of pork chops can vary considerably, depending on how near the center of the loin they are cut. If center-cut pork chops are priced one month and end-cut the next month, the price of pork chops might seem to have gone down. But in fact this would reflect a difference in quality, not a change in price. In attempting to hold quality constant in measuring price changes from month to month, the Bureau draws up detailed specifications to describe the qualities of the articles priced each month. These specifications are carefully built up with the advice of manufacturers and retailers who know these commodities. . . .

The Construction of the Index

What quantities of various commodities and articles actually go into the market basket, or the shopping list? As stated previously, the quantities used in the computation of the index for each city are based upon the 1934-36 actual purchases of that city's families in terms of pounds, yards, cans, dozens, etc. These quantities have been kept constant since that time. When the quantities of each item are multiplied by their average prices in the period 1935-39, the total makes up the cost of the market basket in the base period (which we call 100). These same quantities multiplied by their average prices in May 1948, add up to the current cost of the market basket. This recent cost is about 70 per cent higher than the average for 1935-39. Therefore, the index in May 1948 was about 170.

The quantities in the market basket have been held virtually unchanged for more than a decade, but we know that incomes have risen, and consumers may have changed their pattern of expenditures. Thus, they might buy larger quantities of food but still spend a smaller proportion of total expenditures for food and more for rent, clothing, amusements, etc. How does the Bureau take such changes into account? The method of meeting this problem is to check periodically on the buying habits and expenditure patterns of moderate-income urban families. Beginning in 1945, the Bureau has conducted studies of a small sample of families in 3 cities each year. In these studies it discovers what articles and in what quantities people are actually buying. In the postwar period a total of 9 cities have been completed, and it is planned to do 3 more in 1949. The findings are analyzed to determine the extent to which the buying habits of American families today differ from those of 12 to 14 years ago. The results may necessitate revision of the weights which are used in the computation of the index. If the studies show that these changes would have an important effect on the index, we may have to speed up the sample studies, doing more than 3 cities each year, or perhaps doing all 34 cities simultaneously as was done in 1934-36. . . .

[*Author's Note*

Beginning in November 1949 a comprehensive three-year revision of the consumers' price index, based on new surveys, was undertaken by the Bureau of Labor Statistics.]

Appendix B

Excerpts from the Mills Committee Conclusions on Technical Issues Before It [2]

QUESTION 1. *Are the prices reported by the Bureau those actually paid by customers of reporting retail stores?*

. . . [The BLS] method of collecting prices has led to the criticism that the quotations reported will be higher or lower than actual prices according to whether it is to the interest of the retailer to appear to be holding prices above or below the true market. . . .

ANSWER: We have tested reported food price quotations through actual purchases at 159 independent stores and 37 chain stores in 17 cities. . . .

We believe that these checks confirm the essential accuracy of the food prices reported to the Bureau. The observed discrepancies indicated a margin of reporting error of less than 2 per cent. . . .

QUESTION 2. *Are the retail stores included in the Bureau's sample representative of those patronized by wage earners and lower-salaried workers in metropolitan areas covered by the Bureau's compilations?*

[2] Office of Economic Stabilization, *Report of the President's Committee on the Cost of Living,* Washington, 1945, pp. 101-108.

. . . Some users of the index believe that migrations of labor during the war have changed the purchasing habits of the workers so drastically that the group of stores priced by the Bureau is no longer representative. . . .

ANSWER: . . . We conclude that food price reports from the retail stores included in the regular Bureau sample are representative of prices prevailing in stores patronized by wage earners and lower-salaried workers in the cities covered by the tests made and in suburban sections of the metropolitan areas tested. In particular, we find in this evidence no support for the opinion that prices in independent stores in suburban districts are consistently higher than prices in independent stores in neighboring large cities. . . .

QUESTION 3. *To what extent is the Bureau's index of living costs affected by the omission of black-market prices?* . . .

ANSWER: We distinguish between black markets proper, in which rationed goods are sold without exchange of ration coupons, and retail stores in which some goods are sold at above-ceiling prices, with surrender of ration coupons by customers. . . . Transactions in rationed goods effected without exchange of ration coupons should not be represented in an official index of living costs. The Bureau does obtain above-ceiling prices charged in ordinary retail outlets, with customary exchange of ration coupons, and these prices are included in the index. . . . We conclude that there is probably an error in the index because of the under-reporting of above-ceiling prices by ordinary retail outlets, but that for food products this error does not exceed 2 per cent.

QUESTION 4. *Does the index of living costs measure hidden price increases due to quality deterioration?*

. . . Critics of the index argue that this sort of hidden increase in prices has been very large and is not reflected in the index.

ANSWER: The Bureau of Labor Statistics seeks to hold quality factors constant by pricing goods with specified characteristics. For many types of consumer goods it is able to do so today. For other goods and services quality deterioration is an inevitable accompaniment of the war effort. . . .

With reference to the cost-of-living index, our concern is with the price equivalent of quality change. We believe that consumers' goods and services, in the aggregate, have since 1939 suffered some loss of quality that is not reflected in reported prices. No dollar value can be put on this loss. In large part it is an intangible and unmeasurable element of the war. Consumers cannot be compensated for it. The cost-of-living index takes incomplete account of it.

QUESTION 5. *Are the rents reported to the Bureau those actually paid by tenants?*

Some users of the index have been under the impression that rentals are still obtained from rental agents, who are under pressure from the rent control authorities, and that the rent reports are, therefore, biased downward.

ANSWER: We have made no field check on this point, but we have examined the Bureau's procedure. We find that all rental reports are now obtained directly from tenants by agents who visit their homes. We believe that the rents thus reported are free from bias and may be accepted as accurate.

QUESTION 6. *Are the housing facilities included in the sample representative of those occupied by wage earners and lower-salaried workers in large cities?*

ANSWER: . . . In our opinion the new samples are satisfactory representations of family dwellings in the cities represented in the general index. We do not believe that these 34 cities adequately represent the diversity of urban housing conditions in the country as a whole. We recommend that advantage be taken of rental surveys now in process or being planned by the Bureau and the Office of Price Administration to increase the coverage of the index. . . .

QUESTION 7. *Does the Bureau's rent index accurately measure recent changes in the cost of housing to wage earners and lower-salaried workers living in large cities?*

ANSWER: We believe that for the areas covered by the Bureau's sample the index of rents provides an acceptable measure of changes in the cost of housing for urban workers who live in the same communities and in residences of the same general types as those occupied before the defense and war effort. . .

QUESTION 8. *Are the goods and services priced now typical of those purchased by wage earners and lower-salaried workers in large cities?* . . .

ANSWER: . . . There is no completely satisfactory solution of the problem faced by makers of a cost-of-living index when the character of consumption is changing. We believe that the adjustments made by the Bureau represent a reasonable compromise between the desire to reflect current consumption and the desire to maintain an index that measures with accuracy average changes in the unit prices of consumer goods and services.

We would add that changes in the kinds and quantities of goods consumed by average families in the United States have not as yet been very great. Mass consumption is slow to change. Purchases of new durable goods are, of course, smaller, but such goods constitute in normal times only some 10 per cent of consumer outlay for families with moderate incomes. For wage earners and salaried workers in the country at large, the distribution of expenditures for food, clothing, and rent has not been substantially modified. . . .

QUESTION 9. *Does the index of living costs measure changes in average family expenditures on consumer goods and services?*

This question reflects the popular interpretation of the phrase "cost of living" as representing the total amount families spend for goods and services.

ANSWER: No. The index is designed to measure only those changes in family expenditures resulting from changes in unit prices. It is not designed to measure alterations in family expenditures resulting from changes in manner of living, whether the changes are due to choice or necessity. Such alterations can be measured only by other statistical devices . . . The distinction between changes in family expenditures due to price movements and those due to shifts in the way of living is of special concern today when the pattern of living is being altered for a great many consumers. Rising incomes are giving many families opportunities to live on higher levels than they have known before.

QUESTION 10. *Does the Bureau's index provide an acceptable approximation of recent changes in the cost of living for urban workers?*

ANSWER: Yes.

. . . The various tests we have made indicate that these measurements define with satisfactory accuracy changes in the prices of the goods and services purchased by urban workers. . . .

We have said that the index provides an acceptable approximation to recent changes in living costs. We believe that as a measure of price changes affecting urban workers in large cities it is a good approximation.

Bibliographical Note

The classic publication of the controversy over the BLS index is:

Office of Economic Stabilization, *Report of the President's Committee on the Cost of Living*, Washington, 1945.

This includes: the letter of transmittal and report by Chairman William H. Davis, "Comments on the Chairman's Report," by R. J. Thomas, George Meany's letter on the report, and "Wartime Cost of Living," the report of the industry members of the President's Committee on the Cost of Living. The volume is also valuable because of a supplementary section containing some correspondence pertinent to the Report of the President's Committee and, among others, the following basic documents:

An Appraisal of the U. S. Bureau of Labor Statistics Cost-of-Living Index, by a Special Committee of the American Statistical Association; October 10, 1943 (Mills Committee Report)

The Cost-of-Living Index of the Bureau of Labor Statistics: A review and appraisal of the "cost-of-living" report by George Meany and R. J. Thomas, labor members of the President's Committee on the Cost of Living, made by the Bureau of Labor Statistics at the request of the Chairman of the Committee, William H. Davis; February 25, 1944 (BLS Review and Appraisal)

Prices and the Cost of Living in Wartime—An Appraisal of the Bureau of Labor Statistics index of the cost of living in 1941-44: Report of the technical committee appointed by the Chairman of the President's Committee on the Cost of Living, by Wesley C. Mitchell, chairman, Simon Kuznets, and Margaret G. Reid; June 15, 1944 (Mitchell Committee Report)

Not included in the Office of Economic Stabilization volume are the two principal union reports on the index:

George Meany and R. J. Thomas, *Recommended Report for the Presidential Committee on the Cost of Living*, Washington, D. C., 1944.

Philip Murray and R. J. Thomas, *Living Costs in World War II, 1941-44*, Washington, D. C., 1944.

A critique of the index by a labor research director not in agreement with the Meany-Thomas views is found in:

Lazare Teper, "Observations on the Cost of Living Index of the Bureau of Labor Statistics," *Journal of the American Statistical Association*, Vol. 38, September 1943, pp. 271-286.

Wage stabilization during World War II is treated both historically and analytically in various sections of the three-volume *Termination Report* of the National War Labor Board. The various executive orders, laws, key cases (such as the *Little Steel* case), and other relevant source materials are reprinted in Volume II of this *Report* (Washington, 1947).

Some thoughts and proposals on the operating and public relations problems of Federal statistical agencies are in the following reports of the Commission on Organization of the Executive Branch of the Government (Hoover Commission):

Task Force Report: *Statistical Agencies*, Washington, 1949.

Commission Report: "Statistical Activities" in *Budgeting and Accounting; Statistical Activities*, Washington, 1949; also published in *The Hoover Commission Report*, (McGraw-Hill), New York, 1949.

The correspondence and verbatim minutes of the President's Committee on the Cost of Living, as well as exhibits presented to the Committee, are in the Industrial Records Division of the National Archives, Washington, D. C.

INDEX I—Agencies

Except where specifically noted otherwise, all agencies listed are agencies of U. S. Federal Government. The U. S. Senate and U. S. House of Representatives are referred to as U.S.S. and H.R., respectively.

State and local governments are listed but not individual state and local agencies.

INDEX II—Topics